All the Years
of American Popular Music

ALL
THE YEARS
OF AMERICAN
POPULAR
MUSIC

David Ewen

Prentice-Hall, Inc., Englewood Cliffs, New Jersey

All the Years of American Popular Music by David Ewen

Copyright © 1977 by David Ewen

All rights reserved. No part of this book may be reproduced in any form or by any means, except for the inclusion of brief quotations in a review, without permission in writing from the publisher.
Printed in the United States of America
Prentice-Hall International, Inc., London / Prentice-Hall of Australia, Pty. Ltd., Sydney / Prentice-Hall of Canada, Ltd., Toronto / Prentice-Hall of India Private Ltd., New Delhi / Prentice-Hall of Japan, Inc., Tokyo / Prentice-Hall of Southeast Asia Pte. Ltd., Singapore / Whitehall Books Limited, Wellington, New Zealand
10 9 8 7 6 5 4 3

Library of Congress Cataloging in Publication Data

Ewen, David.
  All the years of American popular music.

  Includes index.
  1. Music, Popular (Songs, etc.)—United States—History and criticism. I. Title.
ML3561.P6E95   780'.42'0973   77-6733
ISBN 0-13-022442-1

To the memory of Dr. David M. Bressler
1907—1974
in gratitude for the cherished memories that cling to a friendship
that stretched across half a century

Preface

Of books on American popular music there seems to be no end. The accumulation keeps mounting: biographies of popular musicians; books on jazz, rock, the blues, country and western music, Soul, popular songs, the big bands; books on the music of the Broadway theater and the motion-picture screen; encyclopedias and discographies.

Why, then, still one more book on popular music?

The reason is simple. Though the bibliography of books in any single area of popular music is plentiful, no book so far has attempted to cover the entire world of popular music in all its varied facets within a single volume. The time had come, I felt, for a book to survey popular music in its totality, to see it whole as well as steadily. *All the Years of American Popular Music* is making that effort.

Many areas have here been cultivated. Every style and field of popular-music creativity has been covered: national ballads and war songs; sentimental ballads and novelty songs; popular songs of the Tin Pan Alley variety and show-business songs; ragtime and the blues; jazz and rock; rhythm and blues and Soul; hillbilly music and country and western music; symphonic jazz. In addition, since the songs the American masses have sung through the years go even further afield, I found it necessary to also cover the history of American folk music; the songs of the American labor movement; the songs of the civil rights movement.

To better understand how this music developed, other fields beyond the music itself are touched upon. This book, then, is not only the history of popular songs and popular composers; it is also the history of the musical theater—from the ballad opera of Colonial days through extravaganzas, minstrel shows, operettas and comic operas, vaudeville, burlesque, the revue, musical comedy, musical plays, rock musicals. The performance history of musical productions are included, together with brief biographies of the principal composers, librettists and lyricists. Similarly, other facets of show business are reviewed from their earliest history: motion pictures, radio, recordings, television.

Byways and alleys, as well as the broad highways, are explored in order to present a complete picture. In this book will be found material on discotheques and Muzak; disc jockeys and payola; the big bands and the small rock groups; theme songs, singing commercials and singing telegrams; the song lyric; the dubbing of voices on the screen sound track; Oscar-winning songs and the evolution of background music and scoring for the screen; the history of musical plagiarism and famous lawsuits; festivals and awards; social dancing; ASCAP and BMI.

No history of American popular music can be complete without a discussion of the careers of the many men and women who helped to bring songs to prominence. Biographies of numerous performers are included from Ed Christy and Bert Williams to Eddie Cantor and Al Jolson; from Lillian Russell and Nora Bayes to Sophie Tucker, Mary Martin and Ethel Merman; from the Hutchinson Family to the Carter Family; from Bessie Smith and Billie Holiday to Janis Joplin, Barbra Streisand and Bette Midler; from Frank Sinatra, Bing Crosby and Rudy Vallee to Perry Como, Andy Williams and Tony Bennett.

Additionally, places are explored where popular music incubated and was allowed to flourish: Storyville and Preservation Hall in New Orleans; Newport and Woodstock; 52nd Street, the street of Swing, and 28th Street, come to be known as Tin Pan Alley; Nashville and Bakersfield; the Avalon Ballroom and the Fillmore Auditorium in San Francisco; the Palace Theater, Roseland Ballroom, Barney Josephson's Café Society in New York.

Popular music does not exist in a vacuum; it is the outgrowth of social and political forces of which it is frequently the voice. A history of popular music must, finally, take into account, however briefly, the society in which it flourished. As we course through the years in American popular music, the changing mores, customs, political forces that shaped the lives of Americans are recalled to give added meaning to the popular music of different epochs. As Carl Sandburg put it so well: "The song history of America gives the feel and atmosphere, the layout and lingo of regions, of breeds of men, of customs and slogans, in a manner and air not given in regular history. There is a human stir in these songs with the heights and depths to be found in Shakespeare. A wide human process marches through them."

Contents

9
THE MUSICAL THEATER: FROM EXTRAVAGANZA TO OPERETTA

10
WAY DOWN YONDER IN NEW ORLEANS:
THE BIRTHPLACE OF JAZZ

11
THE END OF A CENTURY

PART THREE: 1900—1920

12
A NEW CENTURY: NEW VISTAS FOR POPULAR MUSIC

13
THE MUSICAL STAGE IN TRANSITION: VAUDEVILLE, BURLESQUE,
REVUE, EXTRAVAGANZA, OPERETTA, MUSICAL COMEDY

19
THE ASCAP AND BMI STORY

20
HILLBILLY MUSIC

21
THE ERA OF THE GREAT DANCE BANDS

22
HEYDAY OF THE MUSICAL THEATER

23
THE SILENT SCREEN ERUPTS INTO SOUND

PART SEVEN: SINCE 1960

PART ONE
1620-1865

1

A New Nation
Conceived in Liberty . . .

1

They came to the New World with song memories of their native lands to supplement the autochthonous repertory of the sometimes haunting and sometimes frenzied music of the American Indian.

The Separatists (or Pilgrims) and the Puritans sang psalms and hymns at church, town meetings, and at home. The English gentlemen representing the London Company at Jamestown, Virginia, kept alive the ballads of the British Isles. The slave ship that introduced slavery to the colonies in 1619 carried in its hold the chants, rhythms and rites of Africa.

French traders and explorers, Spaniards, the Dutch, the Germans and Irish—all of these people brought with them the songs of the old world into the new.

Many of these songs have been forgotten, such as "En Roulant ma Boule" and "Voyageur's Song" brought in by the frontier French, or the "Corn Grinding Song" of the Spanish. Others songs have become permanently fixed in the American repertory. The song with which Americans now celebrate Thanksgiving—"We Gather Together"—was brought to the new world by settlers who came from Holland in 1626 to found New Amsterdam. The authorship is sometimes credited to Adrianus Valerius, in whose collection, the *Nederlandtsche Gedenck-Clanck*, it was first published in Haarlem, Holland, in or about 1621. In Holland the song had celebrated a solemn day of thanksgiving by farmers for a fruitful harvest. After the first public Thanksgiving day was celebrated in the Massachusetts Bay Colony on February 22, 1631, the song's adoption by the New England colonies seemed inevitable.

"Auld Lang Syne," with which Americans celebrate New Year's Eve and which has also been sung lustily at reunions, graduations and farewell ceremonies, was brought to young America by the Scottish either in the late eighteenth or early nineteenth century. The phrase "auld lang syne" appeared in print in Scotland as early as 1694, and the earliest version of the poem with that title can be found in James Watson's *Scots Poems* in 1711. But the version Americans now know was written by Robert Burns, the verse first published in Edinburgh in 1796–1797. The melody itself had appeared in various guises and in sundry publications from 1687 on, most recognizably in "O Can Ye Labor Lea, Young Man," issued in *The Scots Musical Museum* in Edinburgh in 1792–1793. The first appearance of the Robert Burns poem with the now-familiar melody took place in *A Select Collection of Original Scottish Airs*, published in London in 1798. The melody of "Auld Lang Syne" was for many years borrowed by Princeton University for "Old Nassau," and by Vassar College for "The Rose and Silver Gray." In our own time, Guy Lombardo has helped to make the playing of "Auld Lang Syne" a New Year's Eve ritual.

But like seeds, foreign songs were dropped on the fertile soil of the colonies to take firm root. From these seeds there sprouted the varied blossoms of American popular and folk music.

The first songs to gain wide circulation in the colonies were the New England psalm tunes and hymns favored by the Separatists and the Puritans. Psalmody had come to the new world before the Separatists sailed into Plymouth. French Huguenots introduced French psalmody to the Carolinas in 1572. During a few weeks' stay in the California coast in June 1579, Sir Francis Drake's men practiced English psalmody. But it was with the Separatists and the Puritans that a continuous tradition was established.

The Separatists brought with them on the *Mayflower* only a single book. It was Henry Ainsworth's *Psalter*, a volume of thirty-nine psalm and hymn tunes to texts translated from the Hebrew, published in Amsterdam in 1612. These melodies, as Ainsworth revealed, were lifted from English, French and Dutch sources. Some of the English tunes had been taken from the pages of the Sternhold and Hopkins psalter, the first complete edition of which appeared in England in 1562. For a time, the Puritans were faithful to Sternhold and Hopkins while the Separatists preferred Ainsworth.

Dissatisfied with the English translations in Sternhold and Hopkins, the Puritans decided in 1640 to publish a psalm book of their own. Thus *The Whole Booke Of Psalmes Faithfully Translated into English Meter*, now commonly identified as *The Bay Psalm Book*, was the first book to be published (Cambridge, Massachusetts) in the English-speaking colonies of the New World; seventeen hundred copies were sold for twenty-three pence apiece. (In 1947, a copy of this first edition was purchased in New York for $151,000, believed to be the highest price ever paid for a book up to that time.) Originally, *The Bay Psalm Book* consisted exclusively of texts, but the ninth edition in 1698 contained thirteen melodies.

After the Separatists and the Puritans were united into a single colony in 1691, the Ainsworth psalter was discarded. The new tunes in the 1698 *The Bay Psalm Book* were dull and stereotyped in comparison to some of those in Ainsworth. As Gilbert Chase remarked in *America's Music*, the tunes of the Ainsworth collection "have considerable metrical variety and rhythmic freedom. Only a few of the psalms in Ainsworth's version use the four-lined ballad stanza (so-called 'common meter') that later became so tiresomely prevalent in English psalmody. Stanzas of five, six, eight and twelve lines are frequently used by Ainsworth, and he has no less than eight different rhythms for the six-syllable line alone." Waldo Selden Pratt further adds in his *Music of the Pilgrims*: "This music represents the folk-song style, with its symmetrical and echoing lines, each with a definite unity and all fused into a total enveloping unity. But it is the folk song that has retained great freedom of inner structure. It may be that these thirty-nine melodies illustrate more than one strain of folk-song tradition."

Out of Ainsworth's psalter came "Confess Jehovah," "I Laid Me Down and Slept," "Who Is the Man?" and, most famous of all, "Old Hundred." The last (originally called "The Old Hundredth," because it was the hundredth psalm in the Anglo-Geneva psalter of 1561) is still sung as the doxology to the words "Praise God from Whom All Blessings Flow."

2

There was also secular music in New England, mostly of the kind that the English publisher, Playford, issued in London in 1561 in his collection, *The English Dancing Master*. Hardly a boat sailed from England to the colonies without bringing some recent English songs and song collections. Playford's anthology undoubtedly arrived with them. Thus the still familiar "Greensleeves" and "Sellingers' Round" became popular in Massachusetts before the end of the seventeenth century.

Popular songs in the colonies were first distributed through broadsides: a sheet containing some newly written verses, the work of a local poet, usually on a subject of topical or local interest, intended to be sung to a familiar tune. The first broadside appeared in New England only a decade after the arrival of the *Mayflower*. Broadsides were hawked in the streets for a penny apiece, eagerly snatched from the hands of the salesman as soon as he reached the streets. Cotton Mather, the Boston clergyman, condemned those "foolish songs and ballads which hawkers and peddlers carry into all parts of the country." But the popular appeal of the broadside could not be arrested. It was not long before broadsides became the most convenient way to spread news and propaganda.

The first song to get its promotion through the broadside was the ballad "Brave Wolfe," the author of the words and the source of the melody not known. The hero of this topical song was the English general, James Wolfe, who led the British Army against the French forces of Marquis de Montcalm at Quebec on September 12, 1759, and who was killed in battle in his hour of victory. In the ballad, General Wolfe inquires from his aide-de-camp: "How goes the battle?" When told that victory was at hand, he replies: "Then I die with pleasure."

"Yankee Doodle" was another song whose initial distribution and popularity came about through the use of the broadside. For a long time it was taken for granted that the melody of "Yankee Doodle" came from a British, Dutch, Irish or German source. Many present-day musicologists still are inclined to believe so. But Professor S. Foster Damon made a strong case for "Yankee Doodle" as a thoroughly American product in a paper delivered at the annual meeting of the Bibliographical Society in October 1959. Because of the eminence of Professor Damon as a scholar and because of the extensiveness of his investigations, his conclusions deserve serious consideration. Professor Damon traced the words of "Yankee Doodle" back to 1745 and found that *both* the words and the music were in general circulation in the colonies by the 1760s. The song was interpolated into the first American ballad opera, Andrew Barton's *The Disappointment*, published in 1767. There the chorus is instructed to sing "Yankee Doodle" as it makes its exit from the stage. In 1768, "Yankee Doodle" was commented upon for the first time in the press when the *Journal of the Times* in Boston reported: "The British fleet was brought to anchor near Castle William. . . . Those passing in boats observed great rejoicing and that the 'Yankee Doodle' song was the capital piece of band music."

After having explored all possible origins, Professor Damon became convinced that both the words and the music of "Yankee Doodle" were born and bred in the colonies. "Its jauntiness and fantasy," wrote Professor Damon, "its cocksureness combined with self-criticism and its satire based on sympathy instead of contempt, all fit the American character today. . . . Thus early did we find ourselves." This, too, now is fact: The English nursery rhymes sometimes said to have provided the tune for "Yankee Doodle"—"Lucy Locket" and "Kitty Fisher"—appeared long after "Yankee Doodle" had become famous in the colonies.

It is true that "Yankee Doodle" first became popular with the British troops. They sometimes sang it to taunt the colonists by chanting it outside church during religious services. For John Hancock, that passionate advocate of revolt, British soldiers improvised the following mocking parody in 1775:

> "Yankee Doodle came to town
>   For to buy a firelock;
> We will tar and feather him
>   And so we will John Hancock."

And when Lord Percy's troops marched to Lexington in April of the same year to try to capture John Hancock and Samuel Adams, the soldiers sang "Yankee Doodle" en route.

As if in retribution, the colonists appropriated the song from the British as their own battle cry of freedom after Bunker Hill. When Washington took command at Cambridge, Edward Banks adapted it on a broadside as a war song, "The Yankee's Return from Camp." Throughout the Revolutionary War, "Yankee Doodle" remained popular with the fighting colonists. The tune was probably played by a band when Cornwallis surrendered at Yorktown. A British band performed it when the victorious colonists marched their prisoners across New England—a final gesture of nose-thumbing at the enemy.

The verses we now associate with "Yankee Doodle" are probably a post-Revolutionary War adaptation and variation of words used up to that time. They begin with the lines:

> "Yankee Doodle came to town
>   Riding on a pony.
> Stuck a feather in his cap
>   And called it macaroni."

The origin of the word "Yankee" is still in doubt. Some say it is an Indian mispronunciation of the word *English* or the French *Anglais*. The word "doodle" refers to a foolish fellow or simpleton. A "macaroni" was an eighteenth-century English fop who assumed well-bred European mannerisms.

"Yankee Doodle" was published in London in 1777, the first American song released in Europe. This was also the first occasion upon which the song was issued with both the words and the music. The long title on this publication read: "Yankee Doodle, or as Now Christened by the Saints of New England, the Lexington March." No author was credited. The sheet music instructed the performer that the words were "to be sung through the nose and in the west-country drawl and dialect."

The first American publication of both the words and the music took place in Philadelphia in 1798, issued by the house of G. Willig. Meanwhile, the melody had been used in the *Federal Overture*, an orchestral medley of patriotic airs arranged by Benjamin Carr, published both in Philadelphia and New York in 1795. There were also piano adaptations, one of which was a set of variations, and another a rondo within a formal piano sonata.

In America's first stage comedy—Royall Tyler's *The Contrast*, written in 1787—one of the characters sings "Yankee Doodle." "Yankee Doodle" continued to be played and sung in American theatres after that. When the song was not formally scheduled in a performance, audiences would sometimes call for it.

One of the reasons "Yankee Doodle" was able to retain its popularity through the years was the frequency with which the melody was borrowed for appropriate new lyrics as campaign songs during Presidential elections. In 1800 "Yankee Doodle" became "The American Spirit." In ensuing Presidential contests "Yankee Doodle" was changed to "Harrison," "Farmer Clay," "Rough and Ready" (for General Zachary Taylor), "The Latest Yankee Doodle" (for General Winfield Scott), "Breckinridge and Lane," "Labor's Yankee Doodle" (in 1888), "Taft and Sherman," and others as well.

"Yankee Doodle," then, is a native and not a foreign product. Almost in reciprocity, another item—those delightful songs for children gathered in *Mother Goose*—is not American at all, as some writers have suggested, but an English importation. Those writers claiming an American origin, maintained that such juvenile bonbons as "Jack Spratt," "Peter Peter, Pumpkin Eater," "Little Boy Blue," "A Frog He Would a-Wooing Go" were the work of a Boston lady named Elizabeth Goose who invented them for her grandchildren. They further explained that Elizabeth Goose's son-in-law, Thomas Fleet, recognizing the potential market for these ditties, collected them under the title of *Songs for the Nursery, or Mother Goose Melodies for Children*, which he published in Boston in 1719. A copy of this alleged publication has never been located. This fact, combined with the knowledge that Charles Perrault had published in France in 1697 a volume of ten stories under the title of *Mother Goose (Contes de ma mère l'oye)* discredits both the story about Thomas Fleet and his inventive mother-in-law, and the belief that these lovable childhood songs are American.

3

Wherever there was an audience for public entertainments in the colonies, there songs could be heard.

There was no dearth of entertainment: concerts with varied musical attractions; puppet shows; jugglers, acrobats and dancers; productions of musical plays and nonmusical plays with interpolated songs.

The first auditorium in the colonies used for public entertainment was The Palace Green, built in 1716 in Williamsburg, Virginia. Other places of entertainment arose in other parts of the colonies thereafter—in empty stores or warehouses, courtrooms and spacious meeting places. From the 1730s on, performances of one kind or another were continually taking place in various types of buildings.

The first musical production in the colonies took place in a courtroom. The city was Charleston, South Carolina; the time, the evening of February 8, 1735; the production, a one-act condensation of an English ballad opera, *Flora, or the Hob in the Well*. It was presented without scenery, costumes, footlights or limelight. The prototype of all English ballad operas—and the greatest in this genre—was, of course, John Gay's *The Beggar's Opera*. This was first produced in the colonies in New York on December 3, 1750. Subsequently, ballad operas in general, and *The Beggar's Opera* in particular, were performed by numerous companies throughout the colonies.

Not long after *The Beggar's Opera* was first introduced to the New World, an American turned his hand to the writing of a native ballad opera. He was Andrew Barton, and his opera was *The Disappointment* (the one already mentioned in which "Yankee Doodle" was sung). It was never produced, though it did get several rehearsals, and was published in 1767. A projected premiere was canceled because its satire was regarded as too provocative and offensive.

In ballad operas, airs and songs were interpolated into the spoken text, the melodies for the most part being tunes then most popular with the general public, adapted to new lyrics. Simple in style and approach, usually concerned with everyday subjects written in the people's English, and filled with popular songs mostly of English origin, the ballad opera was the distant foreign ancestor of American musical comedy.

The pasticcio was another form of musical production favored in the colonies. This was a comedy in which musical numbers by various composers were incorporated. The first successful pasticcio, and one that retained its popularity for many years, was *Love in the Village,* by Bickerstaffe and Arne, performed in 1766 in both Charleston and Philadelphia. A historian is tempted to look upon the pasticcio as the forerunner of American comic opera.

The year of 1766 also marked the construction in Philadelphia of the first building used exclusively for theatrical entertainments thereby becoming the first real theater in the colonies. After that, theaters were opened in cities large and small to feed the public hunger for entertainment. The largest theater in the colonies was built in Charleston in 1773.

Popular songs were prominent not only in ballad operas and pasticcios but also in serious plays. Sometimes they were placed within the text itself, but most often they were heard as between-the-acts diversion for those in the audience uninterested in going to the lobby for food and drink. Because songs were so important a part of the production of serious plays, every actor in legitimate dramas was required to have a pleasant singing voice.

4

The English Cavaliers in Virginia did their best to preserve the refinements and gentility of old-world living. The men dressed in flowing capes and collars, shoes decorated with gold or silver buckles, and hats with swaying plumes. These men liked to sport ample moustaches, Van Dyke beards, and long flowing powdered hair carefully groomed daily by a barber. Ladies also had elaborate headdresses which, before a ball, would sometimes take two days to prepare.

Gentlemen and ladies danced the minuet, the gavotte, the jig and a dance called the "Sir Roger de Coverley" which was soon to become known as a Virginia reel. These cavaliers sang and played on the virginal, the sixteenth-century ancestor of the piano, so-called probably because it was most often performed upon by genteel young ladies. The music of the cavaliers was not only airs from the English ballad operas, but also a vast repertory of English, Irish, Welsh or Scottish ballads which they helped to preserve in the New World.

The ballads all told a story. The gentle, lilting, highly formal and neatly balanced melodies served in a strophic format to spin a narrative in a long series of verses. The most celebrated of these ballads was "Barbara Allen," a seventeenth-century English ballad mentioned in Samuel Pepys' diary. The song told how, in the month of May, Sweet William lay on his deathbed. His last request was for his beloved Barbara Allen to come to him, a plea that went unheeded. When Barbara Allen heard the tolling of funeral bells and discovered they were ringing for Sweet William, she begged to have his grave dug wide and deep so that she might lie there with him. "I'll die for him in sorrow," she said plaintively. After they were buried together, there grew from Sweet William's grave a blood-red rose, while from the grave of Barbara Allen came a briar. In time the rose and the briar were entwined into a lover's knot.

More lachrymose still is the tale of "Lord Thomas and Fair Eleanor," whose melody comes out of Scotland. Our hero is Lord Thomas, a bold young man in love with fair Eleanor. His mother insists he marry a brown-skin girl who owns land and a house. Jealous that Lord Thomas is in love with Eleanor, this brown-skin girl, in a fit of rage, plunges a knife in Eleanor's heart. Lord Thomas avenges this murder by cutting off the head of the brown girl with his sword. "Dig my grave both wide and deep," he begs his mother, for he longs to have fair Eleanor buried at his side, and the brown girl at his feet.

Many a ballad has come to be known as a "riddling song," because it uses the technique of dialogue, or a question-and-answer method. "Lord Randal" from Virginia sometime before 1750, is one such. It is an exchange between mother and son in a series of verses each of which ends with the line: "Make my bed soon, for I'm sick at heart, and I fain would lie down." Upon questioning, Lord Randal informs his mother that while he plans leaving his brother silver and gold, for his sweetheart he is bequeathing only a rope to hang her.

"Lord Ronald" is a variation on the stark theme found in "Lord Randal." In "Lord Ronald," a ballad from the British isles, the hero is asked by his mother where he has dined, what he has eaten, and also what he plans to leave his father, mother and sweetheart as a heritage. Lord Ronald replied to all but one of these queries kindly and sadly, always ending with the refrain: "And I'm weary, weary hunting, and fain would lie down." But when asked about his sweetheart, he replies grimly he plans to leave her a gallows tree from which to hang.

Once again mother and son engage in a question-and-answer repartee in "Edward," a Scottish ballad. The mother wants to know why there is blood on Edward's knife. At first he tells her it comes from a mare. Upon further questioning he tells her it is the blood of a dog, and after that the blood of a fox. But in the end he is compelled to admit that he has killed his own brother because the victim had cut down a holly bush. To other questions, Edward discloses he plans to sail the ocean round never again to return. To his mother's final query as to what she is to do, he answers hotly that the curse of hell should fall upon her because it was she who had given him counsel.

Singing and dancing were favored forms of entertainment in the homes and taverns of Virginia. Sometimes the songs were performed by professional minstrels, but most of the time they were sung by laymen. Faulty memories, a not always precise ear for rhythm and pitch, the occasional tendency to contribute personalized embellishments, all were responsible for the appearance of numerous variants of each ballad. Conditions in which people lived, suffered or thrived—conditions unique to the new world—also caused frequent changes in lyrics and melodies. There were over a hundred versions of "Barbara Allen" alone, and all the other ballads also have many different variants. In the process of this transformation, the ballads from the British isles acquired an American identity.

5

William Billings, America's first professional composer, brought to the culminating point the age of New England psalmody.

Fate had not been kind to him. Born in Boston on October 7, 1746, he came to the world with one blind eye, withered hands, legs of uneven length, and a rasping voice. As he grew to manhood, he helped Nature in making him into a physical monstrosity by assuming a slovenly and outlandish dress, behaving like a boor, and never concerning himself unduly with cleanliness. Despite his native and assumed disfiguration he managed to convince two women to marry him (the first in 1764, the second a decade later) and bear him six children.

As a boy he received some singing lessons from a local pastor. Music became a passion. When he was fourteen, the death of his father compelled him to become an apprentice to a tanner. He neglected his work to spend hours scribbling tunes with chalk on the hides of his tannery. At other times he devoured psalm books and sought technical guidance in composition by memorizing Tans'ur's *Musical Grammar.*

Eventually he gave up tannery for music, and by doing so became America's first native-born professional musician. Outside the door of his home, near the White Horse Tavern, he hung the sign of his new calling as a singing teacher which read simply: "Billings—Music." Since he was convinced everybody should sing, and since he was violently opposed to the haphazard singing practices then so widely prevalent in New England, he formed in 1774 a singing class in Stoughton, the first of its kind in the colonies. (After his death this group became the nucleus of the Stoughton Musical Society, America's first significant performing musical organization.) The example he set in forming a singing class then led to the creation of several singing schools by others where Americans were taught to read music. Billings, father of the American singing school, was also a pioneer in other musical practices. He was the founder of the American church choir, directing two of them, one at the Brattle Street Church, and the other at the Old South Church. He was also the first in the colonies to use a pitch pipe and to introduce a violoncello into church services.

None of his varied activities provided him with much of a livelihood. He died as he had lived, in poverty. Not even occasional concerts given for his benefit, nor his publications, could relieve him of ever pressing financial distress. He died a pauper on September 2, 1800, and was buried in the Boston Common in an unidentified grave.

He was a prolific composer of psalms, hymns and anthems for four-part chorus which heralded a new age in American psalmody. They were published in six volumes: *The New England Psalm Singer* (1770); *A Volume of Anthems, Fuges and Choruses* (1770); *The Singing Master's Collection* (1778, with several other editions published in 1779, 1781, and between 1786 and 1789); *Music in Miniature* (1779); *The Psalm Singer's Amusement* (1781); and *The Suffolk Harmony* (1786).

His music had much of the raw authenticity of the man who wrote it. In his writing, as in his appearance, Billings defied convention, formality and the status quo. It is true that he often sidestepped rules of composition because he was poorly schooled. But it is equally true that by temperament and nature he was an iconoclast, and by instinct an innovator. He did not like the trim, well-ordered stately kind of church music then getting sung in New England. Billings sought a more robust kind of music. As he explained in the preface to his first collection of psalms and hymns: "For my own part, I don't think myself confined to any rules. . . . I think it is best for every composer to be his own learner. . . . Nature lays the foundation. Nature must give the thought." His musical writing, as he himself recognized, was "more than twenty times as powerful as the old slow tunes, each part striving for mastery and victory." For the most part he was partial to a fast tempo, rugged rhythms, a strong harmony, and a bass that moved with an athletic stride. His harmonic and contrapuntal writing, filled with practices then forbidden by authorized texts, was as vigorous as it was uncouth. Such psalms and hymns as the canonic "When Jesus Wept," "David's Lamentation," "The Lord Is Risen," "Creation" and "Be Glad Then America"—to single out a few—was no longer English psalmody but a rough and homespun product of the colonies.

"When Jesus Wept" is a fuguing tune (or as Billings preferred to spell it, "fuging tune"), a method this composer favored in his many compositions. To Billings, a fuguing tune was not one utilizing a fugal style, but one in which the first voice offers a phrase which is then repeated successively by three other voices. Sometimes this method is found at the beginning of a piece, sometimes in the middle, sometimes at the end—preceded or followed, as the case may be, by all the voices in harmony.

His free and independent spirit, so characteristic of America's early settlers, refused to be bridled. Sometimes he introduced into his religious music the rhythms of dance tunes. This happened in "I Am a Rose" and in his Christmas carol, "A Virgin Unspotted," in each of which a jiglike passage appears. Billings had both the daring and the gift to indulge in vivid imagery. He could simulate musically the sound of laughter for the phrase "shall laugh and sing," or the flight of a bird for the words "should I like a tim'rous bird." He could be realistic, as when he instructed his singers to clap their hands when the words spoke of hand clapping. And in "The Lord Is Risen" he could be highly descriptive, as Douglas Townsend remarked in his liner notes to a Columbia recording of Billings' music. "In one phrase, for example, the ear is presented with a tonal picture of the rise of Christ (highest note of the melody) until He becomes 'the first fruits of them that slept,' described by the lowest notes of the melody, which is also, a symbolic touch, the first and last note of the phrase."

Billings also produced secular songs in four-part harmony: "Consonance," "Morpheus," "Connection," together with such unusual and provocative items as "Modern Music" and "Jargon." In each of these last two he again proved himself to be an original. The words of "Modern Music" suggest the kind of music he wrote for them, for his music is a literal translation of the instructions found in the text Here are some of the lines:

> "And since we all agree
> To set the tune on E
> The Author's darling key
>
> He prefers to the rest,
> Let the bass take the lead
> And firmly proceed
> Till the parts are agreed
> To fuge away, then change
> To a brisker time
> And up the ladder climb
> Then down again, then mount the second time
> And end the strain, then change the key
> To pen five tones and flow in treble time
> The Note exceeding low deep down a while.
> Then rise by slow degrees,
> The process surely will not fail to please
> Since Common and Treble we jointly have run,
> We'd give you their essence compounded in one;
> Although we are strongly attached to the rest,
> Six-four is the movement that pleases us best."

"Jargon" was Billings' acidulous response to his many critics who, better trained than he, mocked him for his musical crudities, sloppiness, awkwardness and ignorance, and who mistook his originality for caprice. As an expression of derision, a few of his contemporaries one day hung two cats by their tails on Billings' signpost—the howling of the victims intended by the perpetrators of this prank as an example of the kind of music Billings was writing. The composer laughed right back at his critics by writing "Jargon." It is filled with excruciatingly discordant harmonies from first measure to last. When Billings published this piece he added an explanatory manifesto to which he fixed the title of "Goddess of Discord."

He wrote: "In order to do this piece justice . . . let it be performed in the following manner. Let an ass bray the bass, let the filing of a saw carry the tenor, let a hog who is extremely weak squeal the counter, and let a cartwheel, which is heavy-loaded, and that has long been without grease, squeak the treble. If the concert should appear to be feeble you may add the cracking of a crow, the howling of a dog, the squalling of a cat, and . . . the rubbing of a wet finger upon a window pane."

Billings, and not his critics, had the last laugh. Before Billings' death, few psalm collections in America failed to include at least one of his compositions, nor was there a singing group of any importance that was not performing some of his pieces. By 1790, Billings had written a war song that was so influential in arousing the martial spirit of the rebel colonists against mother England that it has come to be described as the "Marseillaise" of the American Revolution. The song was "Chester," and it won for Billings the right for consideration as America's first genuine composer of popular music.

6

As rebellion against England passed from hot words to still hotter deeds, the tensions of the times found an outlet in song. Thus, in New England, the political song joined the religious in public favor.

The Sons of Liberty interrupted their terrorism to write and spread songs like "A New Song" which denounced tyranny. Samuel Adams organized singing groups in Boston where "The Liberty Tree" (words by Thomas Paine) and "Sons of Liberty" were heard. These and other lyrics, written either in the white heat of anger or in cool deliberation for the purpose of propaganda, were printed and distributed on broadsides.

Surely it is ironical that most of the political lyrics expressing defiance of England should have been set to English melodies! The prevailing practice was to borrow the tune of a well-known English song and set it to new incendiary verses. Thus, through the medium of English-born melodies, the colonies denounced the Stamp Act, the dictatorial Writs of Assistance, the Townshend Acts with their crushing duties on importations, the Boston Massacre and other abuses which became the steps leading to revolution.

"The Liberty Song" was one of the most inflammatory of these songs. John Dickinson wrote the words and set it to the melody of William Boyce's English hymn of praise to the British Navy, "Heart of Oak." "The Liberty Song" has come to be recognized as America's first political song. It was inspired by the refusal of the Massachusetts Legislature to rescind the Circular Letter of February 11, 1768, which imposed duties and taxes on the colonies. "I enclose you a song for American Freedom" wrote Dickinson to James Otis of Massachusetts. "I have long renounced poetry, but, as different songs are very powerful on certain occasions, I venture to invoke the deserted muse." His words were first published in the *Boston Gazette* on July 11, 1768. With Boyce's music it first appeared in Bickerstaff's *Boston Almanac*. After that the Sons of Liberty adopted it as their official song.

"Come, join in hand, brave Americans all
  And rouse your bold hearts at fair Liberty's call;
  No tyrannous acts shall suppress your just claim,
  Or stain with dishonour America's name.

In Freedom we're born, and in Freedom we'll live,
    Our purses are ready,
    Steady, friends, steady
Not as slaves but as Freemen our money we'll give."

So popular did "The Liberty Song" become that the Tories responded in kind with numerous parodies. One of these claimed that "not as men but as monkeys the token you give." Another—following the evacuation of two British regiments in the wake of the Boston Massacre of 1770—warned the "simple Bostonians" to "beware of your Liberty Tree," that "if *we* chance to return to this town, your houses and stores will come tumbling down."

Each and every issue that aroused the colonists and united them against the Crown was sung about to hastily concocted lyrics just as speedily circulated on broadsides. The Stamp Act led to the writing of Peter St. John's "American Taxation" and to "What a Court Hath England" to the tune of the English "Derry Down." The Townshend Acts brought on "Young Ladies in Town" which exhorted American women to boycott English textiles. "Fish and Tea" and "Castle Island" were two other song satires on English taxation.

Once the shot was fired at Lexington, the Revolution was on. In a large sense it was a people's war and as such it found expression in populist songs. From the very beginnings of the conflict, "Yankee Doodle" (as has already been noted) was a favored song of the colonists. But England was attacked far more often with her own melodies than with native ones. "God Save the King" became "God Save the Thirteen States." Other well-known English melodies were used for "Liberty's Call," "The Burning of Charleston" and "Americans All" in 1775, and for "War Song and Independence" in 1776. After Washington and his men crossed the Delaware to drive the Hessian mercenaries from Trenton and Princeton to regain control of New Jersey, "The Battle of Trenton" commemorated this turning point in the war. And when General Burgoyne surrendered at Saratoga on October 7, 1777, this decisive occasion found voice in song with words of unknown origin adapted to the Scottish melody of "Brennan on the Moor."

"Free America" was one of the most fiery of the war songs. Joseph Warren, who wrote the words, was a minute man who helped launch Paul Revere's ride and who died at the battle of Breed's Hill, or Bunker Hill, in 1775. Using the melody of "The British Grenadiers," Warren hurled an admonition to the colonists to "oppose, oppose, oppose, oppose for North Americay." The melody of "The British Grenadiers" was also used for "Lord Cornwallis' Surrender," after Cornwallis and his army were defeated at the battle of Yorktown on October 19, 1781.

The colonists fought, and they sang. Joel Barlow, writer of patriotic verses who became a Chaplain in the Revolutionary army, wrote in 1775: "I do not know whether I shall do more for the cause in the capacity of Chaplain than I would in that of a poet; I have great faith in the influence of songs; and I shall continue, while fulfilling the duties of my appointment, to write one now and then, and to encourage the taste for them which I find in the camp. One good song is worth a dozen addresses or proclamations."

And so martial songs written to English melodies described battles, engagements, sieges, victories: "Bunker Hill," "The Ballad of Trenton," "Burgoyne's Defeat" are characteristic. Songs sang the praises of Washington, Lafayette, John Paul Jones and Nathan Hale among other heroes. The songs of the American Revolution were further supplemented by fife songs. These were heard on the battlefield played by fife and drum. "My Dog and Gun," "On the Road to Boston" and "The Girl I Left Behind" are three of many. The last had been brought to the colonies from Ireland, had been popular in the New World from 1650 on, and was first published there in 1770. Before the year of 1770 was over it was parodied in "I'm So Lonesome Since My Monkey Died." During the Presidential campaign of 1840 it returned as "Hard Times" and in that of 1892 as "The Independent Man." Its melody was also used for many years as a march for the graduating class at West Point. "The Girl I Left Behind" is frequently associated in the minds of many Americans with Archibald Willard's painting *Spirit of '76.*

   Throughout the Revolution "Yankee Doodle" was not only heard in its original form but also in amusing parodies. One of the most famous was that of Francis Hopkinson—a statesman, a friend of George Washington, and one of the signers of the Declaration of Independence who was, coincidentally, one of America's first serious composers. His verses to the tune of "Yankee Doodle" concerned an amusing incident. David Bushnell (inventor of a man-propelled submarine that proved inoperative) devised a scheme to attack British ships. He filled kegs with powder and floated them down the river towards those enemy vessels anchored in Delaware River outside Philadelphia. When the British saw the kegs come floating towards them they began firing wildly. This sight proved so amusing to Hopkinson that he concocted a set of satirical verses, "The Battle of the Kegs," meant to be sung to the strains of "Yankee Doodle." There is good reason to believe he sang them to George Washington and his staff at their army headquarters in Virginia.

> "Gallants, attend and hear a friend
>   Trill forth harmonious ditty;
> Strange things I'll tell which late befell
>   In Philadelphia city.
>
> " 'Twas early day, as poets say,
>   Just when the sun was rising,
> A soldier stood on log of wood
>   And saw a sight surprising.
>
> "As in amaze, he stood to gaze;
>   The truth can't be denied, sirs,
> He spied a score of kegs—or more,
>   Come floating down the tide, sirs.
>
> "From morn to night these men of might
>   Displayed amazing courage.
> And when the sun was fairly down
>   Returned to sup their porridge."

But not all of the songs of the American Revolution borrowed English melodies. There was, once again, "Yankee Doodle." Two other distinguished war songs were also native. One was "The American Hero," lyrics by Nathaniel Niles, with melody taken from Andrew Law's "Bunker Hill." Both the words and the music date from 1775. Modeling his melody after the patterns of an English ballad, Law had created in "Bunker Hill" a tune that sounded like a mournful processional. Nevertheless, when joined to the spirited words of Niles' "The American Hero" it became a rallying cry for rebels ready to die for their freedom. The song reflects the hopes and fears of the colonists when, after Bunker Hill, they came to realize they had come to grips with a great military power.
   The most important song of the American Revolution came from the New England psalmodist, about whom we have already spoken—William Billings. As a friend of Samuel Adams and Paul Revere, Billings allied himself with the cause of the Revolution from its very inception. He enlisted his music in the struggle by writing new lyrics to the melodies of his psalms, hymns and anthems. These were distributed on broadsides in army camps. "Many of

the New England soldiers . . . who were encamped in southern states had his popular tunes by heart and frequently amused themselves by singing in camp to the delight of all those who heard them," recorded a writer in the *Musical Reporter*. The colonists "wept as they remembered Boston," to the tune of Billings' psalm, "By the Waters of Babylon." Other Billings melodies became stirring war songs with "Retrospect," "Independence," "Columbia" and most important of all, "Chester." "Chester" originated as a hymn in the *Singing Master's Apprentice*. The new martial words began as follows:

> "Let tyrants shake their iron rod
> And slav'ry clank her galling chains.
> We fear them not, we trust in God,
> New England's God forever reigns."

The stately melody, with its even meters and formal cadences, betrayed its church origin and hardly made it suitable for belligerent lyrics. But the new words caught and fixed the spirit of the times, and "Chester" spread throughout army camps to become America's first great war song.

2

In Freedom
We'll Live:
The First Half Century

1

With peace, Americans found the singing of popular songs a welcome diversion—at home, quilting bees, ceremonies of all kinds, and public meetings. The new Americans learned their songs from broadsides which continued to flood the streets; from printed sheet music issued by such early American music publishers as Draper and Folsom in Boston, G. Willig and Benjamin Carr in Philadelphia, James Hewitt in New York, and from songsters, the first of which was *The American Miscellany* in 1789. A songster was an inexpensively priced collection of popular verses intended to be sung to familiar melodies; it was a pamphlet in a small octavo or vest-pocket size.

In the early post-Revolutionary War period, the subjects covered by songs ranged over a wide spectrum. There were ballads of unfulfilled or unrequited love; songs about fires, storms, shipwrecks and other disasters; songs about the gaiety and pitfalls of city life or the rewards of rural existence; songs in praise or denunciation of alcohol; songs about contemporary fashions, fads, diversions and problems; humorous songs and songs overflowing with sentiment.

Political subjects continued to serve as valuable song material. Many songs reflected America's preoccupation with the manifold problems of building a new state. In the first decade of the nineteenth century, songsters were full of lyrics interpreting or commenting upon the political events of the time. Some songsters were devoted exclusively to political subjects, for example *The Nightingale of Liberty* or *The American Naval and Patriotic Songster. The Missouri Songster*, issued in Cincinnati in 1808 and widely circulated at camp meetings, was also largely political. Young Abraham Lincoln and his sweetheart, Ann Rutledge, used this songster at the Rutledge Tavern in New Salem.

The Declaration of Independence was sung about in "Independence Day," words by Jonathan M. Sewall to an unidentified melody, also in "Song for the Fourth of July" and "Freedom Triumphant." The ratification of the Constitution was the subject of "The New Roof," words by Francis Hopkinson to the melody of "To Anacreon in Heaven." "A New Federal Song" and "Rise Columbia" (the latter sung to the strains of "Rule Britannia") sang the praises of the new Republic.

"To Anacreon in Heaven" was an English song, its music probably written in or about 1770 by John Stafford Smith to words by Ralph Tomlinson for the London Anacreontic Society, a group of aesthetes and art lovers. The first appearance in America of this melody took place in 1798 when a Thomas Paine—not *the* Thomas Paine—used the melody for his lyrics to "Ye Sons of Columbia." After that the melody was used several times by political lyricists before Francis Scott Key set his words for "The Star-Spangled Banner" to it and made the melody immortal. It has also been used a number of times since Key.

There were songs honoring George Washington for his birthday and inauguration, and later to mourn his death. Among those most favored were "Washington," "God Save the Great Washington," "A Toast to Washington," "Elegy on the Death of General Washington" and "Union and Washington." "God Save the Great Washington" utilized the melody of "God Save the King." "Union and Washington"—words by Eli Lewis with original music by Edward Tyler—was first published in the Pennsylvania *Packet and Daily Advertiser* on August 5, 1788.

Other songs besides "Union and Washington" boasted melodies originating in the young country. "Ode for the Fourth of July" (not to be confused with "Song for the Fourth of July") came in 1789 with music by Horatio Garnett and words by Daniel George. The deacon, Jezaniah Sumner, wrote both the words and the music for "Ode on Science" in 1798 in which science serves as the symbol of freedom. Written fifteen years after the American independence, about which it spoke, this song enjoyed widespread popularity. "All haughty tyrants we disdain," run the last two lines, "and shout, 'Long live America!' "

Many a song lyric was devised to promote Presidential candidates, most often borrowing familiar tunes. When Robert Treat Paine wrote the words for "Adams and Liberty" he used the melody of "To Anacreon in Heaven." It appeared in 1798 at the behest of the Massachusetts Charitable Fire Society and earned for its author a fee of $750.00, by no means an insubstantial sum at that time. Paine also wrote the lyric for another pro-Adams song, "The Green Mountain Farmer."

Songs began playing a prominent role in American elections in 1800 when the candidacy of Adams was promoted by "Adams and Liberty," while the Jeffersonians rallied to his support with "The Son of Liberty." A parody of "Yankee Doodle" was also circulated for Jefferson.

With successive political campaigns, songs assumed increasing importance. Presidential campaigns provided a welcome form of entertainment. At barbecues, mass meetings, torchlight parades, songs proved as influential as speeches in swaying the sentiments of an electorate. The words of "Madison, Union and Liberty" were distributed in a broadside in 1808 to an unspecified melody. "Monroe Is the Man" was sung to Joseph Mazzinghi's "Young Lochinvar" in 1816. Andrew Jackson's campaign in 1824 (in which John Quincy Adams was voted to office even though Jackson earned the greater popular and electoral vote) was enlivened with "The Hunters of Kentucky" in which Samuel Woodworth's words were linked to the popular tune, "Unfortunate Miss Bailey." The 1828 campaign in which

Jackson finally emerged victorious over John Quincy Adams saw a lively exchange of songs: for Adams there was "Little Wat Ye Wha's A-Comin' " (to the Scottish melody, "Highland Muster Roll") and "Adams and Clay" (to the tune of "The Star-Spangled Banner"); for Jackson, "Jackson Toast" (to the melody of "Auld Lang Syne") and "The Hickory Tree" (melody not specified).

"Adams and Liberty" and "Adams and Clay" were only two of several Presidential campaign songs using the melody of "The Star-Spangled Banner." Two later ones were "Buchanan and Breckinridge" in 1857 and, in 1860, "Stand By the Flag."

2

Like a sensitive thermometer recording temperature, the popular songs reflected the political storms and stresses of the times. Toward the close of the eighteenth century, the problem of "foreign entanglements" produced a rich crop of political song literature.

Thomas Jefferson was the champion of both the common man and liberty. As a vigorous opponent of the Alien and Sedition Acts, he inspired the writing of "Jefferson and Liberty" in 1800. The author of the lyrics was Robert Treat Paine, who earlier had sung the praises of Adams in "Adams and Liberty." "Jefferson and Liberty" was probably sung publicly for the first time soon after Jefferson's inauguration, in Connecticut on March 11, 1801. "The gloomy night before us flies," read the opening lines. "The reign of terror now is o'er." It is significant to remark that the melody of this song—which became Jefferson's musical identification and after that, in 1804, his campaign song—came from an Irish source, the reel "Gobby-O." Jefferson's supporters were largely made up of immigrant laborers and farmers, many of whom were Irish.

Patriotism stirred other Americans into writing political songs. A few of these were "The Federal Constitution and the President Forever," "Brother Soldiers, All Hail," "Madison and Liberty" and "The American Star." The last had words by John McCreery and was sung to the melody of D. C. Hewitt's "The Wounded Hussar." It was first published in 1800 in J. Hewitt's collection, *Musical Repository*.

The first American national ballad to survive to the present came out of the political and international storms of 1798: "Hail Columbia," words and music of American origin. Joseph Hopkinson (son of Francis) was invited by a Philadelphia singer, Gilbert Fox, to write for him some patriotic verses. Fox wanted to use a patriotic song as the tour de force in the finale to Borden's comedy, *The Italian Monk*, at the New Theater in Philadelphia on April 25, 1798. Hopkinson welcomed the assignment, for he was convinced that a patriotic song could very well "get up the American spirit," as he put it, and make Americans "look and feel exclusively for our honor and rights." For his melody, Hopkinson selected the stirring tune of "The President's March" which Philip Phile wrote as an instrumental number to honor George Washington and which had been published in Philadelphia in 1793 or 1794. Since President Adams agreed that the new patriotic song might very well unite the American people in this time of crisis, he joined his Cabinet in attending Fox's concert. To dramatize his performance, Fox was accompanied by a brass band and chorus. A huge portrait of President Adams hung as his backdrop. That evening the ballad was a sensation. Two days later it was published by Benjamin Carr in Philadelphia as "New Federal Song." For a quarter of a century after that "Hail Columbia" was America's national anthem. It was heard on every American ship at the lowering of the colors at sunset. For still another half a century it shared its status as a national anthem with "The Star-Spangled Banner." During the Civil War, "Hail Columbia" was the anthem sung and played most often in the North. From Charles Coffin's *Four Years of Fighting* we learn that in 1861 this song was "everywhere the music of the streets, vocal as well as instrumental."

The successful attack of American troops under General William Henry Harrison on November 7, 1811, against the Indian Headquarters on the Wabash River near Tippecanoe Creek was glorified that same year in "The Battle of the Wabash," words by Joseph Hutton to the melody of "To Anacreon in Heaven." Because of this ballad, Harrison acquired the nickname of "Tippecanoe" which was widely used in slogans and songs during the Presidential campaign of 1841.

In or about 1812, a New York publisher, John Paff, issued a song, "Hail to the Chief," words from Sir Walter Scott's *The Lady of the Lake*, and music by James Sanderson. So successful did this song become that Benjamin Carr's Music Store in Baltimore and G. E. Blake and G. Willig, both in Philadelphia, released it between 1812 and 1814. This piece of music is of particular interest to us today because it is always performed in honor of the President of the United States, particularly at ceremonial occasions. It is not known precisely when this practice was initiated, but we do know that it was performed at the inauguration of President Polk on March 4, 1852. It has long been maintained that John Sanderson was an English composer, thereby making *Hail to the Chief* an English composition. However, as no copy of an English publication has ever been found, and since the melody is unknown in England, there is cause for suspicion that the "John Sanderson" appearing on copies of the early sheet music is not the English John Sanderson, but possibly a pseudonym adopted by an American composer.

3

America's second conflict with Great Britain, in 1812, brought on a spate of war songs. "The American Star," which had been written in 1800, was revived and gained a new lease on public enthusiasm. Samuel Woodward's stormy words to "Patriotic Diggers" sounded a rousing call to Philadelphians to hold strong against the British fleet in Chesapeake Bay; its Scottish-like melody was later borrowed for the school songs of Haverford and Swarthmore colleges. Once hostilities broke out, "Yankee Doodle" reemerged with new fiery words —once again to do combat with the British. Virtually every phase of the war was sung about in ballads and popular tunes. Since major victories came on sea rather than on land, the best songs were devoted to naval encounters. The frigate *Constitution*, affectionately dubbed "Old Ironsides," commanded by Captain Isaac Hull, engaged the British *Guerrière* in combat on August 19, 1812. After two rounds of fire were exchanged, the *Guerrière* surrendered. The American people glorified this engagement in the song, "Hull's Victory," words by Joseph Hutton, music by John Bray, and also in "The *Constitution* and the *Guerrière*." On October 12, 1812, the *President*, under the command of Stephen Decatur, captured the British *Macedonian*. This event was commemorated in W. Strickland's "Decatur's Victory." On February 24, 1813, the *Hornet*—under James Lawrence, whose dying words "don't give up the ship" were immortalized—defeated the *Peacock*. James Hewitt sang about this victory in his "Lawrence the Brave." The defeat of the British flotilla of Admiral Robert Heriot Barclay by the American fleet of Commodore Oliver H. Perry in September 1813 inspired the writing of two songs each called "Perry's Victory," one by Joseph Hutton, and the other by Andrew C. Mitchell.

The war of 1812 gave birth to the song since become America's national anthem, "The Star-Spangled Banner." Many of the specific details surrounding its writing, long handed down as historic truth, have turned out to be more fancy than fact, as P. William

Filby, director of the Maryland Historical Society, discovered after long and patient research. Carefully sifting fact from legend, Mr. Filby, in collaboration with Edward G. Howard, compiled a monograph which offers a definitive history of the writing of "The Star-Spangled Banner"—findings reported at length by Homer Bigart in a front-page story in *The New York Times* on July 4, 1972.

The story begins with Dr. William Beanes (once General Washington's physician) who, in 1814, was held prisoner by the British on Vice Admiral Alexander Cockburn's flagship in Chesapeake Bay off Baltimore. Dr. Beanes' friend, Francis Scott Key, and John S. Skinner, a civilian involved in prisoner exchange, were permitted by President Madison to try to effect Dr. Beanes' release. Under a flag of truce, Key and Skinner sailed from Baltimore on September 5 and two days later reached the British flagship, which was then lying near the mouth of the Potomac River. There they received a promise of Dr. Beanes' freedom. However, since the British were then on the eve of launching an attack on Fort McHenry at Baltimore, the three Americans had to be detained until after the battle. The men were transferred to the *Minden*, a small prisoner exchange boat, anchored eight miles from Fort McHenry. It was from this sloop that Key witnessed the attack on the morning of September 13. All that day and night the fort was heavily shelled. The following dawn, Key saw the American flag still atop the fort—not flying proudly as legend has maintained, but, according to Filby, "wrapped soggily around a pole." As Filby explained: "It would have taken a gale to make the flag wave because of its size and the rainy weather." Nevertheless, Key's excitement found outlet in poetry which he then and there scribbled on the back of a letter (not on an old envelope as has been said; envelopes did not come to general use until 1840). Key did not write out all four stanzas then and there in a white heat of inspiration; probably no more than the first verse was scribbled that dawn, with the others added at a later date. To accompany his words, Key apparently had the melody of "To Anacreon in Heaven" in mind from the very beginning. He knew it well, having used it nine years earlier for another patriotic song, "When the Warrior Returns," one of whose lines read "by the light of the star-spangled flag of our nation."

Though a plaque at the Smithsonian Institution placed the date of September 15, 1814, as the day Key went ashore at Baltimore, Filby has found to his satisfaction that Key did not land until the evening of Friday, September 16. He then went to the Indian Queen Tavern (not the Fountain Inn) where he rented a room and there revised and expanded his poem. He read it to his brother-in-law, Joseph Hopper Nicholson, who thought it deserving of publication. On September 20, Key's verses appeared in the Baltimore newspaper, *The Patriot*, which remarked editorially: "The following beautiful and animatory effusion, which is destined long to outlast the occasion and outlive the impulse that produced it, has already been extensively circulated." Still another Baltimore newspaper, the *American*, printed the poem a day later. On October 18, it was sung publicly for the first time by a Mr. Hardinge (not Frederick Durang).

The anthem became popular throughout the East after the Civil War, and in the rest of the country after the Spanish-American conflict. For many years both the Army and Navy regarded it as America's national anthem, before it was officially adopted by an act of Congress on March 3, 1931.

Periodic attempts have been made to dislodge "The Star-Spangled Banner" as America's official anthem and to replace it either with Katherine Lee Bates' "America the Beautiful" or Irving Berlin's "God Bless America," efforts that proved unavailing. The melody of "The Star-Spangled Banner" was justifiably criticized as being unsingable because of its thirteen-step vocal range. But an even more serious criticism is that our national anthem should glorify peace, not war, and should not commemorate a comparatively minor incident in American history. In addition, say critics, it is offensive to place a friendly power which has been our traditional ally for over a century in the role of an enemy. But "The Star-Spangled Banner" also has its defenders, one of whom is Filby himself who says of it: "It's a wonderfully martial air, and the poetry is not bad at all."

4

The war of 1812 ended with the signing of a peace treaty at Ghent, Belgium, in December 1814. Without knowing that the war was over, Andrew Jackson, veteran of Indian battles, successfully defended New Orleans on January 8, 1815 against an attack by a large British force in which the British were decimated by Jackson's crack riflemen. (Samuel Woodworth's "The Hunters of Kentucky" was an amusing commentary on that battle of New Orleans.) However anticlimactic, this victory made Jackson into a hero and it became his stepping-stone to the Presidency, with "The Hunters of Kentucky" serving as his campaign song.

The New Orleans victory was also celebrated in "The Eighth of January," a fiddle tune from the British Isles. A century and a half later, Jimmy Driftwood, a balladeer, wrote new words for this melody calling his song "The Battle of New Orleans." It became a resounding country and western hit in 1959 after being popularized by Johnny Horton in a Columbia recording.

Samuel Woodworth, who wrote the words to "The Hunters of Kentucky," and several other songs already referred to, was the most significant songwriter to come out of the War of 1812. The first important lyricist in American popular music, Woodworth was a man of varied literary gifts. He was born in Scituate, Massachusetts, in 1784, from where he went to Boston to learn the printer's trade. There he published verses in several newspapers and edited a journal for young people. In 1809 he made New York his permanent home. During the next two decades he engaged in several varied literary and journalistic endeavors. For one year, in 1823, he edited the New York *Mirror*. He edited other journals and newspapers as well, to which he often contributed his own writings. In addition he completed a novel (*The Champion of Freedom*, published in 1816) and several plays (*The Forest Rose*, in 1825, was the most successful). Despite his productivity, and occasional successes, he was reduced to such penury by 1828 that theatrical benefits had to be given to help support him and his family. In 1837 he was victimized by an apoplectic stroke which brought on paralysis. Completely incapacitated, he lingered on for another five years under the most pitiful circumstances, from which he was finally relieved by death on December 9, 1842. Today he is remembered solely for his song lyrics, of which the sentimental ballad, "The Old Oaken Bucket," is the most celebrated.

During the first decades of the nineteenth century, current events often served as material for popular songs. Michael Fortune wrote the words and music for "The Acquisition of Louisiana" in 1812. "Peace" from the *Everyday Songbook* of 1815 commented upon the prosperity of those times while "The Aristocracy of Democracy" and "Hard Times" touched upon the depression of 1837. When, in 1824, General Lafayette returned to visit America, G. Meineke wrote the music for "Lafayette's Welcome" and "The Chivalrous Knight of France," words by Samuel Woodworth and W. H. Hamilton respectively. W. W. Strickland wrote the words of "Come Honor the Brave" to honor Lafayette, setting it to the Scottish melody, "My Heart's in the Highlands."

In 1825 the Erie Canal was opened. For the momentous opening of the canal, Samuel Woodworth wrote "The Meeting of the Waters of Hudson and Erie." Far more familiar today are "The E-ri-e" and "Erie Canal" (or "Fifteen Years on the Erie Canal" or "Low Bridge, Everybody Down"), both by unidentified writers, and both latter-day compositions. "Erie Canal" was particularly popular with mule drivers dragging canal boats past inland towns.

Upon the completion of the construction of the Baltimore and Ohio Railroad in 1828, C. Meineke wrote "The Railroad," and John Godfrey Saxe described the delights of riding through forests and over bridges by rail in "The Railroad Chorus," dedicated to the Baltimore and Ohio.

5

During the post-Revolutionary War period, the musical theater offered plays with music, ballad operas, straight plays with interpolated songs and "burlesques."

Francis Hopkinson composed the first native American musical stage work boasting an amplitude of music—songs, duets, ensemble and orchestral numbers. He described his *The Temple of Minerva*, for which he wrote both text and music, as an "oratorial entertainment," but in essence it was a play overflowing with musical episodes. Hopkinson first published the text anonymously in *Freeman's Journal* in Philadelphia on December 19, 1791. Before the year was over, text with music was performed in Philadelphia in the presence of George Washington and his wife. *The Temple of Minerva* was an allegory in praise of the alliance between young America and France.

The next significant musical production in America was *Tammany*, given in New York in 1794, performed by Tammany Hall of that city to express anti-Federalist sentiments. This, too, was a political production. Mrs. Anne Julia Hatton's text used as its central character a Cherokee chieftain whose name was the title of the play. The music, made up of formal airs, ballads and ensemble numbers, was composed by James Hewitt.

Two years later two more musical productions were introduced, both of them in 1796, and both in New York. Benjamin Carr's *The Archers, or The Mountaineers of Switzerland* was performed on April 18; Victor Pellissier's *Edwin and Angelina*, on December 19. The libretto of the first was William Dunlap's adaptation of Schiller's *William Tell*, while that of the second (by Elihu Hubbard Smith) was based on a novel by Oliver Goldsmith.

Except for a few random pieces—such as the song, "Why, Huntress, Why?" from *The Archers*—none of these scores has survived. All four productions have been euphemistically termed "operas" by some historians, the earliest operas in America, but the truth is that none of these has either the dimensions or the artistic aspirations of grand opera. They should be designated as ballad operas. In any event, they were the ancestral beginnings of American operetta.

Another species of musical theater came into vogue in the early nineteenth century. These were broad travesties or caricatures of famous plays or performers known as "burlesques." Together with dialogue, burlesques stressed song, dance and pantomime. This species first evoked enthusiasm from the American public in 1828 when John Poole presented his burlesque treatment of Shakespeare's *Hamlet* in which he starred. A decade or so later, *La Mosquita* was a takeoff by William Mitchell of the celebrated Viennese ballet dancer, Fanny Elssler, in her famed interpretation of *Tarantella*.

A more bountiful source of popular song literature than that of the ballad opera or the burlesque was the spoken play with interpolated songs. Samuel Woodworth's "The Fortune I Crave," to the Irish melody of "The Cottage on the Moor," appeared in *The Deed of Gift*, produced in Boston in 1822. "The Harp of Love," words by Charles Powell Clinch to a traditional air, was heard in the stage adaptation of the then recently published novel by James Fenimore Cooper, *The Spy*, produced at the Park Theater in New York in 1822. Samuel Woodworth's "Love's Eyes," to the Scottish melody of "Roy's Wife," was included in *The Forest Rose*, given at the Chatham Theater in New York in 1825. "By the Margin of Fair Zurich's Waters," music by James Gaspard Maeder with the identity of the lyricist unknown, was used in *Beulah Spa*, mounted at the Bowery Theater in New York in 1834. Four years later. " 'Tis Home Wher'er the Heart Is," words by Robert Dale Owens to a traditional melody, was used in the tragedy *Pocahontas*, at Wallack's National Theater in New York.

Other stage media popularizing songs were concerts featuring singers appearing either individually or in groups, between-the-acts performers at stage productions, circuses and the variety-type entertainments then beginning to emerge throughout the States.

Henry Russell promoted his own songs and ballads at his song recitals, about which more will be said in a later chapter. Another English-born singer, Joseph Philip Knight, toured America in 1839. On October 9, in a New York recital, he introduced his newly written ballad, "Rocked in the Cradle of the Deep," words by Emma Willard, which became an immediate favorite with audiences and a staple in the repertory of basso profundos.

In the late eighteenth century, white performers with blackened faces began invading the stage with caricatures of Negro song and dance, in such popular numbers as the "Poor Black Boy" and "The Gay Negro Boy." In 1799, Gottlieb Graupner sang "The Gay Negro Boy" to his own accompaniment in *Oroonoko* at the Federal Street Theater in Boston.* Later, James Roberts, a highly regarded blackface performer, featured songs by Micah Hawkins in his act. Hawkins was one of the earliest creators of both humorous and serious Negro songs, though very little is known about him. Among the Hawkins songs featured by James Roberts were "Massa Georgee Washington and General Lafayette" and "Backside Albany" or "The Siege of Plattsburgh" which was written a year after the Battle of Lake Champlain in 1814 which had inspired it.

After the War of 1812, blackface performers lampooned black people in military uniforms. One such routine was "The Guinea Boy" in which a black boy is mustered into service by the British against his will.

Blackface entertainers appeared in circuses. One was George Nichols, a clown in Purdy Brown's Theater and Circus of the South and West. Nichols was most famous for the humorous song, "Clare de Kitchen" (or "De Kentucky Screamer"), whose melody he had adapted from a tune he had heard black firemen sing on the Mississippi. The text is made up of a series of unrelated nonsense verses about a strange conglomeration of animals, among them an old blind horse, a bullfrog wearing a soldier's uniform, and a whippoorwill whose sad destiny was to be eaten. By the time C. Bradlee published this number in Boston in 1835, it had become a standard in the repertory of blackface minstrels throughout the States.

In 1829, George Washington Dixon, one of the earliest blackface entertainers, introduced "The Coal Black Rose" at the Bowery Theater in New York. This song about the struggle between two men for a girl named Rose, was singled out by Foster Damon as "the first burnt-cork song of comic love." It was probably written by White Snyder—whose name appears on the sheet music issued by Maverick in 1829. During the next few decades, hardly a theater anywhere failed to feature it. Dixon had been performing blackface songs from 1827 when he made his first appearances in Albany, New York. Another song which he

---

*This is the same Graupner who made a mark in serious American music by founding a symphony orchestra in Boston early in the eighteenth century.

popularized—and which he insisted he wrote—was "My Long-Tail Blue," an early example of a comic song about a dandy. The sheet music cover shows a foppish black man dressed in swaggering tails and top hat, holding a cane delicately between the fingers of the left hand. The "long-tail blue" in the song title refers to the black man's Sunday dress, but, as the number goes on to explain, the fop is also the proud owner of another jacket which he wears the rest of the week.

Both George Washington Dixon and another highly successful blackface performer of this period, Bob Farrell, are each credited with the early success of "Zip Coon," first published by G. Willig in Baltimore in 1834, to become a classic of early minstrelsy. Dixon and Farrell each claimed to have written it, as did George Nichols. In any case, the melody appears to have been derived from an old Irish folk tune. "Zip Coon" refers to a Broadway fop who pretends to be a "larned skolar." Some of the lines are gibberish, one of which reads: "Sings possum up a gum tree, coony in a holler." As an instrumental number under the title of "Turkey in the Straw," "Zip Coon" has become one of the most famous pieces of square dance music.

The "Bonja Song," published between 1818 and 1821, with words in Negro dialect by R. C. Dallas, refers to an instrument, the *bonja*, a primitive gourd banjo used by black men to accompany their songs. The banjo evolved from the bonja to become one of the few instruments native to America, and the one with which the black man in popular music is most often associated. The transformation of the bonja into the banjo is believed to have taken place when Joel Walker Sweeney in or about 1830 devised this instrument by cutting a cheese box in half, covering it with skin, and stretching across its face five (later four) strings. The sheet music of "What Did You Cum From?", published by Firth and Hall in New York in 1840 and later popular with glee clubs and male quartets, shows a picture of Sweeney's banjo already with four strings; it also credits Sweeney with having sung it "with great applause at the Broadway circus." Another number with banjo accompaniment popularized by Sweeney was "Ole Tar River," published in 1840, some of whose catch phrases reappeared in several of Stephen Foster's ballads.

Thomas Dartmouth Rice (popularly known as "Daddy" Rice) was the crown prince of these early minstrels. He was born in New York City in 1808. Though trained to be a woodcarver he was already dedicated to the theater. After working as a handyman in a theater in Louisville, Kentucky, he made his debut as a blackface performer with a stock company in that city. He was often called upon to render blackface numbers between the acts of stage plays. He made several songs and routines famous: "Gumbo Chaff," which he wrote about a black Mississippi River boat hand; "Dandy Jim from Carolina," which had originally been written by S. S. Steele and J. Richard Myers for the minstrel, "Cool White"; Rice's own version of Nichols' "Clare de Kitchen"; "Sich a Gitting Upstairs," of unknown authorship; and "Long Time Ago," author also unknown, in which the short refrain "long time ago" is repeated after each line beginning with "Oh, I was born in ole Varginee." Rice featured "Long Time Ago" in his own musical production in 1833 which he described as an "Ethiopian opera." At that time, "Ethiopian" was a word often used as a synonym for blackface forms of entertainment and songs. Rice was a prolific writer of "Ethiopian operas," which in actuality were not operas at all but blackface farces or extravaganzas with Negro songs and dances.

The routine that made "Daddy" Rice a historic figure in American popular music, and the most celebrated blackface performer of his time, was "Jim Crow."

In 1818, while appearing in Baltimore (others say it was in Louisville), Rice happened to see an old deformed Negro employed nearby as a stable groom. The old man walked with a peculiar limp, moving his body with strange contortions. Something else about him attracted Rice's interest. As the groom ambled along with shuffling motions, he muttered to himself a ditty beginning with the lines: "Wheel about an' turn about and do jis so, an' ebry time I wheel about I jump Jim Crow."

This scene made such an impression on Rice that he decided to introduce the old slave's strange motions and gibberish chant into a new routine. At the same time Rice adopted an outlandish costume: an ill-fitting suit with patched trousers, a broad-brimmed hat worn at a rakish angle, unlaced shoes through the left sole of which the toe had worn its way. With right hand on hip, and left hand poised in midair, Rice sang the verse of his song with great deliberation:

> "Come listen all you gals and boys
> I'se just from Tuckyhoe,
> I'm goin' to sing a little song,
> My name's Jim Crow."

In the refrain, Rice performed a dance with distorted postures, a halting gait, and shuffling motions, accentuating the rhythm of his song with each movement and gesture:

> "Wheel about and turn about
> And do jis so.
> Ev'ry time I wheel about
> I jump Jim Crow."

At the words "jis so" he jumped high in the air, rolling his left hand roguishly at the audience.

This act caused such a furor of approbation that Rice retained it permanently in his act. When he made his New York debut at the Park Theater in 1833 he performed it during the intermission of two one-act plays. After that he invariably presented it wherever he appeared, including London in 1836. By then, blackface performers were doing Jim Crow routines of their own throughout America. In addition, all kinds of parodies were concocted touching on current events.

"Jim Crow" made history for the American popular stage as well as for American popular music. With it, the songs and routines of the black man became a fixture on the musical stage; the ground was prepared for the emergence of the minstrel show, just as a tradition had begun in American popular music exploiting Negroes and their musical and personal idiosyncrasies. At the same time, "Jim Crow" became permanently entrenched in the American language to designate the policy of discrimination or segregation against Negroes in employment and public places.

Rice's own fortunes were far less felicitous than those of the routine he so made famous. Stricken by paralysis in 1850 he endured poverty and loneliness as well as physical suffering. He died in 1860, following a second paralytic stroke.

3

America
Singing:
Some Early Folk Music

1

Folk music born from the womb of American backgrounds and experiences was still another area of popular music to get cultivated. From the dawn of American history, Americans sang of their aspirations, hardships, despair and tragedies. Inspired by forces far different from those producing the commercial popular song, these folk songs had an identity all their own. They followed the frontier, accompanied industry in its expansion, went out into the fields, mines and forests, aboard ships, and to the building of railroads. As American democracy grew to maturity, a rich and varied repertory of songs was accumulated, expressing and interpreting national growth and change. It was a repertory that initially was influenced by popular songs but which, in the end, exerted a profound impact upon them.

American folk songs were most frequently of foreign origin. Yet, by a subtle chemistry, these foreign melodies became American, transformed by American experiences. Just as the immigrant was to become American through his assimilation of American outlooks, conditions, and way of life; just as, more specifically, the language of England acquired new shadings, accents and inflections on its way towards becoming American, so the foreign song realized its own elements and traits as it passed from the lips of one generation of Americans to the next. Not only did the melody itself undergo change in mood and emotion but the structure of the song changed as well. Such changes made new songs out of old ones—new songs with their own identity and personality.

There were the songs of the streets, ancestors of present-day singing commercials. Since the early eighteenth century, vendors hawked their wares in the streets with personalized street cries. Some of these tunes, like the commodities they advertised, were passed on from seller to buyer. In Boston, in 1799, the street cry, "Come Buy My Woodenware" became a popular tune. Back in 1707, in New York, an attempt was made to forbid street singing by law, but to no avail. Merchants continued to peddle their wares in the streets with such cries as "Oysters, Sir," or "Buy a Broom," or "Any Razors or Scissors?" In Charleston, South Carolina, Negro hawkers strolled through the streets selling fish, vegetables or fruits; their cries became part and parcel of the song literature of those times. Even up to 1840, street cries were so prevalent throughout the States that the New York *Mirror* complained editorially "about tradesmen who make music enough everyday of the week to set every citizen's teeth on edge. . . . You cannot pass a pile of pine boxes without music, or dodge through a defile of empty brandy cakes, without encountering a concert." Less than a century later George Gershwin successfully simulated the street cries of Charleston peddlers in his opera, *Porgy and Bess*.

2

Lumbering had already become a major industry in New England at the turn of the eighteenth century; and in the nineteenth century it moved farther west. The lumberjacks, or shantymen, were a polyglot lot, comprising Scottish, Irish, German and French Canadians. "Into the woods flocked the adventurers. . . ." wrote James Cloyd Bowman in the Michigan *History Magazine*. "Many . . . were drawn into the camps by their love of hardy, out-of-door, roving life with men. Many others were recent emigrants, and came eagerly to try the first chance that fortune offered in the new land of opportunity. Some were natural 'floaters,' dominated . . . by an insatiable wanderlust. Occasionally, one proved a fugitive from justice and took to the friendly forest. And almost every nationality was represented."

Work was hard, beginning at four in the morning and continuing to sunset. Danger was omnipresent, and diversions were few and far between. A favorite form of entertainment for lumberjacks was to listen to minstrels sing songs and tell tall stories after the evening meal. The word "shantyman"—derived from the French word "chanter," meaning "to sing"—points up the significance of song in the life of these lumberjacks; so does the legend of George Burns. One evening, during the height of a blizzard, Burns staggered into a logging camp, frozen and half starved. When he recovered, he asked for food, offering to pay for it with songs. These made such an impression on the men that they insisted he stay with them all winter and entertain them every evening. Burns' shortcomings with an axe were more than compensated for by his gift for song invention. Burns was typical of the wandering minstrel who went from one logging camp to the next practicing his folk art.

The songs of the shantyman were usually about experiences close to him. "A Shantyman's Life" told of his rigid daily routine. "The Little Brown Bulls" spoke of his work on the river while "The Logger's Boast" and "Once More a-Lumb'ring Go" express his pride in his work. "The Jam on Gerry's Rocks" described a logjam, the dread of all lumberjacks. Sometimes the songs narrated stories of legendary lumberjacks. There was the mythical Paul Bunyan and his blue ox "Babe," who inspired a long line of tall tales. Bunyan scooped out the Grand Canyon by dragging his pick, and he worked in such freezing weather that his profanity froze into ice and did not thaw out until the following July. Then there were Jimmie Whalen and Johnny Stiles, actual shantymen, who both met tragic ends in a logjam.

The songs were filled with loneliness, bleakness, nostalgia for home, dreams of romance. Dramatic impact came through the free rhythms and the declamatory nature of the melody. Sometimes old English ballads, sailor chanteys, Negro spirituals or railroad songs were adapted for shantyman songs, but just as often the melody was original with the singers and had the same improvisational character as the lyric. Rough, brusque and masculine in spirit, the songs of the shantyman project emotions self-consciously. Many have the restrained sorrow of sad men too stout of heart to voice their inmost feelings. Poignancy is achieved through understatement. Occasionally, a rough-and-tumble humor is interposed. But whether in sorrow or joy, these songs are the voices of vigorous men leading robust lives, and they have the firm stride and the steellike muscle of such men.

3

The songs of the shantyman were generally concerned with his work, sung retrospectively when the day's labor was over. On the other hand, sailor songs—or chanteys, once again the word comes from "chanter"—were principally work songs sung during the performance of menial tasks.

America built ships that soon rivaled the best built by Europeans, as commerce and whaling were developed. New American ideas of shipbuilding created the Clipper, queen of the seas, unrivaled monarch of the waters until about 1850 when it was replaced by the steamboat.

The work of sailors was arduous; life was unspeakably difficult in the face of discipline often cruel to the point of sadistic. To lighten backbreaking tasks, and spirit-breaking experiences, sailors sang. As Richard Henry Dana noted in *Two Years Before the Mast:* "A song is as necessary to sailors as the fife and drum to soldiers."

As conditions aboard ships worsened in the early nineteenth century, the crew became more and more rugged, gruff and brutal. The men worked hard, drank hard, cursed hard, fought hard. The songs they improvised, invented or adapted had a fiber as tough as those who sang them.

The art of the chantey developed as maritime commerce expanded. The chantey told of the sailor's attitudes towards the sea, his ship, his work, his interests, his dreams, his bitterness, his frustrations. Chanteys became indispensible to the work at hand which had to be done by manpower. Without the precision of rhythmic movement provided by these songs, the men could hardly have achieved the kind of teamwork required for heaving and pulling. The men sang continually at work, and their singing was encouraged by their superior officers. Since these songs adopted the rhythmic pattern of the type of work being done, they were characterized by sharpness of beat and accent and cogency of rhythmic drive.

Chanteys fell into four categories. Songs for tasks requiring short heavy pulls on the bowline (or rope) were called "short drags" or "short hauls." Among them are "Haul Away, Joe" and "Haul the Bowline." Songs for more sustained and heavier tasks, such as hoisting topsails where a steady pull on the bowline is called for, were called "halliards." "Blow, Boys, Blow," "Blood Red Roses" and "Blow the Man Down" had a more even rhythm and meter than the short drag and a more mobile kind of melody. In "Blow the Man Down," the best known of these halliards, the word "blow" means "knock" and Paradise Street mentioned in the opening line was a red-light district. For still more monotonous jobs there were songs sung at the capstan or windlass and consequently identified as "capstans." A capstan is a wheel to which a chain cable is attached; anchors are raised or lowered by turning the capstan by means of bars inserted into it. Capstan chanteys had long sustained melodies with slow marchlike rhythms. In this category we find "A Drunken Sailor," "The Rio Grande," "One More Day" and "Shenandoah." The last is believed to have started out as a ballad about a trader wooing the daughter of an Indian chief whom he later deserts. The song was brought to the sea from lumber camps. In the chantey, the sailor speaks of courting Sally for seven years who rejected him because he was a "dirty sailor"; he finds solace in "drinkin' rum and chewin' terbaccer" as he is bound away " 'cross the wide Missouri." "Santy Anno," another famous halliard, is much later, dating from the Mexican War. It was first heard in southern ports sung by black longshoremen before boarding ship; it is also sometimes identified as "The Plains of Mexico."

Not all chanteys were work songs. There were the songs of the "fo'c'sle"—a contraction of forecastle—that part of the ship's upper deck forward where the crew lived and relaxed. These chanteys sought to entertain the off-duty crew. They are songs about ladies of easy virtue, carousals ashore, getting shanghaied, epics of whaling and fishing, ballads of war and naval heroes, nostalgic songs of love and home. "Blow Ye Winds" was a fo'c'sle ballad about whaling ships and their crews. "Rolling Home" expressed a yearning to return to "dear old England." "The Banks of Newfoundland" described the hardships of storms and gales. "Song of the Fishes" and "Boston, Come Ye All" were tunes about fishing. In "Home, Boys, Home" the sailor reminisces about Boston, "a fine town with ships in every bay."

Fo'c'sle songs were usually accompanied by an instrument—a violin, a harmonica or an accordion. But short drags, halliards and capstans—work songs all—were unaccompanied (a cappella). In each instance, whether songs of work or songs for relaxation, a leader would set the tempo and sing the introductory verses; the rest of the crew joined in the chorus. The leader was given latitude to improvise and embellish upon the solo part, and it was he who usually made up the original tunes or adapted remembered ones. Leaders were chosen for their pleasing voices, and since Irish and Negroes usually boasted good voices, they outnumbered other nationalities and races among these leaders. This is why the stylistic traits of Irish balladry and Negro spirituals predominate in so many chanteys. But other musical sources also provided a fund of melody: foreign and national ballads, songs of the shantyman and ditties from the stage.

4

During the seventeenth and eighteenth centuries, pioneer settlers penetrated the Appalachian and Cumberland mountains of West Virginia, Kentucky, Tennessee, the Carolinas and North Georgia. Due to the difficulty of access, these mountain settlers lived an existence quite distinct from that found on the eastern seaboard. Virtually until the dawn of the twentieth century, the life of these mountain folk was as primitive as it was isolated. Horseback and horse drawn wagons were the mode of transportation, over difficult trails and roads. Working the soil provided a livelihood. Homes were crudely built; lighting came from oil lamps, and the heat from an open fire. Furniture and cooking implements were rudimentary. The existence of these people was simple to the point of austerity. The barter system was the main medium of exchange. Most of these folk had little or no schooling. They spoke an archaic language which was passed on from one generation to the next. In those southern hills, from the late eighteenth century on, everybody sang. Few homes did not own some musical instrument, a fiddle, a dulcimer, a guitar or a banjo.

These mountain folk preserved a wonderful heritage of folklore, and they kept alive a remarkable library of folk songs, many of English or Scottish origin. Long unknown to the rest of America, this music was kept alive in the protection of the surrounding mountains. Then, in the second decade of the twentieth century, several musicologists visited this cloistered world to bring its folk songs out of their obscurity. Loraine Wyman and Howard Brockway published *Lonesome Tunes*; Josephine McGill, *Folksongs of the Kentucky Mountains*; and the most prestigious of all, Cecil Sharp of England edited several monumental collections of American mountain songs, including *English Folk Songs from the Southern Appalachians*, *American-English Folk Songs* and *Folk Songs of English Origin*. Thus, by the end of the decade, a good deal of attention was being focused on these mountain tunes by the world outside the Appalachians and the Cumberlands. One decade more saw further recognition and appreciation of these mountain tunes with the founding of the American Folk Festival (Mountain Dance and Folk Festival), in Asheville, North Carolina. It was first organized in 1928 by Bascom Lamar Lunsford, a fiddler, banjoist and folksinger who began collecting the folk music of the Southern hill country in the early 1920s. He founded the Mountain Dance and Folk Festival at Asheville as a yearly meeting place for devotees of folk music where they could meet, exchange experiences, and listen to each other's performances. Alan Lomax, John Jacob Niles and Carl Sandburg were on the original advisory board. This festival continued to thrive through the next four decades and more, attracting to it not only the foremost exponents of American folk songs but audiences numbering in excess of ten thousand come for this event from different parts of the country.

Some of the mountain songs came to be known as "lonesome tunes," partly because they touched so poignantly on the theme of loneliness, and partly because they were sung solo rather than chorally. "Down in the Valley" is a poignant love song given wide circulation as a popular song in the 1930s. In 1947, Kurt Weill used it in a one-act American folk opera which bore the title of the song. "Cindy" is also a love song, while "Old Smokey" and "Careless Love" are laments by one who has loved and lost. The Decca recording by The Weavers of "Old Smokey" (or "On Top of Old Smokey") sold over a million disks in 1951. "Careless Love" has such a blues quality that W. C. Handy, the king of the blues, adapted it into a commercial song published in Tin Pan Alley in 1921.

"Sourwood Mountain" is a light ditty that became popular at square dances. It has a nonsense refrain of "hey-de-iddle-um-day." A recurring nonsense line is found in the dialogue song, "Lolly Too-Dum": "lolly too-dum, too-dum, lolly too-dum day." Still another dialogue song, "Jennie Jenkins" lapses into nonsense. Here a young man asks his girl what she plans to wear. Red? No, she replies, red is a color she dreads. White? No, white is much too bright. Green? No, that "ain't fit to be seen." She rejects other colors as well with proper explanations. After each of her replies, Jennie ends with "I'll buy me a fol-di-roldy-tildy-toldy, seek-a-double, use-a-cause-a, roll-the-find-me," to which the man answers, "Roll, Jennie Jenkins, roll." Many variants exist of both these ballads.

Some mountain songs were religious, and therefore sometimes called "white spirituals." Of these, "Wayfaring Stranger" and "Wondrous Love" were heard often at camp meetings.

Variants of ballads of English derivation, such as "Barbara Allen," were also basic to this folk literature. Other ballads were exclusive to this mountain region. Some eulogized heroes actual or legendary: Daniel Boone, Mike Fink, David Crockett, Kit Carson. Others elaborated on the tragic fates of womenfolk, like that of "Pretty Polly" who was stabbed in the heart with a knife by Willie, or that of "Darlin' Corey" who killed "that revenue officer that took her man away with her forty-four" and who then was laid "in a lonesome graveyard ground."

5

The Western migration began during the Revolution and gained momentum after the war. An ever swelling army of pioneers crossed the Alleghenies to Iowa, Kansas, Missouri, Texas—and after that beyond, to Oregon and California. In 1788 almost a thousand boats carried 18,000 settlers down the Ohio, driven by the search for fertile soil or the hunger for fresh opportunities. This flow continued uninterruptedly in the nineteenth century.

The flight to the West inspired a wealth of folk music. The bullwhackers, driving their wagons, sang as they traveled. Prospective settlers dreaming of rich, verdant lands and a new life, translated these dreams into songs. Stouthearted pioneers who lived dangerously —always menaced by disease, Indians, animals, starvation—spoke of their hardships in word and melody.

A spirit of independence, love of freedom and equality affected the writing of folk songs. These men looked contemptuously upon the popular tunes of the Eastern seaboard—"Federalist tunes" was the term they used for these songs of an effete and snobbish people. In the East people sang about flirtations, fashions, politics, amusing pastimes, various diversions and current events. For his songs, the frontiersman chose subjects suitable for a common, democratic people. He had no sympathy with sentiment or sentimentality, for parlor pastimes or big-city temptations. The frontiersman brought to his own music a spirit that was proud and free, and he elaborated on themes closest to his everyday experiences. "Way Down Ohio" and "The Jolly Wagoner" told of his travels to the West. "To the West" was a fiery affirmation of his hopes and dreams in a brave new world; and so were "Whitestown" and "Liberty." "Shoot the Buffalo" described one of his favored outdoor activities; "Ground Hog," another. These and similar songs had a vitality and a manly vigor that would have been out of place in the stuffy atmosphere of Eastern homes and auditoriums. The pioneer was unafraid to be original in his musical thinking. The complex rhythmic patterns and accentuations of "The Star of Columbia" were different from the more formal processes of the popular songs of the Eastern urban areas.

The fiddle was the favorite instrument of the frontiersman. Bob Taylor, onetime Governor of Tennessee, wrote: "The fiddle, the rifle, the axe, and the Bible . . . were the trusty friends and faithful allies of our pioneer ancestry in subduing the wilderness and erecting the great commonwealth of the Republic." At their social gatherings, the pioneers would either play old tunes on their fiddles or spontaneously improvise new ones. These social gatherings included square dances and play parties, the latter initiated by the more religious members of the community as a modified substitute for dancing for the young folk. With involved gestures and steps the young people would sing and move to the melody and rhythm of "Here Comes Three Dukes," "Weevily Wheat," "Going to Jerusalem" and "Skip to My Lou."

Originally borrowed from many different sources (usually Irish reels and minstrel show tunes), the melodies of the frontiersman underwent a radical change of feeling, structure and style at the hands of the Western fiddlers. These melodies gained new figurations as the performer allowed his imagination to wander freely around a given tune. Men of strength and individuality had to express themselves in songs that were strong and free. Unorthodox intervals (usually successions of open fifths) would dramatize the lyric line. Rhythms would change abruptly. Before long, borrowed melodies came to be considered original homespun pioneer products and—truth to tell—they had become original in the hands of their performers.

There was primitivism in these social songs as well as in the pioneer's religious music, his "white spirituals." "The Promised Land" and "The Saint's Delight" were rugged, powerful, sometimes crude. There were no formal religious services on the frontier. The circuit rider would come to a settlement to conduct a revival meeting and lead the pioneers in the singing of hymns. Sometimes secular tunes were adapted for religious functions. Where new religious tunes were created they had the passionate and savage feelings often encountered in the pioneer secular song. During sacred worship, the melodies became almost barbaric as the pent-up emotions of the frontiersman found an outlet in religious ritual.

6

In the South, black people were creating a folk music of their own; a music the like of which could be heard nowhere else in the world; a music whose influence on commercial American popular music was decisive.

The first Africans, twenty in number, landed in Virginia aboard a Dutch man-of-war in 1619, just one year before the arrival of the *Mayflower*. Seven years later, eleven more Africans were brought to the colonies. With the arrival in Boston of the ship, *Desire*, in 1638, the slave trade began in New England. There, in 1641, the "body of liberties" laws were enacted giving tacit approval to the institution of slavery. By the early eighteenth century, there were about 75,000 slaves in the colonies; a century later this number swelled to a million.

The slaves brought with them from Africa a gift for expressing their feelings in melody and rhythm, and a flair for dancing. The blacks also imported from Africa various kinds of drums, and an instrument that in its ultimate evolution became the American banjo. Finally, they introduced into the music of the colonies stylistic traits indigenous to African music: syncopated beats, shifting accents, variety of rhythms, and the "call and answer" format of voodoo chants.

Africans frequently sang and danced during working hours. On slave ships bound for the New World, and later on the plantations in the colonies, Negroes were encouraged by their masters to sing, since music was felt to be an opiate dulling the sharp edge of rebellion. Transplanted into a new cruel world where he was despised and rejected, the Negro found solace in songs.

In the New World, the Negro came into contact for the first time with European melody and harmony. Before long, his music making tried to combine European idioms with African rhythms and musical approaches. Still one other powerful New World influence helped give Negro song its personality and character: Christianity. In religion, the Negro found an escape from his own miserable existence; in it he found the promise of a new life in the hereafter to compensate him for his ordeals on earth. And so he sang, "steal away to Jesus . . . I ain't got long to stay here . . . My Lord calls me, He calls me by thunder." The Negro began identifying himself with Christ who had been crucified.

To the Negro in the New World, religion and song often became one and the same. The religious songs of the Negro were sometimes "sorrow songs," the elegiac lamentations of an oppressed people. Often they were "Shouts," orgiastic outbursts of religious ecstasy.

The Negro spiritual employed some techniques that set it sharply apart from other kinds of American folk songs. Generally speaking, the spiritual was at times characterized by mobile changes from major to minor without the benefit of formal modulations; by freedom of rhythm and intonation; by its plangent moods; by the injection of notes, like the flatted third or seventh, foreign to the key; and by the variation of the metric pattern.

Unlike many other American folk songs, the spiritual was created not by an individual, but by groups; it was meant to be sung chorally, not solo. Consequently—almost unique in American folk music—the interest lies not only in the melody but in the harmony. Beyond this, the spiritual was not the creation of specially endowed ballad singers in the way so many of the tunes of the shantyman, sailor chanteys or the songs of the Western pioneers were. More often than not, the spiritual sprang from the heart of an entire race of people. It was born, it grew, it developed, it changed—and there was rarely evident any one identifiable hand in its evolution.

There were three classes of spirituals. One employs the call-and-answer technique found in African tribal song. Here one line is provocatively thrown out by a leader, and is answered by a repetitious word, phrase, or sentence by a group of voices. The tempo is fast, the melodies are spirited, the mood intense. In this class belong "Shout for Joy," "Joshua Fit the Battle of Jericho" and "The Great Camp Meeting."

A second type has a slower tempo, a statelier movement and greater majesty. It is mainly the songs in this group that have come to be known as "sorrow songs." A long sustained phrase is the core of the melody, as in "Deep River," "Steal Away to Jesus," "Nobody Knows De Trouble I've Seen," "Sometimes I Feel Like a Motherless Child," and "Swing Low, Sweet Chariot."

The third kind of spiritual consists of a highly syncopated melody made up of snatches of rhythmic patterns. Here we find "Little David Play on Your Harp" and "All God's Chillun Got Wings."

The most wonderful spirituals—not only for their emotional content but also for the variety of their melodic structure—are those that sprang from the black man's piety. Such a spiritual is the deeply moving "He's Got the Whole World In His Hands," commercialized in 1957 in a popular adaptation by Geoff Love and first successfully recorded in England by Laurie London before it was widely featured by American gospel singers. Religion fired the black man's imagination and set it aflame.

The Crucifixion was a subject close to the hearts of the Negro. When he sang of Christ on the Cross, as in "Crucifixion," he brought to his music the immense and shattering sorrow of one who knows the full meaning of rejection and suffering. Perhaps nothing more noble or moving has been spoken in folk music about the Crucifixion than spirituals like "Never Said a Mumblin' Word" or "Were You There When They Crucified My Lord?" (The pronoun "My" in the second spiritual is significant. To the Negro, Jesus was someone personal to whom he could speak his heavy heart openly, as if to a sympathetic friend, and receive solace.) In spirituals like these, the expression of sorrow is all the more poignant for its restraint and understatement.

The Old Testament also struck a personal note with the Negro, for in the captivity of Jews in Egypt there was a counterpart to slavery. "Let my people go," rings out firm and clear in "Go Down, Moses" because the Negro was here sounding a plea for his own emancipation. Negroes could not speak openly of freedom. But in the appropriate allegory of the Old Testament they could express their inmost hopes without fears of reprisal. "I am bound for the Promised Land," was as much a hope for escape to a place of liberation as it was an affirmation of religious belief in a future world. Frederick Douglass emphasized this point when he wrote: "A keen observer might have detected in our repeated singing of 'O Canaan, Sweet Canaan, I'm bound for the land of Canaan,' something more than a hope of reaching heaven. We meant to reach North, and North was our Canaan. . . . On our lips, it simply meant a speedy pilgrimage to a free state . . . and deliverance from all the evils of slavery."

While many spirituals possessed an awesome majesty, others like "The Old Time Religion" and "I Know the Lord Has Laid His Hand on Me" are rhythmic and passionate. Still others—the "Shouts"—were very closely related to African song. "Shouts" developed during religious services. What would start out with dignity and devotion would end up in mass hysteria. James Weldon Johnson vividly described one of these "Shouts" in *The Book of American Negro Spirituals*: "A space is cleared by moving the benches, and men and women arrange themselves, generally alternately in a ring, their bodies quite close. The music starts, and the ring begins to move. Around it goes, at first slowly, then with quickening force. Around and around it moves on shuffling feet that do not leave the floor, one foot beating with the heel in a decided accent in strict two-four time. The music is supplemented by the clapping of hands. As the ring goes around it begins to take on signs of frenzy. The music, starting perhaps with a spiritual, becomes a wild, monotonous chant. The same musical phrase is repeated over and over, one, two, three, four, five hours. The words become a repetition of an incoherent cry. The very monotony of sound and motion produces an ecstatic state. Women, screaming, fall to the ground, prone and quivering. Men, exhausted, drop out of the Shout. But the ring closes up and moves around and around."

These "ring Shouts" produced much spiritual music that is wild and febrile. Some of these "Shouts" were adaptations of familiar and stately spirituals become primitive and savage during the rite; other songs were improvised during the delirium of worship.

The first spiritual to appear in printed sheet music was "Roll, Jordan, Roll" published in Philadelphia in 1862. After that, a number of other spirituals were published until, in 1867, in Port Royal Island there appeared the first collection of Negro spirituals, *Slave Songs of the United States*, edited by William Francis Allen, Charles Pickard Ware, and Lucy McKin Garrison.

A scattered few of these publications trickled into the North. But before this happened, spirituals arrived by other paths. Passengers bound for the North on the Mississippi riverboats brought back with them the sounds of the strange new music the Negro was producing in the southland. Also, some Negro spirituals were introduced to the North by abolitionists who used them as propaganda at their rallies.

Not until 1871 did the spiritual first come into general popularity throughout the country. This was due to the efforts of "The Jubilee Singers," a group from Fisk University in Nashville, which in 1871 began touring the country in concerts devoted exclusively to Negro songs.

George L. White, treasurer of Fisk University, had been teaching his students to sing in groups. Before long he became convinced that the entire country, whites as well as blacks, would be interested in the poignant music of his race. He had another idea in mind as well. From the time of its founding in 1866 to provide education to liberated Negroes, Fisk University had been harassed by financial problems. Public concerts by the students might, he felt, provide a sadly needed source of revenue. The University authorities reluctantly gave White permission to form a choral group of nine students, but only on the condition that White himself defray all expenses. For two years, White trained this ensemble. On October 6, 1871, it left Nashville for its first tour. "North to Cincinnati they rode—four half-clothed black boys and five girl-women—led by a man with a cause and a purpose," wrote W. E. B. Du Bois. "They stopped at Wilberforce, the oldest of Negro schools, where a black bishop blessed them. They went, fighting cold and starvation, shut out of hotels, and scornfully sneered at, ever northward; and ever the magic of their song kept thrilling hearts, until a burst of applause at the Congregational council at Oberlin revealed them to the world. They came to New York and Henry Ward Beecher dared to welcome them, even though the metropolitan dailies sneered at these 'nigger minstrels.' "

As the tour progressed, and as the music became increasingly familiar, the audiences swelled in size and their enthusiasm mounted proportionately. The road was finally paved with unexpected triumphs. At the Gilmore Music Festival in Boston in 1872 an audience of some twenty thousand rose to its feet and shouted: "Jubilee Forever!"—"Jubilee songs" being the term antedating "spiritual." In 1878, when the Fisk Jubilee Singers returned to the University they brought back with them over $150,000 earned from concerts in the United States and Europe. This was testimony that the spiritual had captured the heart of the world.

The fame of the spiritual kept growing all the time. The New York music critic, Henry E. Krehbiel, spoke for its musical importance and won many converts. One of them was Antonín Dvořák, the distinguished Bohemian composer who had come to America in 1892 to become director of the National Conservatory of Music in New York. Dvořák became an avowed enthusiast of the spiritual. He wrote: "In the Negro melodies of America I discover all that is needed for a great and noble school of music. They are pathetic, tender, passionate, melancholy, solemn, religious, bold, merry, gay. . . . It is music that suits itself to any mood and purpose." Dvořák himself began to use authentic Negro material, or material simulating authentic Negro spirituals, in his serious compositions, notably in the *Symphony from the New World*. In the first movement there is a suggestion of "Swing Low, Sweet Chariot"; and in the second, we hear a famous melody that has the unmistakable character of an authentic spiritual, even though it was original with Dvořák. With words by William Arms Fisher, this beautiful melody was used for the song, "Goin' Home."

The black composer, Henry T. Burleigh, coming under Dvořák's influence, was encouraged by the master to make arrangements of many of the spirituals. This was still another potent factor in the popularization of Negro songs among music lovers. His arrangement of "Deep River," for example, was performed by the Flonzaley Quartet and by Fritz Kreisler, and was sung by Frances Alda—adding further confirmation to the general belief that the spiritual was well on its way towards artistic significance.

Not all Negro songs were spirituals. Negroes always made music for any and every situation in which they found themselves. They not only sang in worship, or in a lamentation over their sad destiny, but also in work and play.

Some Negro songs were born on the banks of the Mississippi. Laboring on the southern docks to load and unload cargo from riverboats, Negroes, known as "roustabouts," accompanied their tasks with songs. These lyrics and melodies were usually improvised. The words spoke of the work at hand and sometimes digressed to comment on the elegance of the riverboats, the personal idiosyncrasies of various boat captains, a love affair, a fight, or trouble with police. Sometimes the lyrics became nonsensical as in the following:

> "Ducks play cards and chickens drink wine
> And de monkey on de grape vine,
> Corn starch pudding and tapioca pie,
> Oh, de gray cat pick out de black cat's eye."

Elements of spirituals are found in some of these songs, particularly in their syncopated beats. But these songs also had a momentum and drive not generally found in other Negro songs. As the Negroes sang, they went through the physical motions of loading and unloading with a peculiar motion and gait: a slouching motion of the body and rhythmic movements of the hands synchronized with slow dancelike footwork.

It is impossible to exaggerate the influence of the Negro song on American popular music. The techniques and idioms, the moods and feelings, the personality and the idiosyncrasies of Negro songs formed the bone and marrow of American popular song expression. The songs and dances of the minstrel show, the ragtime of New Orleans, St. Louis and New York, the blues of St. Louis, the jazz of New Orleans, Chicago and New York, and the commercial melodies of Union Square and Tin Pan Alley—all these owe a profound debt to Negro folk music sources.

4

Mr. Tambo
And Mr. Bones:
The Minstrel Show

1

The minstrel show was the first indigenous form of American musical theater to be acclaimed in Europe.

In the economic depression of 1842, as one theater after another closed its doors, many actors specializing in blackface songs and routines were thrown out of work. Necessity compelled some performers to abandon solo acts and to combine in group performances, the better to compete for the few available bookings.

Among the first of these newly created blackface groups we meet up with was Dan Emmett. He may well be considered a founding father of the minstrel show. He was also the first major composer to come out of it.

The son of a blacksmith, Dan Emmett was born in Mt. Vernon, Ohio, on October 29, 1815. As a child he helped out in his father's blacksmith shop. At thirteen, Dan was apprenticed to a printer, after which he worked for a newspaper. All the while music was his prime interest. "As far back as I can remember," he once wrote, "I took great interest in music. I hummed familiar tunes, arranged words to sing to them, and made up tunes to suit words of my own." He learned by himself to play the violin and the flute. In 1834 he enlisted for three years in the Army by falsifying his age as twenty-one. At Newport Barracks in Kentucky he learned to play the drums, and at Jefferson Barracks in Missouri he was made leading fifer.

When the Army discovered that he had been only eighteen when he had enlisted, it discharged him on July 8, 1835. Emmett then embarked upon a career in show business. In the late 1830s he worked for a circus in Cincinnati for which he wrote his first Negro song, "Bill Crowder," writing just the words and taking his melody from "Daddy" Rice's tune then so much in vogue, "Gumbo Chaff." Bill Crowder, in the song, is a Negro in Cincinnati who becomes embroiled in a fight with a Jewish old-clothes man. When "Bill Crowder" was sung in the circus the performer was a blackface equestrian.

Emmett made his stage debut as a blackface performer with the Cincinnati Circus company by doing Negro impersonations, playing the banjo and singing. In the early 1840s he appeared not only with that company but also with Spalding's North American Circus. Then, in 1842, he formed an act with Frank Brower, a dancer, singer, and one of the earliest known stage performers on the bones. Sometimes together, and sometimes with a third partner, Brower and Emmett were seen in New York variety theaters until, like so many other performers at that time, they became victims of the mounting depression.

Emmett was then living in a boarding house on Catherine Street in New York. Billy Whitlock, a banjo player and singer, dropped in on Emmett one day to try out some numbers. Here is Whitlock's account of what happened. "When we had practiced two or three tunes, Frank Brower came in (by accident). He listened to our music, charmed to the soul. I told him to join us with the bones, which he did. Presently Dick Pelham came in (also by accident) and looked amazed. I asked him to procure a tambourine and make one of the party, and he went and got one. After practicing for a while, we went to the old resort of the circus crowd, The Branch in the Bowery, with our instruments, and in Bartlett's billiard parlor performed for the first time as the Virginia Minstrels."

A more formal debut for the Virginia Minstrels followed at the Bowery Amphitheater on February 6, 1843, where, for one week, the four minstrels presented a "Negro concert" as part of a circus show. The New York *Herald* announced their appearance: "First night of the novel, grotesque, original, and surprisingly melodious Ethiopian band, entitled the Virginia Minstrels, being an exclusively musical entertainment combining the banjo, violin, bone castanets, and tambourine, and entirely exempt from the vulgarities and other objectionable features which have hitherto characterized Negro extravaganzas." The four minstrels then strutted their stuff at several other theaters in New York. Then, on March 7, 1843, at the Masonic Temple in Boston, the four minstrels comprised for the first time a whole evening of entertainment. Their performance was labeled an "Ethiopian concert." Actually it was the first minstrel show ever produced.

"The novel feature of the Virginia Minstrels," says Gilbert Chase in his history of American music, "was the association of four entertainers in a coordinated team, dressed in distinctive costumes, each assigned a specific role in the ensemble, each playing a characteristic instrument and putting on a complete, self-sustained show."

The four men wore the costumes of Negro plantation workers. They were seated on the front of the stage in a semicircle, partly turned to the audience, and partly to each other. Dan Emmett, with his fiddle, and Whitlock, with his tambourine, were in the center. At either end were Pelham with a tambourine and Brower with the bones. In blackface, they played their instruments, sang, and indulged in humorous banter or in question-and-answer routines in Negro dialect. Frequently, between the verse and chorus of a musical number, two of the four men would indulge in an amusing verbal exchange. The evening began with an instrumental piece and ended with a parody written by Emmett in which he was featured as a banjoist.

The Virginia Minstrels became the first of these troupes to perform in England. In May 1843 they arrived in Liverpool where they gave two "Ethiopian concerts." Several appearances in Manchester then led to the London debut at the Adelphi Theater on June 19.

The enthusiasm of the English for this novel and esoteric form of stage entertainment kept mounting with successive performances.

By the time Emmett returned to America, in September 1844, the English public had been completely won over to the minstrel show. From then on, and for several more decades, leading American minstrel troupes found a warm welcome in English theaters. For the Virginia Minstrels, those English appearances were the final curtain. Emmett and Brower formed a new quartet of minstrels in America in 1844. After that, Emmett appeared in theater companies, circuses and several prominent minstrel companies.

2

When the Virginia Minstrels appeared at the Bowery Amphitheater on February 6, 1843, their program included two songs by Dan Emmett: "De Boatman's Dance," described as "a much admired song in imitation of Ohio boatmen," and "Old Dan Tucker," a "Virginian refrain in which the ups and downs of Negro life are described." Both were published in 1843.

"De Boatman's Dance" touched lightly on the carefree life of Ohio boatmen. For years after this number was first introduced it was featured by minstrel troupes in routines suggesting through body motions and gestures the movements of boatmen. As for "Old Dan Tucker"—Dan Emmett got the idea for this song from a ne'er-do-well acquaintance who was always getting into trouble—the title character was a hapless fellow who, in the chorus, is admonished to "get out de way." Not only did "Old Dan Tucker" forthwith become a fixture in the repertory of minstrels everywhere, but only a year after its publication it became, with new lyrics, the battle hymn of a group of New York farmers in their revolt against feudal conditions. A few years later, the song was adopted to abolitionist verses propagandizing emancipation. In time it was parodied for several Presidential campaigns: in "Clay and Frelinghuysen," "Polk, Dallas and Texas," "Get Off the Track," "Old Zack Upon the Track," "Clear the Track for General Weaver," and "Get Out of the Way, You Old Grand Party." It also became a favorite at square dances.

The year 1843 also witnessed the first performance and publication of Emmett's "My Old Aunt Sally," a sententious Negro ballad. More popular is "De Blue Tail Fly" in 1846, today frequently named "Jim Crack Corn." The alternate title is credited to the present-day folksinger, Burl Ives, who explained in an interview: "The lyrics of Dan Emmett was 'Give me cracked corn and I won't care.' Cracked corn was a field corn that cracked when you heated it. That didn't mean much so I changed it to Jimmy Crack Corn—the Gimme to Jimmy. It still doesn't mean anything. It's a nonsense syllable."

And then there is Dan Emmett's classic, "Dixie," in 1859. Emmett wrote "Dixie" for the Bryant's Minstrels, a company of twelve performers which had been formed in February 1858 and which he joined either in October or November of the same year. His obligations with that company were to perform on several instruments, sing, appear in comedy sketches, and write the words and music for "walk arounds," the "walk around" being an effective finale with which the programs of the Bryant's Minstrels always ended. The whole company was involved in these "walk arounds," a routine which Hans Nathan described in *Dan Emmett and the Rise of Early Negro Minstrelsy:* "Near the footlights were a few comedians who became active during the first part of the walk around. They alternately stepped forth and sang a stanza, interrupted by brief, pithy passages of the entire group. Then everyone on the stage sounded the final chorus which followed immediately, and to the concluding instrumental music, the solo performers began to dance in a circle with boisterous and grotesque steps and rowdy gestures. They were probably joined by the rest of the company in the background, who had previously furnished the percussive accompaniment by clapping their hands—sometimes together over their heads . . . or sometimes on their knees . . . and stamping the floor."

Emmett wrote "Dixie" to serve such a walk around. "One Saturday night in 1859," as Emmett himself later recalled, "as I was leaving Bryant's theater where I was playing, Bryant called after me. 'I want a walk around for Monday, Dan.' The next day it rained and I stayed indoors. At first, when I went at the song I couldn't get anything. But a line, 'I wish I was in Dixie,' kept repeating itself in my mind, and I finally took it for a start. Suddenly I jumped up and sat down at the table to work. When my wife returned I sang it to her. 'It's all about finished now, except the name. What shall I call it?' 'Why, call it, "I Wish I Was in Dixie Land" ' she said. And so it was." Emmett was also quoted as having said that the idea for the song first came to him when his wife complained about the Northern winter weather and remarked to him plaintively, "I wish I was in Dixie."

Emmett probably heard the word "Dixie" during his travels in the South where, even long before the Civil War, it served as a synonym for the southland. Various explanations have been offered for the origin of the word. Some maintain it is a convenient contraction of "Mason and Dixon line." Others recall that "dixie" was often used in Louisiana to refer to a ten-dollar bill—the French word "dix" meaning "ten."

Emmett's "Dixie" was first presented by Bryant's Minstrel at Mechanics Hall, then a permanent home for minstrel shows, on April 4, 1859. "It made a tremendous hit," Emmett said, "and before the end of the week everybody in New York was whistling it." The authorized publication of words and music, using as its title "I Wish I Was in Dixie's Land," appeared in 1860 with the imprint of Firth, Pond and Company. Pirated editions of the lyrics were extensively distributed on broadsides, and many another publisher released sheet music of both the words and music without any payment to author or copyright owner. All kinds of parodies were circulated.

After the song had become a stock-in-trade for minstrel companies throughout the North, it invaded the South where at first it was parodied as an anti-Lincoln song during the Presidential campaign of 1860 ("That's The Way We'll Fix 'Em"). Before the end of 1860, the original version of the song was used by the Rumsey and Newcomb Minstrels in Charleston, South Carolina, and was featured by W. H. Peters, a popular singer; a year later the melody was used as march music for Zouaves in a spectacle, *Pocahontas*, produced in New Orleans. Meanwhile, in 1860, a New Orleans publisher issued a pirated edition of words and music on which a J. Newcomb was identified as lyricist and J. C. Viereck as composer. Only after the owner of the copyright—Firth, Pond and Company—raised vehement objections did the New Orleans publisher acknowledge Emmett as the lyricist-composer.

By 1861, a New York newspaperman could say with justification that "this lively tune has become in our city as popular as the most refreshing airs of any operatic compositions." The New York *Clipper* called "Dixie" one of the "most popular compositions ever produced." But Emmett himself profited little from such success and acclaim. He had sold the publishing rights outright to Firth, Pond and Company for one hundred dollars in 1861, and the company purchased from Emmett all other rights for an additional three hundred dollars.

During the Civil War, "Dixie"—once again with new words—became the favorite war song of the South. Its importance now acquired new dimensions which is touched upon when the subject of Civil War songs is discussed.

The writing of "Dixie" represented the high point of Emmett's career both as a composer and as a performer in minstrel shows. His popularity went into a sharp decline after he left Bryant's Minstrels in July 1866. In or about 1867 he lost his voice and tried earning his living by playing the violin in Chicago. Between 1872 and 1874 he owned and managed a saloon but he did not altogether abandon the stage. At the second of two variety performances given for his benefit in 1880 he brought down the house by playing "Dixie" on the violin. Between 1881 and 1882 he worked for Leavitt's Minstrels which toured the eastern states, the South, the Middle West and Canada. According to Leavitt, Emmett received "a tumult of cheers as a great hero and as an exponent of Southern sentiment."

In 1888 he went into retirement in his native city of Mt. Vernon, Ohio, from which he emerged briefly in 1895 to tour with Al G. Field's minstrel company. Then eighty years old, Emmett inspired wild enthusiasm each time he played and sang "Dixie." When the tour ended in Ireton, Ohio, in 1895, Emmett returned to Mt. Vernon to resume his retirement. He died there on June 28, 1904.

3

The success of the Virginia Minstrels inspired other blackface performers to emulate them. Rival companies sprang up all over the country, often with songs and routines borrowed from the Virginia Minstrels. There were the Kentucky Minstrels, the Ethiopian Minstrels, the Congo Minstrels, the Sable Harmonists, the Campbell Minstrels. And then there was the greatest minstrel of them all, E. P. Christy, founder and guiding genius of Christy's Minstrels.

If the Virginia Minstrels offered the bare skeleton of a minstrel show, Christy's Minstrels endowed it with muscles, sinews and flesh, developing the physiognomy by which the minstrel show would henceforth be identified.

Edwin P. Christy was born in Philadelphia in 1815. His first appearances as a blackface performer took place in Buffalo, New York, when he was twenty-seven. There he appeared with four (later six) performers who called themselves "Christy's Original Band of Virginia Minstrels." With this name Christy was trying to steal for himself and his players some of the limelight already focused on the Virginia Minstrels while trying to pass off the legend that it was he who was the originator of this form of entertainment.

In 1843, Christy introduced the song "Farewell, Ladies," which even today is played or sung to announce the conclusion of an evening's activities under the title of "Goodnight, Ladies." The published sheet music in 1847 acknowledged Christy as author of words and music. The second part of "Farewell, Ladies" or "Goodnight, Ladies"—beginning with the words "Merrily We Roll Along"—was appropriated for the popular children's poem, "Mary Had a Little Lamb" in 1868 in H. R. White's *Carmina Collegensia*. The poem had been written almost forty years earlier by Sarah J. Hale and had received its first publication in the Boston magazine *Juvenile Miscellany* in September 1830. As a song completely independent of "Goodnight, Ladies," "Merrily We Roll Along" was published in 1867.

With an enlarged troupe, Christy's Minstrels appeared for the first time in New York at Palmo's Opera House on April 27, 1846. During the next six years, the company gave about five hundred performances in New York, many of them at Mechanic's Hall, besides appearing with enormous success in England. In that time, Christy's Minstrels formalized the routines, established the format, and refined the basic techniques of the minstrel show. As finally crystallized by Christy, the pattern of the minstrel show was adopted by all subsequent troupes.

The Christy minstrels would file on the stage dressed in frock coats (large flowers in lapels), striped trousers, calico shirts, high silk hats and white gloves. All their faces were blackened with burnt cork. From Christy would come the summons that became the traditional opening of minstrel shows: "Gentlemen, be seated!" At a resounding chord from the instruments the minstrels would seat themselves in a semicircle facing the audience. Mr. Interlocuter (played by Christy) sat in the middle. He was the go-between for the two end men at the opposite extremes of the seated row: Mr. Tambo (who banged on a tambourine) and Mr. Bones (who rattled the bones). Mr. Interlocuter asked questions to which either Mr. Tambo or Mr. Bones would respond with puns, double entendres or other amusing responses. A typical exchange:

> Mr. Bones: Mr. Interlocuter!
> Interlocuter: What is it Mr. Bones?
> Mr. Bones: Why does a chicken cross the street at night?
> Interlocuter: Why *does* a chicken cross the street at night?
> Mr. Bones: Why, to get to the other side!

After such a response Mr. Bones would rattle the bones while the other minstrels exploded into loud guffaws.

There were three parts to an evening's entertainment. The first consisted of variety entertainment, or to use a term technical with minstrel shows, the "olio." Here would take place the light banter between Mr. Interlocuter and either Mr. Tambo or Mr. Bones. In between this exchange of gay repartee there would be presented solo songs accompanied on the banjo (now become the basic instrument of the minstrel show), choral numbers and dances.

The second part was called "fantasia." This was a free-for-all, without any set form, in which individual performers were given an opportunity to strut their stuff. The conclusion burlesqued some of the activities and procedures of the first two parts.

Following Christy's lead, minstrel troupes began presenting their shows in the style and format of Christy's Minstrels. Some of these were headed by Cool White (John Hodges), considered one of the most renowned minstrels after only Christy himself. White was involved with the Virginia Serenaders, the Ethiopian Minstrels and the New Minstrels. Other highly esteemed groups in the Christy style were the Harrington Minstrels, organized in or about 1848, the Ordway Minstrels who appeared in 1850, and the Bryant's Minstrels founded in 1858.

Ed Christy went into retirement in 1854, a man of considerable wealth. His company was taken over by George N. Harrington who assumed the name of Christy. Christy's Minstrels continued to prosper for a number of years, but its founder, Ed Christy, unhappily succumbed to occasional seizures of insanity. During one spell he met his death by jumping out of a second-story window of his New York apartment on May 21, 1862.

4

The history of the minstrel show in general, and Christy's Minstrels in particular, is interlocked with the career of one of America's greatest composers, and the supreme creator of Negro songs, Stephen Foster.

Foster was not a trained musician. His knowledge of musical technique was perfunctory, his use of harmony elementary, consisting of little more than basic chords. He lacked self-criticism to a point where he could write a potboiler and a song masterpiece, almost with alternate strokes of the pen, often incapable of accurately evaluating the merits of either. But he was born with the gift of melody. He might have said, as Goethe's minstrel did, "I sing as the bird sings." For him melody was a natural and spontaneous expression.

When inspired, Foster produced beautiful lyricism with facility, simplicity and spontaneity. His lyricism has never failed to touch hearts and stir sentiments. Foster's best songs remain to this day one of the proudest legacies of our musical heritage.

He was a voice of his times. When he wrote his songs, the Negro question was disturbing the conscience of the North. This is why the minstrel show grew so popular there so quickly. By finding amusement in blackface performers, by listening to sentimental songs about the South, by watching Negro dances, Northern audiences found a safety valve for the release of passions aroused by the issue of slavery. Foster's song classics—like the stage medium in which they were heard—reflect Northern sentimental responses to the "Negro question."

If he was a voice of his times, Foster was also their victim. His was a period of enormous economic and industrial expansion. Money-making was the greatest virtue, the single measure of success. In this scheme of things, the making of music was consigned to young ladies who had no better way to spend their time. It was hardly to be expected that young Stephen Foster would be encouraged to develop his unmistakable talent. His father, Colonel William Barclay Foster, was a pioneer who had settled near Pittsburgh when it was a border settlement. He had acquired position and money through his industry and shrewdness as a trader. He believed that the country belonged only to men unafraid to work, and who had the brains and initiative to exploit rich commercial opportunities. Consequently, he had little sympathy for culture, art or book learning, and he did not look sympathetically on his son's musical strivings.

Nor was this an age to give just rewards to a creative artist. Compared to the popular composers of a later decade, Foster earned a pittance. His royalties amounted to about $1,000 a year for eight years; he sold some of his songs outright for as little as $15.00. He was usually in debt, nearly always living on advances from his published or still unpublished (and at times unwritten) songs. Just before his death he was a hopeless alcoholic, living alone in miserable poverty in New York's Bowery.

Stephen Foster was born in Lawrenceville, near Pittsburgh, on July 4, 1826. An early musical influence was the religious songs of the Negro. Stephen was only seven when he was taken by his household slave to a Negro church. The shouts and spirituals he heard there were so indelibly impressed on his young mind that many years later he used some of these melodies in two songs. "Hard Times Come Again No More" and "Oh, Boys, Carry Me 'Long." He was an exceptionally gifted child and tried to satisfy his musical yearnings by playing any instrument that came within reach: a drum, a guitar, a flageolet. At nine, he entertained his little friends by imitating blackface performers in such songs and routines as "Jim Crow" and "The Coal Black Rose."

For his academic education he was sent in 1840 to the Towanda Academy, and later the same year to the Athens Academy at Tioga Point, both in Pennsylvania. To put it mildly, he was no scholar. It was during this period that he set down on paper his first piece of music, "The Tioga Waltz," possibly written for the commencement exercises at the Athens Academy or more probably for a school exhibit at the Tioga Point Church where it was performed on April 1, 1841.

In 1841, he transferred to still a third school in Pennsylvania, the Jefferson College at Canonsburg, where he stayed just one week. "I must regret," wrote father Foster to his brother, "that Stephen has not been able to avail himself of the advantages of a college education. . . . His leisure hours are all devoted to music, for which he possesses a strange talent."

By the fall of 1841, Stephen Foster was through with all schooling, and for a time he concentrated on music. In or about 1842 he wrote "Open Thy Lattice, Love," a love song that became his first publication. The lyrics, by George P. Morris, had been published in a New York newspaper and had previously been set to music by Joseph Philip Knight. George Willig of Philadelphia published Foster's song in December 1844. Ironically, on the title sheet his name is printed erroneously as "L. C. Foster"—an omen of a life and a career never destined to go quite right. "Open Thy Lattice, Love" is a graceful, pleasant, somewhat sentimental melody, hardly original, and giving small indication of the composer's soon-to-bloom lyric powers. Other songs followed, some written for a club of young men that met twice weekly at Foster's home and whose meetings were enlivened with the singing of songs. Foster wrote a few of these—this time to his own lyrics, a custom he continued later with all of his masterpieces—in the style of popular tunes then heard so often in minstrel shows. One was "Lou'siana Belle," another, "Oh! Susanna," a third, "Old Uncle Ned."

Foster tried to interest the minstrel, "Daddy" Rice, in using some of his songs, but at that time Rice preferred featuring his own numbers. But the Sable Harmonists did include some of Foster's early songs in their productions, and so did other minstrel troupes. And it was in the minstrel show that both "Oh! Susanna" and "Old Uncle Ned" were first successful. "Oh! Susanna," a novelty song with banjo accompaniment, represents an excursion into humor and nonsense. "Old Uncle Ned" is important among Foster's songs as being his first about the Negro. Uncle Ned was an old black man who lays down his shovel and hoe to leave for the place "where all good darkies go."

An important publisher, W. C. Peters, became interested in Foster. In 1847, he published "Lou'siana Belle," and in 1848 both "Old Uncle Ned" and "Oh! Susanna." However, unauthorized printings of "Old Uncle Ned" and "Oh! Susanna" in New York preceded the Peters publications by several months. Foster received no payment from Peters for either "Lou'siana Belle" or "Old Uncle Ned"—beyond some free copies of the sheet music. But Peters did pay one hundred dollars for "Oh! Susanna."

Since a career in music was not yet to be considered seriously, Stephen Foster found employment as a bookkeeper in his brother's commission house in Cincinnati late in 1846 or early in 1847. Here he came in contact with the work songs of Negroes loading and unloading Mississippi River boats. Like the religious chants he had heard in childhood, they became an unforgettable memory.

By 1850, Foster seems to have realized that he was no more suited for the business world than for the academic. He returned to Pittsburgh to devote himself entirely to songwriting. His hopes for the future were bolstered by a new affiliation with the powerful New York publisher, Firth, Pond and Company. His first two songs released by this house were "Nelly Was a Lady" and "My Brudder Gum," for which Foster's only payment was fifty free copies of the sheet music. But, in recognition of Foster's potential, Firth, Pond and Company then arranged to pay him a royalty of two cents a copy. The first song appearing under this new arrangement was "Dolcy Jones," which earned Foster a little over twenty dollars. But with subsequent publications sales increased, and in time Foster was insured some kind of annual income from his songs, even though a modest one.

Foster's first major compositions for Firth, Pond and Company were published in 1850. They were "De Camptown Races" (originally called "Gwine to Run All Night") and "Nelly Bly," both further exercises in the writing of nonsense songs. On February 23, 1850, Foster made a bid for Ed Christy's support by offering him "De Camptown Races." "I wish to unite with you in every effort to encourage a taste for this style of music so cried down by opera managers," Foster wrote him. But even before Foster contacted Christy, the minstrel had already been using some of his songs. When the pirated New York edition of "Oh! Susanna" appeared it was described on the title page as "music of the Original Christy Minstrels" because they had sung it with outstanding success. Several publications of Firth,

Pond and Company in 1850 noted that these were Foster's "Ethiopian or Plantation melodies as sung by the Christy Minstrels."

In response to Foster's request, Ed Christy used "De Camptown Races" early in 1850, and several more Foster numbers after that. Christy always paid a pittance for the privilege of performing a song before its publication—ten dollars, for example, for "Oh, Boys, Carry Me 'Long."

It was for Ed Christy that Foster wrote his greatest Negro ballads (the words as well as the music). Christy not only introduced them but passed some of them off as his own compositions. The first was Foster's masterpiece, "The Old Folks at Home" (or "Swanee River").

When he wrote "The Old Folks at Home" Foster had no intention of getting sentimental over the Suwanee River in Florida. It is doubtful that he was even aware of its existence. His original choice was Pedee River, but he soon came to the conclusion that this name was not euphonious. Needing a two-syllable name he began hunting through a map. Thus he came upon the three-syllable Suwanee River, whose source was in Fargo, Georgia, and which coursed into North Florida. The word "Suwanee"—which Foster contracted into two syllables as "Swanee"—had a melodious ring to it, and for this reason he chose an obscure little river for his song.

He sent his manuscript to Christy who is believed to have paid him a flat sum of either fifteen or twenty-five dollars for permission to perform it and to use his own name as composer on the published sheet music. It is interesting that the reason Foster agreed to this peculiar arrangement was not for the fee but because he felt that his Negro—or "Ethiopian"—songs were inferior to his sentimental ballads, and he did not like having his name associated with what he regarded as a mere potboiler. As he wrote to Christy: "I had the intention of omitting my name on my Ethiopian songs, owing to the prejudice against them by some, which might injure my reputation as a writer of another style of music." But apparently he regretted this decision, for six months after "The Old Folks at Home" had been published under Christy's name, he wrote to Christy: "I find that by my efforts I have done a great deal to build up a taste for Ethiopian songs among refined people. . . . Therefore, I have concluded to reinstate my name on my songs and to pursue the Ethiopian business without fear or shame and lend all my energies to making the business live, at the same time I will wish to establish my name as the best Ethiopian songwriter." The money Christy paid him was not all Foster earned from his masterpiece. He was also getting royalties from the publisher, which within six months amounted to about $1,500, and in time earned him well over $2,500.

"The Old Folks at Home," introduced by Christy in 1851, was such an immediate success that in less than a year after its appearance it was, according to the Albany State Register, "on everybody's tongue, and consequently in everybody's mouth. Pianos and guitars groan with it, night and day; sentimental young ladies sing it; sentimental young gentlemen warble it in midnight serenades; volatile young bucks hum it in the midst of their business and pleasures; boatmen roar it out stentorially at all times; all the bands play it; amateur flute players agonize over it every spare moment; the street organs grind it out at every hour; and singing stars carol it on the theatrical boards and at concerts; the chambermaid sweeps and dusts to the measured cadence of 'The Old Folks at Home'; the butcher boy treats you to a strain or two of it as he hands in his steaks for dinner; the milkman mixes it up strangely with harsh ding-dong accompaniment of his tireless bell; there is not a 'live darkey,' young or old, but can whistle, sing or play it."

As was customary at that time, other minstrel troupes took their cue from Christy by featuring "The Old Folks at Home" prominently in their own repertories. The sale of sheet music swelled from the impressive figure of 40,000 copies the first year to 130,000 by 1854. "The publishers keep two presses running on it, and sometimes three; yet they cannot supply the demand." So reported *The Musical World*. Imitations or parodies of the ballad further attested to its enormous popularity— songs such as "Young Folks at Home," "The Old Folks Are Gone," and "Home Ain't What It Used to Be." The total number of sheet music sales of "The Old Folks at Home" from 1851 to the present time is reputed to be over twenty million copies placing it among a small handful of top-selling sheet music of all time.

Between 1852 and 1853, Foster continued to establish himself as "the best Ethiopian writer." Three gems appeared in that time: "Massa's in De Cold Ground" in 1852 and "Old Dog Tray" and "My Old Kentucky Home" in 1853. Christy paid Foster ten dollars for the prepublication performing rights for each of these songs and helped to launch them. All of these songs, in fact every Negro song Foster published after 1852, carried Foster's name on the title page of the sheet music. "Massa's in De Cold Ground" sold 75,000 copies within a short period of time, "Old Dog Tray," 48,000 copies, and "My Old Kentucky Home," 50,000 copies.

The writing of "My Old Kentucky Home" came about as a result of Foster's first visit to the South. In 1852 he came to Federal Home, a mansion near Bardstown, the Kentucky home of one of Foster's relatives. This gracious and stately pillared house was the abode Foster had in mind when he wrote his song classic. But it is not true, as is stated on the memorial tablet in the front hall of the mansion (since become a museum), that Foster wrote the song at Federal Home.

While Foster was writing his best songs, the skein of his private life had become tangled. On July 22, 1850, he married Jane Denny McDowell, who four years later inspired him to write the ballad, "Jeanie With the Light Brown Hair." On April 18, 1852, they had a daughter, Marion. But Foster chafed under the restraints of domesticity, and he and his wife were worlds apart in outlook and personality. She cared nothing about music, objected to his association with minstrels and the musical stage, and stood in horror of his pronounced predilection for alcohol. She had little sympathy for her husband's musical ambitions, and was impatient with his frequent flights into fancies and dreams. She nagged him continually to give up songwriting and settle down to some honorable and well-paying business. She was totally incapable of realizing that a lark can neither be kept from singing nor confined permanently to the ground.

Foster wrote his last great Negro song, and his only one in Negro dialect, in 1860, inspired by a slave belonging to his wife's household. It was "Old Black Joe." From 1860 on, Foster devoted himself primarily to sentimental balladry, with songs like "Poor Drooping Maiden," "Under the Willow She's Sleeping," and "Beautiful Dreamer," the last completed in 1864 just a few days before his death. In these the flame of melodic genius flickered only infrequently. It was at about this time, too, that he left Pittsburgh to settle in New York with his family, possibly to negotiate a new contract with his publishers. Here his physical and moral disintegration was rapid. He took more and more to writing potboilers for a pittance, and they were failures. His popularity, which once had made him a household word, had completely dissipated. As an escape from his mental anguish, from frustrations and disappointments, he turned more than ever to the bottle. He fluctuated between inebriation, which often left him in a stupor, and penitence, in which he groped for any and every remedy that might liberate him from his vice. Finally, his family returned to Pittsburgh while Foster lived in squalor and misery in a sordid room on the Bowery, a man broken in spirit and health.

"In January of 1864," recalled Foster's brother, "he was taken with ague and fever. After two or three days, he arose and while washing himself he fainted and fell across the wash basin, which broke and cut a gash in his neck and face. He lay there insensible and bleeding until discovered by the chambermaid who was bringing the towels he had asked for to the room. She called for assistance and he was placed in bed again. On recovering his senses he asked that he be sent to a hospital. He was so much weakened by fever and loss of blood that he did not rally."

The poet, George Cooper—to whose lyrics Foster wrote some eighteen songs in 1863—gives a slightly different version. Cooper maintained that it was he, and not the chambermaid, who found Foster naked and bleeding on the floor of his hotel room; that it was he who called in the doctor who sewed up the gash in Foster's throat; and that it was he and the doctor who helped get Foster to the hospital.

Foster died in Bellevue Hospital in New York on January 13, 1864. After his death a sadly worn purse containing three pennies and thirty-five cents in scrip were found in a pocket of his frayed suit, together with a slip of paper on which were scrawled the words "dear friends and gentle heart," probably the title of a song he did not live to write.

5

During the first quarter of the nineteenth century, the minstrel show enriched American popular music with still remembered numbers in addition to the treasured contributions of Dan Emmett and Stephen Foster. Many of these minstrel show songs, while becoming the property of minstrels everywhere, are identified with individual performers or companies.

Cool White was the composer of "Lubly Fan" ("Will You Come Out Tonight?") which he introduced with the Virginia Minstrels in 1844. When Christy's Minstrels offered it a few years later the song was called "Bowery Gals," and it was then sung by the Ethiopian Serenaders as "Buffalo Gals." It soon became a practice among various troupes to change the locale in the song title to the name of the place where it was being performed—hence "Louisiana Gals," and "Pittsburgh Gals" and so forth. In 1940, Terry Shand, Jimmy Eaton and Mickey Leader adapted this minstrel tune for "Dance with a Dolly," which was made into a substantial hit by Russ Morgan and his orchestra in a Decca recording.

To George Christy and Wood's Minstrels goes the credit for popularizing "Keemo Kimo," a nonsense song of 1854. Nobody knows who wrote this frivolous little item about a frog who lived in a pool. There is some suspicion that Ed Christy may have been its author, though the first publication mentions only an arranger—a certain Sedgwick. However, there are some who maintain it is an adaptation of an old English folk song, "Froggy Went A-Courting." In the chorus the song descends to outright absurdity:

> "Keemo ki'mo! Dar! Oh whar?
> Wid my hi, my ho, and in come Sally singing
> Sometimes penny winkle, lingtum, nip-cat—
> Sing song Kitty can't you ki'me oh!"

While Foster wrote two "Nelly" songs popular in minstrel shows ("Nelly Bly" and "Nelly Was a Lady"), the most popular "Nelly" song to come out of minstrel shows was Benjamin Russell Handby's "Darling Nelly Gray" in 1856. This was a tearful tale of woe about a black slave girl torn from the arms of her lover to be returned to slavery in Kentucky.

During the Civil War and Reconstruction, the minstrel show continued to pave the way to success for many a song. Dave Reed, who first appeared as a minstrel on the

Mississippi steamboats before joining Bryant's Minstrels in 1863, made famous the Negro dialect songs, "My Polly Ann" and "Nancy Fat," in which the words were his own but the music was by T. McNally. "Reed," wrote Lester S. Levy in *Flashes of Merriment*, "would deliver these numbers dressed in a short dark coat, light striped pants, and a cap that was a travesty of that worn by the Union soldier." Many a minstrel show hit song inevitably brings up the name of Billy Emerson, who in the opinion of many of his contemporaries, was one of the greatest minstrels of the post-Civil War era. Billy Emerson introduced and popularized Billy Newcomb's "Big Sunflower," written in or about 1866. So intimately did Emerson become identified with this number that he always wore a huge sunflower in his lapel as part of his costume. Emerson was also responsible for the early success of the nonsense song "Polly Wolly Doodle" and of "The Old Clothes Man" in the latter of which he combined Yiddish and Negro dialects. Later, as a member of W. S. Cleveland's Minstrels, Emerson presented "Could I Only Back the Winner," a recital of his bad luck at the race track.

Not any one minstrel troupe but many of them around the country featured two other blackface classics of the Reconstruction. "Shew! Fly, Don't Bother Me" (Frank Campbell—Billy Reeves)* was a walk around published in 1869, but introduced widely during the Civil War. Only after its publication did it enter the repertory of such famed minstrels as Cool Burgess and Rollin Howard. The author of "Goodbye, Eliza Jane," which appeared in 1871, is not known, though Eddie Fox is mentioned on the sheet music as arranger. It became a staple of minstrel shows.

The minstrel, Charles A. Reade, billed as "the great German star and Ethiopian comedian," formed his own company, and became celebrated in the 1870s both as a writer and as a performer of German dialect songs. These included "I Lose Me Mine Vife," whose verses were separated by spoken narrative, "I Lose Me Dot Cat," and "Miss Krause Dot Keeps Her Dollar Store."

"Miss Lucy Neale" (James Sanford) and "Belle of Baltimore" (J. G. Evans) were two other songs often heard in minstrel shows during the Reconstruction.

George Evans, Eddie Leonard and Lew Dockstader were the last great minstrels, all of whom had worked with various troupes which carried the minstrel show into the twentieth century.

The company of one hundred minstrels headed by George Evans in the early twentieth century was one of the two most famous minstrel show troupes in the post-Civil War period, the other being the Lew Dockstader Minstrels. Some aficionados of the minstrel show maintain that only Ed Christy's Minstrels was the equal of the companies headed by Evans and Dockstader. George Evans was always billed as "Honey Boy" because he made famous his own song, "I'll Be True to My Honey Boy." A later Evans song—"In the Good Old Summertime" (Ren Shields)—was even more popular. It was first conceived one day in 1902 at the Brighton Beach Hotel in Brooklyn. At that time, Evans happened to remark to Ren Shields, a lyric writer, and the actress Blanche Ring, that he always preferred the good old summertime to winter. Blanche Ring shrewdly suggested that such a sentiment could well be fashioned into a ballad. Evans agreed, wrote the music a few days later, and had Ren Shields prepare the words. The song was introduced on Broadway in 1902 in the musical, *The Defender,* a performance that helped to make the ballad famous and also to carry

---

*From this point on in this book, names appearing in parentheses after a song title are those of the lyricist and the composer, in that order. When a song composer has been otherwise listed with a song, the name in the parentheses will be that of the lyricist—as say, Billy Reeves' "Shew! Fly, Don't Bother Me" (Frank Campbell). In other instances, when a single name appears in parentheses, then the composer and the lyricist are the same. When no parentheses appear after a song title, and no other identification is given, the name of the author is unknown.

Blanche Ring to stardom. Incidentally, "In the Good Old Summertime" was one of the first song hits about a season of the year. A million copy sheet music sale convinced vaudeville performers that this song was just as appealing to audiences during spring, autumn and winter.

As a member of the Primrose and West Minstrels in 1903, Eddie Leonard wrote the words and music of "Ida, Sweet as Apple Cider." At that time, Leonard was about to lose his job. But when the premiere of this song inspired an ovation, the manager of the minstrel company kept Leonard on. From here, Leonard went on to become one of the greatest minstrels of all time, famous not only for his songs, but also for the soft-shoe tap dance.

As a boy performer in Gus Edwards' vaudeville revue, *Kid Kabaret*, Eddie Cantor did an impression of Eddie Leonard singing "Ida, Sweet as Apple Cider." Later, as a star in every medium of show business, Cantor sang it continually as a tribute to his own wife, Ida, so that this song is now more often associated with him than with the man who had created and introduced it.

Even more closely identified with Eddie Leonard is another of his own songs, "Roll Dem Roly Boly Eyes," which he introduced in 1912 in vaudeville where he was billed as "the last of the great minstrels." It was this song that mimics favored most often when they did impersonations of Leonard—pronouncing the word "eyes" as "wa-wah eyes" the way Eddie Leonard used to drawl it out. A Broadway musical in 1919, written as a frame for Eddie Leonard's talents as a minstrel was named *Roly Boly Eyes*, and in it he sang not only the title number but also "Ida, Sweet as Apple Cider."

Lew Dockstader (born George Alfred Clapp) made his stage debut with an amateur group when he was seventeen, and his bow in a minstrel show a year later. After appearing with various minstrel companies he formed a performing partnership with Charles Dockstader. Their act was billed as a brother team, and George Alfred Clapp assumed the stage name of Lew Dockstader. Charles Dockstader's illness broke up the team after a few years but sometime around 1896, Lew Dockstader formed a new performing partnership, this time with the great minstrel, George Primrose. The two, each now at the peak of his career, became the most celebrated duo in minstrel show history. George Primrose was outstanding as a dancer, performer on the bones and storyteller. Lew Dockstader, a huge and burly man wearing a costume of an oversized suit and trick shoes, was an incomparable teller of jokes, and inimitable in doing monologues about and impersonations of political figures, notably Theodore Roosevelt. He made each and every one of his gestures an instrument for the projection of comedy. This felicitous partnership broke up after five years. In or about 1901 Lew Dockstader formed his own minstrel company which toured the country for eleven years, and became the last of the great minstrel show troupes. Young Al Jolson, at the beginning of his stage career, joined the Dockstader's Minstrels in 1908 to become one of its stars. The minstrel show was still reflected in Al Jolson's performances after he left Dockstader to set out on his own as one of the greatest performers of his generation.

When George Evans, Eddie Leonard and Lew Dockstader each left the minstrel show to go into vaudeville they were bowing to the inevitable. By the early 1900s the minstrel show was through, having been superseded by vaudeville in the hearts of the American theatergoing public.

6

The most significant change in minstrel shows in the post-Civil War era came about with the emergence of black groups. Up to the time of Reconstruction, minstrel shows had been exclusively the domain of white people imitating black men in gestures, humor, dance, dialect, song and appearance. The first black troupe was Lew Johnson's Plantation Minstrel Company, appearing soon after the end of the Civil War. Strange to say, though these performers were all black, they followed the practice of their white colleagues by blackening their faces with burnt cork, painting their lips in red and white circles twice the usual size and—stranger still—adopting the exaggerated mannerisms of speech and gestures white people had come to accept as black stereotypes.

The Georgia Minstrels was the first successful black troupe. Originally organized by a black man, Charles Hicks, it grew so popular that a white man, Charles Callender, took over its management. As Callender's Georgia Minstrels it toured America, after which it assumed the name of Haverly's Minstrels for European appearances. Its main importance lay in the fact that it eliminated caricature and provided authentic Negro comedy, songs and dance. Two of its principal performers were Billy Kersands (whose unusual natural physical endowments enabled him to slip a cup and saucer into his mouth) and Sam Lucas. Lucas became one of the foremost Negro personalities in the American theater up to that time. His career spanned half a century, towards the end of which he assumed the role of Uncle Tom in a silent motion picture production of *Uncle Tom's Cabin* in 1915.

In time, Billy Kersands formed a distinguished black minstrel unit of his own. Richard and Pringle, Hicks and Sawyer, McCabe Young were some of the other names appearing in the titles of highly successful black minstrel troupes. In 1893, the Forty Whites and Thirty Blacks, organized by Primrose and West, became the first racially integrated minstrel company.

From the ranks of the black minstrel show came the first major black popular song composer, James A. Bland, the most distinguished creator of sentimental songs about the Negro and the South after Stephen Foster.

He was born in Flushing, New York, on October 22, 1854. His father, one of the first Negroes to be graduated from college, received an appointment as examiner in the United States Patent Office in Washington, D. C. In Washington, James Bland attended the public schools and followed his natural musical inclination by learning to play the banjo with which he accompanied himself in songs. From time to time he gave performances at clubs and at the homes of Washington notables.

Graduated with honors from Howard University, young Bland was directed to law by his father, but the making of music remained a compulsion. He preferred to seek employment in the theater rather than find his future in the law courts. Since black minstrel troupes were beginning to flourish, Negro performers were now able to get jobs. In 1875, Bland joined the Billy Kersands Minstrels and soon after became a member of the Georgia Minstrels. For both these organizations Bland wrote songs.

One day, in 1878, Bland visited a Virginia plantation on the James River, not far from Williamsburg. Enjoying the beauty of this idyllic setting Bland was suddenly reminded of a dream that a girl at Howard University had described to him. She had seen herself being carried back "to old Virginny where I was born." The peaceful scene now before his eyes, and the recollection of that dream, were to be translated into Bland's greatest ballad, "Carry Me Back to Old Virginny," in which an old Negro voices his nostalgia for the place where he was born.

Years later, in 1940, "Carry Me Back to Old Virginny" became the official song of the State of Virginia. In 1946, when a tombstone was erected on Bland's grave in Merion, Pennsylvania, the song was performed, and Governor William A. Tuck said in his address: "James Bland put into ever-ringing verse and rhyme an expression of feeling which all Virginians have for their state. 'Carry Me Back to Old Virginny' tells in inspiring song the innate patriotism and love of native heath of all our people, white and Negro alike."

One year after he wrote "Carry Me Back to Old Virginny" and saw it become successful, Bland completed two other sentimental ballads for which he is remembered and honored. Bland himself introduced "In the Morning by the Bright Light" and "In the Evening by the Moonlight" as a member of the Georgia Minstrels. The first owed its inception to the same peaceful plantation scene near Williamsburg that had inspired Bland to write "Carry Me Back to Old Virginny." The idea for the second ballad came to Bland upon seeing and hearing a group of Negroes singing spirituals outside their cabin accompanied by a banjo.

In 1879 Bland produced a light, jaunty number that became a minstrel show classic: "Oh! Dem Golden Slippers," written as a walk around for the Georgia Minstrels. He followed this, in 1880, with "Hand Me Down My Walking Cane" and "De Golden Wedding."

When the Georgia Minstrels toured Europe in 1881 as Haverly's Minstrels, Bland was a member of the company. The troupe, headed by Bland, brought down the house at its debut in London by performing "Oh! Dem Golden Slippers." After that, success mounted upon success in England. When the tour ended in 1883, and the company returned to the United States, Bland decided to remain in England. He made numerous appearances there, billed as "The Prince of Negro Songwriters," and gave command performances for Queen Victoria and the Prince of Wales.

When the vogue for blackface entertainers subsided in England, bookings for Bland became few and far between. The huge sums of money he had earned had by this time been squandered. He returned to the United States in 1901 a pauper, to spend his last days in Philadelphia, where he died on May 5, 1911. He was buried in a Negro cemetery in Merion, Pennsylvania, in an unmarked grave. Not until 1939 was his grave located and landscaped, and in 1946 a headstone placed over it with funds provided by the American Society for Composers, Authors and Publishers (ASCAP).

5

Of Ballads, Songs and Snatches

1

From America's beginnings, the sentimental ballad found a responsive audience.

John Hill Hewitt was the first major composer of such ballads. He was the oldest son of James Hewitt, that Jack-of-all-musical-trades who had distinguished himself as a violinist, organist, impresario, publisher and, in 1794, was the composer of one of America's earliest operas, *Tammany*. His son, John Hill Hewitt, born in New York City on July 11, 1801, was educated in Boston's public schools. After a brief period as apprentice to a sign painter, he attended West Point, which he left in 1822 without graduating, and where he had received some music instruction. He then joined a theatrical troupe organized by his father. When this company became insolvent, John Hill supported himself by teaching music in Augusta, Georgia. After that, he moved to Greenville, South Carolina, where he founded and edited a political journal.

His first published ballad was also his most famous one: "The Minstrel's Return from the War," written in Greenville in or about 1825. His brother, who published it in 1827, had so low an opinion of its commercial value that he failed to copyright it. Nevertheless, as the composer himself later recalled, the song "was eagerly taken up by the public . . . and was sung all over the world. My brother, not securing the rights, told me he missed making at least ten thousand dollars."

"The Minstrel's Return from the War" is America's first successful ballad of native authorship. Hewitt also earned the distinction of writing two of the earliest successful nostalgic songs about the South: "Take Me Home Where the Sweet Magnolia Blooms" and "Carry

Me Back to the Sweet Sunny South." Among the more famous of Hewitt's other ballads, of which he wrote some three hundred, were "The Knight of the Raven Black Plume," "Our Native Land," "The Mountain Bugle," and a classic of the Civil War, "All Quiet Along the Potomac Tonight."

For two decades preceding the Civil War, Hewitt edited various journals, including *The Clipper* in Baltimore, of which he was part owner, and *The Capitol*, in Washington, D. C. During the war he was a drillmaster for the Confederate troops in Richmond, Virginia. He died at the age of eighty-nine in Baltimore, Maryland, on October 7, 1890.

Henry Russell was Hewitt's successor as a significant composer of American sentimental ballads. He was born and he died in England, but since all of Russell's ballads were written in America—where they gained their first acceptance—Russell's songwriting career justifiably belongs to American popular music history.

He was born in Sheerness, England, on Christmas Eve of 1812. In 1833 he came to America where, for eight years, he occupied the post of organist at the First Presbyterian Church in Rochester, New York. An eloquent speech by Henry Clay was the stimulus for the writing of his first ballad. Russell asked himself: "Why should it not be possible for me to make music the vehicle of grand thoughts and noble sentiments, to speak to the world through the power of poetry and song?"

In all, Russell wrote about eight hundred songs, some of which he himself introduced to his own piano accompaniment during his American tours as a concert baritone. His most famous ballad is "Woodman, Spare that Tree" in 1837, its inspiration what may have been a true incident. Russell and G. P. Morris, a New York journalist and lyricist, were driving in the country where Morris had lived as a boy. They decided to pay a call at Morris' onetime home. Upon their arrival, they saw a farmer with axe in hand about to fell a tree for firewood. This was the tree which as a boy Morris had seen his father plant. Morris pleaded so ardently with the farmer to save the tree that the farmer threw his axe aside.

This episode (which some claim is fictional) provided Morris with a subject for several verses which Russell then set to music. Russell introduced the song at one of his concerts. A highly theatrical performer, Russell delivered his own ballads with a flourish of histrionics. This proved true with his rendition of "Woodman, Spare that Tree." So moved was one member of the audience that he arose and inquired of Russell whether the tree had actually been spared. Upon being reassured, the questioner muttered "Thank God! Thank God! I breath again!" and the rest of the audience burst into applause.

Many other Russell ballads caught the fancy of his audience. "The Old Arm Chair" (Eliza Cook) is in all probability the first "mammy" song ever written, a tearful tribute to a chair that had once belonged to mother. "The Indian Hunter" (Eliza Cook) and "A Life on the Ocean Wave" (Epes Sargent) were also pioneer achievements. The former is an early example of American popular songs about the Indian; the latter, an early treatment in song of the sea.

Russell returned to his native country in 1841, dying in London on December 8, 1900.

2

Many of the early sentimental ballads in America followed the practice of other popular songs in adopting foreign tunes for natively conceived lyrics.

During the summer of 1817, Samuel Woodworth wrote the words for "The Old Oaken Bucket" in which he recalled scenes of childhood. The poem was published in the *Republican Chronicle*, in New York, on June 3, 1818. It carried the title of "The Bucket," and its author was disguised by the pseudonym of "Selim." The first musical setting of the poem is not the one we now know. When words and music were first assembled for publication in Boston, in or about 1833, the melody was a Scottish air, "Jessie, the Flower of Dumblane." But the melody we now sing to Woodworth's words is the work of G. Kiallmark, an English composer. The music had been published in London in 1822 and had been used for Thomas Moore's poem "Araby's Daughter." Woodworth's lyrics with Kiallmark's music appeared together for the first time in *The Amateur Song Book*, published in Boston in 1843.

"Home, Sweet Home" is a beloved American ballad with words by an American, and melody by a foreigner. The lyricist is John Howard Payne, born in New York City in 1791. In early manhood he went to London where for a time he wrote plays and appeared as an actor. He collaborated with Sir Henry Bishop, eminent English composer-conductor, in the writing of an opera, *Clari*, produced in London on May 8, 1823. Its principal aria, "Home, Sweet Home," was sung by Maria Tree at the end of the first act as a nostalgic recollection of her home. Actually, it was Payne himself who was here expressing his inmost feelings, for destiny had made him a wanderer in foreign lands.

Bishop's melody had first been written a few years before *Clari* as a Sicilian air for a collection of folk tunes, *Melodies of Various Nations*. This is why some critics accused Bishop of having stolen a Sicilian melody for "Home, Sweet Home" in *Clari*. He had to go to court to prove his authorship, which he did to its full satisfaction.

In *Clari*, "Home, Sweet Home" proved a showstopper. Then the song was heard throughout England. "Never has any ballad become so immediately and deservedly popular," reported the *Quarterly Musician* in London. Kitty Stephen sang it at festivals in New York and Birmingham in 1832. Mme. Ann Bishop, wife of the composer and a distinguished musician in her own right, included it in her song recitals. The fame of the ballad became worldwide through the efforts of two world-famous prima donnas, each of whom made it one of their concert favorites. Jenny Lind often sang it as the closing number on her program, and Adelina Patti, for four decades, frequently offered it as an encore, providing her own accompaniment at the piano. When Mme. Melba returned to her native Australia for the first time after achieving world renown, her rendition of "Home, Sweet Home," also to her own piano accompaniment, left few dry eyes at her opening concert.

In America, "Home, Sweet Home" was first heard when *Clari* was given its American premiere at the Park Theater in New York on November 12, 1823. That year the song was published in Philadelphia.

Payne never profited financially from the widespread success of his immortal ballad. "How often," he commented sadly in his diary, "have I been in the heart of Paris, Berlin, London, or some other city, and have heard persons singing or hand organs playing 'Home, Sweet Home' without having a shilling to buy myself the next meal or a place to lay my head." But honor (if not hard cash) did come his way. In 1850, two years before his death, the President invited him to the White House to hear Jenny Lind sing it. Had Payne lived twenty-one years more he would have witnessed another tribute. With funds from benefit performances of *Clari*, a statue of Payne was erected in Prospect Park, in Brooklyn, New York, at which time a thousand voices joined in the singing of "Home, Sweet Home."

3

Other distinctive American sentimental ballads, however, had both homegrown music and words.

It should be remembered that Stephen Foster wrote many a touching ballad that had no concern with either black people or the South. Indeed, his career as a song composer began with the love ballad "Open Thy Lattice, Love" (1844) and ended two decades later with the haunting "Beautiful Dreamer" (1864). In between these two polar points came "Farewell My Lilly Dear" (1851), "Jeanie with the Light Brown Hair" (1854), "Come Where My Love Lies Dreaming" (1855) and "Gentle Annie" (1856), each one bearing the imprint of his talent for tender lyricism.

A similar kind of delicacy and sweetness pervades several other ballads of the pre-Civil War decades. "Flow Gently, Sweet Afton," a poem by Robert Burns, acquired an enduring musical setting in 1838 from James E. Spilman, a Philadelphian. Marion Dix Sullivan's "The Blue Juniata" (1844), is a gentle song about a river in Pennsylvania which outlived a lovely Indian girl. "When I Saw Sweet Nellie Home" (Frances Kyle—J. Fletcher) in 1858, and, in 1860, H. S. Thompson's "Ida Lee" and "Annie Lisle" are equally affecting. The latter eventually lent its melody to the words of "Far Above Cayuga's Waters," the school song of Cornell University. Other famous ballads of 1860 were: " 'Tis But a Little Faded Flower" (Frederick Enoch—John Rogers Thomas); "Rock Me to Sleep, Mother" (Florence Percy—Ernest Leslie); "When the Corn is Waving, Annie Dear" (Charles Blamphin). "Aura Lee" (W. W. Fosdick—George R. Poulton) followed in 1861. During the Civil War it was a favorite of the Union Army, and in 1865 its melody was used for the graduating class song at West Point, "Army Blue." (Elvis Presley, in collaboration with Vera Matson, borrowed the melody for "Love Me Tender" in 1956, and Jan Berry and Arnie Ginsburg for "Jenny Lee" in 1958.)

Some of the ballads before the Civil War shed copious tears over the untimely death of some young girl. "Oh, don't you remember sweet Alice?" inquires Thomas Dunn English in his verses, "Ben Bolt," for which Nelson Kneass wrote the music in 1848. Alice, the song goes on to say, now lies under a stone in an old churchyard in an obscure corner. English's poem, *Ben Bolt*, was first published in the New York *Mirror* before receiving three musical settings, the last of which became the most celebrated. Its composer, Kneass, was a minstrel, who confessed he borrowed his melody from an old German song. The song, "Ben Bolt," owes a good deal of its early popularity to the Hutchinson Family which featured it often and prominently on its concert programs. Much of its later fame came from the fact that George Louis Du Maurier, in his novel *Trilby* (1894) used this song for Svengali, the hypnotist, to bring the heroine, Trilby, under his spell.

H. S. Thompson's "Lily Dale" (1852) tells of the grief of loved ones over the death of "sweet Lily, sweet Lily dear" over whose grave blossoms the wild rose in a flowery vale. Death also casts its long shadow over that popular minstrel show ballad of 1856, Benjamin Russell Hanby's "Darling Nelly Gray." "They've taken you away and I'll never see my darling anymore," is the grief-stricken lament of Nelly Gray's lover as he sits by the river weeping.

One of the most successful American ballads ever written was "Listen to the Mocking Bird" in 1855. By the end of the century, it had sold over twenty million copies of sheet music, making it one of the three or four best-selling compositions of all time. It became a fixture in theaters, particularly with stage performers adept at simulating the whistles and calls of birds to be interpolated either between the lines of the chorus or at the end of the chorus. President Lincoln once compared this song to "the laughter of a little girl at play."

The words and music of "Listen to the Mocking Bird" were by Septimus Winner who once confessed he took his melody from a song he had heard a black man sing in Philadelphia. Winner sold out all the rights to his song for fifty dollars, and it was published in Philadelphia in 1855. The name of the author on the title page reads "Alice Hawthorne," a pseudonym Winner had previously adopted for other songs.

Winner was born in Philadelphia on May 11, 1827, where he became an influential musical figure. He opened a music shop; gave lessons on the violin, banjo and guitar; prepared two hundred instruction books for twenty-three instruments; arranged compositions for violin and piano; wrote articles on music for a magazine edited by Edgar Allan Poe; and was a founder of one of the city's most venerable musical organizations, the Philadelphia Music Society.

His first success as a composer came in 1854 with the sentimental ballad "What Is Home Without a Mother," for which he first assumed the pen name of Alice Hawthorne. "Listen to the Mocking Bird" was written a year later. During the Civil War, Winner wrote war songs, one of which gave him the questionable distinction of being the only composer ever to get court-martialed for a song. It was "Give Us Back Our Old Commander (1862), written after General George B. McClellan was ousted by the War Department for failing to follow up his victory at Antietam. Expressing as it did the strong pro-McClellan sentiment among the people, the song sold over one hundred thousand copies of sheet music within a brief period. Edwin Stanton, the Secretary of War, issued an order to court-martial any soldier heard singing it; at the same time he instituted military court-martial proceedings against Winner for treason. When Winner promised to cease further distribution of the song, the court action was dropped. But it did not end the song's popularity. In 1864 it helped promote the Presidential campaign of General McClellan. Its melody was later used as a Presidential campaign song for Ulysses S. Grant.

During the Civil War, Winner also wrote a nonsense song that has not been forgotten: "Where, O Where Has My Little Dog Gone?" (1864), its melody taken from the German folk song, "Zu Lauterbach." A year later, Winner completed one of his best songs, the ballad, "Ellie Rhee." Winner lived on into the twentieth century, dying in the city of his birth on November 22, 1902. Parenthetically, his brother, Joseph E. Winner (using the pen name of R. A. Eastburn) was the author of one of the most familiar songs extolling the joys of drinking: "The Little Brown Jug" (1869), which in 1939 was revived and has since been identified with Glenn Miller and his orchestra.

4

In the years between the War of 1812 and the Civil War two important national ballads were born: "America" and "Columbia, the Gem of the Ocean."

In 1831, Lowell Mason, a distinguished music educator, brought several volumes of songs to Samuel Francis Smith, a clergyman. Mason suggested that Smith use one of the melodies in these books for a new American patriotic hymn. "Accordingly," recalled Smith, "one leisurely afternoon, I was looking over the books, and fell in with the tune of 'God Save the King,' and at once took my pen and wrote the piece in question ["America"]. It was struck out at a sitting without the slightest idea that it would ever gain the popularity it has since enjoyed. . . . The first time it was sung publicly was at a children's celebration of American independence at the Park Street Church, Boston, on July 4, 1831. . . . If I had anticipated its future, doubtless, I would have taken more pains with it." Since that time, "America" has assumed an importance second only to "The Star-Spangled Banner" as an American national anthem.

It has often been suggested that the melody of "Columbia, the Gem of the Ocean" came from the English "Britannia, the Pride of the Ocean." Yet when "Columbia, the Gem of the Ocean" was first published in Philadelphia in 1843 under the title of "Columbia, the Land of the Brave," the sheet music credited David T. Shaw as the author of both the words and the music, with no mention of the English melody. Shaw was an actor-singer who had introduced this song at the Chinese Museum in Philadelphia in 1843. Soon after the song's publication, Thomas à Becket—an English actor then residing in Philadelphia—brought forward the claim that it was he who had written "Columbia, the Gem of the Ocean" on a commission from Shaw. When a second Philadelphia publisher issued the song in 1844 under its present-day title, the sheet music carried the legend that this was "a popular song . . . adapted and arranged by T. à Becket." If this is not sufficient to confuse us, a publisher in New York released the ballad in 1861 under a new title, "The Red, White and Blue" (the last three words of the lyric) identifying it as a "national song . . . arranged by Thomas D. Sullivan." No mention here is made of Shaw, Becket or "Britannia, the Pride of the Ocean." To this day, the authentic source of the ballad remains in doubt, though many tend to accept Becket as the author of both the words and the music.

5

American history continued to provide the material for popular songs.

The twenty thousand or so Americans who had settled in the then Mexican territory of Texas declared on March 2, 1836, their independence and intention to set up a government of their own. In reprisal, General Santa Anna and his Mexican troops attacked the American garrison at the Alamo on March 6 and massacred its two hundred defenders, including such Texan heroes as Davy Crockett and Commander William B. Travis. With the rallying cry "Remember the Alamo" on their lips, eight hundred Texan troops under General Sam Houston attacked the Mexicans and defeated them at San Jacinto. Santa Anna was taken prisoner and released only after he had signed a secret pact granting independence to Texas, which was then established as a republic with Sam Houston as President. From then on, the movement for annexation of Texas to the United States gained momentum, until, in 1845, Texas officially became the twenty-eighth state.

To Mexico, the joining of Texas with the United States represented an act of hostility. Though there was no overt provocation by Mexico, American political leaders, headed by President Polk, used Mexican resentment as an excuse for military action—the goal being the annexation of all lands necessary to make the Pacific coast the western boundary of the United States. The war with Mexico lasted two years, resulting in an overwhelming American victory. By the terms of the peace signed at Guadalupe Hidalgo, over one million square miles of the new territory was ceded to America by Mexico, including what was eventually to become the states of Nevada, Utah and California, and parts of what was to become Arizona, New Mexico, Wyoming and Colorado.

Though liberals (including Abraham Lincoln, Emerson, Longfellow and Thoreau) opposed the Mexican war, which they regarded as an imperialist conflict, in most Americans it ignited the fire of chauvinist pride. This feeling was expressed in many songs. The skirmish in 1836 popularized "Remember the Alamo," words by T. A. Durriage to the melody of "Bruce's Address"; also "The Death of Crockett," to the melody of "The Star-Spangled Banner." When war with Mexico broke out in 1846, "Remember the Alamo," of a decade earlier, was revived as were such older songs as "Hail, Columbia," "The Hunters of Kentucky," "Yankee Doodle" and "The Girl I Left Behind Me," all of them fitted out with new martial lyrics. Volunteers for the American Army were mustered in to the tune of "Join the Hickory Blues," or "The Song of the Memphis Volunteers" or "To Arms." The war itself produced the "Texan Rangers' Song," words by James T. Lytle (of the McCullough Rangers) to the tune of "I, Afloat"; "Buena Vista," and "Fire Away" (the latter set to the melody of the famous Scottish song, "The Campbells are Coming"). General Zachary Taylor's victory at the battle of Monterey in June of 1846 was acclaimed in "Santy Anno," or "The Plains of Mexico," (later popular on American ships as a capstan chantey).

Irish-American troops sang "Green Grow the Laurels" (subsequently adapted into a western favorite, "Green Grow the Lilacs"). Legend would have us believe that the word "gringo"—used by Mexicans as an epithet for Americans—came from a corruption of the two opening words of "Green Grow the Laurels." But in all probability, "gringo" is derived from the Spanish word "griengo," meaning a foreigner.

The melody of a popular minstrel show song, "Miss Lucy Neale" (James Sanford), published in Philadelphia in or about 1844, was used for several songs during the Mexican-American War, including "The Song of the Memphis Volunteers" and a paean to Texan freedom, "The Song of Texas." Other minstrel songs were also borrowed for that war: "De Boatman's Song" for "The Battle Call" and "Old Dan Tucker" for "Uncle Sam and Mexico." "Yankee Doodle," in one of many versions during the Mexican-American War, became "We're the Boys of Mexico." "The Rose of Alabama" became "Strike for Your Rights! Avenge Your Wrongs!," and the chantey, "A Yankee Ship and a Yankee Crew" was used for "Come Raise Aloft the Red, White and Blue."

6

Political campaigning along modern lines can be said to have originated with the Presidential campaign of 1840 in which William Henry Harrison, a Whig, was pitted against the incumbent, Martin Van Buren, a Democrat. Techniques for creating an image to which voters could respond favorably were being developed for the first time. Electioneering songs were improvised to help arouse enthusiasm for a candidate or to discredit his opponent.

Horace Greeley, America's first prestigious journalist, was largely responsible for bringing songs so prominently into the 1840 campaign. At that time, Greeley was the editor of the Whig paper, *Log Cabin*. During the 1840 Presidential campaign he instituted the practice of including a new campaign song in each issue of his paper.

The Whigs had the best slogans, catch phrases, symbols and songs. And so, Martin Van Buren—dubbed by the opposing Whigs as "the little Van" or "Little Vanny"—was defeated, and Harrison became America's ninth President.

Harrison was built up by his party as a man of the people: a simple, honest, homespun character. A log cabin was adopted as his symbol. But the people were also reminded that he was a hero. To recall Harrison's victory over the Indians at Tippecanoe River in 1811 (which could hardly be called a famous victory!) the sobriquet, "Tippecanoe" became synonymous with the name of Harrison. The log cabin and the name "Tippecanoe" were reproduced on handkerchiefs, flags, medals, almanacs and miniatures to advance Harrison's cause.

The Whigs also conceived the catch phrase of "Tippecanoe and Tyler, Too"—Tyler being John Tyler, Harrison's running mate. This was also the title of the most famous song of this campaign, and one of the most celebrated in the history of American Presidential campaigns. To the marchlike tune of "Little Pigs" (which blackface minstrels had popularized), Alexander Coffman Ross, a jeweler in Zanesville, Ohio, added catchy lyrics in 1840:

> "What's the cause of this commotion, motion, motion,
>   Our country's through?
> It is a ball a rolling on,
>   For Tippecanoe and Tyler, too.
> And with them we'll beat little Van, Van, Van
>   Van is a used up man
> And with them we'll beat little Van."

Ross presented words and music of "Tippecanoe and Tyler, Too" for the first time at a Whig rally in Zanesville where it was received so enthusiastically it had to be repeated several times. Soon afterward, he sang it in New York at another Whig convocation, and once again the audience shouted with delight. Adopted by the Whigs as the principal campaign song for their candidates, it "sang Harrison into the presidency," as the *North American Review* reported.

There were many other pro-Harrison songs. "Harrison" used the tune of "Yankee Doodle"; "The Log Cabin and Hard Cider Candidate" and "Bullet Proof" took the melody of "Auld Lang Syne"; "Old Tippecanoe" was set to the tune of "Old Rosin the Beau." There were anti-Van Buren songs as well: "Van Buren" ("Who is the worst of tyrant's breed? Van Buren!") or "Little Vanny," to the melody of "Old Rosin the Beau." So many songs promoted Harrison that Harrison songsters proliferated: *The Log Cabin and Hard Cider Melodies; The Harrison Medal Minstrel; The Tippecanoe Song Book*.

Democrats also had songs, more in opposition to Harrison than in promotion of Van Buren. Among these were "The Last Whig Song" to the melody of "Old King Cole" and "When This Old Hat Was New," set to a popular song of the same period. But these were lost in the shuffle.

"The Pesky Sarpent," still another 1840 campaign song, is an alternate title for one of America's oldest folk songs from New England, "Springfield Mountain." The folk ballad was inspired by the death of Lieutenant Thomas Merrick, age twenty-two, who met his death in Farmington, Massachusetts, in 1761 from the bite of a rattlesnake. The verses, intended for the melody of "Old Hundred," first appeared on a broadside in 1761, probably the work of Nathan Torrey. A humorous version, renamed "The Pesky Sarpent"—this time with melody borrowed from a Scottish jig—received wide circulation on the stage. It had a refrain made up of nonsense syllables, and was sung with exaggerated inflections and gestures. Published in Boston in 1840, "The Pesky Sarpent" was later that year lifted by both principal parties in that Presidential election.

"Old Rosin the Beau" (or "Old Rosin the Bow")—whose melody was taken for two already mentioned Harrison campaign songs—was a popular tune first published in Philadelphia in or about 1838. This number is the prototype of many later songs about bibulous gentlemen whose lives are drawing to an end. The author of the lyrics and music is unknown; the melody—in slow, three-quarter time—has a recognizable Scottish flavor.

"Old Rosin the Beau" reappeared during the Presidential campaign of 1844 as "The Mill Boy of the Slashes," "Old Hal of the West" and "Two Dollars a Day and Roast Beef," all three for the candidacy of Henry Clay against James K. Polk. This was the election in which President Tyler (who as Vice President had succeeded to the Presidency upon Harrison's death one month after he took office) accepted the renomination as President on the Democratic ticket only to withdraw from the campaign and be replaced by Martin Van Buren. James Polk, the first "dark horse" in national politics, campaigned on a platform favoring the annexation of Texas and the territory of Oregon.

The year 1844 was not the last in which "Old Rosin the Beau" electioneered for Presidents. In 1860 it was used for "Lincoln and Liberty" and, after numerous campaign appearances, reemerged in 1872 as "Straight-Out Democrat" for the independents who opposed the nomination of Horace Greeley.

In the election year of 1844, and again in 1848, such old-time favorites as "Yankee Doodle," "Old Dan Tucker," "Auld Lang Syne," "The Girl I Left Behind Me" and "The Hunters of Kentucky" were once again used for various candidates. "Wait for the Wagon" joined this list in 1852. The first published sheet music, issued in Baltimore in 1851, identifies no lyricist but names George P. Knauff as the composer. But there is a suspicion that R. Bishop Buckley, a member of the Buckley Serenaders, had a hand in its composition. In any event, "Wait for the Wagon," a hit in 1851, became ripe pickings for the Whigs in their search for a good Presidential song, and they rewrote it as "Wait Till November." In 1856, "Wait for the Wagon" served both the Democrats and the newly formed Republican Party. It was sung for the Democrat, John Buchanan, as "Wait for the Wagon, the Old Democratic Party" and "The Union Wagon," and for the Republican, John Charles Fremont, as "We'll Give 'Em Jessie" ("Jessie" referring to the initials, J. C. in Fremont's name).

In 1860, "Wait for the Wagon" became "Lincoln and Hamlin"; in 1884, "Vote for Our Party"; and in 1912, "Wait for the Wagon" espoused the Presidential cause of Theodore Roosevelt.

7

In January 1848, Captain John A. Sutter, who owned a tract of land in Sacramento Valley in California, engaged Marshall, a contractor, to build a mill on the fork of the American River. During this construction, Marshall discovered particles of gold in the water. Without realizing what they were, he sent one nugget to San Francisco as a curio. There, a prospector recognized it and rushed to Sutter's mill. In March he struck a rich deposit of gold. His success inspired others and by May there were two thousand prospectors in Sacramento Valley. In September, the Baltimore *Sun* printed an item about the discovery of gold in California. This news was reprinted in several other papers. By year's end, a few groups started the long journey west.

Then the mad rush began. More than one hundred organized companies left Massachusetts in 1849. They came to California by land on horseback and in wagons. Almost five hundred wagons were counted on a ten-mile stretch along the Platte River. They also arrived by sea, making the long voyage from the East Coast to San Francisco by way of Cape Horn; one such journey from Boston took two hundred and forty days. In 1849, more than seven hundred vessels—many of them unseaworthy, others of primitive construction—passed through the Golden Gate carrying would-be prospectors avid for gold.

Here was one of the great adventures in American history. It brought between forty and fifty thousand prospectors into California in less than a year. By 1850, California swarmed with more than one hundred thousand new settlers, all desperately sifting the waters and combing the earth for the precious metal. Five million dollars' worth of gold was found the first year; by 1853, the sum reached sixty million.

An adventure of such proportions, inspiring monumental hopes and illusions—and just as often bringing disenchantment, frustration, and despair—inevitably brought songs into being. The forty-niners who trekked across the plains and prairies, pursuing the mirage of shining gold, created songs to describe their dramatic quest. Those who came to California over great distances, whether by land or sea, overcame the monotony of travel by improvising songs. Sometimes the lyrics were somewhat bawdy:

> "The miners came in forty-nine
>   The whores in fifty-one;
>   And when they got together,
>   They produced the native son."

Most of the songs of the forty-niners were parodies of well-known numbers, the two used most often by Stephen Foster, "De Camptown Races," which the forty-niners transformed into "Sacramento" and "Oh! Susanna." "I'm off for California with my wash-bowl on my knee," is the way the forty-niners changed the words of "Oh! Susanna" while retaining its melody. "Sacramento" had two versions, one full of hopes and dreams, sung by the prospectors en route to California:

> "We've formed our band and we are all manned,
>   Dooda, dooda.
>   To journey afar to the Promised Land,
>   Dooda, dooda, day!

> "Then ho, boys, ho,
>   To California go!
>   There's plenty of gold
>   So I've been told
>   On the banks of Sacramento!"

The second version struck a plaintive note, the chant of those returning home without gold, bitterness having replaced exhilaration, and hope succumbing to despair:

> "Ho, boys, ho
>   For California O!
>   There's plenty of bones, so we've been told
>   On the banks of Sacramento!"

Many of the songs of the forty-niners were collected into two pocket-sized volumes: *Put's Original California Songster* in 1855 and *Put's Golden Songster* in 1858. Put—or "Old Put" as he was more often called—was John A. Stone who had come to California in 1850 in what proved to be a futile quest for gold. Frustrated, but not defeated, "Old Put" went to San Francisco, which by then had become a wide-open, roaring community where successful prospectors would celebrate with drinking, gambling and whoring. Stage entertainment provided the icing on the cake of such diversions. Shows were put on by visiting minstrels. Performances of gold rush songs were given by disenchanted miners converted by failure from prospectors into troubadours. The most famous of the troubadours was "Old Put." He fashioned the lyrics for some fifty songs that touched upon many facets of the life and times of the forty-niners, adapting them to melodies from the stage or from abroad, from chanteys and from the songs of the shantyman. He popularized these songs with his troupe, The Sierra Nevada Rangers, which appeared in San Francisco and toured mining camps along the banks of the Sacramento.

In the preface to his first songster, "Old Put" tells us something about himself. Writing in the third person, he explains: "Having been a miner . . . for a number of years, he has had ample opportunities of observing, as he has equally shared, the many trials and hardships to which his brethren of the pick and shovel had been exposed. . . . Ever since . . . his crossing of the plains, in the memorable year of '50, he has been in the habit of noting down . . . the leading items of his experiences. . . . His songs may show some hard edges, and he is free to confess that they may fail to please the more aristocratic portion of the community, who have but little sympathy with the details, hopes, trials, or joys of the miner's life. . . ."

"Sweet Betsy from Pike," perhaps the foremost heroine of the gold rush days, was an

"Old Put" invention. The words from the song bearing that title were his; the melody probably came from an English music hall tune, "Vilikins and his Dinah." "Sweet Betsy from Pike" tells how Betsy and her lover, Ike (with two yoke of oxen, a big "yaller" dog, and tall Shanghai rooster) crossed the wide prairies and overcame harrowing hardships before reaching California. Eventually, they got married. But Ike's chronic jealousy spelled ruin for their union. After getting divorced from Ike, Betsy told him: "Goodbye, you big lummox. I'm glad you backed out."

Joe Bowers is the name sometimes concocted for a forty-niner. He is first found in the ballad, "Joe Bowers," the lyrics sometimes credited to "Old Put," sometimes to one of his rival California minstrels, John Woodward, of Johnson's Pennsylvanians, a troupe popular in California. The melody is unidentified. Joe Bowers deserts his mother and his girl friend, Sal, in Missouri, to seek gold in California. He slaves day and night, through fair weather and foul. Finally he makes a strike which he intends turning over to Sal. But his dreams crumble to dust when he learns from his brother that Sal has married the butcher back home.

Tom Moore is another popular Klondike character, found not in a song by "Old Put" but in "The Days of Forty Nine," authors unknown. Tom Moore is a woebegone relic of the days of forty-nine. They call him a "bummer" and a "gin sot." He just wanders from town to town, pining for the good old days. Since many forty-niners resented having so disreputable a character as Tom Moore represent them, another song was conceived in rebuttal by J. Riley Main, "The Good Old Days of 50, 1 and 2," which offers a more heroic and romantic image of the prospector.

Some of the songs of "Old Put" were full of optimism. "Come Yourselves and See" (melody of "The Blue Tail Fly") guaranteed young and old that they would be well paid in the land of gold. Other songs, however, were touched with bitterness. The hardships of the westward trek, whether by land or sea, are described in "The Fools of '49," "Crossing the Plains," and "Coming Around the Horn." Using an elephant as a symbol for hard times and futility, "Old Put" wrote "Seeing the Elephant" (to the melody of "Old Dan Tucker"). "Seeing the Elephant," referred to the cruel realities of a miner's life. These sordid details are elaborated upon in "The Old Settler's Song," whose refrain says simply "And I have been frequently sold" and whose final verse reads:

"When I looked on the prospects so gloomy,
    The tears trickled over my face,
And I thought that my travels had brought me
    To the end of the jumping off place."

6

A House
Divided
Against Itself

1

Beginning in the 1840s, and existing for about half a century, professional groups made up of members of a single family gave concerts of vocal music. These "singing families" became a potent medium for the introduction and popularization of songs. (More than a century later, the "singing family" was reincarnated in American popular music through the King Family, Pat Boone and his family and—in country and western music—the Carter and Ritchie families.)

In the nineteenth century, the Hutchinson Family was the most influential singing group. None of their rivals—not the Bakers, nor the Blakeleys, nor the Cheneys—brought so many songs to the American people and to acceptance.

The first successful singing family, however, was not the Hutchinsons but the Rainers, made up of two men and two women. They came from Switzerland to give concerts of famous Swiss songs, appearing in the costumes of their native country. It was the popularity enjoyed by the Rainers that inspired the Hutchinsons to emulate them. Proud of their own country and their national heritage, the Hutchinsons became convinced that an American group performing American songs could woo and win audiences the way the Rainers had done. One of the Hutchinsons expressed this thought in a verse published in an early concert program of the family. It read:

"When foreigners approach your shores
You welcome them with open doors;
Now we have come to seek our lot
Shall native talent be forgot?"

The Hutchinson Family had already begun to answer its own question by performing its first concert. This took place on Thanksgiving Day in 1839 at the Baptist meeting house in the Hutchinsons native town of Milford, Vermont, and offered a program of hymns and anthems. At that concert thirteen Hutchinsons performed, all of them the children of Jesse and Mary Leavitt Hutchinson. That concert did not put the Rainers into the shade, nor did the second Hutchinson concert in nearby Lynn. After that, most of the Hutchinsons admitted defeat and decided to take up the life of either farmers or business people. Three, however, remained determined to pursue further the musical ambitions of the family. Between 1840 and 1841, Judson, John and Asa Hutchinson—now calling themselves the Aeolian Vocalists—gave concerts in or near Milford. One of their performances attracted only fifty customers who brought a total of $6.25 to the box office.

The three men suspected that what their offering lacked most was feminine attraction. Looking at their little sister, Aby, then only thirteen, they sensed that she might fill the gap. Aby had a pretty round face, large eyes, great charm and an exquisite singing voice. As soon as Aby became the fourth member of this singing group—and once some of the numbers on their program focused attention on her pulchritude and musical talent—success was assured. The quartet's first tour, in 1842, covered New Hampshire, Vermont, Massachusetts and New York, and witnessed a continuous growth in the size and enthusiasm of audiences. It was during this tour, at Albany, New York, that the name of the group was permanently changed from Aeolian Vocalists to the Hutchinson Family.

These four Hutchinsons were born show people. They recognized the publicity value of adopting a song as their musical identification (something nobody before them had thought of doing). Thus, by a half century or more, they were the predecessors of those performers of popular music who assumed a theme song as a musical signature. The Hutchinson Family song was "The Old Granite State," words by Jesse Hutchinson set to an old revival hymn, "The Old Church Yard." They sang it for the first time at the Broadway Temple in New York City in 1843, the year the song was published. For the next half century, the Hutchinson Family—not only the original foursome, but various combinations of Hutchinsons—almost never omitted this song from their program. Sometimes it was heard at the beginning of the concert, sometimes at the end. Since their native New Hampshire was known as "the old granite State" the song was in part—but only in part—a tribute to it. For the rest, the song served to introduce the audience not only to the individual members on the stage but also to the absent members of the Hutchinson brood. "We come from the mountains of the Old Granite State" they sang. The song reached its climax with the Hutchinsons expressing their social and political credo. "Liberty is our motto," and "Yes, we're friends of emancipation," and "we're all teetotalers."

The Hutchinsons were also show people in the kind of songs they featured. Since they knew audiences were partial to the sensational, the melodramatic and the lurid, the Hutchinsons filled their programs with ballads or story songs often gruesome in their realism, or bursting with sentimentality. On their very first tour these numbers already dominated their programs. One was "The Vulture of the Alps," music by Jesse Hutchinson to a poem of unidentified authorship which he had found in an old school reader. This piece was well calculated to raise the hair and accelerate the heartbeat of its listeners. It is a tale of woe in which an agonized parent watches her infant child being snatched by a ravenous vulture. "The Vulture of the Alps" was the first published song by a Hutchinson (1842) and thereafter became a family tour de force.

John Hutchinson was starred in two Henry Russell ballads, "The Maniac" and "The Ship on Fire." John Hutchinson sang the former, as he wrote, "alone to the accompaniment of my brothers. Judson and Asa would commence a prelude. Meanwhile I would be in my chair behind them, with the finger of each hand raising the hair of my head, and bringing it in partial dishevellment. Then I would rise, with the expression of vacancy inseparable from mania, and commence."

When with his rich stentorian voice and his flair for histrionics, John Hutchinson offered "The Ship on Fire" in Canton, Pennsylvania, his rendition proved so vivid that one member of the audience fled from the auditorium to summon the fire engines. Years later, President Lincoln asked the Hutchinsons to sing this ballad for him at a White House reception, disclosing that it had long been one of his own favorites from the Hutchinson repertory.

Then there was "The Snowstorm" (Sheba Smith—Lyman Heath), introduced by the Hutchinsons in New York on May 17, 1842. This is a tragic tale of mother and child. A woman, trudging through a blinding snowstorm in the Green Mountains in search of her husband, is clutching her child, shielding it with her cloak. "Oh, God, she cries in accents wild, if I must perish, save my child!" When a traveler comes upon them, the child is alive, but the mother has frozen to death.

The Hutchinsons also presented songs of a less sensational character, but no less strong in sentiment. Henry Russell's "The Gambler's Wife" allowed Aby to shine as a lonely, harassed, deserted wife of a chronic gambler. The melancholy "Mrs. Lofty and I" (Mrs. Gildersleeve Longstreet—Judson Hutchinson) was another sentimental ballad poignantly sung by Aby, for whom it was written. "My Mother's Bible" (George P. Morris—Judson Hutchinson) was still one more lachrymose ode, about a bible which mother's hands had often clasped and which, on her dying bed, she turns over to her loved ones. "My Mother's Cottage" (Jesse Hutchinson—Judson Hutchinson) proved to be still another variation on the theme of mother. "Ben Bolt" (Thomas Dunn English—Nelson Kneass) also enjoyed a prominent place on their programs following its publication in 1848.

"Excelsior"—in the writing of which all the Hutchinsons participated—is to the text of Henry Wadsworth Longfellow's famous poem. The mood of this song is far less maudlin, but no less dramatic. As Carol Brink noted in *Harps in the Wind*: "Here were all the ingredients of a favorite Hutchinson number: the mountains, the snowstorm, the dramatic climax which John knew so well how to handle, and finally the lofty and noble ideal." When the song was published in 1843 Longfellow contributed a brief paragraph for the title page.

John Hutchinson was spotlighted in dramatic numbers and Aby in some of the more sentimental ones. When there were comedy songs, these were taken over by Judson Hutchinson—songs such as "The Horticultural Wife," written by all the Hutchinsons, and "Go Call a Doctor, or anti-Calomel" by Judson Hutchinson.

What truly set the Hutchinsons apart from other singing families were their crusades against existing evils. As propagandists they electrified their audiences while keeping their programs continually alive with contemporary interest—and consistently provocative. As performers and as songwriters they added a significant chapter to the social and political history of their times, times when a nation was a house divided against itself.

2

Temperance was the first reform movement with which the Hutchinsons became affiliated. In Baltimore in 1840, several reformed alcoholics organized the Washingtonian movement to promote total abstinence from intoxicating liquors. At public meetings, the gospel of temperance fanned out with societies formed in different localities spreading the cause. Through the power of the spoken and written word—and through songs—the reform movement gained sufficient momentum to capture half a million or so dedicated converts, and by 1851 fifteen states had passed legislation prohibiting the sale of intoxicants. Carrie Amelia Nation (whose first husband had been an alcoholic) took on a one-woman campaign in Kansas to destroy saloons, one of many vigorously involved in the temperance cause. Their efforts helped to bring about the birth of the Prohibition Party in 1869. At long last, on October 28, 1919, the eighteenth amendment to the Constitution was passed, prohibiting the manufacture, sale and transportation of intoxicating drinks in any part of the United States, bringing with it the era of the speakeasy, the illicit hip flask, the bootlegger, the racketeer, the gangster empires.

At the urging of a Presbyterian minister, William Patton, an avowed crusader in the Temperance movement, the Hutchinsons attended their first Temperance rally in 1842 at the Temperance Temple in Saco, Maine. After Lyman Beecher, son of Henry Ward Beecher, introduced them to an audience of some three thousand, the Hutchinsons sang several Temperance songs and concluded with "The Old Granite State." Witnessing the impact these songs had on the audience, they realized for the first time the power of music in crusading campaigns. Their appearances and performances at Temperance meetings now became increasingly frequent. More than that, they began to include many of these songs in their regular concert programs, thereby introducing a fresh and exciting feature to their programs.

There was no shortage of Temperance songs, and there were also songs satirizing the movement ("The Striped Pig," and Henry Russell's "The Total S'city"). And there were songs extolling the joys of inebriation. In 1842, William Clifton took the French folk tune, "Malbrouck" and used it for his words for "We Won't Go Home Till Morning," a tribute to the happy state of intoxication. When this song was first published, the sheet music cover portrayed young collegians enjoying the pleasures of drink in a taproom. Eleven years later, Julien Carlen wrote the words and music of "Brandy and Wine" which raised a toast to various liquors, with the refrain, "Drink it down, drink it down," recurring throughout.

But an age that found so much delight in overdramatic and overemotional ballads was far more partial to songs pointing up the tragedy of alcoholism than its blessings. These songs represent a significant addition to the balladry of post-Civil War America. In 1907, Emmet G. Coleman published *The Temperance Song Book*, whose subtitle read: "A peerless collection of Temperance songs and hymns for the Women's Christian Temperance Union, Loyal Temperance Legion, Prohibitionists, Temperance Praise Meetings, Medal Contests, etcetera." It included many of his own songs ("Under the Curse," "The Temperance Train," "Breaking Mother's Heart," and "Father, Dear Father, Come Home") and with them many a song dear to the hearts of those in the Temperance movement, such as "The Drunkard's Lament" (Rollin C. Ward) and "The Temperance Call" (Franz Abt).

Many antiliquor songs were heard even outside Temperance meeting halls. There were "The Drunkard's Child" (A. E. Parkhurst), "Don't Marry a Man if He Drinks," "Father's a Drunkard and Mother Is Dead" (Stella of Washington—A. E. Parkhurst), and "Papa Don't Drink Anymore" (Arthur W. French—Charles D. Blake).

"King Alcohol," words by Jesse Hutchinson to the melody of "King Andrew," was an important number in the Hutchinson repertory of Temperance songs. He wrote it when a distillery in Salem, Massachusetts, was converted into a Temperance hall, in or about 1840—its chorus labeling various types of "spirits" as a "fiendish crew." The Hutchinsons also sang "Drink Nothing, Boys, But Water," "The Temperance Ship Is Sailing On," "Father Bring Home Your Money Tonight," "We Are all Washingtonians" and "The Teetotalers are Coming," the last being another of their own compositions.

3

The Hutchinsons also allied themselves with other causes. When they sang Henry Russell's "The Indian Hunter" they joined its composer in pleading for justice for the native American. With the song, "Tobacco," they inveighed against smoking. The Hutchinsons also promoted woman's suffrage with "Let Us Speak Our Minds if We Die for It" (William Brough—J. G. Maeder), "Western Suffrage Song" and "Vote It Right Along."

But of all their political and social involvements, abolition was the cause about which the Hutchinsons were most passionate. Slavery was the greatest single issue splitting America in the mid-nineteenth century. In the North, the abolitionists worked feverishly to keep emotions at white heat over slavery, exploiting emotions and ideals with an artist's skill, inspiring pity, hatred, defiance.

The abolitionists knew full well the value of songs as propaganda. Antislavery singing societies were formed for which new verses were prepared for well-known tunes; some of these lyrics were the work of William Lloyd Garrison. The borrowed melodies included "Old Hundred," "Auld Lang Syne," the "Marseillaise," "Old Rosin the Beau" and "Oh! Susanna." Assembled in such songsters as *The Anti-Slavery Harp* (1851), they were in general circulation at abolitionist meetings.

Many of these songs gained fame outside the meeting hall. A public fond of sentiment readily took to songs describing the physical and mental cruelties inflicted on blacks. The minstrel shows, of course, provided a welcome forum for songs about black people in slavery, though more in a sentimental than aggressive vein. Exceptions to this are found in the first songs Dan Emmett wrote for Bryant's Minstrels after joining that company: "The Land of Freedom," "Wide Awake" and "Johnny Roach." Unlike so many other songs about the South and the Negro heard in minstrel shows, these were tinged with strong political and social feelings.

The Hutchinsons were a far more forceful instrument for carrying the message of abolition to the American people than was the minstrel show. The father, Jesse Hutchinson, had been a boyhood friend of the dedicated abolitionist Horace Greeley; as boys, they had both learned the printer's trade in New Hampshire. Jesse's son, Judson Hutchinson, had also long known Frederick Douglass, the central figure in a cause célèbre of the late 1830s—Douglass' flight from Southern slavery to find refuge in New England where he lectured at the meetings of the Massachusetts Anti-Slavery Society. Nathaniel P. Rogers, editor of the *Herald of Freedom*—a journal advocating equality among all men—was another friend of the Hutchinsons. Rogers was the one who urged the Hutchinsons to enlist their singing and songwriting talents in the cause of abolition.

All these personal contacts with men deeply engaged in the struggle against slavery helped to influence the Hutchinsons. The family's feelings were further strengthened on November 17, 1842, the day that Jesse, the father, and his son, John, attended an abolitionist meeting at Marlboro Chapel in Boston. The meeting had been organized to support and help free George Latimore. Latimore was a southern slave who had escaped to the North from Norfolk but who had then been imprisoned in Boston under the Fugitive Slave Bill. As the two Hutchinsons entered the meeting room, they sang "O Liberate the Bondsman," a number they had written for this occasion. With this, and several more antislavery songs, they generated such enthusiasm that four hundred dollars was collected to purchase Latimore's freedom from his Southern master.

One day, several of the Hutchinsons visited the Hope Slatter prison in Baltimore where Southern blacks who had fled from slavery were incarcerated. The Hutchinsons recoiled with horror at the sights and smells confronting them. "Our hearts sickened," John said. "We inwardly cursed such an institution and re-resolved to do everything in our power to ameliorate the slaves' conditions and wash from our escutcheon the bloody stain."

After that, the Hutchinsons performed at the meetings of the Anti-Slavery Society at Faneuil Hall in Boston. One session, on January 25, 1843, was opened with their singing of "Blow Ye Trumpet, Blow!" Subsequent sessions were invariably opened or closed with their rendition of antislavery songs, and at times, these songs were also heard between speeches. Antislavery songs also became an important part of the regular concert programs of the Hutchinsons. Some of these songs were written by one or more of the Hutchinsons; a few were among the best of their kind: "The Slave's Appeal," "The Fugitive Slave to the Christian," "The Bereaved Slave Mother," "Jordan," "The Liberty Bell" (using the melody of "Old Rosin the Beau") and "Get Off the Track," to the tune of "Old Dan Tucker" which the Hutchinsons erroneously believed to be an old slave melody. Dan Emmett's "Jordan Is a Hard Road to Travel," still another abolitionist song popular with the Hutchinsons, had its beginnings in the minstrel show before they took it over.

In "Get Off the Track," a steam car, then very much a novelty, symbolized the onrushing forces of emancipation. ("Roll it along, Roll it along, Roll it along, thro' the nation, Freedom's Car, Emancipation!") When the Hutchinsons first sang it at an anti-slavery rally it caused such a furor that the shouting interfered with their performance. At their concerts, "Get Off the Track" created a schism in their audiences, with abolitionists expressing loud approbation, and the opposition howling in disapproval. "When they came to the chorus cry that gives name to the song," wrote Nathaniel P. Rogers in *Herald of Freedom*, "when they cried to the heedless pro-slavery multitude that were stupidly lingering on the track, and the engine 'Liberator' coming hard upon them, under full steam and all speed, the Liberty Bell loud ringing and they standing like deaf men right in its whirlwind path, the way they cried 'Get off the track!' in defiance of all time and rule was magnificent and sublime."

Passions aroused by the songs of the Hutchinsons and the propaganda of the abolitionists were brought to the boiling point with the publication of Harriet Beecher Stowe's *Uncle Tom's Cabin*, first serialized in the *National Era* in 1851, then released in book form in 1852 to achieve a sale of some three hundred thousand copies in its first year. John Hutchinson tried to convince Mrs. Stowe to dramatize her novel, but she insisted it was unsuitable for the stage. Mrs. Stowe's opinion seemed vindicated when, five months after the appearance of the novel, it was dramatized by C. W. Taylor, who also filled the role of Uncle Tom. Sadly truncated and mutilated, the novel proved a complete failure in its dramatic treatment in New York. The play survived just two weeks. But the following autumn, a new stage version was mounted at the Museum Theater in Troy, New York, the work of George T. Aiken. This adaptation—and several others—made the novel one of the most valuable stage properties of the time. The popularity of *Uncle Tom's Cabin* on the stage remained undiminished till the end of the century.

Songs about *Uncle Tom's Cabin* came thick and fast. One was "Little Topsy's Song" (Eliza Cook—Asa Hutchinson), featured successfully by the Hutchinsons. Other songs gained wide popularity without the benefit of performances by the family. These included "Eliza's Flight" (M. A. Collier—E. J. Loder), "Little Eva" (John Greenleaf Whittier —Manuel Emilio), "I Am Going There," (John S. Adams) touching on Eva's death, and "The Death of St. Clare" (M. A. Collier—melody not identified).

4

The 1860 Presidential campaign found the Hutchinson family solidly in the camp of the Republican Party and Abraham Lincoln. Lincoln first heard them in concert in Springfield, Illinois, in 1851, and is known to have heard them many times after.

The *Hutchinson Republican Songster* was published during the Presidential campaign. It included fifty songs advocating Lincoln's candidacy, most of them parodies of familiar tunes. The words of "Freemen Win When Lincoln Leads," used the melody of "Lutzow's Wild Hunt"; "Have You Heard the Loud Alarm?", that of "The Old Granite State"; "Lincoln and Liberty," that of "Old Rosin the Beau." Many numbers in this collection used the candidate's name in the song title: "Hurrah for Lincoln," "A Suit of Lincoln Green," "Abe of Illinois," "Lincoln," "Lincoln and Victory," and "Lincoln, the Pride of the Nation," the last set to the melody of "Columbia, the Gem of the Ocean."

The Hutchinsons were not the only ones to promote Lincoln. In a campaign broadside published by H. De Marsan, the ever popular "Wait for the Wagon" emerged as "Lincoln and Hamlin." "Old Dan Tucker" and "Yankee Doodle" were two other standard melodies heard with new words in the Lincoln campaign. "Old Abe Lincoln Came out of the Wilderness" (author of words not known) lifted its melody from the popular song by J. Warner, "Down in Alabam' " (1858) which is better known to us today as "The Old Gray Mare."

There were also songs for the opposition. The Secessionists sang "Breckinridge and Lane," whose melody was "Yankee Doodle." The splinter Constitutional Union Party was for John Bell and Edward Everett in "Union Dixie," to the melody of "Dixie," and in "Campaign Rally Song," to the melody of "De Boatman's Dance."

Nevertheless, the singing voices of the Hutchinsons and others were highly influential in helping to sweep Abraham Lincoln into the White House. Then when the Civil War pitted North against South—and brought the issue of slavery into somewhat better focus—the Hutchinsons enlisted their talents in the war effort. They continued singing antislavery songs to keep the issue alive on the home front, and they introduced war songs to build up the morale of both civilians and fighting men.

Because of their complete dedication to the Northern cause, on one occasion the Hutchinsons came to grips with some unpleasant realities involving the Union Army. On January 14, 1862, they were allowed to sing for the troops of the Army of the Potomac at Fairfax Seminary. They sang "We Wait Beneath the Furnace Blast," words by John Greenleaf Whittier to the melody of the old Lutheran chorale of Martin Luther, "Ein feste Burg." This song was a defiant response to some proslavery sentiments expressed by General McClellan, who like some other Northern generals opposed abolition. When the Hutchinsons came to the lines "what whets the knife for Union's life—Hark to the answer, Slavery!" the men in uniform broke out noisily, some in cheers, and others with hisses, depending upon their personal prejudices on the subject of abolition. General Kearny summoned the Hutchinsons after the concert and forebade them to sing again for the Army, exclaiming: "You are abolitionists. I think as much of a rebel as I do of an abolitionist!" The heated protests of the Hutchinsons brought this controversial affair to the attention of Brigadier General Franklin who, upon reading the Whittier lyrics, decided that the song was "incendiary" and that further performances would "demoralize the Army." He was backed up by General McClellan. In the end President Lincoln became involved. The President maintained that this was "just the character of song that I desire the soldiers to hear." The Hutchinsons were once again given permission to sing for the troops only upon the invitation of a specific command-ing officer.

The personnel of the Hutchinson Family kept changing, as different members of the family replaced others, and a new generation succeeded the preceding one. But the intensity with which they kept on fighting social and political battles remained undiminished. As Mrs. Elizabeth Cady Stanton, one of the founder's of woman's suffrage, wrote in 1881 in *The History of Woman's Suffrage*: "It is now forty years that the various branches of the Hutchin-son family have been singing the liberal ideas of their day on antislavery, Temperance, and Woman's Rights platforms, and they are singing still with the infusion of new blood in the second and third generations." The Hutchinsons left no doubt about where they stood. At a woman's suffrage program in Philadelphia in 1876—given as part of the centennial celebra-tion of the signing of the Declaration of Independence—they closed their program with "A Hundred Years Hence," which they themselves wrote. In it they summed up their hopes for a future society built on the foundations of the causes and reforms they had been promoting through the years:

> "One hundred years hence, what a change will be made
> In politics, morals, religions and trade. . . .
>
>   . . . .
>
> "Then woman, man's partner, man's equal shall stand
> While beauty and harmony govern the land,
> To think for oneself will be no offense,
> The world will be thinking, a hundred years hence.
>
> "Oppression and war will be heard of no more
> Nor the blood of a slave leave his print on our shore,
> Conventions will then be a useless expense,
> For we'll all go free suffrage, a hundred years hence.
>
> "Instead of speech-making to satisfy wrong,
> All will join the glad chorus to sing Freedom's song;
> And if the Milennium is not a pretense,
> We'll all be good brothers—a hundred years hence."

5

The Civil War produced a rich literature of songs reflecting the emotions in both camps —the ardor and the bitterness, the exaltation and despair, the hopes and frustrations, the nostalgia and the chilling loneliness. There was hardly any aspect of the conflict, or its principles or protagonists or events, that did not find an outlet in song.

After General Beauregard's Confederate batteries fired on Fort Sumter on April 12, 1861, and the Union forces retaliated the following July with an attack at Bull Run, the South appropriated "Dixie" to inflame patriotism, to arouse the fighting spirit, and to aggravate sectional pride. Dressed up with new martial lyrics, "Dixie" proved more effective in generating these feelings than hundreds of editorials, slogans and speeches.

As a Confederate war song, with new words by Albert Pike, "Dixie" was transformed into:

> "Southerns, hear your country call you
> Up! less worse than death befall you!
> To arms! To arms! To Arms! In Dixie.
>
>   . . . .
>
> "Advance the flag of Dixie!
> Hurrah! Hurrah!
> For Dixie's land we'll take our stand,
> And Live and die for Dixie!
> To arms! To arms! And conquer peace for Dixie.
> To arms! To arms! And conquer peace for Dixie."

Nobody knows exactly when "Dixie" first became the Confederate Army's song of songs. But we do know that even before the outbreak of the war, the South had looked with favor on Emmett's "Dixie," for it was played at the inauguration of Jefferson Davis as President of the Confederacy in Montgomery, Alabama, on February 18, 1861. We also know that, after Bull Run, "Dixie," spread throughout the entire Confederacy, though this time with the new martial lyrics. It was sung in army camps everywhere, and then on the field of battle. General George Pickett ordered that it be played at the charge of Gettysburg. It even incubated a widely sung parody, "The Officers of Dixie," the words of which were by a man who assumed the pen name of "A. Growler."

The fact that a Northerner had written the melody was conveniently forgotten in the South. The authorship was ascribed in the South to an unidentified Negro expressing his attachment to his Southern homeland. Up North, however, Dan Emmett was often subjected to attacks in the press for having fathered the South's battle song. In vain did he protest that "if I had known what use they were going to put my song, I would be damned if I'd have written it!" Unable to convince his critics he was innocent of "treason" by writing "Dixie"— that the South had confiscated his innocent minstrel show melody for its own purposes without his permission or knowledge—he prepared new lyrics for his melody exhorting the North to meet "those Southern traitors with iron will" and "to remember Bunker Hill." Another Northern lyricist, whose identity has never been discovered, also tried to make "Dixie" into a Union war song by writing "Union Dixie." But neither of these two new versions caught on, and "Dixie" remained the war hymn of the Confederacy. Abraham Lincoln confirmed this Southern identity of "Dixie" when, after the surrender at Appomattox, he remarked that since the rebel army had been conquered so had "Dixie." He exhorted a band outside the White House to play it for him. "It did," writes Hans Nathan in his book on Emmett, "but that 'Dixie' thus actually became a trophy of the North, the South never admitted."

Second in importance only to "Dixie" among the war songs of the Confederacy was "Maryland, My Maryland." The lyrics were by James Ryder Randall, professor of English literature at Pydras College in Louisiana. Randall had been aroused by a newspaper account of Northern troops being fired upon as they passed through Baltimore. "My Southern blood was stirred to fever point," he recalled. "My nerves were all unstrung. I could not dismiss what I had read from my mind. About midnight, I arose, lit a candle, and went to my desk. Some powerful spirit seemed to possess me, and almost involuntarily I proceeded to write the verses of 'My Maryland.' . . . The whole poem was dashed off rapidly when once begun. It was not composed in cold blood, but under what may be called a conflagration of the senses. I was stirred to a desire for some way of linking my name to that of my native state."

Completed on April 1, 1861, the poem was first published five days later in a Louisiana paper, then on May 31, in *The South*, a prosouthern journal in Baltimore. It forthwith was widely circulated through broadsides.

Soon after the appearance of the broadside, Jennie Cary of Baltimore held a meeting at her home for advocates of the Southern cause. One of the attractions was a singing group led by Miss Cary. When she expressed the desire to feature on her program some song to rally the people of Baltimore to the Confederate side, her sister showed her Randall's poem. Jennie Cary provided for it the melody of "O Tannenbaum," the German folk song written in 1824 and popular in America both as a college song and as a Christmas carol. This was truly an unintentional happy marriage of words and music. The song aroused so much enthusiasm when performed at Miss Cary's home that people in the streets flocked to the windows of her house to see what was happening.

Words and music were first published in Baltimore in 1861, and after that in the South. Jennie Cary, and her sister Hetty, sang it for the troops of General Beauregard at a concert at the Fairfax County House in Virginia during the summer of 1861. It was on this occasion that the popularity of the song began to soar. "The refrain," said Hetty Cary, "was speedily caught up and tossed back to us from hundreds of rebel throats. . . . There surged forth from the throng a wild shout, 'We will break her chains! Maryland will be free!' "

"Maryland, My Maryland," lost face after the state allied herself with the North, and after General Lee's first invasion of Maryland failed. But with many a Southerner the song remained a favorite. In a later generation it became the official song of the State of Maryland, and was also adopted as the theme music for the annual Preakness race at Pimlico Park at Baltimore.

"The Bonnie Blue Flag" and "The Yellow Rose of Texas" were two animated songs calculated to buoy up the spirits of the South. The words of "The Bonnie Blue Flag" are believed to have been written by Annie Chambers-Ketchum, while the music by Henry Macarthy, an English-born performer in American variety theaters, was based on an old Irish tune, "The Jaunting Car." Some writers maintain that the song's inspiration had been the blue flag with the white star adopted by the State of South Carolina when it became the first to secede from the Union. Others suggest that Macarthy wrote his song after recalling a dramatic episode at the Mississippi Convention of January 9, 1861, when a Southerner entered the hall waving a blue flag with white star his wife had just sewn. Whatever the stimulus—and it may have been nothing more dramatic than Macarthy's wish to introduce some exciting material into his variety act—he performed it in Jackson, Mississippi, during the spring of 1862. Later the same year, while appearing before an audience of Confederate soldiers in New Orleans, he used it as march music for his finale.

Several parodies of "The Bonnie Blue Flag" were written and popularized. The most celebrated was "The Homespun Dress," also known as "The Southern Girls." The words, attributed to Carrie Bell Snyder, were written in 1862 or 1863. Extensively sung in the South during the Civil War, "The Homespun Dress" entered the repertory of Southern folklore, particularly in Mississippi where, as Arthur Palmer Hudson noted in *Folksongs of Mississippi*, "almost every woman and many of the men who lived through the period of the Civil War or grew up with the generation after the war could sing it."

"The Yellow Rose of Texas" came to the South by way of Northern minstrel shows. When first published in 1853, its author was identified merely as "J. K." The song grew popular as a Confederate marching song, both in its original version and in parodies. One of these parodies was "The Song of the Texas Rangers." Another gives an account of the disaster attending the Tennessee campaign of 1864. In a twentieth-century adaptation by Don George, "The Yellow Rose of Texas" was successfully revived in 1955 and became a best-selling recording.

Other war songs sent the South rallying around their flag. Some were written by James Hill Hewitt who had first become famous with his ballad "The Minstrel's Return from the War" some thirty-five years earlier. The Civil War made him the southland's song laureate. As soon as the war broke out he wrote "Southern Song of Freedom" and soon after that "The Young Volunteer."

Many of the stirring war songs of the South were written to borrowed melodies. "The Valiant Conscript" and "The Confederate Yankee Doodle" both were sung to the melody of "Yankee Doodle"; "The Southern Wagon" (a salute to the seceding States) to the melody of "Wait for the Wagon"; and "We Conquer or Die," words by James Pierpont, to the melody of "Jingle Bells."

In a sentimental mood, the South sang "Lorena" (H. D. L. Webster—J. P. Webster). So popular did it become that for decades after the war, many girl babies in the South were named after the heroine of this ballad, and so were several pioneer settlements and even a steamship. John Hill Hewitt was the composer of two other beloved Civil War ballads of the South. "Somebody's Darling," (Marie Ravenal de la Coste) was one of the few Southern ballads to gain favor in the North. This song was mentioned in Margaret Mitchell's famous Civil War novel, *Gone With the Wind*. But Hewitt's masterpiece in sentimental ballad form was "All Quiet Along the Potomac Tonight," about which a good deal of misinformation has been disseminated in song histories and reference books. A true-life incident was long said to have been the source of this ballad. As this story goes, John Moore, on guard duty in the Confederate Army, lit a fire one night to warm himself. The light exposed his position to the opposite bank of the Potomac where a Union picket saw and shot him. His friend, Major Lamar Fontaine, rushed to his side and noticed a newspaper near his body with a headline then often used by the press to denote a lull on the Potomac battlefront, "All quiet on the Potomac tonight." This story continues to relate how one day after this tragedy, Fontaine wrote five stanzas of a poem about his dead friend in which, allowing his imagination free rein, he told how at the moment of death Moore was pining for wife and home. John Hill Hewitt then wrote music for Fontaine's words. The fame of this song among Confederates was further said to have brought about a ban on the lighting of campfires during guard duties.

But the research of several notable song historians, including Richard B. Harwell, the author of *Confederate Music*, gives the lie to this sad tale. No such incident apparently occurred; what is more, Lamar Fontaine was not the author of the verses to which Hewitt set his music. The words were written by Mrs. Ethel Lynn Beers, a Northerner, who picked her subject from a brief news item reporting the fatal shooting of a Confederate soldier on guard duty and bearing the headline of "All quiet on the Potomac tonight." She published her verses in *Harper's Weekly* on November 30, 1861, and it was soon thereafter set to music by several different composers, one of whom was W. H. Goodwin, and another, John Hill Hewitt whose version became the most famous of all.

The songs of the South were good, but those of the North were better still. In the battle of songs, as on the field of conflict, the North emerged victorious. Shortly after the surrender of General Lee, a few Northern soldiers performed a potpourri of Northern war songs for several Confederate officers. A Southern Major remarked; "Gentlemen, if we had had your songs, we'd have licked you out of your boots."

One of the first, and one of the best, of these Northern war songs was "The Battle Hymn of the Republic." Only its lyrics were written during the war. The melody appeared in the middle 1850s as a camp meeting song popular with black congregations, "Say, Brothers, Will You Meet Us?" sometimes attributed to William Steffe. As was often the custom with well-liked tunes, this Methodist hymn was the basis of innumerable parodies, some of them topical, others, ribald. The most celebrated of these parodies was "John Brown's Body," a discussion of which is imperative before we pass on to the history of "The Battle Hymn of the Republic."

"John Brown's Body" came from the second battalion of the Boston Light Infantry, Massachusetts Volunteer Militia. The "John Brown" in this song is not the man who headed the historic band of antislavery zealots in an attack on Harper's Ferry on October 16, 1859, and was hung in Charleston, Virginia on December 2. Rather, he was a Scot, the battalion sergeant. The fact that this fellow bore the same name as the notorious zealot—added to the fact that the sergeant was also disarmingly naive and simple minded—made him a helpless butt for taunts and jests. This John Brown was a member of the battalion chorus, one of whose numbers was the Methodist hymn, "Say, Brothers, Will You Meet Us?" To this tune, members of the battalion improvised lyrics mocking the hapless Scotsman. This "John Brown's Body" version became such a popular marching song with the 21st Regiment that it was used to celebrate the receiving of colors on the Boston Common on July 18, 1861. One week later, the regiment sang it while marching along Broadway in New York en route to the battlefields of Virginia; and on March 1, 1862, the regiment sang it in Charleston, Virginia, at the very place where the abolitionist John Brown had been executed for his insurrection.

The spreading fame of "John Brown's Body" was of course due entirely to the fact that the namesake of the song was mistaken by the general public for the passionate and dedicated abolitionist. It became an outstanding number in the antislavery song repertory of the times. Many parodies were invented. "The President's Proclamation," words by Edna Dean Proctor, was inspired by the Emancipation Proclamation; "Marching Along," words by William B. Bradburg, became one of the familiar marches of the Union Army; and "Marching Song of the First Arkansas Regiment"—words by a white officer, Captain Lindley Miller—was in honor of the first black regiment called to the colors in the spring of 1862, and was a particular favorite of the First Arkansas Colored Regiment.

One day, in December 1861, Julia Ward Howe—poet, pioneer suffragette, and the wife of a noted physician—heard "John Brown's Body" and was impressed by it. When asked by one of her friends, a minister, to write some new and more suitable words for this melody she complied willingly. That very night, at the Willard Hotel in Washington, D. C., the opening line suddenly came to her in her sleep: "Mine eyes have seen the glory of the coming of the Lord." With this as a starting point, she wrote the rest of her lyrics by candlelight, completing them before dawn. Her poem was published in the *Atlantic Monthly*, in February 1862, for which she received the payment of five dollars. Soon after it was republished in several magazines and Army hymn books, and issued as sheet music by at least three publishers with the melody of "John Brown's Body." After the chaplain of the 122nd Ohio Regiment of Volunteers taught it to Union soldiers, "The Battle Hymn of the Republic" became one of the most frequently sung war hymns in the Union Army. It is said that when Lincoln heard it sung for the first time he wept and begged that the performance be repeated. Since then, the song has served as Lincoln's identification, beginning with the 1864 Presidential campaign when the melody was also used by the Democrats to attack Lincoln in "White Soldiers' Song."

"The Battle Hymn of the Republic" outlived the Civil War and the 1864 campaign. Its melody became a Presidential campaign song in 1872 ("Hurray! Hurrah! for Grant and Wilson"), in 1888 ("The Collar and the Kerchief"), in 1900 ("When Bryan is Elected"), in 1920 ("The Campaign Hymn of the Republic"), in 1932 ("Battle Hymn of the Republican

Party") and in 1944 ("Republican Battle Hymn"). During World War II, Major William Harris, a paratrooper, wrote a parody which was sung by many of his fellows. It was called "Paratrooper's Lament, or Blood on the Risers," and its refrain went: "Gory, gory, what a helluva way to die! . . . And he ain't gonna jump no more!".

In the post-World War II years, the song made the news time and again. When President Lyndon B. Johnson was inaugurated in January 1965, "The Battle Hymn of the Republic" was sung by the Mormon Tabernacle Choir following his address. This became a front-page news item because several Southern senators objected violently to its performance on the grounds that this was a "Union song." Ten days later, the song was heard at the funeral services of Sir Winston Churchill in London, selected by his widow and members of his immediate family in tribute to Sir Winston's American mother. When the funeral train carried the body of Senator Robert Kennedy past the railroad station in Baltimore, Maryland, in June 1968, en route to its burial place in Washington, D. C., the crowds which had gathered to pay their last respects to the assassinated presidential aspirant suddenly and spontaneously erupted into singing "The Battle Hymn of the Republic." The melody was used by James Smith in 1971 for "The Battle Hymn of Lieutenant Calley" to protest his conviction of a court-martial jury to life imprisonment for his role in the 1968 massacre at My Lai in Vietnam. In 1972, in Miami, Florida, after Senator George McGovern delivered his acceptance address upon being nominated for the presidency at the Democratic National Convention, the strains of the hymn were sounded by all those present. On January 26, 1973, at the burial services for President Lyndon B. Johnson at the LBJ Ranch in Texas, it was sung by Anita Bryant who explained that after she had sung "The Battle Hymn of the Republic" for Johnson at his ranch he told her: "Honey, I want you to sing that when they lower me in the ground." Mrs. Johnson overheard his remark and asked her to do so. When, on January 20, 1977, Jimmy Carter was inaugurated President of the United States and "The Battle Hymn of the Republic" was played and sung, no objection to this "Union song" was vocalized by any Southerner.

"The Battle Hymn of the Republic" is one of many distinguished surviving war songs of the North. "When Johnny Comes Marching Home" was written by the famed bandleader of the Union Army, Patrick S. Gilmore. Apparently, he thought so little of this effort that he published it in 1863 under the pseudonym of Louis Lambert. He later confessed he had written the words but had used the melody of a traditional Negro folk song. It is more probable, however, that Gilmore's source was an Irish tune he had heard soldiers sing during the war. Union soldiers liked "When Johnny Comes Marching Home" and sang it frequently. The Confederacy took cognizance of its popularity by using the same melody for a comic verse, "For Bales," words by A. E. Blackmar, popular in New Orleans in 1863, its subject referring to the unsuccessful attempt by Union soldiers to capture bales of cotton stored up Red River. After the Civil War, "Johnny Comes Marching Home" was revived several times. It lent its melody to "Abe Lincoln Went to Washington," a tribute to the President after his assassination. During the Spanish-American War, "When Johnny Comes Marching Home" grew so popular that it became one of the songs most often associated with that conflict. The song returned during World War I in the modern dress of a fox-trot. Its melody was later given symphonic treatment by two distinguished American composers, Roy Harris and Morton Gould.

The war in the North inspired the writing of several songs about Abraham Lincoln. Septimus Winner wrote "Abraham's Daughter," and C. E. Pratt wrote the words, and Frederick Buckley the music, for "We'll Fight for Uncle Abe." Lincoln's call in 1862 for 300,000 volunteers inspired "We Are Coming, Father Abraham" (James Sloan Gibbons

—Luther Orlando Emerson). That year Stephen Foster also completed the words and music of a song with the same subject and the same title. The Emerson song had considerable sobriety reflecting the gravity of the times.

Sobriety and gravity are also prevalent in "Tenting on the Old Camp Ground," one of the most poignant ballads of the Civil War. It was written in 1863 by Walter Kittredge, a singer who had given concerts accompanying himself on a melodeon. The writing of "Tenting on the Old Camp Ground" became for Kittredge an emotional release from his apprehensions upon being called up for the draft. The thought of leaving his wife, their child and their newly acquired house in New Hampshire, stirred within him sober thoughts and painful feelings. These became crystallized in his mind the night before he had to report for his physical examination in a line which came to him as he looked sadly out of his window: "Many are the hearts that are weary tonight, wishing for the war to cease." That night he wrote both the lyrics and the music. The following morning he was turned down by the Army, since one year earlier he had been afflicted with rheumatic fever. Kittredge then went to Boston to market his song. One publisher, to whom he offered it for fifteen dollars, turned it down as too lugubrious, and too lacking in martial spirit. From Boston, Kittredge went to Lynn, hoping to get the support of the Hutchinson Family. Asa Hutchinson not only offered to interest the publishing house of Oliver Ditson but also assured Kittredge that the Hutchinson Family would feature it prominently on its programs. He remained true to his word. The Hutchinson Family introduced it at High Rock in 1863, and a year later Oliver Ditson published it. The sheet music sold so well that within a short period Kittredge earned over a thousand dollars in royalties (which he divided with Asa Hutchinson, probably the earliest example in American popular song history of "payola"). By 1864, Asa was drawing more royalties from this one song than from all his other published numbers combined.

Its popularity did not die with war's end. The song was continually sung during the post-war years, at campfires and picnics, political meetings and elections, and at soldier rallies. It was heard at the Philadelphia centennial celebration in 1876. Kittredge joined John Hutchinson in singing it at a soldier's reunion in Washington, D. C. in 1892. A year later a chorus of five hundred voices performed it at the Chicago Columbian Exposition.

Somber, too, is "Weeping, Sad and Lonely," or "When This Cruel War Is Over" (Charles Carroll Sawyer—Henry Tucker). Here a young girl recalls the time when her beloved stood before her proudly in his blue uniform vowing to remain true both to her and to their country. In thought she sometimes sees him lying wounded on the field of battle with none to hear his call for help or whisper words of solace. The song was written in 1863 and performed that same year by the Woods Minstrels in New York. It was then published in several different editions, in time amassing a sale of about a million copies.

Despite the grimness of war and war's hardships, comedy songs were being written and circularized. In 1862, H. C. Work wrote "Grafted into the Army," which humorously touched upon the Conscription Act then passed by Congress, calling for the draft of every ablebodied male between the ages of twenty and forty-five. A draftee could buy his way out of service either by paying the government $300 or providing a substitute candidate for the uniform. In Work's lyrics, which are filled with amusing malapropisms, a widow comments sardonically on the fact that her son, Jimmy, was "grafted" into the army—a play on the word *drafted*.

Hardships attending the war in the South led to the writing of such comedy songs as "Goober Peas" and "Short Rations." The economic problems in the South were depicted comically in the North in "Hard Times in Dixie" ("M. K."—"Eugarps"). The North also responded gleefully to the capture of Jefferson Davis on May 10, 1865, with "Jeff in Petticoats" (George Cooper—Henry Tucker), Davis having erroneously been rumored to have been caught disguised in women's clothes.

"Farewell to Grog" was a mock lament over the prohibition of grog, a mixture of rum and water, among the men of the American Navy on September 1, 1862. On the eve when this prohibition was to take effect, the men of U.S.S. *Portsmouth* held a wake. For this occasion, one of the seamen, Caspar Schenck, wrote a parody of an English drinking song, "Landlord Fill the Flowing Bowl," calling it "Farewell to Grog."

"Drink It Down" was not in a comic vein, but its lighthearted tribute to various beverages—port, sherry, whiskey, cider, brandy, ale, punch and even water—represents a striking change of pace and style in the song literature of the Civil War years. Long after the war, the song was popular at drinking fests.

The principal military confrontations, both on land and sea, contributed subjects for a treasury of war songs both in the North and the South. The foremost sea engagement took place off Newport News in Chesapeake Bay on March 8, 1862, when the Confederate *Merrimac* sank the Union's *Cumberland*. "The Cumberland and the Merrimac" and "The Cumberland Crew" tell of this Confederate victory. The first significant military clash between the North and South, the Battle of Bull Run in which the Union Army suffered a disastrous defeat, is the subject of "Flight of the Doodles," sung to the tune of "Root, Hog, or Die." "The Battle of Shiloh" (melody based on a Southern Appalachian folk song) and "The Battle of Shiloh Hill" (words by M. B. Smith of the Second Regiment, Texas Volunteers, and the music, the melody of the "Wandering Sailor") are about one of the war's bloodiest battles at Pittsburgh Landing in Western Tennessee in April 1862. "Virginia's Bloody Soil" touches on the Battle of the Wilderness in May 1864, a Union victory, though a highly costly one. General Sherman's historic march to the sea inspired the writing of "When Sherman Marched to the Sea" (S. B. Meyers—M. E. Mack) and the far more famous "Marching through Georgia" by H. C. Work. Eugene J. Johnson wrote the words for "The Fall of Charleston" to the melody of "Whack Row de Dow."

Henry Clay Work, George Frederick Root, and Will S. Hays were three popular song composers whose early creativity and fame were nurtured by the Civil War.

George Frederick Root was born in Sheffield, Massachusetts, on August 30, 1820, and received his musical training both in Boston and in Europe. Upon returning to the United States he became interested in music education. He helped found the New York Normal Institute for the training of music teachers and initiated conventions where music teachers could discuss methods of teaching class singing.

His admiration for Stephen Foster led him in the early 1850s to write popular songs, though not without self-consciousness and condescension, since he released these efforts under the pseudonym of "Wurzel" ("Wurzel" being the German word for "root"). First came two ballads between 1853 and 1855: "The Hazel Dell," which he sold to a publisher for a small cash payment, and "Rosalie, the Prairie Flower," for which he received a royalty that brought him several thousand dollars. The success of "Rosalie"—and that of a sacred evangelical hymn, "The Shining Hour"—convinced him he need no longer hide behind the anonymity of an assumed name.

In 1859, Root came to Chicago where he worked as a printer for Root and Cady, a publishing house which his brother had founded a year earlier. Three days after Fort Sumter was fired upon, Root wrote his first war song. "The First Gun Is Fired," a call for a military response from the North. He soon followed this with other appeals for action—"God Bless Our Brave Young Volunteers" and "Forward Boys, Forward"—and his first sentimental war ballad, "The Vacant Chair" (Henry S. Washburn). Reading about a lieutenant who was killed just as he received leave to come home for Thanksgiving gave Washburn, the lyricist, the idea for "The Vacant Chair," which told about a chair left vacant at a family dinner table through the sudden death in battle of a loved one.

In 1862, Lincoln made his call for volunteers for forty Army regiments and for the Navy. This sent Root to his worktable. In a single morning he completed words and music of "The Battle Cry of Freedom" (at first more popularly named "Rally 'Round the Flag"). Just that day Frank and Jules Lombard, a singing duo, came to Root and Cady in search of a good war song for a program scheduled for a rally at the Chicago Court House Square on July 24, 1862. Root showed them his manuscript, on which the ink was not yet dry. The Lombards liked the song, and took it for their concert. The audience reacted so enthusiastically upon first hearing that it insisted upon joining in the refrain after one or two repetitions. Several days later, the Hutchinson Family offered the song at a war rally at Union Square, New York. The vociferous response led them to repeat the song several times on that program and to feature it prominently during the war at their concerts.

It is hardly possible to exaggerate the influence that "The Battle Cry of Freedom" had on the fighting spirit of Union soldiers. When the morale of these men plunged to the depths of despair in 1863, a glee club sang it for some of the troops. One unidentified soldier remarked that the song "ran through the camp like wildfire. The effect was little short of miraculous. It put as much spirit and cheer into the camp as a splendid victory. Day and night you could hear it by every campfire in every tent." One Confederate soldier recorded, after hearing some captured Union soldiers sing it: "I shall never forget the first time I heard 'Rally 'Round the Flag.' It was a nasty night during the 'seven days' fight and if I remember it rightly it was raining. I was on picket when, just before taps, some fellow on the other side struck up the song and others joined in the chorus until it seemed to me the whole Yankee Army was singing. . . . I am not naturally superstitious but I tell you that the song sounded like the knell of doom. . . ."

"The Battle Cry of Freedom" filtered through the Confederacy, inspiring two parodies. In "Battle Song" enough alterations were made in the lyrics to change the song into a Southern anthem. In another parody, with new words by William H. Barnes and a musical adaptation by Herman L. Schreiner, the changes were much more radical.

Within two years of its sheet music publication, "The Battle Cry of Freedom" sold over three hundred thousand copies. When Major Anderson raised the American flag at Fort Sumter at the end of the war, the sound of a band playing "The Battle Cry of Freedom" could clearly be heard across the bay. "You have done more than a hundred generals and a thousand orators," President Lincoln told Root. The melody had particular significance for Lincoln, since, during the Presidential campaign of 1864, it was used for "Rally 'Round the Cause, Boys" to enlist further support for the Northern war effort, and for "Rally for Old Abe" to further Lincoln's second bid for the Presidency.

After the war, "The Battle Cry of Freedom" continued to be heard, though in parodies more usually than not. In its original form it was performed at the Presidential convention of the Republican Party in 1868 and became a powerful propaganda weapon in capturing the nomination for General Ulysses S. Grant. During that election year, however, new words were fitted out for its melody and it became "Ulysses Forever," Grant's campaign song. During the 1876 Presidential campaign the melody promoted devaluation in "Rally to the Call, Boys" and in the 1880 campaign the Southern Democrats used the melody for " 'Tis Slavery Forever." As "The Plumed Knight" it served for the Presidential candidacy of James G. Blaine in 1884, and as "Sound Money and Protection" it performed a similar function for William Jennings Bryan. In 1896, a monument to Root was erected and dedicated in Chicago at which time Jules Lombard emerged from retirement to sing "The Battle Cry of Freedom."

Root continued writing war songs, sometimes martial and sometimes sentimental, until the end of the war. Among the martial tunes were "On, On, On the Boys Came Marching," a sequel to "The Battle Cry of Freedom," and "Tramp, Tramp, Tramp." The latter served to fill an empty page in a Christmas catalogue issued as a house organ for Root and Cady. When he saw the manuscript Root's brother remarked: "You've certainly written better numbers." Nevertheless, the song became Root's second greatest song success.

Root's sentimental ballads included "Just Before the Battle, Mother" in which he took note of the fame of "The Battle Cry of Freedom" by referring to it in his lyrics; also "Starved in Prison," which depicts a Union captive who is fated never again to see home or family.

The war had apparently been the necessary stimulus Root needed to create. In peace time he abandoned composing for publishing and teaching. His achievements as a songwriter were over but they were surely not forgotten. When he died at Bailey's Island off the coast of Maine on August 6, 1895, Charles A. Dana, the editor of the New York *Sun* wrote: "George Root did more to preserve the Union than a great many brigadier generals, and quite as many brigades."

Henry Clay Work was driven to the writing of some of his most effective war songs by his profound abolitionist and Unionist sentiments. As Root did, he wrote his own lyrics.

Work was the son of an active abolitionist whose home served as a station in the Underground Railway through which over four thousand slaves escaped. Born in Middletown, Connecticut, on October 1, 1832, Work was apprenticed to a printer in Hartford where he came upon an old melodeon in a room above the shop. He acquired enough of the basics of music by experimenting on that instrument to be able to write songs. His first was "We Are Coming, Sister Mary," which Ed Christy purchased for twenty-five dollars for his minstrels and which Firth, Pond and Company published in the early 1850s.

In 1855, Work arrived in Chicago where he was employed as a printer. Seven years later, he wrote an antislavery song which was his first step to success: "Kingdom Coming." He brought it to George Root at the office of Root and Cady who found it "full of bright, good sense and comic situations in its darky dialect, the words fitting the melody . . . and the whole exactly suited to the times." Root and Cady published it that year and Christy's Minstrels introduced it on April 23, 1863. Negro troops adopted it, chanting it while marching into Richmond in the closing days of the war. So popular did this song become that it inspired several imitations. Two of these were written by Work himself: "Babylon Is Fallen!" in 1863 and "Wake Nicodemus!" in 1864.

After General Lee invaded Pennsylvania, Work wrote "The Song of a Thousand Years." Apprehensive about the fate of the North in the war, he expressed his feelings in "God Save the Nation."

The song with which Work's name will always be associated came in the last months of the war in 1865. It was "Marching Through Georgia." The South has always resented this number which memorializes its defeat. Nevertheless, the song prospered through the years. Its melody ultimately propagandized woman's suffrage, the Populist party, "free silver," Prohibition and the Presidential candidacies of McKinley and Theodore Roosevelt. The song has been played at square dances and, with appropriate words, it has been used as a Princeton football song. During World War I, British troops chanted it while leaving for France, and during World War II, Americans sang it while marching into Tunis.

When he wrote "The Drummer Boy of Shiloh," Will S. Hays was broaching a subject dear to the hearts of many a Civil War songwriter: that of the drummer boy, too young to fight, but not too young to go unarmed into battle beating on his drum and often coming face to face with death. Again and again the song literature of the Civil War eulogizes the drummer boy and laments his untimely death, as in "Drummer Boy of Vicksburg," "Drummer Boy of Nashville," "The Dying Drummer Boy" and H. C. Work's "The Little Major." Hays's "The Drummer of Shiloh" is the best of this genre.

Will S. Hays—the initial stands for Shakespeare—was born in Louisville, Kentucky, in July 1837. For a time he worked as a clerk in a Louisville music shop and as a staff writer for the Louisville *Courier Journal*. In or about 1856 he wrote the words and music of his first songs, "Little Ones at Home" and "I'm Looking for Him." But not until 1862 did any of his songs achieve publication. This happened in 1862 to "Evangeline," with a text by Longfellow. In that year he also wrote "The Drummer Boy of Shiloh" which was sung both in the North and the South.

As a Louisville resident, close to the Southern border, Hays had ambivalent feelings about the war. In "My Southern Sunny Home," written during the war, a Southerner is nostalgic for home—a curious song for a Northerner to write during the war. But then "Oh! I Wish the War Was Over" had already betrayed the composer's impatience with the war in general, and the Northern effort in particular. In 1864, Hays wrote a campaign song for General McClellan who opposed President Lincoln's reelection; in it Hays promoted a peace that was to be achieved not by victory in battle but by a compromise with the South.

Once the war ended, both Work and Hays turned their songwriting talent to the production of sentimental ballads, some of which are among the best and most successful of their time. These will be discussed in later chapters.

PART TWO
1865 – 1900

7

The
Cruel War
Is Over

1

The minstrel show was the first significant type of indigenous stage entertainment for which Americans wrote popular songs, and it served as the springboard from which many songs leaped to success.

During Reconstruction the minstrel show continued to flourish. But several other stage forms also came into being. One was the spectacle, or extravaganza, which first blossomed in New York in 1866 with *The Black Crook*. This was the first musical production to establish some of the rituals of later American musicals.

The term "extravaganza" makes its initial appearance in the American theater in 1857. At that time a visiting European ballet company produced in New York *Novelty, with the Laying of the Atlantic Cable*. This was a lavish production abounding in spectacular scenes. Though a failure, *Novelty* was the precursor in the American theater for the extravaganza. Almost a decade later, *The Black Crook* became the first successful extravaganza in America. And with it, this form of stage entertainment achieved public acceptance.

Accident and coincidence played important roles in the birth of *The Black Crook*. In the 1860s, two New York impresarios—Henry C. Jarrett and Harry Palmer—imported some expensive stage sets from Europe. At the same time they contracted a troupe of French dancers. Their intention was to produce an elaborate French ballet at the Academy of Music in New York. Late one night, in 1865, the Academy burned to the ground, and the projected French ballet lost its home. The two impresarios now entered into negotiations with William Wheatley, owner of Niblo's Gardens, for the use of his theater.

When Wheatley was approached by Jarrett and Palmer, he had just acquired the rights to *The Black Crook*, a melodrama by Charles M. Barras. It was a masterpiece of hokum. Its complicated plot involved magic spells, transformations and enchantments. An often confusing story concerned a black crook, Herzog, who sold his soul to the devil in exchange for supernatural powers. He uses these powers for evil, and in the end is damned by the devil. Wheatley, a veteran showman, knew the full value of novelty. He came to the conclusion that a triple union of the Barras drama, the imported stage sets, and the French dancers might very well result in an attraction which, as he put it mildly, "will certainly arouse curiosity."

As coproducer, Wheatley began planning along Gargantuan lines to make his production the largest, the most lavish and the most expensive ever mounted in New York up to that time. He rebuilt the stage of Niblo's Gardens to make room for the elaborate sets and the complicated apparatus required for the extravagant stage effects. He fitted out the girls of the French ballet in expensive and unusually transparent Parisian silks and laces. He spent what at that time was regarded as a fabulous sum—$55,000—before the curtain went up on September 12, 1866.

It was a stunning production, lasting five and a half hours, revealing to the startled eye such spellbinding effects as a demon ritual, a hurricane in the mountains, a carnival, a "ballet of gems," a march of Amazons and a splendiferous finale with angels and fairies. Suggestive dances and partially undraped females added spice to this sumptuously prepared dish. A new quality of sex insinuation was introduced in dance and song, starting the American musical theater on its long journey towards sex exploitation. The girls did the cancan, an importation from France witnessed in America for the first time. Milly Cavendish stepped lightly in front of the footlights, wagging a provocative finger at the men in her audience as she sang in a high-pitched baby voice "You Naughty, Naughty Men" which had been written for her by T. Kennick (words) and G. Bicknell (music). "You may talk of love and sighing, Say for us you're nearly dying, All the while you know you're trying, To deceive, you naughty, naughty men!"

The Black Crook turned out to be a gilt-edged investment. It had a continuous run of sixteen months (474 performances) up to 1866, the longest of any theatrical entertainment in New York. It earned $600,000 for each of the three producers and $60,000 for its author, Barras. Virtually to the end of the century, it enjoyed numerous revivals. In the twentieth century, in 1929, *The Black Crook* enjoyed a highly successful revival in Hoboken, New Jersey, in an adaptation by Christopher Morley. A quarter of a century later, the circumstances surrounding the first production of *The Black Crook* became the textual source of a Sigmund Romberg musical, *The Girl in Pink Tights*.

The show's tremendous appeal did not rest exclusively in its dazzling sights and sounds. No less important to its triumph was the widely circulated rumor that this was devil's brew. The production was bitterly attacked both in newspapers and the pulpit as an immoral, degrading spectacle. "The police should arrest all engaged in such a violation of public decency," editorialized James Gordon Bennett in *The Herald*. From a platform at the Cooper Union Institute, the Reverend Charles B. Smythe described "the immodest dress of the girls," apparently in the naive expectation that this was a way of discouraging spectators from the play: the girls appeared with "thin, gauze-like material allowing the form of the figures to be discernible. The attitudes were exceedingly indelicate. . . . When a danseuse was assisted by a danseur, the attitudes assumed by both in conjunction suggest to the imagination scenes which one may read describing the ancient heathen orgies."

Such denunciations aroused the curiosity of New Yorkers and sent them in droves to the theater. Everybody, it seemed, wanted to see this "degrading spectacle" for himself. Respectable women disguised themselves with veils, but they came. Many returned several times.

As might be expected, the monumental success of *The Black Crook* led to imitation. Extravaganzas invaded the American theater in increasing numbers. One of the best was *Humpty Dumpty* in 1868. Its book was, for the most part, the work of George L. Fox, who was also the star in the production. The music consisted primarily of adaptations of existing songs. Spectacle was the order of the day: elaborate ballets, some featuring a five-year old danseuse; a lavishly mounted scene with dancers on roller skates; a spectacle set in a subterranean fairy grotto; an ice-skating episode on a moonlit pond; a Neapolitan marketplace. *Humpty Dumpty* lasted in New York even longer than did *The Black Crook*—483 performances. It was revived so often, in and out of New York, that George L. Fox appeared in it over a thousand times.

The Brook, in 1879, though officially described as a "musical farce," was also an extravaganza. This was one of the first American musical productions to attempt to integrate musical numbers into the text. Nate Salsbury was the guiding genius of this production: the author of book and lyrics; the adapter of the music; the star. A comparatively simple plot line tied the whole thing together into a neat package. Five principal characters, called the Salsbury Troubadours, go off by boat for a picnic. That picnic becomes the background for pantomimes, topical material, humorous sketches, caricatures and songs when the revelers find theatrical costumes in their baskets and decide to put them on. Music sprang naturally from all these proceedings. The popularity of *The Brook* extended beyond the Atlantic Ocean, when it was brought to London where it was the first American musical ever given there.

Burlesques—that is musical productions emphasizing travesty, parody and caricature—began to assume the investiture of extravaganzas, and soon came to be known as "burlesque extravaganzas." One was *Evangeline*, in 1874; another, *Adonis*, a decade later. The first was a takeoff on Longfellow's famous poem with book by Edward E. Rice and J. Cheever Goodwin. This was the first American stage production that officially called itself a "musical comedy," a serviceable term that would soon be an umbrella covering most musical presentations. *Evangeline* also earned a place in the history of the American theater because it was the first American musical in which the score was written specifically for it. The music (also the work of Edward E. Rice) consisted of topical songs, comedy numbers, ballads, a waltz, a march and various ensemble and choral pieces. One of its best numbers was the ballad, "Thinking, Love, of Thee" sung by Evangeline.

Adonis, in 1884, parodied the theme of Pygmalion and Galatea. This production also profited from a score by Edward E. Rice written expressly for this occasion. Henry E. Dixey was the star of a merry escapade that saw him monopolizing the limelight with his singing, dancing, pantomiming and improvisations. Striking in appearance, with his well-shaped figure encased in silk tights, he was a matinee idol inspiring romantic dreams in women. *Adonis* became the first New York musical to achieve a consecutive run of over five hundred performances—actually 603.

Some of the most successful burlesque extravaganzas of the Reconstruction period were the long series of "Mulligan plays," books by Edward Harrigan and Tony Hart. These productions dominated the New York stage from 1879 until Hart's death in 1891. This series had its modest beginnings as a variety sketch which Harrigan and Hart offered at the Academy of Music in Chicago on July 15, 1873. They sang a number called "The Mulligan Guard" (Ed Harrigan—David Braham), a sardonic comment on the splinter organizations bedecking themselves with military uniforms that sprang up as an aftermath of the Civil War. Dressed in a ragged, outlandishly mismatched military costume, Harrigan and Hart reduced to a shambles the pretenses of these pseudo-military organizations. The song "The Mulligan Guard" became a rage not only in America but in Europe as well. In America, as E. H. Kahn wrote, "newsboys, policemen, hot corn vendors, the oyster sellers at their street-corner stalls and hokey pokey men who sold ice cream, whistled it as they performed their various chores. . . . Throughout America, children who in other eras might have chanted 'Ten Little Indians' could be found chanting a variation on that theme called 'Ten Little Mulligans.' " In Europe, Rudyard Kipling mentioned it in *Kim* as a song popular with the English Tommies in India, and the Viennese operetta composer, Karl Milloecker, quoted it in the first-act finale of *The Beggar Student*.

All this encouraged Harrigan and Hart to build a whole show around the character of Dan Mulligan, the protagonist of their variety sketch and song. They called it *The Mulligan Guards' Picnic*, and it came to New York in 1878. It set the pattern for a whole series of similar productions for which Ed Harrigan and Tony Hart wrote the books, Harrigan the lyrics, and David Braham the music. Ed Harrigan was cast as Dan Mulligan. Tony Hart sometimes assumed the leading female part and sometimes secondary male roles. Other characters included Mulligan's wife Cordelia (a role in which Annie Yeamans became a star), their son, Tom, and their black maid, Rebecca. With broad satirical strokes, the authors created, and the performers enacted, various types familiar to New York's lower strata of society, such as an Irish grocer, a German butcher, and a black maid. These characters were placed in complicated situations yielding an earthy kind of humor. At the same time, these productions became the first American musicals to offer not only characters but also locales familiar to their audiences, together with the speech, manners, habits, customs and diversions that were part and parcel of the everyday life of New Yorkers.

During the next few years, Harrigan and Hart wrote, produced and starred in one Mulligan burlesque after another. Immediately after *The Mulligan Guards' Picnic*, came *The Mulligan Guards' Ball*, *The Mulligan Guards' Chowder*, *The Mulligan Guards' Christmas*, and *The Skidmore Fancy Ball*, all in 1879. In 1880, the Harrigan and Hart series comprised *The Mulligan Guards' Surprise*, *The Mulligan Guards' Nominee*, and *The Mulligan Guards' Silver Wedding*. In 1881, Harrigan and Hart opened the New Theater Comique, their own playhouse for their ethnic satirical burlesques. Its first production was *The Major* in which Harrigan temporarily deserted Mulligan to play Major Gilfeather. More Harrigan and Hart burlesques followed. A fire destroyed the New Theater Comique in 1884, and one year later, after *The Investigation*, the Harrigan and Hart partnership ended, their harmonious relationship on the stage having been destroyed by offstage discords.

David Braham, the musical director of all the Harrigan and Hart productions, also wrote their music. Born in London in 1838, he was eighteen when he arrived in America, after having studied the violin and made some concert appearances in his native country. He first earned his living in America by playing in pit orchestras; later he was a conductor. In the 1870s, after he had written the music for "The Mulligan Guard" for Harrigan and Hart, he achieved some minor success as a popular song composer with lyricists other than Harrigan: "You're the Idol of My Heart" (George K. Hyde), "Over the Hill to the Poorhouse" (George L. Catlin), "The Eagle" (G. L. Stout) written as a patriotic song for America's centennial celebration, "Flirting in the Twilight" (Jennie Kemble) and "To Rest Let Him Gently Be Laid" (George Cooper). In addition to the music he was writing for Harrigan and Hart acts in variety theaters, he was also collaborating with Harrigan on songs not intended for this burlesque team. Among them were "Are You There Moriarity?" and "Money, the God of the Purse."

In 1879, Braham came with Harrigan and Hart to New York to assist them in their first full-length burlesque extravaganza, *The Mulligan Guards' Ball*. Many a successful popular song came out of the Harrigan and Hart burlesques after that. Some were of Irish content and interest, successfully tapping a vein which, for the next quarter of a century or more, the American popular song would favor. The best of Braham's songs for the Harrigan and Hart productions, all of them to Harrigan's lyrics, included "Poverty's Tears Ebb and Flow" from *Old Lavender* in 1878; "The Babies on Our Block" and the title song from *The Skidmore Fancy Ball* in 1879; "The Full Moon Union" from *The Mulligan Guards' Surprise*, "Locked Out after Nine" from *The Mulligan Guards' Picnic*, and "The Skidmore Masquerade" from *The Mulligan Guards' Nominee*, all in 1880; "Paddy Duffy's Cart" from *Squatter Sovereignty* in 1881; "I Never Drank Behind the Bar" from *McSorley's Inflation* in 1882; and "My Dad's Dinner Pail" from *Cordelia's Aspirations* in 1883.

While the partnership of Harrigan and Hart ended with *The Investigation* in 1885, the tradition of their burlesque extravaganzas continued for another decade or so, with Dan Collyer replacing Hart as Harrigan's collaborator. From *The Grip* in 1885 through *The Merry Malones* in 1896, ethnic city characters continued to be enmeshed in homey, everyday situations and incidents, told with gentle irony and humor and embellished with Braham's winning songs. The Braham song output for these musical travesties included the engaging waltz that helped make Emma Pollack famous and which she introduced in *Reilly and the Four Hundred*, "Maggie Murphy's Home" in 1890; the title song of *The Last of the Hogans* in 1891; "They Never Tell All What They Know" from *The Woolen Stocking* in 1893; and "Danny by My Side" from Harrigan's final production, *The Merry Malones*, in 1896. The last of these songs was beloved by New York's Governor Alfred E. Smith, who sang it in 1933 during ceremonies attending the fiftieth anniversary of the opening of Brooklyn Bridge in New York.

Braham was not only Harrigan's musical collaborator but also his son-in-law, having married Harrigan's sixteen-year-old daughter in 1876. Braham's death in New York on April 11, 1905, preceded that of Harrigan by six years. Tony Hart died in 1891, not long after his breakup with Harrigan.

2

Vaudeville—which was also destined to perform a powerful service to popular songs—was another form of American musical stage entertainment to become crystallized during the Reconstruction. Vaudeville had its antecedent in variety, of which it was an extension, just as variety itself had been the logical outgrowth of the fantasia section of the minstrel show. In all probability the word "vaudeville" came from the French term, "vau-de-vire." In fifteenth-century France, there was a place in the province of Normandy called Val (or Vau) de Vire—Valley of the River Vire. After the work day ended, the natives of this community habitually entertained one another with drinking songs (many the work of Olivier Basselin, a mill owner) and dances. The fame of these performances spread throughout France until this form of diversified entertainment came to be known as "vau de vires," which in time was corrupted to the word "vaudeville."

Vaudeville was first used to identify variety entertainment on February 23, 1871, at Weisiger's Hall in Louisville, Kentucky, where a troupe headed by H. J. Sargent called itself "Sargent's Great Vaudeville Company from Chicago." Then, in the early 1880s, a company of variety performers toured the States, naming its form of stage presentation not variety but vaudeville. During this same period, a theater in San Antonio, Texas, became the first to call itself a vaudeville house.

If any single person can be said to have been responsible for evolving vaudeville out of variety, he is Antonio Pastor, a graduate from circuses and minstrel shows, and one of the most successful popular song composers of his time.

Pastor was born in New York on May 28, 1837. "There is a divinity that shapes our ends," Pastor once philosophized. That divinity led him straight to the theater. When he was eight he made his first public appearance as a singer at a temperance meeting at the Old Dey Street Church and became an impresario by organizing a circus show in his own backyard. He then opened up a peep show for adults which went into bankruptcy when he was fined twenty dollars for conducting a performance without a proper license. In 1846, he joined Barnum's Museum where he blackened his face with burnt cork and played the tambourine. Before a year had passed, he strutted across the stage as a minstrel man. A year after that he sang comic songs with the John J. Nathan Circus where, besides doing turns as a blackface minstrel, he rose to the position of ringmaster. In 1851, he served as ringmaster and performer in dramatic sketches at the Bowery Amphitheater, and in 1857, he appeared as a clown at the Nixon Palace Gardens. He was a man of varied talents, the best of which were yet to flower.

After 1858, Pastor abandoned burnt cork and, after 1860, the circus, to become a performer in variety. He made his official variety debut at Frank River's Melodeon in Philadelphia in 1860. As his costume, he wore boots with high heels and a full-dress outfit, and held a folded silk top hat in hand which he would snap open and place jauntily on his head cocked over one eye. He proved so successful at the Broadway Music Hall on Broadway near Broome Street (which he had helped to open on the evening of March 22, 1861) that he was kept there a year. Then he inaugurated his own variety theater at 444 Broadway where his songs, dances and sketches brightened the stage for the next four years.

At the Broadway Music Hall, on the eve of the Civil War, he created a new genre of popular music with which he would henceforth be associated: the topical song. Accident, rather than plan, was responsible for its introduction. On his way to the theater he learned that the Civil War had just broken out. During his act he interrupted his regular performance to make a brief patriotic speech which he ended by singing "The Star-Spangled Banner." The ovation that followed this interpolation gave him an idea for his act which was largely responsible for making him one of the top variety performers of his time. He would introduce into his act songs of his own composition which commented upon the news of the day while that news was still hot. During the war, the principal battles and events were covered by Tony Pastor in "The Monitor and the Merrimac," "The North and the South," "The Union Volunteers" and "Corcoran's Irish Brigade." After the war, Pastor discoursed musically on kidnappings, fires, elections, assassinations, political corruption, the invention of electricity and current fashions. It has been written that much of Abram S. Hewitt's victory in getting elected Mayor of New York City in 1866 came about through a Tony Pastor song in which was born a catch phrase used throughout that mayoralty campaign: "What's the matter with Hewitt? He's all right!".

The topical song made Pastor a top-ranking songwriter as well as performer. But he was also a skilled performer of songs by other writers, responsible for the popularity of many songs, sentimental and comic. In the former category we find "The Poor Girl Didn't Know" (John Cooke), telling of the indiscretion of a poor female innocent who had not been long in New York when she strayed into a saloon instead of church. Among the latter is "Oh Fred,

Tell Them to Stop" (George Meen). The title is provocative, but this comic number is about a girl riding on a swing and pleading not to be pushed too high.

Pastor's preeminent achievement in the theater was neither as songwriter nor performer but as an impresario of vaudeville entertainment. On March 21, 1865, he opened a variety theater in Paterson, New Jersey, to carry out one of his long-held beliefs: namely, that the theater could interest a large, new clientele—women and children—if smoking and drinking were prohibited in the auditorium and if the entertainment was consistently wholesome. His first venture in this direction, at Paterson, was not a success. Newspapers referred to him derisively as the "self-appointed pastor of the theater," and women remained hesitant about entering, and bringing their children into, a precinct so long regarded as profane ground. But Pastor was not discouraged. Later that same year, he took over an auditorium at 201 Broadway which he named Pastor's Opera House. In a further attempt to attract women and children he offered door prizes of dress patterns, groceries, pots, pans, toys and sewing materials. These lures began attracting women into the theater, and they brought their children with them. Once inside, they were delighted by the varied assortment of acts gathered by the ingenious impresario: ballad singers and comedians, jugglers and acrobats, animal acts, performers in burnt cork and one-act sketches. "I am quite serious in saying," wrote James L. Ford in *Forty Odd Years in the Literary Shop*, "that the most important moment in the history of the development of the theater in this country was that in which Tony Pastor gave away his coal, flour, and dress patterns to secure the patronage of respectable women."

Tony Pastor had to move in 1875 to larger quarters, further uptown to 585 Broadway, where he remained six years. It was during this period that he became the first impresario to send variety entertainers on tour. On October 24, 1881, he opened the house that became one of New York City's theatrical showplaces, a cathedral of clean variety entertainment now to be officially christened vaudeville, the Tony Pastor Music Hall on East 14th Street off Union Square in the Tammany Hall building. In the *Dramatic Mirror*, Pastor himself described his Music Hall as "the first specialty vaudeville theater in America, catering to the polite tastes, aiming to amuse and fully up to the current times and tops." He presented eight acts in all on his first bill covering a wide gamut of entertainment. Pastor himself was featured singer and master of ceremonies. The program was highlighted by Ella Wesner; a male impersonator who sang English ditties and did monologues; Don Collyer, a character actor; the French Twins; and with them an acrobat, a female instrumentalist, a dramatic sketch and a grand finale.

Upon the stage of the Tony Pastor Music Hall appeared many who were already established stars, but also others who were still unknown but soon to become bright lights on the theatrical marquee. Upon that stage, too, were introduced many of the songs a nation would sing as long as this theater was in its full glory.

Less than two months after the Music Hall opened, Lillian Russell made her vaudeville debut there, on November 22, 1881. Born in Clinton, Ohio, in 1861 as Helen Louise Leonard, she had early prepared herself for an operatic career by studying voice with Dr. Leopold Damrosch. In 1879, she abandoned all idea of becoming a prima donna and joined the chorus of a Brooklyn Gilbert and Sullivan company in performances of *H. M. S. Pinafore*. She stayed with the company only two weeks and about a year later she auditioned for Tony Pastor at the theatrical boarding house where she was living. Pastor liked the way she looked—her rich blond hair and voluptuous hourglass figure. "She radiated a serene beauty and a calm confidence in her own loveliness," was the way Allen Churchill described her in *The Great White Way*. Pastor also liked the way she sang, the way she "delivered with dignity or humor and sang in a voice which high-domed James Gibbons Huneker compared to a teakettle," in Churchill's words. But what Tony Pastor did not like was her name, Helen Louise Leonard. He coined a new one for her, Lillian Russell, and booked her for his theater, billing her as an "English ballad singer." At her opening performances, Pastor introduced her to the audience as "the beautiful English ballad singer whom I've imported at great trouble and expense. Ladies and gentlemen, I give you a vision of loveliness with a voice of gold, Miss Lillian Russell." In so doing, he started her off on a career that would contribute much of the luster and glamour to the nineties.

Lillian Russell was the first of many stars to receive their first real recognition at the Music Hall. Others were Weber and Fields, the Four Cohans, the first Pat Rooney, the Three Keatons (one of whom was Buster, later the star of silent film comedies), Eddie Foy, Sam Bernard, Nat Goodwin, Lottie Gilson, May Irwin and Sophie Tucker.

In the end, Tony Pastor became a victim of his own success. Competitors sprang up who had learned from him how to present clean vaudeville week after week that was also topflight entertainment. With ramifications and embellishments of their own, they succeeded in wooing away his audiences. Not far from the Music Hall, the Union Square Theater was taken over by B. F. Keith as a vaudeville house. It offered high grade vaudeville at admission prices that were half what Pastor charged. Excellent vaudeville fare was also available at Koster and Bial's on Sixth Avenue and 23rd Street. After trying unsuccessfully to regain his audiences by drastically reducing prices at the Music Hall, Tony Pastor decided to call it quits. He closed his theater in 1908, and as if he had lost the will to live at the same time, he died soon after at Elmhurst, New York, on August 28, 1908.

3

Some of the songs heard on the stage during the Reconstruction tell us a good deal about the diversions, pastimes and amusements through which Americans escaped from the problems and adjustments of a postwar era. The increasing popularity of the circus helped make "The Man on the Flying Trapeze" a hit in 1868. In that year, three different publishers issued its sheet music, none identifying either the lyricist or the composer. Several years later, however, George Leybourne and Alfred Lee were named as lyricist and composer respectively in the Saalfield Song Collection, *Comical, Topical and Motto Songs*. Leybourne, an English performer who became successful in America as a singing comedian, was in all probability the lyricist of "The Man on the Flying Trapeze," but it is extremely doubtful that Alfred Lee was its composer. To this day, the real creator of the music has never been certified. John Allen made this song his specialty in vaudeville theaters in the 1870s. More than half a century later, the song was revived in the motion picture classic, *It Happened One Night* (1934) and it was further popularized over radio by Walter O'Keefe.

Americans enjoyed the game of croquet and so, in 1867, the song "Croquet" (C. H. Webb—John Rogers Thomas) became popular. Baseball began to take hold as a national pastime. "The Home Run Gallop," by a Mrs. Bodell of Washington, D. C., and "The Baseball Quadrille," by Henry von Gudera, were published in 1867, followed in 1869 by "Hurrah for Our National Game" and "The Red Stockings Polka" (honoring baseball's first professional team, in Cincinnati), and in 1877 by John T. Rutledge's "Tally One for Me." "That Game of Poker," by Charles MacEvoy, suggests that this indoor sport was already gaining wide acceptance in the year this song was published, 1877.

Now, as before, Americans liked to sing and listen to ballads touching the heart. Prominent among the writers of sentimental ballads were two who had previously gained attention and distinction for their Civil War songs, H. C. Work and Will S. Hays.

Work had written a sentimental ballad about the scourge of alcohol in 1864 while the Civil War was still on. Called "Come Home, Father," it was based on a story by Timothy Shay Arthur, *Ten Nights in a Barroom* which was published in 1854 and made into a stage melodrama by William W. Pratt four years later. In the song, a child comes to a saloon to plead with her father to come home since her little brother, Benny, is sick in his mother's arms and "there's no one to help but me." The father, steeped in alcohol, is deaf to the child's tearful request. The steeple clock tolls the passing hours ominously. Benny dies—his last words "I want to kiss papa good night." The fame of this ballad grew prodigiously after the end of the war, particularly after it was interpolated into the William W. Pratt melodrama as its emotional high point. The ballad was ultimately adopted by the National Prohibition Party as its official song when the Party was organized in Oswego, New York, to advance temperance.

After the Civil War, Work made the writing of sentimental ballads his specialty. His best were "The Lost Letter," "The Ship That Never Returned" and—one of the most durable of all sentimental ballads of the Reconstruction—"Grandfather's Clock." Written in 1876, it told of a clock that stood for ninety years after having been purchased on the day grandfather was born and which stopped ticking the moment he died. The ballad was introduced in the year of its composition by Sam Lucas, then appearing with the Hyer Sisters Colored Minstrels in New Haven. From there the song went on to sell a million copies of sheet music, a phenomenon for its time.

Work was also a gifted writer of comedy or novelty songs in which he usually had a chorus interject amusing or illustrative comments. One of the best was "Poor Kitty Popcorn," in which the chorus repeatedly enters with "Meyow!"

The death of three children, and the tragedy of his wife's affliction with a mental disorder, broke Work's health and spirit in his closing years. He had also lost all his money in a disastrous land investment. Death released him from his miseries on June 8, 1884, in Hartford, Connecticut. In 1975, an album of fourteen of Work's ballads, humorous and novelty numbers, was released by Nonesuch under the musical supervision of William Bolcom: *Work: Who Shall Rule This American Nation?*

Will S. Hays did not come fully into his own as a songwriter until after the end of the Civil War—the fame of his drummer boy war song notwithstanding. In 1866, he wrote one of his most famous ballads, "Nora O'Neal," which was one of three of his songs that year to sell a quarter of a million copies each, the other two being "We Parted on the Riverside" and "Write Me a Letter." He had four more hits in 1871, one of them "Mollie Darling." By the time he died in his native city of Louisville, Kentucky, in July 1907 he had written several hundred songs. His later successes included the two ballads, "Oh Give Me a Home in the South" and "Take This Letter to Your Mother."

There were other composers and lyricists prominent in the production of sentimental ballads. In 1866, James Austin Butterfield wrote the music for "When You and I Were Young Maggie." Butterfield was an Englishman, born in 1837, who came to America in 1856. He first earned his living as a music teacher in Chicago before embarking on a career as a publisher in Indianapolis. His avocation was writing songs of which he completed some one hundred and fifty. "When You and I Were Young Maggie"—still a strong favorite at community sings—is his only song still remembered.

Butterfield came upon the lyrics in a collection of poems, *Maple Leaves*, by a Canadian schoolmaster, George W. Johnson. The "Maggie" in the poem was a Canadian girl with whom Johnson had fallen in love. They used to meet at a mill on a creek near her home, as the poem tells. In 1865, they were married and set up a home in Cleveland where

Johnson was employed as a teacher. His marital happiness was short-lived, for Maggie died soon after her marriage. Johnson wrote his poem as a tribute to her and a token of his undying love.

The untimely death of still another young lady soon after her happy marriage was the subject of another celebrated sentimental ballad of the time, "Sweet Genevieve." Its lyricist was George Cooper, that distinguished poet and lyricist who had provided many a nineteenth-century American composer with effective lyrics, including Stephen Foster. Cooper lost his bride, Genevieve, in 1869; his poem was an expression of his overwhelming grief. Henry Tucker, a composer specializing in sentimental tunes whose Civil War ballad, "Weeping Sad and Lonely" has already been commented on, bought the poem for five dollars and set it to music. The song was first widely disseminated by minstrel troupes, and only later became a standard in the repertory of barbershop quartets and community sings.

Among the most highly esteemed sentimental ballads of the 1870s were "I'll Take You Home Again, Kathleen" and "Silver Threads Among the Gold." For a long time it was conjectured that a personal tragedy led to the writing of "I'll Take You Home Again, Kathleen." It was thought that Thomas Paine Westendorf, author of both the lyrics and the music, created it because of his concern for his wife, suffering from a serious illness. But all this is apocryphal. Westendorf wrote his ballad in 1875 when he became lonely for his young wife who had just gone to visit her family in another town. In the song he despatched her not to another town but across the sea.

"Silver Threads Among the Gold" is the chef d'oeuvre of Hart Pease Danks, a highly productive songwriter. Born in New Haven, Connecticut, on April 6, 1834, Danks studied music in his boyhood. He engaged in carpentry in Chicago while continuing to follow his musical inclinations by serving as a choir leader, conducting musical societies, singing and composing. His first fruit as a composer was a hymn which was followed in 1856 by "Anna Lee" and "The Old Lane," two ballads for which he wrote words as well as music. In 1864, he came to New York where he supported himself by directing musical groups and appearing in song recitals. In 1870 he achieved his first success as a songwriter with the ballad, "Don't Be Angry With Me, Darling."

One day he came upon a poem by Eben E. Rexford in a Wisconsin farm journal. He was so taken with it that he offered to buy it for three dollars. Rexford was so delighted with Danks's interest in his work that for the same price of three dollars he sold him the rights not to one but to several poems, one of which was "Silver Threads Among the Gold." Danks set it to music in 1872 as an expression of hope that he and his beloved wife might survive to a ripe old age. Ironically, they separated soon after the ballad was published.

Danks sold his song outright for a few dollars to C. W. Harris who published it in 1873. He lived to see "Silver Threads Among the Gold" become one of the most widely heard sentimental ballads of the nineteenth century, selling well over two million copies of sheet music, and being adopted by virtually every silver-tongued singer in vaudeville. Danks unhappily died in abject poverty in a rooming house in Philadelphia on November 20, 1903.

"Silver Threads Among the Gold" had a second lease on life after Danks' death. Revived in 1907 by Richard J. José, then a star of the Primrose and West Minstrels, it caught on a second time; a new printing of the sheet music sold an additional million copies.

Three more composers of sentimental ballads of this period deserve attention. They are Joseph P. Skelly, Harry Kennedy and Charles A. White.

Skelly was a shiftless plumber continually in debt because of his weakness for alcohol. His publisher, Frank Harding, once said: "I used to buy beautiful songs from J. P. Skelly for from six to twenty-five dollars, excellent manuscripts." Invariably, these transactions took place when Skelly did not have the price of a drink. He managed, in spite of his addiction, to write some four hundred songs. His first success came in 1877 with "My Pretty Red Rose," followed two years after by "If My Dreams Would All Come True." His most famous ballad was "Why Did They Dig Ma's Grave So Deep?" (1880), for many years a fixture in the repertory of boy sopranos. Skelly was also the composer of "Strolling on the Brooklyn Bridge" (George Cooper), written to celebrate the opening of Brooklyn Bridge in New York on May 24, 1883.

Harry Kennedy was another composer with an insatiable thirst for hard liquor. By profession a ventriloquist who worked with two dummies in a minstrel show, Kennedy spent his leisure time writing songs. He gained his first recognition with two sentimental ballads, "A Flower from Mother's Grave" in 1878 and "Cradle's Empty, Baby's Gone" in 1880. The New York *Herald* noted on November 9, 1884, that "Cradle's Empty, Baby's Gone" had "a tremendous run among the shop girls of this city." Some of Kennedy's biggest hits came toward the end of his life. They were "Molly and I and the Baby" (1892) and "Say Au Revoir but Not Goodbye" (1893). The second exploited echo effects which vaudevillians enjoyed interpolating during the singing of the chorus. One of its best known interpreters was Helene Mora, called "the female baritone." She sang it over Kennedy's fresh grave after he had succumbed to tuberculosis.

Charles A. White was a Bostonian who entered the music publishing business after having served on the faculty of the Naval Academy in Newport, Rhode Island. As the head of the reputable White-Smith Publishing Company he became a power in the industry. One of his early songs, "The Widow in the Cottage by the Seaside," was published in 1868 by Oliver Ditson, but by 1870, with "Come, Birdie, Come," White became his own publisher. Two of his best sentimental ballads were about dying children, "Put Me in My Little Bed" and "In Her Little Bed We Laid Her." His song of songs was "Marguerite" in 1883. He sang it for Denman Thompson backstage at the Old Boston Theater where Thompson was then appearing in *The Old Homestead*. So taken was the actor with this song, and particularly with its echo effects, that he used it in *The Old Homestead* and started it off on its journey to success.

Comedy songs provided a welcome antidote to the sighs and tears of sentimental balladry. Three of the best were "Reuben and Rachel" (now often called "Reuben, Reuben"), "I Wish I Were Single Again" and "Upside Down." "Reuben and Rachel" (Harry Birch—William Gooch) appeared in 1871. This was a comic dialogue between a man and a woman. The charms of single blessedness are extolled in J. C. Beckel's "I Wish I Were Single Again" (1871). "Upside Down," from this same period, was the work of two character actors, Sol Smith Russel and Howard Paul. Russel became its famous interpreter on the stage. This song describes a wild dream suffered by the writer after he had eaten pickled salmon.

The Reconstruction years gave life not only to new sentimental ballads, comedy songs and songs about recreational pastimes, but also to what is surely the most celebrated American lullaby: "Rock-a-bye Baby," words and music by Effie I. Crockett. Effie was only fifteen when, in 1887, she served as a baby-sitter for a restless child. To lull it to sleep she improvised a melody and used it for a variation of words from an old Mother Goose rhyme, "Hush-a-bye baby on the tree top." Some time later she hummed the tune to her music teacher who, in turn, recommended the song to a Boston publisher. "After he heard it," Effie recalled in later years, "he asked permission to publish it. He did, after I had written three verses to go with the Mother Goose lines. I was afraid my father wouldn't approve, so instead of using my real name, Effie I. Crockett, I used the name of Canning, my grandmother's name. It was not until the song began to sweep the country that I told Father I wrote it." Under the title "Rock-a-bye Baby" the song was published by Charles D. Blake and Company in 1887.

4

During the Reconstruction a notable phase in the growth and development of America was the building and opening of the railroads. Construction of the first transcontinental railroad began in 1863 when the Union Pacific laid tracks westward from Omaha, Nebraska; the Central Pacific extended eastward from Sacramento, California. On May 10, 1869, the tracks, covering some fifteen hundred miles, joined at Promontory, Utah.

In every direction, miles and miles of rails were laid. Where in 1865 there were only about 35,000 miles of railroads in operation, by 1890 there were over 125,000.

The men who drove in the spikes on sunbaked prairies, and who blasted passages through rock and mountains, the men who operated locomotives, and the trains themselves supplied material for a new and rich literature of folk and popular music.

In "The Utah Iron Horse" the Mormons sang about the impact upon Utah of the coming of the railroad. Track gangs laboring on the grading of roadbeds, on the laying of tracks or the digging of tunnels, all provided the subject for "She'll Be Coming 'Round the Mountain," which used the melody of the Negro spiritual, "When the Chariot Comes." The "she" in this folk song is the supply train puffing its way toward the rail workers who sing hallelujahs at its approach. "Nine Hundred Miles," melody once again derived from Negro music, but this time a blues, is about a man nine hundred miles from home who hates hearing the lonesome train whistle but who hopes to reach home "tomorrow night, if that train runs right." Inmates of the Texas State Prison were partial to "The Midnight Special," because they used that song to voice their hopes for freedom; they always could hear the whistle of the "Midnight Special" as it sped from Houston to San Francisco. Still another popular railroad song was "I've Been Working on the Railroad," which had originated as "The Levee Song."

Many of the men working on the railroads were Irish which is why some of the railroad songs have a strong Celtic flavor, and why so many of the characters named in railroad songs are Irish. There is "Paddy on the Railroad"—an Irishman who is sadly abused by a boss who keeps bellowing, "Paddy do this" and "Paddy do that"—and "Paddy Works on the Railway."

But the most famous of all American folk ballads honoring a railroad worker has for its hero not an Irishman but a black man. He was John Henry, a steel driller of uncommon powers, an acknowledged champion in his profession. "He drove steel from his left shoulder and would make a stroke of more than nineteen and a half feet," reads a report about him, "making the hammer travel like lightning. And he could drive ten hours without turning a stroke." One of several folk songs bearing the title of "John Henry" describes how he met death in the Big Bend Tunnel of the C.&O. Railroad in or about 1873 when a huge boulder crushed him. Henceforth, as this ballad spins out the legend, those living near the mouth of the Big Bend Tunnel refused to go there at night because it was haunted by John Henry's ghost driving steel. Another even more imaginative ballad on the theme of John Henry insists that he died not through an accident but in a competition with a steam drill. The steam drill drove only nine feet but John Henry drove fifteen; but Henry drove so hard that he broke "his poor heart and he laid down his hammer and died."

Commercial songwriters, as well as folk song troubadours, found a bountiful source of song material in railroads. Charles Mackay and Stephen Massett anticipated the linking of the Western and Eastern rails at Utah in "Clear the Way," dedicated to the "pioneers of the

Great Pacific Railroad." In 1869, H. C. Work also sang the praises of that railway system in "The Pacific Railroad." In 1870, Harry Frances and Alfred von Rochow paid tribute to the Brotherhood of Locomotive Engineers in "The Iron Horse." A year later, Will S. Hays celebrated the success of the Thatcher Perkins locomotive of the Louisville and Nashville Railroad in "Number Twenty-Nine."

It was, however, long after the Reconstruction days were over—indeed, it was not until the twentieth century—that the two best-known songs of the railroad were written. "The Wreck of the Old '97" told of the wreck of the mail train of the Southern Railway, Train Number 97, near Danville, Virginia, in 1903, that killed its engineer and most of the crew. David Graves George wrote the words to the melody of H. C. Work's "The Ship that Never Returned." An early recording in 1924 by Vernon Dalhart on the Victor label sold over a million disks and earned a profit of over $150,000. Since at that time nobody knew who the author of the lyrics was, Victor advertised for him. Fifty claimants appeared, among them David Graves George. In the ensuing litigation all claimants were dismissed for failure to produce convincing corroborating evidence. David Graves George was thereby denied his share of the financial profits, but not his share of glory, since his authorship of the words is now generally recognized.

Still another wreck was responsible for what surely is the most celebrated of all railroad songs, "Casey Jones" (T. Lawrence Seibert—Eddie Newton). This time the wreck occurred outside the town of Vaughn, Mississippi, on April 29, 1900, when a crack train of the Central Illinois crashed into a line of boxcars. The engineer, Casey Jones, shouted to Sam Webb, the fireman, to jump and save his life. Webb jumped and survived. But Casey became a victim of the crash. When Casey's body was found, one of his hands was on the wheel and another on the air brake lever. This story is told in the ballad, "Casey Jones," which was published by its authors in Los Angeles in 1909, was adopted by railroad workers throughout the country, and was brought to both the stage and the general public by the Leighton Brothers, a vaudeville team.

In 1947, a monument was erected on Casey Jones' grave at Mount Calvary Cemetery in Jackson, Tennessee. The inscription paid tribute to the memory of one who had become "part of the folklore of the American language" and quoted two lines from the song, "For I'm gonna run her till she leaves the rail, Or make it on time with the southern rail."

5

The Reconstruction period was also the heyday of the cowboy and his songs.

Cowboys were a heterogenous lot, including European immigrants, footloose adventurers, second-generation pioneers, happy-go-lucky daredevils, fugitives from justice. Varied origins produced a diversity of song, parodies of popular songs and ballads, and adaptations of English, Irish, Scottish or Negro melodies. The cowboy made these melodies his own. His background and personality, the unique nature of his occupation and life-style all left an indelible impression on his songs. In 1907, Andy Adams described the cowboy songs as "a hybrid between the weirdness of the Indian cry and the croon of the black mammy. It expresses the open spaces, the prairie, the immutable desert."

The cowboy often devised his songs to rally his herd from San Antonio, Texas, to the shipping point in Dodge City, Kansas, and to the grazing fields of Wyoming, the Dakotas and Montana. He sang as he herded, and he sang to lull them to sleep. The cowboy sang songs that were simple, with little variety of structure or rhythm. The cowboy was a lonely and sometimes a sad man, and many of his songs are lugubrious, as is the case with "The Streets of Laredo," one of the two best-known cowboy songs extant. The other is "The Old

Chisholm Trail." The melody of "The Streets of Laredo" came from a British ballad, "The Unfortunate Rake," which told of a soldier dying of syphilis. In the cowboy song, it is a cowboy who is dying from a gunshot in the breast, giving instructions for his funeral and confessing that he's done wrong.

"Poor Lonesome Cowboy," "The Cowboy's Life Is a Dreary, Dreary Life" and "All Day on the Prairie" are three other ballads that reflect the cowboy's loneliness as he does his solitary work in the vast open spaces. "All day in the prairie in the saddle, I ride," he sang sadly, "not even a dog, boys, to trot by my side." Some of the cowboy songs overflow with nostalgic sentiments for a home, a girl, friendship, peace and rest—"The Cowboy's Dream," for example, to the melody of "My Bonnie Lies Over the Ocean." "Red River Valley" was a cowboy torch song; its melody came out of the East where it was heard on the variety stage as "In the Bright Mohawk Valley" (James J. Kerrigan).

The cowboy's best friend was his horse, and some of his songs are about Old Paint or Pinto or Black Bess or Blue Dog: "Goodbye, Old Paint," or "I Ride an Old Paint." The cowboy's one dread was a lonely grave; hence he often sang about dying alone and being buried on an empty prairie: "Bury Me Not on the Lone Prairie," "The Dying Cowboy" and "Blood on the Saddle."

Cowboys also sang around a campfire or in the ranch bunkhouse about the miseries of their life and work, or about cutting loose in Dodge City. "The Old Chisholm Trail," to which new lyrics were continually improvised, is one of the most familiar of all cowboy songs. "It was a dull day on the drive when one of the cowboys did not make a new verse to 'The Old Chisholm Trail'," wrote an unidentified cowboy. The brisk melody was a perfect companion to lyrics describing the life and activities of a cowboy herding his cattle. "The Railroad Corral" spoke of the joy of the cowboy whenever he came to the end of his long trail, and "Git Along Little Dogies" and "The Night Herding Song" were two of his standbys as he herded his cattle; the first is a day call, the second a nocturnal one.

Into many of his songs the cowboy interpolated familiar cowboy calls of "whoopee-yi-yi" or "yipee" or "comma ti-yi-yoppy" or "hi-oo-oo." In some songs the clattering of the horse's hoofs is reproduced in the rhythm.

J. A. Lomax once described "Home on the Range" as the "cowboy's national anthem." Its authorship has long been hotly disputed. There are many supporters of the claim of Dr. Brewster Higley, a homesteader, that he wrote the lyrics in 1873 in a cabin near Beaver Creek, Kansas; and to that of Daniel E. Kelly, a guitar player from Gaylor, a trading post some twenty miles from Beaver Creek, that he fashioned the melody the same year. At that time the song was introduced by Clarence Harlan and the words were published in *The Smith County Pioneer* in Kansas under the title of "Oh, Give Me a Home Where the Buffalo Roam." On March 21, 1874, the words were reprinted under the title of "Western Home" in the *Kirwin Chief* in Kansas. But not until 1904 were words and music published simultaneously, using a new title, "Arizona Home." At that time William Goodwin was named as the composer and lyricist. Others, too, insist they were the legitimate authors, among them being C. O. Swartz, Bingham Graves, Bill McCabe and somebody called "Jim." A court in 1934, following an action instituted by William Goodwin and his wife, decreed that the song was in public domain.

The song's popularity began in 1910 when it was published in Alan Lomax's anthology *Cowboy Songs*. Lomax had heard it sung in Texas by a Negro saloon keeper. In 1925, a Texas publisher issued it in a sheet music edition that further popularized the ballad, and five years after that David Guion, a Texas musician, made an arrangement that gained such wide circulation that Guion is sometimes erroneously named as the composer. Charles Kuralt interviewed David Guion on the CBS night news telecast on December 17, 1973. The interview left the unmistakable impression that the question of the authorship of "Home on the Range" was settled, and that David Guion was the man who wrote it. Guion seemed to corroborate this impression by maintaining that he owns the copyright which is still in force. But the copyright he owns is of his adaptation, and there can be no question—in spite of the inferences of that telecast—that the song existed long before David Guion adapted it.

In the early 1930s, "Home on the Range" was often heard over the radio and was erroneously reputed to have been the favorite song of President Franklin D. Roosevelt. It also became the official song of the State of Kansas. In September 1973, "Home on the Range" made news. During the tour of the Philadelphia Orchestra under Eugene Ormandy in the People's Republic of China that September, the Chinese soloist at one of these performances played "Home on the Range" as an encore. It turned out that the choice of this encore was not his, but that of a Chinese official. And the reason the official made this demand is because he was told that when President Nixon visited China, the President, or a member of his entourage, asked a Chinese band to play "Home on the Range." Thus the idea was born that this was a song of particular importance to Americans, possibly a national anthem.

6

After emancipation, many black men found jobs in the mines and tunnels of Virginia, and in the cotton fields of the South. There they were as much exploited as they had been as slaves. Some black men, unprepared for their liberty, landed on the rock piles of prisons in Georgia, Tennessee and Texas where they bemoaned their sad lot and continually dreamed of escape.

Out of their toil and distress came a rich lode of folklore, the work songs of the blacks. If these songs are neither as imaginative, nor as moving as spirituals, it is mainly because they sprang from the humdrum monotony of physical labor rather than from a profound religious experience. Nevertheless these work songs have considerable interest. Sung out-of-doors, and never to the accompaniment of a musical instrument to set the pitch and guide the intonation, these songs developed their own curious inflections and intonations. The voice was allowed to slide to tones foreign to the scale and to intervals smaller than the half tone. Grunts and groans were interpolated into the melody becoming a part of the melodic texture—grunts and groans inspired by the physical strain of smashing a rock with a hammer or piercing cement with a steel drill. Out of these singular inflections and intonations developed a unique melody and harmony which, many years later, became a distinguishing feature of authentic jazz.

The melody and harmony of these work songs established an atmosphere of bleakness deriving from the feeling of utter hopelessness with which black men did their harrowing jobs. These work songs are often touched with pathos; even humorous verses are frequently set to melancholy melodies. In prison camps, the black man was the victim of barbarous and often sadistic overseers. In work camps, his pay was poor and uncertain, and his treatment at the hands of foremen ruthless.

> "Told my cap'n my hands was cold
> Said, 'Damn your hands, boy
> Let the wheelin' roll.'
> Raised my hand, wiped de sweat off my head,
> Cap'n got mad, Lord, shot my buddy dead."

"I works from kin to cain't"—sighs the Negro, lamenting his long hours. These songs may well be said to have been the precursors of the blues.

Many songs were improvised during the performance of work. The leader raised his voice in the opening refrain of "Boll Weevil" or "Pick a Bale of Cotton," classics of cotton pickers, or "Whoa Buck," the field song of black ploughmen, or "Hammer Song," the song of those who labored on stone, or "Nine Foot Shovel," which originated with the Georgia chain gang. The leader was a specialist who knew not only the techniques of the work at hand but also the songs best suited to accompany it; a good leader could inspire his men to greater effort. After the leader give his cue, the work gangs would chime in with a chorus of convention-defying harmonies. The melody would vary with each repetition, the rhythm always allowed flexible changes. At the end of the song, the melody might finish in a form far different from what it had been at the start. Sometimes new melodies were created for familiar words—as one voice after another would make its own individual contributions after the leader had thrown out a phrase—and sometimes new words were produced for familiar tunes.

The blacks were not the only ones exploited in the years immediately following the Civil War. Perhaps the most flagrant abuse of white labor took place in the coal mines where the work was dangerous, the wages miserable, the hours long. Children—deprived of sunshine, schooling and play—were forced to work with their parents and older brothers so that the pennies earned from long hours of health-destroying work in the pit might help the family make ends meet.

Songs flourished in the mines; sorrow has ever been fertile soil for music. Miners participated in communal gatherings at night, in nearby barrooms or even during the lunch hour in the mine. Minstrels traveled from one mine to the next, circularizing ballads and providing miners with entertainment. These minstrels sang of their own experiences often in melodies lifted from foreign sources, but freely adapted and readapted until these songs acquired an original personality. Mine songs are filled with social implications; they have the sweat of toil in them, and the fear and despair of the exploited worker.

One of the favored miner ballads is "The Old Miner's Refrain," a summary of the frustrations of a miner's life. "I'm getting old and feeble and I can work no more," the ballad begins, and it ends just as dismally with "the only place that's left me is the alms-house for a home, that's where I'll lay this weary head of mine." Another famous song, "Down in a Coal Mine," is a somber description of sunless depths "underneath the ground, where a gleam of sunshine can never be found."

7

The folk balladry of the Reconstruction, and that of the years following, included songs about many who lived on the other side of respectability. Notorious western desperados, such as Jesse James and Sam Bass, became sympathetic characters in song. In "Jesse James," the ballad stood ready to concede that he "killed many a man" and "robbed the Glendale train." But the chorus keeps repeating that he had "a wife to mourn for his life" and "three brave children," and that "the dirty little coward that shot Mister Howard [laid] poor Jesse in his grave." The long succession of verses tells us how Jesse James was betrayed by one of his own men, who shot him "on the sly" and killed him. In the last verse the balladeer identifies himself as "Billy Gashade" which is probably a pseudonym.

"Sam Bass" related how Bass, born in Indiana, came to Texas to work as a cowboy. "A kinder hearted fellow you seldom ever see." Sam and his men held up the Union Pacific, then robbed four more Western trains. Sam Bass met his doom at Round Rock, Texas, in

1878 after a former member of his gang tipped off the Texas Rangers that Bass and his cohorts were going to hold up the town bank. "Poor Sam," the ballad sighs, "he is a corpse, and six foot under clay." As for the traitor responsible for Sam's death: "perhaps he's got to heaven, there's none of us can say, but if I'm right, in my surmise, he's gone the other way."

But "Billy the Kid" makes no attempt to be sympathetic. The word "true" appears in the opening line, "I'll sing you a true song of Billy the Kid," and in a series of verses the true story of the boy bandit unfolds, from the time when he killed his first man at twelve years of age, to his manhood, by which time he was responsible for the death of twenty. He was finally shot down by Sheriff Pat Garrett, whom he had planned to make his twenty-second victim. The ballad ends with a moral:

> "There's many a man with a face fine and fair
> Who starts out in life with a chance to be square,
> But just like poor Billy he wanders astray
> And loses his life in the very same way."

The hero of "Tom Dooley" (Tom Dula) was a North Carolinian who had served with the Confederate Army. Upon returning from the war he discovered that his girl friend had fallen in love with a Yankee schoolmaster. Dooley kills her in 1866, in Wilkes County, North Carolina, but is captured by the schoolmaster who brings him to justice, and to death at the gallows. The song "Tom Dooley" speaks the victim's own confession of guilt. "Hang down your head Tom Dooley," he repeats in the chorus in third person, "poor boy, you're bound to die." We learn from *Folk Song, U.S.A.*, edited by Alan Lomax, that Dooley "sat up in the cart on the way to his hanging ground and sang it in his sour baritone, playing the tune over on his fiddle between every verse." A twentieth-century variant of the Tom Dooley ballad was composed by Dave Guard in 1958 and immediately became popular in a best-selling Capitol recording by the Kingston Trio. A folksinger, Frank Proffitt, maintained that he, and not Guard, had prepared the version made popular by the Kingston Trio; that, as a boy, he had often heard his father sing the original ballad.

To many balladeers, the western desperados appeared in the guise of modern-day Robin Hoods who stole from the rich to give to the poor. The East had its own Robin Hood in Jim Fisk. He was an unsavory character who had amassed wealth in Wall Street and acquired power in New York City politics illegitimately. Involved with pretty Josie Mansfield, he was murdered by a rival for her affections in 1872 outside the Grand Central Hotel. When "Jim Fisk" was published, the music carried the initials "J. S." for the lyricist-composer. Subsequent editions, however, spelled out the name fully. He was William J. Scanlan, born in Springfield, Massachusetts, in 1856. He first made his mark as a ballad singer at temperance meetings and later in variety where he teamed up with an Irish comedian. "Jim Fisk" was Scanlan's first success as a songwriter—if he actually did write the ballad, which some authorities doubt. Later in life, Scanlan starred in musical productions in New York, the best of which were on Irish subjects, and in some of these he introduced several of his songs.

Two other ignoble characters appear in "Frankie and Johnny." Frankie was a prostitute, Johnny a loose character who "done her wrong." Several hundred variants of "Frankie and Johnny" exist and in most of these Frankie finally shoots her man and is acquitted.

It is impossible to say when and where "Frankie and Johnny" first appeared. In *The Covered Wagon*, Emerson Hough places the song as far back as 1840. Thomas Beer says in *The Mauve Decade* that it was sung at the siege of Vicksburg. In *The American Songbag*, Carl

Sandburg fixes the ballad's birth some time in the 1880s.

When "Frankie and Johnny" was made into a motion picture starring Helen Morgan in 1935, an odd litigation ensued. A lawyer from Portland, Oregon, brought suit against Republic Pictures, Helen Morgan and others for defaming the character of his client, a black woman with the name of Frankie Baker. He maintained that this woman had killed her boyfriend in 1899 and was the true source of the famous ballad. The case was dismissed, and the plaintiff had to defray all court costs.

8

A New Breed
of Publisher

1

In the early 1880s, the business of publishing popular songs began to undergo a drastic reappraisal and transformation. Before that time, the publishing of popular songs was a subsidiary function of music shops, or of a publisher whose principal activity was the issuance of serious music and music instruction books. This was true of Oliver Ditson in Boston, and Chicago's Root and Cady and Lyons and Healy, John Church in Philadelphia, J. L. Peters and William A. Pond, both in New York, George Willig in Baltimore, and of most of the smaller firms across the country.

Those publishers were generally a staid and stuffy lot. They did not believe in promotion or advertising to advance their songs, depending mainly on luck and fortuitous circumstances. They waited for performers to visit their offices in search of a song rather than seeking out performers and trying to find ways and means of interesting them. These publishers also did little or nothing to develop songwriters.

But in or about 1880, several new young men entered the popular song publishing arena. They were invaders from alien fields, come to a new one because they realized that this was ground that had not been properly cultivated. These young men brought with them iconoclastic thinking, an adventurous spirit, and the untried ways of newcomers either innocent or defiant of stultifying conventions. One of the innovations they initiated was to concentrate their publishing exclusively on popular songs, and direct all their energy and ambition toward developing this single area fully and profitably.

Such publishers were Will Rossiter in Chicago and Frank Harding in New York, both of whom entered the song publishing business around 1880. Will Rossiter (who issued many of his own songs for which he adopted the pen name of W. R. Williams) was one of the first song publishers in America to seek out audiences for his publications. He took bundles of his songs under his arm to a local retail shop and would then sing the songs to the customers; after that he would peddle the sheet music. In trying to reach out to the buying public, rather than waiting for it to come to him, he was the first publisher to advertise his songs in theatrical trade journals.

Frank Harding entered his father's publishing house on the Bowery in New York in 1879. He created forthwith a firm specializing in popular songs. He did not wait in his office for composers and lyricists to send or bring him their manuscripts. He encouraged them to write songs expressly for his company, paying them the price of several rounds of drinks each time they submitted a usable manuscript. His office became a hangout for songwriters. There they played poker, drank liquor and exchanged small talk. Many were stimulated to write new numbers because they needed the price of a drink. "It was no use giving them more than ten dollars at a time," he said. "A man could get damned drunk on ten dollars." Several songwriters were carefully nurtured in this way by Harding: J. P. Skelly, Charles Graham and Monroe H. Rosenfeld, to single out three. And hits began flowing out of Frank Harding's office: Tony Pastor's "I Have Only Been Down to the Club," Matt Reardon's "Marriage Bells," J. W. Kelly's "Where Did You Get That Hat?" and "Throw Him Down McCloskey," James Thornton's "My Sweetheart's the Man in the Moon" and "Drill Ye Tarriers, Drill" of unknown authorship.

In New York, Willis Woodward and T. B. Harms were two other young upstarts who challenged the status quo in publishing. As Isidore Witmark wrote in his autobiography, *From Ragtime to Swingtime*: "They anticipated in a modest way the future of popular music publishing business by their primitive methods of introducing and 'plugging' songs that showed any signs of life. In fact, they had the call on all the public singers and minstrels as introducers of their respective numbers."

While still a fledgling concern, T. B. Harms, formed by two brothers, Alex and Tom Harms, realized their first substantial sales with "Wait Till the Clouds Roll By" (J. T. Wood—H. T. Fulmer) in 1881, and in 1883, with "When the Robins Nest Again" (Frank Howard). Soon they broke new ground for the publishing business by devoting much of their initiative to issuing and promoting songs that had first been introduced in the musical theater. (The publishing of theater songs was a field which they would soon dominate.) From the presses of Harms came songs from W. J. Scanlan's *Shane na Lawn* and *Mavourneen*, with "Molly O!" from the latter production a major song hit. Also from Harms came songs from *Wang* and *Panjandrum*, two extravaganzas starring De Wolf Hopper. In 1893, the firm reaped a harvest with three giant song successes from the extravaganza, *A Trip to Chinatown*, each of them amassing a sale of several hundred thousand copies: "Push dem Clouds Away," "Reuben, Reuben" (not to be confused with "Reuben and Cynthia") and the still very popular "The Bowery." All three were by Percy Gaunt.

In addition to their theater songs, T. B. Harms boosted independent numbers into large sales figures. In 1884, there was "Always Take Mother's Advice" (Jennie Lindsay). Miss Lindsay was one of the first successful women popular composers in America. That same year also set to music Bank Winter's "White Wings," a ballad of a sailor's return to his sweetheart after a long absence on the high seas. Two other sentimental ballads in 1887 added appreciably to the financial strength of T. B. Harms, "If the Waters Could Speak as They Flow" (Charles Graham) and "The Song That Reached My Heart" (Julian Jordan).

Willis Woodward and Company issued "The Outcast Unknown" in 1887, one of the earliest important ballads by Paul Dresser, the foremost composer of sentimental ballads of the 1880s. Dresser was a three hundred and more pound hulk of a man who oozed generosity and sentimentality from every pore. Whatever he liked to do he did to excess: eating, hard drinking, loving, spending money and writing sentimental ballads.

Paul Dresser was born John Paul Dreiser on April 21, 1857, in Terre Haute, Indiana, by the banks of the Wabash, the river he glorified in his most famous song. His brother. Theodore Dreiser, became the famous American novelist. Their father, a fanatically religious man who ruled the family with iron discipline, planned to have Paul become a priest. For a time, Paul attended a seminary near Evansville, Illinois. But his main interest was music, and since his was an undisciplined nature, he deserted both home and school when he was sixteen to become a blackface performer with a traveling medicine show for which he wrote comedy songs and parodies. After that he joined a minstrel troupe in Cincinnati which billed him as "the sensational comique" in one-night stands. Still later, in New York, he played minor parts at Harry Miner's Bowery Theater and was a blackface end man with the renowned Thatcher, Primrose and West Minstrels. It was then that he changed his name from Dreiser to Dresser, and made his first bid for attention as a songwriter by assembling some of his songs in *The Paul Dresser Songbook*. Two of his songs were beginning to find receptive ears and inspire copious tears, "I Believe It For My Mother Told Me So" and a ballad inspired by one of his own frustrated love affairs, "The Letter that Never Came." Dresser himself, as a member of the Billy Rice Minstrels, introduced "The Letter that Never Came" in Brooklyn, New York, in 1886 and sold it for publication to T. B. Harms.

Pat Howley, a hunchbacked employe in the publishing house of Willis Woodward, was so impressed by "The Letter that Never Came," that he bought another Dresser ballad for his firm, "The Outcast Unknown." On Howley's urging, Dresser gave up acting permanently to concentrate on writing songs for Willis Woodward and Company. Two songs about prison life appeared in 1888 and 1891, "The Convict and the Bird" and "The Pardon Came Too Late." In "The Convict and the Bird" a prisoner pleads with a bird to come to him each day and sing of sunshine and freedom. One day when the bird arrives the prisoner is lying dead in his cell. Death is also the fate of the prisoner in "The Pardon Came Too Late."

After that, and for the rest of the golden decade of sentimental balladry, the flamboyant personality and creative talent of Paul Dresser dominated and enriched the songwriting scene.

2

The way in which many newcomers to music publishing came from humble background, with little or no experience, was brought into focus in the 1880s with the establishment of the house of M. Witmark and Sons, destined to become a major power in the song industry. The firm was founded in 1886 by three brothers, Isidore, Julius and Jay Witmark, aged seventeen, thirteen and eleven, respectively. Isidore and Jay had previously operated a small press at their home at 402 West 40th Street where they earned a modest income printing Christmas cards and advertising throwaways. The third boy, Julius, had been a boy singer of ballads with Billy Birch's San Francisco Minstrels at the Eden Musée on 23rd Street and Sixth Avenue, and then, in 1885 with the Thatcher, Primrose and West Minstrels.

Isidore, who had early learned to play the piano, liked to write songs. Two were published by Willis Woodward and both were introduced by brother Julius, "A Mother Is a Mother After All" and "A Sister's Lullaby." Julius also had a tie-in with the house of Willis Woodward, which had just embarked on the revolutionary practice of paying singers to perform the firm's songs. Woodward agreed to pay Julius a share of the royalties from Jennie Lindsay's "Always Take Mother's Advice" if he used the song in his act. Julius fulfilled his end of the bargain. He not only sang it frequently but was mainly responsible for the song's success. With the sheet music a best-seller, Woodward reneged and refused to pay the young man the rather large sum due him and tried to buy him off with a twenty-dollar gold piece.

This infuriated the Witmark boys who decided to seek vengeance by going into the song publishing business themselves and thus offer Woodward competition. They had no money to invest, but they did have two basic ingredients for the operation of a successful publishing venture. In Isidore, they had a composer who could be counted on to provide fresh new material for their publications. In Julius, they had a singer with an established reputation to promote these songs. They had one thing more: In their small office equipped with a steam printing press they had a place to open their new business.

The Witmarks began their publishing career by setting a precedent. President Grover Cleveland was about to marry Frances Folsom at the White House. For their first release, the Witmarks capitalized on this much publicized event by writing an instrumental composition, *President Cleveland's Wedding March* by Isidore Witmark. "It was an important coup," recalled Isidore Witmark, "and placed the boys firmly upon the music publishing map of the country." Because of its timeliness, the sheet music had a good sale, brought in a profit, and transformed three young, impoverished printers into a publishing house that would henceforth establish new methods of operation.

The Witmark boys thus introduced into music publishing a new procedure which would become a custom: to take song material from front-page news, and manufacture songs for a specific event. With their next two publications they took a cue from Willis Woodward by bribing performers to use their songs. The oldest Witmark, Isidore, became the catalytic agent between his publishing house and entertainers, and also became one of the first of a species soon to be known as song pluggers. The second Witmark publication was "I'll Never Question Tomorrow" (M. J. Cavanagh—Isidore Witmark). This was the first song to bear the imprint of M. Witmark and Sons, as the new firm was now baptized. (The "M" stood for the boys' father who had no financial interest in the concern. Since the boys were all underage, he was required to sign all business documents.) Isidore Witmark arranged for Mlle. René to feature his song on her cross-country tour. She was a French music hall performer then on her first visit to America. In time she married William A. Brady, the American theatrical producer, and became the mother of Alice Brady, star of stage and screen. Then, with their third publication, the Witmarks made a financial coup. Isidore Witmark wrote "Daddy Nolan" for the vaudeville star, Daniel Scully, who not only incorporated it into his routine but also bought fifty thousand copies of sheet music for distribution as souvenirs. Isidore Witmark's biggest song hit was "Too Whoo! You Know" (M. J. Cavanagh), published in 1887. "As the list of Witmark publications lengthened," we learn from Isidore Witmark's autobiography, "he [Isidore Witmark] placed songs with almost every topnotcher at Tony Pastor's." The growth of M. Witmark and Sons demanded larger quarters. In 1888 operations were transferred to 32 East 14th Street. Once again the Witmarks were pioneers; they became the first of many publishers to base their operations in that section of New York known as Union Square.

The house of M. Witmark and Sons published songs by writers other than young Witmark. While still on West 40th Street, it issued "When the Sun Has Set" (Charles K. Harris). This was Harris' first published song. When he received a royalty check for eighty-five cents he came to the conclusion that if he was to earn any money in songwriting he would have to become his own publisher. With a capital of about a thousand dollars provided by two friends, he opened a one-room office at 107 Grand Street in Milwaukee, Wisconsin. After one year he showed enough profit to repay his friends and to transfer his little venture to a more commodious office in the Alhambra Building in Milwaukee; soon after that he extended his publishing activity further by opening a small branch in Chicago. He, too, had become a member of this now rapidly growing army of young, new, go-getting publishers.

Born in Poughkeepsie, New York, on May 1, 1867, Harris interested himself in minstrel show songs when he was a boy. He constructed a banjo from an empty oyster can and some strands of wire, and upon this primitive instrument he strummed his favorite tunes. Before long, Harris was earning his living in small variety theaters in Milwaukee singing minstrel show tunes and accompanying himself on a banjo. When he was sixteen, he attended a performance of *The Skating Rink*, a musical starring Nat C. Goodwin. He was convinced he could write a far better skating song than the one used in that production. He went home, wrote "Since Maggie Learned to Skate," and somehow managed to convince Goodwin to use it instead of the scheduled number. After that, Harris wrote other songs, such as "Creep, Baby, Creep" and "Let's Kiss and Make Up," his eye always fixed on some stage performer or variety entertainer who might be induced to sing it. One or two of his songs were used. "When the Sun Has Set" was sold to Witmark to become his first publication. From all these creative efforts, Harris earned practically nothing, but he did gain the satisfaction of being a songwriter who had been performed and published.

When he opened his own publishing house, Charles K. Harris Company, he hung a sign outside his door reading: "Songs Written to Order." *Songs written to order!* . . . In that humble setting of Harris' cramped office the American song business was beginning to emerge as a factory for the production of musical numbers.

In 1892, Charles K. Harris took the song business another major step by writing and publishing the first popular song to sell several million copies of sheet music. That song was "After the Ball," inspired by an incident he personally witnessed during a brief visit to Chicago. At a dance there, Harris happened to notice a young couple quarrel and separate. The thought suddenly came to him: "Many a heart is aching after the ball." He wrote both the lyrics and the music of "After the Ball" soon after his return to Milwaukee. He described his ballad as a "song story" because the lyric was a long and woeful tale of mistaken identity spun out through three sixty-four measure verses after each of which a thirty-two measure chorus was repeated. An old man explains to his little niece why he never married: Many years ago, at a ball, he saw his sweetheart kiss a strange man. Convinced she was unfaithful, he left her for good. Only many years later did he discover that the stranger was his sweetheart's brother.

"After the Ball" was introduced in a vaudeville theater in Milwaukee in 1892 by Sam Doctor. The song was a failure because midway in his rendition Doctor forgot the words. Then Harris bribed a prominent performer, J. Aldrich Libbey, then starring in the successful extravaganza, *A Trip to Chinatown* in San Francisco, to include it in his show. Harris paid Libbey five hundred dollars in cash and a percentage of sheet music royalties (another early instance of "payola"!). When Libbey finished the first verse and chorus "not a sound was heard," as Harris later recalled in his autobiography. "I was ready to sink through the floor. He then went through the second verse and chorus, and again complete silence reigned. I was making ready to bolt, but my friends . . . held me tightly by the arms. Then came the third verse and chorus. For a full minute the audience remained quiet, and then broke loose with applause. . . . The entire audience arose and, standing, wildly applauded for five minutes."

A few days later, Harris received from Oliver Ditson an order for 75,000 copies of the sheet music. Other orders came pouring in, as performers everywhere began to include it in their repertories. John Philip Sousa played the ballad at the World Exposition of 1893, where it became such an immediate favorite that from then on Sousa included it on each of his Exposition programs. The popular vaudevillian, Helene Mora, made it her tour de force. After only one year, Harris was drawing a profit of $25,000 a week from the sale of the sheet music. Eventually, "After the Ball" sold over five million copies. It laid the foundation for Harris' dual career as songwriter and publisher, though never again was he to write a ballad to equal the triumph of "After the Ball."

3

When "After the Ball" was first published, the Union Square area in downtown New York was the entertainment capital of America. Its main artery was 14th Street which led westward from Third to Fourth Avenues into the Square. It was here that Tony Pastor ran his famed shrine of vaudeville, the Music Hall, only a stone's throw from that temple of opera, The Academy of Music. On this street, too, were the Dewey Theater, home of burlesque shows and Theiss' Alhambra, where extravaganzas were staged. Nearby, too, were other theaters offering live musical entertainment, such as the Union Square Theater, the Theater Comique, the Standard, the Broadway and the Fifth Avenue. Sandwiched between the theaters were eating places, of which Luchow's on 14th Street was the most famous; musical halls, such as Huber's Prospect; numerous penny arcades; beer and dance halls; and brothels.

Such a concentration of live entertainment offered limitless possibilities for the exploitation of songs. With this in mind, Charles K. Harris decided to shift his expanding organization from Milwaukee to Union Square in the early 1890s. But he had been anticipated by several other publishers, the first of which was M. Witmark and Sons who had arrived on East 14th Street in 1888, followed soon afterwards by Willis Woodward, who settled in the Star Building on Broadway and 13th Street. In the early 1890s, F. B. Haviland, an employe of the New York branch of Oliver Ditson, and Pat Howley, the manager of Willis Woodward, formed a publishing partnership of their own. Since they had limited capital, they had to retain their jobs to support themselves until their new venture prospered. They rented a one-room office a short walking distance from Union Square, on East 20th Street, calling their firm George T. Worth and Company to conceal the identity of its two owners from their employers. But Oliver Ditson soon discovered that Haviland had become a competitor and fired him; and Pat Howley decided to devote all his time to his own publishing activities. The new organization was now renamed Howley, Haviland and Company. Pat Howley now offered Paul Dresser a junior partnership to serve as staff composer. Thus Dresser's greatest ballads, and many lesser ones, carried the imprint of Howley and Haviland. A good deal of this firm's prosperity came about through Dresser's songs. Within a few years, Dresser became an equal partner, and the firm once again changed its name, this time to Howley, Haviland and Dresser.

Like iron filings attracted to a magnet, publisher after publisher came streaming to Union Square in the 1890s to set up their offices there. One of them came from Detroit in 1894, the Whitney-Warner Company which then changed its name to the Jerome H. Remick Company. Three others were newly formed organizations, soon to become strongholds of hit songs: Shapiro-Bernstein, Joseph W. Stern and Company and Leo Feist and Company.

Most of these new publishers had very little capital when they started. Frequently, their total assets consisted of a desk, a chair and one or more manuscripts. But these neophytes had drive and initiative. Impatient with the haphazard process by which, in preceding years, a song was written, published and became successful or not, they decided that a song was no different from any other commodity in the market. It had to be manufactured to meet the prevailing taste. These publishers devised formulas by which songs were produced with speed and dispatch—formulas so efficacious that most often these songs were produced by composers who could not write down a note of music. Stereotypes were created for dialect songs, black and other ethnic songs, humorous and nonsense songs, and most significantly, sentimental ballads.

These new publishers also realized that a song, like all other commodities, could only become successful through exposure to the buying public. Consequently, these Union Square publishers not only devised an effective method for producing songs, but also for "plugging" them—that is, selling them to the public. Many of them became their own song pluggers. Among them were Julie Witmark, Pat Howley, Edward B. Marks, Joseph W. Stern and Leo Feist. "In the nineties," wrote Edward B. Marks in his autobiography, *They All Sang*, "a publisher had to know his way about night spots. It was important to get his wares before the bibulous public; so he had to spend a large part of his time making the rounds for plugs and more plugs. In his wanderings he saw as broad a cross section of New York as any man—even broader than a wine agent, because the song plugger hit spots where champagne would have been considered an effeminate affectation. Sixty joints a week I used to make. Joe Stern, my partner, covered forty. What's more we did it every week. . . . The songs were started where liquor flowed and released the impulse to sing. . . . The way to get a song over was to get it sung in the music halls by a popular singer. . . . I bought beer for the musicians and jollied the headliners."

Union Square was the training ground for song pluggers. Their sole responsibility was to place songs with performers. The fate of many a song rested on the plugger's personal charm, contacts and powers of persuasion. The best pluggers were able to lift a song from obscurity to national acceptance—a plugger like Meyer Cohen who was affiliated with Joseph W. Stern and Company, or Mose Gumble who worked first for Shapiro-Bernstein and then for Jerome II. Remick. These men were powerful influences in the placement of songs of their respective firms with stars such as Lottie Gilson (called "the little magnet" because of her drawing power at the box office), George M. Cohan, Weber and Fields, Nora Bayes and many others. But the stars of the stage were not the only ones to be influenced by pluggers and cajoled into using the plugger's songs. Theater managers, orchestra leaders, singing waiters, performers at beer halls, in fact anybody commanding an audience anywhere was ripe pickings for a plugger.

Many and varied were the methods devised by ingenious pluggers to get their songs played or sung. A free meal, a box of cigars, a bottle of perfume, costume jewelry, and sometimes even a modest sum of money, was the price with which a plugger could buy a performer's interest in one of his songs. Pluggers also invaded local music shops or the music section of large department stores, spending hours performing their songs for passing customers and conning them into buying the sheet music. Pluggers would carry "chorus slips" bearing the words of a refrain, and distribute the slips to patrons of beer halls so that they could join the performance by singing the choruses. Pluggers sometimes traveled by truck to a congested area of the city, with the back of the truck becoming a platform from which the plugger sang his songs to the passing crowds. Pluggers would also visit sport arenas.

A new method arrived at in Union Square was to seat the plugger in the audience. When his firm's song was featured on the bill, and after one verse and chorus had been given on the stage, the plugger would rise as if spontaneously from his seat, and with the spotlight focused on him, he would sing several more choruses of the same number until it became branded on the consciousness of the audience. An effective variation of this method was contrived for Lottie Gilson in 1893. Gus Edwards (later the distinguished vaudeville and song composer, but then only fourteen years old) was paid five dollars a week to sing the chorus of a song several times in his sweet piping child's voice after Lottie Gilson had finished presenting it on the stage. The boy Edwards was liked so well by the audiences, that the trick of placing a boy plugger in the audience became a standard practice in vaudeville and burlesque houses. This became the subject of a song, "A Singer in the Gallery" (Harry A. Mayo) published by M. Witmark and Sons in 1895.

Boy singers were not only placed in the audience but also used as water boys. (It was then customary to serve patrons drinking water between the acts.) The first water boy to become a singing stooge was young Joe Santley, later a celebrated vaudevillian, and half of the team of Santley and Sawyer. M. Witmark and Sons placed him in one of the aisles. From that vantage point, young Santley joined the stage performer at Proctor's Fifth Avenue Theater in plugging such sentimental ballads as "When You Were Sweet Sixteen" (James Thornton) and "Absence Makes the Heart Grow Fonder" (Arthur Gillespie—Herbert Dillea).

4

During the 1890s, the sentimental ballad flourished and prospered as never before. The nineties was basically a sentimental decade. It paid lip service to morality, virginity, and basic virtues in unctuous phrases. It regarded the home, the family as sacrosanct; the mother, as a boy's best friend; a sister or a daughter, beyond the touch of sordid realities. Man was the sovereign of his domain. He might visit places forbidden to his wife, daughter or sister. He might toast—with champagne in a lady's slipper in fancy restaurants—women who lived on the other side of respectability; he might even consider it the ultimate in sophistication to consort with the glamorous female stars of the stage. But this in no way interfered with, or was regarded as a contradiction of, his sanctimonious attitude. His wife lived in a world of her own. Possibly as a reaction to the way in which her husband entertained less acceptable companions away from home, a man's wife made a fetish of her respectability. She swathed herself in a multitude of garments, her skirt floating atop layer upon layer of petticoats; her corset strapped around her body like protective armor; her peek-a-boo shirtwaist and mutton sleeves permitting little flesh to be seen. To her, the woman of the night spots—for all their finery and diamonds—were unfortunates to be regarded with a mixture of pity and contempt, because so few of them would ever know the blessings of married life, children, and the security and peace of respectability.

The ballads of the 1890s reflected the era by sentimentalizing home, virtue, parental and filial devotion, while lamenting those who followed a life of sin or sold themselves for gold. Virtue was ever its own reward and vice always met its just punishment. Between the two polar points lay an extensive field for song exploitation: the constancy or fickleness of lovers; the pathos of misunderstandings and separations; the sad plight of abandoned wives or children; the tragedy of death. Many of these ballads not only squeezed every ounce of sentiment they could from a given situation, but went on to build a complete story of woe—with the beginning, middle and end of a short story—through a succession of verses.

That the songs were an echo of the mores of the times was one of the reasons why sentimental ballads of the 1890s went out of their way to glorify the pure and excoriate the wicked. Another reason lay in the fact that the greatest single market for sheet music was the average family, which spent evenings around the piano singing ballads. Since women, carefully sheltered from the unsavory world outside their protected households, dominated the audience, the songs had to appeal to their moral standards and satisfy their partiality for tear-provoking sagas.

5

On the foundation stones of sentimental ballads, many of the new firms in Union Square erected the solid framework of their establishments.

For M. Witmark and Sons, a single sentimental ballad spelled the difference between financial struggle and security. That ballad was Charles Graham's "The Picture That's Turned Toward the Wall," with which the Witmarks became a major publishing company in 1891. Graham had a short life, dying of alcoholism in Bellevue Hospital in 1899 in his early manhood. His first successful ballad was "If the Waters Could Speak as They Flow," published by Willis Woodward in 1887. The Witmarks then published a few more of his ballads before scoring heavily with "The Picture That's Turned Toward the Wall." Graham wrote it after seeing a melodrama by Joseph Arthur, *Blue Jeans*, on 14th Street, in which a farmer turns his daughter's picture toward the wall because she had just run away from home with a lover. This scene provided Graham with an idea for a ballad which he sold to the Witmarks for fifteen dollars. The Witmarks put the manuscript in a file of unpublished numbers and forgot about it. Then, one day, Andrew Mack, an Irish tenor, dropped into the Witmark office seeking a new song. When nothing in the catalogue appealed to him, the Witmarks opened their files of unpublished music and came upon "The Picture" which Mack seized upon. He introduced it in *The City Directory* at the Bijou Theater. Julie Witmark, now a star vaudeville performer, incorporated the song into his own act and helped to spread it throughout the country. The song made the house of Witmark a major institution virtually overnight, as Isidore Witmark confessed in his autobiography. " 'The Picture That's Turned Toward the Wall' was more than a financial success for the Witmarks. It brought them a coveted prestige. Formerly they had sold sheet music by the hundred copies; now they knew sales in the thousands. . . . Jobbers who had scorned to deal with 'children' were camping on their doorstep for copies. Dealers who had refused them displays now buried other songs beneath 'The Picture.' Singers whom they had been obliged to chase now chased them."

Graham's most successful ballad after 1891 was "Two Little Girls in Blue," which was published not by the Witmarks but by another young firm, Spaulding and Kornder, in 1893. Its similarity to Charles K. Harris' "After the Ball" is much too close to be coincidental. In both a lover's quarrel leads to a tragic and permanent separation. This tale of woe, in both ballads, is narrated by an old man: to a niece in "After the Ball," but to a nephew in "Two Little Girls in Blue." Graham sold his ballad for ten dollars, then saw it become a best-seller that brought a fortune to its publisher after Lottie Gilson introduced and popularized it in vaudeville.

Hits came thick and fast from M. Witmark and Sons in the 1890s, now that they had become a firm to reckon with. They used their newly gained power and prestige to good advantage in convincing important stage performers to use their numbers. In 1894, John Russell, of the Russell Brothers, popularized in vaudeville "Her Eyes Don't Shine Like Diamonds" (Dave Marion). A year later, Lottie Gilson brought down the house at the Gaiety Theater with "The Sunshine of Paradise Alley" (Walter H. Ford—John W. Bratton).

Possibly the most successful sentimental ballad to come from the Witmarks was "When You Were Sweet Sixteen" in 1898. It was written by James Thornton, one of the most prolific of the sentimental balladists of the 1890s and a distinguished vaudeville monologist. Born in England in 1861, Thornton came to America when he was eight. As a young man he worked as a singing waiter in Boston and New York, after which he toured the vaudeville circuit. His first number was a mammy song, "Remember Poor Mother," sold to a publisher for $2.50 in 1890. His wife, Bonnie, introduced it at the Bal Mabile Café on Bleecker Street where Thornton was then employed as a singing waiter. Two years later came Thornton's first hit, "My Sweetheart's the Man in the Moon," which Frank Harding purchased for fifteen dollars. The writing involved Bonnie. One night she pleaded with Thornton to come home straight from the theater instead of stopping off in a saloon as was his practice. When he refused, Bonnie inquired if she was still his sweetheart, to which Thornton replied flippantly, "My sweetheart's the man in the moon." Given the idea and a title for a song, and encouraged by Frank Harding, Thornton wrote it the following morning. Bonnie sang it frequently in local cafés.

In 1894, Thornton's ballad about a fallen woman, "She May Have Seen Better Days," was successfully released by T. B. Harms. W. H. Widom introduced it with the Primrose and West Minstrels. This was followed in 1895 by Thornton's "The Streets of Cairo" (or "The Poor Country Maid") published by Harding and introduced by Little Egypt at the Chicago Columbian Exposition. Its verse borrowed a tune from a familiar hootchy-kootchy. Thornton had three more hit songs in 1896: "On the Benches in the Park," "Don't Give Up the Old Love for the New" and "It Don't Seem Like the Same Old Smile." The last received first prize in a song contest conducted by the New York *World*.

But Thornton's greatest song was still to come, a song that sold well over a million copies and further helped to entrench the already solid position of M. Witmark and Sons. The song was "When You Were Sweet Sixteen," written as a love song for his wife, Bonnie.

Thornton originally sold the song to Joseph W. Stern and Company for twenty-five dollars. Stern did not publish it, but allowed it to collect dust in the files. Thornton then sold it a second time, to M. Witmark and Sons for fifteen dollars. Bonnie Thornton introduced it in vaudeville, the first of many vaudevillians to use it in their acts. After the sale of the sheet music began to move, Joseph W. Stern sued the Witmarks for all the profits, claiming prior ownership. A settlement was reached out of court. Joseph W. Stern and Company relinquished all claims to the ballad for a payment of five thousand dollars.

Perhaps the biggest seller of all among Witmark's sentimental ballads was "Sweet Adeline," another example of the echo-type song, the echo produced by repetition of a word, phrase or line, in this case "Sweet Adeline, My Adeline," to a background of barbershop harmonies. Though this ballad was published in 1903, after the Witmarks had moved out of Union Square to greener pastures uptown, its composition belongs to the 1890s, specifically 1896. Harry Armstrong, who sang in vocal quartets, wrote the words in Boston when he was eighteen; at that time he called it "Down Home in New England." After coming to New York, where he was later employed by the Witmarks, he invited Richard Gerard Husch (who used the pseudonym of Richard H. Gerard) to write a melody for his verses. Husch complied. The song now bore the title of "You're the Flower of My Heart Sweet Rosalie." The song manuscript shuttled from one publisher to the next without finding a taker. Husch finally suggested a change of title. By chance, the authors came upon a poster announcing the farewell tour of the prima donna, Adelina Patti. "Let's call the girl in our song Adeline," Armstrong suggested. The new title—condensed to "Sweet Adeline"—apparently turned the trick; Witmark purchased the song. For about a year following its publication, the sheet music failed to move. Then the Quaker City Four, a vaudeville singing quartet, came to Witmark in search of a new number. When "Sweet Adeline" was sung to the Quartet, Harry Ernest, its manager, exclaimed: "That's just what we've been looking for!" The Quartet introduced it at Hammerstein's Victoria Theater in New York in 1903. Before long it entered the repertory of barbershop quartets and became a favorite of people in a happy state of inebriation. In 1906, 1910 and 1914, John J. Fitzgerald of Boston used it as his theme song for three successful mayoralty campaigns. In 1929, the song provided the title for a musical comedy by Jerome Kern and Oscar Hammerstein II, a musical romance of the Gay Nineties. In this musical, James Thornton, the gifted balladist and vaudevillian, appeared as himself in what was his last stage appearance. He died in New York nine years later.

6

Some of the greatest successes from the presses of Howley and Haviland during its first years in business came from the pen of its junior partner and staff composer, Paul Dresser. Dresser's ballads in 1894, "Once Ev'ry Year" and "Take a Seat, Old Lady," were among the firm's first publications. Its first money-maker appeared a year after, "Just Tell Them that You Saw Me," which Dresser wrote after reading a newspaper account about a man ruined by a tragic love affair. So successful was this ballad in its first year of publication that "just tell them that you saw me" became a catch phrase on everybody's lips. One enterprising manufacturer realized a coup by printing this phrase on lapel badges.

Dresser's greatest ballad of all, though not his most financially rewarding, was "On the Banks of the Wabash Far Away." Written in 1897, the song was most often associated with the state of Indiana. There are several versions of how Dresser came to write it. Theodore Dreiser maintained that it was he who suggested the subject of the Wabash to his brother, since rivers always did well in popular songs. Dreiser further insisted that he helped his brother fashion the lyrics. But what is probably a more accurate account came from Max Hoffman, the orchestrator for the Witmark firm. He is quoted by Isidore Witmark as saying: "I went to his room at the Auditorium Hotel [in Chicago] where instead of a piano there was a small folding camp organ Dresser always carried with him. It was summer. All the windows were open and Paul was mulling over a melody that was practically in finished form. But he did not have the words. So he had me play the full chorus over and over again at least for two or three hours, while he was writing down the words, changing a line here and a phrase there until the lyric suited him. . . . When Paul came to the line 'through the sycamores the candlelights are gleaming,' I was tremendously impressed. . . . I have always felt that Paul got the idea from glancing out of the window now and again as he wrote, and seeing the lights glimmering on Lake Michigan. . . . During the whole evening we spent together, Paul made no mention of anyone's having helped him with the song."

Only three months after it was published, "On the Banks of the Wabash Far Away" was played and sung in theaters, at home and in the streets. In 1913 it was officially made the State song of Indiana.

Dresser's next success came with "The Curse of the Dreamer" in 1899. At first entitled "The Curse," it spoke of the composer's bitterness upon learning that his wife, May Howard, the burlesque queen, had deserted him for another man. He had no intention of publishing the song, regarding it as too personal for public distribution. Instead, he used the ballad to try to effect a reconciliation with May, and for a short time he succeeded. But May was inconstant, and before long deserted him again, this time permanently. It was only then that Dresser capitalized on his sorrow by rewriting his song to provide it with a happy ending and endowing it with the new title of "The Curse of the Dreamer."

Though Dresser earned large sums from his songs (in the neighborhood of half a million dollars in less than two decades) he kept very little of it. He always lived in the grand manner, indulging extravagantly his passion for women, food, liquor and grand hotel suites.

This, together with his fabled generosity, made money melt in his hands. By the time he was fifty, he was totally penniless, deserted by friends he had once feasted and at times supported. The sales of his ballads began to decline by 1902. By 1905 his publishing house went into bankruptcy. With the hope of recouping his fame and fortune, he rented a two-room office on West 28th Street (the street soon to become known as Tin Pan Alley). Always dressed in an elegant frock coat and silk top hat—as if clinging tenaciously to the memory of his more prosperous years—he would go to his office daily with the proud stride of one who refused to accept defeat. His colleagues and his onetime competitors were convinced he was through. But Dresser still had a winning card up his sleeve, a ballad that became his greatest success. It was "My Gal Sal," published under his own imprint in 1905. (The Sal in this song was a prostitute with whom he had been in love in his early manhood.) Sad to say, Dresser did not live to taste this triumph. He died of a heart attack in Brooklyn, New York, on January 30, 1906, just a few months before his last ballad started its climb to heights. Louise Dresser, a young entertainer discovered by Dresser, whose name she assumed, introduced it in vaudeville. By the end of 1906, the song had sold several million copies of sheet music. Had Dresser lived, his returns as composer-publisher would have recovered for him the fame and the wealth he feared lost forever. As it was, he died a pauper, a thoroughly broken man.

As long as Dresser flourished as a composer, the publishing house with which he was affiliated, Howley, Haviland and Dresser, flourished with him. When his fortunes declined, so did those of the publishing house. But before this happened, the company profited from several notable sentimental ballads by composers other than Dresser. The best were "In the Baggage Coach Ahead" in 1896 and two years later, "Gold Will Buy Most Anything but a True Girl's Heart."

"In the Baggage Coach Ahead" was by Gussie L. Davis, a black man who had worked as a janitor at the Cincinnati Conservatory of Music where, seemingly by osmosis, he absorbed enough musical knowledge to write songs. The first to be published was "The Lighthouse by the Sea," put out by a small Cincinnati printer in 1886. While holding down various menial jobs including Pullman porter, he wrote and saw published "Wait Till the Tide Comes In" (George Propheter) in 1887 and, in 1893, "The Fatal Wedding" (W. H. Widom). In "The Fatal Wedding"—in which a wedding is interrupted by the arrival of the groom's real wife and their baby, and is brought to a tragic denouement with the groom's suicide—Davis quotes a passage from Mendelssohn's *Wedding March*.

For "In the Baggage Coach Ahead," Davis wrote his own lyrics based on an actual episode he had witnessed as a Pullman porter. A sobbing child disclosed to him that his mother was lying in the baggage car in a coffin. Davis wrote his ballad in 1896 and sold it to Howley and Haviland for a few dollars. Pat Howley placed it with Imogene Comer, a vaudevillian billed as "the queen of song." She introduced it at Howard's Athenaeum Theater in Boston where it stopped the show. She kept it in her act for the next three years.

When Howley and Haviland first published "Gold Will Buy Most Anything but a True Girl's Heart" the sheet music named Monroe Rosenfeld as both the lyricist and the composer. (Subsequent publications identified Charles E. Forman as lyricist.) Rosenfeld was a man of numerous talents. He was a newspaperman, press agent, short-story writer, arranger and adapter of popular songs and composer. The Achilles' heel of his personality was neither liquor nor women, to which so many of his fellow songwriters were chronically addicted. It was the racetrack. More than one of his songs was written to raise the money for a bet on a sure winner. More than once he was reduced to the practice of palming off somebody else's songs to an unsuspecting publisher for some immediate cash. And when these maneuvers proved futile he was not above passing fraudulent checks. The chronic limp from which he suffered in later years came from his jumping out of a second-story window to flee from the police.

In some of his songs he revealed a beguiling sense of humor and satire. Two such songs came out in 1884. In "I've Just Been Down to the Bank" he commented sardonically on a scandal then much in the news: the bankruptcy of the Marine Bank in Brooklyn, New York, in which General Grant and his son had involved themselves with a shady operator, Ferdinand Ward, Jr., through whom they lost their entire fortunes. The title page of the song pictures a well-dressed man carrying a satchel filled with money rushing from the Marine Bank to a nearby harbor. "Take the next boat for Canada, Free Fare to bank presidents," reads a caption. In case the point of the song was not made sufficiently clear by the picture and caption, a dedication on the title page read, "To Ferdinand Ward, Jr." A spoken commentary between the verses of the song further helped to carry the satiric message.

Once again stimulated by a monumental scandal, was Rosenfeld's "Ma! Ma! Where's My Pa?" which he issued in Chicago under the pen name of H. R. Monroe. Here the object of Rosenfeld's satire was Grover Cleveland who, during his drive for the Presidency of the United States, confessed that he was the father of an illegitimate child. To the title's provocative question, the chorus replies: "Up in the White House, darling, Making the laws, working the cause, Up in the White House, dear."

Rosenfeld's big song in 1886 was "Johnny Get Your Gun," in jig time. (Some thirty years later George M. Cohan borrowed the title for the opening words of "Over There.") A humorous topical song in 1888 was "Let Me Shake the Hand that Shook the Hand of Sullivan," a tribute to the then heavyweight boxing champion of the world. Still in a jocular vein was "And Her Golden Hair Was Hanging Down Her Back," published in 1894 as the first hit of the newly formed firm of Leo Feist. Rosenfeld wrote only the words, though when the sheet music first appeared he was also acknowledged as the composer. But Rosenfeld had, in this case, taken the liberty of stealing somebody else's tune, that of Felix McGlennon, whose name graces later editions of the sheet music. In this lighthearted effort, the heroine is a shy country lass come to the big city with "her golden hair hanging down her back." She returns to her hometown with "a naughty little twinkle in her eye."

Rosenfeld's true forte was the sentimental ballad, with which he first achieved some measure of recognition between 1884 and 1885 with "Hush Little Boy, Don't You Cry" (published under the pseudonym of F. Belasco) and "Goodbye, Boy, Goodbye." Greater success with sentimental ballads came from "With All Her Faults I Love Her Still" in 1888, an echo song first popularized by the minstrel, Richard José. (There is some reason to suspect that Rosenfeld filched this melody from a German song by Theodore Metz.)

Rosenfeld's "Those Wedding Bells Shall Not Ring," in 1896, reminds us in its subject matter of Gussie L. Davis's "The Fatal Wedding," by which it was undoubtedly influenced. With "Take Back Your Gold," which Joseph W. Stern and Company published in 1897 during its first year in publishing, Rosenfeld credits another man with writing lyrics which were actually his own. That man was Louis W. Pritzkow, a minstrel who was being bribed to use the song in his act with Primrose and West's Minstrels. But Pritzkow did not make the song famous. That credit goes to Emma Carus. At that time she was a song plugger hired to promote that ballad. Her husky delivery was just right for the ballad's dolorous sentiments, especially in such defiant lines as "She spurned the gold he offered her and said, 'Take back your gold, for gold cannot buy me!'" This ballad was also favored by the sweet-voiced boy tenor, Master John J. Quigley, and by such male balladists as Fred Salcombe.

In "Gold Will Buy Most Anything but a True Girl's Heart," a best-seller in the Howley and Haviland catalogue in 1898, the theme of gold versus true love is further explored by Rosenfeld, though in a somewhat less familiar pattern. Here a wealthy man offers jewels fit for a queen to a poor girl to tempt her not to marry the man she seems to favor. But she tells him proudly, "gold will buy most anything but a true girl's heart."

7

Two years after the firm of Charles K. Harris came to power and affluence with its first publication, "After the Ball," the house of Joseph W. Stern and Company repeated this phenomenon in Union Square by building a major publishing organization on the corner-stone of its first release.

The two heads of Joseph W. Stern and Company were Joseph Stern and Edward B. Marks. Each was more or less a novice at songwriting, and thorough innocents about publishing. Marks was a salesman of sewing hooks and eyes, whalebones and other notions. Stern was a necktie salesman who, as he said, "could play the piano with one hand and fake with the other." Marks had written a few song lyrics which had been set to music by unknowns, despite which some of them managed to get heard in vaudeville, and a few of them were published by Frank Harding. One was "December and May," music by William Lorraine. It was introduced at Tony Pastor's Music Hall by Lydia Yeamans who made it a basic part of her routine.

One day in 1894, Marks met Stern in Mamaroneck, New York. A storm kept them in their hotel. There Marks read a newspaper account of a child lost in the city streets, who was found by a policeman who turned out to be the child's long-lost father. Marks read the item to Stern who agreed that this incident had the makings of a ballad. That day, Sterns and Marks pieced together, "The Little Lost Child," with Marks writing the words and Stern the music. Once they finished writing, they quickly arrived at the decision to open their own publishing house to issue the song.

With a capital of about one hundred dollars, they rented a basement office on 14th Street near Second Avenue. Since Marks still intended pursuing his career as a notions salesman, the firm was called simply Joseph W. Stern and Company. "The Little Lost Child" became their first property. On the day that the sheet music was delivered, Della Fox, a stage star then much in the limelight, dropped into the office seeking new song material. She became infatuated with "The Little Lost Child" and introduced it in vaudeville. After that Lottie Gilson used it frequently in her vaudeville act.

A momentum having been started, the success of "The Little Lost Child" went into high gear through a new method of song plugging which this ballad introduced, the song slide. A Brooklyn electrician had arrived at an unusual effect during the showing of the play, *The Old Homestead*, by flashing a picture on a screen in the rear of the stage while a singer was performing a ballad. This gave the electrician the idea to dramatize popular songs by flashing on a screen not one but a whole series of pictures. For his experiment he chose "The Little Lost Child." Shrewd merchants that they were, Stern and Marks realized the value to their song of this innovation. They provided the electrician with the money to photograph the pictures with which the ballad could be dramatized. The song and the slides were introduced one matinee in 1894 at the Grand Opera House on 23rd Street and Eighth Avenue. Allan May sang the ballad while the pictures of the stray child, the mother and the policeman were flashed on a screen. This novelty caught on, establishing the song slide as a popular form of stage entertainment, promoting the sheet music sale of the ballad to over two million copies, and creating the song slide as a major new medium for song plugging.

Two years later, in 1896, Stern and Marks met with even greater prosperity with the publication of their new ballad, "Mother Was a Lady." Lottie Gilson introduced "Mother Was a Lady" at Proctor's 58th Street. She made it *her* song, though many another vaudevillian used it as well. In time, the sheet music sale surpassed that of "The Little Lost Child."

Before the nineteenth century was over, Joseph W. Stern and Company added to its prestige and wealth with the release of several ballads by writers other than themselves. In 1895, they published "Down in Poverty Row" (Gussie L. Davis—Arthur Trevelyan) and two songs by James Thornton in 1896 and 1897, "Don't Give Up the Old Love for the New" and "There's a Little Star Shining for You." Monroe Rosenfeld's hit, "Take Back Your Gold," was on the Stern lists in 1897, while in 1898 the company mined gold with "She Was Bred in Old Kentucky," which Harry B. Berdan (using the pen name of Harry Braisted) and Frederick J. Radcliffe (under the pseudonym of Stanley Carter) had written to prove to their friends that they were just as adept in writing sentimental ballads as they were comedy numbers, one of which, "You're Not the Only Pebble on the Beach" had been a song hit two years earlier.

8

The sentimental ballad that told a tale of woe or preached a moral was the principal commodity of this new breed of publisher in Union Square. But it was not the only one. Other types of song also found a ready market. There were the simple ballads that were gentle songs of nostalgia and sentiment with no story content.

In its first year, 1894, Howley and Haviland published "The Sidewalks of New York." Its lyricist, James Blake, was a salesman in a hatter's shop who liked to write verses. At the request of Charles Lawlor, a buck-and-wing performer in vaudeville who was also an amateur composer, he wrote some verses about New York to a melody Lawlor whistled to him one day. The two men induced Lottie Gilson to introduce it at the Old London Theater in the Bowery. The audience became so enchanted with it that they joined her in singing a repetition of the chorus. Howley and Haviland then released the sheet music to realize one of its first profitable publications.

Since then "The Sidewalks of New York" has grown into something of an unofficial anthem for the city after which it was named. The political career of New York's dapper Mayor James J. Walker was closely linked with this song. In 1924, when the name of Alfred E. Smith was placed in nomination for the Presidency at the Democratic National Convention in San Francisco, the bandleader struck up the strains of "The Sidewalks of New York." This was the first time that this song became Smith's musical identification, something that continued for the rest of his life. The sudden resurgence to popularity of "The Sidewalks of New York" in 1924 led an enterprising journalist to seek out its authors. He learned that Lawlor was dead, and that Blake was blind and living in poverty in New York. In 1933, the New York *Herald* created a fund to support Blake for the rest of his life. He died two years later.

"Daisy Bell" (or "A Bicycle Built for Two") owed its success to the swelling vogue for bicycle riding in the 1890s. The author of both the words and music was an Englishman, Harry Dacre. Upon visiting the United States in 1891 he brought among his possessions a bicycle for which he was charged duty. A friend, meeting him at the pier, remarked wryly; "It's lucky you don't have a bicycle built for two, otherwise you'd have to pay double duty." The phrase "bicycle built for two" impressed itself on Dacre's mind and became the closing words of the first song he wrote in America.

There was little interest in the song in the United States at first, its initial rise to prominence occurring in a London music hall. Then, late in 1891, a radical change in the structure of the American bicycle made the vehicle easier and safer to manipulate. This brought on a fad for bicycle riding in which women participated. This new interest in cycling led Tony Pastor to sing Dacre's ballad at the Music Hall. After that, Jennie Lindsay caused a furor with it at the Atlantic Gardens in the Bowery, and T. B. Harms published it in 1892.

Another Englishman, Michael Nolan, a performer in English music halls, wrote a ballad which became basic to vaudeville song literature in America in the 1890s and was often used by vaudevillians to accompany clog dances. It was "Little Annie Rooney," published in London in 1889, then in the early 1900s, introduced to America at New York's London Theater by Annie Hart, "the Bowery Girl."

"The Band Played On" was written by John E. Palmer in 1895 after he heard a German street band, such street bands then being popular in New York. He sold the song to Charles B. Ward, a vaudevillian, who published it in 1895 under the imprint of the New York Music Company. At that time he gave Palmer the credit for writing the lyrics while passing himself off as the composer. Ward introduced the ballad at Hammerstein's Harlem Opera House in 1895, following which it was promoted both by other vaudevillians and by the New York *World*, which published both the words and the music to become one of the first newspapers to promote a popular song. The huge sums earned from the sheet music sale brought a fortune to Ward but nothing to Palmer beyond the paltry sum Ward had originally paid him.

9

When Ireland was afflicted with famine between 1846 and 1850 over a million and a half Irishmen emigrated to the New World. The Irish became a favorite ethnic group for stage caricatures and songs. Irish songs and the portrayal of Irish characters were largely responsible for the large and sustained interest in the Harrigan and Hart extravaganzas.

In the 1880s, William J. Scanlan achieved renown both as a performer of Irish roles and as a composer of Irish songs. For the stage musical *Friend and Foe* (1881) he wrote "Moonlight at Killarney" which he himself introduced. In 1883 and 1885 he wrote the songs for, and starred in, *The Irish Minstrel* and *Shane na Lawn*. The latter was where he sang "Peggy O'Moore," "Remember Boy, You're Irish" and "My Paddy's Always Poor." Scanlon's best known Irish song was "Molly O!" from *Mavourneen* (1891).

His successor as an Irish performer and writer of Irish ballads was Chauncey Olcott. Born in Buffalo, New York, on July 21, 1858, Olcott made his first public appearance as a singer of ballads in his native city. After that he performed as a blackface minstrel with the Thatcher, Primrose and West company. Following several performances on the New York musical stage, he went to London where he studied singing and played in light opera. Back in the United States, he wrote the music, and at times the librettos as well, for a number of musical productions of Irish content, among them *Minstrel of Clare* (1896), *Sweet Inniscarra* (1897), *A Romance of Athlone* (1899), *Garrett O'Magh* (1901) and *Old Limerick Town* (1902). He also filled a starring role in each of these productions.

Olcott's best Irish song is "My Wild Irish Rose" (1899), one of the most celebrated American-Irish ballads ever written. He himself introduced it in *A Romance of Athlone*. "Kate O'Donahue," which he sang in *Sweet Inniscarra*, was another of his song successes.

Olcott continued writing songs and appearing in stage musicals until 1925 when his health gave way. He then went into retirement in Monte Carlo where he died in 1932.

One of the most lovable Irish waltzes was "Sweet Rosie O'Grady." Maude Nugent, a singer at The Abbey, a night spot on 38th Street and Eighth Avenue, is said to have written the words and music. She brought her song to Edward B. Marks who turned it down on the grounds that popular songs with a girl's name in the title were no longer marketable. Miss Nugent stalked out of the office of Joseph W. Stern and Company and headed toward Howley, Haviland and Dresser. Marks pursued her, stopped her in the street, and said he had suddenly changed his mind. Then and there he purchased the song for one hundred dollars. He published it in 1896 and saw it become one of his firm's major releases—with the help of Maude Nugent who sang it regularly at The Abbey and after that at Tony Pastor's Music Hall and other vaudeville houses.

"Rosie O'Grady" had a daughter twenty-two years later, but the song, "The Daughter of Rosie O'Grady," was written neither by Jerome nor Miss Nugent. Monty C. Brice wrote the lyrics, and Walter Donaldson the music, and the song was published in 1918. The younger Pat Rooney introduced it at the Palace Theater in New York in 1919. From then on he used it as his musical trademark, always accompanying his singing with a waltz clog.

Rough and tumble Irish songs, as well as sweet ones, also proved popular on the vaudeville stage. The foremost of these were "Drill Ye Tarriers, Drill" (1888), "Down Went McGinty" (1889) and "Throw Him Down, McCloskey" (1890).

We do not know who wrote either the words or the music of "Drill Ye Tarriers, Drill"—"tarriers" being slang for rowdy characters. But we do know that it was first sung by a vocal trio dressed up as ruffians in a musical farce, A Brass Monkey, in 1888. Thomas F. Casey, who had been a blaster and driller in street excavations, then made it the highlight of his vaudeville act at Tony Pastor's. J. W. Kelly and Maggie Cline were two other vaudevillians famous for their renditions of this robust work song.

"Down Went McGinty," was a humorous ditty by Joseph Flynn. Its subject was an Irishman who was so accident prone that he fell in the strangest of places, including into coal chutes, from high walls, or into the river. Flynn, an Irish comedian, introduced the song with his partner, Frank B. Sheridan, at Hyde and Behman's Adams Street Theater in Brooklyn in 1889, and sent the audience into an uproar, launching the song upon a long and successful route in vaudeville.

"Throw Him Down, McCloskey," by J. W. Kelly was a vigorous ballad about a boxing match that was said to have taken place in a saloon. Maggie Cline, whose big voice and robust delivery were perfectly suited for this rowdy number, made this one of her most famous routines for over a quarter of a century. The song fame of McCloskey sent J. P. Skelly to write a song of his own in which the hero bore that name. He called it "McCloskey on the Spree" (1891), but like most imitations it failed to duplicate the popularity of its model.

10

A new brand of popular Negro song was being heard in theaters in the 1890s. It bore the indelicate label of "coon song." Performers of coon songs shouted more often than they sang, magnetizing audiences with the dynamism of their personalities as well as with the robustness of their delivery.

The popular and vulgar usage of the word "coon" (as a term for the black man) in connection with a song or its singer probably began when several songs in the 1880s carried that word in their titles: "New Coon in Town" (Paul Allen) in 1883; "The Whistling Coon" (Sam Devere) in 1888; "Little Alabama Coon" (Hattie Starr) in 1893.

May Irwin was the first outstanding exponent of coon songs, the one who helped develop the techniques and idiosyncrasies of that singing style. She did so first with one of her own songs, "Mamie, Come Kiss Your Honey" which she featured in the stage musical, A

Country Sport, in 1893. Two years later she electrified her audiences with her presentation of "The Bully" (or "The New Bully") in *Widow Jones*. That song and that performance marked the real beginning of the vogue for coon songs (or coon shouts) that lasted for about two decades.

May Irwin came upon "The Bully" while she was traveling by train from St. Louis to Chicago. Aboard the train was Charles E. Trevathan, a sportswriter, who entertained his fellow travelers by singing several numbers to his own guitar accompaniment. One of his songs was "The Bully," which he said he had heard at Babe Connors' famed brothel in St. Louis, sung by Mama Lou, a black performer who made a specialty of Negro songs. "The Bully" described lustily and bawdily how a black man, brandishing a razor, was looking for a bully who had just come to town. By the time the bully is found, he is beyond the services of either a doctor or a nurse but fit only for a hearse. May Irwin became so intrigued with "The Bully" that she had Trevathan write it down for her, with some discreet expurgations in the lyrics. She used it in her very next stage appearance in New York. When "The Bully" was published in 1896, Charles E. Trevathan's name appeared on the sheet music as the author; no mention was made of Mama Lou.

"All Coons Look Alike to Me" was the next major hit among coon songs. It was written by Ernest Hogan, a popular black vaudevillian, whose performances first made the song a success. Hogan once revealed that he borrowed the melody for "All Coons Look Alike to Me" from a syncopated tune he had heard played on a piano in a saloon in Chicago's red-light district. Hogan's real name was Reuben Crowders. He was born in Bowling Green, Kentucky, soon after the Civil War. As a boy he ran away from home and traveled about with summer tent companies and Uncle Tom shows, singing and dancing, and trying to write songs. At one time he was the end man with Bert Williams in minstrel shows before Williams teamed up with Walker. In 1897, Hogan did a cakewalk in *Summer Nights* atop the Casino Roof in New York.

Isidore Witmark, whose firm published the song, wrote that Hogan, later in his life, was ashamed of having written the song, since black people became deeply resentful of the term "coon song" and some of the expressions and sentiments found in many such songs.

The coon songs of Ben Harney, some of the best ever written, though belonging to this period, will come in for consideration in a later chapter when ragtime is discussed. Celebrated among other coon songs of the 1890s was "My Gal Is a Highborn Lady,"written by Barney Fagan and published by M. Witmark and Sons in 1896. Fagan, a graduate of the minstrel show and vaudeville, once disclosed how he came to write his famous song. He was bicycling along Lake Michigan in Chicago when a pedal broke. Its persistent click against the wheel suggested a melody to him which he wrote down the same day. The Witmarks bought it outright for one hundred dollars. Ernest Haverly introduced it with the Haverly Minstrels, and after that Clara Wieland further helped to make it a standout success in vaudeville.

The writing of "At a Georgia Camp Meeting" represented on the part of its creator, Kerry Mills, a gesture of protest against coon songs. As Frederick Allen Mills he had studied violin seriously, became the head of the violin department at the University of Michigan School of Music, taught violin privately at Ann Arbor and occasionally gave violin recitals. As Kerry Mills he stepped out of the world of serious music into that of popular songs. In 1895 he wrote, and himself published, a syncopated two-step march for piano, "Rastus on Parade." His acquaintance with coon songs during this time convinced him that this kind of music denigrated black people. He felt impelled to write a syncopated song presenting the black man in a more favorable light. Using the subject of Southern religious camp meetings, he wrote "At a Georgia Camp Meeting." He then formed his own publishing company

(F. A. Mills) to issue it, first as a two-step march for piano in 1897, then as a song with lyrics, in 1899.

When the vaudeville team of Genaro and Bailey used "At A Georgia Camp Meeting" in their act they accompanied it with a dance called the cakewalk. This was a high-stepping strut across the stage with body bent backward, while they tipped their high hats and fussed with their canes. The cakewalk had first been evolved on plantations before the Civil War. "When there was little work," explained Shephard N. Edmonds, a black man from Tennessee, "both young and old would dress up in hand-me-down finery to do a high-kicking, prancing walk around. They did a takeoff on the high manners of the white folks in the 'big house.' " The word "cakewalk" was adopted for this dance because a cake was given as a prize to the couple performing the most elaborate or original routine.

The cakewalk entered the minstrel show, then invaded other branches of show business. Harrigan and Hart included "Walking for Dat Cake" in one of their productions in 1877, describing it as a picture of Negro life and customs. By the early 1890s, the cakewalk became a rage. Cakewalk contests were held. In 1892, the first annual cakewalk jubilee was instituted at Madison Square Garden in New York, a three-night contest featuring cakewalk competitions for dancers successful in small-town contests. The dance was also becoming increasingly popular in vaudeville, first with Charlie Johnson and Dora Dean in 1893, and most importantly with Williams and Walker who became so successful with it at Koster and Bial's in New York that they became identified with it for the remainder of their successful career in vaudeville.

11

Mama Lou, who had introduced "The Bully" at Babe Connor's brothel in St. Louis, was the first to popularize a nonsense song with ribald suggestions that has become a song classic of the 1890s, "Ta-ra-ra bom-der-e." There are many who believe that Mama Lou wrote it. In any event it was she who made it known long before it was marketed commercially by Willis Woodward in Union Square in 1891. A press agent, Henry J. Sayers, heard Mama Lou sing it. Since he was then handling the publicity for a company of performers, The Tuxedo Girls, he decided to adapt it for his troupe. As he later disclosed: "I had never tried my hand at songwriting but I thought that with a few changes I could clean up the stuff. When I showed it to the boss, he almost threw me out of the office. 'This is unprintable, unsingable, untouchable,' he shouted. I decided to rewrite the lyrics entirely. But they fell flat and remained that way three years."

In 1891 Sayers interested Woodward in publishing it. Soon afterward, Lottie Gilson sang it in London where her striking delivery, accompanied by high kicks and shrieks, created a sensation. "Everywhere," wrote a correspondent from England to the New York *Herald* early in 1892, "one hears 'Ta-ra-ra bom-der-e' and there is hardly a theater in London in which the refrain is not alluded to at least once during the night." The first sheet music published in London sold for a dollar a copy. Competitive publications later brought the price down sharply to two cents a copy, and then it was distributed free with the purchase of a tin of tea. Lottie Gilson introduced it to the American stage at Koster and Bial's in New York, where she duplicated her London triumph.

There were several other nonsense songs delighting the audiences of the 1890s. Frank Addis Kent's "Um-Skit-a-Rat Trap-Si-Si-Do" was about a musician who performed on both the piano and the cornet. His rehearsing was described in a senseless chorus that enabled the composer to quote a few measures from such song favorites as "Auld Lang Syne," "Annie Laurie," "After the Ball" and "My Sweetheart's the Man in the Moon." Two other nonsense songs are associated with Lottie Gilson. They are "La-Didily-Idily, Umti Umti Ay" (Richard Morton and C. M. Rodney—C. M. Rodney) and "Tol Lol Lol" (George Horncastle—Felix McGlennon). A particularly appealing nonsense song was "Zizzy Ze Zum Zum Zum" (Karl Kennett—Lyn Udall) first heard in *Cook's Tours* produced at Koster and Bial's in 1898. The absurdity of this number was intensified by the way in which it was performed with exaggerated facial grimaces and eccentric bodily gestures.

Comedy, rather than outright nonsense, was tapped by Joseph Tabrar in "Daddy Wouldn't Buy Me a Bow-Wow" (1892) through its use of baby talk. A battered old hat found in a discarded theatrical trunk in an attic led to the writing of "Where Did You Get that Hat?" by Joseph J. Sullivan in 1888. Sullivan made the song popular in vaudeville after introducing it at Miner's Eighth Avenue Theater in New York in 1888.

The advice of father to son on how best to succeed in business was treated with levity in "Do, Do, My Huckleberry, Do" in 1893. The Dillon brothers, John and Harry, wrote it for their own vaudeville act. Charles E. Trevathan wrote an amusing ditty, "The Frog Song," for May Irwin and it became one of her standbys.

12

One other song from the 1890s deserves discussion. It is a curiosity. It was never intended for the market, nor did it achieve popularity through the recognized media or sales methods. It was the work of amateurs, and its first appearance was not in sheet music of a Union Square publisher or through presentation on the stage. Yet, achieving an inexplicable momentum of its own, this song grew from obscurity to unparalleled fame. For this song has since been sung by and listened to by more people in America during the past half century than any other.

The song is "Happy Birthday to You."*

The authors were sisters, Patty and Mildred J. Hill, kindergarten teachers by profession. In 1893 they wrote a song called "Good Morning to All," with Patty writing the words and Mildred the music. It was published that same year in a collection, *Song Stories for Children*, issued in Chicago by Clayton F. Summy. Nobody knows just who it was who made a slight change in the lyrics of "Good Morning to All" so that it might become a birthday greeting in song, or just how or when it started to catch on. We do know that since 1910 not a single day has passed by in America without "Happy Birthday to You" being sung thousands of times in thousands of different places.

By 1910, most people thought that "Happy Birthday" was a folk song in the public domain. Because of this misconception, a good many people have innocently become involved in legal action. Just before World War II, Western Union instituted the "singing telegram" by having Western Union boys sing "Happy Birthday" to the recipient of such a greeting, or having a woman sing it over the telephone. The first singing telegram transmitting such a birthday greeting went to Rudy Vallee in 1934, who was then appearing in a New York nightclub. Before long, Western Union received a rude shock when it was dragged into court for infringement of copyright which belonged to Clayton F. Summy. A settlement was reached, but from then on Western Union confined its singing telegrams to songs like "For He's a Jolly Good Fellow" and its birthday greetings to the sending of Raggedy Ann dolls with birthday messages. After having been used by countless millions for almost forty years, the

---

*According to the *Guinness Book of World Records*, "Happy Birthday to You" is the most frequently sung song in the English language. The next two are "For He's a Jolly Good Fellow" and "Auld Lang Syne."

singing telegram quietly expired in California at midnight of June 3, 1974.

Irving Berlin was also sued for infringement of copyright of "Happy Birthday" when, in one of the scenes in the Broadway revue *As Thousands Cheer* (1933), he had a chorus sing "Happy Birthday" to Clifford Webb impersonating John D. Rockefeller. Even Berlin had the erroneous notion that the song was in the public domain. Composers of serious music also got into trouble. Roy Harris used it to honor the fiftieth birthday of the American composer Howard Hanson. Keeping the occasion in mind, Harris brought his composition to a climax with a modern treatment of "Happy Birthday." After Harris' composition had been introduced by the Boston Symphony, Harris was forced to delete the "Happy Birthday" passage from his score.

Of course, there is not much the copyright owner could do about "Happy Birthday" being sung all over the country, every day in the year, at private parties, in homes, and in restaurants while the copyright was still in force. Even a computer could not calculate just how many times it has been sung. The paradox is that the authors not only earned practically nothing from this unprecedented and unequalled success, but that their names are not even remembered.

9

The Musical Theater: From Extravaganza To Operetta

1

The bright, young and energetic men who were publishing songs in Union Square were not slow to discover that gold could be mined from the musical theater.

Random songs from the theater had long been published with varying degrees of success. We have already seen how the greatest songs of Stephen Foster, written for and introduced in minstrel shows, enjoyed substantial sheet music sales for their time when issued by Firth, Pond and Company. After Firth, Pond became William A. Pond and Company, it released the major songs of David Braham from the Harrigan and Hart burlesques. But a full awareness that the theater could be an immeasurably rich source of publishable new songs did not surface until the closing years of the nineteenth century. The house of T. B. Harms became one of the first Union Square publishers to fully exploit the theater for its music. In the middle 1880s, at the start of its history, T. B. Harms became the publishers of William J. Scanlan's principal Irish songs from his stage musicals, and in 1891 it had a giant hit in "Molly O!" from Scanlan's *Mavourneen*. In 1891, Harms also published "Ask the Man in the Moon" (a topical song about New York even though the setting of the operetta is Siam) and the ballad, "A Pretty Girl!" both from the extravaganza *Wang* starring De Wolf Hopper as the regent of Siam, co-starring Della Fox, which opened at the Broadway Theater in New York on May 14, 1891, both with lyrics by J. Cheever Goodwin and music by Woolson Morse.

In 1892, T. B. Harms mined a song lode from the score of *A Trip to Chinatown*, the most successful extravaganza produced in America up to that time. The book was by Charles

Hoyt, and its principal songs were by Percy Gaunt. This production toured the United States for a full year before coming to the Madison Square Theater in New York on November 9, 1891, to begin the longest consecutive run in New York theater history, 657 performances. During that time, two companies offered it simultaneously in New York, while several others were on tour.

Its plot, set in San Francisco, was trite and synthetic. But for the fact that it included satirical and topical allusions to such current events in the news as woman's suffrage and temperance, it would hardly have been capable of winning audiences. However, the fetching songs (combined with some magnificent production numbers) made the show appealing. In fact, one of the songs actually spelled the difference between failure and success for the entire production. When it first opened, A Trip to Chinatown did poorly. Charles Hoyt sensed that a strong musical number would help matters and asked Percy Gaunt to write it. The song was "The Bowery," lyrics by Charles H. Hoyt, about that disreputable slum district in downtown New York, placed with sublime irrelevance in a San Francisco setting. Harry Conor appeared as a rube from the sticks and sang "The Bowery" in squalid surroundings peopled with drunks and thieves. When first performed, the song created such an uproar of enthusiasm that Conor had to repeat all six verses. From that moment, "The Bowery" became the highlight of the production, and was chiefly responsible for enticing audiences to the theater. Since then this song has ranked with "The Sidewalks of New York" as the most frequently sung number about New York, or its environs, ever written.

But "The Bowery" was only one of the four hit songs from A Trip to Chinatown, the others being "Push Dem Clouds Away" (described in the sheet music as "an African cantata"), "Reuben, Reuben," and an interpolation, Charles K. Harris' "After the Ball." T. B. Harms published the three Gaunt numbers, selling about a million copies of sheet music, discovering for the first time what a bountiful source of revenue could come from publishing theater songs. As for Charles K. Harris' "After the Ball," we have already seen that, after being published by Harris himself, it became the most profitable song property in America up to that time.

2

M. Witmark and Sons became a strong entry into the theatrical sweepstakes in 1898 by acquiring an entire catalogue of songs from the burlesque extravaganzas of Weber and Fields.

In the mid-1890s and early 1900s, the Weber and Fields burlesque extravaganza became what the Harrigan and Hart burlesques had been a decade or so earlier, a full reservoir of ethnic humor and characterizations, and an endless source of merriment.

Joe Weber and Lew Fields began adapting the individual characteristics of burlesque to their own special thespian talents in 1877 as an act combining Irish song, dance and comedy in a vaudeville act at Duffy's Pavilion in Coney Island. Seven years later they became the stars of burlesque shows produced by Ada Richmond at Miner's Bowery Theater where they first conceived and developed their caricatures of Germans, as well as some of those comic episodes which became their stage trademarks.

In 1896, Weber and Fields opened their own theater, the Weber and Fields Music Hall on 29th Street, off Broadway. There they presented the first of a series of burlesque extravaganzas, The Art of Maryland. They established a pattern of entertainment which they produced with uncommon skill, combining travesty, slapstick humor, repartee full of malapropisms and burlesque takeoffs on current plays. The Art of Maryland was, in effect, a comic parody of The Heart of Maryland, a stage play starring Mrs. Leslie Carter. In addition to this parody, Weber and Fields offered variety entertainment in the form of an "olio," in which the leading members of the cast (including Lottie Gilson) did their specialties. Weber and Fields introduced their famous pool-game skit, and a novelty in the form of an "animatograph," a primitive kind of motion picture, was introduced.

Both men were cast as Germans. Joe Weber (called Mike) was short and fat; Lou Fields (called Meyer) was tall and thin. Both were dressed in oversized clothes, sometimes checked suits and sometimes evening clothes. Each wore a derby, had a little tuft of beard under the chin, and mutilated the English language. "I am delightfulness to meet you," Mike would say to Meyer, to which Meyer would respond, "Der disgust is all mine." Fields was the bully, Weber his helpless victim. "All the public wanted to see," Weber once complained, "was Fields knock the hell out of me." They would invariably make their entrance by having Weber run out on the stage shouting, "Don't poosh me!" Behind him came Fields, cane in hand pointed menacingly at the poor abused little fellow. Once peace was effected between them they indulged in a ludicrous exchange of dialogue of which the following has become perhaps the most famous joke to come out of show business: "Who vass the lady I seen you with last night?" "That was no lady, she vass my wife!" Horseplay was their stock in trade. They might bring in a canary's cage, but a pig would be in it. They would have a smoking cigar in the lips of a marble bust. More often than not poor Weber ended up with a pie in his face.

Parodies of successful plays added further to the absurdity of the proceedings. Weber and Fields made a mockery of William Gillette's *Secret Service*, J. M. Barrie's *The Little Minister*, Rostand's *Cyrano de Bergerac*; also of *Quo Vadis?*, *Barbara Frietchie* and *Sappho*. In addition to all this, the Weber and Fields burlesque extravaganzas boasted lavish production numbers together with glamorous stars in song and dance. Onto the stage of the Weber and Fields Music Hall stepped some of the most admired personalities of the stage in New York: Lillian Russell, Anna Held, Lottie Gilson, Fay Templeton, De Wolf Hopper, Sam Bernard, David Warfield, Bessie Clayton, Cecilia Loftus, Marie Dressler and the McCoy Sisters.

All the music in the Weber and Fields productions—from *The Art of Maryland* in 1896, through *Hoity Toity* in 1901—and a good deal in *Twirly Whirly* in 1902, came from Joseph Stromberg who also filled the shoes of musical director. His way with a simple, easy-to-remember melody in ballad form was his salient charm. But he also had a distinctive touch in the handling of syncopated rhythms in coon and ragtime songs. His best songs, all of them to the lyrics of either Robert B. Smith, Edgar Smith or Harry B. Smith, were: "Kiss Me, Honey, Do" (sometimes also called "Dinah") sung by Peter F. Dailey in *Hurly Burly* (1898); "When Chloe Sings a Song," the first coon song ever performed by Lillian Russell, heard in her initial Weber and Fields production, *Whirl-i-gig* (1899); "Ma Blushin' Rosie," Fay Templeton's big number in *Fiddle-dee-Dee* (1900) and later on, in other places, an Al Jolson specialty; the sentimental ballad, "I'm a Respectable Working Girl," another Fay Templeton tour de force from *Hoity Toity* (1901); and the ballad by which Lillian Russell must always be remembered, "Come Down Ma Evenin' Star" from *Twirly Whirly* (1902).

John Stromberg (1853–1902) first worked as an arranger for M. Witmark and Sons before turning to songwriting. His first published song, for which he wrote both the words and the music, appeared in 1895, "My Best Girl's a New Yorker." On the strength of this one number Weber and Fields hired him to be the conductor and composer for the burlesque extravaganzas they were then projecting. Stromberg worked for Weber and Fields for the next half dozen years, creating the complete scores for about a dozen productions, and four numbers for *Twirly Whirly*. Before he could complete the remainder of the songs for that production he committed suicide in his New York apartment, depressed because of chronic bad health and his failure in a realty investment. In one of his pockets was found the manuscript of "Come Down Ma Evenin' Star." When Lillian Russell sang this number on the opening night of *Twirly Whirly* (Steptember 11, 1902) she broke down midway and could not continue. This number became her song identification as long as she appeared on the stage.

The remaining songs in *Twirly Whirly* were written by W. T. Francis, who for a time succeeded Stromberg as conductor-composer for Weber and Fields. Maurice Levi wrote the music for the Weber and Fields burlesque extravaganza, *An English Daisy*, in 1904. In 1904, Weber and Fields broke up their partnership. The split became an event of national interest, discussed in the newspapers and a favorite topic of conversation. When the final curtain went down on *An English Daisy* "a demonstration unique in theatrical history" took place as was reported by the New York *Herald*. "An audience which filled the large new theater and composed of representatives of society clubdom, the world of first night, the theater in every walk of life, called for the curtain to rise again. Then in response to demands, speeches were made by members of the company in which the two men who had made Weber and Fields a household word were told they were committing business suicide; were told that they were making a grievous mistake, amid cries of 'Right, right!' A Broadway audience is not particularly sentimental, but the tears that streaked the painted and powdered faces on the stage were multiplied many times in the audience as 'Auld Lang Syne' became the final musical number."

Actually that night was not the last performance by Weber and Fields. Eight years later the partners were reunited for the last time in *Hokey Pokey* (1912) and *Roly Poly* (1913), two shows that time and again brought back memories of old Weber and Fields productions by reviving formerly successful songs, routines and travesties. Onetime favorite performers from the Old Weber and Fields Music Hall were starred, and with them was Lillian Russell singing—to be sure—"Come Down Ma Evenin' Star."

Between 1896 and 1898, Weber and Fields themselves published the principal songs from their shows. But they soon realized that they were not equipped to handle the business end of music publishing and sold out their catalogue to M. Witmark and Sons for ten thousand dollars. Henceforth, the publishing rights to all the songs from the Weber and Fields burlesque extravaganzas belonged to the Witmarks.

3

In 1898, the house of Witmark also entered into an arrangement to publish the music from *The Fortune Teller*. In doing so, Witmark's involvement with the musical theater deepened. For with this publication there began an affiliation between the publisher and Victor Herbert, America's first major composer of comic operas and operettas. This association continued for the next two decades, covering all of Victor Herbert's greatest music for the popular musical stage.

In America, the terms "comic opera" and "operetta" were often used interchangeably, so alike were these two types of production. Both were stage entertainments deriving much of their interest from elaborate staging and costuming, a carry-over from extravaganzas. In both, the libretto departed from reality into a make-believe storybook world in which saber-rattling officers and princes, elegant and beautiful princesses, fine ladies and gentlemen moved in picturesque, exotic or mythical settings. These characters became enmeshed in intrigues from which the virtuous emerged triumphant, while evildoers met their just punishment; in which the hero always won the heroine after numerous vicissitudes and misunderstandings. Sentimental romance was the thread on which to bead the pearls of songs, dances and eyefilling production numbers.

If there is any single difference between comic opera and operetta it is that in one comedic or farcical situations are stressed while in the other sentimentality and romance predominate.

American comic operas and operettas, as distinguished from extravaganzas, first came to the fore in the 1880s after the New York stage had been inundated for several decades by a wave of musical stage entertainment from Europe. In 1867, Offenbach's *La Grande Duchesse de Gérolstein* received its American premiere in New York. After that, opera bouffes, or French comic operas, came into vogue, especially those by the master, Offenbach. Then the American premiere of *H.M.S. Pinafore* by Gilbert and Sullivan arrived at the Boston Museum on November 25, 1878. This ignited a passion for English comic operas. *Pinafore* became such a rage that in its first American season it was performed by ninety companies, five of them performing simultaneously in New York. This phenomenal success led to the presentation of other Gilbert and Sullivan masterpieces, including the official world premiere of *The Pirates of Penzance* in New York in 1879 (under the personal supervision of Gilbert and Sullivan) and the world premiere of *Iolanthe* shared by London and New York on the same day in 1882.

Beginning with the 1870s, the American musical theater also played host to operettas from Germany and Austria, the cream of the crop of the works of Franz von Suppé and Johann Strauss II. When the Casino Theater opened in New York on October 21, 1882, as a home for musical productions, it offered Johann Strauss' *The Queen's Handkerchief*. Between 1882 and 1889, thirty-five European operettas were seen at the Casino. These operettas were also in demand outside New York. In the single season of 1894–1895, fourteen different companies toured the United States with these productions.

Imitation was the flattery American writers paid to this foreign stage entertainment, with Gilbert and Sullivan as the model most often emulated. In 1879, one year after the triumph of *H.M.S. Pinafore* in Boston, John Philip Sousa (later to become world famous as the march king) wrote the music for his first comic opera, *The Smugglers*. It was a failure on the road, which did not dissuade him from writing the music for *Désirée* (Washington, 1884) and the one-act *The Queen of Hearts* (Washington, 1885), both only lukewarm successes. Not until 1896, with his fifth produced comic opera, and his first in New York, did he finally assert his importance in the theater. *El Capitan* was the best of his eleven comic operas; two of its selections were adapted by the composer into the famous march of the same name. "Sousa's operettas, all in English," writes Paul E. Bierley in *John Philip Sousa: A Descriptive Catalog of His Works*, "clearly show the influence of Gilbert and Sullivan. This is particularly true of his early efforts. Sousa adopted their style as characterized by improbable characters and plots, short recitatives, chorus finales and ensemble episodes where the individual singers voice their separate messages contrapuntally. In addition, Sousa's music has Sullivan gaiety."

America's first successful comic opera appeared a decade before *El Capitan*. In 1886, Willard Spencer wrote the book, lyrics and music for *The Little Tycoon*, which had a five hundred performance run in Philadelphia before opening in New York at the Standard Theater on March 29, 1887, for another extended run. All too obviously influenced by *The Mikado*, Spencer's comic opera was a satire on the weakness of wealthy Americans for foreign titles of nobility, with humorous asides on the peculiarities of Oriental dress and conduct. Just as the text has Gilbertian overtones, so the music echoes Sullivan in "Love Comes Like a Summer Sigh," "Doomed Am I to Marry a Lord" and "Sad Heart of Mine."

Spurred on by the success of *The Little Tycoon*, American composers and librettists began industriously to write comic operas, some of them in the Gilbert and Sullivan manner. Willard Spencer himself realized another successful stage venture with *Princess Bonnie*, which played over one thousand performances in Philadelphia before coming to New York, and to appear on road tours and in revivals. *Wang*, an extravaganza produced in 1891, was once again reminiscent of *The Mikado*—book and lyrics by J. Cheever Goodwin and music by Woolson Morse. It was one of the highlights of the New York theatrical season that year. Wang was the Regent of Siam (enacted by De Wolf Hopper) who is plagued by financial problems. They are solved through those devious and singularly unbelievable developments so precious to the heart of comic operas. The often absurd developments of the plot are very much in the vein of Gilbert and Sullivan and so is Wang's topical song, "The Man with the Elephant."

Meanwhile, in 1890, there appeared the first American comic opera that is still remembered, Reginald de Koven's *Robin Hood*, which is closer to Offenbach than to Gilbert and Sullivan. De Koven was born in Middletown, Connecticut, on April 3, 1859. He received his musical training in Germany and Paris, notably with Léo Delibes, the composer of *Lakmé*. De Koven's academic education was completed at St. John's College, Oxford. After returning to the United States in 1882, he settled in Chicago where he was first employed in a bank, and then in a stockbrokerage house. Marriage to an heiress, followed by his own fortunate investments in Texas real estate, made him wealthy. Possessing the means to return to music on a full-time basis, he divided his activity between composition and music criticism.

In his creative work he preferred writing music for the popular theater. He formed a collaborative arrangement with Harry B. Smith, a young man who had worked as a reporter and later as music critic for the Chicago *Daily News*, and after that as a drama critic for the Chicago *Tribune*. In time, Smith became one of the most prolific writers of librettos and lyrics for operettas, comic operas and musical comedies the American musical stage has known. Before teaming up with De Koven, Smith wrote the texts for two stage musicals, both of them failures. In 1887, he completed the libretto and lyrics for De Koven's first comic opera, *The Begum*, another carbon copy of *The Mikado*. This work was also a failure, and so was *Don Quixote* in 1889. But with their third opera, Smith and De Koven had a winner. *Robin Hood* opened in Chicago on June 9, 1890 and in New York City on September 28, 1891. This is the most important American comic opera before Victor Herbert, and one of two from the pre-Herbert era that is still remembered and occasionally revived (the other being *El Capitan*).

One of the reasons *Robin Hood* occasionally returns to the stage is because one of its songs has become an American classic: "Oh Promise Me" (lyrics not by Harry B. Smith but by Clement Scott), a number that has become more or less a fixture at American weddings.

"Oh Promise Me" was not originally written for *Robin Hood*, but had been completed three years earlier and published as an independent number by G. Schirmer, a house specializing in serious music. When a need was expressed for an additional strong song for *Robin Hood*, De Koven decided to use "Oh Promise Me." None of the performers in the show seemed interested in it. The melody, however, stayed in the memory of Jessie Bartlett Davis, a contralto cast in the role of Alan-a-Dale. One day, the producer heard her humming this melody an octave lower than written. He told her: "If you sing it in the show the way you're singing it now, it will be the making of your reputation." Though still unconvinced that the song had merit, Jessie Bartlett Davis sang it in the second-act marriage ceremony scene one night after the premiere of the opera. The audience response convinced her that the song had enormous appeal and should remain in the production. As the producer had prophesied, "Oh Promise Me," which threw all the other songs in the production into the shade, helped make Miss Davis a star.

However much they were obscured by the luster of "Oh Promise Me," two lesser numbers in *Robin Hood* deserve survival, "Brown October Ale" and "The Armorer's Song," both assigned to the character of Little John.

After *Robin Hood*, De Koven and Smith wrote one comic opera after another; hardly a year passed without one of their shows appearing on Broadway. The two best were *Rob Roy* (1894) and *The Highwayman* (1897). *Rob Roy* was set in Perth, Scotland, in 1715, where an attempt was made to restore the Stuarts (specifically, the pretender to the throne of England, Charles Edward Stuart). This cause gained the support of Rob Roy and his men. Two lovely ballads held the musical spotlight, "Dearest Heart of My Heart" and "My Home Is Where the Heather Blooms." The main character in *The Highwayman* is a soldier of fortune who, ruined by his chronic gambling, turns to highway robbery. This is one of De Koven's most consistently tuneful scores, boasting as it does the "Moonlight Song," "The Gypsy Song," "The Highwayman Song" and "Do You Remember Love?".

De Koven's last comic opera was *Her Little Highness* in 1913. After that he turned to more serious avenues of artistic expression by completing two grand operas, *The Canterbury Pilgrims*, introduced at the Metropolitan Opera in New York on March 8, 1917, and *Rip Van Winkle*, given in Chicago on January 2, 1920. He died two weeks after the premiere of his second opera, at his home in New York, on January 16.

Sousa's *El Capitan* appeared six years after *Robin Hood*. It was first produced at the Tremont Theater in Boston on April 13, 1896, and it came to New York on April 20 to the Broadway Theater. It ran almost continuously for four years in the United States and Canada and subsequently was revived intermittently, most recently at the opera house in East Haddam, Connecticut, in 1972, and at Ford's Theater in Washington, D. C., in November 1974. Its esoteric setting is sixteenth-century Peru and the plot has recognizable Gilbertian convolutions. The Sullivanesque echoes in Sousa's score can be detected in its two best numbers, "A Typical Tune of Zanzibar," lyrics by Sousa himself, and the ballad, "Sweetheart, I'm Waiting" (Tom Frost).

4

On November 20, 1894, *Prince Ananias*, produced by The Bostonians in New York, brought a new name to the American musical theater, that of Victor Herbert. Since he became the first American composer for the theater whose best works have survived, whose comic operas and operettas are consistently revived on stage and screen, and whose finest songs have become classics, that date in 1894 is surely a red-letter day both for the American theater and American popular music. By itself, *Prince Ananias* caused no earth tremors. The text, by Francis Neilson, was placed in sixteenth-century France where a group of entertainers are compelled to amuse the king or meet death, a challenge successfully met by its poet, Ananias. The critics did not like the libretto at all. For Victor Herbert's music, however, they reserved some kind words, especially for the ingratiating waltz and march music, and for the song "Amaryllis" (Francis Neilson) that opened the second act. It was Victor Herbert's music alone that kept the comic opera in the repertory of The Bostonians for two seasons, and then on tour.

Prince Ananias was the first Victor Herbert operetta to reach the stage, but it was not his first stage score. It was preceded by *La Vivandière* for which Lillian Russell had commissioned Herbert to write the music. *La Vivandière* was never produced, possibly because the final product did not fully satisfy that queen of the American musical theater, and possibly because, in the final analysis, she was reluctant to gamble her reputation on the unknown ability of an obscure and unperformed composer. The score has since been lost, so that all we know about this maiden effort by Herbert was a report by James Gibbons Huneker for whom Herbert played his music privately. Huneker said that the score was "light and dainty . . . with humor and enthusiasm."

Despite his unpretentious beginnings with one comic opera that was never produced and a second that at best was received only mildly, Herbert's success in the theater was destined. It came early, and it stayed with him till the end. He was born in Dublin, Ireland, on February 1, 1859, and he was three when his father died. He and his mother went to live with his maternal grandfather in a small town outside London. Since his grandfather, Samuel Lover, was a poet, novelist and dramatist, the child Victor was raised in a cultured atmosphere where he early learned to appreciate the arts and the good life. At seven he began studying the piano with his mother, showing such talent that both his mother and grandfather were determined to send him to Germany for intensive music study. This offered no problem since, in 1866, Herbert's mother married a German physician whose home was in Stuttgart. There Herbert received his musical education, specializing in the cello which he studied privately for two years with Bernhard Cossmann. For four years after that Herbert played the cello in various European orchestras, and was appointed first cellist of the Stuttgart Royal Orchestra. For it, he wrote two major works for cello and orchestra, a suite and a concerto, which he himself introduced.

Slim and handsome with a carefully trimmed moustache and curly brown hair falling provocatively over his brow, young Victor Herbert was a man to command attention. He was always well tailored, had wit and courtly manners, and proved himself a man of the world who valued the blessings of good food and fine wine as highly as he did good music. Inevitably the well-bred young ladies of Stuttgart directed admiring and flirtatious glances at him. Theresa Förster, leading soprano of the Stuttgart Opera, found him much to her liking and for that reason, even more than for his musical abilities, hired him as her vocal coach and piano accompanist. Romance blossomed quickly. On August 14, 1886, they were married in Vienna. Two months later they set sail from Bremen for the United States where Fräulein Förster had been engaged for the Metropolitan Opera Company.

Victor Herbert joined the cello section of the Metropolitan Opera orchestra. He did not delay in taking out his citizenship papers. From then on he never again set foot on Irish or German soil, and except for a single hurried visit to England never left the United States.

Fräulein Förster remained only a single full season at the Metropolitan Opera, and during her second season there sang only one performance. After that she was heard only intermittently with other American and European companies. Victor Herbert also deserted the Metropolitan. For a number of years following his arrival to America, he appeared as a cellist in solo performances; he formed and conducted an orchestra in concerts in Boston and New York; he served as musical director of the renowned Twenty-second Regiment Band; he founded and played in the New York String Quartet; and he was a member of the faculty of the National Conservatory of Music. He was not only making a name for himself in American music, he was also earning a good deal of money. This led his wife to abandon her own career and to devote herself completely to that of her husband.

For a time, his efforts at composition were confined exclusively to concert works. The commission from Lillian Russell in 1893 turned him from serious to popular music, and from the concert platform to the stage. Despite his frustration in failing to see La Vivandière produced, he knew that he had found his true métier in writing for the stage. As he told his wife with finality: "I *must* write for the theater." And so, in 1894, he became a composer for the stage officially with the premiere of *Prince Ananias*.

Recognition came with his very next effort, *The Wizard of the Nile* (1895). Book and lyrics were by Harry B. Smith, who had previously collaborated with Reginald De Koven. This comic opera was written for Frank Daniels, a comedian who appeared in the role of Kibosh, a fake magician in ancient Egypt who is called upon to use his necromantic powers to relieve a drought.

After out-of-town tryouts, the show came to the Casino Theater in New York on November 4, 1895, for a thirteen-week stay. After that it toured the country, and then received several successful revivals in New York. However, long before the first run at the Casino Theater had ended, the entire country was whistling, singing, playing and listening to some of the lilting melodies from that score, particularly the infectious waltz-quintet, "Star Light, Star Bright." And the country was also repeating *ad nauseam* a slang expression repeated by Kibosh through the play, "Am I a wiz?"

The Serenade, in 1897, was even more successful. In it a song, "I Love Thee, I Adore Thee" (Harry B. Smith) is the pivot on which the whole plot revolves—the serenade being the means by which Alvardo, a handsome opera singer, wins the heart of Dolores, even though she is being pursued by the Duke of Santa Cruz. Throughout the operetta, the serenade recurs in different guises: as a parody of a grand opera aria, as a monk's chant, as a song of a brigand and as a sentimental waltz.

A new star emerged in *The Serenade*, the winning and winsome Alice Nielsen. She had been a member of the chorus when she was discovered by Herbert's wife who recommended her for the leading female role of Yvonne. Although Hilda Clark, with whom Miss Nielsen alternated roles in the company, also played Yvonne occasionally, the part became identified with Miss Nielsen.

Once she became an established star, Miss Nielsen won the privilege of having Herbert write a new stage work expressly for her, the operetta *The Fortune Teller* (1898), in which she appeared in the dual role of Musette, a gypsy fortune teller, and Irma, a Hungarian ballet student. Musette is called upon to impersonate Irma, the better to allow her to pursue her romance with the Hungarian hussar, Captain Ladislas.

The Hungarian setting offered Herbert the opportunity to write music generously sprinkled with paprika, to lyrics by Harry B. Smith. Numbers like "Romany Life" and "Czardas," which are parts of a quintet, may be only an Irish-German-American's idea of what authentic Romany music is like. They are nonetheless soundly lyrical, wholly musical, alive with gypsy verve and aflame with gypsy passion. The most distinguished song in the score is the serenade popularized by Eugene Cowles in his portrayal of the gypsy musician, Sandor, "Gypsy Love Song" (sometimes also called "Slumber On, My Little Gypsy Sweetheart," after the first line of the chorus). This number, in which the verse is no less appealing in its melodic beauty than the chorus, is reputed to have been Herbert's own favorite among his songs.

In the fall of 1898, Herbert was appointed principal conductor of the Pittsburgh Symphony, an assignment in which he dedicated himself to trying to elevate the musical tastes and standards of that city. In 1899, he completed three operettas, and in 1900, one. None is noteworthy either as a stage production or for the songs it yielded. Then the burdens and obligations of a symphony conductor brought on a three-year hiatus during which Herbert deserted the stage. When he finally returned to it, in 1903, following his resignation as conductor, he held a masterpiece in hand, *Babes in Toyland*, the first of several musicals with which his imperial position as a composer of American operettas was permanently secured.

10

Way Down Yonder In New Orleans: The Birthplace of Jazz

1

Toward the close of the nineteenth century, and early in the twentieth, another branch of popular music was developing in New Orleans. Compared to the hothouse product of Union Square, this music had a natural growth. It derived its personality and characteristics from the songs, dances, religious shouts, blues and work songs of black people. In New Orleans this music was known as ragtime, but in actuality it was jazz—"real" jazz, "hot" jazz.

The word "jazz" was coined in another city and in a later decade—in Chicago in 1914. Some say the word is a corruption of the bawdy Elizabethan term "jass." Others maintain that it is bastardization of the name Charles, contracted to "Chas" or "Jas" (Charles probably being some popular black musician). Still others insist that the word comes from "jasbo," a word bandied about for a long time in minstrel shows.

In any event, in 1915, an ensemble calling itself the Original Dixieland Band performed at the Boosters Club in Chicago. One evening its audience was particularly enthusiastic and kept demanding encores by calling out for "more jass." Soon after this episode, the Original Dixieland Band added the word "jazz" to its name, and several other groups did likewise. *Variety* recognized this trend on October 27, 1916, by stating, "Chicago has added another innovation to its list of discoveries in the so-called 'jazz band.' The jazz band is composed of three or more instruments and seldom plays regular music. The College Inn and practically all the other high-class places of entertainment have a jazz band featured, while the low cost makes it possible for all the smaller places to carry their jazz orchestras." "Jazz," both the word and the music, appeared on a record label for the first time in February

131

of 1917 when Victor released the "Livery Stable Blues" and "Tiger Rag" in a recording by the Original Dixieland Jass [sic] Band.

If any single place can be pinpointed as the birthplace of jazz it is New Orleans, even though the music was not yet known by that name. The city was receptive to the rhythms and sounds of jazz music through contact with the African bamboula danced on Sundays in Place Congo to the accompaniment of throbbing drums. Besides this, the emotional climate in New Orleans was most favorable to jazz's early growth. New Orleans was the only city in America in which prostitution was licensed. After 1897, prostitution was confined by city ordinance to a specific locality known as Storyville. Cradle of vice, Storyville also became the cradle in which jazz was born.

Since New Orleans was tolerant of black men, it became the city toward which many of them drifted after emancipation. Many blacks tried to earn a living by singing songs to banjo or guitar accompaniment in the streets. The black man soon discovered new musical instruments in New Orleans, since for many years that city had been a manufacturing center for wind instruments. These were plentiful and comparatively cheap. With secondhand ones readily available, these instruments came within the limited price range of any black hungry to make music. The ready access of wind instruments led to the formation of many bands. Band music flourished in the streets of New Orleans to accompany funerals, processions, patriotic parades, weddings, lodge parties, excursions and carnivals. Band music was the entertainment on the riverboats plying up and down the Mississippi River. Band music helped to advertise prizefights and bargain sales in stores.

Wind instruments provided the black man with a greater musical satisfaction than he had formerly known from either singing or from playing the banjo or guitar. He took to these new instruments eagerly. Since these novices received no formal instruction, but had to learn their instruments by a process of experimentation, they evolved their own technique of performance together with unorthodox sounds and timbres not encountered in formal exercise books. Even after the black man learned to play well, he frequently could not read a note of music. Compelled to depend upon ear rather than eye, he took familiar popular tunes and gave free play to his musical intelligence and intuition in embellishing these tunes. The kind of music the black man coaxed from his instrument was precisely the kind of music the habitués of the vice palaces of Storyville could respond to. It was music with kinesthetic appeal, full of emotional thrusts. It was music calculated to make the pulse beat faster, the feet grow restless. It was a new kind of music heard nowhere else in the world. It was jazz.

As first evolved in New Orleans, jazz was not a style of composition but a style of performance. It was not written down, it was played. Sometimes through spontaneous and sometimes through calculated improvisations on melodies old and new, these black musicians introduced into their music new color combinations, discords, unusual melodic figurations, highly innovative counterpoint. Sometimes these improvisations appeared in solo passages, as one musician in the band would take the spotlight and allow his musical fancy to take over. Sometimes these improvisations were performed by the entire ensemble in a complex network of counterpoint and rhythm; each man in the ensemble was permitted to pursue his own direction, but without losing contact with the basic melodic or rhythmic structure. These musicians also brought to their playing technical devices found in their folk music. Jazz abounded with marked syncopations, strong accentuations, unexpected intervallic procedures and intonations—qualities found so plentifully in spirituals, shouts and work songs. Since this was a singing people, these black musicians tried to emulate in their instrumental performance the harsh, guttural, throaty sounds of their singing. In so doing they created a new kind of instrumental tone which has since come to be known as "dirty."

In this way, these black musicians helped to bring a new kind of popular music into existence. It was blatant and high-tensioned. It had energy and explosive force. In those years this music would have shocked many other cities, and would have been violently rejected. But it flourished in New Orleans, in such honky-tonks, sporting houses and gambling joints as 101 Ranch, the Tuxedo Dance Hall, Lulu White's Mahogany Hall and Pete Lala's Café. Haunts such as these on or near Basin Street provided the black musician with ample opportunities for employment, such as no other city, or district of a city, could offer at that time. Musicians were not well paid, receiving about two dollars a night; many had to double during the day as waiters, barbers or day laborers to make a living. But as musicians they received a compensation as cherished as money: encouragement in their music making, and sometimes adulation. In Storyville, these musicians were given the stimulation they needed to develop their personalized art in a personal manner. In Storyville the jazz musician was king.

2

The two basic elements of New Orleans jazz were ragtime and the blues.

The word "ragtime" was probably derived from the shuffling clog dance black men called "ragging." Ragtime was characterized by strong syncopation—that is making a weak beat strong or, conversely, the expected strong beat weak—over an oom-pah, oom-pah accompaniment that is rigidly even in rhythm. Syncopation, of course, appeared in such early minstrel show tunes as "Zip Coon" and "Old Dan Tucker," and was a characteristic of the cakewalk and the coon song. But it was the regular rhythm in the bass over the syncopated tune in the treble that converted a syncopated melody into ragtime.

The bands in the streets of New Orleans, and the jazz performers in the saloons and bawdy houses, often "ragged" familiar melodies in so many different ways, and for such an extended period of time, that the listeners would be left limp with emotional fatigue.

The second element of jazz improvisation in New Orleans, the blues, was an outgrowth of the earlier sorrow songs in which black people bewailed their fate. Soon after the end of the Civil War, Negro performers began improvising a new kind of sorrow song on street corners and in saloons. In it, the singer voiced his personal woes in a world of harsh reality: a lost love, the cruelty of police officers, jail, oppression at the hands of white folk, hard times.

The word "blues" was coined in a later day as the official name for this kind of song, but already, in the latter part of the 1880s, some of the stylistic qualities of the blues were already crystallized. The lyric was usually made up of three-line stanzas, the second line always repeating the first as if to emphasize the immensity of the singer's distress; these lines were in classical iambic pentameter. The melody spread over twelve measures in three four-bar phrases. In time, other distinguishing traits were evolved: the flatting of the third and seventh steps of the diatonic scale, henceforth known as "blue notes"; the astringent discords entering the accompaniment when blue notes were lacking; "breaks" in the melody which allowed a singer to interpolate such exclamations as "Oh Lawdy!" or "Oh Baby!", and the instrumentalists to embellish a melody with decorative figurations.

In New Orleans the blues was more popular as an instrumental style than a vocal one. It was true that "New Orleans Willie" Jackson, the big boy with the blues, as he was often called, sometimes sang this brand of music at Brown's Ice Cream Parlor. True, too, that somewhat later Armand J. Piron's orchestra in New Orleans featured the blues as sung by Esther Bigeou and Lizzie Miles. But the influence of such singers was totally obscured by that of the New Orleans instrumentalists.

3

There were several excellent hot bands in New Orleans in the 1880s. Some were led by the drummer, John Robechaux; another, the St. Joseph Brass Band, by the cornetist, Claiborne Williams. But the one generally credited with being the first of the great jazz figures in New Orleans appeared early in the 1890s. He was Charles "Buddy" Bolden, cornetist, a barber by day who, in his spare time, published and edited a scandal sheet. He was, however, essentially a musician who sent Storyville rocking with his ragtime and blues. Tall, slender, strikingly handsome—a hellion with the women—Buddy Bolden was truly a king in New Orleans after he organized his own band in the mid-1890s. According to Louis Armstrong he was "a one-man genius that was way ahead of 'em all." Bolden's was one of the most powerful cornets in New Orleans. "He'd turn his big trumpet toward the city and blow his blues," recalled the New Orleans jazz pianist, "Jelly Roll" Morton, "calling his children home as he used to say. The whole town would know that Buddy Bolden was at the Park, ten or twelve miles from the center of town. He was the blowingest man ever lived since Gabriel." Bolden's ability to embroider a melody with all kinds of tonal filigree was a stunning aural experience. Buddy improvising on a blues like "Make Me a Pallet on the Floor" or "Careless Love," or rags such as "The Idaho Rag" or Scott Joplin's "Maple Leaf Rag" could hold his listeners spellbound. Bolden set and established the organization of the hot-jazz ensemble that became more or less traditional in New Orleans, comprised of six or seven men, with one or two cornets (the spine of the ensemble), clarinet, trombone, double bass, guitar and drums. In or about 1907 Bolden became ill while playing his cornet in a street parade. He was committed to an asylum where he remained until his death in 1931.

He ushered in an era in jazz which saw the appearance of a long succession of artists who helped to make New Orleans the capital of jazz up to about 1917. One of them was Edward "Kid" Ory, who started his professional career in jazz as a trombonist in one of Bolden's combos. A self-taught musician, Ory first learned to play the guitar and banjo on homemade instruments before acquiring a secondhand valve trombone for four dollars. He formed a jazz band of his own when he was thirteen which played at picnics, and at fifteen he began touring as a jazz musician in saloons in or near his birthplace, La Place, Louisiana. In 1907, when he was twenty-one, he came to New Orleans. There, three years later, he formed his own jazz group that became legendary in early jazz history. Jimmie Noone, Joe "King" Oliver, Johnny Dodds and Sidney Bechet were some of the all-time jazz greats who played in his ensemble at one time or another in New Orleans. When Joe "King" Oliver left the band in 1917 to go to Chicago, he was replaced by young Louis Armstrong, then seventeen years old, whom Ory discovered. "I had heard Louis playing in a parade," Ory once reminisced. "I told him if he wanted steady work he should come and see about playing with our band." However, Armstrong's fabled career in jazz did not begin to unfold in its incomparable richness until he had left New Orleans for Chicago.

Ory became famous as a "tailgate trombonist," which John S. Wilson described as a "huff and puff style that primarily supported the other instruments." Trummy Young, himself a trombonist, once said: "Dixieland trombone is punch. It's got to come out and it's got to build. I don't think anyone really knows it outside of Ory."

After Ory left New Orleans in 1919 he continued as a highly active jazz musician with his own and other hot-jazz groups, making personal appearances in America and Europe, doing recordings, and appearing in two motion pictures: *New Orleans* (1947) and *The Benny Goodman Story* (1956). He also composed. His "Muskrat Ramble" became a Dixieland classic. Ory also wrote several blues numbers, among them "Savoy Blues" and

"Society Blues." Though he retired in 1964 at the age of seventy-eight, he continued making appearances at Disneyland in California. He died in Honolulu in 1973.

The name of Sidney Bechet has been mentioned. He became the only jazz artist in New Orleans to achieve fame on the soprano sax, but he was also a clarinetist. Though Bechet remained active as a jazz musician and entertainer until the end of his life in Paris in 1959, the high point of his development as a jazz virtuoso was probably reached during his early years in New Orleans. He first became interested in the clarinet when he was six, having borrowed the instrument from his brother. Self-taught, he was only eight when he sat in on the clarinet with Freddie Keppard's band. One year later he became a protégé of George Baquet, one of the few jazz musicians in New Orleans able to read music; Bechet was sometimes called upon to substitute for Baquet at Ranch 101. After that, Bechet joined Kid Ory's band and in or about 1912 he was a member of the famous Eagle Band. For two years between 1914 and 1916 he toured Texas and other Southern states with a traveling show, but by 1916 he was back in New Orleans, this time playing with Joe Oliver's Olympia Band at Big 25. "Bechet," says Leonard Feather in his *Encyclopedia of Jazz*, "maintained a colorful style with a heavy vibrato and created forceful melodic lines." One of Europe's most highly esteemed symphonic conductors, Ernest Ansermet, expressed enthusiasm for jazz in general, and for Bechet in particular, in an article published in the *Revue Romande* in Switzerland in 1918.

Joe "King" Oliver, in whose band Bechet played, became a legend in jazz history. As a trumpet player, he was strongly influenced by Bolden whom he imitated, but Oliver soon became a jazz stylist in his own right. In the end, the designation of "King," which Bolden had long assumed, became Oliver's—particularly after a memorable night in Storyville. On that occasion, Oliver walked up and down Iberville Street playing on his trumpet the most varied and fanciful improvisations and defiantly pointing the mouth of his trumpet toward the cabarets and honky-tonks where such favored musicians as Freddie Keppard, trumpet, and Emanuel Perez, cornet, held sway. They say that on that night, lovers of jazz music began to drift out of all the honky-tonks to follow Joe Oliver on his march through Storyville into the Aberdeen Café where he was then performing. They overcrowded the place to listen to Joe Oliver playing for hours at a stretch.

Before he left for Chicago early in 1918, Oliver had played with various groups in which some of New Orleans' best loved jazzmen could be found. At one time, at Pete Lala's, he played with the Olympia Band, one of the best groups in Storyville. This group included Freddie Keppard at the trumpet and Alphonse Picou at the clarinet. Sometime later, at the same place, Joe "King" Oliver played in "Kid" Ory's band whose complement at that time comprised Ory himself and "Miff" Mole on trombone among others. At the 101 Ranch, Joe Oliver's jazz groups included Sidney Bechet and Emanuel Perez.

Oliver was the benefactor of young Louis Armstrong, and much that young Armstrong learned about playing the trumpet in his apprentice years in New Orleans was learned from Oliver. Many of Armstrong's first engagements in the honky-tonks of Storyville came about through Oliver. As Armstrong later recalled: "We got all of King Oliver's extra work. Joe was looking out for this boy."

Other jazz band combinations enriched New Orleans jazz. The Tuxedo Band, performing at the Tuxedo Hall, had Freddie Keppard as one of its members. Later on, the band numbered Johnny Dodds, clarinet, and Zutty Singleton, drums. At other times, the Eagle Band boasted Johnny Dodds, Keppard, Bechet, and such famous trumpet players as "Bunk" Johnson and "Mutty" Carey. In 1911, Bill Johnson—the bass player who devised the

technique of slapping the strings with open palm, because one night he broke his bow
—joined the Original Creole Band organized by Freddie Keppard with several members of
the Olympia Band.

And then there was the "spasm" band devised toward the end of 1890 by Stale Bread,
a zither player. It was made up of a harmonica, a zither, a bass constructed from half a barrel
with clothesline wire for strings, a guitar made from a cheese box, a banjo contrived from a
soapbox, and with tin cans and barrels serving as drums.

Competition was keen among bands and individuals. Sometimes two bands crossed
each other in the street, each followed by its own admirers. The bands would soon engage in
a free-for-all in which each tried to outdo the other in timbre and sonority. "Bands in those
days were fighting all the time," recalled "Bunk" Johnson. "During Mardi Gras and parades,
bands got taken around in wagons, and they'd back them, tail gate to tail gate, and play each
other down." "Kid" Ory wrote: "They used to have 'cutting contests' everytime you'd get on
the streets. Freddie Keppard's band whipped us good because he was a stronger trumpet
player than we had at first. Then he started whipping everybody. The public was on my side.
When the other band finished, they'd tie the wagons together. The crowd tied them to keep
them from running away from us." A Decca recording in 1930 by Louis Armstrong of
"When the Saints Go Marching In," which brought this Dixieland classic to popular attention everywhere, was the kind of music played in New Orleans streets to and from a burial at
the turn of the century.

Rivalry between jazz kings was equally sharp. When a competitor appeared and tried
to steal Buddy Bolden's followers, Buddy took a stand in Lincoln Park (a stone's throw from
where his rival was performing) and played rags and the blues with all his heart and soul. The
crowds began flowing back to listen to Bolden. After his performance, in a state of exhaustion, Buddy remarked with gratification, "My chillun's come home."

4

The piano could not be used by jazz groups in their marches and parades, and it was rarely
found in the jazz ensembles in Storyville's night spots. Those few ragtime and blues piano
players that got a hearing in New Orleans generally performed in the city's bordellos.

One New Orleans pianist transformed a Storyville brothel into a temple of jazz to his
many devotees. He was "Jelly Roll" Morton, who in 1885, was born in Gulfport, Louisiana,
with the awesome name of Ferdinand Joseph La Menthe Morton. His musical history began
in 1902 when he was seventeen and visited one of New Orleans' more celebrated night spots,
the Villere and Bienville. All the piano greats of New Orleans habitually gathered in its back
room after working hours to perform themselves or to listen to others. Two jazz pianists
whose influence on Morton was profound came there, and hearing them play gave Morton a
vision of his own musical destiny. They were Sammy Davis, "one of the greatest ma-
nipulators I guess that I've ever seen in the history of the world on the piano," as Morton
recalled, and "Tony Jackson . . . considered among all who knew him the greatest single-
handed entertainer in the world, his memory being something like nobody's ever heard in
the music world." It was not long before Morton began making a career of playing the piano
in the city's brothels and barrel houses. He became, as Hugues Panassie said of him, the
father of the jazz piano, the one from whom subsequent jazz pianists took their inspiration.
"Jelly Roll's style is typically New Orleans," wrote Panassie. "His splendidly constructed
phrases recall the phrases of the great New Orleans trumpets. The passion of this great pianist
is tempered by his relatively delicate touch and his pronounced feeling for melodic curves
gives his playing a delicious freshness and reveals his frank and moving sensitivity." George

Avakian adds, "There are many who will assure you that no greater jazzman ever sat down at the keyboard."

Morton was as given to braggadocio that verged on self-glorification as he was to ostentation in dress (with a diamond embedded in one of his teeth) and flamboyance of behavior. He insisted that it was he, and he alone, who invented jazz. He was inclined to claim every jazz classic ever written as his own creation. Though his claims have sometimes been subjected to ridicule, Morton did make a monumental contribution to jazz literature. Two of his rags are among the best ever written and among the most widely performed: "Tiger Rag," believed to have been derived from a French quadrille; "King Porter Stomp," a tribute to one of the foremost ragtime players in the South, two or more of whose melodic themes Morton is said to have incorporated into his composition. There are other distinguished rags: "Superior Rag," "Frog-i-More Rag," "Kansas City Stomp," "Shreveport Stomp," "The Pearls," "Black Bottom Stomp," "Mr. Jelly Lord," "The Perfect Rag," "Grandpa's Spells" and many others. This is music which is more than the kind of finger exercises practiced by so many other ragtime writers, music that more often than not is multithematic, music that is guided by a subtle intelligence. And then there are Morton's blues: "The Original Jelly Roll Blues," "Wolverine Blues," "London Blues," "Sidewalk Blues," "Cannonball Blues," "Buddy Bolden Blues," "New Orleans Blues," "Don't You Leave Me Here," "Deep Creek Blues," "Dead Man Blues," "Mournful Serenade" (based on "King" Oliver's "Chimes Blues") and "Smokehouse Blues," all with a sophisticated approach to structure, rhythm and harmony. What William Russell said about the "Frog-i-More Rag" applies equally to the best of "Jelly Roll" Morton: "The most typical features . . . are abundantly evident: his wealth of melodic invention and skill in variation; the tremendous swing . . . his feeling for formal design and attention to detail; his effectiveness of pianistic resources; the contrasts of subtle elegance with hard-hitting drive; the variety of harmony, and yet freedom from complication and superficial display."

Between 1909 and 1915, Morton appeared at Tom Anderson's Annex in New Orleans, as well as in many other places in and out of the city. California became his base of operations from 1915 to 1923, Chicago from 1923 to 1928, and New York from 1928 to 1935. Between 1924 and 1926 he made recordings of his own music for Gennett, Paramount, Rialto and Vocalion which reveal him in full command of his creative and performing resources. More remarkable still are his hot band versions of his rags and blues recorded for Victor between September 1926 and October 1930 with his own ensemble, Morton's Red Hot Peppers. Here are found such Morton gems as the "Black Bottom Stomp," "Smokehouse Blues" and "Dead Man Blues."

Morton's fortunes went into a slump in the 1930s. He was now considered "old hat" in comparison to the new voices in jazz and swing then heard. His public appearances were failures and he ended up running a shabby nightclub in Washington, D. C. But Alan Lomax, the folklorist whose *Mr. Jelly Roll* (1950) is a prime source of information about Morton, did not forget what "Jelly Roll" had accomplished. In 1938, Lomax had Morton record at the Library of Congress one hundred and sixteen sides (collected on the Circle label and issued in a limited release) in which "Jelly Roll" played his pieces, and those of some of his famous contemporaries, besides talking about himself and his music, and even doing some singing. He was now an old and sick man, with faltering fingers and delayed reactions. Yet his individualized approach to ragtime and blues and his incredible inventiveness endowed many of these recordings with historical importance.

In 1941 failing health brought Morton to a sanatorium in Los Angeles, from which he was taken to the County General Hospital where he died later the same year.

The survival of "Jelly Roll" Morton's music owes much to Bob Greene who spent thirty years of his life studying Morton's music and personalized manner of performance and who, since 1948, has devoted himself completely to the popularizing of Morton's music. In the summer of 1973, Greene led a band at the Newport Jazz Festival in a concert in which the sound, texture and feel of Morton's Red Hot Peppers was recreated. The same group, under Greene, then was heard at the Alice Tully Hall at Lincoln Center in February 1974 in a program entitled "The World of Jelly Roll Morton." As John S. Wilson remarked in his review in *The New York Times*, Bob Greene and his band succeeded admirably in projecting "the flavor of Mr. Morton's music—the breaks, the slurs, the accents, the coloring—that are such memorable elements in 'Smokehouse Blues,' 'Sidewalk Blues,' 'Jelly Roll Blues' and the whole Morton repertory. . . . It was a thoughtfully prepared concert, brilliantly executed and lovingly received by a house filled with seemingly knowledgable listeners." Bob Greene recorded "The World of Jelly Roll Morton" for RCA in 1974—one more addition to the Morton revival, which also included an album of orchestral transcriptions of Morton's pieces arranged and conducted by Dick Hyman for Columbia.

One pianist whom Morton regarded more highly than others was Anthony "Tony" Jackson whom he often said was the greatest ragtime and blues pianist of all time. (Later in life, in 1916, Jackson gained popularity in commercial musical circles with his song, "Pretty Baby," words by Gus Kahn, and the melody written collaboratively with Egbert Van Alstyne.) Born in New Orleans in 1876, he was intended by his family for the church. His schooling took place at New Orleans College among other places. But a natural aptitude for singing and playing the piano led him finally to renounce religion for music. In his teens he played ragtime and the blues in the honky-tonks of New Orleans, including Mahogany Hall. At one time, he worked with "Bunk" Johnson. By the time Jackson was eighteen he was one of the most highly esteemed performers in New Orleans. Roy Carew, who heard Jackson at Villere and Bienville, never forgot the experience. Many years later he wrote in the *Record Changer*: "It was the most remarkable playing and singing I had ever heard; the songs were just some of the popular songs of that day and time, but the beat of the bass and the embellished treble of the piano told me at once that here was something new to me in playing. And the singing was just as distinctive. . . . High notes, low notes, fast or slow, the singer executed them perfectly, blending them into a perfect performance with the remarkable piano style."

In 1904, Jackson toured with the Whitman Sisters' New Orleans Troubadours as a featured entertainer. He was later heard in Chicago and New York and, from 1917 until his death in Chicago four years later, he was the leader of a jazz band whose members, at one time or another, included Sidney Bechet and Freddie Keppard.

5

Just before America's entry into World War I, Storyville was closed down by an order from Washington, D. C. But New Orleans jazz had been moving northward even before the closing of Storyville. In 1911, the Creole Band, with Freddie Keppard as mainstay, toured the vaudeville circuit. This was the first opportunity the country as a whole had to hear real jazz. In 1914, a vaudevillian named Gorham asked trombonist Tom Brown to organize the Brown Band from Dixieland, made up of white players; a year later it settled down at the Lambs Café in Chicago. This group is sometimes credited with pioneering jazz performances in Chicago. Certainly, its popularity led other Chicago cafés to seek out New Orleans musicians for their own establishments. Another white group, the Original Dixieland Band, found a haven at Schiller's Café while, in 1915, Alcide "Yellow" Nuñez, the gifted clarinetist who had played with Laine's Reliance Band, came to the Athenia Café. Black musicians were also welcome in Chicago. Between 1914 and 1915, a band formed by "Jelly Roll" Morton was heard at the De Luxe Café and the Elite No 2, and in 1916 Emanuel Perez formed a five-piece ensemble for the De Luxe Café.

With the decline and fall of the Storyville empire, the flow of jazz players from New Orleans to Chicago became a veritable exodus. Freddie Keppard established himself in Chicago in 1917 and worked with Sidney Bechet at the De Luxe Café. Joe "King" Oliver appeared at the Dreamland Café and after that at the Royal Gardens where, in 1918, Bill Johnson's Original Creole Band took over. The New Orleans Rhythm Kings, headed by Paul Mares at the trumpet, and including the clarinetist Leon Rappolo and trombonist George Brunis, held sway at the Friar's Inn beginning in 1922. "Jelly Roll" Morton organized his famed Red Hot Peppers, one of Chicago's most distinguished jazz ensembles; the group included "Kid" Ory and guitarist John St. Cyr. When Louis Armstrong formed a band of his own at the Dreamland Café in 1924, and began making his first recordings with a group called The Hot Five, Chicago had become the capital of jazz—just as New Orleans had been before World War I. The traditions of New Orleans were thus being kept alive—not merely at formal performances in cafés and night spots but also informally at The Three Deuces, where the jazzmen would meet after their night's work to engage in cutting contests soon to be called "jam sessions." At the same time a new jazz tradition was being developed, the Chicago tradition.

6

Many years after the fall of Storyville and the flight of New Orleans jazz to the North, an attempt was made to recapture some of the glory that was New Orleans jazz. In the late 1950s several old-time jazz musicians who had been relegated to musical obscurity by radically changed interests and values in popular music, began gathering for jazz sessions in an art gallery in the French Quarter of New Orleans, on St. Peter Street. These were called "rehearsals" because they were spontaneous performances in the old New Orleans manner. People dropped in to listen, and to deposit coins into a passed hat.

In July 1961, the art gallery was renamed Preservation Hall and was taken over by Allan P. Jaffe, a jazz tuba player, and his wife, Sandra. They had come to New Orleans a year earlier and were dismayed to find so little old-time jazz being played, with most black musicians then involved in rhythm and blues. The Jaffes decided to do something about it. They transformed the onetime art gallery into an intimate, informal auditorium for jazz performances on a larger scale and on a more permanent basis than the "rehearsals" previously held there. More and more of the old-time jazz musicians began to participate in improvised concerts. At first the admission was free, with the audience invited to make contributions. Subsequently a charge of one dollar was made.

Writing for the Knight newspapers, Harry Dubin described a typical evening at Preservation Hall. "Like a medieval clarion, the sixty-three year old musician—the 'youngster'—sounded the first note on the trumpet. The six old men who had been sitting alongside him in the small dingy room suddenly began moving—as though some muse were whistling a tune that only they could hear.

"While Humphrey, 73, flexed his shoulders and sounded sweetly on the clarinet, Josiah (Cie) Frazer, 69, lightly tapped the drums. Little Chester Zardis, 73, kicked up his leg and stroked the bass. The piano tinkled, the banjo twanged.

"Then, finally, the senior member of the group, a man celebrating his 81st birthday, stopped his humming and started to slide that old trombone the way some say only Jim Robinson can.

"An elderly black man, but certainly no older than those performing, stood in the back of the white tourist crowd and nudged a bearded out-of-towner who had wandered in through the little St. Peter Street doorway out of sheer curiosity on this Christmas night in New Orleans. 'That's the way jazz used to be played,' the old man whispered approvingly."

11

The End of a Century

1

The rapid growth of industry, the opening up of limitless opportunities for financial advancement through investments and speculation, the giant strides made by science, architecture, journalism—all of these were factors responsible for the swelling of the national ego in the closing decade of the nineteenth century.

A patriotic song in 1898 brought into sharp focus this pride in country. Katherine Lee Bates, a professor of English at Wellesley College, paid a visit to Pike's Peak near Colorado Springs. The grandeur of the sight moved her then and there into writing the verses for "America, the Beautiful," whose opening line read, "O beautiful for spacious skies." This poem was first published in *The Congregationalist*, a Boston magazine, on July 4, 1895. Thomas Bailey Aldrich suggested to Miss Bates that the poem was good enough to become a national anthem and advised that music be written for it. But an existing melody was borrowed, that of "Materna," by Samuel Augustus Ward, which had been written in 1882, and was first published in *The Parish Choir* in Boston on July 12, 1888, as a musical setting for the hymn "O Mother Dear, Jerusalem." Nobody now knows who was the first to join Ward's music to Katherine Lee Bates' poem, but words and music proved perfect mates and combined into one of America's most effective patriotic anthems. Though many attempts have been made to write new music for the Bates poem (including several hundred submitted to a contest promoted by the National Federation of Music Clubs in 1926) the melody of Samuel August Ward remains the only one used for these stirring words.

Another piece of music, reflecting the growth of American power and prestige, came just one year after Miss Bates wrote her poem. In 1896, John Philip Sousa, the celebrated bandmaster, returned from a European trip aboard the *Teutonic*. He was on deck when the strains of a patriotic march leaped to mind. "I could see the Stars and Stripes flying from the flagstaff of the White House just as plainly as if I were back there again" he later recalled. At the same time he compared in his mind "the vast difference between America and American people and other countries and other peoples, and that flag of ours became glorified . . . and to my imagination it seemed to be the biggest, grandest flag in the world, and I could not get back under it quick enough." Back in America, he finally wrote down the march, "The Stars and Stripes Forever," using the melody he had conceived aboard ship. The strong proudly assertive music is the voice not only of its composer in his love of country and flag but also of a people grown conscious of the grandeur of their native land. In 1898, Sousa wrote the following words for his march, apparently intending to use the words and music for a pageant, *The Trooping of the Colors*:

> "Hurrah for the flag of the free!
>   May it wave as our standard forever,
>   The gem of the land and the sea,
>   The banner of the right.
>   Let despots remember the day
>   When our fathers with mighty endeavor
>   Proclaimed as they marched to the fray
>   That by their might and by their right
>   It waves forever."

Despite these words, "The Stars and Stripes" has survived as an instrumental composition, probably the most successful march ever written. From the sheet music sales, Sousa is reputed to have earned almost half a million dollars, a figure more than doubled by royalties from recordings. When the copyright expired in 1953 more than fifty new arrangements were published in the United States alone. Vladimir Horowitz, the world-renowned piano virtuoso, made a dazzingly pyrotechnical arrangement for the piano with which he often delighted his audiences. In 1958, George Balanchine used the march as the climax of his ballet of the same name (which used other Sousa melodies as well), introduced by the New York City Ballet and remaining in its permanent repertory. Two decades after Sousa's death, "Stars and Stripes Forever" was used as the title for a motion picture biography in which Clifton Webb played Sousa.

America's "march king" was born in Washington, D. C., on November 6, 1854, the son of a trombonist in the United States Marine Band. As a boy, John Philip Sousa witnessed the frenetic activity and hysteria attending the outbreak of the Civil War, the marching troops, the flying banners, the military bands, the inflammatory songs. From his father he inherited his love and respect for band music. At ten he began studying the violin, and soon thereafter the trumpet; he also became adept at the cymbals and the triangle. At fourteen, he enlisted in the Marine Corps where he joined the band. Two years later, as a civilian, he continued studying music, mainly harmony, and pursuing varied musical activities such as conducting theater orchestras, playing the violin in the orchestra of the Ford Opera House, and writing light music. As a boy he had written some waltzes, several pieces for violin and piano, and a galop, "The Cuckoo." His first marches were "Review" and "Salutation," in 1873, the former being his first march publication, which he sold to a publisher in return for one hundred copies of the sheet music.

During the summer of 1876, Sousa played the violin in an orchestra conducted by Jacques Offenbach during the French composer's visit to America to participate in the Centennial Exposition at Philadelphia. For these performances, at Offenbach's request, he prepared an orchestral potpourri of national anthems, "International Congress," which opened with a fugal treatment of "Yankee Doodle," ended with "The Star-Spangled Banner," and included anthems from France, Ireland, Germany, Russia, Poland, Australia, Finland, Italy and other countries. Now a resident of Philadelphia, Sousa played the violin for four years in theater orchestras, wrote the music for his first comic opera, *The Smugglers* (1879), and married Jennie Bellis, a young actress who was understudying a role in *Pinafore*.

In 1880 Sousa became the musical director of the United States Marine Band, a post he held with distinction for a dozen years. It was a bedraggled outfit when Sousa took it over, but within a year or so he developed it into such a highly disciplined and musically satisfying unit that its concerts for the first time became musical events of importance in Washington, D. C. It was during this period that Sousa wrote the earliest of his now famous marches. In 1888 came "Semper Fideles" (the motto of the Marines). Sousa wrote it at the request of President Chester A. Arthur who wanted Presidential music more appropriate than "Hail to the Chief." "I wrote 'Semper Fideles,' " Sousa once explained, "one night while in tears, after my comrades of the Marine Corps had sung their famous hymn at Quantico." Sousa dedicated his march to the officers and men of the Marine Corps and gave it an exciting world premiere, as he himself described. "We were marching down Pennsylvania Avenue, and had turned the corner at the Treasury Building. On the reviewing stand were President Harrison, many members of the diplomatic corps, a large part of the House and Senate, and an immense number of invited guests besides. I had so timed our playing of the march that the 'trumpet' theme would be heard for the first time, just as we got to the front of the reviewing stand. Suddenly ten extra trumpets were shot in the air, and the 'theme' was pealed out in unison. Nothing like it had ever been heard there before—when the great throng on the stand had recovered its surprise, it rose in a body, and led by the President himself, showed its pleasure in a mighty swell of applause."

One year later he wrote "The Washington Post" and "The Thunderer," and in 1890, "High School Cadets. "The Washington Post" was composed for a ceremony on the grounds of the Smithsonian Institution on June 15, 1889, for the presentation of awards in an essay contest sponsored for school children by the Washington *Post*. Written to the rhythm of the two-step, then a favorite social dance, Sousa's "The Washington Post" became so popular the world over that in many European countries two-steps were often referred to as "Washington posts." "The Thunderer" was created for the conclave of the Grand Encampment of the Masonic Order held in Washington, D. C., in October 1889. Nobody knows who is being referred to in the title, though one supposition is that one of the men in charge of the arrangements for the conclave might have been nicknamed "the thunderer." "The High School Cadets" was written at the request of the marching cadet corps of the only high school in Washington, D. C.

In 1880, Sousa made his first tour of Europe with the Marine Band. It was on this occasion that the press began to call him "the march king," just as Johann Strauss II was the world's acknowledged "waltz king."

Two years later, Sousa left the Marine Band. In partnership with David Blakely, a wealthy Chicago entrepreneur, he now formed Sousa's New Marine Band. Bedecked in blue and black military uniforms, the band, under Sousa's direction, gave concerts throughout the United States. Sousa now sported a neat, pointed beard, a military uniform with gold braid on the tunic, and white kid gloves. After a year or so, with an expanded instrumental organization and the addition of a chorus, he made triumphant appearances at Carnegie Hall in New York and at the Chicago World's Fair. Since there was government opposition to calling his musicians "New Marine Band"—which had no affiliation with the Marines—the ensemble was renamed simply "Sousa's Band." It gave more than ten thousand concerts, with four extensive tours of Europe between 1900 and 1904. In 1910, Sousa's Band traveled around the world. It made a number of recordings on the Victor label (only ten of which were conducted by Sousa himself, the others by unidentified associates but issued in Sousa's name). During World War I (when he shaved his beard) he served in the Navy as lieutenant for which he organized some one hundred bands over a twenty-month period. Sousa made his first appearance over the radio when he was seventy-four.

He continued writing marches both for his own concerts and for special occasions. Stimulated by a letter from his wife that their son had marched in his first parade, held in Philadelphia to celebrate the return to that city of the Liberty Bell which had been on tour, Sousa wrote "The Liberty Bell" (1893). Sousa and his band introduced "King Cotton" at the Cotton States Exposition in Atlanta, Georgia, in 1895. This new march, reported the Atlanta *Commercial* on November 19, 1895, "has proved a winner. It has been heard from one end of Dixie to the other and has aroused great enthusiasm. . . ."

Sousa's two greatest marches, "El Capitan" and "The Stars and Stripes Forever" followed in 1896. Thematic material for "El Capitan" came from the score of Sousa's comic opera of the same name (1895). The march was played aboard Admiral Dewey's flagship, *Olympia*, when it sailed to attack Manila. And Sousa's band (augmented to one hundred pieces), led by Sousa, played it at Admiral Dewey's victory parade in New York on September 30, 1899.

In 1899, Sousa completed "Hands Across the Sea" as a gesture of international good will. On the front cover of the sheet music appeared the following line by Frere: "A sudden thought strikes me—let us swear an eternal friendship." Sousa and his band introduced it at the Academy of Music in Philadelphia on April 21, 1899, when it proved so successful that it had to be repeated three times and inspired many feet in the audience to beat a tattoo, as reported by the Philadelphia *Inquirer*.

Sousa died of a heart attack in Reading, Pennsylvania, on March 5, 1932, after a rehearsal. The last composition he was destined to conduct was "The Stars and Stripes Forever." By that time, he had left behind a library of marches without precedent in American music—as well as comic operas, an oratorio, vocal music, and numerous odds and ends, together with band arrangements of American national anthems and patriotic hymns. In recognition of his high place in American popular music, and his unrivaled status as a composer of marches, Sousa was elected to the Hall of Fame for Great Americans at New York University in 1973. (The only other popular composer to be so honored was Stephen Foster in 1940. Edward MacDowell, a serious composer, elected in 1960, was the only other musician to enter this hall of fame.)

One familiar piece of march music which Sousa did *not* write but for which he was long given credit was "The Caisson Song," or "The Caissons Go Rolling Along," the official march of the American Field Artillery. Sousa and his band performed it at the Hippodrome Theater in New York in 1918 at a Liberty Loan Drive, using his own band arrangement. Strangely, Sousa appears to have supported the belief that it was he who wrote this music rather than arranged it; the first publication of the march in 1918 gives full credit to the march king. Later research, however, disclosed that both words and music were the work of Edmund L. Gruber, a lieutenant of the Fifth Artillery in the Philippine Islands. He wrote the song in 1908 to celebrate the joining of two units of his regiment which had formerly been separated. His name is found on the sheet music released by Shapiro-Bernstein in 1936. At some later date, the song was adapted by W. H. Arberg as an official number of the United States Army, then called "The Army Goes Rolling Along."

2

During the Spanish-American War, patriotism in America swelled into chauvinism and jingoism. On the night of February 15, 1898, the American battleship *Maine*, despatched to Cuba to protect American interests, was blown up in Havana harbor. "Remember the *Maine*" became a catch phrase arousing the martial spirit of Americans to battle pitch. Powerful members of Congress, eager to see American influence extended outside her own boundary, together with some highly vocal newspapers, thundered the demand that America intervene in the Cuban-Spanish war.

Though there was good reason to believe that, under American pressure, Spain was ready to withdraw its troops from Cuba, Congress recognized Cuban independence on April 19 as a prelude to its entry into the war. The brief Spanish-American War that followed lasted just four months. It was pretty much of an opéra bouffe affair, with the enemy no match for American forces.

The war had cost Americans little either in men or money. The easy victory became a heady wine intoxicating patriots. For such a war, a jaunty, cocky tune was very much in order. Such a song was "When Johnny Comes Marching Home," which struck a responsive chord with Americans everywhere, even though it was written much earlier for the Civil War. When the song was copyrighted on September 26, 1863, in Boston, words and music were credited to Louis Lambert, and this is the name that appeared on the sheet music when it was first published that year. This sheet music also makes note of the fact that the song was "introduced and performed by Gilmore's Band." The conviction among many present-day musicologists is that "Louis Lambert" was the pseudonym for Patrick Gilmore, the eminent bandmaster who introduced it, and that he wrote the song while serving in the Federal Army in New Orleans, probably borrowing his melody from an Irish source. To this day, "When Johnny Comes Marching Home" is far more often associated with the Spanish-American War than the conflict for which it was originally written.

Paul Dresser's jingoistic "Our Country, May She Always Be Right" (1898), and a lively song popular in minstrel shows, "A Hot Time in the Old Town Tonight" were also in tune with the spirit of the times. The latter actually became one of the two most famous songs to come out of the Spanish-American War and, like its rival "When Johnny Comes Marching Home," it antedated that war by a number of years. "A Hot Time in the Old Town Tonight" was written in 1886 by Theodore Metz, bandleader of the McIntyre and Heath Minstrels; a decade later it was published by Willis Woodward and Company. Metz wrote his song after witnessing a fire in Old Town, Louisiana, that was extinguished by several black children. When one of his fellow minstrels remarked, "there'll be a hot time in Old Town tonight," Metz knew he had the idea for a good minstrel show number. He asked Joe Hayden to provide him with appropriate lyrics. (Another, though less acceptable, version of the origin of this song had it that Metz saw a poster advertising a hot time for all who attended a minstrel show.) For some years after its composition, the melody was used as a march by the McIntyre and Heath Minstrels in its street parades, but it never caught on with the general public as an instrumental number. But as a song, with lyrics, it began attracting notice after being used as an opening chorus in minstrel shows and, later, featured in vaudeville by Josephine Sabel. During the Spanish-American War, it became a prime favorite with American soldiers in Cuba, a happy anticipation of their return home; a French newspaper described how, after the victory at San Juan Hill, the Rough Riders sang it boisterously and enthusiastically around a campfire.

Sentimentality was not altogether absent from the songs of this war, the most popular being Charles K. Harris' "Break the News to Mother." In 1897, the composer of "After the Ball" attended a performance of *Secret Service*, a play starring William Gillette. One scene affected Harris strongly, where a wounded Confederate drummer boy, whose life was ebbing away, whispered to the Negro butler at his plantation to "break the news to Mother." The following day, Harris wrote a verse and chorus of a Civil War ballad which he named "Break the News to Mother." He later recalled: "Try as I might, I could not think of a second verse or a climax to the song. How to end the song with a punch puzzled me. While in a barber's chair a thought came to my mind in a flash and I cried out, 'I have it! I'm going to kill him!' . . . I was in a hurry to leave, and in less than two minutes was out of the chair, much to the relief of the barber. I had the last verse."

Nothing much happened to the ballad at the time. As Harris' brother warned him, the song would not have much appeal since "there hasn't been a war since 1865 and another war is a long way off." But at the outbreak of the Spanish-American War, Harris reissued his ballad which suddenly became timely.

3

The field artillery song "Caissons Away" brings up the subject of songs dedicated to or used by the various branches of the armed service.

"Reveille," the military bugle call sounding assembly in the morning after the first call, is a French importation, having appeared in a manual on military music in the French Army published in Paris in 1848. In 1853, it made its first American appearance in print in *Dodworth's Brass Band School*. "Taps," a bugle call sounded at night to order the extinguishing of all lights and sometimes heard as a postlude to a military funeral, is believed to have been composed by General Daniel Butterfield in July 1862 while he was commanding a brigade in the Army of the Potomac in Confederate territory. The General was dissatisfied with the music then used for "Extinguish Lights," wrote a new theme, and had his bugler, Oliver Willcox Norton, play it. Nobody knows just when the word "Taps" was used for this music or why, but the name with the music appear in Emory Upton's *Infantry Tactics* published in New York in 1874.

The Navy's "Anchors Aweigh," was published in 1906. Alfred H. Miles, a member of the 1907 class of the Naval Academy wrote the words while Charles A. Zimmerman, bandmaster of the Academy, created the music for the Army-Navy football game in 1906. In November of that year, "Anchors Aweigh" was sung by the members of the Naval Academy on the football field before game time. Rudolf Wurlitzer of Cincinnati published it in 1907 without the words, offering it as a march and a two-step; a later sheet music edition erroneously names Zimmerman as both lyricist and composer. During the next two decades, the song was heard at the annual Army-Navy football classic. Then, in 1926, Royal Lovell, a midshipman, wrote some additional verses for the song which appeared in the *Trident Literary Society* of the Naval Academy. "Anchors Aweigh," with the additional stanzas, was issued commercially by Robbins Music Corporation. As a Navy song, it gained prime importance during World War II.

The Marine hymn, "From the Halls of Montezuma," appeared in 1918 in an uncopyrighted version "printed but not published by the United States Marine Bureau." The song was copyrighted by the Corps a year later. The melody was lifted from an air (*"Couplets des deux hommes d'armes"*) in an obscure opéra bouffe, *Geneviève de Brabant*, by Jacques

Offenbach. Considerable doubt exists as to who wrote the lyrics. One account (a sheet music edition issued by the Marine Publicity Bureau) claims they are the work of an unidentified Marine, an officer of a battalion of forty men in Mexico City in 1847 during the Mexican War. This is why the phrase "from the halls of Montezuma" opens the song. "To the shores of Tripoli" suggests the conflict of the Marines against the Barbary pirates in 1805. In *The Book Of Navy Songs* (1926), Col. Henry C. Davis of the Marine Corps is named as the lyricist. A Marine copyright of 1919, however, names L. Z. Phillips as the author of the words while *The Quantico Leatherneck* sheet music edition singles out General Charles Doyen. Though the Marine's Hymn achieved its fame during World War II, it had for some time been recognized as the official anthem of that branch of service.

The "Army Air Corps Song" first appeared in 1939. It was the winner of a song contest conducted by *Liberty* magazine, the first prize of one thousand dollars going to Robert M. Crawford, then a teacher of voice at the School of Music at Princeton University. During World War II, Crawford served as a Major in the Air Transport Command. The song was adopted by the Air Force and since 1939 has been identified with it. During World War II, it was used as a recurring theme in the Air Corps production, *Winged Victory*, written by Moss Hart, and successfully presented both on the stage and the screen.

A song now often associated with the infantry came into existence in 1943 during World War II. It was "What Do You Do in the Infantry?" Words and music were by Frank Loesser, then serving in the armed forces. The song was introduced by Bing Crosby.

PART THREE
1900 – 1920

12

A New Century: New Vistas for Popular Music

1

A new century had arrived. "The United States," said *The New York Times* proudly, "is now the envy of the world." America had just emerged from the brief Spanish-American War as a power which had extended its influence not only to Cuba, Puerto Rico and the Philippines, but even further by leasing in perpetuity the Canal Zone for the building of a canal linking the Atlantic and Pacific oceans.

Internally, expansion was the keynote. The country was now made up of forty-five states with a population of just over seventy-five million. Industry, grown to prodigious proportions, had created the billion-dollar trust and the financial baron. Prosperity was brought westward through the successful application of science to agriculture, to the south with the rise of new factories and the development of natural resources, to the east through a dramatic extension of business opportunities. Exports to Europe soared as the demand for American-made machines and products exceeded the supply.

The development of public education and growing literacy brought new strength to the press and made it an all-powerful instrument for the molding of public opinion. Large-circulation magazines and best-selling novels reached a larger public than ever before.

It was an age capable of thinking in terms of immense size, symbolized by the building of New York's first skyscraper, the Flatiron Building, in 1902. It was an age encouraging speed, first with the trolley car in Boston in 1898, then with the subway in Boston and New York in 1898 and 1900, respectively, and finally with the automobile, fourteen thousand of them on the road by 1900. As transport accelerated, man's age-old

151

dream of flying was reaching fulfillment. In 1903, the Wright brothers lifted their airplane from the ground at Kitty Hawk.

The national ego was expanding, and so was the consciousness of things American. Jack London, Edith Wharton, Theodore Dreiser and Frank Norris explored American background and character for their novels. American drama was beginning to emerge with William Vaughn Moody's *The Great Divide* in 1906. American opera was being written by John Knowles Paine (*Azora* in 1903) and by Frederick Shepherd Converse, whose *The Pipe of Desire* became in 1910 the first American opera ever mounted by the Metropolitan Opera in New York. Pointing a finger at American achievement, the Hall of Fame was instituted at New York University in New York and the first volume of *Who's Who in America* was released, both in 1900. To promote American culture, the American Academy of Arts and Letters was founded in 1904. In sports, the Olympic Games were held for the first time in the United States in 1904 and, as if to further underline the new importance of America in the community of nations, T. J. Hicks became the first American to win the marathon. Baseball had unmistakably become the national pastime: the first World Series took place in 1903 in Pittsburgh and Boston. Female pulchritude was glorified through the establishment of the bathing-beauty contest in Atlantic City, New Jersey; the Gibson girl, a centerfold drawing appearing regularly in *Life* drawn by Charles Dana Gibson, became, by the early 1900s, the very model of what a young American girl should look like; and, on the stage, Florenz Ziegfeld glorified the American girl in his *Follies*.

In 1907, George M. Cohan—a real Yankee Doodle Dandy—strutted up and down the stage, a flag draped around him, singing the praises of country and flag.

The 1900s was the birth of a new era and it brought with it new days for popular music as well.

2

By the time the nineteenth century came to a close, Union Square ceased to hold a geographical monopoly on song-publishing. Theaters and other places of amusement had begun to move from 14th Street and its environs further uptown. In 1893, Koster and Bial's had transferred from 23rd Street and Sixth Avenue to 34th Street, taking there its featured attractions of European variety stars. The Casino, the Herald Square, the Knickerbocker, the Broadway, the Republic, Wallack's, the Liberty—theaters where one was likely to encounter musical productions—were located ten streets or more north from the area around 34th Street. Between 44th and 45th streets on Broadway stood Hammerstein's Olympia, an emporium of entertainment housing a music hall, a theater, an Oriental café, a billiard parlor and a roof garden. The music hall and the Roof Garden (which extended over the adjoining Republic Theater) provided the best in vaudeville. Beginning in 1904, vaudeville also flourished at Broadway and 42nd Street at Hammerstein's Victoria.

Within this neighborhood there were also clustered some of the city's most fashionable restaurants, many of which offered salon music: Shanley's Café Martin, the Metropole, Delmonico, and Café des Beaux Arts and, the hub of New York's social life at night, the fabled Rector's, on Times Square adjoining the Hotel Cadillac. "I found Broadway a little lane of ham and eggs," boasted its founder Charles Rector, "and left it a full-blown avenue of lobsters, champagne and morning-afters." This was not altogether a wild boast. Rector's was called Broadway's cathedral of froth and the Supreme Court of frivolity. It became as famous for its clientele as for its filet de sole Marguery or crabmeat Mornay. Diamond Jim Brady and Lillian Russell were habitués, as were Victor Herbert, Paul Dresser, De Wolf Hopper,

O. Henry, Jim Corbett, John L. Sullivan, Rupert Hughes and many other leaders of the
business, social, musical, theatrical and sports worlds.

Ever eager to be close to their market, the publishers of Union Square followed the
theaters and restaurants in their northward trek. Toward the end of the nineteenth century,
Howley and Haviland moved its offices to Broadway and 32nd Street, and Leo Feist established himself on 37th Street. But most of the other publishers became centralized on a
single block, 28th Street between Fifth Avenue and Broadway. The first publisher to set up
shop there was M. Witmark and Sons, who opened his offices at 49 West 28th Street in
1893. Following it were Joseph W. Stern and Company, Jerome H. Remick, F. A. Mills
and Shapiro-Bernstein, all from Union Square. They were joined by Broder and Schlam
from San Francisco and Charles K. Harris from Milwaukee. By 1900, 28th Street had the
largest representation of music publishing houses found anywhere, anytime, on two sides of a
single street.

In or about 1903, this street was baptized "Tin Pan Alley" by Monroe Rosenfeld.
This songwriter and journalist was then preparing an article on popular music for the New
York *Herald*. He came to 28th Street for material. While visiting Harry von Tilzer, the
renowned songwriter turned publisher, Rosenfeld heard the sounds of an upright piano into
which von Tilzer had wound strips of paper through the strings to produce a tinny effect he
favored. Those tinny sounds gave Rosenfeld the idea for the title of his article, Tin Pan Alley.
From the time his piece was published, 28th Street (and coincidentally the popular music
industry in America) came to be known as Tin Pan Alley. Many years later, von Tilzer
insisted that he, and not Rosenfeld, had coined the name, and that it was he who had
suggested it to Rosenfeld for his article. This may have been true, since Rosenfeld was
notorious for filching the ideas of other people. In any event, it was Rosenfeld who first gave
the name circulation.

To maintain a steady flow of songs—a flow which had, by comparison, been merely a
trickle in Union Square but had become a surge in Tin Pan Alley—publishers expanded
their staffs. Piano demonstrators were assigned cramped cubicles in which they exhibited the
latest song products of their respective firms to performers. Arrangers helped illiterate composers put their melodies on paper and harmonize them. Orchestrators adapted the original
piano version for instrumental groups; these orchestrations were distributed free to encourage
performances of the songs. Staff composers and lyricists were employed on a contractual basis
to manufacture songs in quantity—of greater concern in Tin Pan Alley than quality.

More even than in Union Square, songs were produced in Tin Pan Alley as if on an
assembly line. Songwriters relied less on creativity and more on catering to the whims, needs
and interests of their audiences. When the general public became interested in such new
developments as the telephone, the automobile, telegraphy and the flying machine,
songwriters were ready to provide songs on these themes by the dozen. But only one eye of
the songwriter was on public demand. The other was fixed on the competition. In Tin Pan
Alley imitation was a way of life. Should a song grow popular with a girl's name or with
"Goodbye" in the title; should a spelling song or a song on an American-Indian subject gain
popularity, then it was not long before competitive songwriters began producing similar
songs.

The sole yardstick by which Tin Pan Alley measured its success was the number of
copies sold of the sheet music, since the sheet music sale represented the only source of
income for both publisher and writers. That a small fortune could be realized with a single
song had already been proven before the time of Tin Pan Alley by Charles K. Harris' success

with "After the Ball," and by Stern and Marks with "Mother Was a Lady" and "The Little Lost Child." But in Tin Pan Alley, more than ever before, financial bonanzas could be achieved with just a single publication. A sale of a million copies, which had been the exception in Union Square, became almost habitual in Tin Pan Alley. Between 1900 and 1910 there were nearly a hundred songs that sold in excess of a million copies each. Harry von Tilzer's "A Bird in a Gilded Cage" (Arthur J. Lamb) sold two million copies in 1900. "Let Me Call You Sweetheart" (Beth Slater Whitson—Leo Friedman) and "Down by the Old Mill Stream" (Tell Taylor), published in 1910, each sold between five and six million copies. Other songs achieving astronomic sales during that decade were "In the Shade of the Old Apple Tree" (Harry H. Williams—Egbert Van Alstyne) and "Put on Your Old Gray Bonnet" (Stanley Murphy—Percy Wenrich). By July 1913, *Billboard* was beginning to publish a weekly tabulation of the week's biggest sheet-music sales (the first such chart in popular music). For the initial listing, one hundred and twelve retailers and department stores were canvassed, but within a few weeks the list tapped over five hundred reports. Among the ten titles on the first chart were "When I Lost You" and "Snooky Ookums," both by Irving Berlin; "When It's Apple Blossom Time in Normandy" (Mellor, Gifford and Trevor); "The Trail of the Lonesome Pine" (Ballard MacDonald–Harry Carroll); and "That's How I Need You" (Joe McCarthy and Joe Goodwin–Al Piantadosi).

A million-copy sale brought the publisher a profit of about a hundred thousand dollars; and if he was also the author of the song, which was sometimes the case, this sum could be doubled. A composer and lyricist who were not their own publishers also earned about a hundred thousand dollars which they divided between them, since most of the writers now sold their songs on a royalty basis of five percent rather than for a flat fee.

To make the sheet music more readily accessible to potential buyers, Tin Pan Alley opened two new markets outside the music shop, the department store and the five-and-ten-cent store. Late in the nineteenth century, Siegel-Cooper's on 18th Street and Eighth Avenue became the first department store to open up a sheet music section. Macy's on Herald Square followed. By 1900, the department store had become an important artery through which sheet music flowed. At the same time, sheet music counters were placed in five-and-ten-cent stores. Publishers now despatched song pluggers to these store counters to sing and play current releases as an inducement for buying.

The plugger became the kingpin in Tin Pan Alley. On his influence with major stage performers, his gift at salesmanship, his ability to put a song over in public demonstrations, his personal charm, and his ingenuity in placing his songs in former untried territories, lay the difference between success and failure for many a song. In Union Square, publishers themselves often served as their own pluggers. In Tin Pan Alley the art and science of plugging grew so sophisticated and specialized that trained men were employed to fill this role—men like Jean Schwartz (later a successful songwriter), Mose Gumble, Johnny Nestor, Joseph Santley (who graduated to becoming a vaudeville headliner) and Ben Bloom. Sometimes these and other pluggers stood near their offices on 28th Street to keep an alert eye on stage performers who came to the street in search of song material. Confronting them, the pluggers would use every wile and guile in their repertory to induce these performers to enter the offices of their respective publishers and listen to the latest numbers. But other plugging methods were far more subtle and complex. Pluggers had to maintain a personal relationship with the stars of the stage and use their own powers of persuasion to get these performers to use the songs they were promoting. Pluggers went even farther afield by promoting their songs at parades, picnics, political campaigns, circuses, on excursion boats, the boardwalks of Atlantic City and Coney Island, and even at baseball games and the six-day bicycle race at Madison Square Garden. When amateur nights became popular, first in burlesque houses and later in nickelodeons and vaudeville theaters, pluggers hired talented youngsters to pose as amateurs and enter these contests with songs chosen for the occasion by the plugger. When mechanical pianos, with music recorded on cylindrical disks, invaded penny arcades, pluggers would see to it that their songs were placed on the machines, further publicizing them by displaying the sheet music over the machine.

The activity of Mose Gumble, ace plugger, was typical. He was a bald-headed singer who made the rounds of places where people gathered, all the way from Coney Island in Brooklyn to 125th Street in Manhattan, singing the songs he wanted to promote. He enjoyed a huge acquaintance in the trade, cajoling actors with his charm and glib tongue into using his numbers. As a fifteen-dollar-a-week staff pianist for Shapiro-Bernstein, Gumble had demonstrated songs for stars such as George M. Cohan, Nora Bayes, and Weber and Fields. From demonstrating he went on to plugging. He would sometimes board a horsecar on Broadway and shout out his songs to the throngs in the streets. But initially his favorite stamping ground was Coney Island. From evening to the following morning he toured Coney Island dance halls, restaurants and other night spots. Many a time he slept on the beach to be on time for the next morning's rehearsals, and thus put himself in a better position to convince a singer to use one of the pieces he was plugging. Single-handedly he was responsible for starting Jean Schwartz's "Bedelia" (William Jerome) on its three-million copy sale. From then on he was one of the most influential pluggers on 28th Street. He went on to work for Remick (which also employed young Ben Bloom), remaining there for about two decades. One of Gumble's major coups at Remick's was to lift Egbert Van Alstyne's "In the Shade of the Old Apple Tree" (Harry H. Williams) off the ground and send it winging as one of the biggest songs of 1905.

"Ragtime Cowboy Joe" (Grant Clarke–Lewis Muir and Maurice Abrahams) became one of the biggest hit songs of 1912 through the plugging endeavors of Harry Cohen (subsequently becoming the high potentate of Columbia Pictures in Hollywood). "I would sometimes sing it fifty, sixty times a night," he later recalled, "all over New York—at Rector's, Shanley's, Reisenweber's, in dressing rooms, in agents' offices."

In the early part of the century, nickelodeons began offering "flickers"; some four hundred of these theaters were in operation by 1907. Here the song plugger found still another outlet for his merchandise. Pluggers placed songs with house pianists who provided the background music for silent films. Pluggers also appeared as live entertainers on the stage just before the film was presented, or during intermission. The nickelodeon soon became such a happy hunting ground for pluggers that it was not unusual to find one of them working eight of these theaters an evening and many more over the weekend. Sammy Smither (onetime baseball player turned plugger) once boasted he could plug a song fifty times in a single evening.

3

When, in 1905, Paul Dresser (then near the close of his life) opened a two-room office on 28th Street to form his own company with which to retrieve his past fame and fortune, he came to compete with several major popular song composers in the Alley who had become powers by publishing their own music.

The house of Harry von Tilzer, which came into existence on 28th Street in 1902, had its footing in the hits of Harry von Tilzer himself, one of the most prolific, versatile and successful songwriters of his generation. Toward the end of his life he often told interviewers he had written over eight thousand songs, and that three thousand of these had preceded his first hit. But after that his songs sold several hundred million copies.

His name originally was Harry Gumm, and he was born in Detroit on July 8, 1872. In his early boyhood, his family moved to Indianapolis where he satisfied his early love for the stage by attending performances of minstrel and burlesque shows, and haunting the lobbies of local hotels to catch a glimpse of his favorite performers. The lure of the stage led him to run away from home when he was fourteen to join the Cole Brothers Circus. A year later he was a member of an itinerant theatrical troupe for which he played the piano, sang, wrote songs and filled juvenile roles. It was at this point of his career that he discarded his own uneuphonious name to adopt his mother's maiden name of Tilzer and to precede it with a flamboyant "von" to give it added distinction.

While playing with a burlesque company performing in Chicago, von Tilzer met Lottie Gilson, the beloved star of vaudeville. She was impressed with the young man's talent for songwriting, one of his songs by then having been published by Willis Woodward in 1892, "I Love You Both." She urged him to come to New York to become a professional songwriter. Later in 1892 he arrived in New York, supporting himself by playing the piano and singing in a saloon. His song manuscripts now began to accumulate, some used by performers in vaudeville and minstrel shows and one, "De Swellest Gal in Town" being published.

His first song success did not materialize until 1898. When it came, it was of giant dimensions. The song was "My Old New Hampshire Home," for which Andrew B. Sterling, with whom von Tilzer was then sharing a room near Union Square, provided the lyrics. They worked out their song late one night, using the illumination of a street lamp outside their window. They could not use a light in their own room for fear of attracting the attention of the landlady to whom they owed three weeks back rent. One publisher after another turned down "My Old New Hampshire Home." Then a small printer, William C. Dunn, bought it outright for twenty-five dollars and issued it in 1898 under the imprint of Orphean Music Company. An immediate favorite in vaudeville, "My Old New Hampshire Home" had a sheet music sale in excess of two million copies.

William C. Dunn bought from von Tilzer still another song that proved a winner, this time with a sheet music sale of about a million copies, "I'd Leave My Happy Home for You." Von Tilzer got his title and song idea from a wealthy young stagestruck girl who was ready to desert her palatial home if von Tilzer could find a place for her in the theater. Von Tilzer brought this idea to Will A. Heelan who scribbled out a lyric with a slight Negro dialect and an infectiously recurrent "oo—oo" in the refrain: "I'd leave my happy home for you, oo—oo, oo—oo, You're the nicest man I ever knew, oo—oo, oo—oo." Annette Flagler introduced it in vaudeville and Blanche Ring then used it in her act at the Tony Pastor Music Hall in 1899.

On the strength of these two songs, William C. Dunn grew from a printer into an affluent publisher. He then sold out his publishing interests to two young enterprising Union Square publishers, Lew Bernstein and Maurice Shapiro. Shapiro and Bernstein forthwith put von Tilzer on a royalty arrangement for his two hit songs, even though they were not obligated to do so. They also took him in as a partner and renamed their firm Shapiro, Bernstein and von Tilzer. This move proved a gilt-edged investment for Shapiro and Bernstein. In less than two years, von Tilzer produced a new two-million copy smash in "A Bird in a Gilded Cage" (Arthur J. Lamb). It is believed that von Tilzer agreed to write the music to these lyrics only on the condition that the verses made it perfectly clear that the unhappy girl in the song was the millionaire's wife and not his mistress. Amusingly enough, in view of this display of puritanism, von Tilzer did not hesitate to try out his ballad for the first time in a brothel. When some of the girls burst into tears on hearing it, he exclaimed: "If *these* ladies weep real tears over my song, I have composed a hit." A hit, indeed!—one which invariably brought down the house when ballad singers presented it in vaudeville, and sent the buyers of sheet music in droves to the shops.

In 1902, von Tilzer left Shapiro and Bernstein to organize his own publishing house. He started the firm of Harry von Tilzer on 28th Street with a veritable blaze of fireworks, producing seven major hits in his first four years, four of them among the most famous ballads he ever wrote. Of these seven hits, four appeared in the firm's initial season, each one a financial triumph. "The Mansion of Aching Hearts" (Arthur J. Lamb) was a sequel to "A Bird in a Gilded Cage," once again preaching that gold, diamonds and a mansion cannot buy happiness. "Down Where the Würzburger Flows" (Vincent P. Bryan) was written as a drinking song for a Broadway musical, *Wild Rose*, but was not used. Von Tilzer then induced Nora Bayes, still a comparative newcomer to the stage, to try it out in vaudeville. She did so at the Orpheum Theater in Brooklyn. The composer sat in a box and, following sound song-plugging procedure, rose to sing several refrains of his song after Miss Bayes had completed her own rendition. She subsequently used the song so often that she came to be known as "The Würzburger Girl." In 1903, von Tilzer wrote a sequel, "Under the Anheuser Bush" (Andrew B. Sterling).

"On a Sunday Afternoon" occurred to the composer one Sunday at Brighton Beach in Brooklyn. He asked Andrew B. Sterling, who had been his lyricist on several occasions, to write the words, and when these were completed von Tilzer produced a serviceable melody.

Von Tilzer's fourth hit song of 1902 was "Please Go 'Way and Let Me Sleep," for which he wrote his own lyrics. It was first propelled to popularity by plugging. Arthur Deming introduced it in vaudeville while Harry von Tilzer, seated in the audience, pretended to be deep in sleep. Deming feigned that he was being disturbed by von Tilzer's snoring, and called to an usher to arouse the noisy sleeper. Drowsily, von Tilzer rose from his seat and sang the chorus, "Please Go 'Way and Let Me Sleep." This routine delighted the audience and provided the publicity needed to launch a brisk sheet music sale.

Von Tilzer's next million-or-more copy sheet music sale came in 1905 with "Wait Till the Sun Shines, Nellie" (Andrew B. Sterling). Some say this song was inspired by a newspaper account of an impoverished family in which the reporter remarked that the sun would once again shine for the victims after their storm. Others maintain that von Tilzer heard a stranger speak the line "wait till the sun shines, Nellie" in a hotel lobby. Whatever its origin, the ballad was introduced by Winona Winter in vaudeville before becoming a staple in the repertory of other vaudevillians and of male quartets.

In the ensuing decade, Harry von Tilzer was responsible for still another ballad—this time a "mammy song"—that is still remembered, "I Want a Girl Just Like the Girl that Married Dear Old Dad" (William Dillon). Written in 1911, it became a favorite of barbershop quartets.

Harry von Tilzer was a master of more song styles than one. Through the years he wrote ragtime songs such as "Goodbye, Eliza Jane" (Andrew B. Sterling), Irish ballads such as "A Little Bunch of Shamrocks" (William Jerome), nostalgic songs about the South such as "Down Where the Cotton Blossoms Grow" (Andrew B. Sterling) and coon songs such as "Alexander, Don't You Love Your Baby No More" (Andrew B. Sterling). In addition, he wrote one of the first telephone songs to gain popularity, "Hello, Central Give Me 603" (William Dillon) which bears the alternate title of "All Alone"; one of the first popular songs inspired by a social dance, "The Cubanola Glide" (Vincent P. Bryan); and the prototype of those rural songs so often favored in Tin Pan Alley, "Down on the Farm" (Raymond A. Browne).

Though von Tilzer's last song hit, "Just Around the Corner" (Dolph Singer) appeared as late as 1925, his most productive years were the first dozen of the twentieth century when Tin Pan Alley was in its full glory. The decline of Tin Pan Alley as a prime force in the music industry coincided with Harry von Tilzer's both as composer and publisher. Since the type of songs he wrote lost their popularity after World War I, von Tilzer's creativity lapsed after 1925. He died in a hotel in New York City on January 10, 1946.

Harry von Tilzer's younger brother, Albert, also made his mark in Tin Pan Alley as a composer and a publisher. While attending public school in his native city of Indianapolis, where he was born on March 29, 1878, he learned to play the piano. For a time he worked as the music director of a vaudeville troupe. Then in 1899 he went to Chicago for a brief stay, employed there in a local branch of Shapiro, Bernstein and von Tilzer. Soon after the turn of the century, Albert von Tilzer arrived in New York. While earning his living as a shoe salesman in a department store he wrote his first piece of music to be published, a piano composition, "Absent-Minded Beggar Waltz," in 1900. Three years later his brother, Harry, published "That's What the Daisy Said" for which Albert wrote both the words and the music.

In 1903, with still another brother, Jack, Albert von Tilzer formed the York Music Company which issued the following songs by Albert von Tilzer: "Teasing" (Cecil Mack) in 1904; "The Moon Has His Eyes on You" (Billy Johnson) and "A Picnic for You" (Arthur J. Lamb) in 1905; and "Honey Boy" (Jack Norworth) in 1907, which must not be confused with the "Honey Boy" with which the minstrel George "Honey Boy" Evans is identified. Albert von Tilzer's biggest hit was "Take Me Out to the Ball Game" (Jack Norworth) in 1908 which, in time, became the unofficial anthem of America's national pastime, but which von Tilzer wrote twenty years before he saw his first baseball game. The success of this song brought Albert von Tilzer a contract to tour the vaudeville circuit. Other performers, most significantly, Nora Bayes, also adopted this song for their vaudeville acts.

Among Albert von Tilzer's later hits were: "Put Your Arms Around Me, Honey" (Junie McCree), introduced in 1910 by Elizabeth Murray but after that one of many specialties of Blossom Seeley in vaudeville; "I'm the Lonesomest Gal in Town" (Lew Brown) in 1912; "Oh, How She Could Yacki, Hacki, Wicki, Wacki, Woo" (Stanley Murphy and Charles McCarron), a Hawaiian-type number with which Eddie Cantor made his impressive debut as a Ziegfeld star in 1916; "I May Be Gone for a Long, Long Time" (Lew Brown), a World War I ballad introduced by Grace La Rue in the revue Hitchy Koo of 1917; "Oh By Jingo" (Lew Brown), a nonsense song introduced by Charlotte Greenwood in 1919 in the Broadway musical Linger Longer, Lettie; "I Used to Love You But It's All Over Now" (Lew Brown) in 1920; and "I'll Be With You in Apple Blossom Time" (Neville Fleeson), also in 1920, made popular in vaudeville by Nora Bayes.

After the declining popularity of his songs in the later 1920s, Albert von Tilzer abandoned Tin Pan Alley to write songs for the movies. Later he went into retirement and died in Los Angeles on October 1, 1956.

In early Tin Pan Alley days, Theodore F. Morse was another composer capitalizing on his own songs by becoming his own publisher. While few of his songs have survived as many of those by the von Tilzer brothers have, Morse nevertheless was in his time a highly esteemed songwriter. Born in Washington, D. C., in 1873, he ran away from the Maryland Military Academy to go to New York when he was fourteen. He found a job as clerk in a music shop, then as a salesman for the New York branch of Oliver Ditson Company. He was fifteen when one of his compositions was published. In 1897 he formed the Morse Music Company in New York. Three years later he sold his firm to become an associate of Howley, Haviland and Dresser. This was the house that issued Morse's first successful song, "In the Moonlight with the Girl You Love" (Raymond A. Browne), which was interpolated into the operetta *The Toreador*, in 1902, where it was sung by Christie MacDonald. "Dear Old Girl" (Richard Henry Buck) and "Hurray for Baffin's Bay" (Vincent P. Bryan)—interpolated for Montgomery and Stone into the extravaganza *The Wizard of Oz*—followed in 1903.

When Howley, Haviland and Dresser went into bankruptcy in 1904, and Haviland organized the new firm of F. B. Haviland and Company in Tin Pan Alley, Morse joined him as full partner. Some of the strongest numbers in the catalogue of this new organization were written by Morse to lyrics by Edward Madden. These included "Blue Bell," "I've Got a Feelin' for You," "Daddy's Little Girl," "Starlight" and "Down in Jungle Town." To Jack Drislane's lyrics Morse wrote "Keep on the Sunny Side" and "Arraha Wanna," while to lyrics by Howard Johnson he wrote "M-o-t-h-e-r," one of the earliest spelling songs to come out of Tin Pan Alley. Morse also collaborated with a lyricist who adopted the pen name of Dorothy Terriss, but who in private life was Morse's wife, Theodora. Theodora Morse was destined to become a partner in the writing of several solid hits, but none to her husband's music. Two worth mentioning are Julian Robeldo's waltz, "Three O'Clock in the Morning," the Victor recording of which in 1922 by Paul Whiteman and his orchestra sold over a million disks, and Ernesto Lecuona's "Siboney" in 1929, popularized that year by Grace Moore in the motion picture *When You're in Love*.

The one song for which Morse is now remembered most often was not an original with him but a tune he took out of Gilbert and Sullivan's comic opera, *The Pirates of Penzance* ("Pirate's Chorus"). To this melody he wrote new words. The title of Morse's song is the opening line, "Hail, Hail, the Gang's All Here," a number that was on the lips of many American soldiers during World War I.

In addition to the above numbers, Morse was also responsible for writing several ragtime tunes, among them "Another Rag" (D.A. Esrom) in 1911, and "When Uncle Joe Played a Rag on His Old Banjo" (D. A. Esrom) in 1912. Morse died in New York City in 1924.

4

Harry von Tilzer's ragtime song, "Goodbye, Eliza Jane" in 1903 was an early symptom of the ragtime virus soon to infect all of America.

The first time the word "ragtime" was used on sheet music was in 1893 for "My Ragtime Baby" (Fred S. Stone). In January 1897, "Mississippi Rag" by William Krills became the first piano rag to be copyrighted. The first published piano rag was "Harlem Rag" by Tom Turpin (the owner of a St. Louis brothel) which, though written in 1895, did not appear in print until December 1897. Thomas Broady's "Monday Broadway Stroll" and "A Tennessee Jubilee" were piano rags in 1898. This was also the year Scott Joplin, the acknowledged king of piano rags, had his first composition in print, the medley "The Original Rags." A year later, Joplin's "Maple Leaf Rag" became the first ragtime composition to become a sheet music best-seller, detonating an explosion which made ragtime the big noise in American popular music.

Ragtime had its beginnings in New Orleans, as did piano rags. Piano rags also came out of St. Louis and nearby towns in Missouri: from Louis Chauvin, Tom Turpin and Scott Joplin; from Joplin's protégés and disciples, James Scott, Arthur Marshall and Scott Hayden.

Actually, piano rags were composed and played in St. Louis and Sedalia before Joplin's time, when they were called "jig piano" and ragtime bands were dubbed "jig bands."

Scott Joplin, from the St. Louis school of ragtime, was unquestionably the greatest creator of piano rags. Joplin is believed to have written five hundred compositions in all, not only rags, but also marches, waltzes (including syncopated waltzes), cakewalk tunes and various arrangements. In a more spacious format he completed an extended folk ballet, *The Ragtime Dance*, and two operas, the first in popular American idioms. *The Guest of Honor* (1903) is the first ragtime opera ever written. *Treemonisha*, several years later, employed a variety of folk and popular music styles as well as ragtime. In 1908, Joplin completed and had published *The School of Ragtime*, an instruction book of ragtime etudes for the advanced piano student.

The son of Giles Joplin, an ex-slave who was a railroad employe, Scott Joplin was born in Texarkana, Texas, on November 24, 1868. While Scott was still a child the father deserted his family to go off with another woman. Scott and his brothers were raised by their mother, who earned her living as a domestic worker. A woman of rare perception and sensibility, she soon perceived that Scott was unusually musical. It was she who arranged for the boy to play a piano for the first time at one of the homes where she was employed. Scott was seven at the time, and his initial contact with a piano was a case of love at first sight. Despite the poverty of the Joplin family, Scott's mother somehow managed to acquire an out-of-tune piano for her own home upon which the boy started to learn to play tunes by himself with elementary chords. A local music teacher became interested in him and gave him some formal instruction on the piano together with harmony lessons. Scott soon acquired a local reputation as a musical prodigy.

After Joplin's mother died, the boy, aged fourteen, traveled through Texas, Louisiana and the Mississippi Valley playing the piano mostly in honky-tonks. At the same time he was assimilating and absorbing the musical forklore of his people.

When he was seventeen he settled in St. Louis where he remained for the next eight years. There he came under the influence of a black pianist, Louis Chauvin, who is believed to have introduced him to, and aroused his fascination for, ragtime. Joplin played the piano in saloons and bawdy houses along Chestnut and Market streets, as well as in outlying towns and nearby cities. It was then that he began scribbling music on paper; some ballads and waltzes for the piano. In 1893 he went to Chicago where he formed a band which played in the red-light district. In or about 1894 he made his home in Sedalia, across the river in East St. Louis, playing the cornet in the Queen City Band and becoming a member of the Texas Medley Quartet, which he organized. He also found the time, and the inclination, to attend the George R. Smith College, an educational institution for blacks sponsored by the Methodist Church, where he took courses in advanced harmony and composition. Later he was employed as pianist at the Maple Leaf Club, in the "sporting belt" district of Sedalia, which throbbed nightly with the rhythm of ragtime. He was now writing piano rags, the first to be published being *Original Rags* in 1899. He was also playing piano rags constantly. Devotees of ragtime would first visit the Rosebud, the brothel where its owner, Tom Turpin, was the musical attraction, and after that proceed to the Maple Leaf Club to listen to Joplin. Joplin's rags had a cogency all their own, together with originality of harmonic color, a seemingly endless fund of infectious melodies and a natural feeling for syncopation.

One of the many who were intrigued by Joplin's rags was the owner of a local music store and a publisher, John Stillwell Stark. One of the piano rags that particularly captured Stark's imagination and enthusiasm was the "Maple Leaf Rag," about which Joplin himself once said "will make me the king of ragtime composers." Stark bought the piece for fifty dollars and royalties, had it printed in St. Louis, and placed it on the counter of his music shop in September 1899. It sold unbelievably well, considering that it had no advertising or promotion; several hundred thousand copies were disposed of within a dozen years. In time its sale may well have reached the million mark, something without precedent for a popular instrumental number. It undoubtedly helped to make piano ragtime music a national passion.

The huge success of "Maple Leaf Rag" sent Stark to St. Louis where he expanded his publishing operations, primarily by issuing more of Joplin's rags. It also enabled Joplin to get married (a disastrous experience that ended in divorce about 1905), to give up his job as saloon pianist, and to devote himself primarily to teaching and composition. He, too, moved to the greener pastures of St. Louis in 1900. There, three years later, he bought a thirteen-room house and worked harder than ever on his compositions. After going to St. Louis, Joplin completed and published thirty rags. Among the best of these were "Peacherine Rag," "Sunflower Rag," "Paragon Rag," "Euphonic Sounds," "The Entertainer," "Wall Street Rag," "Pineapple Rag," "Rose Leaf Rag," "Easy Winners," "Palm Leaf Rag," "Fig Leaf Rag," "Country Club Rag," "Elite Syncopations," "Solace," "Gladiolus Rag," "Stoptime Rag" and "Sugar Cane." His last such work was "Magnetic Rag" in 1914.

Joplin also extended the horizons of his creativity by writing the ballet, *Ragtime Dance*, in the 1890s and, in 1903, completing the book and music of a ragtime opera, *The Guest of Honor*, which received only one performance in St. Louis. Little is known of this opera beyond its title since it was never published and the manuscript has disappeared. We do know that its failure to gain more than one performance and any kind of recognition was a severe blow to Joplin, and it is possible that he himself destroyed his manuscript.

But we do know a good deal about Joplin's American opera *Treemonisha*, for which he once again wrote his own libretto. This work obsessed him from the time he started working on it until his life's end. In 1905, Joplin moved to New York City where he finally found happiness in his marriage to Lottie Stokes. In New York he tried to find a publisher for his opera. So deeply did he become involved in the writing of *Treemonisha*, and in trying to get it produced that he abandoned teaching, and sharply cut down the output of his compositions. Between 1911 and 1917 only three of his numbers were published. Failing to get a publisher for his opera, he issued it at his own expense in a piano edition. In 1915, he financed a private performance in a Harlem rehearsal hall, presenting it without orchestra or staging, and himself accompanying the singers on the piano. The response of the mostly black audience was one of outright boredom. All hope Joplin may have nursed for a stage production with orchestra was crushed. The bitter disappointment was almost as damaging to his mind and body as the syphilis of which he was a victim. In 1916 he was committed to a mental institution, the Manhattan State Hospital on Ward's Island, where he died on April 1, 1917. He was buried in an unmarked grave at St. Michael's Cemetery in Queens, New York. Almost a half century after his death, in October 1974, a bronze plaque donated by ASCAP was finally placed on his grave. It read simply: "Scott Joplin, American Composer, Nov. 24, 1868–April 1, 1917."

Treemonisha was first revived, after sixty years, at Atlanta, Georgia, on January 28, 1972, mounted by Katherine Dunham. An all-black cast performed it as part of the Afro-American Music Workshop Activities. Largely financed by the Rockefeller Foundation, the opera was produced by Morehouse College and Atlanta University Center. The following summer, on August 9, *Treemonisha* was given once again, this time at Filene Center at Wolf Trap Farm Park near Washington, D. C., in virtually the same production as that in Atlanta. Then, in Gunther Schuller's orchestration and with Frank Corsaro's staging, it was a highlight of the Opera Spring Festival in a performance by the Houston Opera in Texas on May 23, 1975. It was this production of *Treemonisha* that finally came to Broadway, to the Uris Theater on October 21, 1975, after a three-week run at the Kennedy Center for the Performing Arts in Washington, D. C., to earn for Joplin a "special" posthumous award from the Pulitzer Prize committee in 1976.

Joplin had neither the composer's craft to build his music into an integrated operatic score, nor the dramatist's gift for creating character and atmosphere, or building up a sustained theatrical interest. In his music, Joplin was basically a miniaturist. His score was made up of twenty-seven individual pieces with no transitional material to bind them together into a musical unity. No effort was made to enlarge and develop the basic musical ideas. Parts were better than the whole—but many of these parts were decidedly the work of a strongly endowed creator and add up to a memorable musical experience.

Though primarily a period piece, the libretto of *Treemonisha* has contemporary significance as the voice not only of racial tolerance but also of woman's liberation. But it is the music and not the text that gives the opera its fascination. Though long erroneously described as a ragtime opera, *Treemonisha* is music not of one but of many styles, all of them drawing copiously from the vast reservoir of Negro music, folk as well as popular. Some of the most deeply moving music is encountered in the spiritual-like sections for chorus, such as "We Will Trust You as Our Leader," and "Lead Us, Lead Us, and We Will Surely Rise." Monisha's air, "The Sacred Tree," also possesses a spiritual-like quality in its simplicity and in the genuineness of its emotion. "We Will Rest Awhile" is in the style of a barbershop quartet and "We're Goin' Around" is a corn husker's "ring dance."

Joplin provided the endings of his second and third acts with perhaps the most unforgettable music of the opera. The second act concludes with a spiritual, "Aunt Dinah Has Blowed de Horn" which, said Harold C. Schonberg, music critic for *The New York Times*, "hits the listener like an explosion—exultant, swinging, wonderfully spiced harmonically. This is the real thing." And to end the third or final act, Joplin brings "A Real Slow Drag" in that rag idiom of which he was such an acknowledged master ("Dance slowly, Prance slowly, while you hear that pretty rag"). "This slow drag," reported Schonberg, "is amazing. Harmonically enchanting, full of the tensions of an entire race, rhythmically catching, it refuses to leave the mind. Talk about soul music!"

The revivals of this opera marked but one of many manifestations of the remarkable renascence of Joplin's music in the early and mid-1970s. Mr. Schonberg published two feature articles in the Sunday music section of *The New York Times*: "Scholars Get Busy on Scott Joplin" on January 24, 1971, and "The Scott Joplin Renaissance Grows," the following February 13. And the Joplin Renaissance kept growing! Late in 1971, Joplin's music was published in a two-volume set edited by Vera Brodsky Lawrence and launched by the New York Public Library which then went on to offer the first public concert ever devoted exclusively to Joplin's music—on October 22, 1971, at the Library and Museum at Lincoln Center. In 1974, the best-selling novel of E. L. Doctorow, *Ragtime*, was partially inspired by Joplin's music with Joplin and his music getting mention. In 1975, the first Joplin biography was published (*Scott Joplin and the Ragtime Era* by Peter Grammond), and in September of that year both the *New York Times Magazine* and *Time* ran feature stories on Joplin.

One of the strange offshoots of the Joplin Renaissance has been the way in which Joplin's ragtime classics have been embraced by musical elitists. Serious concert artists, such as the pianists Alan Mandel and Joshua Rifkin, and the violinist Itzhak Perlman, played Joplin rags at their recitals. Joplin rags were getting played by symphony orchestras, including the prestigious Cleveland Orchestra under Lorin Maazel, which offered Gunther Schuller's orchestral arrangement of "The Entertainer" on January 11, 1976. From the organ with which E. Power Biggs achieved world fame with the music of Johann Sebastian Bach came the stumbling rhythms of Joplin in an album issued by Columbia. A further mating of Baroque music and Joplin came about with Joplin rags played on the harpsichord, in a Klavier release called *Scott Joplin Ragtime Harpsichord*. Even the world of ballet took cognizance of Joplin: In 1972–1973, the Pennsylvania Ballet offered *Eight Movements in Ragged Time*, choreography by John Jones and with the score made up entirely of Joplin.

The American modernist composer, Gunther Schuller, president of the New England Conservatory of Music in Boston, gathered a dozen of his students to form the New England Conservatory Ragtime Ensemble and led them in performances of the so-called *The Red Back Book*. The "Red Back Book" is a name long given by ragtime musicians to an album called *Fifteen Standard High Class Rags* in which stock orchestral arrangements of Joplin's ragtime numbers were made for dancing and for performances at band concerts. Scott Joplin himself is believed to have made some of these arrangements, with others by John Stark and by D. S. De Lisle, and probably a few others. This anthology was first published in St. Louis by John Stark in or about 1905. At the instigation of Vera Brodsky Lawrence, Schuller decided to perform *The Red Back Book* publicly and on records with a twelve-man group comprising a trumpet, trombone, clarinet, flute, piccolo, tuba, piano, drums and string quartet. All performers were dressed in casual, brightly colored sports clothes; Schuller himself appeared in bright-red slacks and red-striped jacket. They presented *The Red Back Book* in 1973 at Lincoln Center and the Minskoff Theater, both in New York City. They also recorded two albums: *The Red Back Book* and *More Scott Joplin Rags*. The first of these releases, in its first six months of circulation, sold more copies throughout the United States than any classical release in that time.

The recordings of Joplin's music kept multiplying, coming from many different companies and performers, until there was hardly a note by Joplin that had not found its way into the recording studio. One of the most successful has been the soundtrack recording of the Academy Award-winning motion picture, *The Sting*, released by MCA. *The Sting*, though set in the 1930s, had used Joplin's music of preceding decades to wonderful advantage, as adapted by Marvin Hamlisch, sometimes offered solely on the piano, sometimes in orchestral versions. Fifty-five years after his death, Joplin captured an "Oscar," even if only indirectly and with Hamlisch as an intermediary.

All this was further forceful indication that, at long last, Joplin had come to be recognized as one of the most important, if not *the* most important, exponent of piano ragtime. Sedalia, the city where Joplin first became famous, recognized this in 1974 when, between July 25 and July 28, it honored him with the first ragtime festival ever held. The concerts, in which Eubie Blake and the New England Conservatory Ensemble were among the participants, were held both in Sedalia's park (where Joplin had performed) and on the very site where once had stood the Maple Leaf Club.

A prophet was now with honor not only in "his own country" but also "in his own house," his life story dramatized on the screen in *Scott Joplin* (1977).

5

In the writing of classic piano rags, Scott Joplin had disciples. The two most important were James Scott and Joseph Lamb. Scott was a black man from Missouri; Lamb was a white man from New York.

James Sylvester Scott was born in Neohoso, Missouri, in 1886, and spent much of his life in Carthage in southwest Missouri. When he was sixteen he worked as a handyman in

Dumars' music store where, one day, he was discovered playing the piano. When Dumars learned that Scott had been trained musically, he took a new interest in the boy, elevating him to salesman and song plugger and encouraging him in his music making. Increased interest in Scott's music led Dumars to become his publisher. In 1903 he issued two of Scott's piano pieces, "A Summer Breeze" and "Fascinator," and in 1904 "On the Pike March" to celebrate the St. Louis Exposition. These first three Scott instrumentals, according to Rudi Blesh and Harriet Janis, "are finished products that, though reflecting the influence of 'Maple Leaf,' show marked independence and originality. They are characterized by a flowing melodic content of strong Missouri country feeling." Scott remained an employe at Dumars for about a dozen years. In that time he visited St. Louis, met Joplin, and established contact with John Stark who published Scott's piano rags, among them "Frog Legs" in 1906, "Great Scott Rag" in 1909 and "Climax Rag" in 1914.

In 1914, Scott moved on to Kansas City where he married, become a music teacher, and for about a decade from 1916 on was organist and musical arranger at the Panama Theater. He kept writing classic rags, and Stark kept publishing them: "Evergreen Rag" in 1915, "Honeymoon Rag" and "Prosperity Rag" in 1916, "Pegasus—A Classic Rag" and "Modesty Rag" in 1920, and his last piece, "Broadway Rag," in 1922.

"Jimmy never talked about his music," revealed his cousin Patsy Thomas, "just wrote, wrote, wrote, and played it for anyone who would listen. He wrote music as fluently as writing a letter, humming and writing all at the same time. He liked playing as many notes as possible under one beat with the right hand. . . . He sat at the piano with the left leg wrapped around the stool, and his body kept very still, no bouncing with the rhythm as one sees today."

When his wife died in 1926, Scott, then a victim of chronic dropsy, left Kansas City for Springfield. He kept on playing the piano though he was often in pain from swollen fingers. He died in a hospital in Springfield on August 30, 1938. In comparing the classic rags of Scott with those of Joplin, William J. Schaeffer and Johannes Riedel spoke in *The Art of Ragtime* of Scott's "clearer, simpler lyricism," adding: "Scott's rags often sound like Joplin's slightly aerated and simplified, as Handel sometimes seems a sleeker, more architectonic version of Bach."

Though an Easterner and white, Joseph Lamb wrote ragtime that was thoroughly Negro, so much so that almost until the end of his life he was thought to be black. He came from Montclair, New Jersey, where he was born in 1887. For a time he attended Stevens Institute with the intention of becoming an engineer. There he began writing waltzes and songs, some of which were published in Canada. In or about 1907 he became fascinated with ragtime. He visited the office of John Stark to buy some rags. "There was a colored fellow sitting there with his foot bandaged up . . . and a crutch beside him," he told Rudi Blesh. "I hardly noticed him. I told Mrs. Stark that I liked the Joplin rags best and wanted to get any I didn't have. The colored fellow spoke up and asked whether I had certain pieces which he named. I thanked him and bought several and was leaving when I said to Mrs. Stark that Joplin was one fellow I would certainly like to meet. 'Really,' said Mrs. Stark, 'well here's your man.' . . . It was a thrill I've never forgotten." A few evenings later, Lamb visited Joplin at his home and played some of his own rags—"Sensation Rag," "Dynamite Rag," "Old Home Rag." Joplin's response was: "That's good—regular Negro rag." Joplin induced Stark to publish "Sensation Rag" in 1908, then several others, and after that practically everything Lamb wrote for many years. The best were "Contentment Rag," "American Beauty Rag," "Topliner Rag," "Patricia Rag," "The Ragtime Nightingale" and "Hot Cinders."

Lamb spent most of his life in Brooklyn, New York, working in the New York garment district. The last of his rags published by Stark was "Bohemia Rag" in 1919, after which Mills bought a handful of his other rags for thirty-five dollars in which Lamb was influenced by the "novelty" piano rag music of Zez Confrey. After that the publishers would have none of him, but he kept on writing for a time until, discouraged by his failure to get published, he stopped composing completely. In 1949, Rudi Blesh sought him out to get material on him for his book on ragtime. Blesh's book brought Lamb to the notice of ragtime lovers. Encouraged, Lamb started writing again, producing a "completely unique breed of ragtime composition" (as one reviewer wrote in 1973 in reviewing an album of the classic rags of Lamb performed by Milton Kaye and produced for Golden Crest by Rudi Blesh), "rags that no longer limited to the preconception that this was music for dancing, had a freedom in the use of tempo changes that none of his predecessors attempted." Lamb's last composition, "Arctic Sunset," was published in 1964, four years after his death.

6

In the latter half of the present century another spirited renewal of interest in a master of early piano rags took place. He was Eubie Blake who, providentially, lived to enjoy and profit from it. Blake had been in an enforced thirteen-year retirement as pianist, vaudevillian and composer when, in 1959, he returned to professional life by recording for 20th Century-Fox Records the LP, *Wizard of Ragtime Piano*. It took another decade or so, however, before a mounting and sustained enthusiasm for Blake's ragtime was set into motion. This first occurred in the late 1960s at the jazz festival in New Orleans where Blake's piano playing and his music drew an ovation. In 1969 Blake gave a forty-five-minute concert of his music at Rutgers University; in 1970 he recorded a two-disk album for Columbia, *The Eighty-Six Years of Eubie Blake*; and in 1971 he performed in colleges and concert halls in New York, St. Louis, the West Coast and Canada.

If 1971 was a very good year for Eubie Blake, 1972 was even better. Nearing his ninetieth birthday, he gave some thirty concerts in cities throughout the United States, including appearances in Southern California, Carnegie Hall in New York, and at the Newport Jazz Festival, which that summer took place in New York. The following October he was one of thirty black men to receive the then newly instituted Ellington Medal in recognition of his "great art." This presentation was made at New Haven, Connecticut, by Dr. Kingman Brewster, Jr., president of Yale University. A concert by the recipients of these medals included a performance by the old vaudeville team of (Noble) Sissle—also a medal recipient—and (Eubie) Blake, reunited for a nostalgic recollection of some of their old routines. The year ended on a further note of triumph for Blake when, on December 3, he gave a solo concert at Alice Tully Hall at the Lincoln Center.

On his ninetieth birthday, February 7, 1973, Blake was honored with a luncheon sponsored by ASCAP. In a special birthday salute, Biograph Records released two albums of Eubie Blake's rare piano roll performances. A few weeks later, almost as a belated birthday gift, Blake received his first copy of a newly published book, *Reminiscences with Sissle and Blake* by Robert Kimball and William Bolcom, the title of which was borrowed for an intimate revue produced Off-Broadway in New York in 1974.

From early childhood, ragtime was a part of Eubie Blake's musical experiences. Born to two ex-slaves in Baltimore, Maryland, on February 7, 1883, he was affected and influenced by music as far back as he could remember. He says: "I heard it all my life . . . when my mother would go out and wash white folks' clothes, I'd play music lessons the way I liked, and when she came home and heard me she'd say, 'you take that ragtime out of my house, don't you be playing no ragtime.' " He kept on playing ragtime nevertheless, while developing his technique at both the piano and organ. When he was fifteen he would slip out of the house through his window, while his mother thought he was fast asleep, to play the piano in Agnes Shelton's "establishment," which, of course, was a bordello. For the next few years he played the piano in saloons, bordellos and cabarets. In 1899, when he was sixteen, he wrote a piano rag that became his most famous single composition, the "Charleston Rag." Seventy-three years later he recorded it for Biograph in an album, *Black and White Piano Ragtime*.

After traveling with Dr. Frazier's medicine show that toured small towns in Pennsylvania, Blake came to New York where he tried penetrating Tin Pan Alley with some of his piano rags, which were turned down as too difficult for performance. But two of his rags, in a simplified version, were finally issued by Joseph W. Stern & Company in 1914; "Chevy Chase" and "Fizz Water." A third, "Bugle Call," appeared in 1916.

A decisive event in his life came in 1915 with his meeting with, and the beginning of his friendship for, Noble Sissle, a bandleader, singer and writer of song lyrics. "I need a lyricist," Blake told him. They shook hands, and a collaboration was born. With the help of Eddie Nelson they wrote a song, Blake's first, "It's All Your Fault," which Sophie Tucker sang in a vaudeville house in Baltimore. They also worked out a vaudeville routine for themselves. As Sissle and Blake they toured the vaudeville circuit in the Northeast, appearing at the Harlem Opera House in New York, and finally entering the sanctum sanctorum of vaudeville, the Palace Theater, on July 4, 1919. They continued to appear in vaudeville either in the Number Two spot for headliners or as top headliners for the next few years. In 1921, they wrote the songs for the first successful all-Negro revue produced in New York, *Shuffle Along*. In it was the hit song, "I'm Just Wild About Harry," introduced by Florence Mills. They wrote songs for several other Broadway musicals, none of which equaled the successful run of their maiden stage effort. In *The Chocolate Dandies* (1924) is found one of their best songs, "Dixie Moon."

When Noble Sissle went to Europe in 1927 to lead a band there for several years, Blake worked primarily with Andy Razaf as his lyricist. Blake's leading song hit since "I'm Just Wild About Harry" came from *Blackbirds of 1930*, "Memories of You," sung by Minto Cato, and later made famous by Benny Goodman and his band. A secondary hit from the same production was "You're Lucky to Me," introduced by Ethel Waters. A later valuable song by Blake and Razaf was "I'd Give a Dollar for a Dime" from *Tan Manhattan*, a nightclub production.

Then came Blake's lean years: failures of his shows, depleted royalties from sheet music sales, the inability to get bookings for concerts or the theater, the lack of interest of publishers or producers in his new songs. He went into involuntary retirement in 1946, convinced now that he was sixty-three, it would be permanent. At seventy-six, the lost spotlight was recaptured, as a new career as ragtime pianist and composer unfolded. He had never stopped composing, even in retirement. In the 1950s he wrote "Butterfly" and "Capricious Harlem," as well as many other pieces. When he appeared in Carnegie Hall in the summer of 1972, he introduced four new piano rags he had completed that very year, one of which was "Classical Rag."

7

More than any other single person, Ben Harney was a pioneer in spreading the gospel of ragtime to New York in the 1890s. His skin was so light that he was able to pass as white. As long as he monopolized the limelight he was taken for a white man. Though he spent his declining years in the black district of Philadelphia, he was numbered among white ragtime musicians even by authoritative writers. We know now that Harney was black, just as we always knew that he wrote and played ragtime like a black man.

He was born in or about 1872, probably in Middleboro, Kentucky. In his youth he played piano rags in saloons and brothels in Kansas City and Missouri, following which he was heard throughout the West. In 1895 he joined a minstrel troupe with whom he performed dance specialties and sang songs of his own composition. In 1896 he came to New York, making his debut as a performer of piano rags and as a singer at the Union Square Theater. He went on to star billing at Tony Pastor's Music Hall and to tour vaudeville houses in the East and Midwest.

His act included the singing of his own songs, which he delivered in a husky but effective voice. In these he was assisted by a black man named Strap Hill, one of the earliest full-time stooges in vaudeville. Strap Hill would sing the verse of a song from a seat in the balcony. On the stage, Harney would repeat that verse imitating Hill's peculiar inflections and delivery. Strap Hill then would clamber down from the balcony to the stage to sing the whole number through to Harney's syncopated piano accompaniment.

But Harney was even more famous for his performances of piano rags. His repertory included not only his own piano rags, but also the ragging of such familiar items as the major scale, or such semi-classics as Mendelssohn's *Spring Song*, Rubinstein's *Melody in F* or the *Intermezzo* from Mascagni's *Cavalleria Rusticana*. Historically, these were among the first known attempts to rag (or jazz up) the classics. Harney brought further dignity to ragtime by publishing the first primer on ragtime playing, *The Ragtime Instructor* (1897).

Harney's most famous songs appeared between 1895 and 1899. "Mister Johnson, Turn Me Loose" was first published in January 1896 in Indiana when Harry Green was named as its author. Harry Green, a pianist, had heard Harney sing the number and decided to confiscate it, selling it to the Indiana publisher as his own composition. Possibly smitten by conscience, Green decided to dedicate it to Harney, adding on the title page that Harney had sung it "with immense success." In April of the same year, Frank Harding of New York issued the sheet music with Harney properly credited as composer and lyricist. When the music failed to move off the shelves, Harding sold the copyright to M. Witmark and Sons. Harney's success in vaudeville that year—and May Irwin's effective presentation of the song in the musical *Courted in Court*—made it a hit.

Having made a sizable profit from "Mister Johnson, Turn Me Loose," M. Witmark and Sons bought Harney's "You've Been a Good Old Wagon But You Done Broke Down," which had originally been published in Louisville, Kentucky, in January 1895. Again the Witmarks had another solid hit, thanks once more to May Irwin, who sang it repeatedly in vaudeville.

Harney's third ragtime classic was "Cakewalk in the Sky," published by the Witmarks in 1899. Here Harney experimented with the use of syncopation in the lyrics as well as in the music by the way he broke up his phrases.

By the time Harney made his last vaudeville appearance in 1923, ragtime had been superseded by jazz, and he went into permanent retirement. He died in Philadelphia on February 28, 1938.

8

There were many who could never forget that ragtime was born and raised in brothels, saloons and gambling dens. Denunciations of ragtime as degrading and obscene came thick and fast. The *Musical Courier* of New York wrote editorially in 1899: "A wave of vulgar, filthy and suggestive music has inundated the land. The pabulum of theater and summer hotel music is 'coon music.' Nothing but ragtime prevails, and the cakewalk with its obscene posturings, its lewd gestures. . . . Our children, our young men and women, are continually exposed to the contiguity, to the monotonous attrition of this vulgarizing music. It is artistically and morally depressing and should be suppressed by press and pulpit."

In 1901, the American Federation of Musicians passed a resolution urging its members to "make every effort to suppress and discourage the playing of such musical trash"—and by "trash" it was, of course, referring to ragtime. Four years later the *Journal of the International Music Society* said contemptuously that ragtime "suggests the gait of a hurried mule among anthills. . . . The phrases, being no longer presented with regular and recurrent pulsations, give rise to a sense of disorder which combined with the emotional experience of the music, suggests an irresponsibility and a sense of careless jollity. . . ." Ivan Narodny, writing in the New York *Evening Sun* in 1916, said that ragtime suggested "the odor of the saloon, the smell of the backyard and subways. Its style is decadent. It is music meant for the tired and materially bored minds. It is essentially obvious, vulgar and yet shockingly strong for the reason that it ends fortissimo." And the *Musical Courier* of February 1, 1917, quoted an unnamed authority that "ragtime is tonal drunkeness."

But there also were those who spoke in defense of ragtime. Rupert Hughes wrote in the *Musical Record* of April 1, 1899: "If ragtime were called tempo di raga . . . it might win honors more speedily." Then he went on to prophesy, "Ragtime will find its way gradually into the works of some great genius and will thereafter be canonized."

Regardless of criticism, piano rags, and songs in the ragtime idiom, continued to be written, played and listened to for the next two decades. In the early 1900s, ragtime enthusiasts in New York were streaming night after night to 39th Street and Broadway, to the saloon operated by Baron Wilkins, because the word had quickly spread around town that some of the best ragtime music in America could be heard there. Women in high society began hiring black ragtime pianists to provide a fillip to their parties. James Weldon Johnson, who composed "Caprice Rag," "Daintiness Rag" and "Harlem Strut" among numerous other piano rags, and who performed at one of these functions recalled: "The ragtime music came near spoiling the party. As soon as I began, the conversation suddenly stopped. It was a pleasure for me to watch the expressions of astonishment and delight that grew on the faces of everybody."

Between 1910 and the early 1920s, some of the best novelty rags for the piano were composed by Felix Arndt and Zez Confrey. Felix Arndt (1889–1918) was born in New York City where he received his academic education and studied the piano with private teachers. Entering professional life as a popular musician, Arndt wrote special material for Nora Bayes, Gus Edwards, and others, and served as staff pianist for several music publishing houses. He also made over three thousand piano rolls for Duo-Art, Q.R.S. and other companies, together with some records for Victor, all mostly of his own novelty pieces. The best were "Desecration," "Marionette," "Soup to Nuts," "Toots," "Clover Club," "Love in June" and the one number above all others that keeps his name still alive, "Nola." This was written in 1915 as a musical portrait of Nola Locke, a gifted young singer-pianist, with whom Arndt was in love. He presented it to her as his engagement gift, ten months before they married. "Nola" was published in 1916 and soon afterward played by Vincent Lopez and his band at the Pekin restaurant on Broadway. Lopez then made it his theme music and was responsible for keeping this music alive as long as he and his orchestra remained popular. In 1958, Sunny Skylar added lyrics to this melody, but the song never caught on. It was through Arndt's influence on the then young and still unknown George Gershwin that Gershwin not only began making piano rolls in January 1916, but also was stimulated into writing a piano rag of his own, in collaboration with Walter Donaldson, "Rialto Ripples" (1916).

Zez Confrey (1895–1971) carried the art of the novelty ragtime for the piano into the 1920s. Born in Peru, Illinois, with the surname of Edward, which he never used, he received his first piano lessons before he had learned to talk, and his principal musical training at the Chicago Musical College. With his older brother, Jim, he organized and played in a touring orchestra in or about 1915. During World War I, he enlisted in the Navy. While in service he appeared and toured in a Navy production, *Leave It to the Sailors*. After the war, Zez Confrey worked as a pianist and made recordings of his own novelty rags. One of the earliest of these was "Twaify's Piano"—"Twaify" being a night spot in La Salle, Illinois, frequented by Confrey and his friends. Confrey's most celebrated composition is "Kitten on the Keys" which he himself introduced at a concert of Paul Whiteman and his orchestra at Aeolian Hall, on February 12, 1924, on the same program that first gave the world George Gershwin's *Rhapsody in Blue*. Other of Confrey's successful numbers included "Dizzy Fingers" (revived in 1956 in the motion picture *The Eddie Duchin Story*) and "Stumbling," for which he himself wrote the lyrics, and which several decades later was used as a recurring melody in the motion picture musical, *Thoroughly Modern Millie* (1967).

9

The increasing use of syncopation in popular songs as well as in piano music made the ragtime song so popular in Tin Pan Alley that it eventually temporarily displaced the ballad as its most marketable song product.

Throughout his long career in show business, Joe E. Howard used the sentimental ballad, "I Wonder Who's Kissing Her Now" (Will M. Hough and Frank R. Adams—Joseph E. Howard and Harold Orlob) as his musical calling card. But Howard's first success as a songwriter had come ten years earlier, in 1899, with a syncopated song, "Hello, My Baby," which he wrote in collaboration with his wife, Ida Emerson. This number struck a responsive chord with performers and audiences, as did several other syncopated songs by other writers during the next few years. In 1902, Bob Cole wrote "Under the Bamboo Tree," which was introduced in the vaudeville act of Bob Cole and J. Rosamond Johnson. Marie Cahill later incorporated it permanently into her repertory during her tours of the vaudeville circuit. This song is believed to have been inspired by the melody of the spiritual "Nobody Knows De Trouble I've Seen." When first presented, the song bore the title of the first three words of the chorus, "If You Lak-a Me," but when Joseph W. Stern published it, it was called "Under the Bamboo Tree."

Possibly the most famous of those early ragtime songs was "Bill Bailey, Won't You Please Come Home?" which was kept vibrantly alive through several decades by Jimmy Durante and Eddie Jackson, Ella Fitzgerald, Della Reese and Bobby Darin. Bill Bailey was said to have been a black vaudevillian, a member of the team of Bailey and Cowan. One night he was locked out of his apartment by his wife who objected to his late night revels with his friends. One of them, Hughie Cannon, a song-and-dance man, gave him the price of a hotel room, assuring him that once he had found another bed his wife would plead for him to come home. This incident is believed to have given Hughie Cannon the subject for his ragtime song in 1902. John Queen, a minstrel, introduced it in Newburgh, New York. The song grew so popular that it inspired imitations or sequels, such as "I Wonder Why Bill Bailey Don't Come Home" or "Since Bill Bailey Came Back Home."

The writing, distribution and popularization of ragtime songs went into high gear just before World War I. In 1911, Lewis F. Muir published his first hit, "When Ragtime Rosie

Ragged the Rosary." Two years after that he wrote and published one of the two most famous ragtime songs of the decade, "Waiting for the Robert E. Lee" (L. Wolfe Gilbert). Muir was born in 1884, place unknown. His career as a performer of ragtime began in 1904 in the saloons and brothels of St. Louis and at the World Exposition. In 1910 he came to New York where his first published song appeared, "Play that Barber Shop Chord" (Ballard Mac-Donald). Bert Williams was largely responsible for its success by featuring it first in vaudeville in New York and then in the *Ziegfeld Follies of 1910*. Paradoxically, the huge sheet music sale was the cause of the financial collapse of its publisher. When the firm of J. Fred Helf first released the sheet music, it bore the name of William Tracey as lyricist. But when the song proved to be a financial bonanza, Ballard MacDonald went to court to claim authorship. He was able to prove that originally he had been assigned by Muir to write the words; that he actually wrote some of them; that Tracey merely finished the job. MacDonald was awarded damages of $37,000 which sent the publishing house into bankruptcy.

L. Wolfe Gilbert wrote the lyrics of "Waiting for the Robert E. Lee" after watching black men unload freight from a Mississippi riverboat, the *Robert E. Lee*, at Baton Rouge, Louisiana. After Gilbert completed the writing of the words at Muir's request, the song was published by F. A. Mills. A plugger brought the song to Al Jolson, then at the beginning of his fabulous career. After Jolson introduced it at one of his Sunday evening concerts at the Winter Garden in New York, the sale of the sheet music boomed. Other performers contributed to the song's prosperity, notably Ruth Roye, Belle Baker, and the young Eddie Cantor.

The second of the two most famous "ragtime songs" of this period was Irving Berlin's "Alexander's Ragtime Band." Indeed, this is the song, above all others, that helped make ragtime the principal song style in Tin Pan Alley. Yet "Alexander's Ragtime Band" is not, strictly speaking, a ragtime song at all. And syncopation is found in just a single instance, in the chorus at the word "just." Basically, this is a march tune which briefly quotes a bugle call and Stephen Foster's "Swanee River." Nevertheless, "Alexander's Ragtime Band" not only helped make ragtime a nationwide craze but it also established its author as a "king of ragtime."

Irving Berlin had revealed his interest in syncopation in 1909 with "That Mesmerizing Mendelssohn Tune" in which he "ragged" Mendelssohn's *Spring Song*. A year later, he wrote "Stop that Rag," energetically delivered by Nora Bayes in *The Jolly Bachelors*; "That Beautiful Rag," for which Berlin wrote only the lyrics (music by Ted Snyder), which he himself helped to introduce in *Up and Down Broadway* (1910); and "Yiddle on Your Fiddle Play Some Ragtime." In 1911, Berlin preceded the writing of "Alexander's Ragtime Band" with "Ragtime Violin," with which the still unknown Eddie Cantor enlivened his vaudeville act.

Irving Berlin was born Israel Baline in Temun, Russia, on May 11, 1888. Four years later, his family fled in the wake of a pogrom and settled in a bleak, cold tenement on Cherry Street in New York's Lower East Side. Irving spent most of his boyhood on the streets. He sold newspapers and participated in the activities of a street gang. When he was fourteen he ran away from home, at the same time, breaking permanently with academic schooling. For a time he earned fifty cents a day as a street busker, singing sentimental ballads in saloons and on street corners. He went on from there to a regular Saturday night job at Callahan's saloon in Chinatown and at The Chatham on Dover Street. Occasionally, he found additional employment as a song plugger at Tony Pastor's Music Hall promoting the songs of Harry von Tilzer's firm.

In 1906, Berlin acquired a full-time job at Pelham's Café on Pell Street, in New York's Chinatown. From dusk to dawn he served tables, swept floors, and entertained the clientele by singing popular songs. His specialty was the improvisation of topical or amusing lyrics to familiar tunes. It was at this time that he wrote his first song to get published, but only the lyrics. Two waiters of a rival café had written and published in 1906 "My Mariuccia Take a Steamboat" (George Ronklyn—Al Piantadosi). The proprietor of Pelham's Café insisted that his own men follow suit. The café pianist, Nick Michaelson, wrote a melody for which Berlin fashioned the words. Their song was "Marie from Sunny Italy," and Joseph W. Stern & Company published it in 1907. Berlin's income from his share of the collaboration was thirty-seven cents. It was on this publication that the boy born as Israel Baline appeared for the first time as Irving Berlin.

The next stop in Berlin's songwriting career was Union Square. For a time he was a singing waiter at Jimmy Kelly's restaurant, just a few steps from Tony Pastor's Music Hall. Then he worked as a song plugger for Leo Feist. All the while he was writing song lyrics. One day, in 1908, a vaudevillian paid him to write some topical verses. Berlin complied with "Dorando"—Dorando being a marathon runner then much in the news through his defeat by Johnny Hayes in the Olympic games. When the vaudevillian decided not to use these verses in his act, Berlin tried marketing them to a Union Square publisher. Ted Snyder, a young composer who had recently opened his own publishing house, the Seminary Music Company, offered twenty-five dollars for "Dorando" but only on the condition that Berlin would supply it with a melody. Since Berlin was musically illiterate, he dictated a hurriedly concocted tune to an arranger and consummated the sale. So it came about that Irving Berlin wrote his first melody.

From time to time, he wrote other melodies, mainly to his own lyrics, but sometimes to the lyrics of other writers. On other occasions he provided lyrics to other composers, principally to his publisher Ted Snyder, at whose firm he was now employed as staff lyricist with a drawing account of twenty-five dollars a week. Berlin's first successes came in 1909 with two ragtime numbers, "That Mesmerizing Mendelssohn Tune" and "Yiddle on Your Fiddle"; also with "Sadie Salome Go Home" (lyrics by Edgar Leslie), a takeoff in Yiddish dialect of opera. These realized a combined sheet music sale of several hundred thousand copies. With "Sadie Salome," Fanny Brice, then a coon shouter in burlesque, was re-fashioned into a comedienne and a prime interpreter of Yiddish dialect songs.

Further indication of Berlin's rapidly growing prestige as a songwriter came in 1910 when Fanny Brice made her debut at the *Ziegfeld Follies of 1910* singing his "Goodbye, Becky Cohen" and "Doing the Grizzly Bear"; and when the Shuberts engaged him and Ted Snyder to appear in the revue *Up and Down Broadway*. In that revue, the two songwriters were seen as collegiates, dressed in sweaters and holding tennis rackets under their arms. They sang two songs written for the occasion by Berlin and Snyder, "Sweet Italian Love" and "That Beautiful Rag."

In 1911 Berlin began assuming that dominant position in American popular music he would maintain for the next half century. Several of his songs were interpolated into four Broadway musicals, including the *Ziegfeld Follies* where Bert Williams sang "Woodman, Woodman, Spare that Tree," one of his specialties. That year, too, Berlin wrote "Everybody's Doin' It," which almost singlehandedly made the Turkey Trot a dance craze, and "The Ragtime Violin" introduced by Eddie Cantor. And it was also in that year that his "Alexander's Ragtime Band" exploded in the song business.

Berlin wrote "Alexander's Ragtime Band" as a vehicle for his own appearance in the *Frolics*, a revue put on by the Friar's Club in New York to which he had just been elected a member. He never appeared in the revue, however, and the song was placed in the Columbia Burlesque on Broadway where it went unnoticed. Then Emma Carus, that specialist in coon shouts and ragtime, offered it in her vaudeville act in Chicago. She scored with it so decisively that in a few days' time everybody in Chicago, it seemed, was humming the tune.

Other star vaudevillians used it in their acts, the most important of whom was Sophie Tucker. Within a few months' time, the song sold a million copies of sheet music, and several hundred thousand piano rolls. It became one of the most frequently performed popular songs in the country.

Because the public was deluded by the title into thinking that this was a ragtime song, "Alexander's Ragtime Band" made ragtime an American craze. Songwriters began producing ragtime numbers by the carloads. Louis A. Hirsch wrote "The Gaby Glide" (Harry Pilcer) for the American debut of the French dancer, Gaby Delys, in *Vera Violetta* (1911). In 1912, Theodore F. Morse wrote "Another Rag" (D. Esrom), and "When Jose Plays a Ragtime on his Banjo" (D. Esrom). The big ragtime number of 1913 was Chris Smith's "Ballin' the Jack" (Jim Burris), among the early songs describing a social dance. It was introduced in vaudeville in 1913 by Billy Kent and Jeanette Warner and was first made popular by Eddie Cantor in vaudeville. Its interpolation in the screen musical *For Me and My Gal* (1942) put it on radio's "Your Hit Parade" that year. After that, it was used effectively by Danny Kaye in his one-man appearances in theaters and in his movie *On the Riviera* (1951). Shelton Brooks' "The Darktown Strutters' Ball," in 1917, was made into a ragtime classic by Sophie Tucker in her many vaudeville appearances. "Dardanella" (Fred Fisher—Felix Bernard and Johnny S. Black), in 1919, sold over a million and a half copies of sheet music and more than a million records in a Victor release performed by Ben Selvin's Novelty Orchestra.

Irving Berlin proved to be one of the more productive of ragtime composers. In 1912 he wrote "Ragtime Mocking Bird," "Ragtime Soldier Man," and "Ragtime Sextet," the last a satirical rag version of the sextet from *Lucia di Lammermoor*. That same year he introduced "Ragtime Jockey Man" and "That Mysterious Rag" in the Broadway revue, *The Passing Show of 1912*. In 1913 he was billed as "the ragtime king" at the Hippodrome in London where he sang his newly written "International Rag." When he finished his prepared act he offered to sing as encores any of his ragtime pieces that had not been included in the scheduled program. The audience responded with numerous requests for songs Berlin had never written, under the mistaken notion that every ragtime song in existence was his work.

It was as a writer of ragtime songs that Irving Berlin was called upon to write his first full score for the Broadway theater. This revue, *Watch Your Step*, billed as a "syncopated musical," opened at the New Amsterdam Theater on December 8, 1914. Its stars were the dancing idols of America and Europe, Vernon and Irene Castle, for whom Irving Berlin wrote "The Syncopated Walk." "More than anyone else," wrote an unidentified critic, "*Watch Your Step* belongs to Irving Berlin. He is the young master of syncopation. . . . He has written a score of his mad melodies, nearly all of them the tickling sort, born to be caught up and whistled at every street corner and warranted to set any roomful a-dancing." Besides "The Syncopated Walk" Berlin's infectious tunes for this revue included "The Minstrel Parade" and "They Always Follow Me."

One of the acts in *Watch Your Step* had the Italian master of opera, Giuseppe Verdi, protesting over the way in which his melodies were continually "ragged." But this routine ended with Verdi finally coming to the conclusion that his melodies, after all, sounded much better that way!

10

The deification of Vernon and Irene Castle was the immediate consequence of the passion for social dancing that seized America in the years preceding America's involvement in World War I.

Before 1911, such social dances as the polka, the waltz and the schottische, taxed physical endurance. Consequently, only the young danced, and even they required rest periods between dances. But the 2/4 and 4/4 rhythm of ragtime made dancing much simpler. These dances were easy to learn and perform. Anybody capable of walking could dance —whether a fox trot, a turkey trot, a grizzly bear, a bunny hug, a lame duck or a camel walk. Syncopation was so stimulating to both the senses and the feet that the old joined the young in the fun. To satisfy this mounting madness for social dancing, some restaurants (which until then had concerned themselves primarily with cuisine) had to give food a place of importance second to dancing. The first to do so was the celebrated Bustanoby's, whose salon orchestra was conducted by Sigmund Romberg, a young European musician then recently come to America to seek his fortune, which he eventually acquired through his operettas. The salon orchestra, conducted by Romberg, was initially used to provide background music for dining. But, one evening, Romberg played several ragtime numbers. These inspired a few couples to rise from their tables and begin dancing. The novelty of dancing between courses of a meal caught on quickly.

Other restaurants rushed into competition by offering dance music with meals: the Café de l'Opéra, Reisenweber's and Murray's, to single out three. Such renowned hotels as the McAlpin and the Waldorf-Astoria followed suit, and so did tea rooms and Chinese restaurants. Some factories introduced dancing during the lunch hour, and a few department stores instituted dance teas in the afternoon. The demand for after-theater dancing brought the American nightclub into existence. The first was Lee Shubert's Palais de Danse near Broadway, which soon found an imitator in Williams Morris' Jardin de Danse atop Loew's State Theater. "Dance clubs" also came into existence. These were a subterfuge to outwit curfew law which made it illegal for nightclubs to stay open all night. Couples now made it a practice to do "dance crawls" from sunset to sunrise; it became the "in" thing among the smart set.

"Rag" dancing contests were featured in ballrooms and vaudeville. Dancing schools opened and thrived, and dance instructors reaped a financial harvest by giving private lessons to those in high society, often charging as much as a hundred dollars a session. Newspapers disclosed that John D. Rockefeller was taking private lessons and that Mrs. Stuyvesant Fish had commissioned the creation of a new ragtime dance, "The Innovation," for one of her social functions. Ragtime dances were glorified in the theater. Dancers became stars of the first magnitude, but none greater than Vernon and Irene Castle.

Vernon Castle was an Englishman whose real name was Blythe. He came to America in 1906 and appeared as an eccentric dancer in *The Girl Behind the Counter* (1907) in which Lew Fields was starred. (This was the show in which Paul Lincke's well-known popular German song, "The Glow Worm" was introduced to America.) He met Irene Foote, a New Rochelle girl, at a swimming party, fell in love with her, and used his influence to get her a small part in the musical *The Hen Pecks* (1911) in which he appeared. Later that year, on May 28, they were married. Discouraged that they were not getting ahead in the theater as quickly as they would have liked, they went to Paris. There they endured appalling poverty, even though for a time they found small parts in a French revue. A chance engagement brought them to the Café de Paris where their dancing met with a sensational response. After appearances at the swank casino in Deauville, they became the talk of France. They then returned to America to repeat their French conquests, first at Louis Martin's restaurant, where they initiated a tea dance every afternoon. They were then starred in the musical *The Sunshine Girl* (1913) where they gave an electrifying presentation of the Turkey Trot, and where Vernon Castle and Julia Sanderson enchanted audiences with the tango. Before the year ended, Vernon and Irene Castle were swept to the heights of fame and wealth on the wave of the national enthusiasm for social dancing. *Watch Your Step*, with Irving Berlin's score, was written for them in 1914. They founded the Vernon Castle School of Dancing; Castle House, an ultra luxury dance palace for the elite; nightclubs (the Castle Sans Souci and Castles in the Air); and even their own resort, Castles by the Sea, in Long Beach, New York.

They popularized one dance after another so thoroughly identified with them: the Castle Walk, the Castle Classic Waltz, the Castle House Rag, the Castle Lame Duck, the Castle Maxixe, the Castle Innovation Waltz, the Castle Tango, the Castle Hesitation Waltz. During one-night stands on the vaudeville circuit they earned $30,000 a week. When they finished the formal part of their vaudeville routine they conducted a dance contest on the stage.

Irene Castle changed the habits and appearance of American women. She bobbed her hair, and women everywhere bobbed theirs. She replaced the conventional hobble shirt with a simple flowing gown, and flowing gowns became fashionable. She favored Dutch bonnets, and Dutch bonnets were the style. Because she was slim and svelte, she transformed the American concept of female pulchritude from the buxom Gibson girl to a boyish, sylphlike figure.

Vernon Castle met his death during World War I while serving with the British Air Force, the victim of an airplane accident at Fort Worth, Texas. Irene later wrote a biography of her husband, entitled *My Husband*, which in 1939 became the source of a motion picture musical, *The Story of Vernon and Irene Castle*. The times and the songs of the Vernon and Irene Castle years were nostalgically recreated, and with them some of the more famous Castle dances, performed by the Vernon and Irene Castle of the 1930s, Fred Astaire and Ginger Rogers.

Immediately after the death of her husband, Irene went into permanent retirement. Almost coincidentally—though this was no cause and effect—the popularity of ragtime songs seemed to have died as well.

11

Like so many other songwriters in Tin Pan Alley, Irving Berlin became his own publisher soon after the resounding triumph of his "Alexander's Ragtime Band." In 1912, Waterson, Berlin and Snyder was formed which in their first year became enriched by two giant Berlin hit songs. One was the kind of syncopated tune in which he had already proved himself a master: "When the Midnight Choo-Choo Leaves for Alabam'," which became a staple in vaudeville. The other, "When I Lost You," found Berlin strumming a far different kind of tune. This was a sentimental ballad, inspired by personal tragedy.

Early in 1912, Berlin married Dorothy Goetz, sister of the Broadway producer. Returning from a Cuban honeymoon to their new home on Riverside Drive, the Berlins settled down to a happy marital life all too soon shattered. Dorothy succumbed to typhoid, contracted in Cuba. Berlin's grief sent him to the writing of the first of his personal ballads, "When I Lost You," which became a success rivaling that of "Alexander's Ragtime Band," selling well over two million copies of sheet music. The ballad—particularly the autobiographical ballad to which Berlin confided his most personal feelings—henceforth became one of Berlin's strongest suits as a songwriter; this was particularly true in the 1920s, during his frenetic and much publicized romance with Ellin Mackay, the daughter of the head of Postal Telegraph, whom he finally married.

As his own publisher, Berlin also issued a song in another style to which from time to time he was partial: using two different melodies for two different sets of lyrics for one and the same chorus. He first tried this technique with "Play a Simple Melody" which Sallie Fisher and Charles King introduced in Berlin's first full-length stage musical, *Watch Your Step* (1914).

Two songs in 1913 from the presses of Waterson, Berlin and Snyder were typical of a third strain in Berlin's creativity, his sense of humor: "Somebody's Coming to My House" and "My Wife's Gone to the Country." For the latter, Berlin collaborated on the lyrics with George Whiting while the music was written by Ted Snyder. So popular did this song become that the New York *Evening Journal* commissioned Berlin in 1913 to write two hundred additional verses.

In 1915, Waterson, Berlin and Snyder published two more Berlin songs of special interest, "When I Leave This World Behind" and "I Love a Piano." The first of these has a curious history. A lawyer, Charles Lounsberry, was publicized as having left a will in which he bequeathed to his heir "the dandelions in the field and the daisies thereof . . . the long days to be merry in . . . the right to choose a star that shall be his." Reading about it, Berlin was moved to write a ballad, "When I Leave This World Behind" which he dedicated to the memory of Lounsberry. Only much later did Berlin discover that there had never existed any such person and that the story of the will had been manufactured by an imaginative journalist.

"I Love a Piano" appeared in the Broadway musical *Stop, Look and Listen* (1915), sung by Harry Fox and the ensemble. While Berlin has consistently refused to single out those of his songs which are his favorites, he once confided to this writer in a letter that if he were compelled to make a single selection it might very well be "I Love a Piano."

In 1919, Berlin intruded more boldly into Tin Pan Alley as composer-publisher by leaving the firm of Waterson, Berlin and Snyder, and organizing his own house, that of Irving Berlin, Inc. This event was commemorated throughout the United States with an Irving Berlin week. The Loew vaudeville circuit had two current Berlin songs on every program at each of its theaters; Irving Berlin himself appeared that week at the Palace Theater in New York; music stores had special displays of his best-known songs. From 1919, Berlin had a monopoly of the choicest property in Tin Pan Alley, the songs of Berlin himself. The first important Berlin songs to appear with the Irving Berlin, Inc. imprint, all of them 1919 publications, were "A Pretty Girl Is Like a Melody" and "Mandy" which were featured in the *Ziegfeld Follies of 1919*, and "Nobody Knows—and Nobody Seems to Care." But the firm also published the music of many other songwriters. In 1921, for example, it became the publisher of Walter Donaldson's "My Mammy" (Joe Young and Sam Lewis), an Al Jolson favorite. So profitable did the firm of Irving Berlin, Inc. become from its very beginnings that within eighteen months Berlin was able to realize from it a profit of $200,000. Three decades later, the Berlin house was earning for him nearly a million dollars a year.

12

Though many songwriters in Tin Pan Alley served as their own publishers, there were many who preferred to concentrate on creation and to leave the publishing to others.

Jean Schwartz soared to Tin Pan Alley fame in 1903 with the ballad Mose Gumble promoted into a three-million copy sale for Shapiro-Bernstein, "Bedelia." Schwartz was of Hungarian origin, born on November 4, 1878. When he was fourteen he came to America where he found employment as a demonstrator of songs in the sheet music department of Siegel-Cooper. After that he worked as a song plugger for Shapiro-Bernstein. Schwartz's first publication was a piano cakewalk, "Dusky Dudes" (1899). In 1901, he formed a collaborative arrangement with William Jerome, a highly esteemed lyricist and the husband of Maude Nugent. That year they wrote "When Mr. Shakespeare Comes to Town," which was interpolated into the Weber and Fields extravaganza, *Hoity Toity*; also a comedy song, "Rip Van Winkle Was a Lucky Man," popularized by Harry Bolger in the musical, *The Sleeping Beauty and the Beast*. Soon thereafter came another comedy song, "Mister Dooley," which Thomas Q. Seabrooke introduced in the extravaganza, *A Chinese Honeymoon* (1902), together with "Hamlet Was a Melancholy Man," introduced in 1903 by Eddie Foy in a Chicago extravaganza, *Mr. Bluebeard*. This was also the year of "Bedelia," with which Blanche Ring would regularly bring down the house in *The Jersey Lily* (1903). Schwartz's best songs after that included "Chinatown, My Chinatown," interpolated into the revue *Up and Down Broadway* (1910) four years after its composition, and "When the Girl You Love Is Loving," placed in the *Ziegfeld Follies of 1908*.

When the partnership of Schwartz and Jerome was dissolved in 1914, the composer worked with several lyricists, among whom were Grant Clarke, Harold Atteridge, Anne Caldwell, and Sam M. Lewis who also worked with Joe Young. Two songs, lyrics by Lewis and Young, became Jolson specialties: "Hello, Central, Give Me No Man's Land" and "Rock-a-bye Your Baby with a Dixie Melody," both featured by Jolson in *Sinbad* (1918).

Between 1913 and 1928, Schwartz contributed the scores to many a Broadway revue, extravaganza and musical comedy. He died in Los Angeles on November 30, 1956.

When Shapiro-Bernstein published "Navajo" (Harry H. Williams—Egbert Van Alstyne) in 1903, it was not only presenting one of the earliest successful songs on Indian names and subjects in Tin Pan Alley, and creating a trend in that direction, but was also bringing its young composer, Egbert Van Alstyne, his first song success. Born in Chicago on March 5, 1882, Van Alstyne received his musical training at the Chicago Musical College and his academic education in Chicago's public schools and at Cornell College in Iowa. When his schooling ended, he appeared in vaudeville in an act with Harry H. Williams, who soon began writing the words to Van Alstyne's melodies. They came to New York in 1900 where Van Alstyne found a job as staff pianist in Tin Pan Alley. "Navajo" brought him into the limelight three years later, after being introduced by Marie Cahill in the Broadway musical *Nancy Brown*. Williams and Van Alstyne boasted an even greater success in 1905 with "In the Shade of the Old Apple Tree," which they wrote while employed as song pluggers for Jerome H. Remick, its publisher. Van Alstyne once explained that the song came to him one day in Central Park, a curious fact, if true, since there were no apple trees in Central Park.

Van Alstyne's later hit songs to lyrics by Williams were also published by Remick: "Won't You Come Over to My House?" and "I'm Afraid to Come Home in the Dark," in 1906 and 1907, respectively. After 1917, Van Alstyne worked principally with Gus Kahn as his lyricist. "Pretty Baby"—for which Van Alstyne collaborated with Tony Jackson in writing the melody, with Gus Kahn responsible for the lyrics—was introduced by Dolly Hackett in the Broadway revue, *The Passing Show of 1916*. "Your Eyes Have Told Me So" was presented by Grace La Rue in vaudeville. Van Alstyne remained productive virtually to the end of his life, which came in Chicago on July 9, 1951.

Remick was also the publisher of Percy Wenrich's "Put On Your Old Gray Bonnet" (Stanley Murphy) one of its banner hits in 1909. Wenrich came from Joplin, Missouri, where he was born on January 23, 1887. He had two songs published in Chicago, and had worked as a song plugger in Milwaukee, before he came to New York in 1908. There, that year, he wrote "Up in a Balloon" (Ren Shields), a pioneer song effort on the subject of aerial navigation. One year later he wrote "Put On Your Old Gray Bonnet" which he himself sang to Remick one afternoon. Remick felt it did not have popular appeal and turned it down, but a few days later he called Wenrich to tell him that the tune kept running through his head. "Any song that even I can't forget must become a hit," he told the composer. It sold over two million copies of sheet music and became a favorite of vaudevillians and community sings. Remick also published Wenrich's next success, "On Moonlight Bay" (Edward Madden) in 1912, while Wenrich's "When You Wore a Tulip" (Jack Mahoney) came from Leo Feist's firm. After a long retirement as composer and vaudeville entertainer, Wenrich died in New York City on March 12, 1952.

Ernest R. Ball was one of the principal writers of ballads in Tin Pan Alley during its early years. From his professional beginnings, Ball was the exclusive (and the highly valuable) property of M. Witmark and Sons. Ball was a melodist in the grand tradition who knew well how to write "honestly and sincerely of the things I knew about and that folks generally know about and are interested in." He was born in Cleveland, Ohio, on July 21, 1878. Showing aptitude for music, he was given a thorough training at the Cleveland Conservatory. He was fifteen when he wrote his first piece of music, a march. In the early 1890s he came to New York where, for a time, he was a pianist at the Union Square Theater. A few years later he was hired as a demonstration pianist by Witmark for twenty dollars a week.

One night, in the spring of 1903, he met James J. Walker, then a State Senator and many years later the Mayor of New York City. Walker gave him a crumpled sheet of paper on which were scrawled the words of a song lyric. "I put the paper in my pocket, and for the next two months carried the scribbled lines around with me," Ball revealed many years later. "Bit by bit, I worked out a tune that somehow seemed to fit and finally I wrote the music to the words. The result was 'Will You Love Me in December As You Do in May?' I awoke one morning to find that I had written a piece of music that was being sung from one end of the country to the other." The song made so much money that Witmark at once signed Ball to a twenty-year contract. Jimmy Walker earned over ten thousand dollars for his lyrics; he was still receiving royalties thirty years after publication. It became Walker's song identification, played at his wedding to Janet Allen in 1912, during his tenure as New York's Mayor, and for the last time at his funeral in 1946.

The success of "Will You Love Me in December" convinced Ball that his talent lay with songs that came from the heart and appealed to the heart. In line with this he wrote "Love Me and the World Is Mine" (Dave Reed, Jr.) in 1906, one of the decade's leading ballads, which repeated its American success in foreign lands in many different translations. It was first sung at Proctor's Fifth Avenue Theater but was skyrocketed to fame in performances by Maude Lambert and Truly Shantuck in vaudeville.

Ball continued writing successful ballads, but it was some years before he produced anything quite as good as "Love Me and the World Is Mine." Then, in 1910, in collaboration with Chauncey Olcott, Ball wrote "Mother Machree" (Rida Johnson Young) which Olcott used in the Irish musical, *Barry of Ballymore*. It entered the permanent repertory of Irish tenors and proved a particular favorite of the beloved concert tenor, John McCormack. Later ballads kept Ball in the front rank of Tin Pan Alley composers: "Till the Sands of the Desert Grow Cold" (George Graff, Jr.); "When Irish Eyes Are Smiling" (Chauncey Olcott and George Graff, Jr.), introduced by Olcott in the Irish musical *The Isle o' Dreams* (1912); "Turn Back the Universe and Give Me Yesterday" (J. Keirn Brennan); and "Let the Rest of the World Go By" (J. Keirn Brennan).

From 1905 on, and for many years thereafter, Ball was a vaudeville headliner in an act made up of his own ballads. He suffered a fatal heart attack in his dressing room immediately after a performance at Santa Ana, California, on May 3, 1927. "He will live forever," John McCormack said of him on hearing about his death.

13

The Musical Stage
In Transition:
Vaudeville, Burlesque,
Revue, Extravaganza,
Operetta, Musical Comedy

1

The most effective way to bring new songs to the public was to have them performed in the theater. The right song sung by the right performer before appreciative audiences—this was the seemingly foolproof formula for musical success.

In the early 1900s, vaudeville was the most potent stage medium for song distribution. Vaudeville theaters were beginning to blanket the country, due to the enterprising efforts of a new generation of Tony Pastors, headed by B. F. Keith and E. F. Albee. Both Keith and Albee had served their theatrical apprenticeships in the circus. They teamed up to present a pirated version of *The Mikado* in Boston and on a road tour charging twenty-five cents admission, where regular presentations of *The Mikado* usually cost a dollar and a half. In 1885, Keith and Albee opened their own theater, the Bijou in Boston, a run-down house which they refurbished. There they made vaudeville history by initiating a policy of continuous entertainment (as opposed to the prevailing two-a-day) beginning at 11:00 A.M. and running until 11:00 P.M. For an admission charge of ten cents (later increased to twenty-five cents), audiences could see Weber and Fields, the Four Cohans and other vaudeville stars. Keith and Albee did so well here that they soon extended their activities as vaudeville impresarios to Philadelphia, first at the Bijou, then at the Chestnut Street Theater. In New York, in 1893, they took over the Union Square Theater and transformed it into a vaudeville house competing with Tony Pastor's nearby Music Hall. In 1893, they also built the most palatial theater thus far dedicated to vaudeville, the Colonial in Boston, at a cost of a million

178

dollars. This theater became the capital of an empire that by 1914 embraced a chain of some four hundred theaters in the East and Midwest, all of them owned and operated by Keith and Albee. While spreading their influence by the acquisition of theaters, they also developed a vaudeville exchange, the Keith-Albee circuit (later called the United Booking Office) which in time handled the bookings for vaudevillians in over three hundred theaters.

Elsewhere others were expanding the horizons of vaudeville. The Western circuit was known as the Orpheum circuit since its hub was the Orpheum Theater in San Francisco. It had been a bankrupt saloon when Martin Beck took over its management and gave it financial and theatrical respectability. Soon there were three successful Orpheum Theaters operating in California under Martin Beck's wing, including one in Los Angeles. Beck extended his influence and power by joining up with John J. Murdock of Chicago. Murdock first gained fame by booking star acts at the Masonic Temple Roof in Chicago. Then, in 1906, he opened the opulent Majestic Theater for vaudeville, the first million-dollar house in Chicago. Murdock and Beck helped to develop the Western Vaudeville Association which controlled vaudeville bookings in the Midwest.

Keith-Albee and the Western Vaudeville Association represented "big time" for vaudevillians. But "small time" circuits were also influential. The Pantages Circuit covered about thirty theaters in the Mid and Far West. The Sun Circuit boasted about two hundred theaters by 1909, mostly in smaller towns in Ohio, Pennsylvania and adjoining states. Marcus Loew, a onetime operator of penny arcades, opened his first vaudeville theater in the Bronx, New York, in 1910, featuring there "surprise nights" when unannounced stars would make unscheduled appearances. Loew then went on to build theaters all over the country, and by acquiring two small circuits (the Sullivan and the Considine) he became the Mogul of "small time" vaudeville. His one hundred and fifty or so theaters, of which the State in New York was the most important, stretched from coast to coast.

F. F. Proctor, who operated a chain of vaudeville houses in several Northern cities, opened Proctor's Twenty-eighth Street Theater in New York in 1889. Here he became the first to present continuous performances in New York from 11:00 A.M. to 11:00 P.M. in emulation of Keith-Albee in Boston. ("After breakfast go to Proctor's; after Proctor's go to bed," was its slogan.) In New York, Proctor also brought vaudeville to the 125th Street Theater and to the Fifth Avenue Theater. In 1907, he joined Keith in forming the Proctor Amusement Company that comprised several hundred vaudeville houses throughout the United States.

Vaudeville, of course, also held sway in New York in various other houses, such as Tony Pastor's Music Hall, Koster and Bial's, the Orpheum, and Hyde and Behman's on Adams Street in Brooklyn. There were also the vaudeville theaters owned by Oscar Hammerstein (the grandfather of Oscar Hammerstein II, the writing partner of Richard Rodgers). Hammerstein made millions from an assortment of inventions, ranging from cigar-making machines to a primitive vacuum cleaner, and from investments in real estate. To help promote his real estate investments in Harlem he opened the Harlem Opera House in 1889. After that he opened the Columbus in East Harlem, then in 1895 the Olympia on Broadway and 45th Street, and in 1899 the Victoria on Broadway and 42nd Street. The Olympia proved such a financial disaster that it virtually wiped out the fortune Hammerstein had accumulated. But the Victoria succeeded in rehabilitating him financially so that he could now embark on his distinguished (and expensive) career as an opera impresario on 34th Street at the Manhattan Opera House in competition with the Metropolitan Opera a few streets away.

The Victoria opened on March 2, 1899, with a bill headlining the Dutch comedians, the Roger Brothers, and including a musical theater star, Georgia Caine, an Italian dialectician, George Marion, and a comedienne, Maud Raymond. For this opening, Oscar Hammerstein composed a march, "Victoria Festival"; he also appeared on the bill to make a welcoming speech. "The Victoria," wrote the drama critic of the *American*, Alan Dale, "at a bird's eye view, looks like a big, tinkling pearl box—all in white and gold with the opals of electricity studding it in profusion, gorgeous carpets, splendid lounges, and all of the ultra-elegance of an ultra-elegance-loving metropolis. . . ."

During the seventeen years of its existence, the Victoria earned over twenty million dollars, bringing in a profit of over five million. Its manager was Oscar Hammerstein's son, William (father of Oscar Hammerstein II), a shrewd showman who knew the full value of sensation. Anybody making the newspaper headlines could get a bid from William Hammerstein to headline his bill at the Victoria: boxing, wrestling and cycling champions; glamorous women involved in highly publicized breach-of-promise or divorce suits; even women involved in lurid murder trials. Evelyn Nesbit Thaw headed the bill at the Victoria for eight weeks at a salary of $3,500 a week. She was the wife of Harry K. Thaw, who murdered Stanford White, the architect, to avenge the honor of his wife. Florence Burns, a murderess from Brooklyn who had killed her young lover, got $750 a week to appear. Ethel Conrad and Lillian Graham, who collaborated in the shooting of the millionaire W.E.D. Stokes, were also a headliner act, and so was Nan Patterson, the onetime "Florodora girl" who, though acquitted of killing her boyfriend, was luridly billed as "The Singing Murderess." Such headline personalities sang, danced, whistled, or were featured in sketches. But of performing talent they had little, and their sole appeal rested on the fact that they had just stepped onto the stage of the Victoria from newspaper headlines.

The decline and fall of the Victoria, which shut its doors in 1915, was brought about through the rise of a formidable competitor, the Palace Theater on 47th Street and Broadway. It was built by Martin Beck who tried to gain a foothold in New York by creating there America's leading vaudeville theater. But, incapable of loosening the stranglehold E. F. Albee maintained on the vaudeville industry in the East, Beck had to satisfy himself with only a minor interest in the new theater while turning over its control to Albee. The Palace opened on March 24, 1913, as one of the most beautiful auditoriums in New York, if not all America. As Max Gordon, the theatrical producer, recalled in his autobiography, *Max Gordon Presents*, "From the curved marble rail in the rear you could hear a whisper from the stage, and wherever you sat in the eighteen-hundred seat theater . . . you could see the stage clearly. . . . Seats . . . were upholstered in a beautiful flowered cretonne. The two crystal chandeliers suspended from the ceiling bespoke the grandeur of royalty."

The opening bill wandered into esoteric fields, including as it did an "Arabian pantomime," an exotic dancer, La Napierkowska, a two-scene operetta, *The Eternal Waltz*, and a Spanish court violinist, Ota Gygi. Among the other attractions were a singing comedy duo, McIntyre and Harty (replaced after the first performance by the distinguished actor of the legitimate theater, Taylor Holmes), a one-act skit by George Ade, *Speaking to Father*, a famous cartoonist, Hy Mayer, the Four Vannis, and a comedian who occupied a lowly place on the bill and was advertised in type so small as almost to escape the eye—Ed Wynn, described as "the King's jester." The Palace started off on a bad footing. The reviews were decidedly negative. *Variety* headlined its story: "Palace's $2 Vaud a Joke; $7,000 Variety Program in New York's Most Extravagant Theater Falls with a Thud—No Praise and No Attendance."

The attendance was so poor at the Palace during the first five weeks that it seemed certain that the end of that season would also mark the end of vaudeville there. The first week represented a loss of about $8,500, and the next four weeks were even worse. But the sixth week saw a turn for the better. The bill offered the famous dancer, Bessie Clayton, the comedy team of Dooley and Sales and, as headliner, Ethel Barrymore, already the first lady of the American theater. Business spurted. Reviews began to grow more cheerful. When Sarah Bernhardt was brought from Paris to appear on May 5 in what was her initiation into vaudeville, the house was overcrowded. With her company she appeared in scenes from the French plays in which she had become world famous, including the closing of Dumas' *The Lady of the Camelias*. Though few in the audience knew enough French to understand what was being said on the stage, the response was so overwhelming that Miss Bernhardt was induced to extend a contracted two-week stay for an additional week and a half. She was paid $7,000 a week, a sum without precedent in vaudeville and possibly in any branch of the American theater, in spite of which the Palace showed a sizable profit from her engagement.

During the 1913–1914 season, after a summer hiatus, the Palace began a consistent program of offering each week the best in vaudeville entertainment. The brilliance of its weekly presentations made business at the competitive Victoria slacken. The new season opened with Fritzi Scheff, climaxing her act with the Victor Herbert waltz, "Kiss Me Again" which she had introduced a few years earlier in *Mlle. Modiste*; also Victor Moore, in association with his wife, Emma Littlefield, in their famous comedy sketch, "Change Your Act." The stars came each week to be seen and heard—and they conquered. Nora Bayes, fresh from the *Ziegfeld Follies*, sang "Shine on Harvest Moon" (Jack Norworth—Nora Bayes) which she had introduced in the *Follies of 1908* and which already was her musical trademark. Gus Edwards and his schoolboy act brought the talent of fresh, young personalities who, in time, would become some of the greats of vaudeville. George Jessel introduced his Mama telephone routine ("Hello, Mama. This is Georgie. Your son, Georgie.") Belle Baker, who made the Jewish popular song "Eili Eili" a vaudeville showstopper, introduced two Irving Berlin songs, "Michigan" and "Cohen Owes Me Ninety-Seven Dollars." Vernon and Irene Castle did their suave and sophisticated dance routines. Will Rogers, also fresh from the *Ziegfeld Follies*, delivered his dry commentary on people, places and things while twirling his lasso. Ruth Roye, held over for fourteen weeks, introduced and instantly popularized a nonsense song about a monkey honeymoon, "The Aba Daba Honeymoon" (Arthur Fields—Walter Donovan). She also brought down the house with "Waiting for the Robert E. Lee" (L. Wolfe Gilbert—Lewis F. Muir). Eddie Foy brought his Seven Little Foys and his repertory of song hits that included "I'm Tired" (William Jerome—Jean Schwartz). Sophie Tucker gave her lusty renditions of "There's a Girl in the Heart of Maryland" (Ballard MacDonald—Harry Carroll), Irving Berlin's "International Rag," and the "Who Paid the Rent for Mrs. Rip Van Winkle?" (Alfred Bryan—Fred Fisher), a song that irritated the puritanical Albee. Eva Tanguay stormed across the stage singing "I Don't Care" (Jean Lenox—Harry O. Sutton) and indulged in risqué double entendres that made Albee wince but drew shouts of delight from audiences. Blossom Seeley, billed as "the Hottest Girl in Town," offered songs with which she was always identified, "Somebody Loves Me," (B. G. De Sylva and Ballard MacDonald—George Gershwin), "Way Down Yonder in New Orleans" (Henry Creamer—J. Turner Layton), "Put Your Arms Around Me, Honey" (Junie McCree—Albert von Tilzer), "Smiles" (J. Will Callahan—Lee S. Robert), "I Cried for You" (Arthur Freed—Gus Arnheim and Abe Lyman). Blanche Ring gave her inimitable rendition of an English comedy song in which an Irish girl marries an Oriental nabob on St. Patrick's Day in "I've Got Rings on My Fingers" (Weston and Barnes—Maurice Scott), which carries the hard-to-believe subtitle of "Mumbo Jumbo Jijiboo O'Shea." The constellation of stars seemed as infinite as those of the solar system: Eddie Cantor, Fanny Brice, the

Marx Brothers, Clayton, Jackson and Durante, Bill Robinson, Mae West, Burns and Allen, Nazimova, Douglas Fairbanks, Anna Held, Houdini, Weber and Fields, Elsie Janis—the list could go on almost indefinitely.

So many topflight performers were being featured on each of its bills that a program note in 1917 assured audiences that the position of an act on the bill was no reflection of its merit. The program added proudly: "When a bill is made up almost exclusively of headliners—a state of affairs not unusual at the Palace—every number is frequently worthy of a 'star spot' on ordinary vaudeville bills." The Palace became the goal of every vaudevillian, the zenith of his career; and the approbation of its audiences—especially of those that gathered on Monday afternoons made up mostly of theater professionals—the highest accolade.

There were usually between eight and ten acts on the Palace bill, and the format was one which all major vaudeville houses copied. The most important performer, the headliner, appeared in the next-to-closing act; the second principal performer was seen prior to the intermission. The show invariably opened and closed with the so-called "dumb act"—magicians, animals, acrobats, skaters, jugglers, trick bicycle riders, stilt walkers. The rest of the program was a potpourri of varied permutations and combinations of the following: a concert, operatic, operetta or popular singer; monologist; one-act play; miniature revue; song-and-dance team; comedy act; blackface performer.

From time to time the Palace featured songwriters as attractions. Jack Norworth, the husband of Nora Bayes, appeared without his wife in January 1914 using his own song "Smarty" (Jack Norworth—Albert von Tilzer) as the staple of an act that also recalled memories of "Honey Boy" (Jack Norworth—Albert von Tilzer), "Take Me Out to the Ball Game" (Jack Norworth—Albert von Tilzer) and "Shine On Harvest Moon" (Jack Norworth—Nora Bayes). In 1915, Harry Carroll presented some of his songs that, during the three previous years, had made him a composer to reckon with in Tin Pan Alley. He had rung up his first hit in 1912 with "On the Mississippi" (Ballard MacDonald) in which Arthur Fields assisted him in the writing of the melody. "There's a Girl in the Heart of Maryland" (Ballard MacDonald) was for Carroll a solo effort as far as the melody went, as were his later song hits. "By the Beautiful Sea" (Harold Atteridge) and "On the Trail of the Lonesome Pine" (Ballard MacDonald) were made successful by Muriel Window in *The Passing Show of 1914*.

L. Wolfe Gilbert, who in a long and active career wrote the lyrics for armfuls of song hits, had an act at the Palace (with the assist of Fritzi Layton and Harry Donnelly) in which he went through the "and then I wrote" routine, culminating with his greatest triumph, "Waiting for the Robert E. Lee," music by Lewis F. Muir. Some of Gilbert's most famous songs were written to the music of Anatole Friedland (1888–1938) with whom he formed an act that played the Palace in 1917 and which served as the frame for "Lily of the Valley," "My Own Iona" and "My Sweet Adair." Friedland also appeared at the Palace in a solo act singing his own hits while accompanying himself at the piano, and sometimes he was seen as the central character of miniature but elaborately staged revues using his music.

James Thornton came to the Palace not as a songwriter but as a monologist. Wearing a black cutaway coat and striped trousers and glasses he would make his entrance on the stage holding a newspaper in one hand while pointing an upraised forefinger toward the ceiling, while he exclaimed: "One moment please." He would then go through a repertory of monologues. But he also included in his act a few of his songs and when, at performance time, he was in his cups, which was not infrequent, he always plodded through a sentimental rendition of "When You Were Sweet Sixteen."

Noble Sissle, lyricist, and Eubie Blake, composer, were on the Palace bill in 1919, though at that time they had not yet written their best-known hit, "I'm Just Wild About Harry." Irving Berlin also appeared at the Palace that year. And Ernest R. Ball and Gus Edwards each were Palace attractions on many occasions.

All of these acts, with the exception of Irving Berlin, toured on one or another of the circuits that linked together the one thousand major vaudeville houses in America (the "big time") and the four thousand lesser theaters (the "small time") of which the Palace was the summit. This, of course, was true for all vaudevillians. Frequently one act served a vaudevillian for several years, since the route from New York to California, on one of the major circuits, took about a year, and this route was traversed several times; an act, consequently, need not be changed for several years. Songs performed in acts were carried on these circuits to cities large and small throughout the country, kept alive and popular from coast to coast for years on end. A publisher often knew which act was playing in which city by the way the sheet music sale of a certain song suddenly spurted there.

The value of having a prominent vaudevillian use a song on the Keith-Albee or Orpheum circuit—and even on the lesser circuits—was inestimable, as Tin Pan Alley realized. Bribes of cash or jewels bought for a publisher the favor of a star performer. Some performers demanded a percentage of the royalties on any song they featured. By 1905, Tin Pan Alley was paying out about a half a million dollars in cash or commodities to stars. In this way the vaudeville circuit became the road upon which many a song traveled to national fame.

2

The most important songwriter to come out of vaudeville was Gus Edwards. His best songs were written specifically for an act which he wrote and directed, and in which he starred for many years in vaudeville. He was born in Germany on August 18, 1879, and at the age of eight he was brought to America. As a boy he worked as a tobacco stripper in his uncle's cigar store. His evenings were spent in Union Square where he often sneaked into its theaters. Somehow he managed to meet and attract the interest of Lottie Gilson. Discovering that Gus had a pleasant singing voice, she used him as a boy stooge in her act. For a salary of five dollars a week, young Edwards was required to sit in the balcony of Hurtig and Seamon's burlesque house. From that vantage point, he would follow Miss Gilson's performance of "The Little Lost Child" with his own poignant rendition. He continued working in this role for other performers as well—Emma Carus, Maggie Cline, Imogene Comer, Helene Mora—at such places as Tony Pastor's Music Hall, Miner's Bowery Theater and Koster and Bial's. M. Witmark and Sons at one time paid him to plug its songs. His popularity as a boy stooge led to the writing of a popular song, "A Song in the Gallery."

It was not long before Edwards progressed from his seat in the balcony to the stage. He joined an act, "The Newsboy Quintet" in which the boys (like characters out of Horatio Alger's novels) appeared in rags and with dirty faces to sing the day's popular ballads. With an assist from Paul Dresser and George M. Cohan, who gave him some basic instruction, Edwards now started writing songs. His first was "All I Want Is My Black Baby Back" (Tom Daly), which was used in the newsboy act in 1898. Since he did not know how to write down a note of music, he had Charles Previn notate the melody for him. May Irwin sang that number in vaudeville.

During the Spanish-American War, Edwards was despatched to Camp Black to help entertain troops bound for Cuba. There he met Will D. Cobb, a department store salesman, whose hobby was writing song lyrics. Edwards and Cobb decided to work together on songs.

In 1899 they wrote "I Couldn't Stand to See My Baby Lose," introduced by May Irwin, and in 1900, Howley and Haviland published "I Can't Tell Why I Love You, But I Do." Their next collaboration was "I'll Be with You when the Roses Bloom Again" in 1901 which was sung in vaudeville. With "Goodbye, Little Girl, Goodbye" in 1904 and "If a Girl Like You Loved a Boy Like Me" in 1905, they further extended their success, and came to be known in the trade as "Mr. Words and Mr. Music."

Edwards worked fruitfully with other lyricists, one of them Vincent P. Bryan. In 1905, they wrote "Tammany" for a party held by the National Democratic Club of New York for which Edwards had been engaged as master of ceremonies. For this occasion, "Tammany" satirized some of the less creditable practices of the Democratic Party. (At the same time it was a takeoff on songs with American Indian subjects then so much in fashion in Tin Pan Alley.) Before using it on their program, Edwards was cautious enough to sing it for several political leaders who assured him that nobody in the Democratic Party would find the song offensive. In fact the song was so well received at the social event that the Party decided to make it the official theme song of New York's Tammany Hall. The song was sung by Lee Harrison in the extravaganza, *Fantana* (1905), and was then popularized by Jefferson de Angelis.

Another Bryan-Edwards number in 1905 was one of the first about automobiles. It was "In My Merry Oldsmobile," inspired by the first transcontinental trip ever attempted by an automobile, with two Oldsmobiles making the journey from Detroit to Portland, Oregon, in forty-four days. This song was promoted in vaudeville, sometimes by singers wearing the traditional motorist garb of the period—long white coat, visored white cap and goggles.

The rich financial returns that both "In My Merry Oldsmobile" and "Tammany" brought to their publisher, M. Witmark and Sons, convinced Edwards that he should be publishing his own songs. He formed his own company in Tin Pan Alley. "Sunbonnet Sue" (Will D. Cobb) in 1906, followed immediately by "I Just Can't Make My Eyes Behave," (Will D. Cobb) which became one of Anna Held's greatest song successes, each sold more than a million copies. The new firm of Gus Edwards Publishing Company was thus solidly established.

In 1907, Gus Edwards initiated a vaudeville act which made him as famous as a vaudevillian as he had by now become as a songwriter. In one variation or another, and under one title or another, he continued producing and appearing in that act for the next two decades on the vaudeville circuit. His first act was called "School Boys and Girls," with Edwards appearing as the only adult in the act, filling the role of a schoolmaster heading a classroom of kids who sang, danced and did comedy bits. Young Herman Timberg was in that production. "Kid Kabaret" introduced little Eddie Cantor and Georgie Jessel; "Band Box Revue" had Lila Lee and Georgie Price; "Blonde Typewriters" introduced Johnny Stanley; and "Carleton Nights" marked the debut of Ray Bolger. Many of the new songs used in these acts were written by Edwards himself. "School Days" (Will D. Cobb) in 1907, had a sensational three-million copy sheet music sale. "By the Light of the Silvery Moon" (Edward Madden) was sung by Georgie Price in 1909 as a stooge in the audience. Later the same year Lillian Lorraine made it her song theme after featuring it in the *Ziegfeld Follies of 1909*. Two other Edwards hit songs given their first hearings in his revues were "If I Were a Millionaire" (Will D. Cobb) and "Jimmy Valentine" (Edward Madden).

Edwards' emphasis on juvenile talent inspired a remark often heard on Broadway in his time, "Pull in your kids—here comes Gus Edwards." Through the years, the act became the nursery for future stars of vaudeville and musical comedy. Even a partial list of these discloses Edwards' remarkable instinct for detecting latent talent. Besides those already mentioned were Eleanor Powell, Groucho Marx, Jack Pearl, Charles King, Mae Murray, Eddie Buzzell, Bert Wheeler, Ann Dvorak and the Duncan Sisters.

Gus Edwards presented his last children's revue in the early 1930s. By then vaudeville was in its final days. Both as a vaudevillian and as a songwriter Edwards expired when vaudeville did. He retired in 1938, living long enough to witness his life story glamorized in the motion picture *Star Maker* (1939), starring Bing Crosby. Edwards died in Los Angeles on November 7, 1945.

3

Bert Williams, probably the greatest black comedian to come out of vaudeville, also wrote the music for many of the songs he made famous. The bedraggled character he projected so poignantly (of which his later comic roles in the *Ziegfeld Follies* were merely extensions) were developed, refined, polished, perfected and made famous in vaudeville. The act of Williams and Walker came to Koster and Bial's on April 23, 1896. This was their first appearance in big time after an apprenticeship in lowly music halls and variety theaters in San Francisco. They were so successful in New York that they remained at Koster and Bial's for six months. After that they toured the Keith vaudeville circuit. The headline spot they reached by the end of 1897 was retained for the next decade in most of America's major vaudeville houses, including Tony Pastor's Music Hall. They danced, sang, exchanged comic repartee, did pantomimes, strummed the banjo and performed the cakewalk. In short, theirs were the routines which audiences had come to expect not only from black performers but also from white performers in blackface.

Bert Williams started out by imitating the caricature of black men favored by white minstrels. But in time he progressed from caricature to character portrayal. As finally delineated in vaudeville he was a hapless, shiftless, beaten fellow—half pathetic, half comic —in a world he never quite understood. He was a striking contrast to his partner, George Walker, who always dressed flamboyantly (off stage as well as on). Walker was tall, self-assured to the point of arrogance, and given to sophisticated attitudes. Bert Williams was short, shuffling, awkward, confused. He wore a kinky-haired wig. His face was blackened with burnt cork (in the minstrel tradition) with lips broadened into white ellipses. His costume consisted of a onetime frock coat with tails shorn off, top hat and white gloves. Wrinkled socks hung loosely in oversized scuffed shoes. A large collar was detached from the shirt. He moved deliberately, lazily, and spoke in a slow drawl. His gestures were clumsy, his face sagged, his lips drooped with the sadness of defeat. Williams neither sang nor danced well, and his gesturing left much to be desired, but somehow he managed to convert these deficits into assets for the portrait he was projecting. He was, in effect, the black counterpart of "the little tramp" a decade or so before Charlie Chaplin conceived him. The tears Bert Williams inspired in audiences came not only from irrepressible laughter but from heartache. W. C. Fields once said of him that he was "the funniest man in the world, and the saddest."

The way he entered the stage at once established the mood for his character portrayal. The limelight would be focused on the wings of the stage. Suddenly in the center of the light a white-gloved hand would be seen. Slowly an arm became visible, and then a shoulder. Finally, a shabbily dressed, melancholy black man came hesitantly into full view.

Songs were basic to his portrayal, and the one that is most frequently brought to mind when the name of Bert Williams is mentioned is "Nobody," for which he wrote the music to Alex Rogers' words. He sang it for the first time in vaudeville in New York in 1905. To start its presentation he went through the stage business of hunting in the pocket of his ragged frock coat for a little notebook. He began turning the pages ever so slowly until he came upon the one he was seeking. Then in a chant that was half song and half recitative, he began to sing: "When life seems full of clouds and rain, and I am full of nothin' but pain, who soothes my thumpin', bumpin' brain?. . . . Nobody!" The first rendition in 1905 proved a smash. "Nobody" remained in Bert Williams' act, and subsequently was used by him in virtually every important appearance. When he made his debut in the *Ziegfeld Follies* in 1910, "Nobody" was one of his highlights. "Before I got through with 'Nobody,' " Bert Williams once complained, "I could have wished that both the author of the words and the assembler of the tune had been strangled or drowned. . . . For seven whole years I had to sing it. Month after month I tried to drop it and sing something new, but I could not get anything to replace it and the audiences seemed to want nothing else." The popularity of this song died with Bert Williams. Nobody could project the feeling of haunting loneliness in a comedy number the way Williams did. Bob Hope revived it (none too effectively) in the motion picture, *The Seven Little Foys* (1955).

"Nobody" may have been Williams' song triumph, but it was not the only one of his songs in whose writing he had a hand to appeal to audiences. Many of his songs—beginning with "I Don't Like No Cheap Man" in 1897—were written in collaboration with George Walker. Among these were "The Medicine Man," "The Fortune Telling Man," and "When It's All Goin' Out and Nothin' Comin' In" (in which Walker was aided by James W. Johnson in writing the lyrics). Other Bert Williams song specialties, for which he wrote the melodies, were fashioned to the words of various lyricists. These included "Let It Alone" (Alex Rogers), "Somebody Lied" (Jeff T. Brainen and Evan Lloyd), "I'd Rather Have Nothin' All the Time than Somethin' for a Little While" (John B. Lowitz). Williams also popularized songs by other composers: "My Castle on the Nile" (J. W. Johnson, Bob Cole—Rosamond Johnson); "I'm a Jonah Man" (Alex Rogers); "I May Be Crazy but I Ain't No Fool" (Alex Rogers); and "You're in the Right Church, but the Wrong Pew" (Cecil Mack—Chris Smith).

The partnership of Walker and Williams had to break up in 1909 when Walker became a victim of paresis brought on by syphilis. From then on, Bert Williams went it alone, first in vaudeville, then in the *Ziegfeld Follies* as well as in vaudeville. Until the end he remained a star of stars, a performer who succeeded in freeing the black performer from the stereotypes and clichés to which he had so long been subjected, and the first black man to become a star in the *Follies*. Williams collapsed from pneumonia in 1922, while touring with *Under the Bamboo Tree* where he was the only black man in a company of whites. He was brought back to New York where he died.

<h1 style="text-align:center">4</h1>

Vaudeville stars helped make songs into hits, and conversely, hit songs helped make many a vaudevillian into a star.

Sophie Tucker was a maker of hits. Born in Russia in 1888, she began her stage career as a contestant in an amateur night contest in New York in 1906. She then appeared in small-time vaudeville theaters. Because she was both big and unattractive she was advised to blacken her face and concentrate on "coon" songs. At Tony Pastor's Music Hall she was billed as a "Coon shouter" and her repertory included Albert von Tilzer's "Honey Boy" (Jack Norworth). Accident forced her to desert burnt cork. For an engagement at the Howard Atheneum Theater in Boston, a burlesque house, her trunk of costumes and makeup failed to arrive in time. She was compelled to appear in white face. Her natural vigor and personal magnetism, especially when she sang "That Lovin' Rag" (Victor H. Smalley—Bernie Adler), proved so infectious that the audience forgot her less attractive features. Immediately after this appearance she renounced blackface for good. "I can hold an audience without it," she announced. "I've got them eating right out of my hand." She now concentrated on ragtime songs, and was billed on the Morris circuit as "The Mary Garden of Ragtime." She became a star with "Carrie" (Junie McCree—Albert von Tilzer), "The Cubanola Glide" (Vincent P. Bryan—Albert von Tilzer) and other ragtime numbers. As a star, she took an unpublished song by an unknown composer and lifted it to the heights of popular success. It stayed her theme song for the remainder of her long career. That song was Shelton Brooks' "Some of These Days."

Sophie Tucker's maid was responsible for bringing her "Some of These Days." The maid insisted that she meet and listen to Shelton Brooks, a black songwriting entertainer specializing in impersonations of Bert Williams. One day in 1910, he sang "Some of These Days" for Sophie Tucker in her dressing room in a Chicago vaudeville theater. She liked it instantly, and did not delay introducing it in her act. She never stopped singing it after that, up to her final appearances as "the last of the red hot mamas." As she wrote: "I've made it . . . my theme. I've turned it inside out, singing it in every way imaginable, as a dramatic song, as a novelty number, as a sentimental ballad, and always audiences have loved it and asked for it."

A social gathering at the San Francisco Exposition was the source of a later Shelton Brooks hit song, a ragtime classic, "The Darktown Strutters' Ball," which the Original Dixieland Jazz Band introduced in the year of its composition (1917) and which Sophie Tucker used successfully in vaudeville.

Sophie Tucker was the immediate inspiration for "I'm the Last of the Red Hot Mamas" (Jack Yellen—Milton Ager), written especially for and about her in 1929. She introduced it in vaudeville, then sang it when she made her motion picture debut in *Honky Tonk* (1929).

Sophie Tucker made an unknown song into a giant hit, but on the other hand, there are songs which were responsible for raising formerly unknown or little known performers to stardom.

One of them was Emma Carus. She was a big woman who was aware of her physical shortcomings and openly acknowledged them. She liked to open her vaudeville act with the self-deprecating comment, "I'm not pretty, but I'm good to my folks." But she had a way with a song which she belted out with a big, cultivated voice whose range went from a sweet contralto to a booming baritone. Born in Berlin, Germany, in 1879, she was brought to the United States as a child. Her first singing job was in a New York "museum" which put on eighteen shows a day from which she graduated into various other musical productions. She was eighteen when she made her debut in vaudeville singing Monroe Rosenfeld's "Take Back Your Gold" (Louis W. Pritzkow), the first time she revealed her special gift for a personalized style of song delivery. "Take Back Your Gold" became a hit ballad in 1897 because of Emma Carus, and Emma Carus became a vaudeville headliner because of this ballad. Fifteen years later, as a recognized star, she was to bring Irving Berlin's "Alexander's Ragtime Band" for the first time to the forefront of national consciousness.

Eva Tanguay, born in Quebec, Canada, in 1878, was probably the most uninhibited vaudeville performer of her time. A song helped make her one of the most provocative, exciting, talked-about and highest paid vaudevillians of her day. That song was "I Don't Care" (Jean Lenox—Harry O. Sutton). ("I don't care! I don't care! What they may think of me. I'm happy-go-lucky, Men say that I'm plucky, So jolly and carefree.") Mose Gumble, Remick's ace song plugger, had brought this song to her attention in 1905. Realizing that it neatly compressed into lyrics her own hedonistic concept of life, she sang it in vaudeville in 1905 when she was twenty-seven. From then on she was labeled the "I Don't Care Girl." (When her biography was screened in 1953 it was called *The I Don't Care Girl*.)

She made her stage debut with the Francesca-Redding Company in Holyoke, Massachusetts, when she was eight, and for five years she toured with that company in juvenile leads. Her first appearance on Broadway took place in 1901 at Hammerstein's Paradise Roof Garden in a musical called *My Lady*, starring Eddie Foy. Four years later, "I Don't Care" made her the talk of the town.

Her voice was not much to listen to, and her dancing not much to watch. What she did have was inexhaustible energy that exploded each time the limelight was focused on her. She swept across the stage like a hurricane. She used the stage as a forum from which to berate her audience, her management, or anybody else who at that given moment was an annoyance to her. She shamelessly exploited sex, the way she provocatively wiggled her body, with her sassy innuendos and double entendres, her spicy and suggestive comments in prose and verse, and in her songs. "I have one foot in New York," she yelled out, "and one foot in Chicago. And between them I make my living." The audience caught its breath and gasped, but it loved her. At one time on the stage she poured a bottle of champagne over her head. She did Salome's dance in a costume that left little to the imagination. "I also did something else that no one else had thought of," she explained in discussing her Salome routine. "Instead of dancing around holding the papier mâché head I hired a Negro boy with big eyes. I sat him on the side of the stage, all covered up. As I began to dance, I uncovered his head which, to the audience, appeared to be resting on a silver tray. As I moved about the stage his huge eyes also moved, following me. The audience was electrified. But . . . the Mayor of New York . . . sent word to me to put some clothes on or he'd close the show." In contrast to her minimal costume as Salome, another one weighed forty-five pounds, made up entirely of coins. (No vaudevillian ever spent more money on costumes and props than she.) The songs she wailed (many written for her) represented the beliefs of a fully emancipated woman: "I Want Someone to Go Wild with Me," "It's All Been Done Before but Not the Way I Do It," "I've Got to be Crazy," "Go As Far as You Like" and "Nothing Bothers Me." She caused tempests not only on stage but behind the scenes with her perpetual feuds with managers, booking agents and fellow performers. Off stage she remained in character, perpetually involved in scandals, escapades, lawsuits and continually providing newspapers with juicy story material. The candle she burned at both ends did not make a wondrous light at the end. She was destroyed by her indiscretions and extravagances, ending up half blind, crippled by arthritis and totally impoverished. She who had been one of the highest priced single acts in vaudeville, drawing at times as much as $3,500 a week and who had been reputed to have earned over two million dollars, was compelled in 1930 to accept a fee of $150 for a three-day appearance at the Bushwick Theater in Brooklyn. By the time she died of a cerebral hemorrhage in 1947, "The Girl Who Made Vaudeville Famous," "Cyclonic Eva Tanguay," "The Evangelist of Joy," "Mother Eve's Merriest Daughter," "The Electrifying Hoyden" and "Vaudeville's Greatest Drawing Card" (as she was frequently hailed in the press and on billboards) was virtually forgotten, living the last ten years of her life in seclusion and obscurity in Hollywood, California.

Nora Bayes' first important step toward stage popularity was with the Harry von Tilzer song, "Down Where the Würzburger Flows." That step led to stardom in vaudeville, musical comedies, the *Ziegfeld Follies* and her one-woman shows. Born Nora Goldberg in 1880, probably in Joliet, Illinois, she went to Chicago when she was eighteen, married her first husband, an undertaker, and began her professional theatrical career singing "coon" songs and sentimental ballads at the Hopkins Theater and the Old Chicago Opera House. Her New York debut took place in a musical farce, *The Roger Brothers in Washington* (1901). An engagement at Tony Pastor's Music Hall after that brought her engagements in Eastern vaudeville houses.

In 1902, she was appearing at the Orpheum Theater in Brooklyn where she introduced "Down Where the Würzburger Flows." The first time she presented this number she broke down and seemed incapable of continuing. Harry von Tilzer, in a box, took over the singing until she recovered. The audience was so taken with this impromptu performance that the management decided to keep this routine in the act throughout her engagement. It is certainly well within the realm of probability that the whole business had been neatly contrived beforehand; von Tilzer always had a boundless inventiveness in plugging a song. If this was so, the outcome exceeded all expectations. Nora Bayes became a magical name at the box office, and the song became a best-seller in sheet music.

In her appearances during the next half dozen years, Miss Bayes made this number one of her musical standbys. "The Würzburger Girl" as she came to be called, had a low, husky voice and a lively and infectious personality, both of which had a hypnotic effect on audiences. She was a stately figure on the stage. She would stride up and down, swinging her hips, a fine lace handkerchief or a fan in her hand. She would stop center stage to deliver a recitation or a rhymed quip. Above all else she was a grand lady of song—be it sentimental, comic or ragtime: songs like "Has Anybody Here Seen Kelly?" (C. W. Murphy and Will Letters, adapted by William C. McKenna), "Take Me Out to the Ball Game," (Jack Norworth—Albert von Tilzer), "When It's Apple Blossom Time in Normandy" (Mellor, Gifford and Trevor), George M. Cohan's World War I anthem, "Over There," Irving Berlin's "Tell Me Pretty Gypsy," "I'll Be With You in Apple Blossom Time" (Neville Fleeson—Albert von Tilzer), "The Japanese Sandman" (Raymond B. Egan—Richard A. Whiting) and the song that replaced "Down Where the Würzburger Flows" as her theme, "Shine on Harvest Moon" (Jack Norworth—Nora Bayes). She is reputed to have written it in collaboration with the second of her five husbands, Jack Norworth, though there is reason to suspect the song was actually composed by Dave Stamper, staff composer of the *Ziegfeld Follies*, with Norworth merely providing the lyrics and Miss Bayes just her approval. In any event, she introduced it in the *Ziegfeld Follies of 1908*, and from that time on made it the high spot of her act, billed as "the Empress of Vaudeville." When the screen biography of Nora Bayes and Jack Norworth was filmed in 1944, it bore the title *Shine On Harvest Moon*. Her last appearance was at Tom Noonan's Bowery Mission in March 1928. A few days later she died in a Brooklyn hospital following an abdominal operation.

5

Where vaudeville appealed to the entire family with its wholesome entertainment, another kind of variety show was feeding the prurient appetites of males in the 1890s. It was burlesque, not to be confused with the travesties or parodies of the early 1800s, nor with the ethnic burlesque extravaganzas of Harrigan and Hart and Weber and Fields. In the 1890s, burlesque began to mean girls in various stages of undress, together with the titillating hootchy-kootchy. From these developed the off-color humor, the bumps and grinds of the show girls, and the art and science of undress called the striptease which brought burlesque into disrepute and into the arms of the law.

Burlesque had its beginnings with the girls in pink tights doing the cancan in *The Black Crook* in 1866. Three years later, *Ixion* arrived to New York from London, a spectacular production built around mythological characters, starring Lydia Thompson and featuring her British blondes. Lydia Thompson played the title role, while the attractive Pauline Markham (the mistress of the then Governor of South Carolina) was Venus. Though this was an eyeful as to scenery, costuming and staging, and though it provided a delightful musical interlude with Lisa Weber singing "Walking Down Broadway" (W. H. Lingard—Charles E. Pratt), the main attractions of *Ixion* were the girls in tights, their provocative poses and attitudes, the suggestive dancing of Ada Harland, and the double entendre humor. Those girls who did not wear tights were seen in skirts slit down the middle to reveal shapely legs and well formed thighs. Critics expressed shock, and clergymen, indignation, but the audience howled with delight.

The success of *Ixion* in New York and on tour led to the formation of all-female minstrel troupes. Companies such as The Red Riding Hood Minstrels, Mme. Rejane's Female Minstrels or May Fiske's English Blondes all glorified female anatomy within an improvised minstrel show format, often by having girls on a trapeze or a swing soar over the audience while removing some of their clothes.

The word "burlesque" appears in the name of a company formed by Michael B. Leavitt in New York in the late 1870s, the Rentz-Santley Novelty and Burlesque Company. This may very well by why Leavitt is often considered as the first important pioneer in the presentation of American burlesque shows. Taking his cue from *Ixion*—while borrowing elements from vaudeville, the minstrel show and the extravaganza—Leavitt presented Mme. Rentz's Female Minstrels, the name "Rentz" borrowed from a then popular European attraction, the Rentz Circus. Leavitt starred an American beauty, Mabel Santley. Females not only preempted the stage, but also the other side of the footlights by serving as box-office attendants, ushers, doorkeepers and ticket takers. This show did so well that from then on, season after season for a decade, Leavitt offered what came to be known as the Rentz-Santley Shows. Mabel Santley was the leading female ornament in these feminine minstrel shows, but not the only one. Out of these productions stepped Ada Richmond and May Howard. Miss Howard—who married and then deserted Paul Dresser—earned the distinction of becoming the first to bear the title of "burlesque queen." After leaving Leavitt, May Howard became the star of Bob Manchester's Owls, and in 1888 she formed her own troupe, the May Howard Burlesque Company. Ada Richmond also branched out by forming the Ada Richmond Burlesquers.

Sam T. Jack added the spice of salaciousness to burlesque entertainment. He was the manager of Leavitt's touring Rentz-Santley shows who came to Chicago where he opened his own burlesque theater. There he pulled out all the stops as far as sex exploitation went. The humor in his productions was bawdy and vulgar. Girls often appeared totally nude in "living pictures." They also tantalized audiences with the cancan, and with its burlesque successor, the hootchy-kootchy. The hootchy-kootchy was introduced to America in 1893 by Little Lady Egypt in *The Streets of Cairo*, a production mounted at the Midway Plaisance at the Chicago World's Fair. Dressed in Oriental garb, Little Egypt performed an exotic dance calling for athletic gyrations of an exposed stomach, together with quivers of other parts of the anatomy. The Oriental dancer, and the hootchy-kootchy, now became a vogue, encouraging others to imitate Little Egypt at tent shows, museums and burlesque houses. Sam T. Jack made the hootchy-kootchy a major burlesque attraction.

For a time each burlesque theater was an independent operation, usually with a stock company that changed its bill every week. Then, as with vaudeville, circuits (or "wheels" as they were called in burlesque) were developed to facilitate bookings for traveling units. The Eastern Circuit of House Managers—which later became the powerful Eastern, or Columbia, Wheel, with Sam A. Scribner as president—covered the East. The West belonged to the

Empire Association, or Western Wheel. Between them they played virtually every important burlesque theater so that a troupe traveling the circuit could be assured uninterrupted performances for thirty-five weeks. A third "wheel," the Mutual Burlesque Association, was added in 1922.

Most of the ritual of burlesque was crystallized by the early 1900s: the risqué black-outs, the vulgarities, the German and Jewish comedians, the slapstick, the half dressed girls, the aphrodisiac dances. To Bernard Sobel, author of A *Pictorial History of Burlesque*, the decade between 1900 and 1910 was "the golden age." He wrote: "This decade marked the heyday of burlesque, when entertainment was substantial and comedians robustious, star-bound for Broadway. Managers were proud of their shows, flourished in their rivalry, introduced novelties, perfected book, score and production, and made audiences happy."

Some of the stars of this decade included "Sliding" Billy Watson, Alexander Carr, Ben Welch, "Bozo" Snyder, Al Shean, Bickel and Watson, Millie de Leon, Billy "Beef Trust" Watson, and Blaze Starr. This was the decade when amateurs as well as professionals brightened the burlesque stage, for it was in burlesque that "amateur night" came to the theater. This happened at Miner's Bowery Theater in 1903. From then on, amateur night became a regular Friday evening feature at Miner's and was carried over in vaudeville and motion picture theaters. It was at one of these amateur nights at Miner's that Eddie Cantor, then fifteen, made his stage debut, winning first prize. It was also at one of these amateur nights that the phrase "get a hook" was first heard as a response to a rank performance. *The Actor's Fair Bulletin* tells the story: "A particularly bad amateur was inflicting upon a patient audience an impossible tenor solo. Despite howls, groans, catcalls, the artist persisted in staying on, when Tom Inner, who was running the show, chanced to see a large old-fashioned crook-handled cane which had been used by one of the Negro impersonators. Quickly he had the . . . stage manager lash it to a long pole. With this he stepped to the wings, without getting into the sight of the audience, deftly slipped the hook around the neck of the singer and yanked him off the stage before he knew what happened. The next amateur who was giving an imitation of Booth, announced he would impersonate Richard Mansfield, when a small boy yelled 'Get the hook!' The audience roared and the actor fled in dismay."

Fanny Brice, Joe Cook and George White were several others to enter the theater by way of amateur nights at burlesque, though not at Miner's. It was during this decade that Sophie Tucker made the change from blackface to white under circumstances already described. Just as the decade was ending, Fanny Brice, appearing in the burlesque *College Girls' Show*, made a transformation of her own. She was then billed as a "coon" singer and as an interpreter of ballads, and not as a comedienne. One day she was called upon to do a specialty number. She asked Irving Berlin (then still a neophyte songwriter) for material. As she tells the story: "Irving took me in the back room and he played 'Sadie Salome' . . . a Jewish comedy song. . . . So, of course, Irving sang 'Sadie Salome' with a Jewish accent. I didn't even understand Jewish, couldn't speak a word of it. But, I thought, if that's the way Irving sings, that's the way I'll sing it. Well, I came out and did 'Sadie Salome' for the first time ever doing a Jewish accent. And that starched sailor suit is killing me. And it's gathering you know where, and I'm trying to squirm it away, and singing and smiling, and the audience is loving it. They think it's an act I'm doing, so as long as they're laughing I keep it up. They start to throw roses at me." This incident changed Fanny Brice into a comedienne, and a supreme interpreter of Yiddish comic songs was born. Florenz Ziegfeld heard her sing one of those songs at the burlesque house and forthwith signed her to appear in the *Ziegfeld Follies of 1910*.

Many later stars of the musical theater, vaudeville and motion pictures had their beginnings in burlesque, though not necessarily in the decade of 1900–1910. The first time Al Jolson, aged fourteen, appeared as a performer in a theater was with the Villanova Touring Burlesque Company where he worked as a boy singing stooge for the burlesque queen, Aggie Baller. She was billed as "Jersey Lily," and during her bumps and grinds, the boy Jolson would sing "You Are My Jersey Lily" from his seat in the audience. He also did reprises of her vocal numbers. In 1901, still as a boy soprano, he appeared in several touring burlesque productions including *The Little Egypt Burlesque Show*, before progressing to vaudeville.

W. C. Fields was a juggler in a down-at-the-heel touring burlesque company before he advanced to vaudeville and from there to the *Ziegfeld Follies*. Emma Carus got her theatrical start in Leavitt's Rentz-Santley Shows. Other stars graduating from burlesque to show business greatness included Abbott and Costello, Eddie Cantor, Leon Errol, Willie Howard, Bobby Clark, Jimmy Savo, Al Reeves, Red Skelton, Jack Haley, Rags Ragland, Red Buttons, Jay C. Flippen, Fay Templeton, Phil Silvers—and, of course, many others.

Billy Minsky was the leading burlesque producer, his heyday being from late 1910 up to the time the flame of burlesque was totally extinguished by the police some two decades later. He first presented stock burlesque at the National Theater Winter Garden on East Houston Street in New York, then spread out to theaters throughout New York and elsewhere, including the Republic in Times Square and the Apollo in Harlem. It was with Billy Minsky that the striptease became the climactic attraction of burlesque shows in the 1920s and later. The peeling of clothing to a state of seminudity was not a burlesque invention, to be sure. Many an actress had inspired a glint in male eyes by recreating Salome's Dance of the Seven Veils. Eva Tanguay had done it in vaudeville, and Theda Bara on the silent screen. But the slow and sensual way in which it was performed to the accompaniment of appropriately languorous music was exclusively a burlesque creation. The first striptease to be performed in any theater was probably that of Gaby Deslys in the Broadway musical, *Stop, Look and Listen*, in 1915. There she disrobed while singing an Irving Berlin song that began: "Take off a little bit, if that don't make a hit, take off a bit more." The striptease, as a burlesque feature, had to wait another half dozen years or so before it was developed into personalized art form by Ann Corio, Gypsy Rose Lee, Margie Hart and Georgia Sothern, who could be seen at the Irving Place Theater in downtown New York, at Harlem's Apollo, the Republic in Times Square or at the Star Theater in Brooklyn.

In burlesque, music was purely functional, serving as a background or as transition music or as filler material for singers. Consequently few songs were first introduced on the burlesque stage and fewer still were written directly for it. Nevertheless Tin Pan Alley found the burlesque "wheel" one additional channel through which popular songs could be successfully introduced throughout the country. As Bernard Sobel noted, to place a song in a burlesque show was "the infallible method, in the nineties and long afterward, of establishing a hit and insuring great profits. The runs were long and by the time one show after another presented a song the whole country knew the tune by heart."

6

Vaudeville gave rise to a new form of musical theater in the 1890s—the revue. The revue was a conception of George W. Lederer, who felt that vaudeville, in an ambitious frame, could command a far higher price at the box office than the paltry fifty cents or twenty-five cents charged by vaudeville houses. What Lederer had in mind was a combination of vaudeville, extravaganza and burlesque with sumptuous sets and elaborate costuming. He offered this new kind of musical stage entertainment at the Casino Theater in New York on

May 12, 1894, calling it *The Passing Show* (not to be confused with later revues of the same name produced by the Shuberts). Lederer spared no expense in providing a sumptuous setting for his diversified attractions which included an acrobatic act, a sketch, burlesques of prominent actors and actresses, travesties of current plays, beautiful girls posing in "living pictures," spectacles, production numbers and songs. The songs were the work of Ludwig Englander (1859–1914) with lyrics by Sydney Rosenfeld. The best of these were "Old Before His Time," a takeoff on the problem plays and naturalistic dramas then popular on Broadway, and the ballad "I Love My Love in the Springtime." All the songs in the show were written expressly for this production, a practice nonexistent in vaudeville and burlesque, where each act used whatever material it wished. Writing songs directly and exclusively for a revue became the usual procedure, though often outside song material would be interpolated.

So popular was *The Passing Show* that for the next few years many imitations were mounted on Broadway. Two of them had music by Gustave Kerker (1857–1923): *In Gay New York* (1896) and *The Whirl of the Town* (1897). By 1900, the revue became a fixture with a familiar pattern. It was a feast for the eye and a treat for the other senses. It glorified female beauty, though more discreetly than burlesque; it emphasized costuming, scenery and stage technology. Overall effect was given precedence over detail. For years, the revue provided entertainment through glamor and splendor; stimulating and intellectual originality were left to other branches of the theater.

More than any other single person, Florenz Ziegfeld was responsible for the character and personality of the Broadway revue in the first two decades of the twentieth century. Father of the *Follies*, which for two decades was the criterion toward which all other revues aspired, he was a producer in the grand manner. His was the courage to think and plan within grandiose designs; his, the recklessness to ignore budgets while mounting incomparably lavish productions. He once paid an actress $650 a week and had her wear a $1,200 gown just to walk across the stage in a single scene. He ordered a setting at a cost of $25,000 only to discard it because he found it too garish. He purchased the finest talent available without worrying about the price tag, and he paid salaries rarely heard of in his time, not only to the stars but also to the girls of the chorus. He was never one to compromise with his ideal. As the years passed, his revues grew ever more ambitious, ever more opulent, ever more extravagant with talent and feminine beauty.

Born in Chicago in 1868, he was the son of Dr. Florenz Ziegfeld, the president of the Chicago Musical College which he had founded just a year before his son's birth. The younger Florenz served his apprenticeship as a showman at the Chicago World's Fair in 1893, first as the impresario of several acts he had imported from Europe, and then as the manager of Sandow the Great, the strong man. Ziegfeld then began dreaming of bringing to America the idol of the Parisian stage—petite Anna Held, with the wide luminous eyes, the personification of Gallic naughtiness and charm. Though he certainly did not have the wherewithal to sign her to a contract—he went to Paris and managed to corral her for *A Parlor Match*, which came to the Herald Square Theater on September 21, 1896. There she enchanted her audiences with her unique blend of baby-faced ingenuousness and infectious sexiness. In 1897 she became Mrs. Florenz Ziegfeld, her husband continuing to be her producer for *The Parisian Model* (1906) where she sang "It's Delightful to Be Married" (Anna Held—Vincent Scotto) and Gus Edwards' "I Just Can't Make My Eyes Behave" (Will D. Cobb). She now became the much publicized darling of the musical theater who made news with her milk baths and who carried her husband to wealth and a place of consequence in the theater.

A new dream now obsessed Ziegfeld: to create for America the equivalent of Paris' Folies Bergères—a spectacular revue celebrating the greater glory of female beauty. (This idea was believed to have originated with his wife, Anna Held.) He first experimented with such a production on the roof of the New York Theater on July 8, 1907. He crowded the stage with "the Anna Held Girls" (sans Anna Held herself), fifty of the most beautiful women (according to Ziegfeld) ever gathered at the same time in one theater, some imported from Paris. The stage also overflowed with stars. Annabelle Whitford, in bloomers, appeared as "the Gibson Bathing Girl." Mlle. Dazie performed a Jiu-Jitsu waltz. Grace La Rue and Emma Carus were the featured singers. Dave Lewis did novelty numbers, and Bickel and Lewis, burlesque routines. One of the production numbers had the chorus marching up and down the aisles beating on snare drums. "Mr. Ziegfeld," reported an unidentified critic, "has given New York the best melange of mirth, music, and pretty girls that has been seen here in many summers."

This was the *Follies of 1907*. Until 1931 (with hiatuses in 1926, 1928 and 1929) Ziegfeld continued producing his *Follies*. In 1908 he moved it to Erlanger's Theater. After 1911, Ziegfeld called his revue the *Ziegfeld Follies* and in 1913 it moved into the New Amsterdam Theater on 42nd Street, which now became its permanent home. Through these revues he became one of the foremost showmen of his generation. From one edition to the next he grew increasingly ambitious in scope and aims, and increasingly financially extravagant. Where the first edition in 1907 had required an overall expenditure of $13,000 before the curtain rose, and a weekly payroll of $3,800 after that, the *Ziegfeld Follies of 1919* had a production cost of $100,000 and a weekly payroll of $20,000. He made every effort to provide a dazzling background for his girls, to make the "Follies" girl a synonym for the ultimate in feminine glamour and beauty. Out of the Ziegfeld chorus line stepped such later stars of stage and screen as Mae Murray, Nita Naldi, Harriet Hoctor, Olive Thomas, Ann Pennington, Marion Davies and Lilyan Tashman.

And from the cast of leading and minor performers there also emerged some of the all-time greats of the American theater, many of them unknown when Ziegfeld found and used them. He used to say that, since he demanded the best, he was not interested in making stars but only in buying them. He gladly paid the price for Eva Tanguay, Lillian Lorraine, Bert Williams, Bessie McCoy, Leon Errol, W. C. Fields, Ed Wynn, Van and Schenck, the Dolly Sisters. But the truth is few producers did more than Ziegfeld to lift unknowns to heights. He had a uncanny flair for detecting performing genius in the raw.

He found Fanny Brice in a shabby burlesque house, brought her to the *Follies of 1910* and had her sing a ragtime number, "Lovey Joe" (Will Marion Cook—Joe Jordan) and Irving Berlin's Yiddish dialect song, "Goodbye, Becky Cohen." Ziegfeld had signed her for $75.00 a week, but the morning after her successful debut in the *Follies* he tore up the contract and gave her one befitting a star. She remained a Ziegfeld star for many years thereafter, appearing in every edition (except one) between 1910 and 1923, and after that in the Shubert sponsored *Ziegfeld Follies* in 1934 and 1936. Her facial contortions, her gawky gestures, her expressive eyes all made her rendition of comedy numbers unique. Her best numbers in the various editions of the *Follies* were Irving Berlin's "Ephrapham" and "I'm a Vamp from East Broadway," (lyrics by Bert Kalmar and Harry Ruby), "Second Hand Rose" (Grant Clarke—James F. Hanley), and "I'm an Indian" (Blanche Merrill—Leo Edwards). In 1921 she stepped out of her comedic character to sing "Mon Homme" or "My Man," a French ballad adapted for America by Channing Pollock. The song had been intended for the American debut of Mistinguett, but when Ziegfeld decided not to use her in his *Follies* he shrewdly turned the song over to Fanny Brice, since the ballad pointed up so poignantly

Miss Brice's then ill-fated marriage with the convicted gambler, Nicky Arnstein, to whom she remained devoted even after he was imprisoned for fraud. Leaning against a lamppost, and dressed in tattered clothes, her throbbing presentation of "My Man," created a furor in the audience, as Ziegfeld knew full well it would.

In signing up Eddie Cantor, Ziegfeld acquired a show business nobody who had made appearances in vaudeville without causing any storms and, in 1916, appeared in *Canary Cottage*, a musical produced on the West Coast. In the *Midnight Frolics*, a revue Ziegfeld was producing atop the New Amsterdam Theater in 1916, Cantor presented a Hawaiian type number, "Oh, How She Could Yacki, Hacki, Wicki, Wacki, Woo" (Stanley Murphy and Charles McCarron), preceding it with some stage business that caught the fascinated interest of the audience. He invited three gentlemen from the audience to the stage; they turned out to be (no less), William Randolph Hearst, Diamond Jim Brady and Charles Dillingham. They were asked to draw a card from a deck and hold it overhead. Each did so, and while the three men were thus frozen into this posture, Cantor proceeded to sing one chorus after another of his Hawaiian song. When Cantor finished singing, he took the cards from the upheld hands, quietly thanked the men, and asked them to return to their seats. The stunt brought howls from the audience and stopped the show. Ziegfeld, who was notorious for sending telegrams even when the recipient was right at hand, sent one that night to Cantor: "You'll be here a long time," it read.

An orphan boy in New York's East Side, where he was born in 1892, Cantor was raised by a doting grandmother who earned a threadbare existence as a peddler. Capturing first prize in the amateur night contest at Miner's whetted Eddie's already voracious appetite for the stage. During the next few years he worked as a singing comedian for a burlesque company, was a singing waiter in Concy Island, and was one of the talented boys in Gus Edwards' schoolboy act in vaudeville. It was with Gus Edwards that Cantor first sang, "Ida, Sweet as Apple Cider" (Eddie Leonard), mimicking the way Eddie Leonard sang it. For the remainder of his long career, Eddie Cantor kept singing that number, as a tribute to his wife, Ida.

It did not take Cantor long to move down from the roof of the New Amsterdam into the theater itself, and from the *Frolics* to the *Ziegfeld Follies*. He did so in 1917 when his audience, each evening, insisted that he give twelve or more repeats of "That's the Kind of a Baby for Me" (Alfred Harrison—Jack Egan), which became his first recording, on the Victor label. He was now a full-fledged Ziegfeld star and he remained that not only through several editions of the *Ziegfeld Follies*, but also in a few musicals which Ziegfeld mounted for him, the most successful of which were *Kid Boots* (1923) and *Whoopee* (1928).

With eyes virtually popping out of their sockets and through the large, white, horn-rimmed glasses (*sans* glass) and clapping his hands as he jumped kangaroo-like back and forth across the stage, Eddie Cantor delighted the audiences of the *Ziegfeld Follies* when he sang Irving Berlin's "You'd Be Surprised" in 1919, and "My Blue Heaven" (George Whiting—Walter Donaldson) in 1927. "You'd Be Surprised," which Cantor recorded for Emerson in December 1919, became Cantor's first disk to sell about a million copies. It also enjoyed a million-copy sale in sheet music within a year of publication, and sold over one hundred and fifty thousand piano rolls. In presenting "My Blue Heaven" Cantor personalized it by interpolating into its lyrics several lines about his own five daughters—the "crowd" in his own blue heaven.

Most of the music for the *Ziegfeld Follies* during its twenty-four years on Broadway was fashioned by such reputable Tin Pan Alley craftsmen as Raymond Hubbell (1879–1954), Louis A. Hirsch (1887–1924) and Dave Stamper (1883–1963). These men could always be counted upon to produce skillfully and with despatch the kind of functional music needed for the production numbers and solos to suit the individual talents of the stars. Dave Stamper wrote his first song for the *Ziegfeld Follies* in 1912; "Daddy Has a Sweetheart and Mother Is Her Name" (Gene Buck). After 1912 there was hardly an edition of the *Follies* without some Stamper songs. One of his most opulent scores was written with Louis A. Hirsch, to Gene Buck's lyrics, for the 1922 edition. There Gilda Gray (who helped popularize the shimmy) regularly released a storm of approval in the audience with "It's Getting Dark on Old Broadway," Mary Eaton sang "Throw Me a Kiss," and Evelyn Law and Andrew Tombes were heard in "My Rambler Rose." Another melodic embellishment that year was " 'Neath the South Sea Moon." For the 1919 edition, Stamper wrote "Tulip Time," and "Sweet Sixteen," and for 1921, "Sally, Won't You Come Back" and "Raggedy Ann." All of Stamper's songs were to Buck's lyrics.

Louis A. Hirsch did the songs for the editions of 1915, 1916, 1918 and 1922. In 1915, Ina Claire and Bernard Granville sang "Hello, Frisco." "I Want that Star" was heard in 1916, "Garden of My Dreams" and "Syncopated Tune" in 1918, and "Hello, Hello, Hello" in 1922, all once again to lyrics by Gene Buck.

Raymond Hubbell provided the basic scores for the editions between 1911 and 1914 inclusive and that of 1917. The following numbers, lyrics by Buck, had special interest: "Take Care, Little Girl," sung by Bessie McCoy in 1911, "Romantic Girl" and "The Broadway Glide" in 1912, "In the Beautiful Garden of Girls" and "Just You and Me" in 1917.

The name of Gene Buck has been mentioned again and again. Besides being the principal lyricist for the *Ziegfeld Follies*, he also often wrote, or assisted in writing, the books. Buck had his beginnings in Tin Pan Alley as a designer of sheet music covers. "Daddy Has a Sweetheart and Mother Is Her Name," to Stamper's music, was not only his first lyric to be heard in the *Ziegfeld Follies*, but actually the first he ever wrote. This began his seventeen-year association with Ziegfeld, which ended with the *Ziegfeld Follies of 1931*.

At various times, Jerome Kern, Victor Herbert, Rudolf Friml, Gus Edwards and Irving Berlin wrote songs for the *Ziegfeld Follies*. After placing many of his songs as interpolations from 1910 on, Irving Berlin finally wrote the basic score in 1919, and again in 1920 and 1927. His "A Pretty Girl Is Like a Melody" was introduced by John Steel in 1919 for a production number in which the girls represented classical musical compositions. It became a theme song for the *Ziegfeld Follies* after that, and also for various fashion shows and beauty contests. This 1919 edition also included two other Berlin staples: "You'd Be Surprised," made famous by Eddie Cantor and "Mandy." "Mandy" had been written for Irving Berlin's World War I all-soldier revue, *Yip, Yip, Yaphank*. Placed in the *Ziegfeld Follies* after that, it was used for a first-act finale recalling the old-time minstrel show, in which Marilyn Miller was dressed as the minstrel, George Primrose, and where Van and Schenck sang the song.

Songs, like stars, were made in the *Follies*. In his initial season with Ziegfeld, Bert Williams sang his by now firmly established trademark, "Nobody." But in later editions, Williams introduced and popularized new numbers, among these being Irving Berlin's "Woodman, Woodman, Spare That Tree" in 1911 and "Dat's Harmony" (Grant Clarke—Bert Williams) and "My Landlady" (F. E. Mierich and James T. Bryan—Bert Williams) in 1912. In 1914 he performed a routine that became as celebrated as his rendition of "Nobody," his poker pantomime.

Lillian Lorraine (whom Ziegfeld once described as the most beautiful woman he had ever seen) cruised about in a toy flying machine over the heads of her audience scattering flowers as she sang "Up, Up, Up in My Aeroplane" (Edward Madden—Gus Edwards) in

1909. Three years later she introduced "Row, Row, Row" (William Jerome—James V. Monaco). "Peg O' My Heart" (Alfred Bryan—Fred Fisher) and "Rebecca of Sunnybrook Farm" (Seymour Brown—Albert Gumble) were both introduced in 1913 by José Collins, an English singer. Gallagher and Shean introduced a topical song, "Gallagher and Shean," which they themselves wrote. With it they practically stole the show in 1922, though the same edition also boasted "Oh, Gee, Oh Gosh, Oh Golly I'm in Love" (Olsen and Johnson—Ernest Breuer) sung by Eddie Cantor.

Taking their cue from the master, several producers became wealthy putting on annual revues of their own, obviously imitative of the *Ziegfeld Follies*. The Shuberts began producing their annual *The Passing Show* at the Winter Garden in 1912, most of its music written by Louis A. Hirsch. Jean Schwartz wrote the principal songs for the 1913 edition and between 1914 and 1924 Sigmund Romberg was its principal composer.

In their bid to rival Ziegfeld, the Shuberts acquired some of the stars of the *Ziegfeld Follies* for *The Passing Show*: Marilyn Miller, Lillian Lorraine, José Collins, Ed Wynn. Others became stars in *The Passing Show*: Willie and Eugene Howard, Charlotte Greenwood, Walter Woolf King, Jefferson de Angelis, Bessie Clayton, George Jessel and Fred and Adele Astaire.

The Astaires started out as stage child prodigies. They were both born in Omaha, Nebraska, their original name being Austerlitz—Adele in 1898, Fred in 1899. At a tender age, they were propelled into dancing school by their mother. Fred was seven, and Adele eight, when they made their debut in the theater, in a vaudeville act billed as "Juvenile Artists Presenting an Electrical Musical Toe-Dancing Novelty" which played the Orpheum circuit for twenty weeks and brought them as far west as Los Angeles. They tried to make the New York stage that year (1906) but were barred by legislation forbidding the exploitation of children. When they finally did come to New York a few years later they were allowed to make their debut at a benefit show at the Broadway Theater. In 1911 they were booked for Proctor's Fifth Avenue Theater for a comedy sketch, "A Rainy Day," written, staged and produced by Ned Wayburn, in which they proved a dud. Within the next few years, however, as a dancing duo, they outgrew small-time bookings in the Midwest to return to the Orpheum circuit as headliners. They became so famous by 1917 that in that year they were featured in a Broadway musical, *Over the Top*, with a score by Sigmund Romberg. It was here that they made their bow in the legitimate theater. Though this show was a failure, Fred and Adele Astaire made their presence felt with their original dance routines. "One of the prettiest features of the show," reported Lewis Sherwin in the *Globe*, "is the dancing of the two Astaires. The girl, a light, sprite-like little creature, has really an exquisite floating style in her capering, while the young man combines eccentric agility with humor." On the strength of this performance, the Astaires were signed for *The Passing Show of 1918*. "In an evening in which there was an abundance of good dance," wrote Heywood Broun in his review in the *Tribune*, "Fred Astaire stood out. He and his partner, Adele Astaire, made the show pause early in the evening with a beautiful, careless, loose-limbed dance, in which the right foot never seemed to know just what the left foot was going to do, or cared, either. It almost seemed as if the two young people had been poured into the dance." In the *Evening World*, Charles Darnton called the Astaires "the hit of the show."

The strongest musical numbers from the various editions of *The Passing Show* did not come from the composers of the basic scores, but were interpolations. In the very first edition, the standout song was Irving Berlin's "The Ragtime Jockey Man," introduced by Willie Howard. The first real hit from the succeeding editions were Harry Carroll's "By the Beautiful Sea" (Harold Atteridge) and his "The Trail of the Lonesome Pine" (Ballard Mac-

Donald) in *The Passing Show of 1914*. In 1916 came "Pretty Baby" (Gus Kahn—Tony Jackson and Egbert Van Alstyne) which profited from Dolly Hackett's winsome rendition. The greatest hit song of all to come out of *The Passing Show* was "Smiles" (J. Will Callahan—Lee S. Roberts), sung in 1918 by Nell Carrington and a female chorus.

"Smiles" was born at a convention of music dealers in Chicago attended by Lee Roberts, a composer. One of the speakers there expounded on the subject of the importance of a smile in business dealings. This led Roberts to remark casually: "There are smiles that make us happy, and smiles that make us blue." That day he wrote a melody appropriate to this thought and dispatched it to J. Will Callahan for the lyrics. When "Smiles" was turned down by publishers in Tin Pan Alley, the songwriters formed their own company to issue it, then sought out several dance bands to plug it. It was also placed strategically in *The Passing Show of 1918*. The song caught on quickly—possibly because it was a welcome antidote to the problems and stresses of World War I in which America was then thoroughly involved. Within six months of its publication, "Smiles"—by then a Remick publication—sold over two million copies of sheet music.

Not until 1922 did *The Passing Show* come up with a song to match the success of "Pretty Baby" and "Smiles." This was also an interpolation, Walter Donaldson's "Carolina in the Morning" (Gus Kahn). Bill Frawley had introduced it in vaudeville, but Willie and Eugene Howard, in *The Passing Show*, were mainly responsible for its immense success.

The last edition of *The Passing Show* was produced in 1924. By then, the Shuberts were mounting two other annual revues, the *Greenwich Village Follies* and *Artists and Models*. In addition, George White was presenting the *Scandals*, Earl Carroll, the *Vanities*, and Sam Harris and Irving Berlin, the *Music Box Revue*.

7

Both the extravaganza and the operetta remained popular after 1900—the extravaganza until shortly after World War I, and the operetta for another decade after that.

One of the highlights of the early 1900s helped to open a new theater in New York, the Majestic, on Columbus Circle, on January 21, 1903. The offering was an extravaganza, the musical fantasy *The Wizard of Oz*. L. Frank Baum's book and lyrics were based on his own popular children's novel *The Wonderful Wizard of Oz*, published three years earlier. The music was a collaborative effort by A. Baldwin Sloane (1872–1926) and Paul Tietjens (1877–1943). This was a child's world evoked with elaborate stage pictures and stunning stage effects. The emphasis was on the stage effects; for example, the cyclone that opened the production and a scene crowded with poppies in which the poppies turn out to be girls. But comedy was not lacking, projected mainly by Fred Stone and David Montgomery as Scarecrow and Tin Woodman respectively here achieving stardom for the first time. The main song came neither from Sloane nor Tietjens but was an interpolation, a nautical comedy number, "Hurray for Baffin's Bay" (Vincent Bryan—Theodore F. Morse), sung by Montgomery and Stone.

Extravaganza acquired a sumptuous new home in 1905, the Hippodrome Theater on Sixth Avenue and Forth-third Street. For about two decades, extravaganzas were produced there. Almost two million dollars were spent in making the Hippodrome the largest and best equipped theater in the world, large enough to accommodate five thousand patrons. Its immense stage had provisions for some six hundred performers and fifty animals.

The Hippodrome opened on April 12, 1905, with *A Yankee Circus on Mars*, an elaborate circus show. This was followed by a ballet. After the intermission, a spectacular war drama was presented in two tableaux, *Andersonville*.

After that, the Hippodrome boasted some of the largest casts and the most startling stage effects on view anywhere. A naval battle was reproduced in *Battle of Port Arthur* (1908) and an airplane battle (*The Battle in the Skies*) in *Sporting Days* (1908). A tornado and an earthquake brought drama to *Under Many Flags* (1912), while incidents from the French Revolution, the Civil War, and several other military engagements were staged in *Wars of the World* (1914). Other effects and attractions were sui generis for the Hippodrome, such as spraying perfume throughout the theater, a mystifying tank act in which bespangled girls descended into a forty-foot tank filled with water without reappearing, a Fifth Avenue fashion parade, a skater's ballet in St. Moritz, Switzerland, a rush hour scene at Grand Central Station, stampeding herds of deer and elephants—the stage wonders seemed endless. Stars of international fame added luster to these spectacular goings-on: the clowns Marcelline and Toto; the famed Russian ballet dancers, Pavlova, Fokine and Fokina; Sousa and his band; the opera tenor Orville Harrold; the swimmer Annette Kellerman; Houdini, the fabulous magician and "escape artist."

The kind of entertainment the Hippodrome dispensed required functional music, rather than songs, to serve the varied demands of the spectacles and divertissements. This music was composed from 1905 through 1914 by Manuel Klein (1876–1919), who also served as the theater's music director, and by Raymond Hubbell who contributed the scores between 1915 and the last Hippodrome extravaganza, *Better Times*, in 1922, with the exception of 1918 and 1921.

One hit song, however, did come from the Hippodrome, though more by chance than by design, "Poor Butterfly" (John Golden—Raymond Hubbell). In 1916, an Oriental singer had been engaged for *The Big Show*. Under the misconception that the singer was Tamaka Miura, a Japanese prima donna who had received considerable publicity for her performance in Puccini's *Madama Butterfly*, Hubbell and Golden wrote a popular song inspired by the Puccini heroine, Cio-Cio-San. But the contracted singer turned out not to be Japanese, but a Chinese American who had come out of vaudeville rather than opera. The song stayed in the show however, and the Chinese singer performed it—very badly as it turned out. Within a few days she was removed from the cast and replaced by Sophie Bernard. Miss Bernard's poignant rendition put the song over solidly. It went on from the stage of the Hippodrome to sweep the country and sell several million copies of sheet music. Later on, as a successful producer, John Golden recalled in his autobiography the phenomenal success of his song. " 'Poor Butterfly' was strummed, hummed, whistled and wept over by as many voices and hands as there were pianos, ukuleles, typewriters and tenors in the land. . . ."

Extravaganza found a second home on Broadway in 1911, in the Winter Garden at 51st Street, whose rich history from its very beginnings was recalled on April 20, 1975, at the presentation of the Tony Awards telecast over the ABC network. At the Winter Garden song and singer were glorified as well as spectacle. Built by the Shuberts to house their musical productions, the Winter Garden opened on March 20, 1911, with a triple bill. First came a Spanish ballet, then a three-scene Chinese opera, and finally, *La Belle Paree*, an American extravaganza with a French setting and characters.

Stage history was made that evening in *La Belle Paree*. Its music was written by a young composer whose songs until then had been interpolated into numerous Broadway musicals but who was now contributing the major portion of a stage score for the first time. He was Jerome Kern. His five numbers, however, gave no indication that within a few seasons he would become one of the most gifted and productive composers of the Broadway theater. But about Jerome Kern—more, much more later.

There was still another Broadway debut in *La Belle Paree* of no small moment, that of Al Jolson. Here he proved decisively that he was star material. The son of a synagogue cantor in Washington, D. C., Al Jolson (born Asa Yoelson in St. Petersburg, Russia, in 1886) became stagestruck in early boyhood. He wormed his way to a gallery seat at the Bijou Theater in Washington where Eddie Leonard was the headliner. After Eddie Leonard had completed a verse and chorus of one of his favorites, "Ida, Sweet as Apple Cider," he invited the audience to join him in singing it. Al sang, his sweet, high-pitched voice soaring over the mumble of the rest of the audience. His performance was greeted with an outburst of applause. This was Al's first contact with an audience, with which he was to carry on a love affair that lasted all his life.

Still a boy, he found jobs in burlesque houses and small-time vaudeville theaters. By the time he was twenty-two he was getting star treatment with one of the last of the great minstrel show troupes, the Lew Dockstader Minstrels, where he sang "It's a Long Way Back to Dear Old Mammy's Knees," his first try at a "mammy song." When the troupe appeared in New York at the Fifth Avenue Theater in 1909, *Variety* took notice of the way in which audiences responded to him by saying: "Haven't seen a demonstration for a single act, or any act for that matter, as was given Al Jolson."

That same year he was featured at Hammerstein's Victoria in New York. Here, for the first time, he indulged in a practice he would pursue through the years: departing from the set routine of an act to indulge in impromptu remarks to the audience and singing whatever songs struck his fancy at the moment. Already he was the cocksure performer convinced of his own extraordinary ability, and supremely confident of his capacity to hold audiences. Already he had the bravado to do his thing as his instincts dictated. On his opening night at the Victoria he stopped midway in his act and called for the houselights. Stepping to the front of the stage, and addressing his audience as if it were a friend in his living room, he said, "Ya know folks, this is the happiest night of my life. . . . I want to sing and sing and sing. . . . Ya wanna lissen?" Stimulated by the audience's enthusiastic response, Jolson went through one number after another—comedy songs, ragtime songs, sentimental songs.

He did the same thing one night at the Winter Garden in *La Belle Paree*, transforming disaster into triumph for the Winter Garden. The first night audience was so bored by *La Belle Paree* that some made a retreat out of the theater long before the final curtain. Al Jolson, in blackface as Erastus Sparkler, singing Kern's "Paris Is a Paradise for Coons" (Edward Madden) failed to dispel the monotony of the proceedings. The following morning the critics were annihilating. At the next performance, a Thursday matinee, Jolson decided to dispense with the nonsense of the rehearsed show to do those things he did best, in his own way. He interrupted the production to make some impromptu comments about the way the critics had treated the show that morning. "Lots of brave folks out there," he remarked good-humoredly as an aside. "Either that—or they can't read." He stopped for a moment to let the chuckle subside. Then he added, "Come to think of it, there's a lot of brave folks up here on the stage." Increased laughter. He then asked the audience if it preferred to hear him sing instead of watching the rest of the show. An affirmative answer sent Jolson into his own act, singing his heart out to his audience—the songs *he* liked, not the songs he was required to sing. The newspapers the next day took note of this innovation. Crowds began swarming to the Winter Garden. And that is the way it would be for the rest of the decade whenever he appeared—crowds overflowing the Winter Garden just to see and hear Jolson.

Before the end of that year, Jolson was starred in another Winter Garden production, *Vera Violetta*. Once again this was just one third of a triple bill. But now it was Jolson in

Vera Violetta who attracted the crowds. As a blackface waiter, Claude, in an extravaganza with a European setting, he was given more opportunities to sing, tell jokes and speak asides to the audience in his inimitable manner. There were others in that show worthy of attention. Gaby Deslys came from Paris for her American debut, in a number written expressly for her, "The Gaby Glide" (Harry A. Pilcer—Louis A. Hirsch). And José Collins resuscitated "Ta-ra-ra-bom-der-e." Attractive as these two were, it was Jolson who completely captured the limelight—Jolson interpolating songs not in the basic score by Edmund Eysler and Louis A. Hirsch, songs like "That Haunting Melody" (George M. Cohan) and "Rum Tum Tiddle" (William Jerome—Jean Schwartz) which were the first numbers Jolson recorded, for Victor on December 22, 1911.

In his next Winter Garden production, *The Whirl of Society*, early in 1912, Jolson created a character who would return in subsequent extravaganzas, Gus, a naive, often blundering black man always doomed to be the underdog in a succession of adventures usually in exotic or unusual places. *The Whirl of Society* was once more one of three attractions in the evening's entertainment, and once again it was Jolson who was the magnet attracting audiences to the theater. For this production, he prevailed on the Shuberts to build him a runway leading from the stage to the rear of the theater down the middle aisle, so that he could run up and down singing his songs in an even closer contact with his audiences. In this way he introduced Irving Berlin's "Ragtime Sextet" (with the collaboration of several other stars), "My Sumuran Girl" (Harold Atteridge—Louis A. Hirsch) and "On the Mississippi" (Ballard MacDonald—Arthur Fields and Harry Carroll), the last becoming one of the hit songs of the year because of Jolson.

In recognition of Jolson's mounting popularity, and at his own urging, the Shuberts inaugurated Sunday evening "concerts" at the Winter Garden early in 1912 where Jolson was allowed to hold sway as king in his own palace. Not only did his army of admirers flock to the Winter Garden, but also his colleagues came to watch, listen, study and envy. He appeared on those nights in white-face. When he came on the stage "it is as if an electric current has been run along the wires under the seats where hats are stuck. The house comes to a tumultuous attention." Those lines were written by Robert Benchley in *Life* about a Jolson performance in an extravaganza, but they certainly apply equally to his Sunday evening concerts. "He speaks, rolls his eyes, compresses his lips, and it is all over. You are a member of the Al Jolson Association. He trembles his underlip, and your heart breaks with a loud snap. He signs a banal song and you totter out to send a night letter to your mother. Such a giving off of vitality, personality, charm, and whatever all those words are, results from a Jolson performance." He would remove his jacket, loosen collar and tie, and while singing would run up and down his beloved runway addressing himself to his audience and making each of them feel that Jolson was singing to him alone.

In 1913, the Shuberts gave Jolson a seven-year contract guaranteeing him $1,000 a week for a thirty-five week period and a bonus of ten thousand dollars. (The rest of the year Jolson played the vaudeville circuit at a salary of $2,500 a week.) The triple bill format was permanently abandoned at the Winter Garden in favor of extravaganzas occupying the entire evening, tailor-made to suit Jolson's personality and talents. With a sublime irrelevance which delighted his audiences, he would frequently step out of character in the final half hour of the show, to become Al Jolson instead of Gus. He monopolized the limelight and the attention of his audience, reminding his listeners from time to time that "you ain't heard nothin' yet."

The music for *The Honeymoon Express* (1913) was written by Jean Schwartz (lyrics by Harold Atteridge), but as usual with Jolson, the songs making the strongest impression were those that were interpolated. One of these was "You Made Me Love You" (Joseph McCarthy—James V. Monaco).

One evening, Jolson was suffering from an ingrown toenail. To relieve the pressure on his ailing foot he went down on one knee. Then he threw out his arms toward his audience as if in a huge embrace. This gesture proved so effective that from then on Jolson used it with other songs, particularly his "mammy songs," and made it a gimmick which all Jolson mimics would adopt.

Jolson was starred in *Robinson Crusoe, Jr.* in 1916 (where, for the first time, he was billed as "the world's greatest entertainer"), in *Sinbad* (1918) and *Bombo* (1921). Into each he continued to interpolate songs other than those Sigmund Romberg (with Atteridge as lyricist) had written for these productions. Sometimes these interpolations were used during the Broadway run of the show, sometimes out of town, and many were first tried out at the Sunday evening concerts. More often than not the songs became giant hits. The Jolson delivery proved such a guarantee of success that publishers bribed him to use their numbers with valuable gifts, or cash, or a cut in the song's royalties. Invariably, this investment proved gilt-edged.

He sang "Where the Black-Eyed Susans Grow" (Dave Radford—Richard A. Whiting), "Yacka Hula Hickey Dula" (E. Ray Goetz and Joe Young—Pete Wendling) and "Where Did Robinson Crusoe Go with Friday on Saturday Night?" (Sam M. Lewis and Joe Young—George W. Meyer) in *Robinson Crusoe, Jr.* In *Sinbad* he sang "Rock-a-bye Your Baby with a Dixie Melody" (Sam M. Lewis and Joe Young—Jean Schwartz), "My Mammy" (Sam M. Lewis and Joe Young—Walter Donaldson), and "Swanee" (Irving Caesar—George Gershwin). Into *Bombo* he brought "California, Here I Come" (Al Jolson and B. G. De Sylva—Joseph Meyer), "Toot, Toot, Tootsie" (Gus Kahn and Ernie Erdman—Dan Russo), "I'm Goin' South" (Abner Silver—Harry Woods), "April Showers" (B. G. De Sylva—Louis Silvers) and "Yoo-Hoo" (B. G. De Sylva—Al Jolson).

8

When Victor Herbert returned to the writing of operettas in 1903, after a three-year layoff, he sought to exploit the success of *The Wizard of Oz* by writing music for a similar kind of extravaganza. It was *Babes in Toyland*, book and lyrics by Glen MacDonough. The setting was Mother Goose land; its colorful characters stepped out of the pages of nursery rhymes and fairy tales. Opening on October 13, 1903, *Babes in Toyland* represented for Herbert not merely a return to the stage but also to stage success. In fact, it became his most successful operetta up to that time, and one of a handful of his durable operetta creations. "The songs, the dances, the processions, the fairies, the toys, the spiders, and the bears!" wrote the eminent critic, James Gibbons Huneker, upon its premiere. "Think of them all set in the midst of really amazing scenery, ingenious and brilliant . . . and all accompanied with music a hundred times better than is customary in shows of this sort." A musical highlight was the second-act instrumental piece, "The March of the Toys" that opened with a piquant fanfare for toy trumpet. Equally appealing were "I Can't Do the Sum," sung by the schoolchildren as they tap out the rhythm with chalk on their slates, and the tuneful "Toyland." In addition, Herbert once again demonstrated his gift for parody when, in "Rock-a-bye Baby" he imitated the styles of various composers of divergent idioms from Donizetti to Sousa.

Before 1903 was over, Herbert had another operetta on Broadway, *Babette*, whose sole claim to interest rests in the fact that it consummated the transfer of Fritzi Scheff from grand opera to operetta. Since *Babette* was a failure, Fritzi Scheff had good reason to regret her decision to abandon the Metropolitan Opera for the Broadway theater. But two years later, on December 25, 1905, she was crowned a queen of operetta in a new Victor Herbert work, *Mlle. Modiste*, written expressly for her. Cast as Fifi, she played the part of a humble employe in a milliner's shop on the Rue de la Paix in Paris who becomes a famous prima donna and in the process also captures the man she has long loved, but who, up to then, has proved elusive.

Fritzi Scheff gave such a winning performance that from then on she and the role of Fifi became synonymous. The song triumph of the operetta was that immortal waltz, "Kiss Me Again" (Henry Blossom). As originally planned in *Mlle. Modiste*, "Kiss Me Again" was meant to be satiric rather than sentimental. It was one of several refrains for a number entitled "If I Were on the Stage" in which Fifi demonstrates her versatility by singing various types of songs: a gavotte, a polonaise, a waltz and so forth. Each was actually a caricature of the genre. But such was the acclaim given to "Kiss Me Again" on opening night that the following day Herbert decided to lift the melody out of its context, to precede it with a specially written verse, and to use it as a self-contained love ballad. This waltz, more than any single element in the operetta, was responsible for making Fritzi Scheff a star, and *Mlle. Modiste* a success. Two other numbers in the score with lyrics by Henry Blossom, though obscured by the popularity of "Kiss Me Again," deserve mention. One is a vigorous tune, "The Mascot of the Troop," assigned to Fifi and a male chorus in which the "Marseillaise" is briefly quoted. The other is a comedy number, "I Want What I Want When I Want It."

In 1906, Herbert wrote *The Red Mill* to exploit the comedy talent of the stars of *The Wizard of Oz*, David Montgomery and Fred Stone. Cast as Kid Conner and Con Kidder, respectively, they were two Americans stranded at an inn in Holland who become involved in the romantic entanglements of Gretchen, the daughter of the Burgomaster.

This was one of Herbert's best scores, overflowing with wonderful songs, all to Henry Blossom's lyrics. The happiest melodic inspirations were a duet of Gretchen and Van Damm, "The Isle of Our Dreams," and Gretchen's tender "Moonbeams" as she pines for the man she loves. In a lighter vein is "Every Day Is Ladies' Day" and the spirited "The Streets of New York," closing the operetta.

This score also included a Herbert song to which, to this day, mystery clings. In the wedding scene for Gretchen and the Governor of Zeeland, Con and Kid come disguised as Italian street merchants in their effort to disrupt the ceremony. They sing "Good-a-bye, John." The words of the first refrain and the melody of the refrain, as well as the title of the song itself, are the same as those in a song by Harry Williams and Egbert Van Alstyne published a year earlier by Jerome H. Remick. Did Herbert stoop to outright plagiarism? It is difficult to suspect this of one as gifted as Herbert, who never lacked for musical invention. Besides, neither the songwriting team of Williams and Van Alstyne nor the publishing house of Remick made any move to sue Herbert or to prevent the performance or publication of the song. If this was plagiarism—as all evidence indicates—it was probably done in all innocence, a fact apparently recognized and respected by the aggrieved parties.

Like *Mlle. Modiste*, *Naughty Marietta* (1910) was written with a specific star in mind, Emma Trentini, a member of Oscar Hammerstein's Manhattan Opera House Company. The setting of her operetta debut was eighteenth-century New Orleans, to which Marietta, a highborn Neapolitan lady played by Miss Trentini, had come to avoid an undesirable marriage. A song becomes the catalyst between her and the dashing Captain Dick Warrington who has fallen in love with her.

The song that serves as a pivot on which the plot revolves, and which helps to consummate the love of Marietta and Captain Warrington, is "Ah, Sweet Mystery of Life" (Rida Johnson Young). Herbert first wanted to use the melody of its refrain as an instrumental intermezzo. But Orville Harrold, an opera tenor playing Dick Warrington, recognized its potential as a ballad and urged Herbert to have a lyric written for it. This was destined to become the most popular song in the operetta and one of Herbert's most resounding hits. When it was published, the house of Witmark was in such financial distress that for a time it seemed it would collapse into bankruptcy. But the giant sheet music sale of "Ah, Sweet Mystery of Life" brought salvation to the Witmarks.

The score of *Naughty Marietta* contained three other Herbert song classics, all to Rida Johnson Young's lyrics. "I'm Falling in Love with Someone" is a ballad in which Dick Warrington expresses his love for Marietta. In "Italian Street Song," Marietta recalls nostalgically her life in Naples. "'Neath the Southern Moon" is a romantic, idyllic number, and "Tramp! Tramp! Tramp!" a rousing marching tune.

After *Naughty Marietta*, Herbert seemed incapable of recapturing the formula that up to then had made him so successful. *Sweethearts* (1913) had some delightful music and a tender love story set in old Bruges, in Belgium. Herbert himself felt that the finest score he ever wrote was that for *Eileen* (1917) which included one of his most beautiful love ballads, "Thine Alone" (Henry Blossom). "Thine Alone" became so popular that of all Herbert's songs its sheet music and record sales were rivaled only by "Ah, Sweet Mystery of Life." But *Eileen* was a box-office failure.

His operettas kept on appearing on Broadway up to the end of his life. He also wrote music for special productions, including various editions of the *Ziegfeld Follies* between 1918 and 1923. He was still very much in demand, still regarded with veneration by his peers. More than that, he still had his own special gift for composing appealing, sentimental numbers such as "Thine Alone" and "A Kiss in the Dark" (B. G. De Sylva), heard in *Orange Blossoms* (1922). But his sun as an operetta composer had set. He belonged to the age of the waltz. This was the new day of jazz, and new styles found new composers. "My day is over," he told a friend. "They are forgetting poor old Herbert."

In 1924, while working on special numbers for a new edition of the *Ziegfeld Follies* Herbert fell suddenly ill, and collapsed in his doctor's office. He died of a heart attack on May 26, 1924, in New York.

His death came a few years too soon. Had he lived another decade he would have heard his music played more often (through that new medium, radio) than that of any other American, living or dead. Had he lived another dozen years he would have witnessed revivals on Broadway of *Babes in Toyland* and *Mlle. Modiste*, whose music inspired new accolades from the critics. Had he lived two decades more he would have witnessed the longest run ever enjoyed by a Herbert operetta—531 performances of a revival of *The Red Mill* on Broadway in 1945. He would also have seen some of his famous operettas transferred to the screen (*Babes in Toyland* twice) and found his own career glorified in song, dance and story in the motion picture musical *The Great Victor Herbert* (1939). He also would have heard one of the greatest coloratura sopranos of our times, Beverly Sills, recording an album of his most famous melodies, with the support of the London Symphony Orchestra under André Kostelanetz, in an Angel album released in 1975.

Victor Herbert died thinking of himself as a has-been. But he actually became a classic.

While Herbert was in his heyday, the Broadway stage was enriched with the music of several other important composers of operettas. The best were Gustave Kerker, Karl Hoschna, Gustav Luders, Ivan Caryll, Rudolf Friml and Sigmund Romberg.

Kerker was born in Hereford, Germany, on February 28, 1857. He came to the United States when he was ten. Before writing the music for *The Cadets* (1879), his first operetta, he played in and led several theater orchestras. Upon coming to New York he was engaged as conductor at the Casino Theater.

His first Broadway operetta was *The Pearl of Pekin* (1888); his first success, *Castles in the Air* (1890), in which De Wolf Hopper had his first starring role, supported by Della Fox. Kerker's best remembered production opened at the Casino Theater on September 28, 1897—*The Belle of New York*, in which Edna May became an overnight star as a Salvation Army lass who falls in love with the son of a New York vice crusader. *The Belle of New York* proved far more successful in London than in New York, playing at the Shaftesbury Theater for almost seven hundred performances. The musical numbers that helped make Edna May the toast of both New York and London were "She Is the Belle of New York" and "They All Follow Me," lyrics by Hugh Morton. Kerker died in New York City on June 29, 1923.

Gustav Luders, the composer of *The Prince of Pilsen* (1902) was also of German extraction, born in Bremen on December 13, 1868. After receiving his musical training in Germany he came to Milwaukee in 1899 where he found employment as the musical director of several theater and light opera companies. Charles K. Harris induced him to come to Chicago. He worked as arranger and orchestrator for Witmark's Chicago branch, where he made an excellent piano arrangement of Barney Fagan's ragtime classic, "My Gal Is a Highborn Lady" when that number was first published.

Luders' first stage work, a comic opera, *Little Robinson Crusoe*, was produced in 1899. Henry W. Savage then contracted him to write the music for *The Burgomaster* (1900), book by Frank Pixley. This was so well received when it opened in Chicago that it made permanent the collaboration of Pixley and Luders and encouraged some critics to refer to Luders as "another Victor Herbert." Its principal song was "The Tale of the Kangaroo," the first of several Pixley-Luders songs using "The Tale" in its title. Pixley and Luders later completed the songs for *King Dodo* (1902), starring Raymond Hitchock as the ruler of Dodoland who seeks the return of his youth so that he can win the love of fair Angelina. There were three excellent numbers, the ballad "Diana," the march "The Lad Who Leads," and "The Tale of a Bumble Bee." In 1903 *The Prince of Pilsen* became their crowning achievement. Its story revolves around a Cincinnati brewer who is mistaken for a prince on the French Riviera, a status he enjoys to the full. The actual prince is more than satisfied at this turn of events for it allows him to engage incognito in a romance with the brewer's daughter. Its principal songs were "Heidelberg Stein Song," "The Tale of the Seashell," and one of the most successful of all Luders' songs, the waltz duet, "The Message of the Violet."

By 1913, Luders had written the music for thirteen operettas. The number thirteen proved fatal. *Somewhere Else*, produced on January 20, 1913, closed after three performances because of the hostile reaction of the critics. Luders died of a heart attack one day after the operetta closed.

Karl Hoschna's triumph came with *Madame Sherry* (1910). A native of Bohemia, where he was born on August 16, 1877, Hoschna received his musical training at the Vienna Conservatory. In 1896 he came to the United States and played the oboe in an orchestra conducted by Victor Herbert. He then worked for M. Witmark and Sons as arranger and orchestrator. In the early twentieth century he wrote three operettas, but none of these reached Broadway.

In 1908, Charles Dickson, an actor and playwright, acquired the rights to *Incog*, a farce he planned to adapt into an operetta. He asked Isidore Witmark to recommend a composer and librettist. For the music, Witmark suggested Hoschna, while for the book and lyrics, Witmark named a young man still inexperienced in the ways of the theater, Otto

Hauerbach. Hauerbach was born in Salt Lake City, Utah, on August 16, 1873, and had taught English and public speaking at Whitman College in Walla Walla, Washington, before coming to New York in 1901. In New York he became first a newspaper reporter, then an advertising copywriter. (Later, Hauerbach contracted his name to Harbach and became one of Broadway's most distinguished and prolific writers of musical comedy books as well as a highly skilled fashioner of song lyrics.)

Hoschna and Hauerbach were each paid a flat fee of one hundred dollars to transform *Incog* into an operetta. Now renamed *Three Twins*, it opened on June 15, 1908, with Bessie McCoy as star. The three twins in the title were the twin brothers Harry and Dick Winters and their friend Tom Stanhope, who disguised himself as Harry Winters, the better to pursue Kate. As Kate, Bessie McCoy sang "Cuddle Up a Little Closer" and "The Yama-Yama Man" (the latter with lyrics not by Hauerbach but by Collin Davis). These two songs helped make her a star henceforth identified as "the Yama-Yama girl." Curiously, neither of these two songs was originally meant for this play. Hoschna had written "Cuddle Up a Little Closer" for a vaudeville sketch, while "The Yama-Yama Man" was hurriedly introduced in *Three Twins* after it had begun rehearsals

During the next three years, Hoschna and Hauerbach wrote eight operettas for Broadway. *Madame Sherry* was their best, coming to the New Amsterdam Theater on August 30, 1910. The story concerned a man-about-town who hoodwinks his rich uncle into believing that an Irish landlady is the glamorous Madame Sherry. The tuneful score had a resounding hit number in the tantalizing "Every Little Movement," and lesser successes in two waltzes, "Girl of My Dreams" and "The Birth of Passion." Hoschna died a little over a year following the premiere of this operetta, on December 23, 1911.

Ivan Caryll was born in Liège, Belgium, in 1860, and began his career as a composer of operettas in London in 1893. For the ensuing seventeen years he wrote a considerable amount of music for the London stage. Some of his operettas were sufficiently attractive to warrant their importation to New York. Acclaimed in New York, but originating in London, were *A Runaway Girl* (1898), *The Girl from Kay's* (1903), *The Earl and the Girl* (1905) and *The Orchid* (1907). Caryll emigrated to the United States in 1911 where he became an American citizen and remained until his death. His first American operetta proved to be the supreme achievement of his career, *The Pink Lady*, which smashed attendance records at the New Amsterdam Theater. Other box-office records were broken during an extensive national tour. Because of the operetta's popularity, the color pink came into fashion for women's clothes in 1911.

Hazel Dawn was "the pink lady," one of Lucien's girl friends. He tries to pass her off as the wife of a fictitious furniture dealer when he meets his fiancee in a fashionable restaurant. To Hazel Dawn, Caryll assigned his best numbers—two waltzes with the same melody, "My Beautiful Lady" and "The Kiss Waltz," both to words by C. M. S. McLellan.

After *The Pink Lady*, Caryll's major American operettas were *Oh, Oh, Delphine* (1912), *Chin-Chin* (1914) and *The Girl Behind the Gun* (1918). His last operetta was *Tip Top* in 1920. Caryll died in New York on November 28, 1921.

Rudolf Friml was the one above all others who may be said to have inherited Victor Herbert's mantle as Broadway's leading operetta composer. Appropriately enough, it was Herbert who—at least indirectly—was responsible for Friml's first appearance on Broadway. Arthur Hammerstein, the producer, was planning a new Victor Herbert operetta for Emma Trentini following her triumph in *Naughty Marietta*. Since star and composer were no longer on speaking terms, each refused to work with the other. When Herbert definitely withdrew from the project, a new composer had to be found. The publishers, Rudolf

Schirmer and Max Dreyfus, came up with a name new not only to Broadway but also to Tin Pan Alley—that of Rudolf Friml. Thus far, Friml had written only serious pieces for the piano and some art songs. The publishers, however, persuaded Hammerstein to take a chance on the new man, since he had shown a marked gift for writing vocal music. To engage an inexperienced and unknown composer for a major Broadway production was a gamble. How that gamble paid off can be judged by the fact that Friml's first operetta was *The Firefly*.

In writing his music for *The Firefly*, Friml (like Herbert before him) was faithful to the traditions of the European musical theater. Once again like Herbert, he would remain loyal to those traditions for the rest of his career, even while the musical theater around him was undergoing a drastic change. As long as foreign traditions prevailed on New York's popular musical stage, Friml was productive and successful. Between 1912 and 1926 he wrote the scores for four of the most highly acclaimed operettas of their time: *The Firefly*, *Rose-Marie*, *The Vagabond King* and *The Three Musketeers*. But when the European traditions passed, Friml was also through. After 1930 he contributed only two shows to Broadway, both failures. After 1943 he was comparatively silent. When he concentrated his activity in Hollywood on the movies, he was engaged not in new, modern productions, but mostly on adaptations of his old operettas.

It is perhaps understandable why he should work best within European patterns, since he had steeped himself in European music before writing his first operetta. Born in Prague on December 7, 1879, he attended the Prague Conservatory, after which he toured Europe as pianist in joint recitals with the violin virtuoso, Jan Kubelik. When the violinist came to America in 1901, Friml was with him. After a second American tour in 1906, Kubelik and Friml parted. The pianist had by now decided to stay in America, there to pursue his own career. During the next few years he appeared as a concert pianist and wrote music. He might have remained permanently a semi-obscure and little noticed pianist-composer —competent, respected, but not particularly brilliant— if chance had not thrown the book of *The Firefly* in his lap in 1912.

The Firefly—book and lyrics by Otto Hauerbach—opened at the Lyric Theater on December 2, 1912. It was custom built for Emma Trentini. She appeared as a street singer, Nina, who disguises herself as a boy and stows away on a Bermuda bound ship so that she may be near the man of her heart, Jack Travers. Two years later, Nina emerges as a famous prima donna who finally wins Jack's heart with her singing at a garden party.

Friml knew how to write for the voice as few others on Broadway could. He knew how to make an ingratiating, ear-caressing melody emphasize the best qualities of a large operatic voice. Singer and song became one. It is difficult to say which won the audiences more completely—melodies like "Giannina Mia," "Love Is Like a Firefly," "The Dawn of Love" and "When a Maid Comes Knocking at Your Heart," or the beguiling way Mme. Trentini sang them. The score had an additional winner in the highly appealing "Sympathy."

Now a composer much in demand, Friml did not lack for assignments. His best operettas during the 1910–1920 decade were *High Jinks* (1913), *Katinka* (1915), *You're in Love* (1917), *Sometime* (1918) and *Tumble In* (1919). From these came some superior songs, all of them to Hauerbach's lyrics: "Something Seems Tingle-Ingleing" and "The Bubble" from *High Jinks*, and the title song from *You're in Love*. To lyrics by Rida Johnson Young, the outstanding numbers of *Sometime* were the title number and "Any Kind of Man."

Friml did not appear with another major stage success to rival *The Firefly* until 1924 when he wrote the music for *Rose-Marie*.

Sigmund Romberg was the next giant of American operetta. He was also the last. When he died in 1951, a dynasty in the American musical theater came to its end.

Romberg's versatility ran the gamut from inoffensive sentiment, and at times a delicate sweetness, to gaiety, froth and lighthearted irresponsibility; from grace and refinement to vigor and robustness. It is hard to say which was his best vein. Are "Auf Wiedersehn" (Herbert Reynolds) and "When I Grow Too Old to Dream" (Oscar Hammerstein II) more characteristically Romberg in their gentle loveliness and feminine allure than such sterner items as "Stout-Hearted Men" (Oscar Hammerstein II) or "Drinking Song" (Dorothy Donnelly)? Is the Schubertian mobility of melody in songs like "Lover, Come Back to Me" (Oscar Hammerstein II) and "One Alone" (Otto Hauerbach and Oscar Hammerstein II) a better measure of his gifts than such insouciant trifles as "Three Little Maids" (Dorothy Donnelly) from *Blossom Time* or "Jump Jim Crow" (Rida Johnson Young) from *Maytime*? It is hard to say. To whatever style or mood he turned, Romberg was able to bring a charm uniquely his.

Romberg's best music is essentially Viennese. He never forgot, nor did he tire of recalling nostalgically, the times he had spent in Viennese cafés, salons and theaters. The world he knew as a young man was the one he loved to write about in his music.

It is true that he produced a carload of songs in an American style and tempo. The first two songs he wrote and published were American one-steps: "Some Smoke" and "Leg of Mutton" in 1912. The hundreds of songs he pieced together for forty-six musicals and revues produced by the Shuberts were typical Tin Pan Alley products, no better and no worse than most of the run-of-the-mill items then turned out by the Alley for Broadway consumption. Yet when he wrote with his heart, what emerged was invariably Viennese in personality.

It was that way when he wrote the score for his first operetta, *The Blue Paradise*, an adaptation of a Viennese musical; and it was like that when he wrote the music for such subsequent operettas as *Blossom Time* (the Vienna of Franz Schubert), *May Wine* (psychoanalysis in a latter-day Vienna) and *The Student Prince* (Heidelberg—but in a Viennese style). It was also that way when he fashioned such unmistakably Viennese waltzes in the style of Johann Strauss II or Franz Lehár as "The Desert Song" (Otto Hauerbach and Oscar Hammerstein II), "Will You Remember?" (Rida Johnson Young) or "One Kiss" (Oscar Hammerstein II)—songs appearing in plays not set in Vienna. Finally, it was still that way when he wrote his first original score for the talking screen: *Viennese Nights*, whose hit song was appropriately called "I Will Remember Vienna" (Oscar Hammerstein II).

Toward the end of his life Romberg told his wife: "I'm two wars away from my time. My time was pre-World War I. I've got to get away from Vienna. That's all passé. . . . I think I'll refuse anything from now on without an American background." In line with such thinking he wrote music for the screen adaptation of *The Girl of the Golden West* in 1938, the score for a resounding Broadway success, the musical comedy *Up in Central Park* in 1945, and another Broadway musical, *The Girl in Pink Tights*, produced posthumously in 1954. But the sad truth was that he was never completely at ease as a musician, nor happy as a man, when he worked in any manner other than Viennese.

He was born not in Vienna, but in a small Hungarian border town on July 29, 1887. Intended for engineering, he was sent to various preparatory and engineering schools in Hungary and Vienna. In Vienna he also studied music. After eighteen months of service in the 19th Hungarian Infantry Regiment stationed in Vienna he gave up all thoughts of engineering. He came to the United States when he was twenty-one, worked at first in a pencil factory, then played the piano in several New York cafés and restaurants. In 1912 he was made the conductor of his own orchestra at Bustanoby's Restaurant where he performed salon music and music for social dancing.

In 1913, Joseph W. Stern published Romberg's first songs, and soon after J. J. Shubert contracted him to succeed Louis A. Hirsch as staff composer for the Shubert enterprises.

Romberg's introduction to Broadway came in 1914 with *The Whirl of the World*, the Al Jolson extravaganza at the Winter Garden. After that, the Shuberts placed the full burden of their musical needs on the young man's shoulders. Since that burden consisted of writing music for about four productions a year, the wonder is not that Romberg failed for a time to rise above the level of mediocrity then prevailing in the musical theater, but that he was able to function without collapsing under the pressure of his assignments. Between 1914 and 1917, Romberg wrote 175 numbers for seventeen Shubert musicals, fifteen of these productions coming within a twenty-two month period. The music for all these, save one, was the kind of functional commodity Tin Pan Alley was then dispensing.

Romberg took stock of himself and was dissatisfied with the inventory. He had approached only one assignment with exhilaration, *The Blue Paradise*, an adaptation of a Viennese operetta with a Viennese background by Edgar Smith. It came to the Casino Theater on April 5, 1915, with Vivienne Segal, then a novice, making her stage debut in the leading feminine role of Mizzi, a flower girl in a Viennese garden restaurant. It was for this production that Romberg wrote "Auf Wiederschn" (Herbert Reynolds), the first Romberg song with a nostalgic old-world flavor, the first of his unforgettable waltzes, and his first song success.

Romberg decided, at last, that to save his artistic soul he must break with the Shuberts and venture on his own with the kind of musical productions capable of providing him with larger scope for his talent. When Romberg explained to Shubert what was bothering him, the producer urged him to reconsider his decision, promising to find him a book capable of proving his musical powers.

Shubert was as good as his word. In 1917 he turned over to the composer a text which Rida Johnson Young had adapted from a German operetta. Now bearing the title *Maytime*, it had a nineteenth-century American setting with American characters.

This was the first time Romberg had a play in which music was planned as a major element. *Maytime* opened on August 16, 1917, and proved such a box-office success that to accommodate the demand for seats a second company had to open in a nearby theater (one of the rare instances in Broadway history that two productions of the same musical ran simultaneously). There was no question in the minds of either critics or audiences that it was Romberg's music that was largely responsible for the triumph. The waltz "Will You Remember?" recurred throughout the play as a kind of catalyst binding together the action spanning three generations. A modernized conception of a minstrel show tune, "Jump Jim Crow," and "The Road to Paradise" and "Dancing Will Keep You Young," the last with lyrics by Cyrus Wood rather than by Rida Johnson Young, were other infectious numbers.

Maytime notwithstanding, Shubert sent Romberg back to writing the routine assignments that crowded his office: extravaganzas like *Sinbad* for Al Jolson (where the song interpolations by other composers proved stronger than Romberg's contributions); revues like *The Passing Show* and *Over the Top*, the latter with Fred and Adele Astaire. Romberg was growing increasingly restive with such chores, impatient to test his wings again in the ambitious flights. But he had to wait. The year was 1918, and Romberg had to serve in the United States Army, writing music for Army shows and going from camp to camp entertaining the troops. When World War I ended, he finally broke his ties with the Shuberts and set up his own producing firm to present the kind of shows in which he had faith. Two musicals were both disasters. Now heavily in debt, Romberg meekly returned to the Shuberts to resume his old duties.

Happily the first new assignment he received was a play in the style of *Maytime*. It was *Blossom Time*, an operetta based on the life of Vienna's immortal composer, Franz Schubert. With *Blossom Time*, in 1921, Romberg entered upon the richest phase of his career as an operetta composer.

9

Even while Friml and Romberg were writing their operettas, that stage medium was slowly being nudged into oblivion by musical comedy. Musical comedy was a native product. The operetta was partial to foreign or exotic settings, to plots far removed from the real or the contemporary, to stock characters involved in stock situations, and to music that borrowed its three-quarter time lilt or two-quarter or four-quarter time pulses, as well as its lyricism, from the Continental stage. On the other hand, musical comedy usually had an American background and American characters together with an American flavor in the brisk rhythms and breezy melodies of its music.

The first time the term "musical comedy" was used was for a burlesque, *Evangeline*, in 1874. Its composer, Edward E. Rice, expressed the hope that his play would foster "a taste for musical comedy relieved of the characteristic and objectionable features of the opera-bouffe."

When musical comedy was slowly evolving in the 1900s, it took over some of the approaches, methods and techniques of earlier species of the musical theater. The large production numbers and elaborate costuming and sets came out of extravaganzas. Satire, slapstick and travesty were borrowed from burlesque. The occasional irrelevant interpolation of songs, dances, comedy routines and large scenes within the plot was a heritage from operetta. To these familiar elements musical comedy added something new—a thoroughly native identity. In 1900, America's musical theater began drawing settings and characters from native sources far more freely than heretofore. At the same time, a new vigor and brashness, and an accelerated tempo entered into the writing of dialogue, lyrics and music.

We find the first flowering of American musical comedy with George M. Cohan.

Something novel and fresh entered the American musical with this explosive personality. At the turn of the century, Cohan was the living, vibrant present; he was the new era. Cocksure, egocentric, chauvinistic, energetic, gigantic in scheming and planning, he was a symbol of the new day in America.

With the boisterous self-assurance and feeling of inward power that marked these years, George M. Cohan was virtually a one-man Trust of the musical theater. He wrote his own plays, and the words and music of their songs. He devised his own dances, and staged, directed and often produced his own shows. Frequently he was also the star. He was not equally gifted in every department, nor was he ever profound or particularly imaginative. But he *did* know the theater and his audiences. He was a born song-and-dance man whose long presence on the stage from childhood on had taught him how to establish instant contact with his audience. He was a showman second to none, and everything he said and did had the showman's flair. And it was as a showman, rather than a creative force, that he injected such a vital spark into the American theater.

The blood of the theater flowed in his veins. He was born in Providence, Rhode Island, on July 4, 1878 (although his birth certificate says July 3), the third child of two veteran vaudevillians. In his ninth year, George made his bow as actor when, billed as "master Georgie," he spoke some lines in a sketch presented by his parents in Haverstraw, New York. In 1888, at the B. F. Keith Bijou in Boston, the Cohan parents, the boy George, and his sister, Josephine, first became known as "The Four Cohans." George played the violin, Josephine performed skirt dances, and the elder Cohans enacted one of the father's facile sketches.

It was not long before George began playing an increasingly significant role in the stage affairs of the Cohans. He started doing a specialty of his own, appearing as a bootblack; he combined this routine with songs, sentimental recitations and buck-and-wing dances. When he was eleven he wrote a sketch that was used in the act. From then on he always had a hand in the writing of new material.

He was only thirteen when he started writing songs, the words as well as the music, which henceforth became his practice. In his sixteenth year, "Why Did Nellie Leave Her Home?" was purchased by Witmark for twenty-five dollars and proved such a failure that Cohan had to seek out another publisher. A year later he wrote "Hot Tamale Alley," which sold moderately well since it was introduced and promoted in vaudeville by May Irwin. By the time Cohan was twenty he boasted a substantial hit in "I Guess I'll Have to Telegraph My Baby" (one of the earliest popular songs about wireless telegraphy). It was presented in vaudeville by a singing comedienne, Ethel Levey, who little realized she would some day become Mrs. George M. Cohan.

It was not long before the Four Cohans became headliners all over the country, from the Orpheum in San Francisco to Tony Pastor's Music Hall in New York. They drew the then quite substantial weekly salary of one thousand dollars for their act. By the time the nineteenth century was over, a fifth Cohan joined the act, for Cohan married Ethel Levey in the summer of 1899 and she became a member of the company. A star in her own right, Ethel Levey would now speak George's lines, sing his songs and live more or less in the reflected glow of his fame.

George M. Cohan was now the dominant force in the Four Cohans act, not only its business manager and one of its principal performers, but also the author of its main songs and sketches. After the final curtain he began a practice that became habitual with him of addressing the audience with the following lines: "My mother thanks you, my father thanks you, my sister thanks you, and I thank you."

A vaudeville act could no more contain the varied gifts and the irrepressible drive of George M. Cohan than a drawing room could a hurricane. In 1901 he expanded one of his sketches into a three-act play with a dozen songs, calling it The Governor's Son. With all the Cohans in the cast, it opened in New York that year, but folded after only thirty-two performances. But for two seasons it toured the country, returning to New York for a new run of over sixty performances. In 1903, the Cohans appeared in another vaudeville sketch extended by George M. into a full evening's entertainment, Running for Office. This, too, did badly in New York, but enjoyed a modest success on the road.

In 1904, Cohan joined forces with producer Sam H. Harris. Their first production was a new Cohan musical, Little Johnny Jones, the first time Cohan wrote a complete original book, as well as the songs, for the Broadway stage. It opened at the Liberty Theater on November 7, 1904. George M. Cohan himself appeared in the title role, for which the prototype was Tod Sloan, the American jockey who had gone to England in 1903 to ride for King George in the Derby. Johnny Jones, in the play, rides in the Derby, is falsely accused of having thrown the race, but in the end is cleared. Three of the four Cohans were in the cast; Josephine, now married to Fred Niblo, preferred for the time being to be on her own.

There were many appealing things in *Little Johnny Jones*. There was George's little monologue, "Life's a Funny Proposition," which introduced some homely philosophy. There were two Cohan hit songs by which he—and the musical—will always be remembered: "The Yankee Doodle Boy," with which he made his first entrance in the play, and "Give My Regards to Broadway." There were his breezy portrait of an American jockey and the stirring effect he created when he draped an American flag around his body and strutted up and down the stage in a flag-waving routine.

These attractions notwithstanding, *Little Johnny Jones* closed after fifty-two performances. Cohan remained convinced that the play was too good to fail. He kept playing in it on the road until it finally caught on. In 1905 he brought it back to New York for another three-month run. Later the same year he reappeared in it for another two weeks in New York, and in 1907 for still another two-week stint.

Transforming *Little Johnny Jones* from a failure to success was Cohan's turning point in his career in musical comedy. From then on, Cohan was "Mr. Big" on Broadway, completely dominating the musical theater for the next two decades.

Cohan established a personal identity in his dress, behavior, mannerisms, singing and dancing. He danced with a kangaroo step while holding a bamboo cane under his arm and a hat tipped slightly over one eye. He sang and spoke with a nasal twang out of the corner of his mouth. He talked to audiences as if to his barroom friends, pointing a forefinger at them as he spoke. He was the merchant of corn which he delivered in song, monologue and unrehearsed little addresses.

As a creator, as well as a performer, he brought to the musical comedy stage a dynamic American identity. His characters talked in American slang, and they behaved the way Americans do. They sang the kind of simple, sentimental songs to which Americans were partial. Their problems and complications, as well as their dreams and ideals, were those Americans recognized as their own.

After *Little Johnny Jones* came *Forty-Five Minutes from Broadway*, produced in 1906. The locale referred to in the title was the New York suburb of New Rochelle. Fay Templeton, a burlesque star, played Mary Jane, housekeeper to a miserly millionaire, who inherits his fortune when after his death, his will is found in an old suit of clothes. Mary Jane turns down the inheritance since the man she loves, Kid Burns, refuses to marry an heiress.

Miss Templeton enchanted audiences with her performance, and began a new career in the legitimate theater. The cast included a young comedian, Victor Moore, playing Kid Burns, who stole some of the thunder from Fay Templeton while asserting his own right to stardom. Cohan's two best songs were "Mary's a Grand Old Name" and "So Long Mary."

The first night audience was enchanted with the musical. But the Chamber of Commerce of New Rochelle was outraged, feeling that references in the text denigrated this community and its people. But with the mounting approbation given the musical by critics and audiences, the Chamber of Commerce recognized that New Rochelle was gaining not notoriety but fame, and objections melted into silent approval.

Emphasizing Cohan's unique place on Broadway at this time was the fact that the most serious rival to the popularity of *Forty-Five Minutes from Broadway* was a second Cohan musical, *George Washington, Jr.* In it Cohan starred himself as a super-patriotic American whose chauvinism leads him to assume the name of America's first President.

The characterization of the American portrayed by Cohan enabled him to drape the American flag around himself and race across the stage singing "You're a Grand Old Flag." It would appear that there was nothing either in this song or routine to arouse tempers. Nevertheless something of a minor scandal developed. Cohan got the idea for the song from a G.A.R. veteran who once told him of having been the color-bearer during Pickett's charge on Gettysburg. Pointing to the American flag, the veteran exclaimed: "She's a grand old rag." In his play, Cohan used the line "you're a grand old rag." The day following the premiere, several patriotic societies protested that Cohan was insulting the American flag by referring to it as a "rag." (Cohan himself always suspected that the storm had been unleashed by a critic who had been denied seats for opening night.) Cohan changed the provocative "rag" into "flag," and the protests subsided.

When *George Washington, Jr.* returned to New York after a road tour, the role formerly assumed by his wife was taken over by Vinnie Dale. The change of casting lent proof to a rumor long circulating that Cohan and his wife were splitting up. After his divorce decree became final, Cohan married Agnes Nolan in 1907. They both lived to celebrate thirty-five years of a happy marriage.

Not yet thirty-two in 1910, Cohan already was one of the richest and most powerful figures along Broadway, not only by virtue of his own plays and songs, but also through the successful plays of other writers which he produced through the years in conjunction with Sam H. Harris. It did not seem that there were many more avenues in the theater through which he could travel to triumph. Yet there were. He wrote comedies without songs or dances which became box-office successes on Broadway before World War I; *Get Rich Quick Wallingford* (1910), *Broadway Jones* (1912), and *Seven Keys to Baldpate* (1913). And in 1917 he wrote the most stirring song inspired by World War I, "Over There," about which more will be said in another chapter.

He reached the pinnacle of his profession when his zest for the theater was dampened by an unforeseen development. On August 7, 1919, the Actors Equity Association called a strike to compel theater managers to recognize it as a bargaining representative for its members, and at the same time to remedy some of the more flagrant abuses then suffered by actors. Twelve Broadway shows closed, and in four weeks' time the number doubled. Cohan, like every other producer, was seriously affected. But unlike them he came to regard this strike not as a managerial-employe problem but as a personal attack upon him. For in the vanguard of the Equity forces were many actors whom Cohan had helped time and again, some of whom he had raised to prominence, others whom he had provided with funds. To see them line up solidly against him seemed a betrayal. From that moment on, he refused stubbornly to recognize the validity of the issues involved in the strike, insisting that the theater had no place for unionism, and that performers had no just cause for grievance. He promised to dedicate every dollar he owned to defeat Equity, and threatened to leave the theater for good if he failed.

The war between Equity and George M. Cohan was brief, but while it lasted it was acrimonious. Cohan became the outspoken enemy of many who had been his closest friends for years, and they rejected him as fiercely as he did them. He withdrew his membership from both the Friars and Lambs clubs. He organized the short-lived Fidelity League as a rival to Equity for actors who believed in and with him.

By the time a new season got under way after Labor Day, Actors Equity had won a complete victory. But Cohan kept fighting long after the war was over. He kept using his immense popularity and influence to discredit or undermine Equity; he continued his threats to withdraw from the American theater. He was only shadowboxing, since the position of Equity had become unassailable. In spite of everything he had accomplished, he could not turn back the clock.

He did not retire from the Broadway theater, but he did seem to lose interest in the affairs of the stage. In 1920 he dissolved the still prosperous firm of Cohan and Harris. He traveled and rested more than ever, wrote and acted less frequently. And while Cohan hits did not completely disappear from Broadway, they grew increasingly rare.

He wrote forty plays, collaborated in the writing of forty others, and had a hand in the production of still another one hundred and fifty. He published over five hundred songs, one of them one of the most popular American war songs ever written. Besides all this, he had, in his time, made almost ten thousand appearances as an actor. No wonder that Gene Buck called him "the greatest single figure the American theater has produced."

There is sufficient ammunition with which to attack Cohan's musical comedies if one is so inclined. His stories were always trite, his characters, synthetic, his philosophy, cliché-ridden and his songs simple and ingenuous. James S. Metcalf in *Life*, like so many other critics of Cohan's day, recognized the less pleasing qualities of Cohan's dramatic art. He described Cohan as a "vulgar, cheap, blatant, ill-mannered, flashily dressed, insolent, smart alec who, for some reason unexplainable . . . appeals to the imagination and approval of large American audiences." What so many critics failed to realize in the early 1900s—but what audiences sensed—was that Cohan's musicals struck a completely new and vital note. They brought an invigorating new tempo, spirit, impudence, exuberance and brashness into both book and song. With Cohan's informality, racy language, monumental ego and chauvinism, the American musical approached the threshold of modernity. Indeed, a historian of the American musical theater can hardly resist the temptation of saying that the American musical comedy, as it came to full growth in the 1920s and 1930s, was born with George M. Cohan.

In 1914, Jerome Kern succeeded George M. Cohan as a major composer of American musical comedies. In that year he achieved his first stage success with *The Girl from Utah* and his first song classic with "They Didn't Believe Me" (Herbert Reynolds) which had a two-million copy sheet music sale. Kern had arrived. A year later he helped to revolutionize the American musical comedy with the so-called Princess Theater Shows for most of which he wrote all the music.

He was born in New York City on January 27, 1885. When he was graduated from the Newark (New Jersey) High School, he entered the New York College of Music where he studied piano and theory. There was no questioning his enthusiasm for music, nor his industry and ability. But he was no blazing flame. His level-headed father, consequently, refused to allow Jerome to go to Europe for additional study. Instead, Jerome had to enter his father's business, a fairly prosperous merchandising house in Newark.

Jerome joined his father in 1902, but his career was brief. One day, sent to New York to buy two pianos, he became so spellbound by a super-salesman that he purchased not two but two hundred pianos! With that single stroke he almost ruined his father financially. Now convinced that the world of business was alien to the boy, and probably guided by an instinct for self-preservation, the father decided to send his son to Europe after all. (Actually this affair with the pianos did not turn out so disastrously. After Jerome went off to Europe, his father, faced with the necessity of disposing of two hundred pianos, devised an attractive installment plan which netted him a handsome profit on the whole deal.)

Jerome Kern went to Europe in the fall of 1903. He traveled, listened to a great deal of music, and did some studying with private teachers. In London, faced with the necessity of replenishing his funds, he took a job in the office of Charles K. Frohman, the American producer, then presenting musical shows in London. Kern's duties were to write little songs and musical pieces as opening numbers—an inconsequential and poorly paid assignment, since London theatergoers habitually came late and seldom heard the opening music.

This humble assignment gave Kern the direction he needed. He permanently discarded his onetime ambition to write symphonies and concertos and turned instead to popular music. During this period he wrote a song called "Mr. Chamberlain"—a topical number about an English statesman then in the news (the father of England's later Prime Minister, Neville Chamberlain). It was sung in the London musical *The Beauty and the Bath*. This might be called Kern's first successful song, for the audiences loved it. But its main importance lies in the fact that the lyrics were written by P. G. Wodehouse. A decade later, Wodehouse became famous as a writer of whimsical novels besides serving as an all-important collaborator of Jerome Kern in the Princess Theater Shows. But in 1903 he was twenty-four, not too widely known, a columnist for a London newspaper and a contributor of stories and poems to various periodicals.

In 1904, Kern returned to the United States. Since he wished to make his way in popular music, he decided to learn everything he could about the song business at its source—Tin Pan Alley. For two years he worked first for Shapiro-Bernstein, and then for Harms, accepting whatever assignment, however menial, came his way. Sometimes he worked as a song plugger and sheet music salesman; sometimes he adapted songs of other composers for his firm's catalogue; sometimes he wrote stock numbers.

At Harms he attracted the attention and interest of Max Dreyfus, its manager. Recognizing Kern's creative possibilities, Dreyfus had him write songs, some of which Harms published. (Kern later was published exclusively by Harms, and in time became its vice president.) Dreyfus found a job for Kern as piano accompanist for Marie Dressler. She was then a popular vaudevillian, but later became famous as a character actress on the screen. Dreyfus also helped open doors for Kern leading to the Broadway theater.

Kern received his first stage assignment in 1904 when he was asked to adapt the music of an English musical, *Mr. Wix of Wickham*. That score (into which Kern interpolated four of his own songs) proved so fresh in its melodic and harmonic approach that at least one New York critic sat up and took notice. "Who is this Jerome Kern," inquired Alan Dale in the *American*, "whose music towers in an Eiffel way above the average primitive hurdy-gurdy accompaniment of the present-day musical comedy?"

After *Mr. Wix of Wickham*, Kern moved energetically forward in his profession. In 1905, his song, "How'd You Like to Spoon With Me?" (Edward Laska) was heard in the Broadway musical *The Earl and the Girl*. Though an interpolation, it became the leading musical number of the show—"the most successful . . . ever produced here," reported the *Dramatic Mirror* in an excess of enthusiasm. Kern was now the proud parent of his first American hit song.

For the next half dozen years, Kern's sole affiliation with musical theater was through further interpolations of his songs into the scores of other composers. It was everyday practice in those days to add one or more songs by various composers to a musical production whose basic music was the work of somebody else. Between 1905 and 1912, about a hundred of Kern's songs were heard in some thirty Broadway musicals. Then, in 1911, the Shuberts contracted with him to write half the score (six songs) for *La Belle Paree*, which opened at the Winter Garden. A year later, Kern completed his first original Broadway score for *The Red Petticoat*, a failure. The next two Broadway productions with Kern's music also did poorly. Finally, in 1914, appeared *The Girl from Utah* and with it the song classic, "They Didn't Believe Me." Kern's place on the Broadway scene was now firm.

The Girl from Utah was an English musical for whose American adaptation Kern prepared about half the score. Julia Sanderson starred in the American production as Una Trance, come to London from Utah to avoid becoming one of the many wives of a Mormon. In London she falls in love with Sandy Blair.

"They Didn't Believe Me" was Julia Sanderson's song not only because she introduced it, but because Kern wrote it with her voice and style in mind. From the two hundred
and more songs Kern had written up to this time, this one stands out with beacon-like
brilliance. Kern no longer submitted meekly to the song conventions of his day, but bent
them to his own creative needs. He could digress from the norm, yet his melody remained
fluid and graceful, falling naturally on the ear. He subtly changed rhythm and key within the
refrain. At one point he introduced an altogether new melodic thought when none was
expected. Yet the song remained all of one piece, progressing with inexorable logic.

With a song like this one, Kern stood on the threshold of individuality and greatness
as a composer for the popular musical theater. He crossed the threshold in 1915 with his first
Princess Theater Show.

These shows were so named because they were housed in the Princess Theater in
New York, an auditorium seating only three hundred. Its manager, Elizabeth Marbury,
had difficulty booking shows into such a small house. She hit upon the plan of creating for
that auditorium economically budgeted, small-sized and intimate musicals.

She called upon Jerome Kern to write music for the project and suggested Guy Bolton
for book and lyrics. Bolton was a young Englishman who had been trained as an architect in
France and who, after coming to New York, helped to design the Soldiers and Sailors
Memorial on Riverside Drive. In 1912, when he was twenty-six, he collaborated on a play
that had just two performances. By the time Miss Marbury brought him to Kern, Bolton had
written and seen produced two more plays, neither particularly eventful. He had also
contributed some sketches to *The Smart Set*.

Before beginning to work on their first Princess Theater Show, Kern and Bolton
joined to write a large-scale musical more traditional in format and design. It was *Ninety in
the Shade*, in which Bolton received an assist in the writing of the libretto from Clare
Kummer. Marie Cahill, a performer now well past her prime, was given the starring role.
Despite some amusing moments in the text, and a few hummable tunes, this musical
survived for just forty performances in 1915.

Now Kern and Bolton turned to the job of writing an intimate show for Miss Marbury. They adapted an English musical which they renamed *Nobody Home* (1915). It was an
informal production, modest in intentions, but studded with bright lines and amusing
episodes. With broad strokes it caricatured an Englishman, Freddy Popple, recently come to
the United States, who gets involved with a Winter Garden prima donna. The plot was slight
and it called for just two sets, a handful of characters (none played by a recognizable star), a
chorus line of only eight girls (used sparingly) and an orchestra of ten. Stage mechanics,
costuming and scenery were reduced to basics. As Guy Bolton outlined the intent of the
authors, they sought to create "a straight, consistent comedy with the addition of music.
Every song and lyric contributed to the action. The humor was based on the situation, not
interjected by comedians. . . . Realism and Americanism were other distinguishing traits."
Witty dialogue, freshly conceived melodies and dances, sophisticated attitudes, novel twists
in developing the elementary story line were the main attractions, not girls, stars or production numbers.

Jerome Kern's songs included two gems: "You Know and I Know" and "The Magic
Melody," both to Schuyler Greene's lyrics. So consistently adventurous was Kern in his
melodic and harmonic writing that even so distinguished a musicologist as Carl Engel could
take note of him. He wrote: "Unless I am very much mistaken, 'The Magic Melody' by Mr.
Jerome Kern was the opening chorus of an epoch . . . which marked a change, a new regime
in American popular music."

Budgeted at $7,500, *Nobody Home* was able to turn a small profit even after a run of only 135 performances. Elizabeth Marbury became assured of the validity of her innovation. She gave Kern and Bolton the encouragement to proceed along similar lines with a second show. It was *Very Good Eddie*, which appeared toward the end of 1915, stayed on for over a year, and earned a profit of more than one hundred thousand dollars. Its financial success, abetted by the approbation of the critics, forthwith established the Princess Theater Show as a Broadway institution.

Everything about it was compact and economical; the tone was intimate, the manner, informal. Acting, singing and dancing were pitched in a low key. Together with *Nobody Home*, it established a new genre in the American musical theater that departed radically from the accepted pattern of extravaganza and revues. Music, dance and dialogue in *Very Good Eddie* were ebullient in spirit, and so was Kern's music whose best songs, to Schuyler Greene's lyrics, were "Nodding Roses" and "Babes in the Wood." (The lyrics of "Nodding Roses" was written in collaboration with Herbert Reynolds; those of "Babes in the Woods" with Kern.) *Very Good Eddie* lost none of its pristine charm when it was revived first at the Goodspeed Opera House in East Haddam, Connecticut, in the summer of 1975, and later on Broadway at the Booth Theater on December 21 where it was a resounding success.

A third partner was soon added to the Bolton-Kern team, an addition making it one of the most successful trios in the musical theater of the pre-World War I era. He was P.G. Wodehouse, who by 1915 had become famous for such novels as *Psmith in the City* and *Psmith, Journalist*. In 1915 Wodehouse was paying his third extended visit to the United States to serve as a drama critic for *Vanity Fair*. In this capacity he attended the opening night of *Very Good Eddie*, where Kern suggested to Wodehouse that they revive their London writing association. The decision was finally reached to have Wodehouse assist in the writing of the next Princess Theater Show by serving as the lyricist, with Bolton confining himself exclusively to the book. Thus the Princess Theater Show gained a third writer who could gracefully enter into the spirit of this venture; a writer capable of matching Kern's music with sparkling lyrics years ahead of their time in skill of versification, grace of rhyming, subtlety of phrasing, and the precious art of being simple without descending to triviality.

This trio of writers succeeded in bringing further vivacity and sophistication to the Princess Theater with *Oh, Boy!* (1917). It had a Broadway run of 463 performances (122 more than that of *Very Good Eddie*). A second company was set up at the neighboring Casino Theater, and four companies went on the road. Bolton's text had an American college town as a setting for a gay boudoir escapade.

Kern's nimble pen leaped with agility from humor to sentiment, always with a spontaneous flow of graceful lyricism. In a takeoff on a sentimental ballad of 1912, "When It's Apple Blossom Time in Normandy" (Mellor, Gifford and Trevor), Flatbush, Brooklyn, is used as the locale in "Nesting Time in Flatbush." Tender sentiment permeated "Till the Clouds Roll By," a song become so famous that its title was used in 1946 for Kern's screen biography.

The last Princess Theater Show by Kern, Bolton and Wodehouse (and the penultimate production in this memorable series) was, *Oh, Lady! Lady!* The title came from a phrase often bandied about by Bert Williams in the *Ziegfeld Follies*. It opened on February 1, 1918, and while not quite so popular as its predecessors, it nevertheless brought in a comfortable profit during its run of over two hundred performances. Three songs are memorable: "Before I Met You," "You Found Me and I Found You" and the title number. A fourth number has become a song classic but, though written for *Oh, Lady! Lady!* it was never used in it. This was the ballad "Bill," which finally turned up triumphantly in *Show Boat* some seven years later.

The last Princess Theater Show was *Oh, My Dear!* (1918) with music by Louis A. Hirsch, but with Bolton once again providing the book, and Wodehouse, the lyrics. Kern, apparently, was sorely missed. *Oh, My Dear!* lacked the sparkle, effervescence and freshness of the earlier productions. Though the Princess Theater Show came to an end on less than a note of triumph, its contribution to the American theater proved far-reaching. It pointed the way to a new kind of musical stage presentation in which originality and subtlety of text and music took precedence. Out of the style, technique, nuances and approaches of the Princess Theater Show came the delightful intimate revues of the 1920s and 1930s, as well as the unconventional musical comedies of Rodgers and Hart of the same period.

14

New Sounds, New Voices in Tin Pan Alley

1

The blues invaded Tin Pan Alley in 1914 brought there by W. C. Handy, who composed the first commercial blues to be published, and after that the most widely performed and admired blues ever conceived. The son of a pastor, William Christopher Handy was born in Florence, Alabama, on November 16, 1873. He was only a child when he saved pennies earned from odd jobs and bought a guitar despite parental objections. His father ordered him to return the guitar and exchange it for a dictionary. "My son," he told him sternly, "I would rather see you in a hearse than have you become a musician." But the boy's musical urge could not be denied. He fell in love with the trumpet when he heard it for the first time. He tried fashioning one from a cow's horn, and failing, acquired a real trumpet for a dollar from a visiting circus musician. Without any instruction he learned to play it.

He soon fled home and his intransigent father to join a traveling minstrel troupe. When that company was stranded on the road, William made his way home as best he could by hopping freight trains. Sobered by this experience, he temporarily renounced music to take up teaching, graduating from the Teachers Agricultural and Mechanical College in Alabama in 1892. His miserable pay induced him finally to abandon the classroom and take a job in a steel foundry, where he organized and led a brass band. When the economic crisis closed down the foundry, Handy made a second attempt at becoming a professional musician. He played the cornet at the World's Fair in Chicago in 1893. Three years later he found employment as cornetist, arranger and bandleader with Mahara's Minstrels.

He stayed with the Minstrels seven years, after which he organized the Negro Knights of Pythias Band in Mississippi with which he gave concerts throughout the South. He heard his first blues at a deserted railroad station where an aged black man was crooning a blues sorrowfully, as if to himself. Somewhat later, Handy heard a local band in Cleveland, Mississippi, perform some New Orleans blues and ragtime to an enthusiastic audience. "This had the stuff people wanted," he realized. "Their music . . . contained the essence. Folks would pay more money for it. . . . That night a composer was born, an *American* composer. Those country black boys had taught me something that could not possibly have been gained from books." Whereas Handy had up to then been trying to write Tin Pan Alley songs, he now became imbued with the mission of writing music that sprang from the heart and the experiences of his race.

Handy wrote his first blues in 1909. The impetus was a mayoralty campaign in Memphis, Tennessee, where a candidate named Crump was running on a reform ticket. To help advance Crump's campaign, Handy decided to write a song rallying the votes of the black people of Beale Street. The melody he used was a blues, a style he knew these people could understand and respond to. The song "Mr. Crump" not only helped to sweep its namesake into office but remained popular with the blacks of Memphis after the election. In 1912, Handy published it at his own expense as a piano piece, now naming it "The Memphis Blues." A year later, a shrewd New York publisher bought all the rights to this composition for fifty dollars, reissuing it with lyrics by George A. Norton. This was the first blues to come out of Tin Pan Alley. It had a sensational success, bringing a fortune to its publisher, and establishing once and for all the commercial value of the blues as a popular song idiom.

Since he had sold "The Memphis Blues" outright, Handy did not profit from the enormous sheet music sale. He decided to write another blues to capitalize on the success of his first. Renting a room in Beale Street he went to work. In his autobiography, *Father of the Blues*, he described how the successor to "The Memphis Blues" came into being:

"A flood of memories filled my mind. First there was a picture . . . of myself, broke, unshaven, wanting even a decent meal, and standing before the lighted saloon in St. Louis without a shirt under my frayed coat. . . . While occupied with my own miseries during the sojourn, I had seen a woman whose pain seemed even greater. She had tried to take the edge off her grief by heavy drinking. . . . Stumbling along the poorly lighted street, she muttered as she walked, 'My man's got a heart like a rock cast in the sea'. . . . By the time I had finished all this heavy thinking and remembering, I figured it was time to get something down on paper, so I wrote 'I hate to see de evenin' sun go down.' If you ever had to sleep on the cobbles down by the river in St. Louis you'll understand the complaint."

And so Handy wrote the words and music of "The St. Louis Blues," his classic —certainly the best known blues ever played, written or published. Strange to say, in view of the widespread popularity of its immediate Handy predecessor, "The St. Louis Blues" was turned down by every publisher to whom it was submitted. Finally, in partnership with Harry Pace, Handy formed his own company and issued the song in Memphis in 1914. It failed to make much of an impression. Convinced he had a loser, Handy went on to write several more blues. The best were "Yellow Blues" in 1914, "Joe Turner Blues" in 1915, and "Beale Street Blues" in 1916, the last eventually identified with the jazz trombonist and bandleader Jack Teagarden.

After Handy transferred his publishing firm to Tin Pan Alley in New York, several stage stars began featuring "The St. Louis Blues." Sophie Tucker sang it in vaudeville, and Gilda Gray at the Winter Garden. Victor issued a recording that proved so successful that other companies released recordings of their own, and piano roll manufacturers went into the act as well. "The St. Louis Blues" was used in an all-black revue *Change Your Life*

(1930), was the inspiration for a motion picture, and lent its title to three other movies, including one purporting to be the life of Handy. Ted Lewis made it one of his specialties on records, in the movies and in public appearances. Forty years after its first publication, "The St. Louis Blues" was still bringing Handy an annual royalty of about twenty-five thousand dollars.

It became not only an American classic, but one favored abroad. It was the music King Edward VIII asked the pipers of Scotland to play for him, and it was beloved by Queen Elizabeth II. It was played at the marriage of Prince George of England to Princess Marina of Greece. It became the battle hymn of the Ethiopians when that land was invaded by Italy in the 1930s.

Handy wrote many other blues, including "The Harlem Blues," "The John Henry Blues," "Aunt Hagar's Blues" and "East of St. Louis Blues." But "The St. Louis Blues" is his masterpiece, his one piece of music above all others to immortalize his name. It is because of "The St. Louis Blues" that Handy became a hero in Memphis, with public park, schools, theaters and swimming pools named for him. In 1969, his face appeared on a stamp commemorating the sesquicentennial of Memphis. A foundation for the blind bears his name. At the New York World's Fair in 1939 he was listed as a leading contributor to American culture. On his sixty-fifth birthday he received a touching tribute on the stage of New York's Carnegie Hall. In 1958 he was given Hollywood's ultimate tribute when his life was dramatized on the screen in *The St. Louis Blues* with Nat King Cole appearing as Handy.

Though blind the last two decades of his life, Handy made numerous appearances on radio and television. He died in New York City on March 28, 1958. The centenary of his birth was commemorated in 1973 with the mayors of New Orleans, St. Louis and Florence, Alabama, naming November 16 as "W. C. Handy Day," and with commemorative concerts of his compositions at the Yale University School of Music and at Howard University in Washington, D. C., among other places. The city of Memphis held a full week of celebration in which Diane Crump, granddaughter of the man who had inspired "The Memphis Blues" participated. Massed bands of every high school in Memphis paraded through the streets, playing "The St. Louis Blues" and ending their march at Handy Park, where Handy's statue stands.

2

In 1917 there came out of Tin Pan Alley a song called "Everybody's Crazy About the Doggone Blues" (Henry Creamer—Turner Layton). The message had validity: Everybody, it seemed, was writing blues for popular consumption. W. C. Handy had opened the floodgates. The tidal wave of blues inundated the song industry.

Some of the commercialized blues came from men who had known New Orleans well, Spencer Williams and Clarence Williams (no relation) for example. Spencer Williams was born and had spent his impressionable years in New Orleans before coming to New York to promote his career as a composer. He had his first song hit with "I Ain't Got Nobody," words by Roger Graham, and music written with Dave Peyton. Published in 1916, this was a number in the style and spirit of the blues. Among his other popular songs was "Squeeze Me," which he wrote with Thomas "Fats" Waller—Waller's first composition, published in 1925. Spencer Williams also wrote instrumental blues in the traditional structure and idiom, "Basin Street Blues," "Tishomingo Blues," "Dallas Blues" and "Arkansas Blues."

Early in his career, Spencer Williams collaborated with Clarence Williams. One of their first efforts was "Royal Garden Blues." Clarence Williams spent his boyhood playing

222222
1900—1920

the piano in honky-tonks of New Orleans' Storyville where he became professionally affiliated with Sidney Bechet and Bunk Johnson among other jazz notables. Williams turned to composing in or about 1913, and achieved recognition in 1919 with "Baby, Won't You Please Come Home" (Charles Warfield). In a more orthodox blues style he wrote "West Indies Blues" and "Sugar Blues."

Most of the blues being written for the general market, however, came from Tin Pan Alley's native songwriters. "I've Got the Army Blues" (L. Wolfe Gilbert—Carey Morgan) appeared in 1917 as a lament over the draft in World War I, and "The Alcoholic Blues" (Edward Laska—Albert von Tilzer) bemoaned Prohibition. Tin Pan Alley kept on producing blues throughout the 1920s. Jerome Kern wrote two blues in 1920 and 1921: "Left Alone Blues" for the musical *The Night Boat* in 1920 and, a year later, "The Blue Danube Blues" for *Good Morning, Dearie*, both to Anne Caldwell's lyrics. Irving Berlin wrote the lyrics for "Home Again Blues" to a melody by Harry Akst (then Berlin's secretary) in 1920, words and music for "The Schoolhouse Blues" in 1921, and "Shaking the Blues Away" for the *Ziegfeld Follies of 1927*. George Gershwin wrote "The Yankee Doodle Blues" (Irving Caesar and B. G. De Sylva) in 1922 and "The Half of It, Dearie, Blues" (Ira Gershwin) for *Lady, Be Good!* in 1924. Blues harmonies and melodies were prominently used by Gershwin in his symphonic works and in his folk opera, *Porgy and Bess*.

The song hits of 1921 included "The Wabash Blues" (Dave Ringle—Fred Meinken), "The Wang, Wang Blues" (Leo Wood—Gus Mueller, "Buster" Johnson and Henry Busse), and "Cry Baby Blues" (Sam M. Lewis and Joe Young—Henry Busse). The year of 1922 brought "Doo Dah Blues" (Fred Rise—Ted Fiorito) and "Lovesick Blues" (Irving Mills—Cliff Friend). "Hometown Blues" (Dave Ringle—J. Fred Coots) appeared in 1923, "Washboard Blues" (Fred Callahan and Mitchell Parish—Hoagy Carmichael) in 1926, "How Long, How Long Blues" (Ann Enberg—Leroy Carr) in 1929 and "Bye, Bye, Blues" (Fred Hamm, Dave Bennett and Chauncey Gray) in 1930, which was introduced by and became the signature music of Bert Lown and the Hotel Biltmore Orchestra.

The highlight of *George White's Scandals of 1926* was a lavish production built around the song "The Birth of the Blues" (De Sylva, Brown and Henderson). The subject of this spectacular scene was a battle between the blues and the classics. The blues was represented by Handy's "The Memphis Blues" and "The St. Louis Blues," sung respectively by Margaret McCarthy and Dorothy McCarthy. The Fairbanks Twins represented the classics through two compositions, one by Robert Schumann, the other by Franz Schubert. The conflict arrived at a peaceful compromise with Gershwin's *Rhapsody in Blue*, a part of which was played as the climax of the scene.

3

It is not difficult to find fault with the Tin Pan Alley of the early years of the twentieth century. It produced songs in quantity with assembly line techniques. Larceny was condoned as tunes or song ideas were freely stolen. Many of the men producing hit songs were musically illiterate.

Yet in one respect Tin Pan Alley cannot be dismissed or laughed at, and that was as a cradle where young composers were raised from infancy to the maturity of self-fulfillment. Legion is the number of outstanding songwriters who served their apprenticeship in Tin Pan Alley as song pluggers, salesmen, arrangers, demonstration pianists and stock clerks. Already we have written of Ernest R. Ball, Jean Schwartz, Irving Berlin and Jerome Kern, each of whom learned his trade in Tin Pan Alley. During the first two decades of the twentieth century, many others grew from humble Tin Pan Alley jobs to become master songwriters.

Fred Fisher was the office manager of Harms and Leo Feist; Richard A. Whiting and Egbert Van Alstyne worked for Remick. Harry Ruby was a song plugger for the publishing houses of Gus Edwards and Harry von Tilzer, and Milton Ager, for Waterson, Berlin and Snyder. George Gershwin was a piano demonstrator for Remick. In other Tin Pan Alley firms, Harry Carroll started out as an arranger, Walter Donaldson as a demonstration pianist and George W. Meyer as a song plugger.

Fred Fisher (1875–1942) came from Germany in 1900 after spending an adventurous boyhood in the German Navy and the French Foreign Legion. In Chicago he began studying the piano and writing his first songs. He then drifted to New York where for many years he combined songwriting with desk jobs in Tin Pan Alley. Though his speech never lost its German accent, his musical language completely absorbed and assimilated the inflections of American popular music. He learned his lessons in Tin Pan Alley early and well. "Peg o' My Heart" (Alfred Bryan) in 1913 was a ballad in the recognizable Tin Pan Alley mold. Fisher wrote it after seeing Laurette Taylor in the Broadway play of the same name, and he dedicated his song to her. José Collins sang it in the *Ziegfeld Follies of 1913*. As successful as this ballad was in 1913, it proved even more so in its reincarnation in 1947 when it was recorded both by the Harmonicats and by Peggy Lee, each of these recordings selling over a million disks. At that time, too, it reached a top rating on radio's "Your Hit Parade." Two more outstanding Fisher ballads were "There's a Broken Heart for Every Light on Broadway" (Howard Johnson) and "Ireland Must be Heaven, for My Mother Came from There" (Howard Johnson and Joseph McCarthy).

Fisher's versatility enabled him to master many other Tin Pan Alley styles besides the ballad. He enjoyed one of his earliest sheet music best-sellers with a "coon song" in 1906, "If the Man in the Moon Were a Coon," to his own words. "Come, Josephine, in My Flying Machine" (Alfred Bryan) was one of the earliest songs about aerial transportation; written in 1910, it was introduced that year in vaudeville by Blanche Ring. In 1914, in *The Belle of Bond Street*, Gaby Deslys introduced Fisher's comedy number, "Who Paid the Rent for Mrs. Rip Van Winkle When Rip Van Winkle Went Away?" (Alfred Bryan). "They Go Wild, Simply Wild, Over Me" (Joseph McCarthy) in 1917 was another of his infectious comedy songs. "Dardanella," in 1919—the song above all others for which Fisher must be remembered—is a ragtime number.

In its first year, "Dardanella" sold almost two million copies of sheet music and over a million disks in a Victor recording by Ben Selvin's Novelty Orchestra. Within a few years, it was believed to have sold six and a half million records. But another claim to its fame comes from a lawsuit in which Fisher sued Jerome Kern for plagiarism, insisting that the boogie-woogie-like recurring bass theme Kern used in his song "Ka-lu-a" (Anne Caldwell) was a steal from a similar device in "Dardanella."

It took a good deal of arrogance for Fisher to sue Kern for plagiarism, since "Dardanella" itself had actually been stolen property involving Fisher in a lawsuit of his own. It started out as "Turkish Tom Tom," a piano rag by Johnny S. Black. Fisher wrote lyrics for it, and became its publisher, now using for this number the new title of "Dardanella." After its initial successes, Felix Bernard, a vaudevillian came forward with a claim that it was he and not Black who had written the basic melody and that he had renounced his prior rights to it for a cash settlement of one hundred dollars. Bernard went to court to claim some of the royalties, insisting that Fisher had defrauded him. Bernard's case was handily dismissed; but all later sheet music publications carried Fisher's name solely as lyricist, while Johnny S. Black *and* Felix Bernard are named as composers.

Though Fisher's principal songs appeared before World War I, he produced several hits in the early 1920s; the best known of them are the sentimental ballad "Daddy, You've Been a Mother to Me" and "Chicago" ("That Toddling Town") for both of which he wrote his own lyrics; "Chicago" was popularized in vaudeville by Blossom Seeley.

Harry Carroll (1892–1962) began earning money from music while attending public school in Atlantic City, New Jersey, where he was born. Late in the afternoons and in the evenings he played mood music on the piano in local movie theaters. After graduating from high school he came to New York. During the day, he toiled in Tin Pan Alley as an arranger, and at night, he played the piano at the Garden Café on 50th Street and Seventh Avenue. He wrote some songs that caught the interest of the Shuberts who hired him to write music for some of their productions. Carroll rewarded their faith with his first smash, in 1912, "On the Mississippi" (Ballard MacDonald), which he wrote with Arthur Fields. It was interpolated that year into two Shubert productions, *The Whirl of Society* and *Hanky Panky*. It had a million-copy sheet music sale, and so did three other Carroll songs in the next two years: "There's a Girl in the Heart of Maryland" and "The Trail of the Lonesome Pine," both to the lyrics of Ballard MacDonald, and "By the Sea" (Harold Atteridge). "The Trail of the Lonesome Pine" was inspired by the popular novel of the same name by John Fox, Jr.; Muriel Window introduced it in *The Passing Show of 1914*. Miss Window also sang "By the Beautiful Sea" in that show, but earlier it had been introduced to the stage in vaudeville by The Stanford Four.

In 1918, Carroll created the complete score for the Broadway musical, *Oh Look!*, lyrics by Joseph McCarthy. Here we find "I'm Always Chasing Rainbows," sung by Harry Fox. The melody of its chorus was lifted bodily from Chopin's Fantaisie-Impromptu in C-sharp minor. Stealing melodies from the masters was nothing unusual in 1918, and it would prove far less so in ensuing years. But until then nobody profited so prodigiously from larceny as Carroll did. Over a million copies of sheet music were sold, as well as a million disks, and all this in less than a year; its fame was kept permanently alive in theaters and in motion pictures. It was the high point of Harry Carroll's revue in which he was starred for many years on the vaudeville circuit, and in his nightclub act in which he appeared as a single. Perhaps overshadowed by the luster of such fame, Carroll's later songs all lapsed into obscurity.

While Richard A. Whiting (1891–1938) wrote some of his best songs late in life for the screen, his career had its important beginnings in Tin Pan Alley. Born in Peoria, Illinois, Whiting had his first hit while working as an office manager for Jerome H. Remick, then based in Detroit. It was "It's Tulip Time in Holland" (Dave Radford) which Remick published in 1915. Whiting thought he had made a financial coup when he accepted a Steinway grand piano as full payment for all the rights to this ballad, since his earlier numbers, published by Remick, had brought him an outright payment of one hundred dollars each. "It's Tulip Time in Holland" sold a million and a half copies of sheet music in half a year, which would have brought Whiting the price of fifty grand pianos had he been on a royalty basis.

After 1915, Whiting was receiving royalties, and consequently was able to profit from the successes of "Mammy's Little Coal Black Rose" (Raymond Egan), "Where the Black-Eyed Susans Grow" (Dave Radford) which Al Jolson featured in *Robinson Crusoe, Jr.*, "Where the Morning Glories Grow" (Gus Kahn and Raymond Egan) and the foremost ballad of World War I, "Till We Meet Again" (Raymond Egan).

Whiting carried his habit of success into the twenties with "The Japanese Sandman" (Raymond Egan), "Ain't We Got Fun," to his own words, and "Sleepy Time Gal" (Joseph R. Alden and Raymond Egan). Nora Bayes often sang "The Japanese Sandman" in vaudeville, and Paul Whiteman and his Orchestra made a hit record of it for Victor. "Ain't We Got Fun" was first heard in the revue *Satires of 1920*, but did not catch on until Ruth Roye used it in her vaudeville act. "Sleepy Time Gal," whose melody was written in collaboration with Ange Lorenzo, was widely circulated by Glen Gray and his Casa Loma Orchestra and by Cliff "Ukulele Ike" Edwards.

Whiting's subsequent song history belongs partly to the Broadway theater but mainly to the Hollywood talking screen.

Egbert Van Alstyne (1882–1951) had been a musical prodigy in Chicago where he was born and received his musical training. Then he toured the vaudeville circuit, and worked in Tin Pan Alley as a staff pianist and song plugger for Remick. He first drew attention to his songwriting talent with one of the earliest Tin Pan Alley exploitations of the American Indian, "Navajo" (Harry H. Williams). Marie Cahill introduced it in the Broadway musical *Nancy Brown* (1903). Two more of his songs, to Williams' lyrics, used the American Indian as subjects, "Cheyenne" in 1906 and "San Antonio" in 1907. But Williams and Van Alstyne proved that they were no less adept with other types of song material. "In the Shade of the Old Apple Tree" in 1905 was one of the giant ballad successes of the decade. "Back, Back, Back to Baltimore" in 1904 was a Negro comedy song popular in vaudeville and minstrel shows. And "Oh, that Navajo Rag" in 1911 was, as its title indicates, a ragtime number.

In 1915, Van Alstyne found a new lyricist in Gus Kahn. Kahn had come from Germany as a child of five, and was brought up and educated in Van Alstyne's hometown of Chicago. While supporting himself by working as a clerk in a hotel supply firm and later in a mail-order house, Kahn began writing lyrics, one of which was published in 1907. It was as a writing partner of Egbert Van Alstyne that Kahn hit his full stride as one of the most prolific and successful lyricists of his time (the subject of the only screen biography devoted exclusively to a lyricist, *I'll See You in My Dreams*, in 1951). In 1915, to Kahn's lyrics, Van Alstyne wrote "Memories," and in 1916, with Tony Jackson as collaborator, "Pretty Baby." Other early successes by Kahn and Van Alstyne were "Sailin' Away on the Henry Clay" which Elizabeth Murray introduced in the musical, *Good Night, Paul* (1917), and "Your Eyes Have Told Me So," where Van Alstyne had Walter Blaufuss as collaborator in writing the melody.

Walter Donaldson (1893–1947), a native of Brooklyn, New York, wrote songs for school productions without the benefit of formal training. After graduating from high school he tried to make his way in Wall Street before he came to the decision to make popular music his lifework. He found a job as demonstration pianist and song plugger in Tin Pan Alley. Writing songs became a passion. He lost one of his jobs in Tin Pan Alley because he was found scribbling his own melodies during working hours. In 1915, Waterson, Berlin and Snyder published Donaldson's first song hit, "Just Try to Picture Me Down Home in Tennessee" (William Jerome) more familiarly known as "Back Home in Tennessee." It has become the song most frequently associated with that state, but Donaldson wrote it without ever having set foot there.

During World War I, Donaldson was an entertainer for the armed forces at Camp Upton, New York. The war gave him fresh material for songs, one being a comedy number, "How Ya Gonna Keep 'Em Down on the Farm?" (Sam M. Lewis and Joe Young) which Sophie Tucker introduced in vaudeville and Eddie Cantor made famous. After the end of the war, Donaldson joined the newly formed publishing house of Irving Berlin, Inc. in an executive position. He remained there a decade, writing for it a long succession of hits which made him a leader in Tin Pan Alley in the 1920s. These hits began with "My Mammy"

(Sam M. Lewis and Joe Young) in 1920. When Al Jolson heard it, it had already been sung on the vaudeville circuit by Bill Frawley. Jolson instantly felt this was his kind of song and interpolated it into *Sinbad*. Performed on bended knee, and with white-gloved hands outstretched, "My Mammy" at once became a Jolson standard. He sang it when he made his screen debut in *The Jazz Singer* (1928), and again on the sound track of his screen biography, *The Jolson Story* (1946).

In 1922, Walter Donaldson began working with the lyricist, Gus Kahn, who by then had become a songwriter of no small consequence in Tin Pan Alley. This partnership was initiated with a smash, "My Buddy," sung to national fame by Al Jolson. The words-and-music partnership of Gus Kahn and Walter Donaldson continued with "Yes, Sir, That's My Baby," still in 1922, and "Carolina in the Morning" three years later. "Yes, Sir, That's My Baby" was written for Eddie Cantor; in fact, the idea for the song lyric was hatched in Cantor's home in Great Neck, Long Island. Kahn was playing with a mechanical toy pig belonging to Cantor's little daughter. As the toy jogged along the floor, Kahn improvised the lines "yes sir, that's my baby, no sir, don't mean maybe" to the rhythm of the toy pig's movements. Cantor told them then and there that those two lines were the beginnings of a good song. Kahn completed the lyric, Donaldson, the music, Cantor introduced it on the stage, and Gene Austin made a highly successful recording of it for Victor.

"Carolina in the Morning" was introduced in vaudeville by Bill Frawley after which it was sung by Willie and Eugene Howard in the revue *The Passing Show of 1922*. Here again, we have a nostalgic song about a Southern state which the composer had never visited.

The Kahn-Donaldson team was also responsible for the complete score of the Ziegfeld produced musical, *Whoopee* (1928) where Eddie Cantor sang "Makin' Whoopee" and Ruth Etting "Love Me or Leave Me." "My Baby Just Cares for Me," another Eddie Cantor favorite, was not written for that stage show but for the movie version produced by Paramount in 1930.

One of Donaldson's most famous ballads, and another staple in the Eddie Cantor repertory, was "My Blue Heaven," lyrics not by Gus Kahn but by George Whiting. It was written in 1924, three years before its publication; Donaldson wrote it one afternoon at the Friars Club in New York while waiting for his turn at a billiard table. George Whiting, then appearing in vaudeville, adapted the lyrics to the melody and used it in his act, but the song failed to attract much attention. For three years it lay in discard until Tommy Lyman, a radio singer, picked it up for use as his theme song. Gene Austin recorded it for Victor, selling several million disks. Only then did Eddie Cantor use it—in the *Ziegfeld Follies of 1927*. It has become one of the most famous songs ever written about marital happiness—ironically by Donaldson, a bachelor!

In 1928, Donaldson left the firm of Irving Berlin, Inc. to join up with Mose Gumble, the veteran song plugger, to establish the new Tin Pan Alley firm of Donaldson, Douglas and Gumble. This house issued the song hits from *Whoopee*, and after that several Donaldson songs to his own lyrics, among them "Just Like a Melody Out of the Sky," "You're Driving Me Crazy" and "Little White Lies."

The songwriting career of Harry Ruby (1895–1974) was also prefaced by training in Tin Pan Alley. Like Irving Berlin he was a boy from New York's East Side, and again like Berlin he received much of his boyhood education in the city streets. After teaching himself to play the piano he worked with a trio in a New Jersey resort when he was sixteen. Some years later he was hired as a demonstration pianist and song plugger for the publishing house of Gus Edwards. Later he held a similar post with Harry von Tilzer.

For a time he also toured the vaudeville circuit as a pianist. While making the rounds of the vaudeville theaters he met and befriended Bert Kalmar, a vaudevillian who was also the owner of a New York music publishing firm. Kalmar prevailed on Ruby to come to work with him as pianist and song plugger. Some time later, when a knee injury incapacitated Kalmar for his vaudeville act and he decided to devote his time to writing lyrics, he asked Ruby to work with him. Their first job was writing songs for Belle Baker's vaudeville act, one of which, "He Sits Around," in 1916, became one of her special features. A year later they wrote a Hawaiian-type song then so much in vogue in Tin Pan Alley—"When Those Sweet Hawaiian Babies Roll Their Eyes." Several comedy numbers were added to their expanding output in 1920, among them "So Long, Oo Long" and "Where Do They Go When They Row, Row, Row?". The latter was a tongue-in-cheek comment on the 1912 hit song, "Row, Row, Row" (William Jerome—James V. Monaco) still very much around in 1920. Kalmar and Ruby wrote their first Broadway score in 1923, for *Helen of Troy, N.Y.*, book by Marc Connelly and George S. Kaufman. Most of the best songs of Kalmar and Ruby during the 1920s came from the musical theater. Eddie Cantor sang "My Sunny Tennessee" in *The Midnight Rounders* (1920); Jack Whiting and Marie Saxon were heard in "All Alone Monday" in *The Ramblers* (1926); Oscar Shaw and Mary Eaton introduced "Thinking of You" in *The Five O'Clock Girl* (1927); and "I Wanna Be Loved by You" was a feature of the boop-a-doop girl, Helen Kane, in *Good Boy* (1928).

On the other hand, "Snoops the Lawyer" in 1921 was popularized in vaudeville after which it helped to launch Beatrice Lillie's career as a comedienne in England. And one of Ruby's hardiest standards, "Three Little Words," was written for the motion picture *Check and Double Check* (1930) where it was sung by Bing Crosby to an instrumental background provided by Duke Ellington and his orchestra.

Sometimes Ruby wrote his music for lyricists other than Kalmar, and sometimes, too, he was either his own lyricist, or he wrote lyrics for other composers. It was as a lyricist rather than composer (with the help of Kalmar) that he created another of his song classics, "Who's Sorry Now," in 1923, music by Ted Snyder, introduced in vaudeville by Van and Schenck. The song was revived in 1957 when Connie Frances interpreted it with a strong beat rather than in a slow and sentimental tempo for an MGM recording that sold over a million disks and brought the then unknown singer into the limelight.

Harry Ruby lived long enough to write many hit songs after "Who's Sorry Now," to witness the publication of *The Kalmar and Ruby Song Book* (1936), to write *Songs My Mother Never Sang* (1943), and to see his life story dramatized in the motion picture *Three Little Words* (1950).

George W. Meyer (1884–1959) was an electrician, accountant and oculist before he turned to song plugging. "Lonesome" (Edgar Leslie) in 1909, written in collaboration with Kerry Mills, was his first successful song, selling over a million copies. The songs that followed were just a prelude to the biggest hit of his career. In 1917 "For Me and My Gal" (Edgar Leslie and E. Ray Goetz) had a three-million-copy sheet music sale. There was hardly a vaudeville star of any eminence who did not perform it, including Al Jolson, Eddie Cantor and Sophie Tucker. A quarter of a century later, in 1942, the song provided the title for the MGM screen musical in which Judy Garland was starred and in which Gene Kelly made his screen debut.

Milton Ager, born in 1893, gained his early musical experience playing mood music in movie houses, providing musical backgrounds for song slides, serving as accompanist to a singer on the vaudeville circuit and doing odd jobs as song plugger for the Chicago branch of Waterson, Berlin and Snyder. He came to New York in 1913 to work in the main office as demonstration pianist and song plugger. In 1920, he initiated a fruitful words-and-music partnership with the lyricist Jack Yellen. Their first success was "Who Cares?" which Jolson interpolated into *Bombo* in 1922. "I Wonder What's Become of Sally?," introduced at the Palace Theater in New York in 1924, had a million-copy sheet music sale; and so did "Ain't She Sweet" in 1927, adopted by Eddie Cantor, Sophie Tucker and Lillian Roth for their respective vaudeville acts after Paul Ash and his orchestra had introduced it at the Oriental Theater in Chicago. The subsequent song accomplishments of Yellen and Ager belong to the musical theater, and after that to the motion picture screen.

4

When George Gershwin, not yet sixteen, was hired for fifteen dollars a week to work as a demonstration pianist for Jerome H. Remick in Tin Pan Alley, he became the youngest employe in the business. He was born in Brooklyn, New York, on September 26, 1898. His childhood and early boyhood were spent in the city streets, mostly on New York's Lower East Side, in the pastimes of the street: roller skating, punch ball, fights. However a sensitive response to things musical was latent in him, and every once in a while something happened to bring it to the surface. He was about six when he heard Anton Rubinstein's *Melody in F* in a penny arcade. "That melody," he later recalled, "held me rooted . . . drinking it all in avidly." About a year later, he would sit for hours on the curb outside Baron Wilkins' nightclub in Harlem, listening to the intoxicating sounds of Jim Europe's jazz music. He was about ten when, playing ball outside his public school in New York, he heard the strains of Dvořák's *Humoresque* played by a violinist. This music was, in his own words, "a flashing revelation." The violinist was one of George's schoolmates, a gifted young musician named Maxie Rosenzweig who later concertized as Max Rosen. George sought out Maxie and they became friends. Maxie often played the violin for George and began to unfold to him the world of great music.

A piano entered the Gershwin household when George was twelve. From then on the boy was tireless in his efforts to draw from the keyboard the popular tunes he knew and loved, and in making up melodies of his own. He began studying the piano with local teachers. The most important was Charles Hambitzer. He introduced Gershwin to what up to then had been for the boy terra incognita: the piano classics from Bach and Chopin to Debussy and Ravel. He fired the boy with his own ardor, and transmitted to him his own enthusiasm. Hambitzer soon encouraged Gershwin to supplement piano study with instruction in composition and theory with Edward Kilenyi. At his teacher's urging Gershwin began going to concerts. He also worked hard at the piano. But he had a mind of his own, and would not allow anything to deflect him from his love for popular music. He was, as Hambitzer once wrote, "crazy about jazz and ragtime." The young Gershwin delighted in playing Irving Berlin's "Alexander's Ragtime Band" and when he first heard Jerome Kern's music—at his aunt's wedding in 1914—he instantly became a passionate Kern enthusiast. "I followed Kern's work and studied each song he composed," Gershwin recalled later. "I paid him the tribute of frank imitation, and many things I wrote at this period sounded as though Kern had written them himself." Yes—the boy Gershwin was already writing popular music: a ballad, "Since I Found You" in 1913 which was never published, followed by "Ragging the Träumerei." Gershwin became convinced that in the hands of a Berlin or a Kern, popular idioms could become important music. Slowly Gershwin acquired the assurance that this was the kind of music he wanted to write. "The boy is a genius without doubt," reported Hambitzer to his sister. "He wants to go in for this modern stuff, jazz and what not. . . . I'll see that he gets a firm foundation in standard music first."

Determined to learn all he could about popular music, Gershwin went to work for Jerome H. Remick. There his duties consisted in playing Remick tunes all day long for potential clients and occasionally going out to department and five-and-ten-cent stores to plug them. "I still recall George's earnestness, his intense enthusiasm for his work, his passionate interest in every phase of the popular music business," recalled Harry Ruby, then a fellow song plugger. "Sometimes when he spoke of the artistic mission of popular music, we thought he was going highfalutin'. The height of artistic achievement to us was a 'pop' song that sold lots of copies. . . ."

Gershwin was learning the song business from the inside, the subtle and complex mechanism that triggered a hit. He was put into direct communication with the best popular tunes of the day, and with many of their creators. And all this time he was writing songs of his own. His serious approach to popular songwriting is best illustrated by an incident. A fellow plugger at Remick's found him one day in his cubicle practicing Bach's *The Well-Tempered Clavier*. "Are you practicing to become a concert pianist?" the plugger inquired. Gershwin replied: "No, I'm studying to be a great popular song composer."

By 1917, he joined the professional ranks of song composers. Sophie Tucker liked his song "When You Want 'Em You Can't Get 'Em" (Murray Roth) and recommended it to Harry von Tilzer who published it. Another song, "The Making of a Girl" (Harold Atteridge) was not only published (this time by G. Schirmer), but was Gershwin's first to be heard on Broadway, in the revue *The Passing Show of 1916*.

Two of Gershwin's songs in 1917, "You—oo Just You" and "There's More to the Kiss than X-X-X" were sung by Vivienne Segal at her concert at the Century Theater. These two numbers linked Gershwin's name with that of the lyricist Irving Caesar. Caesar, a New Yorker, was three years older than Gershwin. Educated in the city public schools and at the College of the City of New York, Caesar worked as a stenographer on the Henry Ford Peace Ship in 1915 that tried to end World War I. Caesar then became a mechanic in one of Ford's automobile plants. His heart, however, was in songwriting; even while working at the conveyor belt he kept thinking about and working out song ideas.

He first met Gershwin at Remick's where he would come from time to time to listen to Gershwin's piano playing. They soon became friends. They joined a social club in downtown New York, played billiards in Broadway pool rooms, sneaked into Carnegie Hall concerts through a back entrance, attended Kern musicals, and collaborated in amusing improvisations for their friends. Working together became a foregone conclusion.

Gershwin was outgrowing his cramped cubicle at Remick's. He left that job and held some others, but none advanced him in his songwriting ambitions. Irving Berlin, one day, gave him an attractive offer to become his musical secretary. "But," Berlin added, "I hope you don't take the job. You're much too talented to be anybody's secretary." Gershwin followed Berlin's advice and turned down the position. Then came a job that promised much more for his future. Max Dreyfus, the head of Harms, offered him a weekly salary of thirty-five dollars to write songs. There were no set duties or hours. All Gershwin was obligated to do was to show Dreyfus everything he wrote, and to listen to the older man's counsel.

With Dreyfus behind him, Gershwin began to advance quickly. In 1918, he wrote the complete score for a revue, *Half-Past Eight*, which opened and closed in Syracuse without Gershwin receiving the fifteen hundred dollars promised him. He had songs in three Broadway productions. In 1919, Alex A. Aarons, a young man engaging in theatrical producing for the first time, signed him to write his first full score for a Broadway musical. It was *La, La, Lucille*, which opened the new Henry Miller Theater in New York on

May 26, 1919, and compiled a run of over one hundred performances before it had to close because of the Actors Equity strike. One of its songs was "There's More to the Kiss than X-X-X," renamed "There's More to the Kiss than the Sound." Another, "Nobody but You" (Arthur Jackson) had a melody with Jerome Kern charm.

In the same year of 1919, Gershwin was the proud parent of his first hit song, "Swanee," that sold over two million records and a million copies of sheet music.

"Swanee" was born in Dinty Moore's restaurant in New York. Gershwin and Irving Caesar were having lunch there to discuss song ideas when they decided to write a one-step in the style of the then popular "Hindustan" (Oliver G. Wallace and Harold Weeks). They chose an American setting, "something like Stephen Foster's 'Swanee River' " as Gershwin suggested. The idea jelled further atop a Fifth Avenue bus, and by the time they reached Gershwin's apartment on Washington Heights, they had clearly in mind the song they wanted to write. They completed it in Gershwin's living room the same afternoon while a poker game was in progress in the adjoining dining room. That game was temporarily interrupted as Gershwin and Caesar tried out their song for the first time, with Papa Gershwin providing an obbligato by whistling into a comb wrapped in tissue paper.

Ned Wayburn used "Swanee" for an elaborately contrived stage production which helped to open the recently constructed movie palace in New York, the Capitol Theater, on October 24, 1919. Sixty chorus girls, electric lights glowing on their slippers, danced to its rhythms on an otherwise darkened stage. The song did not go over, and the sale of sheet music was poor. But one day Gershwin played it for Al Jolson who decided to include it at a Winter Garden Sunday night concert. It made such a hit there that Jolson interpolated it into the musical extravaganza, *Sinbad*, in which he was then appearing. He also recorded it for Columbia on January 9, 1920. "Swanee" now swept the country and raised its still unknown composer to a position of prominence.

In 1920, Gershwin's place on Broadway and Tin Pan Alley was made even more secure when George White engaged him to write the music for the *Scandals*, an ambitious revue which White had launched one year earlier to compete with the *Ziegfeld Follies*. For five editions, Gershwin wrote all the songs used in the *Scandals*. He was now traveling far and fast—farther and faster than even he dared dream about at that time.

15

To Make the World Safe for Democracy

1

On July 28, 1914, on the heels of the assassination of Archduke Francis Ferdinand of Austria by a Serb nationalist at Sarajevo, hostilities broke out between Serbia and the Austro-Hungarian Empire. Despite frenetic efforts throughout Europe to confine the war, Russia, Germany, France and England were drawn into the maelstrom within a week. Like a sensitive seismograph, Tin Pan Alley recorded the vibrations in song.

A major European war stimulated a renewal of patriotism and national pride. In 1915, Americans heard, responded enthusiastically to, and sang "America, I Love You" (Edgar Leslie—Archie Gottler), "Under the American Flag" (Andrew Sterling—Harry von Tilzer) and "We'll Never Let Our Old Flag Fall" (Albert E. MacNutt—M. F. Kelly).

President Wilson firmly declared American neutrality and urged Americans everywhere to be "impartial in thought as well as action." Some songs, however, betrayed the fact that, the President notwithstanding, there were those who leaned strongly toward the Allies. It is not without significance that several English songs associated with the war became popular in America at this time: "Keep the Home Fires Burning," "It's a Long, Long Way to Tipperary," "Pack Up Your Troubles" and "Roses of Picardy."

Sentimental and cultural sympathies with the Allies notwithstanding, Americans were in no mood to get into the fight. This sentiment found voice in a major hit song of 1915: "I Didn't Raise My Boy to Be a Soldier" (Alfred Bryan—Al Piantadosi), which Ed Morton introduced in vaudeville and which became a part of Nora Bayes' repertory. The sheet music cover portrayed exploding shells bursting around an old gray-haired woman protecting her son. In a similar pacifist vein were "Don't Take My Darling Boy Away" (another number made popular by Miss Bayes), and "Our Hats Off to You Mr. President," the latter an expression of gratitude to President Wilson for affirming that "we are too proud to fight."

In 1916, President Wilson was reelected on the slogan "he kept us out of the war." But propelled by uncontrollable forces, events moved swiftly, including growing American favoritism for the Allies, and hostility toward the German "Hun." Pacificism was slowly being corroded by mounting war fever and reports of German arrogance and "atrocities."

Ever responsive to changing moods, songs reflected the feelings of the American people. After the invasion of Belgium, Irving Berlin wrote "Voice of Belgium." The sinking of the *Lusitania* brought "When the Lusitania Went Down" (Albert E. MacNutt—M. F. Kelly). "In Time of Peace Prepare for War" (Eddie Cavanaugh—Bob Allan), expressed an aroused martial spirit. With pacifism gradually becoming taboo, nobody sang "I Didn't Raise My Boy to Be a Soldier" any longer. In its place were numerous parodies more sympathetic to the times: "I Did Not Raise My Boy to Be a Coward," "I'd Be Proud to Be the Mother of a Soldier," and "I Didn't Raise My Boy to Be a Soldier, I'll Send My Girl to Be a Nurse," were three of many.

On April 2, 1917, President Wilson asked a cheering Congress for a declaration of war against Germany. "The world must be made safe for democracy," he said. America was at war. On September 12, 1918, all men between the ages of eighteen and forty-five were compelled to register for the draft so that an army of one million men could be raised.

Machinery for disseminating war propaganda throughout the country was set up with dispatch in Washington, D. C., with the creation of the Committee for Public Information headed by George Creel. The war message was thundered from lecture platforms, street corners and omnipresent posters. Theatrical and motion picture stars appeared at rallies to help sell Liberty Bonds, whose sale was also promoted in motion picture houses. In the nation's schoolrooms the purchase of War Saving Stamps was encouraged ("Lick a stamp and lick the Kaiser.") Hollywood was busily concocting motion pictures about the war, pointing up the atrocities perpetrated on women and children by the Hun. *The Beast of Berlin* was one of the more lurid ones, with other anti-German war motion pictures including *The Spy Menace, My Four Years in Germany* and D. W. Griffith's *Hearts of the World*.

Songs were an all-important part of this deluge of propaganda. In no other American war were songs sung by so many people in so many different places. With many theaters and cabarets closed down because of fuel and power shortage, Americans reverted to seeking their entertainment at home. What better way to while away an evening than by singing war songs? It became the patriotic thing to do. Everybody sang—not only at home, but in theaters, in arranged songfests, at community sings, at Liberty Bond rallies. The Committee for Public Information encouraged singing as a builder of homefront moral by issuing songbooks for distribution to audiences in motion picture and vaudeville theaters to stimulate communal singing. The government even dispatched special song leaders to visit the theaters and animate the audiences into singing. Songbooks were freely circulated to the men in army camps.

With the ranks of professional entertainers sadly depleted by enlistments and the draft, theaters had to seek new forms of public entertainment. One was song competitions in which newly written war songs were introduced before audiences by song pluggers from Tin Pan Alley. The audience was called upon to pick the winner. Another form of entertainment was the amateur night which gained increased momentum during the war.

With machine-like precision and speed, Tin Pan Alley was geared to meet this swelling demand for war songs by producing them on every conceivable subject. There were songs to kindle the fires of patriotism, to arouse the fighting spirit, or to incite hate or contempt for the enemy. There were others which sang of hope, optimism, sentiment, nostalgia for home, the pain of separation from loved ones. There were songs to glorify various branches of the service. There were humorous songs to provide relief from war tensions.

The arch villain in this struggle was, of course, the Kaiser. Tin Pan Alley produced over a hundred anti-Kaiser songs beginning with "We Are Out for the Scalp of Mister Kaiser" on June 7, 1918, and "We Want the Kaiser's Helmet Now" four days later. "We Will Make the Kaiser Wiser," the following September, was sung to the melody of "John Brown's Body." As the war psychosis deepened, Kaiser songs became increasingly savage. In due course were published, performed and sung: "We're Going to Hang the Kaiser on the Linden Tree," "We're Going to Whip the Kaiser," "The Crazy Kaiser," "I'd Like to See the Kaiser with a Lily in His Hand," "We'll Give the Stars and Stripes to the Kaiser," "If I Only Had My Razor Under the Kaiser's Chin," "Shoot the Kaiser" and "The Kaiser Is a Devil." Kaiser songs kept coming even after the Armistice: "Hang the Kaiser to the Sour Apple Tree," "We've Turned His Moustache Down," "We Sure Got that Kaiser, We Did" and "The Kaiser Now Is Wiser."

High on the list of favorite topics for songs were separation and farewell. The best were: "I May Be Gone for a Long, Long Time" (Lew Brown—Albert von Tilzer), "Au Revoir, But Not Goodbye, Soldier Boy" (Lew Brown—Albert von Tilzer), "Send Me Away With a Smile" (Louis Weslyn—Al Piantadosi), "Bring Back My Daddy to Me" (William Tracey and Howard Johnson—George W. Meyer), "Just a Baby's Prayer at Twilight" (Sam M. Lewis and Joe Young—M. K. Jerome), "Hello, Central, Give Me No Man's Land" (Sam M. Lewis and Joe Young—Jean Schwartz). Perhaps the most famous of all were "Till We Meet Again" (Raymond Egan—Richard A. Whiting) and "There's a Long, Long Trail" (Stoddard King—Zo Elliott).

Richard Whiting, the composer, thought so little of "Till We Meet Again" that he crumpled up his manuscript and threw it in the wastebasket. His wife found it there and, without her husband's knowledge, brought it to the attention of the Detroit branch of Jerome H. Remick, where Whiting was then employed. The house tried out the song in a Detroit movie theater in one of the patriotic song contests then so popular. The song won first prize. Remick then published it and had Muriel Window introduce it. It became a runaway best-seller, with several million copies of sheet music disposed of, making it the leading ballad of World War I.

"There's a Long, Long Trail" was actually written before the war. Its authors— Stoddard King, lyricist, and Zo Elliott, composer—were then seniors at Yale where they wrote it for a fraternity banquet. Nobody seemed to have a high regard for it. The following fall, Zo Elliott entered Trinity College at Cambridge, England. He submitted his song to a small publisher who accepted it after Elliott agreed to pay the expenses for the first printing, with the money refundable if the song was profitable. When the war broke out in Europe, Elliott was touring Germany, from which he escaped to Switzerland. There he found a sizable sum of money awaiting him as accrued royalties on his song which, stimulated by the war, had begun to be heard in England. After returning to America in 1914, Elliott induced M. Witmark and Sons to take over the copyright. For about three years the sheet music failed to move off the shelves, but with American participation in the war the sales suddenly began to skyrocket. This ballad was particularly cherished by President Wilson who often sang it after dinner.

Many songs of World War I had a stirring martial ring and message. The cream of the crop were: "We're Going Over" (Andrew B. Sterling—Bernie Grossman and Arthur Lange), "We'll Knock the Heligo-Into, Heligo-Out of Heligoland" (John O'Brien—Theodore F. Morse), "Bing! Bang! Bing 'Em on the Rhine" (Jack Mahoney and Allan Flynn), "Just Like Washington Crossed the Delaware, General Pershing Will Cross the Rhine" (Howard Johnson—George W. Meyer), "We Don't Want the Bacon—What We Want Is a Piece of the Rhine" (Howard Carr, Harry Russell and Jimmie Havens), "Keep Your Head Down Fritzi Boy" (Gitz Rice), "Lafayette, We Hear You Calling" (Robert A. King), "Your Country Needs You" (Al Dubin—Rennie Cormack and George B. McConnell) and "Liberty Bell, It's Time to Ring Again" (Joe Goodwin—Halsey K. Mohr).

Effective as some of these songs were in igniting the flames of war in the consciousness of civilians, none seemed to capture the excitment of the war so completely as did George M. Cohan's "Over There." It became *the* song classic of World War I, possibly the most celebrated American war song of all time.

Cohan himself once described "Over There" as a "dramatization of a bugle call." He wrote it in his office late in the evening of April 8, 1917, the day after President Wilson had signed the declaration of war. (The long held conviction that he wrote it on the back of an envelope on his way to New York City from his home in Great Neck, Long Island, after reading the war headlines that morning, has been disavowed by his family.) The next morning, Sunday, at his New York apartment, he called his family together. "He said," his daughter Mary recalls, "that he had just finished a new song and he wanted to sing it for us. . . . He put a big tin pan from the kitchen on his head, used a broom for a gun on his shoulder, and he started to mark time like a soldier singing, 'Johnnie, get your gun, get your gun, get your gun'. . . . Then he started to walk up and down, swinging one arm vigorously and singing even more loudly: 'Over there, over there, Send the word, send the word over there.' We kids had heard, of course, that the United States was at war, and now here was Dad acting just like a soldier. So I began to sob, and I threw myself down, hanging for dear life to his legs as he marched, begging him, pleading with him not to go away to the war."

When Cohan tried out his song for American soldiers at Fort Myers, near Washington, D. C., the response was disheartening. However, when sung by Charles King at a Red Cross benefit at the Hippodrome Theater in New York, it inspired a thunderous ovation from the audience. Soon after that, Cohan sang it for Nora Bayes in her dressing room. So taken was she with it that she at once interpolated it into the musical in which she was then appearing, (and also recorded it for Victor). Her rendition almost caused a stampede in the theater. She continued singing it up and down America throughout the war.

Leo Feist acquired the publication rights for twenty-five thousand dollars which, as it turned out, proved a mere pittance compared to the income that poured in the moment the song reached the marketplace. By the time the war was over it had sold two million copies of sheet music and over a million records. Even the great Enrico Caruso sang and recorded it in his quaint accent. President Wilson described it as "a genuine inspiration to all American manhood." A quarter of a century later, the song brought Cohan the Congressional Medal from President Franklin D. Roosevelt by a special act of Congress.

Among other war songs were some that sentimentalized American relations with its Allies: "Madelon" (Alfred Bryan—Camille Robert), "Joan of Arc, They Are Calling You" (Alfred Bryan and Willie Weston—Jack Wells), "Lorraine, My Beautiful Alsace Lorraine" (Alfred Bryan—Fred Fisher) and "My Belgian Rose" (George Benoit, Robert Levenson and Ted Garton).

"The Rose of No Man's Land" (Jack Caddigan—Joseph A. Brennan) paid tribute to the Red Cross nurse, while "The Navy Took Them Over and the Navy Will Bring Them Back" (Howard Johnson—Ira Schuster) was a gesture to the men in blue on the high seas. There were songs anticipating the soldier's return home: "When the Boys Come Home" (John Hay—Oley Speaks) and George M. Cohan's "When You Come Back." And, for a change of pace, there was an abundance of humorous songs, many of them poking mild fun at the doughboy's amatory adventures in France. There was the "stammering song," "K-K-K-Katy" (Geoffrey O'Hara), "If He Can Fight Like He Can Love, Goodnight Germany" (Grant Clarke and Howard E. Rogers—George W. Meyer), "I Don't Want to Get Well" (Howard Johnson and Harry Pease—Harry Jentes), "Oh, Frenchy!" (Sam Ehrlich —Con Conrad), Irving Berlin's "They Were All Out of Step but Jim," Walter Donaldson's "How Ya Gonna Keep 'Em Down on the Farm, After They've Seen Paree?" (Sam M. Lewis and Joe Young), Harry Ruby's "And He'd Say Ooh-La-La! Wee Wee" (George Jessel), "When Yankee Doodle Learns to Parlez-Vous Français" (William Hart—Ed Nelson) and "Oui, Oui, Marie" (Alfred Bryan and John McCarthy—Fred Fisher).

2

The war was very much a part of the Broadway musical theater, too. Some musicals assumed martial titles, as did two Sigmund Romberg musicals produced by the Shuberts in 1917 (*Over the Top* and *Doing Our Bit*), Victor Herbert's *Her Regiment* in 1917, and Ivan Caryll's *The Girl Behind the Gun* in 1918. Some of these did not actually have a war text, but the musical *The Better 'Ole* in 1918 was based on Captain Bruce Bairns' experiences in the trenches.

Many production numbers in revues and musical comedies assumed a military character. The *Ziegfeld Follies of 1917* had a patriotic finale which opened with Paul Revere's ride, included George Washington and Abraham Lincoln, and ended with President Wilson reviewing the American troops of 1917. For this scene Victor Herbert wrote "Can't You Hear Your Country Calling" (Gene Buck) which, as Herbert's biographer, Edward N. Waters, wrote, "helped to whip the crowd to a high pitch of excitement." The *Ziegfeld Follies of 1918* had an eye-arresting tableau, *Forward Allies*. The *Passing Show of 1917* offered a stirring production number for the song "Goodbye Broadway, Hello France" (C. Francis Reisner and Benny Davis—Billy Baskette), while the 1918 edition had a takeoff on Salome's dance with Salome dancing around with the head of the Kaiser on a tray.

War songs, the humorous as well as the sentimental, were widely interpolated. For the *Ziegfeld Follies of 1918* Berlin wrote "Blue Devils of France" and "I'm Gonna Pin a Medal on the Girl I Left Behind." In the same edition comedy was represented by the song "Would You Rather Be a Colonel with an Eagle on Your Shoulder, or a Private with a Chicken on Your Knee?" (Sidney D. Mitchell—Archie Gottler). One of the rousing numbers in *Hitchy Koo of 1918* was "Here Come the Yanks with the Tanks" (Ned Wayburn— Harold Orlob).

On May 30, 1918, *Biff! Bang!* came to the Century Theater. This was a revue written and acted by sailors of the Naval Training Station. Later the same year, on December 3, *Atta Boy* presented a revue at the Lexington Theater written and put on by the soldiers of the Aberdeen Proving Grounds. Neither was of even passing interest. But another all-soldier show became a shining theatrical event in 1918, Irving Berlin's *Yip, Yip, Yaphank*.

In 1917, Berlin had been called to uniform and stationed at Camp Upton, New York. General Bell, its commanding officer, asked him to write and produce an all-soldier show to raise $35,000 for a badly needed Service Center. Drawing from his own experiences as a sad rookie, Berlin not only wrote all the songs, sketches and dialogue, but even planned the dance routines and became a principal in the cast. *Yip, Yip, Yaphank* opened at the Century Theater on July 26, 1918. Berlin appeared in one of the scenes as a badly mauled K. P. whining: "I scrub the dishes against my wishes, to make this world safe for democracy." In another scene, he was dragged from his cot by the merciless call of reveille to lament "Oh, how I hate to get up in the morning," which became one of the most successful comedy songs of World War I. A poignant note was introduced in the song "In the Y.M.C.A." where a rookie, overwhelmed by loneliness, writes a letter to his mother. The revue ended with a spectacular finale, "We're On Our Way to France," with the cast in full regalia, embarking for overseas duty.

There was an ovation after the final curtain. General Bell made a brief speech in which he remarked: "I have heard that Berlin is among the foremost songwriters in the world, and now I believe it." *Variety* called the show "one of the best and most novel entertainments Broadway has ever witnessed." *Yip, Yip, Yaphank* played to capacity houses for four weeks, earning $83,000 for Camp Upton's Service Center; the sum grew to more than $150,000 after a short tour of Boston, Philadelphia and Washington, D. C. Eventually, the songs from the show earned many times that amount for the composer. While Berlin drew no additonal salary or royalties during the war from anything connected with *Yip, Yip Yaphank* he was, of course, free to capitalize on his songs once he discarded his uniform. Two passed the million-copy sheet music sale, "Oh, How I Hate to Get Up in the Morning" and "Mandy," the latter interpolated into the *Ziegfeld Follies of 1919.*

3

A compelling need among Americans to escape from time to time from the omnipresent pressures of war created a market for escapist songs. This is why, undoubtedly, Hawaiian-type songs flooded the market from 1916 on. The anguish of the world that Americans were feeling was alleviated momentarily by the exotic beauty of the far-off peaceful island where the main interest centered on the hula dance and hula girls.

The fad for Hawaiian songs began in 1915 with importations from Hawaii of "On the Beach of Waikiki" and "Song of the Islands." In Tin Pan Alley a hardy veteran of the song business, composer Jean Schwartz, with the help of lyricists Bert Kalmar and Edgar Leslie scented a possible vogue. In 1915 they wrote "Hello, Hawaii, How Are You?" With the war in Europe creating new stresses for Americans in 1916, a rash of Hawaiian songs erupted, persisting uninterruptedly throughout the war. Among them were "Oh, How She Could Yacki, Hacki, Wicki, Wacki, Woo" (Stanley Murphy and Charles McCarron—Albert von Tilzer), with which Eddie Cantor made his debut as a Ziegfeld protégé, and "Yacka Hula Hickey Dula" (E. Ray Goetz and Joe Young—Pete Wendling), which Al Jolson sang at the Winter Garden; also "They're Wearing 'Em Higher in Hawaii" (Joe Goodwin—Halsey K. Mohr), "The Honolulu Hicky-Boola-Boo" (Charles McCarron and Lew Brown—Albert von Tilzer), "I Lost My Heart in Honolulu" (Will D. Cobb—Gus Edwards), "My Honolulu Ukulele Baby" (Gerald N. Johnson—Henry Kailmai), "Hawaiian Butterfly" (George A. Little, Billy Baskette and Joseph Santly), "Back to My Sunny Honolulu" (Walter S. Poague —L. J. Finks), "I Can Hear the Ukuleles Calling Me" (Nat Vincent—Herman Paley) and "Hawaiian Sunshine" (L. Wolfe Gilbert—Carey Morgan).

Swept along on this tide of escapism, some songwriters found refuge in other far-off places in "On the South Sea Isle" (Harry von Tilzer), "My Isle of Golden Dreams" (Gus Kahn—Walter Blaufuss), "Hindustan" (Oliver G. Wallace—Harold Weeks) and "Singapore" (L. Wolfe Gilbert—Anatole Friedland).

The musical theater also provided welcome avenues of escape in 1917 and 1918. The beguiling make-believe world of operetta was represented by Rudolf Friml in *Sometime* and by Sigmund Romberg in *Maytime*. The Oriental spectacle, *Chu Chin Chow*, which had proved an opiate for war-weary Londoners was equally popular in New York; and so was the Al Jolson extravaganza, *Sinbad*. Levity, charm, humor—divorced from all possible military or war connotations—were generously distributed in two Princess Theater Shows, *Oh Boy!* and *Oh, Lady! Lady!*.

Two other musicals were immense box-office successes possibly because they offered a respite from the tensions of the times. *Going Up*, with book and lyrics by Otto Harbach and music by Louis A. Hirsch, was a musical farce about civilian aviation in which Edith Day sang the infectious "Tickle Toe" ("Ev'rybody Ought to Know How to Do the Tickle Toe"). *Leave It to Jane* was written by the combination responsible for the Princess Theater Shows—Guy Bolton, P. G. Wodehouse and Jerome Kern—but it was a sharp departure from intimacy, economy and understatement. It was, as a matter of fact, a full-scale musical with a college setting where a siren uses her allure to keep the school's star football halfback from defecting to the team of a rival college. Kern's best songs were the title number "The Siren Song," and a humorous confection, "Cleopatterer." That score was a prime attraction in 1917, and it remained one when this musical was revived Off-Broadway in 1959 for a run of several years.

4

During the war the men in uniform sang hopefully: "We are homeward bound, some day we'll hear that pleasant sound." After the Armistice was signed on November 11, 1918, they sang: "We are homeward bound, at last we hear that pleasant sound." The war to end all wars, the war to make the world safe for democracy, was over. More than one hundred thousand Americans had died, and over two hundred thousand more had been wounded. The immediate cost in dollars was in excess of twenty billion.

But the war was to leave scars that defaced American life. The men back from the war were soon to discover that while they were gone profiteers at home had become millionaires through the war: the number of American millionaires had been increased by four thousand. The returning heroes also learned that the jobs they had left behind had been confiscated by the so-called "slackers," and were no longer available. Many of those who had made inordinate sacrifices in the war effort now faced unemployment, economic depression, and a country indifferent to their plight.

Those returning from the war also discovered that during their absence, on May 1, 1919, reformers had pushed through Congress the Eighteenth Amendment, nationally prohibiting the use of grains for making intoxicating beverages. This was followed by the enactment of the Volstead Act which specified that an intoxicating liquor was any beverage containing one-half of one percent alcohol. "How Dry I Am" became the anthem of those suddenly deprived of stimulating liquors. Nobody knows who wrote those words, but the melody was first used by Edward F. Rimbaults for a religious hymn, "Happy Day," published in 1891.

Deprivation of his right to drink what he wanted was not the only freedom the returning soldier lost while he was abroad fighting for freedom. A new hate was being manufactured by government propaganda machinery to replace an old one, which led to flagrant desecration of the basic personal rights of the American citizen and violated the Fourth Amendment of the Constitution. With the Kaiser safely secreted in Holland and with Germany in total economic and political disarray, crushed financially by the reparations it had to pay, the onetime blistering hatred against the Hun was supplanted by an altogether new hate for the "Red." Those in political and financial power, together with the country's leading newspapers, were looking with dread at a new enemy, Russia, where revolution had put the proletariat into power and the classless society into being. The fear that the virus of Communism might also affect America—a fear nurtured by the proliferation of strikes and the beginnings of a belligerent left-wing movement—led the Attorney General of the United States, A. Mitchell Palmer, to organize in 1919 a series of raids on the homes and offices of American citizens to seize known or suspected Communists and summarily to deport them. The Secretary of Labor was further empowered through an Alien Act to deport any alien believed to be a radical.

Disenchantment with the war, and with the abuses it carried into peacetime, poisoned the air. Americans were looking back to the comparative serenity and normalcy of the prewar years. The old wholesome values acquired a new glamour—love, marriage, home, the simple delights of familiar places. In the immediate postwar period these were the subjects tapped most often, and most successfully, by Tin Pan Alley. Among the leading songs of 1919 were "Love Sends a Little Gift of Roses" (Leslie Cooke—John Openshaw), "Oh What a Pal Was Mary" (Edgar Leslie and Bert Kalmar—Pete Wendling), "Peggy" (Harry Williams—Neil Moret), "I'm Forever Blowing Bubbles" (Jean Kenbrovin and John W. Kellette), "My Home Is a One Horse Town But It's Big Enough for Me" (Alex Gerber—Abner Silver), "I'll Be Happy When the Preacher Makes You Mine" (Sam M. Lewis and Joe Young—Walter Donaldson), "Smilin' Through" (Arthur A. Penn), "The World Is Waiting for the Sunrise" (Eugene Lockhart—Ernest Seitz), "You're a Million Miles from Nowhere when You're One Little Mile from Home" (Sam M. Lewis and Joe Young—Walter Donaldson) and "In My Sweet Little Alice Blue Gown" (Joseph McCarthy—Harry Tierney).

"In My Sweet Little Alice Blue Gown" was heard in the Broadway musical *Irene*, which opened just one week after the Armistice. The book was by James Montgomery, lyrics by Joseph McCarthy and music by Harry Tierney. Its sweet Cinderella plot conjured for its audiences a far happier world than the one it had just experienced and was still experiencing. *Irene* was a box-office smash. It had the longest consecutive run of any Broadway musical up to that time, and sent seventeen companies touring the road.

"In My Sweet Little Alice Blue Gown," sung by Edith Day, was its principal musical number. Americans had then just been made strongly conscious of the color blue because of the gowns worn by Alice Roosevelt Longworth, daughter of Theodore Roosevelt. This song instantly became one of the most popular American waltzes ever written.

Irene, which had followed immediately after the end of World War I, returned to Broadway more than half a century later, after the closing of the longest war in which America was ever involved, that in Vietnam. Once again *Irene* came to serve as an antidote. *Irene* revisited Broadway in 1973—an old-fashioned musical comedy bringing with it a welcome nostalgia, sweetness and innocence that seemed to have disappeared from the mainstream of American life.

PART FOUR

1920–1940

16

The Jazz Age

1

The first decade of the twentieth century turned the corner, disclosing an altogether new ambience and a new social climate. Suddenly and inexplicably, sentimentality, nostalgia, storybook escapism—all this was swept rudely away. In its place came hard-boiled cynicism, reckless abandon, a devil-may-care attitude that proclaimed the gospel "today we live, for tomorrow we die," that "I can do anything I want so long as I don't hurt others," and that repeated Edna St. Vincent Millay's dictum that though her candle burned at both ends, it shed a wondrous light. This was the *real* aftermath of World War I. The young—they were called "flaming youth" after the title of Elinor Glyn's best-selling novel—kissed promiscuously, petted openly, dressed provocatively, used profanity freely, drank liquor copiously and, in essence, flaunted their emancipation. Women bobbed their hair, shortened their skirts to knee length, rolled their stockings below their knees, wore skimpy underclothes called "scanties," smoked in public, began using cosmetics in excess, and reduced their home chores by introducing canned goods into the kitchen. Charles Dana Gibson's "Gibson Girl" of a previous decade was replaced by the flapper in the drawings of John Held, Jr. She was boyish, flat chested, and thin hipped. The young man, called the "sheik" or "cake-eater," was dressed in knickers over blue and gray diamond-patterned golf hose, a coat to match the knickers and a bow tie jutting out from a soft collar.

This was a time for excesses. Too many people played too hard at having a good time and being liberated, drank too much illicit alcohol, gambled too heavily in an overinflated stock market, made too much money and spent it too freely. This was a time when firm values and standards and sacred shibboleths were debunked in magazines like the *American Mercury*, edited by H. L. Mencken and George Jean Nathan, which claimed "to attempt a realistic presentation of the whole, gaudy gorgeous American scene"; in novels like Sinclair Lewis' *Main Street* and *Babbitt*; in biographies debunking American heroes, such as William Woodward's book on George Washington and Edgar Lee Masters' on Lincoln; in that novel-turned-into-play by Anita Loos, *Gentlemen Prefer Blondes* which satirized the gold digger; in the deromanticization of war and the revelation of its uglier face in the play *What Price Glory?* by Maxwell Anderson and Laurence Stallings, in the bitter novel *Three Soldiers* by John Dos Passos, and in a novel from Europe that became the literary sensation of the twenties, Erich Maria Remarque's *All Quiet on the Western Front.*

Sophistication became the wisdom of the day, expressed in irony and wisecracks, with Dorothy Parker as its high priestess and the newly founded journal, *The New Yorker*, as its mouthpiece. Absurdity infiltrated everyday speech with expressions such as "cat's meow," "for crying out loud," "cat's pajamas," "banana oil," "so's your old man," "Dumb Dora" and "hot diggity." Daily comics became not only required reading but material for conversation and quotation. It was considered the height of wit and sophistication to mispronounce "absolutely" as "absotively," and "positively" as "posolutely."

Sex came out of hiding into the full light of day. It dominated the screen, with sex symbols like Clara Bow, the "It" girl, and Rudolph Valentino of the sensual lips and bedroom eyes. It was glorified in Atlantic City with the bathing beauty contest and the crowning of the first Miss America in 1921. It filtered into the press, particularly through the sensationalism with which tabloids (a product of the 1920s) fattened their circulation figures—extensive pictorial and verbal handling of juicy scandals involving Fatty Arbuckle and Virginia Rapp, Daddy Browning and Peaches, the murder trial of Ruth Snyder-Judd Gray and the Halls-Mills murder case. The gossip columnist (also an offspring of the 1920s) provided readers with a prurient glimpse into the extracurricular activities of the famous and the infamous. Petting (frequently in automobiles) had become a favorite sport of the young and the not-so-young; "companionate marriage"—trial marriage without benefit of clergy—was advocated by Judge Benjamin Barr Lindsay; the exchange of jokes and epithets between the sexes would have brought a blush even to a roué a decade earlier.

There seemed no ceiling to prosperity, either in the land boom in Florida (at least for a time), or on Wall Street, or in Hollywood where profits and salaries assumed astronomical figures. Movies were bigger, better and more spectacular than ever. There were eighteen thousand theaters in the country where the public made gods and goddesses of Gloria Swanson, John Barrymore, Norma Talmadge and Richard Barthelmess, among many others. There were idols in the sports world as well—Babe Ruth, Jack Dempsey, Bobby Jones, Red Grange, Bill Tilden, and Gertrude Ederle who became the first woman to swim the English Channel.

Stunts and fads took hold: flagpole sitting, marathon dancing, ouija boards, crossword puzzles, miniature golf, autosuggestion, marriage ceremonies in airplanes, capsule education through one-volume outlines of philosophy, history, literature and music.

Nobody captured more accurately the hedonistic times and their impact on the gay set than did F. Scott Fitzgerald. Representations of the 1920s, whether in books or on stage or screen, show that period as an incessant carnival—gay, giddy, reckless, noisy and brash, with everybody hell-bent on having a good time.

The decade has been called "the roaring twenties," the "teeming twenties," the "lawless twenties," the "turbulent twenties." Gertrude Stein referred to it as "the lost generation." But others have also identified it as "the jazz age." The word "jazz," in this instance, refers not only to that indigenous product grown in New Orleans, Missouri, Chicago and New York. In the twenties, "jazz" became a generic term covering virtually all forms of popular music, including the songs of Tin Pan Alley and Broadway, as well as concert music then being written utilizing jazz techniques and idioms.

2

Let us trace the progress of jazz after it left New Orleans in 1917 to make its way to Chicago. With so many New Orleans musicians active on the Chicago jazz scene, the traditions of New Orleans were kept very much alive. Younger jazzmen prominent in Chicago not only carried on this Dixieland tradition but created one of their own. Several of the newer jazz personalities achieved popularity and importance in Chicago equal to, and in some instances even surpassing, that of their distinguished New Orleans predecessors.

First and foremost was Bix Beiderbecke, the cornetist, one of the few white jazzmen whom blacks at that time flattered not only with adulation but imitation. Beiderbecke was a soft-spoken, cultured man almost as familiar with the music of Debussy and Stravinsky as he was with that of his jazz idols. He lived so completely in the world of his own making that the amenities and values outside the world of his music had little relevance for him. He lived in a kind of dream state from which he seemed to awaken only when he put cornet to lips. In his music-making he was a classicist. His playing was subdued and disciplined, combining sweetness with strength. His clear, pure tones and artistic phrasing made him one of jazz's true aristocrats.

He came from Iowa—born in Davenport in 1903—where he began learning to play the cornet without formal instruction when he was fourteen. From then on the cornet became his alter ego. While attending high school in Davenport he sat in with various jazz bands, then played with a jazz group at Terrace Gardens. In 1921, he enrolled at the Lake Forest Military Academy in a suburb of Chicago, from which he was expelled a year later for failure to maintain acceptable academic standards. He formed a school jazz band. When he was not playing, he was listening to and studying jazz music wherever and whenever he could find it. He spent hours listening to recordings of the Original Dixieland Jazz Band and trying to imitate the cornet playing of Nick La Rocca.

After leaving the military academy, he took his first full-time professional assignment playing with a band on an excursion boat on Lake Michigan. After that, in 1923, he joined a jazz band, the Wolverines, one of the first major jazz ensembles to come up in the Chicago area. It was founded by Dick Voynow, a drummer, for an engagement at a roadhouse called the Stockton Club. Besides Bix on the cornet, the group included Jimmy Hartwell (clarinet), Al Grande (trombone), Bobby Gillette (banjo), George Johnson (tenor sax), Min Leibrook (bass) and Bob Conzelman and Voynow (drums). Bix was the band's heart and soul. It was Bix and his cornet that made Chicago's jazzmen sit up, take notice and shake their heads in disbelief. Hoagy Carmichael never forgot the sound of Bix's cornet in the King Oliver classic, "Dippermouth Blues," even though Bix's contribution in the "break" in the chorus consisted of just four notes. "These notes weren't blown," recalls Carmichael, "they were hit, like a mallet hits a chime, and his tone had a richness that can come only from the heart. . . . Those four notes that Bix played meant more to me than everything else in the books."

Bix made his first recordings with the Wolverines for Gennett. These disks included "Jazz Me Blues" (Tom Delaney), "Copenhagen" (Walter Melrose—Charles Davis), "Riverboat Shuffle" (Dick Voynow and Hoagy Carmichael), and that New Orleans standard, "Tiger Rag." In these and subsequent recordings, Bix's playing was something to listen to and treasure. Some jazzmen waxed poetic trying to describe him. Frankie Trumbauer, with whose band Bix played the cornet in 1925 at the Arcadia Ballroom in St. Louis, wrote: "To describe in print the work of Bix is almost like trying to describe the color in the beautiful flowers that we see all around us, or the beautiful clouds we see in the sky, or the varicolored leaves in the fall." Frankie Trumbauer and his band recorded "Singin' the Blues" (Sam M. Lewis and Joe Young—Con Conrad and J. Russell Robinson) with Bix doing the ad lib solos which were meticulously studied and copied by many a jazz cornetist.

In 1924, the Wolverines appeared in New York at the Cinderella Dance Hall near Times Square. Bix came with them, but did not remain long. He soon drifted back to Chicago and at various times was heard with Charles Straight's orchestra, Jean Goldkette's band, Frankie Trumbauer's ensemble and several other groups. When Jean Goldkette's band broke up in 1927 and some of its principals joined the Paul Whiteman Orchestra in New York, Bix went with them. He stayed with the Whiteman orchestra several years, and with them he made a number of recordings. Some of these disks betray how his now chronic alcoholism and declining health were corroding his art. But occasionally Bix's style shines through like fluorescent lighting. This occurred, for example, in "Sweet Sue" (Will J. Harris—Victor Young).

But Beiderbecke's artistic and physical resources were becoming sadly depleted. For a year he dropped out of the Paul Whiteman Orchestra to take a "cure" (while Whiteman generously maintained him on full salary). Upon Beiderbecke's return to Whiteman, he was more erratic than ever. In spite of good intentions and promises of reform, Beiderbecke drank more prodigiously than ever, while his health deteriorated. He made some recordings in 1930, and took on some odd jobs in 1931. He was in a state of physical exhaustion when he played with a band in Princeton, New Jersey, in June 1931. He caught a cold which developed into fatal pneumonia. After his death on Long Island in 1931 he became a legend. An excellent novel was inspired by him, *Young Man with a Horn*, by Dorothy Baker (1938), made into a motion picture in 1950 starring Kirk Douglas. In 1974 two biographies were published, *Remembering Bix: A Memoir of the Jazz Age* by Ralph Berton and *Bix: Man and Legend* by Richard M. Sudhalter and Philip R. Evans with William Dean-Myatt. Beiderbecke's best records have become treasured collector's items. "I'd give my right arm if I could live to hear another Bix," Paul Whiteman once said. "I think my arm's safe enough."

Others contributed generously to Chicago jazz. A number of jazz-crazy kids from Austin High School became inflamed with the passion for jazz upon hearing King Oliver's records. These youngsters included Jimmy McPartland, trumpet, Frank Teschemacher, clarinet and the saxes, and Bud Freeman, tenor sax. These became the backbone of another brilliant Chicago jazz group, The Blue Friars. Two other distinguished jazz ensembles in Chicago were the Chicago Rhythm Kings led by Teschemacher and The Chicagoans formed by Eddie Condon, guitarist. Among individual performers to become prominent in Chicago were Muggsy Spanier, cornet; Coleman Hawkins, tenor sax; Earl "Fatha" Hines and Jess Stacey, piano; Eddie Condon, guitar; Gene Krupa, drums; and Mezz Mezzrow, clarinet and saxes.

A large jazz unit, led by Erskine Tate, was heard at the Vendome Theater between 1918 and 1929. Among the luminous names on the roster of its players were Freddie Keppard, Earl "Fatha" Hines, "Fats" Waller (piano) and Louis "Satchmo" Armstrong.

Though Louis Armstrong was born in New Orleans in 1900 and there received his initiation into jazz, it was in Chicago that he reached artistic maturity and greatness.

After his father had deserted his family in New Orleans, the child Louis helped to support his mother and sister by delivering coal to prostitutes and lifting food out of hotel garbage cans and selling it. When he was ten he fired a pistol in the street in celebration of New Year's Eve. This offense brought arrest and confinement in the Colored Waifs Home for Boys. "It was," he later said, "the greatest thing that ever happened to me. Me and music got married at that home." There and then Peter Davis, a music instructor, began teaching Louis to read music and play the bugle and cornet. Louis soon joined the Home's brass band which performed at picnics, funerals and other events. After his release from the Home Louis worked as a newsboy and in a junkyard. All the while he was playing the cornet in various honky-tonks. One night, Bunk Johnson failed to show up at Madranga's. Louis sat in for him and was heard by none other than the king himself—Joe Oliver. Oliver liked what he heard, took Louis under his wing, and gave him cornet lessons. Armstrong always looked back upon Oliver as the greatest jazz performer he had ever known and the greatest single influence upon his own development. "Joe Oliver taught me more than anyone," Armstrong recalled.

When he was seventeen, Louis married Daisy Parker, a prostitute. The marriage was turbulent and brief. Soon after his separation from his wife, when Joe "King" Oliver went North, Armstrong replaced him with the Kid Ory band. After that he was heard with Fate Marable's group on riverboats, and for some months with Zutty Singleton's ensemble at the Orchard Cabaret in the French Quarter.

By 1922, Oliver had established himself in Chicago as the leader of King Oliver's Creole Jazz Band. He asked Armstrong to join him as second cornetist. Together they made incomparable music, as each inspired the other to unparalleled flights of musical fancy. They went through a "break" with stunning virtuosity and a beautiful sense of coordination. Armstrong made his first records with Oliver's band on the Gennett label: "Canal Street Blues" (Joe "King" Oliver), "Sobbin' Blues" (Art Kassel and Victor Burton), "Riverside Blues" (Thomas A. Dorsey) and "Dippermouth Blues" (Joe "King" Oliver), among others.

In 1924, Armstrong married Lillian Hardin. She was a pianist who had studied music at Fisk University but who turned from the classics to jazz soon after her arrival in Chicago. She was a prime force in getting Armstrong to leave Oliver's band, feeling as she did that the time had come for Armstrong to emerge as a jazz personality in his own right. Between 1924 and 1925, Armstrong played solos, switching from cornet to trumpet, with the Fletcher Henderson Orchestra at the Roseland Ballroom in New York which Louis J. Becker had opened up at 1658 Broadway on December 13, 1919, and where over a period of several decades many a distinguished jazz ensemble would perform for the dancing pleasure of young and old, the famous and the unknown. In New York, Armstrong made more recordings. In "Sugar Foot Stomp" (Walter Melrose and Joe "King" Oliver) his playing pierced through the texture of the orchestra like a sharp blade.

He was back in Chicago in 1925. For the next four years he made jazz history there. First he played in his wife's band, Lil's Hot Shots. Then he formed his own jazz group, the Hot Five, which in addition to Armstrong himself included Kid Ory (trombone), Johnny Dodds (clarinet), Lil Armstrong (piano) and Johnny St. Cyr (banjo). They played at the Dreamland Café in 1925 and 1926 and made recordings for Okeh which many jazzmen used as a basic course for their own further education. The earliest of these releases were "Come Back Sweet Papa" (Paul Barbarin and Luis C. Russell), "Gut Bucket Blues" (Louis Armstrong), "Jazz Lips" (Lillian Hardin Armstrong), "Muskrat Ramble" (Kid Ory), "Don't Forget to Mess Around when You're Doing the Charleston" (Louis Armstrong and Paul Barbarin) and "Heebie Jeebies" (Boyd Atkins). The "Five" became seven in 1927, with the addition of Baby Dodds (drums) and Pete Briggs (tuba), and then was once again reduced to five.

Armstrong was now at the pinnacle of his fame and artistry, with few equals. His skill at the trumpet was in a class by itself with those dazzling successions of high C's, the breathtaking glissandos, the piercing sonorities. His art at improvisation was so formidable that even Virgil Thomson, the distinguished serious composer and music critic, was led to remark that it combined "the highest reaches of instrumental virtuosity with the most tensely disciplined melodic structure and the most spontaneous emotional expression, all of which in one man you must admit is pretty rare." Even today we can listen with admiration to those 1927 Okeh recordings of "Wild Man Blues" (Louis Armstrong and "Jelly Roll" Morton), "Potato Head Blues" (Louis Armstrong) or the 1928 recording of "West End Blues" (Clarence Williams and Joe "King" Oliver). These and other recordings of this period find Armstrong at the peak of his powers.

It was in Chicago that Armstrong initiated his "scat" singing—singing nonsense syllables in place of words and vocally simulating instrumental sound. Some say this came about accidentally when, during a 1926 recording session, Armstrong forgot the lyrics of a song and had to improvise vocal sounds. Scat singing henceforth became one of the highlights of Armstrong's performances.

Some of Louis Armstrong's prodigious trumpet performances in Chicago were in collaboration with the pianist, Earl "Fatha" Hines, who has been called "the father of the modern jazz piano." The give and take between piano and trumpet in several different groups headed by Armstrong was as striking an excursion into jazz virtuosity and improvisation as could be heard in Chicago. Almost as if oblivious to the other men of the ensemble, the two synchronized as few duos in jazz ever did before, understanding each other's most subtle aims with seemingly infallible instincts, and inciting each other to breathtaking passages of creative improvisation. Hines' association with Armstrong, and his close artistic partnership with him through many years, were largely responsible for the "trumpet style" that has characterized Hines' piano performances. This style was described by Stanley Dance in *Stereo Review*: "In the treble he simulated vibrato with tremolos and played stabbing single notes. His phrasing often resembled a trumpet player's, with momentary suspensions suggesting breath pauses. He had early developed an octave technique in the right hand that enabled him to cut through the clamor of jazz horns in the days before amplification. Added to a strong, incisive touch, all this gave his playing an unusually bright, brassy quality. More important, there was also a new feeling of rhythmic freedom, quite at variance with the disciplined approach of the stride school, and breaking irrevocably with the methodical ragtime tradition that still lingered in jazz."

Hines was born in Duquesne, Pennsylvania, in 1905, and received a thorough grounding in classical piano music before he embraced jazz. In 1923 he went to Chicago, and for the next five years played at the Elite Club No. 2 where his individual piano style made him a prime attraction. In 1928, his fame was enhanced through records for Vocalion and Okeh with Louis Armstrong and Jimmy Noone, the clarinetist, and the piano solos he recorded with such a personalized style for Q. R. S., including his own "A Monday Date" and "Fifty-Seven Varieties" and "I Ain't Got Nobody" (Roger Graham—Spencer Williams and Dave Peyton). Discussing Hines' rendition of "I Ain't Got Nobody," the *Jazz Record Book* says, "In a contemplative style, 'Nobody' has unusual swing due to Hines' forceful accents and timing—traits doubtless brought to perfection during his long association with Louis Armstrong. Even some of the motival development suggests Louis' trumpet figures—yet Hines' style is ideally pianistic." In 1929, Earl Hines formed his own orchestra which played intermittently for about a decade at the Grand Terrace in Chicago, and became one of the best jazz orchestras in the country, famous for its renditions of its theme music, "Deep Forest" (Reginald Foresythe), "Rosetta" (Earl Hines and Henri Woode), his own "Jelly,

Jelly" and "The Earl" and some Duke Ellington standards. It was while broadcasting over the radio from the Grand Terrace that the nickname "Fatha" was born. While Earl Hines was playing his theme music, the announcer departed from his script to improvise the following greeting: "Here comes 'fatha' Hines through the 'Deep Forest' with his children." Between 1947 and 1951, Earl Hines was once again playing with a group headed by Louis Armstrong, and in the mid-1950s he went into semiretirement. He returned to the jazz scene triumphantly, this time as a solo pianist, with three concerts at the Little Theater in New York in 1964, and in subsequent years made sensational appearances at Carnegie Hall and the Newport Jazz Festival. In 1973, *Variety* singled him out as the "sensation" of the Newport Jazz Festival in New York, and the critics' poll by *Down Beat* magazine chose him as top jazz pianist of the year.

To return to Louis Armstrong: by the time Armstrong deserted Chicago permanently for New York in 1929, he was already recognized as one of the all-time jazz greats. In New York he played at Connie's Inn in Harlem, and in his first Broadway show, *Hot Chocolates* (1929) where his first romance with commercialism may be said to have begun. It was in that all-black revue that Armstrong achieved his first giant commercial success in his performance of "Ain't Misbehavin' " (Andy Razaf—Thomas "Fats" Waller). He made many other songs into hits after that: "S-h-i-n-e" (Cecil Mack and Lew Brown—Ford Dabney), "After You've Gone" (Henry Creamer—Turner Layton), "When It's Sleepy Time Down South" (Leon and Otis Rene—Clarence Kluse), among many. His greatest singing triumph came late in his career, in 1964, when he kindled into a veritable conflagration a perfunctory show tune, the title song from the broadway musical *Hello, Dolly!* (Jerry Herman).

Soon after his divorce from Lillian in 1932, Armstrong embarked on his first tour of Europe. His records had made him so famous by now that wherever he went he packed the house and sent it into convulsions of enthusiasm. During his first appearance in London, at the Palladium, the nickname of "Satchmo," which clung to him thereafter, was coined by P. Mathison Brooks, editor of the London *Melody Maker*. The word "Satchmo" was an erroneous garbling of "Satchel mouth," the epithet long associated with Armstrong because of the ample expanse of his mouth.

After that first tour, he went on to conquer every medium of entertainment: the theater, concerts, nightclubs, records, radio, television. He circled the globe three times. He had merely to sound the first few notes of some of his particular standbys to cause a furor, numbers such as "Ol' Man Mose" (Louis Armstrong and Zilner Randolph), "Muskrat Ramble," "I'll Be Glad When You're Dead, You Rascal You" (Sam Theard), "When the Saints Go Marching In," besides "Ain't Misbehavin' " and, after 1964, "Hello, Dolly!." Over one hundred thousand listeners went wild when he sounded the first notes on his trumpet in Accra, Ghana. In Leopoldville he was carried on a canvas throne to the city stadium by tribesmen.

He maintained his popularity up to the time of his death on July 6, 1971, at his home in Corona, Queens, in New York, which he had been sharing with his third wife, Lucille Wilson, from the time they were married in 1942. He deserved that popularity because of his incomparable contributions to jazz. But he was able to maintain it because he had become a showman second to none, skilled in the art and science of wooing and winning audiences. The public went wild over his grin, his mugging, his ad lib wisecracks, his exhibitionism, his scat singing. But through those opportunistic shenanigans (which upset so many of his most fervent admirers and disciples) there managed to filter through the essence of the artist who made jazz history.

Chicago was not only the birthplace of new jazz performers but also of new jazz styles. Boogie-woogie came into existence in Chicago's South Śide in the 1920s. It was first heard at monthly parties, sometimes referred to as "pitchin' boogie" parties, to raise rent money. At these affairs, the music consisted of exciting piano improvisations soon to be called boogie music or boogie-woogie. The term itself first came into general use in pieces by Pinetop Smith (1904–1929), a pioneer of piano blues, and a composer of one of its best numbers "The Pinetop Boogie-Woogie." The style itself, an outgrowth of the blues, placed emphasis on rhythm rather than melody. A brief, rhythmic figure, usually with eight beats to the bar repeated without variation, furnished the background for a blues melody to create a powerful rhythmic momentum. Outstanding exponents of boogie-woogie after Pinetop Smith were Jimmy Yancey (1894–1951), composer of "Yancey Stomp," "State Street Special" and "Eternal Blues"; Albert Ammons (1907–1949), who just before his death was invited to perform at the inauguration ceremonies of President Harry S Truman; and probably the most important of all Meade Lux Lewis (1905–   ), composer of such boogie-woogie favorites as "Honky Tonk Train," "Blues Whistle," "Chicago Flyer" and "Bear Cat Crawl." Boogie-woogie attracted national attention for the first time at a concert entitled "From Spirituals to Swing" at Carnegie Hall on December 23, 1928, featuring Meade Lux Lewis and Albert Ammons. Following that, these same pianists, and boogie-woogie, attracted enthusiasts to Café Society in Greenwich Village.

3

The jazz empire in Chicago was breaking up in the 1920s. Many of its leading personalities began streaming toward New York. In 1924, Bix Beiderbecke came to play at the Roseland Ballroom, and Louis Armstrong arrived to perform with the Fletcher Henderson Orchestra. Sidney Bechet came in 1926, and "Jelly Roll" Morton in 1928. In 1928, too, Jimmy McPartland, Gene Krupa, Eddie Condon, Bud Freeman and Frank Teschemacher formed an ensemble in New York to perform with the vaudevillian Bea Palmer.

But before this happened, Dixieland jazz had invaded New York's musical life. This took place in 1915 when the Louisiana Five, led by Alcide Nuñez, rocked Bustanoby's restaurant. On January 16, 1917, the Original Dixieland Band, headed by Nick La Rocca, started a successful engagement at Reisenweber's restaurant, featuring such New Orleans classics as "Tiger Rag," "Sensation Rag" and the "Livery Stable Blues." The loud, nervous, seemingly disorganized music so puzzled the clientele at Reisenweber's that for a time nobody made a move to dance to its strains. Only after the proprietor announced that this music was "jazz" and that it was intended for dancing, did some of the patrons move out to the floor.

In 1917, the Victor Company tried to induce Freddie Keppard to record several jazz numbers. He refused because he did not want his "stuff" to be stolen by other jazz musicians. Victor then gathered several members from the Original Dixieland Band, added the word "Jazz" to its name, and produced several disks including performances of the "Livery Stable Blues" and "Tiger Rag." Thus a white group was the first to make jazz records. In 1921, Kid Ory pressed his first disks for a small company, and James P. Johnson recorded for Okeh the first jazz piano solo ever committed to shellac. A year later, Gennett had Joe "King" Oliver and some of his men make records in Richmond, Indiana. The Fletcher Henderson Orchestra was the first New York ensemble to make recordings.

The Fletcher Henderson Orchestra was one of the first major organizations to come out of New York. It was also the first significant black group in New York, and the first large jazz organization with a full complement of brass, reeds and rhythm instruments. Before he became a musician, Henderson had graduated from Atlanta University where he had majored in chemistry. In 1920, he came to New York for postgraduate work. Gradually he shifted to music, first by working part-time for W. C. Handy's publishing house, then by serving as a house pianist for Black Swan, a small record company. At Black Swan he assembled his first orchestra for the purpose of accompanying Ethel Waters on tour. Then, in 1923, he organized a band for Club Alabama. A year later he formed for the Roseland Ballroom the orchestra that became famous; it appeared on and off at that ballroom during the next fifteen years.

An excellent pianist and arranger, Henderson introduced a more formal kind of jazz music than that formerly heard either in New Orleans or Chicago. With Henderson, carefully prepared orchestrations replaced ad lib solos and group improvisations. From time to time many of the most outstanding jazz artists of the time found a place in the Henderson orchestra, including Coleman Hawkins and Don Redman (saxes), Buster Bailey (clarinet), Miff Mole (trombone), Joe Smith and Tommy Ladnier (trumpets) and Louis Armstrong. Henderson's prepared orchestrations used some of the techniques and devices of real jazz, but to these he added a new richness of harmonic coloring, a lush sonority and some beautiful solo writing. After his orchestra broke up in the 1930s, Henderson made arrangements for various bands, including those led by Isham Jones, the Dorsey brothers and Benny Goodman.

While Henderson's music was being heard at the Roseland Ballroom, that of Paul Whiteman and his Orchestra was drawing the crowds to the Palais Royal nightclub. Whiteman had preceded Henderson in presenting carefully prepared arrangements for a large ensemble. But Whiteman's was not essentially a jazz ensemble, though many distinguished jazzmen played in it—not unless we are willing to follow the practice of the twenties to designate all popular music as jazz. Whiteman's prime contribution was to offer popular music in attractive arrangements that borrowed instrumental techniques, colorations, and harmonic and rhythmic elements from jazz.

Whiteman was the son of a music educator in Denver, where Paul was born in 1890. After studying the violin, he became a member of the Denver Symphony. At this time he sometimes gathered some of the orchestra men for impromptu rag sessions. After an additional period as the violinist of the San Francisco Symphony, Whiteman abandoned serious music for popular. A further push to this decision was hearing a jazz band in a San Francisco dive. He described his reaction in his autobiography: "It screeched, it bellowed at me from a trick platform in the middle of a smoke-hazed beer-fumed room. And it hit me hard. Raucous? Yes. Crude—undoubtedly. Unmusical—sure as you live. But rhythmic, catching as the small-pox and spirit lifting."

Whiteman now found a job with a small jazz combo, the John Tait Café Band, then lost it because he was incapable of mastering the jazz style. For the next few months he worked hard at understanding and assimilating this idiom. In 1917 he formed a jazz band of his own but before it could give many performances America was at war and Whiteman was mustered into the Navy. There he organized and led an orchestra of some forty men at Bear Island in California. After the war, Whiteman assembled a civilian orchestra to fill engagements in California. His performances at the Alexandria Hotel in Los Angeles made him a favorite of the movie colony. He stayed on for about a year, the real beginnings of the Paul Whiteman Orchestra.

At this decisive moment in his career, when he approached the threshold of success for the first time, Whiteman met Ferde Grofé. Grofé, like Whiteman, was the son of a serious musician. He was born in New York City in 1892, spent his childhood studying music, then in 1909 joined the Los Angeles Philharmonic as a violist. For a time he combined work with symphony orchestras with engagements with ragtime groups. Then he left symphonic music to form his own jazz unit. He was conducting it in a Los Angeles dance hall in 1919 when Whiteman heard him performing some of his own arrangements. These led Whiteman to engage Grofé as an orchestrator and pianist. From then on, through 1924, Grofé wrote all of Whiteman's orchestrations which were performed in carefully prepared renditions. Grofé's imaginative musical settings, which revealed a sure understanding of jazz-orchestral sound and the capabilities of each instrument, combined with Whiteman's suave performances, created a new era for the presentation of popular music.

While at the Alexandria Hotel in Los Angeles, the Whiteman Orchestra was heard by S. W. Straus who was so impressed that he engaged the orchestra to open a new hotel, the Ambassador in Atlantic City, New Jersey. During this engagement, the Whiteman Orchestra embarked on its long and rewarding recording affiliation with Victor. The first disk was "The Wang, Wang Blues" (Leo Wood—Gus Mueller, "Buster" Johnson and Henry Busse). The second, "Whispering" (John Schonberger, Richard Coburn and Vincent Rose) coupled with "The Japanese Sandman" (Raymond M. Egan—Richard A. Whiting) sold nearly two million records in its first year. Two years later, in 1922, Whiteman enjoyed another million-and-more disk sale with "Three O'Clock in the Morning" (Dorothy Terriss—Julian Robeldo). Other successful Whiteman records of the early 1920s were "San" (Lindsay McPhail and Walter Michels), "When Buddha Smiles" (Arthur Freed—Nacio Herb Brown and King Zany) and "China Boy" (Dick Winfree and Phil Boutelje).

Paul Whiteman came to New York in 1920 and started an eventful engagement at the Palais Royal nightclub on October 1. The orchestra now progressed from one triumph to another, and from one medium to the next. In 1921 Paul Whiteman and his Orchestra were headliners at the Palace Theater. In 1922 it was featured in the *George White Scandals*, and in 1923 the Orchestra made a successful debut in London. Early in 1924, it shaped popular music history with a concert in Aeolian Hall, New York, an auditorium heretofore reserved for classical music. At this time Whiteman gave the world premiere of Gershwin's *Rhapsody in Blue*. He was now crowned by press and public as "the King of Jazz," which became the title of a motion picture written for and built around him and starring him in 1930.

In the 1930s, Whiteman and his Orchestra were frequently heard over the radio, and in 1943 he was named musical director of the Blue Network (later become the American Broadcasting Company). Largely inactive in his last years, he died in 1967.

Beginning with 1927, Whiteman and his Orchestra became more closely oriented with real jazz by including among its personnel such jazz artists as Bix Beiderbecke, Red Nichols, Jimmy and Tommy Dorsey and Joe Venuti. But other ensembles in New York proved much more true to Dixieland and Chicago jazz than was Whiteman: bands, for example, led by Red Nichols, Jean Goldkette, Ben Pollack and, most importantly, Duke Ellington.

Red Nichols came from Utah where he had played the cornet in a band led by his father. He was expelled from the Culver Military Academy when he was seventeen after he was caught smoking. Coming East, he played the cornet with various bands, some of which he himself organized. He also made some recordings for Gennett in Richmond, Indiana, in 1922. He then formed the group that made him a preeminent exponent of Dixieland music: The Five Pennies, so called even though from time to time there were six to ten men in his ensemble. It began making extraordinary recordings for Brunswick and Okeh in 1926 and 1927, including the best-selling, "Ida, Sweet as Apple Cider" (Eddie Leonard) and "Five Pennies" (Red Nichols). Among the jazz greats who were members of the Five Pennies were Jimmy Dorsey, Miff Mole, Benny Goodman and Glenn Miller.

Ben Pollack's orchestra—among the first large white jazz ensembles anywhere—also had its fair share of distinguished jazz performers: Glenn Miller, Jimmy McPartland, Charley Spivack, Harry James and Muggsy Spanier. Pollack brought to New York the traditions of Chicago jazz which he had learned firsthand by serving as drummer with the New Orleans Rhythm Kings at the Friars Inn. Pollack made some jazz records for Gennett between 1922 and 1923, and formed his own band in California in 1925 where he hired sixteen-year-old Benny Goodman. Returning to Chicago early in 1926, Pollack gained recognition with his ensemble at the Southmoor Ballrooms, the Rendezvous and The Blackhawk. He brought his men to New York, opening at the Little Club in March 1928, then becoming a fixture at the Park Central Hotel and at the Silver Slipper. He combined commercialized popular music with a true Dixieland style and feeling which characterized the recordings he made for Victor between 1926 and 1929.

Late in 1926, Jean Goldkette and his band came to the Roseland Ballroom in New York where its performances created a stir. Goldkette was a Frenchman who had come to the United States in 1911 to pursue a career as concert pianist. Changing over to popular music, he played with a small combo at the Lamb's Club in Chicago before forming his first band in Detroit in 1921 and beginning to make records for Victor in 1924. In Detroit, he held sway at the Greystone, Detroit's leading ballroom, where he was billed as "The Paul Whiteman of the West." In 1926, Goldkette began assimilating and exploiting the talents of Joe Venuti, Frankie Trumbauer, Bix Beiderbecke and the Dorsey brothers to create an orchestra of true distinction. It was this highly developed organization that invaded New York to enrich its jazz activities. But its history in New York was brief. By late 1927 the orchestra broke up, with many of its leading players going over to Paul Whiteman. From time to time, Goldkette formed other bands, and made some records, but his best days were over. His greatest achievements belonged to the mid-1920s, and most particularly his performances at the Roseland in New York and his 1926 recordings.

Some of the most original jazz music heard in New York in the twenties was played by Duke Ellington and his orchestra. He was born Edward Kennedy Ellington in Washington, D. C., in 1899. The nickname "Duke" was conferred on him when he was just a kid by one of his friends because of his dapper clothes and debonair behavior, a nickname that clung to him thereafter for these same reasons. In his boyhood, Ellington revealed a gift not only for music but for art. As a high school student he won first prize in a poster contest sponsored by the National Association for the Advancement of Colored People. In 1917, he was offered a scholarship by the Pratt Institute of Applied Art, but he declined it because he was already convinced he preferred music. He had begun studying the piano when he was seven, the lessons he received at this time being the only formal piano training he ever received. As a boy he participated in performances of jazz music. While employed after school hours as a soda jerk at the Poodle Dog Café in Washington, he wrote his first composition, "The Soda Fountain Rag." Later he organized his own jazz band which played around the Washington area at parties, dances and other social functions. He paid a brief visit to New York in 1922 hoping to establish himself there musically but, failing, returned to Washington to continue making jazz music with his own men. During that visit to New York he heard the jazz piano performances of Willie "the Lion" Smith and James P. Johnson, among others, which made such a deep impression upon him that they were to influence his own style of piano playing.

In 1923, Ellington reappeared in New York with several men of his band. As the Washingtonians they found an opening at Baron's in Harlem. The band then was being led by its banjoist, Elmer Snowden, but when the group moved downtown to a basement café on

Broadway and 39th Street—the Hollywood Club, soon renamed the Kentucky Club —Ellington took over the group. It remained there for four and a half years, and as the Washingtonians, recorded for Brunswick one of the earliest instrumentals to reveal Ellington's developing creative talent, "Black and Tan Fantasy." In 1927, the Ellington ensemble swelled into a fourteen-member group and was renamed the Kentucky Club Orchestra. Its members included such outstanding jazz virtuosos as Joe "Tricky Sam" Nanton at the trombone, Bubber Miley at the trumpet, Rudy Jackson at the clarinet and tenor sax, Sonny Greer at the drums and Ellington himself at the piano.

In 1927, Ellington and the Kentucky Club Orchestra moved on to the Cotton Club in Harlem when Joe "King" Oliver and his band suddenly bowed out of a scheduled engagement. It was there that Ellington began to step out as a major spokesman for real jazz in New York, and to achieve national renown through regular radio broadcasts direct from the Cotton Club as well as through recordings. A new jazz style was being evolved —growling, stark and tense—that would become identified with Ellington's name and become known as "the jungle style." "We tried new effects," Ellington later reminisced to an interviewer. "We put the Negro feeling and spirit in our music." Some of the recordings between 1929 and 1932 show how successful Ellington was in infusing this Negro feeling and spirit into jazz through stunning arrangements (for many of which he himself was responsible), unique use of the brass to produce growling effects, and variety of coloration. "East of St. Louis Toodle-o" (Bubber Miley—Duke Ellington) became Ellington's radio-theme music in the 1930s. Among other notable Ellington recordings of this period was "The Mooch" (Duke Ellington and Irving Mills) coupled with "Dreamy Blues" (Duke Ellington). The latter, with lyrics by Irving Mills and Albany Bigard, became in 1931 one of Ellington's finest songs, "Mood Indigo." In addition there were "Rockin' in Rhythm" (Duke Ellington, Irving Mills and Harry Carney), "Saturday Night Function" (Albany Bigard and Duke Ellington) and the following pieces written by Ellington alone: "Dicty Glide," "The Duke Steps Out," "The Creeps," "Birmingham Fantasy" and "Immigration Blues."

Ellington now occupied a prime place in New York jazz. In live performances in nightclubs and theaters, over the radio, on records and in motion pictures, he reached millions of listeners many of whom became permanent converts to the jazz cult because of him. Without succumbing to showmanship gimmicks, Ellington managed to accumulate success upon success. He made his first tour of Europe in 1933 when he gave a command performance at Buckingham Palace. In 1930, he and his orchestra were featured in the first of many motion pictures, *Check and Double Check*. He extended his artistic horizon with appearances at Carnegie Hall between 1943 and 1950, and at the Lincoln Center in 1964. In 1963, he opened up for himself an altogether new avenue of creativity in San Francisco with the first of his "jazz-sacred concerts" at the Grace Cathedral in San Francisco which brought jazz into the church and for which Ellington wrote religious music in a jazz style. He wrote the music for two more sacred concerts after that, the third given at Westminster Abbey in London. His fame became worldwide through numerous foreign tours, some sponsored by the State Department, to Europe, the Middle East, Africa, South America, the Orient, Australia, New Zealand and the Soviet Union.

He was overwhelmed with tributes and honors. In national polls by *Down Beat* he was chosen top man in jazz in 1944, 1946 and 1948. In 1969, on his sixtieth birthday, President Nixon conferred on him the Presidential Medal of Freedom. In 1971 he became the first American in popular music to be inducted into the Royal Swedish Academy. A year later, Yale University established in his honor the Afro-American Fellowship Fund "to preserve and perpetuate the Afro-American musical spirit," and two African countries, Chad and Togo, released postage stamps with his picture. In 1973, President Georges Pompidou of France bestowed on him the Legion of Honor, and Columbia University conferred on him an honorary degree.

There were also setbacks, a serious one during the 1940s and in the first years of the 1950s, when Swing took center stage and forced Duke Ellington to the sidelines. But Ellington continued playing and writing his own kind of jazz. Then at the Newport Jazz Festival in 1956 he and his orchestra sent the audience dancing in the aisles. This started a new era of prosperity for Ellington which continued to grow and expand up to the time of his death.

There was another momentary setback in 1965, with the Pulitzer Prize Committee voting a special citation to Ellington for "the vitality and originality of his total productivity" only to have it summarily turned down by some higher authority (never identified). The fuss that followed resulted in the resignation in protest of two members of the Committee, Winthrop Sargeant and Robert Eyer. Ellington himself took his defeat stoically. He said, "Fate is being kind to me. Fate doesn't want me to be famous too young."

For Ellington's seventy-fifth birthday in 1974 there were worldwide tributes beamed in thirty-six languages over radio and television by the United States Information Agency. At Carnegie Hall, thirty-five jazz groups and various soloists performed his music in a gala concert in his honor. At the Central Presbyterian Church, parts of the music he had written for the three sacred services were heard. A definitive biography, Stanley Dance's *The World of Duke Ellington* and an autobiography, *Music Is My Mistress*, published in 1970 and 1973 respectively, attracted new interest. Verve released a special commemorative album entitled *A Tribute to Duke Ellington—We Love You Madly*, in which leading jazz organizations and artists performed Ellington. Unhappily, Ellington was unable to be present at any of the public concerts and demonstrations in his honor, since he was confined to a hospital bed at the Columbia Presbyterian Medical Center's Harkness Pavilion for treatment of cancer of both lungs. He died of pneumonia at the hospital on May 24, 1974.

He left behind him not only his famous orchestra, which was taken over by his son, Mercer, to carry on the Ellington tradition, but also a wealth of recordings made during half a century beginning with 1924 and comprising over two thousand titles. Even after Ellington's death, recordings (never before released commercially) kept coming. One set made in 1945 came from the private collection of Mel Tormé, the singer, and was issued in 1976. Broadcasts Ellington had made during World War II from various clubs throughout the United States, and featuring all of the great Ellington soloists, were issued publicly for the first time in 1976 in eight volumes on the Fairmont label, with still more albums promised for a later release.

In addition to all this, Ellington left behind him the enormous repertory of jazz music which he himself created, some six thousand compositions in all—popular songs, short jazz instrumental pieces, extended jazz works, sacred music, music for the theater and music for motion pictures. Some of his compositions profited from either the collaboration or arrangements of Billy Strayhorn (1915–1967), the brilliant young musician who worked with Duke Ellington and his orchestra from 1939 until his death, and who wrote some of the music featured prominently by Duke Ellington through the years, including "Take the A Train," later used by the Ellington orchestra as its theme.

Throughout his life, Ellington's fame as composer kept pace with that as performer. His "It Don't Mean a Thing" (Irving Mills), and "Sophisticated Lady" (Mitchell Parish and Irving Mills), became hits in their respective years in 1932 and 1933 and standards after that. "Solitude" (Eddie De Lange and Irving Mills), another standard, received the ASCAP Award as the best popular song of 1934. After that came a shower of exceptional songs: "I Got It Bad" (Paul Francis Webster), "Just Squeeze Me" (Lee Gaines), "Satin Doll" (Johnny Mercer—Billy Strayhorn and Duke Ellington), "Day-Dream" (John La Touche—Billy Strayhorn and Duke Ellington), "I Let a Song Go Out of My Heart" (Henry Nemo, John Redmond, Irving Mills—Duke Ellington), "Caravan" (Irving Mills, Juan Tizol and Duke Ellington) and "Don't Get Around Much Anymore" (Bob Russell).

Some of Ellington's most important compositions are those cast in a mold larger than the song form, in which jazz assumed symphonic stature. "Black and Tan Fantasy," written with Bubber Miley in 1927, was the first of his important jazz instrumentals. *Reminiscing in Tempo*, a twelve-minute composition, came in 1934 and *Blue Belles of Harlem* was written soon afterward on commission for Paul Whiteman and his Orchestra. He wrote *Black, Brown and Beige*, a fifty-minute work, for his first Carnegie Hall appearance in 1943. He later introduced in Carnegie Hall other spaciously designed orchestral works, including *Deep South, Liberian Suite* (written on commission from the Liberian government), *New World A' Comin'* and *Night Creature*. *Harlem* was written for an Ellington concert at the Metropolitan Opera House in 1951. *Golden Broom, Green Apple* and *A Blue Mural* from *Two Perspectives* were first heard at his appearance at Lincoln Center in 1964. *Suite Thursday*, based on John Steinbeck's novel, *Sweet Thursday*, was commissioned for the Monterey Jazz Festival in 1960. Other orchestral works included *Such Sweet Thunder* (inspired by the Shakespeare Festival in Stratford, Ontario, in 1957), *Toga Brava*, written in honor of the African country, Togo, and *Perfume Suite*, in collaboration with Billy Strayhorn.

In addition, Ellington wrote the music for a ballet, *The River*, presented by the American Ballet Theater at Lincoln Center in 1970; music for the stage—*Jump for Joy*, produced in Los Angeles in 1941, and *Beggar's Opera*, a jazz adaptation of John Gay's ballad opera, seen on Broadway in 1947 with John La Touche providing the lyrics; and music for several motion pictures, among them *Anatomy of a Murder* (1959), *Paris Blues* (1961) and *Assault on a Queen* (1966).

Several of Ellington's jazz classics were tapped for a three-segment ballet, *Three Black Kings*, introduced at the Alvin Ailey Center Dance Theater in New York in August 1976.

Summing up Ellington's creative contribution to American music, Ralph J. Gleason, the distinguished jazz critic and historian wrote: "Ellington has created his own musical world which has transcended every attempt to impose category upon it and has emerged as a solid body of work unequalled in American music. His songs have become a standard part of the cultural heritage, and his longer compositions a part of the finest art of our time."

4

The jazz age of the twenties was the time when singers of the classic blues first gained nationwide prominence.

Early in 1920, Perry Bradford, a songwriter, urged Fred Hager, manager of Okeh Records, to cut two of his songs, "That Thing Called Love" and "You Can't Keep a Good Man Down." Hager consented, but on the condition they were sung by Sophie Tucker. When Miss Tucker proved unavailable, since she was under exclusive contract to another record company, Bradford induced Hager to gamble on Mamie Smith, an unknown young black singer. Though recordings by black performers were not commercial at the time, the Mamie Smith release did well enough to have her press a second Okeh disk on August 10, 1920, "Crazy Blues" (Perry Bradford). "Crazy Blues" was a new title given to a song first named "Harlem Blues" which Mamie Smith was then singing in the stage musical

Maid of Harlem. The change in title on the disk was made with the hope of reaching a market larger than one exclusively black. But the Negro character of the song was adhered to by providing Mamie Smith with the backing of a black group, Johnny Dunn's Original Jazz Hounds.

August 10, 1920, is a momentous date in the jazz history of the twenties, for the recording made that day of "Crazy Blues" is the first vocal blues every consigned to a disk; it made Mamie Smith the first black singer to record a solo performance, and its sale (over one hundred thousand copies) initiated a new vogue in the then still young recording business for gifted black singers. Small competitive firms soon invaded the new market. Arto cut records by Lucille Hegamin; Emerson Records, those of Lillyan Brown; Okeh Records, disks by Helen Baxter and Sara Martin. Black Swan was founded in New York City by W. C. Handy and Harry Pace to become the first black-owned record company. It brought out the blues singing of Alberta Hunter and Ethel Waters. Paramount Records, a Chicago subsidiary of the Wisconsin Chair Company, released the records of Ida Cox, Monette Moore and Ma Rainey. The larger companies also got into the act. Frank Walker of Columbia Records contracted with Bessie Smith and, in February 1923, issued her first disk. It was "Down Hearted Blues" (Alberta Hunter—Lovie Austin) which had previously been sung by Alberta Hunter for Black Swan, coupled with "Gulf Coast Blues" (Clarence Williams).

With Mamie Smith's records selling at the rate of about seventy-five thousand disks a month, and other blues recordings doing almost as well, the vogue for blues records took root. But for a long time they were popular only among Negroes. Convinced that only black audiences were interested in the music of blacks, record companies beginning with Okeh listed their blues disks as "race records," preferring the less specific word "race" to "Negro," and aiming their promotion and distribution exclusively to the black market. But this market proved rich enough to encourage disk companies to build up their catalogues of race records, creating a wonderful and permanent library of blues singing.

Though she was not the first to be recorded, Ma Rainey is often singled out as the earliest of the great singers of the classic blues. "Classic blues" were described by Le Roi Jones in *Blues People* as "music that seemed to contain all the diverse and conflicting elements of Negro music, plus the smoother emotional appeal of the 'performance.' The first Negro music that appeared in a formal context as entertainment though it still retained the harsh, uncompromising reality of the earlier blues forms." In essence, classic blues borrowed a popular singing style, and at the same time, carried authentic blues style into the rendition of popular songs.

Ma Rainey was a squat, pudgy woman with ample physical endowments. She looked like a caricature, with her large gold-capped teeth, her necklace of twenty-dollar gold pieces, and a fan of ostrich feathers in her hand. Some of her black colleagues called hers "the ugliest face in show business," but this was an overstatement since her Puckish features and her gentle expressive eyes had instant appeal. She sang the blues, for which she wrote both the words and the music, with a big contralto voice and an earthy, vigorous delivery touched with melancholy. Her song styling influenced some of her contemporaries, the most important of whom was Bessie Smith. This was a style which embraced, in the words of Barry Ulanov, "carefully placed two-bar fill-ins and introductions, the little melodic variations, the tricks of voice and rhythmic accent, the twists of phrase with which to entwine the double meanings."

Ma Rainey was born Gertrude Pridgett in Columbus, Georgia, in 1886, where she made her singing debut in a tent show when she was fourteen. The name of Rainey came from Will Rainey, who had come to Columbia with a traveling show and married the

eighteen-year-old Gertrude. The "Ma" was affixed to her name much later, probably because of her matronly appearance. With her husband, Ma Rainey formed the team of Rainey
and Rainey which toured the South for several years until they separated not only as
performers but also as life partners.

She was sixteen when she heard her first blues, sung by a girl in a small Missouri
town. Ma Rainey soon began inventing blues of her own which she introduced as encores
before making them the core of her singing act in Negro cabarets, tent shows and meeting
houses. Her fame as a singer of blues spread throughout the South. Paramount Records, in
search of new performers for its race catalogue, became interested in her. In 1923 she
recorded some of her standbys, "Booze and Blues," "Boweavil Blues," "Counting the
Blues," "Moonshine Blues" and "Southern Blues."

If Ma Rainey was "the mother of the blues" (as her record company identified her),
the incomparable Bessie Smith was its empress. The world of the blues in the twenties was
populated with many a Smith—Mamie, Clara, Laura, Trixie as well as Bessie. All were
black, and none were related by family ties. But, without denigrating the contributions of
Mamie, Bessie was the greatest of the Smiths.

She was a woman acquainted with grief. Throughout her life she was haunted by
memories of an unhappy childhood and youth and consumed by an insatiable appetite for
liquor and sex. Fame and success failed to rid her of her loneliness which became chronic
after her stormy marriage to an illiterate night watchman was permanently shattered. She was
a bundle of exposed nerves which life seemed continually to aggravate. Her outward bluster
and rough-and-tough manner, and her profanity, were a facade concealing an exquisite
sensitivity that was easily and frequently wounded. In success, as in failure, she was devoured
by a towering rage she could not control.

When Bessie sang the blues in her slow, languorous and incomparably touching way,
she was not only expressing the hurt that afflicted her race of which the blues was a voice, but
also her own inner torment that never seemed to find a peaceful resolution. The poignancy
of Bessie Smith's art lay not only in the subtlety of her phrasing but in the fact that in singing
the blues, and the more commercial torch songs to which she brought the blues style, she
was singing about herself.

She was born in Chattanooga, Tennessee, probably in 1894, and was raised in
poverty by a sister, since their father had died soon after Bessie was born, and her mother, a
few years after that. As a child, Bessie sang in the streets of Chattanooga. She later joined a
traveling show with which Ma Rainey was affiliated. A friendship was struck up between
these two blues singers, but it is fiction and not fact that Ma Rainey discovered Bessie Smith
and taught her how to sing the blues. After that Bessie Smith appeared with other touring
companies in honky-tonks, gin mills, little theaters, and on the black vaudeville circuit. By
1922 she had acquired a considerable following which brought her to the attention of Frank
Walter, in charge of the race department of Columbia Records. He had Bessie Smith record
two sides on February 17, 1923, "Down Hearted Blues" and "Gulf Coast Blues." To the
amazement of all involved, it sold 780,000 disks in less than six months.

Making more records became a foregone conclusion. Bessie Smith recorded twenty-
nine more sides before 1924 was over, including "Haunted House Blues" (J. C. Johnson),
and "Weeping Willow Blues" (Paul Carter), as well as several numbers accompanied by
Fletcher Henderson. Early the following year she made some monumental recordings
backed by Louis Armstrong's trumpet: "The St. Louis Blues" (W. C. Handy), "Reckless
Blues" (Bessie Smith) and "Cold in Hand Blues" (Jack Gee and Fred Longshaw). These were
followed, though without the benefit of Louis Armstrong's collaboration, by "Dixie Flyer

Blues" (Bessie Smith), "Nashville Woman Blues" (Fred Longshaw), "The Gin House Blues" (Henry Troy—Fletcher Henderson), "Young Woman's Blues" (Bessie Smith) and "Empty Bed Blues" (J. C. Johnson) among others. The huge sales accumulated by her records in 1924 and 1925 were largely responsible for rescuing Columbia Records from imminent bankruptcy.

The success of her records spread her fame throughout America and established her as a star in professional theaters where she was billed as "the greatest and highest salaried race star in the world." She bestrode the stage with regal dignity, every inch the empress. Carl Van Vechten, who heard her in 1925, described her impact in *Jazz Records*: "Walking slowly to the footlights, to the accompaniment of the wailing, muted brasses, the monotonous African pounding of the drum, the dromedary glide of the pianist's fingers over the responsive keys, she began her strange, rhythmic rites in a voice full of shouting and meaning and praying and suffering . . . but seductive and sensuous, too . . . inspired partly by the powerfully magnetic personality of their elemental conjurer woman. . . . The crowd . . . burst into hysterical, semireligious shrieks of sorrow and lamentations."

The twenties was Bessie Smith's decade of triumph. The end of that decade plunged her from the heights into the abyss. The blues had begun to lose their appeal among the general public, the record industry was in the doldrums, the theater was afflicted by depression. Her own indiscretions had aged her beyond her years. She continued making records, and singing in night spots, for a pittance. Having squandered her money recklessly when she was earning it by the barrel, she was now forced to hold rent parties to subsist. "Nobody Knows You When You're Down and Out" (Jimmy Cox) she wailed more than once in one of her most famous blues which she waxed in 1929. Once again—Bessie Smith was singing about herself.

For a time, in the 1930s, it seemed as if she would lift herself out of the depths. Some appearances in such night spots as Connie's Inn in Harlem and Wander Inn Café in Philadelphia proved successful. There were plans afoot for her to make more records, now that the industry was beginning to recover from the ravages of depression, to make a movie in Hollywood, and to appear on the Broadway stage, none of which materialized.

She was planning a Southern tour with *Broadway Rastus* when early in the morning of September 26, 1937, her car, speeding south from Memphis on Route 61, plunged into a parked car. Bessie's car was overturned. She was found lying in the open road, one of her arms nearly severed from her body. A passing surgeon did his best to attend her while awaiting an ambulance which finally took her to the Afro-American Hospital in Clarksville, but Bessie Smith was dead-on-arrival.

Following her death a story was widely circulated that Bessie Smith bled to death because she had been denied admission to a white hospital in Clarksville. This controversial material was the basis for Edward Albee's play, *The Death of Bessie Smith* (1960). But the facts, carefully sought out, prove otherwise. Dr. Hugh Smith, who had been on the scene of the tragedy, pointed out that "down at the Deep South cotton country, no ambulance driver, colored or white, would have thought of putting a colored person off in a hospital for white folks. There were two hospitals—one white, one colored—one-half a mile apart. I suspect that the driver drove just as straight as he could to the colored hospital." The driver of the ambulance provided confirmation.

Thirty-three years after Bessie Smith's death a gravestone was finally placed on her unmarked grave at Mount Lawn Cemetery in Sharon, Pennsylvania. The epitaph read: "The Greatest Blues Singer in the World Will Never Stop Singing." In 1970, Columbia Records launched a giant project to reissue almost everything Bessie Smith had recorded (including disks never before released) in five double album sets. The first of these received the Grand Prix du Disque in 1971 at the Montreux Jazz Festival. Two others were given Grammy awards by the National Academy of Recording Arts and Sciences as the best albums in their specific categories. Some three hundred thousand copies of these albums were sold within a short period of time, and they kept on selling.

Bessie Smith was also remembered on the stage. Her story, told in words and in many of the songs with which she was identified, unfolded in *Me and Bessie*. This was more of a collage than a musical play, virtually a one-woman show (though two other characters were identified respectively as "man" and "woman," and all were backed by a band), starring Linda Hopkins. Conceived and written by Will Holt with Miss Hopkins, dances arranged by Lester Williams, and under the direction of Robert Greenwald, *Me and Bessie* came to Broadway on October 22, 1975, at the Ambassador Theater after having tried out at the Mark Taper Forum in Los Angeles.

Thus Bessie Smith's art survives to influence new generations of blues singers, of whom Billie Holiday, "Lady Day," became the one most deserving to inherit her empress' crown. Among a later generation of blues singers, there was Janis Joplin who studied Bessie Smith's recordings in Texas long before she ventured on her own career. She confessed that Bessie Smith "showed me the air and taught me how to fill it." And Mahalia Jackson, the devout gospel singer (who might be expected to be less than tolerant to Bessie Smith as a human being or to the kind of songs she made famous) called her "my favorite" adding, "her music haunted you even when she stopped singing."

5

Jazz became a sophisticated lady when it assumed symphonic raiment, became symphonic jazz, and entered the serious concert hall. More than any other single person, George Gershwin was responsible for bringing to popular music in general, and to jazz idioms in particular, the richness and discipline and structure of serious music.

Gershwin never intended to abandon popular music for classical composition. To bring artistic validity to the popular song was for him as much of a compulsion as to write good serious music in a popular idiom. In 1920, Gershwin was engaged by George White to write all the music for his annual Broadway revue, *Scandals*. The songs Gershwin wrote for five editions—and others of his songs interpolated into various other Broadway musical productions—played no small part in making jazz a sophisticated art. Songs like the infectious "Do It Again" (B. G. De Sylva) which Irene Bordoni introduced in *The French Doll* in 1922, "Stairway to Paradise" (B. G. De Sylva and Ira Gershwin) and "Somebody Loves Me" (Ballard MacDonald) from the *Scandals* of 1922 and 1924 respectively, were in a class all their own. "Somebody Loves Me" possessed a fresh and personal lyricism that always seemed to pervade a Gershwin ballad. Other Gershwin songs showed an inventiveness of rhythmic technique, a dexterous use of changing meters and staggered accents, and at times an unorthodox harmonic approach, that set them sharply apart from most of the other popular songs of that day. No wonder, then, that even so serious a musician as Beryl Rubinstein, a concert pianist and later the director of the Cleveland Conservatory, could as early as 1922 speak of Gershwin as "a genius." "With Gershwin's style and seriousness, he is not definitely of the popular music school, but is one of the really outstanding figures in this country's serious musical efforts. . . . When we speak of American composers, George Gershwin's name will be prominent on our list."

Recognition of the artistic importance of Gershwin's popular songs came from still another and equally unexpected corner. On November 1, 1923, Eva Gauthier, the celebrated concert singer, gave a recital in Aeolian Hall, New York, in which she performed works by such old masters as Byrd, Purcell and Bellini, and such moderns as Schoenberg, Milhaud and Hindemith. With remarkable courage and independence, she interpolated into her program one group devoted to American popular music, the first time any concert artist had dared make such a move. In this group she included Berlin's "Alexander's Ragtime Band," Jerome Kern's "The Siren Song" (P. G. Wodehouse), Walter Donaldson's "Carolina in the Morning" (Gus Kahn), and three songs by George Gershwin, "Stairway to Paradise" (B. G. De Sylva and Ira Gershwin), "Innocent Ingenue Baby" (A. E. Thomas and Brian Hooker) and "Swanee" (Irving Caesar). She sang a fourth Gershwin song, "Do It Again" (B. G. De Sylva), as an encore and it was received so enthusiastically it had to be repeated.

"It seemed to one listener," wrote Deems Taylor in the New York *World* the following morning, "that the jazz numbers stood up amazingly well, not only as entertainment but as music. . . . What they did possess was melodic interest and continuity, harmonic appropriateness, well-balanced and almost classically severe form, and subtle and fascinating rhythm—in short the qualities that any sincere and interesting music possesses."

For this popular song group, Mme. Gauthier called upon George Gershwin to be her accompanist. Deems Taylor continues: "The singer reappeared, followed by a tall, black-haired young man who was far from possessing the icy aplomb of those to whom playing on that platform at Aeolian Hall is an old story. He bore under his arm a small bundle of sheet music with lurid black and yellow covers. The audience began to show signs of relaxation; this promised to be amusing. . . . Young Mr. Gershwin began to do mysterious and fascinating rhythmic and contrapuntal stunts with the accompaniment."

Carl Van Vechten was another to recognize the significance of this event which for the first time carried George Gershwin into a serious concert auditorium: "I consider this one of the very most important events in American musical history."

It was, perhaps, inevitable for the three American exponents of symphonic jazz —Paul Whiteman, Ferde Grofé and George Gershwin—to team up for a single all-important musical occasion. When they did, another slice of popular music history was carved.

Paul Whiteman had, of course, been playing Gershwin's songs since 1920, and Grofé had been orchestrating them for Whiteman. But Whiteman entered into a more direct collaboration with Gershwin in 1922 when the Whiteman orchestra played in the pit of the *Scandals*. For the 1922 edition, Gershwin wrote the music for a one-act Negro opera, *Blue Monday*, libretto by Buddy De Sylva. Since Whiteman and his orchestra were in the pit, the conductor had to work with Gershwin in preparing the opera for performance, which took place at the Globe Theater on August 29, 1922, with a cast including Lester Allen, Jack McGowan and Coletta Ryan.

The opera's libretto lacked credibility. If the opera had any interest it was for a few high moments in Gershwin's score, the poignant "Blue Monday Blues," the moving spiritual, "I'm Going to See My Mother," the blues, "Has Anybody Seen My Joe?" In songs such as these a perceptive listener could detect suggestions and anticipations of the later *Porgy and Bess*. But *Blue Monday* as a whole was an apprentice effort; it lacked integration and dramatic truth; it suffered from a lack of musical continuity; its recitatives were naively conceived and awkwardly put together.

Blue Monday disappeared from the *Scandals* after the opening night. George White felt that the somber mood of the opera chilled the audience to a point where it was incapable of enjoying the revue numbers that followed. Besides, the New York reviews were unfavorable. Several years later, on December 29, 1925, Paul Whiteman revived the opera in a Carnegie Hall concert. Now renamed *135th Street*, it was given with a new cast headed by Blossom Seeley and Benny Fields. Whiteman again revived the opera a decade after that in Carnegie Hall. It was introduced over television on the "Omnibus" program on March 29, 1953. A fragment was seen in the Gershwin screen biography, *Rhapsody in Blue* (1945). And the opera was given in its entirety in a semi-staged production during a three-day Gershwin festival in Miami, Florida, in 1970.

For a second revival of *135th Street* in 1936, it was given a new orchestration by Ferde Grofé. But more than a decade earlier Grofé had joined forces with Whiteman and Gershwin to create what historians acknowledge to have been a red-letter day in American music, the premiere of the *Rhapsody in Blue*.

The story of how the *Rhapsody in Blue* came to be written has often been told, but not always accurately. The basic facts are these. Late in 1923, Whiteman planned to take his orchestra into a serious concert hall with a program devoted entirely to American popular music. His purpose was to prove that "jazz" was an idiom commanding respect. To give his concert added significance he asked Gershwin to write a new work for him in a jazz style, for Whiteman had a favorable impression of *Blue Monday*. Gershwin said he would write such a work for Whiteman, but being burdened by various commitments for the theater he soon forgot that promise. One day late in the winter of 1923, he read a brief notice in the New York *Herald Tribune* that he was writing a "jazz concerto" for Whiteman's forthcoming concert at Aeolian Hall on February 12, 1924. That announcement, and the imminence of the concert, set him to work. Some ideas for a large orchestral work in a jazz idiom had already occurred to him, and he had jotted them down in a notebook. He now took to his worktable in earnest, choosing the rhapsody because its free and elastic form allowed him greater freedom in working out his ideas. He began a two-piano version on January 7, 1924, and completed it in three weeks. Ferde Grofé's orchestration for jazz orchestra and piano was ready on February 4. Ira Gershwin christened the new work *Rhapsody in Blue*.

Whiteman's historic concert took place at Aeolian Hall on Lincoln's Birthday of 1924.

This was Whiteman's complete program:

I. True Form of Jazz
    a. Ten years ago—"The Livery Stable Blues"
    b. With modern embellishment—"Mama Loves Papa". . .   Baer

II. Comedy Selections
    a. Origin of "Yes, We Have No Bananas". . .   Silver
    b. Instrumental Comedy—"So This Is Venice". . .   Thomas
       (Adapted from *The Carnival of Venice*)

III. Contrast—Legitimate Scoring vs. Jazzing
    a. Selection in True Form—"Whispering". . .   Schonberger
    b. Same Selection with Jazz Treatment

IV. Recent Compositions with Modern Score
    a. "Limehouse Blues". . .   Braham

      b. "I Love You". . .   Archer
      c. "Raggedy Ann". . .   Kern

V. Zez Confrey (piano)
    a. Medley of Popular Airs
    b. "Kitten on the Keys". . .   Confrey
    c. "Ice Cream and Art". . .   [no composer listed]
    d. "Nickel in the Slot". . .   Confrey
      (Accompanied by the orchestra)

VI. Flavoring a Selection with Borrowed Themes
    Russian Rose. . .   Grofé
    (Based on the *Volga Boat Song*)

VII. Semi-Symphonic Arrangement of Popular Melodies
    a. "Alexander's Ragtime Band". . .   Berlin
    b. "A Pretty Girl Is Like a Melody". . . Berlin
    c. "Orange Blossoms in California". . .   Berlin

VIII. A Suite of Serenades. . .   Herbert
    a. Spanish
    b. Chinese
    c. Cuban
    d. Oriental

IX. Adaptation of Standard Selections to Dance Rhythms
    a. "Pale Moon". . .   Logan
    b. "To a Wild Rose". . .   MacDowell
    c. "Chansonette". . .   Friml

X. George Gershwin (Piano)
    Rhapsody in Blue. . .   Gershwin
    (Accompanied by the Orchestra)

XI. In the Field of the Classics
    Pomp and Circumstance. . .   Elgar

This program—in which Victor Herbert's Suite, Zez Confrey's "Kitten on the Keys" and Gershwin's *Rhapsody in Blue* were world premieres—was a strange, almost indiscriminate potpourri of the good and the bad in the popular music of the 1920s. It was not a program able to sustain the interest of a discriminating audience; the similarity of style and orchestral coloring in the various numbers and the lack of any genuine continuing musical interest, made the concert, after a while, a bore. But for the *Rhapsody in Blue* the event might well have proved a failure. Up to the moment the Gershwin *Rhapsody* was given on the long program, the audience showed increasing signs of fatigue and restlessness. Then came the opening clarinet portamento of the *Rhapsody in Blue*, and the audience was suddenly magnetized. This was a definitely new sound, a refreshing, even exciting, change from the dull routines that had preceded it. The opening clarinet yawp plunged into the first theme—a brash, impudent, saucy subject that not only set the mood for the entire work but was the voice for the frenetic and convention-shattering 1920s. Other musical ideas, no less infectious, followed, culminating in the broad rhapsodic slow section for strings which has since become one of the most celebrated melodies in serious American music, and Whiteman's signature theme. The *Rhapsody* closed with a brief, dramatic coda.

The *Rhapsody in Blue* pointed to the future of symphonic jazz and suggested its possibilities. Single-handedly, the *Rhapsody* transformed Whiteman's concert from an exotic novelty, to be shortly forgotten, into a musical event of first importance.

The reaction of the critics was varied. There were those whose enthusiasm knew no limits. Henry O. Osgood, assistant editor of *Musical Courier*, said that the premiere of the *Rhapsody in Blue* was a more important event than that of Stravinsky's *The Rite of Spring*. Equally excessive in his praises was Henry T. Finck who felt that Gershwin was "far superior to Schoenberg, Milhaud and the rest of the futurist fellows." W. J. Henderson described the music as "highly ingenious." Gilbert W. Gabriel said of the composition that "the beginning and the ending of it were stunning. . . . Mr. Gershwin has an irrepressible pack of talents, and there is an element of inevitability about his piece."

At the opposite pole stood critics like Lawrence Gilman and Pitts Sanborn. "How trite and feeble and conventional the tunes are, how sentimental and vapid the harmonic treatment, under its disguise of fussy and futile counterpoint," lamented Gilman. Sanborn complained that the music "runs off into empty passage work and meaningless repetition."

The critics may analyze, dissect, praise or blame. But in the last analysis it is the listening public that elevates a musical work to the status of a classic. The entire world has assigned the *Rhapsody in Blue* a position of significance among the outstanding works of the twentieth century. It is doubtful if any other serious American musical work since 1900 has been played as often as Gershwin's, is loved so universally, is so well known in so many different places and in so many different guises. It has been arranged for solo piano, two pianos, eight pianos; for piano and symphony orchestra and violin and symphony orchestra; for solo harmonica and an orchestra of harmonicas; for a mandolin orchestra. It has been used as the background music for a Grecian ballet, a modernistic ballet and a tap dance. In 1930, the Roxy Theater in New York paid Gershwin $10,000 a week to appear on its stage to play the work; while in the same year Fox paid the highest figure ($50,000) offered up to then for a musical composition to be used in a motion picture. In 1946, the Rhapsody gave its name as a title for Gershwin's screen biography. The royalties from the sale of sheet music, records, and performance rights totaled over $250,000 in a quarter of a century. The *Rhapsody in Blue* not only helped make Gershwin affluent but also gave him world recognition as a composer.

More important even than its immense financial success and its universal appeal is its influence on the music of its generation. The *Rhapsody in Blue* liberated jazz from Tin Pan Alley; it brought jazz into the free open world of serious music where from this time on it would assume a place of honor.

The *Rhapsody in Blue* was by no means the first piece of serious American music to use popular American idioms. In or about 1900, Charles Ives used ragtime effects in his first piano sonata, and in his song "Charlie Rutledge." American popular music first invaded the concert auditorium on March 11, 1914, when Jim Europe led a Negro orchestra in a concert at Carnegie Hall. In 1919, young Gershwin made tentative experiments to carry a basic style of popular music into serious composition by writing *Lullaby*, for string quartet, whose main melody was a blues-like quality. In the early 1920s, John Alden Carpenter wrote a delightful jazz score for a ballet, *Krazy Kat* (1921). But none of these symphonic jazz compositions or performances had quite the impact that the *Rhapsody in Blue* had on the world of music. Gershwin's *Rhapsody* brought acceptance to American popular music among many serious musicians who had formerly held it in disdain. Henceforth, celebrated composers in America would not hesitate to use jazz techniques and styles for their serious efforts. Jazz, regarded by so many composers as an ungainly stepchild before 1924, suddenly assumed dignity and propriety.

Soon after the premiere of the *Rhapsody in Blue*, Gershwin was commissioned by Walter Damrosch, the conductor of the New York Symphony Society, to write a new jazz orchestral work for his organization. Gershwin chose to write a piano concerto. He completed his *Concerto in F* on November 10, 1925, this time doing his own orchestration, a practice he followed for all subsequent serious works. The following December 3, the Concerto was introduced in Carnegie Hall at a concert of the New York Symphony Society, Walter Damrosch conducting, with the composer as soloist.

Jazz was no less prominent in the *Concerto* than it had been in the earlier *Rhapsody*. The new work opened with an abandoned Charleston theme in the kettledrums and woodwinds. It continued in this vein with other racy jazz ideas, including a poetic subject for muted trumpet with which the second movement opens, and an expansive melody for the strings in the same movement that is the heart of the entire work; both of these, for all their aristocratic loveliness, were obviously born on the other side of the musical tracks.

The *Concerto* showed a definite advance in Gershwin's symphonic jazz writing. There is a greater variety and richness of thematic material than in the *Rhapsody*, and these ideas are worked out with greater elasticity and technical assurance. The progress in musical know-how and the artistic growth are evident in all later serious works by Gershwin. In 1926, he wrote three jazz *Preludes* for piano which he himself introduced at a concert at the Hotel Roosevelt in New York, in which he was the assisting artist to the operatic contralto Marguerite D'Alvarez. The first *Prelude*, in B-flat major, is a skillful blend of the tango and the Charleston. The second, in C-sharp minor, is a blues melody, and the most famous of this set, familiar not only in its original version by also in transcriptions. By contrast, the third *Prelude*, in E-flat major, is effervescent with leaping jazz rhythms.

Less than two lears later, during a vacation in Europe, Gershwin worked on an orchestral composition, the tone poem *An American in Paris*. It was introduced by the New York Philharmonic Orchestra under Walter Damrosch on December 13, 1928. Describing the feelings of an American tourist as he strolls along a Parisian boulevard, *An American in Paris* was Gershwin's most successful effort to combine jazz with symphonic writing. Jazz is found in the brisk trombone tune early in the score; in the wailing blues melody for muted trumpet which is the core of the work; and in a piquant Charleston melody for two trumpets. Modern symphonic writing appears in the brisk walking theme, in the harmonic writing often overlaid with modernism, and in the brilliant orchestration which included the actual sounds of two Parisian taxicab horns.

The *Second Rhapsody* (1931) grew out of a brief orchestral sequence Gershwin wrote for his first motion-picture assignment, *Delicious*. Here he gives a tonal portrait of the sights and sounds of a large city. The *Rhapsody* opens with an incisive rhythmic subject descriptive of riveting, and has for its principal melody a blues first heard in the strings and then in the brass, one of the most spacious and expansive themes Gershwin ever wrote. The *Second Rhapsody* was introduced by the Boston Symphony under Serge Koussevitzky, with the composer at the piano, in Boston on January 20, 1932.

The *Cuban Overture* (1932)—originally entitled *Rhumba*—and the *Variations on I*

Got Rhythm (1934) show impressive forward strides by the composer in the use of counterpoint in the first work, and in the art of thematic development in the second. The *Cuban Overture* was the outcome of a brief holiday which Gershwin spent in Havana where he was fascinated by its native rhythms and percussion instruments. In this overture he incorporated both elements, the rhythms of the rhumba and the habanera, and such Cuban instruments as the claves, the gourd, and the maracas. The *Cuban Overture* was first heard at a concert at the Lewisohn Stadium in New York, on August 16, 1932, Albert Coates conducting.

Gershwin wrote the *Variations on I Got Rhythm* for a concert tour he was making with an orchestra in 1934 in a program made up of his own works. The *Variations* was introduced in the first of these appearances, in Boston, on January 14, 1934. "I Got Rhythm" is, of course, one of Gershwin's best-known and most dynamic songs; it comes from the musical comedy *Girl Crazy* (1930). In this work for piano and orchestra, Gershwin subjects this vigorous theme to many subtle changes of mood, atmosphere and feeling: from a melancholy dirge to a brilliant eruption of pyrotechnics; from a dolorous blues lament to an athletic melody full of spirit and joy of life.

Gershwin's last serious work and his greatest—the folk opera, *Porgy and Bess* (1935) —will be discussed together with his other stage works in another chapter.

In his symphonic works, Gershwin pointed the way which many American popular and serious composers followed. This was the direction Duke Ellington took with his bountiful repertory of small and large orchestral works. This was also the direction taken by Ferde Grofé. In the year of the *Rhapsody in Blue*, 1924, Grofé wrote the *Mississippi Suite* for Paul Whiteman in which jazz colors and idioms are adroitly used, particularly in his tonal description of Huckleberry Finn. More celebrated, though, is Grofé's *Grand Canyon Suite* (1931). This is a five-movement portrait of one of America's natural wonders. The names of the respective movements give the clue to their programmatic content: "Sunrise"; "The Painted Desert"; "On the Trail" (the best known section of the set, long utilized by Philip Morris cigarettes as its musical signature on radio and television); "Sunset"; and "Cloudburst." Here the use of jazz elements is more discreet than in the *Mississippi Suite*; but both the melodic and rhythmic content is unmistakably of jazz origin.

Like Grofé, Robert Russell Bennett (1894–   ), earned his living as an orchestrator of other people's music. He has been for many years a top orchestrator for the Broadway musical stage. In between his more profitable Broadway chores, he found the time to write many serious musical works. Some are filled with those popular elements he had assimilated from the musical stage, and these include: *Charleston Rhapsody* (1926), *March*, for two pianos and orchestra (1930); *Concerto Grosso*, for jazz band and orchestra (1932); and *Variations on a Theme by Jerome Kern* (1933), the theme being Kern's song "Once in a Blue Moon" (Anne Caldwell) from the musical *Stepping Stones* (1923).

Jerome Kern was encouraged by André Kostelanetz, the celebrated conductor, to write two works in forms more spacious than the songs to which he had hitherto confined himself. *Scenario* (1941) was an extended symphonic work made up of the principal songs from the Broadway musical play *Show Boat* (1927), an adroit integration of the basic musical materials from that show. About a year later, Kern wrote a second large orchestral work for Kostelanetz, this time with original thematic ideas, *Mark Twain: A Portrait for Orchestra*. This was a four-section composition treating various episodes in Mark Twain's career. Both works are filled with that gentle, charming and personal lyricism Kern brought to his best songs, and both are the sum of ingratiating lyric parts.

Serious composers also discovered from Gershwin that jazz techniques and styles could be effective within the patterns and formats of the most serious classical works. Aaron

Copland (1900–   ), at the dawn of a career that eventually brought him to a leading position among serious American composers, discovered jazz and wrote two major works in that style, *Music for the Theatre* (1925), an orchestral suite in which the "Dance" and "Burlesque" movements were rooted in the jazz style and techniques of the early 1920s, and the *Piano Concerto* (1926), where there was an even more extensive exploitation of jazz writing. John Alden Carpenter (1876–1951) wrote an important ballet in the jazz style called *Skyscrapers*. It was introduced at the Metropolitan Opera House in 1926. Jazz appears in the music of other serious American composers: in *Daniel Jazz* (1923) and the *Jazz Suite* (1925) by Louis Gruenberg (1884–1964); in *Jazz Symphony* (1927) and the Opera *Transatlantic* (1930) by George Antheil (1900–1959); in *New Year's Eve in New York* (1929) by Werner Janssen (1899–   ); in *Chorale and Fugue in Jazz* (1931) and *Swing Sinfonietta* (1936) by Morton Gould (1913–   ); and in the ballet, *Fancy Free* (1941) by Leonard Bernstein (1918–   ).

6

Jazz—the sophisticated lady of New York—became a voice loud, clear and often in the popular music of the 1920s, 1930s and 1940s. Jazz concerts in serious auditoriums became the practice as Vincent Lopez brought his orchestra to the Metropolitan Opera House, Paul Whiteman, Benny Goodman and Duke Ellington their respective ensembles to Carnegie Hall. Jazz orchestras, specializing in a quasi-symphonic treatment of popular music, multiplied and flourished throughout the United States, led by such acclaimed musicians as Lopez, Whiteman, Abe Lyman, Leo Reisman, Guy Lombardo, Stan Kenton and many others.

Whether jazz had artistic validity or was a demoralizing and decadent force was a hotly fought issue. One educator said that "its influence is as harmful and degrading to civilized races as it always has been among savages from whom we borrowed it. If we permit our boys and girls to be exposed indefinitely to this pernicious influence, the harm that will result may tear to pieces our whole social fabric." A physician discovered that: ". . . jazz affects the brain through the sense of hearing, giving the same results as . . . alcoholic drinks taken into the system. . . ."

The President of the Christian and Missionary Alliance Conference charged that ". . . American girls are maturing too quickly under the hectic influence of jazz." John Roach Straton denounced jazz from his pulpit in New York as "music of . . . intellectual and spiritual debauchery, utter degradation." A city ordinance banned jazz in Zion City, Illinois, together with other sinful practices. The American composer and educator, Daniel Gregory Mason, said of jazz: "It is not a new flavor, but a kind of curry or catsup strong enough to make the stale old dishes palatable to unfastidious appetites. . . . It is the musical counterpart of the sterile cleverness we find in so much . . . contemporary conversation . . . theater and books."

Others spoke up for jazz with equal conviction and fervor. Within the august halls of Harvard University there took place a symposium on jazz conducted by Professor Edward Burlingame Hill. The League of Composers in New York—guardian of the most serious principles and aims of contemporary music—held a jazz conference. Outstanding musical artists came vigorously to its defense, among them Fritz Kreisler and Leopold Stokowski. Mrs. Charles S. Guggenheim said in an interview that a chair of jazz should be established at the American Academy of Rome. Actually a course in jazz music *was* instituted at the New School for Social Research in New York. In 1925, Alfred Frankenstein, the eminent music critic, published one of the earliest critical evaluations of jazz in *Syncopating Saxo-*

phones, the forerunner of many valuable analytical and historical volumes of jazz issued both in the United States and in Europe.

The respectability of jazz was soon further confirmed through the establishment of jazz festivals from Newport in Rhode Island to Monterey in California; through the publication of scholarly jazz journals; through valuable anthologies of historical recordings; through the syndication of critical jazz columns in newspapers; and through the opening up of courses on jazz in leading American colleges and universities.

"I like to think," said Hiram K. Motherwell in the 1920s, "that it [jazz] is the perfect expression of the American city, with its restless bustle and motion, its multitude of unrelated details, and its underlying rhythmic progress towards a vague Somewhere. Its technical resourcefulness continually surprises me, and its melodies, at their best, delight me."

17

Tin Pan Alley Abandons 28th Street: The Popular Music Industry in the 1920s

1

As a geographical entity on 28th Street between Fifth Avenue and Broadway, Tin Pan Alley ceased to exist after World War I. But as a way of life for American popular music, as a finely constructed mechanism triggering hit songs, and as the developing medium for talented new composers and lyricists, the Alley was still very much alive in the twenties.

The decentralization of the music publishing business had begun to take place even before World War I. With the theater district becoming increasingly concentrated around Broadway between 42nd and 50th streets, publishing houses started to move closer to this all-important scene of operations. The house of Waterson, Berlin and Snyder moved to the Strand Theater Building on Broadway. When Irving Berlin broke away from that firm in 1919 to organize his own establishment, Irving Berlin, Inc., he located nearby, once again in the heart of the theatrical district. By the middle 1920s, other major firms had deserted 28th Street. Leo Feist and J. H. Remick now operated on West 40th Street; F. B. Haviland on West 44th Street; Harms on West 45th Street; Charles K. Harris on West 47th Street. The newer companies organized in the twenties were also scattered around the Main Stem: Jack Mills, Inc., Fred Fisher Inc., Yellen and Bornstein (soon to be renamed Ager, Yellen and Bornstein), Edward B. Marks (an outgrowth of Joseph W. Stern & Company), and Maurice Richmond Company (soon to become known as Richmond-Robbins). Many small firms, most of them newcomers to the business, found offices in the Brill Building at 1619 Broadway—an "old gray building," as William H. A. Carr and Gene Grove described it in the New York *Post*, "in which the offices run the gamut from plain to dingy, from ordinary to tiny."

By the mid-1920s, the Broadway musical theater had become the prime showcase for the merchandise of Tin Pan Alley. Vaudeville was dying. In 1926, there were only twelve theaters in America devoted exclusively to vaudeville and by 1932 even these few closed. The Palace Theater, so long vaudeville's Taj Mahal, presented its last week of straight vaudeville between July 9 and 16 of 1932. After that it at first combined vaudeville with movies, and then the screen took over completely. Radio, talking pictures and the Depression were the lethal blows from which vaudeville was never to recover. Burlesque was also a dying institution. In its increasingly bolder sex exploitation, nudity and outright pornography, burlesque was involving itself in a continual game of hide-and-seek with the law. In the end the law caught up with it.

But the musical theater was prospering as never before. In the 1920s there were eighty legitimate theaters in New York. Between forty and fifty musicals were being produced each season, with sometimes as many as four premieres an evening. Though staging and costuming were ever more lavish, and though more and more stars were recruited for each production, the costs to mount a musical and the overall budget to run it were still below the possible take at the box office of an even moderately successful undertaking. A run of two hundred performances represented a financial profit, and a run of three hundred meant a considerable financial return for the investment. The percentage of box-office successes was never before, or since, so high.

A song well placed in a hit show was its surest route to success, carrying along with it not only large sheet music sales but also other subsidiary income. Some of the foremost hits of the twenties were born on the Broadway stage, with a famous star serving as midwife. Conversely, a hit song often made it possible for a musical to survive imminent disaster and emerge triumphant. The box-office success of *Irene*, in 1919, for example, was primarily the result of the popularity of its lovable waltz, "In My Sweet Little Alice Blue Gown" (Joseph McCarthy—Harry Tierney). *Mary*, a musical in 1920, owed its prosperity almost entirely to its hit song, "The Love Nest" (Otto Harbach—Louis A. Hirsch), and *Little Jesse James* in 1923 to "I Love You" (Harlan Thompson—Harry Archer). The Rodgers and Hart musical, *The Girl Friend* (1926) was a box-office dud until its two principal songs began to take hold outside the theater, the title number and "Blue Room." And in the early thirties, *Gay Divorce* (1932) became known as the "Night and Day" show because of that Cole Porter song classic, while *Take a Chance*, the same year, was often referred to as the "Eadie Was a Lady" show (B. G. De Sylva—Nacio Herb Brown).

2

What had been true earlier in Tin Pan Alley remained valid in the twenties. Some of the most important songwriters of this decade received their basic training in music publishing houses.

Fred E. Ahlert (1892–1953) had worked as an arranger for Waterson, Berlin and Snyder before his songwriting career began to flourish with "My Mammy's Arms" (Sam M. Lewis and Joe Young) in 1920. His greatest hit in the twenties was "I'll Get By" (Roy Turk) which sold a million copies of sheet music and just as many records, and has since beome a standard. This number, as well as Ahlert's "Mean to Me" (Roy Turk) are most often associated with the singer Ruth Etting. Ahlert went on to even greater success in the early 1930s. Bing Crosby introduced Ahlert's "Where the Blue of the Night Meets the Gold of the Day" (Roy Turk and Bing Crosby) in the motion picture musical, *The Big Broadcast of 1932*, and then adopted it as his radio theme song. "Walkin' My Baby Back Home" (Roy Turk and Harry Richman) became Harry Richman's specialty. "I'm Gonna Sit Right Down and Write

Myself a Letter" (Joe Young) was first popularized in the mid-1930s by "Fats" Waller and then revived a quarter of a century later by Bill Haley and the Comets in their best-selling Decca recording.

Louis Alter (1902–   ) was an arranger for Shapiro-Bernstein and after that piano accompanist for Nora Bayes. What first brought him to the limelight as a composer was an instrumental piece, "Manhattan Serenade," inspired by the sights and sounds of New York City. He wrote it originally for the piano, and later orchestrated it. It became something of a minor classic in the jazz repertory after Paul Whiteman and his Orchestra recorded it for Victor. It has often been heard in the movies and over radio and television when music is needed to suggest or portray Manhattan. Beginning with 1928, Alter contributed songs to Broadway musicals, and after 1929 to motion pictures. "Twilight on the Trail" (Sidney D. Mitchell), from the movie *The Trail of the Lonesome Pine* (1936) was such a favorite with President Franklin D. Roosevelt that Alter presented the manuscript of the song, together with Bing Crosby's recording, to the Roosevelt Memorial Library in Hyde Park, New York.

Joseph A. Burke (1884–1950) was also an arranger in Tin Pan Alley before he became a composer. He had to wait almost a decade for recognition, which came in 1925 with "Oh, How I Miss You Tonight" (Benny Davis and Mark Fisher) which Davis introduced into his vaudeville act. Three years later came "Carolina Moon" (Benny Davis), first recorded by Gene Austin for Victor, and further popularized by Guy Lombardo and his Royal Canadians before Morton Downey used it as his radio theme song. After 1929, Burke wrote extensively for motion pictures, but some of his famous songs originated in Tin Pan Alley rather than in Hollywood. "Dancing with Tears in My Eyes" (Al Dubin) was first performed over the radio by Rudy Vallee. "Moon Over Miami" (Edgar Leslie) was introduced by Ted Fiorito and his orchestra after which it became the theme music for Dean Hudson and his orchestra.

Hoagy Carmichael (1899–   ) contributed to Tin Pan Alley, before the 1920s closed, a song destined to become one of its all-time classics: "Star Dust," written while he was still a comparative novice in the music business. Born in Bloomington, Indiana, he completed there his high school education as a preliminary to law study. To earn his keep, he played the piano in jazz bands, some of which he organized. In 1924, he wrote "Riverboat Shuffle," an instrumental number published a year later under the title of "Free Wheeling" when it was introduced by the Wolverines in a Gennett recording. In 1939, Dick Voynow, Irving Mills and Mitchell Parish wrote lyrics for it and restored its original title. Meanwhile, in 1925 Carmichael wrote "Washboard Blues" (Fred B. Callahan and Irving Mills), which became a best-selling recording in a performance by Red Nichols and his Five Pennies for Brunswick and in Paul Whiteman's release for Victor with Carmichael himself doing the vocal.

While practicing law in Miami, Florida, Carmichael became convinced by the success of Red Nichols' recording of "Washboard Blues" that his destiny was music. He returned to Bloomington and worked as a piano demonstrator for the local branches of several Tin Pan Alley firms. He also played the piano in orchestras led by Jean Goldkette and Don Redman.

In his autobiography, *Stardust Road* (1946), Carmichael describes how he wrote "Star Dust." One night in 1929, he was sitting on the so-called "spooning wall" at the University of Indiana musing about a girl he had once loved and lost. As he was thinking and dreaming, he looked up at a star-studded sky. A melody suddenly came to mind. He rushed over to the University book nook, which had a piano, and wrote down his song. When one of Carmichael's former schoolmates first heard the melody he instantly baptized it "Star Dust" because, as he said, "it sounded like dust from the stars drifting down through the summer sky." Carmichael confesses that he had no real notion what the title meant but he liked the sound of it and felt it suited his music.

In its first version, "Star Dust" was a piano instrumental in fast tempo. As such it was introduced by Don Redman and his orchestra. Jimmy Dale, an arranger, recognized its commercial possibilities if it were played in a slower tempo and with sentimental feeling. Victor Young prepared such an arrangement and in this new format the song was played by Isham Jones and his orchestra and after that by Emile Seidel's orchestra with Carmichael at the piano. Now a sweet, sentimental tune, "Star Dust" cried out for a lyric, which was provided by Mitchell Parish who was then employed by the house of Irving Mills, which published the song in 1929. That year it was sung for the first time at the Cotton Club in New York. In the early 1930s, "Star Dust" was played by many outstanding bands, among them one led by Artie Shaw, whose recording sold over two million copies within a five-year period. André Kostelanetz and Eddy Duchin were two others who helped to establish it as an all-time song favorite. Since then "Star Dust" has been recorded over five hundred times in forty-six different arrangements and translated into forty languages. It is perhaps the only popular song ever recorded on two sides of a single disk in two different performances, one by Tommy Dorsey and his orchestra and the other by Benny Goodman and his band.

While "Star Dust" was soaring to nationwide popularity, Carmichael settled in New York where he wrote "Rockin' Chair" to his own lyrics in 1930. It was introduced by Mildred Bailey and became her theme song. Miss Bailey also introduced "Lazybones," whose melody came from "Washboard Blues" but with new lyrics by Johnny Mercer, and "Georgia on My Mind" (Stuart Gorrell). The popularity of "Lazybones" was greatly enhanced through performances by Rudy Vallee, while "Georgia on My Mind" enjoyed a triumphant revival in 1960 with Ray Charles' recording for ABC-Paramount which received Grammys from the National Academy of Recording Arts and Sciences as the best rock 'n' roll recording and the best male vocal performance. With "Lazy River" (Sidney Arodin) in 1931, Carmichael added a footnote to jazz history with a Victor recording by a band which he had assembled and which included the Dorsey brothers, Jack Teagarden, Gene Krupa, Bud Freeman, Benny Goodman, Joe Venuti and Bix Beiderbecke. Other Carmichael songs of the thirties were "One Morning in May" (Mitchell Parish) and "Heart and Soul" (Frank Loesser), the latter introduced by Larry Clinton and his orchestra in a movie short, *A Song Is Born* (1938) and performed by Gene Krupa and his orchestra in the motion picture *Some Like It Hot* (1939). Carmichael wrote a good deal of other music for the movies and contributed his distinctly individual singing style and Hoosier accent in featured speaking and singing roles in various motion pictures, and over the radio and television.

Born in New York's East Side as Konrad A. Dobert, Con Conrad (1891–1938) came to Tin Pan Alley by way of the vaudeville stage where he had been appearing since his sixteenth year. His first published song, "Down in Dear New Orleans" (Joe Young) was interpolated into the *Ziegfeld Follies of 1912*. He formed a publishing partnership with Henry Waterson, the Broadway Music Corporation, that issued his "Oh, Frenchy" (Sam Ehrlich). But "Palesteena," which he wrote in collaboration with J. Russel Robinson, was published by Shapiro-Bernstein in 1918. It was introduced by the Original Dixieland Jazz Band and popularized by Eddie Cantor. In 1920, Conrad enjoyed a resounding success with "Margie" (Benny Davis), melody written with J. Russel Robinson. The "Margie" in this song was the five-year-old daughter of Eddie Cantor. Cantor introduced it at the Winter Garden before interpolating it into the revue *The Midnight Rounders* (1921). Between 1921 and 1924, Conrad's hits included "Ma, He's Making Eyes at Me" (Sidney Clare), "Barney Google" (Billy Rose), inspired by a popular newspaper cartoon, a song written for Eddie Cantor but more often identified with Olsen and Johnson, and "Memory Lane" (B. G. De Sylva) which he wrote with Larry Spier.

J. Fred Coots (1897–   ) started out as a song plugger. His reputation was established with the stage musical, *Sally, Irene and Mary*, which had a two-year run on Broadway. During the rest of the twenties, Coots contributed either the full scores or individual songs to many other Broadway musicals, the last of them *Sons o' Guns* (1929). In the 1930s, Coots was productive as a composer for motion pictures and nightclubs, but his greatest song successes came out of Tin Pan Alley: "I Still Get a Thrill" (Benny Davis), introduced in 1930 by Hal Kemp and his orchestra; "Love Letters in the Sand" (Nick and Charles Kenny), introduced in 1931 by Dolly Dawn, first recorded by Russ Columbo, became the theme song of George Hall and his orchestra, and finally, in 1957, became more popular than ever through Pat Boone's recording for Dot; "Santa Claus Is Coming to Town" (Haven Gillespie) sung to nationwide fame over the radio by Eddie Cantor in 1934; and "You Go to My Head" (Haven Gillespie), first performed by Glen Gray and the Casa Loma Orchestra before becoming the theme song of Mitchell Ayres and his orchestra.

Sammy Fain (1902–   ), born in New York City, became a song plugger and staff pianist for the firm of Jack Mills, after which he toured the vaudeville circuit with Artie Dunn. His first published song was "Nobody Knows What a Red-Headed Mama Can Do" (Irving Mills and Al Dubin) in 1925.

In 1927, Fain met Irving Kahal, a young vaudevillian, whose passion was writing song lyrics. For seventeen years, up to the time of his death in 1942, Kahal wrote the lyrics for Fain's music, though sometimes in collaboration with others. The first year of the partnership of Kahal and Fain brought them a hit with "Let a Smile Be Your Umbrella," in which Kahal was assisted by Francis Wheeling on the lyrics, and which Fain and Dunn introduced in vaudeville, and the Duncan Sisters sang in the motion picture *It's a Great Life* (1929). During 1927, Kahal and Fain completed the score for their first Broadway musical, *Manhattan Mary*, starring Ed Wynn. Willie Raskin and Kahal were the lyricists for Fain's hit song of 1929, "Wedding Bells Are Breaking Up that Old Gang of Mine," and Pierre Norman Conner and Kahal were his lyricists for "When I Take My Sugar to Tea," which was interpolated into the Marx Brothers' extravaganza film *Monkey Business* (1931).

Joseph Meyer (1894–   ), no relation to George W. Meyer, came from California where he had pursued a mercantile career while studying music and playing the violin in a café orchestra in San Francisco. His purpose in coming to New York in 1922 was to engage more actively in writing music. Soon after his arrival he published "My Honey's Lovin' Arms" (Harry Ruby). Al Jolson interpolated Meyer's "California Here I Come" (B. G. De Sylva) into the Winter Garden extravaganza *Bombo*, and instantly made Meyer a composer of some account in Tin Pan Alley. Jolson also introduced Meyer's "If You Knew Susie" (B. G. De Sylva) in *Big Boy* in 1925. Actually, Jolson did not like this song particularly and soon turned it over to Eddie Cantor who, he felt, was better suited to sing it. Cantor first performed it at a benefit in New York and brought down the house. "If You Knew Susie" remained Cantor's song thereafter, one of the mainstays of his large repertory.

There were two other song successes by Meyer in the twenties: "A Cup of Coffee, a Sandwich and You" (Billy Rose and Al Dubin), introduced by Gertrude Lawrence and Jack Buchanan in the sophisticated English revue imported to New York, *Charlot's Revue of 1926*, and "Crazy Rhythm" (Irving Caesar), written in 1928 with Roger Wolfe Kahn and introduced that same year by Ben Bernie in the musical *Here's Howe*. In the 1930s, Meyer contributed songs to the *Ziegfeld Follies of 1934* and to several motion pictures.

Harry Tierney (1895–1965) completed his music education in New York, after which he went to London in 1915 to work as staff composer for an English music publisher. Back in the United States in 1916, he wrote "M-i-s-s-i-s-s-i-p-p-i" (Bert Hanlon and Benny Ryan), a spelling song introduced by Frances White in the *Ziegfeld Midnight Frolics* (1916). A year later Anna Held scored with Tierney's "It's a Cute Little Way of Me Own" (Alfred Bryan) in *Follow Me*.

As a staff composer for Jerome H. Remick in Tin Pan Alley, Tierney wrote songs interpolated into the *Ziegfeld Follies*, George M. Cohan's *The Royal Vagabond* and several other Broadway productions. His first complete score for a Broadway musical, and the one that made him sought after as a composer for the stage, was *Irene* in 1919, which boasted "In My Sweet Little Alice Blue Gown" (Joseph McCarthy). After that, Tierney devoted himself to Broadway, writing songs for smash box-office successes produced by Ziegfeld. For *Kid Boots* (1923), starring Eddie Cantor, he wrote "If Your Heart's in the Game" and "Someone Loves You, After All," lyrics by Joseph McCarthy; and for *Rio Rita* (1927), the highly popular title number, lyrics by McCarthy. Tierney also contributed songs to the *Ziegfeld Follies*, editions of 1919, 1923, 1924 and 1927, with "My Baby's Arms" (Joseph McCarthy) introduced by Delyle Aida and John Steel in 1919.

3

The moral and emotional climate of the twenties is reflected in many of the songs of that decade. The feverish quest for good times is captured in "Ain't We Got Fun?" (Gus Kahn and Raymond Egan—Richard A. Whiting). Ruth Roye and Van and Schenck each made it a high point of their vaudeville acts in 1921. The spirit of reckless abandon finds a voice in "Runnin' Wild" in 1922 (Joe Grey and Leo Wood—A. Harrington Gibbs), which Art Hickman and his orchestra helped make popular. The pervading optimism induced by the conviction that this was the best of all possible worlds and the best of all possible times is sounded loud and clear in the song made famous by Al Jolson, "I'm Sitting on Top of the World" (Sam M. Lewis and Joe Young—Ray Henderson) in 1925. The twenties gave assurance that there are hidden benefits in adversity (Jerome Kern's "Look for the Silver Lining," lyrics by B. G. De Sylva) and that rain is sure to be followed by sunshine (Louis Silvers' "April Showers," lyrics by B. G. De Sylva).

The appetite of the twenties for the outlandish and absurd was fed by Tin Pan Alley with a steady diet of nonsense songs. Among them were: "Who Ate Napoleons with Josephine when Bonaparte Was Away?" (Alfred Bryan—E. Ray Goetz); "Barney Google" (Billy Rose—Con Conrad); "Does the Spearmint Lose Its Flavor on the Bedpost Overnight?" (Billy Rose and Marty Bloom—Ernest Breuer); "Horses" (Byron Gay—Richard A. Whiting); "I'm Just Wild About Animal Crackers" (Freddie Rich, Sam Coslow and Harry Link); "Diga Diga Doo" from the *Blackbirds of 1928* (Dorothy Fields—Jimmy McHugh); "Who Takes Care of the Caretaker's Daughter While the Caretaker's Busy Taking Care?" (Paul Revere and Chick Endor); "I Faw Down and Go Boom" (James Brockman and Leonard Stevens —James Brockman); and "I Got a 'Code' in My 'Doze' " (Arthur Fields, Fred Hall and Billy Rose).

One nonsense song proved sensational: "Yes, We Have No Bananas" (Frank Silver and Irving Cohn), written in 1923 after the songwriters happened to overhear a Greek fruit peddler say this to a customer. Frank Silver's Music Masters introduced it in a New York restaurant, but it did not catch on. Then Eddie Cantor, while touring with the revue *Make It Snappy*, interpolated it into that production in Philadelphia. On its first hearing it so captured the audience that repetitions were demanded for over a quarter of an hour. The song stayed in the show, and in Cantor's permanent repertory. His best-selling Victor record was one of many to help make the song into something resembling a national passion.

They still sang of love in Tin Pan Alley in the twenties, and Irving Berlin was writing the best songs about it. His melodic gift seemed capable of evoking the most sensitive and tender moods. In 1921 he wrote and published "All by Myself," introduced at the Palace Theater by Charles King, and "Say It with Music," from the *Music Box Revue*. Then, in 1924, Berlin fell in love with Ellin Mackay, daughter of the tycoon of Postal Telegraph. They were of different religions and social stations. It is now a thrice-told tale how the father renounced Berlin in no uncertain way as a possible son-in-law and did everything in his power to break up the love affair. The year of 1924 was one of great emotional stress for Berlin, a period in which he wrote love ballads for Ellin born of frustration and hurt. "What'll I Do?" was sung for the first time anywhere by the diva Frances Alda, in a broadcast honoring Irving Berlin in 1924; this was before it was interpolated for Grace Moore and John Steel into the *Music Box Revue*. On that same radio program, John McCormack, the beloved Irish tenor of the concert hall, introduced a second Berlin autobiographical ballad, "All Alone," which was also included in the *Music Box Revue* for Grace Moore and Oscar Shaw. Two more Berlin love songs for Ellin followed in 1925, "Remember" and "Always," the latter introduced in vaudeville by Gladys Clark and Henry Bergman.

On January 4, 1926, Irving Berlin and Ellin Mackay were married secretly in City Hall, in New York. After a honeymoon in Atlantic City they went to Europe. As his wedding gift to his bride, Berlin turned over all his rights to "Always." His ballads in 1926 were still autobiographical, but now spoke of marital happiness: "At Peace with the World," "Because I Love You," "How Many Times," and "Blue Skies." "Blue Skies" was written for Belle Baker who sang it in the musical *Betsy* (1926).

4

In seeking out fresh new subject matter for songs, Tin Pan Alley found an overflowing reservoir of ideas in silent motion pictures.

Motion pictures made their first flicker on October 6, 1889, at Thomas Edison's The Kineographic Theater (or "The Black Maria" as it was dubbed) in West Orange, New Jersey. On April 4, 1894, Edison exhibited in New York the kinetoscope, the first motion picture machine.

By 1896, flickers—or moving pictures—were being exhibited in penny arcades through a viewer into which a coin was inserted to activate the machine. For about a minute, fifty feet of film offered a succession of photographs in motion simulating action. One of these attractions showed Fred Ott (sometimes referred to as movie's first actor) in the process of sneezing. Another presented May Irwin and John C. Rice in the act of kissing. The appeal of these flickers was not so much in what was being portrayed as in the novelty of seeing pictures move.

A year or so later, successful experiments were made to project the pictures on a screen, making a performance available to a large audience. Through these projection machines, moving pictures entered vaudeville houses and were usually shown at the end of the live show. One production had the Empire State Express run off the screen apparently right at the terrified audience. Films were now being produced on a regular basis by such firms as Edison, Essanay, Vitagraph and Biograph.

Biograph, which began operations in 1903, became the first to use an indoor studio and artificial lighting. From Biograph came motion picture's first great director and the one most responsible for its early technical developments. He was D. W. Griffith, who had directed his first motion picture, *The Adventures of Dollie,* in 1908 before he moved on to become the head of Biograph. There he introduced to the screen sixteen-year-old Mary Pickford (who had been seen on the stage from her fifth year on) in *Her First Biscuits* (1909) and *The Violin Maker of Cremona* (1910). Griffith's Biograph films after that were *Enoch Arden* (1911), *Man's Genesis* (1912) and *The New York Hat* (1912), the last two just two years before his monumental *The Birth of a Nation,* starring Lillian Gish (another Griffith discovery). From Biograph also emerged another of filmland's early stars, Florence Lawrence, known as "the Biograph Girl" in such films as *Miss Jones Entertains* (1909) and *Resurrection* (1910).

The first theater devoted exclusively to motion pictures opened in Los Angeles in 1902. A year later, Edwin C. Porter of Edison Studios, produced the first motion picture with a story line, *The Great Train Robbery.* This marked the real beginning of motion pictures as a nationwide source of entertainment and encouraged the filming of other "story pictures." In November 1905, *The Great Train Robbery* opened in a theater designed exclusively for motion picture entertainment in Pittsburgh, the admission price five cents. This was so profitable that other nickel theaters—or nickelodeons—were opened all over the country; by 1908 there were four hundred.

Within half a dozen years the nickelodeon expanded into the movie palace, Clune's Auditorium in Los Angeles, and the Strand and the Rialto in New York City. The one-reel attraction was extended to four, five, six or seven reels. One of the earliest and most important of these several-reel films was *The Squaw Man* (1913), the first production of Samuel Goldwyn (born Goldfish) who had come from Warsaw by way of Germany and England to the United States in 1895 as a thirteen-year-old orphan. Using savings earned in the glove business, and convincing some of his friends (including Jesse Lasky) to do likewise, Goldwyn produced *The Squaw Man* in Flagstaff, Arizona, in eleven days, with Cecil B. De Mille doing his first chore as a motion-picture director. The huge success of *The Squaw Man* brought into existence the Jesse L. Lasky Feature Play Company, with Jesse Lasky as president and Samuel Goldwyn as treasurer and general manager. Before long the Jesse L. Lasky Feature Play Company merged with Adolph Zukor's Famous Players to become The Famous Players Lasky Corporation, with Goldwyn still one of the powers. After that Goldwyn withdrew to form his own company, the Goldwyn Pictures Corporation.

The popularity of the several-reel film brought on the production of *Brewster's Millions* (1913) and, in the same year, the importation from Europe of *Quo Vadis,* which boasted spectacular scenes and effects. "If a feature moving picture production can fill a Broadway theater," remarked a critic for *The New York Times,* "*Quo Vadis* ought to be able to do it." *The Squaw Man, Brewster's Millions* and *Quo Vadis* created a gold rush on box offices everywhere, and so did David W. Griffith's epoch-making *The Birth of a Nation,* which opened at Clune's Auditorium in Los Angeles on February 8, 1915. The nickel admission charged by the one-reelers had grown into the top dollar price for *The Birth of a Nation.*

The movie star was beginning to become a national institution. In addition to Mary Pickford, Lillian Gish and Florence Lawrence there were others: Theda Bara, whose sultry performances introduced the "vamp" to the screen; Charlie Chaplin, who began making one-reel slapstick comedies for Mack Sennett in 1913 and less than three years later was commanding a salary of over half a million dollars a year as the sad and lovable little tramp; William Faversham, who starred as Jim Carson in *The Squaw Man,* the screen's first actor to make women's hearts throb; Francis X. Bushman, the screen's first matinee idol, who made his film debut in 1911 and went on to star in *The Magic Wand* (1912), *The Spy's Defeat* (1913) and *Romeo and Juliet* (1916); Pearl White, the heroine of serials.

Tin Pan Alley immediately realized that moving pictures could be a major ally. When nickelodeons began to spring up all over America, song pluggers knew they had acquired a new shop in which to exhibit their wares. They did so with song slides, song fests, and amateur nights. Song pluggers often invaded the auditoriums themselves to provide live entertainment by singing the current numbers from their respective firms. By the early 1910s, one plugger, Sammy Smither, boasted he could plug a song fifty times an evening by making the rounds of nickelodeons.

But a more significant way of promoting the songs of Tin Pan Alley was having them played on the piano as background music for the movies. The music required to set moods, intensify emotions, build up tensions and climaxes was left to the discretion of the performing pianist. Certain numbers became so convenient for portraying given situations musically that they soon became clichés: Tobani's "Hearts and Flowers" for sentimental or tragic sequences; brio passages from overtures by Rossini or Franz von Suppé for storms, climaxes or suspense; Sinding's "The Rustle of Spring" for bucolic scenes. But other types of music were also needed to fill out the musical canvas, and popular tunes of the day provided this material. It was up to the song plugger's powers of persuasion, and his bribes, to convince these pianists to use his songs which, through repetition, became impressed on the consciousness of audiences.

With Griffith's *The Birth of a Nation*, the background music was for the first time no longer left to the whims and wishes of the accompanying pianist. This was the first occasion upon which an original score was conceived for a motion picture. This score was written by Joseph Carl Breil (1870–1926), a serious composer whose opera *The Legend* was to be produced at the Metropolitan Opera House a few years later (1919). The principal number of his motion picture score was "The Perfect Song" (Clarence Lucas) which, in the 1920s, was used by Amos 'n' Andy as their radio theme song. The score was played not on a piano but by an orchestra. (The first symphony orchestra to enter a movie theater to accompany the silent film had been used by S. L. Rothafel in 1913 when he was the manager of the Regent Theater on 116th Street and Seventh Avenue.)

The original music for the sequel to *The Birth of a Nation*, *The Fall of a Nation* in 1916, also a D. W. Griffith production, was prepared by Victor Herbert. To the critic of *Musical America*, Herbert's music proved far more significant than the picture itself. "It is not only synchronized with the picture but its rhythms are in absolute accord with the tempo of the action. Mr. Herbert's stimulating score clearly indicated the marked advance that music is making in the domain of the photoplay and should prove encouraging to composers who have not yet tried their hand at this type of work."

The writing of background music for the screen soon engaged the services of competent musicians who made it their specialty to adapt, arrange or conceive the proper kind of music to meet the varied, changing needs of a film story. Among the leaders were Hugo Riesenfeld (1879–1939), William Axt (1888–1959), David Mendoza (1894–1975) and Erno Rapee (1891–1945).

There were other ways in which motion pictures and Tin Pan Alley were affiliated. Songwriters began to borrow motion picture titles and subjects for songs. In 1914, "Poor Pauline" (Charles McCarron—Raymond Walker) was inspired by Pearl White and her serial, *The Perils of Pauline*. (This song was revived in 1947 for Betty Hutton in her talking picture, *The Perils of Pauline.*) During this period, songs were written about Charlie Chaplin ("Oh, Those Charlie Chaplin Feet"), Mary Pickford ("Sweet Little Mary Pickford"), and even the Mack Sennett comedy two-reelers ("Those Keystone Comedy Cops"). The first million-dollar screen production—*Civilization* (1916), portraying "the physical horrors of war"—led to the writing of movie's first title song. The first theme song—a recurrent melody running throughout the background score—appeared in 1918. It was "Mickey" (Harry H. Williams—Neil Moret) written to help promote the picture of the same name, then used recurrently in the background music and in 1947 successfully revived by Ted Weems and his orchestra in a Decca recording.

The writing of theme songs for motion pictures became a profitable activity in Tin Pan Alley in the twenties, bringing rewards to both the music and the motion picture industries. For Tin Pan Alley this meant the creation of songs that sold many copies of sheet music and phonograph records, helped along by the promotion a successful movie was able to give. To the movie industry, a theme or title song—frequently one and the same—was a potent agency for the promotion of a motion picture.

To Erno Rapee goes the distinction of becoming the first successful composer of movie theme songs. Rapee came not out of Tin Pan Alley but a movie palace, since he was a serious musician who for more than a quarter of a century was employed as principal conductor of orchestras at the Rivoli, Capitol, Roxy, and finally the Radio City Music Hall, all in New York City. In 1926, he took a melody he had written in Hungary a dozen years earlier and refashioned it as "Charmaine" (Lew Pollack), as a theme song for the silent motion picture, *What Price Glory*, in which Dolores Del Rio was starred as the heroine Charmaine. It was incorporated into the background score, of which it became the heart—a score also prepared by Rapee, no longer played by a pianist or an orchestra in the pit but reproduced by an unidentified female singer and orchestra on the sound track. The popularity of the motion picture helped make the song "Charmaine" a national hit. It is equally true that the success of the song was no small help in bolstering the box-office returns wherever the movie was made. (When *What Price Glory* was remade as a talking picture in 1952, "Charmaine" was once again used as a recurrent theme.)

"Charmaine" was largely responsible for the contagious outbreak of movie theme songs that followed. Rapee, with Pollack as his lyricist, wrote two of the most successful in the twenties. "Diane" was sung by an unidentified singer on the sound track of *Seventh Heaven* (1927) in which Janet Gaynor was starred and for which she won an Oscar, an award instituted that year. "Angela Mia" served as the recurring theme in the synchronized score for *Street Angel* (1928), once again starring Miss Gaynor.

The most successful movie theme song of the twenties was "Ramona" (L. Wolfe Gilbert—Mabel Wayne). It had been commissioned by the studio to help promote the motion picture of the same name starring Dolores del Rio. Before this picture was released in 1927, Paul Whiteman and his Orchestra (with Dolores del Rio doing the vocal) broadcast the song on a coast-to-coast radio network. What was particularly eventful about this performance (above and beyond the fact that it marked the premiere of one of the giant hit songs of the decade) was that Paul Whiteman and his Orchestra were broadcasting from New York, and Miss del Rio from California. This was the first time an orchestra and its soloist were separated by three thousand miles. Soon afterward, Miss del Rio promoted the song on a transcontinental tour of leading motion picture houses, and Gene Austin recorded it for Victor to realize a two-million disk sale.

In the closing years of the twenties, the screen erupted not only into sound, but into speech and song. The talking picture made the silent screen obsolescent. Songs in general, and theme songs in particular, now acquired an even more significant status in Hollywood studios, creating a revolution that forever changed the character and makeup of the popular music industry.

18

The Phonograph
and Radio Invade
the American Home

1

The million disk sale—an impossible dream in the recording business a decade earlier —became a reality by 1920. By the middle 1920s, some 130 million records were sold annually. For Tin Pan Alley this meant a bountiful new source of revenue, as well as a productive way of promoting and distributing new songs.

This recording boom came at a crucial hour in Tin Pan Alley's history. In the 1920s, sheet music sales were lessening. Americans no longer seemed to find entertainment by grouping themselves around the living room piano and singing popular tunes. Community sings were also losing their appeal. Thus the market for sheet music went into a precipitous decline. A song hit of the 1920s was regarded as solid success if it amassed a sale of several hundred thousand copies. The million-and-more-copy sale had become a rarity and a phenomenon.

Beginning in 1920, and increasingly so from then on, a hit song began to be measured more by the number of records it sold than by copies of sheet music. For survival, a publisher was increasingly dependent on the recording business.

A few dates provide the basic outlines for a history of recorded music. On December 15, 1877, Thomas A. Edison filed a patent application for a machine to be used in office dictation, called the phonograph, which reproduced sound on a cylindrical disk. On September 26, 1887, Emile Berliner developed the flat disk revolving on a turntable, a more practical and efficient way of mass producing records than the cylindrical disk of Edison. Soon after this, Berliner established the Berliner Gramophone Company in Philadelphia in competition with a company started by Edison himself. Columbia Records was formed in 1887, and the Victor Talking Machine Company in 1901. From these events emerged the present-day record industry.

As early as 1897, Tin Pan Alley had a glimpse of the possibilities of this new machine to promote songs. That year Joseph W. Stern and Company opened the Universal Phonography Company, a recording studio where "coon songs" were cut on cylindrical disks by May Irwin and Lottie Gilson. In 1898, for the Berliner company, Alice Nielsen recorded Victor Herbert's "Always Do as People Say You Should" (Harry B. Smith) from *The Fortune Teller* and Cissie Loftus did impersonations of Edna May, among others. Edna May herself recorded three songs for Berliner, two of them from her musical stage success, *The Belle of New York*, "They All Follow Me" and "The Purity Brigade" (Hugh Morton—Gustave Kerker). In the first year of its operation, the Victor Talking Machine Company had Bert Williams record fifteen songs between October 15 and November 8. And in 1902, J. Aldrich Libbey made a half a dozen records for Edison including one of Harry von Tilzer's "On a Sunday Afternoon" (Andrew B. Sterling), grown popular that year.

Up to about 1903, performing artists looked upon recording as a toy. The artistic and commercial possibilities of recording were ignored. But Enrico Caruso changed all that. In 1902, F. W. Gaisberg, an executive with the Gramophone and Typewriter Company in London, engaged Caruso to record ten arias in a single afternoon for about fifty dollars a record. These were released in London in time for Caruso's London debut at Covent Garden on May 14, 1902. Nobody expected that these records would sell as well as they did. Then the Victor Talking Machine Company bought out the Gramophone and Typewriter Company, thereby acquiring not only these Caruso masters but Caruso himself. Less than three months after his debut in America on November 23, 1903, Caruso's first American recordings began to appear. Their sensational success not only established for the first time the financial success of the early phonograph, but endowed recording with a dignity and an artistic value it had never before known. From then on virtually every major performer began making records, popular performers as well as opera and concert stars. On October 27, 1903, Richard José, the onetime minstrel, recorded for Victor "Silver Threads Among the Gold" (Eben E. Rexford—H. P. Danks), beginning an affiliation with Victor that resulted in almost one hundred disks by 1910, including several remakes of "Silver Threads Among the Gold." Vesta Victoria began making records in 1903, first for Columbia and later on for Edison, Pathé and Victor; but not until 1907 did she finally do for Victor the song she made famous, "Waiting at the Church" (Fred W. Leigh—Henry E. Pether). Emma Carus sang "Navajo" (Harry H. Williams—Egbert Van Alstyne) and "In Zanzibar—My Little Chimpanzee" (Will D. Cobb—Gus Edwards) for Columbia in 1904. One of the last of the great minstrels, Lew Dockstader, recorded the then current comedy hit, "Everybody Works but Father" (Jean Havez) for Columbia in 1905 together with half a dozen other numbers. For Columbia, Chauncey Olcott recorded in 1906 "When Irish Eyes Are Smiling" (Chauncey Olcott and George Graff, Jr.—Ernest R. Ball), "My Wild Irish Rose" (Chauncey Olcott) and other Irish ballads with which he was identified. Blanche Ring could be heard in her famous rendition of "I've Got Rings on My Fingers" (Weston and Barnes—Maurice Scott) on a Victor disk in 1909. Also in Victor recordings, in 1910, Nora Bayes did her favorites, "Shine On, Harvest Moon" (Jack Norworth—Nora Bayes) and "Has Anybody Here Seen Kelly?" (C. W. Murphy and Will Letters, adapted by William C. McKenna). Sophie Tucker became an Edison recording star with "That Lovin' Rag" (Victor H. Smalley—Bernie Adler) and several other of her rag favorites. George M. Cohan, Lottie Gilson and Al Jolson made their bow on records in 1911, and Weber and Fields in 1912. By the end of World War I, Eddie Cantor, Ernest R. Ball, Fanny Brice, Ruth Roye and Van and Schenck were among the many stage stars entering America's living rooms through records.

How potent the phonograph record had become as an arm of the songwriting business first became evident in 1919. That year George Stoddard induced the Victor Company to record his song "Mary," which was then still in manuscript and unperformed. In three months time this record sold three hundred thousand disks, bringing its composer a royalty of fifteen thousand dollars. This was the earliest indication that a record could transform an unknown song into a success.

The year 1919 continued to demonstrate the power of records in promoting songs. Victor released the first popular dance disk ever to sell an estimated million copies. It was "Dardanella" (Fred Fisher—Felix Bernard and Johnny S. Black) in a recording by Ben Selvin and his orchestra. Ben Selvin, a violinist, bandleader and record executive, was twenty-one when he recorded "Dardanella." He then went on to become the most prolific bandleader in the record business, responsible for almost ten thousand disks recorded under nine different names for nine different companies. Among the other best-selling records of 1919 were Eddie Cantor's performance of Irving Berlin's "You'd Be Surprised" for Emerson, while early in 1920, Al Jolson cut for Columbia Gershwin's "Swanee" (Irving Caesar). Cantor's success in 1919 brought him a five-year contract from Brunswick, guaranteeing him a quarter of a million dollars in royalties.

With Paul Whiteman's two-million Victor disk sale of "Whispering" (John Schonberger—Richard Coburn and Vincent Rose), coupled with "The Japanese Sandman" (Raymond Egan—Richard A. Whiting) in 1920, followed two years later by the million-disk distribution of the Paul Whiteman recording of "Three O'Clock in the Morning" (Dorothy Terriss—Julian Robledo), the power of records to make songs into decisive hits was proved once and for all. That power was further demonstrated in 1924 with "The Prisoner's Song," also called "If I Had the Wings of an Angel," the only song ever written by Guy Massey. He sent his manuscript to Shapiro-Bernstein where it caught the interest of Louis Bernstein. A plugger for the publishing house promoted the song for a Victor recording, sung by Vernon Dalhart. To help in the promotion, the publishers created the fiction that the songwriter had spent a term in jail. The record sold about a million copies, as did the sheet music.

In the twenties, other estimated million-disk sales—estimated because in those years no official figures were available—included recordings of "Ida, Sweet as Apple Cider" (Eddie Leonard) by Red Nichols and his Five Pennies for Okeh; Al Jolson's recording for Brunswick of "Sonny Boy" (De Sylva, Brown and Henderson) coupled with "There's a Rainbow 'Round My Shoulder" (Billy Rose and Al Rose—Dave Dreyer); "Piccolo Pete" (Phil Baxter) performed for Victor by Ted Weems and his orchestra, and believed to be the first novelty song to achieve a million-disk sale; and Gene Austin's recordings for Victor of "My Blue Heaven" (George Whiting—Walter Donaldson) and "Ramona" (L. Wolfe Gilbert—Mabel Wayne). Sales of several hundred thousand disks each were realized by Frank Crumit's Victor recording of "A Gay Caballero" (Frank Crumit and Lou Klein) and Frank Munn's Brunswick recording of H. T. Burleigh's 1917 ballad, "Little Mother of Mine" (Walter H. Browne).

Frank Crumit, who had sung with Frank Biesel's Orchestra before he came to New York and became a musical comedy star in *Tangerine* (1921), was one of the most prolific popular recording artists of the 1920s. He made several hundred records in those ten years, first for Columbia and after December 14, 1923, for Victor. In some of these he was joined by Julia Sanderson, who had starred with him in *Tangerine*, became his wife in 1927, and in 1935 his co-star on the Blackstone Cigar Show over radio.

But if Crumit was one of the most prolific recording artists of the decade, Gene Austin was the most successful, besides being the first singer to gain fame initially through records. He was a crooner, one of the first, anticipating Rudy Vallee by a few years. His sweet tenor voice and subdued styling became one of the most cherished sounds to come from the phonograph loudspeaker. His Victor recordings, which also numbered in the hundreds, are reputed to have sold eighty-six million copies in all, an accomplishment with few precedents among recording singers. He came from Texas, grew up in Louisiana and Baltimore, and soon after World War I, studied dentistry and law before he began in earnest to pursue a career in singing. He was twenty-four when he made his first records for Vocalion in 1924, none of them particularly eventful. On January 30, 1925, he began his long and prosperous association with Victor by recording "When My Sugar Walks Down the Street" (Gene Austin, Jimmy McHugh and Irving Mills), a best-seller. His best-seller the following year was "Yearning" (Benny Davis—Joseph Burke). But all this was just a portent of greater things to come. He accumulated formidable sales within the next few years with the following, each of which is believed to have sold at least a million disks: "My Blue Heaven" (George Whiting—Walter Donaldson) later his radio theme song, "Girl of My Dreams" (Sunny Clapp), "Ramona" (L. Wolfe Gilbert—Mabel Wayne), "Sleepy Time Gal" (Raymond Egan and Joseph R. Alden—Ange Lorenzo and Richard A. Whiting), "My Melancholy Baby" (George A. Norton—Ernie Burnett), "Carolina Moon" (Benny Davis—Joseph Burke) and "The Lonesome Road" (Gene Austin—Nathaniel Shilkret). The last of these was written for the first screen adaptation of Jerome Kern's musical play *Show Boat*, produced by Universal in 1929.

2

In the early twenties, radio started out as a crystal set toy for amateurs. By 1930, it had become a multimillion dollar industry, certainly the most powerful single entertainment medium. In 1922 the annual sale of radios amounted to sixty million dollars; by 1929 the figure was over eight hundred million dollars. The federal census revealed that over twelve million families owned radios, a radio in every third home.

Dr. Frank Conrad, an employee of Westinghouse Electric Company, conducted an all-important experiment in "wireless telephony" in a barn in East Pittsburgh early in 1920. In March of the same year, Lee De Forest installed a transmitter on the roof of the California Theater in San Francisco. Before the year was over, commercial broadcasts on a limited scale were initiated by the Detroit *News* using the call letters WWJ, and Westinghouse Broadcasting opened KDKA, a radio station in Pittsburgh, with the transmission of the Presidential election returns on November 2. After that, still in 1920, Westinghouse opened WJZ in Newark, New Jersey.

Radio passed directly from infancy to full maturity. In 1921, radio stations mushroomed so rapidly throughout the United States—by 1922 there were five hundred of them spread from one coast to the other—that the government had to step in and regulate the new industry by initiating the licensing of broadcasting stations. By the mid-1920s, over a thousand radio stations were in operation (a number reduced in 1927 to 708 by the newly instituted Federal Radio Commission whose mission was to control and regulate the airwaves). Rapid developments gave warning of the character radio broadcasting would eventually assume. Radio produced its first singing stars on October 18, 1921, when Ernie Hare and Billy Jones, soon to become known as the "Happiness Boys," sang popular ballads, humorous songs and duets, and exchanged jokes for ninety minutes over WJZ to begin a radio career lasting eighteen years. They adopted "How Do You Do" (Phil Fleming, Charlie

Harrison and Cal De Voll) as their theme song, and during the twenties were responsible for making hits of several songs, among them "What Has Become of Hinky Dinky Parlay Voo?" (Al Dubin, Irving Mills, Irwin Dash and Jimmy McHugh) and "I Love to Dunk a Hunk of Sponge Cake" (Clarence Gaskill).

The first sponsored program appeared in 1922 when the Queensborough Corporation, a real estate outfit, presented a program over WEAF, New York, which at the same time introduced radio's first commercial. That year, radio also relayed for the first time an event from an outlying district remote from the studio by means of telephonic communication, when a New York station broadcast a football game from Chicago between the universities of Chicago and Princeton.

Radio announcing opened a new profession for performers in 1923 when Milton Cross, Ed Thorgenson and Phil Carlin served in that capacity for programs of the A & P Gypsies, starring Harry Horlick's orchestra over WEAF, New York, sponsored by the Great Atlantic and Pacific Tea Company. The first linking of several stations into a single chain was effected on November 3, 1924, to carry President Coolidge's speech over twenty-seven stations spanning the country. On November 15, 1926, the first radio network was formed, the National Broadcasting Company, an event commemorated with a gala program of serious and popular music as well as comedy, starring Will Rogers, Mary Garden, Weber and Fields, Titta Ruffo, Harold Bauer, the New York Symphony and the Oratorio Society of New York under Walter Damrosch, all broadcasting from newly opened studios in New York. Henceforth, it was possible to bring an entertainer to an audience of many millions during a single broadcast.

Necessity was the mother of the inventions that served as guidelines for early broadcasting. Since most of the small radio stations had limited funds, they had to seek out programs calling for no payment. Thus microphones were set up in hotels, dance halls and other places in which dance bands appeared; both the bands and the auditoriums cooperated gladly for the sake of the publicity involved. The first remote radio pickup of a dance band took place in 1921 with regular broadcasts from Hotel Pennsylvania in New York of Vincent Lopez and his orchestra, a development largely responsible for this band's early successes in New York. In 1923, the music of Ben Bernie and his orchestra was picked up by remote from the Roosevelt Hotel. Fred Waring and his Pennsylvanians made their first broadcast in 1924 over WWJ in Detroit, and Paul Whiteman and his Orchestra were sponsored for a regular radio series in the mid-1920s. Rudy Vallee and his Yale Collegians had their performances at the Heigh-Ho Club in New York, broadcast over WABC, then a local station in New York.

Radio in the twenties brought fame not only to bands but also to many singers and many songs. Vaughn De Leath, who had been a concert singer in her teens,, was the first woman singer to gain recognition over radio, for which reason she came to be called "the original radio girl." She made her first radio appearance in January 1920 singing Stephen Foster's "Swanee River" in Lee De Forest's studio, and in 1921 she helped to open WJZ. Hers was a soft, crooning style, a manner of performance which she can be said to have originated, but which was later fully exploited by competitive males. She sang "I'm Just Wild About Harry" (Noble Sissle—Eubie Blake), "Nobody Knows What a Red-Headed Mama Can Do" (Irving Mills and Al Dubin—Sammy Fain), "Where'd You Get Those Eyes?" (Walter Donaldson), "Looking at the World Thru Rose-Colored Glasses" (Tommy Malie and Jimmy Steiger) and many other of the hits of the day together with some classical blues, all of which she recorded from 1921 on for Okeh, Gennett, Edison and Columbia.

Wendell Hall became a singing star on one of radio's earliest variety shows, "The

Eveready Hour," launched on December 4, 1923, sponsored by the National Carbon Company. During his first year on this program he introduced his most famous song, "It Ain't Gonna Rain No Mo'," a modernization of an old Southern melody to comical verses. He recorded it for Edison on October 1, 1923.

Other singers elevated to stardom by radio during the twenties included the "Sweethearts of the Air" (Peter de Rose and "the ukulele girl," May Singhi Brun), Will Osborne, Johnny Marvin, Little Jack Little, "Whispering" Jack Smith, Lanny Ross (called "the Troubadour on the Moon"), Jessica Dragonette, "The Silver-Masked Singer" on the Goodrich program whose identity was meticulously concealed for a long time but who turned out to be Joseph M. White, and radio's first great child star, Baby Rose Marie, who was heard over NBC in 1926 when she was only three.

Over the radio in the twenties, Will Osborne introduced "Just Me and My Radio" (Will Osborne and Al Woods); Jack Little, "I'm Gonna Let the Bumble Bee Be" (Addy Britt—Jack Little); 'Whispering' Jack Smith, "Cecilia" (Herman Ruby—Dave Dreyer). "Mexicali Rose" (Helen Stone—Jack B. Tenney) was introduced and familiarized as the theme song of the Clicquot Club Eskimos over NBC.

3

With so much music being dispensed free into the American home every day, the record business seemed doomed. The annual sale of records plunged from over a hundred million disks a year in the late 1920s, to just six million in 1932. The price of a single disk was in many instances reduced from seventy-five cents to thirty-five cents in the hope of rebuilding a shattered market.

But by the mid-thirties a remarkable upsurge in record sales began to take place. From then on sales began to rise annually to new peaks. By 1939, the annual record sales exceeded one hundred and forty million disks. What the record companies had long been advertising about their product in a concerted effort to combat radio competition had validity: "Music you want *when* you want it." Hearing a good song or a favorite singer over the radio was one thing. To renew that pleasure at will through a record was quite another. The public began proving this by buying records they had just heard over the air, or those of performers who sang them, in increasing numbers. Once this record buying habit was restimulated, the public also sought out in records new songs by their preferred performers, and even new performers being introduced on disks.

Victor, Columbia and Brunswick were the main recording companies between 1930 and 1934. A new entry in 1934 was Decca Records, a European outfit that opened its American branch with Jack Kapp (then recording head of Brunswick) as its director. With his brother, Dave, Kapp soon developed Decca into a major recording power. Their first major coup was to lure Bing Crosby from Brunswick; among his first Decca recordings in 1934 were "Love In Bloom" (Leo Robin—Ralph Rainger), "I Love You Truly" (Carrie Jacobs Bond), "Just a-Wearyin' for You" (Frank Stanton—Carrie Jacobs Bond), "Two Cigarettes in the Dark" (Paul Francis Webster—Lew Pollack) and "Love Is Just Around the Corner" (Leo Robin—Lewis Gensler). By 1937, Bing Crosby realized his first million-disk sale for Decca with "Sweet Leilani" (Harry Owens) which he had introduced that year in the motion picture *Waikiki Wedding* and which had received an Academy Award. Bing Crosby was now Decca's big money-maker, but the company struck gold with other artists as well. In 1935, Guy Lombardo and his Royal Canadians (up to then Columbia artists) joined the Decca lists and came up with the first of many best-sellers in 1937 with "It Seems Like Old Times" (Charles Tobias—Sam H. Stept), soon to become Arthur Godfrey's radio theme song. In

1935, Decca released a giant money-maker in "The Music Goes 'Round and 'Round" as performed by its authors, "Red" Hodgson, Edward Farley and Michael Riley. After that Decca best-seller lists included recordings by the Dorsey brothers, Hoagy Carmichael's own recording of his "Georgia on My Mind" (Stuart Gorrell) and, in 1938, Ella Fitzgerald's first successful record with which she hit the bigtime, "A-Tisket, A-Tasket" (Ella Fitzgerald and Al Feldman).

As a recording helped bring Ella Fitzgerald for the first time the recognition she deserved, so it did a similar service for two of the most successful singing groups of the thirties. In 1931, the Brunswick recording of "Tiger Rag" backed by "Nobody's Sweetheart" (Gus Kahn, Ernie Erdman, Billy Meyers and Elmer Schoebel) became the first by a vocal quartet selling a million disks or more. They boasted two more solid hits soon after that: "Dinah" (Sam M. Lewis and Joe Young—Harry Akst), still in 1931 and, in 1932, their theme song, "Good-Bye Blues" (Jimmy McHugh and Dorothy Fields—Arnold Johnson). That quartet was the Mills Brothers (John, Herbert, Harry and Donald), a black group from Piqua, Ohio. The four men were the sons of John Mills, Sr., who doubled as a barber and a concert singer. Donald was only ten, Harry twelve, Herbert thirteen, and John fifteen when they began their professional career as a singing quartet in vaudeville. There they sometimes used kazoos for special effects, but on one occasion when no kazoos were available they simulated kazoo sound effects vocally by cupping their hands over their mouths. This innovation drew attention to them, and brought them an engagement with WLW, a radio station in Cincinnati, where they appeared for ten months. After that, they toured Ohio and neighboring states, a road that led them to New York City, appearances with the Columbia Broadcasting System, and a contract with Brunswick Records. Their first recordings a smash, the Mills Brothers went on to motion pictures (beginning with *The Big Broadcast* in 1932), nightclubs, network radio programs, and to London, England, where they gave a Royal Command performance. When one of the brothers, John, died in 1936, John Sr. took his place, and when the father retired in 1957, the group became a trio. They went on from there to celebrate their fiftieth anniversary in show business in 1975 with a gala concert at the Dorothy Chandler Pavilion in Los Angeles (supported by stars with whom they had once appeared on radio) and with a parade on Hollywood Boulevard. By then they had made over one thousand recordings. Some of their greatest successes came between 1941 and 1946 on the Decca label: "Paper Doll" (Johnny Black), which achieved the staggering total of six million disks; "I'll Be Around" (Alec Wilder); "Till Then" (Eddie Seiler, Sol Marcus and Guy Wood); and "You Always Hurt the One You Love" (Allan Roberts and Doris Fisher).

On November 24, 1937, the Andrews Sisters recorded "Bei Mir Bist Du Schoen" (Sammy Cahn and Saul Chaplin—Sholom Secunda). This was the first disk by a female group to sell a million copies, and with this one record not only the song but the performers burst upon the popular music scene as successes of the first order. The Andrews Sisters (Patti, Maxine and Laverne) made their first professional appearances as children in a revue first put on at the Orpheum Theater in Minneapolis where they were born, and then touring the RKO circuit for a year. After that they were a singing trio with various dance bands, one of which left them stranded in New York without funds. They were about to give up their singing career when they made their record "Bei Mir Bist Du Schoen." This was not their first recording. Eight months earlier, in March 1937, they had pressed four sides for Brunswick, and in October 1937, two more sides for Decca, but as they confessed, "only our relatives bought our first records."

There are two different versions of how they came to record "Bei Mir Bist Du Schoen." One of them has their agent, Lou Levy, bringing to the attention of the Andrews Sisters the

Yiddish song of Sholom Secunda with the thought that three gentile girls singing a Yiddish song might go over in New York City. This version goes on to say that when they first cut the song, they used only the Yiddish lyrics, a fact that made Jack Kapp of Decca stop them cold midway in the session to insist that English words be used. At this point, Levy prevailed on Sammy Cahn to make the adaptation.

But Sammy Cahn tells another story, probably accurate, in his autobiography *I Should Care* (1974). Cahn heard the song one evening in 1936 at the Apollo Theater in Harlem performed in Yiddish by two black men. Cahn was startled to see how well the song went over with the black audience that couldn't understand a word of the lyrics. He made it his business to acquire a copy of the sheet music. It was lying on the piano in his apartment when his friend, Lou Levy, brought the Andrews Sisters for a visit. The sheet music attracted the interest of the trio, who borrowed it. When the Andrews Sisters later tried to induce Jack Kapp of Decca Records to allow them to record it, he agreed, but only on the condition that the song have English lyrics. At this point, Sammy Cahn was brought back into the picture to prepare these lyrics, which he did with the collaboration of Saul Chaplin, and in this new version the Andrews Sisters recorded it. Only then did Cahn take the trouble to acquire the rights from the publisher for an outright payment of $150.

Released late in 1937, the record went on to earn over three million dollars for Decca. A success of this magnitude led Cahn and Chaplin to try to duplicate it. In 1938, they adapted another Yiddish song, "Joseph, Joseph" (music by Nellie Casman and Samuel Steinberg), which became another highly successful Decca release in a performance by the Andrews Sisters. A second million-disk sale did not materialize, however, until 1944 when they recorded for Decca "Rum and Coca-Cola" (Morey Amsterdam—Jeri Sullavan and Paul Baron).

Victor and Columbia also had their generous share of million-disk sales and best-sellers during the thirties, topped by Gene Autry's Columbia release of "That Silver-Haired Daddy of Mine," which Autry, later famed as an interpreter of cowboy songs, wrote with his father-in-law, Jimmy Long. But among the records to top the best-seller lists most consistently were those of the great dance bands of the thirties: "The Peanut Vendor" (L. Wolfe Gilbert and Marion Sunshine—Moisés Simons) by Paul Whiteman and his Orchestra; the "St. Louis Blues" (W. C. Handy) by Ted Lewis and his band; "Little White Lies" (Walter Donaldson) and "You're Driving Me Crazy" (Walter Donaldson) by Guy Lombardo and his Royal Canadians, while Lombardo was still a Columbia artist; "I'm Gettin' Sentimental Over You" (Ned Washington—George Bassman) by Tommy Dorsey and his band before it became their theme song; "Stormy Weather" (Ted Koehler—Harold Arlen) by Leo Reisman and his Orchestra; "Marie" (Irving Berlin) by Tommy Dorsey and his band; "Begin the Beguine" (Cole Porter) by Artie Shaw and his band; "Ciribiribin" (Harry James, Jack Lawrence and A. Pestalozza) by Harry James and his band before it became their signature; "The Little Brown Jug" (J. E. Winner), "In the Mood" (Andy Razaf—Joe Garland), "Sunrise Serenade" (Jack Lawrence—Frankie Carle) and "Moonlight Serenade" (Mitchell Parish —Glenn Miller), by Glenn Miller and his band, with "Moonlight Serenade" becoming Glenn Miller's theme song; and "Three Little Fishies" (Saxie Dowell) by Kay Kyser and his band.

By the mid-1920s, recorded music was being heard not only in homes, but—thanks to the jukebox—also in bars, honky-tonks, ice-cream parlors, restaurants, taverns and social halls. Offering dancing as well as listening pleasure, the jukebox was a modernized version of the nickelodeon in the old penny arcades, a coin-operated phonograph in an elaborate and gaudy cabinet in which any one of a number of records could be played by pushing the appropriate button. This machine was probably called "jukebox" because it was first first used extensively in "juke" houses, "juke" house being the Southern designation for a brothel or roadhouse. By 1939, two hundred and twenty-five thousand of these instruments were in operation, and were said to have been responsible for the sale of thirteen million records a year. When, in the early 1940s, the war dried up the supply of live entertainment, more and more jukeboxes were used to fill the void. It is believed that it was largely the jukebox that was responsible for the record successes of "The Music Goes 'Round and 'Round" ("Red" Hodgson, Edward Farley and Michael Riley), "A-Tisket, A-Tasket" (Ella Fitzgerald and Al Feldman) and "Three Little Fishies" (Saxie Dowell). Though in later decades, radio broadcasts by disc jockeys often replaced the jukebox in public places, there still were some six hundred thousand of these machines in operation in 1974, according to E. G. Doris, executive vice-president of Rock-Ola, a major jukebox manufacturer. Nevertheless, the Wurlitzer Company, which over a forty-year period had built over 750,000 jukeboxes, announced in 1974 it was discontinuing this operation in favor of electric organs, having been convinced that the jukebox was becoming obsolete.

4

The economic depression of the early 1930s brought attrition to the theater box offices all over the United States. On Broadway the total number of productions each season had diminished by one third. Many Broadway shows, in the 1930s, had to find their customers in Leblang's drugstore where, at curtain time, tickets were disposed of at half the box-office price. In 1934, only ten musicals were mounted, as opposed to thirty-two in 1930, and all of those in 1934 were failures. Attendance at movie houses declined forty percent. Not even bingo games and bank nights could substantially bolster the declining box-office take. Vaudeville had vanished from the amusement scene, and burlesque was on its last legs.

For entertainment, America was turning more and more to radio, which had become by the 1930s the fourth largest industry in the country. It was estimated that some thirty million people were glued to their chairs in front of the radio dial and speaker every evening of the week.

The new medium created its own phenomena. There was the "soap opera"—protracted serials slanted for the female market sponsored by soap products. By 1938, seventy-eight of these serials were bringing in an income of over twenty-five million dollars to the two major networks. The most preferred were "Stella Dallas," "One Man's Family," "Pepper Young's Family," "David Harum," "Life Can Be Beautiful," "The Romance of Helen Trent," "John's Other Wife." There were also comedy serials starring Amos 'n' Andy, The Goldbergs, Fibber McGee and Molly, The Aldrich Family, Myrt and Marge and Easy Aces. There were the mysteries, the supernatural or western adventure series, such as the "Inner Sanctum," "The Shadow," "The Green Hornet," "Buck Rogers in the 25th Century" and "The Lone Ranger." There was the singing commercial: "The Voice of RKO," by Tom Kennedy, heard on the RKO Radio Hour, which Variety maintains was radio's first theme song; "Barbasol, Barbasol, no brush, no lather, no rubin' " sung by Harry Frankel as Singin' Sam, the Barbasol Man; the melody of "Smile for Me" (Phil Baxter) for Fitch Shampoo; "Pepsi-Cola, hits the spot, twelve full ounces that's a lot" (its tune taken from the old English ballad, "John Peel"), sung on the Pepsi-Cola program by the Tune Twisters, a vocal trio.

A catchword or a catch phrase used by radio stars on their programs for identification entered the everyday speech of the people. East side, west side, all around the town you could hear people quoting Amos 'n' Andy ("I'se regusted"), Jack Pearl ("Vas you dere,

Sharlie?"), Henry Aldrich ("Coming, Mother!"), Ben Bernie ("Yowsah, yowsah"), Jimmy Durante ("I've got a million of them"); Gracie Allen ("Oh, George, I'll bet you say that to all the girls").

One radio phenomenon had particular significance for American popular music. It was the disc jockey or "deejay." Nobody knows who coined this term or precisely when. In the early 1930s "radio jockey" was in general circulation and by the late 1930s it was supplanted by "disc jockey."

Who was the first disc jockey? Was he Reginald A. Fessenden, an electrical engineer employed by Edison, who on Christmas Eve of 1906 transmitted a recording of Handel's "Largo" from his laboratory in Brant Rock, Massachusetts (picked up by a bewildered radio operator aboard a ship on the Atlantic Ocean)? A few months after that, Lee De Forest, radio's pioneer of pioneers, broadcast a recording of Rossini's *William Tell Overture* from his own laboratory atop the Parker Building in New York City. But if the single transmission of one recording does not make a disc jockey, then, perhaps, the first of this breed was Charles D. "Doc" Herrold. In 1910, he played recordings over his own radio station in San José, which, in 1929, acquired the call letters of KQW. Also, at about this time, Thomas E. Clark broadcast records to Lake Erie steamers equipped by him with telephone receivers. In 1911, Dr. Elman B. Myers broadcast eighteen hours of recorded music a day over a small experimental station in New York. And during World War I, Frank Conrad opened an experimental radio station in his garage in Wilkinsburg, Pennsylvania, 8XK, where he played records for radio "hams." A local music shop offered to provide him with the recordings for his program in return for plugs. These commercials increased business not only for that music shop but for others in that city as well.

But disc jockeys did not become a real force in radio until 1932, when Al Jarvis began playing records and making ad lib comments about them on a one-hour noonday program over KJWB in Los Angeles, on a show called "The World's Largest Make-Believe Ballroom." In 1934, the Jarvis program was enlarged to a three-hour morning production with numerous sponsors. A year later, Martin Block initiated his own "Make Believe Ballroom" over WNEW in New York, by playing five records by Clyde McCoy to create the illusion that they were coming live from a ballroom. Those musical selections alternated with imaginary conversation with an absent McCoy. Within a year, four million faithfuls were tuning in daily to this program which now consumed two and a half hours of air time, and had its own theme song written for it, "It's Make Believe Ballroom Time" (Martin Block and Mickey Stoner), which Glenn Miller and his orchestra recorded. Block's ad lib commercials had incredible selling power: Fact and not fiction has it that during the blizzard of 1938 he sold three hundred refrigerators for a Newark department store. Other disc jockeys also wooed and won success. Jack Cooper, the first black disc jockey, specialized in race records in Chicago. Arthur Godfrey began his long life in radio as its "Huck Finn" by playing Dixieland records and ad libbing humorous commercials over WMAL in Washington and then, beginning in 1934, over WJSV in that city. Bill Randle started out at WERE in Cleveland where two decades later he helped to discover Elvis Presley and Johnnie Ray.

Since smaller stations were unable to hire live talent for their daily schedules they resorted to filling in their hours with phonograph music and appropriate commentaries. They built up such a large audience response that these broadcasts soon proved commercially profitable. Even the larger stations profited from this practice, with the disc jockey able to fill the late hours when sponsorship for any other kind of program was unavailable.

The widespread use of records by jockeys caused consternation among record companies who saw in this a serious inroad into record sales. Bandleaders and popular singers joined in the revolt against the disc jockey, feeling that such free exposure greatly damaged their earning capacity on live radio programs and in public appearances. Lawsuits were instituted against radio stations to end what the plaintiffs regarded as piracy. One was filed in 1938 by Paul Whiteman in conjunction with RCA Victor against WNEW. In a decision of far-reaching implications in 1940, Judge Learned Hand of the Second U.S. Circuit Court of Appeals reversed an earlier decision of Federal Judge Vincent L. Leibell which had restrained WNEW from playing Paul Whiteman's records. Justice Hand maintained that "the common-law property of orchestra leader and corporation manufacturing phonograph records ended with the sale of the record, so that the radio broadcasting company could not be restrained from using records in broadcasts."

In spite of the widespread appeal of the disc jockey show, it did not supplant live musical entertainment which was now flooding the airwaves. Out of these live shows came the singing stars who, in a single broadcast, were able to reach an audience far larger than they had known in a lifetime of public theatrical appearances and who, for that very reason, could make a song (or a forgotten one) sweep the entire country.

Rudy Vallee began dominanting the air waves only after he had acquired his first network sponsored program, the Fleischmann Hour, over NBC. Born Hubert Prior Vallee in Island Point, Vermont, in 1901, he chose the first name of Rudy to replace "Hubert Prior" both to conjure up the image of Rudolph Valentino, the sex symbol of the silent screen, and as a tribute to the saxophonist, Rudy Wiedhoft, whom he admired. A saxophonist himself, Rudy Vallee formed his first band while he was still an undergraduate at Yale. After leaving college, he formed the Yale Collegians, which opened at the Heigh-Ho Club on East 53rd Street in New York on January 8, 1928. Up to this point he had entrusted the singing of all vocals to others—sometimes to a trio, sometimes to a solo vocalist—confining himself to leading his band and playing the saxophone. But on the evening of his debut at the Heigh-Ho Club, its manager expressed dissatisfaction with the band's vocalist. Vallee became a last-minute replacement for the singer by taking over one of the choruses of "Rain" (Eugene Ford). Vallee enlisted the service of a megaphone to help amplify his weak and limited voice. "Then and there," as Vallee recalled in his autobiography, *My Time Is Your Time*, "was made the decision that was to send me (through the medium of radio later) to fame and fortune."

Radio Station WABC in New York began to relay the performances of Vallee and the Yale Collegians from the Heigh-Ho Club on a nightly basis, and because it could not afford to use a paid announcer, prevailed on Vallee to do this chore for the broadcast. It was at the first of these broadcasts that Vallee conceived the idea to open his program with the salutation: "Heigh-ho everybody—this is Rudy Vallee announcing and directing the Yale Collegians from the Heigh-Ho Club." He also began to combine announcements of the numbers on his program with informal chats about anything that might spring to mind. Those informal chats, and the salutation of "Heigh-ho everybody—this is Rudy Vallee" became as much his radio trademarks as the megaphone was his musical one.

Three weeks after the WABC broadcasts were placed on a nightly basis, WOR in Newark, New Jersey, also began to broadcast nightly from the Heigh-Ho Club. By the following spring, there were as many as twenty broadcasts emanating from the Heigh-Ho Club each week, including one that was sponsored every Sunday afternoon by a Harlem jeweler.

While still appearing at the Heigh-Ho Club, the name of Vallee's band was changed from the Yale Collegians to the Connecticut Yankees. (Several prominent Yale alumni took offense at the use of the name of the University for a nightclub band; besides, these alumni insisted, the members of the band just did not look like Yale men.) And so, the band was rechristened the Connecticut Yankees, this name occurring to Vallee after he had seen a performance of the Rodgers and Hart musical, *The Connecticut Yankee*, at the Vanderbilt Theater.

In February 1929, Vallee and his Connecticut Yankees made a three-day appearance at Keith's 81st Street Theater in New York. The place was jammed with yelling, stamping, squealing youngsters who caused such a disturbance in their enthusiasm for Vallee and his songs that mounted police had to be summoned to restore order. This was the first time a popular singer ever inspired an outburst of youthful frenzy in a theater, predating the Frank Sinatra pandemonium at the Paramount Theater by thirteen years. Such instant success led the manager of the 81st Street Theater to hold Vallee and his band over for an additional four days, and brought them a contract to tour the vaudeville circuit, with an appearance at the Palace Theater that April.

After leaving the Heigh-Ho Club, Vallee and the Connecticut Yankees became the star attraction of the Versailles Club on East 60th Street in New York which was soon renamed the Villa Vallee. From these public appearances both in the nightclub and in theaters, Rudy Vallee immediately went on, still in 1929, to make records, to appear in his first two movies, and to get his first sponsored network show. His first recording was "Deep Night" (Rudy Vallee—Charlie Henderson) for Victor, whose melody was based on a prom song from Amherst College. And his first sponsored network program was the Fleischmann Hour, initiated in October 1929, during the week of the stock market crash. For his first broadcast Vallee adopted the signature music that would open and close his radio programs for the next decade: "My Time Is Your Time" (R. S. Hooper—H. M. Tennat). This was an English song Vallee had heard in London in 1925 and to which he had acquired the American rights. He sang it for the first time with the Yale Collegians in Yale's dining hall, and in 1927 he played and sang it at the Heigh-Ho Club. When the Fleischmann programs were being planned, Vallee was advised to use as his theme song either "Deep Night" or "I'm Just a Vagabond Lover" (Rudy Vallee—Leon Zimmerman), with both of which he was already identified. In fact, the singing of "I'm Just a Vagabond Lover" marked Vallee's debut in motion picture, in the Paramount production *Glorifying the American Girl* (1929) after which, that same year, it helped provide the title for the first motion picture in which he was starred, the RKO production *Vagabond Lover*. Vallee rejected "Deep Night" as a theme song because it was too languid and, as he put it in his autobiography, he was afraid listeners "would fall asleep halfway through the first chorus." And he objected to "I'm Just a Vagabond Lover" because it sounded too egotistic. "My Time Is Your Time," however, seemed just right; in essence it seemed to say, he felt, that "we are here to entertain you for the course of an hour."

By 1929, Rudy Vallee had become such a hot commodity in the music business that the publishing house of Leo Feist put him on a weekly retainer as an adviser, and stood ready to publish anything he recommended. "I'm Just a Vagabond Lover" was one of the first Feist publications under this arrangement, and Rudy Vallee went on to plug that song into a monumental hit in his Victor recording, over the radio, in nightclub and stage appearances, as well as in his first two movies.

For his first two years on the Fleischmann Hour, Vallee's program consisted primarily of the music of the Connecticut Yankees and Vallee's vocals and comments; only incidentally and rarely were guest artists included. But in 1932, Vallee changed his format to a variety show emphasizing not only songs, but comedy, novelty features and even dramatic episodes. Bob Hope, in one of his first radio appearances, was a guest performer and so were

Fanny Brice as "Baby Snooks," Red Skelton, Milton Berle, Lou Holtz, Alice Faye, Dorothy Lamour, Frances Langford and the Mills Brothers. Alice Faye and Frances Langford were completely unknown when they first appeared with Rudy. Appealing as these stars were, the prime attraction of these broadcasts remained Rudy Vallee, singing his songs in his sweet, sentimental crooning style, and making informal and breezy introductions and comments. Coincidentally, the strong suit of these broadcasts were the songs Vallee made famous, sometimes literally overnight.

During the thirties, Rudy Vallee maintained over the air the collegiate image he had earned in nightclubs by having graduated from Yale, by leading a band named after Yale, and by being partial to college or college-type songs. College songs, or songs inspired by college, loomed large in his radio repertory. Over the radio he introduced "Betty Co-Ed" (J. Paul Fogarty and Rudy Vallee), a new song published in 1930. But Vallee drew other college songs for his broadcasts from the past, rather than from the current crop, and made them into hits. "The Stein Song" (Lincoln Colcord—E. A. Fenstad) dated from before World War I when it was sung at the University of Maine. NBC acquired the rights in the 1920s, and Vallee introduced it over the air in 1930. "There's a Tavern in the Town," goes even further back, having been copyrighted in 1883 (authors unknown); later it became a favorite drinking song among college men. Singing it over the air and recording it for Victor, Vallee extended its popularity with the general public. In 1936, Vallee revised and adapted Yale's "The Whiffenpoof Song" (Meade Minnigerode and George S. Pomeroy—Tod B. Galloway) with which Vallee first became acquainted during his years at Yale. This, too, he made into a national success by singing it over the radio and recording it. "Whiffenpoof" was the name of a society at Yale, a branch of the Glee Club, the word taken from the name of an imaginary character in the Victor Herbert operetta, *Little Nemo* (1908).

Many another song started on its way toward popularity from Rudy Vallee's broadcasts. These are some: "Sweet Lorraine" (Mitchell Parish—Cliff Burwell); "If You Were the Only Girl in the World" (Clifford Grey—Nat D. Ayer); "When It's Springtime in the Rockies" (Mary Hale Woolsey—Robert Sauer); "I Kiss Your Hand, Madame" (Sam M. Lewis and Joe Young—Ralph Erwin); Irving Berlin's "Marie"; "Honey" (Seymour Simons and Haven Gillespie—Richard A. Whiting); "S'posin' " (Andy Razaf—Paul Denniker); "Let's Put Out the Lights" (Herman Hupfeld); "When Your Hair Has Turned to Silver" (Charles Tobias—Peter De Rose); "Good Night, Sweetheart" (Ray Noble, James Campbell, and Reg Connelly, adapted by Rudy Vallee); and Irving Berlin's "Say It Isn't So."

The soft, subdued, relaxed singing style known as "crooning," and admirably suited for a radio microphone, made others besides Vallee famous. Two are mentioned with Vallee in a song published by M. Witmark and Sons in 1931, "Crosby, Columbo and Vallee" (Al Dubin—Joe Burke), indicating that in 1931 a young man named Crosby was already attracting interest and admiration through his broadcasts over CBS.

"The groaner," "the gentile cantor," "the boo-boo-boo-boo-boo man," as he has variously been called—or just plain Bing as he came to be known around the world—was born in Tacoma, Washington, in 1904, as Harry Lillis Crosby. The nickname "Bing" was early applied to him because he was such an avid reader of a newspaper cartoon, "Bingville Bugle." At Gonzaga High School, a Catholic institution, he appeared with a small jazz band and sang in school productions. He then enrolled in Gonzaga University for the study of law. There he played traps, sang duets with Al Rinker, and appeared with the seven-piece unit which Rinker had formed. By 1925, Bing Crosby had had enough of law. With Rinker he bought a second-hand car for forty dollars and made his way to Los Angeles where he hoped that Mildred Bailey, the jazz singer, who was Rinker's sister, would open up for them some professional doors. Billed as "Two Boys and a Piano," they found engagements in small night spots in the Los Angeles area, and made a Columbia record on October 18, 1926, with Don Clark and his Los Angeles Biltmore Hotel Orchestra, "I've Got the Girl" (Walter Donaldson). Paul Whiteman heard them late that year and signed them as duo vocalists for his orchestra. They appeared with the Paul Whiteman Orchestra and made a number of Victor Records, but they did so poorly that they were dropped. This singing duo became a trio when Harry Barris joined them; as the Rhythm Boys they returned to the roster of Paul Whiteman and his Orchestra. Dressed in blue flannel jackets and ice-cream trousers, the three men provided the vocals for Whiteman's orchestra for three and a half years and became an important adjunct of that renowned organization. During that time they made highly successful recordings with Paul Whiteman and his Orchestra for Victor, notably in 1927 "Mississippi Mud" (Harry Barris and James Cavanaugh), in which the Rhythm Boys were backed by Bix Beiderbecke and Tommy and Jimmy Dorsey, and in 1928 "My Suppressed Desire" (Ned Miller—Chester Conn) and "From Monday On" (Harry Barris and Bing Crosby). In 1930, the Rhythm Boys went to Hollywood to appear with Paul Whiteman and His Orchestra in the motion picture musical *The King of Jazz*.

Impatient with Bing Crosby's lackadaisical ways and dilatory behavior—Bing himself described his actions as "youthful indiscretions"—Whiteman fired the Rhythm Boys. They stayed on in Los Angeles, appearing with Gus Arnheim and his orchestra at the Coconut Grove, where Crosby began doing solo vocals. Despite his physical appearance—receding hairline, and protruding ears that resembled the handles of a sugar bowl—Crosby soon began to endear himself to audiences with his easygoing and relaxed manner, his pleasant Irish face, and his crooning style into which he was now beginning to interpolate those "boo boo boo boo boos" and the "bay bub do ee do dee dos" (In order, he said, "to make a sound which resembled the human voice with a bubble in it") which he made famous. Night after night he was called upon to repeat one of his numbers, "I Surrender, Dear" (Gordon Clifford—Harry Barris).

"I Surrender, Dear" was responsible for bringing Crosby to radio, and through radio to a success story that lasted over forty years and made him a giant in the entertainment world. He recorded the song for Victor on January 19, 1931, with Gus Arnheim's Orchestra (and Jimmie Grier's excellent arrangement). The song sold so many disks that more than ever Bing Crosby was inextricably associated with it, so much so that he was starred in a movie short built around the number. This short was seen by William S. Paley, president of CBS, who was so taken with Crosby's singing style that he forthwith signed him to a radio contract. A sustaining program in 1931, it soon attracted sponsors—Cremo Cigars, then Woodbury Soap, and after that Chesterfield cigarettes—programs which made Bing Crosby one of radio's outstanding singing attractions in the 1930s, important enough to land him a precedent-shattering twenty-nine-week engagement at the New York Paramount Theater in 1932. That same year he signed a contract to appear in the first of some forty motion pictures, *The Big Broadcast* (1932), where he introduced "Where the Blue of the Night Meets the Gold of the Day" (Roy Turk and Bing Crosby—Fred E. Ahlert) which later became his radio signature, as well as "Please" (Leo Robin—Ralph Rainger).

Crosby continued singing over CBS until 1936 when he shifted to NBC to become the host of the "Kraft Music Hall" for a ten-year stint. Though Crosby introduced some song successes over the radio—Irving Berlin's "How Deep Is the Ocean" and "Just One More Chance" (Sam Coslow—Arthur Johnston), for example—the bulk of Bing Crosby's song repertory originated through the years in motion pictures. As for Crosby's later radio history, he left NBC in 1946 because he insisted on having his programs taped rather than presented live, something which the networks still resisted strongly. ABC, however, was ready to abandon this restriction in order to capture Crosby, and on October 1, 1947, over ABC Bing Crosby appeared with the first magnetically taped show used over radio. Later, when tapings became routine procedure, Crosby returned to his first radio home, CBS.

In the early thirties, Crosby found a strong competitor for crooning honors at CBS. He was Russ Columbo. When Columbo sang his own song, "Prisoner of Love" (Leo Robin—Russ Columbo and Clarence Gaskill) which he introduced over the air in 1931, or his theme songs "You Call It Madness" (Gladys Du Bois, Paul Gregory, Con Conrad and Russ Columbo) and "Paradise" (Gordon Clifford and Nacio Herb Brown—Nacio Herb Brown), or "Auf Wiedersehen, My Dear" (Al Hoffman, Ed Nelson, Al Goodhart and Milton Ager) his style so closely resembled Crosby that at moments it was difficult to identify which of the two men was performing. A feud developed between the two singers as to who was the true originator of the singing style Crosby was making famous, a rivalry Columbo helped to sharpen when he, too, made a recording of "Where the Blue of the Night Meets the Gold of the Day" in 1931. Since Columbo had a large following of his own, the rivalry was for a time a hotly disputed issue. It was finally resolved with Columbo's sudden death on September 2, 1934, when the barrel of a gun exploded accidentally and struck him in the head.

Another battle of radio crooners engaged Rudy Vallee and Will Osborne. Osborne had been a drummer who had been given an important start as a bandleader when Vallee turned over to him the direction of his band while he was busy making movies. Then, as a radio crooner, Osborne popularized over the air "Beside an Open Fireplace" (Paul Denniker—Will Osborne) and "Just Me and My Radio" (Al Woods—Will Osborne). He sought to steal some of Vallee's limelight by maintaining that he, and not Vallee, was the first to devise the art of crooning, ignoring the fact that Gene Austin and Vaughn De Leath had preceded them both. Newspapers were flooded with publicity items about the Vallee-Osborne feud, some of them absurd or outrageous, all of them stressing Osborne's belligerent antagonism to Vallee. On one occasion Osborne challenged Vallee to a boxing match to decide once and for all who deserved to be called the first of the crooners. On another occasion, Osborne planned to sue Vallee for half a million dollars. A third time, Osborne had his lawyers issue an unsuccessful injunction to prevent the publication of Vallee's autobiography. "How this feud is going to end, nobody can guess," noted the New York *Daily Mirror*. Then it added facetiously: "Maybe the boys will hurl plums at forty paces, handfuls of confetti at a city block."

Nobody, however, could contest Kate Smith's right to supremacy as radio's "songbird of the South." Born in Greenville, Virginia, in 1909, she had made her Broadway debut as a comedienne and singer in the Broadway musical, *Honeymoon Lane* (1926), after which she played a minor part in the road company of *Hit the Deck*, and on Broadway, in *Flying High* (1930). Her excessive weight limited her to comedy characters, a fact she resented almost as deeply as she did the caustic remarks of her fellow performers about her appearance. She was almost ready to forget show business for good when Ted Collins, a recording manager for Columbia, became her manager. "You do the singing," he told her, "and I'll fight the battles." He found for her a fifteen-minute sustaining program five times a week over CBS. The time slot was 7–7:15, which ordinarily would have spelled artistic suicide for a performer since it was in competition with Amos 'n' Andy, which enjoyed the largest and most devoted radio audience of any program at that time. Kate Smith's first radio appearance took place on May 1, 1931, and featured that early Crosby favorite, "I Surrender, Dear" and three numbers which owed some of their fame to her, "Dream a Little Dream of Me" (Gus Kahn —Wilbur Schwandt and Fabian Andre), "By the River Sainte Marie" (Edgar Leslie—Harry

Warren) and "Please Don't Talk About Me when I'm Gone" (Sidney Clare—Sam H. Stept). For her theme song, she chose a number she had helped H.E. Johnson and Harry Woods write, "When the Moon Comes Over the Mountain."

Despite the formidable competition offered by Amos 'n' Andy, the Kate Smith program grew so popular that within thirty days it acquired a sponsor in Palina Cigars. Kate now became a radio fixture. In 1936, she was the hostess and star of a radio variety show, "The A & P Bandwagon," and in 1938 she was the sole performer on a three-times-a-week, fifteen-minute show. From there she progressed to the Kate Smith Hour, a daytime program, and the weekly Kate Smith Hour. She had also become a recording star for Columbia, beginning August 17, 1931, when she pressed her theme song, "When the Moon Comes Over the Mountain."

Of all the songs Kate Smith either introduced or popularized over the air, the most significant was unquestionably Irving Berlin's "God Bless America."

Morton Downey, radio's beloved "Irish thrush"—born in Wallingford, Connecticut, in 1902—had worked as a song plugger and singer in modest nightclubs during his teens. He was discovered by one of Paul Whiteman's friends who arranged to have him sing with an orchestra organized in 1922 by Whiteman for the transatlantic liner, S. S. *Leviathan*. After that, Downey was heard with Paul Whiteman and his Orchestra at various engagements, including the first time Whiteman and his orchestra appeared at the Palace Theater in New York. He also made a recording for Edison under the name of Morton James and another one in 1924 under his own. In 1927, Morton Downey starred at the Casino de Paris in London where he so delighted the Prince of Wales with his rendition of the Rodgers and Hart song "You Took Advantage of Me" that the Prince had him repeat it eleven times. Downey made his radio debut in 1930, after which he was sponsored by Camel cigarettes, Woodbury Soap, Bourjois perfumes and Pall Mall cigarettes. In 1932, a national poll singled him out as the best male singer on the air. He was also one of the best paid, drawing over a quarter of a million dollars a year from his radio work alone. While he specialized in Irish ballads (he is reputed to have sung "When Irish Eyes Are Smiling" thousands of times) his silver-toned voice was particularly well suited to American ballads as well. He helped Dave Dreyer and Billy McKenny write one of his two radio theme songs, "Wabash Moon," which he introduced. His other radio theme was "Carolina Moon" (Benny Davis—Joe Burke).

Arthur Tracy became so celebrated as radio's "The Street Singer" that there were many who knew him only by that description and not by name. He studied voice at the Curtis Institute in Philadelphia, and there became a pioneer in radio by broadcasting over a local station in 1923 and 1924. Discovered by a talent scout, he was given the lead in a touring company production of Sigmund Romberg's *Blossom Time*, following which he found engagements in vaudeville, burlesque, the concert hall and with stock companies. In 1929 he came to New York where he returned to radio broadcasting. Within a year he was featured on a regular sponsored program, and in 1931 he was heard regularly three times a week over CBS. He signed on and off with his theme, "Marta," a Cuban song by Moisés Simon with new American lyrics by L. Wolfe Gilbert, which became his first record, pressed by Victor on July 10, 1931. In 1932, he was one of the stars on "Music that Satisfies," sponsored by Chesterfield. In addition to his own theme song, Tracy also popularized "Save the Last Dance for Me" (Walter Hirsch—Frank Magine and Phil Spitalny) which, after introducing it over the radio, he recorded for Brunswick in December 1931.

Maurice Chevalier, star of the Casino de Paris in France, whose bow on the American motion picture screen in *Innocents of Paris* was still a year away, made his radio debut over WABC in 1928 on a weekly program sponsored by Coty Perfumes, receiving the then unprecedented fee of five thousand dollars a program. This was America's introduction to "Valentine," the French song by Albert Willemetz and H. Christine, which Chevalier had made famous in Paris. Later the same year, Chevalier became the star of a new musical variety show sponsored by Chase and Sanborn over WEAF. When Eddie Cantor took over in 1931 he became the highest paid star in broadcasting, and the Chase and Sanborn Hour became radio's show of shows. Sunday evenings was a time when traffic in city streets was reduced to a trickle, when most of the nation's telephones stopped ringing, as Mr. and Mrs. America stayed home for an hour to listen to the comedy and singing of the former Ziegfeld stage star. On these Sunday evening programs, Eddie Cantor frequently revived the songs he had made famous in the theater. But he also introduced many new numbers, among them "Now's the Time to Fall in Love" (Al Lewis and Al Sherman), "When I'm the President" (Al Lewis and Al Sherman) with its recurrent motif of "We Want Cantor! We Want Cantor!" and "Santa Claus Is Coming to Town" (Haven Gillespie—J. Fred Coots). Cantor introduced this last number in 1934, one week before Thanksgiving, at the insistence of his wife, Ida, even though he himself was indifferent to it. He made it an immediate hit, and something of a Yuletide classic. Richard A. Whiting's "One Hour With You" (Leo Robin), which Cantor used as his radio signature with somewhat altered lyrics, had become familiar before Cantor adopted it, having been introduced in 1932 in the movie of the same name starring Chevalier. In addition to introducing new songs and reviving old ones, Cantor's radio hour led to the discovery of fresh singing talent, including Eddie Fisher, Deanna Durbin and Dinah Shore. In addition to his motion pictures appearances, Eddie Cantor continued regularly on radio (and beginning with 1950 on television) until 1953 when a heart seizure sent him to semi-retirement. Cantor died of a heart attack on October 10, 1964.

Radio was the first performing medium to bring recognition to Gene Autry for doing what he did best, singing cowboy songs; the long series of Western movies in which he was starred as a singing cowboy came later. He was born on a tenant farm in Tioga, Texas, in 1908, and learned to sing from his father, a Baptist minister. As a boy of ten, Autry worked with the Fields Brothers Medicine Show, then appeared in a nightclub, accompanying himself on a guitar which he taught himself to play. For a number of years he worked as a cowhand, losing one job after another because of his preoccupation with singing and his indifference to his work. Later he was employed by the St. Louis and San Francisco Railroad in Oklahoma as a roustabout and freight handler, and subsequently as a telegraph operator. While holding these jobs he perfected himself as a guitarist and developed his yodel singing style in the rendition of cowboy songs. Then, over KVOO, in Tulsa, where he appeared without pay, he was billed as "Oklahoma's Singing Cowboy." He made some recordings of cowboy songs for Victor, the first of many companies with which he was affiliated between 1930 and 1934, and was the star of the radio programs, "The National Barn Dance" and "The National Farm and Home Hour," over WLS in Chicago. Beginning in the early 1930s he began to use his own songs. "That Silver-Haired Daddy of Mine," which he wrote with Jimmy Long, a train dispatcher, sold a million records and several million copies of sheet music. In 1934 he appeared in *In Old Santa Fé*, the first of about one hundred motion pictures in which he was either featured or starred, and in which he was heard in some two hundred and fifty of his own songs. In 1940, Autry had a major network radio show of his own, a Western variety program called "Gene Autry's Melody Ranch," sponsored by Wrigley's Doublemint Chewing Gum. It was first heard over CBS in January 1940 as a Sunday afternoon presentation but later transferred to a Saturday evening half-hour spot over CBS.

The most popular female singing group over the radio was the Boswell Sisters

—Martha, Helvetia ("Vet") and Connee (originally Connie). They came from New Orleans, where in their early teens they had won a radio contest. They began making records in 1925, but did not become stars until the 1930s when they appeared regularly on the "Music that Satisfies" program sponsored by Chesterfield over NBC and made some outstanding records for Brunswick with the Dorsey Brothers Orchestra. When they disbanded in 1936, Connee Boswell went on to become a singing star in her own right, even though, having been stricken with polio as a child, she was paralyzed and had to work from a wheelchair. She became one of the regular guests on the Kraft Music Hall program hosted by Bing Crosby over NBC. Whether on records or over the radio, she exerted a far-reaching influence on female pop singers, revealing a style which, as Dom Cerulli wrote in *Down Beat*, "was a clean break from the on-the-beat rather formal type of pop singing in vogue before her arrival." Some of her song favorites were "They Can't Take That Away from Me" (Ira Gershwin—George Gershwin), "The Loveliness of You" (Mack Gordon—Harry Revel), "That Old Feeling" (Lew Brown—Sammy Fain), "Bob White" (Johnny Mercer—Bernie Hanighen) and "Start the Day Right" (Charles Tobias, Al Lewis and Maurice Spitalny), "I Cover the Waterfront" (Edward Heyman—John Green) and "Stormy Weather" (Ted Koehler—Harold Arlen). She is reputed to have sold over seventy-five million records before her death on October 12, 1976.

There were, to be sure, many more singing stars on the radio during the thirties and with them came many songs. For the Pepsodent program, Bob Hope used as his signature, "Thanks for the Memory" (Leo Robin—Ralph Rainger), a song he had just introduced in the movie *The Big Broadcast of 1938*; it has remained his theme song ever since. For the Burns and Allen program, an "oldie" of the twenties was revived for their theme song, "Love Nest" (Otto Harbach—Louis A. Hirsch). But most of the songs growing popular over the air were new ones. Bell Baker introduced "All of Me" (Seymour Simons and Gerald Marks); Lanny Ross, "That's My Desire" (Carroll Loveday and Helmy Kresa); Lee Wiley, "My Love" (Ned Washington—Victor Young); Conrad Thibault, "You and the Night and the Music" (Howard Dietz—Arthur Schwartz) before it was used in the Broadway musical *Revenge with Music* (1934); Hildegarde, her musical signature, "Darling, Je Vous Aime Beaucoup" (Anna Sosenko); Frank Parker and Frances Langford, "Music, Maestro, Please" (Herb Magidson—Allie Wrubel); and Paul Whiteman and his Orchestra, "Deep Purple" (Mitchell Parish—Peter De Rose).

A valuable (though not always accurate) barometer of popular song successes was provided over the radio by "Your Hit Parade" sponsored by Lucky Strike cigarettes over CBS. This was a weekly Saturday-night program that had a run of twenty-eight years, the last three on television, purporting to present the top tunes of the week based on the number of performances those tunes received over the radio, on jukeboxes, in record and sheet music sales and in dance band performances. Precisely what system was employed for the week's selections—processed by Price, Waterhouse and Company—was a carefully guarded secret. Each Friday before the broadcast, a Brinks armored truck collected material from several unidentified key sources and brought it to the producers. More guarded still was the information pinpointing the three top songs of the week, information kept secret from the performers themselves until the last possible moment. The idea, of course, was to build suspense, and the strange thing is that week after week—even when the top choices were obvious —dramatic interest was aroused. People everywhere went around wondering what the top tune would be that week on "Your Hit Parade." The story goes that when Frank Sinatra, then a top singer on that program, attended a White House reception in 1944, President Roosevelt tried to elicit from him the title of the top tune on the next Hit Parade broadcast.

Sinatra was unable to supply this information because he did not know it himself.

On the program, a roll of drums preceded the awesome tones of the announcer: "And now the top three tunes in the nation." Number Three was given first, followed by Number Two. Then, once again with an appropriate fanfare, the "top song in the country, Number One on Your Lucky Strike Hit Parade" was announced and performed.

Through the years, from seven to fifteen songs were played on each program, though ten was the usual number. The singing stars over a quarter of a century made a truly formidable array: Lanny Ross, Dick Haymes, the Andrews Sisters, Margaret Whiting, Ginny Sims, Georgia Gibbs, Doris Day, Bea Wain, Frank Sinatra, Lawrence Tibbett, Andy Russell, Johnny Desmond, Kay Thompson, Dorothy Collins, Snooky Lanson, Joan Edwards, Eileen Wilson, Buddy Clark, Barry Wood, Dinah Shore, Martha Tilton, Russell Arms and Gisele MacKenzie. Mark Warnow conducted the orchestra for almost five hundred broadcasts, and when he died he was succeeded by his brother, Raymond Scott. Other conductors through the years were Lenny Hayton, Harry Salter, Carl Hoff, Leo Reisman, B. A. Rolfe and Harry Sosnick.

The first program, on April 20, 1935, was conducted by Lenny Hayton, with Warren Huff doing the announcing. "Your Hit Parade! We don't pick 'em, we just play 'em. From North, South, East and West, we check the songs you dance to . . . the sales of the records that you buy . . . and the sheet music you play. . . . And then, knowing your preferences, we bring you the top hits of the week!" The Number One song that evening was Kern's "Lovely to Look At" (Dorothy Fields and Jimmy McHugh) from the screen musical *Roberta*. Number Two was "Lullaby of Broadway" (Al Dubin—Harry Warren) from the motion picture musical *Gold Diggers of Broadway*. Number Three was "Soon," a Rodgers and Hart song from the movie *Mississippi* where it was sung by Bing Crosby. (This ballad is not to be confused with the 1930 ballad of the same name by the Gershwins.) Jerome Kern had another number on this same program, "I Won't Dance" (Otto Harbach and Oscar Hammerstein II) from the movie *Roberta*.

Among the songs that had the most frequent representation on "Your Hit Parade" between 1935 and 1940 were: "In a Little Gypsy Tearoom" (Edgar Leslie—Joe Burke); "Did I Remember?" (Harold Adamson—Walter Donaldson), an Academy Award nominee from the motion picture *Suzy*; "September in the Rain," from the motion picture *Melody for Two* (Al Dubin—Harry Warren); "My Reverie" (Larry Clinton), a melody lifted from Debussy's *Reverie*; "South of the Border" (Jimmy Kennedy and Michael Carr), an English importation; "The Woodpecker's Song," an Italian song by Eldo di Lazzaro with new American lyrics by Harold Adamson; "Red Sails in the Sunset" (Jimmy Kennedy—Will Grosz), an English song; Jerome Kern's "The Way You Look Tonight" (Dorothy Fields), winner of the Academy Award in *Swing Time*; "It Looks Like Rain in Cherry Blossom Lane" (Edgar Leslie—Joe Burke); "Deep Purple" (Mitchell Parish—Peter De Rose); and "I'll Never Smile Again" (Ruth Lowe) which had first become successful in the Victor recording by Tommy Dorsey and his orchestra, with Frank Sinatra doing the vocal.

From February 1943 through 1944 Lucky Strike presented a supplement to "Your Hit Parade," called "Your All Time Hit Parade," with Tommy Dorsey and his orchestra, and singers Frank Sinatra, Frances Langford and Sophie Tucker as principal participants.

While singers dominated radio music in the thirties, the sound of instruments could also be heard throughout the land. There was George Gershwin's piano playing. On February 19, 1934, Gershwin inaugurated his own program, "Music by Gershwin," sponsored by Feen-a-Mint, a laxative. Twice a week on Monday and Friday evenings from February 19 to May 31 for fifteen minutes over WJZ, and once a week on Sunday evening from September 23 to December 23 for half an hour over WABC, Gershwin offered programs not only featuring Gershwin music played by Gershwin, but also the music of other American composers who had influenced him, and the music of young and still little known popular composers who were getting their first radio hearing—Harold Arlen, Rube Bloom, Vernon Duke, Dana Suesse, Oscar Levant.

Popular songs fitted out in resplendent symphonic dress were being heard regularly over CBS in performances by André Kostelanetz and his orchestra. Kostelanetz made his radio debut in 1924. Five years after that, the Atlantic Broadcasting Company (predecessor of the Columbia Broadcasting System) contracted him to conduct a series of air concerts. In 1932, "André Kostelanetz Presents" became a sponsored coast-to-coast program over the CBS network. From then on, for the next decade or so, Kostelanetz music dominated the air waves on major sponsored programs. His new techniques of using microphones in orchestral performances, his individual way with strings, his lush orchestral colorations all helped bring new dimensions to the performances of popular and semiclassical music. When, in 1935, he conducted "Chesterfield Time" over a network of one hundred and fifty stations, he used the largest orchestra ever assembled over the air for a popular program (sixty-five men). In 1936 and 1937, *Radio Guide* magazine awarded him its medal of merit for consistently providing his listeners with "so much enjoyment" while refusing "to cheapen or compromise the quality of his programs." For four years, his radio program was chosen by *Motion Picture Daily* in a national poll of six hundred music editors and critics as Number One among musical shows. In 1943, another poll—among one hundred and twenty newspapers in the United States and Canada—voted him a place of honor both in popular and serious music, the only musician so far to get recognition in both categories. In the symphonic group, Kostelanetz and his orchestra earned third place, directly behind the NBC Symphony under Toscanini and the New York Philharmonic Orchestra; in popular music Kostelanetz won top honors. And on records, as well as over radio, Kostelanetz and his orchestra reached out to a fabulous audience. No conductor sold more records than he—in time, some fifty million albums!

Popular music was also receiving symphonic treatment over the Mutual network at the hands of Morton Gould and his orchestra. Gould was eighteen when he was discovered by S. L. Rothafel—the motion picture theater impresario better known as "Roxy"—who hired him as a staff pianist for the Radio City Music Hall in New York. Three years later, in 1934, Gould received his first radio assignment to conduct popular music on a sustaining program for WOR, in Newark, New Jersey. After seven years with WOR, Gould became the musical director of the "Cresta Blanca Carnival," a program sponsored over a nationwide hookup. He combined his meticulously prepared performances with his own symphonic arrangements of popular classics that were daring in their harmonic language, exploitation of new sound effects, and in their lush sonorities.

Similarly, popular music was heard in ingratiating orchestral performances on the "Carnation Contented Hour" over NBC by Percy Faith's orchestra; by "The Hour of Charm" which featured Phil Spitalny and His All-Girl Orchestra, with Evelyn and Her Magic Violin over NBC; by the Longines Symphonette, led by Mishel Piastro, sponsored by the Longine-Wittnauer Watch Company over the Mutual network; on the "Voice of Firestone," where Howard Barlow conducted the orchestra over NBC; and on the "Saturday Night Serenade" over CBS, where the orchestra was conducted by Gustave Henschen and then by Howard Barlow.

The air waves were also alive with the music of the dance bands, for the thirties was the decade of the great bands. Every important dance band or jazz unit was getting regular hearings over the air, not only in the now greatly expanded disc jockey shows but also in programs sponsored by Camel cigarettes (Glen Gray and the Casa Loma Orchestra), Twenty Grand cigarettes (Jimmy Dorsey), Raleigh and Kool cigarettes (Tommy Dorsey), Chesterfield cigarettes (Glenn Miller), Lady Esther (Wayne King), Woodbury Soap (Shep Fields), Johnson Wax (Ted Weems), Lucky Strike cigarettes (Kay Kyser), National Biscuit Company (Benny Goodman), Studebaker (Richard Himber), Old Gold cigarettes (Paul Whiteman), Robert Burns Panatella cigars (Guy Lombardo) and many others. In addition, remote relays of one-night stands by the great bands appearing in ballrooms throughout the country was a regular late Saturday night feature, with as many as six different bands heard in a single night from six different localities. On these "remotes" were heard the bands of Glenn Miller, Benny Goodman, Gene Krupa, the Dorsey Brothers, Harry James, Cab Calloway, Vincent Lopez, Paul Whiteman, Abe Lyman, Guy Lombardo, Ted Weems, Wayne King, Hal Kemp, Glen Gray, Ted Fiorito, Eddie Duchin, Shep Fields, Jan Garber and others. This vast radio exposure became an incalculable force in building up the sales of the recordings of these groups, so that records became radio's collaborator in enhancing the popularity of the big name bands.

5

In the mid-thirties, "wired radio" supplemented radio broadcasting in expanding the musical experiences of Americans. Wired radio piped popular music to captive audiences in restaurants, cocktail lounges, hotels and motels, factories, banks, railroad stations, beauty parlors, gas stations, department stores, offices of dentists and physicians, apartment house elevators and other public places as well as in private homes. The idea was first conceived in 1922 by Major General George O. Squier, chief signal officer of the United States Army, who tried to use electric light lines to transmit music and news to homes. Under the name of Wired Music, this project was developed in Cleveland by the North American Company but had to be abandoned because the quality of the musical transmission was impaired by interference from trolley car wires. Then, in 1934, the company was reactivated, this time in New York, as Muzak, then using telephone lines and starting out as a service for restaurants. Three years later, when it was learned that piped music could improve the morale and productivity of workers, Muzak offered its services to factories and other working establishments. By degrees, piped music filtered into one area after another of everyday activity. Subsequently acquired by Teleprompter, a subsidiary of ITT, Muzak was heard by eighty million people a day and earned over four hundred million dollars a year.

Muzak became one of three major organizations providing wired radio, the other two were 3-M in Minneapolis and Seeburg in Chicago. All operated on the same principle. The music they transmitted was intended not as stimulating listening but as soothing background. The music was made up of agreeable standards in popular music played in subdued orchestral renditions; vocal music was too distracting and so were extended solos. Fifteen minutes of uninterrupted music was followed by fifteen minutes of uninterrupted silence. No announcements or advertising intruded. Jazz, blues, protest songs and classical music were all scrupulously avoided, as was anything else either raucous or controversial. The music had to remain below the threshold of attention. Consequently, marked contrasts of tempo, volume or range were taboo. Muzak—which prepared three hundred and sixty-five programs a year without repeating a single tune more than once every nine days on any work shift —distributed three kinds of programs, one for factories, another for offices, and a third for general public places. Three-M sold a rhythmic library slanted for offices and factories, a melodic library for stores and restaurants, and specialized programs of Latin, Hawaiian or sacred music. Seeburg offered fast tempo music for industry and medium tempo music for libraries, offices of dentists and physicians, waiting rooms and similar places. With most reaction being either highly favorable or quietly tolerant, the sphere of activity for wired radio has continually expanded until it affects Americans almost continuously throughout the day, almost everywhere, and has become a giant subliminal force in developing the public taste for popular music.

19

The ASCAP and
BMI Story

1

With so much popular music being performed by so many, in so many places, and through so many media, the music business needed an agency to protect the interests of composers, lyricists and publishers. The first of these was the American Society of Composers, Authors and Publishers (ASCAP). Though it was first founded in 1914, it was not until the twenties and thirties that it began to operate as a licensing agency for the works of its members when they were used for profit either in live or canned performances.

The need for such an organization became apparent before World War I, when most composers and lyricists in Tin Pan Alley depended for their income on royalties from sheet music sales. It sometimes happened that a composer's songs were performed by numerous orchestras and sung by many performers without the sheet music moving in sizable quantities. A composer would then see his work become popular without profiting from this development. Sometimes, too, places of amusement exploited the popular music of the day to promote their business, and derived monetary advantages from it, while the composers and publishers of the music were not compensated. The United States Copyright Act of 1909 supposedly protected the composer by maintaining that any creation is the property of the author and that nobody could use it for his own financial benefit without the author's permission. But the copyright act was generally ignored, and hotels, restaurants and other places of amusement were availing themselves of popular music without making any compensation.

This problem became the subject of a discussion one day in 1913 in New York by three men, Raymond Hubbell, composer, Nathan Burkan, lawyer, and George Maxwell, American representative of the powerful Italian publishing house of Ricordi. They noted that in Europe, since 1871, there existed SACEM (*Société des Auteurs, Compositeurs, et Éditeurs de Musique*) which collected a fee or royalty each time a musical composition was played. Nathan Burkan was convinced that the American copyright law covered the payment of fees for performances anywhere and through any medium, even though no such fees were ever paid. Girding themselves for battle, these three men gained the cooperation of Victor Herbert who, in turn, used his enormous influence to win the support of other popular composers and lyricists.

After a preliminary discussion at the Lamb's Club in New York late in 1913, a meeting was called for composers, lyricists and publishers at Luchow's Restaurant on 14th Street where a gourmet dinner of German specialties and wines was planned by Glen MacDonough, the lyricist and librettist. But it rained on the day of this scheduled meeting, and only a few men were present. These were Victor Herbert, Silvio Hein, Louis A. Hirsch, Raymond Hubbell, Gustave A. Kerker, George Maxwell, Jay Witmark and Nathan Burkan. Disheartened at this meager turnout, the men nevertheless proceeded to enjoy their meal and to map out plans for the founding of an American organization similar to Europe's SACEM. A new meeting was now called for February 13, 1914, at the Hotel Claridge in Times Square. Twenty-two publishers and one hundred and seven composers and lyricists attended, and formally organized the American Society of Composers, Authors and Publishers (ASCAP, for short) electing as its first officers George Maxwell as president, Victor Herbert, vice president, Glen MacDonough, secretary and John Golden, treasurer. Victor Herbert was made vice-president when he stubbornly refused to accept the presidency, and John Golden long maintained that he was made treasurer in absentia while he was in the men's room.

What was now needed was to test the validity of the 1909 copyright law in court as it pertained to live performances. To do so, an action was instituted by an ASCAP publisher against the Vanderbilt Hotel claiming an infringement of copyright in the unauthorized performance of John Philip Sousa's march "From Maine to Oregon" in its dining room. Though the suit was won by the plaintiff in the United States District Court, it met a reversal in the Circuit Court of Appeals, which insisted that the customers had come to the dining room to enjoy food and not to listen to music.

Despite this defeat, which momentarily seemed to spell doom for the fledgling organization, another lawsuit was filed soon afterward on April 1, 1915, by Victor Herbert against Shanley's Restaurant on Broadway and 42nd Street for an unauthorized performance of selections from Herbert's operetta *Sweethearts*. The case was tried on May 1, 1915, before Judge Learned Hand of the United States District Court who ruled against the plaintiff. The Court of Appeals affirmed Justice Hand's decision on the technical legal grounds involving fine points of the copyright. The case was brought to the United States Supreme Court which, on January 22, 1917, reversed the decision of the two lower courts. Justice Oliver Wendell Holmes wrote in part in his decision: "If music did not pay, it would be given up. If it pays, it pays out of the public's pocket. Whether it pays or not, the purpose of employing it is profit, and that is enough."

With this decision, the raison d'être of ASCAP was established, but it took a number of years before the organization could attract enough members to become a power, and it required numerous legal suits before ASCAP could enforce compliance with the law by those using music. At the end of its first year of operation, ASCAP was licensing the performance of its music to only eighty-five New York hotels who were paying an average of $8.23 a month. As late as 1921, the legal and operating costs for ASCAP far exceeded its income, and only thirty-nine new members had been added to its rolls, 231 as against 192 in 1914. Owners of restaurants, cabarets, dance halls, theaters and so forth, were outraged that they were compelled to pay a regular fee for using music that up to now they had been using just for the asking. Some threatened to eliminate orchestras altogether. Since this would mean a loss of jobs, the musician's union put itself on record as opposing ASCAP and urging its members to boycott ASCAP music. This in turn frightened some publishers into abandoning ASCAP and advertising that their music was "tax free."

One of the lawsuits instigated by ASCAP involved the young radio industry. At its beginnings, in the first years of the twenties, radio was given a free license to use ASCAP music in order to encourage the growth of the infant industry. But when radio began to grow rapidly into a lucrative commercial enterprise, ASCAP insisted upon payment for the licensing of its music for broadcasting. In the courts, the radio industry argued that broadcast music did not actually represent "performances" in the technical sense since a broadcast was the emission of radio waves; that even if a performance were taking place, it was given in a private studio before a limited audience that paid nothing for admission. The federal courts finally rejected these arguments and ruled in favor of ASCAP, from which time radio stations everywhere were required to pay an annual fee for the right to use ASCAP music.

In 1924, the motion picture industry became licensees (having lost a suit against ASCAP as being a monopoly in restraint of trade) and by 1929, ASCAP had won over all organizations using music for profit. When wired radio was instituted in the mid-thirties by Muzak, it too, had to pay an annual sum for using the music of ASCAP members.

Thus ASCAP became a powerful agency protecting the financial interests of its several thousand members in the late twenties who divided an annual take of several million dollars a year. By the mid-thirties, ASCAP had almost thirty thousand establishments licensed, which paid ten million dollars a year. Sixty-two percent of this income was paid out by 657 radio stations, twenty-one percent by theaters and movie houses, and the rest by other establishments. The affluence and power of ASCAP kept pace with the expanding economy and continued growth of the music business in all its facets through the ensuing years. By the time ASCAP celebrated its sixtieth birthday on February 13, 1974, it could boast a membership of sixteen thousand composers and lyricists, and six thousand publishers, was receiving an annual income from license fees exceeding seventy-five million dollars and was disbursing almost sixty million dollars to members.

After deductions for running expenses, ASCAP divided its income equally between publishers on the one hand and composers and lyricists on the other. Originally the amount paid each year to a composer or lyricist depended upon an arbitrary rating assigned him, that position varying with his importance. Composers such as Irving Berlin, George Gershwin, Jerome Kern, Cole Porter or Richard Rodgers, and lyricists like Oscar Hammerstein II, Ira Gershwin and Lorenz Hart were given top rating or "AA" positions, and up to World War II their income amounted to about $25,000 a year (twice that if the composer and lyricist were one and the same as was the case with Irving Berlin and Cole Porter). Lesser composers and lyricists drew lower annual incomes since they were placed in lower categories.

After 1950 a more equitable method of distributing ASCAP income was evolved. This new, and somewhat complex, method was dependent on the number of performance hours received by each song through every possible medium. Composers and lyricists gaining the most hearings could now command about $50,000 a year (once again, that sum was doubled if the composers were their own lyricists). Those composers enjoying fewer hearings were placed respectively in the $30,000 a year category, or $20,000 a year, or less. Under this arrangement, a composer and lyricist who was no longer productive or even alive, but whose work was still widely performed, could still earn a commanding fee, assuming that his music or lyrics were played as often as those of his still productive competitors. What this means to a composer or lyricist was once explained by Deems Taylor when he pointed out that Stephen Foster had died with thirty-eight cents in his pocket, but that if he had been alive a century later, he could have counted on anywhere from $20,000 to $50,000 a year income from ASCAP even if he had stopped writing music altogether.

2

Toward the closing years of the thirties a monumental crisis seized radio music. ASCAP now felt that it was in a position to play a strong hand, what with its monopoly of the best songwriters of Broadway and Hollywood and with radio's insatiable hunger for music. In 1940 a five-year contract expired under which radio stations had been paying ASCAP an annual fee of four and a half million dollars. In its new contract, ASCAP demanded twice that amount, a sum that radio executives regarded as so outrageous that they refused to discuss an agreement. A stalemate followed during which all ASCAP music was removed from the air. To fill the vacuum, radio had to use music in public domain, such as the songs of Stephen Foster, hillbilly music, folk songs, and songs by young and inexperienced writers who had no ASCAP affiliation. Radio became a musical wasteland, and it seemed ready to remain so indefinitely. Then in 1941 ASCAP retreated. Under the terms of a new five-year contract, ASCAP agreed to accept even less each year than it had received under the previous contract, three million dollars instead of four and a half.

But ASCAP suffered an even more serious setback than just the loss of dollars. Because of this controversy, a new organization was formed by the radio interests in 1940 to compete with ASCAP and become capable of providing broadcasters with its own continuous supply of music. The new rival was Broadcast Music Incorporated (BMI), formed in 1940, with Neville Miller as president. It sought to get performing rights from its own stable of independent writers and publishers, offering to turn over to them all of its income from the licensing of their music (minus essential expenses) "on the basis of the performance of music on thousands of independent stations as well as countrywide networks."

By the end of its first year, BMI had several hundred writers and publishers on its rolls, and drew an income from license fees of one and a half million dollars. During that first year BMI could already boast several hit songs in its catalogue, among which were: "I Hear a Rhapsody" (George Fragos, Jack Baker and Dick Gasparre), the leading song of 1941 on radio's "Your Hit Parade"; "The Breeze and I," lyrics by Al Stillman to a melody adapted by T. Camarata from Ernesto Lecuona's piano piece, *Andalucia*; "You Are My Sunshine" (Jimmy Davis and Charles Mitchell), a hillbilly type number, one of whose authors, Jimmy Davis, ran successfully for the governor's seat in Louisiana in 1944, his drive sparked by his ballad; and "It's a Big Wide Wonderful World" (John Rox).

In 1940 and 1941, BMI had among its licensed songs such hits as "Amapola," a Spanish song by Joseph M. Lacalle with new English lyrics by Albert Gamse, which Deanna Durbin had sung in her movie *First Love* (1939); "I Don't Want to Set the World on Fire" (Eddie Seiler, Sol Marcus, Bennie Benjamin, and Eddie Durham), the leading song of 1941; "Deep in the Heart of Texas" (June Hershey—Don Swander), an audience participation number in which people clap hands at the end of each of several phrases in the chorus. In 1942 and 1943, BMI hits included "Paper Doll" (Johnny S. Black), which had been written in 1915, was not published until 1930, and had to wait for its fame until 1942 in a best-selling Decca recording by the Mills brothers; "Tico-Tico," a Brazilian song by Zequinha Abreu with new lyrics by Ervin Drake, introduced in the Walt Disney production *Saludos Amigos* (1942), then made popular by Xavier Cugat and his orchestra in nightclubs and recording; "Pistol Packin' Mama" (Al Dexter), another song in hillbilly style, introduced by the composer and his Troopers on an Okeh recording and made into a hit Decca recording by Bing Crosby.

BMI started from weakness, the lack of established and experienced songwriters, the bulk of whom were affiliated with ASCAP. But compelled to build up its ranks from mostly young writers, BMI was freer to exploit new areas, such as hillbilly music which had gained a national audience over the radio during the ASCAP drought, and rock 'n' roll, when it took over the music scene so completely in the 1950s. Hillbilly music and rock brought to the music scene new writers who found BMI more receptive to their work than ASCAP. BMI was more willing to keep step with the rapidly changing times in music than was ASCAP, whose writers, with their orientation in Broadway and Hollywood, compelled them to pursue traditional ways in defiance of the demands of a new, young audience. In meeting these demands, and in fully recognizing the call of a new kind of audience, BMI was able to grow prodigiously. By 1952, 80 percent of all the music played over the radio was licensed by BMI. By the time BMI celebrated its first quarter century of existence, it had more than eight thousand writers and six thousand publishers on its lists, their works licensed to twenty thousand outlets in the United States and Canada, earning about ten million dollars a year in performance payments. Two decades later the income of BMI soared to about thirty-five million dollars a year. Where BMI had had 1,100 writers, 150 publishers, 3 record companies, and 600 radio stations when it first came into existence, by the early 1970s the figures had zoomed to 25,000 writers, 10,000 publishers, 4,000 record companies and 7,000 radio stations.

20

Hillbilly Music

1

The country and western music of the 1960s and 1970s was preceded by the hillbilly music of the twenties and thirties.

The word "hillbilly" had been used from the beginning of the twentieth century to designate the inhabitants of the backwoods of the rural South. It took another quarter of a century for that word to be associated with the music of that region. On January 15, 1925, a string band from the mountain regions of North Carolina and Virginia made six recordings for Okeh. Ralph Peer, recording director for Okeh, baptized this band the "Hillbillies" in catalogues and on labels; the music this group sang and played came to be known as "hillbilly music." Though competitive record companies were at first reluctant to use the word "Hillbilly" for the music of the Southern mountain regions—preferring the phrases "songs of the hills and plains" or "hill country tunes"—the word "hillbilly" gradually gained national acceptance both for the music and for its performers.

These mountain tunes were simple and unsophisticated. The melodies often had a hymn-like character, were in even 2/4 and 4/4 time, with the voice gliding from one note to the next. The lyrics were concerned primarily with tragedies, accidents, personal torments and were identified by guttural sounds and rural inflections. This was music whose traditions and styling had been handed down for generations and whose individuality was preserved by people insulated from the commercial and cultural life of the big city, whose daily life was made up of elementals, and for whom singing and music making were a principal form of diversion.

Radio station WSB, in Atlanta, Georgia, was probably the first high-powered radio station to feature hillbilly music; it did so in 1922. Other radio stations in the South followed this lead, among them WBAP in Fort Worth, Texas, which on January 4, 1923, offered the first radio barn or square dance program, directed by a country fiddler, Captain M. J. Bonner. Such an avalanche of enthusiasm was released by this program that WBAP established a hillbilly barn dance program two or three times monthly after 1927. This 1923 barn dance program was the prototype of many such offerings soon featured by radio stations throughout America, including the "Chicago Barn Dance," devised by George D. Hay, and first broadcast over WLS in Chicago in 1924, which later in the decade, under the new name of "National Barn Dance" became a network presentation.

Mountain and country music was also being recorded, the first in 1922 with performances for Victor by two country fiddlers, Eck Robertson and Henry Gilliland. A year or so later, these same men were heard over WBAP in two numbers they recorded, "The Arkansas Traveler" and "Sally Goodin'," earning the distinction of becoming the first recording artists to plug their own records over the air. For Okeh, John Carson, a singing fiddler, recorded in Atlanta on June 4, 1923, "The Little Old Log Cabin in the Lane" and "The Old Hen Cackled and the Rooster's Going to Crow." The encouraging sales of these two releases led Ralph Peer to place Carson's name on an Okeh contract. Carson became the first performer of hillbilly music to record commercially and to make hillbilly music a profitable commodity in the record business. Other record companies (Columbia, Vocalion, Brunswick, Gennett and Victor) at once went into the competition recording this music. Field units were dispatched to the cities, rural communities, as well as mountain areas of the South to capture on shellac the indigenous songs of native performers, mountain ballads such as "Cumberland Gap" and "Barbara Allen." In 1924, Riley Puckett, a blind hillbilly singer, recorded for Columbia "The Little Old Log Cabin in the Lane" and "Rock All Our Babies to Sleep" to realize the greatest commercial success thus far to come to a hillbilly performer.

Exploitation of hillbilly material by professional Northern performers and songwriters was not slow in coming. Wendell Hall, "the red-headed music maker," famous in vaudeville and radio, accompanying himself on a ukulele, took a hillbilly tune, added some amusing lyrics to it, and came up with a decided Tin Pan Alley hit in "It Ain't Gonna Rain No More," which he recorded for Victor on October 12, 1923. Vernon Dalhart, a singer in light operas in the North, profited even more handsomely from hillbilly music. In 1924, his fortunes as performer were at their lowest ebb when he turned to hillbilly music. That year he recorded for Victor "The Wreck of the Old 97" and "The Prisoner's Song," and with both he entered upon a new and far richer career than he had known so far, this time as a singer of hillbilly songs. He reaped a fortune for himself, for hillbilly music and for the companies for which he made records under his own and assumed names. As a singer, Dalhart added appreciably to both his fame and fortune in 1925 with his recordings on nineteen different labels of "The Death of Floyd Collins" (Andrew Jenkins—Irene Spain). Floyd Collins was a spelunker who had been trapped in a Kentucky cave in 1925.

2

August 1, 1927, was a red-letter day for hillbilly music. Ralph Peer, now representing Victor, had brought his recording equipment to Bristol, on the Tennessee-Virginia border, to seek out new hillbilly music to record. On August 1, on the top floor of a three-story house at 410 State Street on the Tennessee side, he set up his apparatus to record the singing and playing of the Carter Family, and the singing of Jimmie Rodgers. (Jimmy Rodgers of rock 'n' roll fame of later years was a different man, and no relation.) The Carter family specialized in mountain music—the traditional songs, singing style, and instruments of the remote Appalachian mountain region. Jimmie Rodgers was a performer of country music which emphasized solo rather than group singing and whose songs had been influenced by many different idioms—blues, folk and popular music included. Between them, the Carter Family and Jimmie Rodgers may well be said to have marked the first stirrings of country and western music.

The family that made records on August 1, 1927, was made up of A. P. Carter, his wife, Sara, and his sister-in-law, Maybelle Carter. They had come up from Maces Spring, Virginia, and for many years had been performing hill country songs at church, school and other functions. A. P. Carter, who sang bass, was the leader. Sara played the autoharp or guitar and was assigned most of the vocal solos. Maybelle, who sang the tenor in part singing, was a specialist at the guitar who developed her own technique.

An advertisement in the Bristol *Herald* inviting singers and musicians to audition for possible recording brought the Carters to 410 State Street in Bristol, and to Ralph Peer. Their first releases were "Bury Me Under the Weeping Willow," "Little Log Cabin by the Sea," "The Poor Orphan Child," "The Storms Are on the Ocean," "Single Girl, Married Girl" and "Wandering Boy." These did so well that in May 1928 the Carters were brought North by Victor to their studio in Camden, New Jersey. There they made twelve more records. One of them, "Wildwood Flower," with Maybelle playing the guitar, became an all-time Carter favorite.

The Carters made many more recordings after that, some two hundred and fifty songs on a dozen or so labels. In public appearances in theaters and schools, in radio broadcasts, as well as on their disks, they acquired an enormous following, particularly for their heart songs—songs of love and frustrated love—and songs of simple sorrows. Most of them were written (or were reputed to have been written) by A. P. Carter, and the best of them were: "I'm Thinking Tonight of My Blue Eyes," "I'll Be All Smiles Tonight," "Meeting Me by Moonlight Alone," "Little Darlin' Pal of Mine," "Worried Man Blues," "Coal Miner's Blues" and "Foggy Mountain Top."

In the later years, the three Carters were supplemented by Maybelle's three daughters (Helen, June and Anita). Though the older Carters were divorced, they continued to sing with the group for some years, and when they left, the singing Carter family comprised Maybelle and her daughters, who sang over WRNL and WRVA in Richmond, Virginia, made records, and became affiliated with the "Grand Ole Opry" in Nashville, Tennessee. Two of these Carters remained active after 1960. Maybelle occasionally appeared with Johnny Cash, and June Carter not only became Cash's singing partner but his wife as well.

Jimmie Rodgers was the first hillbilly singer to discover that the road of country music was paved with gold, capable of taking a man from poverty to affluence. In his highpitched singing he created a style uniquely his, the "blue yodel." He not only sang the blues, but also country music, western music, cowboy songs, Negro railroad songs, work songs, hobo songs and sometimes even pop tunes. He became the most successful of all hillbilly performers, selling over twenty million records, driving a Cadillac, and acquiring a mansion in Texas he called "The Yodeler's Paradise."

His admirers were legion, most of whom knew him exclusively through his records. His imitators were innumerable. Some of the most successful performers of country and western music of a later decade were influenced by him, and some of them acknowledged their indebtedness. Among them were Elvis Presley and Johnny Cash, Hank Snow and Ernest Tubb, Eddy Arnold and Hank Williams, Gene Autry and Red Foley. Ernest Tubb, the country and western artist, once estimated that perhaps 75 percent of the country and western performers since the time of Jimmie Rodgers were directly or indirectly influenced by him.

His life was all too brief, and much of it was spent in abject misery. He came from Meridian, Mississippi, where he was born in 1897, and where poverty was a way of life. He worked as a water boy for railroad workers, and his daily contact with them made it possible for him to learn their songs and to receive lessons on banjo and guitar. When he was twelve he won first prize in an amateur contest in a local theater by singing "Bill Bailey, Won't You Please Come Home?" (Hughie Cannon) and "Steamboat Bill" (Ren Shields).

He soon became a railroad man himself, serving as an assistant foreman to his father. Jimmie was fourteen years old at the time. A few months later he was a brakeman on a freight yard work train. For the next fourteen years he held various other railroad jobs—call boy, baggage master, flagman. He often entertained his fellow workers by singing to them the folk songs he had been gathering through the years, accompanying himself on the banjo, mandolin or guitar. He also collaborated with black musicians in performances in night spots in Meridian, and was a member of a small jazz combo playing at various public functions.

The small income he was drawing from his railroad work was inadequate to meet the basic needs of his family. (He married in 1920 and had two daughters.) His chronic extravagance made matters worse. In 1923, when he was in New Orleans in search of a more lucrative railroad job than the one he had quit, he had to pawn his banjo to get the fare to come home to attend the funeral of his six-month-old daughter who had suddenly died during his absence.

Greater sorrows lay ahead. Late in 1924, when he was twenty-seven, he suffered a lung hemorrhage. For three days he was on the brink of death in a charity hospital. From then on he suffered from tuberculosis. Since his depleted health precluded working on the railroad any longer he had to find some other way of making a living. All he knew, besides railroading, was singing. In 1925 he joined a medicine show touring Kentucky and Tennessee as a blackface entertainer and banjoist. There was not much money in this, nor in similar efforts, and so, in 1926, he made an abortive attempt to get back to railroading. A flare-up of tuberculosis forced him to admit defeat and give up the railroad for good. He went to Asheville, North Carolina, where he worked as a city detective, a sinecure found for him by a solicitous friend. Refusing to accept such charity, he left the police force to work as a janitor and furnace man in an apartment house.

He was still making music. In Asheville, he formed the Jimmie Rodgers Entertainers, a foursome that gave one-night stands in Southeastern fairs and tent shows and made three appearances a week over WWNC in Asheville. Upon learning that the Victor company was holding auditions in Bristol, he went there in August 1927, met Ralph Peer, and made a test record of "Sleep Baby Sleep," a traditional Southern mountain cradle song, and with it, his own first composition, "Soldier's Sweetheart." For this test he was paid twenty dollars. In November he came to Camden, New Jersey, for a second recording session. On this occasion he recorded "Away Out on the Mountain," "Ben Dewberry's Final Run," "T for Texas," and that old Tin Pan Alley tearjerker, "Mother Was a Lady" (Edward B. Marks—Joseph W. Stern). In "T for Texas" he introduced the "blue yodel" for which he became famous—a yodel interpolated at the end of the final lines of the three-stanzas of a traditional blues.

His first royalty check from Victor was $27.43. Within half a year he was receiving two thousand dollars a month, as his recordings were beginning to find an eager market. In 1928, two of his disks realized a million copy sale each: "Blue Yodel" (now called "Blue Yodel No. 1," because he wrote about a dozen other similar compositions) and "Brakeman's Blues." He wrote both of them himself.

He was now a household name, not only as a result of a continuous flow of best-selling records, but also through his personal appearances in vaudeville, at tent shows, and over the radio in the South. Whether on records or in person he was variously identified as "The Singing Brakeman," or "America's Blue Yodeler." His annual income of about one hundred thousand dollars a year would have been much greater if his illness (which inspired him to write "T. B. Blues") did not make it necessary to restrict his public appearances. Excessive medical costs, together with his chronic extravagance, consumed his finances as rapidly as tuberculosis was destroying his body. In 1933 he spent a month in the hospital, then three months home in bed. He continued making records, almost with his last breath. During his final recording session in New York in May 1933 he was so weak that he had to rest on a cot between record takes. He made his last record only two days before his death, brought on by a hemorrhage at the Hotel Manger (later called Hotel Taft) in New York, on May 26, 1933. His body was transported by train to his hometown of Meridian. When the train approached the town, a continuous low moan came from the train whistle, increasing in volume as it approached the station. Hundreds of his admirers had gathered there, some of them weeping when they heard the funeral whistle.

In death he passed on to legendary fame. Bob Miller wrote "The Death of Jimmie Rodgers" in 1933. A Jimmie Rodgers Society was formed in Lubbock, Texas and in his native town of Meridian, a Jimmie Rodgers museum has been created to house his sheet music and personal papers and his brakeman's kit from his railroad days. An annual country music festival in Meridian never failed to pay him tribute. A monument in his honor was unveiled in Meridian in 1954 before some thirty thousand people, among whom were innumerable musical celebrities and such political notables as Governor Adlai Stevenson and Senator James O. Eastland. It was a bas relief of Rodgers wearing an engineer's cap, a guitar under his arm, giving a thumbs-up sign; near him was a facsimile of Engine 42 (which he immortalized in one of his songs) on which was inscribed the names of the railroad lines for which he had once worked. The inscription read: "His is the music of America. He sang the songs of the people he loved, of a young nation growing strong. His was an America of glistening rails, thundering boxcars, and rain-swept nights; of lonesome prairies, great mountains and a high blue sky. He sang of the bayous and the cotton fields, the wheated plains of the little towns, the cities, and of the winding rivers of America. We listened, we understood."

When the Country Music Hall of Fame was founded in Nashville, Tennessee, in 1961, Jimmie Rodgers was the first to be chosen. His plaque read: "Jimmie Rodgers stands foremost in the country music field as the man who started it all. . . . Although small in stature, he was a giant among men, starting a trend in the musical taste of millions."

His records continued to sell long after his death. Many of them were collected between 1959 and 1965 into the commemorative albums *Never No Mo' Blues, Train Whistle Blues, My Rough and Rowdy Ways, Jimmie the Kid, Hall of Fame, Short But Brilliant Life, My Time Ain't Long*, and *The Best of the Legendary Jimmie Rodgers*. Many of his songs have become staples in the country repertory. Besides those already mentioned there are "My Time Ain't Long," "Mississippi River Blues," "Never No Mo' Blues," "Daddy and Home," "The Land of My Boyhood Dreams," "Waiting for a Train," "Yodeling Cowboy," "Whisper Your Mother's Name" and many more.

3

One of the most potent agencies dispensing hillbilly music was a program that became the oldest continuing show in radio history, "Grand Ole Opry." Its originator was George Dewey

Hay, who had previously been responsible for radio's "Chicago Barn Dance" and the "National Barn Dance." Sometimes referred to as "the solemn ol' judge," Hay had worked as a reporter on the Memphis *Continental Appeal* before becoming the radio editor of station WMC in Memphis. In this capacity he scooped the country with President Warren G. Harding's death in 1923. Hay then moved on to Chicago to become the principal announcer at WLS, where he achieved such distinction that a national poll conducted by *Radio Digest* placed him among the foremost announcers in America. Hay's interest in hillbilly music led him to inaugurate the "Chicago Barn Dance" at WLS in 1924, which enjoyed a top national rating after it went on a network. In 1925, Hay was made director of WSM, a new radio station in Nashville, Tennessee. There he introduced a new barn dance program on November 28, 1925, with Uncle Jimmy Thompson, an eighty-year old fiddler, as star, and with Hay himself serving as master of ceremonies. This program, called simply "Barn Dance," became a fixture at WSM. On December 10, 1927, the show changed its name to "Grand Ole Opry." For several years the show emanated from the studios of WSM, then from the War Memorial Auditorium before moving in 1941 to the Ryman Auditorium, a tabernacle built in the 1880s. It remained there through the evening of March 15, 1974. One evening later, Grand Ole Opry moved into its new fifteen-million dollar opera house in Opry Land, U.S.A., in Nashville, with festivities attended by President and Mrs. Nixon, and relayed to the entire country by a network of two hundred radio stations.

The fiftieth anniversary of the Grand Ole Opry was celebrated on November 11, 1975, with a ninety-minute program emanating from Opryland through the facilities of ABC-TV. Twenty of America's top country performers collaborated in a giant tribute, among whom were such stars as Roy Acuff, Chet Atkins, Johnny Cash, the Carter Family, Roy Clark, Loretta Lynn, Charley Pride, Marty Robbins, Hank Snow and Ernest Tubb. In conjunction with this anniversary two books were published in 1975: an oversized, lavishly illustrated volume by Jack Hurst, *Grand Old Opry*, and a history by Myron Tassin and Jerry Henderson, *Fifty Years with the Grand Old Opry*.

The Grand Ole Opry was the incubator of numerous stars that lit up the skies of hillbilly music, and after that, country and western music. The first was Uncle Dave Macon, dubbed "the king of banjo-pickers" and "the king of hillbillies." He was also king of the Grand Ole Opry for about fifteen years. He had been a farmer, first as a hired hand, and then on his own property in Readyville, Tennessee, before becoming a professional musician in his forty-eighth year. As a boy he had learned to play a five-string banjo. During his farming years he often appeared as an entertainer at barn dances. Discovered by a talent scout for Loew's vaudeville circuit, he was engaged to appear at the Loew's Birmingham Theater in 1918, where he remained on the bill for several weeks. For the next eight years he appeared extensively on the Loew circuit as well as in schoolhouses and various other public auditoriums. With his fame solidified, he was called to appear with the Grand Ole Opry in 1927. He remained a star until his death in 1952.

He was in his prime until about 1940, a star not only at the Grand Ole Opry but also in concert appearances even in motion pictures (*Opry*, produced by Republic pictures, released in 1939). His repertory was made up of songs he had picked up throughout the South, together with numbers he himself created. Those with which he was most often identified were "Cumberland Mountain Deer Race," "Ain't It a Shame to Keep Your Honey Out in the Rain," "The Dixie Bee Line," "All In, Down and Out Blues" and a number in which his skill at the banjo invariably brought down the house, "Uncle Dave's Beloved Solos."

Instrumental rather than vocal music dominated performances at the Grand Ole

Opry, even though the Vagabonds, a vocal ensemble, joined the company in 1931 and the Delmore Brothers, a vocal instrumental duo, in 1932, and were prominent on its programs thereafter. Then Roy Acuff, the singing fiddler, joined the company in 1938. In two years time he inherited the crown and scepter from Macon as "king of Opry." Acuff, born in 1903, was "the Smoky Mountain Boy" from eastern Tennessee who seemed headed for a career in baseball. He played in the minor leagues and was about to sign with the New York Yankees when he became incapacitated by a sunstroke. After his recovery, he learned to play the violin and acquired a repertory of hill tunes by listening to records. For two years he traveled with a medicine show in Virginia and eastern Tennessee. Then, in 1933, he began to be heard regularly over the radio on WROL in Knoxville, Tennessee. He later formed a hillbilly group, "Crazy Tennesseans," which became a feature of WNOX in Knoxville, toured the South in concerts and made some records for Columbia. In 1938, Acuff joined the Grand Ole Opry. Accompanied by a string band, The Smoky Mountain Boys, he became the first singing star of the company, famous not only for mountain songs but for sacred ones. The number with which he is often associated (and his first recording in 1936) was a hymn, "The Great Speckled Bird," words by Reverend Gant set to a melody attributed to A. P. Carter of the Carter Family, "I'm Thinking Tonight of My Blue Eyes." Though he did not sing in the original recorded version, "Wabash Cannon Ball," a hobo song arranged by A. P. Carter about a train carrying the hobo to fantasyland, ultimately became his best-selling disk. Other Acuff standards were "The Precious Jewel," words by Acuff to the melody of a mountain ballad, "The Hills of Roane County"; "Wreck on the Highway" (Dorsey Dixon); the sacred song, "Radio Station S-A-V-E-D;" "Night Train to Memphis" (Beasley Smith, Marvin Hughes and Owen Bradley); and three of his own songs, "Branded Wherever I Go," "It Won't Be Long" and "Unloved and Unclaimed."

Besides earning perhaps the highest income of any country singer up to his time, Acuff extended his influence in country music when, in 1942, he formed the Acuff-Rose Company in Nashville with Fred Rose, a songwriter. This was the first American publishing house devoted exclusively to country music. Acuff also appeared in several motion pictures in the 1940s, including *Hi Neighbor* (1941), *My Darling Clementine* (1943), *Cowboy Canteen* (1944) and *Night Train to Memphis* (1946). His popularity in Tennessee won him the nomination in 1948 for the office of Governor on the Republican ticket, but was not sufficient to gain him the election. In 1962, Acuff became the first living singer elected to the Country Music Hall of Fame in Nashville, as the man who "fiddled and sang his way into the hearts of millions the world over," as the citation said, "oftentimes bringing country music to areas where it had never been before." In 1972, a bronze plaque honoring Acuff was unveiled in the new Grand Ole Opry House, then still under construction. It read in part: "Roy joined the Grand Ole Opry in 1938. He was its first international star. . . . Truly he has earned the title 'the king of country music'." When the new auditorium of the Grand Ole Opry was formally opened at Opryland, U.S.A., Roy Acuff was on the stage to greet and introduce the guest of honor, President Nixon, and to present him with a yellow Yo-Yo like the one Acuff liked to use during his stage performances.

4

A new sound in country music came drifting from the southwestern regions of Texas. It was a marriage of country music and jazz, and it was called "Country Swing" or "Western Swing." Its principal advocate was Bob Wills. He was a country fiddler who worked as a barber until 1929 when he became a member of a medicine show in Fort Worth. As a full-time entertainer, he teamed up with Herman Arnspiger and Milton Brown. In 1933, Wills became a star attraction on three radio stations in Fort Worth. With Arnspiger and Brown he then organized the Texas Playboys which, for a decade, was a five-nights-a-week institution over KVOO in Tulsa, was heard at dances, on records and even in the movies. Among the earliest numbers with which "Country Swing" became standardized, performed by Bob Wills and his Texas Playboys, was their version of a 1923 hit song, "Mexicali Rose" (Helen Stone—Jack B. Tenney), together with two early Bob Wills pieces, "Texas Playboy Rag" and "San Antonio Rose." The last of these grew so popular following its appearance in 1940 that it lent its title to a motion picture in 1941 where it was prominently featured; after that the song was successfully recorded by Bing Crosby.

In *Country Music, U.S.A.*, Bill C. Malone explains that "Country Swing" or "Western Swing" was characterized by "a heavy, insistent beat, the jazz-like improvisations of the steel guitar, and the heavily bowed fiddle. It was rhythmic, infectious music designed for dancing." Malone adds: "Bob Wills left his brand on country music not merely through the spawning of imitative Western Swing bands but in the introduction of certain songs and instrumental rhythms that were adopted by other musicians. Long after the large Western Swing band had declined in popularity, the Bob Wills 'beat' and style of fiddling continued to attract the attention of country musicians. All through the southwestern states, in taverns, dance halls and country nightclubs, countless groups in their choice of songs and styles are a testament to the pervasive Bob Wills influence."

Bob Wills himself composed some of the songs which helped spread the gospel of "Western" or "Country Swing": "Wills Breakdown," "Texas Two Step," "Lone Star Rag" and "Betty's Waltz" among others. Numerous record albums by Bob Wills and the Texas Playboys were pressed by Columbia, MGM, Harmony and Liberty—a vast cornucopia of Western Swing Music. Among the last was *The Bob Wills Anthology* issued in 1973 by Columbia, produced in collaboration with the Country Music Foundation and with research conducted through the facilities of the Country Music Hall of Fame (to which Bob Wills was named in 1968) and the Country Music Museum in Nashville.

Though stricken by a stroke in 1969, which forced him to go into retirement, Bob Wills and members of his old Texas Playboys were able to join Merle Haggard in Dallas in 1973 in the making of Bob Wills' last recording: *Bob Wills and his Texas Playboys: For the Last Time*. In 1975, this album won the Wrangler award from the National Cowboy Hall of Fame and Western Heritage Center.

Bob Wills died of bronchial pneumonia in a nursing home in Fort Worth in 1975. His biography, *San Antonio Rose: The Life and Music of Bob Wills* by Charles R. Townsend, was published in 1976.

21

The Era of the
Great Dance Bands

1

During the twenties, Tin Pan Alley found other areas in which to merchandise its music, besides radio, recordings, the Broadway theater and motion pictures. A major one was the small dance bands which were beginning to appear in dance halls, nightclubs, hotels, theaters and public auditoriums, as well as in recordings and over the radio. Supplementing authentic jazz groups and jazz-oriented bands and orchestras, such as those directed by Louis Armstrong, Duke Ellington, Fletcher Henderson, Ben Pollack, Jean Goldkette and others, there were about fifty thousand small bands offering popular songs in formalized arrangements for both listening and dancing pleasure. An indication of the growing importance of these bands in the popular music business of those years is that many sheet music covers no longer featured the photograph of a prominent stage or vaudeville star but that of a popular bandleader.

Now that records and radio were in every home, social dancing proved a form of entertainment as popular in the home as it was in public places. Naturally, the times—the raucous twenties—and the new jazz, with its emphasis on rhythm, accent and the beat —demanded new kinds of social dances, dances more frenetic than the waltz, the tango or the infinite variety of dances spawned by the one-step and fox trot that were so popular just before World War I. In the twenties, the favorite dances called for the shaking of shoulders and belly, gyrations of the body, swinging of arms, and an athletic pedal dexterity.

There was the shimmy shawobble—shimmy, for short, a ragtime dance calling for the shaking of shoulders and hips. This dance was a vulgarization of the hoochy-koochy. The

313

shimmy was believed to have originated in a Negro café in Chicago (the city that made the hoochy-koochy popular), and was brought to the Broadway musical theater in 1918, though precisely who was the initiator in New York has long been subject to controversy. Some say it was Gilda Gray, who that year performed a shimmy at the Winter Garden to the strains of "The St. Louis Blues." Some say it was Mae West, who did a shimmy in Rudolf Friml's operetta *Sometime* (1918), but who also insisted that she had performed the shimmy earlier in vaudeville. Others affirm it was Bea Palmer who did a shimmy to the song "I Want to Learn to Jazz Dance" (Gene Buck—Louis A. Hirsch). "The World Is Shimmy Mad" (Gene Buck—Dave Stamper) was a song in the *Ziegfeld Follies of 1919*. The world became increasingly shimmy mad in the early twenties. Gilda Gray tore the theater apart in the *Ziegfeld Follies of 1922* with her body convolutions to the music of "It's Getting Dark on Old Broadway" (Gene Buck—Louis A. Hirsch and Dave Stamper). Wherever there was social dancing, the shimmy could be found, with Tin Pan Alley ready and willing to provide appropriate music. People danced the shimmy to Irving Berlin's "You Cannot Make Your Shimmy Shake on Tea" (lyrics coauthored with Rennold Wolf) and to the strains of "I Wish I Could Shimmy Like My Sister Kate" (Armand J. Piron).

By the end of 1922, the shimmy was replaced by the Charleston. The Charleston made its first appearance in cabarets and was later popularized in the all black revue, *Runnin' Wild* (1923) where "Charleston" (Cecil Mack and James P. Johnson) was sung and cavorted to by Elisabeth Welch. This dance dominated the social life of young and old for the next three years. "Kids danced it on side streets and in front of theaters during the intermission for 'throw money,'" reported *Variety*. "In Boston's Pickwick Club, a tenderloin dance hall, the vibrations of Charleston dancers caused the place to collapse, killing fifty." A Charleston marathon at the Roseland Ballroom in New York in 1924 lasted almost twenty-two-and-a-half hours, its winner receiving a one-week engagement at the Rivoli Theater in New York. When people were not dancing the Charleston they were either singing or listening to the music of "Charleston Crazy" (Porter Grainger and Bob Ricketts), "Just Wait Till You See My Baby Do the Charleston Dance" (Clarence Todd, Clarence Williams and Rousseau Simmons), "I'm Gonna Charleston Back to Charleston" (Roy Turk and Lou Handman), "Charlestonette" (Fred Rose and Paul Whiteman) and "Charleston Is the Best Dance After All" (Arthur D. Porter and Charles Johnson). And when they weren't singing or hearing about the Charleston they enjoyed watching it, not only in the theaters but also on the screen. A highlight of the silent motion picture *Our Dancing Mothers* (1928), was Joan Crawford doing the Charleston.

After the Charleston came the Black Bottom, a dance that acquired its name not because one of its movements called for the slapping of the posterior, but because the sluggish foot movements suggested plodding through the mud of the black bottom of the Suwanee River. The dance was said to have been invented in 1926 by Alberta Hunter, who copyrighted it. Billy Pearce and Buddy Bradley taught it to the white clientele of a Harlem nightclub. But it did not become a national craze until Ann Pennington danced it in *George White's Scandals of 1926* to the song "Black Bottom" (De Sylva, Brown and Henderson).

There were other energetic social dances in the twenties that temporarily captured the fancy of the country—Truckin', Sugar Foot Strut, the New Low Down, the Varsity Drag —but none enjoyed the widespread vogue of the shimmy, the Charleston, and the Black Bottom.

2

As long as Americans kept on dancing there were dance orchestras to satisfy this demand. Art Hickman and Ben Selvin, performing at the St. Francis Hotel in San Francisco, are acknowledged to be among the earliest of these dance groups. Florenz Ziegfeld brought the Art Hickman band to New York to repeat its San Francisco success in the *Ziegfeld Follies of 1920* where it introduced "Hold Me" (Art Hickman and Ben Black). In 1921, Art Hickman and his band opened the new Cocoanut Grove at the Ambassador Hotel in Los Angeles. After that engagement, Hickman went into retirement, but his band continued to function for a number of years under other leaders. Toward the end of their career, Hickman and his band helped make a success of "Runnin' Wild" (Joe Grey and Leo Wood—A. Harrington Gibbs).

In New York's Broadway sector, Tin Pan Alley kept a perceptive eye out for straws in the wind. It did not fail to notice that songs like "Runnin' Wild" "Hold Me," "Dardanella" (Fred Fisher—Felix Bernard and Johnny S. Black) and "The Japanese Sandman" (Raymond Egan—Richard A. Whiting) had all been made successful by bands. Jack Robbins, one of the newcomers to music publishing after World War I, was probably the first publisher to realize how important the dance band could be to the song business. He got Paul Whiteman and his Orchestra to record for Victor. He was also responsible for promoting the early career of George Olsen and in getting Vincent Lopez to form his first band.

Olsen organized the first of several bands on the Pacific coast while he was still in college in 1917. Fanny Brice became interested in him soon after the end of World War I and induced Ziegfeld to bring him to New York where he and his band appeared in the Ziegfeld-produced musical *Kid Boots* (1923), starring Eddie Cantor. Olsen remained in New York seven years, performing in other Broadway musicals and in nightclubs. His first hit recording came in 1925 with Jerome Kern's "Who?" (Oscar Hammerstein II and Otto Harbach). In this release, Olsen used a vocal trio. Due to the huge success of this recording, vocal trios were used by rival bands, including those of Vincent Lopez and Paul Whiteman. Among other song hits associated with Olsen and his band were "Horses" (Byron Gay— Richard A. Whiting) and "Doin' the Raccoon" (Raymond Klages—J. Fred Coots). In 1930, Olsen left New York for California where for a number of years he continued leading bands.

Vincent Lopez, the son of a music teacher, at first thought of becoming a priest, but his overpowering interest in music made him change his plans. As a boy, he played the piano in beer halls, saloons and honky-tonks in Brooklyn, New York (where he was born in 1898). In 1917, he became a pianist and bandleader at the Pekin Restaurant on 47th Street and Broadway where he came to be known as "the piano kid." It was there that he introduced Felix Arndt's piano rag, "Nola," which later became his signature music.

On November 27, 1921, Vincent Lopez and his orchestra began an engagement at the Grill Room of the Hotel Pennsylvania in New York which continued for a quarter of a century. Lopez and his orchestra combined their performances at the Grill Room with one-hour-and-a-half nightly broadcasts over WJZ, the first "live" broadcast ever made by a popular band. His opening greeting of "Hello everybody, Lopez speaking" became as much a part of his radio trademark as the rippling measures of "Nola."

In the years that followed, Vincent Lopez and his orchestra also appeared at the Casa Lopez and the St. Regis Hotel. In both he became a favorite of high society, as well as of the general public. His popularity was further enhanced by appearances in vaudeville, concert halls and movie palaces. In 1925 he and his orchestra presented a concert of popular music at the Metropolitan Opera House where the program included a symphonic potpourri, "The Evolution of the Blues," featuring Lopez at the piano playing Scott Joplin's "Maple Leaf Rag" and "Nola." In addition to "Nola," Lopez promoted during his many and varied appearances and recordings Zez Confrey's piano rag, "Kitten on the Keys," an orchestral rag, "Flapperette" by Jesse Greer, and the songs "Avalon Town" (Grant Clarke—Nacio Herb Brown) and "Teasin" (Bob Carleton, J. Brandon Walsh and Paul Biese).

Lopez' long career ended in 1966 when he lost the use of both of his hands following a stroke. He tried to make a comeback some years later but was only able to make a few unsuccessful appearances as a bandleader. His last was at the River Boat in New York's Empire State Building in May 1975, just three months before his death in a nursing home.

The long string of song hits either introduced or popularized by Isham Jones and his orchestra began in 1922 with "Wabash Blues" (Dave Ringle—Fred Meinken), the recording of which (featuring Louis Panico on the trumpet) sold some two million disks. Isham Jones first became prominent in Chicago, where he had gone in 1915 to advance himself as a saxophonist. In Chicago he organized a band which played at the Green Mill, the Rainbow Gardens and the College Inn. The ensemble found a large, responsive and loyal public for its colorful orchestrations, beauty of sound and the virtuosity of its individual performers. From time to time, it was also heard in London, Miami and New York.

Himself an exceptionally gifted popular song composer, Isham Jones introduced and helped make famous many of his own creations during the twenties. The best were: "Broken Hearted Melody" (Gus Kahn), "On the Alamo," (Gus Kahn and Joe Lyons), "Indiana Moon" (Benny Davis), "I'll See You in My Dreams" (Gus Kahn), "It Had to be You" (Gus Kahn) and "The One I Love Belongs to Somebody Else" (Gus Kahn).

Though Fred Waring's performances in the 1930s were individualized through the use of a chorus in conjunction with a band, in a sort of glee club presentation, Waring had been successful a decade earlier with bands minus voices. Soon after leaving college, Waring formed a banjo group with which he launched his professional career by broadcasting over a Detroit radio station. After that he formed a more traditional dance band, calling it the Pennsylvanians, which toured the college and vaudeville circuits. and became a major attraction at the Metropolitan Theater in Hollywood, California. "I Love My Baby" (Bud Green—Harry Warren), a hit song of 1925, was introduced by Fred Waring and his Pennsylvanians. Late in the 1920s Waring's Pennsylvanians began recording for Victor, their first release being "Sleep" (Earl Lebieg), which Waring later used as his signature music. Waring extended both his influence and popularity in the thirties by becoming an institution over the radio where his programs were invariably introduced by his new theme music, "Breezin' Along with the Breeze" (Haven Gillespie, Seymour Simons and Richard A. Whiting).

During the twenties, Ben Bernie, Ted Weems, Abe Lyman, Red Nichols and Ted Fiorito were other dance band leaders who began to form their own organizations and had their first tastes of success.

Ben Bernie, "the ole Maestro," had appeared in vaudeville and worked as a violin salesman in a New York department store before he organized a band in 1922. In 1925, Bernie and his band introduced "Sweet Georgia Brown" (Ben Bernie, Maceo Pinkard and Kenneth Casey), a number which many years later, the Harlem Globetrotters, the black basketball team, used as its theme song in pre-game exhibitions. Many other songs became associated with Ben Bernie and his band during their long and active career at the Hotel Roosevelt in New York, on records, and for some two decades over the radio: " 'Deed I Do" (Walter Hirsch and Fred Rose); "Lazybones" (Johnny Mercer—Hoagy Carmichael); and of course, their opening and closing signatures over the radio. The opening signature was "It's a Lonesome Old Town When You're Not Around" (Charles Kisco—Harry Tobias); the closing one—spoken by Bernie over the played melody—"Au Revoir, Pleasant Dreams" (Jack Meskill—Jean Schwartz).

Ted Weems brought his first band into existence in 1923. Soon thereafter, he and his brother formed a new group that appeared in the Trianon Ballroom in Newark, New Jersey, and which hit full stride not only with one-night stands in ballrooms, but also over the radio and on records. The song most often recalled in connection with Ted Weems and his band belongs to the early thirties. It was "Heartaches" (John Klenner—Al Hoffman). Weems played it one night in Chicago in 1932, then recorded it. "We played it . . . with that corny sort of half-rumba rhythm and with all those effects," Weems recalled in later years. One of those effects was the whistling of Elmo Tanner. "After the broadcast, the writers and the publisher called me and . . . claimed that I was ruining their song, that we had given it the wrong interpretation. . . ." The recording did not create much of a stir so that the authors and the publisher soon forgot their grievance. But the song—and its performance by Ted Weems and his band—was reincarnated in 1947, at which time Ted Weems was long past his prime as a bandleader. That year, a disc jockey in Charlotte, North Carolina, came upon the old Weems record and played it as a novelty. His audience called in for so many replayings that disc jockeys around the country began featuring it on their programs. The old Ted Weems recording was now rereleased by Decca, selling three million copies. This success encouraged Ted Weems to resume his long interrupted career as bandleader and to issue a totally new release of "Heartaches" for Decca.

Abe Lyman introduced "I Cried for You" (Arthur Freed—Gus Arnheim and Abe Lyman) in 1923, "Mandalay" (Earl Burtnett, Gus Arnheim and Abe Lyman) in 1924, and "What Can I Say After I Say I'm Sorry?" (Walter Donaldson and Abe Lyman) in 1926. These were important steps in their ascent to national acceptance. But Abe Lyman and his band became even more intimately identified with another standard of the twenties, "Breezin' Along with the Breeze" (Haven Gillespie, Seymour Simons and Richard A. Whiting). During the twenties, Lyman and his band made significant recordings of "Bugle Call Rag" (Jack Pettis, Billy Meyers, and Elmer Schoebel) and "Everybody Stomp" (Billy Meyers—Elmer Schoebel). For their theme song, Lyman and his band used "California, Here I Come" (Al Jolson and B. G. De Sylva—Joseph Meyer).

The Five Pennies, a jazz band comprising not five but from six to ten men, was the breeding ground for some of the foremost jazz men of the twenties and thirties. Among them were Miff Mole, Jimmy Dorsey, Glenn Miller, Joe Venuti and Benny Goodman. It was organized by Red Nichols, trumpet player, the son of a Utah college music professor. Red began playing the cornet when he was four and in a year's time was already performing in public. In his early boyhood he was a member of small jazz groups. After a single year at a military academy, he played the trumpet full time with various bands, including those of George Olsen, Johnny Johnson and Sam Lanin. In New York in the mid-1920s he made numerous recordings with several of his own groups. The most outstanding was The Five Pennies, which he formed in the mid-1920s, and which made notable recordings for Brunswick. Later Red Nichols led the pit orchestras for two Gershwin musicals in 1930, *Strike Up the Band* and *Girl Crazy*. He toured the country with an enlarged band in the 1930s, besides appearing on major network radio programs. In 1959, his life story was sentimentalized in the motion picture *The Five Pennies* (discussed in Chapter 33) in which Danny Kaye appeared as Red Nichols. The success of this picture gave Red Nichols' career as a bandleader new momentum. He was performing in Las Vegas when he died of a heart attack in 1965.

Ted Fiorito formed his first dance band in St. Louis, and his second in Chicago, both in the 1920s. His first successes were realized with a few of his songs: "I Never Knew That Roses Grew" (Gus Kahn), "I'm Sorry, Sally" (Gus Kahn) and "Laugh, Clown, Laugh" (Sam M. Lewis and Joe Young). As a bandleader, Fiorito first made his mark in Chicago with the Fiorito-Russo orchestra, but after 1928 he led his own orchestra, heard in Chicago's Aragon Ballroom, from where he gained national recognition through network broadcasts. A motion picture contract brought him to California where he further extended his fame in such films as *Twenty Million Sweethearts* (1934), as well as with performances at the Los Angeles Cocoanut Grove and San Francisco's St. Francis Hotel, and on national tours.

3

Most of the big bands and the popular bandleaders of the twenties remained very much in the limelight in the thirties, though now they had to share it with many newcomers. In 1929, three gifted young bandleaders drifted to New York from the West: Glen Gray, Guy Lombardo and Leo Reisman. Glen Gray, who had once played the saxophone with Jean Goldkette, brought his orchestra from the Casa Loma Hotel in Toronto. As the Casa Loma Orchestra, with Gray as saxophonist, it enriched the music scene in New York and made records. In 1937, the group was renamed Glen Gray and The Casa Loma Orchestra. It had two theme songs: "Smoke Rings" (Ned Washington—H. Eugene Gifford), which it introduced and "Was I To Blame for Falling in Love with You." (Gus Kahn and Chester Conn—Victor Young). It made successful recordings of two other numbers: "I Cried for You" (Arthur Freed—Gus Arnheim and Abe Lyman) and "Sleepy Time Gal" (Joseph R. Alden and Raymond B. Egan—Ange Lorenzo and Richard A. Whiting). Besides offering the pop tunes of the day in intriguing arrangements, the orchestra distinguished itself for its novelty instrumentals written or arranged by the band's guitarist, Eugene Gifford.

Guy Lombardo was a native of London, Ontario, in Canada, where he was born in 1902 and where he and his two brothers played in small combos before forming their own jazz group. Lombardo came to the United States with his own band in 1923 and found an engagement at a roadhouse outside Cleveland, the Claremont. On the advice of the owner, Guy Lombardo and his band began developing its slow, sweet, soft styling emphasizing the saxes and punctuating the flow of the melody with harmonies in the other brasses. In 1927, Guy Lombardo took his band to the Granada Café in Chicago when the unit adopted the name it would henceforth bear, Guy Lombardo and His Royal Canadians. A small radio station in Chicago, WBBM, decided to put them on the air direct from the café for a fifteen-minute spot, but when the fifteen minutes were over, Lombardo received a note to keep on playing for the microphone. He played all that evening and, as he played, crowds from all over Chicago began making a beeline to the Granada. Lombardo music—which the Chicago critic, Ashley Stevens, described as "the sweetest music this side of heaven"—was now the "in" sound in Chicago. In 1929, Lombardo and His Royal Canadians went on to New York for an engagement at the Grill Room of the Roosevelt Hotel where they remained seasonally until 1962. Their broadcasts from the Grill Room, as well as their Columbia records, gave them national importance. Their New Year's Eve broadcasts became an annual ritual, climaxed by the playing of the band's theme song, "Auld Lang Syne," on the stroke of midnight. "Little White Lies" (Walter Donaldson) was written for Lombardo who introduced it, as he did another Donaldson standard, "You're Driving Me Crazy." Lombardo played this song on his radio program every night for a week, after which its success was assured. Other songs which Guy Lombardo and His Royal Canadians helped to popularize were "Cryin' for the Carolines" (Sam M. Lewis and Joe Young—Harry Warren), which was introduced in the movie *Spring Is Here* (1930); "Swingin' in a Hammock" (Tot Seymour and Charles O'Flynn—Pete Wendling); "Boo-Hoo" (Edward Heyman—Carmen Lombardo and John Jacob Loeb), adapted from Carmen Lombardo's song "Let's Drink." In his more than half a century of leading bands, Guy Lombardo has sold over 250 million records.

Leo Reisman appeared in New York in 1929 to conduct his orchestra at the Central Park Casino. From 1934 to 1947 he and his orchestra were seasonal attractions at the

Wedgewood Room of the Waldorf-Astoria Hotel. Reisman's slick performances brought a new glow to show tunes and Tin Pan Alley song hits. "Stormy Weather" (Ted Koehler —Harold Arlen)—which Leo Reisman and his orchestra recorded for Victor with the composer, Harold Arlen, doing the vocal—was one of Reisman's earliest record best-sellers. Two others were Cole Porter's "Night and Day," with Fred Astaire doing the vocal, and Vincent Youmans' "Time on My Hands" (Harold Adamson and Mack Gordon), vocal by Lee Wiley.

In the early thirties, Gus Arnheim and his band was the magnet attracting the movie colony to the Cocoanut Grove at the Ambassador Hotel in Los Angeles. Arnheim, a Chicagoan by birth, formed his first band in 1927 (after having worked as a piano accompanist for Sophie Tucker, then with Abe Lyman's band) and began his long residence at the Coconut Grove from which he broadcast nightly on a two-hour stint. When the Arnheim band engaged the Rhythm Boys as its vocal trio in 1930, it gave Bing Crosby his start as a solo vocalist with "I Surrender Dear" (Gordon Clifford—Harry Barris) and "Wrap Your Troubles in Dreams" (Ted Koehler and Bill Molly—Harry Barris). Arnheim left California for Chicago in the mid-thirties to change his style and adopt Swing.

Woody Herman's was the "band that plays the blues." Its founder, Woodrow Charles Herman, began his life in show business as a child prodigy at six, singing and tap dancing in vaudeville theaters in the area of Milwaukee where he was born. After he learned to play the saxophone and clarinet, he included performances on these instruments in an act in which he was billed as "Wisconsin's only professional juvenile." He got his first job with a jazz band—that of Myron Stewart at the Blue Heaven roadhouse outside Milwaukee—while attending St. John' Cathedral Preparatory School. After leaving school, he toured Texas with Joe Lichter's band. For one term in 1930 he studied music at Marquette University, then went back into harness by playing with Tom Gerun's band. In 1933, Herman tried forming a band of his own but failed. Never losing the ambition to form his own outfit, Woody Herman was a sideman with the bands of Harry Sosnick, Gus Arnheim and Isham Jones. When the Isham Jones band disbanded in 1936, Woody Herman took some of its key men and formed a group of his own—a cooperative venture—which made its debut at the Roseland Ballroom in Brooklyn, New York, late that year, then moved on early in 1937 to the Roseland Ballroom in New York City. Though the Herman band advertised itself as "the band that plays the blues," its repertory included pop songs and non-jazz instrumentals, but the blues was his specialty. With "Blue Prelude" (Joe Bishop and Gordon Jenkins) as its first theme song, and "Blue Flame" (Leo Corday—Jimmy Noble and Joe Bishop) as its second, and with Woody Herman's own "Blues on Parade" which he wrote with Toby Tyler, the Woody Herman band achieved recognition for its performance of the blues, not only in public performances but also in Decca recordings. In April 1939, Woody Herman and his band recorded for Decca "Woodchopper's Ball" (Woody Herman and Joe Bishop), which sold a million disks and put the final stamp on Woody Herman and his band as a top jazz outfit in appearances at leading night spots (Meadowbrook Ballroom and the Glen Island Casino), hotels (Hotel Sherman in Chicago and the New Yorker), and on 52nd Street (the Famous Door).

Cab (Cabwell) Calloway, the "hi-de-hi" and "ho-de-ho" showman and scat singer soared to national prominence on wings of the song "Minnie the Moocher" (Cab Calloway, Irving Mills and Clarence Gaskill), which he introduced with his own band at the Cotton Club in 1931 and recorded that year for Perfect. Born in Rochester, New York, and raised in Baltimore, Calloway began his musical career in Chicago in the 1920s as a drummer, and master of ceremonies at local clubs. In Chicago in 1928, he became the head of a band, The Alabamians, which played at the Merry Gardens and for which he did the vocals. He brought the Alabamians to the Savoy in New York in October 1929, the year when he also made his debut in the Broadway theater in the revue *Hot Chocolates*. A year later, Calloway took over the Missourians which did some recording for Victor. In 1930 the band assumed its leader's name, found a booking at the Cotton Club, and grew famous with "Minnie the Moocher." Cab Calloway and his band continued to hold the spotlight in nightclubs, over radio and in stage shows until about 1948. As a star in his own right, Cab Calloway made his motion picture debut in *The Big Broadcast* (1932). He was subsequently seen in *The Singing Kid* (1936) where he introduced "Keep that Hi-De-Ho in Your Soul" (Irving Mills and Cab Calloway), *Stormy Weather* (1943), *Sensations of 1945* and as Sportin' Life in *Porgy and Bess* (1959). In 1967 he was one of the stars in the all-black production of *Hello, Dolly!* on Broadway. He told the story of his career in *Of Minnie the Moocher and Me* (1976) written in collaboration with Bryant Rollins.

The sounds of the great bands of the thirties also included those of Eddie Duchin, who had formerly played the piano for three years with Leo Reisman and his orchestra at the Central Park Casino. Duchin took over that ensemble in 1931. His performances emphasized his brilliant pianism, as in "My Twilight Dream" (Lew Sherwood and Eddie Duchin), adapted from Chopin's Nocturne in E-flat major, which he introduced and made his theme song.

Other bandleaders, other sounds. . . . Shep Fields became famous for his "rippling rhythms" and Freddy Noble's arrangements. Wayne King was "the waltz king"—his theme song, "The Waltz You Saved for Me" (Gus Kahn—Emil Flindt and Wayne King). Les Brown and his "band of renown," founded in 1938 and featured at the Arcadia Ballroom in New York; his theme songs, "Leap Frog" (Leo Corday—Joe Garland) and "Sentimental Journey" (Bud Green, Les Brown and Ben Homer). Jan Garber was called the "idol of the airwaves." Larry Clinton became popular at the Glen Island Casino in New Rochelle overlooking Long Island Sound in 1938, the year in which he introduced and popularized his own "My Reverie," adapted from a Debussy art song; Clinton's theme song was his "Dipsy Doodle," a nonsense song he had written in 1937 when he worked as an arranger for Tommy Dorsey. Russ Morgan ("the wah-wah trombonist") provided music "in the Morgan manner," his theme song, "Does Your Heart Beat for Me?" (Mitchell Parish—Russ Morgan and Arnold Johnson). Kay Kyser became the dean of radio's Kollege of Musical Knowledge—his theme song, "Thinking of You" (Walter Donaldson and Paul Ash) and one of his big song successes, "Three Little Fishies" (Saxie Dowell). Lawrence Welk offered his "champagne music" at the St. Paul Hotel in Minnesota and over KTSP in that city—his theme, his own "Bubbles in the Wine."

And then, of course, there were the fabulous Dorseys—Jimmy and his younger (by one year) brother, Tommy. Together or separately they enriched the sounds of their own bands with their incomparable styling, with Jimmy on the alto sax and clarinet and Tommy on trombone. They came from Shenendoah, where their father, a music teacher and the leader of a brass band, gave them their first music lessons. Jimmy was at first instructed in the playing of the tenor sax, then the alto sax. He later mastered the clarinet without formal lessons. Tommy learned to play the trumpet before he went on to the trombone. The two brothers played with various bands and orchestras in the 1920s including those of Jean Goldkette, Paul Whiteman and Red Nichols. Then they formed two bands, "Dorsey's Novelty Six" and "Dorsey's Wild Canaries," the first broadcasting over Baltimore's earliest radio station. They each worked extensively over the radio, and with various groups on records, achieving considerable renown on their respective instruments. In 1932, with a pickup band, the Dorsey brothers recorded "I'm Gettin' Sentimental Over You" (Ned Washington—George Bassman), which Tommy made his theme song after 1935. The Dorseys formed a band of their own in 1934, comprising eleven men. Its official bow took place at the Sands Beach Club in Los Angeles that summer. Glenn Miller was Tommy's partner on the trombone as well as principal arranger. In *The Big Bands*, George Simon describes how, on first hearing the Dorsey brothers band in 1934, he "stood transfixed in front of the bandstand . . . listening to a band we'd never heard of before and the likes of which we hadn't known until then even existed . . . one of the slickest, most exciting musical aggregations ever to enter our musical lives." The Dorsey brothers band then made some records for Decca, appeared at Ben Marden's Riviera in New Jersey and at the Palais Royal nightclub in New York on May 15, 1935, and then began an engagement at the Glen Island Casino. Bob Crosby was initially the vocalist, but when he left in the summer of 1935 he was replaced by Bob Eberly.

As virtuosos they had their musical differences, as Richard Gehman noted in *The Saturday Review*. "Jimmy was the more ambitious . . . [and] the more agile of the two, musically speaking; he worked his way in and out of choruses like a young pickpocket dodging cops in a crowd. Tommy just seemed to walk down the street, the boss of everyone and everything. Jimmy was the more experimental; Tommy was smoother. Together . . . they made a super combination."

As personalities they were also opposites. Bespectacled Tommy looked like a schoolmaster; Jimmy resembeled a model for a collar ad. Tommy was hyperthyroid, while Jimmy was relaxed. Tommy was aggressive and outgoing, Jimmy was shy. Tommy's metallic hardness of personality and spirit contrasted with Jimmy's gentleness and softness. Tommy was combustible, Jimmy was placid. Their contrasting natures, combined with sibling rivalry, made an explosion inevitable, especially when alcohol provided the ignition. The differences between them grew so sharp that one night, at the Glen Island Casino, they had a fist fight in full view of their audience. Sometime later Jimmy criticized Tommy's tempo in "I'll Never Say 'Never Again' Again" (Harry Woods). Tommy looked at his brother icily, put his trombone under his arm, and walked off the stage.

For a time there was no reconciliation. Each brother went his own way. Jimmy continued to lead the band Tommy had deserted. Often (with Bob Eberly and Helen O'Connell providing vocals) the Jimmy Dorsey outfit achieved additional fame in the late 1930s and early 1940s with performances of "Amapola" (Albert Gamse—Joseph M. Lacalle); "Green Eyes," a Cuban song (E. Rivera and Eddie Woods—Nilo Menendez); "Maria Elena," a Mexican song by Lorenzo Barcelata with English lyrics by S. K. Russell; "So Rare" (Jack Sharpe—Jerry Herst); "Tangerine" (Johnny Mercer—Victor Schertzinger); and the band's theme song, "Contrasts" (Jimmy Dorsey).

Tommy Dorsey formed his own band in 1935 with Bunny Berigan and Pee Wee Erwin (trumpets), Bud Freeman (tenor sax), Johnny Mince (clarinet) and David Tough (drums). Though Jimmy Dorsey's band proved more popular, Tommy's was musically the more spectacular. Indeed, George T. Simon went so far as to maintain that "in retrospect —and in band history—Tommy Dorsey's must be recognized as the greatest all-round dance band of them all. Others may have sounded more creative. Others may have swung harder and more consistently. Others may have developed more distinctive styles. But of all the hundreds of well-known bands, Tommy Dorsey's could do more things better than any other could." Tommy maintained his band at the highest possible artistic level even when personnel changes were made. The later members of his group included Ziggy Elman (trumpet),

Buddy De Franco (clarinet), Buddy Rich (drums). The arranger, initially, was Dean Kin-caide, but he made way for Sy Oliver. The vocalists, from time to time, were Jo Stafford, the Pied Pipers and Frank Sinatra in his professional debut.

The Tommy Dorsey band was unique in the way it sustained moods in ballads, supported by Tommy's warm and sensuous trombone. It was at its best in "I'm Gettin' Sentimental Over You," Irving Berlin's "Marie," "I'll Never Smile Again" (Ruth Lowe) with vocal by Frank Sinatra and the Pied Pipers, "There Are Such Things" (Abel Baer and Stanley Adams—George W. Meyer). But the Tommy Dorsey band was also able to "swing"—as in the numbers Sy Oliver wrote for it ("Swing High," "Singin' on Nothing' " and "Opus No. 1"). But even in Swing, the Tommy Dorsey style was comparatively subdued, a fact that earned him the sobriquet "the sentimental gentleman of Swing."

In 1939, the Jimmy Dorsey band completed an engagement at the New Yorker Hotel with Tommy Dorsey's band beginning one that same night. It was an occasion that brought the feuding brothers together again. A touching reconciliation took place in front of the audience. But not until 1953 (eighteen years after their artistic split) did they combine forces to form another band, the Dorsey Brothers Orchestra. But the hour was too late for making additional jazz history. The day of the big bands was over. Besides, the hours for both men were numbered, young though they still were. Tommy, aged fifty-one, choked to death in his sleep on November 26, 1956. Six months later, on June 12, 1957, Jimmy succumbed to cancer.

4

Tommy Dorsey's was not the only band to start "swinging" in the latter half of the 1950s. Many other sweet bands followed suit, while numerous new ensembles made Swing their specialty. For Swing became the "thing" in jazz on the evening of August 21, 1935, at the Palomar Ballroom in Los Angeles. Benny Goodman was appearing there with his band in stock dance numbers ("society music" it was called) which left audiences apathetic. Disgusted, Goodman decided to fail, if fail he must, in his own way. He and his clarinet, backed by his band, struck up "King Porter Stomp," and some other Fletcher Henderson Swing arrangements. The youngsters in the audience went wild. That roar, Goodman later recalled, "was one of the sweetest sounds I have ever heard." For the rest of his engagement, Goodman emphasized his Swing repertory. This music was carried to the rest of the country by radio. By the time Benny Goodman's engagement at the Palomar ended, Swing was the new sound that jazz enthusiasts were raving about.

Neither the word "Swing," nor the style were basically new when they attracted national interest at the Palomar. Jazz musicians had often used the term to designate improvisations of melodic rhythm. In 1932, Duke Ellington wrote a song, "It Don't Mean a Thing" (Irving Mills).

As a style, Swing was a variation of New Orleans improvisation with this difference: group-notated improvisation usurped the prominent role once occupied by solo improvisation, with the melodic line retaining a definite and clearly enunciated beat while the harmony tended toward discords. Some of the performances of the Fletcher Henderson orchestra in New York in the 1920s, and many of his subsequent arrangements, had a Swing character. But it was Benny Goodman, in Los Angeles, who first brought Swing to the forefront of national consciousness. And it was Benny Goodman who was the commanding figure in Swing music.

When Benny Goodman was ten, in his native city of Chicago where he was born in 1909, his father, a tailor, overheard a boy's band playing in a synagogue. On investigation he discovered that music lessons could be had on borrowed instruments for twenty-five cents a lesson. He shepherded four of his sons to the synagogue to have them begin studying music. Benny because he was the smallest and skinniest of the four, was assigned the instrument commensurate to his size and weight, the clarinet. Within a year Goodman had a clarinet of his own, purchased from a mail-order house, and was receiving classical training from Franz Schoepp. When he was twelve, Goodman began copying Ted Lewis' jazz-clarinet playing by listening to his records. That same year he won five dollars playing a jazz number on the clarinet at an amateur night in vaudeville. That was the first money his clarinet earned for him, and without further ado, Goodman began to contribute to the finances of his family by playing the clarinet professionally.

When he was fourteen, Goodman had a regular job playing with a band at Guion's Parade, a dance hall. One year later, he appeared with orchestras at Midway Gardens and Friar's Inn Society. In 1925 he was hired by Ben Pollack for his orchestra and went with it to the Venice Ballroom in Los Angeles. Back in Chicago with the Pollack orchestra, Goodman made his first recording, "He's the Last Word" (Gus Kahn—Walter Donaldson). Goodman left Pollack in 1929 after a quarrel and went on his own as a free-lance musician in New York. He was in Red Nichols' pit orchestra for the musical *Girl Crazy* in 1930, and that same year, on May 21, made two notable Victor records, Hoagy Carmichael's "Rockin' Chair" and "Barnacle Bill the Sailor" (Carson Robinson and Frank Luther), with a jazz group organized by Hoagy Carmichael that included the Dorsey brothers, Bix Beiderbecke, "Bubber" Miley, Joe Venuti, Gene Krupa and others. Later the same year, Benny Goodman pressed three more sides at Victor with Bix Beiderbecke and other jazz greats. By 1934, Goodman had become a bandleader, with an engagement at the Billy Rose Music Hall, and soon after was sponsored by the National Biscuit Company on a three-hour Saturday night program over NBC, "Let's Dance" (which he shared with Xavier Cugat).

In 1935, Gene Krupa joined the Benny Goodman band and remained with it for three years when he left to form his own jazz band. Krupa—who transformed the jazz band drummer from a time beater to a virtuoso—was reared in Chicago jazz where he had played with local jazz groups and made his first recording on December 9, 1927, with the McKenzie-Condon Chicagoans. Later he worked with Red Nichols, Russ Columbo and Irving Aaronson. He was a member of Buddy Rogers' band when Goodman sent for him. "From the time he joined us," Goodman has said, "Gene gave the band a solidity and firmness as far as rhythm was concerned that it never had before." The Benny Goodman best-selling recording of "Sing, Sing, Sing" (Louis Prima) in 1936 highlighted Krupa in the first extended jazz drum solo in jazz history. Krupa was also a member of the Benny Goodman Trio (with Goodman and the pianist Teddy Wilson), and the Benny Goodman Quartet (with the addition of Lionel Hampton, vibraharpist). Both groups made important recordings: the Trio, in 1935–1936, "More Than You Know" (Billy Rose and Edward Eliscu—Vincent Youmans), Jerome Kern's "Who?" (Oscar Hammerstein II and Otto Harbach), "Nobody's Sweetheart" (Gus Kahn, Ernie Erdman, Billy Meyers and Elmer Schoebel), "Body and Soul" (Edward Heyman, Robert Sour and Frank Eyton—John Green), and "After You've Gone" (Henry Creamer—Turner Layton); the Quartet in 1937–1938, "Dinah" (Sam M. Lewis and Joe Young—Harry Akst), "Sweet Sue" (Will J. Harris—Victor Young), George Gershwin's " 'S Wonderful" and "The Man I Love" (Ira Gershwin), "Sweet Georgia Brown" (Ben Bernie, Maceo Pinkard and Kenneth Casey) and "My Melancholy Baby" (George A. Norton—Ernie Burnett).

Following his sensational appearance at the Palomar Ballroom, Benny Goodman took his band to the Congress Hotel in Chicago, an engagement planned for three weeks but extended to eight months. It was there that Goodman's hot music was finally labeled "Swing". In an advertisement announcing this engagement, and in a report in *Time* magazine that followed, Goodman was spoken of as "the king of Swing." The Congress Hotel engagement ended on April 28, and that summer Benny Goodman appeared in his first motion picture, *The Big Broadcast of 1937*, where he was heard with his band performing "Bugle Call Rag" (Jack Pettis, Billy Meyers and Elmer Schoebel) and "Cross Patch" (Leo Robin—Ralph Rainger), besides backing up some of the stars in one or two other numbers. In October he and his band (which now included Harry James and Ziggy Elman on the trumpets) opened in the Manhattan Room of the Pennsylvania Hotel in New York. An appearance that same year at the Paramount Theater in New York had Swing fans lining up practically at dawn to try to gain admission, and once Benny Goodman and his band started playing, hysteria reigned. This was followed by a concert in Carnegie Hall on January 16, 1937—the first time that Swing invaded those hallowed musical halls, a performance that was recorded live and has become a collector's item—and another regular sponsored program over NBC.

Goodman used "Let's Dance" (Fanny Baldridge—Joseph Bonine and Gregory Stone) as his theme, which he recorded for Columbia. Other Goodman favorites of the thirties were "Goody Goody" (Johnny Mercer—Matt Malneck), "And the Angels Sing" (Johnny Mercer—Ziggy Elman), "China Boy" (Dick Winfree and Phil Boutelje), "Goodbye" (Gordon Jenkins) which Goodman used as a signature music over the radio, "Honeysuckle Rose" (Andy Razaf—Thomas "Fats" Waller), "Memories of You" (Andy Razaf—Eubie Blake), "Sugar Foot Stomp" (Walter Melrose—Joe "King" Oliver), "Sometimes I'm Happy" (Leo Robin and Clifford Grey—Vincent Youmans) and "Blue Skies" (Irving Berlin).

In *The Saturday Evening Post*, Frank Norris described Benny Goodman's Swing sound as follows: "His chief characteristics are definition and power, the rhythm instruments—piano, drums and bass—sound and sure, solidly thumping out the time, while the melody, carried by the concerted brasses and reeds, pulses just a fraction ahead to give the urgent off-beat, the brasses a fine strong burr and the reeds swirling with improvisations on the tune. And then, Goodman's clarinet, clear and unhurried and artful, playing a song that was never written and may never be heard again."

In 1938, the growing passion for Swing brought an audience of over twenty-five thousand to a seven-hour concert by twenty-six bands at Randall's Island, in New York. New Swing bands were being organized all the time. In 1939, Harry James left the Goodman band to form a Swing group of his own. It opened at the Benjamin Franklin Hotel in Philadelphia on February 9. James and his band then cut a few records, one of which was "Ciribiribin," an Italian popular song by Albert Pestalozza, adapted by Harry James, with English lyrics by Jack Lawrence, which became a best seller on the Columbia label and was adopted by James as his band's theme song. In the early 1940s, the James band added to their prestige with the success of "I Had the Craziest Dream" (Mack Gordon—Harry Warren), which James and his band had introduced in the motion picture, *Springtime in the Rockies* (1942) and "I've Heard that Song Before" (Sammy Cahn—Jule Styne), which James and his band recorded for Columbia with vocal by Helen Forrest.

Charlie Barnet, who had been a member of Duke Ellington's orchestra, and had formed a band of his own which was heard at the Glen Island Casino during the summer of 1936 and 1937, became Swing conscious in 1939 with his successful recording of "Cherokee" (Ray Noble), which then became his band's theme song.

Count Basie, the "jump king" and his band came to the Famous Door, a small night spot on 52nd Street, in New York, in July 1938, his beginning as a master of Swing. As Louis

Prima told Arnold Shaw (quoted in Shaw's book *The Street that Never Slept*), "he was a resounding smash from the moment he struck the first opening chords on the piano. . . . There was no band that played with the coordination and precision of Basie's. Those guys didn't just play together. They used to breathe together. That's what gave the band its fantastic punch, no matter how softly they played."

Count Basie, or William Basey more formally, was born in Red Bank, New Jersey, in 1906, where he first learned to play the drums before concentrating on the piano. In his early teens he came to New York's Harlem, where he participated in jazz performances at rent parties and "breakfast dances." In 1926 he moved on to Kansas City, Missouri. As pianist and organist in a movie theater, the dignity of his bearing and manner earned him the sobriquet which clung to him from then on, "Count." For six months he was a member of a jazz band, The Blue Devils, that toured the Midwest and Southwest. Then he played the piano and did the arrangements of Bennie Moten's band, probably the most famous black jazz group in the Midwest. In 1935, Basie formed a distinguished jazz ensemble of his own, which played at "breakfast dances," initiated by Basie in Kansas City, and over radio station WHB in that city. Benny Goodman became interested in this group, and through his influence they obtained an engagement at the Ritz Carlton in Boston. After that came the 1938 appearance at the Famous Door on 52nd Street and at the Paramount Theater in New York. From then on Count Basie's band became a topflight jazz ensemble, in demand in dance halls, hotels, theaters, colleges, on records, over radio and, in the early 1940s, in the movies. Prominent on its program were Basie's own swing instrumentals: "One O'Clock Jump," which he used as his theme, "Every Tub," "Jumpin' at the Woodside," "Good Morning Blues" (written with Ed Durham and James Rushing), "John's Idea" (with Ed Durham), "Swingin' the Blues" (with Ed Durham) and "Baby Don't Tell on Me" (with Lester Young and James Rushing). Among Count Basie's best-selling records in the thirties were "One O'Clock Jump" and "Do You Wanna Jump, Children?" (Al Donahue, James Van Heusen, Willie Bryant and Victor Selsman), the latter with vocal by Jimmy Rushing.

Jimmie Lunceford's Swing band was notable for the quality of its brass and the dynamism of its rhythm section. While teaching at Manassa High School in Memphis, Tennessee, in the late 1920s, Lunceford formed his first band, which played during the summers in Lakeside, Ohio, and broadcast over WREC in that city. From January 1934 on, it found a spot at the Cotton Club. At that time it made some records, one of which, "Jazznocracy" (Will Hudson), became its theme song. With Sy Oliver as principal arranger, the band grew increasingly popular. On November 19, 1940, at a mammoth concert of Swing music at the Manhattan Center in New York in which twenty-eight bands participated in fifteen-minute sequences, Jimmie Lunceford's boys stole the show, even though other participants included Benny Goodman, Glen Miller and Count Basie.

Artie Shaw formed his first band in 1936. After that he changed his personnel almost as frequently as he did wives, forming new ensembles in 1936, 1940, 1941, 1942, 1943, 1949 and 1953. His quixotic temperament and erratic ways, his high-strung nature that brought on more than one physical collapse, were largely responsible for the dispatch with which he dropped bands and built up new ones. But his musical inquisitiveness, his perpetual search for new and different sounds, was also a prime culprit, a search that made him now emphasize strings and now to discard them; now to stress the drums; even to introduce into his group such an esoteric instrument as the harpsichord; to plan (though never to realize) an ensemble of fifty-two musicians.

Shaw was doing free-lance work as a clarinetist on records and over the radio in New York when, in 1936, he was invited to form a group of his own for a Swing Concert at the

Imperial Theater. There he made such a good impression that he decided to form a permanent Swing unit of his own which included strings. It was heard at the Lexington Hotel during the summer of 1936, featuring Tony Pastor on the sax, Lee Castle on the trumpet, and Shaw on clarinet. A year later, Shaw reorganized the band, omitting the strings; its debut took place in Boston in April 1937. Fame came that year with a recording of Cole Porter's "Begin the Beguine" for Bluebird, a subsidiary of Victor. Recording that number had been an afterthought. "Begin the Beguine" had been introduced in the musical *Jubilee* in 1935 and by 1938 few remembered it. Artie Shaw and his arranger, Jerry Gray, had not forgotten it. In their first session for Bluebird, Artie Shaw and his band needed a number for the flip side of a Swing version of Rudolf Friml's "Indian Love Call" (Otto Harbach and Oscar Hammerstein II), this being regarded as their big number. They decided on "Begin the Beguine" because, as Shaw disclosed, they felt it "would make at least a nice quiet contrast to 'Indian Love Call.' " But it was "Begin the Beguine" in Jerry Gray's arrangement that sent the record to a two-million disk sale, one of the largest selling instrumentals of any American band up to then. That record helped to make "Begin the Beguine" one of Cole Porter's best-known songs, and it was, as Shaw himself conceded, "the real turning point of my life."

During the next two years Artie Shaw made more memorable recordings, particularly "Any Old Time" (Jimmie Rodgers) with vocal by Billie Holiday; "Back Bay Shuffle" (Teddy McRae and Artie Shaw); "Non-Stop Flight" (Artie Shaw); and Artie Shaw's theme song, "Nightmare" (Artie Shaw). In 1940, his recordings of Hoagy Carmichael's "Star Dust" (Mitchell Parish) and in 1941, that of "Frenesi," a Mexican song by Alberto Dominguez with English lyrics by Ray Charles and S. K. Russell, each sold about two million disks.

Of the newer Swing bands, the one that challenged the fabulous popularity of Benny Goodman most seriously was that of Glenn Miller. His sound—the way his band used the reeds, and the way the clarinet soared over the saxes—charmed and romanticized the late 1930s in such Glenn Miller unforgettables as his theme, "Moonlight Serenade" (Mitchell Parish—Glenn Miller), "In the Mood" (Andy Razaf—Joe Garland), "Chattanooga Choo Choo" (Mack Gordon—Harry Warren), and that Septimus Winner hit song of 1896 which Glenn Miller revived so successfully in Bill Finegan's Swing adaptation, "The Little Brown Jug."

Before forming his own band, Miller had achieved distinction both as a trombonist and as an arranger. He played in Ben Pollack's orchestra in 1926 and in the pit of several Broadway musicals in the early 1930s, before joining the Dorsey Brothers band as trombonist and arranger in the spring of 1934. After leaving the Dorseys, Miller worked for Ray Noble and Glen Gray. Early in 1937 he decided to organize his own combo, with which he made some Decca recordings, including the Glenn Miller arrangements of "Peg o' My Heart" (Alfred Bryan—Fred Fisher), "How Am I to Know?" (Dorothy Parker—Jack King) and "Moonlight Bay" (Edward Madden—Percy Wenrich). He also appeared with his band in the Blue Room of the Roosevelt Hotel in New Orleans and at the Raymore Ballroom in Boston from which he made his first coast-to-coast radio broadcasts. Internal strife and personal misfortunes seemed to spell doom for Glenn Miller's career as bandleader at this time. In January 1938 his group was disbanded. Two months later, however, he formed a new and better ensemble, retaining only four men from his earlier band, and engaging Ray Eberle and Marion Hutton as vocalists. This new outfit was heard in ballrooms around the Boston area and during the summer of 1939 at the Paradise Island in New York, before capturing the prized assignment of appearing at the Glen Island Casino in New Rochelle. The band also started making important recordings for Bluebird, including its theme, "Moonlight

Serenade," which was coupled with Frankie Carle's theme, "Sunrise Serenade" (Jack Lawrence—Frankie Carle).

Miller wrote the melody of "Moonlight Serenade" while he was still working for Ray Noble; it was for Miller an exercise in composition when he was studying with Joseph Schillinger. Edward Heyman wrote some lyrics for the melody entitled "Now I Lay Me Down to Weep." When Glenn Miller decided to use his composition as his band's theme he sought new words for it, regarding those of Heyman too lugubrious. George T. Simon provided him with "Gone with the Dawn" but this, too, Miller found unsuitable. Finally, Mitchell Parish's lyrics, "Moonlight Serenade," struck the proper note and was accepted.

That other Glenn Miller standby, "In the Mood," had originally been intended as an eight-minute instrumental for Artie Shaw, who performed it frequently. But it was too long a piece for one side of a record and Shaw finally relinquished it. Its composer, Joe Garland, now brought it to Glenn Miller who adapted it into a four-minute item which, from the time of Miller's first recording, became a fixture in his repertory.

The fame of the Glenn Miller band was soaring all the time. It became one of the most sought after and highest paid jazz ensembles in Swing music—over the radio, on records, in public appearances and in the movies. It was at the peak of its fame when, in 1942, during World War II, Glenn Miller volunteered for Army service. As captain, he organized an all-star, all-service band that toured the United States and played over the radio in coast-to-coast broadcasts. As major, Miller formed several ensembles in England which were heard in service camps and over the air. He was en route in a single engine aircraft from Bedford, England, to Paris, on December 14, 1944, to make arrangements for his band's appearance there, when his plane disappeared and was never accounted for.

Glenn Miller was pronounced "officially dead," but his band carried on, performing in Paris in 1945 under the direction of Jerry Gray and Ray McKinley. After the war, several bands were organized imitating the Glenn Miller sound and carrying on the Glenn Miller traditions, one of which was fronted by Tex Beneke who had played tenor sax in Miller's band. In 1956, a new Glenn Miller band was organized, with the approval of the Glenn Miller estate, fronted by Ray McKinley. Meanwhile, in 1954, Universal released *The Glenn Miller Story*, in which James Stewart played Miller; on the sound track the Glenn Miller orchestra was heard in such Miller favorites as "Moonlight Serenade," "Little Brown Jug," "In the Mood," and "Tuxedo Junction" (Buddy Feyne—Erskine Hawkins, William Johnson and Julian Dash). The trombone playing of James Stewart, as Glenn Miller, was dubbed on the sound track by Joe Yukl. Since 1972 two books on Glenn Miller have appeared: in 1972, *Moonlight Serenade: A Bio-Discography of the Glenn Miller Civilian Band* by John Flower; in 1974, a definitive biography, *Glenn Miller*, by George Simon.

5

The era of the great dance bands was significant not only for instrumental sounds but also for the human voice. "Vocals by————" became a vital adjunct of dance band music. Some of the greatest singers in popular music history were alumnae of the dance bands of the thirties. They were all young, unknown and comparatively inexperienced when they started their singing careers with dance bands; they emerged as solo vocalists who have left their mark on American popular music as indelibly as the trumpets of Bix Beiderbecke and Louis Armstrong, the clarinets of Benny Goodman and Glenn Miller, the trombone of Tommy Dorsey, the piano of Count Basie, the drums of Gene Krupa.

Mildred Bailey was the first woman to find permanent employment as a vocalist with a dance band. She was also the first white singer to win acclaim as a jazz singer. "Mildred was an audience spellbinder," wrote Barry Ulanov in A *History of Jazz in America*, "with her exquisite phrasing, the intrinsic loveliness of her voice, and her rocking beat." She was born Mildred Rinker in 1901, in Tekoa, Washington, one of four children, all of whom were musical, and one, Al Rinker, became one of the Rhythm Boys with the Paul Whiteman Orchestra. She sang from childhood on, her inspiration being the great blues singers of the twenties, Bessie Smith and Ethel Waters. After making her first recording as a vocalist with Eddie Lang's Orchestra on October 5, 1929, she toured the West Coast with the Fanchon and Marco revue, and then began singing solo over the radio. On January 12, 1931, in Chicago, she recorded for Vocalion "Trav'lin All Alone" (J. C. Johnson) with Jimmie Noone's Apex Club Orchestra, and the following September, for Brunswick, four sides with the Casa Loma Orchestra: "You Call It Madness" (Gladys Du Bois, Paul Gregory, Con Conrad and Russ Columbo) together with "Blues in My Heart" (Benny Carter and Irving Mills), "When It's Sleepy Time Down South" (Leon René, Otis René and Clarence Muse) and "Wrap Your Troubles in Dreams" (Ted Koehler and Billy Moll—Harry Barris). That same year, 1931, she sent a demonstration record of her singing to Paul Whitman, who was so taken with it that he engaged her as a vocalist, even though no dance band or orchestra had up to now employed a female vocalist. Her first recordings with Paul Whiteman and his Orchestra, made between October and December 1931, included "When It's Sleepy Time Down South," "Georgia on My Mind" (Stuart Gorrell—Hoagy Carmichael), "All of Me" (Seymour Simons and Gerald Marks). "Georgia on My Mind" became one of her strongest numbers as was Hoagy Carmichael's "Rockin' Chair," which she introduced and made her theme song.

In 1933 she married Red Norvo, the brilliant jazz performer on the xylophone and vibraphone who was also a Whiteman musician, but who was then planning to form his own band. Mildred Bailey left the Whiteman orchestra to become the vocalist of her husband's band; the two of them soon came to be known as "Mr. and Mrs. Swing." She kept on making records with some of the best jazz musicians right through the 1940s—with Bunny Berigan, Ted Wilson, Ziggy Elman, Artie Shaw, Johnny Hodges and others—as well as with the Norvo band: "It's So Peaceful in the Country" (Alec Wilder), with the Delta Rhythm Boys; "More than You Know" (Billy Rose and Edward Eliscu—Vincent Youmans); "Squeeze Me" (Thomas "Fats" Waller and Clarence Williams); "There'll Be Some Changes Made" (Billy Higgins and W. B. Overstreet); "Don't Take Your Love from Me" (Henry Nemo); "Please Be Kind" (Sammy Cahn—Saul Chaplin); "Blame It On My Last Affair" (Henry Nemo and Irving Mills). In 1944, 1945 and 1946 she received the Esquire Award as leading female vocalist, and in the mid-1940s she had a radio show of her own over CBS. A *Mildred Bailey Serenade*, an LP issued in 1950, the year when she was hospitalized with her last, fatal illness, provided testimony to the vast and unique scope of her interpretative gifts. She died about a year later.

Billie Holiday was a vocalist with the Count Basie Band in 1937, and with Artie Shaw's in 1938; but a few years before that she made some random recordings with the bands of Benny Goodman and Teddy Wilson. She was adulated in her lifetime by perceptive jazz fans keen enough to recognize that she was something special and unique. Those who heard her in person have never forgotten that experience. Those who know her solely through her records have come to realize that the superlatives heaped upon her were not overstatements.

She was called a blues singer, one of the greatest of all time. But she did not sing the traditional blues but rather conveyed the spirit and feeling of the blues to the popular song repertory. She used her voice as if it were a brass instrument, pouring out her small, cool tones the way Louis Armstrong did with his horn. She would improvise on a given melody; she would concentrate on rhythmic subtleties by anticipating a beat or following it, or floating over it with a sure instinct for timing; she would mold and shape her phrases the way the great jazz men of New Orleans and Chicago used to do. She would give the words of a song the same fastidious attention to phrasing and detail that she gave to the melody, the better to bring out their dramatic or emotional content, endowing them with intense emotion.

She was best in those songs reflecting her personal agonies, rages, phobias, bitternesses, frustrations. Those she herself wrote were autobiographical: "Fine and Mellow," "God Bless the Child," "Don't Explain" and "Billie's Blues." Other songs (some written for her and introduced by her; most of them standards in the pop repertory) touched upon experiences she had undergone. For her, the songs she sang were all adventures of the heart. In her autobiography, *Lady Sings the Blues*, she said: "If you find a tune and it's got something to do with you, you don't have to evolve anything. You feel it, and when you sing it other people can feel something, too. Give me a song I can feel, and it's never work. There are a few songs I feel so much I can't stand to sing them, but that's something else again." Singing such songs revealed her innermost feelings about things that affected her deeply: in "Strange Fruit" (Lewis Allen), "Lover Man" (Jimmy Davis, Roger "Ram" Ramirez and Jimmy Sherman), "Trav'lin' Light" (Johnny Mercer—Jimmy Mundy and Trummy Young), "Deep Song" (Douglass Cross—George Cory), "Crazy, He Calls Me" (Bob Russell—Carl Sigman), "When a Woman Loves a Man" (Johnny Mercer—Bernard Hanighen and Gordon Jenkins), "Them There Eyes" (Maceo Pinkard, William Tracey and Doris Tauber), "Good Morning Heartache" (Irene Higginbotham, Ervin Drake and Dan Fisher), Gershwin's "The Man I Love" (Ira Gershwin), John Green's "Body and Soul" (Edward Heyman, Robert Sour and Frank Eyton), Sigmund Romberg's "Lover Come Back to Me" (Oscar Hammerstein II), Cole Porter's "Night and Day", Jerome Kern's "Why Was I Born?" (Oscar Hammerstein II) as well as his "Yesterdays" (Otto Harbach), "Gloomy Sunday" (Sam M. Lewis—Rezső Seress), "All of Me" (Seymour Simons—Gerald Marks), "Mean to Me" (Roy Turk—Fred E. Ahlert), "I Cried for You" (Arthur Freed—Gus Arnheim and Abe Lyman) and so many others.

Billie Holiday knew the insecurity of having been the illegitimate child of a thirteen-year-old mother and a fifteen-year-old father who deserted his family. She knew the indignity of hunger and life in a slum. At ten she was the victim of an attempted rape which—in the strange ways things worked out for blacks—landed her, and not her assailant, in jail. She was in prison several times after that, suffering the humiliations, degradations and brutality of life behind bars. She experienced the horrors of prostitution and drug addiction. To the end of her days she was hounded (sometimes justifiably, and sometimes without cause) by the law. She was victimized by ruthless race persecution and more than once betrayed by friends. Her affairs with men more often brought pain than ecstasy. These experiences left her with a crippling inferiority and self-doubts, that made it impossible for her to believe that she was endowed with special gifts not granted to many popular singers. Songs touching on any of her deep-rooted hurts made her a performer whose art could neither be emulated nor imitated because it sprang from the profoundest depths of her being.

When she appeared in the lowly dives and night spots of Harlem to start her singing career, her fellow employees derisively referred to her as "lady," because she refused to perform those vulgar gymnastics with parts of the anatomy by which performers would snatch money left on the edge of tables as tips. But it was not long before the term "lady" was being used respectfully, a tribute to the way she moved, the way she conducted herself, the way she behaved as a performer. She was a true lady from the top of her head, which she always adorned with gardenias, to the tips of her toes. Later on, Lester Young, the saxophonist who provided her with fanciful instrumental backings for some of her early recordings, named her "Lady Day." To fellow performers and her admirers she remained "Lady Day," however disreputable her personal life, because as an artist she was a lady to the manner born.

She was only six, in Baltimore, where she was born in 1915, when she started earning her living by scrubbing the doorsteps and the bathrooms of her neighborhood, sometimes bringing home as much as ten dollars a day. "Home" for her was the little old house of her grandparents and her cousin Ida, Billie's mother having gone to New York to work as a maid. Cousin Ida had a sadistic streak and took delight in tormenting her. Music was a solace. By running errands for a nearby brothel she was permitted to play their gramophone and listen to recordings of Bessie Smith and Louis Armstrong, from both of whom she acquired stylistic details that were to characterize her own performances. The attempted rape, when she was ten, brought her for the first time inside a prison. She was tried and found guilty of "enticement" and placed in a Catholic institution for reformation.

When she was thirteen she came to New York to join her mother, but not before she had been victimized by a second rape attempt that left her bleeding and almost lifeless. In Harlem, she worked as a maid (a chore she despised) and later as a prostitute (which she tolerated coolly). Refusing to service one of the clients at the brothel, a man who happened to be a political power in Harlem, brought her another jail sentence, this time for four months. Once out, she decided to make her way more respectably—by singing. She was hired by one down-at-the-heel Harlem night spot and progressed to other Harlem night-clubs, including some frequented by name musicians and actors, many of them powers in the music business. One of them was John Hammond, the distinguished jazz critic who, listening to Billie, could not believe his ears. "No chick I'd heard sounded like this—like an instrument," he said, and he used his influence in the jazz industry to promote her career. Another to be enraptured by her singing was Benny Goodman who, in 1933, invited her to make with him her first record, "Your Mother's Son-in-Law" (Mann Holiner—Alberta Nichols). Nothing much came of that recording debut, beyond a fee of thirty-five dollars. Then John Hammond had her cut half a dozen sides with Teddy Wilson and his band, in-cluding "I Only Have Eyes for You" (Al Dubin—Harry Warren), which Dick Powell and Ruby Keeler had that year introduced in the motion picture musical *Dames*; "I Cover the Waterfront" (Edward Heyman—John Green), written to exploit a motion picture of that name in 1933; and "Miss Brown to You" (Leo Robin—Richard A. Whiting and Ralph Rainger). This batch earned her thirty dollars. For eleven years, between 1933 and 1944, she continued making records for a flat fee—twenty-five, fifty or seventy-five dollars a side—instead of a royalty. She cut over two hundred sides that brought her only a negligible finan-cial return. Only after 1944 did she begin to profit from her recordings, signing a contract with Decca that guaranteed her royalties.

Her life, full of pain as it was, was further complicated by race prejudice, whose ugliness and viciousness she encountered time and again when she toured the country as vocalist for Count Basie in 1937 and, in 1938, with Artie Shaw.

To the singing of "Strange Fruit," Billie Holiday carried her anguished recollections of man's inhumanity to man as translated into race prejudice. She sang it for the first time during her two-year engagement at Barney Josephson's Café Society, Downtown, at 2 Sheri-dan Square in New York which she helped to open in 1938. It was a maverick night spot that was the first integrated nightclub in America, a place that helped carry boogie-woogie, the blues and gospel out of the hinterlands to the metropolis, and which was the starting gate from which not only Billie Holiday but many other famous pop singers, including Lena Horne and Sarah Vaughan, raced into the winner's circle. Billie Holiday's engagement at Café Society first established her as a singing superstar, and "Strange Fruit" was one of the songs that helped make her one.

When Lewis Allen wrote this anti-lynching song he had Billie in mind, and showed it to her one evening at Café Society. She was instantly responsive, not only because of her own sad experiences but also because her father had recently died in misery and neglect for failure to get a hospital to attend him. When Billie introduced it, "I was scared people would hate it," she revealed in her autobiography. "The first time I sang it I thought it was a mistake. . . . There wasn't even a patter of applause when I finished. Then a lone person began to clap nervously. Then suddenly everyone was clapping. It caught on after a while and people began to ask for it." How much effort and pain the performance of this song cost her was also disclosed. "When I sing it, it affects me so much I get sick. It takes all the strength out of me." She recorded the song for a small company, Commodore, on April 20, 1939. The record became a collector's item before the general public was aware of its existence. It was Billie's first successful record; only "Trav'lin' Light," a Capitol release in which she was backed by Paul Whiteman and his Orchestra, did better. Two other Holiday records sold well, "Fine and Mellow" (Commodore) and "Lover Man" (Decca).

Billie Holiday did not reap much of a financial harvest from her recordings. But as a performer in nightclubs and theaters after 1940 she did extraordinarily well, sometimes earning between three and four thousand dollars a week, and well beyond a million dollars in a decade. But she was always out of funds because she was drained by people who exploited her generosity, by her addiction to drugs, by her love affairs, and by her own innocence in handling money.

After a short period in a sanatorium in an attempt to kick the drug habit, she was once again imprisoned, this time on drug charges in 1947, and sentenced to a year and a day at the Federal Woman's Reformatory at Alderson, West Virginia. Because of this prison sentence she was denied a license to sing in nightclubs (her principal source of income), an unreasonable restriction that was as bitter to her as gall. But she was heard in various theaters; at a historic midnight concert in March 1948 in Carnegie Hall which was jammed full with her admirers; on Broadway in a revue, *Holiday on Broadway*, that lasted just three weeks; on records; and in a successful tour of Europe. She even seemed to have found—at long last!—marital contentment with Louis McKay. But she remained for all that a tormented woman, pursued as relentlessly by her fears and doubts and searing memories as by narcotics agents. Those agents were at her bedside when she lay in a coma in an oxygen tent at the Metropolitan Hospital in June 1959. Regaining consciousness, she whispered to a friend: "You watch, baby, they are going to arrest me in this damn bed." And this is precisely what happened. When heroin was found in her handbag, the police arrested her, even though she was on the hospital's critical list. Death spared her another siege in prison. She died on July 17, 1959, in her hospital bed. "Her motor just wore out," explained her booking agent.

Billie Holiday's story was told on the screen in 1972 in *Lady Sings the Blues*, based on her autobiography of that title (1956), written in collaboration with William Duffy. Diana Ross of the Supremes (in her motion picture debut) was "Lady Day." This can hardly be claimed as an authentic biography since so much of it is fiction, most of it sentimentalized, while the unraveling of a complex personality rushing headlong to self-destruction is oversimplified and generalized. But the assets of this film compensate for its liabilities: the acting and singing of Diana Ross; and most of all, the songs for which Billie Holiday is remembered in performances by Miss Ross which, without attempting to be carbon copies of Miss

Holiday's style and sound, nevertheless do manage to capture something of her inimitable phrasing and emotional depth. "Strange Fruit" is heard here, and so are "God Bless the Child," "Good Morning Heartache," "Fine and Mellow" and other Holiday standbys.

Billie Holiday was also immortalized in a ballet. This took place at the New York City Center on December 3, 1974, when the Alvin Ailey Center Dance Theater introduced John Butler's *Portrait of Billie*, a terpsichorean interpretation of Billie's degeneration through drugs and sex. The musical setting was made up of some of Billie's most famous recordings.

Fate has dealt more kindly with Ella Fitzgerald. In lifting her out of the depths of poverty and childhood misery to the peaks as "the first lady of song," it did not plant exploding mines in the path of her progress. Few singers have been more lavishly honored; few singers have earned so much admiration from their peers; few have enjoyed such a prolonged success throughout the entire music world. She has worn her fame and prosperity—just as she has worn her greatness—with regal dignity, nimbly sidestepping personal tragedies and never allowing them to destroy her or upset her career, and fulfilling herself artistically to the fullest extent of her enormous talent.

She was orphaned early in her childhood in Newport News, Virginia, where she was born in 1918, and was consigned to an orphan's home in Yonkers, New York. She was sixteen when, in 1934, she appeared in an amateur night at the Apollo Theater in Harlem. She had been listed as a dancer but stage fright froze her legs and she went on as a singer instead. Without any training, she sang with a graceful ease and an instinctive feeling for the phrase. Chick Webb, a bandleader, was so struck that then and there he hired her for his group as vocalist and became her legal guardian. Her presence on his bandstand during the next few years proved no minor factor in bringing the Chick Webb orchestra the popularity it enjoyed. On June 12, 1935, Ella Fitzgerald made her first record, with the help of Chick Webb and his orchestra, "Love and Kisses" (George Whiting and Nat Schwartz—J. C. Johnson). She then made several more disks, but not until "A-Tisket, A-Tasket" (Ella Fitzgerald and Al Feldman) which she recorded for Decca with Chick Webb and his orchestra in 1938, did her fame begin to catch up with her talent. Best-selling records now started to accumulate: "Wacky Dust" (Stanley Adams—Oscar Levant), "My Wubba Dolly" (Kay Werner and Sue Werner) and "Into Each Life Some Rain Must Fall" (Allan Roberts and Doris Fisher), in the last of which she sang with The Ink Spots.

When Chick Webb died in 1939, Ella Fitzgerald took over his band, renamed it Ella Fitzgerald and Her Famous Orchestra, and toured with it for three years. After that she went on to carve for herself a career as solo vocalist. She sang with the leading bands and jazz virtuosos; made extensive tours around the world; became a prolific recording artist, her records through the years selling in excess of thirty million disks; she began making movies, beginning with *Pete Kelly's Blues* in 1955.

She started out specializing in rhythm and novelty numbers, then went on to ballads, show tunes and standards, to scat singing and to Swing numbers. But to whatever style she applied herself she brought an inborn musicianship, a meticulous feeling for tempo and rhythm, a fastidious attention to detail, that placed her among the elect of jazz singers. It would be difficult to choose from her many and varied performances those that have proved most memorable. But these may serve as a sampling: "Oh, Lady Be Good!" (Ira Gershwin—George Gershwin); "That's My Desire" (Carroll Loveday—Helmy Kresa); "How High the Moon" (Nancy Hamilton—Morgan Lewis); "Flying Home" (Sid Robin—Benny Goodman and Lionel Hampton), Lionel Hampton's theme song; "It's a Pity to Say Good-night" (Billy Reid), recorded with The Delta Rhythm Boys; "A Foggy Day" (Ira

Gershwin—George Gershwin); "But Not for Me" (Ira Gershwin—George Gershwin); "Mack the Knife" (Marc Blitzstein—Kurt Weill); "I'm Beginning to See the Light" (Don George, Johnny Hodges, Duke Ellington and Harry James); " 'Taint What You Do" (Sy Oliver and James "Trummy" Young); "It's Only a Paper Moon" (Billy Rose and E. Y. Harburg—Harold Arlen); and "Stone Cold Dead in the Market" (Wilmoth Houdini). All these, plus the iridescent jewels of George and Ira Gershwin, Irving Berlin, Rodgers and Hart, Cole Porter and Duke Ellington which she recorded in the respective *Song Books* for Verve Records.

She has scooped up honors and tributes with both hands. She was chosen as the leading female vocalist by more critics and popularity polls than any other singer: by *Down Beat* for eighteen consecutive years beginning with 1937; *Esquire*, in 1946 and 1947; *Metronome*, in 1954 and 1956; *Down Beat* Critics Poll, each year between 1953 and 1959; *Playboy*, between 1957 and 1960 inclusive. She has also captured numerous prizes from the National Academy of Recording Arts and Sciences (the much coveted Grammy): In 1958, for the best solo vocal performance by a female (*Ella Fitzgerald Sings the Irving Berlin Song Book*) and the best jazz performance by an individual (*Ella Fitzgerald Sings the Duke Ellington Song Book*); in 1959 for the best vocal performance by a female—"But Not for Me"—and the best jazz performance by an individual (*Ella Fitzgerald Swings Lightly*); in 1960, for the best vocal performance by a female in a single disk—"Mack the Knife"—and in an album (*Ella in Berlin*); in 1962, for the best vocal performance by a female (*Ella Swings Brightly With Nelson Riddle*).

In 1967, *Harper's Bazaar* listed her among one hundred women of accomplishment, the National Association of Television and Radio Announcers chose her as "woman of the year," and ASCAP presented her with the Pied Piper trophy for "her continued and successful efforts to stimulate interest in the good music of today and in the great songs of our musical past." When, in 1968, she was honored with "Ella's Night" at the New York Coliseum, she received the Cultural Award of New York City for "exceptional achievement in the performing or creative arts," and she became the first entertainer to be made an honorary member of the prestigious black sorority, Alpha Kappa Alpha. Despite eye surgery in 1971 and 1972, her career continued to flourish in concerts, recordings and appearances on television. An Ella Fitzgerald night was one of the high spots of the Newport Jazz Festival in New York in 1973, and her fifty-four city tour of Europe in 1974 was a continuous march of triumph. In October 1974, the University of Maryland dedicated the Ella Fitzgerald School of Performing Arts—the first such institution in the United States named after a black singer.

Before Ethel Waters became a star of the Broadway musical theater and a dramatic actress both on the stage and the screen, she had joined that aristocracy of blues singers which numbered Bessie Smith and Billie Holiday. While Ethel Waters never held a permanent post as vocalist with any band, she had made records with various jazz groups in the 1920s, including Fletcher Henderson's orchestra, and made some appearances with Duke Ellington and his orchestra, and through her records and public appearances she proved to be a maker of hit songs.

She came from a slum in Chester, Pennsylvania—born in 1900—the illegitimate child of a twelve-and-a-half-year-old girl who had been raped. She herself suffered a disastrous marriage when she was only thirteen. "I stole food to live on when I was a child," she revealed in her autobiography, *His Eye Is On the Sparrow* (1950). Her spiritual fiber, severely tested by the sordid conditions surrounding her, helped her to resist the blows of an unkind fate: the example of a proud and strong-willed grandmother who raised her, the guidance of the Sisters at the Catholic school which she attended, and the deep religious convictions aroused in her when at twelve she attended a revival meeting.

As a young girl she worked as a chambermaid and laundress for a Philadelphia hotel for about five dollars a week. On the evening of October 23, 1917, when she was seventeen, she attended a Halloween party at Jack's Rathskeller where two of her friends induced her to get up and sing. She complied with "When You're a Long, Long Way from Home" (Sam M. Lewis—George W. Meyer). Two vaudevillians were in the audience and offered her ten dollars a week to appear in their act. She made her professional debut with them that year at the Lincoln Theater in Baltimore. One of her numbers was Handy's "The St. Louis Blues" which she had heard from a female impersonator and the performance rights for which she acquired from the publisher. She became the first woman, and the second performer, to present this classic publicly.

Tall and scrawny, she was billed as "Sweet Mama Stringbean," and since her rendition of "The St. Louis Blues" was creating a powerful impact on black audiences in small vaudeville theaters, she was prominently featured as "Sweet Mama Stringbean singing 'The St. Louis Blues.' " She kept on singing the blues, together with the day's popular ballads, at the Lincoln Theater in Harlem, at Edmond's Cellar on 132nd Street that originally catered solely to blacks but which, through her drawing power, began attracting a white clientele, and at Rafe's Paradise, which drew an exclusively white audience. "I used to work from nine until unconscious," she once told an interviewer. In addition to these appearances she toured the vaudeville circuit in the big time and in a traveling show, *Oh, Joy!*, where for the first time she became a name performer. And she was beginning to make records: first a single disk for Cardinal; then between 1921 and 1923 "That Da Da Strain" (Mamie Medina —Edgar Dowell), "Dying with the Blues" (W. Astor Morgan—Fletcher Henderson and W. Astor Morgan), "You Can't Do What My Last Man Did" (J. C. Johnson and Allie Moore), and "Tell 'Em 'Bout Me" (Sidney Easton) for Black Swan; then, in 1923, "Georgia Blues" (Billy Higgins—W. Benton Overstreet) for Paramount and "Pleasure Mad" (Rousseau Simmons—Sidney Bechet) for Vocalion.

In 1925 she substituted for Florence Mills at Salvin's Plantation Club in New York where she introduced "Dinah" (Sam M. Lewis and Joe Young—Harry Akst), originally a bouncy tune which she transformed into a languorous blues. This song became the first hit to emanate from a nightclub, and Ethel Waters was responsible for it. A few years later she also introduced "Trav'lin' All Alone" (J. C. Johnson), which became a favorite with many blues singers including Billie Holiday.

The Broadway theater called to Ethel Waters. She appeared in *Africana* (1927), *Blackbirds* (1930) and *Rhapsody in Black* (1931) as the preface to her first stage triumph in Irving Berlin's revue *As Thousands Cheer* (1933), where she regularly drew ovations for "Heat Wave" and a bitter song about lynching, "Supper Time."

In 1933, Harold Arlen, the composer, prevailed on Ethel Waters to introduce his blues, "Stormy Weather" (Ted Koehler) in a revue at the Cotton Club in New York. He had written it for Cab Calloway, but when Calloway's engagement at the Cotton Club was not realized, Arlen decided that Ethel Waters—now internationally renowned for her singing of the blues—would be its ideal performer. She was that, and much more. Singer and song became one. In singing this blues, "I was telling the things I couldn't frame in words," she wrote in her autobiography. "I was singing the story of my misery and confusion, of the misunderstandings in my life I couldn't straighten out, the story of the wrongs and outrages done to my people I had loved and trusted. . . . Only those who are being burned know what fire is like. I sang 'Stormy Weather' from the depths of my private hell. . . ."

In 1926, Ethel Waters began recording for Columbia, backed by some of the foremost jazz musicians of the day, among them Bunny Berigan, Tommy and Jimmy Dorsey, Jack Teagarden, Benny Goodman, Fletcher Henderson, Joe Venuti and Gene Krupa. On shellac she gave performance to the songs she had introduced and made famous, and to many others that carried the unmistakable imprint of her artistry: "Go Back Where You Stayed Last Night" (Sidney Easton and Ethel Waters); "My Special Friend Is Back in Town" (Andy Razaf and Bob Schafer—J. C. Johnson); "Sweet Georgia Brown" (Ben Bernie, Maceo Pinkard and Kenneth Casey); "My Baby Sure Knows How to Love" (Andy Razaf —J. C. Johnson); "True Blue Lou" (Sam Coslow—Richard A. Whiting); "I've Found a New Baby" (Jack Palmer—Spencer Williams); "Heebie Jeebies" (Boyd Atkins); "My Handy Man" (Andy Razaf); "I Just Couldn't Take it Baby" (Mann Holiner—Alberta Nichols); "Kind Lovin' Blues" (Ethel Waters, Fletcher Henderson and Lewis Mitchell); "Maybe Not at All" (Ethel Waters and Sidney Easton), and "You Can't Stop Me from Lovin' You" (Mann Holiner—Alberta Nichols).

22

Heyday of the Musical Theater

The plush Broadway revue came into its full glory in the 1920s. This happened in spite of the fact that the *Ziegfeld Follies*, the glamorous yardstick by which other revues measured their own merits, had lost a good deal of its former luster. One by one, the bright performing lights that had illuminated the New Amsterdam Theater, the home of the *Follies*, with such an incandescence, were extinguished. Bert Williams left the *Follies* after 1919. Fanny Brice appeared for the last time under Ziegfeld's aegis in 1923. Will Rogers left after 1924, and W. C. Fields after 1925.

Ziegfeld, however, remained unsparing in his extravagance in making his *Follies* the ultimate in stage entertainment. The *Follies of 1927* was the costliest, though far from the best, almost three hundred thousand dollars having been spent by the time the curtain rose. This was the first edition in which virtually the entire score was the work of a single man, Irving Berlin, instead of a conglomerate of songwriters. It was also the first edition to concentrate on a single superstar, Eddie Cantor, instead of a bevy of stars. (A newcomer, the singer Ruth Etting, did manage to steal some of the limelight with Berlin's "Shaking the Blues Away.") Eddie Cantor's big song that year was not by Irving Berlin but an interpolation: Walter Donaldson's "My Blue Heaven" (George Whiting). During the run of this edition, Cantor's wife gave birth to their fifth daughter. Cantor announced this happy event to the audience from the stage. Then, singing "My Blue Heaven," he improvised the lines: "But five is a crowd, for crying out loud, we're crowded in my blue heaven."

There was no further edition of the *Ziegfeld Follies* until 1931, the last to be produced by the great Ziegfeld himself. It had something old and something new. Something old was a revival of the ballad "Shine On, Harvest Moon" (Jack Norworth and Nora Bayes), made famous at the *Follies* more than a quarter of a century earlier, now recalled by Ruth Etting. Something new appeared with the first master of ceremonies in *Ziegfeld* history, the suave and sophisticated Harry Richman.

Ziegfeld died in 1932. Four editions of the *Follies* were seen after that. Those of 1934 and 1936 were nominally produced by Ziegfeld's widow, Billie Burke though actually by the Shubert brothers, and both starring Fanny Brice. In 1934, the songs included two hits by Billy Hill sung by Everett Marshall, "The Last Roundup" in the style of a cowboy ballad, and "Wagon Wheels" in the manner of a western folk song. The revue also boasted an excellent number by the then comparative newcomer to Broadway, Vernon Duke, whose "What Is There to Say?" (E. Y. Harburg) was sung by Mr. Marshall with Jane Froman. In 1936, Miss Brice was joined by Bob Hope in comedy sketches and song, with Bob Hope introducing a Vernon Duke standard, "I Can't Get Started with You" (Ira Gershwin). In his autobiography, *Have Tux, Will Travel* (1955), Bob Hope noted that this was the song that put him in pictures, explaining: "Mitchell Leisen and Harlan Thompson [two Hollywood writers who were preparing a script for the *Big Broadcast of 1936*] saw me do the number [with Eve Arden] and hired me." This number was later popularized outside the *Follies* by bandleader-trumpeter Bunny Berigan who made it his theme song.

The *Follies of 1936* marked Fanny Brice's last appearance on the Broadway stage. Her career after that was in radio. As Baby Snooks she was still one of radio's supreme stars when she died of a cerebral hemorrhage on May 29, 1951.

The last two *Follies* were produced in 1943 and 1957. That of 1943 had the longest consecutive run of any *Follies* edition, 553 performances. It starred Milton Berle and had songs by Ray Henderson and Jack Yellen. The 1957 edition was planned to celebrate the fiftieth anniversary of the *Follies*. Though its star was that initimable English comedienne, Beatrice Lillie, the *Follies* proved but a shadow of its onetime glowing self. In his review, Louis Kronenberger remarked sadly: "The spirit had all but vanished; the songs had no tunefulness, the lyrics no bounce, the sketches no crackle, and though the dances had moments of color, they quite lacked distinction." With a run of just 123 performances, the *Ziegfeld Follies* expired.

In 1919, a rival had arisen to challenge the supremacy of Florenz Ziegfeld and his *Follies* in the field of revues, the *Scandals*, produced by George White. When George White set out to compete with Ziegfeld, he was coming to grips with his onetime employer, since as a hoofer George White had appeared in the *Ziegfeld Follies of 1915*. By that time White had made his mark in several musicals as a performer, in one of which he was reputed to have advanced the popularity of the Turkey Trot. With little financial backing to speak of, he decided in 1919 to rush in where angels feared to tread, the domain so thoroughly dominated by the *Ziegfeld Follies*. He was determined not only to out-spectacle and out-star the *Follies*, but also to surpass it in the very area the *Follies* had made its own, the presenting of the most beautiful girls in the world.

Some of White's lofty ambitions were realized in the first edition of the *Scandals* in 1919. White had lifted Ann Pennington—she of the dimpled and rouged knees, the rouged chin, and the petite figure—out of the *Ziegfeld Follies* where she had started in 1913 as a forty-dollar-a-week chorus dancer and by 1919 a featured performer drawing over a thousand dollars a week. In the *Scandals* of 1919, her star as a dynamic dancer rose even higher when she performed the shimmy. In that same edition, Lou Holtz, in his Broadway stage debut, provided comedy, and Yvette Rugel sang. Most of all, the *Scandals* was a lavish feast for the eye, filled with spectacular scenes worthy of Ziegfeld, who now realized that he had a formidable rival. After the opening night of the *Scandals*, Ziegfeld wired White offering him two thousand dollars a week to appear with Miss Pennington in the next edition of the *Follies*. White, with the smugness of one fully aware he was a winner, wired back an offer for Ziegfeld and his wife, Billie Burke, to appear in the *Scandals* for seven thousand dollars a week.

George White was truly a winner. That first edition brought him a profit of four hundred thousand dollars. Planning his second edition, White set out to remedy the principal shortcoming of his maiden effort—the music department. The nondescript songs for the 1919 edition were provided by Richard A. Whiting and Arthur Jackson. For the 1920 edition, White engaged young George Gershwin. With various lyricists, Gershwin wrote all the songs for five consecutive editions of the *Scandals*, from 1920 to 1924 inclusive, in which he reached maturity as a song composer and made his first bid for recognition as a serious composer with the writing of a one-act opera. Among those appearing in those five editions were Ann Pennington, W. C. Fields, Paul Whiteman and his Orchestra, Winnie Lightner, Tom Patricola, Will Mahoney and Helen Morgan. Of the forty-five songs Gershwin contributed, he made a bid for greatness with two, "I'll Build a Stairway to Paradise" (B. G. DeSylva and Ira Gershwin), used as a production number in the 1922 edition, described by Carl Van Vechten as representing "the most perfect piece of jazz ever written" and "Somebody Loves Me" (B. G. DeSylva and Ballard MacDonald), sung by Winnie Lightner in 1924 (later a favorite of Blossom Seeley).

When George Gershwin left the *Scandals* in 1924 to concentrate on musical comedies and serious music, George White found a valuable replacement in a remarkable trio of songwriters, Lew Brown, Buddy De Sylva and Ray Henderson. The first two were lyricists, the third, a composer. Their first score was for the 1925 edition. For the next half dozen years or so, the three men worked so intimately and harmoniously that it was not always clear where the work of one ended and that of the other two began. There were times when the composer, Ray Henderson, helped to write lyrics, and when the two lyricists provided ideas to the composer. And, to complicate matters further, there were times when Buddy De Sylva collaborated with someone else in preparing the texts. Consequently, in talking about the songs of DeSylva, Brown and Henderson it is necessary to speak of them as a single creative entity.

Lew Brown was five when he and his family came to the United States from their native Russia, where Lew was born in Odessa in 1893. While attending New York public schools he would scratch song lyrics on paper, some of them parodies of current hits. Brown entered the ranks of professionals with "Don't Take My Lovin' Man Away," for which a publisher paid him seven dollars and which Belle Baker sang in vaudeville. Brown's first hit appeared in 1912 with "I'm the Lonesomest Gal in Town," music by Albert von Tilzer, with whom he continued a productive and successful partnership that lasted several years. In 1922, Lew Brown met Ray Henderson, a newcomer to the songwriting game, with whom he wrote "Georgette" which Ted Lewis and his band introduced in the *Greenwich Village Follies of 1922*, and "Humming."

Ray Henderson, born in Buffalo, New York, in 1896, was trained as a serious musician at the Chicago Conservatory. While there he played pop tunes on the piano at parties and with jazz groups, and filled engagements as the piano accompanist for a vaudeville act made up of an Irish tenor and a Jewish comedian. Once out of the Conservatory, Henderson deserted serious music to become a song plugger for Leo Feist. After that he worked as an arranger and staff pianist for Fred Fisher, Inc., and for Shapiro-Bernstein.

Louis Bernstein became an ally in furthering his songwriting career, and introduced him to the lyricist, Lew Brown, so that they might form a working partnership.

When Lew Brown and Ray Henderson joined forces with Buddy De Sylva to write the songs for the *Scandals of 1925*, Buddy De Sylva was the most prestigious of the three men, having behind him several years of outstanding song successes. He was born in New York as George Gard De Sylva in 1895, the only son of a vaudevillian. The family moved to Los Angeles during Buddy's infancy. There, as a child prodigy, he did a song-and-dance routine at the Grand Opera House, after which he toured the Keith vaudeville circuit. While attending the University of Southern California he made further public appearances, this time as a vocalist with a Hawaiian band. Writing song lyrics had by now become his favorite avocation. Since Al Jolson was the leading light in the musical theater, Buddy De Sylva sent him some of his lyrics, to one of which " 'N Everything" Jolson contributed a melody of his own and then introduced it. Other of Buddy De Sylva's lyrics began to crop up at Jolson's Winter Garden Sunday night concerts and extravaganzas. In *Sinbad* (1918), De Sylva was represented by five songs, including "By the Honeysuckle Vine" and "Chloe," both with music by Jolson. When De Sylva received his first royalty check, for sixteen thousand dollars, he realized his future fortune was in New York writing songs. He arrived in 1919, and for a time worked as a staff lyricist for Jerome H. Remick. That year, in collaboration with Arthur Jackson, he wrote the lyrics for George Gershwin's first Broadway musical comedy, *La, La, Lucille*. A year later, De Sylva's lyrics were set to Jerome Kern's music in *Sally* (1920), whose hit song was "Look for the Silver Lining." With George Gershwin as composer, Buddy De Sylva next wrote the lyrics (often with collaboration) for the five editions of the George White *Scandals* between 1920 and 1924. At the same time, he continued to provide Jolson with the lyrics for songs which, with the magic of Jolson's delivery, became smash hits, among them "April Showers" (music by Louis Silvers) and "California, Here I Come" (music by Joseph Meyer). "It All Depends On You," which Al Jolson interpolated into *Big Boy* (1925) was the first song in which De Sylva teamed up with Brown and Henderson.

De Sylva, Brown and Henderson wrote all the songs for the *George White Scandals* editions of 1925, 1926, and 1928. Their first score, in 1925, was inconsequential. But in 1926, they provided a veritable cornucopia of song riches. In it were "Black Bottom," danced by Ann Pennington in a routine largely devised by George White, "Lucky Day," sung by Harry Richman, "The Girl Is You," shared by Richman and Frances Williams, and a masterpiece, "The Birth of the Blues," the background music for a brilliantly conceived and imaginative production number.

There was no edition of the *Scandals* in 1927. For the 1928 edition, De Sylva, Brown and Henderson wrote "I'm On the Crest of the Wave," sung by Harry Richman, and "Pickin' Cotton" for a dance routine for Ann Pennington. After that, the history of De Sylva, Brown and Henderson belonged to musical comedy and not to the revue.

There were editions of the *George White Scandals* in 1929, 1931, 1935 and 1939. In 1931, Ray Henderson worked only with Lew Brown, a partnership that showed no signs of let-up in spite of the defection of Buddy De Sylva to Hollywood. Ethel Merman and Rudy Vallee were among the stars, and for them Henderson and Brown fashioned such gems as "Life Is Just a Bowl of Cherries," "This Is the Missus" and "My Song." Two other song delights—"The Thrill Is Gone" and "That's Why Darkies Were Born"—were assigned to Everett Marshall. This bountiful score provided a footnote to recording history. It is an early instance in which the main songs of a Broadway musical production were pressed in a single release, sung by Bing Crosby and the Boswell Sisters on two sides of a twelve-inch Brunswick record.

After that, the *George White Scandals* went downhill. The last two editions were failures—the first with a score by Ray Henderson and Jack Yellen, and the second by Sammy Fain and Jack Yellen. A hit song, however, emerged from the last of the *Scandals* with "Are You Having Any Fun?", introduced by Ella Logan.

During the year 1919 in which the *Scandals* was born, H. L. Jones and Morris Green (The Bohemians, Inc.) entered the revues sweepstakes with a new competitor, the *Greenwich Village Follies*. It first opened downtown New York—appropriately, in the Greenwich Village Theater—to bring the spirit and ambiance of the bohemian life of the Village into a revue through song, dance and satire. John Murray Anderson was the director, sketchwriter and author of the song lyrics, with A. Baldwin Sloane serving as composer.

One of the stars of this production was Ted Lewis, with his battered top hat, clarinet, hot band and salutation of "Is Everybody Happy?" He adopted the stage name of Ted Lewis as a boy while playing in a vaudeville theater in South Carolina. The badly mutilated top hat (his sartorial identification) which he rolled off his head and down his arm, was won in a crap game in New York in or about 1916. It became his good-luck charm for the rest of his career. One year later, when he opened at Rector's in New York for his first big break in show business, he spontaneously asked his audience "is everybody happy?" after his first number. He was greeted with such an explosion of enthusiasm that he made it his practice to ask that question to each of his audiences after that.

He needed one more personal item to round out his act in the *Greenwich Village Follies*, his theme song, "When My Baby Smiles at Me" (Andrew B. Sterling and Ted Lewis—Bill Munro). He had introduced it in 1918 before presenting it with his band in the *Greenwich Village Follies* of 1919.

That first edition of *Greenwich Village Follies* proved so appealing that the show had to seek out larger quarters uptown six weeks after opening night, at the Nora Bayes Theater. When the second edition was produced in 1920, it returned to Greenwich Village, only to be compelled once again to find a larger house in the Broadway district. After that the *Follies* remained uptown. There were eight editions in all, the last in 1928 at the Winter Garden. Among its stars, in addition to Ted Lewis, were Frank Crumit, Irene Franklin, Sam White and Eva Puck, the Dolly Sisters, Moran and Mack, Benny Fields, Blossom Seeley and Grace La Rue.

Louis A. Hirsch wrote the music in 1922 and 1923, Cole Porter, then still a novice, and Jay Gorney in 1924, and sundry other composers in 1925 and 1928. The best songs were invariably interpolations. They included Irving Berlin's "I'll See You in C-U-B-A" introduced by Ted Lewis and his band in 1919; "Three O'Clock in the Morning" (Dorothy Terriss—Julian Robledo) in 1921; "Georgette," in 1922, introduced by Ted Lewis; and Cole Porter's "I'm in Love Again," sung by the Dolly Sisters in 1924.

Two new revue series found their way to Broadway in 1923. They were *Artists and Models* produced by the Shuberts, and the *Earl Carroll Vanities*. Both went a step beyond Ziegfeld in glorifying the female body and by exploiting seminudity. In the first edition of *Artists and Models*, the girls appeared in varying stages of undress and in provocative poses. Nudity became even more pronounced in 1924 and 1925. The three editions offered Frank Fay, Frances Williams, Phil Baker, Gertude Hoffman, Billy B. Van and Lulu McConnell. Music was by Jean Schwartz, J. Fred Coots and Sigmund Romberg, among others, with lyrics by Harold Atteridge, Sam Coslow and Clifford Grey.

The stress placed on female pulchritude by Earl Carroll in his *Vanities* was pointed up by the sign above the stage door: "Through these portals pass the most beautiful girls in the world." In his first edition, in 1923, Earl Carroll was not only the producer, but also the author of all material (musical as well as textual) and the stage director. In addition, he gave his name to the theater in which the revue played. But it was always the girls who held center stage. In "The Birth of a New Revue," the opening number of the first edition, each of Broadway's famous revues was personified by a stunning beauty. The most beautiful of these girls, as completely nude as the law allowed, represented the *Vanities*. "Living curtains" offered girls draped in curtains of silks, feathers or velvet, but not sufficiently to conceal their states of undress. The star of the first edition was Dorothy Knapp, "the most beautiful girl in the world."

Nudity continued to dominate the *Earl Carroll Vanities* through the years. By 1930, Robert Benchley came right out and labeled it a "dirty show." What disturbed him most was an undersea scene in which a male pursued water nymphs, all seemingly nude, though wearing flesh-colored tights. The police were more concerned with a sketch in which Jimmy Savo, as a department store window dresser, tantalizingly removes one female garment after another from a mannequin. After some modifications in Savo's routine, the police were placated.

There were eight editions of the *Earl Carroll Vanities* between 1923 and 1932 (with a hiatus in 1927 and an *Earl Carroll Sketch Book* in 1929), and one in 1940 that survived just twenty-five performances. Beginning in 1925, Carroll began to leave the writing of songs and sketches to other hands, and began to stud his casts with stars. Among those appearing from 1925 on were Ted Healy, Julius Tannen, Moran and Mack, Yvette Rugel, Lillian Roth, Ray Dooley, Jimmy Savo, Jack Benny, Patsy Kelly, Will Mahoney, Milton Berle, Helen Broderick and Harriet Hoctor. The music was assigned principally to Clarence Gaskill and Jay Gorney in 1925, Morris Hamilton in 1926 and 1928, Jay Gorney again in 1930, Burton Lane in 1931 and Harold Arlen and Richard Myers in 1932—though there were always interpolations of songs by other writers. An early Harold Arlen standard was heard in the *Vanities of 1932*, "I Gotta Right to Sing the Blues" (Ted Koehler), presented by Lillian Shade but soon to become a specialty of Billie Holiday and the theme song of Jack Teagarden. "My Darling" (Edward Heyman—Richard Myers) was another distinctive number in this edition. "Goodnight Sweetheart" (Ray Noble, James Campbell and Reg Connelly) was given in 1931, also destined to become a standard after being promoted by Rudy Vallee.

Some of the best written, best performed, best conceived and most handsomely mounted revues of the twenties could be seen at the Music Box Theater between 1921 and 1924 inclusive. The Music Box was a new theater built by Sam H. Harris and Irving Berlin on 45th Street at a cost of about a million dollars. For its opening, on September 22, 1921, Sam H. Harris produced *The Music Box Revue*, all of whose songs were the work of Irving Berlin. Almost two hundred thousand dollars was spent on a production which starred William Collier, Sam Bernard, Joseph Santley, Ivy Sawyer, the Brox Sisters and Wilda Bennett. The costuming, scenery, tableaux and production numbers were elegant—"a piling of Pelion on Ossa of everything that is decorative, dazzling, harmonious, intoxicatingly beautiful in the theater," reported Arthur Hornblow in *Theater* magazine. The Irving Berlin score yielded two diamonds, the ballad "Say It With Music" sung by Wilda Bennett and Paul Frawley, and a captivating syncopated number introduced by the Brox Sisters, "Everybody Step." With a five-dollar top price—the highest asked so far on Broadway—the *Music Box Revue* grossed $28,000 in its first week, and through its 440 performances earned a profit of half a million dollars.

Irving Berlin's songs continued to distinguish the other three editions, though there was never a lack of performing or staging pleasures. In 1922, John Steel introduced "Lady of the Evening," Grace La Rue was heard in "Crinoline Days" and the McCarthy Sisters presented "Pack Up Your Sins" as part of an elaborate first-act finale, "Satan's Palace." In 1924, during the run of the 1923 edition, Berlin's ballad, "What'll I Do?" was interpolated for John Steel and Grace Moore, the latter making her Broadway debut before her triumphs at the Metropolitan Opera House. In the 1924 edition, "All Alone" was interpolated for her and Oscar Shaw. The principals in the casts of the last three editions included Clark and McCullough, Grace La Rue, William Gaxton, Charlotte Greenwood, the Fairbanks Twins, Frank Tinney, Robert Benchley (delivering his famous monologue, "The Treasurer's Report"), Phil Baker, the Brox Sisters and Fanny Brice.

In 1927, Irving Berlin wrote virtually the entire score for the *Ziegfeld Follies* and in 1933 for one of the most successful revues of that decade, *As Thousands Cheer*, book by Moss Hart and Berlin. Current events were tapped for sketches, songs and dances. Clifton Webb impersonated Douglas Fairbanks, Gandhi and the senior John D. Rockefeller. Marilyn Miller (in her last Broadway appearance) mimicked Joan Crawford and Barbara Hutton. The changing administration at the White House in Washington and the impact of radio sponsorship on the Metropolitan Opera House were gaily lampooned in satirical sketches. The entire revue was fashioned after the daily newspaper, the various scenes intended to simulate a newspaper's sections, such as the front page, society page, lonely hearts column, the comics and so on. Through trick lighting, newspaper headlines were flashed on a backstage screen preceding each principal number.

Its best song was adapted from a number Berlin had written in 1917 and which as "Smile and Show Your Dimple" had been a failure. Now with new lyrics, and renamed "Easter Parade," it was used for the first-act finale recreating an Easter Day parade on Fifth Avenue, sung by Clifton Webb and Marilyn Miller. Other songs were new. One was "Heat Wave" with which Ethel Waters added several degrees to the temperature with her torrid rendition; another, "Not for All the Rice in China," offered by Clifton Webb, Marilyn Miller and the ensemble. Completely off the beaten track for a revue was the song "Supper Time," unforgettably sung by Ethel Waters, which told of a black woman preparing supper for her children whose husband has just been lynched.

As far as revues went, *Shuffle Along* in 1921, was also a rarity, conceived by Flournoy Miller and Aubrey Lyles, with songs by Noble Sissle and Eubie Blake. This was the first all-black musical to become a box-office success, with 504 consecutive performances in New York, and three road companies on tour in white theaters and to mixed audiences. This was the parent of many subsequent all-black shows adorning the Broadway scene in the twenties. There was a good deal of apprehension when this project was first conceived. Eubie Blake recalls: "We were afraid everyone would think it was a freak show, that it wouldn't appeal to whites. Some people thought that if it was a colored show it might be dirty." But the audiences and critics in New York dispelled all such fears. A typical reaction was that of the New York *American:* "Talk of your pep! There was enough pep for two average musical comedies!" So infectious and individual were the dances that both Ziegfeld and George White hired the show girls of *Shuffle Along* to teach their steps to the white chorines of the *Follies* and the *Scandals*.

Though it used a slender story line about a mayoralty campaign in a small Southern town to justify the songs, dances and comedy, *Shuffle Along* was basically a revue. After a preliminary tour before black audiences, *Shuffle Along* opened in New York in a former lecture hall that had been converted into the 63rd Street Music Hall. Whites now joined the parade uptown to 63rd Street. In *Shuffle Along*, Florence Mills (a replacement after the show had opened) became a singing star, and the song "I'm Just Wild About Harry" a nationwide hit. (In 1948, the song was used to help Harry S Truman in bringing about the greatest upset in the history of American presidential campaigns.) Two other appealing numbers were "Bandana Days" and "Love Will find a Way."

There were two later editions of *Shuffle Along*, in 1933 and 1952, both failures.

The most successful all-black revue after *Shuffle Along* was *Blackbirds of 1928*. It was here that "Bojangles" Bill Robinson was acclaimed for the first time on Broadway when he sang "Doin' the New Low-Down" (Dorothy Fields—Jimmy McHugh) and nimbly tap dancing to its strains across the stage and up and down a flight of stairs. Others in the cast included Aida Ward and Adelaide Hall, both making their Broadway debuts.

The revue not only brought deserved prominence to some of its performers but also to the songwriting team of Dorothy Fields, lyricist, and Jimmy McHugh, composer, who wrote all the songs. McHugh was born in Boston in 1894 where for a while he studied classical music. When his serious music study ended he worked as rehearsal pianist at the Boston Opera House. Deciding to switch to popular music, he found employment as staff pianist and song plugger at the Boston branch of Irving Berlin's publishing house. In 1921, McHugh came to New York, where he worked for the Mills Publishing Company. His first published song was "Emaline" (George A. Little) in 1921. Three years later came his first hits, "When My Sugar Walks Down the Street" (Irving Mills and Gene Austin) and "What Has Become of Hinky Dinky Parlay Voo" (Al Dubin, Irving Mills and Irwin Dash). Jimmy McHugh and Irving Mills, calling themselves the Hotsy Totsy Boys, introduced McHugh's "The Lonesomest Girl in Town" (Al Dubin and Irving Mills) over the radio in 1925. "I Can't Believe That You're in Love with Me" (written with Clarence Gaskill) was interpolated for Winnie Lightner in the revue *Gay Paree* (1926).

For a number of years McHugh wrote songs for the revues produced at the Cotton Club in Harlem. In 1927, at the Mills Publishing Company where he was employed, he met Dorothy Fields, a budding lyricist. She came from a celebrated theatrical family: her father was Lew Fields of Weber and Fields renown and subsequently a producer, and her brothers, Herbert and Joseph, each was distinguished as a writer of musical stage books. Dorothy Fields was earning her living teaching art in a New York high school, when J. Fred Coots, the composer, suggested she try writing some lyrics. To a Coots melody she pieced out a lyric which she later confessed was simply "terrible." But Coots did not lose faith, and took her by the hand to various publishing houses trying to find work for her. Being the daughter of a famous theatrical personality did not help. One and all asked the same question: If she had talent for songwriting why didn't her own father give her a helping hand? Then at the Mills Music Company she found her first paid assignment, fifty dollars to write a lyric for a song planned to honor Ruth Elder, an aviatrix then expecting to fly across the Atlantic. "I wrote the lyric overnight," she recalled. "Ruth Elder never made it, and neither did my song." Soon after that, Dorothy Fields penciled two lyrics for two instrumental numbers. Nothing much came of that either, except the hundred dollars she was paid.

The publishing house of Mills became the meeting ground where Dorothy Fields and Jimmy McHugh came to know each other and decided to form a songwriting duo. Their initial effort was a song for *Harry Delmar's Revels* which was thrown out of the show by opening night. Then Lew Leslie contracted with them to do the whole score for an all-black revue, *Blackbirds of 1928*. The song rejected by Harry Delmar for *Revels* was now placed in this new context. It was "I Can't Give You Anything But Love, Baby," which Aida Ward, Bill Robinson and Willard McLean helped to make one of the top numbers of the revue. Another top tune was "Diga Diga Doo," a Zulu number dynamically projected by Adelaide

Hall. These two items, in a show that was a box-office triumph, proved the making of the songwriting team of Dorothy Fields and Jimmy McHugh that lasted for about ten highly productive years, and the making of Dorothy Fields as one of the top-ranking song lyricists of her time.

To capitalize on the popularity of *Blackbirds of 1928*, a new all-black revue was produced on Broadway in 1929, *Hot Chocolates*, book and lyrics by Andy Razaf, and music by Thomas "Fats" Waller and Harry Brooks. Waller was by no means an apprentice composer when he went to work on the score for *Hot Chocolates*, but a man with rich experiences and a healthy measure of success behind him. The son of a clergyman, he was born in New York in 1904, worked as a nighclub pianist when he was sixteen, at seventeen pressed his first records and made his first piano rolls, and at nineteen started broadcasting over the radio. For several years, beginning in 1924, he toured the vaudeville circuit besides playing in jazz bands, and at times serving as an accompanist for Bessie Smith and other blues singers. As a songwriter he made his first official bid for success in 1925 with "Squeeze Me," the words and music of which he wrote with Clarence Williams; the melody was based on a New Orleans jazz number sometimes attributed to Buddy Bolden. Three years after that, this time working with J. C. Johnson, Waller wrote the score for the all-black revue, *Keep Shufflin'*, whose most important number was "Willow Tree" (Andy Razaf), sung by "Fats" Waller and James P. Johnson.

Waller's two most famous songs appeared in 1929. One was "Honeysuckle Rose" (Andy Razaf), heard in a revue mounted at Connie's Inn, a New York nightclub, and soon afterward made successful over the radio and in a Victor recording by Paul Whiteman and his Orchestra. The other was "Ain't Misbehavin' " (Andy Razaf), the most important song to come out of *Hot Chocolates*, the melody written with Harry Brooks. Andy Razaf has revealed: "I remember one day going up to Fats' house on 133rd Street to finish up a number based on a little strain he'd thought up. The whole show was complete, but they needed an extra number for a theme, and this had to be it. He worked on it for about forty-five minutes and there it was—'Ain't Mishavin'.' "

When Louis Armstrong joined *Hot Chocolates* early in its run to play in its pit orchestra and later to come up on the stage, the song "Ain't Misbehavin' " was turned over to him. That song marked the beginnings of Armstrong's international fame. That same year he recorded it for Okeh, and from then on it was one of his most requested numbers.

2

During the twenties a reaction set in against the orgy of settings and costuming, the extravagant stage effects, and the glorification of feminine beauty in revues. Dissatisfaction was being expressed in many quarters with the way the revue was slighting many other important elements of the musical theater—wit, satire, sophistication. Out of this dissatisfaction came a new trend in the production of revues, away from ostentation toward simplicity, a freshness of material and most of all, adult intelligence.

This revolution first took place not on Broadway, but further downtown, on the East Side, in a little theater called the Neighborhood Playhouse on Grand Street. A group of little known and inexperienced writers and performers collaborated there in 1922 to produce what they described in their first program as a "lowbrow show for highgrade morons"—a satirical revue, *The Grand Street Follies*. Partly out of economic necessity, partly by intention, this *Follies* avoided lavish sights and sounds, large groups of performers and stars. The emphasis was on the laughter inspired by satire, parody, mimicry and caricature. The first edition made sport of stage stars (Irene Castle), ballerinas (Anna Pavlova), opera singers (Feodor

Chaliapin). It ridiculed current dances, and even went so far afield as to mock the poetry of Walt Whitman.

The show had so much sparkle and originality that the theatrical trade began moving downtown from Broadway to Grand Street. A second edition was mounted in 1924, presenting irreverent caricatures of such famous stage personalities as John Barrymore and Emily Stevens (by Albert Carroll), and of Elsie Janis, Beatrice Lillie, Fanny Brice and Rudolph Valentino by other members of the young, talented cast. The Russian Art Theater, a recent visitor to the United States, was made to perform a hillbilly sketch. A medieval musical comedy is honored with the "ignoble prize."

The *Grand Street Follies* remained downtown in 1926 and 1927, then it moved to the Booth Theater in the Broadway sector for its last two editions in 1928 and 1929. Each season brought new victims for the devastating caricatures and parodies of Albert Carroll and Dorothy Sands; hilarious takeoffs of current plays and ballets; impudent satires on opera and the classic theater. *The Wild Duck of the 18th Century* suggested how Ibsen would have written his play in an earlier era, and *The Siege of Troy* demonstrated what would have happened had David Belasco produced that ancient historic event. Albert Carroll mimed Ethel Barrymore and Harpo Marx, Dorothy Sands impersonated a typical Town Hall concert singer. "Glory, Glory, Glory" ridiculed the Ziegfeld girl. In small parts were Jessica Dragonette (soon to become radio's queen of song), and James Cagney (future screen star) doing a tap dance. And all this hilarity was supplemented by little melodies and bright lyrics, often accompanied by ingeniously contrived and cleverly presented dances and production numbers. Everything was in a modest design—everything that is, but the imagination, enthusiasm and talent of the performers and writers.

One of the unknowns contributing songs to *The Grand Street Follies* was Arthur Schwartz, then a young lawyer. Four of his songs were used, including "A Little Igloo for Two" (Agnes Morgan). Schwartz was born in Brooklyn, New York, in 1900. He attended the Brooklyn public schools, New York University from which he was graduated with a Bachelor of Arts degree in 1919, and Columbia University where in 1921 he received the degree of Master of Arts. At New York University, Schwartz composed school marches and football songs. For a time he contemplated a literary career, having done some writing for his college paper. Finally he bowed to the wishes of his father by studying law, supporting himself by teaching English in a New York high school.

Wearing a Phi Beta Kappa key, Schwartz was admitted to the bar in 1924. He practiced law for four years and did quite well. He also composed popular songs. Songs for *The Grand Street Follies* were the first to be heard in a theater. For some time thereafter Schwartz ghost-wrote songs for an ill-fated production that never reached Broadway; doctored songs for another show that opened and closed out of town; and wrote half the score for a revue, *The New Yorkers* (1927) that was a failure. In spite of such disappointments, he became convinced that his talent lay in songwriting. In 1928 he deserted law for music. Only a year after that he proved decisively the wisdom of that decision by becoming one of the composers of *The Little Show*.

Broadway soon felt the impact of *The Grand Street Follies*. While the more elaborate revues continued to flourish, a new kind of production, far less lavish in scope, began to seek and win discriminating audiences. Unquestionably it was from the Neighborhood Playhouse in Grand Street that the Junior Group of the renowned Theatre Guild got the happy idea of putting on *The Garrick Gaieties* in 1925.

This Junior Group was made up of bright, young, talented performers who appeared in bit parts in Theatre Guild productions. In 1924–1925, the Theatre Guild, which up to then had been using the Garrick Theater for its productions, built for itself a stately new mansion on 52nd Street. The Junior Group came up with a plan to put on a show to raise the money for two expensive tapestries for the auditorium. With the Theatre Guild as sponsor, providing the five thousand dollars required for the entire budget, and free use of the Garrick Theater, the Junior Group decided to present their modest offering for two Sunday performances. Philip Loeb became director, Herbert Fields, dance director, Harold Clurman, stage manager. The women of the cast helped to sew the costumes, while the men lent a hand in painting the scenery and building the sets. Several young writers, among them Morrie Ryskind and Newman Levy, provided sketches. When the cast was finally assembled it included not only those who had been among the first to conceive the project but also others whose presence in the theater would some day be strongly felt—performers such as Romney Brent, June Cochrane, Hildegarde Halliday, Betty Starbuck, Lee Strasberg and Libby Holman.

The Garrick Gaieties opened on Sunday, May 17, 1925, for a matinee and evening performance. A sprightly note in the program set the tone for the entire production. *"The Garrick Gaieties* is distinguished from all other organizations of the same character . . . in that it has neither principals nor principles. *The Garrick Gaieties* believe not only in abolishing the star system; they believe in abolishing the stars themselves."

The opening number was "Guilding the Guild," after which came a procession of skits, parodies, songs, dances. Successful Theatre Guild productions were outrageously parodied, with Romney Brent impersonating Alfred Lunt, and Edith Meiser mimicking Lynn Fontanne. There were sketches about the police and manners in the subway, and even a little jazz opera.

Audiences were delighted; the critics, rhapsodic. Alexander Woollcott described the show as "bright with the brightness of something new minted." Robert Benchley called it "the most civilized show in town."

The Guild was encouraged to offer four performances in June (all matinees, all sold out). Then it was put on for a regular run that lasted twenty-five weeks. One year later a second edition was produced at the Garrick Theater with satires on Nijinsky, Queen Elizabeth and several Broadway plays. The third and last edition came to the Guild Theater in 1930.

It was in the first two editions that the songwriting team of Rodgers and Hart first became known to the public through two hit songs, "Manhattan" in the first edition, and "Mountain Greenery" in the second. This was a writing duo whose contributions to the Broadway musical theater, and to popular music, would be of epic dimensions during the next decade or so.

Lorenz Hart, lyricist, and Richard Rodgers, composer, were opposites in personality, temperament and outlook as well as in their living and working habits. Yet it is doubtful if any team in the musical theater worked together with such singleness of thought and harmony of purpose as they did (that is, until Hammerstein joined Rodgers in a later era).

The impact of Hart's lyrics was felt strongly from the very first. When Hart started writing, the lyric was, generally speaking, a sadly neglected and often nearly illiterate stepchild of Tin Pan Alley. For the most part it combined shopworn clichés, bromides and naive sentiments with bad prosody, poor grammar and halting meters and rhythms. Before Hart, the best lyrics of P. G. Wodehouse, Irving Berlin and Ira Gershwin had a cultivated air, but they were exceptions to the prevailing mediocrity and banality.

Hart changed all that. He had a virtuoso's ability to use not only the more formal poetic procedures but also tripping exterior and interior rhymes, glib male and female rhymes, and other clever devices found in good light poetry. He had a way with a phrase that was highly personal, a feeling for figures of speech that avoided the trite and the obvious. His wit and sophistication took unexpected directions. And when he was sentimental, as every commercial lyricist had to be at times, it was usually with restraint and good taste. Frequently his lines leaped with the agility of a dancer, then came to rest easily and gracefully.

His freedom and dexterity of movement and thought would certainly have been arrested, if not completely blanketed, had he not been lucky enough to find an ideal musical collaborator. Richard Rodgers was a composer with an elastic range of idea and feeling, the resiliency to turn to many different styles, the skill to arrive at a fresh thought with simplicity and directness, the independence to think for himself instead of echoing the ideas of other men. He refused to function within those routine patterns and styles that served composers for the theater under many different circumstances and in many different contexts. As he kept on working with his collaborator, and developing and growing with him, he began to conceive of the musical comedy score as a whole rather than a collection of individual parts, each part having a subtle affinity with every other part, a family resemblance so to speak. Rodgers felt strongly—and so did Hart—that a song which did not derive its immediate stimulation from the play for which it was intended could not be integral to the play, and a song that was not integral to the play was superfluous.

They were both novices in the theater when in 1918 they met for the first time. Hart was twenty-three, Rodgers only sixteen. Richard Rodgers was born in 1902 in Hammels Station near Arverne, Long Island, where his parents were spending the summer. Since his father was a successful physician, and his mother a woman of exceptional cultural endowments, the Rodgers household was both comfortable and gracious.

Rodgers once said that he could not remember the time when he did not want to be a composer. In this he received full encouragement from both parents. He started picking out melodies on the piano when he was four; at six he started taking piano lessons and began attending the Broadway theater. He was still a boy when he saw one of Jerome Kern's Broadway shows for the first time. Kern's songs proved a revelation. "The influence of the hero on such a hero-worshiper is not easy to calculate," Rodgers has said, "but it was a deep and lasting one. His less successful musical comedies were no less important to a listener of thirteen or fourteen."

Rodgers seemed to be making music all the time—at home, at assemblies in the public schools he attended, during the exercises when he graduated from public school in 1916. He wrote his first song, "Campfire Days," in 1914 while at a summer camp, following it a few months later with "The Auto Show Girl." In 1917, while attending De Witt Clinton High School, he contributed six musical numbers to an amateur show put on by the Akron Club, a boy's athletic group to which his older brother belonged. As *One Minute Please* it was performed at the Hotel Plaza in New York on December 29, 1917.

One of the members of the Akron Club, Philip Leavitt, was impressed by Dick's musical gifts and felt that those gifts deserved better lyrics than those which the boy had been using up to now. Leavitt was thinking specifically of Lorenz Hart, a young man of uncommon literary and intellectual powers who had a sparkling gift for making up verses. Leavitt suggested to Rodgers that he consider a working arrangement with Hart, and to help bring this about, he brought Rodgers to Hart's home on 119th Street one Sunday afternoon in 1918.

At the first meeting, Rodgers was awed by the fact that Hart was already in his early manhood, being seven years older, and in addition, better schooled and already endowed with a backlog of cultural and intellectual experiences about which Rodgers was still quite innocent. Born in New York City in 1895, Hart had been educated principally in New York's private schools and at Columbia College which he entered in 1913. After a year, he enrolled in Columbia's school of journalism. In 1915 and 1916 he wrote skits and satirical lyrics for the college varsity shows. besides appearing in them as a female impersonator. He left Columbia without a degree in 1917, after which he earned his living translating German operettas into English for the Shuberts, and working during the summer putting on shows at a boys' camp. His ambition was first and foremost the professional theater, and this was the common ground on which he and his young visitor, Dick Rodgers, stood when first they met in 1918.

During that meeting Rodgers was deeply impressed by Hart's knowledge of the theater and poetry, and his personal and unique ideas about how song lyrics should be written. In return, Rodgers sat down at the piano and played for Hart some of his own tunes. Before that day was over, each knew that he must work with the other.

They started working on songs soon after that first meeting, and some of these songs found a receptive ear in Lew Fields, who had recently become a Broadway producer. One day, Rodgers played for Fields some of the numbers he had recently written with Hart. "Any Old Place With You" appealed to the veteran showman, who decided to interpolate it into his musical, A Lonely Romeo, then already running on Broadway. This was in 1919. Lew Fields, then, had the historic role of introducing Rodgers and Hart to the Broadway theater, one of the rare instances in which a seventeen-year old composer was getting a hearing on the professional stage in New York.

In the fall of 1919, Rodgers entered Columbia College where he wrote the music for the Varsity show, Fly With Me, the first time a freshman had ever been called upon to do the music for one of these productions. This musical was seen at the Hotel Astor Ballroom in the Spring of 1920. Lew Fields liked it so much he bought the songs for a musical he was then planning for Broadway, The Poor Little Ritz Girl. It opened on July 28, 1920, half of the score written by Rodgers and Hart, and the other half by the veteran, Sigmund Romberg (with lyrics by Alex Gerber). What attracted most favorable attention was not the music but Hart's lyrics. Heywood Broun wrote in the World: "The neglected lyric gets more of its due than usual, for the song entitled 'Mary, Queen of Scots' seems to us the most rollicking ballad we have heard in a twelve month."

Rodgers and Hart collaborated on a second Columbia Varsity show, and on other songs that were neither published nor performed. Somewhat discouraged, Rodgers decided to study music at the Institute of Musical Art in 1921. A temporary break in these studies enabled him to conduct a tabloid version of a Lew Fields musical which the Shuberts were sending on the road. As for Hart, he returned to the job he had held before collaborating actively with Rodgers, translating and adapting Viennese operettas for the Shuberts. He used the money to produce two Broadway shows without music, both of them failures.

After Rodgers left the Institute of Musical Art in 1923, he and Hart wrote several musicals for which Herbert Fields contributed the book. None found interested producers. While awaiting recognition, Rodgers and Hart wrote about thirty amateur shows for churches, synagogues, schools and clubs, getting only a pittance for such efforts. They also wrote a three-act comedy, The Melody Man, using the thinly disguised pseudonym of "Herbert Richard Lorenz." It was produced by and it starred Lew Fields in the spring of 1924. Since it was a failure, Rodgers, now in debt, decided to quit the theater for good.

He was about to take a job as a salesman of baby's underwear, and forget all about songwriting, when a friend telephoned him and described the project then being hatched by the Junior Group of the Theatre Guild. Rodgers and Hart were induced to write its songs.

The Garrick Gaieties lifted Rodgers and Hart out of obscurity. Their songs, like the overall production, had vivacity and freshness. *Variety* reported that they clicked "like a colonel's heels at attention." Formerly elusive producers now sought out Rodgers and Hart with contracts. With their first Broadway musical in which the score was exclusively theirs, *Dearest Enemy* in 1925, they were well on their way toward changing the destiny of American musical comedy.

The frugal, smart and intimate revue so far had appealed to a comparatively limited audience of sophisticated theatergoers. None of the editions of the *Grand Street Follies* had a run of more than 172 performances and the longest run of any of *The Garrick Gaieties* was 211. *Americana* (1926) also passed the two-hundred performance mark, still only a modest success at best, even though it saw the stage debut of Charles Butterworth as a comedian; for the first time perched the songstress Helen Morgan atop an upright piano to moan a throbbing blues, "Nobody Wants Me" (Morrie Ryskind—Henry Souvaine); and offered a song by George and Ira Gershwin ("The Lost Barber Shop Chord") and a pleasing song item, "Sunny Disposish" (Ira Gershwin—Phil Charig). There were three editions of *Americana*, the second in 1928, the third in 1932, both box-office fiascos. The third edition, however, is remembered for the Depression anthem, "Brother Can You Spare a Dime?" (E. Y. Harburg—Jay Gorney).

In 1929, a new intimate revue became not only a substantial succes d'estime but also box-office magic. The first *Little Show* came to the Music Box Theater on April 20 and remained there a year (331 performances). With the *Little Show*, the informal, sophisticated revue became an integral part of show business. Several unknowns in its case here gained their first recognition. Fred Allen, onetime juggler and ventriloquist, stopped the show regularly with his deadpan and his nasal voice as he delivered wry monologues and commentaries in front of a drawn curtain. Libby Holman established herself as a striking torch singer with her sultry presentations of "Moanin' Low" (Howard Dietz—Ralph Rainger) and "Can't We Be Friends?" (Paul James—Kay Swift). The veteran of the company was Clifton Webb. His debonair way of delivering "I Guess I'll Have to Change My Plan" (Howard Dietz—Arthur Schwartz) and his and Miss Holman's torrid dancing in the "Moanin' Low" sequence brought a welcome change of pace. "I Guess I'll Have to Change My Plan" so neatly suited Webb's style and personality that it is startling to discover that Schwartz had written this melody two years earlier for an amateur production at a boy's camp. At that time it bore the title of "I Love to Lie Awake in Bed," with lyrics by Lorenz Hart, then still very much an amateur at songwriting.

Sketches and lyrics for the *Little Show* were by Howard Dietz, who from this point on would make major contributions to the musical theater, most frequently as Arthur Schwartz's collaborator. Born in New York in 1896, Dietz was a fellow student of both Lorenz Hart and Hammerstein at Columbia College. As a student there Dietz contributed verses to school magazines and to newspaper columns. After leaving college, he served in the Navy during World War I, after which he became successful as an advertising executive. In 1924 he was made advertising director and promotion manager for Metro-Goldwyn-Mayer, with whom he remained thirty years, rising to the office of vice president. While pursuing this career in advertising and promotion, he continued to write song lyrics. In 1924, Dietz wrote the lyrics for the Jerome Kern musical, *Dear Sir*, and in 1927 helped write book and lyrics for an intimate revue, *Merry-Go-Round*. In 1928, Arthur Schwartz persuaded him to become his lyricist. The *Little Show*, to which they contributed most, but not all, of the songs, became the first of a series of collaborations that continued for many years.

There were two other *Little Shows* in 1930 and 1931, the second with sketches and lyrics by Dietz and music by Schwartz. Neither revue had the ingratiating charm and freshness of the original. *The Second Little Show* starred Al Trahan and Jay C. Flippen. Schwartz's music here was modest, and the best numbers came from others—Herman Hupfeld, for example, who supplied words and music for "Sing Something Simple," a plea for songs without tricky rhymes and meters. *The Third Little Show* was dominated by the personality of Beatrice Lillie, who introduced to the American theater Noël Coward's "Mad Dogs and Englishmen." The rest of the numbers were the work of other composers and lyricists, the most amusing being Herman Hupfeld's "When Yuba Plays the Rhumba on the Tuba," sung by Walter O'Keefe.

Much more in the style, tempo and design of the first *Little Show* was *Three's a Crowd* (1930). Once again, Fred Allen, Libby Holman and Clifton Webb were the stars (the "crowd" in the title) and once again Dietz and Schwartz provided materials with the spice and savor of the original. Allen's drawling monologues and Webb's sleek savoir faire in song and dance lost none of their subtle timing. Libby Holman's now famous low moanin' was at its best in Schwartz's "Something to Remember You By" (Howard Dietz) and in "Body and Soul" (Edward Heyman, Robert Sour and Frank Eyton—John Green). "Something to Remember You By" started out as a comedy number called "I Have No Words" for a London musical. It was still planned as a comedy number, though with a change of title and lyrics, when Dietz and Schwartz decided to use the melody in *Three's a Crowd*. Dietz, however, was convinced the song had greater validity as a torch ballad, and that's the way Libby Holman sang it. "Body and Soul" was placed in *Three's a Crowd* after it had been successfully introduced in England by Jack Hylton's orchestra, which recorded it. Max Gordon, the producer of *Three's a Crowd*, acquired the American rights for his revue where, besides being sung by Miss Holman, it was danced to by Clifton Webb and Tamara Geva.

An even higher standard was realized by Dietz and Schwartz in *The Band Wagon* (1931), frequently singled out as one of the best revues ever produced. Here, in the writing of the book, Dietz had the support of George S. Kaufman who helped endow the sketches, characterizations and quips with his own very personal brand of wit.

In 1930, Kaufman had already become a celebrity as playright, musical comedy librettist and newspaperman. He was born in Pittsburgh in 1889. Upon completing his education in the public schools, he worked as a stenographer, traveling salesman and surveyor. All the while, his witty pieces kept appearing in the distinguished newspaper column conducted by Franklin P. Adams (F. P. A.) who was responsible for landing Kaufman his first newspaper job, a column in the Washington *Times* called "This and That." Kaufman moved on to New York in 1914 to write a humorous column for the *Evening Mail*, then worked as a reporter for the New York *Herald* and *The New York Times*. His first appearance as a writer for the stage took place in 1918 with *Someone in the House*, of which he was co-author. As co-author with various playwrights he became outstandingly successful in the twenties with *To the Ladies, Dulcy, Merton of the Movies, Beggar on Horseback* and *The Royal Family*. He also wrote the books for the musical comedies *Helen of Troy, New York* (1923) and the Marx Brothers extravaganza, *The Cocoanuts* (1925).

In *The Band Wagon*, Adele Astaire bowed out as a dancing partner of her brother, Fred, and at the same time as a stage performer. Here, too, Fred Astaire revealed a highly developed adeptness at comedy. Schwartz's opulent score included one of his best songs, "Dancing in the Dark" (Howard Dietz), sung by John Barker before it was danced to by Tilly Losch. (So popular did this song become that its title was used for a motion picture screen musical in 1949 and for Howard Dietz's autobiography published in 1974.) Other Dietz-

Schwartz numbers of especial interest were a polka, "I Love Louisa," for a fetching Bavarian scene, and "New Sun in the Sky" introduced by Fred Astaire.

Flying Colors (1932) was more ambitious in format and scope than either the *Little Show* or *Three's a Crowd*. But it still possessed some of the ingredients that made the two earlier revues so stimulating, principally the songs of Dietz and Schwartz, and the performance of Clifton Webb. Of Schwartz's songs three have become standards: "Alone Together" (danced by Clifton Webb and Tamara Geva), "Louisiana Hayride," used for an arresting production number, and "A Shine on Your Shoes." The cast included Charles Butterworth, Imogene Coca, Vilma and Buddy Ebsen, and Larry Adler and his harmonica.

The next two revues with songs by Dietz and Schwartz were also more pretentious and ambitious than the usual intimate revues. They were *At Home Abroad* (1935) and *Inside U.S.A.* (1948). Both were basically a frame for the clowning of Beatrice Lillie. In the former, the best songs were "Love Is a Dancing Thing" and "Farewell, My Love," together with a blues, "Thief in the Night" sung by Ethel Waters. In *Inside U.S.A.*, the most prominent songs were "Haunted Heart" and "Rhode Island Is Famous for You."

Since nothing on Broadway breeds imitation like success, producers, stimulated by the *Little Show* and *Three's a Crowd*, began competing with one another in the mounting of intimate revues. For *Walk a Little Faster* (1932), starring Beatrice Lillie and Clark and McCullough, Vernon Duke wrote his first full score for Broadway. Since the score included "April in Paris" (E. Y. Harburg)—the song invariably regarded as Duke's best—he was now the proud author of a classic.

Duke's talent as a composer of American popular songs was incubated in the intimate musical revue. His first songs to be heard in the American theater had been "I Am Only Human After All" (Ira Gershwin and E. Y. Harburg), "I'm Grover" (Newman Levy) and "Shavian Shivers" (E. Y. Harburg), the last originally called "Too, Too Divine." All of these appeared in the third edition of *The Garrick Gaieties*. This was in 1930 when another Duke song, "Talkative Toes" (Howard Dietz) was interpolated into *Three's a Crowd*. Two other Duke songs were placed in revues, one in *Shoot the Works* (1931) and the other in *Americana* (1932).

Vernon Duke was born in 1903 in Russia. His name originally was Vladimir Dukelsky which, for many years, he reserved for his serious musical compositions. Music study began when he was seven; composition, a score for a ballet, came only one year later. In 1918, the revolution in Russia drove him from his native land. Taking a circuitous route by way of Constantinople he arrived in America in 1921 hoping to make his way in popular music. This ambition first stirred in him at the Y.M.C.A. in Constantinople when he came upon the sheet music of Gershwin's "Swanee" (Irving Caesar). In New York, he contacted George Gershwin, who gave him criticism and a helping hand, and who also coined for him the name of Vernon Duke, henceforth used for Duke's popular compositions. Duke's beginnings as a popular composer took place at the Paramount studios in Astoria, Long Island. In 1930 he entered the musical theater with two songs in *The Garrick Gaieties*. At the same time he put a foot in Tin Pan Alley by signing a composer contract with Harms.

Walk a Little Faster (1932)—Duke's first complete Broadway score—was no unusual production nor a particular success. It would undoubtedly have been long since forgotten but for the fact that it was the birthplace of "April in Paris." The song was written while the show was rehearsing. There was a need for a romantic interlude. A chance remark, "Oh, to be in Paris now that April's here," gave Duke and his lyricist, E. Y. Harburg, the idea for a romantic number. The song was added to the show during the Boston tryouts, serving as the pivot for a scene set in Paris' Left Bank. Evelyn Hoey, to whom the song was assigned, suffered from laryngitis and could not be heard in the further reaches of the auditorium. This, and the song's subtle melodic structure, mitigated against instant appreciation. Only after *Walk a Little Faster* had closed did the song slowly catch on.

A second Vernon Duke standard, "Autumn in New York," with the words by the composer, was featured in the revue *Thumbs Up* (1932).

Two other prime song favorites written by Duke were performed in the *Ziegfeld Follies* of 1934 and 1936. "What Is There to Say" (E. Y. Harburg), introduced by Jane Froman and Everett Marshall in 1934 and "I Can't Get Started With You" (Ira Gershwin) in 1936 already have been commented upon.

In 1934, Leonard Sillman presented the first of his intimate revues designed to provide an opportunity for unknown or little known performers and writers to get a hearing on Broadway. He called his revue *New Faces*. Among the new faces in that first edition were Imogene Coca, Henry Fonda and Hildegarde Halliday. There were other editions in 1936, 1952, 1956 and 1968. The best of these, and the most successful, was that in 1952 when Eartha Kitt was discovered and where she sang "Monotonous" (June Carroll and Ronnie Graham—Arthur Siegel). "She sang the song sullenly . . . hissing most of it in an absolute paralysis of boredom," recalled Leonard Sillman in his autobiography. *Here Lies Leonard Sillman, Straightened Out At Last* (1961), "until the very end when she really let loose. . . ."

3

The twenties and thirties were decades for creative giants in musical comedy. Never before or since did the musical theater produce such an aggregation of major talents. In music there were Jerome Kern, Richard Rodgers, George Gershwin, Irving Berlin, Vincent Youmans, Ray Henderson, Arthur Schwartz, Cole Porter, Kurt Weill, Rudolf Friml, Sigmund Romberg. Among the librettists and lyricists were Guy Bolton, Otto Harbach, Oscar Hammerstein II, Lorenz Hart, Ira Gershwin, E. Y. Harburg, Howard Dietz, B. G. De Sylva, Lew Brown, George S. Kaufman, Moss Hart, Morrie Ryskind. From those awesome creators sprang some of the greatest American musical comedies and operettas ever produced.

A Jerome Kern Musical?

The twenties began auspiciously, as far as the American musical theater was concerned, with Kern's *Sally* (1920), magnificently produced by Ziegfeld with Marilyn Miller in the title role. The book was by Guy Bolton, and the lyrics by Buddy De Sylva and Clifford Grey. As Sally, Miss Miller was a dishwashing waif who crashes a Long Island party as a "Russian dancer" where her success propels her to a dancing career climaxed by appearances in the *Ziegfeld Follies*. To her role she brought a radiance that illuminated the show's principal song, "Look for the Silver Lining" (B. G. De Sylva), which Kern had previously written for *Brewster's Millions*, a musical that was never produced. She brought to it, as to her overall performance as Sally, what Guy Bolton has described as "an enchantment that no reproduction in other lands or other mediums ever captured." When Miss Miller's screen biography was filmed and released in 1949 it bore the title of this song which she made so famous. Of secondary interest among the songs in *Sally* were the title number (Clifford Grey), "Whip-poor-will" (B. G. De Sylva), both sung by Miss Miller, and "The Little Church Around the Corner" (B. G. De Sylva).

Five years later, in 1925, Marilyn Miller starred in another Kern musical, *Sunny*. The luster of her singing and dancing remained undiminished. As a circus horseback rider in

England who falls in love with an American, she stows away on the ship that is bringing him home. As in *Sally*, she filled the stage with the incandescence of her personality which touched her every song and dance with magic.

Sunny became the crossroads where Jerome Kern and Oscar Hammerstein II (co-author with Otto Harbach of its libretto and lyrics) met creatively for the first time. The grandson of the famous impresario, whose name he carried, and the son of William Hammerstein, manager of New York's Victoria Theater, Oscar Hammerstein II was born in New York City in 1895, Though he came from show people, he was at first directed toward law. As a student at Columbia College (a classmate of Lorenz Hart, Howard Dietz and Morrie Ryskind) he appeared in and wrote sketches for several of the annual varsity shows. In 1917, he went on to law school at Columbia, but his stay there was brief. Before his first year was over he was working where his heart had been for years—the theater—by becoming an assistant manager for the Broadway musical *You're in Love* (1917), produced by his uncle, Arthur Hammerstein. Oscar's hobby had always been writing, and so he wrote a song lyric that was neither published nor performed, a four-act play that opened and closed out of town and, in 1920, the book and lyrics for a musical comedy, *Always You* (music by Herbert Stothart) which was a financial fiasco. Success, for Hammerstein, was not far off, however. In 1920 he collaborated with Otto Harbach and Frank Mandel in writing the book and lyrics for *Tickle Me* (1920)—music by Stothart—which had a run of over two hundred performances. And *Wildflower* (1923)—book and lyrics by Hammerstein and Otto Harbach, and music by Herbert Stothart and Vincent Youmans—was a financial triumph, running for a then spectacular run of 477 performances.

Hammerstein was already well on his winning streak as a writer for the Broadway theater when he first met the redoubtable Jerome Kern in 1924. Before long they talked of working together, and vague conversations were translated into a specific project, *Sunny*.

Working with Hammerstein, Kern soon discovered how valuable a partner he had acquired. One day he turned over to the lyricist a melody whose refrain began with a single note sustained through nine beats for two and a quarter measures; this refrain was repeated five times. It soon became apparent to both men that a single word was required to maintain interest in this sustained note. Hammerstein solved the problem by using "who," which Kern always insisted was the principal reason his song "Who?" became such an enduring success.

Between 1920 and 1927, Kern functioned more or less within the accepted framework of the Broadway musical comedy with writers other than Hammerstein. The two most successful productions starred Fred Stone, his wife, Allene, and their daughter, Dorothy. The first, tailor-made for them and aptly entitled *Stepping Stones* (1923), had two fine Kern songs to lyrics by Anne Caldwell, "Raggedy Ann" and "Once in a Blue Moon." A follow-up to *Stepping Stones* for the performing Stones was *Criss Cross* (1926).

Kern's need to go beyond the restrictions of formal musical comedy was becoming compulsive. He wanted to write the music for a text that was not a synthetic product manufactured for specific stars and their specialties and filled with audience-appealing routines most of which were not particularly germane to the plot. He sought a play that had distinction, plausibility of story, validity of characterizations, authenticity of atmosphere. Kern became convinced that good entertainment need not be sacrificed for good art and vice versa.

With such ideas swirling in his head, Kern seized upon Edna Ferber's novel *Show Boat* as choice material for a new kind of musical, one that was far more than just eye-filling and ear-arresting entertainment, but a bold new concept of what the musical theater could be at its best.

It did not take him long to convince Oscar Hammerstein II to write book and lyrics for the musical stage adaptation, since Hammerstein had also arrived at the conviction that the time had come to jettison some of the hackneyed conventions and practices of musical comedy. For Hammerstein, as for Kern, the writing of *Show Boat* became a labor of love. "We couldn't keep our hands off it," Hammerstein said. "We acted out scenes together and planned the actual direction. We sang to each other. We had ourselves swooning."

Up to this time hardly more than a skillful craftsman, Hammerstein achieved in *Show Boat* a new grace, humanity and poetry. His book became a rich, colorful chapter from America's past filled with dramatic truth, gentle pathos and authentic national character.

Kern's score was studded with exquisite gems. However much he had proved himself a master of aristocratic melodies, Kern never before had been so abundantly lyrical and so varied in his invention. Joe's immortal hymn to the Mississippi, "Ol' Man River" was a modern-day Negro spiritual with the fervor and spontaneous feeling of the authentic product. The wondrous love music of "Make Believe," "Why Do I Love You?", "Can't Help Lovin' Dat Man" and "Bill" (the last with lyrics not by Hammerstein but by P. G. Wodehouse, since the number had been written for another and earlier musical). Each had as distinct an individuality as the characters for which they were intended.

"Ol' Man River" was meant to convey to audiences the impact that the Mississippi River had in the Edna Ferber novel, a character song with the feel of the river in it. Hammerstein himself described it as "a song of resignation with a protest implied, sung by a character who is a rugged and untutored philosopher." Hammerstein's words have the eloquent simplicity of true folk lore; such phrases as "it just keeps rollin' along" and "tote dat barge, lif' dat bale" have acquired permanence in the English language. Prime Minister Churchill, early in World War II, compared the alliance between the British Empire and the United States to the Mississippi. "It just keeps rolling along," he said. "Let it roll . . . inexorable, irresistible."

When Kern first played the melody of "Ol' Man River" for Miss Ferber, "the music mounted, mounted, mounted," as she revealed in her autobiography, *A Peculiar Treasure* (1939), "and I give you my word my hair stood on end, and the tears came to my eyes, and I breathed like a heroine in a melodrama. This was great music. It was music that would outlast Kern's day and mine."

Wodehouse had written the lyrics for "Bill" ten years or so before *Show Boat* for a Princess Theater Show, *Oh, Lady! Lady!* It was not used, and it remained in discard because a suitable singer for it could not be found. When Kern heard Helen Morgan sing "Nobody Wants Me" (Morrie Ryskind—Henry Souvaine) in *Americana*, perched atop an upright piano, he knew that, at long last, "Bill" had found its interpreter. Miss Morgan—a dark, tousled-haired, dewy-eyed singer with a throbbing voice—was cast forthwith as Julie, a role that made her a star; and "Bill" became her big number.

The text had the daring to enter upon a sensitive area formerly considered taboo by escapist theater—miscegenation. The show also dispensed with a chorus girl line, and those bits of humor and burlesque inserted artificially to bring about a change of pace and mood. Nothing was allowed in *Show Boat* that was contrived exclusively for the convenience of stars and their specialties. The plot and the situation was never twisted out of shape to accommodate an attractive piece of stage business. The first and basic consideration was the play and the play alone, with everything else—song, dance, humor, costuming, sets, performers—totally subservient to the aesthetic and dramatic demands of the play.

Opulently produced by Ziegfeld, with a cast that included Helen Morgan, Howard Marsh, Norma Terris, Charles Winninger, Edna May Oliver and Jules Bledsoe, *Show Boat* sailed into the Ziegfeld Theater on December 27, 1927. The critics responded with a unanimity of enthusiasm. To Robert Garland it was "an American masterpiece"; to Richard Watts, Jr. "a beautiful example of musical comedy." Alison Smith wrote in the New York *World*: "It is a complete demonstration of the composer's and lyric writer's dependence on their basic idea . . . a fidelity unrecognized by most musical comedy book makers." In the New York *Sun*, Stephen Rathbun reported: "From any angle, costumes, score, story, singing or acting, *Show Boat* deserves the highest praise."

The public reacted in kind. During its initial run of 572 performances it grossed an average of about $50,000 a week. Later it embarked on an extensive national tour, playing to sold out houses. A triumph when first produced, *Show Boat* has since become a classic. It has often been revived in many parts of the United States; on three occasions it was adapted for the screen—in 1929 as a part talking picture with Laura La Plante, Joseph Schildkraut and Alma Rubens; in 1936, with Allan Jones, Irene Dunne and Helen Morgan; and in 1951 with Howard Keel, Kathryn Grayson and Ava Gardner. It entered the opera house when, in 1954, the New York City Opera included it in its regular repertory. Its melodies also invaded the symphony hall, adapted by Kern into a tone poem, *Scenario*, which was introduced by the Cleveland Orchestra under Artur Rodzinski in 1941.

Two later Kern musicals further developed the musico-dramatic concept first realized by *Show Boat*. In 1931, with *The Cat and the Fiddle*, Kern temporarily parted company with Hammerstein to resume an old collaboration with Otto Harbach. Once again, as in *Show Boat*, the chief concern of the authors was to project a musical play without interference by chorus girl routines, synthetic humor or set numbers. The action moved fluidly. Harbach's book, set in Brussels, centered on a love affair between a serious Roumanian composer and an American girl crazy about jazz. Kern's tuneful score grew naturally out of the action, its finest songs being "The Night Was Made for Love," "She Didn't Say Yes," "Poor Pierrot," and "One Moment Alone." Even after *Show Boat*, John Mason Brown could say in his review that this was "the loveliest, most ambitious score that Mr. Kern has yet written," and Gilbert Gabriel could maintain that "Broadway has not heard lovelier music in all its life."

Music in the Air (1932), for which Oscar Hammerstein II returned to write book and lyrics, was described by its authors as "a musical adventure." This adventure takes place in the little Bavarian mountain town of Edendorf and involves the stormy romance of Karl Reder, the local school teacher, and Sieglinde, a would-be singer.

"Gemütlich" is perhaps the word best describing text and music. The picturesque background of Edendorf is enhanced by such songs as "In Egern on the Tegern See" which has the flavor of a German folk song, and the vivacious German beer hall vocals offered by the Edendorf choral society. The play gains radiance from the background music, notably the first act "Scene Music." Other unforgettable melodies contribute further enchantment; the duet of the two lovers, "I've Told Ev'ry Little Star" and the serenade, "The Song Is You."

So admirable is the fusion of music and play, so naturally do the various parts fit the overall pattern, that the production represented to Brooks Atkinson of *The New York Times* "the emancipation of the musical drama." Atkinson still thought highly of the music when *Music in the Air* was revived on Broadway in 1951.

Kern did not altogether abandon the more traditional musical comedy, the kind with which he had received so much acclaim in the first two decades of the twentieth century. Between *Show Boat* and *The Cat and the Fiddle*, he wrote the music for *Sweet Adeline* (1929), a gay and sentimental romance of the nineties starring Helen Morgan and Charles Butterworth. Here the authors of *Show Boat* (with Oscar Hammerstein II once again functioning as librettist-lyricist) were turning back the theatrical clock by writing a show in the stylized manner of their earlier musical comedies. Two Kern gems have survived, both poignantly presented by Helen Morgan, "Why Was I Born?" and "Here Am I."

Roberta (1933) was once again a reversion to styles of the past. With book and lyrics by Otto Harbach, based on Alice Duer Miller's novel, Gowns by Roberta, it had a Parisian background—a fashionable modiste shop owned by a woman called Roberta, played by Fay Templeton in her farewell to the stage. An American fullback, John Kent, and the shop's chief designer, Stephanie, a Russian princess, take over its management, and in time fall in love.

Roberta owed its success largely to a single song, "Smoke Gets in Your Eyes," one of the most beautiful Kern ever wrote. From opening night on, whenever Tamara, as Stephanie, sang this second-act ballad she stopped the show cold. The song swept the country, accumulating one of the largest sales in sheet music and records of any Kern number. Two other songs—"Yesterdays" and "The Touch of Your Hand"—lent further eminence to a production which otherwise would have been quite humdrum, with its action continually arrested by parades of fashions. Bob Hope was seen here in a subsidiary role and was heard in another appealing Kern number, "You're Devastating."

If a song masterpiece could make Roberta attractive at the box office, it proved ineffectual for Kern's last Broadway musical, Very Warm for May (1939), book and lyrics by Oscar Hammerstein II. It told a trite story about a badly managed New England stock company and the love complications of each of two young people (offspring of two of the company's performers) for people in high society. "The book," reported Brooks Atkinson, "is a singularly haphazard invention, that throws the whole show out of focus and makes an appreciation of Mr. Kern's music almost a challenge." A shame!—for "All the Things You Are" belongs not only with the best of Kern but with the best in American popular music. Despite the subtlety of its structure and the comparative complexity of its enharmonic changes, "All the Things You Are" had immediate appeal and achieved formidable figures in sheet music and record sales. Popular though this song was, it was unable to save the production. Very Warm for May stayed on for just fifty-nine performances and passed unlamented.

And so, Kern's historic association with Broadway ended after almost thirty years with a box-office and critical fiasco. After 1939, Kern worked almost exclusively for motion pictures.

A George Gershwin Musical?

While George Gershwin was justifying the high hopes the concert world held for him by writing the Rhapsody in Blue, the Concerto in F and other serious compositions, he did not neglect the musical theater.

Upon leaving the Scandals in 1924, Gershwin completed the music for his first musical comedy since La, La, Lucille of 1919. It was for Lady, Be Good! starring Fred and Adele Astaire in a book by Guy Bolton and Fred Thompson, in which Gershwin revealed new creative powers in the writing of popular songs. "Fascinating Rhythm," presented by the Astaires in song and dance, used changing meters with virtuoso skill. The title number, "Oh, Lady Be Good!", sung by Walter Catlett and a chorus of flappers, ingeniously utilized triplets in cut time. "So Am I," introduced by Adele Astaire and Alan Edwards, disclosed new depths of feeling in Gershwin's lyricism. But the best song in the score was deleted during out-of-town tryouts because it delayed the play's action and was judged by the producer to lack popular appeal. (The Gershwins later tried unsuccessfully to place it in two other shows. It never did appear in a Gershwin musical, and was issued as an independent number.) The song, "The Man I Love" (Ira Gershwin), is memorable for its contrapuntal background of a descending chromatic figure to a melody made up of a six-note blues progression. The song first grew popular with jazz orchestras in London and Paris. Not until about a half a dozen years after it was written did it gain acceptance in the United States, first in performances by Helen Morgan. It has become one of the most treasured of Gershwin's standards; Gershwin once singled it as one of his own favorites among his popular songs.

Lady, Be Good! became a milestone in Gershwin's stage career because it was the first Gershwin musical comedy for which his brother, Ira, wrote all the lyrics. They had previously worked together on some random songs. The first to get a public hearing was "The Real American Folk Song," which Nora Bayes interpolated in 1918 into Ladies First.

But in Lady, Be Good!, Ira was George's sole lyricist. From then on, the Gershwin brothers went on to become one of the most successful words-and-music partners Broadway and Hollywood has known, with Ira consistently providing George with smart, deft, neatly turned verses capable of stimulating a brilliant composer's imagination.

Ira was two years older than George, born in New York City in 1896. He was the bookish member of the Gershwin family. At Townsend Harris Hall, a New York high school for superior students, he wrote a column for, and was the art editor of the school paper. At the College of the City of New York, he collaborated with Erwin Harburg (later the famous lyricist, E. Y. Harburg) in editing a column for the college weekly; he also contributed small items to New York City newspapers. After two years at college, Ira transferred to night courses, while working during the day as a cashier at a Turkish bath. His writing activity remained undiminished. He sold a humorous piece to Smart Set edited by H. L. Mencken and George Jean Nathan (for one dollar!) and wrote criticisms on vaudeville for The Clipper (with no payment). By 1917 he began turning his talent to song lyrics. The first was a parody of an 1890 type of song, "You May Throw All the Rice You Desire, But Please, Friends, Throw No Shoes," which Don Marquis published in his column in the New York Sun. Ira also wrote the words for some songs for which brother George fashioned the music.

After "The Real American Folk Song" became the first lyric by Ira to reach the stage, he moved fast. In 1921, five songs by George and Ira Gershwin were interpolated into a musical, A Dangerous Maid, which failed to reach Broadway after out-of-town tryouts. Ira's first success came in the same year with lyrics for Two Little Girls in Blue—music by Vincent Youmans and Paul Lannin—where he disguised himself under the pen name of Arthur Francis so as not to capitalize on the rapidly increasing fame of his brother. But in 1924 he emerged from pseudonymity with lyrics for some of the songs in Be Yourself, a musical with book by George S. Kaufman and Marc Connelly and music by Lewis Gensler and Milton Schwartzwald. And it was as Ira Gershwin that, later the same year, he became his brother's full-time collaborator in Lady, Be Good!

After Lady, Be Good!, the Gershwins were represented on Broadway by a dozen musicals, whose basic importance lay in their best songs. Tip-Toes (1925)—starring Queenie Smith in a book by Guy Bolton and Fred Thompson—had "That Certain Feeling," "Sweet and Low Down" and "Looking for a Boy." Oh, Kay! (1926)—book by Guy Bolton and P. G. Wodehouse—starred Gertrude Lawrence in her first appearance in an American written musical, with the comedy support of Victor Moore cast as a bootlegger passing himself off as a butler on a Long Island estate. This score overflowed with musical treasures: "Someone to Watch Over Me," made so memorable by Gertrude Lawrence; the insouciant "Do, Do, Do," boycotted by the radio for many years because the lyrics were considered too suggestive; two numbers in Gershwin's felicitous rhythmic vein, "Clap Yo' Hands" and "Fidgety Feet"; and "Maybe." In Funny Face (1927)—book by Paul Gerard Smith and Fred Thompson

—Fred and Adele Astaire introduced the title number and "Let's Kiss and Make Up." In addition, its well-endowed score included " 'S Wonderful," "He Loves and She Loves," "My One and Only," and one of Ira Gershwin's most brilliant sets of lyrics, "The Babbitt and the Bromide."

The year 1930 was a banner year for the Gershwins. It brought *Girl Crazy*, a box-office success, and the second version of *Strike Up the Band*, an artistic one.

Girl Crazy—book by Guy Bolton and John McGowan—placed a Park Avenue playboy on a dude ranch in Custerville, Arizona.

There were many attractions in *Girl Crazy*. First and foremost were the songs, still another potion of Gershwin magic. The score had one of Gershwin's most poignant love ballads in "Embraceable You," which Ginger Rogers offered in this her second major appearance on Broadway. A secondary ballad no less affecting was "But Not for Me." "Bidin' My Time," sung by a cowboy quartet accompanying themselves with a harmonica, jew's harp, ocarina and tin flute, was a charming takeoff on hillbilly tunes, and "Sam and Delilah" was a satire on the "Frankie and Johnny" type of folk ballad. "Boy! What Love Has Done to Me!" was sophisticated and "I Got Rhythm" had high voltage dynamism.

The orchestra in the pit included some of the all-time greats in jazz, led by Red Nichols: Benny Goodman, Glenn Miller, Jack Teagarden, Jimmy Dorsey and Gene Krupa.

There was the lovable Ginger Rogers to capture audience interest, cast as a sweet ingenue, and there was the comedy and mimicry of Willie Howard as the Jewish taxicab driver who brings the hero in his cab from New York to Custerville.

But surely not the least of the pulses in *Girl Crazy* was the volcanic performance of Ethel Merman in her musical comedy bow. When she appeared on the stage and hurled her big brassy voice across the footlights in "Sam and Delilah" and "I Got Rhythm"—holding the high C in the chorus of "I Got Rhythm" for sixteen measures while the orchestra continued with the melody—the impact of singer on audience was cataclysmic.

A onetime stenographer who was born Ethel Zimmermann in Astoria, New York, in 1909, Miss Merman had preceded *Girl Crazy* with appearances at weddings, parties and in small nightclubs. During an appearance at the Brooklyn Paramount Theater, she attracted the interest of Vinton Freedley, then on the eve of producing *Girl Crazy*. He brought her to George Gershwin who auditioned her in his Riverside Drive apartment. She sang "Little White Lies" (Walter Donaldson) and "Exactly Like You" (Dorothy Fields—Jimmy McHugh) and several other numbers. Gershwin responded by going to the piano and playing for her the songs he had planned for Kate Fothergill, wife of the man who runs the gambling concession at the dude ranch. Without saying so, Gershwin was taking it for granted that Ethel Merman would play Kate. The day after the premiere of *Girl Crazy* Gershwin took Ethel Merman to lunch and was amazed to discover she had not read any of the reviews, all of which raved about her performance. "You're in with both feet," he told her.

Strike Up the Band preceded *Girl Crazy* by nine months, arriving early in 1930. This was the second version of a musical comedy that had played out of town before it decided to close shop for lack of audience interest. The first version had a book by George S. Kaufman which, in the second, was greatly altered by Morrie Ryskind to make it appealing to a wider public. The first version had been a bold, devastating attack on war in which the expected accoutrements of musical comedy were discarded in order to treat international diplomacy, big business, tariffs, war and war profiteers with malice toward all and charity toward none. "Satire," George S. Kaufman once quipped, "is what closes on Saturday night." And satire is what closed down the first version of *Strike Up the Band* in Philadelphia.

In the new version, the satire was muted through the introduction of farcical material written for Bobby Clark and Paul McCullough. Clark (with his omnipresent equipment of cigar, cane and painted eyeglasses) was the unofficial spokesman of the United States, while his comedy partner, McCullough, was cast as the head of the enemy army. Despite the introduction of broad comedy to make the original pungent dish more palatable, *Strike Up the Band,* in its elaborate rewriting, remained adult fare well spiced with satire. It was one of the few musical productions of the period to reveal a strong political consciousness. For even adulterated, *Strike Up the Band* remained a keen political travesty highlighting a war between the United States and Switzerland over the issue of the tariff on chocolates. This theme provided the authors with an opportunity to regard war, big business, diplomacy, and the seemingly lofty ideals for which wars are fought, with mockery. And there was a healthy dose of malice in the music as well. Martial pomp was deflated in the marches "Strike Up the Band" and "Entrance of the Swiss Army"; American chauvinism is reduced to proper size in "A Typical Self-Made American." Several other numbers, however, are in Gershwin's winning lyrical manner, particularly the ballad, "Soon," and the duet, "I've Got a Crush on You." (The latter song had previously been heard in an earlier Gershwin musical, *Treasure Girl,* in 1928.)

With *Strike Up the Band,* the authors veered toward a new direction in the musical theater. Good as it was, *Strike Up the Band* was just a hint of better things to come. One year later, the same authors of text and music came up with a new musical satire in *Of Thee I Sing,* a shattering musico-dramatic commentary on American political life. The heart of its book was a presidential campaign in which Wintergreen and Throttlebottom, played by William Gaxton and Victor Moore, run and are elected as president and vice-president of the United States on a "love ticket," with Wintergreen required to marry a "Miss White House," chosen in an Atlantic City beauty contest.

The story digresses frequently to point a finger of ridicule at the comedy-of-errors of the Washington political scene, at political rallies, the Senate and the Supreme Court and the often forgotten man of politics, the vice-president. Ira Gershwin's breezy lyrics neatly captured the spirit of the text in some of his most nimble and needle-sharp verses of his career, and so did George Gershwin's music. At every point songs helped underline the satirical suggestions and implications of the play. "Wintergreen for President" lampooned political campaign songs, with its neatly interpolated quotations of "Hail, Hail the Gang's All Here," "The Stars and Stripes Forever," "Tammany," "A Hot Time in the Old Town Tonight." The title song struck a blow at patriotic songs and Tin Pan Alley with one swing, beginning as it does as a solemn hymn but suddenly lapsing into Tin Pan Alley sentiment with "of thee I sing—*baby*." In several other instances two birds are destroyed with a single stone: Viennese waltzes and American motherhood in "I'm About to Be a Mother," grand opera and the dignity of the Senate in the Senate scene. But the score is also noteworthy for songs capable of standing apart from the overall texture: the title song, "Who Cares?" and "Love Is Sweeping the Country."

Of Thee I Sing had the longest Broadway run of any Gershwin musical (441 performances) and was the only Gershwin musical with two simultaneous productions, the second a national touring company. It was the first musical comedy in theater history to receive the Pulitzer Prize in drama, and the first American musical comedy to have its book published without the music (by Alfred A. Knopf, Inc.). The musical has often been revived in many different places, especially during years of presidential elections, including a television production in 1972.

Gershwin's last musical was the zenith of his career as both a popular and a serious composer, his folk opera *Porgy and Bess,* first performed by the Theatre Guild in Boston and

New York in the fall of 1935. Du Bose Heyward's libretto was based on the play *Porgy*, written with his wife, Dorothy, which had been successfully produced by the Theatre Guild. Du Bose Heyward shared with Ira Gershwin the task of writing the lyrics for the opera.

Much in *Porgy and Bess* makes use of jazz and other popular elements, together with styles and techniques of grand opera. As I wrote in my biography of Gershwin, *George Gershwin: His Journey to Greatness*, the folk opera "represents, at last, the meeting point for the two divergent paths he [Gershwin] had all his life been pursuing to those of serious and popular music. The serious musician is found at his best in the musically distinguished tone speech, in the powerful antiphonal choruses, in the expressive dissonances and chromaticisms, in the brilliant orchestration, in the effective atmospheric writing, in the skillful use of counterpoint in the duets, and particularly in the last-scene trio. The popular composer emerges in the jazz background of several choruses . . . in the two songs of Sportin' Life, "It Ain't Necessarily So,' and 'There's a Boat Dat's Leavin' Soon for New York,' and in Crown's sacrilegious blues ditty, 'A Red Headed Woman Makes a Choochoo Train Jump Its Track.' Yet there is no feeling of contradiction, no sense of incongruity, in this mingling of the serious and the popular, for the popular is as basic to Gershwin's design as the serious, with its own specific function."

Gershwin's music drew sustenance from Negro folk sources as well as from jazz and Tin Pan Alley. Interspersed in the score are shouts, spirituals, street cries, work songs. This might have been expected in a text about Negroes calling, for the most part, for black performers in a setting like Catfish Row, a tenement in Charleston, South Carolina.

At the premiere, the black cast was comprised mostly of newcomers, headed by Todd Duncan as Porgy and Anne Brown as Bess. An exception was John W. Bubbles, cast as Sportin' Life, a veteran of vaudeville where he had appeared in an act called Buck and Bubbles. (Ford L. Buck was also in the original cast of *Porgy and Bess*.) Bubbles could not read a note of music, had difficulty remembering his lines, and seemed incapable of understanding his role. But George Gershwin was convinced that Bubbles was ideal as Sportin' Life and expended uncommon patience and energy teaching him the intricacies of the role. Bubbles turned in a masterful characterization, much to Gershwin's satisfaction.

Musical excerpts from the opera became popular long before the opera itself. The premiere in New York, with a run of just 124 performances, provided no indication that in time this would be an opera overwhelmed by critical and public acclaim throughout the civilized world. The individual numbers proved a truly remarkable musical cache: the lullaby "Summertime," with which the opera opens; Porgy's outpouring of exultant joy in life, "I Got Plenty of Nuttin' "; the lament, "My Man's Gone Now"; the love duet of Porgy and Bess, "Bess, You Is My Woman Now"; Sportin' Life's cynical "It Ain't Necessarily So" and his enticing, "There's a Boat Dat's Leavin' Soon for New York."

The opera's progress to world triumph must surely be one of the most dramatic and unique experiences in music history. Revived in New York on January 22, 1942, almost five years after Gershwin's death, *Porgy and Bess* had the longest run of any revival in Broadway musical history. Between 1952 and 1956, an American Negro company then toured with it throughout Europe, the Near East, the Soviet Union, countries behind the Iron Curtain, South America and Mexico to an enthusiastic response with few parallels in opera history. After that, *Porgy and Bess* was mounted by many European and American companies in their repertories, was recorded almost in its entirety, and in 1959 was made into a lavish motion picture produced by Samuel Goldwyn, and starring Sidney Poitier, Dorothy Dandridge and Sammy Davis, Jr.

On June 25, 1970, *Porgy and Bess* was produced for the first time in its own locale of

Charleston, South Carolina, in commemoration of the three hundredth anniversary of the founding of the city. The performance was given in a desegregated theater and at the party that followed the black cast mingled socially with whites, the first time such an event had ever happened in Charleston.

When we consider how many productions *Porgy and Bess* has enjoyed worldwide since its premiere in 1935, and that it has been recorded several times and has been made into a movie, it comes as a shock to discover that this opera had to wait forty years to get heard in its entirety the way Gershwin originally wrote it. When *Porgy and Bess* was first produced, cuts were made not only to reduce the running time from the almost three hours called for by the mammoth 559-page score, but also to spare Todd Duncan in the singing role of Porgy. In Boston, during the tryouts, George Gershwin told his brother, Ira: "You won't have a Porgy by the time we reach New York. No one can sing that much eight performances a week!" In this process, the important "Buzzard Song" was removed from the first act together with several lesser segments. Since that time, *Porgy and Bess* has always been given with cuts. Even the excellent Columbia recording in 1955 produced by Goddard Lieberson, purporting to be "complete," had deletions, though the "Buzzard Song" was restored. The "Buzzard Song" was also included in the historic Blevins-Breen production of the 1950s that toured abroad, though shifted to the third act; and in this production sung recitatives were replaced by spoken dialogue.

The first complete performance of *Porgy and Bess*, with recitatives instead of spoken dialogue, was finally given at the Blossom Music Center in Cleveland on August 16, 1975, in a concert presentation by the Cleveland Orchestra, the Cleveland Orchestra Chorus, and distinguished soloists, Lorin Maazel conducting. A complete recording by the same performers was released by London Records in 1976. Here, after the orchestral introduction, the opera does not begin with "Summertime" but with the "Jazzbo Brown Blues" played on the piano, followed by a chorus singing "Da-doo-da, Wa-wa." The "Buzzard Song" and a patter song for Maria were restored, and so were the introductions to the second and third scenes of Act III. Other long omitted odds and ends throughout the opera were returned to their original design, notably "Oh, Doctor Jesus," "O Hev'nly Father" and "Oh, Dere's Somebody Knockin' at de Do'." In reviewing the recording of this now complete version, Edward Greenfield, writing in the London publication, *Gramophone*, emphasized how much better *Porgy and Bess* sounded as Gershwin originally conceived it from the way it was subsequently produced. "It emerges here," said Mr. Greenfield, "triumphantly on the grand operatic side of the fence, a work in its way as moving and revealing of human nature as *Wozzeck* on the one hand, and *Peter Grimes* on the other. . . . The bigness can here be appreciated fully for the first time."

This complete *Porgy and Bess*, but now compressed from three acts into two, was given its first stage presentation in Houston, Texas, by the Houston Grand Opera Company in the spring of 1976. Following a summer tour, this production was brought to New York on September 25, 1976, and in 1977 was recorded by RCA.

After *Porgy and Bess*, Gershwin transferred his musical activity from Broadway to Hollywood.

A Vincent Youmans Musical?

Vincent Youmans belongs with the giants of the American musical theater of the 1920s. He wrote the scores for two of the leading stage successes of that decade, *No, No, Nanette* and *Hit the Deck*. Some of his songs because a permanent part of the popular repertory. His creative imagination, gift for a neatly turned melodic phrase, economy and precision all gave many critics of the 1920's good cause to place him with America's foremost popular composers.

This assurance comes to us from his successes. But, strangely, it comes just as strongly from his failures. Musical plays like *Rainbow* (which had only twenty-nine performances in 1928) and *Through the Years* (twenty performances in 1932) hint at a new concept of the musical theater, a musico-dramatic concept that remained to be realized by others. But Youmans must be considered a pioneer in this virgin territory.

He was born in New York City in 1898. Piano lessons began when he was four. Though he proved immensely musical, his father, a successful businessman, insisted he be trained for the world of commerce. In 1916, Vincent worked as a messenger for the Guaranty Trust Company in Wall Street. But his bent was for music, and after three weeks he left Wall Street for Tin Pan Alley to work as a piano demonstrator for J. H. Remick (the same time that young George Gershwin was employed there).

During World War I, Youmans enlisted in the Navy. At the Great Lakes Station he produced musical shows for which he sometimes wrote songs; he also played the piano in a Navy band. John Philip Sousa, then conductor of Navy as well as Army bands, liked one of his numbers and performed it frequently; other Navy bands followed suit until it became familiar to sailors everywhere. Ten years later this song grew even more popular in *Hit the Deck* as "Hallelujah."

After the war, Youmans was employed as a song plugger for Harms. There he renewed his early friendship with George Gershwin who successfully used his influence to get Youmans an assignment to write for the Broadway stage. This happened soon after Youmans' first publication appeared in 1920 with the Remick imprint, "The Country Cousin" (Alfred Bryan). Youmans' Broadway assignment was to collaborate with Paul Lannin in writing the music for *Two Little Girls in Blue* (1922), Ira Gershwin as their lyricist. With a cast headed by Oscar Shaw and the Fairbanks Twins, *Two Little Girls in Blue*, though no blockbuster, enjoyed a profitable run. One Youmans song clicked, "Oh Me, Oh My, Oh You."

In 1923 came *Wildflower*, an impressive success with its Broadway run of 447 performances. Book and lyrics were by Oscar Hammerstein II and Otto Harbach, while the music was a collaborative effort between Youmans and Herbert Stothart. This score had two salient musical items, the title song and "Bambalina," the latter describing a country fiddler who delights in confusing his dancers by stopping unexpectedly in the middle of a phrase.

No, No, Nanette (1925) was an even greater overall success, though when it was first seen in Detroit in 1924 it had all the earmarks of failure. A major overhaul followed in which the text was extensively revised by Otto Harbach and Frank Mandel, a few new songs were added by Youmans, and the cast was strengthened with Louise Groody as Nanette, Charles Winninger as her guardian, Jimmy Smith, who has a weakness for young girls, and Wellington Cross as Billy Early. Completely revamped, the musical moved on to Chicago where it stayed a year before finally settling at the Globe Theater in New York on September 16, 1925, to begin a 321-performance run. In London it stayed for a remarkable string of 665 performances. Seventeen companies toured South America, New Zealand, the Philippines and China. *No, No, Nanette* was unquestionably one of the most successful musicals of the twenties.

Vincent Youmans' songs (with lyrics by Irving Caesar and Otto Harbach) were some of the best he had written. A disarming simplicity concealed the skill of their structure, the ease with which a melodic line moved, the natural way in which accents fell, the subtlety of the rhythmic pulse and syncopation. This economy marks the two hit songs, "Tea for Two" and "I Want to Be Happy," both to Caesar's lyrics. The melody of "Tea for Two" had been written long before *No, No, Nanette* was conceived; in fact, while Youmans was still in the Navy. Later he used a fragment from this tune for one of his songs in *Two Little Girls in Blue* ("Who's Who with You?") While working on *No, No, Nanette,* after the Detroit debacle, Youmans resurrected this melody and developed it into a new song. He played it one night for Irving Caesar, insisting that Caesar produce his lyric then and there. To satisfy Youmans, Caesar improvised a dummy lyric, intending to discard it for a more satisfying one the following day. But Youmans was so delighted with it that the dummy lyric became the actual one.

As for *No, No, Nanette,* history repeated itself a generation later. In 1971, *No, No, Nanette* soared to triumph as perhaps the most successful revival of a musical comedy ever seen on Broadway (861 performances).

Youmans' next major Broadway musical was staged in 1927. Herbert Fields made a musical adaptation of the Broadway comedy *Shore Leave* (1922), calling it *Hit the Deck.* It was a nautical affair, with Louise Groody again playing the stellar role as the proprietess of a coffee shop in Newport, Rhode Island, near a Navy installation.

With Youmans doubling as composer and coproducer, *Hit the Deck* exceeded the original Broadway run of *No, No, Nanette* by thirty-one performances. The songs (with lyrics by Leo Robin and Clifford Grey) included two all-time Youmans favorites, "Hallelujah," a male chorus, and the duet, "Sometimes I'm Happy," shared by Louise Groody and Charles King.

Between 1927 and 1932, Youmans was heard on Broadway in a succession of box-office disasters, two of which he himself produced, though he was temperamentally unsuited to fulfill this function. But he did not have to be ashamed of two of these failures since each, in its own way, represented a courageous attempt to bring a new spaciousness and artistic validity to the musical stage. *Rainbow,* produced in 1928, was a romantic play with text by Laurence Stallings and Oscar Hammerstein II, set in California during the Gold Rush days of 1849. If any single musical deserves recognition as the precursor of *Oklahoma!* this is it. *Through the Years,* which Youmans himself produced in 1932, was another attempt to write a musical play rather than a musical comedy. This was Brian Hooker's adaptation of *Smilin' Through,* a sentimental play produced on Broadway in 1919, which achieved additional radiance through Youmans' music. Two of its songs, lyrics by Edward Heyman, are famous, the title song (the composer's own favorite among his compositions) and "Drums in My Heart."

How Edward Heyman wrote the lyric for "Through the Years" was described by the lyricist in a letter to this author: "Youmans expressed the importance of this song and told me that of all the melodies he had ever written that this was by far his favorite. He lived in a penthouse apartment in the West Forties, and the night was a rare New York one in which the moonlight actually filtered into the room. He turned out all the lights, opened the terrace doors, and sat me in a large chair facing the piano. For a little over one half an hour, he played the melody over and over without stopping . . . and then I asked him to stop because the lyric was finished. There was not one word ever changed in the lyric and as it is heard today, it was written then."

Individual songs, rather than the productions in which they were set, brought value to others of Youmans' musicals. A few of these numbers further reveal the composer's mastery of his technique, his assurance in achieving exactness of musical expression, compactness of form and thorough articulateness. *Great Day* (1929) had "More than You Know" (Billy Rose and Edward Eliscu), while out of *Smiles* (1930) came "Time on My Hands"

(Harold Adamson and Mack Gordon), introduced by Paul Gregory and Marilyn Miller. "Rise 'n Shine" (B. G. De Sylva), in the style of a revivalist hymn, found a place in *Take a Chance* (1932), a musical for which Richard A. Whiting and Nacio Herb Brown wrote most of the music, and sung with deserving fervor and intensity by Ethel Merman. This was Youman's last contribution to the Broadway stage. In 1933 he went on to Hollywood to write the music for *Flying Down to Rio*.

A Rodgers and Hart Musical?

Kern's *Show Boat*, *The Cat and the Fiddle* and *Music in the Air*, Gershwin's *Strike Up the Band* and *Of Thee I Sing*, and Youmans' *Rainbow* were attempts by the musical theater of the 1920s and early 1930s to establish a closer relationship not only between the words and melodies of songs, but also among songs, dance and book in the overall production.

One pair of writers proceeded toward this same goal consciously, endowed with the talent and imagination necessary to bring it off. That pair was Rodgers and Hart, who had first come to public recognition with *The Garrick Gaieties* in 1925. Rodgers and Hart went on from there to become the most successful words-and-music pair in the theater of that period. They wrote twenty-eight musicals (not to mention nine scores for motion pictures) and several hundred songs. Fifteen of their musicals were box-office successes, and nine were made into motion pictures. Fifty and more of their songs belong with the best in American popular music.

Their success with *The Garrick Gaieties* suddenly made them very much in demand, and they met the interest of producers with extraordinary industry. In 1926 five Rodgers and Hart shows were on Broadway; between 1926 and 1932 they averaged three shows a season.

In some of these productions they profited from the collaboration of Herbert Fields, a librettist well able to keep step not only with their varied invention but also with their passion for attempting the untried. Fields was a member of that distinguished stage family headed by father Lew Fields, the comedy partner of Weber and later a producer, and including sister Dorothy, the lyricist, and brother Joseph, librettist. Born in New York City in 1897, Herbert Fields was educated in the New York City public schools and at Columbia College. He wanted to become an actor, an ambition his father encouraged by allowing him to appear in bit parts in some of his productions. Then in 1919 Rodgers and Hart convinced him to try his hand at writing. The three young men joined forces for a musical, *Winkle Town*, which was never produced, for a nonmusical play (with some interpolated songs) that was a failure when mounted on Broadway in 1924, and for some amateur productions.

Their first collaborative effort to strike gold was *Dearest Enemy* which opened on Broadway on September 18, 1925 (while *The Garrick Gaieties* was still running). Herbert Fields' text broke new ground for a musical comedy book by going to American history for the story, a source musical comedy so far had carefully avoided. The subject was an episode during the American Revolution when Mrs. Robert Murray, and several other patriotic ladies, exploited the endowments with which nature had blessed them as females to delay British troops in New York long enough to permit George Washington and his Continental army to make a strategic retreat. At one point, when the ladies realize they are going to be compromised, they reply stoically: "War is war."

Though the score boasted a hit in "Here In My Arms," it was not so notable for its songs as for the spaciousness of the overall musical writing that embraced duets, trios, choral numbers and even an eighteenth-century gavotte. From then on, Rodgers was to demonstrate his talent for thinking in dimensions larger than the popular song. Through ballets, dream sequences, marches and extended recitatives he would henceforth endow his scores with a scope not usually encountered in the musical theater of the 1920s or 1930s. Beyond all this, Rodgers revealed an instinct for good theater and a taste for dramatic writing that made it possible for him to understand and sympathize with the subtlest demands of his collaborators. For their own part, both Lorenz Hart and Herbert Fields revealed a sound critical sense for music and were well able to comprehend and respond to Rodgers' intentions. These two co-workers, Hart and Fields, not only ploughed their own literary fields, but often provided important suggestions for musical treatments, even as Rodgers had the astute intelligence and the sure dramatic instincts to offer an assist to his writing partners whenever necessary.

Peggy-Ann (1926) was another venture into an unmined area. It was the first Broadway musical to touch on Freudian and psychoanalytical ideas. *Peggy-Ann* is a dream fantasy in which the heroine escapes from her humdrum life in Glens Falls, New York. Surrealistic is the way in which, throughout this dream sequence, fish are made to speak with an English accent, race horses are interviewed, policemen wear pink moustaches, and a wedding ceremony has Peggy-Ann appear dressed in step-ins and uses a telephone book instead of a Bible.

Together with traditional songs—the best of which are "A Tree in the Park," "Where's that Rainbow?" and "Maybe It's Me"—the score included atmospheric and ballet music capturing the free-flowing spirit of the text. Accepted musical comedy practices are shattered in the opening and closing sequences. For the first fifteen minutes there was no singing or dancing, something without precedent on Broadway; and the musical ended in an equally unorthodox manner with a slow dance sequence on a darkened stage, instead of a big closing production number with full cast.

The reason *The Girl Friend* (1926) did so well financially on Broadway was because two of its songs quickly gained popularity around the country so that, inevitably, curiosity was aroused in an otherwise undistinguished musical. The two songs were the title number and "Blue Room."

The year 1927 brought to Broadway another unusual Rodgers-Hart-Fields musical in *A Connecticut Yankee*, a modern adaptation of the Mark Twain story, *A Connecticut Yankee in King Arthur's Court*. The musical comedy begins in the present with the hero (played by William Gaxton) being hit on the head with a champagne bottle by his fiancée. Losing consciousness, he slips dreamward back to the sixth century, to Camelot. There he becomes "Sir Boss," an office in which he proceeds to introduce such twentieth-century refinements as telephones, radio, American slang, advertising billboards, efficiency experts and so forth. Hart was never more agile in his versification or wittier than here. Amusing is the way in which pseudo-Arthurian phraseology is blended with American jargon in "Thou Swell"—"thous" and "wouldsts" coexisting with "lalla paloosa" and the like. "On a Desert Island with Thee" boasts some of the most scintillating lyrics to be found in any song lyric of the 1920s.

"My Heart Stood Still" from *A Connecticut Yankee* is one of the best love ballads Rodgers and Hart ever wrote. The lyric came to Hart after a perilous taxi ride in Paris when his girl friend had exclaimed: "Oh, my heart stood still." The song was completed in London, and was heard for the first time in *One Dam Thing After Another*, a London revue produced by Charles B. Cochran in the spring of 1927. The song quickly became a favorite in England, especially after the then Prince of Wales (later the King of England and after that, Duke of Windsor) asked that it be played for him one evening at the Royal Western Yacht Club in Plymouth, England. Further interest in the song was aroused by the rumor, later proved false, that Ziegfeld wanted to buy it for one of his own productions in America. Recognizing its value, Rodgers and Hart acquired the American rights to their song from

Cochran (by accepting a lower royalty for their score to *One Dam Thing After Another*) and used it in *A Connecticut Yankee*.

If it took about a decade for Rodgers and Hart to write another musical comedy as good or as successful as *A Connecticut Yankee*, it was not for lack of trying. They had seven musicals produced in New York and one in London. All were minor efforts, more entertaining than original. If they are remembered today it is solely because of their best songs: "You Took Advantage of Me" in *Present Arms* (1928); "With a Song in My Heart" (later to become Jane Froman's theme song and the title of her screen biography in 1952) in *Spring Is Here* (1929); "A Ship Without a Sail" in *Heads Up* (1929; and "Ten Cents a Dance" the lament of a taxi dancer, made famous by Ruth Etting in *Simple Simon* (1930).

After *America's Sweetheart* (1931), a satire on Hollywood and its star system, Rodgers and Hart worked for the screen for four years. They returned to Broadway in 1935 with *Jumbo*, a spectacle combining circus with musical comedy. It was produced by Billy Rose at the Hippodrome Theater with book by Ben Hecht and Charles MacArthur and the direction by George Abbott, in his initiation to musical comedy. This was a very small step forward. At best, however, it provided some breathtaking circus stunts, some welcome comedy involving Jimmy Durante, and a wonderful score that included three Rodgers and Hart classics, "My Romance," "The Most Beautiful Girl in the World," and "Little Girl Blue."

But Rodgers and Hart had not abandoned their onetime ideal to shape the musical comedy along revolutionary and innovative lines. Back from Hollywood, they were talking about "musical plays" as distinguished from musical comedies. As Hart explained, they now wanted their songs to be "a definite part of the show and not extraneous interludes without rhyme or reason." They aspired to make humor, song and dance spring naturally from the textual situations, each to be a "plot number." They wanted all the music to carry the action forward, not delay it. They were also thinking of paying more attention to ballet and less to vaudeville-type tap dances and musical comedy girlie routines.

Their first effort in this direction, following their return to Broadway, was *On Your Toes* (1936). This was the first time that Rodgers and Hart had a share in writing the text, in which they were assisted by George Abbott. In *On Your Toes* musical comedy entered the world of ballet, spotlighting the backstage life of a Russian ballet troupe saved from bankruptcy by a onetime vaudevillian who has the company produce a jazz ballet and star him in it. For 1936 this was unusual material for a musical comedy, and to do it justice, George Balanchine, former master of the Diaghilev Ballet and the Ballet Russe de Monte Carlo, was contracted to do the choreography, his first such chore in the popular musical theater. He conceived two principal ballets, "La Princesse Zenobia," a satire on formal Russian ballets based on the subject of Scheherazade, and the other a ballet in an American style and tempo, "Slaughter on Tenth Avenue," the climax of the entire musical.

Much in *On Your Toes* betrayed its age when it was revived in 1954, but not "Slaughter on Tenth Avenue," probably Rodgers' best music in a more ambitious format than the song. As Richard Watts, Jr., wrote in 1954; "A sizable number of jazz ballets have passed this way since its appearance, but it is still something of a classic in its field." The song, "There's a Small Hotel," has proved more popular and been heard more frequently through the years than "Slaughter on Tenth Avenue." But if the true value of a piece of music is measured by artistic validity rather than popularity, "Slaughter on Tenth Avenue" is the musical jewel of *On Your Toes*. Mr. Balanchine acknowledged as much in 1968 when he and the New York City ballet featured it on a serious program of ballets, the only other attraction being one inspired by Igor Stravinsky's *Requiem Canticles*.

Babes in Arms (1937) was the first musical in which Rodgers and Hart received no outside help in the writing of the book. This, too, was unique in coalescing text, song, dance and humor into a single artistic entity. Here we come upon the escapades of several young-sters, the offspring of traveling vaudevillians who, left by themselves on Long Island, produce a show to raise the money to keep them from being herded off to a work camp. George Balanchine once again carried the choreographic burdens. In one of his ballets, "Peter's Journey," characters appear as Marlene Dietrich, Clark Gable and Greta Garbo. "Calhoun's Follies" is an amateur show in which the young people are the participants. The score has four distinguished songs: "Where or When," "Johnny One Note," "The Lady Is a Tramp" and "My Funny Valentine." As Robert Coleman said in his review in the *Mirror*, "Rodgers and Hart thrust aside the conventional musical comedy format in favor of novelty, surprise and freshness."

In *I'd Rather Be Right* (1937) Rodgers and Hart teamed with George S. Kaufman and Moss Hart in the writing of a political satire in the manner of *Of Thee I Sing*. The Gershwin musical had availed itself of a presidential campaign with fictitious characters. *I'd Rather Be Right* had one character portraying an American President who looked, talked and behaved like Franklin D. Roosevelt, penetratingly portrayed by George M. Cohan in one of the outstanding stage characterizations of his career. As president of the United States he comes, in a dream sequence, to Peggy and Phil, a young couple too financially pressed to get married. Borrowing actual names in the news and commenting sardonically on current events, this musical proved a source of none too innocent merriment. Only one song stood out, "Have You Met Miss Jones?" The score was much better as a whole than in individual parts. In numbers such as "A Homogeneous Cabinet," "A Little Bit of Constitutional Fun," "We're Going to Balance the Budget" and "Off the Record," composer and lyricist made a conscious attempt to interrelate music and play more indivisibly than they had previously done.

After coming to grips with the realities of Washington politics, Rodgers and Hart returned to ballet and fantasy, for which they had already revealed a deft touch. They adapted a Hungarian play by Janos Vaszary. *I Married an Angel* (1938) was one of the happier efforts of Rodgers and Hart. It starred Vera Zorina, an alumna of the Ballet Russe, as the angel, and provided her with ample opportunity to exhibit her terpischorean art, particu-larly in the "Honeymoon Ballet." Though emphasized, ballet was well integrated into the whole tapestry. An ideal balance between fantasy and broad humor was another attraction of this musical, while the title song and "Spring Is Here"—together with some delightful musical interludes—contributed appreciably to the overall charm.

Some of the musicals engaging Rodgers and Hart after *I Married an Angel* pointed to their growing audacity in selecting texts, a healthy effort to provide the musical theater with new horizons through the exploitation of unusual subjects. *The Boys from Syracuse* (1938), book by George Abbott, took its plot from *The Comedy of Errors*, the first time, but assuredly not the last, that Shakespeare provided material for the popular American musical theater. Eddie Albert and Jimmy Savo starred as Antipholus of Syracuse and his servant Dromio and their look-alikes of the same names in Ephesus played by Ronald Graham and Teddy Hart. Complications pile on complications, some of a bawdy nature, in this confusion of identities. Two of Rodgers' most beguiling songs were introduced; "This Can't Be Love" and "Falling in Love with Love."

It took courage and independence for musical comedy writers to dip into Shakespeare for their characters and plot. But it took even greater fortitude for Rodgers and Hart to write the musical *Pal Joey* (1940). *Pal Joey* originated as a series of sketches, in letter form, by John O'Hara published in *The New Yorker*. The main character, (played by Gene Kelly who here became a star for the first time), was an opportunistic nightclub hoofer who realized his ambition to own a nightclub by becoming the lover of a wealthy, hard-boiled matron, Vera. In the end he loses his nightclub, Vera, and his girl, Linda. As adapted for the musical stage by O'Hara, *Pal Joey* uncovered some of the less palatable facets of life on Chicago's South Side, including blackmail, illicit love, downright skullduggery, hypocrisy and double-dealing. This was not the kind of material that lent itself to escapist musical theater. Rodgers and Hart recognized this when they induced O'Hara to adapt his pieces into a musical comedy text. Yet they were convinced that the O'Hara stories might introduce a new virility to the musical stage through a closer identification with everyday life. "If it is possible to make an entertaining musical comedy out of an odious story, *Pal Joey* is it," wrote Brooks Atkinson. "Although *Pal Joey* is expertly done, can you draw sweet water from a foul well?" Apparently, theatergoers, for the most part, felt the way Mr. Atkinson did. They rejected *Pal Joey* for its vivid realism and its unpalatable characters.

During the original run of *Pal Joey*, its hit song was "I Could Write a Book." Vera's song, "Bewitched, Bothered and Bewildered" passed unnoticed, but became successful in Paris under the title *"Perdu dans un rêve immense d'amour."* In the late 1940s, "Bewitched, Bothered and Bewildered" began to circulate in American nightclubs, on records and over the radio, and by 1950 it actually made the top spot on radio's "Your Hit Parade" one week. This popularity of a nine-year-old song tempted the farsighted executive of Columbia Records, Goddard Lieberson, to record the score in 1951 which, in turn, inspired a 1952 Broadway revival that ran for more than five hundred performances and broke all preceding box-office records for a revival. The New York Drama Critics Circle now selected it as the season's best musical, and it captured eleven of sixteen Donaldson Awards. In 1957, *Pal Joey* became an attractive movie musical starring Frank Sinatra, Rita Hayworth and Kim Novak. On June 27, 1976, it was once again revived in New York at the Circle in the Square Theater.

In the last of the Rodgers and Hart musicals, *By Jupiter* (1942), they turned to classical antiquity by adapting Julian F. Thompson's comedy, *The Warrior's Husband*, where women are the warriors and the men tend to the household. The main songs were "Careless Rhapsody," "Wait Till You See Her" and "Nobody's Heart."

The run of *By Jupiter* (427 performances) was the longest of any Rodgers and Hart musical. It would have run much longer than that, since it was playing to capacity houses, but the show had to close because its star, Ray Bolger, was to make a flight to the South Seas to entertain American troops during World War II, and Bolger was irreplaceable.

This was the last *new* musical by Rodgers and Hart, but not the last Rodgers and Hart musical to be produced during Hart's lifetime. In 1943, *A Connecticut Yankee* was revived. For it, Rodgers and Hart wrote six new songs, among them being "To Keep My Love Alive," written for and introduced by Vivienne Segal.

Then the partnership was over. Always somewhat shiftless, irresponsible, oversensitive and disorderly in his daily living and working habits, Lorenz Hart grew increasingly undisciplined with the coming of fame and prosperity. Working with him had become a torment to Rodgers. Besides, Hart was mentally and physically ill, an alcoholic. During the writing of *By Jupiter* he had to be hospitalized; work on the musical went by fits and starts, often in the hospital itself. After the opening of *By Jupiter*, Hart went off to Mexico for a few months, a futile attempt to run away from himself. He returned wearier than ever, more depressed and more inclined to find escape in drinking. He had lost all interest in his success, in his talent, and even in the theater itself. When, in 1942, the Theater Guild asked Rodgers and Hart to adapt Lynn Riggs' dramatic folk play, *Green Grow the*

Lilacs, into a musical, Hart bowed out gently but definitely. After all these years, Rodgers had to find a new collaborator.

Having lost the will to work, Hart soon lost the will to live. On March 31, 1943, the musical made from *Green Grow the Lilacs*—*Oklahoma!*—opened at the St. James Theater to inaugurate not only a new musical stage partnership, that of Rodgers and Hammerstein, but also a new era in the musical theater. A few months later, on November 17, *A Connecticut Yankee* was revived. On opening night, Hart disappeared from the theater while the performance was still on. Forty-eight hours later he was found unconscious in his hotel room. He died a few days later, on November 22, of double pneumonia. He was only forty-eight .

"The great thing about Hart's work," wrote P. G. Wodehouse, "was its consistency, even more than its brilliance. Larry Hart was always good. If there is a bad lyric of his in existence, I have not come across it. It seems to me he had everything. He could be ultrasophisticated and simple and sincere. He could handle humor and sentiment. And his rhyming, of course, was impeccable. . . . He brought something quite new into a rather tired business."

The glory that had been the epoch of Rodgers and Hart in the American musical theater was recalled nostalgically on May 13, 1975, with the production of *Rodgers and Hart*, described as a "musical celebration," at the Helen Hayes Theater on Broadway. This production was a concept by Richard Lewine and John Fearnley, choreography by Donald Saddler and staging by Burt Shevelove. The score was a cornucopia of Rodgers and Hart song classics.

A De Sylva, Brown and Henderson Musical?

With the scores of two editions of *George White's Scandals* behind them, De Sylva, Brown and Henderson (with an assist from Laurence Schwab who helped in the writing of the book) went to work on *Good News*, their first musical comedy. In the 1920s, people had an inordinate interest in college life—not, to be sure, the life of the classroom, but the football field, the fraternity and sorority houses, class dances and college romances. Going to the college football game, a hip flask of bootleg liquor for sustenance, was *the* thing to do. This absorption in matters collegiate helped make the song "Collegiate" (Moe Jaffe—Nat Bonx) a hit in 1925; it helped to arouse public adulation for Rudy Vallee, a Yale alumnus, and for his first band, The Yale Collegians.

Good News, in 1927, catered to this vogue for things collegiate. Its setting was Tait College where the emphasis was on football and fraternities rather than the curriculum. The ushers in the theater wore college jerseys. The men in the pit orchestra (George Olsen Band) ran down the aisles of the theater to their places before curtain time letting loose with collegiate "rah-rahs." Throughout the evening, the college spirit was intensified by rousing tunes: "The Varsity Drag," which made the Varsity Drag a popular social dance in the mid-1920s; "On the Campus," "Flaming Youth" and "The Girls of Pi Beta Phi."

In line with the optimistic, Pollyannaish outlook of the 1920s, the principal love song of this musical was "The Best Things in Life Are Free." In 1956 it was used as the title for the screen biography of De Sylva, Brown and Henderson.

Hold Everything! (1928) once again lampooned the contemporary scene, this time the prizefight game and "clean sportsmanship." Bert Lahr was cast as a badly mauled pugilist, and Victor Moore as his hapless and much victimized manager. One of the foremost songs by De Sylva, Brown and Henderson from this score was "You're the Cream in My Coffee."

Follow Thru (1929) saw Jack Haley cavorting in a swanky golf club to offer a pungent commentary on country life and the golfing set. It brought Eleanor Powell her first Broadway success as a step toward even greater triumphs in screen musicals. Text and music were in the happiest De Sylva, Brown and Henderson vein, with the score enriched by "Button Up Your Overcoat" (its rhythms neatly tapped out by Miss Powell's quicksilver toes after it had been sung by Jack Haley and Zelma O'Neal), "My Lucky Star" and "I Want to Be Bad," the last closely identified with Zelma O'Neal.

The last of the DeSylva, Brown and Henderson musicals, *Flying High* (1930), was, like its predecessors, a box-office smash. It concerned itself with airmail pilots and their ambition to overcome the obscurity of their humdrum lives by establishing flying records. Comedy was contributed by Bert Lahr, and an excellent score included "Thank Your Father," "Good for You, Bad for Me" and "Wasn't It Beautiful While It Lasted?"

Hollywood and motion pictures broke up the winning combination of De Sylva, Brown and Henderson, but not before it had created some of the earlier successes of talking pictures. De Sylva became a motion picture producer, occasionally returning to Broadway to put on stage musicals. When he died in Hollywood in 1950 he was still a top man in show business on both coasts. While De Sylva was in Hollywood, Brown and Henderson collaborated on two musicals, neither particularly appealing. For a while after that, Brown and Henderson parted company, Brown going out to the coast as a producer in Hollywood, while Henderson completed some musical chores for Broadway, including the *George White Scandals of 1935* and the *Ziegfeld Follies of 1943*, besides making some contributions to the screen. Eventually, Brown and Henderson reestablished their partnership by opening a publishing firm in New York. Brown died in New York City in 1958, Ray Henderson in Greenwich, Connecticut, in 1970.

In 1944, a De Sylva, Brown and Henderson song, "Together," which had been published as an independent number in 1928, was interpolated into the nonmusical motion picture *Since You Went Away* and was selected as one of the ten best songs of that year. In 1947, a new screen adaptation of *Good News* was filmed (an earlier one had been made in 1930). In 1956, *The Best Things in Life Are Free* brought the life story of De Sylva, Brown and Henderson to the screen, studded with their best songs. In 1974, *Good News* was successfully revived on Broadway with Alice Faye and Gene Nelson. All these were reminders of the heyday of De Sylva, Brown and Henderson.

An Irving Berlin Musical?

After writing the music for the fourth, and last, edition of the *Music Box Revue* in 1924, and for the *Ziegfeld Follies of 1927*, Irving Berlin lapsed into a five-year period of silence, as far as the stage was concerned.

A year or so after his marriage to Ellin Mackay, Berlin wrote "The Song Is Ended." It was almost as if he had a prophetic glimpse of what was lying in store for him. For after completing this song, Berlin was mysteriously paralyzed creatively. He destroyed much of what he wrote; whatever he tried writing seemed trite and repetitious. To make matters worse, during this period, he saw his fortune decimated by the economic debacle that followed the stock market crash of 1929. He needed new hit songs, not only to satisfy his creative urges and to bolster his sagging self-confidence, but also to make a living.

The road back to financial security began in 1932 when two of his old ballads, never before published, were lifted from oblivion: "Say It Isn't So," resurrected by Rudy Vallee over the radio and in a Victor recording, and "How Deep Is the Ocean?". The rehabilitation of Berlin's finances was further solidified with the musical comedy *Face the Music* (1932), book by Moss Hart. Moss Hart was then a comparative newcomer to the Broadway theater, having recently emerged from obscurity and poverty into the limelight of public acceptance and prosperity with the farcical takeoff of Hollywood and talking pictures, *Once in a Lifetime* (1930), written collaboratively with George S. Kaufman. *Face the Music* was Hart's second Broadway production, and his first musical. His text made a shambles of the shenanigans of politicians and corrupt policemen in an uproarious yarn about a crooked officer of the law trying to dispose of his illicit cash by investing in a Broadway musical that seems destined for disaster but which turns out to be a huge financial success. One of the songs, "Let's Have Another Cup O' Coffee," threaded together such Pollyannaish clichés as "there's a rainbow in the sky," and "trouble's just a bubble" to prove that, dark though these days may be, all will turn out well in the end. "I Say It's Spinach" ("and the hell with it") equated the Depression with that unpopular vegetable. Romance took over in the lovely ballad "Soft Lights and Sweet Music."

Berlin's next encounter with the musical theater, his last for a decade, was with the topical revue *As Thousands Cheer* (1933). Seven years later he was back in musical comedy with *Louisiana Purchase*.

A Cole Porter Musical?

Cole Porter epitomized the 1920s in song and lyrics. In him we find the response of that decade to romance and love, remote from the cloying sentimentality and antiseptic cleanliness of so many Tin Pan Alley love ballads. Cole Porter was the cynic whose love was often for sale; who could be true to you only in his fashion; to whom that seemingly crushing love affair was just one of those things.

If his attitude toward love and romance reflected the spirit of the 1920s, so did his partiality for dilettantism and catchpenny philosophies. Through his lyrics he sprinkled, with a crackling succession of scintillating rhymes, all kinds of cultural, literary and geographical allusions. His suave and well-groomed melodies, like his lyrics, eschewed the tender and the sentimental for sensuality and throbbing excitement.

His personal and artistic credo was "anything goes"—even as it was the banner under which the 1920s marched to catastrophe. Like a character from an F. Scott Fitzgerald novel, Porter was the ultra-sophisticate—the carnation sported in his lapel like a legion-of-honor symbol of a faithful sybarite—searching ceaselessly for the fullest riches life could yield; he was the high priest of life's pleasures. Fortunately he was also something of a genius, with a genius's compulsion to create.

Cole Porter was born to wealth on a seven-hundred-acre fruit farm in Peru, Indiana, in 1891. His mother early directed him to the study of the violin and the piano. Though he detested music lessons and exercises, he revealed a strong feeling for music by composing a song when he was ten, and soon after that "The Bobolink Waltz," a piano piece published in Chicago. At thirteen he was enrolled in the Worcester Academy in Massachusetts where he remained three years and where much of his free time was devoted to playing the piano and writing humorous or whimsical songs about members of the faculty. Between 1909 and 1913 he attended Yale. There he led the glee club, wrote music for and helped to produce college shows, and wrote football songs. Two of his football numbers were published and became famous at Yale, "Bingo Eli Yale" and "Yale Bulldog Song." He also wrote a popular song, "Bridget," which J. H. Remick published in 1910.

After a brief stay at Harvard Law School, he transferred to its School of Music where, for the next three years, he received a comprehensive training in piano, theory, music history and orchestration. Despite this application to serious music, he continued writing popular songs. In 1915, two of them found a place in a Broadway musical, *Miss Informa-*

tion, whose basic score was by Kern. Another Porter song was placed in a Sigmund Romberg musical, *Hands Up*.

The first Broadway show made up entirely of Cole Porter's songs was *See America First* (1916). It was a fiasco. Porter wryly remarked that this failure was responsible for sending the author of the book to the priesthood "possibly in penance." As for himself: "I had to leave town until the smell of my first Broadway show had disappeared." Out of this disaster came a song that was a portent of things to come. It was "I've a Shooting-Box in Scotland," whose lyrics touched upon the many exciting foreign or exotic places where the author would have liked to make a home for himself. After the closing of *See America First*, Fred and Adele Astaire used this number in their vaudeville act.

During World War I, Porter saw service in France with the 32nd Field Artillery Regiment and with the Bureau of the Military Attaché of the United States. He acquired a luxurious apartment in Paris and, though in uniform, became famous as a host. Once out of service, in 1919, he remained in Paris to extend his activities as a full-fledged member of the international set. His parties—and the crisp, smart and frequently sexy little songs he wrote and performed for his guests—attracted the elite of Paris to his swank home on the Rue Gounod. One of those most strongly drawn to him was an American socialite, Linda Lee Thomas, one of the most beautiful women and one of the most celebrated hostesses in Paris. She was the divorced wife of the publisher of the *Morning Telegraph*. Linda and Cole fell in love, and were married on December 18, 1919. They set up home on the Rue Monsieur where the parties were long and brilliant. Guests came for the evening and sometimes stayed through the weekend. The Porters hired the Monte Carlo Ballet for one of their festivities. On another occasion, at a moment's whim, all the guests were transported by motorcar to the French Riviera.

In 1923, the Porters transferred their gay life to Venice, to the Rezzonico Palace where Robert Browning had once lived. They had a floating nightclub constructed which accommodated over a hundred guests. They had Elsa Maxwell plan elaborate games, such as a treasure hunt through the canals, or arrange sumptuous balls. The 1920s were here, and the Porters were doing their best to set the tone for the era.

How music did not get lost in all these feverish celebrations and frenetic diversions remains something of a miracle. Porter continued writing songs, including ten numbers for *Hitchy Koo of 1919*, a Broadway revue produced by Raymond Hitchcock. One of its numbers became Porter's first hit, though a minor one: "An Old Fashioned Garden" to which Porter himself remained partial all his life.

Porter contributed six songs to *Hitchy Koo of 1922* (which opened and closed in Boston) and five to the *Greenwich Village Follies of 1924*. He also wrote some risqué but sophisticated songs exclusively for the delectation of his friends, songs like "Settembrini" in which there appears the pithy comment that "those Lido boys are mere decoys." His friends—the Prince of Wales, Noël Coward, the Princesse de Polignac, Cecil Beaton, Baron Nicholas de Gunzburg, Monty Woolley, Howard Sturges, Elsa Maxwell—admitted he had creative talent, but also insisted that it was of the kind that could not readily be offered for sale. "The reason is as plain as the nose on my face," Elsa Maxwell once told him. "You are too good. Your standards are too high. The wit and poetry of your lyrics are far beyond the people. But one day you will haul the public up to your own level, and then the world will be yours." She was, of course, right.

At the Lido, in Venice, E. Ray Goetz, the Broadway producer, moved into the Porter·orbit. Goetz was then planning *Paris*, a musical starring his wife, Irene Bordoni, which called for the kind of slick and suave songs Porter wrote so well. He assigned the score to Porter. The book placed a young man from Boston into the conniving hands of a French actress. He is rescued by his oversolicitous mother, with the actress finding consolation with her leading man. Three of Porter's songs were in the subtly suggestive vein frequently the hallmark of his best songs. They were "Let's Do It," introduced by Miss Bordoni, "Let's Misbehave," which was dropped from the show by the time it reached New York, and "Two Little Babes in the Wood."

Paris (1928) did moderately well, with 195 performances and some flattering notices. *Fifty Million Frenchmen* (1929) did even better. Herbert Fields, fresh from his successes with Rodgers and Hart, prepared a book in which a wealthy American playboy in Paris disguises himself as an impoverished guide so that he may win Loulou's love not for his wealth but for himself alone. The story was an excuse for offering the city of Paris in its many and varied attractions and beauties. Among the Porter songs were "Find Me a Primitive Man," "You've Got That Thing" and "You Do Something to Me." In a newspaper advertisement which he himself paid for, Irving Berlin called these songs "the best collection of . . . numbers I have listened to."

Between 1929 and 1930, two other Porter song standards were on Broadway. A revue, *Wake Up and Dream* (1929), was the showcase for "What Is This Thing Called Love?" whose melody is believed to have come to Porter while he was listening to native music in Marrakesh. In 1930, a book show, *The New Yorkers*, became memorable for Porter's "Love for Sale," one of the rare instances, and the only successful one, in which the world's oldest profession is the subject; for many years this song was banned from the radio airwaves.

Porter's identity as a songwriter was now established. With a wry and frequently sardonic air, and always an elegant manner, his lyrics passed, as Fred Lounsberry remarked, "from the esoteric to the lowbrow, the idealistic to the inconoclastic, the sophisticated to the sentimental." Porter's individuality as a composer was fixed: the frequently long sweeping lyric line, almost Semitic in character, and in a languorous minor mode, refusing to stop to breathe after the sixteenth bar; the nervous throbbing of an irresistible rhythm in the background; the deep purple moods and the sensually exciting climaxes.

Once he had settled down to the business of being a professional songwriter there was nothing of the dilettante about Porter. He became a careful and methodical worker, capable of intense preoccupation with the job at hand, fastidious about meeting deadlines. By 1930, the playboy had become a composer who had won the respect of his colleagues, the enthusiasm of critics, and the admiration of a large public. His songs were among the smartest and most original, both in subject matter and in treatment, heard in or out of the Broadway theater of that period. He had succeeded in doing what Elsa Maxwell had prophesied he would: lift the public to his own level. But he had only begun. After 1930, he participated in more successful musical productions, and was responsible for a longer string of song hits than anyone, with the exception of Irving Berlin or Richard Rodgers.

The reign of "King Cole" on Broadway began officially in 1932 with *Gay Divorce* (the movies added an extra "e" to the last word), a frothy bedroom comedy in an English seaside resort in which an actress, seeking a divorce, is scheduled to be compromised by a co-respondent. A writer, Guy, happens to be in love with this actress and is mistaken for her co-respondent. Fred Astaire played Guy in his usual debonair style. But *Gay Divorce* is primarily remembered as the birthplace of one of the most distinguished songs by an American, "Night and Day," the idea for which came to Porter in Morocco when he heard a Mohammedan priest in prayer. The mounting success of that song was a box-office stimulant, so much so that the musical had to be moved to a larger theater to meet the demand, and the show came to be know as the "Night and Day" musical. "Night and Day" served in 1946 as the title for Cole Porter's screen biography.

Two years later came *Anything Goes* (1934), looked upon by some Broadway commentators as the high point of Cole Porter's career. The first version of its book—by P. G. Wodehouse and Guy Bolton—assembled a strangely mismatched group of characters on a gambling vessel that becomes shipwrecked. Then an actual disaster, the burning of the *Morro Castle* off the coast of New Jersey with a loss of one hundred and thirty-four lives, made the subject of shipwrecks a highly sensitive one, and certainly not one for humor. Howard Lindsay and Russell Crouse were summoned to rewrite the book, the first time that these two men (who would make stage history with *Life with Father*) worked together. Crouse was a newspaperman who wrote a daily humor column for the New York *Evening Post* between 1924 and 1929, and later was employed by the Theatre Guild as press agent. His first two attempts at writing books for musical comedies, in 1931 and 1933, were failures. In spite of Crouse's sorry track record Vinton Freedley, the producer of *Anything Goes*, called upon him to work with Lindsay on that musical. Lindsay came to this assignment after a long and successful career in the theater as actor, director and collaborator in several Broadway plays. *Anything Goes* was his first musical comedy.

The final version placed a curious assortment of characters aboard a luxury liner bound for Europe. They included Public Enemy No. 13 fleeing from the law disguised as a Reverend, played by Victor Moore; a dynamic nightclub entertainer, a role assumed by Ethel Merman; and a young man, played by William Gaxton, who stows away to be near a girl passenger he loves.

The choicest treasures in this musical were Porter's songs. The sardonic attitudes, ecstatic moods, sophisticated poses and sexual suggestions with which he was already identified were found in the title number, in "All Through the Night" and in "I Get a Kick Out of You," the last profiting greatly from Miss Merman's lusty presentation. There were other types of songs, too: a song with lighthearted wit and gaiety, a parody of sailor chanteys, "There'll Always Be a Lady Fair"; a patter song with the neatness and dispatch of Gilbert and Sullivan, "You're the Top," an exchange of superlatives between Ethel Merman and William Gaxton; and a song with bold brass and vigor, written with Miss Merman in mind, "Blow, Gabriel, Blow."

It took Porter another four years to become involved in a musical as satisfying and as successful as *Anything Goes*. In 1938, Bella and Samuel Spewack adapted their stage success *Clear All Wires* into the musical *Leave It to Me!* Victor Moore, who almost stole the show in *Anything Goes*, did just that in *Leave It to Me!*, though he had formidable rivals in Sophie Tucker, Tamara and Mary Martin in her Broadway bow. Moore appeared as a sadly befuddled American ambassador to the Soviet Union, eager to get home again to enjoy double banana splits, and who instigates all kinds of incidents with the hope that he might be recalled.

Though Victor Moore contributed the cream of performances, as well as the cream of the jest, one other cast member captured the spotlight. She was Mary Martin, a little girl from Weatherford, Texas, born there in 1913. She operated a dancing school in her native town, then made her first public appearance in small nightclubs and over the radio. When she performed at the Trocadero in Hollywood, she was discovered by the producer of *Leave It to Me!* and brought into the cast of that show for a small part.

Shedding her ermines in a simulated striptease by the side of a Siberian railroad, this unknown performer sang in a childlike voice: "While tearing off a game of golf, I may make a play for the caddy; but when I do, I don't follow through, 'cause my heart belongs to daddy." A minor role suddenly assumed major proportions through Miss Martin's incomparable rendition of "My Heart Belongs to Daddy." This was a number written by Porter as an afterthought, for the purpose of filling in a stage wait during a scene change. An obscure young actress suddenly became one of the all-time greats of the musical comedy stage.

Leave It to Me! ushered in a new cycle of successes for Porter that continued in 1939 with *Du Barry Was a Lady*. The book, by Herbert Fields and Buddy De Sylva, enmeshed Louis XV (played by Bert Lahr) and Madame Du Barry (Ethel Merman) in frustrated amatory involvements at the Petit Trianon. "Friendship," a song exchange between Miss Merman and Bert Lahr, and "Katie Went to Haiti," torridly sung by Miss Merman, were the top songs. "Well Did You Evah!" helped to introduce Betty Grable to show business.

A Kurt Weill Musical?

Before coming to the United States, Kurt Weill was successful in pre-Hitler Germany as a serious composer, particularly of operas. Immediately after coming to New York he redirected his energies and extraordinary talent to the Broadway musical theater. Within a short time he became one of its major composers, one of the best equipped technically, and one of the most knowledgable about the demands and needs of the stage.

He was born in Dessau, Germany, in 1900, and received his musical training at the Berlin High School for Music and, privately, from Ferruccio Busoni, one of the most esoteric musical thinkers of his time. Weill's first opera, *The Protagonist*, was based on a surrealistic text by Georg Kaiser and produced successfully in 1926 by the Dresden Opera. The Berlin State Opera then commissioned him to write *The Royal Palace* (1927) in which the book and staging utilized actual motion pictures. Here, too, Weill began experimenting with the use of popular American musical idioms, a bent that grew ever bolder in his next opera, *The Czar Has Himself Photographed* (1928), which one German critic dubbed a "jazz opera." Next came a one-act opera, *Mahagonny* (1927) which was expanded to full length under the title of *The Rise and Fall of the City Mahagonny* (1930). Mahagonny is a fictional town in the State of Alabama in the United States where three ex-convicts build a new kind of society where everything is permissible and pardonable. In line with its American setting, Weill included in his score elements of jazz, the blues and ragtime. The hit number was "Alabama Song," its lyrics in gibberish English that makes no sense whatever and yet carries echoes reminiscent of Tin Pan Alley.

Weill achieved a monumental success with *The Threepenny Opera* (1928), Bertolt Brecht's modernization of John Gay's *The Beggar's Opera*, pointing up the moral decadence and corruption of Germany in the late 1920s. After its premiere in Berlin, all of Germany was smitten with *"The Threepenny Opera* fever." Its tunes were played everywhere. A bar, called *The Threepenny Opera*, was opened to play only its music. In its first year, the stage production was given over four thousand performances in over one hundred German theaters; in five years it was seen ten thousand times in Central Europe, and was translated into eighteen languages. It was seen several times in the United States both on the stage and on the screen. An Off-Broadway revival in 1954 had the longest run up to that time of any Off-Broadway production. That revival provided a surprise entry into the sweepstakes of American hit songs with "Mack the Knife" or "Moritat," with new English lyrics by Marc Blitzstein. In 1955 it was recorded in more than twenty different versions and was represented on "Your Hit Parade." Among these best-selling records were those by Louis Armstrong, Ella Fitzgerald and Bobby Darin, with Darin's Atco release disposing of over two million disks and being largely responsible for establishing the success of that young singer. Another song from a Weill opera that became popular in America was "The Bilbao Song" from *Happy End* (1929), successfully performed and recorded by Andy Williams with Johnny Mercer's new English lyrics.

When Hitler came to power, Weill fled Germany and, after a short stay in Paris, came to the United States in 1935 to write the music for *The Eternal Road*, a pageant of Jewish History by Franz Werfel, directed by Max Reinhardt. The production of *The Eternal*

Road hit one snag after another and did not reach the stage until 1937. Consequently, when Weill made his first entry into the American musical theater, it was with a play entirely different from the religious spectacle for which he wrote mystical, spiritual and at times Semitic music.

Weill's first American musical was *Johnny Johnson* (1936), text by Paul Green. This was an antiwar fable produced by the Group Theater, "a medley of caricature, satire, musical comedy, melodrama, social polemic and parable," as Richard Watts, Jr., described it in his review in the *Herald Tribune*. The time is World War I, when a peace-loving America is seized by war hysteria. Johnny Johnson gets into uniform and goes through a series of absurd, surrealistic experiences that make him a total pacifist.

Songs and musical incidents were integral to the story development. Resiliently, the European Weill became the complete American, writing Tin Pan Alley songs and American-type ballads and folk tunes. Like the text, the music combined satire, caricature and burlesque, sometimes overlaid with bitterness.

Weill next wrote music for *Knickerbocker Holiday* (1938). Its book and lyrics were by Maxwell Anderson, the distinguished playwright who here associated himself with musical comedy for the first time. This was a musical with political consciousness. Using New Amsterdam of 1647 as his setting, Anderson sees the dictatorial rule of Peter Stuyvesant as a counterpart to the fascist movement in Germany and Italy of the 1930s. One of the songs, "How Can You Tell an American?" identifies the true American as the man who loves and supports liberty.

Together with its timely text, *Knickerbocker Holiday* had two other attractive assets. One was Walter Huston, who gave a hearty, infectious portrait of Peter Stuyvesant. The other was Weill's music, the most tuneful score he had so far written, and one which included perhaps the best known song of his entire career, "September Song."

The way he wrote "September Song" reveals something of his method, with the needs of the theater always uppermost in mind. When Weill learned that Huston was to star in this play, he wired the actor inquiring the range of his voice. Huston replied tersely: "No voice. No range." Subsequently, Weill heard Huston sing on a broadcast from Hollywood—at any rate, the rasping, husky sounds Huston passed off as singing. Weill recognized that Huston's way of singing could be effective in a special kind of sad song with unusual progressions in the melody. He wrote "September Song" for Huston keeping in mind the individual quality of his voice. Because voice and song suited each other so naturally, both achieved relevance within the play.

4

Though musical comedy in the twenties was slowly edging operetta from public favor—a process virtually completed in the 1930s—Broadway audiences still remained faithful, for the most part, to Rudolf Friml and Sigmund Romberg, operetta's two most distinguished practitioners.

A Friml classic—his greatest success since *The Firefly* in 1912—appeared in 1924 with *Rose-Marie*. The primitive and awesome Canadian Rockies served as the background for the fabled exploits of the Mounted Police and the amatory adventures of Rose-Marie and Jim Kenyon, performed by Mary Ellis and Dennis King. The program carried the following note: "The musical numbers of this play are such an integral part of the action that we do not think we should list them as separate numbers." In spite of the intentions of the authors, Otto Harbach and Oscar Hammerstein II, the score and book were by no means an inextricable entity. Several songs stood out prominently from the overall dramatic and musical texture, and they still do when the operetta is revived: the title number, "Indian Love Call," "The Door of My Dreams" and "Totem Tom-Tom," the last written in collaboration with Herbert Stothart.

Rose-Marie had a substantial run of 557 performances. Only a year later, Friml wrote another operetta that passed the five-hundred-performance mark: *The Vagabond King*, adapted by Brian Hooker, Russell Janney and W. H. Post from J. H. McCarthy's story, *If I Were King*, with lyrics by Hooker. The central character was the fifteenth-century French vagabond poet, François Villon who heads a rabble crowd of loyalists to defend the king from the insurgent Duke of Burgundy, and pursues and wins the love of Katherine de Vaucelles. The rousing "Song of the Vagabonds," by Villon's followers, captured the spirit of the play. It was, in the words of Alexander Woollcott, "a great roaring chorus that cut loose magnificently," a welcome change of pace from the gentler music of the ballad "Only a Rose," the "Huguette Waltz" and the romance, "Some Day."

Another swashbuckling play with a French background became Friml's last Broadway success, *The Three Musketeers* (1928), the Dumas romance translated into an operetta book by William Anthony McGuire, with lyrics by P. G. Wodehouse and Clifford Grey. The emphasis is on the romance of D'Artagnan, played by Dennis King, and Constance Bonacieux, portrayed by Vivienne Segal. The familiar alternation of Friml bravura with Friml tender sentiment once again characterized his score. There was rich, red blood in the stirring chorus, "March of the Musketeers," and the drinking song, "With Red Wine," and romantic feelings in "Ma Belle," "Heart of Mine" and "Queen of My Heart."

The ingredients Friml used in 1912 for a successful stage broth were still a pretty good recipe in 1928—but not for much longer. The musical theater was changing. Friml discovered he was getting out of touch with his audiences. After writing the music for two stage failures in the early 1930s he made a discreet bow out of Broadway for Hollywood where he helped adapt some of his operettas for the screen and wrote some new songs for various productions. But his creative output was losing its vitality. He continued writing abundantly until the end of his life, but little of it got performed. Whenever he appeared before audiences as pianist in all-Friml programs, none of his new works were featured, only those of the distant past that called up nostalgic memories. On December 7, 1969, his ninetieth birthday was celebrated by ASCAP in New York with a party and concert at the Shubert Theater. The finale found Friml at the piano reviewing his never-to-be-forgotten songs of a bygone era, almost as if in admission that creatively his life had ended many years ago. The actual end came three years later, on November 12, 1972, in a hospital in Los Angeles.

For Sigmund Romberg, the twenties was a time of continual triumphs, beginning with *Blossom Time* (1921). The Shuberts had acquired the American rights to a European operetta, *Das Dreimäderlhaus*, whose principal character was the immortal Viennese composer Franz Schubert. When the score of the European production was found unsuitable for American consumption, the Shuberts asked Romberg to write new music. This was an assignment into which Romberg could put his heart: an operetta with a Viennese background, the gay and lovely city of Franz Schubert, one of the greatest melodists the world has known. Dorothy Donnelly's American adaptation of the book was far from biographical truth, involving Schubert in a frustrated love affair with somebody called Mitzi. Romberg's music also takes liberty with that of Schubert. From the treasure-house of Schubert's compositions, Romberg picked up some of the most familiar and characteristic jewels, but provided them with new settings within the stilted formal patterns of the American popular song. Thus, to lyrics by Miss Donnelly, Romberg wrote "Song of Love," adapted from the beautiful cello melody in the first movement of the *Unfinished Symphony*; "Tell Me,

Daisy," taken from the second movement of the *Unfinished Symphony*; "Three Little Maids," lifted from the ballet music to *Rosamunde*; and "Serenade," based on the famous art song of the same title.

Blossom Time did so well at the box-office that within a few months of its opening on Broadway, where it remained for 592 performances, four road companies were touring the country.

In 1924, the Shuberts decided that the time had come to make a musical version of one of their biggest dramatic hits, *Old Heidelberg*, in which Richard Mansfield had starred in 1902. The book was adapted for the American stage by Dorothy Donnelly, who also wrote the lyrics, and was renamed *The Student Prince in Heidelberg*. The "student prince" is Karl Franz, come to Heidelberg from the mythical kingdom of Karlsberg. In this university town he falls in love with Kathi, a waitress. Their love is aborted when Karl must return home to ascend the throne of his kingdom and marry a princess.

When the Shuberts turned over to Romberg the writing of the music for *The Student Prince*, he recognized it as the most ambitious project he had thus far undertaken, and was determined to keep faith with it. The Shuberts considered the kind of music he was sketching out as too highbrow for Broadway, and often told him so. Romberg, nevertheless, insisted on doing numbers with a broad melodic span enriched with an inventive harmonic texture: "Serenade," which the Prince sings to Kathi; their love duet, "Deep in My Heart, Dear"; the nostalgic "Golden Days." Romberg demanded the innovation of an all-male chorus of forty voices for his spacious choral pieces, "Drinking Song" and "Students Marching Song." ("You mean pretty girls can't sing?" one of the Shuberts asked Romberg angrily. "Forty men singing that crap? Who needs it?"). And he fought stubbornly against the advice of Lee Shubert to abandon the sad ending of the text. ("People don't like sad ends in musicals," Shubert insisted.) The Shuberts grumbled that such procedures spelled doom on commercial Broadway. But Romberg was intransigent, and he had his way.

The Student Prince opened at the Jolson Theater on December 2, 1924, where it played to capacity houses for about two years. It was just as successful outside New York, in performances by nine touring companies.

Romberg continued to write operettas in the European style. The locales of the various books might shift from Vienna or Germany to French Morocco or eighteenth-century New Orleans, but the music never lost its Continental flavor.

In 1926 came another Romberg classic, *The Desert Song*, in which he worked for the first time with Oscar Hammerstein II. In *The Desert Song*, Hammerstein collaborated with Frank Mandel and Otto Harbach. New York warmly welcomed this colorful atmospheric and melodious romance of a bandit chief in French Morocco who, as the Red Shadow, is the leader of the Riffs in their struggle against the French protectorate and, as Pierre, is the son of the governor. In the words of a critic for the New York *Sun*, the operetta combined "pageantry, romance, ringing music, vitality, and humor." The title song, "One Alone," "The Riff Song" and "The Sabre Song" were the best of Rombert's musical numbers.

The next time Romberg worked with Hammerstein they came up with another giant success, *The New Moon* (1928). It was set in eighteenth-century New Orleans and was loosely based on the life and exploits of the French aristocrat, Robert Misson.

The hit song was "Lover, Come Back to Me," one of Romberg's most beloved melodies, though not his most original, since its middle section makes more than a passing reference to Tchaikovsky's piano piece *June Barcarolle*. Other charmers in this score were "Softly, As in a Morning Sunrise," "One Kiss," "Wanting You" and, in a more virile vein, "Stouthearted Men."

The New York critics gave virtually unqualified praise. Gilbert W. Gabriel described it in the New York *American* as "certainly and superlatively as good as they come." When, a few years after the Broadway premiere, Hollywood bought it for the screen, it paid the highest price thus far given for a Broadway musical.

Now the most successful operetta composer in America, Romberg became logical prey for Hollywood with the arrival of talking pictures. He settled permanently in Beverly Hills, completed the music for several new motion pictures and helped transfer some of his most famous stage operettas to the new medium.

Soon after Pearl Harbor, Romberg left Hollywood to undertake the first of several concert tours with his orchestra, a project that continued till the end of his life. "An Evening with Sigmund Romberg" as these concerts of Romberg and Viennese music were billed, became an assured success wherever given.

But Romberg did not withdraw permanently from writing music for the stage. In his last years, he enjoyed his second best box-office return with *Up in Central Park* (1945). His last musical, *The Girl in Pink Tights*, was produced posthumously in 1954. Good as *Up in Central Park* was, Romberg is best remembered for his operettas through their frequent revivals. That their charm had not faded with time and changing values became evident in 1973 when a Sigmund Romberg festival was launched in Philadelphia. To the critic of *Variety*, if this festival "has proved anything, it has reaffirmed the vitality of the songs in those operettas. . . . The songs are as glorious as ever."

23

The Silent Screen Erupts Into Sound

1

As the birthplace of new songs and new composers, and as a medium for the popularizing of songs, motion pictures assumed prime importance after they acquired a voice.

Experiments with sound had been going on since the beginning of motion pictures. At the turn of the twentieth century, attempts were made to synchronize recorded sound with films by Cameraphone, which released several short subjects in which the sounds from phonograph records were combined with the sights on films. These starred Anna Held, Eva Tanguay, Blanche Ring and several others.

But synchronizing sound with films remained an awkward process for a long time, yielding none too happy results. The invention and perfection of the Audion tube brought up the possibility of a new and more rewarding kind of synchronization, that of recording sound directly on film. Dr. Lee De Forest, who had invented the first Audion tube in 1906, formed Phonofilms in 1922, which issued a series of one reel talking or singing pictures recruiting the services of Eddie Cantor, George Jessel, Weber and Fields, Vincent Lopez and his orchestra, Pat Rooney III, Harry Richman and others. On April 15, 1923, a program of Phonofilms was given at the Rivoli Theater as part of a program including a full-length silent motion picture, Pola Negri in *Bella Donna*. Advertised as "films that actually talk and reproduce music without the use of phonographs," these Phonofilms presented Eddie Cantor, Weber and Fields, Sissle and Blake, Phil Baker and Eva Puck and Sammy White.

Though the practicability of applying sound to films had been proved by 1925, Hollywood moguls were either thoroughly skeptical of this innovation or in horror of it. They insisted the public would never take to it, and they feared it might result in the collapse of their highly profitable industry. They wanted none of this new-fangled nonsense. The exceptions to these skeptics were William Fox and the Warner brothers. In 1925, Fox leased the use of the Swiss Tri-Ergon sound system, and on January 21, 1926, he produced a short with sound under the company name of Movietone. On April 20, 1926, the four Warner brothers, Samuel, Harry, Albert and Jack, formed the Vitaphone Company for the presentation of sound pictures, entering into an agreement with the Western Electric Company. The Warners transformed Manhattan Opera House on 34th Street in New York into a sound studio for the making of singing and talking shorts.

The first public demonstration of Vitaphone films took place at the Warner Brothers Theater in New York on August 6, 1926. After Will H. Hays, president of the Motion Picture Producers and Distributors of America, delivered a brief address from the screen, Vitaphone offered a series of short subjects with sound featuring such serious musical artists as Mischa Elman, Giovanni Martinelli, Anna Case and the New York Philharmonic Orchestra conducted by Henry Hadley. The second part of the program was a silent picture, *Don Juan* starring John Barrymore. What made this picture unique was the inclusion of some sound effects during a duel scene and the use of a synchronized musical score on disks written expressly for this production by Edward Bowes, David Mendoza and William Axt.

A program of Movietone shorts followed on January 21, 1927, starring Raquel Meller and Frieda Hempel, as a supplement to the motion picture *What Price Glory?* Later that year Movietone presented another program of sound shorts as preliminary to the silent motion picture *Seventh Heaven*. In 1927, synchronized scores were written by Erno Rapee and added to *What Price Glory?* and *Seventh Heaven*. With these two scores, the movie theme song became institutionalized in Hollywood, for from Rapee's synchronized score to *What Price Glory?* came "Charmaine" and from *Seventh Heaven*, "Diane," both with lyrics by Lew Pollack.

There were farsighted individuals in Hollywood who recognized that the future of the movies lay with sound, but most remained skeptical. These men realized that before sound films could be distributed, theater owners everywhere would have to go to the formidable expense of wiring their theaters; that expensive Hollywood equipment would overnight become obsolete, and so would a huge backlog of expensively produced silent films; many glamorous stars of the silent screen, valuable properties to their studios, would lose their magic once they opened their mouths to speak. Even William Fox, pioneer though he was in the production of sound, was somewhat skeptical of its value "on a large scale."

But the four Warner brothers remained convinced that sound was here to stay, and they were ready and willing to gamble on their judgment. They not only set up a program to produce such films but even went to the expense of wiring several of their own theaters for sound. Grudgingly, and in response to public demand, other producers began following the lead of the Warner brothers, though still doubtful if sound was anything but an ephemeral fad.

The cynics and the doubters were silenced on October 6, 1927, when the Warner brothers presented *The Jazz Singer* in New York based on a Broadway play of that name by Samson Raphaelson, which had starred George Jessel in 1925. When the Warner brothers offered Jessel the screen role he turned it down because (some say) he refused to accept stock in the Warner company in place of a huge fee or (as others suggest) he preferred appearing in strictly silent films. Al Jolson was then chosen to replace Jessel as the cantor's son who rejects the synagogue to become a jazz singer, only to substitute for his dying father at the Day of Atonement services. (This human interest Jewish story was reminiscent of Jolson's own biography, save, of course, for the sentimental Day of Atonement ending. In fact, many believe that Samson Raphaelson had Jolson in mind when he wrote his play.)

The Jazz Singer was planned as a silent film with synchronized background music performed by the Vitaphone Orchestra under Louis Silvers. But an experiment was tried, midway in the film, to inject novelty by having Jolson appear in a café scene and sing "Dirty Hands, Dirty Face" (Edgar Leslie, Grant Clarke and Al Jolson—James V. Monaco). The sudden break in the silence, the infusion of Jolson's magnetic singing style, forthwith made the silent picture obsolete, launched the age of talking pictures, and established Warner Brothers as an empire in the celluloid industry. When this song was first filmed on the set, Jolson spontaneously abandoned the script to shout out to the extras in the café scene one of his pet stage cries, "Wait a minute! Wait a Minute! You ain't heard nothin' yet!" The spoken line seemed effective, and it was left in the picture. Other songs by Jolson, and a touching dialogue scene between him and his screen mother, were also sound interpolations. Jolson sang some of his favorites, among them, "Toot, Toot, Tootsie" (Gus Kahn and Ernie Erdman—Ted Fiorito and Robert A. King), "My Mammy" (Sam M. Lewis and Joe Young—Walter Donaldson) and Irving Berlin's "Blue Skies," together with "Mother, I Still Have You" (Al Jolson—Louis Silvers). In the final scene, he gave a poignant rendition of the old Hebrew prayer for the Day of Atonement, the "Kol Nidrei." (Joseph Rosenblatt, the world-famous cantor, had been contracted to dub in the singing of "Kol Nidrei" for Jolson. But Jolson's own style proved so moving that he was allowed to sing it himself. Rosenblatt was used in a special concert hall sequence.)

The Jazz Singer grossed what was then without precedent—three million dollars. When the first all-talking (but no singing) picture, *Lights of New York* (1928), grossed another two million dollars, Hollywood had to concede that sound was highly commercial. A mad scramble now ensued among Hollywood producers to wire their studios for sound; to acquire properties that could be quickly converted to this new medium; and to make sound pictures without further delay. But Warner Brothers (who had also produced *Lights of New York*) had stolen a march and was in the lead. In 1929, from the Warner Brothers studios came Fanny Brice in her film debut, *My Man*, named after the song she had made famous on stage in the *Ziegfeld Follies*. It was a dud. But a new Jolson picture, *The Singing Fool* (1929) once again left no doubts about the capacity of sound films to please audiences and make money. It was the first movie ever to play the Winter Garden in New York, the scene of so many Jolson successes, the first motion picture to charge a top admission price of three dollars, and the first motion picture to gross over four million dollars.

In *The Singing Fool*, Jolson interpolated two numbers by De Sylva, Brown and Henderson written sometime earlier for the stage, and a new number created expressly for the picture. The old songs were "It All Depends on You" and "I'm Sitting on Top of the World." The new one, "Sonny Boy," was the first song written for the talking screen that became a giant success. It was a last-minute replacement for another number which was judged unsuitable. Jolson frantically telephoned De Sylva, Brown and Henderson from California, reaching them in Atlantic City, New Jersey, where they were working on a show. Jolson urged them to write a special number that would fit in with the plot of the movie: a widowed father who is deeply devoted to his little son who dies. De Sylva, Brown and Henderson wrote their song hastily, passing it off to Jolson as a serious effort at sentimental balladry, but actually intending its maudlin lyric and saccharine melody to satirize sentimental songs. Jolson took it seriously and sang "Sonny Boy" in the film where it became so popular that it was largely responsible for the giant box-office draw of the picture.

The first "all talking, all singing, all dancing" screen musical—the dawn of a new epoch in Hollywood—took place on February 1, 1929, with *The Broadway Melody*, an MGM production opening at Grauman's Theater in Hollywood, and one week later in New York. *The Broadway Melody* was a behind-the-scenes story of Broadway show business and the experiences of two sisters in the chorus and their singing boyfriends. It introduced some of the elements that provided Hollywood with a formula for future screen musicals (a formula delightfully satirized in 1968 by the stage musical, *Dames at Sea*): the obscure chorus girl who gains sudden stardom by substituting for an ailing performer; the glamour of Broadway that conceals the heartbreak backstage; the carefully contrived dance spectacles exploited by camera angles and trick camera effects; the contrived ways of bringing in a song.

The Broadway Melody brought to the fore the first songwriting team made famous by the talking screen, Nacio Herb Brown, composer, and Arthur Freed, lyricist. By writing the title number, "The Wedding of the Painted Doll," "Love Boat," "Boy Friends" and "You Were Meant for Me," Brown and Freed opened the door to success for many comparatively unknown composers who would henceforth become identified with screen music.

Both Nacio Herb Brown and Arthur Freed were more or less novices in the songwriting field when they wrote for *The Broadway Melody*. Brown came from Deming, New Mexico, where he was born in 1896. In 1904 he made his home in Los Angeles where he completed his education. After touring the vaudeville circuit for a year as a piano accompanist, he opened a tailoring establishment in Hollywood that drew its clientele from motion picture stars. In 1920, Brown began investing his money in Beverly Hills real estate, an activity that made him a millionaire. That same year he also had his first published composition, "Coral Sea," which he wrote with King Zany and which became moderately successful after it was introduced by Paul Whiteman and his Orchestra. In 1921, Brown wrote another instrumental, "Doll Dance," which was interpolated into a Los Angeles revue, and a song, "When Buddha Smiles," with which his partnership with Arthur Freed began.

Freed was twenty-seven when he wrote the lyrics for "When Buddha Smiles." He started out as a demonstration pianist for a music publisher in Chicago. He then toured the vaudeville circuit with the Gus Edwards revues and the Marx Brothers, then mere youngsters being shepherded around the country by their mother. While serving in the Army during World War I, Freed staged camp shows. After the war he returned to vaudeville in an act with Louis Silvers with whom he wrote material for revues mounted in restaurants. After 1921, he supplemented these activities with lyric writing. His biggest hit before he came to Hollywood was "I Cried for You" in 1923, music by Gus Arnheim and Abe Lyman.

In planning *The Broadway Melody* as the screen's first all-talking, all-singing musical, Irving Thalberg, the head of production at MGM, decided to have its basic songs written just for this production, rather than using numbers already in circulation, the first time this was done in Hollywood. He called upon Nacio Herb Brown and Arthur Freed to write those songs, launching them on their productive careers as songwriters for the screen.

2

On May 16, 1929, several hundred Hollywood personalities gathered at the Hotel Roosevelt for festivities attending the presentation of screen awards soon to become known as "Oscars." The name Oscar for the statuette presented to award winners is said to have been concocted in 1931 by an employe of the Motion Picture Academy of Arts and Sciences who named it after her uncle. These awards, or Oscars, were presented by the Motion Picture Academy to winners in each of several branches of the picture industry. For the year 1927–1928, *Wings* was selected as the best picture, Janet Gaynor as the best actress, and Emil Jannings as the best actor. Awards for a song or a musical score were not made until 1934. An obeisance to the age of sound was made in 1929 through the presentation of an honorary award to Warner Brothers for *The Jazz Singer* as "the pioneer outstanding talking picture which has revolutionized the industry."

An awareness of the importance of music to sound films came the following year, on April 3, 1930, when, for the second season of Oscar presentations, *The Broadway Melody* became the year's outstanding motion picture. In its second year, the Academy Award already possessed a singular aura. That *The Broadway Melody* captured an Oscar helped to put to rest whatever fears still lingered that the talking picture was a passing fancy.

Talking pictures—and specifically musicals—now began to flood the market. In 1929–1930, over one hundred screen musicals were produced, with every major studio represented. These films included one in which color was used for the first time, the Warner Brothers production, *The Gold Diggers of Broadway*.

In a rush to lay their hands on properties that could be made into screen musicals, Hollywood raided the Broadway musical theater. Among the first to make the journey from Broadway to talking pictures in Hollywood was Romberg's *The Desert Song*, in 1929, a Warner Brothers production starring John Boles and Carlotta King. This was for the most part a faithful translation of the stage original in which the basic stage score was used. Between 1929 and 1930, *Rio Rita*, an RKO motion picture starring Bebe Daniels; *The New Moon*, an MGM production with Grace Moore and Lawrence Tibbett; and *The Vagabond King* from Paramount, with Jeanette MacDonald and Dennis King, also all left the stage scores virtually intact. But as more of Broadway's musical comedies and operettas were adapted for the screen, the temptation of producers and directors to try to make a good product even better on the screen proved irresistible—often with catastrophic results. Texts were radically rewritten, often beyond recognition. More damaging still was the way in which the music—the very element that had made most of these productions so attractive in the first place—were either slighted or totally bypassed in favor of newly written and far less attractive scores by writers who had never been involved in the original Broadway productions. In many instances only one, two or three songs of the stage score were retained, supplemented by new creations. This happened to the Rodgers and Hart musicals *Spring Is Here* (five songs), and *Heads Up* (two songs); to Jerome Kern's *Sally* (three songs) and *Show Boat* in its 1929 production (one song); to De Sylva, Brown and Henderson's *Follow Thru* (two songs with an additional number by Rodgers and Hart); to Vincent Youmans' *Hit the Deck* (two songs, but a new one was written for the film by Vincent Youmans and Sidney Clare). In some instances, the entire score was discarded. This happened to Vincent Youmans' *No, No, Nanette*, De Sylva, Brown and Henderson's *Hold Everything* and George Gershwin's *Song of the Flame*. Sometimes, even the title was changed to make the disguise more complete: *Manhattan Mary*, which had starred Ed Wynn on Broadway, was called *Follow the Leader*, still with Ed Wynn, and with Ginger Rogers in her screen debut; *Lady in Ermine*, a successful Broadway musical of 1922 was renamed *Bride of the Regiment*. The height of absurdity in this early Hollywood practice of buying a musical property without using the material for which it paid a high price was reached when Paramount acquired the screen rights to Maurice Ravel's symphonic piece, *Bolero*, a recent sensation in American concert halls, and then discarding it when *Bolero*, starring George Raft, was filmed with Hollywood-concocted background music.

Encouraged by the success of *The Broadway Melody*, Hollywood studios started to concentrate on music written specifically for the screen. Some of these musical productions were revues, a convenience in which the studio could make use of its stable of stars in their specialties, though sometimes a slight plot served as the thread to tie together the disparate parts. This cycle started with the *Hollywood Revue* (1929), an MGM production going the gamut of entertainment from a scene from Shakespeare's *Romeo and Juliet*, enacted by Norma Shearer and John Gilbert, to the comedy of Jack Benny in his screen debut. Here Cliff Edwards, dressed in a slicker and rain hat, strummed on his ukulele while introducing "Singing in the Rain" (Arthur Freed—Nacio Herb Brown). Fox entered the revue competition with the *Fox Movietone Follies;* Paramount with *Paramount on Parade;* Warner Brothers with the *Show of Shows,* and *On with the Show* in which Ethel Waters gave her memorable rendition of "Am I Blue?" (Grant Clarke—Harry Akst).

Other screen musicals in 1929–1930 had a well developed, though often highly synthetic, story line. Some, such as *Sunny Side Up* with Janet Gaynor and Charles Farrell and *The Love Parade* with Maurice Chevalier and Jeanette MacDonald in her screen debut, were real charmers. *Hallelujah!,* a King Vidor production for MGM with songs by Irving Berlin, broke new ground by becoming the first all-black talkie. Several musicals were manufactured to fit the fame and talent of a performing star imported from New York, but fell apart at the seams: *My Man* with Fanny Brice; *The Vagabond Lover* with Rudy Vallee; *Is Everybody Happy?* with Ted Lewis; *Honky Tonk* with Sophie Tucker; *Song o' My Heart* with John McCormack; *Melody Lane* with Eddie Leonard.

The sound of music was regarded so indispensable for films in 1929 and 1930 that even in non-musical productions songs were injected, some of them among the best then being written for the screen. Ramon Novarro introduced "Pagan Love Song" (Arthur Freed—Nacio Herb Brown) in *The Pagan;* Gloria Swanson, "Love, Your Magic Spell is Everywhere" (Elsie Janis—Edmund Goulding) in *The Trespasser;* Nancy Carroll, "A Precious Little Thing Called Love" (Lou Davis—J. Fred Coots) in *Shopworn Angel;* "Paradise" (Gordon Clifford—Nacio Herb Brown) in *A Lady Commands.*

The theme song, a fad in the silent days, became a basic element in talking pictures. Hollywood moguls insisted that songs be written carrying the name of the pictures in their titles for publicity purposes. *Varsity Girl* had "My Varsity Girl, I'll Cling to You" (Al Bryan—W. Franke Harling); *The Wild Party,* "My Wild Party Girl" (Leo Robin—Richard A. Whiting); *Madonna of Avenue A,* "My Madonna" (Fred Fisher—Louis Silvers); *Annapolis,* "My Annapolis and You" (Charles Weinberg and Irving Bibo); *Woman Disputed,* "Woman Disputed I Love You" (Bernie Grossman and Ed Ward). It took Dorothy Parker to reduce this practice to absurdity. Contracted to write the lyrics for *Dynamite Man,* she submitted the words for a song called "Dynamite Man I Love You," whose tongue-in-cheek approach was not appreciated by the producer who rejected it.

The satiation point for screen musicals was soon reached. Audiences had seen too many of them, and too many of them had little more to commend them than sound itself. Only two dozen or so musicals were produced in the years 1931 and 1932. A few did quite well, because they managed to avoid most of the stereotypes to which screen musicals had succumbed. The most successful were those starring Maurice Chevalier—*The Smiling Lieutenant, Love Me Tonight* and *One Hour With You*—and with them, *The Big Broadcast* and George Gershwin's first musical, *Delicious.* But most other musicals of these two years were soundly rejected. Some theaters were now advertising the fact their attractions had "no songs."

The public, however, was not weary of screen musicals as much as they were of musicals assembled by formula. When better musicals were made, with slicker and more imaginative approaches to camera work and direction, with suave and elegant performances and with a fresher approach to story, character and dialogue, they were box-office magic. This was proved in 1933 with the sudden resurgence of the popularity of screen musicals initiated by *Forty-Second Street.*

Forty-Second Street, a Warner Brothers production, once again was a story of back-stage life: how a Broadway musical is produced after overcoming harrowing conditions, and how a sweet innocent manages to capture both stardom and a boyfriend. The formula is the same as before, but it was given an altogether fresh interest through the performance of a new song-and-dance girl-boy duo destined to become screen idols, Ruby Keeler and Dick Powell, and through grandiose dance routines in intriguing patterns and designs, from unusual camera angles, devised by Busby Berkeley. Those Busby Berkeley dance routines were not only the hallmark of *Forty-Second Street,* but also of some of the best musicals produced by Warner Brothers during the next three years. In fact, most musicals of other studios imitated Busby Berkeley's methods.

The best songs of *Forty-Second Street* were the title number, "Shuffle Off to Buffalo" and "You're Getting to Be a Habit with Me." They brought prominence to a new songwriting pair which henceforth would enrich motion picture music with their exceptional gifts. They were Harry Warren, composer, and Al Dubin, lyricist. Warren, born in Brooklyn, New York, in 1893 to Italian parents, came to Hollywood by way of Tin Pan Alley. There, in 1920, he was a song plugger and piano demonstrator, rising in 1923 to the post of staff composer for the firm of Shapiro-Bernstein. His career as songwriter began in 1922 with "Rose of the Rio Grande" (Edgar Leslie), a hit which he wrote in collaboration with Ross Gorman, and continued with such other successes as "Nagasaki" (Mort Dixon) and "Where the Shy Little Violets Grow" (Gus Kahn). In the early 1930s, some of his songs were heard on the Broadway stage: "Cheerful Little Earful" (Ira Gershwin and Billy Rose) and "Would You Like to Take a Walk?" (Mort Dixon and Billy Rose) in the revue *Sweet and Low* (1930), and "I Found a Million Dollar Baby" (Mort Dixon and Billy Rose) in *Billy Rose's Crazy Quilt* (1931). Warren also wrote the complete score for the musical *The Laugh Parade* (1931) starring Ed Wynn, which included "Ooh That Kiss" and "You're My Everything," lyrics by Mort Dixon and Joe Young. A Warren song published independently in 1931, but written a decade earlier, became his greatest success up to that time, "By the River Sainte Marie" (Edgar Leslie) sung to fame over the radio and on records by Kate Smith.

Though Warren had placed some of his songs in motion pictures as early as 1929 he did not go to work in Hollywood until 1932. Settling there, he was selected by Darryl Zanuck, then a producer at Warner Brothers, to write the music for *Forty-Second Street.* Zanuck suggested that he work with Al Dubin, a lyricist under contract to Warners. Dubin was already a songwriter with a long string of credits, and was the first lyricist ever to receive a studio contract in Hollywood. His most important songs before his Hollywood engagement were "A Cup of Coffee, a Sandwich and You," lyrics written with Billy Rose to music by Joseph Meyer, introduced by Gertrude Lawrence and Jack Buchanan in *Andre Charlot's Revue of 1926;* "Nobody Knows What a Red-Headed Mama Can Do," music by Sammy Fain; and "The Lonesomest Girl in Town," music by Jimmy McHugh and Irving Mills. Then, as contract writer for Warner Brothers, Dubin worked with Joe Burke with whom, in 1929, he wrote the songs for *The Gold Diggers of Broadway,* among them "Tip Toe Through the Tulips With Me" and "Painting the Clouds with Sunshine." Dubin continued working with Burke until 1932 when he became Warren's writing partner.

With *Forty-Second Street* the dearth of screen musicals was over, and a flood followed. Harry Warren and Al Dubin provided songs for several of the more successful screen productions that followed. For *Gold Diggers of 1933* they wrote "We're in the Money" (sung by Ginger Rogers and a gold digger chorus), and "Shadow Waltz" (introduced by Ruby Keeler and Dick Powell). In *Gold Diggers of 1935* was one of Warren and Dubin's most famous numbers, "Lullaby of Broadway," for which Busby Berkeley employed a hundred beauties playing on a hundred pianos for one of his more splendid spectacles. This song won an Oscar, a category for screen songs having been added to the list of Academy Awards one year earlier when "The Continental" (Herb Magidson—Con Conrad) was honored.

Toward the end of the thirties, Warren and Dubin separated, to work with other collaborators, but not before they had contributed more notable songs to the screen including "About a Quarter to Nine," introduced by Al Jolson in *Go Into Your Dance* (1935), "With Plenty of Money and You," sung by Dick Powell in *Gold Diggers of 1937*, and "September in the Rain," offered by James Melton in *Stars Over Broadway* (1935).

During this resurgence of the screen musical, Arthur Freed and Nacio Herb Brown remained productive. They followed their initial triumph in *The Broadway Melody* with two more screen musicals bearing the same name, *Broadway Melody of 1936* and *Broadway Melody of 1938*, both starring Eleanor Powell. "My Lucky Star" (or "You Are My Lucky Star") and "Broadway Rhythm" were assigned to Frances Langford in the 1936 production, while "I'm Feelin' Like a Million" was presented by Eleanor Powell and George Murphy, and "Your Broadway and My Broadway" by thirteen-year-old Judy Garland in *Broadway Melody of 1938*.

From childhood, Judy Garland had been groomed to be a star—and a neurotic. She was born Frances Gumm in Grand Rapids, Michigan, in 1923, the youngest of three daughters. Her parents, Frank Avent and Ethel Marion Gumm, were performers in small-town theaters, billed as "Jack and Virginia Lee, Sweet Southern Singers." With the drive of a person with limited talent, the mother was determined to realize through her daughters the stage successes she was incapable of achieving for herself. She had the fierce determination and ruthlessness of the traditional stage mother.

When the team of Jack and Virginia Lee broke up, with the father buying and managing a small movie house, the mother had her two older daughters appear in a song-and-dance act in a movie theater in Grand Rapids. There, at the age of two, Judy made her stage debut by bursting uninvited into her sisters' act and singing "Jingle Bells." It was not long before Judy, with her two sisters, was being herded from theater to theater on one-night stands, ending up in Los Angeles, where the mother aspired to make them into movie stars. A separation between the father and mother left Judy in the care of her mother, with serious consequences. "Actually," Judy later recalled, "Mother was no good for anything except to create chaos and fear." If Judy's timing was a bit off in one of her performances, the mother would pack her bags and threaten to abandon the child alone in the hotel room. The child would succumb to a fit of terror which was, perhaps, the root of her latent insecurity and her chronic fear of being alone.

Going from one theater to another, with arduous rehearsals in between, robbed Judy of her childhood, but it made her into a seasoned trouper. Noël Coward put it this way years later when Judy Garland was one of the world's greatest entertainers: "Whenever I see her before an audience now, coming out with the authority of a great star and really taking hold of an audience, I know that every single heartbreak she had when she was a little girl, . . . every disappointment went into the making of this authority. But that, of course, is the way to learn theater."

The three Gumm Sisters (reunited for an extensive vaudeville tour after the parents had become reconciled) were appearing at the Oriental Theater in Chicago when George Jessel, who was on the same bill, was responsible for the change of Frances Gumm's name to

Judy Garland. Jessel suggested that she merely change her uneuphonious second name, selecting Garland because the New York drama critic, Robert Garland, happened to be backstage at the time. Judy herself selected a new first name, choosing "Judy" because she had become infatuated with the popular song of that name (Sammy Lerner—Hoagy Carmichael).

When the Gumm sisters appeared at the Cal-Neva Lodge on Lake Tahoe in 1934, Judy sang "Dinah" (Sam M. Lewis and Joe Young—Harry Akst), with the composer at the piano, for an intimate group that included a Hollywood agent. Though at first glance Judy was an unlikely candidate for movies—she was too dumpy and overweight to be cute, too old to play children's parts, too young and unattractive for romantic roles—the agent caught something in her singing that made him recommend her for an audition at the MGM studios. After Judy sang "Zing! Went the Strings of My Heart" (James F. Hanley), Louis B. Mayer himself was summoned. The result was a contract without even a screen test.

At MGM, Judy, aged twelve, experienced a new tyranny to supplement her mother's. The studio heads knew they had found valuable property and were determined to develop it fully. They instituted a severe regimen of study, practice and rehearsals calculated to crush one of far stronger nervous equipment than a hypersensitive and much abused child. To slim her down she was put on a starvation diet that often left her faint. Later, when she started to be gold at the box office, they gave her pills to help keep her weight down, amphetamines to pep her up during her working hours, and sleeping pills to calm her down. The stage was set for the later tragic years of dope and alcohol addiction, nervous breakdowns, attempted suicides, broken romances and marriages, and a conglomeration of emotional problems that brought about her premature death at the age of forty-seven.

Judy had made her screen debut as a child in a short with the Gumm sisters. Her second film was an MGM two-reeler, *Every Sunday*, in 1936, in which she shared the singing with another potential starlet, Deanna Durbin. Judy sang popular numbers, and Deanna the classical songs. Deanna's option was allowed to lapse after this appearance, sending her off to Universal Studios where she instantly became a singing star in *Three Smart Girls* (1937), a picture for which its producer, Joe Pasternak, first tried to get Judy Garland, but failing, settled on Miss Durbin. MGM stuck to Judy. To give her some needed cinematic experience she was loaned out to Fox for her first full-length feature, *Pigskin Parade* (1936), a college story starring Betty Grable and Jack Haley. Here she was heard singing "It's Love I'm After," "Texas Tornado" and "Balboa"—music by Lew Pollack, lyrics by Sidney D. Mitchell. *The New York Times* took note of her by describing her as "cute, not pretty, but a pleasingly fetching personality, who certainly knows how to sell a pop."

Her next assignment at MGM was *Broadway Melody of 1938*, where all the hopes, dreams and ambitions that had been concentrated upon her by her mother and the studio became fulfilled when she tearfully sang "You Made Me Love You" (Joseph McCarthy —James V. Monaco) to a photograph of Clark Gable. The insertion of this number for Judy was a sudden late decision. Judy sang it for the first time at a birthday party for Clark Gable. For this occasion, Roger Eden, a musical director at MGM, wrote a special new verse about Gable to precede the chorus of "You Made Me Love You" which Judy sang at the party that night. Louis B. Mayer, who was in attendance, was so deeply affected, as was everybody else there including the "King," that he insisted Judy do it in the *Broadway Melody of 1938* then being filmed on the MGM lot. And a star was born.

3

Other composers supplemented Nacio Herb Brown and Harry Warren in enriching screen music in the early 1930s and at the same time became primarily identified with motion pictures.

One was Harry Revel, born in London in 1905. As a young man he played in Parisian jazz bands and Hawaiian-type ensembles. Even then an ardent admirer of American popular music, and before setting foot on American soil, he wrote "I'm Going Back to Old Nebraska" which was published in London and sold over a million copies of sheet music. In 1929 Revel came to the United States where he met Mack Gordon, a vaudevillian and lyricist, with whom he toured the vaudeville circuit. They began writing songs in 1931, some of which found their way into Broadway musicals, including the *Ziegfeld Follies*. By 1933, Gordon and Revel were in Hollywood. One of their first screen efforts was a winner, "Did You Ever See a Dream Walking?", sung by Ginger Rogers and Art Jarrett in *Sitting Pretty* (1933). A year later, Gordon and Revel wrote the songs for *We're Not Dressing*, starring Bing Crosby, two of which had particular merit, "Love Thy Neighbor" and "Good Night, Lovely Little Lady." After that Gordon and Revel provided Crosby with his songs for *She Loves Me Not* (1934), and *Two for Tonight* (1935) in which Crosby introduced "From the Top of Your Head to the Tip of Your Toes."

Songs by Gordon and Revel also appeared in two screen musicals starring Shirley Temple, the child darling of movie audiences in the 1930s. They were *Poor Little Rich Girl* (1936), out of which came "A Star Fell Out of Heaven" and *Stowaway* (1936). But the songs which helped make Shirley Temple one of the greatest, if not *the* greatest, child star the screen has known, came from pens other than those of Gordon and Revel. "Baby Take a Bow" (Lew Brown—Jay Gorney) was heard in Shirley's first movie, *Stand Up and Cheer* (1934); "On the Good Ship Lollipop" (Sidney Clare—Richard A. Whiting) in *Bright Eyes* (1934); and "Animal Crackers in My Soup" (Ted Koehler and Irving Caesar—Ray Henderson) in *Curly Top* (1935).

Other screen musicals also profited from the songwriting talent of Gordon and Revel. Lanny Ross introduced "Stay As Sweet As You Are" in *College Rhythm* (1934); "I Feel Like a Feather in the Breeze" was heard in *Collegiate* (1936); "Never in a Million Years" and "There's a Lull in My Life" were in the score of *Wake Up and Live* (1937); Tony Martin sang "The Loveliness of You" in *You Can't Have Everything* (1937); and "In Old Chicago" was the title song of a motion picture in 1938. An indication of the formidable success of Gordon and Revel as songwriters for the screen came 1935 when ASCAP gave them special awards for nine of their songs.

As a staff composer at the Paramount studios between 1930 and 1942, Ralph Rainger also wrote for Bing Crosby a handful of tuneful numbers for various appearances on the screen. Ralph Rainger (1901–1942) came from New York where at first he specialized in law. He became involved in music professionally by playing the piano with a dance group, by working as a rehearsal pianist for a Broadway musical, and by officiating as the piano accompanist for the vaudeville act of Clifton Webb and Mary Hay. He was employed as the rehearsal pianist for the *Little Show* in 1929 when a need was expressed for a specialty song for the two stars, Clifton Webb and Libby Holman. To Howard Dietz's words Rainger came up with "Moanin' Low." This was Rainger's first published song, his first to be heard on Broadway, and his first hit. On the strength of its success he was brought to Hollywood in 1930 to work at the Paramount studios where he remained up to the time of his untimely death in an airplane crash.

At Paramount, Rainger, working with Leo Robin as his lyricist, wrote the following hit songs for Bing Crosby: "Please" in *The Big Broadcast* (1932); "June in January" and "With Every Breath I Take" in *Here Is My Heart* (1934); "Love in Bloom" in *She Loves Me Not*

(1934), later to become Jack Benny's theme song; "Blue Hawaii" and "Sweet Is the Word for You" in *Waikiki Wedding* (1937); and "You're a Sweet Little Headache" in *Paris Honeymoon* (1939). In addition, Rainger and Robin fashioned a surefire number for Bob Hope's screen debut in the *Big Broadcast of 1938*, a song that brought its authors an Academy Award and Bob Hope his theme song, "Thanks for the Memory."

Johnny Mercer was still another songwriter to realize his first successes through the movies. He came from an old and stately Southern family, born in Savannah, Georgia, in 1909. As a boy he studied piano and trumpet; when he was fifteen, he wrote his first song, "Sister Susie Strut Your Stuff." In 1927 he came to New York to engage professionally in the music business. One of his lyrics, "Out of Breath" (music by Everett Miller) was used in *The Garrick Gaieties of 1930*. At about this time, Mercer won first place in a singing contest sponsored by Paul Whiteman and his Orchestra. When the Rhythm Boys left Whiteman, Mercer was hired as solo vocalist not, as Mercer explains, because he had an exceptional voice, but "because I could write songs and material generally." For about two years, Mercer wrote special material for Whiteman's orchestra, besides serving as a vocalist, and sometimes as a master of ceremonies. After that Benny Goodman hired him for his band, and Bob Crosby for his orchestra. By this time, Mercer had become an industrious writer of song lyrics, an activity that finally brought him an offer to go to Hollywood to write for the screen. Teaming up with the composer, Richard A. Whiting, he wrote songs for three Hollywood musicals released in 1937. In *Hollywood Hotel*, Dick Powell introduced "I've Hitched My Wagon to a Star"; in *Ready, Willing and Able*, Wini Shaw and Ross Alexander sang "Too Marvelous for Words"; and in *Varsity Show*, Dick Powell was heard in "Moonlight on the Campus" and Priscilla Lane in "Have You Got Any Castles, Baby?".

Two more of Johnny Mercer's songs were once again introduced by Dick Powell in *Cowboy from Brooklyn* (1938), "Ride, Tenderfoot, Ride" (music by Richard A. Whiting) and the title song (music by Harry Warren). Now working with Harry Warren and assisted by Al Dubin, Mercer went on to write the words for "Love Is Where You Find It" and "Confidentially" for *Garden of the Moon* (1938) and his greatest success up to then, "Jeepers Creepers" for *Going Places* (1938). All three lyrics were written without collaboration. Louis Armstrong and his band gave Dick Powell a strong assist in the presentation of "Jeepers Creepers" in that film, after which Armstrong and his band made a best-selling recording for Capitol. Mercer was now well on his way toward becoming one of the top lyricists of all time, as well as a gifted composer in his own right, and so he remained up to the time of his death in 1976.

One of Johnny Mercer's last contributions to popular music was helping to found and to serve as the first president of the Songwriters Hall of Fame. The first annual presentation of miniature pianola trophies was made in 1969, and by the time the Songwriters Hall of Fame was opened in Times Square, New York, on January 11, 1977, to house memorabilia of America's greatest songwriters, 164 had been elected—117 deceased and 47 living.

4

Some of the smaller studios in Hollywood, such as Republic and Monogram, made a specialty of Westerns, in many of which the singing cowboy was the hero.

Among the first groups to disseminate cowboy songs to the general public was the Oklahoma Cowboys, a string band formed in the 1920s by Otto Gray. For about a dozen years it was heard on the stage in the West, including the vaudeville circuit, featuring such cowboy classics as "The Dying Cowboy." The Oklahoma Cowboys also broadcast over the radio in the late twenties and early thirties, as did Gene Autry and Tom Mix and his Straight Shooters, who used as their radio theme "When the Bloom Is on the Sage" (Fred Howard and Nat Vincent), and Tex Ritter. But it was the movie Western, even more than radio, that was responsible for the prodigious growth in popularity of cowboy songs all over the country in the thirties. With Westerns becoming a highly salable commodity in the movie market, cowboy music entered the mainstream of American popular music, promoted by such adulated singing cowboys as Gene Autry, Roy Rogers, Tex Ritter and Tex Williams.

Autry's successes over the radio brought him a movie contract in 1933. He had only a subsidiary part in his first motion picture, *In Old Santa Fe* (1934), where he sang one of his own numbers, "Some Day in Wyoming," written with Smiley Burnette. A year later, Autry assumed his first starring role at the Republic Studios in *Tumbling Tumbleweeds*. Here he introduced the title song, written by Bob Nolan. Together with Bing Crosby's best-selling Decca recording in 1940, Autry helped to make this cowboy song into a standard. In later movies, Gene Autry introduced and popularized many of his own songs, most of them written in collaboration with others. "You're the Only Star in My Blue Heaven" was heard in *The Old Barn Dance* (1938), *Mexicali Rose* (1939) and *Rim of the Canyon* (1949); "Born in the Saddle" (with Johnny Marvin) in *In Old Monterey* (1939); "Be Honest With Me" (with Fred Rose), an Academy Award nominee, in *Ridin' on a Rainbow* (1941). Autry's theme song, "Back in the Saddle Again" (with Ray Whitelcy), was written in 1940, but Autry did not sing it in a motion picture until 1952, in *Wagon Train*. "Tweedle-o-Twill" (With Fred Rose) was introduced by Autry in *Home in Wyoming* (1942) and repeated in *Whirlwind* (1951).

But Autry did not confine himself to those cowboys songs in the writing of which he had had a hand. "Mexicali Rose" (Helen Stone—Jack B. Tenney) was an "oldie" from the twenties which had been popularized over the radio by the Cliquot Club Eskimos, and later made into a successful Decca recording by Bing Crosby. Autry sang it in 1939 in the motion picture of the same name. "South of the Border" (Jimmy Kennedy and Michael Carr) was an English song written for Autry which he introduced during a public appearance tour in England in 1939; after that he recorded it for Columbia to pile up a three-million disk sale in two years. Autry sang Billy Hill's "The Last Round-Up" in *The Singing Hill* (1941) and Hill's last published song, "Call of the Canyon" in the motion picture of that name in 1942.

Roy Rogers was a stout competitor to Gene Autry both in the number of Westerns in which he was starred and in his success as a cowboy singer. He was born Leonard Slye in Cincinnati in 1912 and was raised in Duck Run, near Portsmouth, Ohio. In his late teens he came to Los Angeles where he supported himself by picking peaches and driving a truck. Having by this time learned to play the guitar, and having acquired a storehouse of country songs, Rogers often entertained his fellow workers. After joining various musical groups, Rogers became the lead singer in The Sons of the Pioneers formed in 1934 to specialize in country music, some written by its members. This group made several successful recordings including one of Bob Nolan's "Cool Water." Rogers' own recording of Billy Hill's "The Last Round-Up" was a best-seller, and helped bring him a movie contract. *Come on Rangers* (1938), *Shine On Harvest Moon* (1938) and *Under Western Skies* (1938) were the first of some hundred or so films in which Rogers was starred. In 1937, Rogers joined the Republic studio to make *Wild Horse Rodeo*. During the next two decades there he shared the throne of king of cowboy singers with Gene Autry, often appearing with his wife, Dale Evans, sometimes with the Sons of the Pioneers, and invariably with his horse, Trigger.

Many of the songs Rogers used in his various motion pictures were those that others had introduced and made famous, but whose popularity was further enhanced with his performances: Johnny Mercer's "I'm an Old Cow Hand" in *King of the Cowboys* (1943), Bob Nolan's "Cool Water" in *Hands Across the Border* (1943) and in *Along the Navajo Trail*

(1945), Nolan's "Tumbling Tumbleweeds" in *Silver Spurs* (1943) and Billy Hill's "The Last Round-Up" in *Don't Fence Me In* (1945). One of the most important cowboy songs introduced by Rogers, however, Cole Porter's "Don't Fence Me In," was not originally in a Western, though it was later heard in the film of that name.

Beginning in 1936, Tex Ritter made seventy-eight motion pictures. He was a Texan, born in 1907, who had attended the University of Texas for five years where he studied voice with Oscar J. Fox, a composer of cowboy songs. Ritter's interest in Western folk music, and cowboy songs in particular, was developed through his personal contacts with folklorists John A. Lomax and J. Frank Dobie. Ritter devised a program, "The Texas Cowboy and his Songs"—combining stories with music—which he presented throughout the West. For a year, as a student at Northwestern Law School, he thought of law as a career, but dropped it as his fascination for folk music grew. In 1929 he appeared on KPRC in Houston, and in 1930 he traveled with a musical troupe in one-night stands in the South and Midwest. In 1931 he was starred in New York in the Theatre Guild production of *Green Grow the Lilacs* in which he sang several Western folk ballads. He began making frequent appearances on the radio in New York, including performances on "The Lone Star Ranger" program over WOR, the first Western radio show emanating from New York. Here, as well as in concerts and lectures, he became the first performer to achieve recognition in New York for country music, and was largely responsible for the vogue for cowboy songs that seized New York in the early 1930s. His fame brought him a Hollywood contract in 1936. Two years later he was starred in *The Utah Trail* at the Grand National studios and *Where the Buffalo Roam* at Monogram, and in 1939 in *Down the Wyoming Trail*, *Rollin' Westward* and *Song of the Buckaroo*, as well as in *Roll Wagons Roll* and *Sundown on the Prairie*. In 1940 he sang "You Are My Sunshine" (Jimmie Davis and Charles Mitchell) in *Take Me Back to Oklahoma*. Subsequent starring roles were in *Golden Trail* (1940) and *Pals of the Silver Sage* (1940), together with other films. He combined his screen success with appearances in theaters, rodeos, state fairs, over radio and television and at the Grand Ole Opry in Nashville. His best-selling records, all for Capitol, included the following: "There's a New Moon Over My Shoulder" (Jimmie Davis, Ekko Whelan and Leo Blastic); "Jealous Heart" (Jenny Lou Carson); "You Two-Timed Me Once Too Often" (Jenny Lou Carson); "Rock 'n' Rye Rag" (Tex Ritter, Frank Harford and Edyth Bergdahl); and "I Dreamed of Hillbilly Heaven" (Hal Sothern—Eddie Dean). The most famous song with which Ritter was associated was "High Noon" (Ned Washington—Dimitri Tiomkin) which he introduced on the sound track of the film of the same name in 1952. His eminence in country music was recognized when he was twice elected president of the Country Music Association, and when in 1946 he entered the Country Music Hall of Fame. His motion picture career ended, he made a bid for a seat in the United States Senate in 1970 which failed, and in 1973 he toured England in concerts. "I'd like to do films again," he said at the time, "but nobody's waiting on my doorstep. . . ." He died in Nashville in 1974. *The Tex Ritter Story* by Johnny Bond appeared in 1977.

Tex Williams made his first movie in 1941. After that Williams appeared and sang in some fifty pictures, most of them at the Universal-International lot. He further distinguished himself in country music as the organizer of the Western Caravan, a twelve-piece combo which performed in ballrooms and theaters throughout the United States as well as on network television shows. Williams was the first president of the Academy of Country and Western Music. He made several hit records in the mid-forties: "California Polka" (Dale Fitzsimmons); "Smoke! Smoke! Smoke!" (Merle Travis and Tex Williams), the first Capitol record ever to achieve a million-disk sale); and "Texas in My Soul" (Ernest Tubb and Zeb Turner).

Because of the growing demand for cowboy songs, stars of screen musicals who had not even a remote affiliation with the West, began singing these songs in their movies. Dick Powell introduced "Ride, Tenderfoot, Ride" (Johnny Mercer—Richard A. Whiting) in *Cowboy from Brooklyn* (1938), and Bing Crosby sang Johnny Mercer's "I'm an Old Cow Hand" and Billy Hill's "Empty Saddles" in *Rhythm on the Range* (1936). Cowboy songs were interpolated even in non-Western musicals, as when Roy Rogers introduced Cole Porter's "Don't Fence Me In" in *Hollywood Canteen* (1944). Porter had written that song in the 1930s for a movie, *Adios Argentina*, that was never released, and not until a decade later was it used to become what Sidney Skolsky called "the most instantaneous song hit Cole Porter ever had." Recordings by Roy Rogers, by Kate Smith, and by Bing Crosby with the Andrews Sisters sold millions of disks. In 1944 the song climbed to the top spot of radio's "Your Hit Parade" to stay there a number of weeks. A year later, a Western movie appropriated its title. Cole Porter got the idea for his song from a poem by a Montana cowboy, the rights to which Porter acquired for $150.00. In his song, Porter used just the poem's title and a few phrases. The oft-repeated story that Cole Porter wrote "Don't Fence Me In" to satirize cowboy songs is apocryphal.

5

The large market for screen musicals of all types in the 1930s put a heavy premium on popular music, creating new and seemingly insatiable demands for songs. These demands were far too great to be met adequately by the new generation of songwriters developed in Hollywood. Consequently, the motion picture industry had to reach out to New York—to Tin Pan Alley and to Broadway—for its most experienced, gifted and successful lyricists and composers.

Beginning in 1929, songwriters came out to California in droves. Among the first arrivals were Irving Berlin, De Sylva, Brown and Henderson, Walter Donaldson and Richard A. Whiting.

The first time Irving Berlin became affiliated with talking pictures was with the song "When My Dreams Come True" used in the Marx Brothers farcical extravaganza, *The Cocoanuts* (1929). This was a new song; the ones Berlin had previously written for that stage production had all been eliminated. Still in 1929, Berlin wrote two songs for the King Vidor all-black production, *Hallelujah!*; the title song for *Coquette*, a nonmusical production starring Mary Pickford, and used to promote that film; the theme song for *Lady of the Pavements* ("Where Is the Song of Songs for Me?"); and the title number, together with two other songs, for *Puttin' on the Ritz* (1930), starring Harry Richman, the title song soon to become Richman's theme. In 1931, Berlin provided a title song for *Reaching for the Moon* starring Douglas Fairbanks, Sr. All of these songs were more or less incidental in Berlin's overall musical production. Not so the score he wrote in the latter part of the 1930s, five numbers for *Top Hat* (1935) starring cinema's king and queen of song and dance, Fred Astaire and Ginger Rogers. This is the score that brought us "Top Hat, White Tie and Tails," "The Piccolino," "Isn't This a Lovely Day" and one of Berlin's most beautiful ballads and biggest moneymakers, "Cheek to Cheek," a nominee for an Academy Award.

For the next Ginger Rogers–Fred Astaire musical, *Follow the Fleet* (1936) Berlin contributed seven numbers, among them "I'm Putting All My Eggs in One Basket" and "Let's Face the Music and Dance." For *On the Avenue* (1937), starring Dick Powell and Alice Faye, he wrote nine songs, one of them being "I've Got My Love to Keep Me Warm."

Irving Berlin's giant stature in American popular music was recognized at the studios of 20th Century-Fox in 1938 with the production and release of *Alexander's Ragtime Band*, a veritable horn of plenty of Irving Berlin's song classics that, in addition to the famous title song, included such Berlin favorites as "Easter Parade," "What'll I Do?", "Say It with Music," "A Pretty Girl Is Like a Melody," "Blue Skies" and "All Alone." This was the first time a motion picture score was made up almost exclusively of the standards of a living composer. Berlin wrote the story himself covering the years of 1911 through 1938 and the crosscurrents in the lives of several show people played by Tyrone Power, Alice Faye, Don Ameche, Ethel Merman and Jack Haley. But this story was just a framework for the Berlin songs—the greatest of his career so far—together with three new numbers.

The year 1938 saw the release of one more Ginger Rogers–Fred Astaire musical delight, *Carefree*, with new Berlin songs, the best of which were "Change Partners" and "The Night Is Filled with Music." In Berlin's *Second Fiddle*, Tyrone Power introduced "I Poured My Heart into a Song," an Academy Award nominee.

De Sylva, Brown and Henderson came to Hollywood in 1929 after having written "Sonny Boy" for Al Jolson in *The Singing Fool*. Their first Hollywood assignment was a major screen musical, *Sunny Side Up* (1929), starring Janet Gaynor and Charles Farrell. Much of the lovable and gentle quality of this motion picture was the result of songs such as "Keep Your Sunny Side Up," "If I Had a Talking Picture of You" and "I'm a Dreamer." Three later motion pictures utilized songs by De Sylva, Brown and Henderson *Say It with Songs* (1929), *Follow the Leader* (1930) and *Just Imagine* (1930). Then the partnership of this gifted writing trio was permanently dissolved.

Into *Glorifying the American Girl* (1929) was interpolated "Sam the Old Accordion Man" which Walter Donaldson had written two years earlier and which had been popularized by Ruth Etting. For *Hot for Paris* (1929) Donaldson wrote three new songs to lyrics by Edgar Leslie. Then, for a four-year period, Donaldson parted company with the movies. Upon his return, and for the remainder of the thirties, his songs embellished several important screen musicals, such as *Kid Millions* (1934) starring Eddie Cantor, who sang "When My Ship Comes In" (Gus Kahn); *Reckless* (1935) with Jean Harlow; *Suzy* (1936), starring Jean Harlow and Cary Grant from which "Did I Remember?" (Harold Adamson), dubbed on the sound track by Virginia Verrill for Jean Harlow, was an Academy Award nominee; and *The Great Ziegfeld* (1936) in which "You" (Harold Adamson) was introduced.

Between 1929 and 1932, Richard A. Whiting wrote songs for about half a dozen musicals. Three starred Maurice Chevalier: *Innocents of Paris* (1929), *Playboy of Paris* (1930) and *One Hour With You* (1932). A graduate of the Paris music halls and the Folies Bergères, Chevalier made his live American debut with a program of songs in the last midnight revue produced by Ziegfeld on the roof of the New Amsterdam Theater in July 1929. Chevalier's bow on the American musical screen took place the same year in *Innocents of Paris*, where he introduced "Louise" (Leo Robin—Richard A. Whiting). Chevalier instantly ingratiated himself with Americans as the epitome of Gallic charm and sex appeal. He went on in 1930 to star in *The Big Pond* where he sang "You Brought a New Kind of Love to Me" (Irving Kahal—Pierre Norman Connor and Sammy Fain). Singing Whiting's songs once again, he was heard in "My Ideal"—lyrics by Leo Robin, melody written with Newell Chase—in *Playboy of Paris* and in the title song of *One Hour With You*, lyrics by Leo Robin, which Eddie Cantor soon adopted as his radio theme song.

The songs Whiting wrote with Johnny Mercer for *Hollywood Hotel*, *Varsity Girl* and *Cowboy from Brooklyn* have already been commented upon, as has "The Good Ship Lollipop" which he wrote for Shirley Temple. One other Whiting movie song of the thirties deserves mention, "When Did You Leave Heaven" (Walter Bullock), an Academy Award nominee introduced by Tony Martin in *Sing, Baby, Sing* (1936).

In 1930 another caravan of distinguished New York songwriters invaded Hollywood. Jimmy McHugh arrived with his lyricist, Dorothy Fields, to write the songs for *Love in the Rough* (1930), one of which was "Go Home and Tell Your Mother." After this, McHugh's pen was one of the busiest among Hollywood composers. The wide range of his creativity and the ample span of his success as screen composer are demonstrated by songs such as these, all written in the thirties to Dorothy Fields' lyrics: "Cuban Love Song" from the motion picture of that title starring Lawrence Tibbett in 1931; "Don't Blame Me," used as a promotional song for *Dinner at Eight* (1933); "Thank You for a Lovely Evening" and "Lost in a Fog," both originally written for New York nightclub acts but then interpolated into *Have a Heart* (1934); and "I'm in the Mood for Love," introduced by Frances Langford in *Every Night at Eight* (1935).

Sigmund Romberg's first Hollywood assignment was *Viennese Nights* (1930) which had "Will You Remember Vienna" (Oscar Hammerstein II), sung by Vivienne Segal and Alexander Gray. A year later, Romberg's songs were used in *Children of Dreams*, another movie with a Viennese setting. Both pictures are forgotten, and so would *The Night Is Young* (1935) but for the fact that it was the origin of one of Romberg's most beautiful ballads, "When I Grow Too Old to Dream" (Oscar Hammerstein II), heard as a duet by Evelyn Laye and Ramon Novarro. Romberg's last Hollywood score was for *The Girl of the Golden West* (1938).

Harry Ruby had a winner with his very first song for the screen. It was "Three Little Words" (Bert Kalmar), introduced by Duke Ellington and his orchestra with The Rhythm Boys (one of whom was Bing Crosby) in *Check and Double Check* (1930). As one of Ruby's most successful songs, "Three Little Words" was used in 1950 as the title of his motion picture biography. In the 1930s, Ruby's songs appeared in (but did not greatly interfere with the antics of) the Marx Brothers in *Animal Crackers* (1930), *Horse Feathers* (1932) and *Duck Soup* (1933), with "Hooray for Captain Spaulding" (Bert Kalmar) from *Animal Crackers* becoming Groucho Marx's television theme song.

George and Ira Gershwin also came West in 1930 to the Fox studios to write songs for *Delicious* (1931), which starred Janet Gaynor and Charles Farrell. Together with the music for six songs (none top-drawer Gershwin, but the best being "Delishious") George Gershwin also composed a six-minute orchestral sequence descriptive of the sounds and movements of the city as background music, of which only a single minute was used. This sequence served Gershwin as material for his *Second Rhapsody*, for orchestra.

After this single assignment, George and Ira Gershwin stayed away from Hollywood for five years. When they returned they planted their roots in California soil, permanently as it turned out. Their first new screen score was a lively affair for Fred Astaire and Ginger Rogers, *Shall We Dance* (1937), memorable for the title number, "Let's Call the Whole Thing Off," "They Can't Take That Away from Me," "Slap that Bass" and "They All Laughed." "They Can't Take That Away from Me" became the only Gershwin song ever nominated for an Academy Award which, that year, was won by "Sweet Leilani" (Harry Owens) from *Waikiki Wedding*.

In 1937, the Gershwins wrote the score for a second musical for Fred Astaire, this time paired with Joan Fontaine. This was *A Damsel in Distress*, the showcase for "A Foggy Day" and "Nice Work if You Can Get It." Samuel Goldwyn then contracted the Gershwins to write songs for a magnificently mounted musical, *The Goldwyn Follies*. George Gershwin was able to complete only four of these numbers, two of them, "Love Walked In" and "Love Is Here to Stay," among his finest ballads. He collapsed while working on this assignment. A tumor of the brain caused him to suffer excruciating head pains and melancholia for several months. George Gershwin succumbed at the Cedars of Lebanon Hospital on July 11, 1937, following exploratory brain surgery. "George Gershwin will live as long as music lives," said Eva Gauthier, the singer. Vernon Duke remarked on learning of Gershwin's death: "Death can be kind and it can be just; but it had no business taking our George who was in full flower of his fine youth and who was unquestionably doing his best work."

Sammy Fain's first affiliation with the screen came with "You Brought a New Kind of Love to Me" (Irving Kahal), melody written with Pierre Norman Connor, a song that further endeared Maurice Chevalier to American audiences in *The Big Pond* (1930). From then on, Fain's songs were heard with increasing frequency in films. He had songs in three motion pictures in 1933, and in nine in 1934. The best was "That Old Feeling" (Lew Brown) in *Walter Wanger's Vogues of 1938* (1937), an Academy Award nominee, and a favorite of Jane Froman.

Rodgers and Hart reappeared in Hollywood in 1931 with a film disaster called *The Hot Heiress*. This unhappy experience led them to write their Broadway musical, *America's Sweetheart* (1931), a satire on the movie business. When they returned to California in 1932 they made amends for their earlier failure by working for *Love Me Tonight*, which starred Maurice Chevalier and Jeanette MacDonald in a saucy, sophisticated musical featuring three Rodgers and Hart songs, "Mimi," "Lover" and "Isn't It Romantic?"

Other assignments assumed by Rodgers and Hart in Hollywood were *The Phantom President* (1932) in which George M. Cohan made his debut in talking pictures; a dull Al Jolson movie, *Hallelujah, I'm A Bum* (1933), whose novelty and main interest lay in the experiment of Rodgers and Hart with rhythmic dialogue; and an early Bing Crosby movie, *Mississippi* (1935), one of whose attractions was the song "Easy to Remember."

By the time Jerome Kern worked at the RKO studios with his lyricist, Otto Harbach, on songs for *Men in the Sky* in 1931, the public had begun to reject musicals. When *Men in the Sky* was released in 1932 none of the Kern-Harbach songs were used, though some of the musical material was used as a discreet background. Disenchanted, Kern stayed away from the movie capital for two years. Upon his return he went to work once again for RKO, this time on the screen adaptation of *Roberta* (1935), starring Irene Dunne and Fred Astaire, with a score that included "I Won't Dance" (Otto Harbach and Oscar Hammerstein II) and "Lovely to Look At" (Dorothy Fields and Jimmy McHugh), both written for this film version of the stage musical. *I Dream Too Much* (1935) starred the prima donna, Lily Pons, her coloratura voice heard in the title number and "The Jockey on the Carousel" among others. In this assignment, Kern initiated a collaboration with Dorothy Fields, the lyricist, with whom he wrote songs for three more screen musicals in the 1930s: *Swing Time* (1936), starring Fred Astaire and Ginger Rogers; *When You're in Love* (1937), with Irene Dunne; and *Joy of Living* (1938), with Irene Dunne and Douglas Fairbanks, Jr. A fourth Kern musical, *High, Wide and Handsome* (1937), had lyrics by Oscar Hammerstein II.

Swing Time was the cream of this Kern crop, blessed with a script studded with sprightly dialogue and rapier-edge wit, stunning dance routines by Ginger Rogers and Fred Astaire, and some of the best songs Kern ever wrote for the screen. "The Way You Look Tonight" won the Academy Award that year, but it did not overshadow other excellent songs, namely "A Fine Romance," "Bojangles of Harlem" and "Pick Yourself Up."

From Kern's other screen musicals the most memorable numbers were "Our Song" (Dorothy Fields) from *When You're in Love* and "Can I Forget You?" (Oscar Hammerstein II) from *High, Wide and Handsome*.

When Vincent Youmans came to Hollywood in 1933, it was to write songs for *Flying Down to Rio*, a musical of more than passing significance since it was the first to join Ginger

Rogers and Fred Astaire. Here they were given only subsidiary roles, but they stole the show with their crisp repartee, their singing and their dancing. For them Youmans wrote "Carioca" and "Orchids in the Moonlight," lyrics by Gus Kahn and Edward Eliscu.

Though Youmans lived another dozen years and wrote more songs, none were used on either the stage or the screen. *Flying Down to Rio* was his swan song as a composer. After 1934, a victim of tuberculosis, he spent many years in Colorado, sometimes in a sanatorium, sometimes in a private apartment. His finances worsened along with his health. In 1943, with ample financial backing, he returned to the theater, not as a composer but as the producer of an overly ambitious ballet-revue enlisting the services of outstanding dancers, choreographers and performing artists. *The Vincent Youmans Ballet-Revue,* as he called it, opened in Toronto in 1943, then played for a week in Baltimore, where it proved a ponderous bore. It closed down in Baltimore with a loss of $400,000. Youmans knew he was through professionally, and the knowledge was destroying him. He returned to Colorado where his health continued to deteriorate until, on April 5, 1946, he died in his hotel suite.

After their impressive screen debut as a song and dance team in *Flying Down to Rio* in 1933, Ginger Rogers and Fred Astaire were given starring roles in *The Gay Divorcée* (1934), a screen version of Cole Porter's stage musical, *The Gay Divorce.* All the songs except one, "Night and Day," were eliminated in the screen adaptation to make room for four interpolations. One of these was "The Continental" (Herb Magidson—Con Conrad). When, in 1934, a new category was introduced into the Academy Awards to cover screen songs, "The Continental" became the first recipient.

Cole Porter himself did not get to Hollywood until 1936, his first assignment, *Born to Dance,* starring Eleanor Powell. Its principal song, an Academy Award nominee, was "I've Got You Under My Skin." *Rosalie* followed in 1937, once again with Miss Powell, two of whose songs, "In the Still of the Night" and the title number, were introduced by Nelson Eddy. The title song is a curiosity. Porter wrote and submitted five different songs called "Rosalie" to the studio heads, all of them rejected as too sophisticated. In a contemptuous mood, Porter wrote a new song in which words and melody consciously employed the trite sentiments, clichés and maudlin phraseology usual with screen love ballads. This was the one that was accepted and, to Porter's amazement, went on to become a hit.

6

The highest honor to come to a screen song was the winning of an Oscar once this award had been instituted in 1934 and won by "The Continental." We have already noted that "The Lullaby of Broadway" won the Oscar in 1935, "The Way You Look Tonight" in 1936, "Sweet Leilani" in 1937 and "Thanks for the Memory" in 1938. There remains only one more Oscar-winning song in the thirties to require consideration, "Over the Rainbow" (E. Y. Harburg—Harold Arlen), in 1939.

With "Over the Rainbow," Harold Arlen joins the company of the musical greats in the Hollywood of the thirties. His name originally was Hyman Arluck when he was born in Buffalo in 1905, the son of a synagogue cantor. As a child, Harold sang in the synagogue choir, absorbing the strains of the plaintive songs of his race which later on would assert themselves in his own melodic thinking. Formal piano study began when he was nine with a local piano teacher. When Arlen was twelve he became infatuated with piano rags— specifically with "Indianola" (Domenico Savino). Ragtime sent him to the exploration of jazz and the blues through recordings. By the time he was fifteen, he dropped out of high school after a single year to participate in performances of popular music with local dance bands in cafés, roadhouses and steamers, and as a pianist in movie houses. He next formed "The Snappy

Trio" which grew into a five-man contingent renamed "Southbound Shufflers" that played on a Lake Erie boat and at the Lake Shore Manor near Buffalo. His first song was written at this time (1924), "My Gal, My Pal." Arlen left the "Southbound Shufflers" to form the "Yankee Six," a group popular at college campuses and society parties. Expanding into an eleven-man ensemble it changed its name to "The Buffalodians," for which Arlen played the piano, sang vocals and made arrangements. In 1924–1925, this group was heard in Cleveland, Pittsburgh and in a New York nightclub. Once in New York, Arlen became arranger and vocalist for the Arnold Johnson band featured at the Park Central Hotel and in the pit of *George White's Scandals of 1928*. One of his songs was now published, "The Album of My Dreams," written with Lou Davis, and recorded by Rudy Vallee.

In 1929, Arlen got a small part in the Vincent Youmans musical, *Great Day*. Fletcher Henderson was its rehearsal pianist and when, one day, Henderson was ill, Arlen was called in to substitute for him. During pauses in the rehearsal, Arlen improvised a melody based on a "vamp" from one of the numbers. The choral director, Will Marion Cook, was impressed with what Arlen was playing and urged him to develop it into a song. Through the composer Harry Warren, Arlen got Ted Koehler to write the lyrics for his melody, which was now called "Get Happy." It was introduced in 1930 in the first-act finale of an intimate musical, the *9:15 Revue*, sung by Ruth Etting. The show was a flop, closing after just seven performances on Broadway, but "Get Happy" survived, to become Arlen's first song success, and to mark his real beginning as a professional songwriter.

On the strength of this one song, Arlen was hired by Jerome H. Remick as staff composer for fifty-five dollars a week—his job, just to write songs. He did, and made rapid headway. In 1931, he made his bow as Broadway composer with his first full-length score, for *You Said It*, lyrics by Jack Yellen. For about three years, up to 1934, with Ted Koehler as lyricist, he provided the songs for shows produced at the Cotton Club at 142nd Street in Harlem. In 1931, Aida Ward introduced "Between the Devil and the Deep Blue Sea," and that same year "I Love a Parade" was used for a production number, performed by Cab Calloway and his orchestra. In 1932, Arlen and Koehler wrote for the Cotton Club revue "I've Got the World on a String," and "Minnie the Moocher's Wedding Day," the former for Aida Ward and the latter as a specialty for Cab Calloway. In 1934, Lena Horne, then only sixteen and a newcomer to show business, sang "As Long as I Live," and Aida Ward was heard in "Ill Wind."

Though Arlen mastered many different song styles, he was most partial to the blues. His first blues was written in 1932, "I Gotta Right to Sing the Blues" (Ted Koehler), actually his only one in an authentic blues style; Lillian Shade introduced it in *Earl Carroll's Vanities of 1932*, and later Jack Teagarden used it as his theme music. Subsequent Arlen blues sidestepped the traditional structure and technique of the genuine folk or New Orleans product; some did not even contain the word "blues" in the title. But all convey the plangent spirit of the blues, in the Harold Arlen manner.

One of these Arlen blues is a classic, "Stormy Weather" (Ted Koehler), one of the most famous commercial blues since Handy's "The St. Louis Blues." Arlen wrote "Stormy Weather" for Cab Calloway, bearing in mind Calloway's "hi-de-ho" singing style. When Calloway was replaced by Duke Ellington, Arlen prevailed on Ethel Waters to do the number. But even before the revue opened at the Cotton Club, "Stormy Weather" had become a best-selling record in a performance by Leo Reisman and his orchestra with Arlen doing the vocal. "Stormy Weather" is unconventional in that it has no verse, and the song itself extends for thirty-six measures. ("Ill Wind" also has no verse, and runs for forty measures.)

Other Arlen songs were getting hearings in the Broadway theater. During 1932, the year in which "I Gotta Right to Sing the Blues" was interpolated into *Earl Carroll's Vanities*, another Arlen blues, "Satan's L'il Lamb," was featured in the intimate revue, the third edition of *Americana*. Its main significance lies in the fact that the lyrics were written by two men who would soon work fruitfully with Arlen for many years. One was Johnny Mercer, the other, E. Y. Harburg, better known as "Yip" Harburg ("Yip" being a contraction of "yipsel" or squirrel). Again in 1932, with Harburg and Billy Rose as his lyricists, Arlen wrote "If You Believe in Me" which was placed in a nonmusical Broadway play that year, *The Great Magoo*. One year later, as sung by June Knight and Buddy Rogers in the motion picture *Take a Chance*, this song became famous as "It's Only a Paper Moon," Arlen's first song heard on the screen. In 1934, this time with lyrics by Ira Gershwin and E. Y. Harburg, Arlen contributed nineteen songs to a successful Broadway revue, *Life Begins at 8:40*. In 1936, "Song of the Woodman" (E. Y. Harburg) became a tour de force for Bert Lahr in the Broadway revue *The Show Is On*, and a year after that Arlen, still with Harburg as lyricist, prepared the entire score for the Broadway musical *Hooray for What* starring Ed Wynn.

Arlen was also making his mark in motion pictures. After his debut with "It's Only a Paper Moon," Arlen wrote his first song specifically for the screen, the ballad, "Let's Fall In Love" (Ted Koehler) for the motion picture of the same name (1934). After that, Arlen placed several more songs, none of them of particular moment, in various motion pictures including the *Gold Diggers of 1937* (1936).

In 1938, Arthur Freed, now an MGM producer, planned with Mervyn Le Roy to film L. Frank Baum's *The Wonderful Wizard of Oz*. The studio made fabulous offers to Shirley Temple to assume the starring role of Dorothy, the farm girl. Only after young Miss Temple turned down the role did the producers look into their own backyard and choose Judy Garland, fresh from her recent success in *Broadway Melody of 1938*. Feeling the need of a new score, rather than the one used on Broadway back in 1903 when Baum's novel had been made into a stage musical, Freed and Le Roy called upon Harold Arlen. With Harburg providing the lyrics, Arlen completed twelve numbers, one of which was "Over the Rainbow."

The principal melody of the chorus of "Over the Rainbow" struck Arlen while he was driving to Grauman's Chinese Theater in Hollywood, and he hurriedly wrote it down. The release of the chorus was worked out the next day. When Arlen played the finished song for his lyricist, Harburg was critical. "That's for Nelson Eddy," Harburg said, "not for a little girl in Kansas." Harburg meant that the song was much too pretentious in style, with its slow and stately melody richly harmonized, to be appropriate for *The Wizard of Oz*. Arlen and Harburg sought out the judgment of Ira Gershwin. Gershwin liked what he heard, but agreed that a quicker tempo and a slighter harmonic texture was called for. Those revisions were made and the character of the song thereby transformed. At the studio, there were new difficulties. As Judy Garland later recalled: " 'Over the Rainbow' was deleted from the print of *The Wizard of Oz* three times; after each deletion Arthur Freed would storm into the front office and argue it back into the film. Further opposition came from the publisher, who objected to the difficult-to-sing octave leap in the melody on the word 'somewhere' and to the simple middle . . . 'Why it's like a child's exercise.' But Freed and Arlen stood up to the powers and the song remained."

It became, as we now know, the shining light in that bright score, and went on to win the Academy Award. There is so much of Judy Garland's personality and history in this number that it is difficult to think of the song without remembering the performer. This was the song closest to her heart, the one always calculated to bring down the house in her many personal appearances, particularly in her late years when her life was in disarray. When, after personal tragedies and emotional upheavals had almost destroyed her, she made her dramatic comeback at the Palace Theater in New York for a four-week engagement in August 1967, she created a storm with her tearful presentation of "Over the Rainbow," sitting on the apron of the stage, her feet dangling over the orchestra pit, a single spotlight illuminating her face.

With *The Wizard of Oz*, and specifically with "Over the Rainbow," sixteen-year-old Judy Garland joined the constellation of MGM stars. MGM did not wait long after *The Wizard of Oz* to exploit her new status. They co-starred her with Mickey Rooney in *Babes in Arms* (1939), an adaptation of the 1937 Rodgers and Hart Broadway stage musical. In addition to her participation in two Rodgers and Hart numbers from the stage show, "Where or When" and the title number, she was also heard in "Good Morning" (Arthur Freed —Nacio Herb Brown), "God's Country" (E. Y. Harburg—Harold Arlen), Stephen Foster's "Oh Susanna," "By the Light of the Silvery Moon" (Edward Madden—Gus Edwards) and "I'm Just Wild About Harry" (Noble Sissle and Eubie Blake). In addition she was assigned two solo numbers, "I Cried for You" (Arthur Freed—Abe Lyman and Gus Arnheim) and a novelty song by Roger Edens, "Figaro." In the 1940s, the motion picture musicals, *For Me and My Gal* (1942), *The Harvey Girls* (1944), *Meet Me in St. Louis* (1944) and *Easter Parade* (1948) made her one of the greatest singing stars the motion picture screen has known.

Harburg, who wrote the lyrics for *The Wizard of Oz*, was a New York boy, born in 1898, and educated in its public schools and at the College of the City of New York. He then went to South America as a representative of an American firm which went bankrupt soon after Harburg's arrival. For several years, Harburg held down various jobs in South America. Back in the United States in 1921, he organized an electrical supply company that became successful, until it failed in the Depression.

The writing of song lyrics had been a pet hobby even when he was in business. To Jay Gorney's music he wrote six songs for the Earl Carroll revue, *The Sketch Book*, in 1929. After his electrical supply firm went into bankruptcy, Harburg involved himself more deeply than ever before in lyric writing. "I had my fill," he said at the time, "of this dreamy abstract thing called business and I decided to face reality by writing lyrics." He wrote some songs for several Broadway little shows and intimate revues. "April in Paris" from *Walk a Little Faster*, with Vernon Duke's music, became a standard, and "Brother, Can You Spare a Dime?" from *Americana* (1932), music by Jay Gorney, grew into something of an unofficial theme song for the Depression years.

7

Screen biographies about songwriters and musical performers through the years have provided a convenient catchall for songs old and new, as well as story material, for musicals. Four of them in 1939, initiated this cinematic biographical cycle—three about composers and one on performers.

The Great Victor Herbert, *The Star Maker* and *Swanee River*—the first two from Paramount and the other from 20th Century-Fox—were supposedly the life stories of three famous American popular composers. Walter Connolly played Victor Herbert. *The Star Maker* had Bing Crosby as Gus Edwards, songwriter and vaudevillian. In *Swanee River*, Don Ameche was Stephen Foster. As would become standard procedure with such composer–biographies on the screen, each of these three films played fast and loose with biographical verisimilitude, allowing romantic fancy to play havoc with facts. But at least in two of these—*The Great Victor Herbert* and *Swanee River*—screen biographies provided an excuse for the presentation of a wealth of old-time songs—sixteen by Herbert in *The Great Victor Herbert*, eight by Foster in *Swanee River*. *Swanee River* provided the opportunity to hear an unfamiliar Stephen Foster song, "Ring, Ring de Banjo," together with Foster classics, while the score of *The Great Victor Herbert* offered (together with Herbert standards) such less-familiar Herbert fare as "Someday" (William Le Baron), "Al Fresco" (Henry Blossom), "Absinthe Frappé" (Glen MacDonough), "Rose of the World" (Glen Mac-Donough) and "There Once Was an Owl" (Harry B. Smith).

The fourth screen musical biography in 1939 was the story of the dancing idols, Irene and Vernon Castle, told in the RKO production, *The Story of Vernon and Irene Castle*. More ideal casting could hardly be imagined, with Ginger Rogers and Fred Astaire called upon to portray the Castles. In the musical style of those dancers, Ginger Rogers and Fred Astaire did the Castle Walk, the Maxixe, the Castle House Rag, the waltz and other dances with which the Castles enchanted their contemporaries. Seventeen popular songs of the time provided the musical background, and sixty-three other popular tunes of the decade were heard either in part or entire.

8

The man most often referred to as "the king" of motion picture musicals of the 1930s was Fred Astaire.

Just two and a half weeks before the release of *Flying Down to Rio* in 1933, in which he was paired for the first time with Ginger Rogers, Astaire made his screen bow with a few brief dance sequences and songs in *Dancing Lady* (1933), starring Joan Crawford. Between *Flying Down to Rio* and *The Story of Vernon and Irene Castle* (1939) he was starred in ten musicals, each a winner, and eight of them co-starring Ginger Rogers.

The magical moments from each of these films invariably came when Astaire was dancing—with or without a partner. His virtuosity as a tap dancer, which had few if any equals in the world, was matched only by the imagination, daring and originality of his conceptions. He introduced new dances: "The Carioca" (Gus Kahn and Edward Eliscu —Vincent Youmans)—danced atop seven pianos—in *Flying Down to Rio*; the Academy Award-winning "The Continental" (Herb Magidson—Con Conrad), a seventeen-minute sequence in *The Gay Divorcee* (1934); "The Piccolino" (Irving Berlin) in *Top Hat* (1935); "The Yam" (Irving Berlin) in *Carefree* (1938). In "Top Hat, White Tie and Tails" (Irving Berlin) in *Top Hat*, his cane became a machine gun with his tapping feet beating out the rhythms of machine gun fire. In "I'd Rather Lead a Band" (Irving Berlin) in *Follow the Fleet* (1936), his solo tap dance simulated a series of close order drills. In "Bojangles of Harlem" (Dorothy Fields—Jerome Kern) in *Swing Time* (1936), he appeared in blackface, dressed in derby and loud sports jacket, tapping away in fromt of a screen on which his reflection was magnified into several giant shadows following him every step of the way. In *Shall We Dance* (1937) he did a tap dance on roller skates; in "Let's Call the Whole Thing Off" (Ira Gershwin—George Gershwin) in the same production he performed a drum dance, playing on an assortment of drums not only with sticks but also with his agile toes; for *Carefree* (1938) he devised a golf dance in "Since They Turned Loch Lomond into Swing" (Irving Berlin), skillfully coordinating tap dancing, golf club swinging and harmonica playing. And then there were the elegant, smooth, ethereal dances for which Astaire and Ginger Rogers became so famous: "Smoke Gets in Your Eyes" (Otto Harbach—Jerome Kern) in *Roberta* (1935), "Cheek to Cheek" (Irving Berlin) in *Top Hat* and the "Missouri Waltz" (James Royce —Frederick Knight Logan) in *The Story of Vernon and Irene Castle*.

These and other dances in the Astaire screen musicals of the 1930s were so sensational that they tended to obscure how gifted Astaire also was as a singing performer. Few screen stars have introduced so many songs that have become classics as Astaire. The durability of these musical numbers, of course, attests to the high quality of the song material provided him by some of the greatest popular composers of the time. But the fact that each of these songs became an instant success when first heard on the screen was in large part due to Astaire's effective delivery. Granted that his voice was a small one, with a limited range and an undistinguished tone, nevertheless he was able to bring to his singing his personal charm and sophistication together with an instinctive gift for phrasing and timing in the projection of both the lyrics and the music. These are some of the songs he introduced and first made popular in the 1930s: Irving Berlin's "Cheek to Cheek" in *Top Hat*; Berlin's "I'm Putting All My Eggs in One Basket" and "Let's Face the Music and Dance" in *Follow the Fleet*; Jerome Kern's Academy Award-winning "The Way You Look Tonight" and "A Fine Romance" (Dorothy Fields) in *Swing Time*; George Gershwin's "Let's Call the Whole Thing Off" and "They Can't Take That Away from Me" (Ira Gershwin) in *Shall We Dance*; Gershwin's "A Foggy Day" and "Nice Work if You Can Get It" (Ira Gershwin) in *A Damsel in Distress*; and Irving Berlin's "Change Partners" in *Carefree*.

This list extends into the 1940s to include many other songs that have become standards: Jerome Kern's "Dearly Beloved" (Johnny Mercer), with Cugat's orchestra, in *You Were Never Lovelier* (1942); Harold Arlen's "One for My Baby" (Johnny Mercer) in *The Sky's the Limit* (1943); Irving Berlin's "It Only Happens When I Dance with You" in *Easter Parade* (1948).

In the words of Irving Berlin, quoted in *The New York Times* (November 19, 1976), "You give Astaire a song, and you could forget about it. . . . He sang it the way you wrote it."

Ginger Rogers complemented Fred Astaire perfectly in song, dance and repartee. As far as motion picture musicals were concerned, the thirties might reasonably be regarded as the decade of Fred Astaire and Ginger Rogers, so completely did they dominate the musical screen in that period. They were starred in eight musicals in the thirties: *Flying Down to Rio* (1933), *The Gay Divorcee* (1934), *Roberta* (1935), *Top Hat* (1935), *Follow the Fleet* (1936), *Swing Time* (1936), *Carefree* (1938) and *The Story of Vernon and Irene Castle* (1939). For one decade after that Ginger Rogers was replaced by other partners in Fred Astaire's musicals, and usually with far less happy results. Then, in 1949, Fred Astaire and Ginger Rogers were reunited for the last time in *The Barkleys of Broadway*.

As Virginia Katherine McMath, Ginger Rogers was born in Independence, Missouri, in 1911. When her mother divorced and remarried, Virginia assumed her stepfather's name of Rogers. A stage mother, Lelia Rogers was determined to bring her daughter into the theatrical limelight. As a child, Ginger appeared in local amateur productions in Hollywood, California. Her first professional appearance came in early girlhood when she appeared as a substitute dancer for Eddy Foy's act. When the Charleston became a dance craze throughout the United States in the twenties, Ginger Rogers won so many Charleston contests that a vaudeville producer built an act around her which he named "Ginger and Her Redheads." It was from this time on that Virginia Rogers became Ginger Rogers. As Ginger Rogers she was seen doing the Charleston throughout Texas on the Interstate Circuit. And it was as Ginger Rogers that she appeared as a vocalist with Paul Ash and his orchestra at the Oriental Theater in Chicago.

Still in her teens, she made her way to New York where she appeared in nightclubs and vaudeville, and landed a small part in the Broadway musical *Top Speed*, which opened at the 46th Street Theater on December 25, 1929, where it remained for 104 performances.

She attracted sufficient attention to win a movie contract, making her screen debut in *Young Man of Manhattan* (1930) where she sang "I've Got It But It Don't Do Me No Good" (Irving Kahal, Pierre Norman and Sammy Fain) and spoke a line that became a nationwide catchphrase, "Cigarette me big boy!"

In quick succession in 1930 there came several more movies and, far more significantly, her first starring role in a Broadway smash musical, Gershwin's *Girl Crazy*. A handful of important roles in the movies between 1931 and 1933 included those in *The Gold Diggers of 1933*, where she sang "We're in the Money" (Al Dubin—Harry Warren) in Pig Latin, and *Forty-Second Street*, both at the Warner Brothers studio. In 1933, under contract to RKO, she was assigned a starring role in *Flying Down to Rio* opposite Fred Astaire.

Until this first screen mating of the talents of Ginger Rogers and Fred Astaire, Astaire had not been regarded too highly as a performer in motion pictures. Indeed, when he made his first screen test at RKO, the report read: "Can't act. Slightly bald. Dances a little." In spite of such lack of enthusiasm, RKO signed him to a contract. Then, after loaning him out to MGM for his motion picture debut in *Dancing Lady*, RKO decided to star him with Ginger Rogers in the Vincent Youmans screen musical, *Flying Down to Rio*.

Ginger Rogers helped to surface the latent gold in Fred Astaire. The first time this happened was with the dance "The Carioca" (Gus Kahn and Edward Eliscu—Vincent Youmans) in *Flying Down to Rio*. "The Carioca" proved the making of Ginger Rogers and Fred Astaire. The inclusion of this dance in the motion picture had been something of an afterthought; it was merely a convenience to get Ginger Rogers and Fred Astaire to do at least one dance number in the film. That made all the difference, not only for the song itself (which was nominated for an Academy Award) and for the motion picture (which became a giant box-office success), but most significantly for the motion picture careers of Ginger Rogers and Fred Astaire. As Ginger Rogers later recalled: " 'The Carioca' tore up the screen. Nobody had ever seen a dance team like that. Not on the screen anyway. And we were off."

9

In 1934, the year the Academy of Motion Picture Arts and Sciences first introduced a category for popular songs among its annual awards, it also recognized the importance of music other than songs for the cinema by creating a second musical award, this time for scoring—orchestral arrangements by a screen musician of somebody else's music. Louis Silvers was the first to be so honored for his scoring for *One Night of Love* (1934). But the musical was not the only cinematic medium requiring music, just as the popular song was not the only type of music the cinema could use. By the early 1930s, the importance of background music was recognized: an *original* score, generally for a nonmusical production, helped to establish a mood, suggest setting and time, and build climaxes. Some of the background music of the 1930s resorted to musical stereotypes for given situations and feelings, freely imitative of the romantic repertory of Tchaikovsky, Chopin, Brahms, Puccini or Mahler. But other background scores were conceptions of great imagination, and at times originality. Some of the music was used for the principal and concluding titles, as filler material for dead spots calling for sound but whose music had little relevance to what was happening on the screen, and for those intermittent episodes requiring music for emotional intensification. As the awareness grew of how significant music could be in the projection of a screen drama, background music developed from little snippets into scores of symphonic dimensions, calling for a musician's fullest resources of orchestration, thematic development and atmospheric writing.

The Warner Brothers, who had had the vision to realize that sound would revolutionize the making of motion pictures, also had the foresight to recognize how important music would become in the industry. "Films are fantasy," said Jack L. Warner, "and fantasy needs music." With this in mind, early in its history as a maker of talking pictures, Warner Brothers established a music department on its lot in 1929 and placed at its head Leo F. Forbstein, who had previously devoted himself to conducting orchestras in movie theaters, most recently at Grauman's Metropolitan Theater in Hollywood. Forbstein stayed with Warners for twenty years, during which time he was largely responsible for making his the most creative and influential music division in the entire movie industry, both as to the production of screen musicals and in the placement of original music within nonmusical productions. He himself conducted the orchestras in some of the triumphant screen musicals produced by Warner Brothers in the early 1930s. Then he gave up conducting in the mid-1930s to devote himself completely to the business of building up and running his studio music department. As the musical director of Warner Brothers he was responsible for bringing to his studio two composers whose influence on the development of screen music in the 1930s was decisive and permanent. They were Max Steiner and Erich Wolfgang Korngold.

Max Steiner (1888–1971) wrote or arranged music for about one hundred and fifty productions, averaging about eight scores a year, each score a forty- or fifty-minute symphonic concept. Instinctively he recognized that writing music for the screen called for an operation far different from that of writing music for the stage, and he evolved techniques and methods unique to cinematic music that became general practice in the entire industry. He invented the Click Track, a metronomic device for split second timing of musical episodes within a given scene, allowing sound engineers to compute mathematically the number of clicks per second to each bar of music and to adjust that music according to the given amount of time consumed by that scene. Steiner would look once or twice at a movie for which he was to write the music, then map out those sequences calling for music, together with the amount of time each musical sequence should consume. He then drew up a timing sheet for these specific sequences calling for split second timing. Only then did he start composing, always remembering that his music was there to serve the screen and not vice versa. Bearing this in mind, he concocted all sorts of little motives and musical sequences within his overall context, which gave a literal tonal translation of something the screen was trying to portray. At the same time he had the lyrical gift to spin a sensitive melody when the story allowed, or to paint a tone picture for atmospheric scenes. He was practically the inventor of symphonic background music which, in his hands, became a new musical art form.

He came from Vienna where his grandfather, also named Maximilian Steiner, had been director of the Theater-an-der-Wien and was responsible for getting Johann Strauss, the waltz king, to write his first operetta. As a student at the Academy of Music in Vienna, the younger Maximilian Steiner completed a four-year course in one year and, in addition, won a gold medal. When he was twelve he conducted an American operetta, Gustave Kerker's *The Belle of New York,* in one of his father's Viennese theaters. At fourteen, he himself wrote and conducted the music for an operetta, *Beautiful Greek Girl,* performed at the Orpheum Theater in Vienna where it had a one-year run. In 1904 he moved on to London. There for the next seven years he conducted musicals in leading London theaters and in 1911 he conducted musicals in Paris. With the outbreak of World War I, he was interned as an enemy alien, but was soon released and allowed to come to the United States, arriving in December 1914. For the next fifteen years he worked as an arranger, orchestrator and conductor in the Broadway musical theater. When Harry Tierney, the composer, was called to the RKO studios in Hollywood to assist in the movie production of *Rio Rita*, Tierney suggested that Steiner also be hired, since Steiner had orchestrated and conducted the Broadway production of that musical.

Steiner's first original music for the screen was *Cimarron* (1931) for which he was not listed in the screen credits. Since music was not yet given much importance in a nonmusical film, Steiner was given only a ten-piece orchestra and a three-hour recording period. The scraps of music Steiner managed to include in the movie impressed some of the powers at RKO with the importance of music. Steiner was now given more elbow room in the writing of background music for his succeeding films: *Symphony of Six Million* (1932); *A Bill of Divorcement* (1932), starring Katharine Hepburn in her film debut and John Barrymore; *Little Women* (1933); *King Kong* (1933); and that screen classic directed by John Ford, *The Informer* (1935). In addition, Steiner did the scoring and conducting for a number of musicals produced at RKO, including several starring Fred Astaire and Ginger Rogers. Steiner's last assignment on the RKO lot was scoring and conducting the Irving Berlin screen musical with Astaire and Ginger Rogers, *Follow the Fleet*, in 1936.

It was in *King Kong* that Steiner first revealed his mastery and originality in writing music for the screen. From the opening descending chords that instantly evoked a sense of impending doom, Steiner's music became an important asset in making *King Kong* a cinematic triumph of fantastic horror. Recognition of Steiner's importance in the overall operations at RKO was conceded when he became the first composer in Hollywood ever called upon to consult with the author of the script before the filming of a motion picture. This happened with *The Informer*, for whose background music Steiner received the Academy Award in 1935.

In 1936, Leo Forbstein lured Steiner from RKO to Warner Brothers, Steiner's first assignment for his new studio being the background music for *The Charge of the Light Brigade*. During the next four years he composed music for numerous films, including two starring Bette Davis, *Jezebel* and *Dark Victory*, and others starring Janet Gaynor in the second version of *A Star Is Born* (1937), Paul Muni in *The Life of Emile Zola* (1937), climaxed by one of the most successful motion pictures ever filmed, with one of the best motion picture scores ever written, *Gone With the Wind* (1939), for Selznick International.

The score for *Gone With the Wind*, with its wonderful "Tara" theme that became famous in instrumentals apart from the motion picture, was Steiner's monumental achievement. His score was made up of sixteen main themes and almost three hundred separate segments to make up three hours of music time. It took Steiner twelve weeks to write the score, in which he was assisted by five top Hollywood orchestrators. "Few scores have been woven so thoroughly into the fiber of a movie as Max Steiner's magnum opus," wrote a reviewer for *High Fidelity* in commenting upon a 1973 rerelease by RCA Red Seal of the entire score.

No musician in Hollywood in the 1930s brought a richer background, experience, compositional know-how and world recognition to his screen assignments than did Erich Wolfgang Korngold (1897–1957). By the time Forbstein brought Korngold to Hollywood, and to Warner Brothers in 1934 to do the scoring for the Max Reinhardt screen production of *A Midsummer-Night's Dream*, Korngold was a serious composer of world renown. He became the first serious composer of international significance to be called to Hollywood, and in the twelve years he spent creating eighteen scores, he was one of the highest paid. He brought to screen music a style and technique highly resilient for the pictorial and transitional requirements of the medium, treating each screen subject as if it were an opera libretto calling for his fullest resources. He also brought innovation, such as the experiment of pitching his music just underneath the voices of the actors to achieve a more subtle and sensitive balance between music and the spoken word. The scores he wrote for the screen in the thirties were full evidence of his creative powers: *Captain Blood* (1935); *Anthony Adverse* (1936) for which he received his first Academy Award; *The Prince and the Pauper* (1936); *Another Dawn* (1937); and *The Adventures of Robin Hood* (1938) that brought him his second Academy Award. Korngold held so high a regard for some of this music that he used portions in a serious work, his Concerto for Violin and Orchestra (1945), which took its thematic material from the scores of *Anthony Adverse, The Prince and the Pauper* and *Another Dawn*, as well as from later film productions. "Not only did Korngold's scores establish mood, which any good film score must do," wrote Royal S. Brown in *High Fidelity*, "they also provided a certain element of abstraction that counterbalanced the relatively straightforward and drama-oriented cinematic style." Korngold wrote his scores with such symphonic breadth and creative imagination that they make excellent listening even divorced from the films, something of which little motion picture background music could boast. This was proved in 1972 when RCA Red Seal released an album of "the classic film scores of Erich Wolfgang Korngold," the scores for a dozen films. (A second volume of Korngold's film music was released one year later.) "Everything here," writes Mr. Brown, "is stamped not only with Korngold's totally distinct style but also with the period from which it grew. A great deal of Korngold's music is often bigger—intentionally so—than the film, for it is frequently the music that provided almost single-handedly the esthetic emotion that supplements the dramatic emotion. From this point of view, the warm, often sumptuous romanticism of Korngold's writing could not be more appropriate. The scores . . . abound in extraordinary lyrical richness."

Born in Brünn, Czechoslovakia, in 1897, the son of a renowned music critic, Erich Wolfgang Korngold was a wunderkind who was educated in Vienna and spoken of there as "another Mozart." When he was eleven he composed a musical pantomine produced by the Vienna State Opera, and at thirteen he completed writing a piano sonata that Rudolf Ganz, the distinguished piano virtuoso, performed in the United States. By his nineteenth year, Korngold had two one-act operas produced in Munich. World fame came to him with his full-length opera *The Dead City* produced simultaneously in Hamburg and Cologne in 1920 before coming to the Metropolitan Opera in New York on November 19, 1921. In the 1920s he wrote another full-length opera together with a considerable amount of concert music that placed him in the forefront of European composers.

When Alfred Newman first came to Hollywood in 1930 it was with the intention of staying just three months and completing one movie assignment. He stayed for the rest of his life, doing the scoring for about three hundred films while winning nine Oscars, and conducting the orchestra for many of them. Already in the thirties he enjoyed, with Korngold and Steiner, a top rating among Hollywood composers, particularly after receiving the Academy Award for his scoring of Irving Berlin's *Alexander's Ragtime Band* in 1938.

Born in New Haven, Connecticut, in 1901, Alfred Newman began to study the piano early. Since his family was too poor to own a piano he had to travel ten miles each day to practice on an instrument at the home of a family friend, while studying with a local teacher who charged him twenty-five cents a lesson. When he was eight he was already playing the piano for various clubs and organizations. With his savings he went to New York a year later to study piano with the distinguished teacher, Sigismond Stojowski, who groomed him for his first public recital, in New York, sponsored by Paderewski. The poverty of Newman's family finally compelled him to give up serious music study and earn money. He worked for Gus Edwards and his revue for a time, then when he was thirteen he undertook a vaudeville tour of his own with an act in which he dressed as Little Lord Fauntleroy. In time he turned to conducting orchestras; when he was seventeen he conducted the pit orchestra for *George White's Scandals*. For the next dozen years he worked as a conductor for various Broadway musicals.

Irving Berlin was responsible for bringing Newman to Hollywood in 1930 as musical director for the motion picture, *Reaching for the Moon* (1931), for which Berlin wrote the title song. Newman had every intention of returning to his conducting chores on Broadway when this job was done. But a delay in the production of the movie sent him on loan to Samuel Goldwyn where he wrote the background music for *Street Scene* (1931). During the thirties his scoring or background music was heard in numerous motion pictures, among them *Kid Millions* (1934), *The Mighty Barnum* (1934), *Clive of India* (1935), *The Hurricane* (1937) and *Wuthering Heights* (1939). From *The Hurricane* came the song hit, "Moon of Manakoora" (Frank Loesser—Alfred Newman). In addition, Newman did the scoring and conducting for two films by Charlie Chaplin, *City Lights* (1931) and *Modern Times* (1936). In 1939 he became the general music director of 20th Century-Fox where he remained twenty-one years. David Raksin, himself a distinguished composer of film music who worked under Newman at Fox in the 1940s, said of him: "He was a totally remarkable musician with an amazing sense of theater and timing. . . . Al was a self-regenerating man—just when everyone thought he had said all he had to say about film music, he would surprise everyone and come up with a great score. . . . I think he was more instinctive than profound musically, but what he did have was an unfailing sensitivity to the dramatic meaning of a film scene and the ability to translate that meaning into the language of music."

10

The death of Tin Pan Alley coincided with the birth of talking pictures. The two events were not unconnected. By the time *The Jazz Singer* had established the validity of talking and singing pictures, and was sending the silent film to permanent oblivion, sheet music sales had sunk to the lowest levels in Tin Pan Alley history, about 75 percent below what was considered normal a few decades earlier. Most hit songs sold fewer than a hundred thousand copies. A publisher, therefore, had to realize that he could no longer keep the machinery of his business oiled through the profits from sheet music publication. Royalties from recorded music provided some relief, but it was not enough to fill the gap created by the vanishing sheet music business. The situation in Tin Pan Alley had grown so serious toward the end of the 1920s that nine publishers talked of a giant merger (with backing from banks) in the hope that disaster could be averted by a centralization of their activities and market. Then talking pictures arrived, and the plan was forgotten. The enormous demand for music by talking pictures represented welcome manna from heaven to a starved industry. The insatiable appetite of the screen for songs soon led a number of Hollywood's most important motion picture studios to buy firms in Tin Pan Alley. By doing so, they got a rich backlog of songs from which to draw; at the same time they acquired the services of experienced and successful composers and lyricists who were contractually affiliated with those publishers. Warner Brothers paid ten million dollars for three houses—Harms, Witmark and Remick—which were assembled into one giant organization and renamed the Music Publishers Holding Corporation. Other movie studios followed suit. Metro-Goldwyn-Mayer, for example, acquired Leo Feist, Robbins and one or two lesser firms. Similarly, many other New York publishers were swallowed up by the Hollywood studios. By 1939, 65 percent of the income from performances of popular music collected by ASCAP went to publishers owned by movie interests.

In this way, some of Tin Pan Alley's historic and powerful publishing houses became offshoots of the movie industry, subservient to the needs and demands of the screen. It was now the studio executive who called the tune, figuratively as well as literally. He told the composers and lyricists the type of material needed for specific productions. Once these songs were written, their publication became an automatic procedure in which the publisher himself had little say.

This was the first significant change in publishing, and one that doomed Tin Pan Alley. In the Alley, the publisher had been the central force around which everything connected with songs gravitated—writers, performers, salesmen, pluggers. It was the publisher who selected what songs were to be printed, and he picked them because he liked them and felt that the public would like them. Then he set about the necessary business of getting the songs performed and popularized. Of all the people in the trade, it was primarily the publisher who sought out talent and nursed it to fulfillment; the publisher who told a performer about a song suited to his particular gift; the publisher who worked out methods of promotion.

But now in the new pattern created by the movie industry, the publisher was dictated *to*. He resigned not only his basic function of selecting songs for publication but also of determining the best ways to make them popular. One publisher put it this way, wistfully: "All we do now is clip coupons like bankers, where once we were the makers of song hits and great composers. The thrill and glamour of old Tin Pan Alley are gone forever."

Something more than just a tradition passed away when Tin Pan Alley died in or about 1930. The end of Tin Pan Alley was also the ending of a rich, incomparable epoch in American popular music that had been brought about mainly through the open-door policy that made publishers receptive to manuscripts by unknowns and by composers and lyricists who had still to make their reputations. After 1930 this door was shut tight. Publishers became interested only in the song that had come from a movie, or that had found an outlet on Broadway, over the radio or on records. Now a song had to be big time before the publisher was interested; a composer had to be big time before he was taken under a publisher's wing. In Tin Pan Alley an obscure song, by an equally obscure composer, which grew into a million-copy hit, was so frequent as to be almost normal; since 1930 it has been a fluke, happening at long intervals.

Traditions built up for half a century do not usually die easily. But, after 1929, the impact of the motion picture industry on the song business became a sledgehammer that reduced old methods, procedures and values to dust, and created new and not always better ones.

24

The Troubled Thirties— Workers of America Arise

1

There is, says the Book of Ecclesiastes, a "time to dance and laugh" and a "time to weep and mourn." The twenties brought laughter and dancing, a surrender to hedonism. The thirties was a time for weeping. The intoxication of the twenties brought on the hangover of the thirties. As the twenties drew to their close, the stock market dropped on October 24, 1929. Attempts by bankers to bolster the slump failed. The following Thursday, appropriately described as "black," the bottom fell out of the market. "Wall Street Lays An Egg," was the headline in *Variety* on October 30. Fortunes toppled, and tycoons became paupers. Eddie Cantor tried to make laughter out of his own losses by writing *Caught Short*.

The aftermath of the stock market disaster was a cataclysmic economic depression. Businesses folded, almost thirty thousand by 1931. Nearly twenty-five hundred banks failed. Unemployment spread. Some ten million were jobless in 1931, and the number kept growing weekly.

The ugly signs of the Depression were everywhere: in the migrations of workers in a futile search for nonexistent jobs; in bread lines, soup kitchens and free milk depots; in the shanties which the displaced and the impoverished called home in places named "Hoovervilles"; in the growing army of panhandlers; in the ragged veterans of World War I who descended on Washington, D. C. to demand a bonus only to be dispersed at gunpoint by the militia; in the proliferation of strikes (including that new variety called "sit-down"); in the confrontation of police and workers; in the growing left-wing movement.

A monumental discontent, born in panic and fed on fear and apprehension, seized

409

the nation—a discontent that swept a new Administration into Washington bringing with it a "new deal," a new social philosophy, a new sense of responsibility of government to its citizens. The "one hundred days" following President Roosevelt's inauguration saw a barrage of new bills and messages that permanently changed the social structure of the country. Acts, agencies, practices and laws were hurriedly introduced to stem the tide of economic disaster.

Such conditions brought on a new sobriety. Economic, political and social problems became prime concerns of the everyday citizen.

Poverty, which had become endemic, was the theme of many a hit song of the thirties, with numerous variations. When prosperity rained from the skies it did not bring gold or jewels but pennies—"Pennies from Heaven" (Johnny Burke—Arthur Johnston), introduced by Bing Crosby and an Academy Award nominee in the motion picture of the same name. There was no money to spend on fun, so the only thing to do was to turn out the lights and go to bed—"Let's Put Out the Lights" (Herman Hupfeld), introduced by Rudy Vallee in Atlantic City in 1932. You could find the girl of your dreams as easily in humble places as in palatial ones—"I Found a Million Dollar Baby in a Five-and-Ten Cent Store" (Mort Dixon and Billy Rose—Harry Warren). A shanty in Hooverville could be as good a breeding ground for romance as a mansion—"In a Shanty in Old Shanty Town" (Joe Young, John Siras and Little Jack Little), introduced by Little Jack Little but made successful by Ted Lewis. Love could even thrive on poverty—"Love and a Dime" (Brooks Bowman). The song, "I've Got Five Dollars" (Lorenz Hart—Richard Rodgers) complained about debts "beyond endurance" and about coats and collars "which moths adore." "Ten Cents a Dance" (Lorenz Hart—Richard Rodgers) was the lament of taxi dancers in cheap ballrooms. "Brother Can You Spare a Dime?" (E. Y. Harburg—Jay Gorney), first made popular by Bing Crosby, became the anthem of the Depression, "as characteristic and as familiar," wrote Mark Sullivan, "as bank closings, money-hoarding, and seedy genteel men selling apples on street corners." The hero of this song was described by its lyricist as "a man who had built his faith and hope in this country. . . . Then came the crash. Now he can't accept the fact that the bubble has burst. He still believes. He still has faith. He just can't understand what could have happened to make everything go wrong."

A song imported from Hungary was thoroughly in tune with the somber mood of these years. It was "Gloomy Sunday," promoted by its publishers as a "suicide song" because it was reputed to have encouraged the suicidal tendencies of the tormented and the harassed of the early thirties. The English words were by Sam M. Lewis to Rezsó Seress' music and the English version appeared in 1936 and initially circulated in performances by Paul Robeson. Then, five years later, it became a Billie Holiday classic in a best-selling recording.

Other songs of the Depression years sought to boost sagging morale with pep talks about finding benefit in adversity. Since "potatoes are cheaper, tomatoes are cheaper . . . now's the time to fall in love" was the admonition of "Now's the Time to Fall in Love" (Al Lewis and Al Sherman), popularized by Eddie Cantor on his radio program. "Wrap Up Your Troubles in Dreams" (Ted Koehler and Billy Moll—Harry Barris) was Bing Crosby's advice to listeners to his network radio program. Fred Allen, then still a newcomer as a radio wit, used "Smile, Darn Ya, Smile" (Charles O'Flynn and Jack Meskill—Max Rich) as his radio theme. "If I never had a cent, I'd be rich as Rockefeller" is a line from "On the Sunny Side of the Street" (Dorothy Fields—Jimmy McHugh), sung by Harry Richman in *Lew Leslie's International Revue* (1930).

In his inaugural address in 1933, President Roosevelt said that there was nothing to fear but fear itself. By 1933 people were trying to dismiss their chilling fears by singing

"Who's Afraid of the Big Bad Wolf?" (Frank E. Churchill and Ann Ronell). This song was written for the Walt Disney animated cartoon, *The Three Little Pigs* (1933). The Depression was the big bad wolf against which the financially oppressed children of the early thirties built their house of bricks.

"Happy Days Are Here Again" (Jack Yellen—Milton Ager) also tried to buoy up the spirit of the times. It was written in 1929 for *Chasing Rainbows*, a screen musical produced by MGM, used in a scene in which World War I soldiers first get the news of the Armistice. Before this picture was released, Yellen and Ager published this song and took it to George Olsen, whose band was then appearing at the Hotel Pennsylvania in New York. The band introduced it on "Black Thursday," when the stock market collapsed. "In the big dining room of the hotel," Jack Yellen wrote in recollection, "a handful of gloom-stricken diners were feasting on gall and wormwood. Olsen looked at the title of the orchestration and passed out the parts. 'Sing it for the corpses,' he said to the soloist. After a couple of choruses, the corpses joined in, sardonically, hysterically, like doomed prisoners on their way to a firing squad. Before the night was over, the hotel lobby resounded with what had become the theme song of ruined stock speculators as they leaped from hotel windows." When George Olsen and his band played the number at the Roosevelt Hotel in Hollywood, California, a few years later one of those present was Irving Thalberg, the head of MGM. He inquired why a song as good as this one was not being used in an MGM picture, only to be informed by an embarrassed underling that it was, indeed, in an MGM picture, one still unreleased. At Thalberg's insistence, a whole scene was reshot with new sets to give the song greater prominence. This did not help the picture much, which was a sorry product to begin with, but it did help to further the popularity of the song. During the Presidential campaign of 1932, "Happy Days Are Here Again" was chosen as the principal song for Franklin D. Roosevelt's campaign—a token of better things to come with a new administration. During the dark months that followed, the song helped to provide such optimism as the harassed country could muster. "Happy Days Are Here Again" has since remained a kind of unofficial anthem for the Democratic Party, and served as campaign songs for Harry Truman and John F. Kennedy.

2

With *Face the Music, I'd Rather Be Right, Johnny Johnson* and *Knickerbocker Holiday* the musical theater was reacting to and commenting upon the social, political and international pressures of the troubled thirties. But it was left to the intimate, sophisticated revue to become the real musical interpreter of the times.

The intimate revue first entered the political arena on November 27, 1927, when a new production boldly faced the problems of the laboring class, racial intolerance and international tensions, through song, dance and sketches with sentiment and laughter. That revue was *Pins and Needles*. It actually did not come from the professional theater, though it eventually made stage history there. It was conceived and created by and for the International Ladies Garment Workers Union with a cast recruited from the ranks of union members. As a product with a union label, *Pins and Needles* identified itself unequivocally with a progressive and at times a leftist point of view. "Sing me a song with social significance, all other songs are taboo. . . . Sing me of breadlines, tell me of front page news." This was a kind of leitmotif for the entire production.

Pins and Needles was originally planned as an exclusively amateur production to be performed on weekends in a small theater with the admission price of one dollar for union members and their friends. The theater was the Princess, the same house where the Princess Theater Shows of an earlier decade had helped change the course of musical comedy. The enthusiasm of critics and audiences for *Pins and Needles* encouraged the Union to keep the show on a regular run. It remained at the Princess Theater, later renamed Labor Theater, for three years becoming one of the foremost box-office successes of the American musical theater, and piling up a consecutive run of 1,108 performances. Sketches lampooned government censorship, American chauvinism, proletariat drama, the D.A.R., totalitarianism and—late in the run of the revue—the capitulation to Nazi Germany of Prime Minister Chamberlain at Munich. Songs also reflected a strong political and social consciousness, not only "Sing Me a Song with Social Significance," but also "It's Better with a Union Man," "Doin' the Reactionary," "It's Not Cricket to Picket" and "One Big Union for Two." The hit song, and winner of an ASCAP award in 1937, was "Sunday in the Park," sentimentalizing the simple pleasures of the working man on his day off.

Pins and Needles made the socially and politically oriented revue a vogue on Broadway. It also introduced a new, major songwriter to the Broadway scene, Harold J. Rome. Rome wrote all the songs for *Pins and Needles*, words as well as music. For some time thereafter his songs were filled with social and political implications, prominently displayed and well received in Broadway musical productions with a strongly progressive political slant.

Born in Hartford, Connecticut, in 1908, Rome was a child of the great Depression. He studied law at Yale, but law bored him and after one year he moved on to the School of Architecture from which he was graduated with a degree of Bachelor of Fine Arts in 1934. All these years he engaged in musical activities, earning his way through college by playing the piano in jazz bands. At Yale he took some courses in music and joined the college orchestra on its tour of Europe.

In 1934 he went to New York to try earning a living as an architect. To gain experience, he had to take on a job without pay. To earn money he turned his hand to writing popular songs, sometimes lyrics, at other times melodies, occasionally both. Gypsy Rose Lee helped get some of his lyrics published, and another of his songs was used by the Ritz Brothers in a movie. Encouraged, Rome decided to give up architecture permanently for songwriting.

In the summer of 1935 he found a job at Green Mansions, an adult summer camp in the Adirondack Mountains of New York. In its theater, original musicals were put on weekly written by staff men and performed by a resident company. Rome was hired to write some of the material and assist in the overall production. He worked at Green Mansions for three summers when he wrote the lyrics and music for about ninety songs.

One of his collaborators was Charles Friedman. Friedman had been asked by the International Ladies Garment Workers Union to put on an amateur musical show with union personnel. He needed songs, and he asked Rome to write them. The amateur show, *Pins and Needles*, carried Rome to Broadway and fame.

Now identified with left-wing popular songs, Rome was contracted by Max Gordon, the producer, to write the music and lyrics for a new political revue, *Sing Out the News* (1938). The book by Charles Friedman (with additional sketches by George S. Kaufman and Moss Hart) was antiwar, anti-Fascist, antireactionary, though not with the bite and sting of *Pins and Needles*. Standing out in bold relief from all the other songs was "F.D.R. Jones," sung by Rex Ingram in a Harlem block party scene celebrating the birth of a new member to a black family.

Disguising himself under the pseudonym of Hector Troy, Harold Rome collaborated with Robert Sour in writing the lyrics for "Papa's Got a Job," music by Ned Lehac, for another politically oriented revue, *Sing for Your Supper*, produced by the Federal Theater in 1939. The musical "sleeper" in this revue came at the end of the show, "The Ballad of Uncle Sam," words by John La Touche and music by Earl Robinson, which soon afterwards became famous as "Ballad for Americans."

Harold Rome confined his words-and-music social and political dissent to revues. Marc Blitzstein (1905–1964) did a similar service for the thoroughly social and political musical comedy of this same period. He had been thoroughly trained as a serious musician at the Curtis Institute in Philadelphia, and in Europe with Arnold Schoenberg and Nadia Boulanger. Back in America, he aligned himself with the musical avant-garde, but the political and social climate soon transformed him into a composer writing music for and about the masses in their class struggle, and in a simple, popular Kurt Weill manner. His song "A Nickel Under My Foot," was the plaint of a streetwalker which Blitzstein sang in 1935 for Bertolt Brecht, the librettist of Kurt Weill's *The Threepenny Opera*. Brecht suggested that Blitzstein expand upon this idea to demonstrate how prostitution existed in many different guises—in politics, religion, big business and so forth. This marked the birth of an idea that led to the writing of an opera, *The Cradle Will Rock*. By the end of 1936 Blitzstein had completed the writing of the libretto, lyrics and music, and it was accepted for production by the W.P.A. Federal Theater, with John Houseman as producer, and Orson Welles as director.

The opening night, June 15, 1937, was one of the most dramatic in the performing history of the American musical theater. A few hours before curtain time, the Federal Theater, pressured by groups aroused by the anticapitalist, antiestablishment book, banned the performance. The first-night audience had already begun to file into the Maxine Elliott Theater when the ban was announced. The cast proceeded to entertain the audience while the producer went scurrying in search of another theater. Having found the nearby Venice Theater available, the audience was directed there. But the production could not be mounted as planned, since the scenery, costumes and orchestra were now unavailable. So the company wore everyday street clothes, on a stage bare of scenery, music provided by Blitzstein at the piano. To make the play more comprehensible, Blitzstein informally explained to the audience what was happening before each scene. This unique manner of presentation seemed to add to rather than detract from the text and the overall impact of the opera. Brooks Atkinson described *The Cradle Will Rock* as "the most versatile artistic triumph of the politically insurgent theater," and to Virgil Thomson it was "the most appealing operatic socialism since [Charpentier's opera] *Louise*."

Encouraged by the enthusiastic reaction of audience and critics, Sam Grisman, a Broadway producer, put *The Cradle Will Rock* on a regular Broadway run that lasted 124 performances. The venture proved financially profitable, since the overall budget was miniscule. But more than that, *The Cradle Will Rock* became one of the most provocative and exciting theatrical events of the season.

The action transpired in a night court, pitting the steel workers against their employers in the workers' attempt to form a union. Mr. Mister, the capitalist—who dominated church, school, press and the courts—formed a Liberty Union to smash the Union, but in the end the workers were victorious. The story is carried along by recitatives, patter songs, popular tunes, parodies, torch songs, tap-dance numbers and the blues. "Junior's Gonna Go to Honolulu" was a spoof of the Hawaiian-type song so long popular in Tin Pan Alley, and

"Croon Spoon" was a parody of the Tin Pan Alley variety of love ballad. The influence of Kurt Weill—particularly the Kurt Weill of German operas—was obvious in the way popular elements of the musical stage were combined with sophisticated musico-dramatic resources.

3

The social upheaval induced by the Depression led to the burgeoning of unionism, the proliferation of strikes, the flexing of muscles by the expanding Communist party, and the absorption into the militant left of intellectuals, creative artists, bohemians and other persons of goodwill opposed to bigotry and exploitation. After 1935, all these elements were covered by the umbrella of "the popular front." As the thirties progressed, the class struggle found voice in the songs of working people intended primarily not as stage entertainment but as a potent weapon of leftist propaganda. On the picket line, at leftist political rallies, at Union meetings, in labor summer camps, at labor colleges and during clashes between strikers and the police, the songs were heard.

Some of these songs were carryovers from the past, from the early 1900s when the Industrial Workers of the World (I.W.W.) gathered into its fold agricultural workers, copper miners, migratory workers, lumberjacks, longshoremen and seamen, all of them nicknamed "Wobblies," and all dedicated to the principles of industrial unionism and the class struggle. To carry their message to the masses, they fashioned militant lyrics set to familiar folk or popular melodies. Ralph Chaplin, a poet and artist who worked as an organizer for the I.W.W., was one such lyricist. His "Solidarity Forever," to the tune of "John Brown's Body" became the most famous anthem of the American labor movement. The idea for his poem came to him in West Virginia during the coal miners' strike in Kanawha Valley, but he did not get down to writing the six verses until January 17, 1915, sometime after he had returned home. "I wanted a song to be full of revolutionary fervor and to have a chorus that was singing and defiant," he explained. As taken up by the labor movement only three of his six verses were used.

To the popular tune "Darling Nelly Gray" (Benjamin Russell Hanby), Chaplin wrote "The Commonwealth of Toil," which looked forward to the time when "each man can live his life secure and free when the earth is owned by Labor."

Harry McClintock was another versifier for the Wobblies. He is credited with the words of "Hallelujah, I'm a Bum" to the hymn melody "Revive Us Again." McClintock wrote his lyrics in or about 1897 and he recorded them with the hymn melody in 1926. During the Spanish-American War he sang it in army training camps in Tennessee, whose men then spread it around the country until it became a favorite of hoboes riding the rails and of homeless wanderers everywhere. It was sung at the 1908 convention of the I.W.W. in Spokane, Washington, but its greatest popularity came in the thirties when unemployment sent thousands upon thousands scrounging for meals and riding the rails. As "Hallelujah, I'm a-Travelin' "—words by an anonymous Southern black farmer—it became a protest against Jim Crow.

Most famous of all Wobbly lyricists was Joe Hill. He was born Joel Emmanuel Hagglund in Sweden in 1879 and came to America in 1901 where he changed his name to Joseph Hillstrom, shortened later to Joe Hill. He rode the rods of freight cars while hoboing around the country before settling in San Pedro, California, where he worked as a longshoreman. Sometime around 1910 he joined the I.W.W. on the West Coast, became an organizer and an active participant in various labor disputes. From that time on until his death, he wrote labor propaganda songs promoting the interests and ideals of the I.W.W. and fitting his words to popular melodies. They were sung at Union meetings and on picket lines;

thirteen were included in the 1913 edition of *The Little Red Book*, the songbook of the I.W.W. The most celebrated (the one that immortalized the phrase "pie in the sky") was set to an old hymn, "Sweet Bye and Bye," new words mocking the promises of preachers to their congregations that they will "eat by and by in that glorious land beyond the sky" and urging them meanwhile to "work and pray and live on hay." Hill's song exhorted workers everywhere to unite if they wanted to eat, not to look for "pie in the sky." This labor movement song classic is entitled "Pie in the Sky," though sometimes called "The Preacher and the Slave."

It was Joe Hill's death, even more than his songs, which made him a legend in labor history. He became a cause célèbre when, in Salt Lake City in January 1914, he was arrested on the charge of having murdered a grocer. Despite the weak thread of circumstantial evidence, he was found guilty—mainly due to the anti-I.W.W. and antilabor hysteria then creating a climate in which a fair trial was impossible. Not even appeals by world leaders, including President Wilson, could save him. He met his death bravely on November 19, 1915, his last statement to an I.W.W. leader being: "Don't waste your time mourning. Organize!" His body was brought to Chicago where thirty thousand mourners joined the funeral procession and eulogies were delivered in nine languages.

He was not forgotten. In the thirties, Earl Robinson wrote his poignant ballad, "Joe Hill," to a poem by Alfred Hayes, which was sung in left-wing circles the country over. In 1966, a version of "Joe Hill" by Phil Ochs was recorded by him in the album *Tape from California*. In August 1969, Joan Baez sang Robinson's ballad, "Joe Hill," at the Woodstock festival in New York. In 1970, an opera titled *Joe Hill, The Man Who Never Died*—libretto by Barrie Starvis, music by Alan Bush including four of Joe Hill's songs—was introduced by the Staatsoper in Berlin. In 1971, Joe Hill's story was told on the screen in *Joe Hill*, directed by Bo Wilderberg, on whose sound track Miss Bacz once again sang the Robinson ballad. And in 1976 Gibbs Smith added to Joe Hill's immortality by writing the biography *Joe Hill: Labor Martyr*.

Aunt Molly Jackson was another greatly revered troubadour of the labor movement. She was born and raised in the coal-mining Clay County region of Kentucky. She was five when she first joined a picket line in the company of her father, brothers and sisters. Intensification of her union activities brought her a jail sentence during her teens, but once released she became more active than ever. In time she turned to songwriting as one way to do battle against the frightful conditions in which her relatives and friends in Clay County lived and worked, conditions which brought blindness to her father and one of her brothers, and death to another brother. Her "Poor Miner's Farewell," was her elegy to her dead brother. "Hard Times in Colman's Mines" was a song attack against a mine owner and a plea to miners to strike for better conditions. Her bitterness against mine owners spilled over again in "The Death of Harry Simms," while her loyalty to unionism found voice in "I Am a Union Woman."

In the early 1930s, because of her prolabor and prounion activism, she was compelled to leave Kentucky. She became a singing heroine at union meetings in New York, and was discovered by folklorists, John and Alan Lomax, who had her make many recordings of her own labor songs for the Archive of American Folk Songs. She continued writing prolabor, antimanagement songs up to the time of her death in 1960, though she had to give up singing them, and a year after her death *The Songs and Stories of Aunt Molly Jackson* was recorded and released by Folkways, sung and narrated by John Greenway.

Merle Travis also came from a family of coal miners, and also came to know the full meaning of labor exploitation. "I have known the fruits of strikes," he recalled in the *United*

Mineworker's Journal. "Taylor, my oldest brother . . . practically broke every rib in his body in a mine accident and it changed his whole life." Travis' best songs recalled the occupational sufferings of miners—for example, "Dark as a Dungeon" and "Sixteen Tons," the latter quoting a line he often heard his father speak, "I owe my soul to the company store." Merle Travis first recorded "Sixteen Tons" in an album, *Folk Songs of the Hills* in 1947 for Capitol, but not until eight years later did it become nationally known when Tennessee Ernie Ford sang it on his television show and then recorded it for Capitol in a release that sold over a million copies. At that time "Sixteen Tons" also made the program "Your Hit Parade"—perhaps the only time a pronounced prolabor, antimanagement song ever became commercially successful.

A strike in the coal regions of Harlan County, Kentucky, sent Mrs. Florence Reece, the wife of a union leader and miner, to write "Which Side Are You On?" adapted from the Baptist hymn "Lay the Lily Low." Also born in the coal mines was a song second in popularity to "Solidarity Forever." It was, "We Shall Not Be Moved," based on an old gospel hymn, "I Shall Not Be Moved." It was widely sung among the members of the West Virginia Miners' Union.

The labor crises of the late twenties and throughout the thirties brought on a new flurry of propaganda songs. Many were forged in the furnace, or sharpened on the whetstone, of strikes: "On the Line" (melody taken from the minstrel show tune, "Polly Wolly Doodle") during the textile strike in Passaic, New Jersey, in 1926, for example. From the cotton mill strike in Marion, North Carolina, in 1929, in which six workers were killed and twenty-five wounded, came "We Are Building a Strong Union," based on the hymn "We Are Climbing Jacob's Ladder."

In Gastonia, North Carolina, an attempt to organize mill workers and gain union recognition in 1929, brought the strikers into a bloody conflict with the police. Ella May Wiggins—herself to become a mortal victim in this struggle with guns used by vigilantes—turned to Southern mountain folk songs for such propaganda songs as "Come and Join the I.L.D.—Ye." This and others of her songs deploring the plight of the Gastonia textile workers, and praising their determination to improve their conditions through unionization, were circulated in the North at left-wing rallies and protest meetings by the singer Margaret Larkin and were published in left-wing journals.

To give wider distribution to prounion, antiestablishment worker songs, various songbooks were published to provide material to left-wing singing groups. One was the *Red Song Book* in 1932; another, the *New Workers Song Book* in 1933; and a third, intended for children and comprising parodies of Mother Goose Rhymes, *Songs for Workers and Farmers* in 1933. Within a few years, recordings of prolabor songs were put on the commercial market; among the first was an album released by Timely Records of picket line songs.

Maurice Sugar was one of the songwriters most often represented in workers' songbooks. He was a Detroit union attorney. His verses, to borrowed melodies, became basic to left-wing song repertory in the latter half of the 1930s. One was "The Soup Song," to the tune of "My Bonnie Lies Over the Ocean." The protagonist in this lyric is a worker who spends his nights in a flophouse and his days on the street, and all he gets to eat is a bowl of soup. "During the meal time in the plant kitchens, in the factories," Sugar has written, "long lines of workers would stand with soup bowls in their hands . . . singing the 'Soup Song' with gusto." To help automobile workers organize, Sugar wrote "I Belong to the Company Union," "Be a Man" and "Sit Down," the last inspired by the wave of sit-down strikes inundating the country early in 1937.

4

Besides producing a treasury of labor songs to further the cause of unionization, the radical left also lifted American folk music out of the class of esoterica and brought it to the working masses, providing a platform at its various gatherings for folksingers and folk songs. The leftist movement took to the American folk song with good reason. Many of these songs—especially those of black origin—were social documents lamenting bigotry and the exploitation of the poor by the powerful. These songs were ideologically suited for left-wing convocations. They were simple in structure, easy to listen to and just as easily committed to memory, and they required nothing more than a solo singer accompanying himself on a guitar.

Folk troubadours were widely promoted by the left-wing circles of the thirties. There was Leadbelly or, more formally, Huddie Ledbetter, a black man from Louisiana who sang rural blues, work and slave songs, and songs about the exploitation of the blacks—"The Boll Weevil," "The Rock Island Line," "Green Corn," "Good Morning Blues," "Cotton Fields at Home," "Midnight Special" and "Pick a Bale of Cotton." He picked up folk songs and improvised many of his own while traveling throughout the South with his twelve-string guitar and his gun. He was always getting into trouble with women and the law. At fifteen he fathered an illegitimate child; at twenty, he assaulted a woman who had turned him down and he landed on the chain gang. He was released after one year, only to be dragged back to the rock pile, sentenced for thirty years, because he had fatally shot a man over a woman. Pardoned seven years later he was soon back in jail once more, again for homicide. In Louisiana State Prison he was discovered by John A. Lomax, the folk song archivist, who had him record for the Library of Congress. After leaving prison in 1934, Leadbelly worked for Lomax as chauffeur and was promoted by him as a folksinger in colleges, prisons, left-wing organizations and on records. Toward the end of his life, Leadbelly was singing at the Village Vanguard and other night spots in New York's Greenwich Village. His last days were spent in poverty and sickness, and when he died in Bellevue Hospital in New York in 1949, he was on relief. Had his withered and emaciated body been able to survive another year or so he would have known comparative affluence, for one of his songs, "Goodnight Irene," became a best-seller in several different recordings, accumulating a several million disk sale. He had written it while serving in Louisiana State Prison, where John Lomax had him record it. As adapted by Lomax, this song was revived in 1950 in a Decca recording by Gordon Jenkins and his orchestra and The Weavers, followed by other successful releases by Frank Sinatra, and by Ernest Tubb with Red Foley. Leadbelly's life story and many of his songs were immortalized in a book, *Negro Folk Songs as Sung by Leadbelly*, edited by John and Alan Lomax, published in 1936, material from which was used for a splendid screen biography, *Leadbelly*, released by Paramount in 1976. Leadbelly's biography was romanticized by Richard M. Garvin and Edmond G. Addeo in *The Midnight Special* in 1971. One of Leadbelly's last performances, at the University of Texas in June 1949, was recorded and released by Playboy Records after his death.

The blues and songs about lynching, Jim Crow, slums and poor housing in the repertory of Josh White first began to find favor with radical groups in the late thirties, even before White achieved national fame as a folksinger. Josh White, in fame and success, remained true to songs of social significance, and by the same token the radical left continued to regard him as their favorite son in the forties. The son of a preacher in Greenville, South Carolina, where he was born in 1908, he was named Joshua by his parents in the hope that he, too, would become a preacher. He early learned to sing spirituals and to play the guitar. As a boy he traveled around the country with two blind minstrels, Joel Taggart and Blind Lemmon Jefferson, learning from them a rich repertory of folk songs, and at times accompanying their singing on his guitar. "Roaming the roads, never certain where I'd sleep, and almost always hungry, I heard plenty of bad talk, too, and at first I was too young to understand it," he later recalled. "But the music—the songs and the guitar, somehow made up for everything." He was only eleven when he made his first recording, but several years later, in or about 1933, he began recording spirituals for Columbia, calling himself "The Singing Christian." Under an assumed name, Pinewood Top, he also made recordings of blues, work songs and songs of protest. For a nine-month period he sang with a folk group, the Southernaires, over the NBC network, and further extended his fame as a folksinger with appearances at left-wing gatherings, singing "John Henry," "Hard Time Blues," "Outskirts of Town," "Strange Fruit," "Evil-Hearted Man."

His career was temporarily arrested when he cut his right hand on a milk bottle, severing the muscles of three fingers, making it impossible for him to play the guitar. For several years he worked as an elevator operator in New York to support himself, his wife and their daughter. It took three years for his hand to become sufficiently rehabilitated to allow him once again to play the guitar and resume his folksinging career. His major successes came in the 1940s: in the Broadway theater, beginning with a small part in 1940 in *John Henry* starring Paul Robeson, and continuing with *Blue Holiday* (1945) and *A Long Way from Home* (1948); over the radio; on records; and in night spots, including Barney Josephson's Café Society Downtown where he made the first of many highly successful appearances in 1943. He introduced and made popular a number one would not associate with his repertory, an amusing pop song that became a best-selling record and one of the specialties of the inimitable pantomimist, Jimmy Savo, "One Meat Ball" (Hy Zaret—Lou Singer). This lament of a man who has only the price of one meat ball and is therefore not entitled to bread, was chosen by Josh White because it reminded him of poverty-filled days in the early years of the Depression.

Josh White made the first of three appearances at the White House in 1940, was sent by the United States government on a goodwill tour of Mexico in 1941, and in the fifties made several successful tours of Europe. He became inactive in 1966 following a serious automobile accident while on a singing tour. Three years later, he died in a hospital in Manhasset, Long Island, while undergoing heart surgery.

Even if he had not claimed to be a card-carrying member of the Communist Party and had not been a columnist for the *Daily Worker*, Woodrow Wilson Guthrie, more popularly known as Woody Guthrie, would have assumed a special place of esteem in the left-wing movement of the thirties. This lanky, thin troubadour with a sensitive face, sad eyes and raspy voice, drew deep from the well of his personal experiences to write and sing songs about the Depression, injustice, poverty, dust storms, intolerance, exploitation, migrant workers, unionization and fascism—subjects all close to the radical left. On hobo trails all over America from his early boyhood—while holding down such jobs as filling station attendant, sign painter, junk dealer, shoeshine boy, spitoon cleaner and milkman—he made up a thousand or so songs about what he had seen and experienced in waterfront cafés, dives, Hoovervilles and migrant camps. "Someday," wrote Clifton Fadiman in *The New Yorker* in the early forties, "people are going to wake up to the fact that Woody Guthrie and the ten thousand songs that leap and tumble off the strings of his music box are a national possession like Yellowstone and Yosemite, and part of the best stuff this country has to show the world." One of the best was "So Long, It's Been Good to Know Yuh," a "dust bowl ballad," written after Guthrie had witnessed a dust storm in Pampa, Texas, on April 14, 1935. Guthrie recorded it in a Victor album, *Dust Bowl Ballads*, in the late 1930s, and in 1951 it became a best-selling record performed by the Weavers for Decca. Die-hard unionists cherished Guthrie's "Union Maid" (Guthrie's words to a folk melody, "Red Wing"), one of the best labor movement songs about women. Guthrie's inspiration came at a union meeting in Oklahoma City in 1940, where he was performing. Some thugs invaded the hall to break up the meeting. When they did not make a move, Guthrie conjectured that they had been restrained by seeing so many women and children. The thought that this meeting was like a family affair led Guthrie the following morning to write two verses of "Union Maid" (Millard Lampell later added a third) about a girl unafraid of "goons and ginks" and ever ready to stand her ground at a union meeting.

"Hard Traveling" was based on Guthrie's own experiences as a wanderer. It is, Guthrie himself explained, "the kind of song you would sing after you had been booted off your little place and had lost out, lost everything, hocked everything down at the pawnshop. . . . It is a song about the hard traveling of working people. . . . It tells about a man who has ridden the flat wheels, kicked up cinders, dumped the red-hot slag, hit the hard-rock tunneling, the hard harvesting, the hard-rock jail."

There are many other Guthrie songs to remember, but mention of a few more must suffice: "You've Got to Go Down," a rallying call for all to join the union, parodying the spiritual "I've Got to Walk My Lonesome Valley"; "Blowing Down this Old Dusty Road" and "Do Re Mi" about the trials of migratory workers; the antifascist song, "Round, Round Hitler's Grave," of which he was part author; songs about the wonders of the American scene; "Oklahoma Hills," "Pastures of Plenty" and "This Land Is Your Land."

Commenting upon those songs by Guthrie in which he touches on the majesty of America, an obituary notice on Guthrie in *The New York Times* noted: "He also sang of the beauty of his homeland—a beauty seen from the open doorway of a red-balling freight train or from the degradation of the migrant camps and the Hoovervilles of the Depression years. . . . His vision of America was bursting with image upon image of verdant soil, towering mountains and the essential goodness and character of its people."

For his melody to "This Land Is Your Land" Guthrie went to two American folk tunes in the repertory of the Carter Family, "When the World's On Fire" and "Little Darling of Mine." The Weavers introduced the song in the mid-1950s, and in 1961 the song was propelled to new popularity in the best-selling Columbia recording by the New Christy Minstrels.

Guthrie learned his first folk ballads and blues in childhood from his mother and his father, a professional guitarist, in Okemah, Oklahoma, where he was born in 1912. The family was financially secure until a series of disasters struck: the bankruptcy of the father's land trading business; the destruction of three of the family's houses through fire and cyclone; the death of Woody's sister in an oil stove explosion; the mental breakdown of his mother who had to be institutionalized. From then on, the boy Woody had to seek whatever job was available to support himself. After that he hit the trail for many years, earning his way not only with a variety of menial occupations, but also by singing folk tunes and songs of his own invention to his guitar accompaniment at rodeos, carnivals and dances. In California, he began making appearances over several radio stations. Then, with Will Geer, he performed for labor unions with whom he became a prime favorite in the 1930s. Alan Lomax sought him out and had him record his songs for the Archive of American Folk Songs of the Library of Congress. In the early 1940s, Guthrie joined Lee Hays, Pete Seeger and Millard Lampell in the Almanac Singers which performed extensively throughout the United States for labor organizations, factory workers and at antifascist meetings. Guthrie continued to concertize by himself for several years after that, besides making numerous recordings, until Huntington's chorea, a serious hereditary nervous ailment, permanently hospitalized him. He died at Creedmore State Hospital in Queens, New York, in 1967. Guthrie's autobiography, *Bound for Glory*, published in 1943, is a rich distillation of his picaresque experiences. It became the prime source of an excellent motion picture also named *Bound for Glory* (1976), directed by Hal Ashby, with David Carradine giving a portrayal in depth as Guthrie. Throughout, the motion picture remained faithful not only to its principal character and his songs (the music adapted and conducted by Leonard Rosenman) but also to the Depression years which produced them.

As a folksinger, Burl Ives also found his first audience among left-wing groups in the latter part of the thirties. Ives' American ancestry reached back to the seventeenth century. His father was a tenant farmer in Hunt Township, Jasper County, Illinois, where Burl Ives was born in 1909 and baptized Burl Icle Ivanhoe Ives. In the Ives household everybody sang. From his grandmother, Burl Ives learned folk songs, including "The Blue Tail Fly," "Barbara Allen," "Lord Thomas and Fair Eleanor," and "The Wayfaring Stranger," which later became part of his permanent repertory. "I don't remember when I started to sing," he once told an interviewer. "There wasn't any beginning." When he was four he sang "I Am a Jolly Carpenter" at the local schoolhouse on Christmas Day and soon after was heard in "Barbara Allen" and "Lord Thomas and Fair Eleanor" at a picnic. But, as a child, his crowning ambition was to become a preacher. When he was about nine he became a boy evangelist. Then at a school dance he heard a jazz band play "Wabash Blues" (Dave Ringle—Fred Meinken) and saw people dancing to it. "There they were," he later reminisced, "adancin', and asingin' and alaughin'. I said to myself, 'Boy this ain't religion. It's music.' And I decided not to become a preacher."

He went through Hunt High School, where he was made all-conference guard on the football team, working his way through school by waiting on tables, and at times earning additional money by singing at the Rotary Club, accompanying himself on the banjo. After graduating from high school in 1927, he went to Eastern Illinois State College at Charleston, Illinois, where his extracurricular activities included singing in the college quartet, playing the banjo in the college jazz band and playing football. He dropped out of college after two years to "bum around" the country for three years because "I was curious to see what America looked like." He added sadly: "I found out the hard way." He traveled in every state except Oregon and Washington, supporting himself by being a waiter, dishwasher, preacher and singing folk songs, many of which he picked up during his wanderings. He was back in college by 1931, but not for long. The wanderlust seized him, and once again he hit the road, this time for two years. In 1933 he temporarily took root in Terre Haute, Indiana, singing there over the radio. Then he was on the loose once more, visiting steel mills and logging camps, and at one time becoming a singing member of a traveling company of evangelists. By slow degrees he made his way to New York in 1933. There he lived and worked as a busboy in International House near Columbia University, on Sundays singing solos at the nearby Riverside Church and the Church of St. Mary the Virgin, and from time to time finding odd jobs singing American folk songs and ballads in bars, cafés and night spots in Greenwich Village.

When the Spanish Civil War broke out in 1936, Ives, like many other liberals in America, was sympathetic to the Loyalist cause. To help raise funds for the Abraham Lincoln Brigade of American volunteers fighting on the side of the Loyalists, liberal as well as radical groups gave parties. At one of these Ives was invited to provide entertainment. He kept singing for left-wing groups for about two years. But this flirtation with left-wing politics did not develop into a serious love affair. By 1938 he began drifting more toward commercial areas of entertainment by performing with the Rockbridge Theater, a stock company in Carmel, New York, and appearing on Broadway in the small part of the tailor's apprentice in the Rodgers and Hart musical *The Boys from Syracuse*. In 1940 he came to CBS on the radio programs "Back Where I Came From" and "American School of the Air." Service during World War II interrupted his career, but he had not altogether abandoned the stage since he was a member of the female chorus in Irving Berlin's all-soldier revue, *This Is the Army*. After his release from the Army, Ives got a radio series over CBS, "The Wayfarin' Stranger," started making recordings, and was one of the principals in the Broadway musical *Sing Out Sweet Land* (1944) whose score was made up exclusively of American folk songs. Greater triumphs on the stage and screen, but as an actor and not a singer, now lay ahead for him.

5

In the last years of the thirties, Earl Robinson (1909—   ) emerged as the song laureate of the radical left. He was a young composer who fashioned his music after the style and structure of folk songs, but exclusively with his own material. He was a thoroughly trained musician who had received his Bachelor of Music degree at the University of Washington, studied composition privately with Aaron Copland, and in 1940 received a Guggenheim Fellowship in music to provide a musical setting for Carl Sandburg's *The People, Yes*. But in the late thirties he came to the conviction that the writing of abstract music slanted solely for aesthetic appeal in the concert hall was out of tune with the times; that a socially conscious musician had to ally his art to the labor movement and the class struggle; that a composer had to use the simplest and most easily assimilable terms in his music-making in order to communicate with the masses. Robinson came from Seattle where he finished his academic education. He then found a job as pianist with a ship's orchestra en route to the Orient. Back in America, he bought a secondhand car and traveled across the country from California to New York, earning his way by singing folk songs to his own guitar accompaniment, many of which he had assimilated during his travels. After coming to New York, he served as musical director of a cooperative little theater group for whose productions he wrote the music and in which he sometimes appeared as singer and actor. This company became affiliated with the Federal Theater when that project was launched by the W.P.A.

At this time he allied himself with the Communist party, and enlisted his music-making to the class struggle. In 1938 he wrote two ballads which made him popular with radicals. One was "Joe Hill," the other, "Abe Lincoln." "Joe Hill" was written to propagandize unionism as well as to glorify its hero. "Abe Lincoln" was in line with the Communist popular front line, in the latter part of the thirties, which reached out for support to antifascist and prolabor liberals. A conscious attempt was made by the Communist party to free the American revolutionary movement from the apron strings of the Soviet Union and to ground it in American history, background and experiences. "Abe Lincoln" was the first of several such songs by Robinson. Alfred Hayes' text referred to Lincoln as "a great big giant" who knew "right from wrong." The chorus was Lincoln's pronouncement that "this country with its institutions belongs to the people who inhabit it. . . . They can exercise their constitutional right of amending it, or their revolutionary right to dismember or overthrow it."

In 1942, Earl Robinson wrote another tribute to Lincoln, this time a threnody, "The Lonesome Train," text by Millard Lampell. Its premiere over the CBS network, directed by Norman Corwin, proved so successful that it brought Robinson a Hollywood contract. Upon the sudden death of President Roosevelt in 1945, "The Lonesome Train" was sung in left-wing circles to his memory.

Meanwhile, in 1939, Robinson's fame spread outside radical and liberal groups to reach the general public with another of his pro-American songs, "Ballad for Americans." He wrote it as an extended cantata to the lyrics of John La Touche for the W.P.A. musical, *Sing for Your Supper*, which opened on April 24, 1939, where it went unnoticed. But in 1940, the song was revived by Paul Robeson on Norman Corwin's CBS program, "The Pursuit of Happiness." Immediately after the performance, so many congratulatory telephone calls were made to radio stations featuring that program that the switchboards were jammed for hours. Thousands of telegrams and letters were also received. All this inspired a repetition of the program. The song was now recorded by three major companies; that of Paul Robeson for Victor held the top spot on the recording best-selling list for months. At the RCA Victor exhibit at the New York World's Fair in 1940, so many requests were made for this song that it was soon featured regularly three times a day. The ballad was also heard in concert halls sung by such artists as Lawrence Tibbett and James Melton, and by such symphonic organizations as the New York Philharmonic, the Los Angeles Philharmonic and the Detroit Symphony. Before the year's end, the ballad was heard as the opening feature of the Republican party national convention.

"The House I Live In" (text by Lewis Allen), a few years later, again brought Earl Robinson to audiences outside the left-wing movement. This was another document in praise of American democracy that offered a plea for tolerance. Robinson himself introduced it in a socially oriented Broadway revue, *Let Freedom Sing* (1942), which had a run of about a week. Then Frank Sinatra became interested in it, singing it for the first time at a high school assembly in Gary, Indiana, in 1945. He then starred in a movie short directed by Mervyn Leroy, with screenplay by Albert Maltz, built entirely around this song. It received a special award from the Academy of Motion Picture Arts and Sciences and at the same time launched Sinatra as a crusader for tolerance.

6

Domestic problems were not the only serious concern for Americans during the thirties. The cloud of totalitarianism was darkening much of Europe. Benito Mussolini brought Fascism to Italy, Hitler and Nazism had come to power in Germany, and a civil war had put Francisco Franco as the Fascist head of state in Spain.

All this, combined with the Stalin reign of terror in the Soviet Union and the increasing exportation to America of pro-Stalin and pro-Soviet propaganda, caused grave concern to Americans, however deeply they were involved in the social, political and economic dislocations at home.

As so often had happened in the past in times of international crisis, Americans, in the late thirties, became forcefully conscious and appreciative of the blessings of their country. That is why songs such as Earl Robinson's "Ballad for Americans" and "The House I Live In," slanted for a small partisan audience, were so enthusiastically embraced by the general public. Patriotism also found expression in the popular song. Harold Arlen wrote the stirring "God's Country" (E. Y. Harburg) for the Ed Wynn antiwar musical, *Hooray for What!* (1937) which in 1939 was interpolated into the motion picture *Babes in Arms*. "This Is My Country" (Don Raye—Al Jacobs), first introduced by Fred Waring and his Pennsylvanians in 1940, now become even more popular. (In 1972 it was sung at the opening ceremonies of the Democratic Presidential Convention in Miami Beach.) And one of the most successful popular songs of the late 1930s was Irving Berlin's "God Bless America."

"God Bless America" had been written during World War I for a finale which Irving Berlin had intended for his all-soldier show, *Yip, Yip, Yaphank*. He deleted it because he felt it was "like painting the lily . . . to have soldiers singing 'God Bless America' as they marched down the aisle of the theater, off to war." He wrote a new finale, "We're On Our Way to France" and shoved "God Bless America" into his well-stocked trunk where it remained forgotten for over a quarter of a century. In 1938, Kate Smith, in tune with the times, planned a patriotic program for her radio broadcast on Armistice Day, and asked Irving Berlin to write a song for her. Having recently returned from a European trip and having seen the shadows of fascism and imminent war lengthen across Europe, Berlin had gained a new awareness of the meaning of American liberty and a renewed feeling of pride in his country. But he seemed incapable of putting down on paper the kind of sentiment he felt could echo his innermost feelings about his country. Then he remembered the song he had written for *Yip, Yip, Yaphank* in 1918, retrieved it from the bottom of his trunk, and gave Miss Smith the exclusive performing rights without asking for any compensation. Kate Smith introduced it on the last peacetime Armistice Day celebrated in the United States before World War II. After that, she made a best-selling recording for Columbia. The song caught fire. In 1939, both major political parties used it as the key song for their Presidential nomination conventions. A year later the National Committee for Music Appreciation gave it a special citation. The song was now heard extensively in theaters, and at athletic events and patriotic gatherings throughout the United States and assumed the status of a second national anthem. On February 18, 1955, President Eisenhower was authorized by Congress to present Irving Berlin with a gold medal "in recognition and appreciation of services in composing many popular songs including 'God Bless America.' " Refusing to capitalize on his patriotism, Berlin created the "God Bless America Fund" in 1940 to allocate all proceeds (over $300,000) to the Boy Scouts, the Girl Scouts and the Campfire Girls.

Europe moved to the brink of war when on August 23, the Soviet Union and Nazi Germany signed a nonaggression pact. Less than two weeks later, on September 1, Nazi Germany invaded Poland. Two days later both England and France declared war on Germany. Americans expressed their sympathy with the Allies by singing "There'll Always Be an England" (Ross Parker and Hughie Charles), "A Nightingale Sang in Berkeley Square" (Eric Maschwitz—Manning Sherwin) and "The White Cliffs of Dover" (Nat Burton—Walter Kent), all imported from England and two of them ("The White Cliffs of Dover" and "A Nightingale Sang in Berkeley Square") made popular in America by Glenn Miller and his orchestra. Soon after the fall of France in June 1940, Americans sang and listened to "The Last Time I Saw Paris" (Oscar Hammerstein II—Jerome Kern), a homemade product.

It had always been Hammerstein's practice up to this time to write his lyrics only after the melody had been conceived. And Hammerstein had never written a lyric that had not been intended for stage or screen presentation. "The Last Time I Saw Paris" broke both of these long-standing rules. Having known Paris long and well, Hammerstein was so painfully moved by the news that the Nazi troops had occupied the city, that he felt impelled to write some verses as an emotional release. At the time he had no composer in mind. When he finished his lyric he asked Kern to write appropriate music. Kern, too, knew and loved Paris. This, together with the poignancy of Hammerstein's words, and his own melodic facility, enabled him to complete the song in a single day, and virtually in a single sitting.

Kate Smith introduced it on her radio program in 1940, then recorded it for Columbia. Noël Coward (to whom the song was dedicated), Hildegarde (whose recording was personally supervised by Kern) and Sophie Tucker all used it in their nightclub acts. In 1941, the song was interpolated for Ann Sothern into the screen musical, *Lady, Be Good!* (the only Kern number in an otherwise Gershwin score). The song received the Academy Award, a fact which aroused Kern's fury. Characteristic of his integrity as man and musician, Kern pointed out that his song did not deserve the award since it had not been written specifically for a screen production but was just an interpolation. In addition, he had strong feelings that the best screen song of the year was not his own, but that of Harold Arlen, "That Old Black Magic" (Johnny Mercer) which Jimmy Dorsey and his orchestra, with vocals by Bob Eberly and Helen O'Connell, introduced in *The Fleet's In* (1942). Kern became a prime force in changing the rules of the Academy so that henceforth only songs written expressly for motion pictures would be eligible for the award.

In the early part of Europe's involvement in World War II, with the Soviet Union neutralized by its pact with Nazi Germany, the militant left was writing and performing songs opposing American intervention. The Soviet-Nazi Pact blunted the sharp edge of its hostility to fascism in general and Nazism in particular. Leftist folksingers and writers of folk songs openly espoused for America the same policy of strict neutrality favored and maintained by the Soviet Union. A peace vigil outside the White House organized by the leftist-oriented American Peace Mobilization in 1939 led Woody Guthrie to write "Why Do You Stand in the Rain?" After Pete Seeger, Lee Hays and Millard Lampell formed the Almanac Singers in December 1940 to promote the singing of leftist songs in the writing of which all three collaborated, and after the Almanac Singers made its first appearance (at the National Youth Congress in Washington, D. C., in 1941), the three men joined the propeace movement. Collaboratively they wrote songs for the American Peace Mobilization, some of which they recorded in 1941 in the album *Songs for John Doe*. The opposition to the Selective Service Act of October 16, 1940, the first peacetime draft in American history, was vocalized by them in "The Ballad of October 16" (to the tune of "Jesse James"), "Billy Boy" (to the melody of the folk ballad of the same name) and "C for Conscription." "Plow Under" excoriated the use of militarism to promote prosperity. "Franklin, Oh Franklin," was the lament of one who did not want to go to war, and "The Strange Death of John Doe" touched sadly on the war's senseless waste of human life.

Once the Soviet-Nazi pact was scrapped by the invasion of the Soviet Union by Hitler's armies on June 22, 1941, followed on December 7 of the same year by the Japanese attack on Pearl Harbor and America's engagement in World War II, the left-wing folksingers abandoned their pacifist posture. The prevailing theme of left-wing songs became a complete and unqualified support for the war effort. The Almanac Singers, under the direction of Earl Robinson, issued a record album in 1942, *Dear President*, containing "war songs for Americans" in the writing of which all of them had a hand. The title song called for national unity in this time of grave peril. The most popular number in the album was "Round and Round Hitler's Grave," lyrics by Pete Seeger, and music by Woody Guthrie and Millard Lampell, adapted from the melody of the old square dance "Old Joe Clark." This was the song, sung by the Almanac Singers, which was featured over CBS when America became a participant in World War II, and this was the song broadcast once again over the CBS radio network on V-E Day when the hostilities in Europe ended.

PART FIVE

1940–1950

25

The War Years

The unprovoked attack on Pearl Harbor, Hawaii, and other American outposts in the Pacific, on Sunday, December 7, 1941, by Japanese carrier-based planes, swept the United States into a war it had long known it could not avoid. On December 8, the United States declared war on Japan, and two days later a similar declaration was made against Germany and Italy.

The war sent American songwriters into a flurry of activity in the production of militant songs. The first to be written was "We Did It Before" (Charles Tobias—Cliff Friend). It was conceived on the very day Pearl Harbor was bombed. Two days later, Eddie Cantor (Tobias' brother-in-law) hurriedly interpolated it into *Banjo Eyes*, the Broadway musical in which he was then starring, and offered it as a stirring martial production number that brought down the house.

"Remember Pearl Harbor" (Don Reid—Sammy Kaye) was also written before the smoke above Pearl Harbor cleared. A few months later it became a best-selling record as performed by Sammy Kaye and his orchestra. Ten days after Pearl Harbor, J. Fred Coots wrote and published the words and the music of "Goodbye Mama, I'm Off to Yokohama."

With Americans recoiling from the shock of Pearl Harbor and bracing themselves for a long and hard war, the German national anthem was adapted by Belford Hendricks into "Marching Through Berlin," introduced by Ethel Merman in the film musical *Stage Door Canteen* (1943). "We Must Be Vigilant" (Edgar Leslie—Joe Burke) took its melody from "American Patrol," a march by E. H. Meacham written a half century earlier. "There's a

427

Star-Spangled Banner Waving Somewhere" (Paul Roberts and Shelley Darnell) became best-selling records in performances by Hank Snow and by Elton Britt. And government war agencies borrowed the melody of the George and Ira Gershwin title song from *Strike Up the Band* and, with new words, used it to propagandize their own activities.

The first major song hit inspired by American participation in World War II came from a novice as far as the writing of melodies went. He did not remain a novice long; indeed, Frank Loesser went on to become one of the giant creative figures in American popular music. Up to 1941, Loesser had concentrated his songwriting on lyrics. He made his first solo flight as composer immediately after Pearl Harbor with "Praise the Lord and Pass the Ammunition."

Born in New York City in 1910, Loesser came from a musical family. His father was a piano teacher; his older brother, Arthur, was a musical prodigy who later distinguished himself as a pianist, teacher and critic. Frank Loesser's own interest in music was revealed when he was six and was constantly found at the piano improvising. That same year he wrote a song, "The May Party." Resistant to the discipline of study, Loesser avoided formal music instruction, while pursuing his academic education at the Speyer School, Townsend Harris Hall, and for one year at the College of the City of New York. He dropped college to make his way in the world of business. For a time he worked as an office boy in a wholesale jewelry house, then as a reporter for a New Rochelle newspaper, and after that as a process server for a lawyer, an inspector for a chain of restaurants, a salesman of advertisements for the New York *Herald Tribune*, a vaudevillian whose act comprised making caricatures, a press representative for a small movie company, and as the knit-goods editor for *Women's Wear*. He changed occupations frequently and erratically because his heart was not in the world of commerce. His interest lay in songwriting, in which he had been dabbling for a number of years. He sold one of his lyrics, "Armful of You," for fifteen dollars to a vaudevillian, and he picked up random assignments to provide special material for several other performers of stage and radio. Then he landed a forty-dollar-a-week job in Tin Pan Alley with Leo Feist, Inc., his job being to provide the composer, Joseph Brandfon, with lyrics. Since none of his lyrics were used he was fired after one year. In 1931, one of his songs was finally published. It was called "In Love with the Memory of You," published by Feist; its melody was the work of a young man eventually destined to earn for himself a lustrous name and place in serious American music, William Schuman.

It took three more years for Loesser to gain even modest recognition for one of his lyrics. "I Wish I Were Twins," music by Joseph Meyer, written collaboratively with Eddie De Lange, did moderately well after "Fats" Waller recorded it for Victor in 1934. But success for Loesser was still out of reach. A revue for which he wrote most of the lyrics lasted just seven performances on Broadway. To earn a living, Loesser had to play the piano and sing pop tunes in a New York night spot, the Back Drop, on 52nd Street.

In 1936 he went to Hollywood to work for Universal. A few of his songs were used but for the most part Universal found his work unsatisfactory and released him after a year. Then in 1937 Loesser had his first taste of success with "The Moon of Manakoora," music by Alfred Newman, which Dorothy Lamour sang in *The Hurricane*. Several more creditable efforts came after that: "I Fall in Love with You Every Day" (music by Manning Sherwin and Arthur Altman) in *College Swing* (1938); "The Boys in the Back Room" (music by Frederick Hollander) introduced by Marlene Dietrich in *Destry Rides Again* (1939); and the title song of *Kiss the Boys Goodbye* (1941), music by Victor Schertzinger, sung by Mary Martin. Good lyrics all, revealing their author to be a meticulous craftsman, but hardly indicative that Loesser, during the forties, would become one of Hollywood's ace lyricists and top moneymakers. Nor, of course, could they provide a clue that he had in him the makings of one of America's best popular composers.

The attack on Pearl Harbor, and a remark reputed to have been made by Navy Chaplain William Maguire during that holocaust, provided Loesser with the subject for a new lyric, "Praise the Lord and Pass the Ammunition." He had no intention of writing a melody for it, planning to turn it over to a professional composer as was his custom. But in order to try out the rhythmic pulse and flow of his lines, Loesser improvised a dummy melody which he expected to discard once he committed his lyric to paper in its final form. Upon trying out his song for several friends, they were unanimous in urging Loesser to retain his own melody which, they insisted, had an infectious folk song quality ideal for the words. Convinced, Loesser had his song published in 1942 and it was introduced at Leon and Eddie's nightclub on East 52nd Street by Robert Rounseville. Immediately thereafter Kay Kyser recorded it for Columbia in a release that disposed of more than a million disks. But for the fact that some members of the clergy complained about the juxtaposition of the Lord with the passing of ammunition, and that Father Maguire expressed displeasure at being associated with the now famous slogan, the song might well have become one of the half dozen or so most successful American war songs ever written. As it was, it was still played so often, and in so many versions, that the Office of War Information requested radio stations to limit its use to no more than once every four hours. In addition to selling several million disks in various recordings, the song sold about a million copies of sheet music.

"Praise the Lord and Pass the Ammunition" was Loesser's first contribution to the war effort. That contribution soon grew prodigiously. As Private First Class in Special Services, Loesser helped write soldier shows (to which he contributed all the songs, music as well as words), shows that were packaged and distributed to army camps everywhere. For one G. I. revue, *About Face*, he wrote "First Class Mary Brown" in collaboration with Peter Lind Hayes, and "Why Do They Call a Private a Private?" Loesser also wrote individual songs for various branches of the services, such as "Salute to the Army Air Force," "Sad Bombardier," "The WAC Hymn" and "What Do You Do in the Infantry?" The last became famous first in a Bing Crosby recording and later as the unofficial song of the infantry during the war.

Before the war was over, Loesser wrote one of its most poignant ballads, "Rodger Young." He wrote it at the request of the infantry, which wanted to publicize the heroism of infantrymen. Loesser wrote to Washington for a list of infantrymen who had been awarded the Medal of Honor posthumously. Rodger Young's name was one of them. He was a twenty-five-year-old soldier who, in 1943, singlehandedly attacked a Japanese pillbox in the Solomons, sacrificing his life to save those of his comrades. Like "Praise the Lord and Pass the Ammunition" this ballad had the homespun quality of an American folk song. Meredith Willson introduced it on his NBC radio network program in 1945 in a starkly simple and unpretentious solo performance by Earl Wrightson accompanying himself on a guitar. At the first rehearsal, everybody in the studio "got goose pimples," as Willson recalled in his autobiography, *Eggs I Have Laid* (1955). So did the radio public, for the immediate response by telephone, telegram and letter was a deluge of enthusiasm. Numerous recordings were soon released; the most successful were those by Burl Ives for Decca, Nelson Eddy for Columbia and John Charles Thomas for Victor.

2

Frank Loesser was not the only songwriting hero of World War II. Irving Berlin, at the zenith of his fame and talent, was another. Even before Pearl Harbor, Berlin had assumed the unofficial position of songwriter laureate of World War II not only with "God Bless America" but also with "Any Bonds Today?" to promote the sale of war bonds. Immediately after Pearl Harbor he wrote "Angels of Mercy" for the Red Cross," "I Threw a Kiss in the Ocean" for the United States Navy Relief, "Arms for the Love of America" for the civilian war effort. For those and similar patriotic songs he followed the pattern he had set with "God Bless America" by contributing all royalties from these songs to charities.

His greatest World War II ballad—and one of the most successful songs ever written—was not intended as a war song. But American soldiers fighting in the swamps and jungles of Pacific islands seized upon "White Christmas" as a nostalgic recollection of home and Yuletide peace and goodwill to cherish when the going was roughest. Berlin could have little suspected the impact this ballad would have on American fighting men the world over when he wrote it for Bing Crosby for the motion picture *Holiday Inn* (1942), nor the extent of its popularity on the home front where it became the longest running song in the history of "Your Hit Parade" with eighteen appearances in 1942–1943, ten in first place. After the war, it became an all-time Yuletide classic, second in popularity only to "Silent Night, Holy Night." In its first year it sold over a million copies of sheet music and through several recordings—notably those by Frank Martin and his orchestra for Victor, Frank Sinatra for Columbia and Bing Crosby for Decca—several million disks. By December 1976 it had sold over 108 million records in the United States and Canada alone with twenty-five million more records abroad in about thirty languages other than English; Bing Crosby's recording alone sold over twenty-five million disks. In addition, the song sold over five million copies of sheet music, and a million copies of instrumental arrangements, octavos and orchestrations. It has become, in the words of *Variety*, "probably the most valuable song . . . copyright in the world."

Berlin's greatest single effort for World War II—just as it had been in the first world war—was in the writing and producing of an all-soldier show. The idea came to him soon after Pearl Harbor, when he recognized the acute need among American soldiers for entertainment. Army officials, faced with the grim business of quickly transforming civilians into seasoned troops, frowned on his suggestion to cast a show with soldiers. But he persevered in this aim, and finally won a grudging consent from the Pentagon.

He was assigned a small room in a barracks in Camp Upton (the same camp where he had been stationed during World War I and had produced *Yip, Yip, Yaphank*) so that he might gain firsthand Army experiences. He found materials for his acts, routines, sketches, songs and production numbers on the training field, in the service club, the Army canteen, the mess hall and the PX. Since the army insisted that this must be no goldbrick assignment for the men, rehearsals usually had to take place after the regular army details and duties had been completed. Often in fits and starts, and often late into the night, the show was slowly whipped into shape. Starring Sergeant Ezra Stone, Corporal Philip Truex, Private Julie Oshins and Mister Irving Berlin, and including a cast of about three hundred, most of whom were amateurs, *This Is the Army* opened on Broadway on July 4, 1942, presenting a picture of Army life in song, dance and humor. In the opening scene, inductees dressed in long underwear heard in song what they can expect in "This Is the Army, Mr. Jones." After that came comedy songs, "The Army's Made a Man Out of Me"; songs in tribute to branches of military services other than the infantry, "American Eagles," "How About a Cheer for the Navy?"; songs strong on sentiment and loneliness, "I Left My Heart at the Stage Door Canteen" and "I'm Getting Tired So I Can Sleep." One song filled with nostalgia, recalled poignant memories of World War I, and this was the song that invariably brought the show to a halt with audience enthusiasm. It was "Oh, How I Hate to Get Up in the Morning," revived from *Yip, Yip, Yaphank* and once again sung by Irving Berlin, wearing his World War I uniform.

So great was the demand at the box office that a four-week engagement was extended to twelve weeks. A nationwide tour followed, culminating in Hollywood where the production was made into a motion picture by Warner Brothers. The tour swung back east and across the ocean to England, Scotland and Ireland. By special permission it then visited the combat areas of Europe, the Near East and the Pacific. Two years and three months after it had opened, *This Is the Army* gave its last performance in Honolulu on October 22, 1945. It had earned ten million dollars for the Army Relief Fund and another $350,000 for British War Charities. It had also brought the joy of song, laughter and dance to some two and a half million war-weary American soldiers. In recognition of this monumental achievement, Irving Berlin was presented the Medal of Merit by General George C. Marshall.

3

The ballads with the greatest appeal to both civilian and military audiences were those strumming the strings of loneliness, separation and hopeful reunions. "I'll Be Seeing You" (Irving Kahal—Sammy Fain) had been written before World War II, in 1938, when it was introduced by Tamara in the revue *Right This Way*, without causing much of a stir at the time. It lay neglected for five years. World War II gave lyrics and music a timely interest. Recordings by Hildegarde and Frank Sinatra became best-sellers. In 1944-1945 the song appeared twenty-four times on "Your Hit Parade," ten times in the Number One position. Liberace later used it as the closing theme of his radio and television shows.

"You'll Never Know" (Mack Gordon—Harry Warren) had twenty-four appearances on "Your Hit Parade." Alice Faye introduced it in the motion picture *Hello, Frisco, Hello* (1943), and it won the Academy Award. Dick Haymes' recording for Decca sold a million disks.

The melody of "Don't Sit Under the Apple Tree" (Charles Tobias and Lew Brown—Sam H. Stept) was first used for a lyric entitled "Anywhere the Bluebird Goes," but as "Don't Sit Under the Apple Tree" it was introduced in the Broadway musical *Yokel Boy* (1939). The Andrews Sisters popularized it, first in the motion picture *Private Buckaroo* (1942), then in a Decca recording.

"Sentimental Journey" (Bud Green, Les Brown and Ben Homer) became successful in a Columbia recording by Les Brown and his orchestra, with Doris Day doing the vocal. This was the first best-seller for both Les Brown and his orchestra and for Doris Day. Les Brown later used the song as his orchestra's theme, and the song title was borrowed in 1946 for a motion picture title.

"When the Lights Go On Again" (Eddie Seiler, Sol Marcus and Bennie Benjamin) became a record best-seller in performances by Vaughn Monroe and his orchestra for Victor and Lucky Millinder and his orchestra for Decca. Its title, too, was used for that of a motion picture (1944).

Perhaps the most touching sentimental ballad of World War II was "I'll Walk Alone" (Sammy Cahn—Jule Styne), which was nominated for an Academy Award after Dinah Shore introduced it in *Follow the Boys* (1944). Her recording for Columbia, and Frank Sinatra's for Capitol, each became million-disk sellers, while the sheet music sold well over a million copies. Its authors—lyricist Sammy Cahn and composer Jule Styne—were then comparatively new names in the song business, but they were now destined to occupy a place of no little consequence on the musical scene.

Jule Styne, born in London in 1905, came to the United States when he was eight. In Chicago, he was a child prodigy who appeared as piano soloist with symphony orchestras. Upon completing his music study at the Chicago Musical College, Styne began playing the piano in jazz bands (one of which he himself had organized in 1931) besides making their arrangements. He came to Hollywood where he was employed as a vocal coach, arranger, and composer of background music and songs. Before tying up with Sammy Cahn, Styne's best song was "I Don't Want to Walk without You" (Frank Loesser), introduced in *Sweater Girl* (1942) and made into successful recordings by Bing Crosby and by Harry James and his orchestra.

Styne was working as a vocal coach at 20th Century-Fox when, in 1942, a movie producer introduced him to Sammy Cahn, then employed as a lyricist at Republic Pictures. At that time, Cahn was breaking off a working arrangement with Saul Chaplin and was in need of a composer. At their first meeting, Styne and Cahn met on the common ground of having written hit songs, a circumstance that made them highly receptive to the idea of forming a creative relationship.

Sammy Cahn, whom we have already mentioned as the lyricist of "Bei Mir Bist Du Schoen" in 1937, and "Joseph, Joseph" in 1938, was a boy from New York's East Side, born in a ghetto tenement in 1913. At the East Side public schools and at Seward Park High School he was no shining light. Invariably, he played truant to work in a pool parlor to raise the price for admission to the movies to which he was passionately devoted. Soon after his confirmation, he left school for good to play the violin in the pit orchestra of burlesque houses. At about this time he also entertained himself by writing parodies of popular songs of the day, and by completing both the words and the music for some thirty songs. Then he wrote the lyrics to Saul Chaplin's music, Chaplin being a pianist in the orchestra in which Cahn was employed as violinist. Eventually, Chaplin and Cahn found a market for their songs among singers, bands and comedians in need of special material. "Rhythm Is Our Business" was written for Jimmie Lunceford and his orchestra who used it as their signature music. This was in 1935, when Cahn and Chaplin wrote "The Glen Gray Casa Loma Orchestra Corporation" for the first appearance of Glen Gray and the Casa Loma Orchestra at the New York Paramount Theater. For Andy Kirk and his band, Cahn and Chaplin revised a song by Mann Holiner and Alberta Nichols; as "Until the Real Thing Comes Along" it helped to bring the Andy Kirk band its first recognition. Prosperity first came to Cahn and Chaplin with "Shoe Shine Boy," written in 1936 for the nightclub revue *Connie's Hot Chocolates of 1936*, introduced by Louis Armstrong at Connie's Inn in Harlem.

Their further success with "Bei Mir Bist Du Schoen" and "Joseph, Joseph" brought Cahn and Chaplin a Hollywood contract, first at Warner Brothers, then at Republic. At Warner Brothers they failed to get a single assignment for the duration of their contract. At Republic, they managed to sell a story which was filmed and into which they interpolated a few of their songs. But their headway in the movie capital was proceeding at such a snail's pace that they finally decided to break up. At this point Cahn met and began working with Jule Styne.

It was a happy marriage of words and music from the very beginning. Their first song was a giant hit, "I've Heard that Song Before" which Frank Sinatra, with Bob Crosby and his orchestra, introduced in the movie *Youth on Parade* (1942) when it was nominated for an Academy Award, and which Harry James and his orchestra made into a million-disk sale recording for Columbia. "I'll Walk Alone" was their next hit of the first magnitude during a year (1944) which saw the birth of several other Cahn-Styne song hits that were either introduced or popularized, or both, by Frank Sinatra: "Saturday Night Is the Loneliest Night in the Week" in a Columbia recording; "I Fall in Love Too Easily," an Academy Award nominee in the movie *Anchors Aweigh* (1944); and "As Long as there's Music" in the movie *Step Lively* (1944).

Among World War II songs we find not only sentimental ballads but also militant and comedy songs. Among the more militant, a strong impact was made by: "Smoke on the Water" (Earl Nunn and Zeke Clements) which looked forward to the day of victory when Japan would be transformed into a graveyard; "Comin' In on a Wing and a Prayer" (Harold Adamson—Jimmy McHugh), an Air Force song inspired by a letter written by a pilot to McHugh describing an almost ill-fated mission to North Africa when he came in "on one engine and a prayer," and introduced by Eddie Cantor at an Air Force base; "Say a Pray'r for the Boys Over There" (Herb Magidson—Jimmy McHugh), a message from the home front to the fighting troops abroad and an Academy Award nominee in the motion picture *Hers to Hold* (1943) where it was sung by Deanna Durbin; and the Jerome Kern song, "And Russia Is Her Name" (E. Y. Harburg) written for the motion picture *Song of Russia* (1943) as a tribute to the Soviet Union, now an Ally against the Axis.

And then there were comedy songs. In view of the preponderance of anti-Kaiser numbers during World War I, it is strange to find so few comedy songs about Adolf Hitler. One that did become a hit was "Der Fuehrer's Face" (Oliver Wallace). It was written for an animated cartoon, *Donald Duck in Nutzy Land*, after which it was recorded by Spike Jones and his City Slickers. Up to this time, Spike Jones's madcap band was little known. This recording made both the song and the performers celebrated. A good deal of the humor in this recording comes through the use of a rubber "razzer" that simulates the sound of Bronx cheers, sounded each time the name of Hitler is mentioned.

Also comedic, though not about Hitler, is "They're Either Too Young or Too Old" (Frank Loesser—Arthur Schwartz), the humorous lament of a frustrated female. Bette Davis sang it in the movie *Thank Your Lucky Stars* (1943) in one of her rare appearances as a singer. The song was a nominee for an Academy Award. Comic, too, was a bawdy song heard among Allied soldiers in North Africa, then brought home to the United States in an expurgated version: "Gertie from Bizerte" (James Cavanaugh, Walter Kent and Bob Cutter).

A relief from the agonizing pressures of the war years came from the singing of nonsense and novelty songs that had not even a remote kinship to the war. There had been a resurgence of this type of songwriting during the thirties with "The Flat Foot Floogie" (Slim Gaillard, Slam Stewart and Bud Green); with "Three Little Fishies" (Saxie Dowell), identified with Kay Kyser and his orchestra; with "Hut Sut Song" (Leo V. Killion, Ted McMichael and Jack Owens) in which Swedish double-talk is simulated, and a song made popular by Freddy Martin and his orchestra; with "A-Tisket, A-Tasket" (Ella Fitzgerald—Al Feldman); and with "The Music Goes 'Round and 'Round" (Red Hodgson, Edward Farley and Michael Riley). The vogue for the ridiculous, the childish, the absurd in songs grew during the war years. Possibly the most famous was "Mairzy Doats" (Milton Drake, Al Hoffman and Jerry Livingston), whose lyrics were sheer gibberish. The song idea came to Milton Drake when he heard his four-year-old daughter saying to herself "cowzy tweet and sowzy tweet and liddle harsky doisters." Al Trace and his orchestra introduced the song and the Merry Macs recorded it for Decca, making it such a rage in 1944 that even a singer with the prestige of Grace Moore used it in her vaudeville act.

Originating also in the world and the speech of children was "Swinging on a Star" (Johnny Burke—James Van Heusen) and "Ac-cent-tchu-ate the Positive" (Johnny Mercer —Harold Arlen). The first came from the Academy Award-winning movie, *Going My Way* (1944). Sung by Bing Crosby it captured an Oscar as the best screen song of the year. The context of this novelty number occurred to Johnny Burke, the lyricist, when he was a guest at Bing Crosby's home where, upset by the childish behavior of one of his sons, Bing scolded him severely for behaving "like a mule." Burke expanded this thought into a lyric about a child, stubborn as a mule, who refused to better himself, following this with the mention of other types of animal and fish.

Bing Crosby was also the man who introduced "Ac-cent-tchu-ate the Positive," an Academy Award nominee, in the motion picture *Here Come the Waves* (1944), and a best-seller in a Decca recording by Bing Crosby and the Andrews Sisters. Here is how this song came to get written. Johnny Mercer and Harold Arlen were driving to the studio one day. Mercer became amused by the simplistic tune that Arlen was humming to himself. In some mysterious way, this tune reminded Mercer of a line he had continually repeated as a schoolboy without ever having comprehended the meaning, "You've got to accentuate the positive, and eliminate the negative." Since these words seemed to suit the tune Arlen was singing, Mercer continued to fit them and other words to it. By the time the two men reached the studio, Mercer and Arlen had the words and music down pat for "Ac-cent-tchu-ate the Positive."

4

In the making of original musicals for the screen during the war years, Hollywood maintained a delicate balance between pictures that touched directly on the war or were influenced by it, and others that scrupulously avoided the war through light, escapist entertainment. Some of the war-oriented musicals were revues, many employing the studio's leading stars, and just as frequently making copious use of the song standards in the publishing lists then owned by the studio. *Hollywood Canteen* (1944) offered a glittering cast headed by Bette Davis, Joan Crawford, Jack Benny and Eddie Cantor, in which the standards included Bob Nolan's "Tumbling Tumbleweeds" together with a new number, Cole Porter's "Don't Fence Me In." *Thank Your Lucky Stars* (1943) presented Bette Davis, Eddie Cantor, Errol Flynn, Ann Sheridan and John Garfield. Its music, by Arthur Schwartz to Frank Loesser's lyrics, included "They're Either Too Young or Too Old." The all-star cast of *Thousands Cheer* (1943) had Judy Garland, Eleanor Powell, Mickey Rooney, Gene Kelly, Lena Horne and Ann Sothern, with Miss Horne heard in the standard, "Honeysuckle Rose" (Andy Razaf—Thomas "Fats" Waller). Helen Hayes, Gertrude Lawrence, Katharine Hepburn, Gracie Fields, Ethel Merman and Tallulah Bankhead were the luminaries appearing as guest stars in *Stage Door Canteen* (1943), which had an original score by James V. Monaco (lyrics by Al Dubin) together with a new Rodgers and Hart number, "The Girl I Love to Leave Behind."

Many of the plot musicals were concerned with men in uniform. In *You'll Never Get Rich* (1941), in which Fred Astaire was paired with Rita Hayworth and to which Cole Porter contributed an undistinguished score, a theatrical producer has to overcome the problem of being conscripted into the Army while trying to put on a show. *The Sky's the Limit* (1943) finds a war hero, enacted by Fred Astaire, falling in love during his leave in New York. This film musical had several outstanding songs by Harold Arlen, with Mercer's lyrics, the best being "One for My Baby" and "My Shining Hour," both introduced by Astaire, and the second, an Academy Award nominee. The amorous adventures of two sailors on leave in Hollywood (played by Frank Sinatra and Gene Kelly) unfolds in *Anchors Aweigh* (1944), where Frank Sinatra was heard singing "I Fall in Love Too Easily" (Sammy Cahn—Jule Styne), an Academy Award nominee. The shoreside encounters of two young men in blue form the warp and woof of the stories of two more musicals: *Two Girls and a Sailor* (1943) with Van Johnson, June Allyson and Jimmy Durante and a score made up of songs old and new, and *The Fleet's In* (1942) with a cast headed by Dorothy Lamour and William Holden and songs by Victor Schertzinger and Johnny Mercer. In *Here Come the Waves* (1944), a crooner (played by Bing Crosby) joins the Navy, and in *Follow the Boys* (1944), a hoofer (played by George Raft) helps the war effort by touring the U.S.O. circuit to entertain the troops. *Here Come the Waves* had "Ac-cent-tchu-ate the Positive" (an Academy Award nominee) together with other songs by Harold Arlen and Johnny Mercer, while *Follow the Boys* availed itself of standards. In *Up in Arms* (1944) Danny Kaye was cast as a sadly befuddled rookie in the movie that made him a screen star, and in *Something for the Boys* (1944), set in a home for war wives, Perry Como made his screen debut singing "I Wish I Didn't Have to Say Goodbye" (Frank Loesser—Jimmy McHugh), among other numbers.

Escapist screen musicals provided flight from the war to more placid or remote times and often to exotic places far removed from bursting shells. A step backward in time was made by one of the most delightful musicals of those years, *For Me and My Gal* (1942) where Gene Kelly, fresh from his Broadway success in *Pal Joey* and making his screen debut, was coupled with Judy Garland as a vaudeville team involved in a romance during World War I. The score was made up of standards, with Gene and Judy sharing the title song (Edgar Leslie and E. Ray Goetz—George W. Meyer). World War I was also the period of *Tin Pan Alley* (1940) where a pair of songwriters, Jack Oakie and John Payne, are the rivals for the love of a singing star played by Alice Faye. Once again songs of the pre-World War I and World War I eras provided the musical material, for the scoring of which Alfred Newman received an Oscar.

Going back still further in America's past were *Hello, Frisco, Hello* (1943), *Sweet Rosie O'Grady* (1943), *Coney Island* (1943) and *Meet Me In St. Louis* (1944). The first was a Barbary Coast yarn about a saloon keeper dreaming of graduating to Nob Hill and about the girl he loves. Alice Faye was the girl. Singing into the mouthpiece of a telephone she was heard in the Academy-Award winning song "You'll Never Know" (Mack Gordon—Harry Warren). In *Sweet Rosie O'Grady* and *Coney Island*, Betty Grable had ample opportunities to exhibit her fabled legs while singing new songs as well as standards. Of the former, the most important was "My Heart Tells Me" (Mack Gordon—Harry Warren), in *Sweet Rosie O'Grady*. *Meet Me in St. Louis* was a turn-of-the-century story where Judy Garland was heard delivering a few "oldies" including the title song (Andrew B. Sterling—Kerry Mills) and new songs by Ralph Blane and Hugh Martin: "The Trolley Song," which received the Academy Award, "The Boy Next Door" and "Have Yourself a Merry Little Christmas."

In 1940, Bing Crosby, Bob Hope and Dorothy Lamour initiated their song-and-laugh journeys to exotic lands in *The Road to Singapore*. By 1945 they had traveled in their "road" films to Zanzibar and Morocco, and in years to come they would invade Utopia, Rio de Janeiro and Hong Kong. Victor Schertzinger, with Johnny Burke as lyricist, wrote the songs for the first of these "road" escapades, but for the others, James Van Heusen was the composer.

James Van Heusen was born Edward Chester Babcock in Syracuse, New York, in 1913. He invented the name which he made legal long before he became a famous songwriter, while working as a radio announcer in Syracuse when he was fifteen. He found the Van Heusen on a billboard advertisement for collars, and he put James in front of it because he felt it had the proper sobriety for a name as dignified as Van Heusen. As a boy he studied piano and wrote songs, and as a young man he received additional training in piano and some lessons in voice at Syracuse University. His first break as a composer came when Harold Arlen, also a native of Syracuse, brought Van Heusen to New York in 1933 as his replacement as composer of the Cotton Club revue while he went off to Hollywood on an assignment. The numbers Van Heusen wrote for the Cotton Club did not do well, though one was published, and Van Heusen had to seek his fortune as a songwriter elsewhere. While trying to market his songs he supported himself by operating a freight elevator at the Park Central Hotel. None of the publishers he contacted were interested in him, but the hotel orchestra was induced to play one of his tunes which he had written with Jerry Arlen, "There's a House in Harlem for Sale," and the Santly Brothers Music Publishing Company published it.

For a number of years after that Van Heusen was employed as staff pianist for various firms in Tin Pan Alley. At Remick's, in 1938, he met Jimmy Dorsey, to whose lyrics he wrote the music for "It's the Dreamer in Me" which sold almost a hundred thousand copies of sheet music—Van Heusen's first success. Then, with Eddie De Lange as lyricist, he wrote "Deep in a Dream" in 1938 that sold over two hundred thousand copies of sheet music after being recorded by Guy Lombardo and his Royal Canadians and, in 1939, "All This and Heaven Too" which, serving as a promotional song for the motion picture of the same name, was even more successful. In 1939, Van Heusen with Eddie De Lange also wrote all the songs for a Swing version of Shakespeare's A *Midsummer Night's Dream*, produced on Broadway as *Darn That Dream*.

In 1939, Van Heusen acquired a new lyricist in Johnny Burke, with whom he wrote "Oh, You Crazy Moon" in 1939 and in 1940 "Polka Dots and Moonbeams" and "Imagination." The first two were introduced by Tommy Dorsey and his orchestra, and the third by Fred Waring and his Pennsylvanians. Tommy Dorsey recorded "Polka Dots and Moonbeams" with Frank Sinatra doing the vocal. This was the first time Sinatra sang a Van Heusen number; after that, throughout his career, Sinatra would promote Van Heusen's songs and, in many instances, be responsible for their popularity.

Van Heusen's star was rising, a fact made evident when in a single week three of his songs were heard on "Your Hit Parade," probably the only time such a thing ever happened to a composer. Hollywood—or, more specifically, the Paramount studios—took note of his mounting success and brought him out to California. After two minor assignments, Van Heusen and Johnny Burke wrote the songs for *The Road to Zanzibar* (1941), one of which was a hit, "It's Always You." They continued to write songs for those "road" pictures, most of which were introduced by Bing Crosby: the title number and "Moonlight Becomes You" in *The Road to Morocco* (1942); "Personality" and "Put it There, Pal," in *The Road to Utopia* (1946); "But Beautiful" and "You Don't Have to Know the Language" in *The Road to Rio* (1948).

Not in a road picture, but still introduced on the screen by Bing Crosby were other outstanding Van Heusen songs, all of them with Johnny Burke's lyrics. There was "Sunday, Monday, or Always" in *Dixie* (1943); "Swinging on a Star," for which Van Heusen received his first Oscar, in *Going My Way* (1944); "Aren't You Glad You're You" in *The Bells of St. Mary's* (1945), an Academy Award nominee. After World War II, Crosby introduced and popularized the title number of *Mr. Music* (1950) and "Sunshine Cake" in *Riding High* (1950).

James Van Heusen was a newcomer to the musical screen. Older, established songwriters also had a share in the making of the film musicals which were able to help audiences temporarily forget the war. Cole Porter wrote songs for a backstage story, *Something to Shout About* (1943), in which Don Ameche and Janet Blair introduced "You'd Be So Nice to Come Home To," an Academy Award nominee. Jerome Kern, whose winning of the Academy Award for "The Last Time I Saw Paris" (Oscar Hammerstein II) has already been mentioned, provided opulent scores for *You Were Never Lovelier*, (1942), starring Rita Hayworth and Fred Astaire, *Cover Girl* (1944), pairing Miss Hayworth with Gene Kelly, and *Can't Help Singing* (1944) starring Deanna Durbin. In all three, Kern successfully tapped that sensitive and rich melodic vein that was so uniquely his: with "Dearly Beloved" (Johnny Mercer) in *You Were Never Lovelier*, an Academy Award nominee; "Long Ago and Far Away" (Ira Gershwin), an Academy Award nominee in *Cover Girl*; and "More and More" (E. Y. Harburg) in *Can't Help Singing*.

Though Kern's last score for the screen, *Centennial Summer* (1946), was released after V-J Day, it was filmed while the war was still on. Its music was typically Kern in its melodic freshness and original approach, the best being "In Love in Vain" and "Two Hearts Are Better than One," both to lyrics by Leo Robin and "All through the Day" (Oscar Hammerstein II). After this assignment, Kern wrote only one more song, "No One But Me" (Oscar Hammerstein II) for a revival of *Show Boat* in New York. He came to New York to help supervise this revival when, on November 1, 1945, he collapsed on 57th Street and Park Avenue from a heart attack. He never regained consciousness. A week later, on November 11, he died in Doctor's Hospital, with only Oscar Hammerstein II at his side.

Throughout the war, Irving Berlin was preoccupied with *This Is the Army*. But before he became engaged in this all-soldier production that toured the world, he wrote a song that made popular music history, "White Christmas," a part of his score for *Holiday Inn* (1942) in which Bing Crosby and Fred Astaire were starred. Some of Berlin's songs of an earlier vintage were also heard here, ("Lazy" and "Easter Parade"), but the others were new and, together with "White Christmas," included "Be Careful, It's My Heart" and "Happy Holiday."

Harold Arlen was directly involved with *Blues in the Night* (1941) and only indirectly with the all-black screen musical, *Stormy Weather* (1943). When *Blues in the Night* was first projected in Hollywood the plan was to give serious treatment to jazz and jazz musicians in a script called *Hot Nocturne*. For one of its principal scenes, a Negro in a prison cell, Arlen, with Johnny Mercer as lyricist, wrote "Blues in the Night," a song that became so popular before that picture was released that the name of *Hot Nocturne* was discarded and *Blues in the Night* substituted. In place of a sober and penetrating appraisal of jazz within a serious story context, and almost in a documentary style, *Blues in the Night* became a formalized movie with a stilted plot and synthetic characters. Its prime significance lay in the fact that it produced a song classic, which deserved the Academy Award but failed to win it, though nominated.

Arlen's sole connection with *Stormy Weather* was the title which appropriated that of Arlen's famous blues. "Stormy Weather," the song, had of course been written earlier and for a different medium. In this motion picture it was sung by one of its most famous interpreters, Lena Horne. The film was further distinguished by the "Fats" Waller presentation of his own "Ain't Misbehavin'" (Andy Razaf) and "I Can't Give You Anything But Love, Baby" (Dorothy Fields—Jimmy McHugh).

The only original score Rodgers and Hammerstein ever wrote for the screen, *State Fair* (1945) came in the wake of the inauguration of the Rodgers and Hammerstein epoch in the Broadway theater with their sensational *Oklahoma!* (1943). *State Fair* was a musical remake of an earlier talking picture (1933) that had starred Will Rogers and Janet Gaynor. Since the movie's locale was a small town far out West, the executives of 20th Century-Fox considered the authors of *Oklahoma!* eminently suited to make the adaptation, which starred Dick Haymes, Jeanne Crain and Vivian Blaine. When *State Fair* was released, Kate Cameron, the critic, remarked: "The audience literally floats out of the theater on the strains of the Rodgers music." This was the best original score Rodgers ever wrote for the screen. Three of the six songs were hits in varying degrees: "That's for Me," "It's a Grand Night for Singing" and "It Might As Well Be Spring." The last of this delectable trio won the Academy Award. Both in words and music, it was one of the most unusual and captivating of the Rodgers and

Hammerstein song creations. When, in November 1945, "It Might As Well Be Spring" and "That's for Me" were joined on "Your Hit Parade" by "If I Loved You" from the Rodgers and Hammerstein musical play *Carousel* (1945), it was the first time that this radio program featured three songs by the same composer and lyricist on the same evening. A giant box-office success in the mid-1940s, *State Fair* returned in 1962 in an altogether new screen adaptation (with Pat Boone, Bobby Darin, Pamela Tiffin and Ann-Margret), containing some new Rodgers melodies with his own lyrics added to the old favorites.

Screen biographies of musical personalities also made a rich contribution to screen escapism during the war years by restoring memories of older times and providing nostalgic recollections of older songs. *The Dolly Sisters* (1945) told the romantic story of a pair of singing sisters who had been stars of the *Ziegfeld Follies* and the *Greenwich Village Follies*, played by Betty Grable and June Haver; the motion picture overflowed with oldtime song favorites. *My Gal Sal* (1942) was the screen biography of Paul Dresser, portrayed by Victor Mature, embellished with Dresser ballads including, of course, the title song.

Two of the most successful film musicals of these war years were screen biographies of composers, those of George M. Cohan (*Yankee Doodle Dandy*) and George Gershwin (*Rhapsody in Blue*).

For George M. Cohan, the triumph of *Yankee Doodle Dandy* (1942) provided vindication after the humiliation he had previously suffered from Hollywood. In 1932 he had starred with Jimmy Durante and Claudette Colbert in a Rodgers and Hart musical, *The Phantom President*. He was not long in Hollywood before discovering that he, once a legend on Broadway, was just one more actor in the movie capital. Some people there knew only vaguely what he had accomplished, others did not know anything about him, still others mistook him for somebody else. A gatekeeper would not allow him to park his car on the lot; a junior executive took him severely to task for daring to submit some ideas for the picture in pencil on yellow paper. Even those who remembered him could not forget that he was stepping into a new medium about which he knew nothing. Cohan learned that he would have no control over the lines he spoke or the songs he sang. Only one old Cohan routine was interpolated, "You're a Grand Old Flag," but even here the director insisted in teaching him how to do the number. He regarded this Hollywood adventure as "the most miserable I have ever had in my life." When he returned from California, he said, "If I had my choice between Hollywood and Atlanta, I'd take Leavenworth."

But a decade later Hollywood made amends by giving him a full measure of his importance through a screen dramatization of his life. Jimmy Cagney was starred as Cohan in *Yankee Doodle Dandy*, a role that brought him an Academy Award. Ten of Cohan's song classics were used, as well as the old flag-waving routines and those singing and dancing mannerisms which Cohan had made so famous on the stage. The picture became a box-office blockbuster. At its New York premiere the audience paid almost six million dollars in war bonds as the price of admission. After that, the picture grossed over a million dollars in less than six months. The same fall, a London audience purchased almost a million pounds in war securities to attend the English premiere. There could be little question that the personality of George M. Cohan, and the golden aura of his fabulous theatrical career, was what made this picture so attractive to so many. Mayor La Guardia recognized this fact when he declared July 3, 1942, George M. Cohan Day in New York. For Cohan himself it was the closing chord. Weakened by an abdominal operation, he nevertheless compelled his nurse to take him by taxi to Broadway so that he might catch one more glimpse of one of the scenes of *Yankee Doodle Dandy*. He died soon after, on December 5, 1942, in his New York apartment. But he remained a vibrant living presence in show business. In 1959 his statue was unveiled at Duffy Square in the heart of Broadway. In 1968 the musical called *George M!*, starring Joel Grey, brought Cohan's life and songs to the Broadway stage, a musical subsequently given a television production. And, in 1970, a new award named in his honor, the "Georgie," was instituted and presented by the American Guild of Variety Artists (AGVA).

In *Rhapsody in Blue* (1945), Robert Alda was George Gershwin and Herbert Rudley, Ira Gershwin. The screen play, by Sonya Levien, Howard Koch and Elliott Paul, mixed some truth with a good deal of fiction. The unifying theme in the story was basically sound: Gershwin's struggle to reconcile his passion for jazz with his ideal of writing serious music; his conflict of purpose in producing hits on the one hand and good art on the other. Less convincing was the fabricated love interest. On the positive side was the Gershwin music: nineteen songs, with Al Jolson singing "Swanee," and excerpts from *135th Street*, *Porgy and Bess*, *Rhapsody in Blue*, Concerto in F and *An American in Paris*. The piano playing of Robert Alda on the screen was dubbed on the sound track by Ray Turner; the vocals, presumably sung by Joan Leslie, who played Gershwin's soul mate, Julie Adams, were by Louanne Hogan.

5

Some of the Broadway musicals between 1940 and 1945 touched upon the war, but most of them avoided it.

Irving Berlin's all-soldier revue, *This Is the Army*, was followed a year later by a similar project by the air force, conceived and written by Moss Hart, *Winged Victory* (1943), songs by David Rose to Leo Robin's lyrics, with the inevitable interpolation of the "Army Air Corps Song" (Robert M. Crawford).

Two of Cole Porter's musicals in the early 1940s had war-oriented plots. *Let's Face It* (1941) was a modernization of a Broadway play of 1925, *Cradle Snatchers*, in which three inductees at Camp Roosevelt are recruited as gigolo lovers for three society women at nearby Southampton on Long Island. As one of these inductees, Danny Kaye provided the cream of the jest, particularly with a routine written for him by his wife, Sylvia Fine, "Melody in Four F," a tongue twisting number in double-talk, and with Danny Kaye's inimitable gift at pantomime, which described the adventures of a newly conscripted soldier. Cole Porter's best song here was "Ace in the Hole." In *Something for the Boys* (1943), Ethel Merman was seen and heard as Blossom Hart, a onetime chorus girl who, because of the war, has become a defense worker. An outstanding comedy piece, "By the Mississinewah" and "Hey, Good Lookin' " were Porter's top musical numbers for Miss Merman.

One of the outstanding musicals of 1944 was *Follow the Girls*, book by Guy Bolton and Eddie Davis, lyrics by Dan Shapiro and Milton Pascal, and music by Phil Charig. Gertrude Niessen appeared as Bubbles La Marr, a striptease burlesque queen who, because of the war, is impelled to sacrifice her career and work in a servicemen's canteen. As Goofy Gale, Jackie Gleason won his first laurels as comedian on the Broadway stage. The romantic ballad, "Where Are You?" and the somewhat bawdy number, "I Wanna Get Married" were the attractive songs.

But the best musicals, and the most successful, were those that sidestepped the issues of the war. Within the framework of the musical comedy—as distinguished from musical plays—were Irving Berlin's *Louisiana Purchase* (1940), Cole Porter's *Panama Hattie* (1940), the Rodgers and Hart musical *By Jupiter* (1942), Kurt Weill's *One Touch of Venus* (1943), Harold Arlen's *Bloomer Girl* (1943), Cole Porter's *Mexican Hayride* (1944), Leonard Bernstein's *On the Town* (1944) and Sigmund Romberg's *Up in Central Park* (1945).

In *Louisiana Purchase*, a United States Senator (a role filled by Victor Moore) is dispatched to New Orleans to investigate a shady company and its slick lawyer. Two ballads are recognizably Berlin, "It's a Lovely Day Tomorrow" and "You're Lonely and I'm Lonely."

Panama Hattie and *Mexican Hayride* had scores by Cole Porter. Panama Hattie, a brassy part written for Ethel Merman, runs a bar in the Panama Canal Zone where she overhears and thwarts a plot to blow up the Canal and endears herself to the man she loves. The song hit of the show was "Let's Be Buddies," shared by Miss Merman with an eight-year-old girl played by Joan Carroll. A certain spot in the production called for such a number but the law forebade a child from singing and dancing. Consequently, Porter wrote his song, as he explained, so that it could be "walked to, in order to compensate for Joan having been prevented by law from dancing, and . . . so that Joan could recite instead of court jail by singing." Brooks Atkinson reported: "Gruff old codgers are going to choke a little this winter when tot and temptress sing 'Let's Be Buddies' and bring down the house."

In *Mexican Hayride*, a lady bullfighter from the United States, an American chargé d'affaires with whom she falls in love, and an American fugitive from justice who concocts a fake lottery, are placed in the exotic and colorful setting of Mexico. Here is heard one of Cole Porter's better love ballads, "I Love You," as well as a song with Mexican flavor to which Porter himself was partial, "Sing to Me, Guitar."

On the Town was Leonard Bernstein's first Broadway musical. This Leonardo da Vinci of the twentieth century has broached every area of music—conducting, composing, playing the piano, lecturing, writing books—and in each he has proved a talent which, in some of these areas, touches on genius. Giving further dimension to his formidable versatility is his eminence in both serious and popular music. Born in 1918 in Lawrence, Massachusetts, Bernstein revealed a remarkable gift for music from his childhood on. He was given a musical training together with his academic education that was completed at Harvard College. After studying conducting with Serge Koussevitzky at the Berkshire Music Center in Lenox, Massachusetts, Bernstein made a sensational debut as symphony conductor when, in the fall of 1943, he was a last-minute substitute for Bruno Walter at a concert of the New York Philharmonic Orchestra. This was the beginning of a baton career that brought him an acclaim rivaled by few others. At the same time he wrote serious musical works, beginning with the *Jeremiah Symphony*, which placed him in the vanguard of important young American composers.

One of his more serious works was a ballet, his first, *Fancy Free*, introduced by the Ballet Theater on April 18, 1944, in which Jerome Robbins made his bow as a choreographer. *Fancy Free* was about three sailors on leave, on the hunt for girls. *On the Town* was an amplification of this same subject with text by Betty Comden and Adolph Green. Musically, too, *On the Town* evolved from *Fancy Free*. Bernstein's experiments with a popular style in the ballet score continued with renewed zest in the musical comedy. In *On the Town* he struck a happy medium between time-tested formulas and provocative innovations, particularly in the ballads "Lonely Town" and "Lucky to be Me," while his wit and satire had a rapier edge in "Carried Away" and "I Can Cook, Too," all to lyrics by Betty Comden and Adolph Green. The opening number, "New York, New York," a breezy, infectious tribute to that city, has since become almost as often identified musically with it as "The Sidewalks of New York" (James W. Blake—Charles B. Lawlor). The opening scene had a spacious design as did a fantasy on the subway ride to Coney Island. In his music for these and other ballet sequences Bernstein was able to use his advanced compositional technique and his symphonic thinking to good advantage, producing some of the best musical sequences in the theater in the early 1940s. He also collaborated in writing the lyrics for "I Can Cook, Too."

On The Town boasted a momentous debut for others besides Leonard Bernstein. This was the first musical for which Betty Comden and Adolph Green wrote text and lyrics and they henceforth occupied a position of considerable consequence in the musical theater. Both were born in New York City, Green in 1915, Miss Comden in 1918. Betty Comden attended New York University where she participated in performances of the Washington Square Players. At this time, through mutual friends, she met Adolph Green, whose academic education had ended with his graduation from De Witt Clinton High School. Somewhat later, they met a second time, when both were trying to make headway in the theater. They formed a nightclub act, "The Revuers" (one of whose members was Judy Holliday, later a distinguished comedienne of stage and screen). For it they wrote most of the material. "The Revuers" began attracting the interest and enthusiasm of an elite group of intellectuals at a Greenwich Village night spot, The Vanguard. Leonard Bernstein was one of their close friends. To him, one day in 1944, they confided their ambition to make *Fancy Free* into a musical comedy, a suggestion that was greeted by Bernstein with unqualified enthusiasm.

On the Town infected the theater world with its youthful energy, verve, breathless pacing, excitement and freshness. It was a box-office as well as theatrical success. It received the Page One Award of the Newspaper Guild as an outstanding achievement in the theater. It was sold to the movies for an MGM musical production starring Gene Kelly and Frank Sinatra, released in 1949. In 1959 it was revived simultaneously in two Off-Broadway productions, in 1963 it was performed in the London theater and in 1973 it returned to Broadway for a short run.

A statue of Venus in a museum of modern art comes to life in the Kurt Weill musical *One Touch of Venus*. Mary Martin, as Venus, sings "Foolish Heart" and joins the young barber who has fallen in love with her in "Speak Low," the two outstanding songs in the score, lyrics by Ogden Nash.

Harold Arlen made his return to Broadway, after seven fat years in Hollywood, with *Bloomer Girl*, whose two-year run on Broadway made it the sole stage triumph of Arlen's theatrical career. This was a sentimentalized portrait of America during the Civil War era, dominated by the arresting personality of the feminist, Dolly Bloomer, whose espousal of bloomers as opposed to hoop skirts provokes a crisis in her personal life. Arlen's music, with lyrics by E. Y. Harburg, contained several numbers as good as some he had previously written for Hollywood: the ballads "Right as the Rain" and "Evelina"; the blues, "I Got a Song"; "T'morra" and "I Never Was Born."

In *Up in Central Park*, Sigmund Romberg abandoned the foreign style operetta which had made him famous. *Up in Central Park* was an American musical comedy which brought Romberg the second best box-office returns of his career, with a Broadway run of fourteen months. Few of his preceding stage successes brought him the satisfaction this one did. For some years, whispers had been circulating around Broadway and Hollywood that Romberg was through as a composer, that he was incapable of adapting himself to new times and to the demands of musical comedy. A few failures in the 1940s seemed to confirm these suspicions. Yet when Romberg was called upon to write music for a thoroughly American stage work, and for a book entirely different from those he had worked with in the past, he once again put down a winning hand. The background of *Up in Central Park* was New York in the 1870s during the infamous reign of the Tweed Ring. To this play Romberg contributed a score with four top songs with lyrics by Dorothy Fields: "Close as Pages in a Book," "Carrousel in the Park," "It Doesn't Cost You Anything to Dream" and "April Snow." In addition he created the background music for a spellbinding ice-skating ballet in a Currier and Ives setting.

Romberg's valedictory to the stage, *The Girl in Pink Tights*, once more to a thoroughly American book based upon the production of *The Black Crook* in 1866, was produced posthumously in 1954. *The Girl in Pink Tights* was neither good nor successful, but Romberg did not live to discover this. He died in New York City on November 10, 1951.

While musical comedy was flourishing, the musical play that had had its inception with such productions as *Show Boat* and *Of Thee I Sing* was gaining headway during the war years. Vernon Duke's *Cabin in the Sky* (1940) was one of the most sensitive and perceptive pictures of Negro life and psychology to be found in the musical theater. Every element in the production maintained the quiet dignity and integrity of the Lynn Root play which described the contest between Lucifer, Jr., and the Lawd's General to gain control of the soul of Little Joe, a humble black man. The earthy lyrics and balladry of John La Touche, the choreography of George Balanchine, and the music of Vernon Duke all were in character with the simple folklike play. This was the first plot musical for which Vernon Duke wrote an entire score, all his previous commitments having been for revues. His music tapped a rich creative vein. "Taking a Chance on Love" and "Honey in the Honeycomb" have the overtones of Negro folk music, the first sung by Ethel Waters, the other by Katherine Dunham.

Lady in the Dark (1941) was Kurt Weill's first musical play, as differentiated from musical comedy. Moss Hart's unusual text entered the world of psychoanalysis, and its treatment was novel and daring. The story moves on two levels. On one, Liza Elliott pursues her career as editor of *Allure*. She is a woman of neurotic behavior, physical ailments and inner torment who seeks the help of a psychiatrist. The second level of the play contains dream sequences and the world of her subconscious, through which she is able to realize herself finally as a fulfilled woman. The virtuoso performances of Gertrude Lawrence as Liza and of Danny Kaye in his Broadway stage debut in the subsidiary role of a magazine photographer, were major factors in the remarkable artistic success of this play. But Weill's music also contributed handsomely. His atmospheric music was so perfectly attuned to the dream sequences that it was an inextricable part of the overall drama; and the recurring song, "My Ship," was beautifully suited to these sequences with its individual, haunting melodic structure. But Weill's music also consisted of many outstanding individual numbers, all with lyrics by Ira Gershwin, like the sultry "The Saga of Jenny," "The Princess of Pure Delight" and "Oh Fabulous One, In Your Ivory Tower." Yet even these numbers were so much a part of the dramatic pattern that *Lady in the Dark* remains what Moss Hart originally called it, "a play with music."

"The Saga of Jenny," which appeared in one of the dream sequences, was a tour de force for Gertrude Lawrence who performed it with burlesque bumps and grinds. This was not the kind of song for which Miss Lawrence had become distinguished, and there was considerable doubt in the minds of many involved in the production whether she could carry it off. But she did, to the utter delight of her audiences.

Danny Kaye, in his first Broadway appearance, instantly became a comic star of stars, and one of his numbers that helped was "Tschaikowsky." This was a novelty number, admirably suited for Danny Kaye's unique brand of tongue-twisting delivery, in which the names of forty-nine Russian composers were strung together. Kaye made his electrifying delivery in thirty-nine seconds. This was an obvious showstopper, intended as such, and fear that it might eclipse the star of the show, Miss Lawrence, led to the writing of "The Saga of Jenny" to follow it immediately so that the limelight might once more be focused squarely upon her.

The full realization of the musical play concept was achieved just one year later, in

1943, the first musical on which Richard Rodgers and Oscar Hammerstein II collaborated, and their first masterwork. An all-important chapter in Richard Rodgers' career ended in 1942 when his long and fruitful collaboration with Lorenz Hart was terminated with the writing of *By Jupiter*. But an even more significant chapter opened a year later when he found a new collaborator in Oscar Hammerstein II.

By 1943, Hammerstein had spent about a quarter of a century in the musical theater. He had written or collaborated in the writing of texts and/or lyrics for about twenty-five stage productions, and had been responsible for several hundred songs. He had been a partner in the creation of several operettas and musical comedies that had become major events in the American theater, Vincent Youmans' *Wildflower*, Rudolf Friml's *Rose-Marie*, Sigmund Romberg's *Desert Song* and *The New Moon*, Jerome Kern's *Show Boat* and *Music in the Air*.

He had had, then, his share of triumphs before 1943. But when he joined Rodgers he had suffered three disasters in succession, not to mention several minor calamities in London. When, at long last, he recovered his winning stride through his first collaboration with Rodgers he ran an advertisement in *Variety* with the following headline: "I've Done It Before and I Can Do It Again." But under that heading Hammerstein listed not the succession of his triumphs but his recent failures: *Very Warm for May* (seven weeks); *Ball at Savoy* (five weeks); *Sunny River* (six weeks); *Three Sisters* (six weeks); and *Free for All* (three weeks).

In Hollywood his track record was equally lamentable. He had suffered so many failures on the screen that a Hollywood producer paid him $100,000 to scrap a four-picture contract. Both on Broadway and in Hollywood the conviction prevailed that Hammerstein's creative juices had dried up, that he was incapable of keeping pace with the rapidly changing values in the musical theater.

At this critical juncture in his career, he was asked by the Theatre Guild, one day in 1943, to work with Richard Rodgers in adapting the folk play by Lynn Riggs, *Green Grow the Lilacs*, into a musical. Lorenz Hart had firmly bowed out as Rodgers' collaborator, and the Guild suggested that Hammerstein replace Hart.

Hammerstein and Rodgers were no strangers. They had met for the first time in 1915 when Hammerstein appeared in a Varsity Show at Columbia College and young Dick Rodgers was in the audience; after that performance, Dick went backstage and was introduced to Hammerstein. Four years later, Rodgers and Hammerstein wrote several songs for an amateur production, and a year later they wrote the song "There Is Always Room for One More" for a Columbia Varsity Show. After that they met often, exchanging encouraging words for each other's activities. Richard Rodgers' father was the obstetrician for Hammerstein's two children by his first marriage. But though they knew each other well, Rodgers and Hammerstein did not get to work on a professional musical production until the Theatre Guild brought them together for the Riggs play.

Tentatively entitled *Away We Go*, the proposed production inspired little enthusiasm among potential backers. Parties organized to raise the $85,000 needed for the production costs were fruitless; only $2,500 trickled in. The remainder of the sum was procured through entreaties, cajolery, tears and insistence. Most of the money came from friends of the Guild who regarded their contribution as an outright gift rather than an investment.

The new musical had all the earmarks of disaster. There were no stars in the cast to lure the public into the theater. There was no humor in the unconventional folklike text. The climax of the plot was—of all outlandish things as far as musicals went—a murder. Chorus girl routines were replaced by highbrow ballets. There were no production numbers as such.

The preview performances in New Haven on March 11, 1943, were a dud. "No

Girls, No Gags, No Chance" was wired back to New York. Drastic revisions became necessary, with some mild humor introduced where it could be basic to either plot or character. The show now assumed the new title of *Oklahoma!* These and other changes seemed to have worked a minor miracle, for in Boston the critics began to sing its praises, praises which swelled into raves by the time *Oklahoma!* arrived in New York on March 31. Lewis Nichols perhaps crystallized the critical reaction best by calling it a "folk opera."

Oklahoma! had as strong an appeal to audiences as it had to critics, for while reaching for art Rodgers and Hammerstein had not lost the popular touch. The show shattered every record that had previously existed in the theater for a musical. It remained on Broadway five years and nine months, amassing the staggering total of 2,212 performances and accumulating the then unprecedented sum of seven million dollars at the box office. A national company toured for ten years in some two hundred and fifty cities before audiences estimated at ten million. When the original company closed in New York, it went on a fifty-one week tour of seventy cities. After that, the musical was seen throughout Europe, Scandinavia, Australia, South Africa and, in a special company organized to tour Army camps, in remote places in the Pacific. In London, it remained three and a half years, the second longest run in the history of the London musical stage. In all, it grossed in the neighborhood of forty million dollars. The recording of the complete score—the first time a musical was recorded in its entirety by the original cast—sold over a million albums; the published music disposed of another million or more copies. In 1955, *Oklahoma!* found still a new audience of many millions in its screen adaptation in the then new Todd-AO process. Each of the original investors in the stage production was rewarded by a five thousand percent profit.

Oklahoma! was honored with a special award from the Pulitzer Prize committee. When the touring company brought the musical to the State of Oklahoma for the first time, a state holiday was proclaimed. An *Oklahoma!* songfest was produced in 1955 in Central Park, in New York, before an audience of more than fifteen thousand. And in 1968, to celebrate the twenty-fifth anniversary of the birth of *Oklahoma!*, it was presented in concert form, with spoken documentary, at Philharmonic Hall at Lincoln Center.

Unknowns, when they first stepped into their roles, were transformed into stars by the time *Oklahoma!* had run its course. They included Alfred Drake, Celeste Holm, Joan McCracken, Bambi Linn, Howard Keel and Shelley Winters.

The play from which the musical was taken, set in Oklahoma Territory at the turn of the century, was the stuff of which folklore is spun, and the musical remained faithful to the original concept of Lynn Riggs. Hammerstein's text and lyrics maintained the flavor of American folklore which was further enhanced by settings and costumes, by Agnes de Mille's choreography, and by the music of Richard Rodgers. For Rodgers, *Oklahoma!* represented a departure from earlier methods. Adapting himself resiliently to the folk play, and to the poetry of Hammerstein's lyrics, Rodgers came up with melodies so fresh in their approach, so simple in style and content, so wholesome in manner that they assume the personality of folk songs. In this vein are "The Surrey with the Fringe on Top," "Kansas City," "The Farmer and the Cowman," the title number "Oklahoma!" and "Oh, What a Beautiful Mornin'." Other songs also expressed the Rodgers identity. The principal love song, "People Will Say We're in Love," became a hit in 1943 and was heard on "Your Hit Parade" for thirty weeks. "Many a New Day" and "Out of My Dreams" were also recognizable Rodgers. Yet whether in his own song style or in a folk idiom, each of Rodgers' songs were inextricably bound up with characters and situations to create a perfect integration of text and music.

More than any single musical before it, even *Show Boat, Oklahoma!* made the musical play an established institution in the American theater that would grow and develop in scope and style in ensuing years. Its success undoubtedly gave its authors both the courage and stimulation to continue working with unusual books and to treat then in an unorthodox fashion.

After an intermission in Hollywood to write the music for *State Fair*, Rodgers and Hammerstein returned to Broadway in 1945 with their second musical play, *Carousel*, which in many ways was finer, more deeply sensitive, and more poetic than its predecessor. *Carousel* was Ferenc Molnar's *Liliom* transferred from early twentieth-century Hungary to New England in 1873. There are tragic and touching overtones to the musical play not often encountered on the musical stage up to this time. Nostalgic moods, spiritual moods and tender moods all combined into theater magic. Part fantasy and part realism, *Carousel* tells the story of Billy Bigelow, an irresponsible young man who marries Julie Jordan, a simple, lovable girl, and who gets killed in a holdup in which he tries to get money for his still unborn child. After fifteen years in Purgatory, Billy is allowed to return to earth for a single day to try to redeem his soul.

Ever deeper and richer grows the poetry of Hammerstein's lines whether in dialogue or in the lyrics. Richard Rodgers' music also gains new stature. Together with songs of the hit-parade variety—"June Is Bustin' Out All Over" and "If I Loved You"—there is a remarkable seven-minute recitatative, "Soliloquy" made up of eight different musical ideas; an effective set of symphonic waltzes played under the opening scene; and a stirring inspirational number, "You'll Never Walk Alone." And Rodgers' overall musical writing now gains expansiveness with extended musical sequences combining song, dialogue, recitatives and orchestral episodes.

6

A pincer movement on the city of Berlin, from the east by Soviet troops, and from the west by the Allied forces under General Eisenhower, spelled the end of the Third Reich. Hitler committed suicide in his bunker on April 29, 1945, just eight days before the German army surrendered unconditionally. All the might of the Allied forces was now centered on Japan. On August 6, the first atomic bomb reduced Hiroshima to ashes, killing over eighty thousand Japanese. Three days later, Nagasaki was totally destroyed by a second atomic bomb. One day later, the Japanese sued for peace on Allied terms and on September 2, 1945, the Japanese surrender to the Allies was signed aboard the battleship *Missouri* in Tokyo Bay.

The most devastating and costliest war in history was over. There were to be no more war songs for America as it returned to a peacetime economy and way of life; and, for that matter, almost no peace songs as well. One or two paid passing tributes to the soldiers returning home, "It's Been a Long, Long Time" (Sammy Cahn—Jule Styne) and "I'm Gonna Love that Guy" (Frances Ash).

One Broadway musical production took cognizance of peace with one of the last of the distinguished socio-political intimate revues. It was *Call Me Mister* (1946), sketches by Arnold Auerbach and Arnold Horwitt, songs by Harold Rome. Its overall theme was the readjustment of the G.I. to civilian life. The problems facing the returning veteran were described in songs like "Goin' Home Train" and "Red Ball Express," the latter pointing to the further difficulties of a black man once he took off his uniform. Army life was recalled mockingly in "Little Surplus Me" and "Military Life." "The Face on the Dime" was a black man's poignant tribute to the memory of President Roosevelt. "The Senators' Song" was a caricature of three reactionary Southern Senators.

The song that stole that show, however, had no connection with the Army, demobilization, or any social or political problem. But, then, this song had not been written for *Call Me Mister*, but several years earlier. It was "South America, Take It Away," provocatively sung by Betty Garrett. Rome had written it during a prevailing craze for Latin-American dances and rhythms, but never was able to find a place for it in any of his shows. It was pulled into *Call Me Mister* because a feature was needed for Miss Garrett, and this number seemed to fit her singing style and personality. The decision to use it was made hesitantly because of its irrelevance in the main theme of the revue. But it turned out to be the musical's shining light, and the only number to achieve hit status.

26

The Gentle Art
of Tune Lifting

1

The year of Pearl Harbor, 1941, might reasonably be identified as the Tchaikovsky year in American popular music. This was the year Freddy Martin and his orchestra made a best-selling recording for Victor of "Tonight We Love" (Bobby Worth—Ray Austin and Freddy Martin), music taken from the first movement of Tchaikovsky's Piano Concerto No. 1 in B-flat minor. This was also the year of "The Things I Love" (Harold Barlow and Lew Harris) taken from "Mélodie," Op. 42, No. 3; of "The Story of a Starry Night" (Al Hoffman, Mann Curtis and Jerry Livingston) and "Now and Forever" (Al Stillman—Jan Savitt), each borrowing their main melody from the *Symphonie pathétique*; of "Concerto for Two" (Jack Lawrence), another popular adaptation of a theme from the first movement of the Piano Concerto No. 1.

The classics of other composers also provided material for popular songs in 1941, principally, Rachmaninoff's Concerto No. 2 in C minor from whose first movement came "I Think of You" (Jack Elliott and Don Marcotte), introduced in a Victor recording by Tommy Dorsey and his orchestra with vocal by Frank Sinatra; Anton Rubinstein's "Romance" which became "If You Are But a Dream" (Moe Jaffe, Jack Fulton and Nat Bonx); and Isaac Albéniz's Tango in D minor, transformed into "Moonlight Masquerade" (Jack Lawrence —Toots Camerata).

This practice of lifting melodies from the musical classics for popular songs was, of course, not new in 1941, though by then it had become something of a standard procedure. The gentle art of lifting tunes from the classics in public domain was as old as Tin Pan Alley itself. This practice had become so prevalent in the early part of the twentieth century that the successful lyricist, Vincent Bryan, told an interviewer for the New York *Herald* in 1905: "Filching is the only thing that counts in the songwriting business. All you need to compose a song that will sell is a good memory." Still another distinguished lyricist of that period, Will D. Cobb, remarked wryly: "It's a wise song that knows its own father."

In the closing years of the nineteenth century there had been more than one instance of popular song composers reaching into the musical classics and lifting out of them choice melodies. Monroe Rosenfeld's "Johnny Get Your Gun," in 1886, sounded as if its composer remembered "The Arkansas Traveler." Joseph J. Sullivan's "Where Did You Get that Hat?" in 1888 consciously or otherwise took a leitmotif from Wagner's *Lohengrin*. Percy Gaunt's "The Bowery" in 1892 and the Neapolitan folk song, "La Spagnola," have a family resemblance.

Victor Herbert was the plaintiff in a much publicized lawsuit in 1902 against Marc A. Blumenberg, editor of the *Musical Courier*, who had accused Herbert of frequently and deliberately stealing his melodies from the musical classics. In the July 17, 1901, issue he wrote: "All of Victor Herbert's 'written to order' comic operas were pure and simple plagiarisms. . . . Everything written by Herbert is copied; there is not one original strain in anything he has done." Victor Herbert was usually an amiable, genial, happy-go-lucky, live-and-let-live man. But aroused he was a tiger. This editorial aroused him. He sued *Musical Courier* for libel, asking fifty thousand dollars in damages.

The trial began on October 22, 1902, to become, as Herbert's biographer, Edward N. Waters described it, "one of the most remarkable cases in musical jurisprudence." On the witness stand Blumenberg tried to prove his case by pointing out similarities between the classics and various pieces by Herbert. He found, for example, a parallel between Fauré's song, "The Palms" and something in the Herbert operetta *The Singing Girl*, and between the opening of Beethoven's Ninth Symphony and a passage in *The Wizard of the Nile*. "Authorities" were summoned to substantiate Blumenberg's accusations. Under the withering cross-examination of Herbert's lawyer, Nathan Burkan, their testimony was quickly reduced to absurdity.

Herbert's principal witness was Walter Damrosch, one of America's most highly revered conductors and musical personalities. Damrosch insisted that the similarities existing between some of the classics and some of Herbert's music was no more flagrant than those found among the classics themselves. He maintained that he could find "hundreds of resemblances" in different classical compositions and he emphasized that in no way could these similarities be regarded as plagiarism.

In his column in the New York *Tribune* the eminent music critic Henry E. Krehbiel became particularly upset at Blumenberg's attempt to see borrowings by Herbert from Beethoven's Ninth Symphony. "It was a silly device, and so bunglingly done that it was easy for Walter Damrosch to testify that the alleged quotation from Herbert was not within a mile of the Ninth Symphony."

Blumenberg's lawyer, Gilbert Ray Hawes, saw that the case was going badly for his client. He therefore tried in his summation to soften the imminent blow by insisting that Blumenberg had no intention of accusing Herbert of "theft" but only of "reminiscences." "We have the kindest and best feelings toward Mr. Herbert personally," he said. Then he sought refuge in the "privileged" nature of editorials, insisting that Blumenberg's editorial was a justifiable form of public criticism in a reputable journal.

If Hawes had any hope that his summation would sway the jury, it was forthwith shattered by the charge of Judge Truax. He warned the jury that, far from being privileged,

Blumenberg's editorial had been libelous; that Herbert was entitled to compensation even though his income or his career had not suffered as a result of the editorial. "I know of no law," Judge Truax said, "that gives the publisher of a paper a right to say an untruthful thing about a private individual or a public individual."

After two hours of deliberation, the jury awarded Herbert damages of fifteen thousand dollars. Though in later appeals, the judgment was reduced to five thousand dollars, the cause of irresponsible criticism and journalism had suffered a humiliating defeat.

The practice of tune lifting went into high gear in Tin Pan Alley in the second decade of this century. "Marcheta" by Victor Schertzinger, a hit song of 1913, borrowed its melody from the main theme of Nicolai's Overture to *The Merry Wives of Windsor*. Harry Carroll achieved his greatest song success in 1918 with "I'm Always Chasing Rainbows" (Joseph McCarthy). He never tried to conceal the fact that he had found his melody in Chopin's Fantaisie Impromptu in C-sharp minor. This was the first time that the conscious, deliberate borrowing of a melody from the classics had yielded a financial bonanza. But an even more profitable exercise in tune lifting was performed in 1921 when Sigmund Romberg adapted Franz Schubert's melodies for the songs in the operetta *Blossom Time*. Romberg is reputed to have earned one million dollars from his effort. The crowning paradox of this situation is that during his entire lifetime all that Schubert earned for all his music was five hundred dollars.

A minor epidemic of tune lifting erupted in the 1920s. A notable example was "Avalon," whose melody by Vincent Rose, with the collaboration of Al Jolson, was stolen unashamedly from the aria "E lucevan le stelle" from Puccini's opera *Tosca*. Puccini's publisher, Ricordi, instituted suit against Remick who had published "Avalon" in 1920. The defense tried to prove that the *Tosca* melody had often been used before Puccini's time. The plaintiff had a trio play "Avalon" at the same time that a gramophone record presented the *Tosca* aria. Though "Avalon" was in a major key, and the opera aria in the minor, and despite a flat or two difference, the two numbers sounded virtually the same. Puccini and his publishers were awarded damages of twenty-five thousand dollars and all future royalties from "Avalon" were turned over to Ricordi. One of the smaller record companies, convinced that "Avalon" had the makings of a big hit, had staked all its assets on the recording, promotion and release of this song. On the basis of the court action, the company had to go out of business.

But this unfortunate episode did not keep other Tin Pan Alley tunesmiths of the 1920s from cultivating the fertile area of classical music in the public domain. César Cui's "Orientale" became "Oriental Eyes" (Leo Wood and Irving Bibo—Paul Whiteman and Ferde Grofé) and Rimsky-Korsakov's "Song of India," "Play that Song of India Again" (Leo Wood and Irving Bibo—Paul Whiteman), both performed by Paul Whiteman and his Orchestra. An organ piece by Edwin H. Lemare, the Andantino in D-flat, was made into "Moonlight and Roses Bring Mem'ries of You" (Ben Black and Neil Moret). The Negro spiritual "Deep River" was used for "Dear Old Southland" (Henry Creamer—Turner Layton). Sigmund Romberg usurped Tchaikovsky's "June Barcarolle" for piano for the middle section (release) of his song "Lover Come Back to Me" (Oscar Hammerstein II). Rimsky-Korsakov's *Scheherazade* and "Hymn to the Sun," Ponchielli's "Dance of the Hours" from *La Gioconda*, Liszt's *Liebestraum* and Edward MacDowell's *To a Wild Rose* were other classics to be syncopated, and abbreviated to conform to the sixteen-measure verse and thirty-two measure chorus of popular song structure, besides being fitted out with lyrics.

The music of the masters—esoteric items as well as the thrice-familiar ones—continued to provide Tin Pan Alley with song material in the late thirties. From Tchaikovsky, in 1939, emerged "Moon Love" (Mack David, Mack Davis and André Kostelanetz) and "Our Love" (Larry Clinton, Buddy Bernier and Bob Emmerich), the first from the second movement of Symphony No. 5, the other from the overture-fantasy, *Romeo and Juliet*. Still in 1939, Eddy Duchin got the theme song for his band from Chopin's Nocturne in E-flat in "My Twilight Dream" (Lew Sherwood and Eddy Duchin). Liszt's *Second Hungarian Rhapsody* was changed into "Ebony Rhapsody" (Arthur Johnston and Sam Coslow) in 1934. Less familiar territory was also being pillaged: Claude Debussy's "Reverie" in "My Reverie" (Larry Clinton); Mozart, the opening theme of whose Piano Sonata in C, K. 525 became "In an Eighteenth Century Drawing Room" (Jack Lawrence—Raymond Scott); Maurice Ravel's *Pavane pour une Infante défunte* remade into "The Lamp Is Low" (Mitchell Parish—Peter De Rose and Bert Shefter).

The harvest of hit songs in 1941 derived from the musical classics helped make the early years of World War II a heyday of musical larceny in Tin Pan Alley. In addition to those already mentioned, the early 1940s brought prominence to "On the Isle of May" (Mack David—André Kostelanetz), one more contribution by Tchaikovsky, this time from the Andante Cantabile from the String Quartet in D major; "I Look at Heaven" (Bobby Worth—Ray Austin and Freddy Martin) taken from Grieg's Piano Concerto in A minor; two items from Lecuona's suite, *Andalucia*, "The Breeze and I," lyrics by Al Stillman and music adapted by T. Camerata, and "At the Crossroads," lyrics by Bob Russell; and the song that gave Perry Como his first million-disk sale, "Till the End of Time" (Buddy Kaye and Ted Mossman) from Chopin's Polonaise in A-flat major.

2

In the early forties, two major Broadway musicals also profited from this now chronic custom. In 1943, Oscar Hammerstein II hit upon the happy idea of taking Bizet's opera *Carmen* and modernizing its text into a twentieth-century American all-black play, and using the Bizet score virtually intact but with appropriate new lyrics. The result was what Robert Garland called "a memorable milestone in the upward and onward course of the great American showshop." The locale of the Bizet opera was transferred from eighteenth-century Seville, in Spain, to a Southern American town during World War II. In place of the bullfighter Escamillio we get Husky Miller, a boxer, and Don José, the Spanish corporal of dragoons in the Bizet opera, is replaced by Joe, a black corporal in the United States Army. Carmen Jones is a seductive young black girl who entices Joe to abandon his girl friend, go AWOL, and escape to Chicago with her where she abandons Joe for Husky Miller. She then becomes the fatal victim of Joe's vengeance outside the arena in which Husky is boxing for the championship.

In taking over Bizet's arias, duets and ensemble numbers, Hammerstein fitted them out with new words and titles to conform to his story, locale and characters. Thus the "Habanera" becomes "Dat's Love"; the Seguidilla, "Dere's a Café on De Corner"; the Gypsy Song, "Beat Out dat Rhythm on a Drum"; the Toreador Song, "Stan' Up An' Fight"; the Flower Song, "Dis Flower"; and Micaëla's air, "My Joe."

The music of Edvard Grieg served Robert Wright (1914—) and George "Chet" Forrest (1915—), the composers of *Song of Norway*, which was for 1944 what *Blossom Time* had been in 1921, an operetta about a world-famous serious composer utilizing his music in popular transformations. Playing as fast and loose with biographical facts as *Blossom Time* had done, *Song of Norway*, in 1944, was devoted principally to the love affair between Grieg and Nina Hagerup (fact) and the attempts of a seductive prima donna to win him away (fiction).

In the manner of Sigmund Romberg in *Blossom Time*, Wright and Forrest here reshaped the beloved melodies of a great classical composer into Tin Pan Alley stereotypes. The most famous song in *Song of Norway* is "Strange Music," whose melody came from Grieg's *Wedding Day in Troldhaugen* and Nocturne, both for the piano. The Norwegian Dance No. 2 becomes "Freddy and His Fiddle"; the art song, "I Love You" is fashioned into a popular song with the same title; themes from the Violin Sonata No. 2 and the Waltz, Op. 12, enter into "Now"; the Piano Concerto in A minor contributed the melodies to "The Legend" and "Hill of Dreams."

In subsequent decades, Wright and Forrest continued to ransack the classics for their musical stage scores. One of these was a giant success, *Kismet* (1953), which exploited the music of Alexander Borodin. From this score came three hit songs: "Stranger in Paradise" (from the *Polovetsian Dances* in *Prince Igor*); "And This Is My Beloved" (from the Nocturne in the String Quartet in D major); and "Baubles, Bangles and Beads" (from the scherzo in the same string quartet). One decade later, in 1965, Wright and Forrest attempted to use the music of Rachmaninoff similarly, but their operetta, *Anya*, was a failure.

3

With *Kismet* and *Anya* we have sidestepped chronology and passed briefly beyond the early forties into the fifties and sixties.

After World War II, but still in the 1940s, we come upon the "Anniversary Song" (Al Jolson and Saul Chaplin) which was one of the song highlights of the screen musical *The Jolson Story* (1946); "Anniversary Song" makes felicitous use of one of the melodies from J. Ivanovici's waltz, *Danube Waves*. The main theme from the first movement of Rachmaninoff's Second Piano Concerto became "Full Moon and Empty Arms" (Buddy Kaye and Ted Mossman) in 1946. In 1947, Brahms' Hungarian Dance No. 4 became "As Years Go By" (Charles Tobias—Peter De Rose); in 1948, Leoncavallo's art song, "La Mattinata" became "You're Breaking My Heart" (Pat Genaro and Sunny Skylar); and in 1949, the famous Neapolitan song, "O Sole Mio" was made into "There's No Tomorrow" (Al Hoffman, Leo Corday and Leon Carr).

In the fifties and sixties, "My First and Last Love" (Remus Harris and Marvin Fisher) found its melody in Rimsky-Korsakov's *Scheherazade*; "The Angels Sing" (Paul Francis Webster—Irving Aaronson) in Brahms' Fourth Symphony; "Tell Me You Love Me" (Sammy Kaye) in the aria, "Vesti la giubba" from Leoncavallo's opera *I Pagliacci*; "You" (Sunny Skylar—Morton Frank) and "Don't You Know" (Bobby Worth) in Musetta's waltz from Puccini's opera *La Bohème*; "Alone at Last" (Johnny Lehmann) in Tchaikovsky's Piano Concerto No. 1; "Wild Horses" (Johnny Burke) in the Robert Schuman piano piece, *Wild Horseman*; "No Other Love" (Bob Russell and Paul Weston) in Chopin's Etude in E major; "Here" (Dorcas Cochran—Harold Grant) in the aria "Caro nome" from Verdi's opera *Rigoletto*; "To Love Again" (Ned Washington—Morris Stoloff and George Sidney) in Chopin's Nocturne in E-flat major; "Hot Diggity" (Al Hoffman and Dick Manning), of which Perry Como made a hit record, in Chabrier's *España*; "Moonlight Love" (Mitchell Parish—Dominico Savino) in Debussy's *Clair de lune*; "Song Without End" (Ned Washington—Morris Stoloff and George W. Duning) in Liszt's "Un Sospiro"; "Surrender" (Doc Pomus and Mort Shuman) from the Italian art song, "Torna a Sorrento"; "It's Now or Never" (Aaron Schroeder and Wally Gold) in the Neapolitan song, "O Sole Mio"; and "This Day of Days" (Hy Gilbert) and "The Minute Waltz" (Lan O'Kun) from a Chopin etude and waltz respectively.

In the seventies, Bach's "Jesu Joy of Man's Desiring" was given rock treatment by a group called Apollo 100 on Mega Records, and the celebrated opening theme of Beethoven's Fifth Symphony earned a gold record for Walter Murphy and the Big Apple Band for "A Fifth of Beethoven" on a Private Stock release.

4

It is only a short step from lifting tunes from the musical classics, a safe and sometimes profitable venture if the music is in public domain, to lifting tunes from copyrighted sources, which at times can inflict penalties on the perpetrator.

During World War II—in 1944 to be specific—a song called "Rum and Coca-Cola" (Morey Amsterdam—Jeri Sullavan and Paul Baron) was introduced by Jeri Sullavan at the Versailles nightclub in New York, following which it was made into a best-selling record by the Andrews Sisters to become one of the hit songs of the year. Thereby hangs a dramatic tale involving an infringement of copyright, a story detailed in Louis Nizer's book, *My Life in Court*, in 1961. Mr. Nizer was the attorney for the plaintiff, Maurice Baron, the publisher of a music folio, *Calypso Songs of the West Indies*, by Massie Patterson and Lionel Belasco. In it appeared *"L'Année passée,"* a number Belasco had written as a boy in Trinidad in 1906. This was the melody the authors of "Rum and Coca-Cola" used in the mistaken belief that it was in public domain. Morey Amsterdam had heard the melody in Trinidad, had Paul Baron and Jeri Sullavan adapt it for the American market, and wrote some new English lyrics for it which he published in America together with the melody. The plagiarism suit instituted by Maurice Baron was a victory for the plaintiff, and remained one even after the defendants had appealed to the Circuit Court of Appeals. A settlement followed in which the plaintiff surrendered all his future property rights as well as all writer and publisher credit, in return for a substantial financial payment.

Plagiarism suits were an affliction of the popular music business long before 1944. In the early 1890s a publishing outfit in Chicago did a landslide business on its song sheets, which reprinted lyrics without bothering to get permission from the copyright owners. This outfit worked sub rosa; it did not even identify itself on its publications. Witmark was one of the publishers whose lyrics were being outrageously exploited without compensation. Deciding to do something about it, a Witmark executive called upon Sol Bloom, himself a onetime music publisher (and later a distinguished member of Congress) to study the situation. An astute and resourceful young man, Bloom went to Chicago and by means of some slick detective work, located the illicit publishers. He managed to convince them that he was the head of a combine ready to place an order for twenty-five thousand song sheets. When the printing job was done, Bloom had the sheriff seize the shipment. Damages to the publishers would have amounted to a dollar a song sheet, or twenty-five thousand dollars in all. But when the case came to trial, the expected did not take place. Isidore Witmark, who went to Chicago for the trial, tells the story in his autobiography: "The lawyer for the other side . . . was Arndt, a big, blustering fellow, leaning on a pair of crutches for effect . . . Arndt hobbled painfully on his crutches up and down before the jury box, immediately gaining the sympathy of the jurors. He made a speech as far distant from copyright as the North Pole is from the South, emphasizing all his points in farm language, talking more about straying cows than copyright (the jury was made up of farmers and small storekeepers) and managing somehow to put the shoe on the other foot. He ended his long harangue by accusing Sol Bloom of being the culprit! He told these men, in language they understood, that Sol had deliberately ordered the copies in a diabolical scheme to make an innocent man do wrong. The jury brought in a verdict for the defendant, and the judge even thought there might be a case of conspiracy against the plaintiff. The twenty-five thousand song sheets which were to bring to Sol Bloom's employers twenty-five thousand dollars or more were solemnly burned in the furnace of their office building. The Witmarks, to all intents and purposes, had violated their own copyright!" Actually the Witmarks profited in the end, since unauthorized song sheets disappeared.

Then there was the case of the composer who could have successfully contested a plagiarism suit instituted against her if she had been willing to confess that she, in turn, had borrowed her melody from an earlier song. The music that started this controversy was "Starlight" (Joe Young—Bernice Petkere). After its successful publication in 1931, an amateur California songwriter emerged with evidence (including a copyright stamp and a dated manuscript) of having written an unpublished song that resembled "Starlight" in details. During the ensuing court action, Sigmund Spaeth, the "tune detective," pointed out that there was no basis for this action by revealing that both songs had a common ancestor in "Violets" (Ellen Wright) which, published in 1900, was already in public domain. Indeed, "Violets" and the two later songs in question were just about identical. If Petkere were ready to concede that she had known "Violets" and had lifted its melody, the suit would have been dismissed. But Petkere was insistent that she had never heard the earlier number. By doing so, she lost her case and, on a decision by Judge Alfred Coxe, had to pay damages of ten thousand dollars.

Not cash but acknowledgment went as damages to a composer who proved decisively in court that he was the composer of "I Wonder Who's Kissing Her Now," the song long attributed to Joe E. Howard. Through the years, "I Wonder Who's Kissing Her Now," had been bringing Howard immense prestige and profits. Then the startling revelation emerged, after a bitterly contested legal battle, that Joe E. Howard had not written the ballad after all—it was the work of Harold Orlob.

In 1909, Orlob had been employed by Howard as an arranger. On this job he wrote the melody of "I Wonder Who's Kissing Her Now" (Will M. Hough and Frank R. Adams) to be used by Joe E. Howard in his Chicago production of the musical *The Prince of Tonight*. Because Orlob was a paid employe who had composed the melody as a job assignment, Howard regarded it as his property, lock, stock and barrel. He saw nothing wrong in using his own name as composer when Charles K. Harris published the song. In fact, this kind of appropriation was done so frequently then that Orlob did nothing about claiming authorship; he maintained silence during all the years that the song was selling millions of copies of sheet music and that Joe E. Howard was passing it off as his brainchild. But when the motion picture biography of Joe E. Howard was being released in 1947, Orlob sued to establish his rights as the author. He did not ask for any financial redress. A compromise was effected whereby Orlob was given collaboration status wtih Howard, in return for which Howard was not required to compensate him.

The proof was incontestable that the melody of Joseph H. Santly's hit song, "There's Yes Yes in Your Eyes" (Cliff Friend), published by Remick in 1924, was lifted from the earlier song, "Without You the World Doesn't Seem the Same," by an obscure composer named Wolf. Both melodies were alike. Nor could Santly maintain he had never heard the Wolf song since he had plugged it when he worked for the publisher George Head. Nevertheless, Judge Bondy gave the plaintiff modest damages of two hundred and fifty dollars, maintaining that the first published song had never made any money and that Remick deserved to profit from being able to market the second song so successfully.

A similar situation involved two other composers, Al Piantadosi and Cohalin. Cohalin had written "How Much I Really Cared," which he could prove had been performed publicly in the spring of 1914. Later the same year, Piantadosi composed his great hit, "I Didn't Raise My Boy to Be a Soldier," whose melody was so similar to that composed by Cohalin, that the latter sought redress in court. When it was shown that Piantadosi had worked for the publishing house that had issued "How Much I Really Cared," and therefore had access to it, the court ruled in favor of Cohalin.

The charge of plagiarism that Fred Fisher, the lyricist of "Dardanella" (Fred Fisher—Felix Bernard and Johnny S. Black) brought against Jerome Kern, composer of "Ka-lu-a" (Anne Caldwell) was somewhat more difficult to substantiate. Fisher, who was also the publisher of that song, sued on the grounds that the bass accompaniment, *not* the melody, was the same in both numbers; that, because the success of "Dardanella" had depended so greatly on its recurring bass rhythm, Kern's use of the same device in "Ka-lu-a" was an invasion of his private domain. Artur Bodanzky (conductor of the Metropolitan Opera), Leopold Stokowski (conductor of the Philadelphia Orchestra) and Victor Herbert all testified that this rhythmic concept was not original with Fisher. Realizing he had no case, Fisher offered to settle with Kern for a token payment—a suit of clothes. Infuriated that he had been accused of pilfering somebody else's musical ideas, Kern refused to accept the settlement. Judge Learned Hand ruled damages to Fisher of two hundred and fifty dollars, adding that the whole court action had been "a waste of time for everyone concerned." In all probability, the only reason Kern had to pay anything at all was that he proved so hostile and acrimonious on the witness stand that he had prejudiced the court against him.

When the blues began flooding the song market, Leo Feist sued Roger Graham, a minor competitor, maintaining that the "Livery Stable Blues" which Graham had published was stolen from the Feist publication, "The Barnyard Blues." He did not prove his case and consequently received no damages. But the suit is remembered for a remark made by one of the witnesses, supposedly a blues expert. The court wanted to know for its own information just what the blues were. The expert hardly clarified the issue with his answer: "Why, your Honor, the blues are the blues, that's what the blues are."

If we may once again look beyond the 1940s, we come upon a copyright infringement that brought what is believed to have been the largest damages ever awarded—in excess of half a million dollars. This happened when "Hello, Dolly!" (Jerry Herman), the title song of that phenomenally successful musical comedy (1964), was accused in court by Mack David and the Paramount-Famous Music Company of being an infringement of the copyright on David's song of 1948, "Sunflower," which had been popularized in 1949 by Russ Morgan and his orchestra in a Decca recording, and adopted as the state song of Kansas. There could be no question about the similarity of the two songs. In return for an enormous financial settlement out of court, Herman was allowed to retain the rights to it and the identification as its author. It would be absurd to suggest that Herman consciously stole David's song, since the more or less commonplace melody of "Hello, Dolly!" is something that a composer as gifted as Jerry Herman could produce effortlessly whenever he wished. One can only surmise that Jerry Herman had heard "Sunflower" in 1948 or 1949, and that the melody had sunk into his consciousness. When, almost twenty years later, he had to shape a melody to his lyrics for "Hello, Dolly!" the old melody surfaced without his having the slightest suspicion that it had been written by somebody else many years earlier.

27

The Swing Era
Becomes the Sing Era

1

The postwar boom was on, and the record business was thriving. In 1946, the first full year of peace, twice as many records were sold as in the previous year. For the remainder of the decade, the monthly sales figures averaged ten million disks. Most came from the big three (Columbia, Victor and Decca) but some also from companies grown successful in the latter half of the forties. One of these was Capitol which was organized late in 1942 by Johnny Mercer, Buddy De Sylva and a record store owner, Glenn Wallachs. Two other newcomers in the late 1940s were Mercury and MGM. Through the resources and efforts of these companies, large and small, million-disk sales became increasingly frequent. Where only twenty-six records had sold a million copies or more each in the 1930s, sixty-eight were million or more sellers between 1940 and 1945, and eighty-two from 1945 to 1950. Best-sellers averaged a five-hundred-thousand disk sale or more, and the numbers of these also swelled noticeably. These sales were translated into huge profits for all involved in the making and selling of records.

Carefully tabulated lists of best-sellers were compiled by trade journals and newspapers, with *Billboard* instituting its "Honor Roll of Hits" in 1945. The "top ten," or "top twenty" or "top forty" became not only a valuable barometer of the public's buying tastes in records but also in itself a potent spur to the sales of these records. Many disc jockeys now started the practice of building their programs from the entries on these lists, thereby making likely a longer presence and higher position of these successful records on those lists. Record buyers around the country were falling into the habit of going to the stores and asking for records not by title or performer but by their position on the best-selling tabulations.

The postwar economy was not the only reason the record market was expanding. Another lay in the remarkable improvements in sound reproduction. "High Fidelity" recordings were taking advantage of the advances made by the radio microphone, speaker and amplification in enhancing the quality and fidelity of reproduction.

On June 21, 1948, in New York City, the Columbia Broadcasting System, parent body of Columbia Records, demonstrated the long-playing microgroove recording, 33-1/3 revolutions per minute instead of 78. This made it possible to press twenty-three minutes of music on a single twelve-inch disk. A simple, inexpensive turntable could be purchased as an attachment to the regular phonograph capable of playing this new type of record. The cumbersome album of former days made up of single ten- or twelve-inch disks was now replaceable by a single long-playing record, an economy in storage space as well as in overall price. Victor countered this with an innovation of its own in microgroove recording: a seven-inch record playing at 45 revolutions a minute. While this did not offer more playing time than the older ten-inch disk it was a convenience in that it could easily be stored on an ordinary bookshelf.

Microgroove recordings brought further progress in the quality of sound as well as greater durability in the record itself, which had formerly been highly vulnerable to breakage, warping or surface damage.

The 45 r.p.m. seven-inch disk played a piece of music for four minutes, and as such was highly suitable for popular songs. The longer disk—33-1/3 r.p.m. either on a ten-inch or twelve-inch disk—was ideal for classical music, since it made possible the recording of a complete symphony, concerto or chamber music work on one disk. But popular music also found the 33-1/3 r.p.m. record useful for the collection—on the two sides of one twelve-inch record—of some eight to ten songs, a forty-minute recital by a popular singing artist. More valuable still, the 33-1/3 r.p.m. records now allowed the full score of a musical stage production to be pressed on a single disk. This opened up an entirely new area for record exploitation which performed no small role in the huge annual sales figures being compiled by the industry each passing year.

Probably the first attempt ever made to reproduce on a record music from the stage in a performance by members of the original cast took place in England, in 1920, when numbers from the London production of *Irene* were recorded by Edith Day and others. (After the successful revival of *Irene* on Broadway in 1973, this historic recording was repressed and rereleased by Monmouth-Evergreen.) In 1929, the original cast of the London production of Sigmund Romberg's *The New Moon*, starring Evelyn Laye, recorded selections from that operetta (once again revived and rereleased in 1973 by Monmouth-Evergreen). There probably were several more such recordings in London. In the United States, in 1931, Brunswick released a twelve-inch disk of hit songs from *George White's Scandals of 1931*, sung by Bing Crosby and the Boswell Sisters. The first album of top songs from a Broadway musical with the original cast came one year later, *Show Boat*, performed by Paul Robeson and Helen Morgan. Then, in 1937, Decca released an album of three twelve-inch records of some of the highlights of the original Theatre Guild presentation of the Gershwin folk opera, *Porgy and Bess*. A monumental forward stride in recording music from Broadway original-cast productions was made by Decca six years later when, for the first time, the entire score of a Broadway musical was recorded with the original cast, that of *Oklahoma!* It made up an album of six ten-inch 78 r.p.m. disks selling for five dollars, produced at a cost of twelve thousand dollars. In a year and a half, a half million albums were sold; in time one million albums were disposed of; and after the coming of the long-playing record, the matrix was transferred to a single 33-1/3 r.p.m. disk selling another million and a half copies. From

1943 on, major companies competed with each other in transferring Broadway musicals with or without original casts on disks. Columbia's release in 1949 of all the music from the Rodgers and Hammerstein classic, *South Pacific*, with its original performers, sold a million copies within a few years, about two and a quarter million copies by 1960, and almost three million by 1963. It reached the best-seller lists at once in 1949 and stayed there for 427 weeks.

The invention of magnetic tape, which followed the appearance of the long-playing record, became another electronic event of far-reaching consequence to the recording industry. The earlier method of recording on wax, or acetate, had been both costly and cumbersome, two deficits eliminated when it became possible to record on magnetic tape and transfer the recording to disks. But something more was gained beyond economy and practicability. Magnetic tape made possible editing, and the introduction of novel sounds and effects, which the record business was not slow to exploit.

"More than ever an inanimate object—a platter . . . is king of Tin Pan Alley," remarked Abel Green in *Variety*. "The popular music business seems to revolve almost entirely around the revolving biscuit."

The gauge of a song's success was now measured exclusively by the number of records it sold and on its place in the "top ten" lists. More than even the stage and motion pictures, records had the power to make songs into hits, and singers into stars. Many of the songs receiving a top spot on radio's "Your Hit Parade" between 1945 and 1949, inclusive, began that climb through best-selling records. In 1945 it was "Sentimental Journey" (Bud Green, Les Brown and Ben Homer) in the Columbia recording by Les Brown and his orchestra with vocal by Doris Day; "Till the End of Time" (Buddy Kaye—Ted Mossman), inspired by the motion picture biography of Chopin, *A Song to Remember* (1945), and based on Chopin's Polonaise in A-flat major, in Perry Como's recording for Victor; Cole Porter's "Don't Fence Me In" in the Decca recording by Bing Crosby and the Andrews Sisters. In 1946 it was "To Each His Own" (Jay Livingston and Ray Evans), written to publicize the picture of that name (1946), in a Decca recording by the Ink Spots, and in a Majestic recording by Eddy Howard; "Symphony" (Jack Lawrence—Alex Alstone) in a Victor recording by Freddy Martin and his orchestra; "Five Minutes More" (Sammy Cahn—Jule Styne) in Frank Sinatra's Columbia recording. In 1947 it was the revival of a 1913 hit, "Peg o' My Heart" (Alfred Bryan—Fred Fisher), by the Harmonicats for Mercury; "Mam'selle" (Mack Gordon—Edmund Goulding), from the motion picture *The Razor's Edge* (1947), in Art Lund's recording for MGM; the revival of a 1931 ballad, "That's My Desire" (Carroll Loveday—Helmy Kresa) by Frankie Laine for Mercury; "Ballerina" (Bob Russell—Carl Sigman) in a Victor recording by Vaughn Monroe and his band; "Nature Boy" (Eden Ahbez) in Nat King Cole's recording for Capitol. In 1948 it was "A Tree in the Meadow" (Billy Reid) in Margaret Whiting's recording for Capitol; "It's Magic" (Sammy Cahn—Jule Styne) from the motion picture *Romance on the High Seas* (1948), where it was nominated for an Academy Award, in a Columbia recording by Doris Day who had introduced it in the film; "Now Is the Hour" (Maewa Kaihan and Dorothy Stewart—Dorothy Stewart and Clement Scott) in Bing Crosby's recording for Decca; "On a Slow Boat to China" (Frank Loesser) in a recording by Kay Kyser and his orchestra for Columbia. In 1949 it was "Again" (Dorcas Cochran—Lionel Newman) from the motion picture *Road House* (1949) in Vic Damone's recording for Mercury; "Far Away Places" (Joan Whitney and Alex Kramer) in the Decca recording by Bing Crosby and the Ken Darby Choir; "Cruising Down the River" (Eily Beadell and Nell Tollerton) in the MGM recording by Blue Barron and his orchestra and the Decca release by Russ Morgan and his orchestra with the Skylarks; "You're Breaking My Heart" (Pat Genaro and Sunny Skylar), melody based on Leoncavallo's art song, "La Mattinata," in Vic Damone's recording for Mercury (then Vic Damone's theme song); "Dear Hearts and Gentle People" (Bob Hilliard—Sammy Fain) in Bing Crosby's recording for Decca and Dinah Shore's for Columbia; "Riders in the Sky" (Stan Jones) in Vaughn Monroe's recording for Victor; and "Mule Train" (Johnny Lange, Hy Heath and Fred Glickman), an Academy Award nominee in the motion picture of the same name (1950), in recordings by Frankie Laine for Mercury, Bing Crosby for Decca and Ernie Ford for Capitol.

These records helped make major hits out of new songs and old ones, unknown songs and forgotten songs, but occasionally they did something else, too. Some of these recordings became the stepping stones from obscurity to fame for their performing artists: for Doris Day, Perry Como, Frankie Laine and Vic Damone, for example. For Jay Livingston and Ray Evans, the recording of "To Each His Own" was the start of a successful songwriting career.

The history of "Rudolph the Red-Nosed Reindeer" (Johnny Marks)—one of the most successful popular songs ever written—also began with a recording. It was made by Gene Autry for Columbia in 1949, selling almost two million disks the first year, another million and a half the second, and over six million in all. Columbia never had a bigger seller than this one, and only Irving Berlin's "White Christmas" surpassed it in total record sales. Over one hundred and thirteen million records (thirty-three million abroad) in more than four hundred different versions of "Rudolph the Red-Nosed Reindeer" have passed over the counters through the years up through 1976; ninety different arrangements were made for every possible instrument, combination of instruments, or chorus; more than three and a half million copies of sheet music were sold; numerous tie-ins were made with toys and other commodities; for over a quarter of a century it has remained a perennial Yuletide favorite; and it was made into a color TV Special, starring Burl Ives, presented since 1964 as an annual feature by CBS. Johnny Marks got his inspiration for his song from a story by Robert L. May, written in 1939, and published that Christmas by Montgomery Ward and Company, where May was employed, with a distribution of several million copies.

The capability of the rotating disk to make songs into hits and singers into stars placed uncommon power in the hands of the director of popular artists and repertory (known in the trade as the "A and R director") of each recording company. He was, in the description of Goddard Lieberson, then president of Columbia Records, "a combination of musician, creative man, businessman with a flair for all these." He chose what song should be recorded and who was best suited to perform it. He was the discoverer of new songs and new performing talent. He devised new recording effects through overdubbing, splicing, doctoring of tapes and introduction of extra-musical sounds. He thought up new ideas for albums. He never hesitated to make changes in the music or the lyrics if he felt an improvement or greater salability would follow.

In the late 1940s and the 1950s, among the top A and R men were Mitch Miller, Mannie Sachs, Harry Meyerson, Bob York, Dave Krapalik, Don Costa, Milt Gabler, Charlie Green, Joe Carlton and Andy Wisnell. Mannie Sachs, at Victor, discovered Dinah Shore, Charley Spivack, Harry James, Les Brown and his band of renown. Mitch Miller at Columbia—he with the beard—was largely responsible for the early successes of Rosemary Clooney, Tony Bennett, Johnnie Ray, Johnny Mathis, Guy Mitchell, Doris Day, and Jo Stafford; for such hit songs as "Yellow Rose of Texas" (adapted by Don George) and the "River Kwai March" (Malcolm Arnold) in recordings with his own orchestra; and for introducing into popular music the esoteric sounds of a cracking bullwhip, a tinkling harpsichord, a barking dog and the sonorous tones of French horns.

Men such as these were the new rulers of the music business.

2

The best-selling record lists were monopolized by singers who had usurped the exalted place formerly held by the big bands. During the war, enlistments and conscription had depleted the personnel of every band with a consequent deterioration in the quality of performances; many bands had to close up shop altogether. Wartime restrictions limiting travel denied bands the public exposure that one-night stands and extended tours allowed, bringing about a sharp decline in their popularity. Further damage was inflicted in 1942 when the American Federation of Musicians, hungry for a slice of the profit pie, initiated a crippling strike against the record companies. For thirteen months, from August 1, 1942, to September 18, 1943, the recording field was forbidden territory for bands, creating an inevitable dissipation of their influence and popularity. Using vocal instead of instrumental accompaniments, some singers were able to fill the vacuum left by the disappearing big bands. Since no other popular records were available, these new vocal records found a ready and willing public. Dick Haymes, for example, cut four sides with the Song Spinners on June 3, 1943, and Frank Sinatra, also backed by voices instead of instruments, recorded "You'll Never Know" (Mack Gordon—Harry Warren) on June 7, 1943. Then, on November 11, 1944, the recording companies capitulated to the American Federation of Musicians, the agreement providing for the payment to the union of a royalty on each record, an annual sum of some two million dollars to be used for the benefit of unemployed members. The passage of the Taft-Hartley Act, however, made the renewal of this royalty agreement illegal, and the union was suddenly deprived of a source of welfare revenue. This loss motivated a new ban on the making of phonograph records and transcriptions of any kind by members of the American Federation of Musicians on January 1, 1947, when the contract with seven hundred and seventy-one recording companies expired. This time the recording companies were not caught napping. To meet this new crisis, the major record companies had spent the preceding six months on a feverish twenty-four-hour-a-day recording schedule to create a huge stockpile which more than sufficed to satisfy the market until a new compromise was finally arrived at fifteen months later.

Basically, the reason the public was turning away from bands to singers during the war was because a point of satiation had been reached. The public, seeking new diversions, grew weary of big band sounds and began to seek out a new form of musical entertainment. They found it in the more personalized, more intimate art of the singing stars who were beginning to usurp the limelight during the war years. As George T. Simon noted: During the war "the girls at home and the boys overseas or in camps were equally lonely, equally sentimental, and for the most part preferred to listen to Frank Sinatra crooning instead of Harry James blaring, or to Peggy Lee whispering instead of Gene Krupa banging the drums. The time was ripe for singers."

Indeed, the bands themselves were partially responsible for creating a public for singing stars. Originally, the big bands confined themselves to instrumental sound. Then some bands added a vocal trio. After that, a vocalist, sometimes male, sometimes female, often both, became indispensable; no band could afford to be without a singer. As the public began to manifest an increasing interest in vocalists, bands began to feature them more and more prominently until singers took over center stage of public attention and in the end almost supplanted the big band completely in public favor.

Almost all—but not quite—of the new singing stars who made best-selling records in the postwar years received their apprenticeship as vocalists with bands, a valuable and intensive training ground for their future careers as solo performers. Bing Crosby worked with Paul Whiteman and Gus Arnheim; Doris Day for Les Brown; Frank Sinatra for Harry James and Tommy Dorsey; Peggy Lee for Benny Goodman; Ella Fitzgerald for Chick Webb; Dinah Washington for Lionel Hampton; Mildred Bailey for Paul Whiteman and Red Norvo; Dick Haymes for Freddy Martin and Orrin Tucker; Perry Como for Ted Weems; Dinah Shore for Ben Bernie; Lena Horne for Charlie Barnet; Rosemary Clooney for Tony Pastor; Jo Stafford for Tommy Dorsey; Bea Wain for Larry Clinton; Billie Holiday for Count Basie and Artie Shaw; Sarah Vaughan for Billy Eckstine; Margaret Whiting for Freddie Slack; Billy Eckstine for Earl Hines; Pearl Bailey for Cootie Williams. Even Merv Griffin and Mike Douglas, both of whom became celebrated as talkmasters and performing vocalists on their syndicated television shows, started out as singers with big bands.

By the time the war was over, many of the big name bands of the thirties were out of existence. Eight of them disbanded later within a few weeks' time in 1946, including those of Benny Goodman, Harry James, Tommy Dorsey, Les Brown and Jack Teagarden. The Swing era had been displaced by the Sing era.

Some of the older singing stars, those whose reputations had already become solidly entrenched by 1940, were still top sellers on records. Bing Crosby was proving to be a seemingly inexhaustible gold mine for Decca, with an incredible sixteen records in the 1940s each selling a million copies or more. Al Jolson, restored to fame by his motion picture biography, *The Jolson Story* (1946), returned to the best-selling records lists in the latter part of the 1940s with a handful of his old song favorites, each enjoying a sale of a million disks or more. Gene Autry hit the million-disk sweepstakes with "Here Comes Santa Claus" (Gene Autry and Oakley Haldeman), "Peter Cottontail" (Steve Nelson and Jack Rollins) and, of course, "Rudolph the Red-Nosed Reindeer" (Johnny Marks). Kate Smith joined this august company with "Rose O'Day" (Al Lewis and Charles Tobias), Ella Fitzgerald with "Into Each Life Some Rain Must Fall" (Allan Roberts—Doris Fisher).

Most of the singing stars of the 1940s who piled up impressive record sales, however, were newcomers. Perry Como, in 1946, was the first popular singer ever to sell two million records each of two releases issued simultaneously: the Rodgers and Hammerstein ballad from *Carousel*, "If I Loved You" and the Chopin-derived ballad "Till the End of Time" (Buddy Kaye—Ted Mossman). *Variety* described him that year as "that maker of songs" but more appropriate still would have been the phrase "maker of hit records." Six more songs recorded by Como in the 1940s surpassed the million mark. Cool, detached, relaxed and quiet in his delivery he was equally at ease with novelty songs as with ballads, with numbers like "Dig You Later" or "A Hubba-Hubba-Hubba" (Harold Adamson—Jimmy McHugh) which he had introduced in the motion picture *Doll Face* (1945), or ballads like "Temptation" (Arthur Freed—Nacio Herb Brown), "Prisoner of Love" (Leo Robin—Russ Columbo and Clarence Gaskill) and "I'm Always Chasing Rainbows (Joseph McCarthy—Harry Carroll) all three successfully revived from past years.

Perry (originally Pierino) Como was born in 1913 in Canonsburg, Pennsylvania, where his father was a mill hand. From the time he was twelve, Perry worked as a barber, acquiring his own shop when he was sixteen after having finished high school. Since he had always had a sweet singing voice he was challenged by one of his friends to audition for Freddie Carlone's band. The audition was successful, and from 1934 to 1937 he toured with it in the Midwest. In 1937, Ted Weems signed him for his own band with which Como remained five years. In 1943, when Weems was drafted and his band broke up, Como returned to his hometown to resume his former occupation of barber. But before he reopened his shop, he was given a sustaining program on the local radio outlet of CBS. This, in turn, brought him engagements at the New York nightclubs, the Copacabana and the

Versailles, and after that at the Paramount and Strand theaters. In the summer of 1943 he signed a recording contract with Victor, his first release being "Goodbye Sue" (Lou Ricca, Jimmy Rule and Jules Loman) backed by "There'll Soon Be a Rainbow" (Henry Nemo and David Saxon). It sold well, as did "Lili Marlene" in 1944. This was a sentimental German marching song popular during World War II, appropriated by the British Eighth Army, and after that popularized in the United States by Marlene Dietrich. With the release of his two million-disk sellers in 1946, Perry Como was well on his way as one of the top recording artists in America, as well as a prime singing attraction on radio and in public appearances.

Best-selling records that sometimes reached, and sometimes surpassed, the million figure also became the solid base upon which Frankie Laine and Nat King Cole built their formidable singing careers.

Born Frank Paul Lo Vecchio in Chicago in 1913, Frankie Laine had his first singing experience as a boy member of a church choir, and his first taste of professionalism when, at fifteen, he performed at the Mary Garden Ballroom. While attending high school, he sang in small nightclubs in Chicago. While trying to further develop his career he supported himself by working as a machinist, car salesman and bouncer in a beer parlor. He was holding down a five-dollar-a-week job singing over WINS, a small radio station in New York, when he Anglicized his name to Frankie Laine. One evening, Hoagy Carmichael became so impressed with Laine's rendition of Carmichael's "Rockin' Chair" that he induced the owner of the Vine Street Club in Hollywood to hire Laine for seventy-five dollars a week. A few days after his first appearance there, Laine introduced on his program a distinctive and personalized arrangement of "That's My Desire" (Carroll Loveday—Helmy Kresa) with a belting, foot-stamping style that became Laine's trademark. An executive from Mercury Records heard him and signed him up for what became his first hit record, "We'll Be Together" (Frankie Laine and Carl Fischer), in 1945. Laine's recording of "That's My Desire" a year or so later, sold three hundred thousand disks and brought Laine a royalty check of $36,000. In swift succession came several more records, each selling a million disks or more, the most outstanding of which were "Mule Train" (Johnny Lange, Hy Heath and Fred Glickman), "The Cry of the Wild Goose" (Terry Gilkyson) and "That Lucky Old Sun" (Haven Gillespie—Beasley Smith).

Between the time Nat King Cole recorded his first best-seller, "Straighten Up and Fly Right" (Irving Mills—Nat King Cole) in 1944 and his death twenty-one years later, he is reputed to have sold fifty million records. As the most successful and highly esteemed male black performer of romantic songs, he was responsible for helping make Capitol Records a giant organization. By the time he died, Nat King Cole had joined Frank Sinatra, Bing Crosby and Perry Como as the foremost singing stars of their time and, like them, he had become a millionaire. But unlike Sinatra, Crosby and Como, Nat King Cole (despite his nightclub appearances and some motion pictures) owed his fame and fortune almost exclusively to records.

The son of a minister, he was named Nathaniel Adams Cole at the time of his birth in Montgomery, Alabama, in 1919. In Chicago, where his family moved when he was five, Nat received his first music instruction from his mother, after which he was given a thorough training at the piano. As a boy he played the piano in various combos, including one which he organized. Later, he was the pianist in the pit orchestra for the touring company of *Shuffle Along*. The company broke up in Los Angeles in 1937, and Nat King Cole went to work as a pianist in several small nightclubs. At one of these, the manager suggested he organize a small ensemble. He formed the King Cole Trio made up of guitar, string bass and piano. At this time he assumed the name of Nat King Cole—the idea of "king" given him one day when the manager placed a golden paper crown on his head and mockingly referred to him as "old King Cole." As an exclusively instrumental ensemble the trio found a following among jazz enthusiasts at Hollywood night spots, and after that in nightclubs elsewhere.

One evening while performing at the Swanee Inn in Los Angeles, Nat King Cole was prevailed upon, by an insistent inebriated patron, to sing a refrain of "Sweet Lorraine" (Mitchell Parish—Cliff Burwell). Though he had never sung publicly before, Cole complied. His performance was so well received that he was encouraged from time to time to do vocals with his group.

Not long after Capitol Records was founded, the Nat King Cole Trio was signed for recordings. The first was Cole's own song, "Straighten Up and Fly Right," which he had written, based on a sermon his father had once delivered. Released in November 1943, the record sold about half a million disks in its first year to become not only Nat King Cole's first solid hit record, but also the first successful release of the fledgling company. Cole had even greater success with his recordings of "The Christmas Song" (Mel Tormé and Robert Wells) and "Nature Boy" (Eden Ahbez) in 1946, from which time the trio assumed secondary importance to Nat King Cole's singing until Cole went it alone. In 1949, his recording of "Mona Lisa" (Jay Livingston and Ray Evans) boasted a sale of three million records.

Another black male singer of romantic ballads to make hit records in the 1940s was Billy Eckstine, "the fabulous Mr. B.," beginning in 1945 with "A Cottage for Sale" (Willard Robison—Larry Conley). Though Eckstine, who was born in Pittsburgh in 1914, had sung at a church bazaar when he was eleven, and had had some lessons on the piano and trumpet, he never received any instruction in singing. In Washington, D. C., to which his family moved, Eckstine distinguished himself in sports at Armstrong High School. The first indication he gave of a talent for singing came when he was seventeen and won first prize in an amateur contest in which he imitated Cab Calloway. Though for one summer after that Eckstine was a vocalist for a band led by Tommy Miles, sports remained his principal activity. He played football at St. Paul University in Lawrenceville on an athletic scholarship until he was forced to give up the game permanently after breaking his collarbone. Deciding to take up singing professionally, he appeared in several nightclubs in the East and Midwest until 1939 when he was engaged as a regular vocalist with Earl Hines and his band, where he remained four years. In 1943, at an engagement at the Onyx Club in New York, he started his career as a solo performer. He was temporarily deflected into another musical area in 1944 when he formed the remarkable Billy Eckstine Big Band, which created a considerable stir in jazz circles. Even while he was deeply engrossed in performances of modern jazz, Eckstine made two records in 1945 which made him a singing celebrity and demonstrated he was outgrowing eccentricities which had marred his performances with Earl Hines. They were "A Cottage for Sale" and "Prisoner of Love" (Leo Robin—Russ Columbo and Clarence Gaskill). After Billy Eckstine disbanded his jazz group in 1947, he once again went solo, developing his singing style and delivery and becoming one of the most successful popular singers of his time. "Everything I Have Is Yours" (Harold Adamson—Burton Lane) in 1947, with which Eckstine shifted to the MGM label, became his third record to achieve a million-disk sale. It was followed in 1948 by "Blue Moon" (Lorenz Hart—Richard Rodgers) and, in 1949, by "Caravan" (Irving Mills—Duke Ellington and Juan Tizol). Billy Eckstine's string of record successes spilled over into the first years of the fifties with "My Foolish Heart" (Ned Washington—Victor Young) and "I Apologize" (Al Hoffman, Al Goodhart and Ed Nelson). "His voice," writes Barry Ulanov, "is almost always a thing of beauty. . . . Because of its masculine strength, it moves from note to note with vigor and never falls into the whispering faint that makes listening to the swooners and crooners so disturbing. Because its master, Mr. B., is a natural musician . . . the voice is in tune and makes its cadences with musicianly effect, occasionally lengthening a melodic line beyond its written limits into a statement that has the quality as well as the quantity of a first-rate instrumental jazz solo."

3

Frank Sinatra's first best-selling record was "I'll Never Smile Again" (Ruth Lowe) in 1940, a Victor recording by Tommy Dorsey and his band with Sinatra doing the vocal. This was a rarity among big-band recordings in that the entire side was devoted to Sinatra's singing, a recognition on Tommy Dorsey's part not only of the singular talent of his vocalist but of the growing importance of singing in big-band music. This song, Sinatra's first step on his stairway to greatness as a popular singer, deserves some attention for its strange history. It had been publicized as its author's elegy for the death of her husband which took place only a few months after their marriage. But the discovery that an earlier recording by another artist of this song had been made before the death of Miss Lowe's husband put to permanent rest this sentimental yarn. The earlier recording had been a failure and the song remained in obscurity until Frank Sinatra recorded it with Tommy Dorsey, and later sang it with the Tommy Dorsey band in the motion picture *Las Vegas Nights* (1941).

Sinatra's first million-disk sale came in 1941 with "There Are Such Things" (Abel Baer and Stanley Adams—George W. Meyer), a song with strong optimistic overtones written to offset the gloom of America's first years in World War II. The impact of Sinatra's recording with the Tommy Dorsey orchestra, vocally supported by The Pied Pipers, was reflected in the song's standing on "Your Hit Parade," where it appeared for six consecutive weeks.

By the time his next million-disk record was released, "All or Nothing At All" (Jack Lawrence and Arthur Altman) Sinatra was well on his way toward becoming the most adulated singer of his generation. This record had been cut in 1939 when Sinatra was still an unrecognized and unappreciated vocalist with Harry James and his orchestra. It was a flop, and soon forgotten. Then, in 1942, when the American Federation of Musicians instituted their ban on recordings, the record companies were compelled to reissue old recordings to fill the vacuum. Mannie Sachs, Columbia's A and R man, decided to revive the old Harry James recording of "All or Nothing At All" in 1943, since Sinatra had by then become a sensational attraction. With the new label reading "Frank Sinatra" in large type, followed by Harry James and his orchestra in smaller letters (it had been the other way around in 1939) it went on to amass the largest sale Sinatra had thus far known, and the song became one of Sinatra's perennial favorites (he recorded it again in 1961 and 1966).

With no musical training, Sinatra had to depend entirely on his intuition, his listening, his native musical intelligence, his painstaking concern for detail and his capacity for hard work. His styling was molded by the influence of three popular musicians. The first was Bing Crosby, Sinatra's boyhood idol, whose casual, unostentatious and subdued manner, both vocally and physically dictated to Sinatra the singing stance he would adopt. From Tommy Dorsey, Sinatra learned how to sustain an eight or sixteen measure phrase seemingly without catching his breath, and how to produce a beautifully sculptured melodic arch. And from Billie Holiday, whom he always conceded to have had the greatest influence upon him, he learned how to communicate personally to his audience in his songs and how to emotionalize them. Everything else he developed himself, including his concern for the lyrics, how best to phrase them, how to inject effective pauses within the melodic structure and how to contrast textures.

Born in Hoboken, New Jersey, in 1915, Sinatra's academic schooling ended when he was sixteen and had completed his sophomore year at Demarest High School in Hoboken and spent a brief period in a business school. He sang well but had no musical instruction whatsoever. However, in March 1932, he heard his idol, Bing Crosby, in a personal appearance in Loew's Journal Square Theater in Jersey City. He left the theater vowing that he would become a professional singer, and from then on had no other direction or goal.

He appeared in two amateur contests, one in Jersey City where he won first prize, and the other in Manhattan. Then as the lead singer of a vocal group, The Hoboken Four, he appeared on the Major Bowes Amateur Hour in New York on September 8, 1935, emerging once again with the first prize. The group was then engaged by Major Bowes to appear with one of his traveling units. It broke up in Hollywood a few months later, after which Sinatra was on his own. Back in Hoboken, he found some engagements with a local club and sang frequently over small radio stations in New York and New Jersey. This led to an eighteen-month engagement at the Rustic Cabin, a roadhouse near Alpine, New Jersey, where he served as master of ceremonies, sang with a vocal trio, and sometimes even waited on tables. His salary was fifteen dollars a week, but this engagement brought a far richer compensation, a job as vocalist with Harry James and his orchestra. Harry James had heard Sinatra at the Rustic Cabin, liked the way he fashioned his lyrics, and signed him to a two-year contract for seventy-five dollars a week. Sinatra's first appearance with Harry James was at the Hippodrome Theater in Baltimore during the week of June 30, 1939, when, among other numbers, he sang "Wishing" (B. G. De Sylva), a song hit of 1939 and a nominee for an Academy Award, having been introduced by Irene Dunne in the motion picture *Love Affair* (1939). Two weeks later Sinatra cut his first records with the James orchestra. "All or Nothing At All" was recorded the following August 31. All these recordings went unnoticed.

The unhappy fact was that Harry James and his orchestra were not doing too well, not only on records but also in their public appearances, and though he was contractually bound, Sinatra realized he had to make a change. This change was effected by Tommy Dorsey, who had heard and been impressed by the recording of "All or Nothing At All," and who succeeded in hiring Sinatra away from Harry James.

Singing with Tommy Dorsey and his band, Sinatra evolved a singing style which emulated Dorsey's instrumental sound. It was not long before Sinatra's vocals became the talk of the Tommy Dorsey fans—in such songs as "South of the Border" (Jimmy Kennedy and Michael Carr) and "This Love of Mine" (Frank Sinatra—Sol Parker and Henry Sanicola). *Billboard* now remarked: "He's developing into a first-rate singer." Sinatra's best-selling records with Dorsey of "I'll Never Smile Again" (Ruth Lowe) and "Polka Dots and Moonbeams" (Johnny Burke—James Van Heusen) provided confirmation. Early in January 1942, a national poll conducted by *Down Beat* placed Sinatra as the top vocalist of 1941, displacing Bing Crosby who had occupied this position for four consecutive years between 1937 and 1940.

By 1942, Sinatra became convinced that the time had come for him to break loose not only from Dorsey but from all big bands and began solo singing. With Tommy Dorsey's grudging consent, he made some solo recordings of standards on the Bluebird label (a Victor subsidiary). Though none of these did well, Sinatra was firm in his decision to go on his own. With the tie cut, he made a few public appearances and was given a three-minute spot in a motion picture, *Reveille with Beverly* (1943). For a few months he seemed to be going nowhere. And then the explosion—or series of explosions—was let loose that raised him to the very top of his profession.

That first came without warning at the Mosque Theater in Newark, New Jersey, in November 1942. The audience was made up mostly of kids, and whenever he began a new number they began to squeal, scream and howl. Almost two months later, Sinatra was billed as an "extra added attraction" at the Paramount Theater in New York, on a live program starring Benny Goodman and his band and Peggy Lee. Sinatra created pandemonium among the younger set in the audience, so much so that Benny Goodman and Peggy Lee had to take a back seat. After they left the show to be replaced by minor and less glamorous attractions, Sinatra was kept on for eight weeks. The attendance kept growing, and with it the excitement in the theater. Many in the audience refused to leave when the complete show ended, staying on through repetitions of the feature film so that they could listen again to Sinatra. Extra ushers and guards were hired to keep matters under control when the mounting enthusiasm of the youngsters approached hysteria. "Not since the days of Rudolph Valentino," remarked *Time*, "has American womanhood made such unabashed love to an entertainer."

The third and most volcanic explosion took place once again at the Paramount Theater in New York beginning on Columbus Day of 1944. By then Sinatra had already made considerable progress toward becoming the best loved singer of his time. He had been made one of the leading singers of "Your Hit Parade" program, making his first broadcast on February 6, 1943. He had shifted from Victor to Columbia, becoming one of their leading solo vocalists and, in the ensuing decade, cut 281 songs, his earliest successes being "People Will Say We're in Love" (Oscar Hammerstein II—Richard Rodgers), "You'll Never Know" (Mack Gordon—Harry Warren), "Sunday, Monday, or Always" (Johnny Burke—James Van Heusen), and Irving Berlin's "White Christmas." He had signed a movie contract with RKO, his first starring role in *Higher and Higher* (1943) where he introduced "I Couldn't Sleep a Wink Last Night," an Academy Award nominee, "The Music Stopped" and "A Lovely Way to Spend an Evening," all by Jimmy McHugh with Harold Adamson's lyrics. This was followed by *Anchors Aweigh* (1944) which had an Academy Award nominee in "I Fall in Love Too Easily" (Sammy Cahn—Jule Styne). And he had completed a triumphant ten-week engagement at the Riobama nightclub in New York which, singlehandedly, he saved from bankruptcy. At one of his appearances there a woman fainted from the heat, and an ingenious publicist planted a story in the newspapers that Sinatra's ardent singing of a romantic ballad had brought this on. In the story the word "swoon" was used. Further publicity began to identify Sinatra as "the swooner" or as "Swoonlight Sinatra." He was also called "The Voice that Thrills," a phrase soon contracted into just "The Voice."

But all this, remarkable though it was, failed to provide a warning of the uproar at the Paramount Theater one October day in 1944. It began before dawn at 6:00 A.M. Though the wartime curfew of 9:00 P.M. was in effect for juveniles, almost a thousand girls were waiting on the queue outside the box office. Within an hour after that, the line stretched from Seventh Avenue halfway toward Eighth. The house was instantly filled to capacity after the box office opened at 8:30, filled with three thousand four hundred excitedly buzzing youngsters completely oblivious of the motion picture on the screen which they repeatedly interrupted with the cry: "We want Frankie!" When, finally, Sinatra appeared, the theater became bedlam. Sinatra pleaded with the youngsters to be quiet so that he could continue with his program, and only when he threatened to leave the stage did the din subside. But after each of his numbers, the quiet was shattered by screams, moans and swooning.

The next day was even more hectic. There were ten thousand youngsters extending three abreast from the box office; over twenty thousand more milled around the streets in the

Times Square area. When the box office opened, the booth was destroyed by the onrush, windows of nearby shops were smashed, passers-by near the theater were trampled upon and some girls fainted. Times Square became impassable both for pedestrians and vehicles. Four hundred and twenty-one policemen, two hundred detectives, seventy patrolmen, twenty patrol cars, and fifty traffic cars were among the forces summoned to maintain a semblance of order. Within the theater, fifty additional ushers were on duty. The more than three thousand in the audience, most of them young girls, remained glued to their places throughout the day and evening, expressing their delirium whenever Sinatra was on the stage, waving their undergarments at him, giving every indication of being under something akin to a hypnotic spell. And still these bobby-soxers did not have enough of him. After the last performance they waited for him in mobs outside the theater for a closer glimpse, perhaps a touch; his clothes were shredded into souvenir patches. They even bribed the cleaning woman in his hotel to be allowed, for one precious minute, to lie in his unmade bed.

The suspicion that all this had been manipulated by the skillful hand of George Evans, Sinatra's publicity man, refuses to die. It is more than possible that this altogether unprecedented display of mass infatuation had been the result of a carefully calculated press agent's maneuver. But one can ignite a fuse without much happening unless dynamite is present. The dynamite was Frank Sinatra himself, the way he looked, the way he crooned, the way he projected his deepest emotions, the way he created a personal relationship between himself and each of those aroused youngsters—wooing each separately with his sexy vocalizations. The war was at its height, and young girls were emotionally starved by the absence of young men. Sinatra released their emotions—with his lean and hungry look, hollow cheeks, frail figure and sunken blue eyes, he was very much the boy-next-door image whom a girl wanted to smother with love, sympathy and protection.

After that, in public appearances, on records, over the radio and in the movies he became one of the most potent salesman of songs popular music has known. He had his own radio program after leaving "Your Hit Parade"; the "Frank Sinatra Show" over CBS in 1943 sponsored by Max Factor, and from 1945 to 1947 "Songs by Sinatra," sponsored by Old Gold Cigarettes—his signature, "Put Your Dreams Away" (Ruth Lowe—Stephan Weiss and Paul Mann). He was largely responsible for making hits out of "Homesick—That's All" (Gordon Jenkins), "Day by Day" (Sammy Cahn—Alex Stordahl and Paul Weston), "The Coffee Song" (Bob Hilliard and Dick Miles), "Five Minutes More" (Sammy Cahn—Jule Styne), "The Things We Did Last Summer" (Sammy Cahn—Jule Styne) and "Full Moon and Empty Arms" (Buddy Kaye and Ted Mossman). For the rest of the 1940s he remained America's leading male vocalist. Then, in the early 1950s, his luck and his fortunes seemed to have run out. With his voice almost gone, and his popular appeal with it, he appeared doomed to total oblivion, only to win a new and stronger lease on success and popularity. His Academy Award-winning performance in the nonsinging role of Maggio in *From Here to Eternity* (1954) was the start of the most sensational comeback in show business history. "Since *Eternity*," noted *Variety*, "everybody wants Sinatra on TV." And not just television, but also nightclubs, movies and records—then on the Capitol label. The new heights he scaled made even the older ones seem like hills. He was now to occupy those heights permanently, to become one of the most powerful men in show business.

4

The distaff side was well represented in the swelling ranks of pop singers in the forties.

Doris Day—born Doris von Kappelhoff in Cincinnati, Ohio, in 1924—acquired her professional name from a song, "Day after Day" (Howard Dietz—Arthur Schwartz) with which she auditioned for Barney Rapp, a bandleader. When Rapp hired her as his vocalist, he suggested she change her Germanic name and she selected "Day" from the song that had brought her her first important singing job. She studied dancing with a view to making it a career. She won a five-hundred-dollar prize in a dance contest in Cincinnati, then was employed as a dancer by the Fanchon and Marco company. A serious automobile accident in Hamilton, Ohio, which hospitalized her for fourteen months, put an end to her dancing ambitions and turned her to singing. After taking some lessons, she found a nonpaying job with a small radio station in Cincinnati before auditioning for and being placed with Barney Rapp. She then sang with the Bob Crosby band, the Fred Waring orchestra and, for three years, with the Les Brown orchestra with which she achieved her first best-selling record, "Sentimental Journey," (Bud Green, Les Brown and Ben Homer) in 1945. This release sold a million disks, and she enjoyed two more such successes in the 1940s with "I Confess" (Bennie Benjamin—George Weiss) and "It's Magic" (Sammy Cahn—Jule Styne). As a top-ranking singer she appeared in several swank nightclubs, in one of which, the Little Club in New York, she was discovered by a Hollywood scout who put her into motion pictures. Her first films were *Romance on High Seas* (1948) where she introduced "It's Magic" (Sammy Cahn—Jule Styne), an Academy Award nominee, and *It's a Great Feeling* (1949) from which came the title song, another Academy Award nominee. But her greatest success on the screen came not in singing roles but in smart, sophisticated comedies or suspense dramas. In one of these, she introduced the hit song with which she henceforth became identified and which she used as her theme on television. It was "Whatever Will Be, Will Be" or "Que Sera, Sera" (Jay Livingston and Ray Evans), winner of the Academy Award in the Alfred Hitchcock production, *The Man Who Knew Too Much* (1955). Her recording of that song for Columbia proved to be another million-disk seller. In the early 1950s, Doris Day had two more records that sold a million or more disks. They were "A Guy Is a Guy" (Oscar Brand) and "Secret Love" (Paul Francis Webster—Sammy Fain), the last winning the Academy Award in the motion picture *Calamity Jane* (1953) starring Miss Day.

Dinah Shore also took her professional name from a song. As a Nashville, Tennessee, girl named Frances Rose Shore, born in 1917, she became Dinah Shore early in her singing career because of "Dinah" (Sam M. Lewis and Joe Young—Harry Akst). It is open to contention whether she became Dinah Shore because she had "Dinah" as her theme song when she appeared on a fifteen-minute radio program over WSM in Nashville, as some say, or because she auditioned with that song when she applied for a singing job with Martin Block over New York's radio station, WNEW. In any event, she had sung it often before she adopted it for her first name during her first radio appearances in New York. After six months with Martin Block (where she sometimes shared the microphone with another young and struggling artist, Frank Sinatra) she was hired by Leo Reisman, in January 1939, to appear with his orchestra at the Strand Theater in New York. Soon after that, she made her first recordings, as a vocalist with Xavier Cugat and his orchestra. Her radio appearances now assumed national scope with spots with Ben Bernie and his orchestra over NBC, the Chamber Music Society of Lower Basin Street and "Your Hit Parade." By 1940, two polls named her the most important "new star of radio." The way she sang "Yes, My Darling Daughter" (Jack Lawrence), adapted from a Ukrainian folk song, so appealed to Eddie Cantor that he engaged her for his prestigious network radio show with which she remained three years. This in turn brought her, in 1942, a coast-to-coast sponsored radio program. She now made her first records selling a million disks each: "Yes, My Darling Daughter," "Blues in the Night" (Johnny Mercer—Harold Arlen), an Academy Award nominee, and "Buttons and Bows" (Jay Livingston and Ray Evans). This was introduced by Bob Hope in the motion picture *The Paleface* (1948) where it received the Academy Award. Other of her highly successful recordings in the 1940s were "Shoo-Fly Pie and Apple Pan Dowdy" (Sammy Gallop—Guy Wood), Irving Berlin's "Doin' What Comes Natur'lly," "The Anniversary Song" (Al Jolson and Saul Chaplin), "Dear Hearts and Gentle People" (Bob Hilliard —Sammy Fain) and "Lavender Blue" (Larry Morey—Eliot Daniel), an Academy Award nominee adapted from an old English folk song which she introduced in the motion picture *So Dear to My Heart* (1948).

Margaret Whiting's first record to sell a million copies was "Moonlight in Vermont" (John Blackburn—Karl Suessdorf), which she recorded for Capitol in 1944 with Billy Butterfield's orchestra. As the daughter of the distinguished popular song composer, Richard A. Whiting, Margaret was born in Detroit, Michigan, in 1924, and raised in Hollywood where she came into personal contact with most of the screen's songwriting greats. One of them was Johnny Mercer, who had written many a song with her father and who invited her, when she was fourteen, to appear as a guest on his radio program. She did so well that Mercer kept her as a regular member of his show. Other radio appearances were with "Your Hit Parade," the Eddie Cantor show and "Club Fifteen." As a vocalist with Freddie Slack's band she had her first hit record in "Ain't That Just Like A Man?" (Don Raye—Gene de Paul) in 1943. When Johnny Mercer helped to form Capitol Records he signed up Margaret Whiting, a move that proved strategic and profitable for the young company. Her first record on the Capitol label was "My Ideal" (Leo Robin—Richard A. Whiting) which her father had written for Maurice Chevalier for the motion picture *Playboy of Paris* (1930). After "Moonlight in Vermont" placed her with the top female recording artists in 1944 she made many more best-selling disks.

By the time Peggy Lee graduated into her first million-record sale with "Why Don't You Do Right?" (Joe McCoy) in 1942, a song she had introduced in the motion picture *Stage Door Canteen* (1943) with Benny Goodman and his orchestra with whom she also made her recording, she had gone through an intensive schooling by serving as a vocalist for various bands. She knows well the value of such an experience, for she says: "I learned more about music from the men I worked with in bands than I've learned anywhere else; they taught me discipline and the value of rehearsing and even how to train." In a farm town in North Dakota, where she was born as Norma Dolores Engstrom in 1920, she began her singing career in early girlhood in the church choir, in the high-school glee club and with college bands. From this she progressed to a small nightclub in Hollywood, California, but her failure to get ahead compelled her to work for a living as a waitress and a carnival spieler. She soon got a job singing over WDAY, a radio station in Fargo, North Dakota, at which time, on the advice of the station's manager, she changed her name to Peggy Lee. With a new lease on her singing career she sang at hotels in Minneapolis and Palm Springs and with the bands of Sev Olsen and Will Osborne, all the while developing her distinctive singing style: a subdued intimate delivery. Benny Goodman became interested in her and engaged her as his regular vocalist in 1941. For two years she toured with Benny Goodman's orchestra in theaters, hotels, nightclubs, and on radio programs, and in 1942 she had her first giant record success. In 1944, she left Goodman to become a solo vocalist. At this time she signed a contract with Capitol Records, for whom she recorded "It's a Good Day" (Peggy Lee and Dave Barbour), "Golden Earrings' (Jay Livingston and Ray Evans—Victor Young) and "Mañana" (Peggy Lee and Dave Barbour), among many other hits. The Dave Barbour who collaborated with her in the writing of many of her songs was a guitarist in the Benny Goodman orchestra when he married Miss Lee in 1943.

In the forties, Sarah Vaughan and Dinah Washington belonged in the company of

Ella Fitzgerald as outstanding jazz singers. As Leonard Feather noted in his *Encyclopedia of Jazz*, Sarah Vaughan "brought to jazz an unprecedented combination of attractive characteristics: a rich, beautifully controlled tone and vibrato; an ear for the chord structure of songs, enabling her to change or inflect the melody as an instrumentalist might; a coy, sometimes archly naive quality alternating with a sense of great sophistication." Newark born in 1924, Miss Vaughan began studying music when she was seven, took lessons on the piano for eight years, and on the organ for two. While attending the public schools she played both instruments in school productions. In October 1942, when she was eighteen, she entered an amateur contest at the Apollo Theater in New York's Harlem, sang "Body and Soul" (Edward Heyman, Robert Sour and Frank Eyton—John Green) and walked off with the first prize of ten dollars and a week's engagement at the Apollo. Billy Eckstine, then a vocalist with Earl Hines, induced Hines to hire her as a singer. Her debut with the Hines band took place at the Apollo Theater in April 1943. The following year she was made a vocalist with the distinguished jazz ensemble assembled by Billy Eckstine. Dizzy Gillespie, the trumpeter of that band, brought a demonstration record of her singing to the attention of Leonard Feather, the distinguished jazz critic, who, in turn, used it to get her a recording date with a small outfit on New Year's Eve in 1944. She recorded four vocals for twenty dollars each, and after that continued to make more records for such small companies as Guild, Cotham and Crown, which made a profound impression on jazz enthusiasts. Between 1945 and 1946 she was the vocalist with John Kirby's band at the Copacabana nightclub in New York. She then made solo appearances in other nightclubs, including a six-month engagement at Café Society Downtown and appearances at the Onyx on 52nd Street. Among her most successful recordings, now for Musicraft, were "Body and Soul," "Don't Blame Me" (Dorothy Fields—Jimmy McHugh), "Tenderly" (Jack Lawrence—Walter Gross), "I Cover the Waterfront" (Edward Heyman—John Green), "It's Magic" (Sammy Cahn—Jule Styne) and, in the late 1950s, her greatest seller of all, "Broken-Hearted Melody" (Hal David —Sherman Edwards). On her fiftieth birthday she was extolled on the floor of the House of Representatives by the Honorable Thomas M. Rees, who said in part: "She is not merely a vocalist but a brilliant interpretative musician able to improvise, leave her audience breathless with her fantastic versatility, whether in person or via her many recordings."

Dinah Washington was born Ruth Jones in Tuscaloosa, Alabama, in 1924, and raised in Chicago where she became immersed in gospel music and played the piano for a church choir. As a popular singer, she won an amateur contest at the Regal Theater in Chicago when she was fifteen. Three years later she was working in the women's washroom at the Down Beat Room on Randolph Street in Chicago when its owner, Joe Sherman, gave her a chance to sing with one of the early evening groups. She did so well that she was kept on as a singer and, at Sherman's suggestion, changed her name from Ruth Jones to Dinah Washington—"Dinah" after Dinah Shore, then already one of the most popular female vocalists, and "Washington" after America's first President. Joe Glaser, the artist's manager, caught her act one evening and recommended her to Lionel Hampton. Between 1943 and 1946 she was the vocalist for Hampton's band, and in 1943 she made her first recordings. Leonard Feather, who produced her earliest records, said of her: "Her gutty, forthright blues style, combining jazz qualities with more than a hint of her religious singing background, was later applied to pop and standard tunes, which extended her renown beyond the rhythm and blues field." After 1946 she carved for herself an impressive career as a solo singer, a preeminent interpreter of rhythm and blues, both in public appearances and on Mercury Records. In the early 1950s she began recording pop tunes for the black market, before invading the popular field entirely. Her greatest recorded successes came after 1949, with two numbers recorded with Brook Benton—"Baby You've Got What It Takes" (Murray Stein and Clyde Otis) and "Rockin' Good Way" (Brook Benton, Clyde Otis and Luchi De Jesus); also with "Unforgettable" (Irving Gordon) and "What a Diff'rence a Day Makes" (Stanley Adams—Maria Grever). Both her art and her popularity were on the ascent when she died suddenly in 1967.

Mabel Mercer, who was born in England and achieved her first recognition in Paris as the songstress of the "lost generation" of the 1920s at such night spots as Bricktop's, became an integral part of the American popular song scene from the 1940s on. Since then she has been hailed as a "singer's singer," an artist of exquisite musical sensibilities, flawless diction, meticulous phrasing, a concern for the words of a song, and a capacity to transform songs into miniature dramas. An entire generation of American popular singers have been influenced by her. Margaret Whiting once confessed that after hearing Miss Mercer for the first time "my whole world of music singing changed." Frank Sinatra has been quoted as saying: "Mabel Mercer taught me everything I know." Nat King Cole, Peggy Lee, Johnny Mathis, Tony Bennett and Barbra Streisand are others whose artistic growth has been nurtured by Miss Mercer's art. "There is no one who cannot learn from her," said that exalted prima donna, Leontyne Price.

Many a popular composer has sought her out as an interpreter of their songs because of her empathy with their own artistic vision. "Let Me Love You" (Bart Howard), "Year after Year" (Bart Howard), "The End of a Love Affair" (Edward C. Redding) and "While We're Young" (Bill Engvick—Alec Wilder and Morty Palitz) are just four of the many songs written for her and which she has introduced. "Little Girl Blue" (Lorenz Hart—Richard Rodgers), "Hello, My Lover, Good-bye" (Edward Heyman—John Green), "My Resistance Is Low" (Harold Adamson—Hoagy Carmichael), "Remind Me" (Dorothy Fields—Jerome Kern), "Lucky to Be Me" (Betty Comden and Adolph Green—Leonard Bernstein), "Staying Young" (Bob Merrill) and "Mira" (Bob Merrill) are some of the numerous songs which she has revived to save them from an oblivion they did not deserve. "The ability to find precious gems lost in a quarry of abandoned rocks," wrote Rex Reed for *Stereo Review*, "is just one of Mabel's laudable attributes." And to the familiar standards of George Gershwin, Cole Porter and Harold Arlen, among others, she has continually brought a new dimension that has made them sound as fresh and new as if they had just been written. As Leonard Bernstein has said: "She is the eternal guardian of elegance in the world of popular song."

She was born in 1900 in Burton-on-Trent, in Staffordshire, England, and first became prominent in Paris in the 1920s where she was the darling of such American expatriates as Cole Porter, F. Scott Fitzgerald, Gertrude Stein and Ernest Hemingway. She left Europe in 1938 and received her first engagement that year at the Ruban Bleu in New York. The war years kept her in the Bahamas. Then, marrying Kelsey Pharr, a black American musician, in 1941, she came back to the United States which from then on remained her permanent home.

During the 1940s, she was the magnet drawing singers and composers to Tony's on 52nd Street where she appeared for a number of years. Other engagements not only in night spots but also in theaters in New York made her something of a cult, though it was not until March 1960 that she embarked on her first coast-to-coast tour. She has remained a cult ever since, a star in some of the most plush night spots in America. Her seventy-fifth birthday was celebrated with a swank party on the St. Regis Roof in New York on February 3, 1975, with some of America's foremost popular singers and songwriters attending. *Stereo Review* presented her with its first award of a Certificate of Merit for Significant Contributions to the Quality of American Musical Life. Atlantic Records released a boxed set, *A Tribute to Mabel*

Mercer on the Occasion of Her 75th Birthday, in which four of her albums of the 1950s (covering fifty-five songs) were reissued. Stanyon Records followed suit with *Mabel for Always*, a reissue of her Decca recordings during this same period. Reviewing these two albums, Rex Reed wrote: "Mabel Mercer is still reminding us of the beauty and wisdom there can be in popular music . . . Mabel Mercer is seventy-five years old. She will bury us."

28

The Sound of Jazz in the Forties

1

While the popularity of singing stars, together with prevailing conditions, pushed jazz into the shade in the 1940s, jazz was not in total eclipse. Passionate aficionados saw to it that the embers of what had been a fire a decade earlier were kept burning. *Esquire* kept interest in jazz alive by conducting an annual poll among jazz experts to determine the foremost representatives of every facet of jazz, and presented the winners in live concerts in New York. Milton Gabler, owner of the Commodore Music Shop on 42nd Street, the rendezvous of jazz performers and buffs, offered jam sessions at Jimmy Ryan's on 52nd Street for a number of years in which the foremost jazzmen of the time performed for appreciative audiences. These were the first commercial jazz concerts in New York, the immediate predecessors of the John Hammond jazz concerts at Carnegie Hall and the Eddie Condon—Ernie Anderson concerts at both Carnegie and Town Halls. The jam sessions at Jimmy Ryan's also were responsible for bringing jazz concerts to Los Angeles. When Norman Granz, a film editor at the MGM studios in Hollywood, heard one of Gabler's concerts during his visit to New York he decided to initiate a similar venture in Los Angeles. On July 2, 1944, he gave the first of his informal jazz evenings at the Philharmonic Auditorium, calling it "Jazz at the Philharmonic." A year later he took a group of jazz musicians on tour in the West and Canada.

Jazz was also kept alive in the forties by small record companies that promoted jazz music and jazz performers on such labels as Dial, Savoy, Guild, Bluenote, King, Okeh, Gotham and Crown.

Jazz was still being heard in many places and under various auspices, even though its popularity was on a decline with the general public. What is more, some new jazz bands were being formed, and one or two were successful. One was organized by Vaughn Monroe in 1940, even though well established jazz organizations were on the verge of dissolution, and managed to remain popular through the forties. Monroe had studied trumpet as a boy and, when thirteen, won a statewide trumpet contest in Milwaukee, Wisconsin. While attending the Carnegie Institute of Technology, which he entered in 1929, he continued playing the trumpet in dance bands. He quit college in 1932 to embrace music completely, joining Austin Wylie's band in Cleveland and, six months later, becoming a vocalist and trumpet player with Larry Funk's orchestra with which he remained three and a half years. In 1936, he joined Jack Marshard's orchestra which performed in New England, then fronted one of Marshard's units that commuted between Boston in the summers and Miami in the winters. He formed his own band in 1939, concentrating on sweet music. For lack of public support this group was dissolved, and in 1940 Monroe formed a new group with the intent of providing, as he explained, "the jump and rhythm that intrigue the millions of young music fans." By swinging sweet numbers he hit the right tone for the times, particularly among the young. In 1941, in a poll conducted by *Billboard* at 171 colleges and universities, the Vaughn Monroe orchestra was chosen the most popular jazz group in the country. Monroe now began getting frequent hearings in public places and over the radio, adopting "Racing with the Moon" (Vaughn Monroe and Pauline Pope—Johnny Watson) as his theme, as well as on records. In 1943, Monroe and his orchestra introduced "Something Sentimental" (Frank Ryerson, Irving Taylor and Vaughn Monroe). Among his successful recordings for Victor were "Are These Really Mine" (Sunny Skylar, David Saxon and Robert Cook), "The Story of Two Cigarettes" (Mickey Stoner, Fred Jay and Leonard K. Marker), "Passing Fancy" (Bob Hilliard and David Mann) and "Matinee" (Bob Russell—Carl Sigman). During these years Vaughn Monroe also distinguished himself as a solo vocalist, particularly in his recordings of "Let It Snow! Let It Snow! Let It Snow!" (Sammy Cahn—Jule Styne) and "Ballerina" (Bob Russell—Carl Sigman). It is as a vocalist that Vaughn Monroe is now best remembered, since this is the career he developed fruitfully after he quit leading his orchestra.

2

The greatest conglomeration of jazz bands and jazz players, and the most continuous outpouring of great jazz music in the 1940s, came out of 52nd Street, between Fifth and Sixth Avenues in New York, a place come to be known as "the street of Swing." The jazz fame of 52nd Street began in 1938 when Count Basie and his band appeared at the Famous Door, whose nightly capacity was overtaxed by jazz enthusiasts as well as jazz performers who came to enjoy the rhythmic vitality of Basie's performances and the originality of Basie's own swing instrumentals, in "One O'Clock Jump," "Jumpin' at the Woodside," and "Every Tub," the last written with Ed Durham.

Throughout the forties, jazz flourished on 52nd Street as in no other geographical area. Small combos were made up of some of the finest jazz artists available: small, because the war had depleted the supply of available musicians; small, too, because the electrification of instruments now enabled such small groups to produce large sounds. At the Onyx, the Famous Door, Jimmy Ryan's, Downbeat, Three Deuces, the Yacht Club and (one block further east on 52nd Street) Kelly's Stables there could be heard Coleman Hawkins, Erroll Garner, Dizzy Gillespie, Charlie "Bird" Parker, "Fats" Waller, Art Tatum, Louis Prima and his New Orleans gang, the Red Norvo sextet, the Nat King Cole Trio, Mildred Bailey, Ella Fitzgerald, Billie Holiday, Maxine Sullivan (swinging "Loch Lomond"), Sarah Vaughan,

Charlie Barnet and his band, Woody Herman and his "herd," Lester Young, Zutty Single-ton, "Mezz" Mezzrow and the Dorsey brothers.

A new jazz style winged its way out of the Onyx and the Three Deuces in 1944–1945, promoted by a small combo headed by Dizzy Gillespie on trumpet. This style was first called Rebop, then Bebop, then simply Bop. The name was coined from the nonsense syllables sung by Dizzy Gillespie to a triplet, the last two notes of which carried the sounds "Bu-dee daht" and "Bu-re-bop." The syllables "re-bop" stuck in the memory of those who heard Gillespie and they came to call the music he played Rebop. Others, inclined towards alliteration, preferred Bebop, and those who preferred condensations used merely the word Bop. But whether Rebop or Bebop or Bop, this new kind of jazz was a kind of whirlwind music avoiding a definitely articulated melody; where, despite the velocity, the notes were clearly articulated; where the accentuation usually fell on the upbeat; and where the harmony changed frequently, sometimes in a single measure. In the New York *Herald Tribune* of December 14, 1947, Rudi Blesh described Bebop as "fantastic music that produces a peculiar nervous excitement . . . deriving far more from manner than from matter. . . . Phrases in incoherently broken rhythms, successive and disparate instrumental solos are projected against short 'modern' chordal sequences. . . . Bebop offers no coherent development of idea. A capricious and neurotically rhapsodic sequence of effects for their own sake, it comes perilously close to complete nonsense as a musical expression." This music was often wedded to lyrics filled with double-talk and gibberish.

Lennie Tristano, the brilliant jazz pianist and composer, distinguished Bebop from Swing by saying: "Swing was hot, heavy and loud. Bebop is cool, light and soft. The former bumped and chugged along like a locomotive; this was known in some quarters as drive. The latter has a more subtle beat which becomes pronounced by implication. At this low volume level many interesting and complex accents may be introduced effectively. The phraseology is next in importance because every note is governed by the underlying beat. This was not true of Swing."

Dizzy Gillespie was the man who first made Bebop a vogue. Born in Cheraw, South Carolina, in 1917, he began studying the trombone when he was fourteen, and trumpet a year later. For a number of years he was a free-lance trumpet player with various jazz outfits until 1939 when he joined the Cab Calloway orchestra and became one of its shining lights. With the Earl Hines band, which he joined in 1943, he began developing some of those musical characteristics that were soon to identify Bebop, often supported in these innovations by Charlie Parker who played alto sax, "Little Benny" Harris who played the trumpet, and the band's vocalist, Billy Eckstine. When Billy Eckstine formed a remarkable jazz band of his own in June 1944, Gillespie and Parker were hired. Both of these men were now given further opportunities to experiment with their new style. Thus the bands of both Earl Hines and Billy Eckstine were the incubators of Bebop.

After appearing at the Onyx, Dizzy Gillespie formed a new jazz group that was heard at the Three Deuces. Bebop became entrenched as a major new jazz style with performances by Gillespie and his group of "Salt Peanuts" (Dizzy Gillespie—Kenny Clarke); a Bebop treatment by Tadd Dameron of Cole Porter's "What Is This Thing Called Love?" renamed "Hot House"; "Blue 'n Boogie" (Dizzy Gillespie and Frank Paparelli); and two compositions by Dizzy Gillespie without collaboration, "Groovin' High" and "Dizzy Atmosphere." All these were recorded for Guild by Gillespie and his Sextet. This music made not only Bebop but also Dizzy himself into something of a fetish. Gillespie's devotees affected his eccentric dress—beret, heavy spectacles, beard. As perhaps an inevitable consequence of this craze for Bop, many popular songs were written in the mid-forties in a Bebop style. Three of these were "Be-Baba-Luba" (Helen Humes), "Hey! Ba-Ba-Re-Bop" (Lionel Hampton and Curley Hamner) and "E-Bob-O-Lee-Bop" (Tina Dixon).

Gillespie's disciples and colleagues preached his gospel of Bebop. Thelonious Monk, one of the most innovative jazz pianists of his time, who had briefly played with Dizzy, went on to form his own Bebop combo in the mid-1940s. He made best-selling records of his own pieces "Well You Needn't," "Ruby, My Dear," "Blue Monk" and "In Walked Bud" in 1947 and 1948—pieces of such melodic and harmonic inventiveness that they have become jazz standards and led the jazz critic, Martin Williams, to speak of Monk as "the first major composer in jazz since Duke Ellington."

Earl "Bud" Powell was another exciting Bebop pianist, heard at the Three Deuces playing with "Fats" Navarro (trumpet) and at the Stable with Clark Monroe's combo. Powell also worked with Dizzy Gillespie. In 1945 he suffered the first of several nervous breakdowns and had to be confined to a mental institution.

The most important of Gillespie's followers, and one of the most influential jazzmen of all time, was Charlie "Bird" Parker. Miles Davis went so far as to say: "The history of jazz can be told in four words: Louis Armstrong and Charlie Parker." Nicknamed "Bird" (because he was fond of chicken, says his biographer Ross Russell) and "Yardbird" (because as a boy he used to hang around the yards and alleys outside night spots waiting for his favorite jazzmen to come out), Charlie Parker played the alto sax with Dizzy's combo at the Three Deuces where he soon formed a combo of his own that included Miles Davis at the trumpet. Parker was born in 1920 in Kansas City where his mother worked as a cleaning woman to support her family, since her husband had deserted her. With her meager savings she was able to buy her son a secondhand saxophone when he was thirteen. Two years later he was already playing in local bands and looked upon as a prodigy. Crazy about jazz, he would haunt the night spots and honky-tonks of Kansas City to listen to musicians he revered—Lester Young, Count Basie, Art Tatum, "Hot Lips" Page. When Jay McShann and his orchestra came to Kansas City in 1937 Parker joined it. In 1938 Parker was in Chicago where Budd Johnson heard him play for the first time and later recalled the circumstances: "Billy Eckstine and I were together in a little nightclub on 55th Street off Michigan Avenue. We had a sax player we called Goon. Bird had hoboed up from Kansas City, and he walked in and said to Goon, 'Mind if I give you a little rest on the alto?' Fine with Goon. He could go have a few drinks. Bird got up there and played so much horn Goon said, 'I'll never get this horn to sound right again.' So Goon gave him his horn."

Parker settled in New York about a year after that. His first experiment with a bop technique came at a chili house in Harlem in December 1939. This is how he tells about it: "I'd been bored with stereotyped changes that were being used all the time . . . and I kept thinking there's bound to be something else. I could hear it sometimes, but I couldn't play it. Well, that night I was working over "Cherokee" (Ray Noble) and, as I did, I found that by using the higher intervals of a chord as a melody line and back them with appropriately related changes, I could play the thing I'd hear. I came alive." His first Bop-style recording came in 1942, "Hootie Blues" (Jay McShann and Charlie Parker) which he recorded with Jay McShann and his orchestra for Decca.

In 1943, he played with the Earl Hines band, where he performed with Dizzy Gillespie; in 1944, with Dizzy, he moved over to join Billy Eckstine's band. His now remarkable gift for improvisation, his equally extraordinary rhythmic sense and his seemingly infallible intuition began to command attention and admiration. He further helped to develop Bebop, though his approach to it differed from Gillespie's. As John Malachi, the pianist in Eckstine's band, noted: "Whenever we'd jazz before or after an engagement, Diz would always ask me to call out the chord changes to a new tone so he'd know exactly where he was going. But Bird said, 'Just let me hear them. My fingers will fall into place.' " Parker was able to improvise fifteen, twenty and more choruses without repeating himself, often taking the top notes of a chord and using them as the starting point for further musical explorations.

Wrote Burt Korall in *The New York Times*, "Most important, Parker brought greater flexibility, freedom and subtlety to jazz rhythm, frequently suggesting a polyrhythmic expression."

After leaving Dizzy Gillespie, Parker formed his own group with which he recorded for Savoy his own "Driving from a Riff," an improvisation based on the chord progressions in the popular song, "How High the Moon" (Nancy Hamilton—Morgan Lewis). This was in 1945. A year later, with the Charlie Parker Septet, he recorded it under the title of "Ornithology" (Charlie Parker and Benny Harris) for Dial. For Dial he also recorded his celebrated "Yardbird Suite" in 1946, and for Savoy his "Now's the Time." His Savoy recordings of his own "Donna Lee" in 1947 and "Ah-Leu Cha" in 1948 were further demonstrations of his musical powers.

His addiction to heroin, from the age of fifteen, and his overindulgence in alcohol, food and sex proved physically and mentally corrosive. He had a nervous breakdown from which he recovered; then he tried to commit suicide. He was besieged by woes, not only as a black in an abusive and intolerant society, but also as a musician. Many of the jazzmen around him, refusing to accept growth or change, had no use for his kind of music making, and this hurt him. Other musicians freely lifted his musical inventions and profitably offered them as their own property. Once, when a fellow musician took him to task for his dependence on heroin, he replied bitterly: "Wait till everybody gets rich off your style and you don't have any bread and then lecture me about drugs." He ended up totally disintegrated, a man who spent many of his waking hours drugged or drunk; a man who heckled potential customers outside that palace of Bebop named Birdland in his honor; a man riding subway trains through the night. He died at the age of thirty-four, in 1955, of a heart attack, cirrhosis of the liver and pneumonia.

For a time he was forgotten by all save a few jazz buffs and those using his material for their own profit. But within two decades he was being remembered through his records which offered a complete documentation of his art, with his own Onyx recording, *Charlie Parker: His First Recordings* covering the years 1940, 1942 and 1945, released in 1974 and the recipient of a Grammy award in 1975; the Savoy recordings of 1944–1948; the Verve recordings of 1948 and 1954; in 1974, the Dial recordings of 1946–1947, a six-volume edition on the Spotlite label covering eighty-five versions of thirty-nine titles, and two volumes of "Supersax: Supersax Plays Bird" from Capitol.

His life was novelized in *The Sound* by Ross Russell who, in 1973, also published a biography, *Bird Lives*. The beat poet, Gregory Corso, eulogized him in a poignant poem, *Requiem for Bird Parker*. At the sixteenth annual Monterey Jazz Festival in California in 1973 each of the five concerts paid tribute to Parker, with one full evening designated as "Bird Night." On April 9, 1973, a concert in his honor was performed by his musical "heirs" (as they called themselves) at the Theater de Lys in New York. About two months later, the opening event of the ten-day Newport Jazz Festival in New York was "The Musical Life of Charlie Parker," an evening in which many of the jazzmen who had played with him at one time or another gathered in Carnegie Hall to pay him homage: Dizzy Gillespie, Billy Eckstine, Budd Johnson, Earl "Fatha" Hines, Jay McShann. And a birthday tribute to Charlie Parker was given on August 24, 1975, at Avery Fisher Hall at Lincoln Center.

The street was also alive with the sound of piano music: the extraordinary pianism of Art Tatum and Erroll Garner. Tatum, born in Toledo, Ohio, in 1910, began his musical training on the violin before turning to the piano. In his teen years he made his first piano appearance on a local radio amateur show which led to a job as staff pianist over WSPD in Toledo. There he initiated a fifteen-minute morning program that was picked up by NBC. Tatum made his first appearance in New York in 1932 as accompanist for singer Adelaide Hall. But it was not long before he set forth as a solo pianist, making his first recordings in the 1930s for Brunswick and Decca. His musical mentor was "Fats" Waller from whom, says Barry Ulanov, he borrowed "the left-hand pattern of alternating single notes and chords called 'stride' piano . . ." together with a touch that was "soft, sinuous and classically disciplined." To these he brought a prodigious and effortless technique (which earned the praises of such world-renowned virtuosos as Rachmaninoff and Horowitz) and a boundless gift for harmonic invention and variation. On 52nd Street, Tatum was heard at the Onyx and Downbeat, among other places. Almost blind, he continued to play the keyboard to the end of his days with nothing less than twenty-twenty musical vision. He died of uremic poisoning in 1956 at the age of forty-six. His recordings of W. C. Handy's "The St. Louis Blues," Harold Arlen's "Get Happy" (Ted Koehler), Arlen's "Stormy Weather" (Ted Koehler), "Body and Soul" (Edward Heyman, Robert Sour and Frank Eyton—John Green) and "Chloe" (Gus Kahn—Neil Moret) remain permanent reminders of a jazz keyboard art equalled by few and surpassed by none.

Though he was the son of a pianist—born in Pittsburgh in 1923—Erroll Garner never learned to read or write music. For this reason, when he was in his prime, he depended upon improvisation rather than formal training in renditions of popular-song favorites which he embellished with the most fanciful arabesques. Equipped with an extraordinary ear and retentive memory, Garner was able to play the piano well enough by the time he was seven to perform for his neighbors; when he was eleven he was already employed by Fate Marabale's riverboat band. Garner came to New York in 1944 and for a number of months played the piano at such places as the Rendezvous on St. Nicholas Avenue and the Melody Bar on Broadway without attracting attention. A frequent visitor to 52nd Street to listen to the Bebop of Dizzy Gillespie and Charlie Parker, Garner soon drifted into its musical orbit. He started his career on 52nd Street at Tondelayo's, after which he worked at the Three Deuces. While on 52nd Street, Garner wrote his first successful instrumental, "Play, Piano, Play." By the time he left 52nd Street in 1946, his reputation as a jazz pianist had been solidified. *Esquire* singled him out that year for its New Star Award and his LP, *Concerto by the Sea*, became a best-seller. "At a time when Bebop was just taking shape," Leonard Feather later wrote in an obituary statement, "altering the nature and direction of jazz, Erroll found a new avenue that was unrelated to it; a left hand that chugged away like a happy-go-lucky local train, while the right hand soared into those flurries of single notes with their delayed-action beat, or cascades of jubilant chords that seemed to tell you, 'Boy am I having a ball!' " Garner's best-known piece of music is "Misty," which started out as an instrumental in 1954, a best-seller in a Columbia recording by Garner and Mitch Miller's orchestra. With lyrics by Johnny Burke, "Misty" achieved a million-disk sale in Johnny Mathis' Columbia release. This song was the inspiration for the motion picture *Play Misty for Me* (1971). Erroll Garner continued to dominate the jazz scene up to the time of his death in 1977 through his recordings, his appearances on TV and in concert and through the music he wrote for motion pictures.

3

Woody Herman's "the band that plays the blues" was a fatality of the war years. Then, in

1944, he formed a new group which became known as "the first herd." The blues were now abandoned for a more progressive kind of jazz combining modern arrangements by Ralph Burns, in the manner of Duke Ellington, with a generous infusion of Bop. As long as it survived, which was not long, "the first herd" was the best new jazz band of the 1940s. Its brass section was second to none; it had an extraordinary rhythm section; and there were stunning solo performances by members of an ensemble that included Neal Hefti at the trumpet, Ralph Burns at the piano, and Woody Herman at the clarinet and alto sax. Some of the big instrumental numbers by this new Woody Herman band, all recorded for Columbia, were "Apple Honey" (Woody Herman), "Caledonia" (Fleecie Moore), "Your Father's Moustache" (Bill Harris and Woody Herman) and a "rhumba a la jazz" called "Bijou" (Ralph Burns). At the same time, fresh, novel and invigorating treatment was given to current pop songs: "Laura" (Johnny Mercer—David Raksin), the theme melody of the motion picture of the same name (1944); "I Wonder" (Cecil Gant and Raymond Leveen); and "Happiness Is Just A Thing Called Joe" (E. Y. Harburg—Harold Arlen), an Academy Award nominee introduced by Ethel Waters in the motion picture adaptation of *Cabin in the Sky* (1943).

In public appearances, in the movies, on records and over the radio the Woody Herman band became a major attraction at a time when big bands had to struggle for survival. It received top honors in polls conducted by *Esquire*, *Down Beat* and *Metronome*. It was sponsored over the air by Wildroot, the hair tonic, for whose programs Herman wrote another of the band's popular numbers, "Wildroot." Igor Stravinsky was so taken with Woody Herman's performances that he accepted a commission to write a new jazz work for the band. It was a three-movement work, *Ebony Concerto*, introduced by Woody Herman and his men, with Herman as solo clarinetist, in Carnegie Hall, New York, on March 25, 1946.

In December 1946 Woody Herman called it quits. He was tired, there had been sickness in his family, and he wanted to spend more time with his wife and daughters. There was consternation in jazz circles. "Only once before was a band of such unequivocal standards and evenness of musicianship organized," commented *Metronome* editorially. "That was the Ellington band. It still is, but Herman is not. . . . Woody Herman's magnificent band is dead. Requiescat in pace."

This panegyric was premature. Restive in retirement, unhappy with his effort to keep himself professionally occupied as a disc jockey, Herman formed a "second herd" in 1947 which remained in top form until its demise two years later. Then there was a "third herd" in 1951 which toured Europe and South America. The recession of the late 1950s doomed this one, but a "fourth herd" emerged in the early 1960s, and other herds after that. Woody Herman has faithfully kept alive the big band tradition through his appearances in Europe and America and in his recordings, two of which, *Giant Steps* and *Thundering Herd*, captured the Grammy award as the best jazz LP by a big band in 1973 and 1975 respectively. In the words of *Time*, Herman's performances have retained "a near symphonic fusion of rock and toe-tapping, old-gold sound that was a trademark of his earlier bands."

On November 20, 1976, Woody Herman celebrated his fortieth anniversary as a bandleader at Carnegie Hall with an aggregate of musicians described as "the ultimate herd."

4

The progressive approach to jazz—emphasizing arrangements in which the harmonic, rhythmic and idiomatic resources of serious modern music are combined with a flavoring of Bop, and in which stress is placed on improvised solo work—was advocated by all of

Herman's "herds." It was also the gospel according to Stan Kenton and his band in 1944.

The boyhood ambition of Stan Kenton, who was born in Wichita, Kansas, in 1912, was to become a baseball player, but his mother wanted him to be a pianist. Hearing two of his cousins, trained musicians, play jazz made the boy a convert to music. After studying piano with his mother and organ with a local musician, Kenton played the piano publicly, first in high school, and then in 1934 for Everett Hoagland whose band was performing at the Rendezvous Ballroom at Balboa Beach, California, for whom Kenton also prepared arrangements. Kenton worked with several other bands before forming one of his own, a fourteen-piece outfit, which appeared at the Rendezvous Ballroom in Balboa in June 6, 1941. Kenton's novel arrangements, with their strong syncopations and unusual chord structures, made professional musicians sit up and take notice. The band stayed on at the Rendezvous the whole summer, with many of its performances relayed over the air as the "Balboa Bandwagon" over KHJ. Then it was even more successful at the Palladium in Hollywood. In 1942, Kenton and his band came East, appearing at the Roseland Ballroom in New York City. It was a case of the wrong place for the wrong music, and Kenton's attempts to be commercial were nothing short of disaster. What had been intended as an eight-week engagement lasted just eight days. At this point Kenton realized that "my style had become antiquated. There was nothing really new, no new sounds, just a lot of rhythmic accenting. . . . That's what was wrong with my band. It was much too stiff, I have learned, I have felt that music . . . is a natural pulsating sound."

The new Kenton could first be heard in the recordings he made for Capitol on November 19, 1943, of "Do Nothin' Till You Hear from Me" (Bob Russell—Duke Ellington), a best-seller, and "Artistry in Rhythm" (Stan Kenton) which became the theme music for Kenton's band and which was highlighted by the remarkable work of Shelley Manne at the drums. The Kenton style was further developed in 1945 with a Duke Ellington specialty, "Just A-Sittin' and A-Rockin' " (Lee Gaines—Billy Strayhorn and Duke Ellington), with "Are You Living Old Man" (Redd Evans, Irene Higginbotham and Abner Silver), and with "And Her Tears Flowed Like Wine" (Joe Greene—Stan Kenton and Charles Lawrence).

Though he was becoming increasingly experimental, Stan Kenton and his band were gaining acceptance. In January 1946, *Look* selected Kenton's as the band of the year, and a year later *Metronome* and *Down Beat* followed suit. Engagements at the Sherman Hotel in Chicago, at the Pennsylvania Hotel and the Paramount Theater in New York City were enormously successful. "The Artistry in Rhythm Band," as the Kenton group was sometimes identified, was dissolved in 1947, even though it was still very much in demand. It broke up because Kenton's exhaustion brought him to the brink of a nervous breakdown. He had given too much of himself to his music making, at the expense of his physical resources and the well-being of his family.

But he could not stay away from music permanently. He fronted various groups, enlisting the brilliant arrangements of Pete Rugolo and Gerry Mulligan. He began to explore the world of ultramodern serious music and sought out a common ground on which it and jazz could stand. The influence of Stravinsky, Bartók and Debussy prevailed, with the use of such then advanced idioms for jazz as the whole-tone scale, unresolved discords, polytonality and polyrhythms. Kenton was now the "king of progressive jazz," his jazz filled, as a critic for *Variety* noted, "with dissonant and atonal chords, barrels of percussion and blaring, but tremendously precise brass."

Once again Stan Kenton and his new music met with the approbation of critics and audiences and once again, on December 17, 1948, he decided he was through. "We're nervous, sick, unhappy," he explained at the time, "and our music is going to become all of those things too if we don't watch out." For a time he planned to become a psychiatrist but by January 1950 he was back in music, at the head of a third Kenton orchestra which took on the description of "Innovations in Modern Music." It was a thirty-eight man ensemble, including traditionally non-jazz instruments such as violins, violas, horns, tuba, English horn, oboe and bassoon. "A certain link with the past was retained by rearranging the old hits," wrote Robert T. Jones, "but emphasis was placed on elaborate new compositions and arrangements, often with a Latin beat. The brilliant results could be heard in the recordings of Neal Hefti's 'In Veradero,' with its flashing brass and rich strings trading sequences over a brisk samba beat, or in the guitar-haunted 'Amazonia,' by the Brazilian composer, Laurindo Almeida." "Innovations in Modern Music" finally collapsed. Kenton poured almost a quarter of a million dollars into it before he admitted defeat and once again his men scattered. After that, Kenton periodically fronted small combos, but his principal accomplishments in jazz were finished.

A more relaxed and dreamy kind of jazz music came into existence in the closing forties, probably as a reaction to bop. Still concerned with advanced harmonic and rhythmic writing, this new music was baptized "Cool jazz," and its major practitioners included Lester Young, tenor saxophonist, Miles Davis, trumpet and Leonard Joseph Tristano, pianist. In "cool jazz" big, rich full tones gave way to lighter subdued ones; dotted eighth and sixteenth note passages were replaced by legato ones with even eighth notes. The cool musician lagged along with the beat rather than pushing ahead of it or being right on top of it. This cool style was first detected in Lester Young's first recording of "Oh, Lady Be Good!" (Ira Gershwin—George Gershwin), which he made with a quintet from Count Basie's band for Columbia in October 1936. Young left Basie in 1940 to form a combo of his own which played at Kelly's Stables on 52nd Street in 1941, at Café Society, and on tour with Norman Granz's Jazz at the Philharmonic. He was the winner of the *Esquire* awards in 1945 and 1947, and came out on top in the *Downbeat* poll in 1944.

"Lenny" Tristano, blind from his nineteenth year after a bout of influenza, had studied at the American Conservatory in Chicago where he received his Bachelor of Music degree and fulfilled the requirements for a Masters degree in music. He played the piano in Chicago saloons from his twelfth year. He came to New York in 1946, appearing with various combos which he organized. One of these made records for Keynote in 1947. Another, a group that included Lee Konitz, Warne Marsh and Billy Bauer, made records for Capitol in 1949, the first being Tristano's own "Intuition." In these records, as well as in his public appearances, Tristano carried out his ideas on extending the harmonic boundaries of improvisation while developing a cool jazz style.

29

The Folksinger and the Folk Song Enter the Mainstream of Popular Music

1

In the 1940s, folk music and the folksinger outgrew the comparatively limited appeal which it had attained a decade earlier. Its popularity and influence began to spread. The National Folk Festival, which had been organized in St. Louis in the early 1930s, spread out geographically to Washington, D. C., in 1942, New York City in 1943 and Cleveland in 1947, a several day event of performances of instrumental folk music and folk dances by professionals and amateurs before music-loving audiences numbering in the thousands. (In 1959, this festival acquired permanent headquarters in Washington, D. C., as the National Folk Festival Association Incorporated.) At another folk music festival, held in Seattle, Washington, in 1941, the word "hootenanny" was coined as a synonym for folk jam sessions. Hootenannies (as well as individual folk concerts) were conducted among labor groups, in colleges and other educational institutions, in summer camps, nightclubs and smoky Greenwich Village basements. In the mid-1940s, hootenannies were run in New York City to raise money to found and publish *People's Song*, the first magazine devoted exclusively to folk music. A few years later, cognizant of the fact that folk music had become a commercial commodity, the magazine formed People's Artists, a booking agency for folksingers with branches in principal American cities.

Folksingers and folk music expanded across the country. Motion pictures offered cowboy and western songs with increasing frequency. Broadway, in 1944, became the scene for the Theatre Guild's musical production of *Sing Out, Sweet Land*, whose music was made up entirely of folk songs. Intimate boîtes and night spots everywhere were featuring folksingers on their programs. Folk songs and folksingers were getting plentiful representation on the lists of large and small record companies, and for the first time some of these were becoming best-sellers, even million-disk sellers. And folk music was getting a hearing regularly over the radio airwaves. From the Ryman Auditorium at Nashville, Tennessee, NBC was carrying a segment of performances of the Grand Ole Opry every Saturday night. In 1947, KRLD, Dallas, began each week to funnel the "Big D Jamboree" on Saturday nights through CBS. CBS also presented on Saturday evenings, the "Old Dominion Barn Dance," beginning in 1946, emanating from WRVA, Richmond, Virginia. "Louisiana Hayride" broadcast weekly from KWKH, in Shreveport, Louisiana, beginning with 1948, was heard throughout the South and Southwest, its programs giving first exposure to such renowned country singers as Hank Williams, Jim Reeves and Elvis Presley. Over ABC, Tom Glazer was heard in "Tom Glazer's Ballad Box," from 1945 to 1947; Josh White had his own regular program over WNEW, New York; Oscar Brand was made coordinator of folk music for WNYC, New York in 1945, where each Sunday evening he presented his "Folksong Festival"; Susan Reed was a frequent guest on NBC network shows.

2

As a larger and larger segment of the American public responded enthusiastically to folk music, more and more folksingers became household names. Burl Ives, Woody Guthrie and Josh White, of the thirties, greatly extended their concertizing in the 1940s outside the partisan left-wing movement, reaching to and winning the general music-loving public, and particularly the young. But in the expanding vogue of folk music in the forties other folksingers came to prominence. The most distinguished were Pete Seeger, Oscar Brand and Susan Reed.

Pete Seeger had strong leftist and socially-conscious convictions which he espoused openly and courageously. This made him a favorite of the left-wing movement and brought him into conflict with the House Un-American Activities Committee in 1955 after which he was indicted on ten counts of contempt of Congress (but dismissed by the United States Court of Appeals in 1962) and for a number of years was blacklisted on television stations. Nevertheless, Pete Seeger's popularity and importance far transcended the political and social scene. Most of those who came to hear him in night spots and the concert hall, or who bought his records, were far more concerned with his music making than with his politics. More than any other folksinger of the 1940s, with the possible exception of Burl Ives, Seeger was responsible for creating a huge audience for folksingers and folk songs.

His ancestral roots reached back to the colonial settlers of New England three centuries ago, most of whom had lived in New England and Pennsylvania as teachers, artists, physicians or businessmen, and also as religious dissenters, abolitionists and Revolutionary War heroes. He was born in New York City in 1919 to a musical family. His father, Charles Seeger, was a distinguished composer, musicologist and professor of music; his mother, a violinist and music teacher. His stepmother, Ruth Crawford Seeger, was also a composer and musicologist of national renown while his half-brother, Mike, and his half-sisters, Peggy and Penny, were all three professional folksingers.

The Seeger family was steeped in classical music and so was Pete during his boyhood. He attended private academic schools where he revealed a talent for drawing and writing. When he was sixteen, his father took him to a folk music festival in Asheville, North Carolina. This was his first significant contact with American folk music and the experience changed his life. For about two years he attended Harvard College as a sociology major. Then, in 1938, he abruptly left school for good. He traveled all over the United States, either hitchhiking or riding the rods, gathering folk songs and, during these Depression years, singing them in migrant camps, hobo colonies and saloons. During these travels he met and became a friend of Woody Guthrie, Leadbelly, John A. Lomax and Earl Robinson, all of whom encouraged him in his folksinging and folk music collecting. He went with Lomax on field trips to record folk songs of outlying areas, and together with Woody Guthrie and Leadbelly he appeared on Lomax's radio program over CBS.

In 1940, with Woody Guthrie, Millard Lampell and Lee Hays, Seeger helped to found the Almanac Singers with which he concertized throughout the United States in performances of folk music, labor and prounion songs, and socially-conscious songs mainly at union halls, migrant camps, antifascist rallies and labor conventions. Then, between 1942 and 1945, he served in the Special Services division of the United States Army, entertaining American troops both in the United States and in the Pacific. Following his separation from the service, Seeger helped to form, and became director of, People's Song, Inc., a union of songwriters and a clearing house for folk music. It grew into an organization numbering three thousand, among whom were found the most prominent folksingers of the time, arranged regularly scheduled hootenannies, promoted folk song literature and served as an agency for its distribution among interested organizations. It published a monthly magazine, *People's Song*, which was the predecessor of the folk music magazine, *Sing Out*, which Seeger founded in 1951 and has since edited, and which celebrated its twenty-fifth anniversary with a concert at Town Hall, New York, February 7, 1976.

His real fame with the general music public started in 1949 when, with Lee Hays, Ronnie Gilbert and Fred Hellerman, he organized The Weavers, a vocal and instrumental folk group that made its debut at the Village Vanguard in New York, in 1949. It was an immediate success and was in great demand for nightclubs, concert halls, theaters, colleges, recordings and radio, giving the folk music trend of the late 1940s further momentum. Its first million-disk record sale was "Good Night, Irene" (Huddie Ledbetter and John Lomax) for Decca in 1950. It was immediately followed by other giant record successes: "On Top of Old Smokey" (arranged by Pete Seeger), "So Long, It's Been Good to Know Yuh" (Woody Guthrie) and "Kisses Sweeter than Wine" (The Weavers and Huddie Ledbetter). All became hit songs. By the time The Weavers disbanded in 1952 (temporarily as it turned out) it had sold over five million disks.

With The Weavers breaking up, Pete Seeger continued to concertize throughout the United States, including a series of six programs entitled "American Folk Music and Its Origin" at the Institute of Arts and Sciences at Columbia University. He made recordings of forty and more albums for Folkways and Columbia Records, and appeared at major folk festivals, among them the Newport, Rhode Island, Festival which he had helped to organize. In 1963, he went on a world tour. Two song hits of the early 1960s were by Seeger, and both were grounded in folk music traditions. They were "Where Have All the Flowers Gone?" (inspired by a passage in Mikhail Sholokhov's novel, *And Quiet Flows the Don*, with additional verses by Jod Hickerson), recorded by the Kingston Trio for Capitol and by Johnny Rivers for Imperial and "If I Had a Hammer" (written with Lee Hays) made into best-selling records by Peter, Paul and Mary for Warner Brothers and Trini Lopez for Reprise.

Oscar Brand (whose book, *The Ballad Mongers*, offers a rich fund of information about the folk music renaissance of the 1940s and 1950s) was a Canadian, born near Winnipeg in 1920, who came to the United States when he was seven, settling first in Minneapolis, then Chicago, and finally New York. From his grandparents and parents, all of them singers, he inherited a love for music which was further developed by listening to records and the radio. He attended the public schools in Brooklyn, New York. Upon graduating from Erasmus Hall High School in 1937 he spent several years hoboing around the country, picking up farm jobs as he went, and at the same time collecting folk songs and learning to sing them to his banjo accompaniment. He came back to Brooklyn for additional schooling at Brooklyn College where he became active in dramatic productions and where he graduated in 1942 with a degree in abnormal psychology. Late in 1942 he was called into military service, eventually becoming section chief of a psychology unit. After his discharge in 1945, he took permanent root in New York City with the intention of becoming a professional folksinger. Late that year he was made coordinator of folk music at New York City's municipal radio station, WNYC, launching a program of his own on Sunday evenings, "Folksong Festival" that stayed on the air for many years and offered programs of folk music both in live performances and on records. His now rapidly growing reputation as a folksinger brought him engagements at concerts and intimate nightclubs throughout the United States, in guest appearances on major radio programs, and at folk festivals. He recorded over fifty albums for various companies including Decca, Folkways, ABC-Paramount and Riverside. His own song, "A Guy Is a Guy" became a best-seller on records in 1952 in Doris Day's Columbia recording and achieved a top place on "Your Hit Parade." This song was Brand's adaptation of an old bawdy ballad that became popular during World War II as "A Gob Is a Slob."

Susan Reed was the daughter of a distinguished actor, playwright and director, Daniel Reed, who was an aficionado of folk music and who often had as houseguests famous folksingers and folklorists, including Carl Sandburg and Huddie Ledbetter. Born in Columbia, South Carolina, in 1927, Susan spent most of her early girlhood and youth traveling around the country with her parents. By the early 1940s the Reed family was settled in New York. There Susan, who had proved her musical capabilities from childhood on, sang in a church choir and, during the war years, entertained wounded servicemen in hospitals. She began her professional career as a folksinger in earnest with a successful appearance at Café Society Uptown, in New York, in 1944, following this with performances in concert halls and nightclubs, appearances over radio and on television, and with a long list of folksong LPs in Victor, Elektra and Columbia recordings. Together with American folk music her repertory embraced ballads from foreign lands, accompanied by herself on the zither and the Irish harp.

Others were also tapping the rich vein of foreign folk music for American audiences. Josef Marais was a South African who came to the United States in 1939. Throughout the forties he appeared with a Dutch girl, Rosa Lily Odette Baruch, whom he married in 1947, and, billed as Marais and Miranda, they familiarized Americans with the haunting songs of the African Veld. Richard Dyer-Bennett, an English-born minstrel, became an American citizen in 1935. During the forties he was heard in nightclubs, concert halls, over the airwaves and on commercial recordings in English ballads, as well as the folk songs of other lands, initially strumming on a lute, and later on a Spanish guitar.

3

Through this widespread interest in folk music in the forties, the tributaries of folk songs, foreign as well as American, flowed into the mainstream of American popular music.

It should be noted that this was not a new tendency. Years before 1940 folk music had entered the world of Tin Pan Alley, though only tentatively and timidly. In the 1920s, W. C. Handy made a commercial blues out of the mountain folk song "Careless Love" and the Negro spiritual, "Deep River" was made into the popular song, "Dear Old Southland" (Henry Creamer—Turner Layton). "Shortened Bread" became "Short'nin' Bread" (Clement Wood—Jacques Wolfe), and a Southern American folk tune was used by Wendell Hall for "It Ain't Gonna Rain No' Mo'."

The intrusion of folk music into Tin Pan Alley grew even more assertive in the 1930s. Folk tunes increasingly provided songwriters with melodies for popular exploitation. In 1932, the railroad folk song, "She'll Be Comin' 'Round the Mountain" appeared in Tin Pan Alley as "She Came Rollin' Down the Mountain" (Arthur Lippman, Manning Sherwin and Harry Richman), introduced and popularized by Harry Richman, and the folk song "Goodnight, Irene" was adapted by Huddie Ledbetter and John Lomax for popular consumption. In addition, song hits were patterned after the style, structure and idiom of western and mountain ballads, cowboy songs, railroad songs and work songs. "Bidin' My Time" (Ira Gershwin—George Gershwin) in the musical *Girl Crazy* (1930) was in the image of a hillbilly song. Cole Porter's "Don't Fence Me In" in that of a cowboy folk song, and so was Johnny Mercer's "I'm an Old Cowhand"; Porter's "There'll Always Be a Lady Fair" from the musical *Anything Goes* neatly imitated the idiom and spirit of American sea chanteys.

In the thirties, Billy Hill was one of the popular composers who most fruitfully cultivated the folk-music fields. Born in Boston in 1899, Hill attended the Boston public schools and was trained musically at the New England Conservatory. When he was seventeen he responded to an innate wanderlust by roaming through the West for several years, riding the rods on freight trains, and holding down such jobs as punching cattle in Montana, working in the mines of Death Valley, and washing dishes in roadhouses. When the mood was on him, he wrote popular songs. On one occasion he organized a jazz band that was employed in a Chinese restaurant in Salt Lake City, believed to have been one of the first jazz bands to originate in the West.

Billy Hill's first two published songs were cut to traditional Tin Pan Alley patterns. They were "Rock-a-bye Your Baby Blues" (Larry Yoell) in 1927 and, to his own lyrics, "They Cut Down the Old Pine Tree," both of which he sold to a publisher outright for a few dollars. To earn his keep while writing songs, Hill formed and played in a jazz band. In the early 1930s he drifted to New York, earning his living by working as a doorman in an apartment house on Fifth Avenue. These were years of such poverty that there were times when he could not pay his rent or gas bill, or provide the funds to get his pregnant wife into a maternity ward in a city hospital. A loan of several hundred dollars from ASCAP helped to tide him over this period.

When success finally came to him for one of his songs it arrived in large dimension. The song was "The Last Round-Up" in 1933, imitative of the style of cowboy songs. Since Bing Crosby's recording of this song, and those of several other performers, sold in the millions, Hill could now afford to live in comparative affluence at the Park Plaza Hotel near Central Park and devote himself exclusively to songwriting. In 1934, Hill wrote the lyrics to Peter De Rose's music for "Wagon Wheels" in the style of a Western folk tune. Everett Marshall introduced it in the *Ziegfeld Follies of 1934* and George Olsen and his orchestra recorded it successfully for Columbia. Other of Hill's songs in a folk song style were now being published and performed, assuring him of financial prosperity which happily continued to the time of his death in New York on Christmas Eve of 1940. In addition to two cowboy songs, "Empty Saddles" and "Call of the Canyon," Hill's best numbers included "The Old Spinning Wheel," which was used by the child singer, Mary Small, as her radio theme.

What had been a tendency in the 1920s and 1930s became a trend in the 1940s: adapting folk music into commercial popular songs or producing commercial popular songs from a folk song matrix. We have already commented upon the popular success realized by

"On Top of Old Smokey" by The Weavers. Other song hits of the 1940s also had folk song beginnings: "The Sinking of the Reuben James" in 1941 was adapted by the Almanac Singers from the folk song "Wildwood Flower" as a memorial to the men of the Navy who died on ships during World War II; "Lavender Blue" (Larry Morey—Eliot Daniel), a modernized version of a seventeenth-century English folk ballad, was introduced by Dinah Shore in the motion picture *So Dear To My Heart* (1948) where it was an Academy Award nominee.

Though many hit songs of the forties came directly from folk music sources, others were so strongly influenced by folk music that they sound as if they had folk origins. The following are significant examples: Gene Autry's theme song, "Back in the Saddle Again" (Ray Whitley and Gene Autry); "Blueberry Hill" (Al Lewis, Larry Stock and Vincent Rose) introduced by Gene Autry in the motion picture *The Singing Hill* (1941) and then popularized by Glenn Miller and his orchestra; the chantey-like "Blow High, Blow Low" (Oscar Hammerstein II—Richard Rodgers) from the musical play *Carousel* (1945); "Buttons and Bows" (Jay Livingston and Ray Evans), winner of the Academy Award in *Paleface* (1948) where it was sung by Bob Hope; "Tennessee Waltz" (Redd Stewart—Pee Wee King), introduced by its authors over a radio station in Louisville, Kentucky, in 1947 before it became the first country and western recording by The Short Brothers and was popularized by Patti Page in her three million or so disk sale for Mercury; "Scarlet Ribbons" (Jack Segal—Evelyn Danzig), which Harry Belafonte popularized in a Victor recording in 1956; "Riders in the Sky" (Stan Jones) which, though introduced by Burl Ives, was made famous by Vaughn Monroe in his Victor recording; "Mule Train" (Johnny Lange, Hy Heath and Fred Glickman), a giant success in recordings by Frankie Laine, Bing Crosby and Tennessee Ernie Ford; and "Mockin' Bird Hill" (Vaughn Horton), made famous both by Les Paul and Mary Ford and by Patti Page in their recordings for Capitol and Mercury.

30

Musical Comedy Versus the Musical Play: 1946–1950

1

During the first postwar years, Broadway audiences divided their support and allegiance between musical comedies and musical plays. The best of the more formal and traditional kind of musical theater were: *Annie Get Your Gun* (1946), *High Button Shoes* (1947), *Where's Charley?* (1948), *Gentlemen Prefer Blondes* (1949) and *Miss Liberty* (1949). The most significant musical plays during these four years were: *St. Louis Woman* (1946), *Allegro* (1947), *Brigadoon* (1947), *Finian's Rainbow* (1947), *Street Scene* (1947), *Kiss Me, Kate* (1948), *Regina* (1949), *Lost in the Stars* (1949) and *South Pacific* (1949).

Following his involvement with *This Is the Army* during World War II, Irving Berlin returned to the Broadway theater with *Annie Get Your Gun*, the greatest box-office success of his entire career (1,147 performances on Broadway). It was also what is undoubtedly his most varied, ingratiating and most successful score. Perhaps his remarkable creativity was given an additional stimulus because he was writing songs for the show's producers, Rodgers and Hammerstein, who were already acknowledged to be among the greatest songwriters the theater has known. Ethel Merman was Annie Oakley, a girl handier with a gun than with a man, in one of her expected strident and irresistible characterizations.

Never before or since did Berlin produce so munificent a score as this one. Three of the songs appeared simultaneously on "Your Hit Parade" for ten weeks. The original-cast record album was a best-seller and so were Perry Como's recording of "They Say It's Wonderful" and Dinah Shore's of "Doin' What Comes Natur'lly."

Good as these and other songs were outside the theater, they sounded better still in the context of the musical. "They Say It's Wonderful" was a simplistic love song for a backwoods girl with no education. To the attractive waltz, "The Girl that I Marry," in which Frank describes the kind of girl that appeals to him, he brings sentiment and charm. In Miss Merman's earthy performance as Annie Oakley, "Doin' What Comes Natur'lly" and "You Can't Get a Man With a Gun," acquire a sharp edge in the humor of the double entendres. But away from the stage, "There's No Business Like Show Business" gained in stature by becoming a kind of unofficial anthem for the profession the title glorifies.

Irving Berlin's next musical was *Miss Liberty*. The book was by Robert Sherwood, one of America's most distinguished playwrights and three times winner of the Pulitzer Prize, who made here his solitary exercise in writing for the musical theater. "Miss Liberty" is the Statue of Liberty which becomes the pawn in a rivalry for circulation between two powerful newspaper editors in New York in 1885, James Gordon Bennett of the *Herald* and Joseph Pulitzer of the *World*. "Let's Take an Old-Fashioned Walk," "Paris Wakes Up and Smiles" and an effective setting (and a highly unusual one for Berlin) of the Emma Lazarus poem on the base of the Statue of Liberty, "Give Me Your Tired" are the three best songs.

The now successful songwriters for the Hollywood screen, Sammy Cahn, lyricist, and Jule Styne, composer, made their highly impressive Broadway debut with *High Button Shoes*. Phil Silvers and Joey Faye were cast as two con men in Brunswick, New Jersey, in 1913. The score has an infectious polka in "Papa, Won't You Dance With Me?"

Jule Styne had another winner on Broadway in 1949 with *Gentlemen Prefer Blondes*, this time with Leo Robin as his lyricist. This had an Anita Loos-Joseph Fields book adapted from Miss Loos' 1926 stage comedy which in turn had been a dramatization of her novel published a year earlier. The blondes are Lorelei Lee and Dorothy Shaw, two gold-digging chorines from the *Ziegfeld Follies* en route to France. "Bye Bye Baby" is the song of farewell her button-manufacturer boyfriend sings to Lorelei when she sets sail from America. As Lorelei Lee, Carol Channing—fresh from her initial stage success in the revue *Lend an Ear* (1948)—became a musical comedy star, especially in her presentation of the two hit songs, "Diamonds Are a Girl's Best Friend" and "A Little Girl from Little Rock," delivered in a provocative Dixie accent and baby voice.

Frank Loesser arrived on Broadway with his first musical comedy, *Where's Charley?*, long after his position in American popular music had been firmed. *Where's Charley?* was adapted by George Abbott from an old chestnut by Brandon Thomas, *Charley's Aunt*, first served hot in 1893 and after that reheated in innumerable professional and amateur revivals. It hardly appeared likely that an appealing production could be produced from such a leftover, even with the introduction of songs. Yet *Where's Charley?* managed to be a highly amusing and entertaining diversion. Most of the credit for this achievement belonged to Ray Bolger as Charley. Disporting in female garb as Charley's Brazilian aunt in Oxford, England, Bolger was hilarious without ever becoming offensive or resorting to those clichés favored in Varsity shows in which men dressed as women. Bolger also had a most genial and ingratiating manner with a song, as in "Once in Love with Amy," in which he had the audience participate. The score also had a second love song for Byron Palmer and Doretta Morrow, "My Darling, My Darling," which became almost as popular as "Once in Love with Amy." For several consecutive weeks in 1949 it held either first or second place on "Your Hit Parade." Noteworthy, too, were a comedy number "Make a Miracle," and a lusty march tune with the unlikely title of "The New Ashmolean Marching Society and Student Conservatory Band."

Harold Arlen followed up the success of his 1944 musical comedy, *Bloomer Girl*, with his first attempt at musical play writing: *St. Louis Woman*, book by Arna Bontemps and

Countee Cullen based on Miss Bontemps' novel *God Sends Sunday*, and lyrics by Johnny Mercer. When first projected, the musical was intended as an honest attempt to create a Negro folk play with music. But by the time it opened on Broadway it had become a vehicle out to win favor by including trappings of musical comedy that were disturbingly irrelevant, and by imitating some of the textual material of Gershwin's *Porgy and Bess*. The setting is St. Louis in 1898, where a jockey, Little Augie, murders his rival for the love of Della. On his deathbed, the rival utters a curse that proves a jinx to Augie in all his subsequent races. Whatever reservations one may have about the book, there are none about Harold Arlen's music, some of his best for the musical stage.

In the subsidiary character of Butterfly, Pearl Bailey assumed her first Broadway role, and in introducing the songs "Legalize My Name" and "A Woman's Prerogative" she was offering the first important popular songs with which she has since become associated. Born in Newport News, Virginia, in 1918, Pearl Bailey made her stage debut in 1933 when she was fifteen in an amateur contest in which she won first prize with a song-and-dance routine that included the song "Poor Butterfly" (John Golden—Raymond Hubbell). She once again captured first prize by singing "Solitude" (Eddie De Lange and Irving Mills—Duke Ellington) in an amateur contest at the Apollo Theater in New York's Harlem. She went from there to appear as a specialty dancer with Noble Sissle's orchestra, as a chorus girl in nightclubs in Washington and Baltimore, and as a vocalist with various bands including one led by Cootie Williams. Still pretty much of an unknown quantity, she was engaged in 1944 to appear at the Village Vanguard, in downtown New York, where she worked with such folksingers as Leadbelly and Richard Dyer-Bennett. It was there that she perfected that slow, leisurely throwaway style that became her hallmark. That hallmark helped make her a singing success of the first order in 1945 at the swank Blue Angel nightclub on New York's Upper East Side, in songs such as "Tired" (Allan Roberts and Doris Fisher) which she sang in the motion picture, *Varsity Girl* (1947) and became one of her outstanding song specialties; "Straighten Up and Fly Right" (Irving Mills—Nat King Cole); and Handy's "The St. Louis Blues." The Blue Angel, and after that the Zanzibar, drew a distinguished show business clientele, some of whom responded enthusiastically to her performances. "Bojangles" Bill Robinson told her: "Little girl, you don't know what you have and I hope you never find out." Frank Sinatra had her make a record with him, but it did not do well. Her recording of "Tired" for Columbia, however, was a best-seller. She was still appearing at the Zanzibar in 1946 when she was contracted to make her stage debut in *St. Louis Woman*, a performance that earned her the Donaldson Award.

While "Legalize My Name" and "A Woman's Prerogative" were two songs that the audiences seemed to like best, perhaps because of the way Miss Bailey performed them, several other Arlen numbers were equally distinguished in a well-rounded score: "Come Rain or Come Shine" which has become a standard, "I Had Myself a True Love," "I Wonder What Became of Me," "Mr. Used-to-Be" and "Sleep Peaceful."

2

After *Carousel*, Rodgers and Hammerstein pursued their goal to further the potential of the musical play art form. New innovations and experiments characterized *Allegro*, for which Hammerstein provided the book. Formal scenery was dispensed with; unusual visual designs and colors were thrown on a large screen to intensify moods; a speaking chorus and a singing chorus were used as interpreters and commentators. To tell the life story of the principal character, a physician, Rodgers employed many large musical forms, cantatas for solo voices, chorus and orchestra, and ballet music for sequences touching on various incidents in the physician's life. Two fine songs were "The Gentleman Is a Dope" and "A Fellow Needs a Girl." But for all its splendid moments and refreshing novelty, *Allegro* was a disappointment not only to the critics but also to audiences who had come to the theater expecting another *Carousel*.

A great deal of publicity and enthusiasm preceded the arrival of *Allegro* in New York. Unfortunately, this production failed to live up to expectations. Even greater hullabaloo and fanfare, and a higher pitch of excitement, set the stage for the premiere of the next Rodgers and Hammerstein musical play, *South Pacific* in 1949. This was a musical play adapted from the Pulitzer Prize-winner in fiction, James A. Michener's *Tales of the South Pacific*, in which Joshua Logan was not only Hammerstein's collaborator in the preparation of the book but also its stage director. The starring roles were assumed by the incomparable Mary Martin and the equally renowned Ezio Pinza, the latter stepping for the first time from the stage of the opera house to that of the popular musical theater. Surely this would prove to be a veritable caravan of theatrical delights en route to New York! And so it proved on that unforgettable night of April 7, 1949, when it unloaded its stage riches at the Majestic Theater. "It is a thrilling and exultant musical play," said Ward Morehouse in the New York *Sun*; "a tenderly beautiful idyll of genuine people," said Brooks Atkinson in *The New York Times*; "pearls, pure pearls . . . rare enchantment," reported Howard Barnes in the *Herald-Tribune*; "an utterly captivating work of theatrical art," commented Richard Watts, Jr., in the *Post*.

South Pacific, with a World War II setting on a Pacific island, represented for its authors a radical departure in plot, locale, characters and overall approach from *Allegro*, just as *Allegro* had been basically different from *Carousel*, and *Carousel* from *Oklahoma!* Against the exotic background of a French-run South Pacific island captured from the Japanese during wartime, the plot engages an American nurse, Ensign Nellie Forbush, in a romance with Emile de Becque, a wealthy, middle-aged plantation owner.

While *South Pacific* did not equal the fabulous Broadway run of *Oklahoma!*, it came close with its 1,925 performances. It did manage to set a new mark at the box office by grossing over two and a half million dollars in its first year. In that time, tickets were in such demand that a book could be written of anecdotes about the frantic efforts to secure a pair of tickets. During its entire Broadway run, *South Pacific* was seen by over three and a half million theatergoers who paid over nine million dollars at the box office. It gathered more prizes than any stage production up to that time, about a dozen in all, including the Pulitzer Prize for drama (the second musical to be so honored), and the Drama Critics, Antoinette Perry and Donaldson Awards as the year's best musical. The original-cast recording by Columbia sold a million albums in its first year, and maintained a position on the best-seller charts for over four hundred weeks (something without precedent) in which time three million albums were disposed of. The sheet music sold well over two million copies. The name "South Pacific" was licensed for cosmetics, dresses, dolls, lingerie and other commercial items. By 1970, *South Pacific* had earned a net profit of over seven million dollars on a $225,000 investment, representing for its backers a return of 1,569 percent on their original investment.

In no other Rodgers and Hammerstein production up to then did the music reflect so sensitively both the background and the characters. Rodgers once explained that in writing many of these songs he was always conscious of the characters who sang them. He said: "I tried to weave his [De Becque's] personality into his songs—romantic, rather powerful, but not too involved." The result was "Some Enchanted Evening" and "This Nearly Was

Mine." Rodgers said further: "Nellie Forbush is a Navy nurse out of Arkansas, a kid whose musical background probably had been limited to the movies, radio, and maybe a touring musical comedy. It gave me a chance for a change of pace, and the music I composed for her is light, contemporary, and rhythmic." And so Nellie sings "I'm Gonna Wash that Man Right Outa My Hair" and "A Wonderful Guy." In the same way "Bali Ha'i" and "Happy Talk" are as natural to Bloody Mary as the color of her Tonganese skin; and there is equal affinity between Lieutenant Cable and such songs as "Younger than Springtime" and "Carefully Taught," the latter a courageous effort on the part of its writers to introduce a plea for racial tolerance in the popular musical theater. Three of these songs from *South Pacific*, "Some Enchanted Evening," "Bali Ha'i" and "Younger than Springtime," took turns in usurping the top position on "Your Hit Parade" over an eight-week period.

In 1947, the musical play twice made excursions into musical fantasy with most rewarding consequences. The components that went into making up the delights of *Finian's Rainbow* were a crock of gold able to perform three miracles, an Irishman and his daughter come to Rainbow Valley in the American state of Missitucky, a leprechaun who has an inordinate weakness for human women, a deaf and dumb mute who communicates through dancing, sharecroppers and black men who are in danger of being robbed of their land, and a reactionary Southern Senator who is transformed by the crock into a Negro evangelist and thus gets a taste of being black in a white society. In this delectable text by E. Y. Harburg and Fred Saidy, Irish mythology is blended with a sardonic commentary on American social and political life.

With consistently bright lyrics by E. Y. Harburg and with equally brilliant music by Burton Lane, the songs range from romantic and sentimental ballads tinted with Irish green, to songs of iridescent wit and satire: "How Are Things in Glocca Morra?" (a hit song in 1947–1948), "Old Devil Moon," "Look to the Rainbow," "Something Sort of Grandish," "When I'm Not Near the Girl I Love" and "When the Idle Poor Become the Idle Rich."

In 1947, Burton Lane was no new name either in Tin Pan Alley or the Broadway theater, but *Finian's Rainbow* brought it new luster. The son of a successful real estate operator, Burton Lane was born in New York in 1912, and studied piano and theory in boyhood when he also wrote pieces for the piano. He was only fourteen when the Shuberts engaged him to write some music for an edition of the *Greenwich Village Follies*. He complied with forty numbers, but none of these was heard at the time because that edition was canceled due to the illness of one of the stars. Between 1927 and 1929, Lane worked as a demonstration pianist at Jerome H. Remick when he received valuable advice and guidance from George Gershwin. Two of Lane's songs, with lyrics by Howard Dietz, were interpolated into the revue *Three's a Crowd* (1930); one into *The Third Little Show* (1931); and five into the *Earl Carroll Vanities* (1931). From 1934 on Lane wrote songs in Hollywood, working for several years on the Paramount lot where he wrote, among many other songs, "Says My Heart" (Frank Loesser) for *Cocoanut Grove* (1938) and "How About You?" (Ralph Freed) for *Babes on Broadway* (1942), the latter an Academy Award nominee introduced by Judy Garland and Mickey Rooney. His first complete score for the Broadway stage was *Hold on To Your Hats* (1940), starring Al Jolson, with Jolson singing "Walkin' Along Mindin' My Business," "There's a Great Day Coming, Mañana," and "Would You Be So Kindly," all of them to Harburg's lyrics. With Lane's next full Broadway score for *Finian's Rainbow* seven years later, success, which Lane had been courting so long, was finally attained.

The second musical play fantasy in 1947 was *Brigadoon*, a fable set in a mythical Scottish city that disappeared from the face of the earth in 1747, to return to life one day every century. During one of these reincarnations, the city is visited by two Americans who become enchanted with the place and its people and one of whom falls in love with a local lass.

Brigadoon was the first monumental stage success of the songwriting team of Alan Jay Lerner, librettist and lyricist, and Frederick Loewe, composer. Lerner's tender, sensitive and hauntingly beautiful text hovers delicately between fantasy and reality until the two are fused. Some of Loewe's songs were flavored with a dash of Scotch: "Come to Me, Bend to Me," and "The Heather on the Hill." "Almost Like Being in Love," the hit song of the show, was more typical of Broadway.

When Lerner and Loewe first met in 1942 and decided to join talents, they came from vastly different backgrounds and experiences. Lerner, aged twenty-four, came from a wealthy American family, received his education in private and fashionable schools, and at Harvard College from which he was graduated with a Bachelor of Science degree in 1940. His sole venture in writing for the theater, his pervasive ambition, were some sketches and lyrics for two Hasty Pudding Shows at Harvard, and later preparing scripts for radio programs.

Frederick Loewe was Lerner's senior by fourteen years. He came from Vienna where he was born in 1904, the son of a famous tenor of Viennese operettas. Raised as a musical prodigy, Frederick became the youngest pianist ever to appear as soloist with the Berlin Symphony Orchestra; he was only thirteen. After extensive study of composition with Ferruccio Busoni and piano with Eugène d'Albert, he won the Hollander Award in his eighteenth year. He had also dabbled successfully in the writing of popular music, with a song, "Katrina," when he was fifteen, that sold a million copies of sheet music. In 1942, he came to the United States with the hope of embarking on a career as concert pianist. Failing to make headway in the concert world, he supported himself by playing popular music in theaters and night spots, by working as a busboy in a cafeteria, teaching horseback riding at a resort, participating in professional boxing, working in the West as a gold prospector, delivering mail on horseback and as a cowpuncher. Back East again, he tried to further himself as a popular composer while working as a pianist in a German beer hall. One of his songs, "Love Tiptoed Through My Heart" was interpolated in 1934 into a Broadway play starring Dennis King; another, "A Waltz Was Born in Vienna" was used two years later in *The Illustrators Show*. In 1937 he completed the score for his first musical comedy, *Great Lady*, which opened in St. Louis before coming to New York. It was a failure. Five years later, a Detroit producer became interested in a new musical treatment of Barry Conner's play, *The Patsy*, and approached Loewe. It was at this juncture of Loewe's apprenticeship in the theater that he met Alan Jay Lerner at the Lambs Club in New York and enlisted his services for revamping *The Patsy*, which was produced in Detroit in October 1942, as *Life of the Party*.

After that, they went to work on a new Broadway musical, *What's Up*, a farce starring Jimmy Savo in 1943. It was a failure. Two years later they returned to Broadway with *The Day Before Spring*, a musical that touched lightly on fantasy within an otherwise realistic text. Though this musical also fared badly at the box office, it had enough charm and originality to get some enthusiastic response from the critics. There was something in *The Day Before Spring*, including a few delightful songs, that promised much for the subsequent theatrical career of Lerner and Loewe. That promise was fulfilled a year and a half later with their next musical, *Brigadoon*.

Cole Porter made a momentous step away from stereotyped musical comedies into the much less formalized musical play with the greatest stage success of his life, *Kiss Me, Kate*. The springboard for the text by Bella and Samuel Spewack was Shakespeare's *The*

Taming of the Shrew. The breezy and spirited adaptation shifted nimbly from present-day Baltimore, and the love entanglements of four troupers performing Shakespeare, to Shakespeare's Padua, and the tribulations of Petruchio and Kate. Elizabethan dialogue became a companion to American slang, with Cole Porter's sophisticated lyrics and melodies providing additional savor. Veins tapped successfully in earlier shows by Porter were prominently revealed. Rarely were his moods more deeply indigo than in "Were Thine that Special Face" and "So in Love"; rarely had his flair for parody and satire been more prominent than in "Wunderbar" and "Always True to You in My Fashion"; rarely did he leap from gaiety to broad humor with such agility as in "Brush Up Your Shakespeare" and "I Hate Men"; and rarely did he touch on sex with such deftness and inoffensiveness as in "Too Darn Hot" and "Where Is the Life that Late I Led?" These songs, a scintillating book, the dances of Hanya Holm, the performances of Alfred Drake, Lisa Kirk, Harold Lang and Patricia Morison all added up to a giant success, with a Broadway run of over one thousand performances, productions in foreign capitals in seventeen translations, a best-selling original-cast record album, and an outstanding motion picture adaptation in 1953.

Kurt Weill also made a striking departure from his earlier concepts of the musical theater with two remarkable musical plays, *Street Scene* in 1947 and *Lost in the Stars* in 1949. Each was good enough not only to survive their original productions through many revivals in different places but even to enter the hallowed halls of the opera house.

Street Scene was a musical version of Elmer Rice's powerful Pulitzer Prize tragedy produced in 1929; Rice himself made the musical stage adaptation. The text portrayed the frustrated, complex and tangled lives of an impoverished family in a New York tenement house. Music brought to this compelling realistic drama new depth and dimension. While several songs haunt the memory—"Lonely House," "Somehow I Never Could Believe" and "We'll Go Away Together," all with lyrics by Langston Hughes—no single number or combination of numbers give the show its emotional thrust and its artistic stature, but the integrated musical texture. As Rosamond Gilder wrote in *Theater Arts:* "Kurt Weill turned *Street Scene* into a symphony of the city with its strands of love and yearning and violence, woven into the pattern of daily drudgery. His music reflects the hot night, the chatter and gossiping housewives, the sound of children at play, the ebb and flow of anonymous existence."

Lost in the Stars is once again stirring dramatic art, a touching folk play with music. Maxwell Anderson made the adaptation of Alan Paton's novel, *Cry, the Beloved Country,* a story of racial conflict in South Africa.

The text was moving in its compassion, warm in its humanity, stirring in its promise of a better life of tolerance and brotherly understanding. As in *Street Scene,* music endowed a human and at times profound play with even richer and deeper overtones. Seldom before had the American musical theater provided such moving choral music as that found in this play. Weill uses the chorus to provide commentary: in the overwhelming dirge, "Cry, the Beloved Country"; in a penetrating psychological analysis of an emotional state, "Fear"; in a deeply felt religious statement, "A Bird of Passage." The solo melodies—one is reluctant to call them songs, so fluidly do they arise from and ebb back into the dramatic situation—are equally expressive, reflecting the immense sorrow of the black preacher when he learns that his son Absalom is a murderer, "O Tixo, Tixo" and "Lost in the Stars," and in sharply defining the character of a honky-tonky floozie in "Who'll Buy" and that of Irena, Absalom's sweetheart, in "Trouble Man." So germane is Weill's music to the play, so integral to its overall message and meaning, that many have come to regard *Lost in the Stars* as an opera.

Lost in the Stars was Kurt Weill's last musical. Just a half year after its premiere he died in New York City on April 3, 1950. He was at the height of his creative powers and, only fifty years old, it had seemed that his best work was yet to come.

3

Preceding paragraphs have made mention of the Donaldson, Antoinette Perry and Drama Critics Circle awards. All three were instituted to single out the most distinctive contribution each year to the theater.

The Donaldson Award was founded in 1944 in memory of W. H. Donaldson, founder of *Billboard* magazine. Each year, until 1955, it awarded prizes for the best plays and musicals, first plays, direction, male and female lead performances, settings and costumes. In the musical theater, the first awards in 1944 went to *Carmen Jones* as the season's best musical; to Hassard Short for his direction of that musical; to Bobby Clark and Mary Martin for performances, respectively, in *Mexican Hayride* and *One Touch of Venus*. Musicals selected by the Donaldson Awards as the best of the season between 1945 and 1949 were the revival of *Show Boat* in 1946, *Finian's Rainbow*, *High Button Shoes* and *South Pacific*.

The Antoinette Perry Award, colloquially called the "Tony," was originated in 1947 by the American Theater Wing for "distinguished achievement in the theater." The award was named after Antoinette Perry, onetime chairman of the board and head of the American Theater Wing during World War II. The first musicals selected were *Kiss Me, Kate* and *South Pacific*. Among those who received Tony Awards for productions between 1947 and 1950 were Ray Bolger in *Where's Charley?*, Ezio Pinza in *South Pacific*, Nanette Fabray in *Love Life*, Mary Martin in *South Pacific*, David Wayne in *Finian's Rainbow* and Juanita Hall in *South Pacific*. Awards were also given to Bella and Samuel Spewack and Cole Porter for the book and the score of *Kiss Me, Kate*, to Joshua Logan and Oscar Hammerstein II for their book for *South Pacific*, and to Agnes De Mille, Michael Kidd, Jerome Robbins and Gower Champion for their choreography in *Brigadoon*, *Finian's Rainbow*, *High Button Shoes* and *Lend an Ear*, respectively.

Though the New York Drama Critics Award had been established in 1936, a musical production was not singled out for its kudos until a decade later for *Carousel*. Between 1946 and 1950, this honor also went to *Brigadoon* and *South Pacific*.

31

The Movies, the Radio, and Now Television: The Early Postwar Years

1

The re-creation of Broadway musicals as motion pictures, which had been extensive from the beginnings of talking pictures, was temporarily arrested between 1946 and 1950. The handful of Broadway musicals to become screen musicals in those years, even though greatly emasculated both musically and textually, included the De Sylva, Brown and Henderson musical comedy of the twenties, *Good News*, returning to the screen in 1947 for the second time, with June Allyson and Peter Lawford: Kurt Weill's *One Touch of Venus*, in 1948, starring Ava Gardner and Robert Walker; Sigmund Romberg's *Up in Central Park* in 1948 with Deanna Durbin and Dick Haymes; and in 1949, by far the best of the lot, Leonard Bernstein's *On the Town* in which Frank Sinatra, Gene Kelly and Jules Munshin were the three sailors on leave in hot pursuit of girls, Betty Garrett, Vera-Ellen and Ann Miller, a screen diversion almost as effervescent and vivacious as its stage counterpart.

The emphasis in the screen musicals of the early postwar years was on screen biographies of composers and performers. Jerome Kern's biography was told in *Till the Clouds Roll By* (1946) with Robert Walker as the composer; a story purporting to be that of Cole Porter, in *Night and Day* (1946), Cary Grant playing the principal role; and those of Richard Rodgers and Lorenz Hart in *Words and Music* (1948), with Tom Drake appearing as Rodgers and Mickey Rooney as Hart. In each instance, the prime interest lay in the songs. There were twenty-five of them in the Kern biography sung by a galaxy of stars comprising Judy Garland, Lena Horne, Kathryn Grayson, Frank Sinatra, Tony Martin and Dinah Shore. For the historian of recorded music, *Till the Clouds Roll By* has special significance, since this was the first motion picture sound track to be transferred to disks. In the Cole Porter story, fifteen of his classics were sung mainly by Ginny Simms, but also by Mary Martin ("My Heart Belongs to Daddy") and Monty Woolley ("Miss Otis Regrets"). The Rodgers and Hart screen biography offered another glittering constellation of performers: Ann Sothern, Judy Garland, Mel Tormé, Lena Horne, Gene Kelly, Vera-Ellen and Cyd Charisse who did full justice to some twenty of the greatest songs to come out of the Broadway musical theater of the twenties and thirties.

The lives of other popular composers, though of somewhat lesser stature, were also romanticized on the screen, that of Joseph E. Howard in *I Wonder Who's Kissing Her Now*, and Chauncey Olcott's in *My Wild Irish Rose*, both in 1947, each giving deserved prominence to the title songs.

Among musical performers, the Dorsey brothers were starred as themselves in *The Fabulous Dorseys* (1947), with Paul Whiteman, Charlie Barnet, Ziggy Elman, Henry Busse and Helen O'Connell supporting the Dorseys in performing jazz in the Dorsey manner. And the lustrous career of the enchanting *Ziegfeld Follies* star, Marilyn Miller, was recreated on the screen by June Haver in *Look for the Silver Lining* (1949), who sang Kern's "Who?" and "Sunny" (Otto Harbach and Oscar Hammerstein II), and the title song (B. G. De Sylva) which Marilyn Miller had made so memorable on the stage.

One screen biography of a performer became an unexpected blockbuster, *The Jolson Story* (1946). The idea for this production was born with Sidney Skolsky, the Hollywood columnist, whose boyhood years had been brightened at the Winter Garden. For a long time the project seemed stillborn. Motion picture producers consistently turned a deaf ear and a skeptical eyebrow each time Skolsky tried to persuade them that Al Jolson was a natural for a film biography. The producers argued, not without justification, that the audiences of the postwar era would never respond favorably to the corny sentimentality with which Jolson dramatized his songs; that, in fact, many of those audiences could hardly be expected to know who Joslon was. One producer, however, remembered Jolson, admired him, and felt that the kind of commodity Jolson had once sold to his adoring public was timeless. He was Harry Cohn of Columbia Pictures. Once Cohn agreed to consider the venture, other seemingly insurmountable problems arose. Jolson was now sixty, but with his overdeveloped ego, would not hear of anybody but himself playing "Jolie." To complicate matters further, Jolson was not well, having had one lung removed. Even while the project of his screen biography was under discussion he had to be rushed to a hospital in Los Angeles and placed in an oxygen tent after an attack of malaria. The plans for the picture progressed slowly. Jolson recovered sufficiently to hurl his energies and enthusiasm into the making of the film. He gave his grudging consent for somebody else to portray him on the screen, an unknown, Larry Parks, while he himself recorded all the songs on the sound track. It proved a heaven-made marriage. Larry Parks, young and ebullient, captured every nuance of Jolson's facial, manual and bodily expressions and movements in the delivery of a number; Jolson, in better voice than ever, sang his heart out in his determination to woo and win audiences who had either forgotten him or had never been under his spell.

The story, as with all screen biographies, made compromises with Jolson's actual personal history, but nevertheless was inordinately successful in projecting the Jolson personality in portraying his love affair with audiences and his irresistible compulsion to sing. It was Jolson's singing on the sound track the numbers with which he had once held audiences captive, that gave the picture its uncommon fascination. To these were added a new song that from then on would be a permanent part of Jolson's repertory: "The Anniversary Song" (Al Jolson and Saul Chaplin). "The Anniversary Song" was interpolated into a scene celebrating the wedding anniversary of Jolson's parents. A song strong on nostalgia and sentiment was called for, and none of the old Jolson standbys were suitable. Then Jolson recalled a melody his father used to sing, a melody from a waltz sequence long popular in Eastern Europe, Ivanovici's *The Waves of the Danube*. With Saul Chaplin's help, Jolson fashioned it into a song for a scene that provided one of the more memorable moments in the picture. Jolson's recording (and that of Bing Crosby), both for Decca, each had a sale in excess of a million disks. The song itself appeared several times in a top position on "Your Hit Parade."

The Jolson Story was a huge box-office draw wherever it was seen, following its premiere at the Radio City Music Hall in New York on October 10, 1946. In its first year, it grossed over eight million dollars. The ten-disk 78 r.p.m. Decca album of the songs from the movie sold so prodigiously that only one month after its release, Jolson's royalty was about four hundred thousand dollars (this, in addition to the royalty from the million-disk sale of "The Anniversary Song," which was released on a separate single record.) Jolson was invited to be a guest on the network radio programs of Bing Crosby, Eddie Cantor and Bob Hope until, in October 1947, he became the star of his own radio show, the Kraft Music Hall on NBC.

The remarkable way in which Jolson's singing on the track was synchronized with Larry Parks' movements of lips, eyes, hands and body made practical, once and for all, the dubbing of a voice on the sound track for a performer on the screen, a desirable method of providing a famous and attractive screen star with an equally appealing voice. Dubbing was not new, though it had never before been done so well as in *The Jolson Story*. In 1929, in the first screen version of *Show Boat*, Eva Olivotti sang for Laura La Plante and Johnny Murray sang for Richard Barthelmess in *Weary River*. In the 1930s, Betty Hiestand represented June Lang on the sound track of *Music in the Air* (1934); and in the *Goldwyn Follies* (1938), James O'Brien sang for Douglass Montgomery, and Virginia Verrill for Andrea Leeds. Allan Jones was heard on the sound track in Irving Berlin's "A Pretty Girl Is Like a Melody" for Dennis Morgan in *The Great Ziegfeld* (1936).

In the forties, the science of dubbing gained new sophistication and new importance. Nan Wynn was called upon to sing for Rita Hayworth in *My Gal Sal* (1942), *You Were Never Lovelier* (1942) and *Cover Girl* (1944). In *Youth on Parade* (1942) it was Margaret Whiting, and not Martha Driscoll, who sang "I've Heard that Song Before" (Sammy Cahn—Jule Styne). Eileen Wilson dubbed for Ava Gardner in *One Touch of Venus* (1943); Louanne Hogan, for Jeanne Crain in the first Rodgers and Hammerstein musical version of *State Fair* (1945) and in *Centennial Summer* (1946); Peggy La Centra for Ida Lupino in *The Man I Love* (1946); and Anita Ellis for Rita Hayworth in "Put the Blame on Mame" (Doris Fisher and Allan Roberts) in *Gilda* (1944). Dubbing was used in *I Wonder Who's Kissing Her Now* (1947), Buddy Clark for Mark Stevens; in *Words and Music* (1948), Eileen Wilson for Cyd Charisse; in *Oh, You Beautiful Doll* (1949), Billy Shirley for Mark Stevens. A most curious kind of dubbing was realized in *To Have and Have Not* (1944) where Andy Williams sang Hoagy Carmichael's "How Little We Know" (Johnny Mercer) for Lauren Bacall!

With *The Jolson Story* a winner, Columbia Pictures felt impelled to assemble more elements of Jolson's colorful life story into a sequel, *Jolson Sings Again* (1949), with Larry Parks once again as Jolson, and Jolson again heard on the sound track. In tracing the period in Jolson's life between the time his first marriage broke up and the collapse of his career to the resurgence of his popularity with *The Jolson Story* and his second happy marriage, the story had plenty of fresh dramatic interest to tap. Some of the musical numbers from *The Jolson Story* were reprised together with a new crop of old Jolson favorites.

For Jolson himself, the success of *The Jolson Story* and *Jolson Sings Again* represented one of the greatest comebacks in the history of American entertainment. Virtually in total obscurity for years before *The Jolson Story* was made, Jolson, then past sixty, found himself once again in demand. Not only were his records selling better than ever, but he had also become such a star over the radio that in 1949 CBS signed him to a three-year contract for the exclusive rights to his services on radio and television. And it was as a star of stars in 1950 that he made a tour of the Korean battlefront to perform for American troops, giving forty-two shows in sixteen days. Then, on October 23, 1950, Jolson went to San Francisco to record a radio show with Bing Crosby to be broadcast on November 1. He never made that appearance. On October 23, he died in his room at the St. Francis Hotel. On his deathbed at the age of sixty-four he was still "the world's greatest entertainer," as he had been billed. The producer, Sam H. Harris, remarked, "There's Al Jolson—and then there's the rest of us." Biographies of Jolson were published in 1962 and 1972.

Songs winning Academy Awards between 1946 and 1950 recall some fine screen musicals other than biographies. "On the Atchison, Topeka and the Santa Fé" (Johnny Mercer—Harry Warren) won the Oscar in 1946, after having been introduced by Judy Garland in *The Harvey Girls*. One year later the trophy went to "Zip-a-Dee-Doo-Dah" (Ray Gilbert—Allie Wrubel) which came out of *Song of the South*, Walt Disney's first motion picture with live actors. In 1948, "Buttons and Bows" (Jay Livingston and Ray Evans) was chosen, introduced by Bob Hope in *Paleface*. And in 1949, the song winner was Frank Loesser's "Baby, It's Cold Outside" from *Neptune's Daughter*, sung initially in the film by Esther Williams and Ricardo Montalban, and repeated in a comedy reprise by Red Skelton and Betty Garrett. It should be mentioned that Loesser did not write this Academy Award winning song with *Neptune's Daughter* in mind. He had written it as a diversion for his friends with no thought of commercializing it. But he found a convenient niche for it in *Neptune's Daughter*, and broke down his resistance to introducing the song to the public at large.

2

Throughout the forties, the science of scoring and the art of writing background music gained in subtlety and skill. The old hands from the thirties were still operating successfully. Ray Heindorf received two Academy Awards for his scoring for *Yankee Doodle Dandy* (1942) and *This Is the Army* (1943); Max Steiner for his original music to *Now Voyager* (1942) and *Since You Went Away* (1944); Alfred Newman for the scoring for *Tin Pan Alley* (1940) and *Mother Wore Tights* (1947) and the original background music for *The Song of Bernadette* (1943). For Steiner, the music of *The Song of Bernadette* had the unique distinction of becoming the first motion picture score recorded in its entirety, in a four-record 78 r.p.m. record album (later transferred to LP).

Both Steiner and Newman wrote many other scores for motion pictures in the forties which, without winning Academy Awards, nevertheless rank among the best written for the screen: From Steiner, *The Letter* (1940), *They Died with Their Boots On* (1942), *The Corn Is Green* (1945), *The Big Sleep* (1946), *Johnny Belinda* (1948), *The Treasure of Sierra Madre* (1948) and *Beyond the Forest* (1949); from Newman, *The Mark of Zorro* (1940), *Ball of Fire* (1941), *How Green Was My Valley* (1942), *The Black Swan* (1942), *Wilson* (1944), *Centennial Summer* (1946), *Captain from Castile* (1947) and *The Snake Pit* (1949). *The Snake Pit* was one of the earliest scores to make use of electronic sounds in screen music.

Erich Wolfgang Korngold did not win an Academy Award in the 1940s, in fact he did not even get any nominations. Yet there was no sign of diminution in his creativity as attested by his scores for *The Sea Hawk* (1940), *Sea Wolf* (1941), *King's Row* (1941) and *Deception*

(1946). For *Deception* Korngold further extended the horizon of screen music by writing a cello concerto (the hero of the picture being a cello virtuoso), a work Korngold later expanded into a major concert composition. *Deception* was Korngold's last significant screen score (though he worked on two more motion pictures after that). When his contract came up for renewal in 1946 he turned it down, maintaining that he did not wish to be "a Hollywood composer for the rest of my life," and adding that now that he was fifty and had suffered a heart attack he wanted to get back to his real mission of writing serious music for the concert hall. He did just that for the next decade, completing a violin concerto, a symphony and sundry other compositions. In 1956 he suffered a stroke and on November 29, 1957, he died of a heart attack at the North Hollywood Hospital.

The richness of background music writing and scoring during the fifties was not due entirely to the work of veterans, but also to neophytes as far as screen music went. One of the best motion picture scores of the decade, which did not win an Academy Award though it was nominated, was that which Bernard Herrmann wrote for *Citizen Kane* (1940), the motion picture classic starring and directed by Orson Welles. A year later Herrmann did win the Academy Award, for his score to *All that Money Can Buy* (1941).

Born in New York City, in 1911, Herrmann won a one-hundred-dollar prize for a song when he was thirteen after having taken some music lessons from private teachers. Bent on a career in serious music he studied composition at New York University, and composition and conducting at the Juilliard School of Music. By the time he was eighteen he was a professional musician, having contributed some ballet music to the second edition of the intimate Broadway revue *Americana* (1928) and later by conducting avant-garde concerts with a chamber orchestra he had founded. For several years, beginning in 1933, he was affiliated with the CBS radio network as a conductor and as composer of background music for dramatic and documentary productions. During those radio years he was not idle as a serious composer. A ballet, *The Skating Rink*, was performed at the Radio City Music Hall, its score played by the NBC Symphony under Frank Black. A nocturne and scherzo were introduced by the CBS Symphony under Howard Barlow, and a cantata, *Moby Dick*, received its world premiere in 1940 in a performance by the New York Philharmonic Orchestra under John Barbirolli.

After winning the Academy Award for his music to *All that Money Can Buy*, Herrmann restricted himself to writing no more than one film score a year at most during the forties, invariably maintaining that high level of musicianship and invention that had characterized his first two film projects in *The Magnificent Ambersons* (1942), *Jane Eyre* (1944), *Hangover Square* (1945), *Anna and the King of Siam* (1946) and *The Ghost and Mrs. Muir* (1947). In his music for *Anna and the King of Siam* Herrmann used authentic Siamese scales and melodic interval patterns, because, as he said, he was not interested in having music serve as "a commentary, or an emotional counterpart of the drama" but because he aspired to have it "serve as musical scenery."

Up until the time of his death on December 24, 1975, Bernard Herrmann remained productive. He wrote twenty-two screen scores in the 1950s, and fourteen in the 1960s. Among these were those for *The Snows of Kilimanjaro* (1952), *The Man in the Gray Flannel Suit* (1956), *A Hatful of Rain* (1957), *Vertigo* (1958), *The Naked and the Dead* (1958), *Psycho* (1960), *Tender Is the Night* (1961), *Marnie* (1964), and *Obsession* (1976). The evening before his death he completed his sixty-first film assignment, the scoring for *The Taxi Driver* (1976). The scores to *Obsession* and *Taxi Driver* received Academy Award nominations.

Miklos Rozsa had an armful of Academy Award nominations before he won it in

1945 for his score to *Spellbound*. Two years later he acquired his second Oscar for his music to *A Double Life*. Born in Budapest in 1907, Rozsa began studying the violin when he was five and proved to be a prodigy. His principal musical education took place at the renowned Leipzig Conservatory in Germany from which he was graduated in 1929. One year earlier, the publishing firm of Breitkopf and Hartel became interested in him and signed him to a contract. In 1931, Rozsa moved on to Paris where some of his chamber music had a favorable hearing. There he wrote the *Theme, Variations and Finale* for orchestra with which his career as a composer was further strengthened. This was Rozsa's first piece of music to be heard in the United States, in 1937. Rozsa's ballet, *Hungaria*, performed in London in 1936 by Anton Dolin and Alicia Markova, brought Rozsa to the attention of Alexander Korda, the eminent motion picture producer, who had Rozsa score a half dozen of his pictures beginning with *Knights without Armour* (1937), starring Marlene Dietrich and Robert Donat. While work went on on the Korda production of *The Thief of Bagdad*, World War II erupted in Europe necessitating an immediate transfer of all further activity on the film to Hollywood. Rozsa completed his scoring for *The Thief of Bagdad* in Hollywood in 1940, then took on his first Hollywood assignments in 1941, his music to *Lydia* and *Sundown*; that year, he received his first Academy Award nominations. Other nominations during the forties came to him for *Jungle Book* (1942), *Double Indemnity* (1944), *Woman of the Town* (1944), *Lost Weekend* (1945), *A Song to Remember* (1945) and *The Killers* (1946).

Rozsa's Academy Award-winning score for *Spellbound* was of particular interest for the significant way in which electronic music was utilized to depict hysteria, terror and madness, on an instrument called the Thereminvox. "Its eerie sound," says Tony Thomas in *Music for the Movies*, "blended perfectly with Rozsa's haunting music and contributed mightily to the aural atmosphere of implied madness and mystery." Rozsa adapted this screen score for a concert composition, *Spellbound Concerto*, which has been recorded. Since 1950 Rozsa had been one of the most prolific composers of screen music in Hollywood, with over forty scores to his credit.

Hugo Friedhofer received an Academy Award for his music for *The Best Years of Our Lives* (1946), and nominations for his scores for *Woman in the Window* (1946), *The Bishop's Wife* (1947) and *Joan of Arc* (1948). The son of a cellist, Friedhofer was born in San Francisco in 1902. He dropped out of school, where he majored in art, when he was sixteen and went to work in a lithograph firm while studying painting at night. Though he had begun to study the cello with his father when he was thirteen, music did not assume any significance in his life until five years later when he pursued music study more earnestly and comprehensively. His professional life in music began at twenty when he played the cello in the first of several theater orchestras. While doing so, he extended his musical education with the study of theory, a training that sent him to arranging. As an arranger he went to work for the Fox studios in 1929, his first assignment there being *Sunny Side Up*. He remained with Fox for five years, not only as an arranger but also as an orchestrator and composer. In 1935, Leo Forbstein brought him to Warner Brothers as orchestrator. During his eleven years there, Friedhofer was assigned to write the original music for only one picture, *Valley of the Giants* (1938). But one year earlier, he had received his first screen credit as a composer for his background music to a Samuel Goldwyn production, *The Adventures of Marco Polo* starring Gary Cooper. Friedhofer continued to operate mainly as arranger, adapter or orchestrator, and only occasionally as composer, until 1943, completing some sixty assignments. In 1943 he wrote the complete scores for four motion pictures produced at 20th Century-Fox. During the next seven years he did the scoring or the original music for twenty-three more productions, for two of which he received Academy Award nominations, as well as an

Academy Award itself. Friedhofer completed over forty more scores for the motion picture screen after 1950. Among these were *The Rains of Ranchipur* (1955), *Boy on a Dolphin* (1957), *The Young Lions* (1958) and *One-Eyed Jacks* (1961).

John Green was nominated for his first Oscar for the music to *Fiesta* (1947), following it a year later with the winning of the Academy Award for his scoring for *Easter Parade*. During the next quarter of a century he was to receive Oscars both for his uncommon gift at scoring and his equally impressive creativity in the preparation of background music. Beginning with 1946, he was also called upon to conduct the music at Oscar presentation ceremonies more than ten times.

He was the son of a wealthy banker and builder, born in New York City in 1908. His interest in music dated back to his third year, but his father did not encourage him in it and firmly directed him to a thorough academic education in the Horace Mann School, the New York Military Academy, then Harvard, where he graduated from its School of Economics at nineteen. Through these years, extensive study of the piano and theory helped to nurture and develop Green's innate musical ability. While at college he participated in many of its musical activities, both as a performer and arranger, and was a member of the Harvard Gold Coast Orchestra. He also did some arrangements for Guy Lombardo and his orchestra, an affiliation that was responsible for his first published song, "Coquette." He wrote it collaboratively with Carmen Lombardo, to Gus Kahn's lyrics, inspired by a Broadway play of that name starring Helen Hayes in 1927. Guy Lombardo and his orchestra introduced it over the air and made a hit recording for Columbia.

After leaving Harvard, Green worked for a time as a purchase and sales clerk in a bond house in Wall Street. But he quit his job after six months to team up with Eddie Heyman, lyricist, in writing songs and working as a rehearsal pianist for Gertrude Lawrence. Two of his songs in 1930 gave him status in the Broadway theater, "I'm Yours" (E. Y. Harburg), interpolated into the Rodgers and Hart musical *Simple Simon* (1930) after having been introduced in a movie short, and "Body and Soul" (Edward Heyman, Robert Sour, and Frank Eyton) which became a classic in popular music following Libby Holman's presentation of it in *Three's A Crowd*.

Since movies had always been a major interest, Green applied for and got a job as rehearsal pianist at the Paramount studios in Astoria, Long Island. His first assignment was *The Big Pond*, starring Maurice Chevalier. When its orchestrator fell ill, Green asked to fill in. The first song he arranged was "You Brought a New Kind of Love to Me" (Irving Kahal—Pierre Norman Connor and Sammy Fain). For the next two years he worked in Astoria, arranging the music for twelve films, and between assignments conducting the orchestra at the Paramount Theater in New York. He also had two more song hits to his credit, one of which, "Out of Nowhere" (Edward Heyman) in 1931 was Bing Crosby's first successful record as a solo vocalist. Two years later, once again with Heyman, he wrote "I Cover the Waterfront" to exploit the Paramount motion picture of the same name. Paramount had no intention of using this song in the picture, and it was not used on the sound track of the original first release print. But the song, after being introduced by Ben Bernie and his orchestra over the radio, grew so popular that Paramount decided to include it in the movie, the subsequent film print being rescored for this purpose. In 1934 came another "evergreen" (as he likes to identify his standards), "Easy Come, Easy Go" (Edward Heyman), introduced orchestrally on the sound track of the motion picture *Bachelor of Arts*.

From 1934 to 1940 Green toured the United States as conductor and master of ceremonies of his own band. He wrote the music for and conducted a musical, *Big Business*, the first ever to be broadcast by BBC in London, served either as host or as conductor on many coast-to-coast American radio programs, including the Philip Morris show on which he was starred in 1938 and 1939, and conducted the orchestra for the Rodgers and Hart musical *By Jupiter* (1942) during its Broadway run.

Late in 1942 he signed a contract to be arranger and conductor at MGM. He either adapted or wrote the scores for *Broadway Rhythm* and *Bathing Beauty* in 1944, his first major assignments, and seven more motion pictures in the ensuing five years. He took on musical assignments from other studios as well, such as writing songs for *Something in the Wind* (1947) starring Deanna Durbin at Universal and the score for *The Inspector General* (1949) starring Danny Kaye at Warners.

After gaining his first Oscar for his scoring for *Easter Parade* in 1948, Green was appointed head of the music department at MGM. He stayed there a decade, and, as he recalls, "it was ten years in which I was virtually autonomous—I made the deals as well as the aesthetics."

Franz Waxman did not win an Academy Award until 1950, Dimitri Tiomkin until 1952, Bronislau Kaper until 1953, and Victor Young until 1956. But all four men were eminently active writing music for the screen, and all four men gathered Academy Award nominations while waiting for the prize itself.

To the writing of screen music Franz Waxman carried over the solid technique he had acquired from sound musical schooling in Europe together with the romantic tendencies of many of Europe's serious composers. He gave to his motion picture scores those lush harmonies, overdressed orchestrations, and at times that leitmotif technique that romantic composers of Europe favored in the close of the nineteenth century. Waxman always considered his screen music to be on the serious rather than popular side, and for that reason refused any classification that placed him with popular composers. He was of Polish birth, in Upper Silesia, in 1906. After leaving school he worked for a time as bank teller, studying music during his free hours. When he was seventeen he entered the Dresden Music Academy where he made such progress that he was transferred to the Berlin Conservatory. While pursuing his music studies there he earned his living playing in a jazz orchestra. A meeting with Erich Pommer, the distinguished film producer, brought him to motion pictures and to an assignment to arrange and conduct Frederick Hollaender's score for the Pommer production of *The Blue Angel*, which starred the then little-known Marlene Dietrich. Waxman continued doing the arranging and conducting for German films for about three years, including a film version of Ferenc Molnar's *Liliom*. When the Nazis came to power, Waxman fled from Germany to Paris.

At that time, Erich Pommer was contracted by Hollywood to produce the screen adaptation of Jerome Kern's *Music in the Air* for 20th Century-Fox. He brought Waxman to Hollywood to adapt the music and do the scoring. Hollywood remained Waxman's permanent home after that. During this first year there he studied composition with Arnold Schoenberg while continuing to work for the movies by writing the background music for *The Bride of Frankenstein* (1935). He was now made the head of the music department at Universal where, in a two-year period, he supervised the scoring of about fifty motion pictures, doing the scoring himself for a dozen of them. Late in 1936 he went from Universal to MGM where, in addition to other chores, he was at times allowed to compose original background music. During a six-year period he averaged eight scores a year for MGM. His background music for *Rebecca* (1940), *Dr. Jekyll and Mr. Hyde* (1941) and *Suspicion* (1941) brought him nominations for the Academy Award. Then, in 1943, Waxman went to work for Warner Brothers where his music for *Objective Burma* (1945) and *Humoresque* (1946) earned him two more nominations for the Academy Award.

Dimitri Tiomkin, son of a physician, was born in the Ukraine in 1899, but raised in St. Petersburg. Between 1912 and 1919 he received his musical education at the St. Petersburg Conservatory where he was trained as a pianist. He then settled in Berlin, continuing his music study with one of the most renowned musicians of the time, Ferruccio Busoni, and making his debut as pianist by appearing as soloist with the Berlin Philharmonic. He now formed with Michael Kariton a duo-piano team which gave successful concerts in Paris and which, in 1925, toured the vaudeville circuit in the United States. He then married Albertina Rasch, the ballerina and choreographer, who encouraged him to advance himself as a solo pianist. He made appearances in Europe and America after that, including a performance of Gershwin's Concerto in F in Paris, which was its French premiere. When his wife was hired by the MGM studios in Hollywood to supervise short ballet sequences for the screen, the Tiomkins planted themselves in the movie capital where Tiomkin did some concert work and, in 1930, wrote ballet music for four motion pictures produced at MGM. His first score for a film was for *Resurrection* (1931). Within a few years, Tiomkin became one of the busiest composers in Hollywood, continually called upon to do scoring, or write original background music, or screen songs, or conduct. His first Academy Award nomination came for the scoring for *Mr. Smith Goes to Washington* (1939). During the forties his music for *The Corsican Brothers* (1941), *The Moon and Sixpence* (1942), *The Bridge of San Luis Rey* (1944) and *Champion* (1949) were also nominated, and his background music for *The Westerner* (1940) and *Duel in the Sun* (1946), though not officially recognized, were numbered among his more distinguished accomplishments.

Bronislau Kaper, born in Warsaw in 1902, was headed for a career in law to which he was directed by his father, a successful businessman. But music was his love from the time he first saw a piano when he was seven, and while studying law he also went through a rigorous training at the piano and in composition. In the mid-twenties he made his home in Berlin where, for six years, he was active writing music for German films. After the rise of Hitler, he spent two years in the French capital working for films. In the summer of 1935, Louis B. Mayer, then on vacation in Europe, heard a recording of "Ninon," a European hit song by Kaper and engaged him to work for MGM in Hollywood, an affiliation that lasted three decades. Kaper's title song (Gus Kahn) for *San Francisco* (1936) was his first association with the American motion picture industry and his first American song hit. He wrote for MGM films for four years before he was given his first assignment for a full score for *I Take This Woman* (1940). He did five more scores for MGM that year, including that for *The Mortal Storm*, and during the remainder of the decade was, in one way or another, responsible for the music of almost fifty films, among them *Bataan* (1943), *Gaslight* (1944), *Mrs. Parkington* (1944), *Our Vines Have Tender Grapes* (1945), *Green Dolphin Street* (1947), and *B. F.'s Daughter* (1948). John Green, who, during the forties, was Kaper's colleague at MGM, said of Kaper's screen music: "He is an unequalled master of music that occurs simultaneously with dialogue. . . . He has a built-in computer that somehow records the actual pitch and rhythm and variations of projection and impact of spoken voices. I would study his scores prior to conducting them, and there might be a scene with peppery dialogue—fast, loud, high pitched, rhythmically complicated dialogue. I would see the score he had written for the scene and it would be black with notes— . . . and I would wonder how we could run all this under dialogue. . . . But he had it all in his head—the music would fit in and out, and flow among this dialogue miraculously. . . ."

Victor Young spent twenty years in Hollywood. In that time he was musically involved with some three hundred and fifty motion pictures, nineteen of them nominations for the Academy Award, and one of them a winner, though he did not live to accept the

Oscar. He was born in Chicago in 1900 of Polish ancestry, where his father was an opera singer. Upon his mother's death when he was ten, Victor Young went to live with his grandparents in Warsaw. He attended the Conservatory, specializing in the violin and graduating with honors. He made his concert debut as violinist with the Warsaw Philharmonic, following it with a successful concert tour. On the outbreak of World War I, he returned to the United States, making his American debut in a recital in Chicago. Later he worked as a concertmaster in the Grauman Theater orchestra in Los Angeles. During the remainder of the twenties he was the music director of other motion picture houses and over the radio, besides composing popular songs, the most successful of which was "Sweet Sue" (Will J. Harris) in 1928. During the thirties he formed his own orchestra which was heard in theaters, over the radio and on records. In 1935, one of his songs, "A Hundred Years from Today" (Ned Washington) was used in a motion picture, *Straight Is the Way*, which served as his introduction to the movie industry which he was to serve so fruitfully for the next twenty years. His first original scores for the screen were written for Paramount in 1937, but it was in the forties that his importance was recognized through nominations for the Academy Award for his scores for *Arise My Love* (1940), *Arizona* (1940), *The Dark Command* (1940), *Northwest Mounted Police* (1940), *Hold Back the Dawn* (1941), *Silver Queen* (1942), *Take a Letter Darling* (1942), *For Whom the Bell Tolls* (1943), *Love Letters* (1945) and *The Emperor Waltz* (1948).

David Raksin had always wanted to be a composer for the screen; the concert world, from which so many other Hollywood composers of the forties came and to which they never failed to cast envious eyes, was not for him. He went to Hollywood in 1935 when he was twenty-three because that is where he wanted to establish his musical career—and establish it he did, with one of the best motion picture scores of the forties, for *Laura* (1944). The main theme from this film became a million-disk seller in Woody Herman's recording and after the release of the picture became a song hit with lyrics added by Johnny Mercer.

Raksin was born in Philadelphia in 1912. Having learned from early boyhood to play the piano, organ, several woodwind instruments and the percussion, he organized his own dance band when he was twelve and by the time he was fifteen was an accredited member of the Musicians' Union. While attending the University of Pennsylvania he played in dance bands and in an orchestra broadcasting regularly over WCAU, the Philadelphia outlet of the CBS network. After receiving his degree in music, Raksin came to New York where he was employed by various dance bands (including Benny Goodman's) either as performer or arranger. After two more years as an arranger for the publishing house of Harms he was called to Hollywood by Alfred Newman to assist in the preparation of Charlie Chaplin's music for *Modern Times* (1936). Raksin's first original screen score was for *Tampico* (1944), the year in which his excellent background music for *Laura* brought him recognition and status. Both films were produced by 20th Century-Fox for whom he continued to work for the remainder of the decade as arranger, adapter or composer. His best scores in the forties after *Laura* were for *Forever Amber* (1947) and *Force of Evil* (1949).

3

Figures compiled in 1948 provided no inkling that the decline and fall of the radio empire was near. There were more than thirty-seven million Americans tuning in regularly. Sponsors were expending more than $660,000,000 a year for programs, with a net profit in excess of sixty million dollars to the radio networks and local stations. ASCAP earned about five million dollars that year as revenue for its radio licenses.

Following the war's end, the air waves were alive with the sounds of popular singers, just as, before the war, they had been with those of big bands. Bing Crosby was heard on the Kraft Music Hall until the spring of 1946, after which he was starred on "Philco Radio Time" and the "Bing Crosby Show" sponsored first by Chesterfield cigarettes and then by General Electric. The "Chesterfield Supper Club" presented Perry Como, Peggy Lee, Frankie Laine and Jo Stafford among others. The "Bob Crosby Show," in which Bing's brother led his own band, offered a different female vocalist each week (Peggy Lee, Kay Starr, Jo Stafford and others). The "Club Fifteen" program, hosted by Bob Crosby, used Margaret Whiting, Evelyn Knight, Dick Haymes and Jo Stafford as vocalists. Rudy Vallee was crooning for Drene Shampoo over NBC on the "Rudy Vallee Show" and Frank Sinatra could be heard in "Songs by Sinatra" between 1943 and 1947 and "Songs for Sinatra" in 1947. Al Jolson was starring on the Kraft Music Hall between 1946 and 1948, and Jo Stafford had a show of her own over ABC in 1948–1949.

Popular tunes and show and movie music, of course, provided the basic grist for the mill of radio music. In this department, "Your Hit Parade" continued to tap its private sources to sift each week for radio the leading hit tunes topped by the three most in demand. Between 1946 and 1950 the following songs were the leaders on this program: Irving Berlin's "They Say It's Wonderful" from Annie Get Your Gun (1946); "The Anniversary Song" (Saul Chaplin and Al Jolson) from The Jolson Story (1946); a revival of the 1913 hit song, "Peg o' My Heart" (Alfred Bryan—Fred Fisher); "A Tree in the Meadow" (Billy Reid), an importation from England; and "Some Enchanted Evening" (Oscar Hammerstein II—Richard Rodgers) from South Pacific (1949).

The following songs also made frequent appearances on "Your Hit Parade": "It Might As Well Be Spring" (Oscar Hammerstein II—Richard Rodgers) from the film State Fair (1945); "Symphony" (Jack Lawrence—Alex Alstone); "To Each His Own" (Jay Livingston and Ray Evans), used as the title song for the 1946 film; "Ole Buttermilk Sky" (Jack Brooks—Hoagy Carmichael), an Academy Award nominee from Canyon Passage (1946); "That's My Desire" (Carroll Loveday—Helmy Kresa) revived from 1931; "Heartaches" (John Klenner—Al Hoffman), also revived from 1931; Frank Loesser's "I Wish I Didn't Love You So" from Perils of Pauline (1947); "Buttons and Bows" (Jay Livingston and Ray Evans), the Academy Award winner from The Paleface (1948); "Ballerina" (Bob Russell—Carl Sigman); Frank Loesser's "On a Slow Boat to China"; "Far-Away Places" (Joan Whitney and Alex Kramer); "Bali H'ai" (Oscar Hammerstein II—Richard Rodgers) from South Pacific; "Ghost Riders in the Sky" (Stan Jones); and "Again" (Dorcas Cochran—Lionel Newman) from Road House (1948).

But there was other fare, too, in the radio music of the first postwar years. Country music and folk music were being played over the air. Lush symphonic arrangements of standards and new pop tunes were still heard in performances conducted by André Kostelanetz and Morton Gould. Some bands were still able to find sponsors, despite the sharp decline of interest in such music. A program called "So You Want to Lead a Band," featuring Sammy Kaye and his "Swing and Sway" orchestra, invited members of the audience to step up and conduct the ensemble.

Quiz shows, with or without audience participation, had become popular. Music soon joined in this game. "Beat the Band," hosted by Hildegarde and sponsored by Raleigh cigarettes, required the band to identify songs from clues sent in by the listening public; the prize for having stumped the band was twenty-five dollars and a carton of cigarettes. Kay Kyser's "Kollege of Musical Knowledge" over NBC combined the presentation of musical selections with flippant quizzes of all too easy to answer queries made even simpler by Kyser's broad hints. "Sing It Again" also combined musical selections with musical quizzes.

The musical quiz game became a nationwide passion in 1948 with "Stop the Music" over the ABC network, hosted by Bert Parks. Popular tunes were played by an orchestra conducted by Harry Salter, and sung by Kay Armen or Dick Brown, with key words in the lyrics that provided the song title hummed rather than articulated. A telephone call was then placed from the studio to the listening public, the number chosen at random from telephone books. When the connection was made, Bert Parks shouted: "Stop the music!" If the person contacted could identify the song, he was given a chance to name a "mystery melody" and win a giant jackpot of gifts. It was estimated that some $165,000 in prizes were given away each week, and in the forty-four weeks of broadcasting more than seven million dollars in commodities and services had been distributed.

If the contestant failed to give the correct title of the mystery melody, the song was carried over to the following week. Since an unfamiliar or esoteric song was invariably used, it sometimes took weeks before identification was made. All the while the jackpot kept growing in size, value and diversity. All over the country, the mystery melody became a favorite subject for speculation. The popularity of "Stop the Music" inevitably drew listeners away from competing programs on the other networks. One was the Fred Allen show. To keep his audiences from switching over to "Stop the Music" he offered his listeners an insurance policy guaranteeing them five thousand dollars if they received a call from "Stop the Music" while tuned in to the Fred Allen Show.

4

A new medium of entertainment—the most powerful of all, as it turned out—began to challenge the supremacy of radio in the mid-1940s. It was television. Before many years, television completely displaced radio as America's Number One source of entertainment. As was reported in *Life* magazine, there were only seventeen television stations in the United States, and they were broadcasting to just 136,000 sets. By 1949, the number of stations had grown to fifty, the number of sets in the United States to 700,000, and the potential television audience numbered about four million. In the early seventies, over seventy million sets were in operation into which 750 or more stations were feeding programs seven days a week; over 95 percent of American homes owned at least one set and were using it a minimum of five hours a day.

The repercussions of television on all areas of entertainment were cataclysmic. Radio had to abandon its former concepts of varied programming to stay with what it did best: dissemination of news, disc jockey shows, and, later, talk shows. In the theater, vaudeville and revues were unable to survive the competition of TV variety shows which were liberally studded with stars. The economy of the living theater and motion picture was threatened as the American public, mesmerized by the tube, preferred staying at home.

It took half a century following the momentous discovery by Louis May in 1873 that the element selenium could conduct light, before the first shadowy, flickering pictures were able to be transmitted. On April 27, 1927, Herbert Hoover, then Secretary of Commerce, was televised in an address from a studio in Washington, D. C., the sight and sound of which reached New York, two hundred and thirty miles or so away. This was perhaps the first convincing evidence of the practicability of telecasting. In 1928, the first experimental television station was opened, owned by WGY, in Schenectady, New York, and broadcasting three days a week. In 1930, NBC opened an experimental station in New York (W2XBS). On July 20, 1931, CBS opened its experimental television station (W2XAB) in New York, with a program featuring a talk by James J. Walker, then Mayor of New York, Kate Smith singing "When the Moon Comes Over the Mountain" (Kate Smith, Howard E. Johnson and Harry Woods) and with other musical selections provided by the Boswell Sisters and by George Gershwin. By the end of that year, CBS was telecasting experimentally seven hours a day, seven days a week, devoting its programs mainly to news, shows and intimate revues. In November 1932 it telecast the news of the Presidential election. Still in 1932, a major rival to both CBS and NBC in the infant world of television arrived with the opening of the Dumont TV network, formed by Allen Dumont and Lee de Forest; its first station was W2WXT in Passaic, New Jersey.

Allen B. Dumont began marketing all-electronic TV sets on a national scale. By 1939 there were about eight thousand of them in American homes, most concentrated in New York City. This was the year the first regular schedule of programing was initiated by NBC (W2XBS), the first program on April 30 presenting President Franklin D. Roosevelt opening the New York World's Fair. Other telecasts were made intermittently from the World's Fair grounds, including performances of Billy Rose's Aquacade. During 1939, Dinah Shore could be seen and heard from New York studios, and Imogene Coca (later to become one of television's major comedy stars) appeared in several skits. Meanwhile, theater had come to TV when the play, *Susan and God*, starring Gertrude Lawrence, was telecast by NBC in 1938.

On March 10, 1940, there took place the first American telecast of an opera in New York with a production of a tabloid version of *I Pagliacci* presented by performers of the Metropolitan Opera on the stage of Radio City Music Hall.

Color television was exhibited for the first time in 1940 at a private showing for members of the Federal Communications by W2XAB and a public demonstration the following September 4. But quality color was still some years off, while black and white transmission was slowly gaining a wider public. On July 1, 1941, the first commercial television stations were licensed: WNBT of the National Broadcasting Company (which opened with a telecast of the Dodgers-Pirates baseball game) and WCBW of the Columbia Broadcasting System. Television could now boast its first important newscaster, Lowell Thomas, and its first commercial, for Bulova watches.

The continued growth and development of television programing was slowed after Pearl Harbor. Nevertheless, during the war years, some forward steps were made. CBS inaugurated a music program, "Music Workshop" in 1942 starring the Broadway musical comedy star, Tamara, with Eddie Condon and his orchestra. In May 1943, a performance of the Offenbach opéra bouffe, *The Magic Lantern*, was televised by WRGB in Schenectady, New York, in its entirety. The following December, Humperdinck's opera, *Hansel and Gretel*, was televised in Hartford, Connecticut, by the Hartt Opera Workshops of the Julius Hartt Musical Foundation. In June 1944, Dumont entered the commercial television field by opening its station, WABD-TV, featuring a series of variety shows with Dick Haymes and Fred Waring and his Glee Club; Eddie Cantor made his television debut in 1944.

By the end of 1949, almost two hundred thousand television sets in the United States were tuning in to programs from sixteen stations: "Howdy Doody" for children; "A Woman to Remember," the first television soap opera; Gene Autry in a weekly program of cowboy songs and adventure scenes; "Kukla, Fran and Ollie"; "Meet the Press"; variety on Ed Sullivan's "The Toast of the Town" and "The Admiral Broadway Revue" starring Sid Caesar and Imogene Coca; amateur nights on Arthur Godfrey's "Talent Scouts" and Ted Mack's "The Original Amateur Hour"; theater on the "Philco Playhouse" and "Studio One"; news by John Cameron Swayze on "The Camel News Caravan"; situation comedies on "The Goldbergs" and "The Aldrich Family"; Ed Wynn, television's "the perfect fool"; and, finally, Mr. Television himself, Milton Berle, the irrepressible clown of the Texaco Hour, singing his theme song, "Near You" (Kermit Goell—Francis Craig)—one of the first songs to be popularized over television—and making Tuesday evening sacrosanct for television viewing for virtually all America.

Variety shows were not the only programs offering popular music. Perry Como was heard on the "Chesterfield Supper Club" and Ethel Waters on the "Borden Show." Big band music was seen as well as heard in performances by Paul Whiteman, Fred Waring and Sammy Kaye, the last of whom transferred his radio program "So You Want to Lead a Band" to television. On "The Voice of Firestone" standards and semiclassics were sung and played as regular weekly fare. Serious music was also being televised. On March 20, 1948, television offered symphonic music for the first time—in two concerts presented almost simultaneously by rival networks. Eugene Ormandy conducted the Philadelphia Orchestra from the Academy of Music over WCBS-TV at 5:30 P.M., and the NBC Symphony under Toscanini was telecast from New York over NBC at 6:30 P.M.

To draw national attention to the best in television programing, in 1948 the National Academy of Television Arts and Sciences instituted an award that has come to be called the "Emmy." These presentations were first made in Hollywood, California, in January 1949 to cover the preceding year. At that time only six trophies, or Emmys, were given: one to a performer (Shirley Dinsdale and her puppet Judy Splinters); two to programs ("Pantomime Quiz," a live show, and a film show on "Your Show Time Series"—"The Necklace"); one to a local Los Angeles television station (KTLA), for "overall achievement"; a technical award to Charles Mesak "in recognition of an outstanding advancement in the video field" for his "Phasefader"; and a special award to Louis McManus for his original design of the Emmy. In the musical area, nominations were given to the "Don Lee Music Hall" and "What's the Name of That Song?". The categories were expanded to eleven the following year, when Ed Wynn got two Emmys, one for the "best live show" and another for "the most outstanding personality." That year a nomination went to Fred Waring and his orchestra.

PART SIX

1950–1960

32

Music Is Heard and Seen—
Radio and Television
in the Fifties

1

On Sunday evening, November 4, 1950, radio made a strong (and what proved to be a final) bid to challenge the growing supremacy of television in the field of entertainment. This bid came with a star-studded ninety-minute variety program appropriately named "The Big Show." It emanated from the studios of NBC in Hollywood, hosted by Tallulah Bankhead, with music conducted by Meredith Willson. The first program gave a strong indication of the emphasis to be placed on guest artists of outstanding prominence in show business: Louis Armstrong, Bob Hope, Deborah Kerr, Frankie Laine, Dean Martin and Jerry Lewis, and Dorothy McGuire. Week after week stars of equal luster brightened programs continually punctuated by Miss Bankhead's exclamation of "dahling" to everybody, and ending pontifically with the singing of Willson's "May the Good Lord Bless and Keep You" in which each of the principals in turn delivered one of the lines.

Other new musical programs, though not of equal stature, came to radio. In 1952, the "Musical Comedy Theater," sponsored by MGM offered samples of the Broadway theater over the Mutual Network. Over CBS, from Monday through Friday morning, a songfest was shared by Bing Crosby and Rosemary Clooney. Over the Mutual Network Eddie Fisher was starred on "Coke Time."

But the inevitable was unavoidable. Television was taking over the place of honor from radio in America's homes. More than a thousand sets were being installed daily. By 1950, there were four million TV sets in American homes. NBC was justifiably advertising in newspapers that television was "the greatest medium of mass communication in the world." In recognition of the growing importance of this new medium, some of the large motion picture companies rushed to acquire television affiliations. Paramount owned KTLA in Los Angeles, WBKB in Chicago, and acquired a 29 percent interest in Dumont. 20th Century-Fox made a deal to supply NBC with five TV newsreels a week of Movietone News. Hal Roach announced that he was converting his studios in Culver City to the exclusive production of TV shorts. Stars were deserting radio in droves and heading for the television camera. In 1950 alone, television captured Frank Sinatra, Burns and Allen, Jack Benny, Gary Moore, Groucho Marx, Kate Smith, Roy Rogers and Dale Evans, Vaughn Monroe and Dean Martin and Jerry Lewis. Still in 1950, "Your Hit Parade" joined this invasion (though temporarily without abandoning radio), and Jan Murray hosted "Songs for Sale" a showcase for amateur composers and vocalists.

"Your Hit Parade" remained on television until 1959 when it expired (to return in a new format as a summer replacement in 1974). A look at its long activity both over radio and television is in order. Irving Berlin's "White Christmas" was the song heard most often on this program: thirty-three times, ten times in first position. After that came "People Will Say We're in Love" (Oscar Hammerstein II—Richard Rodgers) thirty times; "Harbor Lights" (Jimmy Kennedy—Will Grosz), a 1937 English song revived in 1949, twenty-nine times; "I'll Be Seeing You" (Irving Kahal—Sammy Fain), twenty-four times; and "You'll Never Know" (Mack Gordon—Harry Warren), twenty-two times. These songs appeared most often in the Number One position: "Too Young" (Sylvia Dee and Sid Lippman)—made famous in 1951 by Nat King Cole in his best-selling Capitol recording, twelve times; "Because of You" (Arthur Hammerstein—Dudley Wilkinson), first published in 1940, eleven times; "I'll Be Seeing You," ten times. Two songs by Richard Rodgers appeared seven times in the Number Two slot: "Bewitched, Bothered and Bewildered" (Lorenz Hart) and "No Other Love" (Oscar Hammerstein II), the last from the 1953 Rodgers and Hammerstein musical, *Me and Juliet*.

Harry Warren was the composer most often represented through the years, with forty-two of his songs selected. After him came Irving Berlin with thirty-three, James Van Heusen, twenty-five, Jimmy McHugh, twenty, Harry Revel, twenty, Richard Rodgers, nineteen, Ralph Rainger, seventeen, Jule Styne, seventeen, and Cole Porter, sixteen. The top lyricist was Mack Gordon with thirty-nine of his songs heard. After him came Irving Berlin with thirty-three, Johnny Mercer, thirty-two, Johnny Burke, twenty-eight, Leo Robin, twenty-six, Sammy Cahn, twenty-five, Al Dubin, twenty-three, and Frank Loesser, twenty-three. Frank Loesser had a distinction all his own: He was the only composer who had two songs alternating in the first and second places for several weeks running, with "On a Slow Boat to China" and "My Darling," in 1948.

The last telecast of "Your Hit Parade" came on April 24, 1959. On that evening the three top tunes were: "Come Softly to Me" (Gary Troxel, Gretchen Christopher and Barbara Ellis), "Venus" (Ed Marshall) and "Pink Shoelaces" (Mickie Grant). All three were either "rock" numbers or "rock" oriented, which goes a long way towards explaining why the time had come for "Your Hit Parade" to close shop. For a long time it had become increasingly difficult for the program to bring the aural and visual variety needed for interest, because of the preponderence of rock music among the leaders. Additionally, the new music audiences were far more fascinated by rock performers than by rock numbers and, consequently, were bored by the same weekly regulars on the program interpreting the rock hits of the week.

After an absence of a quarter of a century, "Your Hit Parade" returned to television on August 2, 1974. Current hits were, of course, highlighted, but the program now depended largely for its appeal on nostalgia. The opening program returned to October 1935 recalling Irving Berlin's "Isn't This a Lovely Day" and "Cheek to Cheek," as well as "Red

Sails in the Sunset" (Jimmy Kennedy—Will Grosz), "I'm in the Mood for Love" (Dorothy Fields—Jimmy McHugh) and "My Lucky Star" (Arthur Freed—Nacio Herb Brown). This program failed to survive that summer season.

The decade of the fifties brought many new musical programs on television. The best of the new variety shows were "Arthur Godfrey and His Friends," the Jackie Gleason Show, the George Gobel Show, the Dinah Shore Chevy Show, the Jack Benny Show, the "Shower of Stars," the "Ford Star Jubilee," "Your Show of Shows" starring Sid Caesar and Imogene Coca, the Perry Como Show, the Red Skelton Show, and the Gary Moore Show.

The leading pop singers with their own television network programs were Perry Como, Eddie Fisher, Frankie Laine, Dinah Shore, Tony Martin, Judy Garland, Jane Froman, Tennessee Ernie Ford, Gordon MacRae, Jo Stafford, Pat Boone, Andy Williams and Teresa Brewer.

There was music of bands and popular orchestras. Freddy Martin and Fred Waring and their respective orchestras appeared on television in 1951. The "Stage Show" in 1954 reunited the Dorsey brothers as a summer replacement for Jackie Gleason. "The Cavalcade of Bands" in 1955 brought back memories of the time when the big bands were in their heyday. The Lawrence Welk Show started its more than a quarter of a century history over television in the summer of 1955 sponsored by Dodge Brothers over TV.

There were other musical features, such as the Liberace show, formerly syndicated among television stations, but a network show in 1952. In 1957, Dick Clark initiated his "American Bandstand," the cradle of many rock stars and rock song hits. There were musical quiz and musical game shows. "Juke Box Jury," in 1953, hosted by Peter Potter, allowed a panel of experts to decide whether a new song would be a hit or a miss. Horace Heidt that same year was in charge of a talent contest show, "Swift Show Wagon." In 1954, "Name that Tune" became a favored television quiz show, hosted by George De Witt. (It returned to television in the mid-1970s.)

There were "Specials" that are memorable still. In 1953, the Ford Fiftieth Anniversary Program, telecast simultaneously over NBC and CBS, paired Mary Martin with Ethel Merman. The musical adaptation of Thornton Wilder's stage play, Our Town, was one of the brightest television evenings in 1955, as was the adaptation of the fairy tale Cinderella into a Rodgers and Hammerstein musical in 1957. In 1958, two distinguished Broadway musicals were adapted for television, Wonderful Town and Kiss Me, Kate. That was the year Fred Astaire made his bow on television in "An Evening with Fred Astaire," assisted by Barrie Chase. And a year later it was Harry Belafonte's turn to make his television debut in "Tonight with Belafonte."

Our Town was a Special with more than transitory musical interest. This was an original musical comedy for TV, presented by Producers Showcase over NBC in 1955, with lyrics by Sammy Cahn, music by James Van Heusen, and starring Frank Sinatra, Paul Newman and Eva Marie Saint. The text was adapted from Thornton Wilder's Pulitzer Prize-winning play of 1938. As an original musical, Our Town was one of the best ever written for television, boasting as it did two outstanding songs, "Love and Marriage" and "The Impatient Years." For the year of 1955, a new category had been included for the Emmy Awards, that of "best musical contribution." There were five nominees, and three of them were for Our Town: the song "Love and Marriage," the complete score by Sammy Cahn and James Van Heusen, and Nelson Riddle's scoring.

Another highly successful original musical in the fifties had the only score written by Rodgers and Hammerstein for a television production. It was Cinderella, produced by a CBS network of two hundred and forty-five stations, the largest ever assembled by any network for a single program. It was presented on the evening of March 31, 1957, reaching an audience of between seventy-five million and one hundred million viewers. Julie Andrews appeared as Cinderella, with the rest of an impressive cast including Howard Lindsay and Dorothy Stickney, Ilka Chase, Kaye Ballard, and a newcomer, Jon Cypher as the Prince. Hammerstein made no basic departure from the Cinderella fairy tale as it had originally been told by Charles Perrault in the seventeenth century. Music had to carry the main burden of providing the fairy tale with fresh interest for a modern-day audience. It did this well. The principal numbers were attractively lyrical: "Ten Minutes Ago," "Do I Love You?", "In My Own Little Corner" and "A Lovely Night." Together with the songs there were three delightful orchestral episodes, a march, a gavotte and a waltz.

Cinderella received a nomination for an Emmy and was subsequently not only repeated over CBS-TV, but also received a completely new television production in 1965. It was also staged in a London theater.

Richard Rodgers made another all-important contribution to television music in the 1950s with his extraordinary background music to *Victory at Sea*. Rodgers' score was the first new instrumental music conceived for the new medium, and to this day it has remained one of the best. *Victory at Sea* was a series of documentaries based on naval engagements during World War II. The first episode was telecast over NBC on October 26, 1952. It took Rodgers eight months to complete the thirteen hours of music required for the entire series, and the final product (orchestrated by Robert Russell Bennett) turned out to be Rodgers' most ambitious and artistically most satisfying compositon apart from the stage. The uniformly high inspiration of the principal sections of this giant score, and the way in which they captured the essence of the pictorial sequences, gave it its importance. Even apart from the pictorial text for which it was intended, the main sections hold up remarkably well, as in a nine-movement orchestral suite arranged by Robert Russell Bennett, recorded by the NBC Symphony under Bennett for RCA Victor, and in such individual items as the "Guadalcanal March," a staple in brass band repertories and occasionally performed at pop concerts. Another musical excerpt is a tango heard in the section entitled "Beneath the Southern Cross." This is a melody Rodgers later used for his song hit "No Other Love" (Oscar Hammerstein II) in the musical, *Me and Juliet* (1953).

Among the honors and praise bestowed on Rodgers' music for *Victory at Sea* was the George Foster Peabody special award in 1952. The George Foster Peabody Awards had been instituted in 1940 for distinguished achievement and meritorious service in radio by the Henry W. Grady School of Journalism at the University of Georgia in Athens, Georgia. For the next eight years, its sole concern with radio music was in the serious field. In 1949, these awards were extended to include television, at which time the "Ed Wynn Show" was honored in the field of entertainment. Jimmy Durante won the award in this same category in 1950. The special award to the music of *Victory at Sea* in 1952—coupled with the regular award to "Your Hit Parade"—were the first instances in which the Peabody recognized popular music. During the remaining years of the fifties, several other popular music programs were singled out for Peabody Awards: Perry Como in 1955; the Dinah Shore Chevy Show in 1957; and "An Evening with Fred Astaire" in 1958.

During the fifties many other original musicals, besides *Our Town* and *Cinderella*, were seen and heard over television. None met the standards demanded by the Broadway stage, and none proved competitive to *Our Town* or *Cinderella* in audience appeal or musical merit. Several other children's tales besides that of Cinderella were used as the material for original musicals, including *Jack and the Beanstalk*, *The Pied Piper of Hamelin* and *Hans Brinker or the Silver Skates*. The Hallmark Hall of Fame, which was the showcase for *Hans Brinker or the Silver Skates* in 1953 (songs by Hugh Martin), also offered that year *The Mercer Girls*, songs by Albert Hague. *The King and Mrs. Candle*, in 1955, had songs by Chuck Sweeney (lyrics) and Moose Charlap (music). *The Helen Morgan Story* was presented by Playhouse 90 over CBS-TV in 1957 with Polly Bergen in the title role, performing the songs most often identified with Helen Morgan. The last score Cole Porter was destined to write for any medium was for *Aladdin*, a TV production in 1958. This was also the year in which Richard Adler wrote the songs for two TV musicals, *Little Women* and *The Gift of the Magi*. None of these musicals received more than a single telecast and it is doubtful they will ever be heard of again.

2

During the fifties many songs and instrumental compositions either had their first hearing on television, or were plugged to success on television, or both. Among the first songs written expressly for television to become hits were "Let Me Go Lover" (Al Hill—Jenny Lou Carson) in 1954, "The Ballad of Davy Crockett" (Tom Blackburn—George Bruns) and "Love and Marriage" (Sammy Cahn—James Van Heusen). "Let Me Go Lover" was the rewrite of a 1953 song, "Let Me Go Devil" (Jenny Lou Carson) recorded that year by George Shaw. At the suggestion of Mitch Miller, "Let Me Go Devil" was redone with new lyrics so that it might be included in a dramatic presentation on "Studio One" over CBS where it was sung by Joan Weber as the pivot on which the plot of the play revolved. Joan Weber's Columbia recording of it sold over a million disks, and records by Patti Page, Teresa Brewer and Sonny Gale did almost as well. "The Ballad of Davy Crockett" was one of several numbers written for the Walt Disney television production *Davy Crockett* (later released as a full-length movie). Fess Parker introduced the ballad in the Disney TV production, and his recording for Columbia, together with those of Bill Hayes for Cadence and Tennessee Ernie Ford for Capitol, amassed a sale of several million disks; in all about ten million disks of this song were sold in twenty-three different recordings, not to mention releases abroad in a dozen languages, with twenty different versions recorded in France alone.

"This Is My Song" (Dick Charles) gained its popularity by serving as Patti Page's theme song, as did the theme song of Perry Como, "Dream Along With Me" (Carl Sigman) and that of Eddie Fisher, "May I Sing to You?" (Charles Tobias—Harry Akst and Eddie Fisher). The enormous popular appeal of Perry Como's television show made it possible for him to make an instant success on his program of the following numbers besides his theme song: "Catch a Falling Star" (Paul Vance and Lee Pockriss), "Round and Round" (Lou Stallman and Joe Shapiro), "Home for the Holidays" (Al Stillman—Robert Allen) and "Papa Loves Mambo" (Al Hoffman, Dick Manning and Bix Reichner). On the television program, *Come to Me*, Johnny Mathis introduced the song of the same name (Peter Lind Hayes —Robert Allen), Giselle MacKenzie introduced "Hard to Get" (Jack Segal) on the dramatic program, *Justice*, Johnny Desmond sang "Play Me Hearts and Flowers" (Mann Curtis —Sanford Green) on a Philco Playhouse program, and on the Gary Moore Show "What Is a Husband" (Bill Katz, Ruth Roberts and Gene Piller) received its first hearing anywhere. "Repeat After Me" (Gordon Jenkins), a best-seller in Patti Page's recording, first came from the nonmusical television play, *Manhattan Tower*; "Song for a Summer Night" (Robert Allen) was introduced by Mitch Miller and his orchestra in a Studio One production of the same name; and Tommy Sands first sang "Teen Age Crush" (Audrey Allison—Joe Allison) on the Kraft Theater over NBC before he recorded it for Capitol.

Other songs owing their birth, their success, or both, to television are "Lilac Chiffon" (Peter Lind Hayes—Robert Allen), sung by Julie London in a Kraft Theater production; "Love Me to Pieces" (Melvin Endsley) introduced by Jill Corey on the Studio One Summer Theater; "Ballad of Paladin" (Johnny Western, Richard Boone and Sam Rolfe), introduced by Johnny Western in the TV series "Have Gun, Will Travel"; "Kookie, Kookie, Lend Me Your Comb" (Irving Taylor) and "Kookic's Love Song" (Mack David and Howie Horowitz), both written for the TV series, "77 Sunset Strip."

Most of the short instrumentals written for television were used as theme or signature music for dramatic series. An exception to this rule was "Tracy's Theme" (Robert Ascher) which was heard in 1959 in the television dramatic presentation of *The Philadelphia Story* before becoming a best-selling Columbia recording in a performance by Spencer Ross and his orchestra.

David Rose was one of the most prolific writers of television instrumental theme music. A national survey in 1959 revealed that Rose's music was used as themes for twenty-two television series including "Highway Patrol" and "Sea Hunt." By this time, Rose had already produced a number of other instrumental compositions, not for television, that became staples in the semiclassical literature; "Dance of the Spanish Onion," and "Our Waltz" which he used as his radio theme, both written in 1942, and the highly popular "Holiday for Strings" in 1943 which he recorded with his orchestra for Victor.

Of English birth in 1910, Rose came to Chicago when he was four. He received his academic education in public schools and his musical training at the Chicago Musical College. For a time he worked as an arranger and pianist for a Chicago radio outlet of NBC and as a pianist for Ted Fiorito and his orchestra. In 1938, Rose made his home in Hollywood, California, assuming the post of music director of the Mutual radio network. For four years, during World War II, he saw service in the American Air Force, when he officiated as composer and music director of Moss Hart's Air Force stage production of *Winged Victory*. This was in 1943, the year "Holiday for Strings" brought him fame as a composer by selling several million records in releases by a dozen different companies.

After the war, Rose conducted extensively over the radio and on records. He is credited with being the first to use an echo chamber for special effects in recording. After serving as music director for numerous radio programs, he fulfilled a similar function for television which was to make abundant use of his creative as well as performing talent. In 1959, Rose won an Emmy in the category of "best musical contribution to a television program" for his musical direction of "An Evening with Fred Astaire" over NBC.

"Peter Gunn" was one of the more distinctive instrumental theme numbers for a television series of the same name, the music nominated for an Emmy in 1959 and success-fully recorded by Ray Anthony for Capitol. Its composer was Henry Mancini, whose initial recognition came from television and his theme for "Peter Gunn." He was born in Cleve-land, Ohio, in 1924 but raised in the steel town of Aliquippa, Pennsylvania, where he studied the piccolo, flute and piano. Recordings of big band music, especially those of Artie Shaw and Glenn Miller, gave purpose to his own musical drifting. He determined to become a jazz musician. With this in mind, he played the flute in several local dance bands. In 1937 he won first prize in flute playing as a member of the Pennsylvania All-State Band. He enjoyed making jazz arrangements, some of which he dispatched to Benny Goodman. Goodman used one of them and advised Mancini to come to New York and work for him. "It didn't take long for both Benny and me to find out I wasn't ready for such an ambitious assignment," Mancini has disclosed. Mancini now realized that his earlier musical training at the School of Music of the Carnegie Institute of Technology and privately with Max Adkin were not enough. He then enrolled in the Juilliard School of Music in New York, specializing in theory and composition. World War II brought his music study to a sudden halt and put him into uniform, first with the infantry, and then the Air Corps. After the war, Mancini worked as pianist and arranger for the reorganized Glenn Miller band which was then directed by Tex Beneke. He worked for Beneke for three years, after which he filled odd jobs making arrangements for nightclub singers and small jazz groups. In 1952 he got a two-week assignment to write the music for a movie at Universal-International. He stayed on that lot for six years, writing background music and doing the scoring for many motion pictures, including one particularly close to his heart, *The Glenn Miller Story* (1953).

Some of the films for which Mancini wrote music were directed by Blake Edwards who, in 1958, received the assignment to direct "Peter Gunn," a mystery series for television. Edwards hired Mancini to write the music. Using a small ensemble, necessary because of the limited budget, and employing a jazz style, which he felt was most suitable for a mystery show, Mancini created, together with the principal theme used weekly, about fifteen minutes of music for each show, all with a strong jazz beat rooted in a blues style. So good was this music that much of it that was pressed on records found wide acceptance. The theme, performed by Ray Anthony and his orchestra for Capitol, was a best-seller in 1959. The Victor recording of some of the principal music from various episodes, performed by Henry Mancini and his orchestra, sold about a million albums and was selected by the nation's foremost disc jockeys in a *Down Beat* pole as the "best jazz record of the year." This recording was also the recipient of two Grammys from the National Academy of Recording Arts and Sciences as the "best album of the year" and as the "best arrangement of the year."

After "Peter Gunn," Mancini wrote the music for "Mr. Lucky," a new television series directed by Blake Edwards. Mancini's own recording for Victor once again was a best-seller and won two Grammys. In 1960, Mancini returned to Hollywood and to motion pictures, for still more impressive achievements in screen music.

In the fifties there were other television programs besides "Peter Gunn" and "Mr. Lucky" to provide attractive theme music. Some of the best television theme music of the fifties came from "Bonanza!" (Jay Livingston and Ray Evans), "M-Squad" (Count Basie), "Rawhide" (Ned Washington—Dimitri Tiomkin) sung by Frankie Laine under the opening titles, "Richard Diamond" (Peter Rugolo), "77 Sunset Strip" (Mack David—Jerry Livingston) and "The Untouchables" (Nelson Riddle).

After 1960, the catalogue of television theme music became formidable, as virtually every major continuing television program—be it a situation comedy, a dramatic production, a talk show or a variety program—had its own musical identification. Among the best of these television themes have been: "Those Were the Days" (Lee Adams—Charles Strouse) for "All in the Family," "Baretta's Theme" (Dave Grusin) for "Baretta," "Ballad of Jed Clampett" (Paul Henning) for "The Beverly Hillbillies," "The Bold Ones" (Peter Rugolo), "Quentin's Theme" (Robert Corbert) for "Dark Shadows," "Dr. Kildaire" (Jerrold Goldsmith and Peter Rugolo), "Gilligan's Island" (John Williams), "Good Times" (Dave Grusin), "Happy Days" (Norman Gimbel and Charles Fox), "Little House on the Prairie" (David Rose), "Mannix" (Lalo Schifrin), "The Man from U.N.C.L.E." (Jerry Goldsmith), "Marcus Welby, M.D." (Leonard Rosenman), "The Mary Tyler Moore Show" (Sonny Curtis), "Maude" (Dave Grusin), "Mission Impossible" (Lalo Schifrin), "The Bob Newhart Show" (Pat Williams), "Petticoat Junction" (Paul Henning and Curt Massey), "Open Highway" (Nelson Riddle) for "Route 66," "Rhoda" (Billy Goldenberg), "Sanford and Son" (Quincy Jones), "Streets of San Francisco" (Pat Williams), "Surfside 6" (Mack David—Jerry Livingston), "Theme from S.W.A.T." (Jack Elliott) for "S.W.A.T.", "Johnny's Theme" for the

"Tonight Show" (Paul Anka and Johnny Carson) and "The Waltons" (Jerry Goldsmith).

Sometimes the theme music had a strong enough popular appeal to become success-ful on records. In the sixties this happened to "Ballad of Jed Clampett" and "Quentin's Theme," both recorded for Columbia by Flatt and Scruggs and to "Quentin's Theme," in a Ranwood recording by Charles Randolph Grean Sounde. Television continued to provide some of its theme music to best-selling records in the seventies. The year 1976 was a particularly eventful one for television theme music on records. The Number One position on the charts in 1976 for many weeks running was John Sebastian's "Welcome Back," in his own recording for Reprise, the theme music for the situation comedy "Welcome Back Kotter." Also high on the 1976 charts were four more television themes: "Theme from S.W.A.T." and "Baretta's Theme" (or "Keep Your Eye on The Sparrow") both in recordings by Rhythm Heritage for ABC, "Happy Days" in a Reprise recording by Pratt and McClain and "Making Our Dreams Come True," recorded by Cyndi Grecco.

Singing commercials on television, as on radio, generally consisted of little more than a brief snatch of melody to some catch phrase selling a product. Sometimes parodies of popular songs were used. From the fifties on, and continuing into the sixties and seventies, this was the case with Cole Porter's "De-Lovely," George Gershwin's "Our Love Is Here to Stay" (Ira Gershwin), Richard Rodgers' "The Lady Is a Tramp" (Lorenz Hart), "There'll Be Some Changes Made" (Billy Higgins—W. Benton Overstreet), "Thank Heaven for Little Girls" (Alan J. Lerner—Frederick Loewe) and Frank Loesser's "Standing on the Corner," all serving to sell automobiles; "Sunny Side Up" (De Sylva, Brown and Henderson) for dog food; "Give Me the Simple Life" (Harry Ruby—Rube Bloom) for canned soups; Cole Porter's "It's All Right with Me" for an airline; "A-Tisket, A-Tasket" (Ella Fitzgerald and Al Feldman) for a biscuit; "Ja Da" (Bob Carleton) for candy; and "Ain't She Sweet" (Hack Yellen—Milton Ager) for ginger ale. Carly Simon was paid fifty thousand dollars for reuse of her "Anticipation" as a commercial and an airline paid a similar amount for Jimmy Webb's "Up, Up and Away."

Occasionally, originally conceived television singing commercials have proved suffi-ciently appealing to warrant being adapted into popular songs. One of the earliest of these, in 1948, was "See the U.S.A. in Your Chevrolet," an advertising jingle for Dinah Shore on her Chevrolet Hour, after which it was adapted by Leon Carr and Leo Corday into a popular song. In later decades, several more singing commercials became popular songs for general distribution: the beer commercial, "If You've Got the Time" and the telephone commercial, "Call Me," the latter recorded by Sammi Smith. A best-seller on records in 1972 was the Coca-Cola commercial, "I'd Like to Teach the World to Sing," written by Billy Davis and Dottie West, selling over a million disks in the Elektra recording by the New Seekers. In 1974, Bell Telephone promoted a new song, "Friendship Is for Keeps" (John Lieberman), which boasted two sets of lyrics, one as a commercial, the other for noncommercial use. Both versions were recorded by Tony Bennett, by The Carpenters and by Valerie Harper. In 1976, Paul Anka wrote and recorded "The Times of Your Life" for Kodak. Paul Williams' song hit, "We've Only Just Begun," started out as a bank commercial.

3

A new crop of popular singers were given prominent exposure over television in the fifties.

When Martin and Lewis came to the television screen on the NBC network on April 3, 1949, the burlesque comedy and zany shenanigans of Jerry Lewis always took prece-dence over the sentimental crooning of Dean Martin, good as he was. Nevertheless, while he was still harnessed to Jerry Lewis' comedy routines, Dean Martin already managed to display a personalized singing charm that sometimes could send a song winging to success.

Born Dino Crocetti in Steubenville, Ohio, in 1917, Dean Martin went through a long and varied list of menial occupations before singing became his profession. Leaving school in the tenth grade, he spent his boyhood years working as a shoeshine boy, filling-station attendant, amateur welterweight prizefighter, steel mill hand, delivery boy of bootleg liquor, cigar store clerk, croupier in a back room gambling dive and dealer in gambling houses. At the encouragement of friends, he took on a nighttime stint as a singer in a Steubenville café which, in turn, landed him a singing job with the Sammy Watkins band at a salary of fifty dollars a week. Now calling himself Dean Martin, he found other singing assignments in various cafés. One of these was the 500 Club in Atlantic City, New Jersey, where, in the summer of 1946, he appeared on a bill including Jerry Lewis. "We started horsing around with each other's acts," Dean Martin later told an interviewer. "That's how the team of Martin and Lewis started. We'd do anything that came to our heads."

After six weeks in Atlantic City, Martin and Lewis opened at the Copacabana in New York where they proved so sensational that they were soon given top billing and a weekly salary of five thousand dollars. They were now a top nightclub attraction and, beginning in 1949, with *My Friend Irma*, stars in motion picture comedies as well. And they went on to conquer the television medium.

Even before he split with Jerry Lewis to go on his own as a solo performer, Martin had revealed how potent was his crooning style (which he had learned by listening to Bing Crosby). He made a hit out of "That's Amore" (Jack Brooks—Harry Warren) which he introduced in the motion picture *The Caddy* (1953), and which brought him his first gold record in a Capitol release in 1954. In 1954, he scored with "Sway" (Norman Gimbel —Pablo Beltran Ruiz) on television and on Capitol records; in 1955, with "Innamorata" (Jack Brooks—Harry Warren) which he introduced in the motion picture *Artists and Models* (1955). In 1955 he was the proud possessor of his second gold record for his Capitol release of "Memories Are Made of This" (Terry Gilkyson, Richard Dehr and Frank Miller) which he further popularized on television.

The separation of Dean Martin and Jerry Lewis in 1956, far from damaging Martin's career, as many suspected it would, gave him the freedom to exploit more fully than ever before not only his singing talent but his acting ability as well. On records, in nonsinging roles in the movies and on television he became a star who made many new songs popular. In 1957, he boasted a new gold record with "Return to Me" (Carmen Lombardo and Danny Di Minno); in 1958, he acquired still another with "Volare" (Mitchell Parish—Domenico Modugno); and in 1959 he had a best-seller with "On an Evening in Roma" (Nan Fredericks —S. Taccani). Subsequently, "Everybody Loves Somebody" (Irving Taylor—Ken Lane), a revival from 1948, became one of Dean Martin's giant record sellers.

Arthur Godfrey's Talent Scouts TV show was the incubator of several new singing stars. In 1950, Rosemary Clooney and Tony Bennett won first and second prizes respectively, which brought them a spot that same year on Jan Murray's TV show, "Songs for Sale."

Rosemary Clooney, born in 1928, came from Maysville, Kentucky. When she was thirteen she was taken to Cincinnati where, together with her sister Betty, she appeared as a duo over WLW, and for three years, between 1945 and 1948, as duo vocalists with Tony Pastor and his band. When Betty withdrew from a professional career in 1948, Rosemary Clooney remained for about a year with Tony Pastor as a solo vocalist. In 1949, she left the band to concentrate on a career as a solo singer. After her first appearances on television with Arthur Godfrey and Jan Murray, Mitch Miller signed her to a Columbia contract. "Beautiful Brown Eyes" (Alton Delmore, Arthur Smith and Jerry Capehart) was a modest success in 1951, but "Come-on-a My House" (William Saroyan—Ross Bagdasarian) that same year was, as far as sales went, a bombshell. The lyrics were by the eminent Pulitzer Prize-winning author and playwright. He was traveling with his cousin, Ross Bagdasarian, in New Mexico when, to pass the time, they decided to write a song, with Bagdasarian providing the tune for Saroyan's whimsical words. The result was "Come-on-a My House" which Saroyan used in his play, *Sons* (1950. When Mitch Miller first proposed to Rosemary Clooney that she record it she was highly skeptical, insisting this was not her kind of material. But Miller was insistent and won out. He conceived a novel instrumental effect by having a harpsichord accompany Miss Clooney. The record, which sold in excess of a million disks, made Rosemary Clooney a singing star. In 1951 she boasted three more million-disk records, "Tenderly" (Jack Lawrence—Walter Gross), "Botch-a-Me" (Eddie Y. Stanley—L. Astore) and "Half as Much" (Curley Williams). Her hit records in 1954 were "Hey, There" (Richard Adler and Jerry Ross), the hit number from the musical *Pajama Game* (1954); "Mambo Italiano" (Bob Merrill); and a novelty song, "This Ole House" (Stuart Hamblen). She was made the star of the "Rosemary Clooney Show" in 1956 which was syndicated to more than one hundred TV stations in as many cities, and in September 1957 she became an NBC television star. In 1976 she shared the stage with Bing Crosby at the Palladium in London and the Uris Theater in New York.

Tony Bennett (born Anthony Dominick Bennedetto in Queens, New York, in 1926) had comparatively little professional singing experience when he appeared on television for the first time in 1950 on Arthur Godfrey's Talent Scouts Show and on Jan Murray's "Songs for Sale." As a boy, Bennett had worked as a singing waiter in an Italian restaurant in Queens, New York, and while serving in the Army during World War II he appeared as a vocalist with several bands. After the war, he worked as an elevator operator at the Park Sheraton Hotel in New York while studying singing and making intermittent appearances. Then his television appearances brought him an important engagement in a Greenwich Village nightclub on a bill headed by Pearl Bailey. Bob Hope heard him there and had him appear with him at the Paramount Theater in New York, and took him with his company on a nationwide tour. When this tour ended, Bennett was further discovered by Mitch Miller at Columbia Records who had him record "The Boulevard of Broken Dreams," a 1950 revival of an Al Dubin, Harry Warren song from 1933. This was Tony Bennett's first successful record. It was rapidly followed by "Because of You" (Arthur Hammerstein and Dudley Wilkinson), "Cold, Cold Heart" (Hank Williams), "I Won't Cry Anymore" (Fred Wise—Al Frisch) and "Solitaire" (Renée Borek and Carl Nutter—King Guion), each a giant seller. In 1951, *Cash Box* singled him out as the leading recording male vocalist of the year. His successes kept mounting, not only on records, but in nightclubs and on television. His recording of "Rags to Riches" (Richard Adler and Jerry Ross) sold over two million disks, with million-disk sales accumulating for "Stranger in Paradise" (Robert Wright and George Forrest) from the Broadway musical *Kismet*, and "Firefly" (Carolyn Leigh—Cy Coleman).

Then, for a time, Bennett's popularity was arrested by the craze for rock numbers for which he had no affinity. But in 1962 his singing career gained a new lease on success with his greatest hit song, "I Left My Heart in San Francisco" (Douglas Cross—George Cory). This song was originally written in 1954. But in 1962 Bennett reintroduced it at the Fairmont Hotel in San Francisco with astonishing results. He then recorded it for Columbia to achieve a more than three million disk sale, a release that received two Grammys. Tony Bennett has remained among the elect of pop singers.

Steve Lawrence (born Sidney Leibowitz in Brooklyn, New York, in 1935) began his singing career as a choirboy in a synagogue where his father was cantor. By the time he was fifteen, Steve was earning his living as a piano accompanist at club dates and amateur nights and in modest bars. He assumed the name of Steve Lawrence (adopting the first names of two nephews) just before he won first prize on the Arthur Godfrey Talent Scouts TV show in 1951 with "Domino," a French song by Louis Ferrari with English lyrics by Don Raye. A year later, he signed with King Records his first recording contract; his initial release, "Poinciana"—a revival from 1936 of a hit song by Buddy Bernier (lyrics) and Nat Simon (music)—sold over one hundred thousand copies. A permanent engagement on the Steve Allen "Tonight" show over NBC in 1954 brought him national coverage. Eydie Gorme (born in New York's Bronx in 1932) was another permanent singer on the "Tonight" show. She had served her vocal apprenticeship with bands led by Tommy Tucker and Tex Beneke; while appearing with Steve Allen over television she made her nightclub debut at the Copacabana in 1956 and her stage debut, a year later, as the singing star of the Jerry Lewis show at the Palace Theater. Steve Lawrence and Eydie Gorme were married on December 29, 1957. Since then they have become one of the most successful male and female singing duos in show business. In 1960, they were awarded a Grammy for "best performance by a vocal group" for their ABC album, *We Got Us Two on the Aisle;* one year later they were among the five recording artists named winners of the Institute of High Fidelity awards for "outstanding contributions to the musical arts." In 1966, Eydie Gorme collected a second Grammy, this time as "best female vocal performance" for her Columbia recording of "If He Walked Into My Life" (Jerry Herman) from the Broadway musical *Mame.* Meanwhile, in 1962, Steve Lawrence enjoyed a giant record sale for "Go Away, Little Girl" (Gerry Goffin—Carole King) which he introduced, and came up with a second record best-seller in 1963 with "Don't Be Afraid Little Darlin' " (Cynthia Weil and Barry Mann) both for Columbia. On February 27, 1964, Lawrence made his Broadway musical comedy debut as Sammy in *What Makes Sammy Run?* in which he received the Drama Critics Circle Award for best male performance of the year and where he introduced "My Hometown" and "A Room Without Windows" (Ervin Drake). Eydie Gorme and Steve Lawrence were then co-starred in the Broadway musical *Golden Rainbow* (1967), out of which came the hit song "I've Got to Be Me" (Walter Marks), another giant seller for Lawrence. Whether singly or as a pair, Eydie Gorme and Steve Lawrence have remained singing stars of the first order.

About two years after the Arthur Godfrey Talent Scouts Show brought Steve Lawrence his first recognition anywhere, Pat Boone won first prize there to start his own professional singing career in earnest. Born in Jacksonville, Florida, in 1934, Boone began singing over the radio on WSIX in Nashville, Tennessee. While attending North Texas Teachers College, he supported himself and his young wife by singing over WBAP-TV in Fort Worth, Texas. This was in 1954, the year he won first prize in Ted Mack's Amateur Hour and in which he gained national attention by repeating this achievement on the Arthur Godfrey Talent Scouts Show. Arthur Godfrey now made him a permanent member of his morning TV shows, and Dot gave him a recording contract. His recording of "Two Hearts" (Otis Williams and Henry Stone) won a place on the charts in 1954. He enjoyed even greater record sales for "Ain't It a Shame" (Antoine "Fats" Domino and Dave Bartholomew) in 1955, and in 1956–1957 with "I Almost Lost My Mind" (Ivory Joe Hunter), "I'll Be Home" (Ferdinand Washington and Stan Lewis) and "Friendly Persuasion," (Paul Francis Webster—Dimitri Tiomkin), the last also known as "Thee I Love," an Academy Award nominee in the motion picture *Friendly Persuasion* (1956). His biggest record success came in 1957 with "Love Letters in the Sand" (Nick and Charles Kenny—J. Fred Coots), a revival of a hit song of 1931.

Then a hot show business property, Pat Boone was made the star of the "Pat Boone Show" on TV and in the motion pictures *Bernadine* (1957) and *April Love* (1957). The title songs from each of these pictures—"Bernadine" (Johnny Mercer) and "April Love" (Paul Francis Webster—Sammy Fain)—became hit records, each selling over a million disks. Boone's subdued and sincere song styling, boyish appearance, sobriety of personal conduct, wholesome family life and his insistence, in spite of his fabulous income, on continuing his academic education at the School of General Studies at Columbia University from which he received his Bachelor of Science degree in 1958, all won him the admiration and following of the older set as well as the adulation of the young.

Andy Williams was an important member of Steve Allen's team on his TV show "Tonight" for two and a half years before he came into his own as a solo vocalist with his first million disk sale of "Butterfly" (Bernie Lowe and Karl Mann) on the Cadence label in 1958. This success was largely responsible for landing him his first show over television on the CBS network a year later.

A native of Wall Lake, Iowa, where he was born in 1930, Williams began his professional career as singer with the Williams Brothers act which appeared in nightclubs with Kay Thompson. He left his brothers in 1952 to become a solo vocalist, his first important assignment being on Steve Allen's "Tonight" Show. Andy Williams' second million-disk sale came in 1959 with a revival of "Hawaiian Wedding Song" (Charles E. King) that had been written and published in 1926. In 1961, Williams left Cadence to become a Columbia artist and to enter upon a more productive phase of his career not only as a recording artist but as a television star. As such, he kept the ballad alive in an age of rock and rhythm and blues, notably with "Moon River" (Johnny Mercer—Henry Mancini) in 1961, and "Days of Wine and Roses" (Johnny Mercer—Henry Mancini) in 1962.

Wayne Newton's singing talent was incubated on television in the fifties. Part Cherokee, he was born in Roanoke, Virginia, in 1942. He began singing in the cradle; his first fee (five dollars) was earned when he was five. While attending public school he was performing in churches and schools in Roanoke. At the same time he started to study the piano, which he learned to play well, even as later he did the banjo, guitar, trumpet, violin and drums.

He was in his early teens when he got his first television job as a singer on station KOOL in Phoenix, Arizona. He did so well that in 1958 he dropped out of school to accept a contract from the Fremont Hotel in Las Vegas. Over a five-year period, he and his brother, Jerry, performed at the Fremont Hotel six times a night, six nights a week.

If television provided Wayne Newton with his first "break" in show business, it was also responsible for bringing him into the national limelight. This happened on the Jackie Gleason CBS–TV show where he appeared as a singing soloist four times in 1962, and four more times in 1963. His youthful chubby appearance, high-pitched soprano voice and emotional stylizations so endeared him to television audiences that he was called upon to make other appearances on major network programs.

He was also called upon to make records, his first single, "Heart" (Jerry Ross and Richard Adler), coming out in 1963. It did only moderately well, but later the same year "Danke Schoen" (Kurt Schwabach and Milt Gabler—Bert Kaempfert) was released by Capitol to become a best-seller. Performances in nightclubs and on television and other best-selling records made Wayne Newton one of the most important singing newcomers of the mid- and late-sixties. Among his best-selling records in the sixties were "Summer Wind" (Johnny Mercer—Henry Mayer), "Dreams of an Everyday Housewife" (Chris Gantry) and a revival of a ballad from 1948, "Red Roses for a Blue Lady" (Sid Tepper and Roy Brodsky). His albums were also high on the best-selling charts, the best of which in the sixties were Danke Schoen, Red Roses for a Blue Lady, Summer Wind, Best of Wayne Newton, Song of the Year and Wayne Newton's Greatest. On the Chelsea label, his album Daddy Don't You Walk So Fast brought him a gold record in 1972.

Though he has sold over sixteen million records, it is in the nightclub that Wayne Newton has become a superstar. The warmth of his personality and the charm of his stage manner have made him an idol of the nightclub circuit, particularly on the Strip at Las Vegas where he has become a box-office attraction in the class of Elvis Presley and Frank Sinatra. A five-year Las Vegas contract, earning him thirty-five million dollars, made him the highest paid performer in nightclub history.

4

Now that the foremost entertainers in popular music had gone over to television, the disc jockey ruled over the radio airwaves with his spinning disks. He, more than any other single force, made unknown singers into stars and unknown songs into gold records. With such power at his command the disc jockey became the autocrat of the popular music business in the fifties.

There were several thousand jockeys playing records over the two thousand or so licensed American radio stations. These jockeys came from many walks of life, from show business, from college campuses and acting studios; some were writers, record collectors, music lovers, or even members of the clergy. They operated in hotels, on college campuses, one-story houses, commercial buildings as well as in the studios of radio stations. The majority of these jockeys built their programs around the leaders in the weekly charts, the most respected of which was "The Top 100" of *Cash Box*, "The Hot 100" of *Billboard* and "The Singles Chart" of *Record World*. *Cash Box* drew up its weekly chart by contacting one hundred fifty radio stations and two hundred music stores; *Billboard* reached sixty-three radio stations and seventy-eight music stores; *Record World* contacted five hundred radio stations and about one thousand record stores. Through these findings, these publications were able each week to chart the course of the records most in demand, and this information was freely tapped when the disc jockeys set about their daily programing. A bullet-shaped symbol next to a record was an indication on the charts that it was on its way up in sales, an all-important sign to disc jockeys in their programing.

The daily programing of the top tunes on the weekly charts is believed to have originated at KOWH in Omaha. Todd Storz, its director, after watching people in an Omaha restaurant pumping coins into a jukebox to hear the current top hits, instituted on his station a daily program of the best-selling records in local stores. In 1953, at his new post at WTIX, New Orleans, Storz extended his scheduling to a twenty-four hour a day operation. "This," remarks Arnold Passman in *The Deejays*, "was certainly not a new approach to radio, but Storz extended the 'Hit Parade' shows to a full-time frenzy at WTIX." After that, Tiger Flowers offered the top twenty tunes of the week at WSDU in New Orleans. The manager of the competing New Orleans radio station, Bud Armstrong of WTIX, took note of the growing popularity of Tiger Flowers' show. "If 'Top 20' pulls that rating," he remarked, "think what we could do with the 'top 40.' " And so, WTIX presented the top forty hits every afternoon from three to six (the slogan of the program being "the top forty at 1450"). On the heels of the success of this programing, disc jockeys on many different stations now began to present their own programs of the top ten, twenty, or forty tunes of the week.

Many jockeys specialized in a specific area of popular music, with some concentrating on folk music, others on rock, country and western, or rhythm and blues slanted towards a black audience.

The top jockeys were supersalesmen not only of the music they played and the records they plugged but also of the products that sponsored them. The top jockeys in America have been: Bill Randle, Bill Gordon, Howie Lund and Bud Weddell in Cleveland; Bob Clayton in Boston; Alan Freed in Chicago; Dick Clark in Philadelphia; Tom Clay in Detroit; Al Jarvis in Los Angeles; Martin Block, Andre Baruch, Sidney Torin (Symphony Sid), Dick Gilbert and Freddie Robbins in New York City; Rege Cordic in Pittsburgh; Bob Crane in Hornell, New York; Rush Hughes and Gil Newsome in St. Louis; Soupy Heinz (later better known as the comedian Soupy Sales) in Huntington, West Virginia; Kurt Webster in Charlotte, North Carolina; "Jazzbo" Al Collins in Salt Lake City; and Wolfman Jack who has been heard on 2,223 stations in forty different countries.

Harry Richmond, an up-and-coming music publisher, was among the first in the business to evaluate correctly the might of the disc jockey. Richmond decided to record the songs he was about to publish, or had just published, for distribution among a select group of disc jockeys. He then called upon them for advice whether the song was worth publishing and promoting. A peripheral benefit from this practice came when some of these jockeys, flattered by this attention, started the ball rolling for Richmond by plugging one or more of the songs he submitted to them.

The successful promotion of several records and songs in the late 1940s provided more than a hint of the clout of the disc jockey in the music business. Richmond, himself, got firsthand evidence of it in 1950 when he published a novelty number "The Thing" (Charles R. Grean), which Phil Harris recorded for Victor. Richmond sent out twenty-five copies of this record (a pressing he made himself) to as many jockeys in key cities. A railway strike in the Boston area held up the delivery of the Phil Harris recording. The record Richmond had placed with Bob Clayton turned out to be an exclusive for that jockey in the Boston area. Clayton took full advantage of this by playing the pressing at least once each hour for several days running. There developed such an enormous demand for the Harris recording in the shops that before the week was over the Victor distributor in Boston sent out his own truck to New York City to pick up twenty thousand disks.

The evidence kept piling up after that that plugs from disc jockeys could zoom a record to the best-seller charts. Bill Randle, at WERE in Cleveland, played a recording in 1951 of the 1926 hit song "Charmaine" (Lou Pollack—Erno Rapee) in a new record performance by Mantovani and his strings. This release not only became an instant best-seller but Randle's plugging, combined with the success of the Mantovani release, started a vogue for string orchestra recordings in general and Mantovani recordings in particular. Bill Randle was also the discoverer of Johnnie Ray's record of "Cry" (Churchill Kohlman), and the one who helped make "The Yellow Rose of Texas" (adapted by Don George) a hit. A local disc jockey in Louisville, Kentucky, in 1951, was responsible for two song hits and, simultaneously, for the emergence to the limelight of a new songwriter, Mrs. Chilton Price. Mrs. Price, a Louisville housewife, wrote two songs with Pee Wee King and Redd Stewart, "Slow Poke" and "You Belong to Me." After the local Louisville jockey played these songs interminably they caught on, and the Pee Wee King Victor recording of "Slow Poke" sold over a million disks. Dewey Phillips, a Memphis disc jockey, was so taken with Elvis Presley's first record, "That's All Right" (Arthur Crudup) backed by "Blue Moon of Kentucky" (Bill Monroe), that he played each side seven times consecutively. A week later six thousand copies of that recording were sold in Memphis, the beginnings of the Presley boom. Alan Freed is credited with putting Chess Records in the black and for bringing Chuck Berry his first recognition. Murray "The K" Kaufman in New York was the first to draw attention to Johnny Mathis.

As soon as record companies, record distributors and music publishers became fully aware of the enormous weight that disc jockeys carried with their audiences, bribery inevitably followed. This practice was baptized by *Variety* as "payola," which the Federal Trade Commission defined as "money or other valuable considerations given to disc jockeys to expose records in which record companies have a financial interest." *Variety* elaborated upon this theme by explaining: "Exposure means playing a record, day after day, sometimes as much as six to ten times daily and substantially increasing its sales. The disc jockeys conceal the fact that they are paid for broadcasting the songs and misrepresent to listeners that they select these records independently and without bias either on each record's merits or public popularity. This deception has the tendency to mislead the public into buying the 'exposed' record which they otherwise might not have purchased, and also to advance these recordings in popularity polls, which in turn tends to increase their sales substantially."

Payment was made in an infinite number of ways: expensive gifts, large cash bonuses, an interest in a publishing house or small record company or a record distributing firm, a regular weekly or monthly income (sometimes paid out on the ruse that the disc jockey was a "consultant" paid to "listen" to given records and give expert advice), paid vacations, expensive travel accounts (with the airplane ticket for a supposed trip often converted into cash), large stocks of free records ("freebees"), Lucullan conventions. Perhaps the most publicized convention was that held in Miami Beach, Florida, during Memorial Day weekend of 1959. One Miami newspaper succinctly described the three-day event as an orgy of the "three B's": Booze, Broads, Brawls. There was such a demand for call girls that those of Miami Beach had to be supplemented with recruits from Chicago, New York and Puerto Rico. Many disc jockeys raided the stores of their hotels, charging their purchases to their hotel bills which, of course, were paid by the record companies. Other jockeys extended their paid-for vacations by one or two weeks. The overall cost to the record companies was astronomic, but behind the scenes, many a new record was being groomed for the charts by extensive national coverage by disc jockeys. The varied enticements and emoluments kept alive the romance between record companies, record distributors, and the disc jockeys. The bribe was the oil for the machinery that kept a record spinning before the radio microphone day after day.

Payola was a dishonest practice, since a disc jockey was presumably well paid to be objective in his choice of records and in the frequency with which he played any given one. Payola represented not only a degeneration of moral and ethical values, but of musical standards as well. Many a song that should have been relegated to the refuse heap as soon as it was recorded was orbited to public acclaim because a number of highly influential disc jockeys were themselves reaping a harvest from this success, a success that they had set into motion in the first place because they were handsomely bribed to do so.

The word payola was new, but not the practice. Long before radio, composers and music publishers had indulged in payola to promote their songs. When Walter Kittredge gave Asa Hutchinson of the Hutchinson Singing Family a share of the royalties of "Tenting Tonight on the Old Camp Ground" in 1863 to get a publisher and to feature it at the concerts of the Hutchinson Family, this was payola; so was the cash payment and the share in royalties that Charles K. Harris paid J. Aldrich Libby in 1892 to place "After the Ball" in A Trip to Chinatown. The name of Louis W. Pritzkow appears on the sheet music as the lyricist of Monroe H. Rosenfeld's "Take Back Your Gold" in 1897 because Rosenfeld was paying him off to introduce the song in one of his minstrel shows. When, in Union Square and early Tin Pan Alley, song pluggers gained the favor of performers through modest gifts and sundry other favors, this was payola. When music publishers provided vaudevillians with paid claques, expensive sets and costumes in return for getting their songs used in the act, this was payola. And when, before long, the evil was extended by having publishers pay entertainers a regular weekly salary of a hundred dollars a week or more to use only the songs of their company, this, too, was payola. By 1905, Tin Pan Alley was paying out half a million dollars a year as bribes to stage stars.

Many music publishers at that time came to realize that bribery was getting out of hand and not always working to the best interests of the industry. Those who did not have an in with performers because they weren't buying their way or paying a high enough price were just not getting their songs placed. This happened to the firm of J. W. Stern and Company which for a time resisted paying performers. But when fewer and fewer of its songs were being heard in theaters, the company admitted defeat. Edward B. Marks instructed his office manager to engage in the prevailing payoff racket. The manager returned to him with the sad tidings that so many acts and performers were by now signed up by competing firms that he could not make a single worthwhile deal.

Those with performers on their regular payroll were rapidly coming to realize that the money being distributed so lavishly week after week was out of all proportion to the value received. These publishers were just not selling enough additional sheet music to absorb this expense. However, they had a tiger by the tail, and could not let go. The publisher knew that if he tried to stop making payments for performances he would leave the field wide open to his competitors and close it completely for himself.

This racket worked badly not only for publishers, but for the performers themselves, however much they benefited financially. The quality of performances in vaudeville and stage musicals—and that of the material being used—suffered serious deterioration. A performer was necessarily partial to the song and the publisher that brought him the highest revenue, even if this number did not suit his style or fit into his act. As a corollary, he often had to turn down another number, from a competitive publisher, that would have served his talent and his act far better.

John J. O'Connor, a writer who had become business manager of *Variety*, was one of those who saw the whole ugly picture.

In or about 1910 he decided to do something about it. He created a new organization, the Music Publishers Protective Association, in which publishers could work as a unit to protect their interests and ban all handouts. Feist, Remick, T. B. Harms, all declined to become members of his organization, insisting that they did not want to rock a boat that was sailing so smoothly. They felt it was expedient to continue along the lines that had been bringing such prosperity to the whole music business, even though they recognized that there was no appreciable ratio between the amount spent on payola and the sales of sheet music. The Music Publishers Protective Association (MPPA) would have been stillborn had not O'Connor devised a stratagem by which to wear down resistance. In 1916, he invited J. J. Murdock, assistant to the theater and vaudeville tycoon E. F. Albee, to attend a vaudeville show at one of the theaters under Murdock's control, the Alhambra in uptown New York. The overture, the music for the acrobatic act, the principal ballad of an Irish tenor, the entrance number for the dramatic act all used the same popular tune—the plugger of that song had done a thorough job in linking up all the acts on the bill. Murdock saw the point O'Connor was trying to make, recognized instantly how this disease had been allowed to fester in the theater. The next day he issued a directive to all the theaters in his circuit that performers were to use only the music of members of MPPA. Feist, Remick, Harms all rushed to join the organization, followed rapidly by other outfits in Tin Pan Alley. The first thing the organization agreed upon was to outlaw any form of payment by its members to performing artists. The Vaudeville Managers Protective Association (VMPA) supported MPPA by barring bookings to any performers known to be receiving payments from publishers.

Payola stopped, but only temporarily. It did not take long for first one publisher, then another, to devise devious ways to influence performers to use their songs. The most effective, and the hardest to pin down as a violation of the rules, was to make a stage star a collaborator in writing a song. This entitled the performer to a share in the royalties. What happened was that a plugger would bring a manuscript to a star seeking advice and criticism. The star might change a word or so in the lyrics or suggest a slight alteration in the melody.

For these miniscule contributions the performer became a collaborator in the song's writing, and was so credited on the sheet music. The fact that the performer thus profited from the song's success made him highly agreeable to including it in his act or show, and to keeping it there as long as the sale of the sheet music kept swelling his or her income.

By the mid-1930s, the music publishers were back at the game of paying performers to get their songs featured by singers or orchestra leaders. Some known to have profited in one way or another were Harry Richman and Paul Whiteman—Harry Richman, by taking an outright fee each time he used a song on a radio broadcast, and Whiteman by serving as a musical "adviser" for Leo Feist. Now it was the song plugger who started a rebellion, sensing as he did that his own efforts in placing songs were being undermined by the bribes of the front offices. Fearing that their jobs were in jeopardy, they joined forces and inflicted fines ranging from one thousand dollars to two thousand dollars on anyone found guilty of bribing performers. Once again the tide was arrested, but payoffs to performers were still so widespread in 1938 that the Federal Trade Commission studied the situation and advised ASCAP that bribery to get songs performed was unethical and had to be discontinued. ASCAP promised to use its influence to remedy this situation which only insured that all such payoffs were henceforth made discreetly.

But all earlier forms of payola in the music publishing business were reduced to insignificance in comparison to the way in which recording companies and distributors were buying the cooperation of the disc jockeys in the 1950s. By that time, the record business was a giant operation; the lucky records that were being snatched up in the stores brought in fortunes in profits. With disc jockeys able to take a new release and in short order plug it to phenomenal success, the recording companies and distributors beat a well-worn path to their doors to gain their favor. As the recording business kept expanding in the years of rock 'n' roll, so did payola until it became the way of life for the radio industry. In December 1950 *Billboard* was already able to report that "payola to disc jockeys is at an all-time peak," adding, "publishers do considerable subsidizing. Much of the money they used to set aside for live remote broadcasts now goes for the spinners. In addition to cash, they send gifts, cut jockeys in on tunes and entertain them on lavish New York junkets. . . ." In *Variety*, a few years later, Abel Green published a series of editorials with the headline: "Payola—Worse than Ever." And disc jockey Howard Miller told an interviewer for the Chicago *Tribune*: "Everyone in the industry knows that payola is running rampant."

In 1959, the lid blew off the pressure cooker, creating an explosion that rocked both the recording and the radio industries to their very foundations.

The scandal was touched off when Tom Clay, disc jockey at WJBK, was openly accused of accepting payola by a promoter of rock 'n' roll. Clay not only admitted it, but went on to discuss the history of payola. Payola, he insisted, was part and parcel of the entire industry and it involved every disc jockey of any consequence. He argued: "It is all right for a man to put down two hundred dollars and leave a record for a deejay. If the deejay honestly thinks it [the record] is good then he is justified in taking the two hundred dollars because after all that money is an investment for the record company. If the deejay turns down the record the two hundred dollars is well spent. It saves the company money—they won't go ahead and make ten thousand records."

Charges and countercharges now kept accumulating. Rumors of big payoffs spread and some were substantiated by fact. Confessions were rampant. A record wholesaler in Philadelphia revealed he had twenty-five local disc jockeys on his payroll. The president of King Records confessed that his payola bill was two thousand dollars a week. One record distributor said that to cover the expense of payola for any given recording he had to sell ten thousand disks. Information leaked out that many disc jockeys had vested interests in the records they played. By owning a percentage in a singer, record company, record distributor, or publishing house, the disc jockey personally profited from the success of a record he was plugging.

The FCC demanded from 5,300 radio stations a detailed accounting under oath of every program for which payment had been made but not disclosed. In Detroit, two stations, WKMH and WJBK, came forward with the information that, given the right price, they plugged records; that they had a deal called "Album of the Week," in which a record or album was broadcast on their disc jockey shows one hundred and fourteen times a week for a payment of $150 a week for a minimum of six weeks. As panic mounted among radio stations, with the fear of losing their licenses, one disc jockey after another, whose guilt of taking payola was more than circumstantial, was relieved of his job either through firing or voluntary resignation. This happened to Tom Clayton and Jack Le Goff in Detroit, Stan Richard, Bill Barlow and Mike Eliot in Boston, and Joe Niagara in Philadelphia among many others. Alan Freed was removed from his job at WABC when he refused to sign a sworn statement that he had never received money or gifts for plugging records.

In November 1959, Frank Hogan, district attorney of New York County, subpoenaed the financial records of many recording companies in an effort to ferret out the truth. Even before he turned over his ledgers, the head of one record outfit came right out and said he possessed a pile of cancelled one hundred dollar checks made out to disc jockeys. President Eisenhower ordered the FTC to make formal charges against offending record companies; three record companies and six distributors were forthwith accused and ordered to appear at a public hearing to present their defense. Congress formed the House Committee on Legislative Oversight, headed by Oren Harris of Arkansas, to hold open hearings of their own. Its investigative unit, with only desultory probing, uncovered the ugly fact that record companies had paid out $263,245 to 207 disc jockeys and other radio personnel in forty-two cities in a single year. Joe Finian of KYW was found to have received $16,000 in 1958–1959 from fifteen record companies "for using his knowledge to evaluate a record's commercial possibilities." Boston disc jockeys got over $40,000 in a three-year period from record companies and distributors. J. Smith of WILD, received $8,565 as royalties on records sold in the Boston area from four companies. Norman Prescott of WBZ acknowledged getting a $10,000 car for pushing certain records. He did not wait to get fired but resigned, admitting disgust at himself and at the entire industry.

The hearings also dealt with the conflicts of interest involving disc jockeys. The most powerful of these jockeys was Dick Clark, who presented a daily two-hour program on ABC-TV, "The American Bandstand," which was reputed to have sold more records than any other single program on radio or television. Clark owned three music publishing companies, had interests ranging from 25 percent to 100 percent in five record companies, owned the musical copyrights to one hundred and sixty compositions, and had a 50 percent interest in a record pressing corporation. From all these involvements he is believed to have earned half a million dollars a year. Clark was never accused of having accepted payola, but the suspicion that he favored the playing of songs and records in which he had an interest could not be stifled. More than one eyebrow was skeptically raised at the fact that where Clark had formerly played "Sixteen Candles" (Luther Dixon and Allyson R. Khent) four times in ten weeks, the song was heard on his program twenty-seven times in thirteen weeks after he had acquired an interest in its publishing company. But Dick Clark insisted he was innocent: "I have never agreed to play a record in return for payment in cash or any other consideration. My only crime was to make a fortune on a nominal investment." And, after he had divested himself of all interests which conflicted with his duties as a disc jockey, he emerged from the scandal comparatively clean.

Alan Freed pleaded guilty to the charge of receiving $30,650 from music companies and was indicted, fined and given a suspended sentence. When he died of uremia in 1965 at the age of forty-three, after holding down a few lesser disc jockey jobs and having been indicted for income tax evasion, he was an impoverished alcoholic.

Legislation in Washington, D.C., made a crime of payola. Tougher regulations were instituted by FCC. Radio companies started to clean out their own stables and to institute programing drawn exclusively from reliable charts. Disc jockeys who survived the holocaust, and the newer men in the industry, were cautious about accepting favors.

But the reform movement proved only temporary. Payola in a more subtle and evasive form continued to contaminate the recording and radio industries until, in 1972, a new giant scandal erupted. It was sparked by Jack Anderson, the distinguished syndicated columnist, who revealed he had uncovered "evidence of a new payola scandal in the billion-dollar record industry." He added, "Disc jockeys and program directors across the country are provided with free vacations, prostitutes, cash and cars as payoffs for songplugging." A month or so later, Clive Davis, president of Columbia Records, and his assistant, David Wynshaw, were removed from their high-paying posts for alleged misappropriation of company funds for personal use. But the trade buzzed with rumors that the firing was also brought on by the company's reputed payola practices involving not only the distribution of large sums of money but also hookers and drugs. A Federal grand jury, in Newark, New Jersey, and the office of Senator James I. Buckley of New York initiated investigations hinting at far-reaching corruption not only among record companies and radio stations but also among disc jockeys. The president of the Recording Industry Association of America, representing fifty-five recording companies, promised full cooperation with all such investigations while recognizing the "possibility that some of the practices reported in the media might be taking place." The upshot of all this was that nineteen indictments were handed down in June 1975 by the Federal government involving three presidents of record companies and six corporations.

Another major upheaval was followed by another period of housecleaning and a new cycle of reforms. But payola, it seems, cannot be totally eradicated, so long as the record business is a more than two billion dollar a year industry, and as long as bribery can work for the greater enrichment of all involved in the industry.

5

Conflict of interest prevailed as well in other areas of the music business. Major record companies were owned by the three giant radio-television networks: Victor by RCA, Columbia by CBS, and ABC-Paramount by ABC. From the beginning of talking pictures, major motion picture studios absorbed the principal music publishing houses. Motion picture studios were also in the record business: Paramount with ABC-Paramount, United Artists, Warner Brothers and MGM with labels of the same names. (In 1963 Warner Brothers acquired Reprise Records, formerly owned by Frank Sinatra.) Some record companies also owned publishing houses, a trend climaxed in the late 1960s with the purchase of Chappell and Company by North American Philips Company for forty-two million dollars. At that time, Philips was issuing Philips Records and Mercury Records and later on it acquired MGM Records. Many singers and bandleaders owned their own publishing houses and, in some instances, record companies. Many a songwriter was becoming his own performer. And several music publishing houses formed their own artist bureaus, and MCA, that giant of artists' representation, eventually acquired Decca Records and the Leeds music publishing company.

Such tie-ins brought on a complex and at times a subtle interrelationship that did not always work for the best interests of popular music. In Hollywood, producers were tempted to use the song copyrights in their possession for any given picture rather than seek out new music that might be more appropriate. In fact, in some instances, music was not being created for the motion picture story. Instead, movie stories were manufactured to make use of the valuable song properties owned by the studios. Leading singers and bandleaders with publishing interests profited directly from the songs they featured. These performers preferred using material published by their own firms rather than those of competitive organizations. A publisher trying to interest a famous singer in one of his new numbers now found the singer to be a competitive publisher. This situation was underscored by William H. A. Carr and Gene Grove in the New York *Post* when they described how one publisher tried to interest a business associate of Frank Sinatra in getting the singer to use one of the company's songs. The associate replied: "The first thing Frank will ask me is if we own the song. If I tell him no, I'll be out of work." In the same way a recording company would far rather record an inferior song from one of its publishing affiliates than a far better song from a rival publisher.

With publishers owning artist bureaus, ways of getting songs performed were simplified. But this development also was likely to compel an artist to favor the publisher's own lists in his programing. Radio networks owning their own record companies could hardly be expected to be indifferent to the products of their affiliates, though they always insisted that this was not the case.

33

The Music Goes
Round and Round—
The Revolving Disk

1

In the fifties the record business was rushing headlong toward an annual sales figure of several hundred million dollars. This was brought about not only by the increased number of singles selling a million copies or more, but by the broadening market for LP albums, which in time would comprise almost three-quarters of all record sales. These albums—eight or more songs on a ten-inch LP, a dozen or more on a twelve-inch—were devoted not only to original-cast recordings of stage shows or to sound tracks from the movies, but also to a package of songs or instrumentals by a single star or group.

The expanding record business saw new companies enter the field and become strong competitors to the established firms of Victor, Columbia, Decca, Capitol, Mercury and MGM. The newcomers best able to share in the wealth of the recording boom of the fifties were Coral, London, Atlantic, Cadence, King, Imperial, Dot, Kapp, Chess, ABC-Paramount, Atco, Sun, Roulette and Chancellor.

Many of the popular singing stars of the 1940s continued to amass enormous sales for their recordings. Later, in 1952, Sinatra shifted from Columbia to Capitol with whom he remained seventeen years. His first Capitol recording in April 1953 was an English song, "I'm Walking Behind You" (Billy Reid) backed by "Lean Baby" (William May—Roy Alfred). It didn't do too well. But when Sinatra acquired the orchestral backing of Nelson Riddle and his orchestra, his fortunes as a recording artist were revived with "My One and Only Love" (Robert Mellin—Guy Wood), with the George and Ira Gershwin standard, "A Foggy Day" and with the Rodgers and Hart classic, "My Funny Valentine." In March 1954 he once again achieved a million-disk sale with "Young at Heart" (Carolyn Leigh—Johnny Richards). This ballad had originated as an instrumental number to which Carolyn Leigh fashioned lyrics. Several leading recording artists—Nat King Cole among them—turned it down, possibly feeling that its subtle melodic progression would preclude mass appeal. James Van Heusen, however, was convinced of its commercial potential and induced Sinatra to record it. *Billboard* selected it as the top single of the year and Sinatra as the year's top vocalist. The song, mainly because of Sinatra, took top place on "Your Hit Parade" and lent its title to a motion picture starring Sinatra with Doris Day in 1955.

The crown and the scepter were now restored to the once deposed king of recording artists. In 1955 both *Down Beat* and *Billboard* placed Sinatra at the head of popular male singers in their all-star polls. By 1958, Sinatra outpolled his closest competitor in the *Billboard* poll by a margin of ten to one. *Metronome* featured him on its cover as "Mr. Personality" and *Jazz* named him the world's leading male vocalist. All this came about through a string of recording successes, each selling a million disks or more: "Love and Marriage" (Sammy Cahn—James Van Heusen), "Learnin' the Blues" (Dolores Vicki Silvers), "The Tender Trap" (Sammy Cahn—James Van Heusen), "All the Way" (Sammy Cahn—James Van Heusen), "Witchcraft" (Carolyn Leigh—Cy Coleman) and "Hey, Jealous Lover" (Sammy Cahn, Kay Twomey, and Bee Walker). All these were singles. Sinatra did equally well with his LP's: *Songs for Swinging Lovers*, *Come Fly With Me*, *Come Swing With Me* and *Only the Lonely*. His capacity to realize gold records still remained strong in 1976 with *Ol' Blue Eyes Is Back* on Reprise even as his powers as a box-office draw in public appearances remained unimpaired—all this in spite of the fact that by the 1970s his voice was betraying ragged edges.

Bing Crosby extended his long list of million-disk sale recordings into the 1950s with "Sam's Song" (Jack Elliott—Lew Quadling) backed up by Irving Berlin's "Play a Simple Melody," in both of which his son, Gary, was his singing partner; also with Cole Porter's "True Love," an Academy Award nominee from the motion picture *High Society* (1956) where his singing partner was Grace Kelly. But it was in his later public appearances, rather than on records, that Bing Crosby revealed how true a master he was of his craft. In London, Dublin and Edinburgh during the summer of 1976—and during a swing of several American cities culminating with his first return to Broadway in over thirty years at the Uris Theater on December 7, 1976—he was at all times in full control not only of his voice but of every stage situation: his voice, richer, deeper and more expressive in the lower register even if it had become somewhat thin at the top; his stage presence exuding that charm, poise and savoir-faire that had formerly made him a superstar on the screen.

Perry Como accumulated other million-disk and best-selling disk recordings in the 1950s in addition to those already mentioned which he had introduced over television. The top Como records were: "Don't Let the Stars Get in Your Eyes" (Slim Willet, Cactus Pryor and Barbara Trammel), "More" (Tom Glazer—Alex Alstone), "Kewpie Doll" (Sid Tepper and Roy C. Bennett) and "Magic Moments" (Hal David—Burt Bacharach). For a number of years in the late 1960s and early 1970s, Perry Como suffered lean years as a recording artist (possibly the result of his now rare appearances on television), but he was once again the proud possessor of a gold record in 1976 with "And I Love You So" (Don McClean).

Many of Nat King Cole's recordings were topping the best-selling lists in the fifties: "Mona Lisa" (Ray Evans and Jay Livingston), winner of the Academy Award in the motion picture, *Captain Carey of the U.S.A.* (1949); "Too Young" (Sylvia Dee—Sid Lippman), which held the top place on "Your Hit Parade" for four consecutive weeks in 1951; "A Fool Was I" (Roy Alfred—Kurt Adams); "Answer Me, My Love," a German popular song by

Gerhard Winkler and Fred Rauch adapted for the American trade with new English lyrics by Carl Sigman; "A Blossom Fell," an English importation (Howard Barnes, Harold Cornelius and Dominic John); and "Time and the River" (Aaron Schroeder and Wally Gold). He made his debut in motion pictures in *The Blue Gardenia* (1953), after which his most important films were *St. Louis Blues* (1958), the screen biography of W. C. Handy, and *Cat Ballou* (1965). In spite of the decline of ballads during the rock years of the 1960s, Nat King Cole's records continued to sell well up to the time of his death in 1965 from cancer; a revival of a 1951 ballad, "Unforgettable" (Irving Gordon), brought him a gold record in 1964. Regrettably, he did not live to see his daughter, Natalie, become a singing star in her own right.

Among Doris Day's best-selling records in the fifties were: "A Guy Is a Guy" (Oscar Brand); "Secret Love" (Paul Francis Webster—Sammy Fain), winner of the Academy Award in the motion picture *Calamity Jane* (1953); and "Whatever Will Be, Will Be" or "Que Sera, Sera" (Jay Livingston and Ray Evans), winner of the Academy Award in the motion picture *The Man Who Knew Too Much* (1956), and later her television theme song.

Sarah Vaughan's best-selling records were "A Lover's Quarrel" (Vic McAlpin and Newt Richardson), "Make Yourself Comfortable" (Bob Merrill), "C'est la Vie" (Edward B. White and Mack Wolfson) and "Broken-Hearted Melody" (Hal David—Sherman Edwards).

Frankie Laine's big records of the fifties were "The Cry of the Wild Goose" (Terry Gilkyson); "Jezebel" (Wayne Shanklin); "High Noon" (Ned Washington—Dimitri Tiomkin), the Academy Award winner in the motion picture of the same name; "I Believe" (Ervin Drake, Irvin Graham, Jimmy Shirl and Al Stillman); and "Moonlight Gambler" (Bob Hilliard—Phil Springer).

Billy Eckstine's hit records included "My Foolish Heart" (Ned Washington—Victor Young) an Academy Award nominee from the motion picture of the same name; and "I Apologize" (Al Hoffman, Al Goodhart and Ed Nelson).

Dinah Shore had a record hit in 1953 with "Blue Canary" (Vincent Fiorino). Among Gene Autry's best-selling records were "Peter Cottontail" (Steve Nelson and Jack Rollins), an Easter song, in 1950 and, in 1951, "Frosty the Snow Man" (Steve Nelson and Jack Rollins).

2

A top-selling record was the aspiration of every young pop singer. A single record often brought fame and prosperity to an unknown. It did so in the fifties for Patti Page with "The Tennessee Waltz" (Freddie Stewart—Pee Wee King); for Eddie Fisher, with "Any Time" (Herbert Happy Lawson), revived from 1921; for Johnnie Ray with "Cry" (Churchill Kohlman); for Teresa Brewer with "Music! Music! Music!" (Stephen Weiss and Bernie Baum); for Connie Francis with "Who's Sorry Now" (Bert Kalmar and Harry Ruby—Ted Snyder); and for Johnny Mathis with "Wonderful, Wonderful" (Ben Raleigh—Sherman Edwards).

When Patti Page came to Tulsa, Oklahoma, in 1939 from her birthplace in Claremore, Oklahoma, her name was Clara Ann Fowler. She was then twelve years old. In Tulsa, after graduation from high school, she sang on a fifteen minute radio program over KTUL sponsored by the Page Company, a local dairy. The program was called "Meet Patti Page," from which time she assumed that name. From Tulsa she went to Chicago, there to make regular appearances as a songstress with the Don McNeill morning radio program, "Breakfast Club," over ABC. In 1948, she made her first recordings for Mercury, in some of which she used the technique of overdubbing, providing herself with her own four-voice harmony. The first of these records were "Confess" (Bennie Benjamin and George Weiss) and "With My Eyes Wide Open I'm Dreaming" (Mack Gordon—Harry Revel). Her New York nightclub debut followed in 1950, and a recording for Mercury of the country and western number,

"The Tennessee Waltz." It sold over two million records in its first year, and seven million within a decade. She followed this stunning success in 1951 with several more best-selling records, among which were "Mister and Mississippi" (Irving Gordon), and "Mockin' Bird Hill" (Vaughn Horton). By the end of 1951 she had sold over six million records. Her major hits after that were her television theme song, "This Is My Song" (Dick Charles), "I Went to Your Wedding" (Jessie Mae Robinson), "That Doggie in the Window" (Bob Merrill), "Changing Partners" (Joe Darion—Larry Coleman), "Cross Over the Bridge" (Bennie Benjamin and George Weiss), "Allegheny Moon" (Al Hoffman and Dick Manning) and "Left Right Out of Your Heart" (Earl Shuman—Mort Garson).

Eddie Fisher, the son of a Philadelphia produce merchant, was twelve years old in 1940 when he began his professional career singing over radio station WFIL in Philadelphia. A year later he won first prize in a children's hour radio contest. A dropout from school in the eleventh grade, he continued to make his way as a singer. When he was seventeen he came to New York as a vocalist with Buddy Morrow's band. Before long he was appearing as an intermission performer at the Strand Theater and at the Copacabana nightclub. In 1948 he was winner of first prize on the Arthur Godfrey Talent Scouts program. A year later, while appearing at Grossinger's famed resort in the Catskill Mountains, he was heard by Eddie Cantor who forthwith hired him to appear with him on a cross-country tour. A recording contract with RCA Victor was negotiated in 1950 with "Any Time," released in 1951, making him such a valuable singing property that he was now headlined at the Paramount Theater. A poll among disc jockeys selected him as "America's most promising vocalist," while Irving Berlin said of him, "something in his voice is the closest thing I have heard to what Al Jolson had in his." His rapidly expanding career was temporarily arrested in 1951 when he was mustered into the Army. As a soloist with the Army Band he made innumerable appearances throughout the United States, Europe and Asia. During his two years in uniform he continued pressing records, realizing ten major record best-sellers with a total sale of seven million disks. The most popular between 1951 and 1953 were "Turn Back the Hands of Time" (Jimmy Eaton, Larry Wagner and Con Hammond); "I'm Yours" (Robert Mellin); "Wish You Were Here" (Harold Rome) from the Broadway musical of that name; "Tell Me Why" (Al Alberts—Marty Gold); an English song, "Lady of Spain" (Robert Hargreaves, Tolchard Evans, Stanley J. Admerell and Henry B. Tilsley); and "Oh, My Pa-pa" (John Turner and Geoffrey Parsons—Paul Burkhard), imported from Switzerland. Soon after his separation from military service, Fisher began a three-week engagement at the Paramount Theater. His boyish appearance—the unruly shock of hair, amiable dimpled smile, and shining eyes—as well as his strong belting singing style made him Sinatra's successor as the idol of squealing youngsters. On April 29, 1953, Fisher became the star of his own television show, "Coke Time," over NBC, and also over the radio on the Mutual Broadcasting System on more outlets than ever given to any performer (some seven hundred). More hit records followed; "Green Years" (Don Reid and Arthur Altman), "Dungaree Doll" (Ben Raleigh—Sherman Edwards), and a song adapted from a Georgia Sea Island chanty, "Cindy, Oh Cindy" (Bob Barron and Burt Long). Following his divorce from Elizabeth Taylor in the mid-1960s, his singing style suffered deterioration and his career plunged into decline.

As a preeminent interpreter of wailing ballads, Johnnie Ray first came fully into his own in 1951 with "Cry." Born in Dallas, Oregon, in 1925, Johnnie suffered a deterioration in his hearing when he was young which left him partially deaf and traumatized. As he told Arnold Shaw in an interview: "I couldn't communicate with other children of my age. I withdrew, was alone a lot. I used to fantasize a lot about being a star." His first important musical influences were gospel, country and western music, and Billie Holiday. When he heard a Billie Holiday record for the first time in 1944, it was, as he says, "like being possessed." When he was seventeen he left home to make his way by playing the piano and singing in night spots in the Midwest, using mostly his own song material. He was discovered in 1951 at the Flame in Detroit by a disc jockey who brought him to an executive from Okeh Records. Ray's first records were his own songs, "Whiskey and Gin" and " 'Til I Say Goodbye." When they began to climb in the charts, mainly due to the plugging of disc jockey Bill Randle, Mitch Miller took Ray to Columbia and had him record "Cry." This was a song written years earlier by a Pittsburgh night watchman at a dry-cleaning establishment. The author entered his song in a contest in Pittsburgh. It was rejected and then stayed forgotten until Johnnie Ray revived it for Columbia at Mitch Miller's request. Ray's record, which included his own "The Little White Cloud that Cried," sold over two million disks, with each of its two sides becoming nationwide hit songs. With Ray's next recording, still in 1951, "Broken Hearted" (De Sylva, Brown and Henderson) revived from 1927, Ray had his second million-disk sale, with three more to follow: "Please Mr. Sun" (Sid Frank—Ray Getzov), "With These Hands" (Benny Davis—Abner Silver), "Walkin' in the Rain" (Johnny Bragg and Robert S. Riley). "Walkin' in the Rain," also known as "Just Walking in the Rain," was a song first introduced and recorded for Sun by a group called The Prisonaires who were inmates of the Tennessee State Penitentiary. Ray developed a singing style all his own, which Howard Taubman, music critic for *The New York Times*, described as follows: "Ray sings like a man in an agony of suffering. Drenched in tears . . . he tears a passion to tatters and then stamps on the shreds. . . . His hair falls over his face. He clutches at the microphone and behaves as if he were about to tear it apart. His arms shoot out in wild gesticulations and his outstretched fingers are clenched and unclenched."

Connie Francis was another who made a specialty of lamentation. She was at the beginning of her singing career—at that time given to excessive bodily gyrations—when in 1957 she made a recording with Marvin Rainwater of "Majesty of Love" (Ben Raleigh and Don Wolf). Later the same year, on the advice of her father, she recorded "Who's Sorry Now" for MGM, with a strong beat rather than in a slow tempo and languorous style. Released later in 1957, this recording at first failed to take fire. But after being plugged on the television program, "The American Bandstand," it rose rapidly to the top of the charts. Born Constance Franconero in Newark, New Jersey, in 1938, Connie Francis began playing the accordion when she was four, made public appearances in vaudeville and sang over the radio. At eleven she appeared on television as a singer-accordionist on "Startime" and at twelve emerged the winner in Arthur Godfrey's Talent Scouts Show on TV. At Belleville High School, in Newark, she took courses in musical theory and orchestration and wrote and produced a musical show. After leaving school, she was hired as a feature vocalist on the NBC program, "Startime" where she remained four years. In 1955 she signed a recording contract with MGM, but not until "Who's Sorry Now" in 1957 did she become a recording star.

She went on from there to become one of the most successful female recording artists of the fifties, a fact confirmed in polls conducted by *Billboard* and *Cash Box*. Within a two-year period she sold a million or more disks of each of ten recordings, a distinction with few parallels in the business. In the single year of 1959 she had three such disks: "My Happiness" (Betty Peterson—Borney Bergantine), a song revived from 1933; "Lipstick on Your Collar" (Edna Lewis—George Goehring) backed by "Frankie" (Howard Greenfield—Neil Sedaka); and "Among My Souvenirs" (Edgar Leslie—Lawrence Wright), revived from 1927. She was starred in three motion pictures in the 1960s: *Where the Boys Are* (1960), *Follow the Boys* (1963) and *When the Boys Meet the Girls* (1965).

Diminutive in size, peppery in personality, with a voice spiced by a nasal twang, Teresa Brewer was described by Bing Crosby as "the Sophie Tucker of the Girl Scouts" and by a TV critic as a "stick of vocal dynamite." Born in Toledo, Ohio, in 1931, she had an active career as a child performer. When she was only two years old she sang "Take Me Out to the Ball Game" (Jack Norworth—Albert von Tilzer) on a children's radio program. Three years later she was a contestant on Major Bowes' radio program, "Amateur Hour." Major Bowes then took her with his company on a several-year tour. When she was twelve she became a regular singer on the "Pick and Pat" radio program. She came to New York in her sixteenth year, capturing top prizes on two radio talent shows, Eddie Dowling's "The Big Break" and the "Talent Jackpot." An assignment as vocalist with the Ted Lewis band at New York's Latin Quarter brought her a Hollywood contract, her first movie being *Those Red-heads from Seattle* (1950) where she introduced "Baby, Baby, Baby" (Mack David—Jerry Livingston). A recording contract with Coral was also at hand that year. One of her first releases brought her stardom: "Music! Music! Music!" which sold over a million disks in its first year and earned for its performer the sobriquet of "Miss Music." Sales figures of her recordings kept growing in the next few years with: "Till I Waltz Again with You" (Sidney Prosen), "Ricochet" (Larry Coleman, Joe Darion and Norman Gimbel), "A Tear Fell" (Dorian Burton and Eugene Randolph), "The Banjo's Back in Town" (Earl Shuman, Alden Shuman, and Marshall Brown), "A Sweet Old-Fashioned Girl" (Bob Merrill), "Bell Bottom Blues" (Hal David—Leon Carr), and "Dancin' with Someone" (Bennie Benjamin, George Weiss and Alex Alstone).

Among black singers, Johnny Mathis' power to sell records and romanticize ballads was second only to that of Nat King Cole. Born in 1935 to poverty in San Francisco, Johnny was the son of an ex-vaudevillian who early taught him vaudeville routines which they performed for family functions. Johnny began studying the piano when he was eight and received his first voice lesson at five years, in both instances specializing in serious music. As a boy he appeared at school and church functions, and in amateur productions, and at an amateur talent contest in which he won first prize. He was even more gifted in athletics, earning six letters in varied sports in high school, and at San Francisco State College where he set a new college record for the high jump and was considered for the Olympics. His aim, however, was to be an English teacher. While attending college he participated as a vocalist in jam sessions at school and at the Black Hawk, a San Francisco nightclub. In 1955, one of the nightclub owners convinced of his talent, persuaded him to devote himself to becoming a singer, taking him under his own managerial wing. Mathis now found engagements in nightclubs, including the Blue Angel and the Village Vanguard in New York, and a recording contract with Columbia where his first release was "Wonderful, Wonderful."

Arnold Shaw, then general professional manager of the publishing house of Edward B. Marks, tells of his reaction to this "strange new voice" in his book *The Rockin' 50s*: "It was young with chesty tenor tones and heady high notes almost falsetto in character. It had no sex or real warmth but it had lift and a sensuous feeling of exhilaration. And when the singer got to the arching, terminal phrase, 'oh . . . so . . . won-der-ful, my love,' the tender and mature love of which he sang became a very palpable reality."

Best-selling records now kept piling up for Johnny Mathis: with "Call Me" (Clyde Otis and Belford C. Hendricks) in 1956; in 1957 with "Chances Are" (Al Stillman—Robert Allen) and "It's Not for Me to Say" (Al Stillman—Robert Allen), from the motion picture *Lizzie*. One year later so many of Johnny Mathis' records monopolized the charts that it was possible for Columbia to release an LP album that year entitled *Johnny's Greatest Hits*, active on the charts for several weeks. In 1959, "Misty" (Johnny Burke—Erroll Garner) became Mathis' fifth single to sell a million disks and his album, *Merry Christmas*, his second to earn a million dollars. There was a continuous flow of gold disks and best-sellers after 1960 with *Heavenly, Warm Open Fire, More Johnny's Greatest Hits, Faithfully, Swing Softly, Open Fire, Two Guitars, Love Is Blue, People*, and *Song Sung Blue*, among others.

3

Vocal groups, of which the Mills Brothers in the 1930s and 1940s had been the first to gain wide distribution on records, shared top honors with solo vocalists on the charts.

In 1950, the Ames Brothers (Joe, Gene, Vic and Ed) came forward on the Coral label with "Rag Mop" (Johnnie Wells and Deacon Anderson), the first of their several million-disk selling records. Among the others new from Victor were: "Undecided" (Sid Robin—Charles Shavers), revived from 1939; "You, You, You," a German song by Lotar Olias with new English lyrics by Robert Mellin; "The Naughty Lady of Shady Lane" (Sid Tepper and Roy C. Bennett); and "Mélodie d'Amour," a French number by Henri Salvador with new English lyrics by Leo Johns.

Les Paul on electric guitar, with Mary Ford doing the vocal, became famous for their multi-track recordings which gave a new dimension and a new sound quality to recording. Their giant sellers were: "Mockin' Bird Hill" (Vaughn Horton); "How High the Moon" (Nancy Hamilton—Morgan Lewis), revived from 1940; a 1919 ballad, "The World Is Waiting for the Sunrise" (Eugene Lockhart—Ernest Seitz); and "Vaya Con Dios" (Larry Russell, Inez James and Buddy Pepper).

In 1951, The Four Aces, headed by Al Alberts, and including Dave Mahoney, Lou Silvestri and Sol Vocarro, made their first record: "Sin" (Chester R. Shull—George Haven). The recording company was Victoria, a small outfit in Chester, Pennsylvania, the city from which The Four Aces came. This record did so well that by the end of the year Decca took over the contract of this singing quartet and released a new best-selling record: "Tell Me Why" (Al Alberts—Marty Gold). After that The Four Aces made hit records of two already popular Hollywood items: "Three Coins in a Fountain" (Sammy Cahn—Jule Styne) and "Love Is a Many Splendored Thing" (Paul Francis Webster—Sammy Fain). When Al Alberts left the group, it dissolved for good.

The Platters was a black group made up of four men—Tony Williams, David Lynch, Paul Robi and Herbert Reed, all of them former parking lot attendants in Los Angeles—and one woman, Zola Taylor. Their first big record was "Only You" (Buck Ram and Andre Rand) for Mercury in 1955. After that they strengthened their popularity and prosperity with "The Great Pretender" (Buck Ram) and, a revival from 1939, "My Prayer" (Jimmy Kennedy and George Boulanger) in 1956, and in 1958 with "Twilight Time" (Buck Ram—Morty Nevins, Al Nevins and Artie Dunn) and Jerome Kern's "Smoke Gets In Your Eyes" (Otto Harbach), both of them revivals. "Harbor Lights" (Jimmy Kennedy—Will Grosz), revived from 1937, was their last hit record (1960). A precipitous decline in their popularity resulted when their lead singer, Tony Williams, left them, and some of the others were arrested on charges involving narcotics and prostitution. With new personnel, the Platters continued to make records and public appearances through the 1960s.

Among the other favorite singing groups on records during the fifties were the Chordettes (Jimmy Lochard, Carol Bushman, Nancy Overton and Lynn Evans) with "Lollipop" (Beverly Ross and Julius Dixon) and "Mr. Sandman" (Pat Ballard); the Kingston Trio (Nick Reynolds, Bob Shane and Dave Guard) with "Tom Dooley" (Dave Guard); and The Crickets

(Buddy Holly, Jerry Allison, Niki Sullivan and Joe Mauldin) with "That'll Be the Day" (Jerry Allison, Buddy Holly and Norman Petty) and "Maybe Baby" (Norman Petty and Buddy Holly).

4

The best-selling record which represented the shortest route to recognition was as eagerly sought after by composers as by performers. Several key composers new to the popular music of the fifties first became known when one of their songs made the best-selling record charts.

Richard Adler and Jerry Ross were two writers who joined their creative efforts in the writing of both lyrics and music. They made an auspicious appearance in 1951 in Eddy Howard's Mercury recording of their song, "The Strange Little Girl." In 1953, Eddie Fisher recorded for Victor "Even Now" (which Adler and Ross wrote with Dave Kapp). Both records sold well, but with "Rags to Riches," in Tony Bennett's Columbia recording in 1953 Adler and Ross hit the jackpot. One day while they were marveling at the meteoric rise to fame of Eddie Fisher, Adler remarked to Ross that Fisher had gone "from rags to riches"—and a song idea was born. After Tony Bennett's million-disk recording, the song also sold a million copies of sheet music, and occupied first place on "Your Hit Parade."

Though Richard Adler (born in New York City in 1921) was the son of Clarence Adler, an eminent pianist and teacher, he received no musical instruction. Richard served for three years in the Pacific in the armed forces during World War II. The war over, he worked for a time in the advertising department of the Celanese Corporation of America while spending his spare time writing songs. His lyrics to "Teasin'," music by Philip Springer, was recorded by Connie Haines for MGM in 1950. In that year, Frank Loesser introduced Adler to Jerry Ross (1926–1955), another songwriting aspirant, suggesting they become collaborators. While waiting to sell the songs they were creating, Adler and Ross contributed special material to the radio program, "Stop the Music," and for such stellar performers as Jimmy Durante, Marlene Dietrich and Eddie Fisher. Songwriting, however, was their prime activity; by 1954 they had completed about one hundred and fifty numbers. Besides "Rags to Riches" their biggest song in the early 1950s was "True Love Goes On and On," successfully recorded for Decca in 1954 by Burl Ives with the Gordon Jenkins Orchestra. After that the history of Adler and Ross became a part of the chronicle of the Broadway musical theater, with *Pajama Game* (1954) and *Damn Yankees* (1955).

Bob Merrill's first big record came in 1950 with "If I Knew You Were Comin' I'd've Baked a Cake," written with Al Hoffman and Clem Watts. Eileen Barton's recording sold over a million disks that year. This was the impressive start of a songwriting career for Merrill which within four years would see eighteen of his songs represented among the leaders in "Your Hit Parade," and a half-dozen songs enjoying a million-disk sale or more.

Bob Merrill, born in Atlantic City in 1921, spent his boyhood years in Philadelphia where he attended its public schools. When he was not at school, he was wandering about the United States filling odd jobs to support himself, working at various periods as a movie usher, a nightclub entertainer, loading boats or picking crops. For a year he studied acting with Richard Bennett at the Bucks County Playhouse. During World War II he served in uniform in Special Services. Upon his separation from the Army, he went to California where for five years he worked as a dialogue director at Columbia Pictures, and appeared in several movies in minor roles. Between 1948 and 1949 he was a casting director for CBS-TV.

He had been dabbling in songwriting for several years without making much progress when, in 1950, the hit record of "If I Knew You Were Comin' I'd've Baked a Cake" made him an overnight musical celebrity. With "Candy and Cake," the same year, he wrote his own lyrics, a practice he would often follow thereafter; Arthur Godfrey recorded it success-fully for Columbia. "Sparrow in the Treetop," in 1951, became a best-selling record in a performance by Guy Mitchell. In 1952, came Patti Page's record of "That Doggie in the Window," and in January 1954, Rosemary Clooney's recording of "Mambo Italiano." Later that year, Jimmie Rodgers' recording of "Honeycomb" was another winner.

After a five-year stint as a television production consultant for Liggett and Myers, Merrill was signed in 1956 to the first four-way contract ever given at MGM: as producer, composer, writer and publisher. One year more and Merrill put his foot solidly in the Broadway musical theater to which, from then on, he would make his major contributions as a songwriter.

Many composers of rock, country and western, and rhythm and blues also realized their first success as songwriters on records.

5

Since the incursion of American folk music into the popular arena continued well through the fifties, popular songs adapted from traditional folk songs were represented in the record listings. Some of these folk song-oriented popular tunes became hits and sold records in the hundreds of thousands or a million and more.

"Kisses Sweeter than Wine" was one of the song hits of 1951. This was an adaptation of an old Irish folk song, "Drimmer's Cow," with new words by The Weavers and the music adapted by Huddie Ledbetter. It was first popularized by The Weavers both in their concerts and in a Decca recording, then in 1957 revived by Jimmie Rodgers in a best-selling Roulette release.

In 1956, Eddie Fisher scored heavily with his Victor recording of "Cindy, Oh Cindy," arranged from a chantey by Bob Barron and Burt Long. That same year, Johnny Mathis found a place in the charts with "Twelfth of Never" (Paul Francis Webster—Jerry Livingston) adapted from the Kentucky folk tune, "The Riddle Song," while Harry Belafonte gave wide circulation to a West Indian folk tune, "Jamaica Farewell" (Lord Burgess) in a Victor release in 1957. "The Battle of New Orleans" (Jimmy Driftwood) became a best-selling record in Johnny Horton's performance on Columbia. This number was derived from a fiddle tune of 1815, "The Eighth of January," celebrating the victory of the United States forces at New Orleans. "Tom Dooley" (Dave Guard) became a smash record success for the Kingston Trio in 1958. This was a new version of a ninety-year-old Blue Ridge Mountain folk song, "Tom Dula," a folk hero in that region who had been involved in a much publicized murder in Wilkes County, North Carolina, in 1866.

These are some other popular songs of the fifties that originated as folk music: In 1950, "The Rovin Kind" (Jessie Cavanaugh and Arnold Stanton), based on the English folk song, "The Pirate Ship," a best-seller in Guy Mitchell's Columbia recording, and "Wanderin' " (Sammy Kaye), derived from a Minnesota folk song discovered by Carl Sandburg and recorded for Columbia by Sammy Kaye and his orchestra; in 1952, "Suzanne" (Harry Belafonte and Millard Thomas), recorded for Victor by Belafonte; in 1956, "Rock Island Line" (Lonnie Donegan), a traditional American folk song first recorded by Leadbelly but popularized by Lonnie Donegan's recording for London; in 1959, "A Worried Man" (Dave Guard and Tom Glazer), a Kingston Trio recording.

6

Between 1958 and 1975, records selling a million disks as singles and record albums earning one million dollars in sales at the manufacturer's level have come to be known as "gold records," since a gold-plated disk is presented by the Record Industry Association of America as a token of achievement. A platinum disk is presented for any LP that sells a million copies and singles selling two million copies. Since 1975, an album has been required to sell five hundred thousand copies to earn a gold record. The former requirement of a million-disk sale for singles for a gold record and a million copies of an LP and two million copies of a single for a platinum record were retained.

Up to 1958, the number of disks sold by each recording was, at best, an educated guess, since companies kept their sales figures a carefully guarded secret. But in 1958 the Record Industry Associates of America, a nonprofit organization for the better development of recorded music, began to award gold and platinum records to those firms willing to provide exact sales figures under proper certification. With virtually every important record company soon complying with this requirement an accurate and substantiated barometer of record sales was provided for the first time.

Four singles were certified in 1958 as selling a million or more disks: Perry Como's recording of "Catch a Falling Star" (Paul Vance and Lee Pockriss); "Patricia" (Bob Marcus—Perez Prado) in a Victor recording by Perez Prado; Laurie London's Capitol recording of Geoff Love's adaptation of the traditional gospel, "He's Got the Whole World in His Hands"; and Elvis Presley's Victor recording of "Hard Headed Woman" (Claude de Metruis) which he had introduced in the motion picture, *King Creole* (1958). The only LP album grossing one million dollars in sales was the original cast recording of the Rodgers and Hammerstein musical play *Oklahoma!*.

In 1959, only one single was certified as a million-disk seller: "Tom Dooley" (Dave Guard), recorded for Capitol by the Kingston Trio. Six albums grossed one million dollars or more: the original cast recording of the Rodgers and Hammerstein musical play *South Pacific* (also awarded a platinum record); the original cast recording of the Broadway musical *Music Man*; Henry Mancini's music for the TV series *Peter Gunn*; *Johnny's Greatest Hits*, an album of Johnny Mathis' best-selling records up to then; a Capitol recording of hymns; and *Sing Along with Mitch*.

Sing Along with Mitch, released in May 1958, was a phenomenon in the record business. A chorus of twenty-eight, under the direction of Mitch Miller, performed standards familiar to all. The lyrics of each song was printed on the jacket of the record to encourage parlor singing, but the album was also intended for listening pleasure. So popular was this release that within fifteen months five more albums were issued, to achieve a combined sale of almost two million albums.

Another yardstick by which the success and importance of recordings was measured came in 1959 when the National Academy of Recording Arts and Sciences made the first of its annual presentations of awards in many different branches of the recording industry. These trophies were called Grammys. Winners were determined by some three thousand voting members of the Academy, each a creative contributor to the business. The basic criterion for judgment was outstanding artistic achievement and technical know-how rather than sales figures. The first of these awards were made on May 4, 1959, to cover the year of 1958. There were nominations in twenty-eight categories in both serious and popular music. In popular music, Domenico Modugno's Decca recording of the Italian importation, "Volare"—also called "Nel Blu, Dipinto di Blu"—with American lyrics by Mitchell Parish to Modugno's melody, was chosen as both the record and the song of the year. Mancini's recording of his own music for *Peter Gunn* was both the year's best album and best arrangement. Best vocal performances by a woman and a man went respectively to *Ella Fitzgerald Sings the Irving Berlin Song Book* on Verve (also chosen as the best individual jazz performance) and Perry Como's performance of "Catch a Falling Star." The Kingston Trio's performance of "Tom Dooley" was the best country and western performance; a Roulette album by Count Basie, the best jazz performance by a group and the best dance band performance; Louis Prima and Keely Smith on Capitol with "That Old Black Magic" (Johnny Mercer—Harold Arlen), the year's best performance by a vocal group; and Billy May's Big Fat Brass on Capitol, the best orchestral performance. Top honors for comedy performance and for children's recording went to Ross Bagdasarian's "The Chipmunk Song" on Liberty. The best rhythm and blues record was "Tequila" (Chuck Rio) performed on a Challenge record by The Champs. The original cast recording of *The Music Man* was the best album of a Broadway or TV production, while the best motion picture sound track of an original score was that of the Lerner and Loewe screen musical *Gigi*, conducted by André Previn for MGM.

For the year 1959, the number of categories was expanded to thirty-two. Bobby Darin was awarded a Grammy as the best new artist, and another for the record of the year, his performance of "Mack the Knife" (Marc Blitzstein—Kurt Weill) on Atco. Frank Sinatra also received two Grammys: for the album of the year (*Come Dance With Me* on Capitol) and the best vocal performance for the same album. The song of the year was "The Battle of New Orleans" (Jimmy Driftwood), recorded for Columbia by Johnny Horton, which was also chosen as the best country and western performance. Ella Fitzgerald received awards as the best female vocalist with "But Not for Me" (Ira Gershwin—George Gershwin) and as the best solo jazz performer in *Ella Swings Lightly*, both on Verve. Duke Ellington was rated the top dance band performer with his own score to *Anatomy of Murder* on Columbia (also selected as the best musical composition to be recorded and the best original sound track album from motion pictures or TV). David Rose and his orchestra, supplemented by André Previn at the piano, gave the best orchestral performance on records with "Like Young" (Paul Francis Webster—André Previn) on MGM. Jonah Jones' recording on Capitol of *I Dig Chicks* was the leading jazz performance by a group. The best rhythm and blues performance was that of Dinah Washington of "What a Diff'rence a Day Makes," (Stanley Adams—Maria Grever), and the best folk performance was that of the Kingston Trio on the Capitol LP, *The Kingston Trio at Large*. Billy May's arrangements in the Sinatra album from Capitol, *Come Dance With Me*, were the best of their kind on records that year. The best original cast album category was shared by *Gypsy* on Columbia and *Redhead* on Victor, while the best sound track recording from motion pictures or TV was that of Gershwin's folk opera *Porgy and Bess*.

Since the National Academy of Recording Arts and Sciences began selecting the year's leading recordings only in 1959, it decided in 1974 to elect each year a number of pre-1959 recordings in both popular and serious music for a recording Hall of Fame. In 1974, these became the first popular records to get elected: Gershwin's *Rhapsody in Blue* by Paul Whiteman and his Orchestra; "Body and Soul" (Edward Heyman, Robert Sour and Frank Eyton—John Green) by Coleman Hawkins and his orchestra; *Carnegie Hall Concert* by Benny Goodman and his orchestra; "The Christmas Song," or "Chestnuts Roasting on an Open Fire" (Robert Wells and Mel Tormé) by Nat King Cole; "I Can't Get Started" (Ira Gershwin—Vernon Duke) by Bunny Berigan and his orchestra; "Mood Indigo" (Duke Ellington) by Duke Ellington and his orchestra; "West End Blues" (Clarence Williams—Joe Oliver) by Louis Armstrong and his orchestra; and "White Christmas" (Irving Berlin) by Bing Crosby.

Four popular recordings were chosen in 1975; Gershwin's *Porgy and Bess* as recorded by Columbia in 1951; "God Bless the Child" (Arthur Herzog, Jr., and Billie Holiday) by Billie Holiday; "Take the A Train" (Billy Strayhorn) by Duke Ellington and his orchestra; and the 1943 original cast recording of the Rodgers and Hammerstein musical play *Oklahoma!* on the Decca label.

34

I've Got Rhythm
and Blues—and Jazz

1

A new term comes into the popular music of the 1950s: "Rhythm and Blues" (or R and B). The name was conceived and adopted by record manufacturers in the late forties in their catalogues as a replacement for "race," and like the race category it covered black music by black performers slanted for a black public. As rhythm and blues it was the urbanization of black folk music, taking technical cues from Dixieland jazz, boogie-woogie and the blues. It was music which, while vocal, was intended primarily for dancing, hence its emphasis on a strongly punctuated beat, driving rhythms and blaring sonorities; hence, too, its indifference to lyrics, which were at times incomprehensible. This was music utilizing the accompaniment of electrified instruments—at first the guitar, then the organ, and after that the bass. This was music that middle-class and upper-class black society tended to look upon as disreputable. From rhythm and blues came rock 'n' roll, when white people took over the idiom; among blacks, rhythm and blues also evolved into a type of gospel music touching on the sorrows of black people and known as "Soul."

Rhythm and blues had its own black disc jockeys over radio stations catering exclusively to black audiences. Many new record companies, specializing in rhythm and blues, became powers: Chess, Jay-Gee, Okeh, Atlantic, Motown, Vee-Jay, Roulette, Stax-Volt, King and Scepter.

Louis Jordan and his Tympany Five were pioneers in rhythm and blues at a time, soon after World War II, when rhythm and blues music as such did not yet exist. Jordan started out in Brinkley, Arkansas, as a blues singer, and later he played the sax in Chick

542

Webb's and Earl Hines' bands. Jordan also did comedy routines, sang songs with risqué lyrics, and presented the kind of caricatures of black men so popular on the stage in past years. Some of his records in the 1940s were million-disk sellers, even though they were intended for the black market. One was his Decca release of the 1947 hit song, "Open the Door, Richard" ("Dusty" Fletcher and John Mason—Jack McVea and Don Howell) which was adapted from a comedy routine popular in black vaudeville houses in the thirties and forties. Other Jordan recordings with the Tympany Five generated some of the excitement and had some of the pulse of later rhythm and blues numbers, while others were portraits of Negro life in the ghetto. His best-selling records were "Caledonia" (Fleecie Moore) and "Choo Choo Ch' Boogie" (Vaughn Horton, Denver Darling and Milton Gabler), "Ain't Nobody Here But Us Chickens" (Joan Whitney and Alex Kramer), "Reet, Petite and Gone" (Louis Jordan and Michael H. Goldsen), "Saturday Night Fish Fry" (Ellis Walsh and Louis Jordan) and "Blue Light Boogie" (Jessie Mae Robinson and Louis Jordan). Bill Haley and B. B. King were two of many to have been profoundly influenced by Jordan.

The rhythm and blues of Chuck Berry, into which he brought the flavoring of country music, was such an all-powerful influence on rock 'n' roll that Lillian Roxon goes so far as to maintain that Chuck Berry "may be the single most important name in the history of rock," adding: "There is not a rock musician working today [the late sixties] who has not consciously or unconsciously borrowed from his sound, the sound that was to become the definitive sound of fifties rock. The Beach Boys made their national reputation with a Chuck Berry song, 'Surfin' U.S.A.' And both the Beatles and the Stones started off in the sixties by 'reviving' Chuck Berry fifties' material, songs that were enormously popular at the height of the rock 'n' roll era, only to be forgotten as the hard-rock sound became more and more watered down."

Born Charles Edward Berry in San José, California, in 1926, and raised in St. Louis, Missouri, Berry learned to play the piano, guitar and sax while attending high school and Poro College. In St. Louis he was a member of the Antioch Church Choir and a lead singer in a religious vocal quartet. In 1952 he formed a combo that was heard at the Cosmopolitan Club in East St. Louis, Illinois. Despite this preoccupation with music, Berry studied to be a cosmetician, a trade he practiced for about six months. He was deflected from it permanently by Muddy Waters in Chicago. Muddy Waters, master of the electric blues style, was described by Dan Morgenstern as a "blend of down-home Mississippi blues with a new big city drive." Berry's brand of blues writing impressed Waters who suggested he contact the Chess brothers, proprietors of a small record company bearing their names and specializing in music for the black trade. Berry brought the Chess brothers one of his own songs, "Ida Red," a wry parody of country music, which had already been turned down by several companies. The Chess brothers encouraged Berry to give the music a strong beat and a rhythmic drive and, when he did so, they had him record it with two sidemen; they also changed the title to "Mabelline," or "Maybellene" (Chuck Berry, Russ Frato and Alan Freed). Alan Freed was one of several disc jockeys to plug it on its way to the number one place in the rhythm and blues charts. Assured by this success, Berry went on to develop his career by writing more songs, appearing in public (endearing himself to his audiences with his duck waddle) and making records. Kids everywhere seized upon Chess recordings of his own songs "No Money Down," "Roll Over Beethoven," "Too Much Monkey Business," "Rock and Roll Music," "Johnny B. Goode," "School Day," "Thirty Days," "Sweet Little Sixteen" and "Almost Grown." Though in his song, "You Never Can Tell," Berry speaks of his obsession with cars, rock and ginger ale, he has insisted that "everything I wrote about wasn't about me, but about the people listening to my songs." In 1963 his "Sweet Little Sixteen" was rewritten as

"Surfin' U.S.A.," with new lyrics by Brian Wilson; and that, too, became a best-selling record in a performance by The Beach Boys for Capitol.

In the early 1960s, Berry's singing and composing career was temporarily halted by a prison sentence at the Federal Penitentiary at Terre Haute. He had been convicted of violating the Mann Act after he had brought a fourteen-year-old Spanish-speaking singer from Mexico to St. Louis to appear with him in his Bandstand club. When he fired her, she turned on him with the accusation that Berry had brought her to the United States for other than musical purposes. After Berry was released from prison he resumed his career, continuing with his successes as if there had been no hiatus. He was still making records, and one of them, "My Ding-a-Ling" in 1972 was a best-seller. On August 9, 1975, he was named to the Rock Hall of Fame.

Rock 'n' roll of the fifties and sixties owed almost as much to Little Richard (Richard Penniman) as it did to Chuck Berry. He wore his hair in a high pompadour combed back in a flowing plume. He favored a baggy suit with twenty-six-inch bottom trousers and on his fingers was a flashy display of rings. Playing the piano, he hammered at the keyboard sometimes from a standing, knock-kneed position. At times he lifted one leg to pound the piano keys with his heel. His singing was an outpouring of religious fervor in a frenzied crescendo that ended up in falsetto cries. "Ohhh! My Soul" was his favorite exclamation during his performance. Brash and bombastic, he could say of himself that he was "the living flame" and that his singing was "healing music, the music that makes the blind see, the lame, the deaf and dumb hear, walk and talk . . . the music of joy, the music that uplifts your soul."

Many of the idolized performers of rock 'n' roll grew up on Little Richard's music and imitated and copied him. Their own idiosyncratic behavior and stage mannerisms were stolen from Little Richard, with modifications or variations, from the high pompadour and the pelvis rotations of Elvis Presley to the frenetic piano exhibitionism of Jerry Lee Lewis, from the "yeah, yeah, yeah" exclamations of the Beatles to the quixotic singing styles, stage presence, behavior and dress of Bill Haley and the Rolling Stones.

Little Richard—born on Christmas Day 1935 in Macon, Georgia—got his first experience in music as a gospel singer in church when he was fourteen. A year later, he traveled with a medicine show as a singer of the blues, dancer and a salesman for a herb tonic. He began making records in 1951 for Victor, but none were of any consequence. After winning first prize in a talent contest in Atlanta, Georgia in 1952, he signed up with Peacock Records in Houston to record several blues, still without making any perceptible progress in his career. He was working as a dishwasher, when Art Rupe, head of Specialty Records, became interested in him. Rupe lent Little Richard the money to buy out his contract from Peacock, then had him record for his own label a number of sides in 1955. One was "Tutti Frutti" (Richard Penniman, Dorothy La Bostrie and Joe Lubin), a number with off-color lyrics cleaned up for this recording. "Tutti Frutti" became successful not in Little Richard's recording but in that of Pat Boone for Dot. However, other of Little Richard's recordings for Specialty between 1956 and 1958 made impressive gains on the rhythm and blues charts: "Long Tall Sally" (Enotris Johnson, Richard Penniman, and Robert A. Blackwell), "Slippin' and Slidin' " (Richard Penniman, Edwin Bocage, James Smith and Albert Collins), "Rip It Up" (Robert A. Blackwell and John Marascalco), "Lucille" (Albert Collins and Richard Penniman). In 1956, Little Richard also appeared in several motion pictures, including *The Girl Can't Help It*.

In 1958, with the world of rhythm and blues in his hand, Little Richard got religion and decided to give up his career. He had, apparently, been in an airplane when fire broke out. He fell on his knees promising God he'd give up "the devil's work" and devote himself to gospel if he survived. (Others have suggested that the Russian Sputnik in outer space was for Little Richard a celestial warning to reshape his life along spiritual lines.) One of his first acts of piety, a spontaneous gesture renouncing worldly goods, was to remove from his fingers all his rings, valued at twenty-five thousand dollars, and discard them in the ocean. By the early 1960s he was back making public appearances and records, apparently none the worse for his religious experience.

B. B. King (Riley B. King) well deserves the name he bears, and the phrase that appears on his business card: "Blues is King—King is Soul." In the world of blues and rhythm—or, if you will, contemporary blues—he has been a monarch.

The contraction of his name from Riley B. King to B. B. King came about in Memphis, Tennessee, where he was a disc jockey at its black station, WDIA. There he was billed as "The Boy from Beale Street," a phrase which soon became "Beale Street Blues Boy" and then, "Blues Boy." B. B. was a contraction of "Blues Boy."

He was born in Indianola, Mississippi, in 1925 on a Delta cotton plantation where, as a boy, he labored long and hard. At that time he was also making music by singing in the church choir, organizing a quartet of spiritual singers, and learning to play an eight-dollar guitar he had purchased with his savings. He learned the blues from Blind Lemon Jefferson and Leroy Carr among others. After a short period in the Army during World War II, he returned to work on the cotton plantation, supplementing his meager earnings by singing the blues on Saturday nights on street corners. In 1947, he went to Memphis where, in 1948, he started singing commercials over WDIA before taking on a job as disc jockey that lasted until 1952. He made some records for Bullet in 1949 before coming up with his first hit record in 1952, this time for RPM, "Three O'Clock Blues" (Jules Taub—Riley King) which for eighteen weeks stayed on the charts, sometimes in first place. He followed this with another record success, "You Know I Love You" (Jules Taub—Riley King). On the strength of his new-found popularity he toured the "chitlin' circuit" for several years, making public appearances, singing the blues to the accompaniment of his electric guitar (to which he gave the name of Lucille).

He extended his fame with some successful recordings: "Woke Up This Morning" (Jules Taub—Riley King), "Please Love Me" (Jules Taub—Riley King), "You Upset Me, Baby" (Maxwell Davis—Joe Josea), "Every Day I Have the Blues" (Peter Chatman) which became his theme song, "Sweet Sixteen, Parts 1 and 2" (Riley King and Joe Josea) and "Partin' Time" (Riley King).

In the early 1960s he suffered a decline in his fortunes because black audiences, to whom he had been addressing himself almost exclusively, were turning away from him. But after an eminently successful appearance before his first white audience, at Fillmore Auditorium in San Francisco in 1966, King found a new clientele for his blues, this time among whites who placed him among the top popular performers of the day, both as a singer of blues and as a pop performer on the electric guitar.

2

Some observers of the jazz scene have referred to the fifties as a "new jazz age." Certainly jazz was enjoying its greatest boom since the era of the big bands. All over America, the sounds of jazz—or, the sounds of the *new* jazz—were being heard. "A flock of nighteries and eateries have switched or converted to a jazz policy," reported *Variety*.

An Institute of Jazz Studies was founded in 1953, and in 1957, a School of Jazz was opened in Lenox, Massachusetts. For the first time, in 1956 the United States government subsidized jazz by authorizing the American National Theater Academy to dispatch a jazz band, headed by Dizzy Gillespie, to the Near and Middle East, the first of many government-sponsored foreign tours for American jazzmen. Television gave jazz its due. In 1955, it reunited the Dorsey Brothers on the weekly program "Stage Show," and Stan Kenton was starred on the series *Music '55*. The first of several national all-jazz shows originated on television in 1957, and in 1958 an educational jazz series was inaugurated on the NBC network.

New jazz groups were mushrooming in different parts of the country under the imaginative and adventurous leadership of such new voices in jazz as Dave Brubeck (the Dave Brubeck Quartet), Gerry Mulligan (the Gerry Mulligan Quartet), Eddie Sauter and Bill Finegan (Sauter-Finegan Band), Art Blakely (the Jazz Messengers), Oscar Peterson (the Peterson Trio), John Lewis (The Modern Jazz Quartet), and Julian "Cannonball" Adderley, alto sax, and his brother, Nat (the Adderley Quintet). California enriched the record market with "West Coast jazz," new combos and new labels. Books on jazz proliferated. In his jazz encyclopedia, Leonard Feather notes that during the five-year period of 1955–1960, "more books on jazz were published . . . than in the entire lifetime of jazz up to that point."

Summer jazz festivals were organized to meet the growing demand for jazz music. The first important one took place at Newport, Rhode Island, in July 1954, the creation of George Theodore Wein, a onetime pianist active in the 1940s with several jazz combos, and the proprietor of several nightclubs featuring jazz, including Boston's Storyville. He conceived and brought to realization the Newport Jazz Festival which attracted to an old open-air casino some three thousand persons. It was a two-day affair. On the first evening Eddie Condon and his Dixieland outfit played "Muskrat Ramble." Dizzy Gillespie appeared with his quintet. Oscar Peterson and his trio were heard in their individualized treatment of "Tenderly" (Jack Lawrence—Walter Gross). Gerry Mulligan and his combo presented "The Lady Is a Tramp" (Lorenz Hart—Richard Rodgers). The formal program went on until after midnight, and was followed by a twenty-man jam session. The following afternoon a forum on the origin and meaning of jazz was held. That evening offered the last of the two concerts, the participants including George Shearing, Erroll Garner and Lennie Tristano.

With the festival proving profitable, a second the following summer was a foregone conclusion. Since city officials withheld the use of the open-air casino, the proceedings moved into Freebody Park. Together with the music of Count Basie, Louis Armstrong, Woody Herman, Dave Brubeck, the Modern Jazz Quartet and Gerry Mulligan, there were lectures on jazz.

There were eighteen festivals in Newport. Its last two years were so harassed by gatecrashers and disturbances that, in 1971, the local officials stepped in and shut down the festival after the first of what had been scheduled as four days of music. George Wein now shifted the festival to New York City in the summer of 1972 and extended its activities with a prodigal hand. Twenty-seven events were heard during a nine-day period, in which some six hundred musicians participated at Lincoln Center's Philharmonic Hall, Radio City Music Hall, the Yankee Stadium, Carnegie Hall, the Staten Island ferry, the grounds of the Brooklyn Museum and along a ten-block stretch on Seventh Avenue in Harlem. Over a hundred thousand jazz enthusiasts attended. The Newport Jazz Festival continued to flourish in New York every summer after that.

The annual Newport Jazz festivals encouraged similar ventures elsewhere. The first all-jazz festival at the Lewisohn Stadium in New York was held in July of 1956 to a capacity audience of over twenty thousand. The Monterey, California, jazz festival was initiated in October of 1958. A five-concert jazz festival was sponsored by *Playboy* magazine in Chicago in 1959. The first annual jazz festival sponsored by the New York *Daily News* took place at Madison Square Garden in 1960.

The 1950s focused the limelight on several new apostles of "cool" and progressive jazz: Gerry Mulligan, Miles Davis and Dave Brubeck.

As a child, Gerry Mulligan, born in New York City in 1927, learned to play the piano, ocarina, clarinet and sax. He also dabbled with composition. He was only seven when one of his popular songs was copyrighted. In 1944 he made his first arrangements, for Johnny Warrington's band over WCAU in Philadelphia. During the next few years Mulligan's arrangements were used by the bands of Tommy Tucker, Gene Krupa, Benny Goodman, Claude Thornhill, Charlie Parker, Miles Davis and Stan Kenton. Mulligan also played the sax with Dizzy Gillespie in Philadelphia. Moving on to California in 1952, Mulligan was encouraged by the producer at the Los Angeles nightclub, The Haig, to form a combo for the club's Monday evening jazz sessions. Mulligan conceived the idea of a quartet without piano, and with himself as bass saxophonist, Chet Baker at the trumpet, Bob Whitlock at the bass and Chico Hamilton at the drums. This group came to national attention with recordings made on the Pacific Jazz label. From this point on, Mulligan distinguished himself not only as a saxophonist and jazz arranger but also as the leader of several combos that won acclaim in Europe as well as America. For a number of years, beginning in 1953, he won top honors in polls conducted by *Down Beat*, from 1954 in polls by *Metronome*, and from 1958 in polls by *Playboy* magazine. In 1957 he was the selection of the critics poll in *Down Beat*.

Miles Davis was that exception to the rule that dictated that a black jazzman had to come from an impoverished background. Born in Alton, Illinois, in 1926, he was the son of a successful dental surgeon and real-estate broker. After the Davis family moved to East St. Louis, Illinois, the thirteen-year old Miles received a trumpet as a birthday gift. Before long he was performing in a high school band, and studying with Eddie Randall. When Billy Eckstine's jazz band came to East St. Louis, Miles sat in for an indisposed trumpet player for three weeks.

After graduating from high school, Miles Davis came to New York. He lived with Charlie Parker while attending the Juilliard School of Music for the study of harmony and theory. Most of his nights were spent on 52nd Street where he absorbed the jazz styles of Charlie Parker, Dizzy Gillespie and Coleman Hawkins. For a time he toured with the Benny Carter band, then, for a five-month period, he played with the Billy Eckstine band on the road. Back in New York in 1948, he organized a remarkable nine-piece jazz ensemble of his own to promote the new sounds of jazz he had assimilated on 52nd Street. In this group were Gerry Mulligan, Kai Winding (trombone), Lee Konitz (alto sax), Johnny Carisi (trumpet), John Lewis (piano), Max Roach (drums), Davis himself on the trumpet, and two instruments new to jazz, the tuba and the French horn. This ensemble, which called itself the Capitol Bank because it was making records for Capitol, had only two brief public appearances, one week at the Clique Club, and two weeks at the Royal Roost, both in New York. But it made some historic recordings with arrangements by Mulligan, John Lewis and Gil Evans —though some of these records were released a number of years later in the album, *Birth of the Cool*. In the 1950s, Davis worked with various small combos both in the United States and Europe, one of which was a nineteen-piece orchestra with which he recorded the album *Miles Ahead*. His trumpet playing was sensitive, understated, lyrical—the very essence of cool jazz. To Bill Coss, Miles Davis' jazz was "the most fragile, though never effeminate, trading of a story line that is somewhat above and beyond him, of almost blown-aside pensive fragments that are always coherent." Between 1951 and 1960 Davis received top honors in polls conducted by *Down Beat*, *Metronome* and *Playboy* magazine.

Having been responsible for many of the innovations in the jazz of the 1950s and 1960s, Miles Davis continued to blaze new trails after that, with a sound that came to be known in the 1970s as "jazz-rock." The Bop acoustical style of the mid-1960s in Miles Davis' music making first gave way to the electronic rock-oriented sounds of the ensuing decade in five Miles Davis albums released by Columbia, in which the piano of Davis was supplemented by the saxophone of Herbie Hancock, the drums of Tony Williams and the bass of Ron Carter. These albums—in which electric piano and other amplified instruments are introduced—stand, wrote Robert Hurwitz in *High Fidelity* magazine, "as a landmark in the history of ensemble jazz." They are *Miles Smiles, Sorcerer, Miles in the Sky* and *Filles de Kilimanjaro*. Jazz-rock became fully crystallized in the Miles Davis albums *In a Silent Way* and *Bitches Brew*, the latter of which became one of the top selling jazz releases of all time, with a distribution of over four hundred thousand albums.

Both as a pianist and as the head of his jazz combo, Dave Brubeck was the darling of the campus, the favored boy of the intelligentsia, and the favorite of jazz polls and jazz editors. He usurped a top spot in polls in *Down Beat, Melody Maker, Cash Box, Billboard* and *Playboy* magazine; he was "editor's choice" in 1952 in *Metronome*; he was "musician of the year" in 1955 in *Down Beat*; and in a poll in California in 1957 he was chosen as one of the five most outstanding young men of that state. A Californian by birth, in 1920, Brubeck underwent a thorough systematic training in serious music from his fourth year on, when he began to study the piano. He also participated early in jazz performances. In his thirteenth year he played the piano with Dixieland and Swing bands. While attending the College of the Pacific in 1941–1942, he organized a twelve-piece jazz unit, and frequently participated with his classmates in jam sessions. During World War II, while in the Army, he played with a jazz band that toured the West Coast and Europe. At this time he was able to continue his music study privately with Arnold Schoenberg. After leaving the Army in 1946, Brubeck resumed the study of composition for three years with Darius Milhaud at Mills College, That same year he formed an experimental jazz octet. Three years later he formed a jazz trio which appeared on Jimmy Lyon's radio show and made some records on the Coronet label which did so poorly that Brubeck bought back the master disks. In 1951, he formed the Dave Brubeck Quartet with Paul Desmond (alto sax), Joe Dodge (drums) and Bob Bates (bass), Brubeck, of course, playing the piano. Through its successful appearances at the Black Hawk in San Francisco it was largely responsible for creating a renaissance of jazz music in that city. Performances at The Haig in Los Angeles extended the popularity of the Quartet along the west coast, while appearances elsewhere in the United States, and recordings on the Fantasy label, acquired for it a national following.

In June 1954 the Brubeck Quartet pressed its first album for a major company, Columbia. It was *Jazz Goes to College* which entered the best-selling charts. *Dave Brubeck at Storyville* was the next Columbia album. In 1956, the quartet's personnel changed with Joe Morello taking over the drums, and Gene Wright, the bass.

In the playing of pop tunes, Dave Brubeck was partial to massive chord structures, elaborate improvisatory passages, powerful rhythmic surges and occasional digressions into atonality and discord. There are some critics who belabor the point that Brubeck's pianism does not possess the capacity for swinging a tune in the manner of his distinguished contemporary, Oscar Peterson. But Brubeck's playing has other qualities, no less attractive: a feeling of excitement, a powerful dynamism, electric sparks that often burst into a bonfire. Playing the piano, as a *Time* cover story revealed in 1954, Brubeck "grabs huge fistful of notes, builds them into a sonata-size movement that ignores the stock thirty-two chorus. The notes grow progressively dissonant. . . . His fingers seem to take on a life of their own. At this point, both musicians and laymen in the audience are apt to wonder whether Brubeck will ever be able to make it back to home base. He creates an illusion of danger. . . . Suddenly the rhythm seems to shift gears. Bits of familiar harmonies reappear. In a few moments it is all over and the music relaxes."

One unidentified reviewer put it well when he said that Brubeck's jazz blends "the sounds of the conservatory and the cathouse." This holds true not merely for Brubeck's performances but also for his own provocative jazz pieces, some of which have not been fully appreciated: "Take Five," "Fugue in Bop Tunes," "Marble Arch," "Basin Street," "Jumping Bean," "On the Alamo," "Over the Rainbow," "Rondo à la Turque" together with his most ambitious composition, the oratorio, *Truth Has Fallen*. Brubeck's music sometimes looks backward to baroque counterpoint and sometimes takes a glimpse into the future through discord, atonality and complex harmonic and rhythmic structures.

In December 1959, the Dave Brubeck Quartet appeared with the New York Philharmonic Orchestra, Leonard Bernstein conducting, in the world premiere of *Dialogue for Jazz Combo and Symphony Orchestra* by Brubeck's brother, Howard. In the early 1960s, Dave Brubeck disbanded his quartet. However, as he still had some engagements in Mexico, he was induced to form a group with Gerry Mulligan, Paul Desmond, Jack Six and Alan Dawson. The felicitous inclusion of Gerry Mulligan in a Dave Brubeck ensemble was George Wein's idea. This combo made many other appearances after that, scoring particular success in European capitals. Some of these concerts were recorded in the albums *Dave Brubeck: We Are All Together Again* for Atlantic and *Dave Brubeck: Live at the Berlin Philharmonic* for Columbia. In the mid-1970s, Dave Brubeck reassembled his Quartet to give it a new lease on life on the jazz concert circuit and on recordings.

In the vanguard of the most important new small jazz combos of the 1950s stood The Modern Jazz Quartet: John Lewis, piano; Milt Jackson, vibraphone; Percy Heath, bass; Kenny Clarke, drums. In April 1952 it recorded four sides for Hi-Lo Records, and early in 1953 it began to attract interest among jazz aficionados with their Prestige album, *The Modern Jazz Quartet with Milt Jackson*. Then, with a single change of personnel in February 1955—Connie Kay replacing Kenny Clarke at the drums—The Modern Jazz Quartet began making numerous concert appearances all over the world, and recordings principally for Atlantic. In their performances they brought a new dignity to jazz, not only in the sound they produced—which acquired new refinements through its associations with classical music—but even in their appearance, stage behavior, and the kind of publicity they allowed to be released. By 1974, after twenty-two years, The Modern Jazz Quartet disbanded, but not before they released an exceptionally meritorious album on the Little David label, "In Memoriam," in which they collaborated with a symphony orchestra. They also made a number of unforgettable farewell appearances climaxed by a concert at Lincoln Center in November 1974 which was given permanence in an Atlantic recording released in 1975.

Experimentation with new sounds in the jazz of the fifties led to the introduction of instruments hitherto confined to the symphony orchestra: the flute in the bands of Frank Weiss and Bud Schank; the French horn, played by Julius Watkins, a member of Les Modes; the oboe, performed by Bob Cooper with the Lighthouse '54. Musical instruments from a wider periphery were also exploited: the Hammond organ by such jazz virtuosos as Bill Davis and Bill Doddgett, the harmonica, by Toots Thielman and Eddie Shu.

Afro-Cuban and Latin-American instruments and rhythms—bongos, conga drums, claves, cimbales and gourds—were adapted for jazz usage, and Cuban and Latin-American rhythms filtered through the texture of some of the jazz performances of this decade. Bands by Stan Kenton, Gene Krupa and Woody Herman hired Cuban drummers. New jazz combos were formed by Cuban popular musicians: Luis del Campo of Machito and Perez Prado. The Duke Ellington orchestra and the bands of Woody Herman and Cab Calloway were now performing mambos.

3

The late 1950s brought to the changing scene a jazz vocalist worthy of joining the hallowed company of Ella Fitzgerald and Ray Charles. He was Mel Tormé, officially Melvin Howard Tormé, born in Chicago in 1925. At the age of four he made his bow as a singer at the Blackhawk Restaurant in Chicago. By the time he reached adolescence he had acted in soap operas over the radio, toured the vaudeville circuit as a vocalist, and written a song, "Lament to Love," which Harry James recorded in 1941. In 1942–1943 he toured as a vocalist with the Chico Marx Band, in 1943 he was in the movies in *Higher and Higher*, and during the early 1940s he also became the leader of a vocal group in California, the Mel Tones, for whom he made the arrangements. Success made him, as he later confessed, a cocky kid who alienated friends and fans, and lost jobs. "I had a chip on my shoulder," he explains. His popularity went into a sharp decline and for a number of years in the 1950s he left the musical scene while unraveling himself from an unhappy marriage and seeking the help of psychiatrists. Then he toured England in 1956 and 1957 to score his first successes as a mature and disciplined artist. From the kind of fuzzy crooning he once favored (which earned him the sobriquet of "velvet fog") he developed into a jazz vocalist adept at improvisations and at scat singing. He also had a way of his own with ballads, which he had not abandoned, his sensitive phrasing of a melodic phrase continually revealing a highly developed and discriminating musical intelligence.

A highly successful engagement in Las Vegas in 1961, his first hit record in many years in 1962, "Comin' Home Baby" (Bob Dorough—Ben Tucker) on the Atlantic label, an appearance at the Monterey Jazz Festival in 1963 and his first concert at Carnegie Hall in New York in December of the same year, all marked his return to a success that would henceforth be his permanently. A man of protean gifts, he is not only a jazz vocalist par excellence, but also a pianist, arranger, producer, drummer, writer and composer. "Christmas Song," also known as "Chestnuts Roasting on an Open Fire," which he wrote with Robert Wells, and which Nat King Cole made into a best-selling record for Capitol, is probably his best known number. But others have also proved popular, among them "Born to be Blue" (with Robert Wells) and "A Stranger in Town."

4

Hollywood, always alert to changing winds of public fancy, took cognizance of this jazz explosion. Some of the giants of jazz were given biographical treatment on the screen. If, as was usual with Hollywood, the facts of biography were played with loosely, at least a studied effort was made to reproduce on the soundtrack, sometimes quite authentically, the music with which each of these jazzmen had been associated and, in the case of jazz performers, the sounds for which these men are remembered.

Young Man with a Horn (1950) was the story of a fictitious trumpet player, modeled after the fabulous Bix Beiderbecke. Kirk Douglas played the Beiderbecke character, while, on the sound track, Harry James' trumpet playing (for Kirk Douglas) is heard not only in standards and jazz classics but also in a new number written expressly for this film, "Melancholy Rhapsody" (Sammy Cahn—Ray Heindorf).

The Glenn Miller Story (1954) had Jimmy Stewart playing Miller, with the Glenn Miller sound effectively reproduced on the sound track by the Glenn Miller band supplemented by Louis Armstrong, Gene Krupa and other jazz greats, and with Joe Yuki dubbing the trombone playing for Jimmy Stewart in the Glenn Miller standards, "In the Mood" (Andy Razaf—Joe Garland), "Sunrise Serenade" (Jack Lawrence—Frankie Carle), "Moonlight Serenade" (Mitchell Parish—Glenn Miller), "Little Brown Jug" (J. E. Winner) and "Tuxedo Junction" (Buddy Feyne—Erskine Hawkins).

Steve Allen played Benny Goodman in *The Benny Goodman Story* (1956). Goodman and his band themselves presented several of the all-time Goodman standbys on the sound track: "And the Angels Sing" (Johnny Mercer—Ziggy Elman), "China Boy" (Dick Winfree and Phil Boutelje), "Goody-Goody" (Johnny Mercer—Matt Malneck), "Jersey Bounce" (Robert B. Wright—Bobby Plater, Tiny Brandshaw and Edward Johnson), "Memories of You" (Andy Razaf—Eubie Blake) and "Moonglow" (Will Hudson, Eddie DeLange, and Irving Mills).

In *The Gene Krupa Story* (1959), with Sal Mineo in the title role, Krupa's wizardry on the drums on the sound track was the highlight.

The Five Pennies (1959) told the story of Red Nichols and his combo, with Danny Kaye playing Nichols and Louis Armstrong playing himself. Red Nichols himself dubbed the horn playing for Danny Kaye on the sound track, while the vocals, supposedly sung by Barbara Bel Geddes as vocalist of the Five Pennies, were dubbed by Eileen Wilson. Among the memorable Five Pennies standards featured in the score were "Runnin' Wild" (Joe Grey and Leo Wood—A. Harrington Gibbs), "Out of Nowhere" (Edward Heyman—John Green), "Indiana" (Ballard MacDonald—James F. Hanley) and the theme song of Red Nichols and the Five Pennies, "Wail of the Winds" (Harry Warren). Louis Armstrong was heard in "Bill Bailey, Won't You Please Come Home?" (Hughie Cannon), "When the Saints Go Marching In," and a jazz version of "The Battle Hymn of the Republic," the last two with Danny Kaye.

Jazz was prominently featured in *Pete Kelly's Blues* (1955), a story about a black cornetist involved with gangsters. Matty Matlock's Dixielanders, with cornet solos by Ted Buckner, performed on the sound track in Matlock's fine jazz arrangements; and the cornet playing of Jack Webb on the screen was dubbed by Dick Cathcart. The title song was new (Sammy Cahn—Ray Heindorf), sung on the sound track by Ella Fitzgerald. But other numbers were familiar, effectively dressed up in new jazz arrangements.

Even in several nonmusical films jazz made its presence felt. Together with Elmer Bernstein's background music in *The Man with the Golden Arm* (1955)—a story of drug addiction starring Frank Sinatra—there was the jazz music of Shorty Rogers and his Giants, with Shelly Manne. This was an Otto Preminger production, as was *Anatomy of a Murder* (1959), a tense criminal trial in which Jimmy Stewart was a lawyer for the defense, George C. Scott, the prosecuting attorney, and Lee Remick, the alleged victim of rape. Duke Ellington's original jazz score made a powerful contribution to the carefully constructed suspenseful plot.

35

The Rock Revolution

1

Rhythm and blues was the matrix which white songwriters and white performers used in molding music to their own image for a predominantly youthful audience. That music was rock 'n' roll.

As a nomenclature for a new style and sound that shook the foundations of popular music and almost demolished the musical establishment, the phrase "rock and roll" appeared in 1951. At that time Alan Freed, a disc jockey at WWJ in Cleveland, was the host of a radio show featuring the best-selling records of the day. The owner of a large Cleveland record shop reported to Freed a phenomenon: the kids were buying recordings of rhythm and blues by the armful. This gave Freed the idea that he might attract youngsters to his program by including rhythm and blues. The response to his innovation exceeded his hopes. He was deluged with requests for more numbers. As a result, Freed, calling himself Moon Dog, initiated a new radio show which he named "Moon Dog's Rock and Roll Party," offering an exclusive diet of rhythm and blues. (Moon Dog was a blind New York street musician who sued Freed for stealing his name. A settlement was made through the payment of five thousand dollars and changing the name of his program to "Rock and Roll Party.") Freed used the term "rock 'n' roll" in preference to rhythm and blues since he felt there was a racial stigma to the latter. He found the words "rock and roll" in the lyrics of a rhythm and blues number. In offering his selections, Freed sometimes shouted in rhythm with the music, sometimes thumped the beat with his fist on a telephone directory, and sometimes emitted cries of "go man, go" or "yeah, yeah, yeah" while the music was playing.

552

The kids loved the music he played and the manner in which he presented it. They responded to the decisive heavy beat which carried such a kinetic impact, to repetitions of the melodic phrases that produced a kind of hypnosis, and to the earthy lyrics discussing love, sex and troubles of all kinds in contrast to the romantic sentimentalizations of the pop tunes to which their parents were partial. In Freed, the kids found a kindred, understanding soul, who, in his between-the-music commentaries, backed them up fully in their rebellion against the domination of parents and society.

Freed's rock and roll program became an even greater force in radio when he moved to WINS in New York in 1954. "I'll never forget the first time I heard the Freed show," said Clark Whelton in *The New York Times*. "I couldn't believe sounds like that were coming out of a radio. In 1954 radio was Gruen watch commercials, soap operas and Snooky Lanson Hit Parade music. . . . Alan Freed jumped into radio like a stripper into Swan Lake. He was a teenager's mind funneled into 50,000 watts. . . . In 1954 there was no one else like him." Within a year, Freed was earning almost three quarters of a million dollars. His radio program not only sold records but also any commodity sponsoring his program. He made public appearances, and he played a part in the movie *Rock Around the Clock* (1956). His imitators could be heard on radio stations throughout the country, all of them pushing rock 'n' roll records and helping to make heroes out of rock 'n' roll performers.

Whites were now beginning to write and play rhythm and blues, and major record companies, with a basically white buying public, began releasing rhythm and blues disks. In 1951, a white combo, headed by Bill Haley, recorded "Rocket 88" (Jackie Brenston) for Essex in Philadelphia. This was a rhythm and blues number that had been recorded a year earlier by its composer for the black company, Chess. In 1952, The Ravens, a totally white-oriented group recorded for Mercury "Rock Me All Night Long" (Jimmy Ricks and Bill Sanford), one of the earliest numbers to use the word "rock" in its title. That same year, Bill Haley wrote "Rock a-Beatin' Boogie," whose lyrics began with the line "rock, rock, rock, everybody, roll, roll, roll, everybody."

It was "rock 'n' roll" and not rhythm and blues that in March 1953 drew eighty thousand youngsters, white and black, to the Cleveland Stadium which had only a ten-thousand seat capacity. The occasion was a ball arranged by Alan Freed. In the ensuing pandemonium the performance had to be canceled. And it was rock 'n' roll that made it possible for Alan Freed, in a personal appearance at the Paramount Theater in Brooklyn, New York, to break box-office records formerly established by Frank Sinatra and to provoke the mass hysteria among the young which only Sinatra before him had been able to arouse.

Among its white admirers and practitioners, rhythm and blues was now being called rock 'n' roll. The large companies did not fail to note that something with far-reaching implications was occurring, that a completely new and affluent market had suddenly opened up for them, that of white teenagers with money to spend and eager to spend it on their favorite records. Large companies now began to take over some of the rhythm and blues pieces already recorded by the blacks for small black companies and reassign them to white performers. This procedure came to be known as "covers." In 1952, Kay Starr recorded for Capitol "Wheel of Fortune" (Bennie Benjamin and George Weiss) after Sunny Gale had done so for Derby. How profitable this practice could be became apparent in 1954 with "Sh-Boom" or "Life Could Be a Dream" (James Keyes, Claude Feaster, Carl Feaster, Floyd F. McRae and James Edwards). First published that year by a small St. Louis house, "Sh-Boom" was then recorded by The Chords for Cat Records, a subsidiary of Atlantic. This release had a profitable sale among blacks, even achieving a place in the rhythm and blues category in the Los Angeles charts. Then The Crew Cuts, a white group, recorded it for

Mercury. The young whites who had become addicted to rhythm and blues seized upon "Sh-Boom" with such avidity that within a few weeks the record climbed to top place in the national charts. Even a parody of this number—written and recorded by Stan Freberg —proved a best-seller.

The phenomenal sales of "Sh-Boom" in the general market rather than in the specialized black areas released a veritable flood. "Covers" filled the catalogues of the major record companies and consistently penetrated the charts. "Goodnight, Well It's Time to Go" (Calvin Carter and James Hudson), first recorded by The Spaniels for Vee Jay as "Goodnight, Sweetheart, Goodnight," was released by Coral, sung by the McGuire Sisters, and by Victor, sung by Johnnie and Jack. This was in 1954, the same year in which "Shake, Rattle, and Roll" (Charles Calhoun), following its release by Joe Turner for Atlantic, was recorded by Elvis Presley for RCA Victor and Bill Haley and the Comets for Decca. "Ko Ko, Mo, I Love You So" (Forest Wilson, Jake Porter and Eunice Levy) became a Perry Como best-seller for Victor after Gene and Eunice had recorded it for Combo. "The Wallflower," also known as "Dance with Me Henry," (Johnny Otis, Hank Ballard and Etta James) rolled up huge sales in the Georgia Gibbs recording for Mercury, following the Etta James release by Modern. Pat Boone did "covers" for Dot of Fats Domino's "Ain't that a Shame," of "At My Front Door" (John C. Moore and Ewart G. Abner, Jr.) and of "Tutti Frutti" (Richard Penniman, D. La Bostrie and Joe Lubin). All three had previously been respectively recorded for the black trade by Fats Domino for Imperial, The Eldorados for Vee Jay, and Little Richard for Specialty. "Rollin' Stone" (Robert S. Riley), recorded by the Fontane Sisters for Dot came on the heels of The Marigolds recording for Excello, and "Tweedle Dee" (Winfield Scott) by Georgia Gibbs for RCA Victor following a recording by LaVern Baker.

The major companies were not only issuing "covers" but also white performances of new rhythm and blues numbers that were now being designated as rock (the term rock 'n' roll soon gave way to the simplified one of rock in general usage). In 1954, "Rock Love" (Henry Glover) was recorded for Dot by the Fontane Sisters. A year later, RCA Victor released Kay Starr in "Rock and Roll Waltz" (Roy Alfred—Shorty Allen) and Coral offered the McGuire Sisters in "Rhythm 'n' Blues" (Jules Loman and Buddy Kaye).

The real opening gun in the rock revolution was fired in 1955 with "Rock Around the Clock" (Max C. Freedman and Jimmy De Knight). It was written in 1953 when it went unnoticed. In 1955, Bill Haley and The Comets recorded it for Decca. This release also found only a limited audience. Then that same year the song was used by Bill Haley and The Comets on the sound track of the motion picture *The Blackboard Jungle*. This still little known rock number was used in the film through the efforts of its composer, Jimmy De Knight (born James Myers). Myers had been hired as a technical adviser for the motion picture, a drama about juvenile delinquency and attempted rape at a vocational training school of a large city. He felt that his "Rock Around the Clock" was a piece of music that would fit in such a context. Suddenly, following the release of *The Blackboard Jungle*, "Rock Around the Clock" acquired a new relevance for young people as an expression of their own feelings of rebellion. This was *their* song, about a world they never made and in which they often felt they were strangers. "To say 'Rock Around the Clock' was a sensation is a rare understatement," wrote Lillian Roxon. "It was the 'Marseillaise' of the teenage revolution. . . . It became the first song to have a special secret defiant meaning for teenagers only. It was the first inkling teenagers had that they might be a force to be reckoned with, in numbers alone." The Decca rerelease of the recording by Bill Haley and The Comets now took off and commanded the top place on charts in America and England to become one of the largest selling singles ever released.

Bill Haley became the first of the rock 'n' roll idols. In the 1950s he was continually mobbed by screaming youngsters. A man in his twenties, chubby, paunchy, married, and the father of five, he hardly seemed a logical candidate for the adulation of the young. His visual trademark was a kiss curl greased on his forehead, with plenty of grease left to plaster down the rest of the hair. He could not be called spectacular when he performed. In fact, he looked a bit silly, with his huge grin and wandering eyes. But he brought to the young the music they wanted to hear and they loved him for it.

He came to rock from other areas of popular music. Born in the suburbs of Detroit in 1927, when he was thirteen he earned a dollar a night playing the guitar. He later appeared over the radio billed as the "Rambling Yodeler." Then, as director of a small radio station in Pennsylvania, he formed and sang with "The Four Aces of Western Swing" and "The Saddlemen," specializing in country and western (or hillbilly) music. By 1950, he was drawn to rhythm and blues, mainly because he had noticed the way it was beginning to appeal to young audiences. Before long, he changed the name of his group to Bill Haley and The Comets and adopted the beat and drive of rhythm and blues. The Comets now began making records of country music and rhythm and blues for Essex, but it was the rhythm and blues numbers that began selling. "Crazy Man, Crazy" (Bill Haley) made the national charts in 1953, and "Shake, Rattle and Roll" (Charlie Calhoun) did even better in 1954. With the latter release, Bill Haley and The Comets were recording for Decca, which then issued "Dim, Dim the Lights" (Beverly Ross and Julius Dixon), "See You Later, Alligator" (Robert Guidry) and the epoch-making "Rock Around the Clock."

Bill Haley always insisted that though Alan Freed may have baptized the new music as "rock 'n' roll," and was the first to promote it, that it was he, Haley, who was its founding father. Certainly, Haley developed some of the distinctive features of early rock. From rhythm and blues he took more of the rhythm and less of the blues, using the hammered beat and emphasizing rhythm with his guitars and drums pounding over the melody. He shouted rather than sang his lyrics, his singing more percussively instrumental than vocal. From country and western, he borrowed the ballad tradition, the simplistic attitude towards melody, the guitar and the repetitious phrasing. He also lifted what was useful to him from pop music, mainly his preference for talking about dolls, angels, dreams, the moonlight. Also in the tradition perpetuated by later rock groups, Bill Haley and The Comets was a small ensemble that sang to its own instrumental accompaniment and depended for its emotional force on shrieking sonorities, heightened and intensified by electric amplification.

2

Rock 'n' roll, as first realized by Bill Haley, was a combination of rhythm and blues, country and western and pop—and that is the way it would remain even after its technique and methods became more sophisticated. Structurally it favored a 4/4 meter made up of eight notes accented on the ground and fourth beat. Old modes rather than modern scales (preferably the Dorian) often endowed the music with an esoteric character. Melodic phrases were not of four, eight or sixteen measure duration (as was conventional with popular songs) but sometimes of seven or nine measures, and a sixteen-measure phrase would be divided not into two eights but into, say, ten measures and six. Sonority and rhythm were basic. Rock 'n' roll was loud music—probably the loudest ever conceived. Its irresistible and implacable rhythmic drive, that never lost momentum, contributed further to its overall excitement.

New devices would continually be introduced to create esoteric sounds: the Fuzz Box which blurred sounds while amplifying them; the Wahwah Pedal which produced nasal twangs; weird often overpowering effects through electrification.

Rock 'n' roll was a narcotic, an intoxicant, an hallucinogenic. It created a catatonic state not only among the listeners but even among the performers themselves.

It was music of protest. The young related to it because they were in ferment, protesting not so much against the evils of society (that would come in the 1960s) as against the moral and ethical standards of the establishment. Of the momentous events that swept the fifties to change the face of American society, the young seemed hardly conscious. What to them were the intensification of the cold war, brinksmanship and threats of massive retaliation, Korea, McCarthyism, the Supreme Court ban on segregation in the schools and the subsequent rise of the civil rights movement? The interests of the young lay in their own insulated world: a coke and a hamburger at a drive-in hangout; sex play in a car in a drive-in movie; the high-school hop; doing the Watusi, the stroll, the Loco-Motion, the Mashed Potato and the Twist; speeding on wheels, whether on motorcycles or second-hand souped up autos. The young adopted a uniform and an appearance separating them sharply from their elders: chinos, sneakers, high-school sweaters, pedal pushers, poodle skirts, black leather jackets, rolled up tee shirts, pegged pants; they wore ducktail haircuts (male) or pony tails (females). This was the beat generation about which Jack Kerouac and Allen Ginsberg wrote, a generation whose celluloid idols were Jimmy Dean and Marlon Brando.

Rock 'n' roll became the first music to be written by youngsters, to be played and sung by youngsters, and to be directed exclusively to youngsters. (In time young people would also publish the songs and own and operate the companies that recorded them.) The subjects selected for rock treatment were things the young were vitally concerned with. Sex was a favorite theme, dealt with not with the romantic illusions of their elders, but realistically, sometimes directly and implicitly ("Baby, Let Me Bang Your Box," or "Drill, Daddy, Drill"). Teenage love, frustrated love, broken love all also offered choice material for rock numbers, and so did current fads. After the Hula Hoop craze was born in California in September 1958, there were four rock numbers written and recorded about it within a matter of days, including "The Hula Hoop Song" (Donna Kohler and Carl Maduri). Words as well as music provided the young with release from their supercharged pent-up emotions; it was their sexual outlet; it was the voice of their inner torments and ecstasies.

3

What rock now needed for it to become a cult among the young was a hero image such as Frank Sinatra had been in the 1930s. They found that image in Elvis Presley, rock's king of kings for more than a decade. He became one of the two or three most successful entertainers show business has known, and in the popular music of the 1950s he was the most influential. "Before Elvis," Nick Cohn wrote in *Rock*, "rock had been a gesture of vague rebellion. Once he'd happened, it immediately became solid, self-contained . . . it spawned its own style in clothes and language and sex, a total independence in almost everything. . . . This was the major breakthrough, and Elvis triggered it . . . he became one of the people who have radically affected the way other people think and live."

He came to rock 'n' roll by way of country and western music and its influence clung even more tenaciously to his music-making than it did to that of Bill Haley. Its presence is strongly felt in most of his motion pictures. His origins lay in the South, in Tupelo, Mississippi, where he was born in 1935, the only surviving son of an impoverished farmer. The Presleys were churchgoers, and young Elvis participated in the singing at church, at camp and revival meetings and at church conventions. When he was ten he entered the annual singing contest at the Mississippi-Alabama Fair and Dairy Show, coming off with the second prize of ten dollars and free admission to all the amusement rides. Soon after that, his mother bought him a thirteen-dollar guitar on which he learned simple chords and accompanied himself as he imitated the singing styles of popular country singers he heard over the radio. Country music was an important early influence, but not the only one. He also learned to sing blues. Borrowings from all three molded his song delivery.

When Elvis was fourteen, his family moved to Memphis where his father found employment in a factory. Times were hard for the family. Elvis had to seek work after school—as a movie house usher, factory hand, mowing lawns, or driving a truck. Already he had adopted his hirsute identification—the shock of hair that ended in a ducktail three inches down to the lobes of his ears and the extended sideburns then pretty much a personal idiosyncrasy but years later a fashion for most men—as well as flamboyant clothes in outlandish colors. He was doing a good deal of singing now. As a gift, his mother had him make a private recording at the Memphis Recording Service, a subsidiary of Sun, a small record company. Sam Phillips, who operated both organizations, became interested in Presley through his record. For several months he had Presley work intensively with Scotty Moore, guitarist and leader of a hillbilly band, to develop and refine his style. After that, Phillips signed him to a recording contract with Sun. Presley's first release was a blues, "That's All Right" (Arthur Crudup), a cover of a recording Crudup himself had made for Bluebird; "Blue Moon of Kentucky" (Bill Monroe) was on the flip side. The record was released in August 1954. Dewey Phillips, disc jockey at WHBQ in Memphis, liked it and played it on his program. Only three hours after this first hearing, fourteen telegrams and forty-seven phone calls asked for its repetition. Within a week, seven thousand records were sold in Memphis.

The success of this recording brought Presley his first professional appearances, and with the two most influential country programs over the radio—the Grand Ole Opry in Nashville and the Louisiana Hayride in Shreveport—together with his first performance before a live audience on a commercial program at an all-country music show held at the Overton Park Shell in Memphis. At the country show, Presley sang country numbers at one of these concerts to an undemonstrative audience. At another performance he decided to try a rhythm number, "Good Rockin' Tonight" (Roy Brown). Accompanying his singing with wriggling contortions of his body, he brought down the house. That shaking and quivering with its sexual suggestiveness, from then on became one of his performing trademarks, and the reason why he would in the future be called "Elvis the Pelvis." Presley insisted that he acquired this bit of stage business when he was a boy by watching singing preachers at revival meetings who would intoxicate the worshippers as much with the gyrations of their bodies as with their voices and prayers. It was equally possible that, consciously or otherwise, he had been impressed by Johnnie Ray's exhibitionism, which had such an electrifying effect on Johnnie Ray's audiences.

Presley's second recording for Sun was "Good Rockin' Tonight" coupled with "I Don't Care if the Sun Don't Shine" (Mack David). *Billboard* now referred to him as a "sock new singer" whose appeal extended not only to enthusiasts of rhythm and blues but also to those of country and western and pop music.

Presley made several more records for Sun, but only three were released under that label. "I'm Left, You're Right, She's Gone" (Stan Kesler) appeared on two national charts, number fifteen on the country and western list, and number eleven on the list of country numbers most often used by disc jockeys. This was one proof that Presley was coming along fast and well. Another indication of his growing popularity was the response of teenage girls during his public appearances in a swing of the Southern rural towns. They shivered, squealed, swooned. It was a case of spontaneous combustion. Nothing like this had happened since the times of Rudy Vallee and Frank Sinatra. An Elvis Presley fan club was formed. And perhaps more out of wish fulfilment than of profit, one young girl went to court to claim he was the father of her child, the first of many paternity suits that were to harass him; it was hastily dismissed.

He now rode in flashy cars or on motorcycles. He dressed ostentatiously, though when he was informal he would roll his sleeves up to show his biceps and pulled up his collar in the back. He kept his hair slick and shiny. For the Southern gals he had become a sex symbol, and he was playing that role to the hilt, more often than not seeking out rather than avoiding the idolatrous female hordes that sought him out wherever he went. When he sang he rolled his hips more than ever, grimaced with pain and punctuated his singing with throbbing hiccups, and lowered his heavy eyelids over his dreamy eyes.

Thus far, Presley's popularity was confined to the South. Was he just a regional phenomenon? Colonel Tom Parker thought not. Parker was a flamboyant, P.T. Barnum-like promoter who had managed Eddy Arnold for a decade and was the head of the Hank Snow Jamboree Attractions. Though Elvis Presley was being managed by Bob Neal of Memphis, Colonel Parker had his eye fixed both on Presley, and on that Neal contract that was due to expire in less than a year. When Arnold Shaw, general professional manager of the Edward E. B. Marks Music Corporation visited Nashville, Parker turned over to him the three Presley recordings, asking Shaw to help him explore Presley's potential in Northern urban areas. "In Georgia and Florida," the Colonel told Shaw, "the girls are tearing off his clothes." In *The Rockin' 50s*, Shaw recalls; "I frankly did not know what to make of the records. They puzzled me but they had a quality despite their crudeness, that intrigued me." He decided to try them out on Bill Randle, the influential disc jockey of WERE, Cleveland. One day later Randle telephoned Shaw excitedly: "I don't know what those Presley records have, but I put them on yesterday and, Arnold, the switchboard lit up like Glitter Gulch in Las Vegas. He hits them [the kids] like a bolt of electricity. My phone hasn't stopped ringing and I haven't been able to stop playing those records."

Things now began happening fast for Presley. Victor bought out Presley's Sun contract together with the unreleased Sun masters for about forty thousand dollars, an additional five thousand bonus going to Presley. Colonel Tom Parker became Presley's manager and shepherded him to unparalleled success. The Elvis Presley Music Inc. was set up as a subsidiary of Hill and Range to issue folios of songs performed by Presley. Presley was signed to a motion picture contract by 20th Century-Fox. Guest shots were found on major television programs: first on the Dorsey "Stage Show" over CBS; then on the Milton Berle show; after that on Steve Allen's Sunday night program; and finally on Ed Sullivan's "Toast of the Town." For three engagements on the Sullivan show he was paid fifty thousand dollars for each appearance, tripling the highest figure Sullivan had thus far paid to any performer. An audience estimated at fifty-four million heard that first Sullivan telecast, and the studio itself reverberated with the shouts and screeches of youngsters. There were noises away from the studio as well, the howls of those who maintained that Presley's bodily contortions and facial mannerisms were obscene, calculated to arouse the latent sex urges of the young.

On December 3, 1955, Victor released on its own label two of the masters Presleys had recorded for Sun: "I Forgot to Remember to Forget" (Stanley A. Kesler and Charles A. L. Feathers) backed by "Mystery Train" (Sam C. Phillips and Herman Parker, Jr.). "The most talked about new personality in the last ten years of recorded music" was the heading Victor used in a full page ad in *Billboard*. In January 1956 came Presley's first recording for Victor. It was "Heartbreak Hotel" (Mae Boren Axton, Tommy Durden and Elvis Presley) backed by "I Was the One" (Aaron Schroeder, Claude de Metruis, Hal Blair and Bill Peppers). It sold over two million records, earning a gold disk, and became the leading seller of 1956 for eight weeks.

Presley's recording history now went on to become an accumulation of startling sales figures and facts unequalled by any other recording artist within an equal span of time. In 1956 alone, his records held the top place in the charts for twenty-five weeks, his first Victor release being supplemented that year by "I Want You, I Need You, I Love You" (Maurice Mysels—Ira Kosloff), "Don't Be Cruel" (Otis Blackwell and Elvis Presley), "My Baby Left Me" (Arthur Crudup), "Hound Dog" (Jerry Leiber and Mike Stoller), "Love Me Tender" (Elvis Presley and Vera Matson) adapted from the Civil War song "Aura Lee" (W. W. Fosdick—George R. Poulton), and "Any Way You Want Me" (Aaron Schroeder and Cliff Owens).

In all, these records sold ten million disks in 1956, the largest sale in recording history for any one performer in a single year; Presley's earnings from them exceeded one million dollars. "Don't Be Cruel" amassed a sale of six million disks, and "Love Me Tender" became the first record ever to get an advance sale of a million copies. In 1957, Presley's records were on the top of the charts for twenty-four weeks. They were: "Too Much" (Bernard Weinam), "All Shook Up" (Otis Blackwell and Elvis Presley), "Loving You" (Jerry Leiber and Mike Stoller), "Teddy Bear" (Bernie Lowe and Kal Mann), "Jailhouse Rock" (Jerry Leiber and Mike Stoller), and "Treat Me Nice" (Jerry Leiber and Mike Stoller). In addition, in 1957, Presley's first LP was issued, and that sold over a million copies.

Within five years of "Heartbreak Hotel" Presley was the proud possessor of thirty-eight gold records (a figure without precedent), each a number one on the charts for weeks running, and with them four platinum disk albums. In that time his recordings earned seventy-six million dollars. Within a ten year period, over 115 million Presley disk units had been sold all over the world, grossing over one hundred and fifty million dollars.

This Presley madness, that made teenagers scoop up each of his records as soon as it was released, expressed itself in other ways, too. Special Projects, Inc., of Beverly Hills, marketed commodities bearing the Presley name, a business grossing about fifty-five million dollars in its first year. This was an all-inclusive line that had every garment worn by young males and females, as well as writing equipment, jewelry, soft drinks, guitars, bookends, dolls, greeting cards, photograph albums, diaries, pillows, stuffed hound dogs, plaster-of-paris Presley busts, and cosmetics.

The youngsters were not only buying Elvis Presley records and commodities, and singing the songs they had learned from his disks, but they were also supporting songs written about him: "My Boy Elvis," Dear Elvis," "My Baby's Crazy 'Bout Elvis," "The Tupelo Mississippi Flash," "Elvis Presley Blues," "I Wanna Spend Christmas with Elvis," "Hey, Mr. Presley," "Elvis Presley for President," "I Don't Want a Bracelet or Diamonds, I Just Want Elvis Instead."

The skeptics said that this Presley phenomenon, remarkable and unprecedented though it was, was a passing fad and nothing more. (They were saying the same thing about rock 'n' roll.) But the high tide of Presley's popularity refused to ebb. His recordings kept on selling in astronomic figures; there seemed to be no end to the demand. Indeed, his recording in 1960 of "It's Now or Never" (Aaron Schroeder and Wally Gold) based on the Neapolitan song, "O Sole Mio," sold five million disks in the United States and nine million globally, remaining on the top of the charts for five weeks in the United States and ten in Great Britain. Each of his movies, with their built-in audiences, was a gilt-edged investment, not only for the studio but for Presley as well, since for his later pictures he was drawing

$250,000 each together with fifty percent of all profits. Within three weeks of its distribution, *Love Me Tender* (1956), his first motion picture, recouped its investment of a million dollars. The long queue of girls that lined up outside the Paramount Theater in New York waiting for the doors to open, when this picture was first shown there, was a reminder of how their mothers had behaved at this same theater when Sinatra was there; and, as in the days of Sinatra, extra policemen and ushers had to be called to prevent an explosive situation from developing among the girls. Each of Presley's public appearances now brought him the-then unheard of figure of twenty-five thousand dollars a night, and even that sum was turned down when he was not in the mood to perform.

Not even the two years he had to spend in the United States Army in a public relations assignment between 1958 and 1960 could diminish his popular appeal. The fires of his teenage worshippers were kept at white heat by his records—those he had recorded before he entered the army, and the new ones he was allowed to make while in uniform—and by his already completed motion pictures. Once out of uniform he was as big as ever, starring with Frank Sinatra on a TV Special, "Welcome Elvis" over ABC on May 12, 1960 which swamped the competition on the other networks in the ratings. *Elvis is Back* was his first new record album, its sales passing the million mark, and his first new single, "It's Now or Never" was one of his greatest successes. *G. I. Blues* (1960) was his next movie. His first new public appearances were benefit performances in 1961 in Memphis and Hawaii. He did not make any more public appearances until 1969, but his motion pictures and records kept flowing.

One unidentified critic had written in 1956: "Elvis Presley is a fad, a fellow a girl turns to for one of those mad impetuous infatuations, whereas Perry Como and Eddie Fisher will still be around, the dependable types, when Presley is back driving his truck."

But thirteen years after this prognostication was published, Presley, in his first public appearance since 1961, was drawing $100,000 a week for a four-week engagement at the International Hotel in Las Vegas. (And where, oh where, was Eddie Fisher?) Less than three years later, some fifty-thousand hysterical admirers packed the auditorium for each of three Presley concerts in Chicago. At Madison Square Garden (Presley's first return to New York in sixteen years) he gave four concerts in three days drawing eighty thousand to each. After that, he taped a public appearance in Hawaii which was televised around the globe to what was surely the largest audience ever to witness a single TV program. A new album, *Elvis Now*, was on the best-seller charts of *Billboard* for over sixteen weeks. His records were still in such constant demand that Victor was now issuing annually an updated pamphlet, *The Complete Catalogue of Elvis Presley Records and Tapes* which, in 1972, filled thirty-two pages and listed forty-eight active titles. And still he was continually adding new figures to the overwhelming statistics he had already compiled, having by now sold over one hundred million singles and fifty-five albums, and having appeared in thirty-two films. In 1975, he was awarded a Grammy for "How Great Thou Art," as the year's best inspirational performance on records, and one of his albums—*Presley—A Legendary Performance, Vol. I*—earned a gold record. In 1976, he was high on the charts with *Elvis: The Sun Sessions*. This was an album made up of Presley's early Sun recordings, the first he ever made, reissued by RCA. "Twenty years," wrote Nik Cohn in a review in *New York*, "they are still the greatest explosions, the most heroic madness, that rock 'n' roll has produced. . . . They are, I think, the rawest, most personal music that he ever created."

And in his late years he was singing better than ever, though now more in a crooning than rock style. Henry Edwards wrote in *High Fidelity* in November 1972: "Since those early days that dramatically changed the direction of pop music, Elvis has sung practically every kind of song. His range is greater than that of almost any other popular singer. His voice is a mellow and expressive instrument."

4

The movie industry became aware of the purchasing power of the young and began to tap that power by catering to the youngsters' total commitment to rock 'n' roll. After having erupted so explosively for the first time on the sound track of *The Blackboard Jungle* with "Rock Around the Clock" rock 'n' roll made an even deeper penetration into motion pictures in 1956 with a film bearing the name of that song. *Rock Around the Clock* was a low-budget production (costing less than a quarter of a million dollars) starring Bill Haley and The Comets in a story faintly suggesting Bill Haley's own career from his humble beginnings in a small town to the time he is discovered by Alan Freed and given prominence through a coast-to-coast telecast. The picture gave Bill Haley and The Comets opportunities to strut their stuff. "See You Later, Alligator" (Robert Guidry) was here introduced. This motion picture caused a storm in movie theaters around the country, sometimes inciting disturbances; and on the campus of Princeton University it even instigated a riot.

Other rock films catered to the youth market. Little Richard could be seen and heard in *The Girl Can't Help It* (1956). Bill Haley and The Comets appeared in 1957 in *Don't Knock Rock. Rock 'n' Roll Revue* (1956)—though starring Duke Ellington and Dinah Washington—shook with rock. In *Rock, Rock, Rock* (1957), LaVern Baker sang "Tra la la" (Johnny Parker) among other rock tunes. *Rock, Pretty Baby* (1957) told the story of a high school band that wins a competition by playing rock music. *Disk Jockey* (1957) and *Jamboree* (1957) both featured Jerry Lee Lewis who sang "Great Balls of Fire" (Jack Hammer and Otis Blackwell) in the latter movie. Tommy Sands was the star of *Sing Boy, Sing* (1958) where he introduced the title song (Tommy Sands and Rod McKuen). Della Reese and Julius La Rosa were the stars of *Let's Rock* (1958); in *Hound Dog Man* (1959) Fabian introduced the title song (Doc Pomus and Mort Shuman).

But in rock movies, as in all other areas of popular music in the fifties, Elvis Presley was the undisputed monarch. The first of his more than thirty screen appearances took place in *Love Me Tender* (1956) in which Presley was cast in a Civil War story as a country boy who marries his brother's fiancée, believing him dead. The country boy's own death resolves this touchy situation after his brother returns from the war. The critics found much to criticize in Presley's acting, but could not deny the impact of his singing in the title number and three other songs. *Time* reported: "But suddenly the figure comes to life. The lips part, the eyes half closed, the clutched guitar begins to undulate back and forth in an uncomfortably suggestive manner. And wham! The mid-section of the body juts forward to bump and grind and beat out a low-down rhythm that takes its pace from boogie and hillbilly, rock 'n' roll and something known only to Elvis and his Pelvis. . . . A bit trembly tender half smile, half sneer, smears slowly across the Cinemascope screen. The message that millions of U.S. teenage girls love to receive has just been delivered."

In his second motion picture, *Loving You* (1957) Elvis Presley played the part of a country lad who becomes a sensational singer with a country band. The title song (Jerry Leiber and Mike Stoller) was one of seven songs that also included "Teddy Bear" (Bernie Lowe and Kal Mann).

Jailhouse Rock (1957) came next, title song by Jerry Leiber and Mike Stoller. *King Creole* (1958) was Presley's last motion picture before his two years of service in uniform, and

G. I. *Blues* (1960) was his first after he left service. There were twenty-five more Presley motion pictures in the 1960s.

(Elvis Presley was the inspiration, and a Presley-like figure was the principal character, in the first important Broadway musical to be influenced by the rock 'n' roll madness—*Bye, Bye, Birdie* in 1960.)

5

Out of country and western music came other heroes of the rock revolution of the fifties. Buddy Holly (Charles Hardin Holly), of Lubbock, Texas, began to study the violin and piano in 1942, when he was four, and the guitar three years later. While attending high school he sang country music over the radio. In 1955 he became the lead singer of The Crickets with whom he recorded "Peggy Sue" (Jerry Allison, Buddy Holly and Norman Petty), "That'll Be the Day" (Jerry Allison, Buddy Holly and Norman Petty) and "Maybe Baby" (Norman Petty and Buddy Holly). (Jerry Allison was the drummer and Norman Petty the recording engineer of The Crickets.) Then Holly went on his own as a solo rock performer, and forthwith won for himself a gold record with "It Doesn't Matter Any More" (Paul Anka) and a best seller in "Early in the Morning" (Bobby Darin and Woody Harris). His promising career was cut short when on February 3, 1959 he met his death in a plane crash.

Jerry Lee Lewis burst upon the rock scene with his explosive singing and his ferocious assaults on the piano. Andy Wickham, onetime A and R man, once called Jerry Lee Lewis' performance at the piano a "rape" adding: "He would play it with his feet, he would sit on it, he would stand on it, he would crawl under it, and he would leap over it, his shivery voice provoking goose pimples, his long crabby fingers assaulting the keys, his feet crashing the pedals like a speed-freak flooding the carburetor of a stalled Ferrari."

Born in Ferriday, Louisiana, in 1935, Jerry Lee Lewis received his academic education at the Bible Institute in Waxahachie, Texas. He learned to play the piano, guitar, violin and accordion by himself. In 1947 he made his professional debut at the Blue Cat Club in Natchez, Mississippi. For the next few years he traveled around as a country and western artist. In 1955 he signed a contract with Sun Records and in two years' time made the grade as a top rock 'n' roller with two gold records, "Great Balls of Fire" (Jack Hammer and Otis Blackwell) and "Whole Lot-ta Shakin' Goin' On" (Dave Williams and Sunny David). Jerry Lee Lewis fell into disrepute and his career was aborted when an unsavory fact of his personal life was disclosed: He was married to his thirteen-year-old cousin.

The Everly Brothers—Phil, born in 1939, and Donald, in 1937—forged ahead in rock 'n' roll in 1957 with two gold disks on Cadence: "Bye Bye Love" (Felice Bryant and Boudleaux Bryant) and "Wake Up Little Susie" (Felice Bryant and Boudleaux Bryant). But long before that they had been a part of the country and western scene. Their careers began during their childhood when they were members of a family singing roup, the Everly Family, headed by their parents; it appeared as a country music group in concerts and over the radio. In their teen years, Phil and Donald appeared in the Grand Ole Opry. They went on from country music to rock soon after they left high school, signing a contract with Cadence Records and placing themselves under the management of Wesley Rose, one of the heads of the powerful Nashville publishing house, Acuff-Rose. After achieving two hits in 1957, they were heard in a long string of best-selling records, many of their songs having been written either by Boudleaux Bryant or by Bryant in collaboration with his wife, Felice. The Everly Brothers had three gold records in 1958: "All I Have to Do Is Dream" (Boudleaux Bryant), "Bird Dog" (Boudleaux Bryant) and "Problems" (Felice and Boudleaux Bryant).

One year later, the Everlys had other gold records with "Take a Message to Mary" (Felice and Boudleaux Bryant) and "I Kissed You" (Don Everly).

After rhythm and blues had been taken over by the young white market, it became increasingly difficult to differentiate between rhythm and blues and rock. The sound of Chuck Berry and Little Richard became part and parcel of the 1950s rock movement. Antoine "Fats" Domino was another black rhythm and blues artist whose first recording, "The Fat Man" (Dave Bartholomew and Fats Domino) sold over a million disks. In the mid-1950s, Fats Domino became one of the dominant figures in the world of rock; the total sale of his records was about sixty million disks and four million albums by 1960, with twenty-two of his releases gaining gold records. (Only two recording artists up to 1960 had collected more gold records than Fats Domino: Elvis Presley and Bing Crosby.)

Antoine Domino had been rocked in the cradle of jazz in New Orleans where he was born in 1928, one of nine children. The blues and ragtime made a deep impression on him during his early years; he was only five when he tried picking out jazz tunes on an old battered piano. A few years later, he played the blues and ragtime in honky-tonks on the weekends, and in his early manhood he formed a jazz band which appeared at the Hideaway Club in New Orleans. Since his music earned him hardly more than a pittance, he had to work in a bedspring factory, and later in a lumber mill.

His talent was detected by Lew Chudd, head of Imperial Records, who signed him to a contract in 1948 as singer-pianist. The first record was a winner, "The Fat Man," a song which Domino wrote about himself, since he weighed two hundred and fifty pounds. By 1952 his rhythm and blues became rock and in 1952, "Goin' Home" (Fats Domino and Alvin E. Young) earned a gold record. Domino had four more gold records in 1953, three of them of songs he wrote collaboratively with Dave Bartholomew—"Going to the River," "You Said You Loved Me" and "I Lived My Life," and a fourth, "Please Don't Leave Me," which he wrote without assistance. Domino's later million-disk sales were also mainly of songs that he wrote with Dave Bartholomew. The exceptions were: "Blueberry Hill," (Al Lewis, Larry Stock, and Vincent Rose), a standard from 1940; "I Still Love You" (Dave Bartholomew, Fats Domino, Watson and Palmer); "Thinking of You" (R. Hall); "Walkin' to New Orleans" (Dave Bartholomew, Fats Domino and Robert Guidry); and "Bo Weevil," which while written by Bartholomew and Domino was based on the old American folk blues song. In all these Imperial recordings, the effect of the rock numbers was heightened by Domino's individualistic presentation, his hammering blows on the piano providing a forceful background to his raspy singing.

The marriage of rock to pop songs in a folk style helped to produce folk rock. Several singing groups grew famous through folk rock, most prominently the Kingston Trio, whose Capitol recording of "Tom Dooley" (Dave Guard) in 1958 brought the singing trio into the performing limelight. This trio was made up of Nick Reynolds, Bob Shane and Dave Guard. They all sang and played the guitar, and Dave Guard also played the banjo. Organized by Dave Guard, the Kingston Trio made its bow in 1957 and soon thereafter was signed to a long-term contract by Capitol. Their first LP, *The Kingston Trio*, included "Tom Dooley." This one cut was seized upon by disc jockeys everywhere and grew so popular that Capitol released it as a single which sold two and a half million disks. If any single number may be said to have launched the vogue for folk rock this was it. "Tom Dooley" was Dave Guard's adaptation of an 1868 folk song from the Blue Ridge Mountain region about a man named Tom Dula who was hanged for murdering his sweetheart.

"Merry Little Minute" (Sheldon Harnick) in 1958 was another of the hit records of The Kingston Trio. This number was a satire on the atom bomb; it had first been introduced five years earlier by Orson Bean in the Broadway revue, *John Murray Anderson's Almanac*, and then featured in nightclubs by Charlotte Rae. In 1959, The Kingston Trio scored again, this time with their recordings of "The Tijuana Jail" (Denny Thompson) and "A Worried Man" (Dave Guard and Tom Glazer), the latter adapted from an American folk song that had been a staple in the repertory of the Carter Family.

6

Some of the new rock performers of the fifties were youngsters whose appeal rested almost as firmly on the fact that they looked like high school kids as on their songs and performances. Paul Anka was just sixteen when the young people took to him. Born in Canada in 1941, the son of a Lebanese restaurateur, Anka paid his first visit to New York when he was fourteen by winning a three-day visit as a prize in a contest. He liked his first taste of New York, and two years later, financed by his father with a hundred dollars, he was back, this time for the purpose of trying to market some of his songs. Somehow he managed to penetrate the recording citadel of Don Costa, the A and R man of ABC–Paramount. Costa reacted so positively and immediately to Anka's songs that he offered him a long-term recording contract. Anka's first record, with himself as its singing performer, was "Diana," which he had written following a frustrated love affair with a girl three years his senior. This one record became the miracle every performer and songwriter dreams of. Released in 1957, it became an instant best-seller, heading the charts for thirteen consecutive weeks, Within a year or so it sold three million disks in America and another six million in the rest of the world. It brought wealth and a worldwide reputation to sixteen-year-old Anka who now became one of the first of that breed of singing performers who were to become such a dominant force in the popular music of the sixties and seventies.

Solely on the strength of "Diana," Anka made his first tour abroad in 1957–1958, visiting Europe, Australia and Japan. Wherever he went he was mobbed by his admirers. In Japan two thousand idolators defied a typhoon to stand in line all day with the hope of gaining admission to his concert. Back in America, in 1958, Anka was deluged with offers to appear on television, at concerts, in theaters and in motion pictures—this in addition to two more extended foreign tours in 1958 and 1959.

"Diana" was no morning glory. Within six years it was pressed on three hundred and twenty recordings in twenty-four countries, with a total sale of thirteen million copies. It amassed the second biggest financial gross in recording history, right behind Bing Crosby's "White Christmas" (Irving Berlin).

Close on its heels, in 1958 and 1959, other Anka performances of his songs swept through the charts as best-sellers: "You Are My Destiny," "Lonely Boy," "Put Your Head on My Shoulder," "It Doesn't Matter Any More," "Let the Bells Keep Ringing," "Crazy Love," "It's Time to Cry," "Teddy" and "Puppy Love." Supplementing these and similar successes was the "Johnny's Theme" which he wrote as signature music for the Johnny Carson "Tonight" Show in 1962 in collaboration with Johnny Carson.

During the sixties, when Presley and the Beatles were usurping the air waves and dominating the record market, Paul Anka's popularity as a composer went into a sharp decline. As he told Arnold Shaw: "I've gotten into the rut of writing for myself, which put me in a terrible groove . . . if I didn't want a song for myself, who else would? One night, I came to the simple idea: I've got to design songs to fit other people." That is how he came to write "My Way" in 1968—an adaptation of a French ballad, *"Comme d'habitude"* for which he had acquired the rights—not only *for* Frank Sinatra but *about* Sinatra's controversial behavior. The song became what Sinatra likes to refer to in his public appearances as "my national anthem," and from 1968 on seemed to be the song audiences everywhere requested most often from Sinatra. Anka wrote songs for other performers as well, such as "She's a

Lady" for Tom Jones. But in addition to writing songs for others, Anka continued to write numbers about himself. "You're Having My Baby" became a gold disk on the United Artists label in 1973, and "I Don't Like to Sleep Alone" was a smash hit in 1975. Two of Anka's albums of songs, in his own performances, received gold disks in 1974 and 1975, *Anka* and *Feelings*. *The Painter*, in 1976, was a best seller.

He was also producing songs as commercials: "The Times of Your Life," written for Eastman Kodak and promoted on TV and radio in Anka's own performance, even did well on the charts in an Anka recording.

On December 8, 1975, *Time* could report that from all such songwriting efforts, from his personal appearances and from his extra-musical business ventures (including in 1976 a million-dollar discotheque in Las Vegas and the auberge, *Chez Paul*, in Sun Valley) Paul Anka had become "one of the richest entertainers in the world."

Bobby Darin was another youngster who made it big with the rock 'n' roll fans of the fifties, both as a singer and as a writer of songs. Born Walden Robert Cassotto in the Bronx, in New York, in 1936, Darin's childhood was unhappy. His father (whom Bobby described as a small-time gangster) died before Bobby's birth. Bobby and his mother lived on relief as best they could. Bobby was a sickly child who for five years suffered recurring attacks of rheumatic fever. Unable to attend school for several years, he had to get his primary education by intensive reading and through coaching by his mother. A musical boy, he taught himself to play the piano, guitar, vibraphone, drums and bass. When he was finally physically capable of attending school classes he proved to be a brilliant student, graduating from the Bronx High School of Science in 1953, and then attending Hunter College where he specialized in speech and drama courses. Impatient to make headway in show business, he left college without a degree. He played the drums, sang, and officiated as master of ceremonies in resorts in the Catskill Mountains of New York. During the winter, he helped write singing commercials for radio and occasionally found a booking as a singer in small New York night spots. In 1956 came his first significant break when he made his television debut on the Dorsey show billed as "the nineteen-year old singing sensation." He was also signed that year to a one-year recording contract with Decca which, when terminated, was replaced by a new agreement with a new recording outfit, Atco.

He was already writing songs, one of his early efforts being "My First Love" written in 1956 with Don Kirshner. One day, the mother of a friend suggested humorously that he write a number called "Splish, Splash." This idea appealed to Darin's sense of whimsy and in collaboration with Jean Murray he wrote the rock number "Splish Splash" which he recorded for Atco in 1958. Within three weeks, a hundred thousand disks were sold, and before much longer it became Darin's first gold record. It was with this release that he adopted the name of Bobby Darin, a name he found by flipping through the pages of a telephone book.

Darin's success continued with "Queen of the Hop" (Woody Harris and Bobby Darin) and "This Little Girl's Gone Rockin' " (Mann Curtis and Bobby Darin), the former gaining Darin his second gold record. In 1959, "Mack the Knife" (Marc Blitzstein—Kurt Weill) and "Dream Lover" (Bobby Darin) realized more gold records. In 1960, in a teenage poll conducted by the Gilbert Youth Research Company, Darin shared with Johnny Mathis the top position as the country's leading male pop singer.

"Mack the Knife" was one of several songs in Darin's album *That's All* recorded in 1959, comprising numbers outside the world of rock with which Darin reached out to audiences other than teenagers. *That's All* sold half a million albums and "Mack the Knife," released as a single, became such a blockbuster that from then on Darin used it as his musical identification. For nine consecutive weeks it was on the top of the charts; it sold more than two million disks and brought Darin two Grammys, one for Darin himself as the year's best singer, and the other one for the record. "Mack the Knife" was a new adaptation by Marc Blitzstein of "Moritat," a number from the Bertolt Brecht-Kurt Weill musical satire, *The Threepenny Opera*, which had sent Germany spinning with enthusiasm in the early 1930s. The new song adaptation was part of the Off-Broadway revival of *The Threepenny Opera* in 1954 with Blitzstein's greatly revised text and new lyrics. "Mack the Knife" became the song hit of that production. It was recorded in 1955 more than twenty times and achieved a top place on "Your Hit Parade." Louis Armstrong's recording for Columbia in 1957 was one of several best sellers, but that of Bobby Darin two years later outstripped the sales of all of its competitors.

In 1960, Bobby Darin was starred in his first motion picture, *Come September*. His leading lady, Sandra Dee, became his wife, but that marriage broke up in 1966. During the 1960s, Darin maintained his popularity not only with youngsters but also with an adult public through his many nightclub appearances, his motion pictures, as well as his records. In 1963 he was nominated for an Academy Award for best supporting actor for his performance in *Captain Newman, M.D.* By 1970, Darin's career had begun to falter. A new television show and successful engagements at Las Vegas appeared to have rehabiliated him in show business before he died in Los Angeles in 1973, the victim of a heart ailment that had plagued him throughout his life.

Ricky Nelson was seventeen when his Verve recording of "A Teenager's Romance" (David Gillam) backed by "I'm Walkin' " (Dave Bartholomew and Fats Domino) brought him a gold record with his very first release. But, despite his youth, he was by no means unknown. Born in Teaneck, New Jersey in 1940, he was the son of Ozzie Nelson, then a bandleader, and Ozzie Nelson's wife, Harriet, the singer in Ozzie Nelson's band. From his eighth year, Ricky was seen on television over ABC on the series, *The Adventures of Ozzie and Harriet*, in which he starred with his father, mother, and his brother David. It had an eighteen-year run, and in it Ricky Nelson proved himself an adept actor. With his first record scooped up by rock fans, Ricky Nelson went on to become one of their singing favorites. He boasted two more gold records in 1957 with "Be-Bop Baby" (Pearl Lendhurst) and "Stood Up" (Dub Dickerson and Erma Herrold), and five more before 1960. For a number of years he failed to produce hits, but in 1972 made a comeback with "Garden Party" which he recorded with his own group, the Stone Canyon Band.

This was one of the phenomena of the rock era: a youngster of high school years, like Ricky Nelson, able to climb to the pinnacle of financial and musical success (often with a single record) and become the object of hero-worship among the young. Fabian was about fifteen when he recorded for Chancellor "I'm a Man" (Doc Pomus and Mort Shuman), "Turn Me Loose" (Doc Pomus and Mort Shuman) and "Tiger" (Ollie Jones) between 1958 and 1959. Frankie Avalon, who had made screen appearances in *Disk Jockey* and *Jamboree* when he was seventeen, became a recording best-seller in 1958 with "Dede Dinah" (Bob Marcussi—Peter De Angelis) and "Ginger Bread" (Clint Ballard, Jr. and Hank Hunter). One year more and three more hit records made him a teenager's idol: "Venus" (Ed Marshall), "Just Ask Your Heart" (Pete Damato and Joe Ricci—Diane De Nota) and "Why" (Bob Marcussi—Peter De Angelis). Bobby Rydell was nineteen in 1959 when he first made his mark with the gold record, "Wild One" (Bernie Lose, Kal Mann and Dave Appell) backed by "Little Bitty Girl" (Fred Tobias—Clint Ballard, Jr.). Annette (Annette Funicello), a graduate Mouseketeer of the "Mickey Mouse Club" over ABC-TV was sixteen when she made her first hit record, "Tall Paul" (Bob Roberts, Bob Sherman and Dick Sherman).

7

Rock made "The American Bandstand" the most extensively viewed (and most imitated) television program for young people and a program that had a giant share in the rapidly spreading influence and popularity of rock music.

"The American Bandstand" grew out of "Bandstand," a Philadelphia television program headed by Bob Horn over WFIL in 1952. In place of live performances, concerts of recorded music were given, supplemented by films provided by managers, record companies and publishers as publicity. Horn got into trouble because of drunken driving at a time when the Philadelphia *Ledger* was in a vigorous crusade against this vice. He was hurriedly replaced by young Dick Clark who, at that time, was employed at WFIL as a disc jockey and announcer.

Clark had come from an upper middle-class family in Mount Vernon, New York. After graduating from Syracuse University in June 1951 he worked for two radio stations in Syracuse where he delivered station breaks and commercials. In Spring of 1952 he moved on to WFIL.

After he took over "Bandstand," the program changed its name to "American Bandstand" and on August 5, 1957 went network over ABC-TV as a daily program. The review *Billboard* gave it when the show received its network premiere was none too encouraging. "As a sociological study of teenage behavior, the premiere was a mild success. As relaxation and entertainment, it wasn't. . . . The bulk of the ninety minutes was devoted to colorless juveniles trudging through early American dances like the Lindy and the Box Step to recorded tunes of the day. If this is the wholesome answer to the 'detractors' of rock 'n' roll, bring on the rotating pelvises."

But the show took hold. Within a year it reached twenty million youngsters over a network of one hundred and five TV stations, not to mention the hundred or so imitators on local TV shows. As a host, Dick Clark proved a winner. He was young, handsome, clean-cut, behaving like a sympathetic big brother to the kids in the studio. His broad grin was infectious. He always appeared casual and relaxed, neatly dressed. Dungarees or jeans were out for girls in the studio-audience, who had to wear skirts; jackets were *de rigueur* for boys. When the kids got on the floor to dance to the recorded music, it was as if they were at a family gathering, with everything quite proper. By emphasizing "cool white" rock—as opposed to the hotter product promoted over the radio by Alan Freed—Dick Clark was making rock music more ingratiating to the ears. Even older folks started to tune in to the program to watch the kids, and felt that the generation gap had become somewhat narrowed.

Clark would play the records and comment on them. The studio audience of kids —three hundred of them picked from thousands of requests—would impulsively start dancing. Invited guests gave their opinions on the new record releases. Leading personalities of the rock world would be interviewed, and so would some of the youngsters who were encouraged to introduce themselves, talk about their personal lives, and give their reactions to the songs that had been played. A highlight was "Dick Clark's Top Ten," Clark's own selection of the ten top-rated rock tunes.

Kids would hitchhike from all over the country to Philadelphia with the hope of getting on the program and dancing. Others would rush to their television sets from school. Careers were given their first important starts on this program, those of Fabian, Frankie Avalon, Connie Francis, Bobbie Rydell and many others. Many new rock dances originated on "The American Bandstand"—the Stroll, the Walk, the Fish, the Slop. It became standard practice for youngsters around the country to adopt the steps and body movements that a few kids of the studio audience were adventurously trying out. Because some of the boys of that studio audience used Butch wax for their hair, Butch wax became a national institution. When some of the girls took to wearing heavy sweaters and heavy rolled socks, this became the uniform of young girls everywhere, even in the sweltering heat of southern Florida and Texas.

As a result of his monumental success on "The American Bandstand" Clark became a formidable power in the music business. When he plugged a song, there was an immediate rush to the shops. Inevitably he was sucked into the "payola" scandal in late 1959 and early 1960, but he survived to celebrate the twentieth anniversary of "The American Bandstand" with a ninety-minute salute over ABC-TV on June 19, 1973 which paid tribute to the program, its host, and the era in which they flourished. The twenty-fifth anniversary of "The American Bandstand" was celebrated over the ABC-TV network—on February 4, 1977, featuring over seventy-five top television and recording artists.

8

Though a segment of the adult public responded favorably to the cool rock offered over "The American Bandstand," the adult community for the most part proved fiercely hostile to rock and its influence on the young. The sounds of rock were regarded as a return to primitivism. More objectionable still were the lyrics, an open endorsement of sex permissiveness, perversion, drugs, disobedience to parents, hostility to society.

Initially, discretion was the better part of valor where the lyrics of rock were concerned. The words of "The Wallflower" or "Dance with Me Henry" (Johnny Otis, Hank Ballard and Etta James) had nothing to do with dancing at first, but to satisfy the sensibilities of objectors to such provocative, double-entendre lines the song's original thought was changed. Early in the history of rock performances, many rock numbers were banned from the airwaves because they were regarded too suggestive. One such was "Honey Love" (Clyde McPhatter and J. Gerald) whose lyric put too much stress on "I need it, when the moon is bright, and I need it when you hold me tight, I need it in the middle of the night, I need your honey love."

But with the passing of time, the barriers to the subject matter of lyrics, and to performances of songs with questionable themes, were broken down (at least for a time). The material youngsters were favoring in their songs—as well as the frenetic way in which it was being extolled musically—sent adult society into a state of shock. Rock was being viewed as an invitation to moral disintegration and juvenile delinquency. Garret Byrne, a Massachusetts district attorney, exclaimed: "Tin Pan Alley has unleashed a new monster, a sort of nightmare of rhythm. Some of our disc jockeys have put emotional TNT on their turntables. Rock 'n' roll gives young hoodlums an excuse to get together. It inflames teenagers and is obscenely objective." The New York *Daily News* accused recording companies and disc jockeys of "pandering to the worst juvenile taste." To the Very Reverend John Carroll of Boston, rock was "like jungle tom-toms readying warriors for battle" whose lyrics "are, of course, a matter for law-enforcement agencies." And A. M. Merrio, associate professor of psychiatry at Columbia University insisted: "If we cannot stem the tide of rock 'n' roll with its waves of rhythmic narcosis, we are preparing our own downfall in the midst of pandemic funeral dances."

Everywhere efforts were made to arrest the epidemic spread of rock 'n' roll. It was banished by the city council from the city swimming pool jukeboxes in San Antonio, Texas because it "attracted undesirable elements given to practising their gyrations in abbreviated bathing suits." The White Citizen's Council of Birmingham, Alabama, joined forces to remove rock 'n' roll records from the local jukeboxes. Mayor Roland Hines of Asbury Park,

New Jersey, prohibited rock concerts in the city dance halls; the city officials of Jersey City canceled a projected rock show at the Roosevelt Stadium; and those of Santa Cruz, California, banned all rock concerts in civic buildings. In Hartford, Connecticut, there was an attempt to revoke the license of the State Theater because Alan Freed was to appear there. A special committee in Boston, after a period of research, found that disc jockeys were "social pariahs" and suggested that they be forbidden to participate in public entertainments.

Even established songwriters (who might be expected to be more tolerant of new trends) combined to attack rock. Some of them, all ASCAP members, appeared before the Celler congressional committee in Washington, D. C., investigating monopoly in broadcasting, to brand BMI as a conspiracy by broadcasters to control the country's popular music. The reason for this attack was not hard to seek. In throwing out its net for new member composers, most of whom were producing rock hits, BMI became a serious threat to ASCAP. With rock and little else getting heard on the air and over TV, and being sold on records, ASCAP members had been caught short, even though some ASCAP standards were getting a rock treatment. Its principal composers and lyricists—to whom rock was untouchable—found to their dismay that much of their lucrative market had been usurped by the young upstarts of rock.

To avoid ASCAP's being accused of sour grapes, several of its top executives disassociated the organization from those dissenting composers and lyricists appearing before the Celler House Committee, insisting that the arguments of these men represented personal opinions and was not the official position of ASCAP.

36

Hillbilly Becomes Country and Western

1

From the ranks of the Grand Ole Opry in Nashville, Tennessee, came the men largely responsible for transforming hillbilly music into country and western: Ernest Tubb, Hank Snow, Eddie Arnold, Hank Williams, and Johnny Cash.

The singing guitarist, Ernest Tubb, joined the Grand Ole Opry in 1943 and earned his way into the Country Music Hall of Fame in 1965. In 1927, Tubb heard a recording of Jimmie Rodgers' "T for Texas" when he was thirteen, and that made all the difference to him. From then on his ambition was to become a country singer. He tried to sing like Rodgers, simulating Rodgers' yodeling style; intermittently he made singing appearances with string bands at square dances. While Tubb was in his teens, his family moved to San Antonio at a time when Rodgers was there, but Ernest never met his idol, something he regretted to the end of his days. But after Rodgers' death, he met Rodgers' widow who, impressed by his talent, presented him with one of her husband's guitars and used her influence to get Tubb his first theater tour and his first recording engagement.

A Texan, born in Crisp in 1914, Ernest Tubb worked as a soda jerk and then for the Works Progress Administration in San Antonio before landing his first radio job at KONO in that city in 1934, a twice-a-week fifteen minute program. He not only modeled his singing style after Jimmie Rodgers but also featured in his repertory many of the songs Rodgers had made famous, including the blue yodels. Among his earliest recordings, on the Bluebird label, a Victor subsidiary, were his own tributes to his idol, "The Passing of Jimmie Rodgers" and "Jimmie Rodgers' Last Thoughts." Working in honky-tonks, plus additional appearances over the radio—together with his growing maturity—enabled Tubb to free himself from the Rodgers influence and develop his own singing style. This personalized manner became evident in his first recording under a new contract negotiated with Decca in 1940, his own "I'll Get Along Somehow," which sold well, and initiated an affiliation with Decca that proved enormously profitable both to Tubb and to the company. Tubb became the most successful country artist on the Decca roster; his own "Walking the Floor Over You" in 1941 became the first of his many records to sell a million disks, and became Tubb's signature music.

With "Walking the Floor Over You" Tubb had arrived as a country artist. He acquired a sponsor for his radio program, was featured in 1942 in two motion pictures (*Fighting Buckaroo* and *Ridin' West*) and, in 1943, was made a member of the Grand Ole Opry company with whom he remained for many years. In that time he was seen in two more motion pictures, *Jamboree* (1944) and *Hollywood Barn Dance* (1947), and in numerous public appearances, including two concerts in Carnegie Hall, in New York, in 1947, the first country musician to appear there. Among the songs which he himself wrote and which he featured successfully over radio, on records and in public appearances were "Our Baby's Book" written on the death of his infant son; "My Tennessee Baby," dedicated to the woman who became his wife; "I'm Bitin' My Fingernails and Thinking of You," written with Roy West, E. Benedict and L. Sanders; "It's Been So Long, Darlin' "; You Nearly Lose Your Mind"; and "Tomorrow Never Comes," written with Johnny Bond. He also recorded successfully the songs of other composers: "Blue Christmas" (Billy Hayes and Jay Johnson), "Don't Rob Another Man's Castle" (Jenny Lou Carson), "Slipping Around" (Floyd Tillman), "Tennessee Border No. 2" (Homer and Jethro—Jimmy Work) and "The Warm Red Wine" (Cindy Walker).

Among Tubb's distinctions were that he was one of the first country performers to make records in Nashville, Tennessee, and one of the first to use an electric guitar—two directions in which many another country singer would follow his lead.

For Hank Snow, who was a mainstay of the Grand Ole Opry for fifteen years, Jimmie Rodgers had also been an inspiration and a model.

Snow was a Canadian—born in Liverpool, Nova Scotia in 1914—who first became interested in hillbilly music through his fascination with western movies. As a boy he studied singing and acquired the beginnings of a country music repertory by listening to Jimmie Rodgers' records. Even after achieving fame in his own right, Snow kept his boyhood adulation of Rodgers (Snow's first son was named Jimmie Rodgers Snow).

Snow sang over the radio in Nova Scotia billed as "Hank, the Singing Ranger." His popularity throughout Canada brought him a contract with Victor in 1936 (an association that would last for over several decades); but not until the mid-1940s did Snow become known in the United States, since his Victor records initially were released exclusively in Canada. But in 1944, a disc jockey in Dallas, Texas, began playing some of Snow's Canadian recordings. This led to Snow's first American bookings, to appearances over the radio, and in 1948 to an eventful national tour. His fame now established, Victor began distributing his records in the United States. One of the earliest was "Marriage Vow" (Jenny Lou Carson), whose label still identified Snow as "Hank the Singing Ranger." In 1950, the "singing Ranger" identification was permanently dropped with two highly successful new releases: "Golden Rocket" and "I'm Movin' On," both written by Snow, and the second a train song, a genre in which Snow particularly distinguished himself. One of Snow's public appearances was in Texas in a show headed by Tubb. It was on Tubb's recommendation that Snow was asked to appear with the Grand Ole Opry. His performances there, as elsewhere, and the records that Victor was releasing so abundantly, placed Snow among the leaders in country music. Among his best-selling records in the fifties were "The Gold Rush Is Over" (Cindy Walker), "I Went to Your Wedding" (Jessie Mae Robinson), "Honeymoon on a Rocket Ship" (Johnnie Masters), "Spanish Fireball" (Daniel James Welch), "I Don't Hurt Anymore" (Jack Rollins—Don Robertson), "Cryin', Prayin', Wishin', Waitin' " (C. Stewart, J. Smith and D. Dill), "Yellow Roses" (Kenny Devine and Sam Nichols), "Stolen Moments" (Sid Wayne—Joe Sherman), "Tangled Mind" (Ted Daffan and Herman Shoss) and "The Last Ride" (Robert Halcomb—Ted Daffan). He continued making best-selling records in the 1960s, together with such albums as *Songs of Jimmie Rodgers, Souvenirs, Everywhere, Railroad Man* and *Favorite Hits.*

Eddy Arnold achieved such renown as a singer of pop songs in the 1960s that one tends to forget that he had earlier been an outstanding exponent of country music and a member of the Grand Ole Opry; that when the County Music Awards were founded in 1967 he was the first chosen as "entertainer of the year." In fact, the designation of "king" which has so liberally been bestowed on country singers was also pinned on him; and that other accolade of the elect of country singers was also his, election to the Country Music Hall of Fame in 1966. Born in Henderson, Tennessee in 1918, Arnold worked as a farmer until the mid-thirties—the reason he chose to call himself "the Tennessee Plowboy" when he became a professional musician. In high school he revealed a gift for singing and playing the guitar. Arnold had to leave school to earn a living, and he worked both on farms and as an assistant in a mortuary. During this period he was often called upon to entertain at public functions and square dances. He made his radio debut in 1936 in Jackson, Tennessee. Within a half dozen years he became a favorite of radio audiences in that state as a major attraction over WTHS, in Jackson. From there he went on to become a singer with Pee Wee King's Golden West Cowboys appearing at the Grand Ole Opry. Beginning in 1948, when he achieved a million-disk sale with his Victor recording of "Bouquet of Roses" (Steve Nelson and Bob Hilliard) he developed into one of the most successful performers of country music in his time. Between 1948 and 1952, many of his recordings were tops on the charts, five of them in 1948 alone. The cream of this crop, together with "Bouquet of Roses," were "Just a Little Lovin" (Zeke Clements and Eddy Arnold), "I'll Hold You in My Heart" (Eddy Arnold, Hal Horton and Tommy Dilbeck), "Then I Turned and Walked Slowly Away" (Arnold "Red" Fortner and Eddy Arnold), "A Heart Full of Love" (Eddy Arnold, Steve Nelson and Ray Soehnel), "My Daddy Is Only a Picture" (Tommy Dilbeck) and "Texarkana Baby" (Cottonseed Clark and Fred Rose). And the country hits continued on into the 1960s to the time when Eddy Arnold changed his artistic course to become a pop singer.

Hank Williams became one of the most dominant figures in hillbilly music after he became a member of the Grand Ole Opry in 1949. He was one of the four musicians elected to the Country Music Hall of Fame when it was instituted in 1961, and in 1974 he was remembered by the Academy of Country and Western Music with a posthumous "Pioneer Award." He was born in Georgiana, Alabama in 1923 and raised on a farm near Montgomery where his mother gave him his first music lessons and introduced him to religious hymns and gospels. When only six, Hank could play the organ so well he was occasionally recruited to perform in church. Two years later he received the gift of a guitar and was given some lessons by a black street singer, his only teacher. Hank Williams soon gained local fame with his guitar playing and in his twelfth year extended his reputation by winning first prize in an amateur contest in a Montgomery theater singing one of his own songs, "W.P.A. Blues." Two years later he formed the Hank Williams and his Drifting Cowboys band which performed at barn dances and other functions. For about a decade beginning in 1937 they were heard over WSFA in Montgomery.

Williams settled in Nashville, Tennessee, in 1946 where his meeting with Fred Rose, the partner in the publishing firm of Acuff-Rose, proved providential. Rose not only signed Williams to an exclusive contract but also arranged to have Williams record for MGM, then a new outfit. (Williams had previously made some records for Sterling, a small company.) His first MGM release in 1947 was a success, his own, "Move It on Over" which he had then recently introduced by KWSH in Shreveport on the Louisiana Hayride program where he had made a number of notable appearances. This record brought Williams an offer to join the Grand Ole Opry in 1949. At his debut there he sang "Lovesick Blues" (Irving Mills and Cliff Friend, revised by Hank Williams), and "stopped the show colder than it had ever been stopped before or since. . . ." "Lovesick Blues," released by MGM in 1949, became Williams first million-disk seller.

During the three years Williams appeared with the Grand Ole Opry he was at the peak of both his success and his creativity. He had four records in 1950 that sold a million disks or more each, all of them his own compositions: "Long Gone Lonesome Blues," "I Just Don't Like This Kind of Livin'," "Why Don't You Love Me?" and "Moanin' the Blues." There were several more million disk-sellers, or records that sold in the hundreds of thousands, after that: "Hey, Good Lookin'," "Baby, We're Really in Love," "Ramblin' Man," "Howlin' at the Moon" and "Cold, Cold Heart," all in 1951 and all by Williams; "Jambalaya," "Your Cheatin' Heart," "Honky Tonk Blues" and "I'll Never Get Out of This World Alive" in 1952, once again all by Williams, though "I'll Never Get Out of this World Alive" was written in collaboration with Fred Rose. Some of these entered the pop lists. Tony Bennett realized a million-disk sale with his version of "Cold, Cold Heart" and Jo Stafford's recording of "Jambalaya" was a best-seller as was Joni James' release of "Your Cheatin' Heart." Hank Williams achieved best-sellers with recordings of songs by other composers: "Crazy Heart" (Fred Rose and Maurice Murray), "Half as Much" (Curley Williams), "Dear John" (Aubrey A. Gass and Tex Ritter) and "Settin' the Woods on Fire" (Fred Rose and Edward G. Nelson).

He could handle success and prosperity no better than he could liquor, women and drugs. All these proved his undoing, together with marital discord, a chronic bad heart, and a bad back from two slipped discs. He became so intemperate in his habits and ways that he was fired from the Grand Ole Opry in September 1952. A second marriage, to Billie Jean Jones, which took place on the stage of the New Orleans Auditorium as part of his show, failed to rehabilitate him. En route to a performance in Canton, Ohio, he died in the back of his Cadillac on January 1, 1953, before his thirtieth birthday; many believe his death was due to an overdose of drugs. In the Canton theater where he was scheduled to appear, the limelight was focused on an empty stage as Hank Williams' voice was heard in his recording of his song, "I Saw the Light." Weeping turned into hysteria at his funeral service at the Municipal Auditorium in Montgomery attended by twenty thousand of his admirers. The "greatest emotional orgy in the city's history since the inauguration of Jefferson Davis" reported Eli Waldron on *The Reporter*.

Though he was dead, his records kept coming, and kept selling: "Kaw-Liga," "I Won't Be Home No More," "Weary Blues from Waitin'," all three by Williams, but "Kaw-Liga" written with Fred Rose, together with "Take These Chains from My Heart" (Fred Rose and Hy Heath). Several dozen of his albums were released in the 1960s in which were collected the one hundred and more songs for which Hank Williams was remembered.

Hank Williams' son—Hank Williams, Jr.—recorded an album of his father's songs never before published or recorded—*Songs My Father Taught Me*, and realized a giant best-seller with his recording of his father's "Long Gone Lonesome Blues." In 1964, the junior Hank Williams was heard singing his father's celebrated songs on the sound track of the motion picture biography of Hank Williams, *Your Cheatin' Heart*, in which George Hamilton appeared as the country singing composer. In 1970, the Hank Williams, Jr. recording of his father's "Cajun Baby" received an award from BMI as one of the most frequently heard country and western compositions within a five-year span, and won a Grammy in a recording by the Nashville Brass. And in 1972 some of the more successful recordings by the original Hank Williams was used on the sound track of *The Last Picture Show* to evoke the feeling and spirit of the 1950s in a small decaying Western town. New Hank Williams albums kept coming in the 1970s and kept making the best-seller lists. *Hank Williams Sr.'s Twenty-four Greatest Hits* sold 150,000 copies between February and December of 1976.

If Jimmie Rodgers and Hank Williams have become legends in country music, Johnny Cash (another alumnus of the Grand Ole Opry) seems likely to become one. There was a time in Cash's career when it appeared he was prone to the same self-destructiveness that ruined the lives of Jimmie Rodgers and Hank Williams when they were in their prime. Fortunately, both for Cash and for popular music, he was able to rise above and conquer his weaknesses and not allow them to destroy his formidable gifts both as a performer and a composer.

Cash, born in Kingsland, Arkansas in 1932, sprang from the same soil of poverty and struggle in which the early lives of Jimmie Rodgers and Hank Williams were rooted. He was the fourth of seven children. In his boyhood, Johnny worked long and hard on the tract of land the government had provided his family. When not thus occupied, he would go in search of rabbits so that the family might have food. A flood brought devastation to the Cash home and land, from which they recovered only after months of harrowing labor. And tragedy was compounded upon poverty with the sudden death of two of Johnny's brothers.

Music provided an avenue of escape from the travail of everyday life. The family joined in singing hymns, accompanied on the piano by the mother. There was also much music making at the home of the maternal grandfather, whose household boasted a guitar, organ and bass viol. Johnny's ears drank in the music he continually heard at home. As he grew up he became infected with the country music he heard over the radio, particularly the singing of Hank Williams. By the time he was twelve, Cash was beginning to write songs, and when he attended high school he made his first appearance over the radio in Blytheville, Arkansas. After graduating from high school, he won the first prize of five dollars in an amateur singing contest, and also began to take singing lessons.

While pursuing these musical activities, Cash was working at sundry menial occupations, such as that of water boy for river gangs and as a factory hand in Detroit. In July 1950, aged eighteen, he enlisted in the Air Force. Trained as a radio operator, he was shipped to Germany. There he purchased a five-dollar guitar, learned to play it, and accompanied himself in appearances in German clubs. He was also writing a good deal of poetry. He left the service in 1954, married Vivian Liberto, a San Antonio girl he first met while in the Air Force and made his home in Memphis, Tennessee, earning his living as a door-to-door salesman of electrical appliances. His ambition was to become a disc jockey, but failing to progress in that direction he decided to develop himself as a singer. An audition for Sun Records was a failure, mainly because he performed hymns. Sam Phillips, the director of Sun Records, advised him to come back when he had better material.

One day, two of his friends came upon some of the poems Cash had written while in the Air Force. They suggested that one of them, "Hey Porter," be set to music. Since these friends were amateur musicians, they also proposed forming a combo. They named it "Johnny Cash and the Tennessee Two" and appeared at various social functions in and around Memphis. They also auditioned for Sam Phillips. One of their numbers, "Hey, Porter," so impressed Phillips that he was ready to have it recorded if Cash would write a new number for the flip side. Cash obliged with "Cry, Cry, Cry." The Sun recording, released in 1955, entered the charts within six weeks, selling about one hundred thousand disks in that time.

Sam Phillips now signed Cash to an exclusive recording contract. Among his new releases in 1956 were "Folsom Prison Blues" and "I Walk the Line," both of which became gold records, the first of many. Cash had written "Folsom Prison Blues" in two hours aboard a plane under the stimulation of having seen the motion picture *Inside the Walls of Folsom Prison*, which had stirred him with a passion for prison reform. Other personal experiences inspired other songs. In "I Walk the Line" Cash remembered his unhappy days as a door-to-door salesman. (In 1970, "I Walk the Line" was used as the title of a motion picture starring Gregory Peck. Cash sang the number on the sound track.) In addition to his gold records, Cash had three more best sellers in 1956, all of them his own compositions, "So Doggone Lonesome," "Train of Love" and "There You Go."

Between 1956 and 1959 each one of Cash's recordings was listed in the "top ten" charts in country and western music. He was the only country composer-performer to accomplish this; over six million of his records were sold in that time. These releases included "Next in Line," "Big River," "Five Feet High and Rising," "Luther Played the Boogie," "The Man on the Hill," all by Cash, and "You're the Nearest Thing to Heaven" which Cash wrote with Hoydt Johnson and Jim Atkins.

In 1959, Cash left Sun Records for Columbia, his first three albums under that label, *Fabulous Johnny Cash*, *Ride This Train* and *The Sound of Johnny Cash* all smash successes. His first Columbia single, "Don't Take Your Guns to Town" stayed on the charts in the number one spot for weeks. This was followed by an extended chain of best-selling records during the rest of the decade, some of whose links were: "In the Jailhouse Now" (Jimmie Rodgers), "Ring of Fire" (Merle Kilgore and June Carter), "It Ain't Me Babe" (Bob Dylan), "Ballad of Ira Hayes" (Peter La Farge) and "A Boy Named Sue" (Shel Silverstein). Cash's recording of "A Boy Named Sue" was chosen as the best single of the year in the Country Music Association Awards in 1969.

By the 1960s, Cash had become a national figure. In addition to his best-selling records he was making appearances with the Grand Ole Opry, giving concerts in the United States and abroad (one at Carnegie Hall in 1961), appearing on guest spots on network TV programs and filling roles in motion pictures. His personal fortune was increased by holdings in real estate and the ownership of two publishing houses. He acquired a mansion on the outskirts of Memphis, drove a large and flashy car, and hired a staff to supervise his business interests and to provide comfort to his home life.

Then he seemed headed for a descent from the heights of success as precipitous as his ascent. As relief from the punishing schedules that were sapping his energies—and domestic squabbles that were tormenting him—he began indulging in tranquilizers and Dexedrine. Driving one night in 1965 from Mexico he was seized at the border and imprisoned for a night in El Paso on the charge of smuggling Dexedrine tablets. That brief stay in jail was not without unexpected dividends since it nourished his long-felt sympathy for prisoners and his horror of prison conditions. In 1968, he issued an album, *Johnny Cash at Folsom Prison*, a recording of a concert he had given there for the inmates. A million of those LPs were sold.

In addition it was awarded a Grammy as the best male vocal performances of the year and the Country Music Association Award as the year's best album. A second prison album, *Johnny Cash at San Quentin*, also won the Country Music Association Award.

That night in a jail cell did something else for Cash. It compelled him to take stock of himself both as a man and as an artist. He would no longer rely on drugs as an escape from emotional tensions and physical fatigue. In 1968 he divorced his wife and married June Carter, a member of the famous singing Carter family. Besides finding love, Cash also discovered the solace of religion, "the coming back to Jesus," as he explained. This spiritual reawakening led him in 1973 to finance and produce a documentary film on the life of Christ, *Gospel Road*, which was filmed in Israel, and in which Cash not only served as narrator but also as a performer of several songs.

In the fall and winter of 1968 Cash broke box-office records with appearances at Carnegie Hall and Madison Square Garden in New York. In 1969 he received the Country Music Association Award as "entertainer of the year." Also in 1969, a ninety-minute television documentary, *Cash!*, was presented over the NET network (and, in a somewhat short-ened version, in movie houses), following which he became the star of his own television program over the ABC network. He appeared in other motion pictures and made many best-selling records. One of his albums was recorded live at the Grand Ole Opry, *Johnny Cash: The Johnny Cash Show*, released in 1970. In 1971, he received another Grammy for his recorded performance with his wife, June, of "If I Were a Carpenter." He was riding high, wide and handsome—his annual income now exceeded two million dollars.

In his appearances on the stage and over television, Johnny Cash opens his program with a forthright self-introduction, "Hello—I'm Johnny Cash." He wears a personalized costume comprised of an outmoded but stylish frock coat, striped trousers, a vest, and a white ruffled shirt giving him the appearance, as Albert Govoni wrote of "a riverboat gambler, a raffish parson, a card shark out of the Old West . . . a New Orleans rakehell on his way to a duel over a woman."

2

The Grand Ole Opry, the founding in 1943 of the Acuff-Rose Company by Roy Acuff and Fred Rose as the first country music publishing house, the arrival of engineers from New York to record local music and musicians, the building of the first local recording studio by Owen Bradley in a quonset hut—these were the first of many steps in the making of Nashville into the capital of country and western music.

In that growth and development, Chet Atkins played an all-important role in the fifties. His importance in Nashville music rests not only on his own music making—those remarkable performances on the guitar—but also upon his accomplishments as a recording producer and executive. As such he was the discoverer of many country musicians such as Charley Pride, Don Gibson and Floyd Cramer, the mainstay of many an established country music star, and the one who is said to have been responsible for the development of "the Nashville sound." "The Nashville Sound," Paul Hemphill explains in a book of that name, "is the loose, relaxed, improvised feeling found in almost anything recorded out of Nashville today, and if any one man could be credited with creating it, the man would be Chet Atkins. . . . It has made Atkins the most respected musician on Music Row today. . . . He is directly responsible for bringing together the right artist and the right song and then seeing that the best possible recording is made." Atkins himself, however, is skeptical that the "Nashville Sound" exists, referring to it merely as a "sales tag." "The studios in Nashville are like the studios anywhere else," he told an interviewer. "If there is a Nashville Sound, it's the musicians. They're mostly from the South and middle west. They have a relaxed quality and they're used to working together. But the sound of country music has become much more refined in recent years. It's a lot more professional . . . because great musicians are coming into Nashville from all over the world."

Atkins was not new either to Nashville or to country music when he became a record producer; he had already long been celebrated at the Grand Ole Opry and on records as one of the finest country guitarists around. On a dirt farm near Luttrell, Tennessee, in 1924, he became fascinated by the guitar when he was only six. He recalls: "My mother and I went to Knoxville and saw a blind man playing guitar on the street for handouts. He was happy, all alone, and just 'digging' time and I loved him. . . . The most important thing in the world, it seemed to me, then, was to be able to play guitar for a living. . . ." The decision to become a guitarist was formed when he was fourteen, Atkins recalls, after hearing Merle Travis play the guitar over WLW in Cincinnati. Country music became a passion with Atkins after he heard some Jimmie Rodgers records and broadcasts of the Grand Ole Opry.

In 1935 he went to live in Columbus, Georgia, where he found a job playing hillbilly music on Parson Jack's program over WRBL. During the early part of World War II he made his way to Knoxville, Tennessee. There he was hired to play the fiddle on the "Jumpin" Bill Carlisle—Archie Campbell radio show over WNOX. It was not long before his talent at the guitar was recognized and he was hired as guitarist on the radio's staff band. For several years he appeared over the radio in various Southern cities both as a solo guitarist and as a member of a group. Some national attention came his way when he played with the Trailblazers on a coast-to-coast radio program emanating from WLW, Cincinnati. Steve Sholes, head of hillbilly music at Victor, became impressed both with Atkins' guitar playing and his transcriptions and offered him a recording contract in 1947 that remained in effect for over a quarter of a century. His first few recordings did poorly, but in 1949 he had a hit with "The Galloping Guitars," and followed this with successful recordings of "Country Gentleman" and "Main St. Breakdown," all his own compositions. He became a featured artist with the Grand Ole Opry where he had made his first appearance in 1946 and where he remained for the next eight years.

In 1949, Atkins was employed as studio guitarist for Victor in Nashville. Two years later he recorded for that company two successful LPs: *Atkins Plays Guitar* and *Chet Atkins in Three Dimensions*. That year he also published the hit number, "Midnight," which he wrote in collaboration with Boudleaux Bryant, and which, in Red Foley's Decca recording, became a giant seller in 1952 and 1953.

When RCA Victor built its own recording studios in Nashville in 1955, Atkins served as assistant to Sholes and as recording engineer. In 1957 he was promoted to part-time producer, after that to managing director of country music at Victor in succession to Sholes and, in 1968, division vice president of country music. The first active performer to assume an executive post at Victor, he personally supervised the recording activity of over forty artists. At the same time he was making numerous appearances as guitarist (including a performance at the White House in 1961 for President and Mrs. John F. Kennedy). For thirteen years running he was named outstanding instrumentalist by Cash Box and, in 1973, he entered the Country Music Association Hall of Fame. His autobiography, *Country Gentleman*, written with Bill Neely, was published in 1974. In 1976, he was awarded a Grammy in the best country instrumental performance category for the album *Atkins–Travis Traveling Show*.

Among Atkins' discoveries in Nashville was the country performer and composer, John D. Loudermilk, whose then budding career was given a significant boost through

Atkins' interest and influence. Born in Durham, North Carolina, in 1934, to an impoverished household, Loudermilk began earning his living while he was still attending elementary school. Through his boyhood and early manhood he was employed as shoeshine boy, carpenter's assistant, steam shovel oiler, telegraph messenger, department store clerk, tobacco farmer, factory laborer, janitor, lifeguard, cotton gin worker, door-to-door salesman, sign painter, window dresser, commercial artist, photographer. Many of these experiences provided him with rich materials for his later songs. Music, however, was not lost in this shuffle to make a living. As a boy he sang in the church choir, listened to the radio broadcasts of the Grand Ole Opry and to the live sound of country music at Saturday night barn dances.

He made his professional debut when he was eleven by appearing on a radio program over a local station; one year later he was a performer on a program telecast from Durham on which Tex Ritter was the master of ceremonies. Having by this time learned to play several instruments, including the guitar, he had ample opportunities performing at square dances and touring with a jazz group.

After graduating from high school, he found a job with a television station in Durham painting sets, performing in a jazz combo, and playing the guitar. One day he presented one of his songs, "A Rose and Baby Ruth." George Hamilton IV, then still a student at the University of North Carolina heard that telecast, liked it, and recorded it in 1956 for ABC-Paramount. The record sold several million disks, made George Hamilton IV into a singing star, and paved the way for Loudermilk's career as a songwriter. Several more of Loudermilk's songs were recorded after that, including "Sittin' in the Balcony," successfully performed in 1957 by Johnny Dee for Colonial and by Eddie Cochran for Liberty.

These successes encouraged Loudermilk to go to Nashville. He met Chet Atkins who became his powerful ally in further developing himself professionally. Cedarwood Publishing Company in Nashville signed Loudermilk and issued his first Nashville songs: "Tobacco Road," in which he recalled his bleak early years and which, some years later, became a best-selling recording in England; "Amigo's Guitar" (written with Kitty Wells and Roy Bodkin), recorded by Kitty Wells for Decca; and "Grin and Bear It" (written with Marijohn Wilkin) recorded by Jimmy Newman for MGM.

In 1961, Loudermilk was taken over by the Acuff-Rose Company which published over five hundred of his songs, fourteen of which became gold records. "Hollywood" and "Dreamboat" were recorded by Connie Francis for MGM; "Ebony Eyes," by The Everly Brothers for Warner; "Bad News" by Johnny Cash for Columbia; "I Can't Hang Up the Phone" by Stonewall Jackson for Columbia; "Paper Tiger," by Sue Thompson for Hickory; "Break My Mind" by George Hamilton IV for Victor; "What a Woman in Love Won't Do" by Sandy Posey for MGM; "I Wanna Live," by Glen Campbell for Capitol.

Fred Rose, Roy Acuff's partner in the founding and running of the publishing house of Acuff-Rose, was also influential in helping to bring to full flower the budding careers of composers. Himself a prolific songwriter, Fred Rose's sympathy for and understanding of composers was second nature. After working as a café pianist in Chicago, and then in nightclubs, and as one of the "Whiteman Twin Pianists" employed by Paul Whiteman and his orchestra, Rose was the star of his own radio show on the CBS network and at WSM in Nashville, Tennessee. Having begun writing songs when he was seventeen, Rose had several hits to his credit during the twenties, including "Honest and Truly" in 1924 and "Deed I Do" two years later. "Deed I Do," written in collaboration with Walter Hirsch, was popularized by Ben Bernie and his orchestra. "Be Honest With Me" and "Tweedle-O-Twill," both written with Gene Autry, were introduced in motion pictures by Autry, the first in *Ridin' on a Rainbow* (1941) where it was nominated for an Academy Award, and the other in *Home in*

Wyoming (1942). Even after helping to launch Acuff-Rose in 1943, Rose continued writing songs. "Blues in My Mind" was recorded by Roy Acuff for Okeh; "Roly Poly" by Bob Wills and his Texas Playboys for Columbia; and "Texarkana Baby," written with Cottonseed Clark, by Eddy Arnold for Victor. In the mid-1940s, Fred Rose turned over many of his publishing chores to his son, Wesley, to allow more time for writing songs. After Fred Rose's death in 1954, he was elected to the Country Music Association's Hall of Fame and in 1976 to the Nashville Songwriters Hall of Fame.

He earned his place in the Hall of Fame not only as a songwriter and publisher but as one who nurtured the creativity of others—particularly Marty Robbins and Boudleaux Bryant.

Marty Robbins had no musical interests in his early years in Glendale, Arizona, where he was born in 1925, or in Phoenix where he was raised. While serving for four years in the Navy during and immediately after World War II, he taught himself to play the guitar so that he could accompany himself singing, including numbers of his own composition. After being released from service, he appeared in small nightclubs in Phoenix singing country and western songs. He then gained a large following through his twice daily appearances on the radio and once a week in the TV series, "Western Caravan." In 1953 he joined the Grand Ole Opry. It was then that Fred Rose became interested in him and gave him a publishing contract. Two of Robbins' earliest publications were "I Couldn't Keep from Crying" and "I'll Go On Alone" in 1953, both of them doing well in recordings by Marty Robbins himself for Columbia and Webb Pierce for Decca. "You Don't Owe Me a Thing" was a best seller in 1956 in Johnnie Ray's Columbia release, and "Please Don't Blame Me" in Robbins' Columbia recording. "A White Sport Coat," recorded in 1957, made Robbins a hero of the teenage set, achieving the top spot in American polls and on the charts. This was Robbins' first gold record, a second coming to him two years later with "El Paso." Hardly a year has gone by since 1959 without at least one of Marty Robbins' songs on the best-selling charts, and usually in a Robbins performance. The best were "Don't Worry," "Big Iron," "It's Your World," "Devil Woman," "Not So Long Ago," "Cowboy in the Continental Suit," "Begging to You," "Tonight Carmen," "Love Is in the Air," "You Gave Me a Mountain," "Camelia" and "My Woman, My Wife." The last of these received a Grammy in 1971 as the year's best country song.

Boudleaux Bryant, born in Shellman, Georgia in 1920, studied the violin for thirteen years in Moultrie, Georgia, where he was raised. After that he played in several symphony orchestras. In 1939 he was engaged to play in a radio orchestra specializing in country music, his first important experience in the popular field. For the next decade he appeared with jazz combos, and with hotel and radio orchestras. In 1945, he married Felice Scaduto, whom he met at the Schroeder Hotel in Milwaukee where she was employed as an elevator operator. A musician herself, having been trained as a singer, Felice encouraged her husband to follow more seriously his hobby of songwriting; she often gave him a valuable helping hand in the writing of the words and the music. During a long period of apprenticeship they encountered failure and frustration in marketing their songs. Then their "Country Boy," recorded by Little Jimmy Dickens for Columbia in 1948, sold over 350,000 disks. At this point Fred Rose became interested in them and became their publisher and the motor behind their drive to success. More and more of their songs were now being recorded by distinguished performers—Carl Smith, Tony Bennett, Billy Eckstine, Eddy Arnold. These numbers included "It's a Lovely, Lovely World," "Have a Good Time," "I've Been Thinking," "Just Wait Till I Get You Alone," "Hey Joe" and "Back Up Buddy." On the strength of these successes, Acuff-Rose signed the Bryants to a ten-year contract as staff writers. Many of their songs under this new arrangement—some by Bryant himself, but most written in collaboration with his wife—were made famous by The Everly Brothers on Cadence Records. Between 1957 and 1960 the best of these Everly Brothers recordings were: "Bye Bye Love," "Wake Up Little Susie," "Bird Dog," "All I Have to Do Is Dream," "Devoted to You," "Problems," "Poor Jenny" and "Take a Message to Mary." "Bye Bye Love," "All I Have to Do Is Dream," "Wake Up Little Susie" and "Bird Dog" were gold records.

After Wesley Rose took over the publishing duties at Acuff-Rose from his father he, too, shepherded many a composer to success. Roy Orbison, born in Wink, Texas in 1936, was one of these. As a boy Orbison led the Wink Westerners over radio station KVWC in Vernon, Texas, while working the oil rigs. At sixteen, Orbison represented Kansas at the International Lions Convention in Chicago as singer and guitarist. While attending North Texas State University he was asked by Sam Phillips of Sun Records to record one of his own songs, "Ooby, Dooby" in 1956. It sold well. When another Orbison song—"Claudette," written as a tribute to the composer's wife—prospered in The Everly Brothers recording for Cadence, Wesley Rose signed him to a publishing contract and looked after his interests. Rose arranged for Orbison to record his own songs for Monument, some of which were immediate winners: "Only the Lonely," "Blue Angel," "Running Scared," "Crying" and "The Crowd," all these written with Joe Melson. In 1962, Orbison boasted so many successful songs as a recording performer-composer that Monument that year released the album *Roy Orbison's Greatest Hits*. Orbison's "Oh Pretty Woman" earned him a gold record. As a performer of other people's songs, Orbison was responsible for other best-selling records, representative of which were "Dream Baby, How Long Must I Dream?" (Cindy Walker), "Candy Man," (Fred Neil and Beverly Ross) and "Mean Woman Blues" (Jerry West and Whispering Smith). Orbison made his motion picture debut in *Fastest Guitar Alive* (1970), and his song "So Young" was used on the sound track of another motion picture, *Zabriskie Point* (1970).

37

The Hollywood Scene in the Fifties

1

The unprecedented box-office returns from *The Jolson Story* (1946) and *Jolson Sings Again* (1949) convinced the moguls of Hollywood of the marketability of movies based on lives of famous popular musicians. Such screen biographies proliferated in the Fifties.

Three Little Words (1950) starred Fred Astaire and Red Skelton as Harry Ruby and Bert Kalmar, the songwriting pair who had written the title song in 1930 as well as many other standards. The cream of these provided the score with all of its song material. Vera-Ellen and Debbie Reynolds were featured, but Anita Ellis dubbed the singing for Vera-Ellen on the sound track, as did Helen Kane for Debbie Reynolds in "I Wanna Be Loved By You."

Another songwriter—this time the lyricist, Gus Kahn—was the hero of *I'll See You in My Dreams* (1951), with Danny Thomas as Kahn playing opposite Doris Day. The many eminent composers who had set Kahn's words to music were liberally represented by their evergreen hits: including Isham Jones, Walter Donaldson, and Egbert Van Alstyne.

I Dream of Jeanie (1952) was one more futile effort by Hollywood to bring to celluloid the life and music of Stephen Foster, with Ray Middleton playing the composer, while the career and the marches of John Philip Sousa were glorified in *Stars and Stripes Forever* (1952) with Clifton Webb as Sousa.

With a Song in My Heart (1952) starred Susan Hayward as Jane Froman, the beloved singing star of radio, nightclubs and recordings who was seriously injured in a plane crash during World War II while en route to Europe with a USO troupe. Her heroic struggle to regain the use of her legs, as well as the momentum of her interrupted career, provided the dramatic interest in a life story richly embellished with the songs with which she achieved fame and which she herself sang for Miss Hayward on the sound track: the title song (Lorenz Hart—Richard Rodgers), "Embraceable You" (Ira Gershwin—George Gershwin), "Blue Moon" (Lorenz Hart—Richard Rodgers), "That Old Feeling" (Lew Brown—Sammy Fain), and a dozen others.

Somebody Loves Me (1952) was the life story of the popular vaudeville team of Benny Fields and Blossom Seeley, the title coming from the George and Ira Gershwin song which had been Miss Seeley's speciality. Among the other standards heard in this score with which either Miss Seeley or Benny Fields made their mark in vaudeville were: "I Cried for You" (Arthur Freed—Gus Arnheim and Abe Lyman), "I'm Sorry I Made You Cry" (N. J. Clesi), "Smiles" (J. Will Callahan—Lee S. Roberts), "Way Down Yonder in New Orleans" (Henry Creamer—J. Turner Layton).

The Eddie Cantor Story (1953) was an attempt to come up with another *Jolson Story*, but with far less happy results. Its main interest lay not so much in Cantor's story but in the way Keefe Braselle looked and cavorted about the stage like Cantor, and in the way Cantor himself recaptured some of his old singing magic on the sound track with his song favorites —fifteen of them, no less.

The heroine of *The I Don't Care Girl* (1953) was, of course, the irrepressible Eva Tanguay, played by Mitzi Gaynor, who, in addition to the title song, was heard in "Hello, Frisco" (Gene Buck—Louis A. Hirsch), "Pretty Baby" (Gus Kahn—Tony Jackson and Egbert Van Alstyne) and "On the Mississippi" (Ballard Mac Donald—Harry Carroll).

Deep in My Heart (1954) was the biography of Sigmund Romberg with José Ferrer cast as the composer. All of Romberg's songs from his operettas worth remembering—and some it is easy to forget—were scrambled together in a score made up of fifteen numbers, including as a curiosity one of his earliest published pieces, "Leg of Mutton."

Bob Hope was Eddie Foy in *The Seven Little Foys* (1955), the Seven Little Foys having been a headlining act in vaudeville for many years. *The Best Things in Life Are Free* (1956) traced, in story and song, the careers of that ace songwriting trio of the Broadway musical theater of the 1920s and early 1930s, De Sylva, Brown and Henderson. Gordon MacRae was De Sylva; Dan Dailey, Ray Henderson; Ernest Borgnine, Lew Brown. The sound track was a generous outpouring of eighteen De Sylva, Brown and Henderson numbers.

In *The Helen Morgan Story* (1957) Ann Blyth was seen as the fabled star of Broadway musicals and nightclubs of the 1920s, with many of the songs Miss Morgan made her personal property sung on the sound track for Miss Blyth by Gogi Grant.

2

With Anita Ellis singing for Vera-Ellen in *Three Little Words*, Jane Froman for Susan Hayward in *With a Song in My Heart*, Eddie Cantor for Keefe Braselle in *The Eddie Cantor Story*, Eileen Wilson for Sheree North in *The Best Things in Life Are Free*, and Gogi Grant for Ann Blyth in *The Helen Morgan Story*, the process of dubbing in a beautiful singing voice for that of an attractive but nonsinging actress became virtually an everyday practice in Hollywood.

Marni Nixon, an outstanding young musician as much at ease in singing the music of the classic masters and the avant-gardists of today as in pop tunes, was a singer used most successfully—and anonymously—for dubbing. Her career as a dubbing artist started in 1949 when she was called upon to sing for Margaret O'Brien in *The Secret Garden*. She was recruited for the sound track of *The King and I* in 1956 to sing for Deborah Kerr. In the 1960s she still functioned in this capacity by singing on the sound track for Rita Moreno in *West Side Story* (1961), for Natalie Wood in *Gypsy* (1962) and for Audrey Hepburn in *My Fair Lady* (1964).

Bill Lee was another singer kept busy making sound tracks for the stars, beginning as far back as 1948 when he sang for Ricardo Montalban in *On an Island With You*. After that he sang for John Kerr in *South Pacific* (1958), for Cary Grant in *Father Goose* (1964), and for Christopher Plummer in *The Sound of Music* (1965).

Similarly, Marie Green sang for Susan Luckey in *Carousel* (1956) and for Pamela Tiffin in the 1962 remake of *State Fair*. Trudi Erwin and Jo Ann Greer were the vocal alter egos of Kim Novak and Rita Hayworth in *Pal Joey* (1957). Carole Richard vocalized for Vera-Ellen in *Call Me Madam* (1953) and for Cyd Charisse in *Brigadoon* (1954) and *Silk Stockings* (1957). On the sound track of *Carmen Jones* (1954) Marilyn Horne, before her triumphs in concert and opera, dubbed for Dorothy Dandridge, and La Vern Hutcheson for Harry Belafonte. Giorgio Tozzi sang for Rossano Brazzi in *South Pacific* where Muriel Smith was heard for Juanita Hall. Lisa Kirk was the sound track singer for Rosalind Russell in *Gypsy*. In Samuel Goldwyn's lavish production of Gershwin's *Porgy and Bess* (1959) Robert McFerrin sang for Sidney Poitier, Adele Addison for Dorothy Dandridge, and Inez Matthews for Ruth Attaway. And in the 1960s, Bill Shirley performed on the sound track for Jeremy Britt, and Jim Bryant for Richard Beymer in *West Side Story*, Gene Merlino for Franco Nero in *Camelot* (1967) and Anita Gordon for Jean Seberg in *Paint Your Wagon* (1969). In most of these musicals, the Hollywood studios did their best to conceal the fact that the featured stars on the screen were not doing their own singing, and for a long time they succeeded. But when the film sound tracks were transferred to records it was impossible to pass off the stars as the singers for that would have been fraud. Subterfuge provided a solution. The Capitol sound track of *Pal Joey*, for example, listed the three major stars of the film without mentioning that two of their singing voices were dubbed. On the label itself the characters performing the songs are identified, but not the singers.

But such devices could not be permanently concealed from the public—not in Hollywood which thrives on leaking well-kept secrets. With the practice of dubbing, and the identity of its practitioners, becoming more and more common knowledge, the studios, in time, gave up the game and stood ready to concede where dubbing was being utilized and to identify those who were performing this essential service.

3

Theme songs and title songs from major nonmusical productions added bountifully to the storehouse of song hits of the 1950s. One of these nonmusical pictures used its principal song as such an important element in the working out of the story that it became largely responsible for the artistic and commercial success of that film, and added a footnote to the history of motion picture music. That picture was *High Noon* (1952), starring Gary Cooper and Grace Kelly. The theme song (Ned Washington—Dimitri Tiomkin) was not on the sound track when the film was first released. At its first run-through, *High Noon* was looked upon as a failure. Dimitri Tiomkin insisted that all that the picture needed was an effective theme song to hint at the plot at the beginning of the film and to help reinforce the emotion and action throughout the course of the story. With the interpolation of Tiomkin's theme song, sung on the soundtrack by Tex Ritter, *High Noon* was previewed and was still found wanting. Convinced that the song had little commercial value, the producers turned over to Tiomkin all publication and recording rights. This proved to be a miscalculation. Frankie Laine's Columbia recording was such a smash success that it helped to change the destiny not only of the song but of the motion picture. Released four months before the motion picture this recording generated considerable curiosity and interest for the picture for which it had been created, with the result that *High Noon* became good box office as well as a classic among Westerns. There was no question in the minds of anyone connected with the production that it was the theme song (sometimes also called "Do Not Forsake Me") that helped to bring this about. "High Noon" won the Academy Award in the song category.

Tiomkin wrote four more important motion picture title or theme songs between 1954 and 1960. Each was a nominee for the Academy Award and each became a hit record. In 1954 there was "The High and the Mighty" (Ned Washington), from the motion picture of the same name starring John Wayne. This number is often referred to as "the whistling song" because the main character whistles the melody throughout the film. "Thee I Love" (Paul Francis Webster) in 1956 was written for *Friendly Persuasion*, with Gary Cooper. Since the producers first intended calling this motion picture *Thee I Love*, Tiomkin's song used the same title. But after the new and final title *Friendly Persuasion* was chosen for the film, "Thee I Love," already written, retained its original title, though it was often identified afterward as "Friendly Persuasion." Pat Boone, then still an unknown quantity as a performer, sang this number on the sound track. Tiomkin had heard him on the Arthur Godfrey television show and felt that his was the ideal voice for the music. Boone was paid only three thousand dollars for this assignment, but his financial rewards were greatly multiplied through the sale of his recording for Dot which disposed of over a million and a half disks. "Wild Is the Wind" (Ned Washington) in 1957 was written for the motion picture of the same name and became a song success in Johnny Mathis' Columbia recording. "The Green Leaves of Summer" (Paul Francis Webster) was heard in *The Alamo* (1960) starring John Wayne, with the Columbia recording by The Brothers Four becoming a best-seller.

Throughout the fifties, instrumental theme music also served motion pictures well and became best-selling records. (In some instances, following their success in films, these instrumental pieces acquired lyrics and became songs.) Highly popular were the instrumental themes from *East of Eden* (Leonard Rosenman) in 1955, *Rebel Without a Cause* (Leonard Rosenman) in 1955, *Picnic* (George Duning) in 1956, to which Steve Allen added lyrics, *The Proud Ones* (Johnny Desmond—Ruth Keddington) in 1956, *Baby Doll* (Kenyon Hopkins) in 1956 and *A Summer Place* (Max Steiner) in 1959. Morris Stoloff's Decca recording of *Theme from Picnic* sold over a million disks, as did Percy Faith's performance of *Theme from A Summer Place* for Columbia.

Many distinguished title songs received considerable acclaim in their own right apart from the motion picture for which they were written and in which they were prominently exploited. Among the most notable were: "The Song from *Moulin Rouge*" or "Where Is Your Heart?" (William Engvick—Georges Auric) from *Moulin Rouge* (1953), the screen biography of Toulouse-Lautrec; "Song from Désirée", also known as "We Meet Again" (Ken Darby—Lionel Newman) played under the opening titles of *Désirée* (1954); "Unchained Melody" (Hy Zaret—Alex North), from the prison motion picture *Unchained* (1955), a nominee for an Academy Award, and its success enhanced through best-selling records by Les Baxter and his orchestra for Capitol and Al Hibbler for Decca; "Love Is a Many-Splendored Thing" (Paul Francis Webster—Sammy Fain), which recurred throughout the motion picture of that title (1955) starring William Holden; it received the Academy Award, and was released in the best-selling disk by The Four Aces for Decca. "The Tender Trap" (Sammy Cahn—James Van Heusen), an Academy Award nominee introduced by Frank Sinatra in the motion picture of that name (1955) and successfully recorded by him for Capitol; "The Song of *Raintree County*" (Paul Francis Webster—John Green), sung by Nat

King Cole on the sound track behind the opening titles of *Raintree County* (1957); "April Love" (Paul Francis Webster—Sammy Fain), a nominee for the Academy Award introduced by Pat Boone in the motion picture of that name (1957); "Tammy" (Jay Livingston—Ray Evans), an Academy Award nominee in *Tammy and the Bachelor* (1957) introduced by Debbie Reynolds whose Coral recording was a gold record; "Song from *Some Came Running*," also called "To Love and Be Loved" (Sammy Cahn—James Van Heusen), an Academy Award nominee sung by Frank Sinatra in *Some Came Running* (1958); and "Gigi" (Alan Jay Lerner—Frederick Loewe) in which Louis Jourdan as Gaston discovers he is in love with the heroine of *Gigi* (1958). In the last of these, the song and the motion picture were both recipients of Academy Awards.

The history of "Three Coins in the Fountain" (Sammy Cahn—Jule Styne)—the Academy Award-winning theme song from the motion picture of the same name (1954)—deserves telling if only to point up once again some of the strange ways in which Hollywood operated where music was concerned. Sol C. Siegel, producer at 20th Century-Fox, asked Sammy Cahn and Jule Styne (then contract songwriters for that studio) to write a song to be named "Three Coins in the Fountain." A picture was in the works called *Believe in Love* and Siegel felt a far better title for it would be *Three Coins in the Fountain*. The only way Siegel could convince the money men in New York to consider the title change was to provide them with a knockout song with the new name. Since no script was available, all Siegel could tell the songwriters about the picture was that it concerned three American girls in Italy who threw coins into a fountain. With nothing more to go by, Cahn and Styne finished their song in two hours. When Siegel proposed that a demonstration record be made and sent to New York, Cahn suggested that Frank Sinatra sing it, since he was then working on the lot. The song, and Sinatra's performance, won the day for Siegel. The film title was changed and the song became its title number and its recurring melody. Besides capturing the Oscar, the song became a best-seller in Frank Sinatra's recording for Capitol. "Three Coins in the Fountain" not only proved the financial making of the film but also helped make the Fountain of Trevi in Rome a prime tourist attraction for Americans.

4

Many other motion picture numbers, other than title or theme songs, hit the best-seller charts as recordings and joined the company of the hit songs of the Fifties. There were, to be sure, the winners of the Academy Award. Some have already been mentioned: "Whatever Will Be, Will Be," or *Que Sera, Sera*," from *The Man Who Knew Too Much* (1956), "High Noon," "Love is a Many-Splendored Thing," "Three Coins in the Fountain." But there were other Academy Award winners as well. In 1951, Hoagy Carmichael, with Johnny Mercer as lyricist, received the Oscar for "In the Cool, Cool, Cool of the Evening" which Bing Crosby and Jane Wyman introduced in *Here Comes the Groom*. "Secret Love" (Paul Francis Webster—Sammy Fain) was introduced by Doris Day in *Calamity Jane* (1953) and successfully recorded by her for Columbia. Sammy Cahn and James Van Heusen received Oscars for songs in 1957 and 1959: "All the Way" and "High Hopes." "All the Way" was the principal number in *The Joker Is Wild* (1957), the film biography of the nightclub comedian, Joe E. Lewis; its score included several standards. As James Van Heusen confided to this writer, "All the Way" was written "to dramatize Joe E. Lewis' loss of voice, and the big jump musically at the end of the second bar to the middle of the third bar was specifically designed to be difficult for him to sing, and he was supposed to break down dramatically." A million disk sale on the Capitol label by Frank Sinatra not only succeeded in making this song a hit in 1957 but was also a powerful stimulus at the box-offices of theaters showing *The Joker is*

Wild. Frank Sinatra also sang "High Hopes" (with the assistance of little Eddie Hodges) in *A Hole in the Head* (1959). This song was written because a somewhat humorous and quasi-nonsensical song was called for in the picture to alleviate the heightened tension of a scene involving father and son.

Nominations for an Academy Award also help single out other notable film songs of the 1950s. Mario Lanza introduced two of them, both by Sammy Cahn and Nicholas Brodszky: "Be My Love" in *The Toast of New Orleans* (1950) and "Because You're Mine" in the film of the same name (1952), both of which became best-selling records in Mario Lanza's recordings for Victor. "Zing a Little Zong" (Leo Robin—Harry Warren) was introduced by Bing Crosby and Jane Wyman in *Just for You* (1952). "That's Amore" (Jack Brooks—Harry Warren) became a Dean Martin favorite after he introduced it in *The Caddy* (1953) and recorded it for Capitol. "The Man That Got Away" (Ira Gershwin—Harold Arlen) became a Judy Garland trademark second only to "Over the Rainbow" (E. Y. Harburg—Harold Arlen). She introduced it in the 1953 remake of *A Star Is Born*. "Something's Gotta Give" (Johnny Mercer) was a number for Fred Astaire in *Daddy Long Legs* (1955) and a recording best-seller for the McGuire Sisters on the Coral label and for Sammy Davis on Decca. "True Love" is one of Cole Porter's most ravishing love ballads. It served as an amorous duet for Bing Crosby and Grace Kelly in *High Society* (1956) with their Capitol recording becoming a gold disk.

Though it was not nominated for an Oscar, "Hi-Lili, Hi-Lo" (Helen Deutsch—Bronislau Kaper) from *Lili* (1953), where it was sung by Leslie Caron and Mel Ferrer, deserves a place with the top film songs of the decade.

Organizations other than the Academy of Motion Picture Arts and Sciences were now giving awards for outstanding achievement in motion pictures. In the realm of film music, an award that became second in importance to that of the Motion Picture Academy was the Golden Globe, an annual motion picture competition which had been instituted by the Hollywood Foreign Press Association in 1944. In its first year, awards were given only in three categories: Best Motion Picture, Best Motion Picture Actor, and Best Motion Picture Actress. In its third annual award, the categories were expanded to five to include Best Supporting Actor and Actress. The first recognition of music was in 1948 when the award for the "best score" was presented for Max Steiner's background music to *Life with Father*. In the fifties, awards for best motion picture scores went to John Green for *The Inspector General* (1949), Franz Waxman for *Sunset Boulevard* (1950), Victor Young for *September Affair* (1950) and Dimitri Tiomkin for *High Noon*. A new category, that of screen musical, was introduced in 1952, the first winner being *With a Song in My Heart*. Later screen musicals in the fifties to be so honored were *Carmen Jones*, (1954), *Guys and Dolls* (1955), *The King and I* (1956), *Les Girls* (1957), *Gigi* (1958) and *Porgy and Bess* (1959). On two occasions, Dimitri Tiomkin was singled out for special honor: in 1955 for "creative musical contribution to motion pictures" and in 1957 with a "recognition award for music in motion pictures." Not until 1962 was a song chosen for one of these awards.

5

In the writing of background music and in scoring, the recognized composers of the forties continued to garner Academy Awards and nominations. Max Steiner was nominated for *The Flame and the Arrow* (1950), *The Miracle of Our Lady of Fatima* (1952), the 1953 remake of *The Jazz Singer* with Danny Thomas, *The Caine Mutiny* (1954) and *Battle Cry* (1954). Franz Waxman was awarded the Oscar for *A Place in the Sun* (1951) and was nominated for

The Silver Chalice (1955) and *The Nun's Story* (1959). Alfred Newman won three Oscars—
for *With a Song in My Heart* (1952), *Call Me Madam* (1953) and *Love Is a Many-Splendored
Thing* (1955)—besides getting nominations for *All About Eve* (1950), *David and Bathsheba*
(1951), *On the Riviera* 1951), *There's No Business Like Show Business* (1954), *Daddy Long
Legs* (1955), *Anastasia* (1956), *South Pacific* (1958) and *The Diary of Anne Frank* (1959).
Miklos Rozsa received the Award for *Ben Hur* (1959) and nominations for *Quo Vadis* (1951),
Ivanhoe (1952) and *Julius Caesar* (1953). John Green captured the Oscar for *An American in
Paris* (1951) and was nominated for *The Great Caruso* (1951), *High Society* (1956), *Meet Me
in Las Vegas* (1956) and *Raintree County* (1957). Victor Young won the Academy Award for
Around the World in 80 Days (1956) and a nomination for *Samson and Delilah* (1950).
Hugo Friedhofer was nominated for *Between Heaven and Hell* (1956), *An Affair to
Remember* (1957), *Boy on a Dolphin* (1957), *The Young Lions* (1958), and *Damn Yankees* (1958);
and David Raksin, for *Separate Tables* (1958).

Both in the writing of background music and in scoring Dimitri Tiomkin stood high
on the achievement list in the fifties with his Oscars for *The High and the Mighty* in 1954
(for title song as well as the background music) and for *The Old Man and the Sea* (1958),
together with nominations for *Giant* (1956), *Wild Is the Wind* (1957) and *The Young Land*
(1959). In accepting his dual Oscars for *The High and the Mighty* in 1955 he sent his
colleagues into an uproar of laughter—and made news in the papers the next day—by
confessing how much he owed, not to his wife or producers or co-workers, but to Brahms,
Beethoven, Tchaikovsky, Wagner and so forth, without whose help, he said, he could not
possibly have achieved the success he was enjoying in Hollywood.

Rivaling these veterans were talented newcomers: André Previn, Alex North, Elmer
Bernstein, Walter Scharf, Ernest Gold and Leonard Rosenman.

André Previn is the nephew of Charles Previn who used to conduct theater orchestras
in and out of New York and who, in the 1930s, wrote music for the screen, winning an
Academy Award in 1937 for his background music to *100 Men and a Girl*. But where
Charles Previn was a native of Brooklyn, New York, his nephew, André, came from Berlin
where he was born in 1929 and where he attended the Conservatory. He was nine when his
family brought him to the United States and settled in Los Angeles. There he combined
academic study in the public schools with the study of musical composition with Mario
Castelnuovo-Tedesco. While attending high school, Previn was brought to the music department of MGM by John Green, his first job to do the arranging for the screen musical,
Holiday in Mexico (1946). "When we hired André," recalls John Green, "he wasn't quite
sixteen and he could only come to work after three o'clock. He was incredible. After about
three years as an arranger we gave him his first score, *The Sun Comes Up* (1948), and from
then on it was: André Previn, composer-conductor." Previn also wrote two songs for this film
(with William Katz): "If You Were Mine" and "Cousin Ebenezer." He retained that post at
MGM until 1960, except for a brief hiatus in 1950–1952 when he served in the Army. At
MGM—and sometimes on loan to other studios—he proved to be one of the most technically adroit and innately gifted writers of screen music available. He did the background
music or scoring and frequently served as musical director as well, for such outstanding
screen productions as *Gigi* and *Porgy and Bess* (for both of which he received Academy
Awards in 1958 and 1959), and for *Three Little Words* (1950), *Kiss Me, Kate* (1953), *It's
Always Fair Weather* (1955), *Elmer Gantry* (1960) and *Bells Are Ringing* (1960), for all of
which he received Academy Award nominations. Before abandoning Hollywood to carve for
himself a new and magnificent career as a symphony conductor, first with the Houston

Symphony in Texas and then with the London Symphony in England and the Pittsburgh Symphony, Previn seized two more Oscars for *Irma La Douce* (1963), and *My Fair Lady* (1964).

Alex North's facility in writing screen music, and the financial rewards his talent brought him, deflected him from a career as a modernist composer for which he had trained himself and towards which he had been heading. He was born in Chester, Pennsylvania, in 1910, and attended the Curtis Institute in Philadelphia and The Juilliard School of Music in New York on scholarships. To support himself in New York he worked as a telegraph operator. Wanting to go somewhere "where my musical education could be subsidized," as he recalls, he applied for a job in the Soviet Union as a "telegraph engineer" in 1934. "The Russians probably thought I would rework their telegraphic system for them, but after a couple of weeks in Moscow I was put to sorting nuts and bolts. They were about to send me home but they were intrigued when I said I was a composer and wanted to study music in Russia. They auditioned me at the Moscow Conservatory and I got in." He came back to the United States in 1936 and continued his music study privately with Ernst Toch and Aaron Copland. Between 1935 and 1940 he was engaged in writing music for ballets, for the Federal Theater Project, and for documentary films for commercial firms. After service in the United States Army during World War II, where he was put in charge of self-entertainment programs for domestic and overseas hospitals, he wrote music for film documentaries for the Office of War Information as well as concert compositions. He contributed the incidental music for the Broadway production of Arthur Miller's play, *Death of a Salesman* (1949), which brought him into personal contact with Elia Kazan, the director. When Kazan went to Hollywood to direct the film version of Tennessee Williams' *A Streetcar Named Desire* (1951), he brought North along to write its background music. This was North's first assignment in Hollywood and his first score to get an Academy Award nomination. It was a departure from the usual scores then being written for the screen since it was jazz oriented, the better to suggest the background of New Orleans. Other Academy Award nominations came to him in the fifties for *Death of a Salesman* (1951), *Viva Zapata* (1952), *The Rose Tattoo* (1955) and *The Rainmaker* (1956), though this does not exhaust the list of his more memorable scores which also include *Member of the Wedding* (1953), *Long Hot Summer* (1958) and *The Sound and the Fury* (1959).

Elmer Bernstein was a New Yorker, born in 1922, who had been trained as a concert pianist by private teachers and at the Juilliard School of Music. During World War II he was in uniform when he made arrangements of folk songs for the Army Air Force Band led by Major Glenn Miller and for radio broadcasts. He was hurriedly called in one day to write the music for a dramatic show, his first such attempt. In 1949, now out of the Service, he wrote the music for *Before Morning*, a radio program produced by the United Nations which impressed Norman Corwin, who engaged him to write the music for one of his radio plays. This, in turn, brought Bernstein a contract from Columbia Pictures in 1950 to do the music for *Saturday's Hero*. He first revealed his gift for screen music with the score for *Sudden Fear* (1954). Here, as Tony Thomas notes in *Music for the Movies*, Bernstein "revealed characteristics that would make his work in this medium—the use of some of the more exotic instruments and the use of solo instruments like the piano and the flute, and the smaller groupings, a thinning out of the concerted form that was prevalent at the time." With his music for *The Man with the Golden Arm* (1955), in which Frank Sinatra was starred as a dope addict, Bernstein received a nomination for an Academy Award. By the end of the 1950s he was one of the most highly esteemed and busiest composers in Hollywood. Already behind him was a long string of successful scores for major productions, among them *The Ten Commandments* (1956), *The Sweet Smell of Success* 1957), *Desire Under the Elms* (1958), *God's Little Acre* (1958), *Kings Go Forth* (1958) and *Some Came Running* (1958).

Walter Scharf, born in 1910, was also a New Yorker. Before going out to Hollywood to work for motion pictures, he had been employed as an accompanist to Kate Smith, had worked with Rudy Vallee both as accompanist and arranger, and had been the musical director of a radio series starring Alice Faye and Phil Harris. In 1952, he was nominated for an Academy Award for his scoring for *Hans Christian Andersen*. Other movies of the fifties using his scoring included *Bundle of Joy* (1956) and *The Joker Is Wild* (1957).

Ernest Gold's career in Hollywood stretched back into the 1940s, but not until the fifties did he give his first indications of superior talent. Born in Vienna in 1921 to a family of musicians, Gold started studying the violin when he was six, and piano two years later. In his late teens he attended the Academy of Music and Performing Arts in Vienna, where his music study was suddenly aborted in 1938 with the annexation of Austria by Nazi Germany. With his father and sister (his mother having died five years earlier) he fled to the United States, arriving with just thirty dollars. His first job in America was as a busboy at the New York World's Fair. Before long he was able to put his musical training to use by working first as a piano accompanist at a private school in New York and then by writing songs for BMI. His first song to get published was "Here in the Velvet Night" (Don McCray) in 1940. "Practice Makes Perfect" (Don Roberts) was his first success, popularized by Billie Holiday and represented on "Your Hit Parade" for seventeen weeks, four of those in first position. Another of his songs, "Accidentally on Purpose" (Don McCray) was also on "Your Hit Parade," this time for four weeks.

Even as a boy in Vienna, and though deeply immersed in the musical classics, Gold's ambition was to write music for the screen, having been fascinated by the work of Max Steiner and Alfred Newman. That ambition remained alive after his arrival in the United States. He went to many movies just to hear the music, and was so entranced by Steiner's score for *The Garden of Allah* (1936) that he saw the movie seven times. His success as a songwriter gave him the entree he needed to Hollywood. In the 1940s, he was signed by Republic, his first score being *The Girl of the Limberlost* (1945). For the next few years he was employed with hack assignments. As he put it: "I learned my trade by working for about a dozen movies (usually in collaboration with others). I never kept any of the pieces for those movies, nor remember their titles." In 1954, he left Hollywood temporarily to work as a rehearsal pianist for the Broadway musical *Plain and Fancy*, but he was soon back. Between 1956 and 1960 he provided background music for a dozen films, in 1957 for *Affair in Havana*, in 1958 for *The Defiant Ones*, and in 1959 for *The Philadelphians*. The music for *The Defiant Ones* consisted of five minutes of rock 'n' roll which Stanley Kramer, its producer, admired. When Kramer started to work on his production of *On the Beach* (1959), and after George Antheil, the composer who had been contracted to write its music, died, he called Gold to take over. That score brought Gold a nomination for an Academy Award, together with the Golden Globe Award and the Downbeat award as the best dramatic film score of the year. One year more and he would achieve still greater renown for his music for *Exodus*.

Leonard Rosenman's first score for motion pictures was for *East of Eden* (1955) and forthwith he demonstrated that unusual gift for musical characterization and atmospheric writing that would distinguish his later screen music. Born in New York City in 1924, he received a thorough training in composition from such masters as Roger Sessions, Arnold

Schoenberg, and Luigi Dallapiccola. As a young man, he served on a fellowship as resident composer at the Berkshire Music Center at Tanglewood, in Massachusetts, where some of his chamber music was heard. One of his private piano students was the motion picture actor, James Dean. When Dean was signed to star in the Elia Kazan production, *East of Eden*, he influenced Kazan to let Rosenman do the music. That score immediately brought Rosenman other assignments. With *The Cobweb* (1955) he became the first composer to write a movie score in the twelve-tone technique, this expressionistic style (which he had learned at firsthand from Schoenberg) being uniquely effective for a film set in a psychiatric clinic. Another of his outstanding scores in 1955 was for *Rebel Without a Cause*, once again starring James Dean. In his music for *Pork Chop Hill* (1959) about the Korean War he incorporated a two-thousand-year-old Chinese lullaby into his score. In his later movies, he would use jazz, Indian music or a post-Romantic idiom to meet the atmospheric and dramatic demands of the cinematic story, thereby revealing a resiliency and versatility which few in Hollywood could rival.

Scoring and writing background music for films had by now developed a modus operandi unique to motion pictures. Before any music gets written, the Hollywood composer joins the producer and director in viewing a rough cut of the film—a run through with no sound—and makes instant decisions on places where music could be spotted. This information is siphoned off to a music editor who prepares a cue sheet on which every piece of action and dialogue is set down in minute detail, accurate to one tenth of a second. This helps the composer to sketch out his music timed perfectly to the various sequences, sometimes with the help of the film itself. The music is then ready for recording. While the music is being played the film is projected, with various visual metronomic devices to guide the conductor in the synchronization of music to film action.

Screen composers have found two techniques of composition most functional in their preparation of the scores. One is the leitmotif, or "leading motive" technique, which Richard Wagner had developed with such superhuman effect in his music dramas. These themes or "motives" are used to identify characters, situations, states of emotion and so forth, and are interwoven into the tonal fabric. "This technique," explains Elmer Bernstein, who has used it extensively, "requires great skill in its execution to avoid extreme banality and is, I believe, one of the most attractive uses of film music since it serves merely to repeat what should be clearly evident in a good film." The other technique is the monotheme, the use of a single melodic idea throughout a score to emphasize a particular emotion or situation or character. It is a method used with incomparable effect by David Raksin in *Laura* (1945), and by Alfred Newman in *Love Is a Many-Splendored Thing* (1955), to single out two of many examples. In *Love Is a Many-Splendored Thing* more than three quarters of the entire score is based on the melodic theme of the title song.

6

Among the best screen musicals of the fifties were many that had been adapted from the Broadway stage. Though such a transfer existed from the beginnings of talking pictures, rarely before had they been performed with such rewarding artistic and financial results. The explanation lies in the later willingness of Hollywood to respect and adhere to the original stage concept as to both music and text without undue desecration and violation, even while taking full advantage of the ability of the camera to go far beyond the confined limits of a three-walled stage. Such faithful translation from stage to screen resulted in cinematic entertainment of the first order in *Kiss Me, Kate* (1953), *Carmen Jones* (1954), *Guys and*

Dolls (1955), *Oklahoma!* (1955), *Carousel* (1956), *The King and I* (1956), *Pal Joey* (1957), *The Pajama Game* (1957), *Damn Yankees* (1958), *South Pacific* (1958) and *Porgy and Bess* (1959).

Musicals originating on the screen during the fifties also represented a new high in cinematic achievement and must be numbered with the best musicals ever filmed.

An American in Paris (1951) took its title from George Gershwin's orchestral tone poem which was used for a twenty-minute ballet sequence danced by Gene Kelly and Leslie Caron. The motion picture was set in Paris and was the love story of an American painter (Kelly) and a Parisian girl (Caron), a romance complicated by the fact that the girl is being pursued by a successful producer while the American is desired by a wealthy female socialite who is promoting his career. The story and setting provide ample opportunities for the presentation of seven old songs by George and Ira Gershwin, including a delightful rendition of "I Got Rhythm," in which Gene Kelly is supported by Georges Guetary and French urchins singing the number in French, and " 'S Wonderful," to which a piquant Gallic flavor is added by including such words as " 'S Magnifique", " 'S Elégant" and " 'S Exceptionnel." *An American in Paris* became the third musical in the history of the Motion Picture Academy Awards to win an Oscar as best film of the year.

Another foreign setting—this time nineteenth-century Copenhagen—brought to *Hans Christian Andersen* (1952) much of its pervading charm as it told of the romance between the beloved Danish storyteller (played by Danny Kaye) and a ballerina. The rest of the charm came from the delightful ballet sequences and the songs of Frank Loesser: "Wonderful Copenhagen," "Thumbelina," "Anywhere I Wander," "No Two People" and "The Inch Worm," all of them sung by Danny Kaye. "Thumbelina" was nominated for an Academy Award.

Singin' in the Rain (1952) has become a classic in its genre. It was a needle-sharp satire on Hollywood of the late twenties when the studios were converting to sound and the first movie musicals were being produced. Enhancing a brilliant script by Betty Comden and Adolph Green were the performances of Gene Kelly and Donald O'Connor as a dance duo, Debbie Reynolds as the romantic interest, and Jean Hagen as a star of the silent screen.

The title song of the film *Singin' in the Rain* (Arthur Freed—Nacio Herb Brown) had been one of the earliest successes of those early talking-singing musicals and as introduced in the new movie it provided Gene Kelly with an opportunity to perform what many critics consider the outstanding solo number of his career. Other songs by Freed and Brown (of the early screen musicals) were also used to full advantage. "Broadway Melody" was used for an eyefilling ballet number while "Should I?" allowed Donald O'Connor to perform a tap dance around the walls and ceiling of a room.

Seven Brides for Seven Brothers (1954) was a thoroughly engaging song and dance package adapted from a story by Stephen Vincent Benét. The plot, while warm and lively, was incidental. It involved a family of Oregon pioneers of the mid-nineteenth century. The oldest of the seven strapping, unkempt, rustic farmers (Howard Keel) comes home with a headstrong and spirited bride (Jane Powell) who not only succeeds in transforming the home, life and habits of these farmers but also inspires her six brothers-in-law to invade the village and kidnap six unwilling maidens as their prospective brides. Michael Kidd's choreography, eight songs by Gene de Paul to Johnny Mercer's lyrics (the best—"When You're in Love," "Wonderful, Wonderful Day" and "Spring, Spring, Spring") and the exuberant performances of Howard Keel and Jane Powell touched the screen with sheer magic.

In *A Star Is Born* (1954) Judy Garland emerged from an extended period of retirement from the screen to give one of her most virtuoso performances. She is the star to the manner born, both in the ballad, "The Man That Got Away" (one of Harold Arlen's later song classics, to Ira Gershwin's lyrics) and in an extended song sequence, "Born in a Trunk" which traces the career of a female singing star and reviews such song standards as "Swanee" (Irving Caesar—George Gershwin), "My Melancholy Baby" (George A. Norton—Ernie Burnett) and "I'll Get By" (Roy Turk—Fred E. Ahlert). The rest of the film—particularly the portrait of the disintegration of a one-time male screen star, enacted by James Mason, who marries the heroine—may border on soap opera, but the make-believe world of Holly-wood is projected with breathless excitement, pathos and occasional touches of satire.

While *It's Always Fair Weather* (1955) is primarily concerned with the reunion in New York of three G.I.'s (played by Gene Kelly, Dan Dailey and Michael Kidd in his motion-picture debut), after a ten-year separation since V-J Day, the bright-paced script by Betty Comden and Adolph Green digresses from the main story line long enough to take devastating cracks at the television business and some of its phony gimmicks. All this, together with Michael Kidd's choreography and André Previn's songs to lyrics by Comden and Green ("I Like Myself," "Thanks a Lot, But No Thanks", "Time for Parting") add up to a delectable screen escapade.

In *Love Me Or Leave Me* (1955), Doris Day is starred as the songstress of the thirties, Ruth Etting, and her entanglement with a racketeer who is brought to screen life by James Cagney. The Academy Award-winning script by Daniel Fuchs and Isobel Lennart succeeds in giving dimension to both of these characters and to create a taut drama. The score is an eruption of song standards with which Miss Etting achieved stardom in nightclubs and the Broadway musical theater.

Gigi (1958) became the first motion picture to corral nine Academy Awards, includ-ing one as the best picture of the year, and another for its title song (Alan Jay Lerner —Frederick Loewe). It set out to be another *My Fair Lady* (Broadway production, 1956), with a different story and characters. Some of the ingredients that helped make *My Fair Lady* an artistic and box-office triumph on the stage were utilized judiciously. The same songwriters were employed, the team of Lerner and Loewe. Cecil Beaton, who had designed the stage sets and costumes, was recruited for a similar chore. The basic story theme was the same though derived from a new source (a story by Colette) with a new setting and with variations. That story was the transformation of a gawky, graceless girl into a woman of beauty and refinement. The place is Paris, the time the 1890s. The principal characters are the heroine, who is being trained by her grandmother and great-aunt to be a courtesan, and Gaston, the young, blasé bachelor who is at first impervious to her charms but ends up falling in love with her. Leslie Caron as Gigi, Louis Jourdan as Gaston, Hermione Gingold as the grand-mother, and Maurice Chevalier as a boulevardier, add spice to this tasty dish. Chevalier sang "Thank Heaven for Little Girls," "I'm Glad I'm Not Young Anymore" and, with Hermione Gingold, "I Remember It Well"; Louis Jourdan was heard in the title song and "The Night They Invented Champagne." All this was delightful entertainment which, as Bosley Crowther reported in *The New York Times*, is not only a "charming comprehension of the spicy confection of Colette, but . . . also a lively and lyrical enlargement upon the story's flavored mood and atmosphere."

Some Like It Hot (1959) looked back to the turbulent era of Prohibition in a hilarious script by I. A. L. Diamond and Billy Wilder. Two young musicians in Chicago, in danger of their lives because they witnessed a gangland massacre, hide out in female garb with an all-girl band in Florida. That the two musicians were played by Tony Curtis and Jack

Lemmon was insurance that the hilarity, under Wilder's brilliant direction, never slackens. Marilyn Monroe plays the glamorous girl with whom one of the two falls in love while he must keep up the fiction that he is a female. Joe E. Brown is a middle-aged tycoon who finds the second musician desirable, believing him a girl. Farcical episodes pile one upon another, and the dialogue remains consistently scintillating up to the closing line. Song standards performed by "Sweet Sue and the Society Syncopators" recreate musically the ambiance and spirit of the twenties.

38

"The Broadway Melody"

1

On Broadway, the 1950s marked the end of the era of Rodgers and Hammerstein. That era was made further incandescent in 1951 by *The King and I* which (as by now had become almost habitual with Rodgers and Hammerstein) represented a striking contrast in content, style, setting, character and methods to anything they had previously attempted. The setting is Bangkok, Siam, during the 1860s where two opposing cultures rub elbows. The characters are Orientals, with the exception of four Caucasians none of whom are Americans. The point of origin is a novel by Margaret Landon, *Anna and the King of Siam*, about a widowed schoolteacher brought to Siam by its king to teach Western culture to his large brood of children. Miss Landon's novel was made into a poignant nonmusical motion picture in 1948 starring Rex Harrison and Irene Dunne. Gertrude Lawrence saw this movie, then read the book, and became intrigued with the idea of playing Anna in a new stage vehicle. She convinced Rodgers and Hammerstein to fashion the story into a musical play, which they did with no little hesitancy. To Hammerstein, the Oriental plot, setting and characters posed innumerable problems. He cringed at the thought of creating an Oriental musical with "girls dressed in Oriental costumes and dancing out onto the stage and singing 'ching-aling-aling' with their fingers in the air." Besides, here was a plot with no love interest between the two principals, and with the major male character dying just before the final curtain. How was it possible to translate this into commercial theater? Rodgers had his own misgivings. "I couldn't write an authentic Far Eastern melody if my life depended upon it. If I could, I

594

wouldn't. A too accurate recreation of Siamese music would have jarred the ears of American audiences and sent them out of the theater . . . shrieking with pain."

Rodgers and Hammerstein met these problems squarely and solved them brilliantly. And with Gertrude Lawrence and Yul Brynner in the leading roles, *The King and I* became a spellbinding experience, representing "a flowering of all the arts of the theater," as Danton Walker described it in the New York *Daily News*.

Without attempting to directly imitate Oriental music, Rodgers often flavored his score with delicate Oriental spices, both in melodic and harmonic structure. The march of the royal Siamese children, Tuptim's "My Lord and Master," and the king's expansive narrative, "A Puzzlement" are cases in point. So is the music for the ballet, "The Small House of Uncle Thomas," in which Jerome Robbins' choreography retells the story of *Uncle Tom's Cabin* in terms of a Siamese dance and in which Rodgers utilizes only percussive effects by ancient cymbals and woodblocks as the background for a spoken chorus. The exquisitely sensitive mood and atmosphere maintained in this ballet are caught and held throughout the musical play, in compelling songs of which the most significant are "I Whistle a Happy Tune," "Hello, Young Lovers," "Getting to Know You," "I Have Dreamed" and "Shall We Dance?".

In *The King and I* a new star was born in Yul Brynner, who played the king. For another star, Gertrude Lawrence, the role of Anna was destined to be her last, in many ways the most radiant of all her interpretations. A half year before *The King and I* came to the end of its 1,246 performances on Broadway, Gertrude Lawrence died on September 6, 1952.

In *Me and Juliet* (1953) and *Pipe Dream* (1955), Rodgers and Hammerstein followed the ritual of the musical theater of the past more strictly than had heretofore been their custom. *Me and Juliet* was a love letter by Rodgers and Hammerstein to the world they knew and loved best—the theater. Here is portrayed the life both backstage and onstage, during the run of a musical comedy. Of the songs, the more memorable ones are "Keep It Gay," "No Other Love" (melody lifted from Rodgers' tango in *Victory at Sea*) and an extended narrative "The Big Black Giant," describing an audience as it appears to the performer.

Pipe Dream, based on John Steinbeck's *Sweet Thursday*, was populated with colorful but disreputable characters in Monterey County's Cannery Row in California. All of them are social misfits, occupants of a place called The Palace Flophouse. Two ballads stood out prominently in an otherwise none-too-distinguished score: "Everybody's Got a Home But Me" and "All at Once You Love Her."

Me and Juliet had a run of only 358 performances; *Pipe Dream*, 246. The critics generally rejected both productions expressing blunt disapproval or the kind of faint praise that is worse than outright denunciation.

The *Flower Drum Song* (1958) once again was more musical comedy than musical play, and once again with a setting, situations, characters and conflicts new to the Rodgers and Hammerstein musical theater. Based on a novel by C. Y. Lee, *Flower Drum Song* takes place in the Chinatown of present-day San Francisco, and throws into conflict two generations of Chinese. The old China is recreated through the scenery, costumes and rituals. These are juxtaposed with such American phenomena as a nightclub striptease, a vaudeville buck and wing dance, and Chinese kids playing with a contraption popular with American youngsters in the late fifties, the hula hoop. In the songs, the old is heard in "A Hundred Million Miracles," with its Oriental melodic structure, and the new in such zestful ballads as "Sunday" and "I Enjoy Being a Girl."

The final curtain on the Rodgers and Hammerstein epoch came down with *The Sound of Music* (1959) which was a compromise between operetta and musical play. It overflowed with tenderness, radiance and sentimentality in telling the history of a singing Austrian family, headed by Baron and Baroness Von Trapp, which toured the music world just prior to World War II. The year is 1938 and the Nazis have marched into and occupied Austria. An anti-Fascist, the Baron is fiercely opposed to to the new regime. After giving a concert in Salzburg, the Von Trapps flee from Austria in the darkness of night, gaining their freedom by climbing the mountains into Switzerland.

Mary Martin portrayed Maria, whose volatile personality is captured in the song "Maria." For her, Rodgers wrote such magical numbers as the title song, "My Favorite Things," and the captivating number which she teaches the children to sing, "Do-Re-Mi." The score also includes music of an ecclesiastical character (the opening choral Preludium) and songs with an Austrian folk song quality ("Edelweiss," "The Lonely Goatherd"). The encompassing charm of youth which pervades "Do-Re-Mi" is also encountered in "So Long, Farewell" and "Sixteen Going on Seventeen," while "Climb Ev'ry Mountain" has religious overtones.

The Rodgers and Hammerstein epoch finished with one of their greatest triumphs. After coming to Broadway with the largest advance sale in theater history (three million dollars), *The Sound of Music* went on to play 1,443 performances on Broadway, to capture six Antoinette Perry Awards, including one for best musical, and to have the sheet music sale of "Do-Re-Mi" exceed that of any Rodgers and Hammerstein song ever published. A touring company played to capacity houses for two and a half years. The London company also had a run of several years. The motion picture adaptation in 1965—starring Julie Andrews and Christopher Plummer—had one of the highest box-office grosses throughout the world of any motion picture. The total sale of the original cast recordings of both the stage production and the motion picture exceeded fifteen million copies, something without precedent.

Less than one year after the opening of *The Sound of Music*, Oscar Hammerstein II died at his home in Doylestown, Pennsylvania on August 23, 1960. His death was mourned wherever his writing had lit up the theatrical skies, which was throughout most of the civilized world. To one man in particular, the loss was irreparable—Richard Rodgers. After a sixteen-year partnership that had changed the face of the American musical theater, Richard Rodgers had to seek out others to work with.

2

The musical comedy and the musical play both continued to flourish during the fifties, with many composers equally adept in both areas.

Frank Loesser's second contribution to Broadway following *Where's Charley?* (1948), was a musical comedy that was a model of its kind and one of the best ever produced: *Guys and Dolls* (1950). In the book by Abe Burrows and Jo Swerling, every farcical episode, routine and song is germane to the plot. Even where musical comedy techniques are employed, these, too, are integral to the text. The bustling opening scene is in the tradition of the musical theater, but in *Guys and Dolls* it became a pantomime of Broadway life and characters, beautifully paced by George S. Kaufman's direction. There is a ballet, choreographed by Michael Kidd— but its theme, in keeping with the characters, is a crap game in a sewer. Even the love ballads, "I'll Know," "If I Were a Bell" and "I've Never Been in Love Before" are the kind of songs Damon Runyon characters would sing. Other Loesser songs develop organically out of the content of the play. They include several humorous numbers, each a gem: the opening "Fugue for Tinhorns" ("I've Got the Horse Right Here"), a three-voiced canon in which horseplayers pick their day's selection; "Adelaide's Lament," bemoaning psychosomatic colds, which Moss Hart once said he considered to be the most original musical comedy number ever written; and the two nightclub routines at the Hot Box, "A Bushel and a Peck" and "Take Back Your Mink."

No less vital is the picturesque, cynical, hard-boiled world of Damon Runyon, whose story provided the material and the characters for this musical comedy. It is Runyon's Broadway characters—and the curious forces and impulses motivating their daily lives and philosophy—that, in the last analysis, dominate *Guys and Dolls* and helped make it as good as it was. And the Runyon characters remained alive and vibrant when an all-black cast brought it back to Broadway on July 10, 1976.

From musical comedy, Loesser progressed to a musical play with *The Most Happy Fella* (1956), which boasts one of the most expansive scores the American popular musical theater has known. Loesser himself made the textual adaptation of Sidney Howard's 1925 Pulitzer Prize play, *They Knew What They Wanted*, his first try at writing the book as well as lyrics and music. The simple, poignant love story of an aging Italian winegrower and a young waitress he has wooed and won through correspondence by sending her not his own photograph but that of his handsome hired hand, is flooded with so much music that critics were at a loss whether to identify the final product as a musical play, a musical drama or an opera. Certainly this is not musical comedy in the way *Guys and Dolls* was—but a play in which music supplies the driving force.

There are so many musical numbers in *The Most Happy Fella*—over thirty—and they are so inextricably a part of the drama that they were not listed separately at the end of the program, as is customary with musical shows, any more than principal arias are listed at the end of an opera program. And the musical material is as varied as it is prolific. There are fat show tunes to remind us that *The Most Happy Fella* belongs to the popular theater. Indeed, disc jockeys were happily spinning "Standing on the Corner" (in the Columbia recording by The Four Lads) long before the show opened; and soon other numbers, like "Big D," "Happy to Make Your Acquaintance" and "Young People" also caught on, though to a lesser degree. Besides show tunes, the score had recitatives, passionate arias and duets, choruses, parodies, dance music and musical interludes of all kinds—every character, situation and mood finding its musical equivalent—to give the musical theater a new depth and dimension.

3

For Alan Jay Lerner and Frederick Loewe, the step from *Brigadoon* (1947) to *My Fair Lady* (1956) was an ascent to the ultimate in artistic and financial success. Midway between these two stage classics, Lerner and Loewe wrote *Paint Your Wagon* (1951), with an original book by Lerner set in California in 1853 during the Gold Rush days. It traced the history of a mining camp from its growth as a bustling boom town to its disintegration as a ghost city. *Paint Your Wagon* did not do well on Broadway and it fared even worse when it was heavy-handedly made into a motion picture two decades later. It deserves a better fate, for it is picturesque in background and characterizations, and boasts some exceptional songs: "Wand'rin' Star," "They Call the Wind Maria" (since become a standard), "I Talk to the Trees" and "I Still See Elisa."

My Fair Lady, five years later, was Alan Jay Lerner's musical version of Bernard Shaw's *Pygmalion*. Many producers had been interested in making a musical out of *Pygmalion*, and many prestigious Broadway composers had taken this project under consideration before *My Fair Lady* became a reality with Herman Levin as producer, Moss Hart as director, Alan Jay Lerner as adapter and Lerner and Loewe as songwriters. The Shaw play was essentially a romance, a fact Lerner did not forget even while preserving in his adaptation

Shavian mockery, irony and satire, together with a personalized touch of humanity and sentimentality. The changes Lerner made in *Pygmalion* were few. "We realized," he said, "we didn't have to enlarge the plot at all. We just had to add what Shaw had happening offstage." In the musical, as in the Shaw play, the main thrust of the plot was the transformation of Eliza Doolittle from a bedraggled and illiterate cockney flower girl into a lady of elegant appearance, beautiful speech, and gracious manners—a transformation brought about by Professor Henry Higgins, a phonetician. Shaw leaves in doubt whether Professor Higgins and Eliza become emotionally involved permanently, but the musical answers that question. In the next-to-the-closing scene, Higgins concedes that he cannot get Eliza out of his mind ("I've Grown Accustomed to Her Face"). When Eliza slips into his house, Higgins takes her presence for granted and orders her to get his slippers.

The magic of *My Fair Lady* was compounded of many unforgettable elements: the performances of Julie Andrews as Eliza, Rex Harrison as Professor Higgins, and Stanley Holloway as Alfred P. Doolittle, Liza's father; Moss Hart's ingenious direction which reached a high point in "The Rain in Spain" number (in which Higgins discovers to his delight that Eliza has lost her cockney accent, which Hart developed into an infectious fandango dance); Hanya Holm's imaginative choreography in the "Ascot Gavotte" and the "The Embassy Waltz"; and the songs of Lerner and Loewe. Two of them were of hit-caliber, "I Could Have Danced All Night" and "On the Street Where You Live." But while tunes like these linger in the mind and on the lips long after the final curtain, there also cling to the memory such witty and sophisticated numbers as Professor Higgins' "I'm an Ordinary Man," "Why Can't the English" and "A Hymn to Him"; Doolittle's two hilarious contributions, "With a Little Bit of Luck" and "Get Me to the Church on Time," and Eliza's "Show Me" and "Wouldn't It Be Loverly?".

Both in New York and in London, *My Fair Lady* enjoyed the longest run of any musical up to that time, the New York run reaching a fabulous total of 2,717 performances. It received the New York Drama Critics and the Antoinette Perry Awards as the season's best musical. It was also produced in twenty-one other countries in eleven translations, including productions in Japan and the Soviet Union. A national company toured for several years. The gross income was in excess of eighty million dollars, with several more millions coming in from the five-million album sale of the Columbia original cast recording (one of fifty different recordings in many languages) and many more millions from the motion picture adaptation in 1964. No musical production up to this time had proved so profitable, and no musical so clearly deserved such rewards.

But the fabulous popular appeal of *My Fair Lady* was not confined solely to the fifties. Returning to Broadway on March 25, 1976, after an absence of two decades—with Ira Richardson as Henry Higgins and Christine Andreas as Eliza—*My Fair Lady* once again touched the Broadway theater with enchantment, proving (if, indeed, such proof were necessary) that it was "a great classical American operetta, one of the finest the world has ever seen," as Clive Barnes reported in *The New York Times* upon witnessing the revival.

4

For Leonard Bernstein, the 1950s was a decade rich with musical stage triumphs, as well as continual victories in the world of serious music. His second musical comedy, *Wonderful Town* (1953), swept Broadway off its feet. This was a musical comedy based on *My Sister Eileen*, stories of Ruth McKenney which had appeared in the *The New Yorker* and been adapted for the nonmusical stage. They told of the Greenwich Village adventures of two young innocents—Ruth, and her sister Eileen—come to New York from Columbus, Ohio, to make their way in the wonderful town, Ruth as a writer, and Eileen as an actress.

The breathless excitement generated by the overture, followed by an equally frenetic ragtag dance of Greenwich Villagers, was the starting point of a production which continued to accelerate in pace until the final curtain. The dynamo responsible for keeping these exciting proceedings continually charged with energy was Rosalind Russell as Ruth—she who had often been the sedate and sophisticated lady on the screen. Together with her sister Eileen (played by Edie Adams) she expressed homesickness in a winsome little number, "Ohio," which Bernstein had intended as a tongue-in-the-cheek parody of hometown songs, but which was taken in all seriousness by audiences and subsequently by radio, record and television performers. There was, however, no mistaking the satirical intent of Bernstein's amusing Irish ballad, "My Darlin' Eileen" or the rowdy humor of "What a Waste" and "Pass That Football"—all to the lyrics of Betty Comden and Adolph Green. Other Bernstein numbers were in a more sentimental vein, and one of these, "A Quiet Girl," was one of the best love ballads he had written so far.

When it was first produced in 1956, Bernstein's *Candide* was a *succès d'estime*, one of those musicals which those who first enjoyed it liked to savor like a choice liquor or wine. A musical play based on Voltaire's famous satirical novel, adapted for the musical theater by Lillian Hellman, with lyrics by Richard Wilbur, John La Touche and Dorothy Parker, it was admirably directed by Tyrone Guthrie. With a cast headed by Robert Rounseville, Barbara Cook, Max Adrian and Irra Petina, *Candide* was a thoroughly winning satire about this best of all possible worlds, the misadventures of Candide in different countries, and his return home a saddened and disillusioned man ready to tend to his own little garden. Bernstein's music met the requirements of every changing situation, the score aglitter with folk songs, music hall ditties, jazz, operatic numbers, choral and ensemble pieces and folk dances of many lands. The best songs were "Glitter and Be Gay" (Richard Wilbur), "Eldorado" (Lillian Hellman) and "It Must Be So" (Richard Wilbur). For all its positive values, *Candide* did not go over with audiences either at its original Broadway run of seventy-three performances at the Martin Beck Theater beginning on December 1, 1956, nor on the national tour that followed, nor at revivals in San Francisco and New York, both in 1971. But then—with an altogether new book by Hugh Wheeler, with extraordinarily inventive and intimate staging by Harold Prince, with some of Bernstein's music refurbished, and with some sparkling new lyrics by Stephen Sondheim—*Candide* was resuscitated in 1974 by the Chelsea Theater Center of Brooklyn, New York, to such ringing hosannas of praise that it was rushed, a month later, to the Broadway Theater for a long, prosperous run. Good as *Candide* had been in 1956—at least to this viewer—it proved immensely better in its new life.

Bernstein's successor to *Candide* was one of the supreme financial and artistic triumphs of the American musical theater: *West Side Story* (1957). The book by Arthur Laurents was based on a conception by Jerome Robbins, who was also responsible for the remarkable choreography. Lyrics were by Stephen Sondheim, achieving renown for the first time as a creator for the Broadway stage which henceforth he would enrich so immeasurably not only as a lyricist but also as a composer.

West Side Story was a grim, turbulent story of life on New York's West Side among teenage gangs. Its tragic love story was a transformation of Shakespeare's *Romeo and Juliet* into modern jargon and symbols. Rarely before or since had the American commercial musical theater turned for its material to so realistic and tragic a tale, concerned with social problems, and timely in its treatment of the problem of juvenile delinquency. The story was projected not only through varied stage techniques but also through several dance sequences such as "The Rumble," "Somewhere" and "Cool." Much of the tension and savagery of the play are reflected in Bernstein's music for these dance sequences. The bitterness of the play seeps into songs like "America" and "Gee, Officer Krupke!" and the play's inherent tenderness and hope are eloquently voiced in "Tonight," "Maria" and "I Feel Pretty."

West Side Story has been revived several times in New York City as well as being performed throughout the United States and Europe, including a presentation at the Viennese opera house, the Volksoper. In 1961 it became a masterly motion picture that captured ten Academy Awards (the highest number to date) including that of best picture.

5

Propelled to Broadway by the success of their hit songs in the early 1950s, Jerry Ross and Richard Adler wrote their first musical stage score in 1954, and came up with a resounding winner. That musical was *The Pajama Game*, book by George Abbott and Richard Bissell based on *7½¢*, Bissell's novel about a small town pajama factory. The cards at first seemed stacked against the survival of *The Pajama Game*. The producers, the choreographer Bob Fosse, and the songwriters were all new to Broadway and unknown to the theater public. A musical that called upon labor troubles for its basic theme and which for the most part utilized the drab settings of a pajama factory and union headquarters was hardly likely to lure audiences into a theater. And as if these were not deficits enough, the musical opened in May; the months preceding summer have always been regarded on Broadway as an invitation to disaster.

Yet *The Pajama Game* did well enough to last more than a thousand performances on Broadway, to win the Antoinette Perry and Donaldson awards as the year's best musical, and in 1957 to be made into an excellent movie starring Doris Day, but using members of the original stage company for the rest of its cast. Sparked by the adroit direction of George Abbott, and energized by galvanic performances by John Raitt, Eddie Foy, Jr., Carol Haney and Janis Paige, *The Pajama Game* was "young, and funny and earthy and fast" (William Hawkins in the *World-Telegram*) and "a royal flush and grand slam all rolled into one" (Robert Coleman in the *Mirror*).

"Hey, There," the song in which Sid, the factory superintendent, first betrays his yearning for Babe, head of the union grievance committee—and which he sings as a duet with himself with the help of a dictaphone—was one of two standout musical numbers. It enjoyed a giant sale of about two and a half million disks in Rosemary Clooney's Columbia recording. The other top song was the tango, "Hernando's Hideaway."

That the songwriting team of Adler and Ross was no flash in the pan as far as Broadway was concerned was proved a year later with *Damn Yankees*. This musical was based on a novel by Douglass Wallop, with George Abbott once again not only helping with the adaptation but also responsible for the direction. The subject of baseball is here combined with the Faust legend: Joe Boyd, a rabid baseball fan in despair at the shabby showing of his beloved team, the Washington Senators, makes a pact with Applegate (otherwise the Devil) to trade his soul for a world series win.

For Gwen Verdon as the temptress Lola, recruited by Applegate to keep Boyd from reneging on his bargain, Adler and Ross wrote a seductive tango, "Whatever Lola Wants", and for the ballplayers of the Washington Senators an inspirational number, "Heart." This became an Eddie Fisher hit record in a Victor release.

With two major shows running simultaneously on Broadway, and selling out the house, and with five songs on "Your Hit Parade," Jerry Ross and Richard Adler loomed as the most important new songwriters on Broadway in several years. Tragically, this happy partnership was prematurely broken up by Jerry Ross' death in 1955 before he reached his thirtieth birthday. He had long been suffering from a chronic bronchiectasis.

Bob Merrill was another songwriter to become successful in the 1950s and then to go on to invade the Broadway theater. His first musical was *New Girl in Town* (1957), George Abbott's adaptation of Eugene O'Neill's 1922 Pulitzer Prize play, *Anna Christie*, with Gwen Verdon in the title role. Bob Merrill, who wrote the lyrics as well as the music, had two fine numbers in "Look at 'Er" and "Sunshine Girl."

Merrill's second Broadway venture was another adaptation of a Eugene O'Neill play, the heartwarming comedy, *Ah, Wilderness!*. *Take Me Along* (1959) was set in Centerville, Connecticut in the early 1900s. Jackie Gleason was starred as Sid Davis, a reporter more interested in the bottle than in the woman who is fond of him. Walter Pidgeon was Nat Miller, the esteemed editor of the town paper, and the father of Richard (performed by Robert Morse in his first stage success), an adolescent whose sentimental attachment to young Muriel causes an upheaval in his staid household. The title song was the hit of this production, with "Promise Me a Rose" of secondary interest.

6

For Cole Porter, the fifties was the end of the road as a composer for the musical stage with *Can-Can* (1953) and *Silk Stockings* (1955). For a man who loved Paris as deeply as Cole Porter did, and who could always look back to his years there as a time of wine and roses, it is eloquently appropriate that his valedictories to Broadway should both have a Parisian background. That of *Can-Can* was Montmartre in 1893, with much of the action taking place in a night spot which surreptitiously features the can-can dance, legally taboo as shocking and immoral. La Mome Pistache, the café proprietress, successfully uses her allure upon the judge to clear the good name of this night spot and legalize the can-can.

For *Can-Can*, Porter composed his most exultant paean to the city of light in "I Love Paris," only one of several numbers with a Parisian flavor, the others being the title song, "C'est Magnifique," "Allez-vous en" and "Montmart'." Cole Porter's suave sophistication could also be enjoyed in "Live and Let Live" and "It's All Right with Me."

Silk Stockings was a musical comedy—the book by George S. Kaufman, Leueen MacGrath and Abe Burrows, based on the nonmusical motion picture *Ninotchka* starring Greta Garbo. The plot is a satire on Soviet officialdom and bureaucracy.

Romance is combined with barbed satire on Soviet life, ways and people. The satire is found in some of the characters, such as the blundering, blustering agents Brankov, Bibinski and Ivanov. It is also encountered in "Siberia," a song takeoff on Russian folk music. The principal love ballad, "All of You," and a new hymn to Paris, "Paris Loves Lovers," are however *echt* musical comedy material.

Silk Stockings was Cole Porter's twenty-fifth musical for Broadway. Before it had ended its run, the composer could look back on a theatrical career that had spanned forty years.

After *Silk Stockings*, Porter completed three more scores, two of them for the movies—*High Society* (1956) and *Les Girls* (1957)—and *Aladdin* for television. That television production, telecast over CBS on February 21, 1958, was Porter's last score for any medium. After that, he lost not only the will to work but even the will to live. After a bone tumor on his right leg required amputation on April 3, 1958, he became a recluse, seeking refuge in alcohol, sleep, self pity and overwhelming despair. Except for a few select friends he divorced himself completely from people. He did not attend a "Salute to Cole Porter" at the Metropolitan Opera House on May 15, 1960, or the commencement exercises at Yale University in June of 1960 where he was conferred an honorary doctorate of humane letters, or his seventieth birthday party arranged by his friends at the Orpheum Theater in New York on June 9, 1962. In October 1964 he was taken to Santa Monica Hospital for the removal of a kidney stone. He never survived that operation, though it was comparatively minor and seemed to have gone well. He died in the hospital on October 15, 1964.

7

The only musical Irving Berlin wrote in the 1950s was *Call Me Madam* (1950) which turned out to be another tour de force for Ethel Merman. Her role was Sally Adams, the American Ambassador to the mythical kingdom of Lichtenburg (a character inspired by Mrs. Perle Mesta who had served as Ambassador to Luxembourg under President Truman). A boisterous and lusty woman, Mrs. Adams becomes enmeshed in political and romantic intrigues in Lichtenburg from which, in the end, she emerges triumphant. "You're Just in Love" was Berlin's leading ballad, a duet with a two-melody chorus, each with its own set of lyrics. Though conceived as a sentimental number, Miss Merman (in partnership with Russell Nype) introduced all sorts of amusing stage business to accompany each encore so that the song assumed comic overtones. Other fine songs were "The Hostess with the Mostes' on the Ball," "It's a Lovely Day Today," "The Best Thing for You," and a song that helped to carry General Dwight D. Eisenhower into the White House, having been used repeatedly during his Presidential campaign, "They Like Ike."

For his two musicals in the fifties, Harold Arlen went to the Caribbean for exotic settings and characters. *House of Flowers* (1954) had book and lyrics by Truman Capote. The "house of flowers" is a bordello in which each of the girls is named after a flower. With two great ladies in the two leading female roles—Pearl Bailey as Mme. Fleur, the proprietress of the bordello, and Diahann Carroll as Ottilie, as her protegée—the musical was performed in grand style. The West Indies, which gave this musical so much of its atmospheric color and appeal are personalized in some of the Arlen songs: "Two Ladies in de Shade of de Banana Tree," "A Sleepin' Bee" and "I Never Has Seen Snow."

In Arlen's *Jamaica* (1957) Lena Horne had her first starring role in a Broadway musical. Here she is Savannah who, in her home of Pigeon Island off Kingston, Jamaica, dreams of coming to New York but is kept on her native island by her love for Koli. In tune with the story and its Jamaican setting, Arlen's music was heavily spiced with the melodic and harmonic condiments of calypso and other West Indian folk idioms and dances, of which "Incompatability," "Take It Slow, Joe" and "Cocoanut Sweet"—all with lyrics by E. Y. Harburg—are memorable examples.

In the 1950s, Harold Rome made the transition from revues, to which he had previously confined his songwriting, to musical comedy. He first did so with *Wish You Were Here* (1952), a musical stage version of Arthur Kober's comedy, *Having Wonderful Time*, about adult camps in New York State and the flirtations, sexual encounters and romances they encourage. In the musical comedy, as in the play, the resort is Camp Karefree in the Berkshire Mountains, and the principal love interest rests with Teddy Stern, a girl from the Bronx, and Chick Miller, a camp waiter. *Wish You Were Here* did not win critical approval, but the audiences loved it, and it stayed on for more than a year. Rome's music and lyrics, much more in the accepted style of the musical comedy theater than those he had once written for smart and usually socially conscious revues, included one of the major hit songs of his career, the title song, which became a gold record in Eddie Fisher's Victor release. "Where Did the Night Go?" was a lesser hit in the show.

The human equations had almost been lost in the scramble to make *Wish You Were Here* an elaborately staged production; indeed, one of the main attractions was a huge, permanent swimming pool on the stage. Miraculously, the human equation survived similar ostentation and fussiness in staging, in Harold Rome's *Fanny* (1954). The heartwarming humanity and compassion found in the three plays by Marcel Pagnol on which *Fanny* was based were carried over skillfully into the new adaptation by S. N. Behrman, one of the ablest writers of stage comedy here making a musical comedy debut, in collaboration with Joshua Logan. This humanity and compassion were captured in the tender, selfless love of Panisse, a wealthy Marseilles owner of a sailmaking establishment, for Fanny, a girl many years younger, whom he marries when she became pregnant with the child of Marius gone off to the sea.

This was one of Rome's best and most versatile scores. Some songs penetrated to the heart of the characters they interpreted: "To My Wife" (Panisse), "Restless Heart" (Marius), "Welcome Home" (César). Sometimes Rome's background music brings mellow overtones to a dramatic scene, while his ballet music consistently has symphonic breadth. Yet in extending his horizon, Rome did not forget his way with a good tune, as we discover in the title song and in "Love Is a Very Light Thing," nor had he lost his sense of humor, which can be found in "Be Kind to Your Parents."

In the inexplicable ways that Hollywood sometimes operates, when *Fanny* came to the screen in 1960 with Leslie Caron, Maurice Chevalier and Charles Boyer, it used none of Rome's fine songs but merely borrowed the melody of the title song as a recurring theme in the background music.

In *Destry Rides Again* (1959), Harold Rome wrote songs for a Western musical, the text having been taken from a story by Max Brand. Destry, a gunfighter, is brought to the cattle town of Bottleneck at the turn of the century to restore law and order. He turns out to be a mild-mannered, diffident young man who is as shy with a gun as he is with girls. Rome's best songs were Frenchy's beguiling ballad, "I Know Your Kind," her duet with Destry, "Anyone Would Love You" and Destry's confession of what love means to a lonely man, "Once I Knew a Fella."

Arthur Schwartz, like Harold Rome, had acquired a pattern for success by writing songs for smart revues, but unlike Rome he had tried writing for musical comedy before 1950. He suffered six successive failures with musicals with a story line before winning his first hand as a composer of musical comedies. That winning hand came with *A Tree Grows in Brooklyn* (1951), adapted from the best-selling novel by Betty Smith. When Shirley Booth, as the amoral and uninhibited Cissie, was on stage, the musical captured some of the ingratiating warmth and tenderness of Miss Smith's novel about the downtrodden Nolan family in Brooklyn New York. While the sympathy of the novel for the harassed Nolans is only passingly realized in the musical, it does have an appealing sweetness. And so do Schwartz's songs, with lyrics by Dorothy Fields, among which were "I'll Buy You a Star," "Love is the Reason" and "Make the Man Love Me."

Schwartz's *By the Beautiful Sea* (1954) counted even more heavily on nostalgia and sentiment than did *A Tree Grows in Brooklyn*, and in *By the Beautiful Sea*, Shirley Booth was once again the strongest character. In Brooklyn, New York, in the early 1900s, Miss Booth appeared as Lottie Gibson, onetime vaudeville trouper, now running a boarding house for show people in Coney Island. With that seaside resort as a backdrop, the romance of Lottie and a Shakespearian actor, Emery, develops. Three songs, to Dorothy Fields' lyrics, are of interest: "Alone Too Long," "More Love than Your Love" and "I'd Rather Wake Up by Myself."

In the fifties, Jule Styne continued to enrich the Broadway musical theater with his music. *Two on the Aisle* (1951) was a revue with sketches and lyrics by Betty Comden and Adolph Green, starring Bert Lahr and Dolores Gray. Miss Gray introduced the three best songs in this score: "If You Hadn't But You Did," "Give a Little, Get a Little Love" and "Hold Me, Hold Me, Hold Me." This was followed five years later by *Bells Are Ringing*, once again in collaboration with Betty Comden and Adolph Green, in which Judy Holliday made her sensational musical comedy debut. Her role was that of an operator in a telephone answering service who gets personally involved in the lives and affairs of her clients. Out of a bountiful score came three hit songs: "Just in Time," "The Party's Over" and "Long Before I Knew You."

Three years after that, in 1959, with Stephen Sondheim as his lyricist, Styne wrote the songs for *Gypsy*. Its book comes from Gypsy Rose Lee's autobiography. Ethel Merman was the stage mother of the two talented show girls, one of whom was Louise (representing Gypsy Rose Lee) and the other June (who became the motion picture actress, June Havoc). Glimpses into the backstage life of vaudeville and burlesque endowed *Gypsy* with its color and much of its vitality sprang from the conviction which Ethel Merman brought to a role uniquely suited to her temperament and talent. She sang (and brought the house down with) "Everything's Coming Up Roses," and participated in "Small World," and "Together Wherever We Go."

8

Among songwriters, some new faces appear. One of them is Stephen Sondheim, the lyricist for *West Side Story* and *Gypsy*. (In the 1960s and 1970s he became one of Broadway's foremost composer lyricists.) Born to wealthy parents in New York City in 1930, Sondheim received his academic education in private schools in or near New York. In one of them, he wrote the book and music for a school musical when he was fifteen. By then he and his mother were living on a farm in Doylestown, Pennsylvania (his mother having become divorced). They lived just a few miles from Oscar Hammerstein II who gave young Sondheim valuable instruction and direction in songwriting. Sondheim also learned much about writing for the stage, doing such chores for Hammerstein as typing scripts and performing minor duties during rehearsals of Rodgers and Hammerstein productions.

At Williams College, from which he was graduated in 1950, Sondheim wrote the book, lyrics and music for two college shows. Though he felt himself ready for a professional career in the theater by the time he left Williams, he continued his music study at Princeton University with Milton Babbitt.

Sondheim's first professional job in show business came in 1953 when he was engaged to write television scripts. A year later he wrote songs for his first professional musical which seemed headed for Broadway but never arrived. When his Broadway debut finally took place in 1956, it was with his incidental music to *Girls of Summer*. Arthur Laurents, the playwright, now asked him to adapt James M. Caine's *Serenade* into a musical comedy text. This production never got off the ground. But soon after that, Laurents brought Sondheim into an ambitious project then being devised by Jerome Robbins and Leonard Bernstein. This is how Sondheim became Bernstein's lyricist for *West Side Story*. *Gypsy* then gave him further prestige as a lyricist, with fame as a composer not far in the future.

Jerry Bock's name first gained significance on the Broadway scene with *Mr. Wonderful* (1956). Though born in New Haven, in 1928, Bock spent his boyhood in the boroughs of Bronx, Brooklyn and Queens in New York. While attending Flushing High School in Queens he took piano lessons. In his last year in high school he wrote the music for an amateur benefit show to raise money for a Navy hospital ship. After graduating, he enrolled in the School of Music at the University of Wisconsin where, in his third year, he wrote the music for a school production that toured the Midwest.

He came to New York in 1949 and for the next three years wrote songs for television shows produced by Max Liebman starring Sid Caesar and Imogene Coca. When television became increasingly reluctant to use original songs, Bock wrote the continuity, dialogue and special material for several television stars, including Kate Smith and Mel Tormé, and contributed three songs (lyrics by Larry Holofcener) to the Broadway revue, *Catch a Star!* (1955). In 1956, Jule Styne, then coproducing the Broadway musical *Mr. Wonderful*, called upon Bock and Holofcener, with George David Weiss, to write its songs. In *Mr. Wonderful*, Sammy Davis, Jr. was starred as a song-and-dance man in Union City, New Jersey, who becomes a nightclub star in an elaborate second act sequence providing Sammy Davis, Jr. with ample opportunities to display his versatility. *Mr. Wonderful* was not only Bock's first full-length Broadway show but also his first Broadway success. The title song became a hit as did "Too Close for Comfort."

"Too Close for Comfort" was sung by Sammy Davis, Jr. Though he was now making his Broadway debut, he was no newcomer to show business, having spent the previous quarter of a century in vaudeville, burlesque houses and nightclubs. Even before *Mr. Wonderful*, the extraordinary gamut of his performing talents had placed him as a top showman. Singer, dancer, pantomimist, impersonator, tap dancer, clown, drummer—all these facets of his performing art had been acclaimed even before he brightened the stage of the Broadway Theater in *Mr. Wonderful*.

Born in New York City in 1926, he was the son of entertainers. Sam and Elvira Davis, his parents, had appeared in Will Mastin's vaudeville act, *Holiday and Dixieland*, which toured the Keith, Loew and Pantages circuit. When the Davises appeared in a new Will Mastin act called *Creole*, Sammy Davis, Jr., aged three, became a member of the company and livened up the proceedings by mimicking the other performers. This act was finally reduced to three members: Sammy Davis, Sr., his son, Sammy, and Will Mastin, who had become the boy's adopted uncle. As the Will Mastin Trio they performed in vaudeville, burlesque houses and cabarets large and small. During these years of rigorous stage apprenticeship, the boy profited no end from the coaching in tap dancing he received from that king of tap dancers, Bill "Bojangles" Robinson.

After Sammy Davis, Jr. had served in the Army between 1943 and 1945, the Mastin Trio was revived. They met their first major success at Slapsie Maxie's nightclub in Hollywood where the younger Sammy often stole the whole show with mimicry, dancing and singing. Booked for a two-week run in a Los Angeles theater, the Mastin Trio stayed on for six months. After that they were headlined with Jimmy Dorsey at the Palace in Columbus, Ohio, with Frank Sinatra at the Capitol Theater in New York, and with Bob Hope and others in a giant benefit for the police in Los Angeles.

The Mastin Trio broke up in 1948. Sammy Davis, Jr., now on his own, could give full play to his many-faceted talents. At Ciro's in Hollywood, the Copacabana in New York, and plush hotels in Las Vegas, he rose to star status. Decca signed him to a recording contract in 1954 (he had previously made some records for Capitol). His first best-selling disk came that year with "Hey, There" (Richard Adler and Jerry Ross) followed one year later by "Something's Gotta Give" (Johnny Mercer).

In November 1954, Sammy was driving to a recording session in Hollywood from Las Vegas where he had been appearing at the Last Frontier. While listening over the car radio to his own recording of "Hey, There" (the first such experience for him) his car collided with another. Sammy ended in a hospital in San Bernardino where, three days after the accident, his left eye had to be removed.

Only a few weeks later, with a patch over his eye and his face badly bruised, he returned to the nightclub scene at Ciro's, in Hollywood, to receive a ten-minute ovation. He made the round of swank nightclubs after that, besides making guest appearances on such major television programs as Ed Sullivan's *The Toast of the Town*, the Milton Berle Show and the Colgate Comedy Hour. And only one and a half years after his accident he was a Broadway star in *Mr. Wonderful*.

Since *Mr. Wonderful*, he has become a superstar in nightclubs, on television, in theater and motion pictures and on records. On records (now on the Reprise label), between the gold disk he had earned for "What Kind of Fool Am I?" (Leslie Bricusse—Anthony Newley) in 1962 and the one he received a decade later for "Candy Man" (Leslie Bricusse—Anthony Newley) he had sold millions of disks. Among his best sellers during this period was "I've Gotta Be Me" (Walter Marks) issued by Reprise in 1968. In the theater he starred in *Golden Boy* (1964). He was Sporting Life in Samuel Goldwyn's motion-picture production of Gershwin's *Porgy and Bess* (1959). Among the other films in which his ability as an actor measured up well to his other performing gifts were: *The Benny Goodman Story* (1956), *Anna Lucasta* (1959), *Ocean's Eleven* (1960), *Pepe* (1960), *Sergeants 3* (1962), *Johnny Cool* (1963), *Robin and the Seven Hoods* (1964) and *Salt and Pepper* (1968). And he added still a new dimension to his creativity with his autobiography, *Yes I Can* (1965), written in collaboration with Jane and Burt Boyar.

But we must return to Jerry Bock's musicals.

Bock's collaboration with Holofcener ended with *Mr. Wonderful*. With *The Body Beautiful*, which lasted just two months on Broadway in 1958, his writing partnership with Sheldon Harnick began. Harnick was a young man from Chicago, born in 1924, who had received a thorough musical training in that city. After serving with the Army Signal Corps, he attended Northwestern University from which he was graduated with a degree of Bachelor of Music and where he wrote lyrics and music for a school production. In 1952, he contributed one song each to the Broadway revues *New Faces of 1952* and *Two's Company*. He continued writing both the words and music for songs used in other revues. Then when, in 1957, he teamed up with Bock, he decided to leave music to his partner and concentrate on the words.

Their first venture on Broadway was a failure; their second, a triumph. *Fiorello!* (1959) seized the three principal awards in the theater—the New York Drama Critics Circle, the Antoinette Perry and the Pulitzer Prize. Jerome Weidman and George Abbott wrote the book based on the career of New York's colorful, dynamic and rambunctious Mayor, Fiorello H. La Guardia. The book traced his career from his law practice in Greenwich Village in 1914 to his election as Mayor on a Fusion ticket. Satire as well as nostalgia and realism, helped make *Fiorello!* an unforgettable stage experience—the satire at its best in songs commenting acidly on graft in politics, "Politics and Poker," and "Little Tin Box." Nostalgia seeps through the ballad " 'Til Tomorrow," and sentiment through the ballad, "When Did I Fall in Love?"

Before he turned his impressive, versatile talents toward the stage, Meredith Willson had been a successful writer of popular songs. He came from Mason City, Iowa. Born in 1902, he learned to play the flute and piccolo while attending high school. In New York, where he arrived in 1919, he continued to study the flute at the Institute of Musical Art. For many years after that he was a flutist with the Sousa Band, Hugo Riesenfeld's orchestra at the

Rialto Theater in New York, and for five years with the New York Philharmonic Orchestra. Moving on to San Francisco in 1929, he was made music director of one of its radio stations and, in 1932, music director of the Western Division of NBC. He settled in Los Angeles in 1937 and was affiliated as music director of major network programs. He also wrote music for the screen, including scores for Charlie Chaplin's *The Great Dictator* (1940) and the Samuel Goldwyn production of *The Little Foxes* (1941). In 1941, his song "You and I" for which he wrote lyrics as well as music, stayed nineteen weeks on "Your Hit Parade" and was used as signature music for the Maxwell House "Good News" radio program of which Willson was music director; it was also made into a successful recording by Glenn Miller and his orchestra with Ray Eberle doing the vocal. Other Willson song hits were "Two in Love," introduced by Tommy Dorsey and his orchestra, with Frank Sinatra doing the vocal on a Victor recording; "May the Good Lord Bless and Keep You," sung after each program by Tallulah Bankhead and her guests on "The Big Show" over radio in 1950; and in 1953 "I See the Moon," introduced on the Arthur Godfrey TV show by The Mariners, that became the song most often requested by American troops during the Korean War.

Willson made a sensational entry into the Broadway musical theater in 1957 with *The Music Man*, a nostalgic, sentimental comedy of small town life in America in 1912, for which he wrote book, lyrics and music. The plot was concerned mainly with the successful effort of a visiting swindler (beautifully realized by Robert Preston) to sell the town of River City, Iowa, on forming a local boys' band. The tuneful score was galvanized by a resounding marching song, "Seventy-Six Trombones". Lilting ballads, "Goodnight, My Someone" and "Till There Was You," were not lacking. During its Broadway run of over 1,300 performances, *The Music Man* grossed over ten million dollars, had a national company touring for several years, was selected by the New York Music Critics Circle and the Antoinette Perry Awards as the season's best musical, and was made into a stunning motion picture by Warner Brothers in 1962.

Albert Hague's first full-length Broadway musical was *Plain and Fancy* (1955), one of the box-office successes of that season. Hague studied piano and composition in Berlin, Germany, where he was born in 1920, and at the Santa Cecilia Academy in Rome. In 1939 he came to the United States, continuing his musical training at the College of Music of the University of Cincinnati from which he was graduated in 1942. After two and a half years in the Air Force, during World War II, Hague turned from serious music to write the score for a musical production in Cleveland in 1946. One of its numbers, "One Is a Lonely Number," became Hague's first song to be heard on a Broadway stage, interpolated in *Dance Me a Song* (1950). But before this happened he had already worked for Broadway by writing the incidental music to *The Madwoman of Chaillot* (1948). For several years Hague wrote music for TV, for a Broadway play (Robert Anderson's *All Summer Long* in 1954), and for a movie short (*Coney Island, U.S.A.*) which won first prizes at the Edinburgh and Venice film festivals in 1951.

Plain and Fancy brought Hague his first significant recognition as a composer for the musical theater. The musical was set in Lancaster County, Pennsylvania, home of the Amish sect which pursues an insular life faithful to Amish speech, behavior, dress, ethics, and special outlook on life. Some of the musical highlights of *Plain and Fancy* were folksy songs describing the Amish way of life: "It Wonders Me" and "Plain We Live." A third song, "Young and Foolish" became one of the hit songs of 1955. All lyrics were by Arnold B. Horwitt.

With Dorothy Fields as his lyricist, Hague wrote the songs for *Redhead* (1959), winner of six Antoinette Perry Awards including that for the season's best musical. Gwen Verdon, fresh from her acclaim in *Damn Yankees* and *New Girl in Town*, virtually stole the show as a redheaded wench, Essie Whimple, who works in her aunt's wax museum in London. Bob Fosse's choreography in a music-hall sequence set to ragtime music, and another highlighting a music hall strut, were some of the visual attractions complementing the song highlights "Look Who's in Love" and "Just for Once."

PART SEVEN

Since 1960

39

Rock Around the Clock . . .

1

The vociferous detractors of rock were confident that rock was just a passing phenomenon, an ephemeral fad with the young. They were wrong. Having found a music of their own, and performers their own age who spoke for them authentically and without inhibitions, young people clung to rock whose influence and importance did not diminish in the sixties and seventies but was greatly augmented. The record business swelled into a two-billion dollar industry. Still more millions were spent by the young on rock concerts and festivals and in the purchase of commodities merchandized to exploit the popularity of rock performers.

Rock music changed radically in the Sixties and Seventies. From its primitive beginnings in the Fifties, it became subtler and more sophisticated. Rock now absorbed some of the idioms of serious modern music and even the electrified instruments (and in the Seventies the electronic ones) of avant-garde composers. It sometimes looked back, utilizing older modes and some of the stylistic practices of baroque music. It also enlisted the resources of such esoteric instruments as the sitar and the dulcimer, and instruments unknown to earlier rock such as the oboe, and on occasion even the harpsichord and baroque trumpet. Vocally it made use of such devices as falsetto, portamento, and *Sprechstimme*, the song-speech which Arnold Schoenberg developed in his expressionist music. It wandered into the Far East by borrowing not only the instruments of India but also the idioms of the Indian raga. Rock lyrics now outgrew the guttural, often indistinguishable diction as well as the sophomoric sentiments of the Fifties. Songs reached toward the poetic, the symbolic, the mystical —all the better to pinpoint the moods of the times. Through such varied means,

611

rock in the Sixties was becoming an art that appealed almost as strongly to the intelligentsia as to the young.

Rock employed many different sounds and techniques, but it remained rock, either as a carryover from the frenetic Fifties (later identified as "hard rock"), or the more subdued and moodier music of the late Sixties that came to be known as "soft rock." There was folk rock and raga rock, acid or psychedelic rock, jazz rock and classical rock, blues rock and soul rock, country rock and glitter rock, sex rock and punk rock.

Just as Elvis Presley dominated rock in the Fifties, and was largely responsible for the character it assumed, so the propelling force of the rock of the Sixties was the Beatles. This foursome from England not only revolutionized the structure, style and techniques of rock but they became a social force, and the most profitable commodity the rock market had so far known. With a somewhat different complement than the one that captured world fame, the Beatles first attracted attention at the Cavern, a jazz club in Liverpool, England. They appeared there almost three hundred times between December of 1960 and February of 1962, and built up a dedicated following. In the summer of 1961, a local disc jockey wrote in a Liverpool "beat" journal: "Why do you think the Beatles are so popular? They resurrected original rock 'n' roll, the origins of which are to be found in American Negro singers. . . . The Beatles exploded on a jaded scene. . . . Here was the excitement, both physical and aural, that symbolized the rebellion of youth. . . . An act which from beginning to end is a succession of climaxes. A personality cult. Seemingly unambitious, yet fluctuating between the self assured and the vulnerable. . . . Such are the fantastic Beatles. I don't think anything like them will happen again."

John Lennon was the group's accepted leader. He played the piano, guitar, harmonica and did vocals. His father deserted the family when John was three, and his mother died in an automobile accident eleven years later. Raised by an aunt who gave him some music lessons, John's interest in music was sparked by Elvis Presley records which made him a dedicated rock 'n' roll enthusiast. For two years he attended the Liverpool College for Art. Although he showed some talent for drawing, his interest and enthusiasm lay elsewhere. In 1958, he and his friend and fellow student, Paul McCartney, organized the Nurk Twins, an act which performed in Liverpool and in southern England and was sometimes described as "the British Everly Brothers." Joined that year by George Harrison and Peter Best, they became the Quarrymen Skiffle Group, and after that were intermittently renamed as the Moondogs, the Moonshiners, the Silver Beatles and finally—at the Litherland Town Hall in 1960—the Beatles. Now a fifth member, Stuart Sutcliffe, bass guitarist, joined the group. The Beatles were heard in Liverpool, in the Reeperbahn, Hamburg's red-light district, and in Scotland. John Lennon who coined the name of "Beatles" explained: "I was thinking about what a good name the Crickets would be for an English group. The idea of beetles came into my head. I decided to spell it Beatles to make it look like beat music, just a joke." They wore boy gear, tight black jeans, a white shirt with black ribbon tie and long hair. Sometimes they wrote their own songs, the work of John Lennon and Paul McCartney. They experimented with unusual effects for rock, such as sounds from a washboard. They cavorted about the stage like a group of hoydens, with many of their stage shenanigans the result of suddenly conceived improvisations.

Paul McCartney—who played piano, guitar, fuzz bass and sang vocals—was fifteen when he met Lennon in 1958. Born in a Liverpool suburb, McCartney was an adept student at school where his strongest course was English literature. For a time he thought of becoming a teacher. But after meeting Lennon, he found music more to his liking and became one of the Nurk Twins. George Harrison also drifted into the McCartney and Lennon orbit in 1958. He was to become the lead guitarist and would experiment with the sitar. The son of a Liverpool merchant seaman, Harrison attended the Liverpool Institute. He enjoyed cricket, soccer and swimming, and taught himself to strum the guitar by listening to the recordings of Chet Atkins and Andrés Segovia. His professional musical career began before he joined Lennon and McCartney when he appeared with small groups in Liverpool, one of which was The Rebels, an apprenticeship that was a valuable asset when he joined Lennon and McCartney to form the Quarrymen Skiffle Group that got a hearing at the Casbah in Liverpool.

As the Beatles, Lennon, McCartney, Harrison, Sutcliffe and Peter Best made some recordings in Germany. One day, in October of 1961, Brian Epstein, the owner of a Liverpool record shop, received a request for a Beatle recording. Curiously, in view of their popularity at the Casbah, Epstein had never heard about this group. Epstein decided to investigate. He visited the Casbah and had his first exposure to the Beatles. "They were not very tidy," he later recalled, "and not very clean. They smoked as they played and they ate and talked and pretended to hit each other. They turned their backs on the audience and shouted at people and laughed at private jokes. But there was quite clearly enormous excitement. They seemed to give off some sort of personal magnetism. I was fascinated by them." He became immediately convinced that they were something big, but only if they could be harnessed and yet left untamed.

Brian Epstein became their manager. His first job was to give them a fresh and presentable image. He had them adopt a new wardrobe: a collarless four button coat, stovepipe trousers and ankle boots, a costume which, combined with their long hairdos, became their trademark. He had them discipline their performance without curbing altogether their innate animal energy. He introduced class and style into their act and got them better bookings in Hamburg and more bookings throughout England. He arranged for them to make their television debut in London in October 1962, and to make recordings for EMI (Electrical and Musical Industries, Ltd.) whose European label was Parlaphone, and American label, Capitol.

Their first English single was "Love Me Do" backed by "P.S. I Love You," both songs written by Lennon and McCartney. It was released on October 4, 1962 and reached number seventeen on the British charts. By the time they had made this record, Stu Sutcliffe had left the Beatles to devote himself to art. (He died soon after of a brain tumor.) One other change had come to the group. At the insistence of a recording executive at EMI, a newcomer replaced Pete Best at the drums. He was Ringo Starr (Richard Starkey, officially), the nickname "Ringo" came to him from his passions for rings. He came from a working class suburb of Liverpool, the son of a house painter. Between his sixth and twelfth years Ringo Starr was a persistent patient in and out of hospitals for various operations; at one time it seemed doubtful he would survive. He left school when he was fourteen, and worked at odd jobs, including playing the drums at dances and in clubs. In 1960, during an engagement in Hamburg, he met the Beatles. Later on in Liverpool he was sometimes called upon to substitute for Pete Best and in 1962 he became a permanent member of the Beatles.

The personnel of the Beatles was now crystallized: John Lennon, Paul McCartney, George Harrison and Ringo Starr. They complemented each other. John Lennon was raucous and flashy. Paul McCartney had an infectious impish quality. George Harrison was arty. Ringo Starr possessed a childlike ingenuousness that made his female admirers want to protect and mother him. Together they had a boyish verve, a youthful excitement, a joy of life, and a disarming disdain for conventional behavior, an effervescent sense of humor, and a likable avoidance of sham and pretense. They were themselves on stage and off it—boisterous, sometimes vulgar, scruffy and thoroughly charming.

In 1963, the Beatles made three more records for EMI: "Please Please Me," "From Me to You" and "She Loves You," all by John Lennon and Paul McCartney. On the day of its release, "She Loves You" had an advance sale of five hundred thousand records, and became the most successful single ever cut by any British performer. (It was in this number that the Beatles introduced the exclamation "yeah, yeah," which they made famous in the world of rock.) Their first LP, *Please Please Me*, was Number One in the British charts.

By the fall of 1963 all England seemed stricken with "Beatlemania." On October 13, 1963, they were the top attraction at the Palladium in London. So unruly were the mobs outside the theater come to pay homage to the Beatles, that newspapermen and television cameras were dispatched to Argyll Street to report the phenomenon. In the theater itself, there were hysterical outbursts before during and after each number. Since the performance was put on tape for television transmission, the audience numbered some fifteen million. "From that day on," said Epstein, "everything changed. My job was never the same again. From spending six months ringing up newspapers and getting 'no,' I now had every national reporter and feature writer chasing *me*."

The Beatles made one-night stands in England and Sweden where, in some instances, police had to use dogs to keep the adulating mobs in check. On November 4, the Beatles brought down the house at the Prince of Wales Theater in London, where they shared the program with Marlene Dietrich, Maurice Chevalier and Sophie Tucker before an audience that included the Queen Mother, Princess Margaret and Lord Snowdon. This show was also televised to some twenty-six million viewers throughout the kingdom.

Beatlemania had many manifestations. One was the eruption of rock groups in Liverpool: the Searchers, Gerry and the Pacemakers, the Mojos, the Swinging Blue Jeans, the Undertakers, the Merseybeats and hundreds more. Beatlemania was young men wearing black jackets or black turtleneck sweaters, the costume then favored by the Beatles, and Beatle wigs that simulated the Beatles hairdo. Beatlemania was the condemnation by some members of the Church of England, with one bishop bitterly describing the Beatles as a "psychopathetic group," and an English vicar facetiously suggesting that the Beatles tape for Christmas a carol, "Oh Come All Ye Faithful, Yeah, Yeah!" Beatlemania was the complaint in Parliament that thousands of policemen had to be recruited from their duties to protect the Beatles wherever they appeared. Beatlemania was Dora Bryan making a hit recording of "All I Want for Christmas is a Beatle," and it was five newspapers serializing their life story within a single week. Beatlemania was the staid and knowledgeable music critic, William Mann, calling John Lennon and Paul McCartney "the outstanding English composers of 1963," and Richard Buckle maintaining in the *Sunday Times* that they were "the greatest composers since Beethoven." Beatlemania was the advance sale of one million disks for their fifth single, "I Want to Hold Your Hand" (again by Lennon and McCartney) which, on the day of its release, immediately zoomed to top place in the British charts. Beatlemania was the advance of two hundred and fifty thousand copies for their second LP, *Meet the Beatles*, probably the largest advance attained by an album up to then. Beatlemania was the sale of two and a half million Beatle records in the single year of 1963, the largest sale for any performer in British pop music, with seven of their records in the top twenty. Beatlemania was *Newsweek* reporting from England that the Beatles produced "a sound that is one of the most persistent noises heard over England since the air-raid sirens were dismantled."

Then, early in 1964, Beatlemania struck the United States. Thousands of screaming youngsters, singing "We Love You Beatles, Oh Yes We Do," swarmed over Kennedy International Airport to welcome the Beatles' arrival in America on February 7 for their first American appearances. Thousands more choked the streets near the Plaza Hotel where the Beatles were staying. At their first public appearance in the United States, twenty thousand jammed the Coliseum in New York. For the first of two television appearances on the Ed Sullivan Show, fifty thousand had requested admission tickets for an auditorium seating seven hundred; it was estimated that seventy-five million people heard and saw that telecast. For their only New York concert, in Carnegie Hall, it was impossible to beg, steal or buy an admission ticket one half hour after the box office opened. Fifty million dollars worth of Beatle commodities were marketed: Beatle sweat shirts, wigs, dolls, posters, buttons, tee shirts, soft drinks, magazines, trousers, electric guitars. In just four weeks time, two and one half million copies of their records were sold by Capitol which now had them on exclusive contract, bringing them a royalty of a quarter of a million dollars. Twelve of the singles topped the best-selling charts.

Beatlemania in the United States was also to exert a terrifying influence upon one group of religious cultists. From *Helter Skelter*, the story of the Manson murders, by Vincent Bugliosi with Curt Gentry, we discover that Charles Manson regarded some of the songs by the Beatles as "prophecy." The Beatles' song "Helter Skelter" contributed the name for the bizarre cult of Manson and his followers; the songs the Manson "family" played most often, besides "Helter Skelter" were "Blackbird," "Revolution I," and "Revolution 9," all written by John Lennon and Paul McCartney, and "Piggies" by George Harrison, each of which seemed to uncover a message that had particular relevance to their cause.

Beatlemania persisted not only in England and the United States but throughout the civilized world as long as the four remained a performing unit, and to some degree after they had split. Their sixth single, "Can't Buy Me Love" (Lennon and McCartney) had an advance sale of three million records in 1964. That year, the Beatles appeared in their first motion picture, *A Hard Day's Night*, which not only was a sensation at the box-office but which surprisingly earned kudos from the critics. For their recording of the title song, the Beatles earned a Grammy for the best performance by a vocal group on records that year.

In the summer of 1964, the Beatles toured Europe, Hong Kong, Australia and New Zealand, and in the fall of the same year they made their first extensive tour of the United States. For a single appearance in Kansas City they were paid $150,000; in that city the pillow slips and bed sheets on which they slept were cut into 160,000 one-inch squares and sold for a dollar a piece. At Shea Stadium in Queens, New York, they grossed over $300,000 for one concert and were paid $160,000. On June 12, 1965, they were made Members of the Order of the British Empire, to the delight of their British fans, and to the horror of members of Parliament. "We are now more popular than Christ," remarked John Lennon with typical Beatle irreverence.

The last of four American tours took place in August 1966, with their final public appearance anywhere taking place in San Francisco on August 29. For a time they continued making records, a TV film *(Magical Mystery Tour)* and motion pictures *(Help!* and *Yellow Submarine)*. The sudden death of their manager, Brian Epstein, in 1967, from an overdose of drugs, led them to create a new firm, Apple, which controlled all their interests in records, films, music publications, merchandising, TV, literature and electronics.

In the latter part of their careers as a foursome, the Beatles experimented with LSD, then gave it up to become involved with the transcendental meditation movement of the Maharishi Mahesh Yogi. Interestingly enough, the year of LSD and the Maharishi was one of their most productive. They wrote and recorded sixteen new songs in a six month period. They produced and appeared in the film for TV, *Magical Mystery Tour*, whose songs became a best-selling record album. Their song, "Michelle" (a part of which McCartney sang in French) and "Eleanor Rigby" (whose instrumental effectiveness was intensified by staccato strings) won Grammys, the former as the best song of the year, and the latter as the best rock vocal performance.

What they had accomplished as recording artists was without precedent. In less than a decade they sold 125 million singles and 85 million LPs, the royalties amounting to 100 million dollars. As their share for the writing of the songs, Lennon and McCartney drew an additional eighteen million dollars in royalties. Even after the Beatles broke up, their records continued to sell astronomically. One year after the dissolution of the group, the combined record product was still drawing twenty four million dollars in royalties.

When Ringo Starr, George Harrison and John Lennon (and Lennon's wife, Yoko) each began making records of their own, the public became aware that the Beatles were breaking up. The breakup became a reality in April 1970 when Paul McCartney announced he was parting company permanently with the Beatles, and then went on to record an album by himself in which he sang and played all the instruments (with his wife, Linda, providing some vocal harmonies). In January 1975, the partnership of the Beatles was dissolved legally by a judge in a private hearing in London.

As long as they were on the rock scene together, the Beatles kept growing artistically, and rock grew with them. At the beginning of their career, they returned to the traditions of rhythm and blues. Later, they brought to rock a dynamism and a kinesthetic appeal that for a time seemed permanently lost. True to the traditions from which early rock emerged were the Beatle performances of "Twist and Shout" (Bert Russell and Phil Medley), Chuck Berry's "Roll Over Beethoven" and "Rock and Roll Music" and that Little Richard specialty, "Long Tall Sally" (Enotris Johnson, Richard Penniman, and Robert A. Blackwell). At the same time, a Beatles song like "I Want to Hold Your Hand" was characteristic of the kind of simple, direct number with little innovation in the music and with an uncomplicated message in the lyrics to which John Lennon and Paul McCartney were at first partial. In this simple ballad category we find such poignant numbers as "And I Love Her" and "If I Fell" from the motion picture and LP album, A *Hard Day's Night*. Their versatility also extended to novelty ("Yellow Submarine"), social comment ("Nowhere Man" and "Eleanor Rigby"), all three from the motion picture *Yellow Submarine*; and even to country and western ("I've Just Seen a Face" from the album *Rubber Soul*).

Under the careful guidance and knowledgeable direction of George Martin, their recording producer, the performing and creative styles of the Beatles underwent continual growth and development. As performers they controlled and disciplined their early style and added professionalism and polish to their stage department. As songwriters, John Lennon and Paul McCartney grew increasingly innovative in seeking out bold harmonies and in experimenting with classic or baroque styles. In one of their finest ballads, "Yesterday," a solo cello accompanies the voice of Paul McCartney. "Penny Lane" called upon cornets to suggest a dimly audible summer-day band concert. "In My Life," from *Rubber Soul*, has instrumental passages that sound as if they came from a harpsichord (produced by accelerating a taped piano performance). In that same album, foreign languages, and such esoteric instruments as the harmonium, fuzz bass, electric piano, and the sitar are introduced. The novel sounds from kazoos and combs, are neighbors to exotic ones from oriental instruments and electronic devices in *Sergeant Pepper's Lonely Hearts Club Band*, an album that won the "Grammy" as the best of the year. Here are opened up not only new vistas for rock music but also for rock lyrics which achieve the symbolic, the allegorical, the mystic and the dadaistic. *Sergeant Pepper* is a song cycle, the first in rock, whose underlying thesis is propounded in the first number, the title song, and continues without a break into the second number, "A Little Help from My Friends," and is reprised toward the end of the cycle. There is no break either between the last three numbers: "Good Morning, Good Morning," the reprise of the opening title number, and the closing song, "A Day in Life." Of one of the songs in this album, "She's Leaving Home," Ned Rorem (probably America's most gifted composer of art songs) insisted that it was "equal to any song Schubert wrote." Of the album as a whole, Nik Cohn said in *Rock:* "*Sergeant Pepper* was . . . the first try ever at making a pop album into something more than just twelve songs bundled together at random. It was an overall concept. . . . It was ideas, allusions, pastiches, ironies . . . Added up, it came to something quite ambitious; it made strange images of isolation, and it sustained."

2

The Beatles was the most prominent of the many English rock groups that crossed the Atlantic to overwhelm the American scene, reversing a tide that had been sending a steady stream of American rock performers to England. Among the most successful of these English groups were the Rolling Stones, Herman's Hermits, the Dave Clark Five, The Who and Led Zeppelin (also Blind Faith, the Animals, Slade, the Zombies, Jethro Tull, and Pink Floyd).

There were five "rolling stones." Mick Jagger was the lead vocalist who also played the harmonica; Keith Richard was lead guitar who did some of the vocals; Brian Jones played the rhythm guitar, the harmonica and the sitar; Charles Watts was the drummer, and Bill Wyman played the bass guitar. They were a tough bunch, hostile, even menacing looking —five youngsters behaving as if they had come to the stage straight from the gutter. They wore their hair even longer than did the Beatles, and were always shabbily attired. They sneered, grunted, groaned and made obscene gestures and grimaces. Lillian Roxon remarked: "Beatles' songs had been rinsed and hung out to dry. The Stones' had never seen soap and water. And where the adorable little windup Beatle moptops wanted no more than to hold a hand, the rasping Stones were bent on rape, pillage and plunder."

They got their name from Muddy Waters' song, "Rolling Stone." The bluesman Muddy Waters was one of their two inspirations, the other being Chuck Berry. The music making of the Rolling Stones, then, was firmly grounded in rhythm and blues, and the blues of black America. The subject matter of their best songs written by two of their members —Mick Jagger and Keith Richard—was a fitting voice for a rebellious generation that felt its freedoms inhibited and chained by conventions and traditions: their greatest song hits, "Satisfaction" "Get Off My Cloud" and "19th Nervous Breakdown."

The five members of the Rolling Stones came to know one another at the Marquee Club in London where they used to congregate to listen to rock. With Ian Stewart, a pianist and maraca player, they formed a rock sextet. Stewart soon withdrew from the performing group to become its road manager. In 1962, the Rolling Stones began an engagement at the Crawdaddy Club, in Richmond, Surrey, where they remained for over a year and became so popular that they were signed to a recording contract by British Decca. Andrew Loog Oldham, a flashy nineteen-year old partial to outlandish clothes, became their manager and skillfully helped them develop the disagreeable and disreputable identities that carried them to world popularity.

Of all the Rolling Stones, it was Mick Jagger who was the cynosure on whom the eyes of the young would be transfixed, and the one who released their hidden emotions and gave substance to their secret fantasies. He was, as *Time* once said of him, "the king bitch of rock" and possibly "the supreme sexual object in modern Western culture." Born in Dartford, Kent, in 1944, Jagger was attending the London School of Economics on a government grant when he became a "rolling stone." He stayed on in school for two years between 1963 and 1965 before he decided to devote himself exclusively to his performing career. Attractive in a boyish sort of way, with his baby face, impish eyes and sensual lips, he seized and held the center of interest both for his gaudy attire (sequined skintight jump suits, huge metal studded belts, gold dust sprinkled over his hairdo) and his even gaudier behavior. He was the personification of sexuality in the jerky movements of his body as he sang, or the way he stuck out his tongue midway in a song, or the lascivious way he would mouth his harmonica.

The first recording of the Rolling Stones came in 1963—"Come On" (Mick Jagger and Keith Richard), number twenty on the British charts. Their second, "I Wanna Be Your Man" (John Lennon and Paul McCartney) reached number ten; their third, "Not Fade Away" (Charles Hardin and Norman Petty), number three; and their fourth, "It's All Over Now" (Mick Jagger and Keith Richard), number one. "Not Fade Away" and "It's All Over Now"—together with "Carol," "Good Times" and "If You Need Me," all of them by Jagger and Richard—were gathered in the first Rolling Stones album, *The Rolling Stones*, released in May of 1964. It stayed in the top spot on the British charts for twelve weeks, selling two hundred thousand copies in its first year. This sale was more than doubled by their second album, *The Rolling Stones Now*, released in February of 1965. In 1965 they had three gold records with "The Last Time," "Get Off of My Cloud" and "Satisfaction" (all again by Jagger and Richard), with "Satisfaction" hitting the top spot on the American charts for six weeks. Within the next two years they got more gold records for "Ruby Tuesday" and the albums *Got 'Live' If You Want It* and *Flowers*. Other best-selling albums in that time were *Out of Our Heads* (which had "Hitch Hike," "The Last Time" and "Satisfaction") in November 1965; *Big Hits* in March 1966 (with "19th Nervous Breakdown," "Not Fade Away" and "The Last Time"); *Aftermath* in June 1966 (with "Paint It Black" and "Under My Thumb"); and *Between Buttons*, in January 1967 (with "Ruby Tuesday").

Aftermath represented a major change of style and pace for them, with some of the rough edges of their delivery smoothed out, their former brute force and vulgarity often replaced by sardonic attitudes, their raucous sounds softened and mellowed by the gentle tones of a dulcimer or a sitar. They made a further attempt at changing style and material with the album *Their Satanic Majesties Request*, released in November 1967, in which they aspired to make a *Sergeant Pepper* album of their own with a not altogether happy venture into psychedelic music.

They made their first tour of the United States in 1964 which was a triumph from first appearance to last, as were each of their performances during the next two American tours in 1965 and 1966. Then, in 1967, the Rolling Stones came upon unhappy days. Jagger, Richards and Jones were all indicted on drug charges, becoming the first important rock performers in England arrested for drug abuse. The attendant publicity, made all the more combustible by the heat of those who were convinced the sentences had been too harsh, halted the further progress of the Rolling Stones—but only temporarily. After Jagger's sentence was reduced by a higher court to a one-year probation, and Richard's conviction was overturned, the Stones started rolling again. Their albums *Beggar's Banquet* and *Through the Past Darkly* (the latter an album of previous hits) in 1968 and 1969 and their single "Honky Tonk Women" in 1969 were all gold records. One of the numbers in *Beggar's Banquet*—which Carl Bernstein of the Washington *Post* called "their rawest, lewdest, most arrogant, most savage record yet," but "beautiful"—was the provocative "Sympathy for the

Devil." A filming of the studio recording of this rock number was used by Jean-Luc Godard in his motion picture *One Plus One* (1970).

A new tour of the United States in 1969 which was paved with still more triumphs ended in disaster. In gratitude for their American successes, the Rolling Stones gave a free concert at the Altamont Speedway near San Francisco on December 6, 1969. A gang of Hells Angels (allegedly hired to protect the Rolling Stones) burst in on their performance on motorcycles, creating bedlam. They beat up some of the audience, stabbed others and killed one of them in their mad stampede. Since violence had attended earlier performances of the Rolling Stones, many held them directly responsible for this outrage, feeling that their performances—and particularly those of Mick Jagger—were an open invitation to riots.

The Rolling Stones did not return to the United States for about a year and a half during which they toured Europe. After a sensational concert at the Royal Albert Hall in London they were given a party where they were presented with twenty gold records representing their million-disk sales. Mick Jagger was starred in two motion pictures released in 1970: *Performance* and *Ned Kelly*. Then, in 1972, the Rolling Stones returned to the United States for their most successful tour up to that time, grossing four million dollars for fifty-two concerts in thirty-two cities. During this national tour, fifteen of their numbers at various concerts were filmed and combined into the color-film concert, *Ladies and Gentlemen, the Rolling Stones*, released in 1974. In 1975, the Rolling Stones embarked upon one of their most ambitious and successful tours, "Tour of the Americas," during which they made their first appearances in Latin America (Mexico, Brazil and Venezuela). Sold-out auditoriums were the rule beginning with the first of their fifty-eight concerts (at Louisiana State University in Baton Rouge on June 1) and ending in Caracas, Venezuela, on August 31. It has been estimated that one and a half million people payed over twelve and a half million dollars to hear them.

Switching record companies to their own label, Rolling Stones, marketed by Atlantic, the Stones released *Sticky Fingers*, *Exile on Main Street* (which brought them a gold record in 1972), *Goats Head Soup* and *It's Only Rock and Roll*, *Made in the Shade* (a gold record in 1975) and *Black and Blue*. On the Abko label they recorded *Metamorphosis* in 1975.

With their cuteness, and their infectious ways, Herman's Hermits were an antidote to the Rolling Stones. Herman's Hermits did little to advance rock, preferring to concentrate on "bubble gum rock," trivial songs about teenage love. American youngsters, pliable in their tastes, doted on the wholesome Hermits even as they did on the Rolling Stones. By the end of 1965, Herman's Hermits sold over fourteen million records in the United States and appeared in two motion pictures produced by MGM.

"Herman" was Peter Noone, a round-faced, ingenuous looking English lad with dimples and buck teeth. He had been the lead singer, as well as pianist and guitarist, of a Manchester rock group called The Heartbeats. His colleagues there called him Herman because he resembled a cartoon character named Sherman in an English television show, and "hermits" was eventually added to Herman because of the pleasing alliteration. The other "hermits" were Keith Hapwood, guitar; Karl Green, guitar and harmonica; Barry Whitwam, drums; and Derek Leckenby, guitar. Mickie Most, an independent record producer, got them a recording contract. Their first release was "I'm into Something Good" (Gerry Goffin—Carole King) in 1964. On the British Columbia label it sold over half a million disks, and on the American MGM release, a quarter of a million disks in its first ten days. Before the passing of many months, this record reached the million mark in global sales. No less than six of their singles in 1965 sold a million disks each, among them "I'm Henry the Eighth, I Am" (Fred Murray and R. P. Weston) and "Mrs. Brown, You've Got a Lovely Daughter" (Trevor Peacock), the latter become one of their most famous numbers. They recorded it only because they needed one more cut to fill out their first American LP, *Introducing Herman's Hermits,* which they released during their first American tour in 1965. That album contained their entire repertory. Since one additional song was needed, Peter Noone decided as an afterthought to include "Mrs. Brown, You've Got a Lovely Daughter" which had been written two years earlier and made popular in a British television play. American disc jockeys were so delighted with this number, and played it so repeatedly, that MGM released it as a single disk which had an advance sale of six hundred thousand disks and sold over a million within four weeks.

Introducing Herman's Hermits was a certified gold record; and so were *Herman's Hermits on Tour* in 1965, *The Best of Herman's Hermits* in 1967, and the single "There's a Kind of Hush" (Les Reed and Geoff Stevens).

The Dave Clark Five made news in English rock circles in 1963 by becoming the first British group to usurp the top place in the British charts from the Beatles. They did it with the Epic recording of "Glad All Over", written by Dave Clark with Mike Smith. Clark was the drummer of the ensemble whose percussion effects combined with the strident sonorities of the other members led to the creation of what came to be known in rock as "the Tottenham sound." A handsome young man with a winning smile and a dashing manner, Clark had been a stunt man and bit player in the movies before he formed his rock group with Lenny Davidson, a clerk, at the guitar, Rick Huxley, a lighting engineer, at the guitar and banjo, Denis Payton, an electronic engineer, at tenor sax, guitar, harmonica and clarinet, and Mike Smith, a finance correspondent, at piano and vibes besides serving as lead vocalist. They met for the first time in a gymnasium where they decided to form a rock group to raise money for Dave Clark's football club. Then, for three nights a week, they were heard in a ballroom in Tottenham, made some records for a small company, and were the recipients of the Mecca Gold Cup as the best band of 1963. Their popularity was enhanced when they were invited to appear at the annual Buckingham Palace Ball, and it was firmly solidified in 1964 with their Columbia recording of "Glad All Over," which held top place on the British charts for two weeks and sold just under a million disks in Great Britain. This success brought them a contract from the promoter, Harold Davison, to appear in concerts, including their first tour of the United States in 1964 during which "Glad All Over" was released under the Epic label to sell over a million disks. Other gold records came their way that same year: "Bits and Pieces" and "Can't You See That She's Mine?" which Clark wrote with Mike Smith, and "Because" and "Any Way You Want It," written by Clark without collaboration. Three more gold records were achieved in 1965 with "I Like It Like That" (Chris Kenner and Allen Toussaint), "Catch Us If You Can" (Dave Clark and Leonard Davidson) and "Over and Over" (Robert Byrd), and in 1966 with the LP, *The Dave Clark Five's Biggest Hits.* In the 1960s, The Dave Clark Five was seen and heard in the motion pictures *Get Yourself a College Girl* (1964) and *Having a Wild Weekend* (1965), both produced in the United States, with the soundtrack of the latter, released by Epic, finding a place in the charts in 1967.

The Who was many things in one. It was the Mod generation obsessed with freakish, frilly, expensive Carnaby Street clothes. It was the Cyrano de Bergerac nose of Peter Townshend and his jacket made from the Union Jack. It was the maniacal goings-on during performance, the smashing of a guitar, the enraged kicking of drums, the tearing of amplifiers and microphones and throwing a mike around a performer's head or smashing it against the head of the drum. It was the release of a smoke bomb, it was feedback, it was raising the decibels of hard rock sound until the ears were split and the head throbbed painfully. But most of all it was the pop songs of Peter Townshend—"My Generation," which virtually became the anthem of the teenage set in England, "Substitute," "Mary-Anne with the Shaky Hands," "I'm a Boy," "I Can See for Miles," "Happy Jack," "Pictures of Lily," "Pinball Wizard"—all of which, when rid of the mayhem and madness that accompanied their performance, proved to be some of the best rock music to come out of England in the Sixties and Seventies.

The Who was a quartet of performers: Peter Townshend, guitar; John Entwistle, bass; Keith Moon, drums; Roger Daltrey, lead vocalist. They first got together as a group in 1963 as Hi-Numbers. Chris Stamp (brother of the distinguished English composer, Constance Lambert) became their manager, changed their name to The Who, and began to fashion them in an image and sound all their own. They clicked big in England, being adopted by the Mods as their own pet group. In 1966 they made their first tour of the United States, but at first made little noise as competitors to the Rolling Stones or Herman's Hermits. But one year later their exhibitionist wrecking act became one of the highlights of the Monterey Pop Festival, and during that same year of 1967 they had their first American hit record with Peter Townshend's "Happy Jack" on Decca. They later acquired gold records for their LPs, *Live at Leeds* in 1970, *Who's Next*, in 1971, *Meaty, Beaty, Big and Bouncy* in 1971 (this one made up of previously released material) and *By the Numbers* in 1975.

Peter Townshend wrote the book, lyrics and music for the rock opera, *Tommy*, to which other members of The Who contributed special numbers. It began as a British TV production in 1968, and in 1968 and 1969 went on to become a smash record album both in England and the United States, in time selling more than ten million copies. It went on from there to be performed on the stage by The Who at the London Coliseum in 1969 and at the Metropolitan Opera House in 1970, and to be produced by symphony orchestras, ballet companies and various troupes in the United States. It ended up as a spectacular motion picture released by Columbia Pictures in 1975, starring Ann-Margret and Oliver Reed, with Roger Daltrey of The Who assuming the title role, other members of The Who in subsidiary parts, and Elton John featured as the Pinball Wizard. Four new members were added to the movie, but the mainstay of its score, as of earlier productions, were "The Acid Queen," "I'm Free," "Pinball Wizard," "We're Not Gonna Take It," and "Listen to Me, See Me, Feel Me," in all of which the beat was strong and loud within a score that, in its amplification in multitrack Quintophonic Sound, was an outburst of orgiastic sounds.

Of the newer English rock groups the most successful by far has been Led Zeppelin which belongs to the money-making class of the Beatles and the Rolling Stones. This is a foursome comprising Jimmy Page, guitarist, Robert Plant, vocalist, John Paul Jones (pseudonym for John Baldwin), bass and keyboard, and John Bonham, percussion. Jimmy Page was the founding father of this group. He was born in Middlesex, England, and he first became fascinated with rock through Chuck Berry's records. When he was fifteen he learned to play the guitar while attending art school in London. Before long he was performing weekend dates with small rock outfits. By the time he was twenty he had become one of the best recording guitarists in London, working with The Who, the Yardbirds and other rock groups, besides doing solo stints. As a member of the Yardbirds, with whom he remained until it was dissolved in 1968, Jimmy Page came to know its manager, Peter Grant, and won his interest in starting a new rock outfit with himself as guitarist and one of his friends, John

Paul Jones, on bass as its nucleus. After Bonham and Plant were added to make up the foursome, Grant made a deal with Atlantic Records. It was for this recording that the group acquired its name of Led Zeppelin. *Led Zeppelin*, their first album which included "Good Times, Bad Times" (Jimmy Page, John Paul Jones and John Bonham), cost $3,800 to produce and in time it grossed seven million dollars, becoming a gold record in the United States in 1969. After the release of this album, Led Zeppelin came to the United States, giving its first performance at the Fillmore East in New York City where their debut proved to be such dynamite that it rocked the auditorium and the audience. The group was forced to play for four hours, stopping only after it had exhausted all of its material. One gold record followed another for the albums *Led Zeppelin II*, *Led Zeppelin III*, *House of the Holy* and *Physical Graffiti*, *Brass Connection*, and *The Song Remains the Same*, the last being the sound track of a motion picture starring the group, released in 1976. Through their records and public appearances in Europe and America, and at most of the major rock festivals including Woodstock in 1969, Led Zeppelin has been grossing about thirty million dollars a year since 1970, with their shrewd manager, Peter Grant, asking and getting ninety percent of the gate gross wherever they appeared.

They come to their public performances equipped with one hundred and fifty lights, including crypton laser beams, a Led Zeppelin neon sign, lighting towers, smoke machines, thunder puffs and an amplifying system that could make them heard a mile away. "Their performance on stage," explains Tony Palmer, "is overwhelming. . . . The tearing, shouting, shrieking sound explodes and explodes, yet its counterpoint remains icily clear. There is no theater like it, no action painting which approaches the constantly fluctuating patterns of light and sound which this lethal combination of talent has managed to unleash." Johnny Page describes this music making as follows: "Ours is the folk music of a technological culture."

3

The stream of rock music that flowed from Great Britain to the United States carried solo vocalists as well as groups. One of them, Elton John, became the first rock superstar of the Seventies. Those who expect to compete with his success story will have a long road to travel. In its cover story of July 7, 1975, *Time* provided statistics proving that this rock performer-composer has become one of the moneymaking elite in popular music. Up through 1976, and over a six-year period, Elton John sold forty-two million albums and eighteen million singles worldwide, earning royalties in excess of eight million dollars; ten of his albums received platinum records. In 1974, he signed a new contract with MCA Records guaranteeing him eight million dollars in royalties within a five-year period. A year later, *Captain Fantastic and the Brown Dirt Cowboy* had an advance sale of one and a quarter million copies before anybody had heard even one of its songs.

A superficial estimate of Elton John might easily place him with some of the eccentrics in rock music who had preceded him. In his performances his extravagant costumes, in a futuristic style, make Liberace's outfits appear conservative by comparison. Elton John's suits are vividly colored (pink, chocolate, flaming red), and embellished with elaborate trimmings of shiny spangles, musical notes, clowns, decorative devices which can light up electrically, feather boas, fur epaulettes. His headgear is exotic, sometimes resembling women's hats bedecked with ribbons and flowers, sometimes consisting of a high hat from which flows an ostrich plume. Occasionally he dyes his hair orange or pink. He favors high heeled shoes or boots. Finally—and this is his most personal identification—he owns a collection of some two hundred eyeglasses, from which he chooses one for each performance. One pair is mink lined; another spells out his name with tiny light bulbs; another is shaped like musical notes linked together with a jeweled bridge bar; another is equipped with windshield wipers.

His stage behavior is often equally excessive. He performs all kinds of acrobatics at the piano, and at times pounds the keyboard with his feet. He may throw tennis balls at the audience, kick the piano stool off the stage, or perform handstands.

What he wears and what he does are not indicative of anger or rebellion but of good fun which his audiences enjoy to the full. He leaves the impression that he is just a boy released of all inhibitions and having the time of his life. "I didn't start enjoying life until I was twenty-one," he has said, "so I'm living through my teenage period now. . . . I'm catching up for all the games that I missed as a child." There is not only enjoyment in what he is doing but also more than a passing suspicion that he is satirizing some of his rock predecessors.

But his phenomenal rise to world fame is not due to his absurdities, however newsworthy. Behind the facade of grandiose sensationalism is a performer of awesome talent who maintains a total rapport with his audience, and a composer with a wide gamut of expressivity. Supported by drummer Nigel Olsson and bass player Dee Muray (with David Johnston, guitarist, added in 1972, and Ray Cooper, as pianist and percussionist in 1974), he has been the purveyor of touching moods and sentiments in his songs of loneliness, rejection and the lack of love to the lyrics by Bernie Taupin. "Half the songs," wrote Albert Goldman in *Life*, "are very plaintive expressions of a very gentle soul who delivers himself in soliloquies that ramble like a schoolboy's letters to his mom." Another writer, Tom Zito, found that beneath these ballads "is a real feeling for the universal experience of a life in harmony with people." Elton Johns' song "Daniel" is about a wounded war veteran who must leave his family because he cannot stand their pity. "I Think I'm Gonna Kill Myself" concerns unrequited teenage love. "Rocket Man" describes the anxious loneliness of an astronaut in space. "There Goes a Well Known Gun" speaks of a pursued outlaw. And "Candle in the Wind" is a comment on the Marilyn Monroe cult and the sadly confused sex goddess who inspired it.

In a contrasting vein, Elton John has written and performed hard rock numbers with a driving momentum and a compulsive background beat that galvanizes audiences: "Burn Down the Mission," "The Bitch is Back," "High Flying Bird," "Saturday Night's Alright for Fighting," "Crocodile Rock" and "Bennie and the Jets."

He was born Reginald Kenneth Dwight in Middlesex, England, in 1947. One of the reasons he changed his name to Elton Hercules John was to disassociate himself completely from his miserable childhood. He was a fat, near-sighted kid whose sense of inferiority made him frightfully introverted. That inferiority was nourished by a despotic father, a squadron leader in the Royal Air Force, who never felt that his son could do anything right. "He never let me do anything I wanted. I couldn't even play in the garden, in case I might change his rose beds. . . . I used to pray that my father wouldn't come home at weekends." And one of the things about which the father was most discouraging was the boy's later ambition to become a rock musician.

Dissension between father and mother, which led to divorce, did not help matters. But music did. As a child, Elton John learned to play the piano by ear and at eleven he won a scholarship to the Royal Academy of Music in London. His mother introduced her son to rock by bringing him recordings by Jerry Lee Lewis and Little Richard. "From then on," recalls Elton John, "rock 'n' roll took over."

When he was seventeen, Elton John quit school to join a rhythm and blues outfit. Between 1964 and 1967 he performed in London and the suburbs with rock 'n' roll groups.

The year 1967 proved fateful. At that time a record company executive advertised for artists, composers and lyricists to submit specimens of their work. Elton John sent in some of his music. Another young fellow, Bernie Taupin, responded with some lyrics. The recording executive brought Elton John and Bernie Taupin together and they became collaborators. Their first single, "Lady Samantha" and their first two albums, *Empty Sky* and *Elton John* appeared in 1969. The last-named album was released simultaneously in England and the United States (in the United States on the UNI label). It was well received by the critics and the record-buying public, with two of its cuts, "Border Song" and "Your Song" invading the hit charts, the latter eventually rising to the Number One position in America.

But it was not until Elton John began singing his songs in public that his fame really began to soar. This first happened in August 1970 with an appearance at the Troubadour Club in Los Angeles before an audience of some of the most powerful men in the record business. Dressed in what he himself called "the most outrageous gear I could find" and releasing all of his inhibitions in his stage behavior, Elton John achieved what John Maitland, president of MCA Records, called "one of the most spectacular openings for an unknown artist I've ever seen." Robert Hilburn of the Los Angeles *Times* called John "staggeringly original."

He continued giving performances at the Fillmore East in New York, at a pop festival in Cannes, France, and during tours of Europe and America. In 1974 he embarked on a forty-four performance, ten-week jaunt through the United States which was culminated at Madison Square Garden on November 29. He was invited to guest appearances on major sponsored television shows; on May 17, 1974, NBC-TV featured an Elton John documentary, *Say Goodbye, Norma Jean*.

All these public performances helped to sell Elton John's records. *Elton John* was certified as a gold disk in 1971, and so were *Tumbleweed Connection*, and Elton John's soundtrack for the movie *Friends*, that same year. *Madman Across the Water* and *Honky Chateau* were the gold disk albums of 1972. Now on MCA Records, "Crocodile Rock", "Bennie and the Jets," "Honky Cat" "Levon," "Tiny Dance" and the albums *Don't Shoot Me, I'm the Only Piano Player* and *Goodbye, Yellow Brick Road* brought John more gold records in 1973; so did *Caribou, Greatest Hits* and "Don't Let the Sun Go Down" in 1974, and "Lucy in the Sky," "Someone Saved My Life" and *Captain Fantastic and the Brown Dirt Cowboy* in 1975; gold records were earned in 1976 with *Here and There, Blue Moves*, and the single, "Don't Go Breaking My Heart."

Still another form of recognition came Elton John's way in August 1975 when the first Rock Music Awards, televised over the CBS network, selected him as rock personality of the year.

In the invasion by English solo performers of the American rock scene we find four who, though they are basically artists of pop music, have had their roots in rock. They are Petula Clark, Tom Jones, Engelbert Humperdinck and Gilbert O'Sullivan.

Petula Clark—onetime child star on the BBC and in British motion pictures, later an idol of the rock set in France—achieved American renown in 1964 with "Downtown" (Tony Hatch). Her recording for Warner sold about two million disks and captured a Grammy as best rock 'n' roll single of the year. In 1965, another rock number "I Know a Place" (Tony Hatch) brought her a second Grammy. Her success carried her to the Copacabana in New York in 1965, followed by guest appearances on major television network programs together with two NBC Specials, "Petula" in 1968 and "Portrait of Petula" in 1969. A career in Hollywood came after that with starring roles in the motion-picture adaptation of the Broadway musical, *Finian's Rainbow* (1968) and the musical version of the motion picture *Goodbye, Mr. Chips* (1971).

Though her success had been won with rock, Petula Clark enlarged her repertory and her audience by entering the pop and country fields, in which she extended her appeal to the older generation. This proved equally true of Tom Jones and Englebert Humperdinck, whose careers were skillfully developed by their manager, Gordon Mills.

Tom Jones was a onetime Welsh hod carrier. Gordon Mills, a songwriter, heard him sing in a local pub where Jones was then billed under his own name of Tommy Scott, "the twisting vocalist." Mills became the young singer's manager, brought him to London, had him change his name to Tom Jones (the motion picture based on Fielding's novel of the same name was then popular) and arranged for him to appear with a small combo in various night spots. "It's Not Unusual" (Gordon Mills and Less Reed) in 1965 was Tom Jones' first record success, on the Parrot label. He then made many more recordings for Decca, appeared on radio and television, won a Grammy in 1965 as the best new recording artist, and in 1967 was picked as Britain's top male singer. In 1968 he made a highly successful tour of the United States. This was not his first visit to America. He had previously sung there three years earlier when he slanted his performances toward teenage audiences with rock numbers. The youngsters rejected him but the older audiences he appealed to in 1968 made him one of their prime singing favorites.

As the star of his own television show in America, "This is Tom Jones" over the ABC network, and as a performer in leading nightclubs and auditoriums, he sent women into almost the same kind of paroxysms of delight and hysteria with which Frank Sinatra and Elvis Presley had affected their mothers. Within two years, Jones sold about twenty-five million records. Four of his albums in 1969 brought him gold records, *Help Yourself*, *Tom Jones Live*, *Tom Jones Live in Las Vegas* and *This Is Tom Jones*. A sixth gold record came that year with his single "I'll Never Fall in Love Again" (Hal David-Burt Bacharach). The pile-up of gold records continued with the releases of *I (Who Have Nothing)*, *Tom Jones Sings She's a Lady*, and *Tom Jones Live at Caesar's Palace*.

As Gerry Dorsey, Englebert Humperdinck had also started out as a rock performer catering to teenage audiences without making headway. Then Gordon Mills took him in hand, changed his name into one that would instantly capture attention (by appropriating that of the German composer of *Hansel and Gretel*) and had him develop a style more universal in its appeal than rock. A country ballad brought Humperdinck his first recognition, a revival from 1954 of "Release Me" (Eddie Miller and W. S. Stevenson) which Humperdinck recorded for Parrot in January 1967. An album bearing this song title brought him his first gold record. His best-selling singles of 1967–1968 included "There Goes My Everything" (Dallas Frazier), "The Last Waltz" (Less Reed and Barry Mason), "Am I That Easy to Forget?" (Carl Belew and W. S. Stevenson) and "A Man Without Love" (Barry Mason, D. Pace, M. Panzeri and R. Livraghi). Three of them were gold disks. All the trimmings of a monumental singing career came after that: more giant hit record albums (*A Man Without Love*, *The Last Waltz*, *Engelbert Humperdinck*, *We Made it Happen*, *Sweetheart*, *Engelbert Humperdinck: His Greatest Hits*), tours, nightclub and television appearances.

With Gilbert O'Sullivan, Gordon Mills drew his third ace. An Irish-born lad from Waterford by the name of Ray O'Sullivan, he came from working-class people, his father having been a butcher. Ray O'Sullivan was fifteen when his father died, leaving behind a family of six children. The mother had to take on jobs as a cleaning woman, and the children subsisted on welfare. Despite his poverty he was able to attend art college in Swindson, England, at which time he started writing songs. After leaving college he supported himself with menial jobs, while continuing to produce songs. He was working as a postal clerk in London when he sent some tapes of his singing and his songs to Gordon Mills who took him on as a client. He had O'Sullivan change his given name to Gilbert to make his full name more recognizable and more easily remembered and he had him assume the stage costume of a varsity sweater instead of that of an English school kid he had previously preferred. In 1972, O'Sullivan's song, "Alone Again," made his name a byword in popular music circles not only in England but also in the United States, selling over three million disks in all including one in his own performance, and some forty different cover versions. He had two more gold records after that, "Clair" and "Get Down." In 1973 he made his first tour of the United States with public concerts and network television appearances; that year he further endeared himself to Americans with his best-selling album *I'm a Writer, Not a Fighter*. Though most of his songs were rooted in the British working class, often filled with British colloquialisms whose meaning he sometimes had to explain, he created an immediate bond between himself and his American audiences. The reason? Joyce Wadler presents an explanation in the New York *Post*: "On stage, Gilbert O'Sullivan looks just like his music sounds: clean-cut, fresh, the cutest sweetie pie in town. On stage, he's about as easy to dislike as a cocker spaniel puppy. But he's a well trained cocker spaniel. He comes out in a black varsity sweater with a big red "G", his five-foot-six, 126 pound, compact Joel Grey body in tight black trousers with red busboy stripes, and he plays it sweet and coy, projecting that peculiarly unthreatening boyish sexuality that's just right for his audience of post-pubescents and youngish to middle-aged housewives. His music is cheerful, up-beat, heavily orchestrated. And even when he rocks, he doesn't rock hard and mean; its more gum-drop bob, sweet rock, Nice rock."

4

San Francisco in the 1960s was called "the Liverpool of the West," for like England's Liverpool it was frenetic with rock activity to which it contributed its own trappings and embellishments. To the lively rock scene, San Francisco added the hippies of Haight-Ashbury, topless waitresses in bars, and two dance auditoriums where rock music was both listened to and danced to and where a rapport was established between the musicians and their admirers: the Fillmore Auditorium, directed by Bill Graham and the Avalon Ballroom, directed by Chet Helms. In each, the stimulation of rock was heightened through psychedelic experiences produced by coruscating colors, strobe lights, electronic equipment, slides, films, drawings, paintings, posters. Absurd or obscene makeup, balloons and streamers further added to the visual excitement. For the Fillmore Auditorium, Bill Graham created a "trips festival," a three-day event intended to simulate an LSD experience.

In these two San Francisco halls—and later in other concert auditoriums where audiences came to listen and not to dance—a new sound in rock emerged, the San Francisco sound, acid or psychedelic rock. Here the music recreated the distorted aural experiences of one who is under the influence of drugs. "It was slower and more languid than hard rock," explains Lillian Roxon, "incorporating much of the Oriental music that was providing background sounds for the drug experiences of the period. Numbers tended to run on longer as though time as we normally know it had lost its meaning. Notes and phrasing lurched and warped in a way that had not, until then, been considered acceptable rock. Lyrics conjured up images previously confined to the verses of poets like Samuel Taylor Coleridge and William Blake." Frequently, acid rock was produced by performers themselves under the influence of hallucinatory drugs, and just as often it was listened to by enthusiasts who were undergoing, or had just emerged from, a hallucinatory drug experience. In the ballrooms and auditoriums, the garish colors and dancing lights helped to reproduce visually the drug-induced experience in the same way that acid rock did aurally.

Within the orbit of acid rock comes "White Rabbit" (Grace Slick), a drug-oriented variation on the theme of *Alice in Wonderland* by the Jefferson Airplane, the first San Francisco group to hit the big time in rock. Grace Slick (who came from Los Angeles in 1965 where she had been a member of The Great Society) was its female vocalist as well as a performer on the bass and rhythm guitar. The other members were: Jorma Kaukonen, lead guitar; Jack Casady, bass; Spencer Dryden, drums; Paul Kantner, rhythm guitar; and Marty Balin, male vocalist. They made their debut at the Matrix in San Francisco on August 13, 1965, but first hit their full stride at the Fillmore Auditorium with their sultry improvisations on folk blues, or jazz, and the piercing voice of Grace Slick in songs about drugs and drug experiences. They became the first San Francisco rock group to land a contract with a major company (RCA Victor), the first to acquire a nationwide hit record, "Somebody to Love" (Darby Slick) in 1966, and the first to get a gold record (for their second album *Surrealistic Pillow* in 1967). Out of *Surrealistic Pillow* came two hit singles, "White Rabbit" and "Somebody to Love." More gold records came their way for the albums *Volunteers, Crown of Creation, The Worst of Jefferson Airplane* and, in 1971, *Bark*. Meanwhile, in 1967, the Jefferson Airplane winged eastward to conquer New York, leaving behind it a San Francisco tradition that was slowly beginning to fade away.

But before that fading was complete, many other new rock groups and personalities became a part of the San Francisco rock scene: the Charlatans, The Grateful Dead, Country Joe and the Fish, The Chocolate Watch Band, Quicksilver Messenger Service, Moby Grape, and the Heavenly Blues Band. Sly and the Family Stone were proponents of "psychedelic soul," first expressed in their album *Whole New Thing* in October 1967, and later in their first gold record, "Everybody People" (Sylvester Stewart).

The most important of these San Francisco rock groups, second only to the Jefferson Airplane, was the Big Brother and the Holding Company. Its main bid for distinction was its lead vocalist—Janis Joplin, the most pervasive, galvanizing, torrential female rock singer of the decade. She joined the group in June 1966, and remained with it until the end of 1968 when she left to carve for herself a legendary career as a solo rock vocalist. In 1970 came her sudden death through an overdose of heroin at the age of twenty-seven.

A hellion on the stage, and even more off it, she sent San Francisco into a delirium with her appearances with the Big Brother and the Holding Company. She was more than a singer. She was a primitive force. *Cash Box* later called her a "kind of mixture of Leadbelly, a steam engine, Calamity Jane, Bessie Smith, an oil derrick and rot gut bourbon, funneled into the twentieth century somewhere between El Paso and San Francisco."

When she sang she would stamp her foot in anger, toss her black hair defiantly so that its strands whipped across her face. At some moments her body movements were corybantic. She used her raspy blues voice and her frenzied howls and shrieks in outbursts of anguish, and there was greater agony still in her moans and whispers. It was almost impossible to believe that one so unseemly in appearance offstage could, when gripped by the emotion of her song, become so arrestingly beautiful, or that one so young could, when singing, appear so old and spent. She wore sleazy costumes made up of furs, feathers, sequins, frowsy hats, bellbottom trousers, and an array of rings, bracelets and necklaces. Apparently, those baubles, bangles and beads were insufficient to satisfy her need for self decoration: a red Valentine was tattooed just above her right breast ("a little something for the boys," she explained) and a Florentine-type bracelet was etched on one of her wrists. But song transformed her into a vision of beauty as well as terror as, through song—which seemed to come from her very guts—she overwhelmed her audiences with emotion and almost seemed to be ravaging them sexually.

She came from Port Arthur, an oil refining town in Texas, where she was the oldest of three children, born in 1943. As a youngster attending Thomas Jefferson High School in Port Arthur she was a misfit. Short, pudgy, pimply, she was called by her schoolmates "pig face." "Can you imagine what that does to a kid?" she once asked. Her behavior and dress were no more palatable than her looks. She was offbeat, or, to use her own words, a "weirdo" and a "beatnik." She outraged her family, neighbors and classmates with her profanities, her willfulness, her unpredictable and unconventional ways and her antisocial attitudes.

Soon after her graduation from high school, she sold her belongings and left home, spending several years of a peripatetic existence attending several colleges for brief interludes, working at odd jobs, and occasionally singing for handouts and beers in small bars, coffee houses and folk-song clubs. In Austin, accompanying herself on an Autoharp, she sang with a hillbilly group, Waller Creek Boys. She did not come off well—her voice was much too shrill at the time—and neither she nor the patrons held out much hope for her future in singing.

She drifted on to San Francisco for the first time in 1962, becoming a hippie in Haight-Ashbury, trying for one week to earn some money as a hooker but finding herself rejected because of her unappetizing appearance, doing some singing in coffee houses and spending some time in a hospital being treated for drug addiction. A shattered love affair added just one more knot to a tangled life.

She was back in Port Arthur, back with her family, seeking rehabilitation. For about a year she tried to conform to a normal life by attending the Lamar State College of Technology. Then, in 1966, she got a call from Chet Helms, who ran the Avalon Ballroom, to come back to San Francisco and become a vocalist with a rock group he was forming, the Big Brother and the Holding Company. Several of its members had been hanging around Chet Helms' pad in Haight-Ashbury, and they decided to organize a combo that, in the words of one of them, Peter Albin, "would speak to all of the children of the nation in their own language."

She arrived in San Francisco on June 4, 1966, and six days later made her first appearance with Big Brother and the Holding Company at the Avalon Ballroom amid swirling psychedelic lights and colors. "It was the most thrilling time in my life. I mean, I had never *seen* a hippie dance before, man, and then I was up there in the middle of one. I couldn't believe it, all that rhythm and power. I got stoned just feeling it. . . . It was so sensual, so vibrant, loud, *crazy!* I couldn't stay still. I had never danced when I sang . . . but there I was moving and jumping. I couldn't hear myself, so I sang louder and louder, and by the end I was wild."

She had never sung rock before, having confined herself solely to the blues. "I didn't know how to sing the stuff. I'd never sung with electric music. I'd never sung with drums. . . . We finally did the song, "Down On Me," a gospel number. . . . The music was boom, boom, boom! and the people were all dancing, and the lights, and I was standing up there singing into this microphone and getting it on, and whew! I dug it."

The music of Big Brother left much to be desired and San Francisco was cold to it. For a few months Janis Joplin as its vocalist—receiving about four dollars an evening—did not fare much better. But an almost continuous involvement with liquor (gallons of beer and cheap wine; when she became affluent it was a quart a day of Southern Comfort, then tequila, gin and vodka), drugs and a seemingly perpetual round of sex (with both men and women) helped to unleash her deepest and most profound emotions: her anger and passion, her fears, her sense of insecurity, her chronic need to be loved, her narcissism. As a singer she began to "explode" (her own word), an explosion that began to rock to the roots those who heard her. To her own individual song styling she added the soul of Otis Redding, whose work she soon came to admire and absorb. The kids began pouring to the Matrix, the Fillmore Auditorium, the Avalon Ballroom—and then away from San Francisco when Big Brother went on the road—yelling, "We want Janis, We want Janis."

Her first all-important exposure to the world of rock came in June 1967 at the Monterey International Pop Festival, attended by several thousand. Big Brother, with Janis, was scheduled for an afternoon appearance. Singing "Ball and Chain" (Willie Mae Thornton) she created a furor. Because of Janis, Big Brother was asked to give an evening performance as well. "That was one of the highest points of my life," Janis Joplin once revealed. (A film documentary of that festival, with Janis singing—*Monterey Pop* produced by D. A. Pennebaker—was released in 1968.)

On the strength of this success, a small recording company, Mainstream, finally decided to release an album that Big Brother and Janis Joplin had pressed earlier that year—*Big Brother and the Holding Company*. It did tolerably well, but earned virtually nothing for either Big Brother or Janis Joplin.

That success at Monterey, however, did bring about a dramatic change of fortune for Janis Joplin. In the audience were Clive Davis, then president of Columbia Records, and Albert Grossman, a rock impresario. Davis brought Big Brother and Janis Joplin under the banner of Columbia for which they recorded live the album *Cheap Thrills* in 1968, that collected some of what by now had become her most famous numbers: her own "Turtle Blues," Gershwin's "Summertime" (Du Bose Heyward), "Piece of My Heart" (Bert Berns and Jerry Ragovoy), "Combination of the Two" (S. Andrew) as well as "Ball and Chain" (Willie Mae Thornton). This was her first gold record (with a million-dollars worth of orders in hand before the release date) and it brought from Steven Lowe a rave review in *High Fidelity*. He called Janis Joplin "the most exciting and openly sensual female singer that rock has produced," possessing "the kind of genuine womanness—uncleansed and intensely real—that Billie Holiday had and that many white vocalists have tried and failed to emulate."

Grossman mapped a national tour for Big Brother and Janis Joplin which brought them to the Electric Factory in Philadelphia, the Psychedelic Supermarket in Boston, the Kinetic Playground in Chicago, the Whiskey a-Go-Go in Los Angeles, the Anderson Theater in New York City (soon to be renamed Fillmore East), and wherever else good rock got heard, including the prestigious Newport Folk Festival in July 1968.

By the end of 1968 Big Brother and Janis Joplin parted. Janis set forth on her own with a new small rock group. Her first national tour began at Fillmore East in New York City on February 12, 1969. She sang some of her now familiar specialties together with numbers fresh in her repertory: "Try" (Jerry Ragovoy and Chip Taylor), "Maybe" (Richard Barrett), "To Love Somebody" (Barry, Robin and Maurice Gibb). Her American tour over, she sang in several European capitals, then made a triumphant appearance at Madison Square Garden in New York on December 19, 1969. Two months before that Columbia released her album *Kozmic Blues* (a gold record again) which contained her own "Kozmic Blues," "Maybe," "Try," and the Rodgers and Hart ballad "Little Girl Blue," among other numbers.

She was now able to command $20,000 to $30,000 an appearance, and well able to indulge herself freely in all the vices that seemed to make life tolerable to her. A woman of prodigious sexual appetites, she even regarded her singing performances as a kind of sexual act, explaining to Hubert Saal of *Newsweek* that it was "all feeling . . . like sex, but much larger in concept. It's that love, lust, warmth, touching thing inside our bodies that everybody digs. . . . When I sing, I'm not thinking. I'm just closing my eyes and feeling, feeling good."

She seemed to be an integrated human being only when she clutched microphone in hand and became involved in a song that touched upon those terrible chronic pains within her, when, as in "Ball and Chain," she sobbed, "An' I say, Oh uh-huh, tell me why, Why does ev'ry little thing I hold go wrong?" Away from the microphone she led a disoriented existence, shunning the sun and thriving during the night hours. She was the existentialist who rejected a repulsive yesterday, refused to contemplate an uncertain tomorrow, but was ready to pay any price for the pleasures of today. The title of the closing song of her last album might well serve as her epitaph: "Get It While You Can." She seemed driven to self destruction by her recollection of past hurts, rejections and frustrations which not even her towering success and fame could obliterate; by paranoia; by an inability to reconcile her megalomania with her self-depreciation and self-contempt.

She tried to remain true to her art to the end. But there *were* defections, and one of these took place at the Woodstock Festival in August 1969. Perhaps the awesome sight of an audience stretching out as far as the eye could see unnerved her, or perhaps the fact that she was being billed as the star of stars at a festival filled with stars, intensified her chronic insecurity. In any event, before going on the stage she emptied a bottle of Southern Comfort and another of vodka and, failing to get from them the reassurance she needed, she locked herself in the toilet to give herself a fix. Her performance was a shambles. After that concert she sobbed: "Man, when you blow it in front of a half a million people, you *really* blow it."

As if in reparation, her last Columbia album, *Pearl* (a gold record) was her best—"Pearl" being the nickname some of her closest friends used for her. No carryover of that Woodstock disaster here! In her own "Mercedes Benz" (a tambourine her solo accompaniment) and in "Me and Bobby McGee" (Kris Kristofferson and Fred Foster) to her own guitar accompaniment, she was at the peak of her artistry. The cut of "Me and Bobby McGee" became her most successful single.

Her last public appearance took place in September 1970 when she returned to Thomas Jefferson High School in Port Arthur to participate in the tenth reunion of her graduating class. In a gesture mingling contempt with defiance for a place and time of past sufferings, she wore a costume outlandish even for her. Her toenails were painted orange. Orange and blue ostrich feathers were stuck slightly askew in her hair. Blue bell-bottoms with rhinestones descended from a see-through blouse to silver slippers. Oversized rose-colored sunglasses covered a good part of her face. That odd appearance was caught and fixed by the motion picture camera in the documentary *Janis*, a Universal production released in 1975.

She came back to Los Angeles early in September of 1970 to record *Pearl*. She was in good spirits. The album promised to be her best yet, and she knew it. She was contemplating marriage with Seth Morgan, a wealthy young New Yorker. And she had not used drugs for a few months. But on October 3, at the Landmark Hotel, she apparently was suddenly seized by depression and called her connection for a supply of heroin. Then she went out into the lobby to purchase cigarettes. Returning to her room, she collapsed, dead from an overdose of heroin mixed with a quart of tequila and two Valiums. Her body was cremated, and her ashes were scattered over the Pacific Ocean off San Francisco.

A song was written about her: "Janis" (Joe McDonald), and three biographies were published. The movie, *Janis*, helped to recall her living image while performing and being interviewed. A two-record album of her greatest hits were released posthumously by Columbia, *Joplin in Concert*, made up of tracks recorded early in 1968 with Big Brother and the Holding Company and at concerts in Calgary, Canada, in June and July of 1970 and at Fillmore West in April of 1970. The Columbia album, *Janis Joplin: Greatest Hits* became a gold record in 1975. She was not forgotten—for both as an artist and as a woman she was not one who was easy to forget.

5

The discotheque, become popular during the rock movement, was brought to California by Elmer Valentine. He was the owner of PJ, a night spot in Los Angeles. While vacationing in Paris, he visited the Whiskey a-Go-Go, a nightclub where the clientele danced to recorded rock music and which was called a "discothèque." He was convinced such a project could be successful in America. On January 15, 1965 he opened the Los Angeles Whiskey a-Go-Go on Sunset Boulevard. He used live music as well as canned, the live performance provided by Johnny Rivers and his rock group. The opening night performance was recorded and became so successful that forthwith Johnny Rivers became the first major star to come out of a discotheque. This album became a force in publicity both for the Los Angeles Whiskey a-Go-Go and the discotheque idea. Hundreds came each evening to the Whiskey a-Go-Go to listen to rock (live and on record) and to dance to it—playing a kind of follow-the-leader game with a "go-go girl" who, in a cage over the dance floor, gave the dancers their cues for changing their routines. Discotheques began to mushroom throughout the United States; in one year, five thousand opened up, twenty of them in Manhattan alone, and others in Chicago, Milwaukee, San Francisco, Atlanta and Los Angeles. In addition, there was a-Go-Go in Aspen, Colorado; a Bucket a-Go-Go in Park City, Utah; a Frisky a-Go-Go in San Antonio; a Champagne a-Go-Go in Madison, Wisconsin; a Blues Note a-Go-Go in Whitesboro, New York. The Go-Go movement even invaded the television screen with "Hollywood a-Go-Go" featured as a regular coast-to-coast program.

The hypertense sounds disgorged sometimes live but mostly from records in discotheques inspired dances with convulsive movements. To dance cheek-to-cheek, body-to-body—traditional with an older generation—was not for the rock era. The kids relegated that kind of dancing to the same limbo to which they had consigned romantic ballads and sentimental love songs of the Irving Berlin or Jerome Kern variety. The compelling need of the rock generation to "do your own thing"—a catch phrase that was like a banner of defiance under which the younger generation of the 1960s marched—even entered into its dancing. The two partners performed their own body movements and rapid-fire footwork. This was solo sex exhibitionism, as well as a display of narcissism, serving more to arouse the performer than the partner. Beverly Nichols expressed his outrage in *New York* Magazine (January, 1962): "The essence of the Twist, the curious perverted heart of it, is that you dance it alone."

The "Twist" became for the 1960s what the Charleston and the Black Bottom had been for the twenties, the terpsichorean expression of the times. Its history begins with a rock song, "The Twist," by Hank Ballard, written in 1958, and introduced a year later by Hank Ballard and the Midnighters on a King recording that had a small sale. Then, in 1961, the Chubby Checker recording for Cameo-Parkway became a runaway best-seller. He was a twenty-year-old singer and dancer from South Philadelphia whose name originally had been Ernest Evans. He was an admirer of Fats Domino, whom he resembled physically; that admiration led him to assume a stage name adapted from that of his idol, using Chubby instead of Fats and Checker instead of Domino. Before going into show business, Chubby Checker had been a chicken plucker who was always entertaining his friends with his

singing. Kal Mann, a songwriter, became convinced that Checker had professional possibilities. He wrote for him "The Class" which Chubby recorded and which went so well
with teenagers that they started buying several more singles Checker had recorded. But it was
"The Twist" that made Chubby Checker an international celebrity, both the song which he
recorded and the dance which he devised for it. On the Ed Sullivan TV show, Checker
performed a solo dance as he sang "The Twist." This performance started a nationwide, then
worldwide, craze for the Twist. Describing this dance, Checker explained: "There are no
basic steps. You move chest, hips and arms from side to side and balance on the balls of the
feet." Shoulders quivered; hips and knees rotated; the whole body rocked. Very little footwork
was involved. Sometimes the partners faced each other; sometimes they worked back to back;
sometimes side to side.

Everybody was doing the Twist—not just the young, but the older folks as well. They
danced it at the Peppermint Lounge where Joey Dee and the Starliters kept playing "The
Twist" all night. It became the favorite hangout of the Jet Set, as overcrowded as the subway
in rush hour. On any given night one might meet there Judy Garland, Noël Coward, Elsa
Maxwell, Tennessee Williams and others, all of them participating in or gaping at the Twist.

Rock numbers other than "The Twist" kept this dance craze alive. For Cameo-
Parkway, Chubby Checker recorded "Let's Twist Again" (Kal Mann and Dave Appell), a
record that received a Grammy as the year's best rock recording, and "Slow Twistin' " (Jon
Sheldon). Elvis Presley sang "Rock-a-Hula Baby" (Fred Wise, Ben Weisman and Dolores
Fuller), a Twist number, in the movie *Blue Hawaii* (1962) and in an RCA Victor recording.
Other popular Twist numbers were: "Twist and Shout" (Bert Russell and Phil Medley),
originally recorded by the Isley Brothers and later by the Beatles; "Twistin' U.S.A." (Kal
Mann); "Twistin' the Night Away" (Sam Cooke), recorded by the composer; "Peppermint
Twist" (Joey Dee and Henry Glover) "Twist, Twist, Senora" (Frank J. Guida, Gene Barge
and Joseph Royster).

The Twist became big business. There was the revenue earned from the sale of
records, and that earned in the night spots and ballrooms where the Twist was the predomi-
nant attraction. The Twist was exploited in a number of movies, among these being *Twist
All Night* (1962) which starred Louis Prima and *Twist Around the Clock* (1962) with Chubby
Checker. Then there was money to be made manufacturing Chubby Checker Tee Shirts,
jeans and dolls; also Twist skirts, Twist raincoats and Twist nighties.

The Twist spawned other dances that were variations; and these dances spawned still
others, some of them incubated in discotheques. They had picturesque names. The Loco-
Motion and the Mashed Potato each came along with a rock number with those titles: "The
Loco-Motion" (Gerry Goffin and Carole King) popularized by Little Eva's recording for
Dimension and "Mashed Potato Time" (John Sheldon and Harry Land), recorded for
Cameo-Parkway by Dee Dee Sharp. Then there was the Limbo Rock, Watusi, the Monkey,
the Chicken, the Waddle, the Fly, the Duck, the Fish, the Popeye or the Hitchhiker, the
Jerk, the Shake, the Pony, the Frug, Walkin' the Dog, and the Hully Gully.

6

The Byrds were among the earliest of several rock groups to come from Los
Angeles, and one of the first groups to promote folk rock. Jim (later Roger) McGuinn was
their principal vocalist as well as leading guitar and banjo player; Chris Hillman played the
bass and the mandolin; Gene Clark, formerly a member of the New Christy Minstrels, was a
vocalist who also played the guitar, harmonica and tambourine; Mike Clarke played the
harmonica and drums; and David Crosby was a vocalist who also played the guitar. They

became The Byrds in August 1964, soon after they made their first recording. That record, on the Columbia label, was Bob Dylan's "Mr. Tambourine Man," which became a gold disk. With a changing personnel, The Byrds were heard at Ciro's on Sunset Strip in Hollywood. Then as a foursome (Roger McGuinn, Jay York at the bass, Clarence White at the guitar, and Gene Parsons at the drums) they appeared at the Village Gate in New York in 1966, now promoting raga rock which was largely responsible for starting a vogue for the sitar in rock music. Their biggest raga rock hit was "Eight Miles High" (Gene Clark, David Crosby and Jim McGuinn) which appeared in their album *Fifth Dimension*. Another of their albums, *The Byrds' Greatest Hits*, in 1968, was a gold record. Besides "Mr. Tambourine Man" and "Eight Miles High" it included "Turn! Turn! Turn!" (Pete Seeger), its words taken from the Book of Ecclesiastes; Bob Dylan's "All I Really Want to Do"; "Mr. Spaceman" (Jim McGuinn); "So You Want to Be a Rock 'n' Roll Star" (Jim McGuinn and Chris Hillman); Bob Dylan's "My Back Pages"; "Five 'D'" (Jim McGuinn); and a few others.

Though the title of Jim McGuinn's "Five 'D'" is a shortened form for "Fifth Dimension", it has no affiliation whatsoever with a black rock group that assumed the name of The 5th Dimension, and comprised Ron Townson, Lamonte Lemore, Marylin McCoo and Florence La Rue, all of them vocalists, together with guitarist Billy Davis, who also participated in the singing. As the Hi-Fi's they had specialized in the blues. In 1966 they changed their name to The 5th Dimension, achieving a hit record on the Soul City label with "Go Where You Wanna Go" (John Phillips). "Stoned Soul Picnic" (Laura Nyro), first recorded by The Mamas and the Papas, was a gold disk in 1968, as were "Up, Up, and Away," (Jim Webb) "Aquarius" backed by "Let the Sunshine In" (Gerome Ragni and James Rado—Galt MacDermott) both from the rock musical *Hair*, and "Wedding Bell Blues" (Laura Nyro). "Up, Up and Away" and "Aquarius" received Grammys as records of the year in 1967 and 1969. Others of their gold records came with the albums *The Age of Aquarius*, *Greatest Hits*, *Love's Lines Angles and Rhymes*, and *Greatest Hits on Earth*, and the singles "One Less Bell to Answer" (Hal David—Burt Bacharach), and "Last Night I Didn't Get to Sleep at All" (Tony Macaulay).

The Monkees was formed as an undisguised attempt to create an American counterpart to the Beatles. A Los Angeles television producer planned a weekly series modeled after the Beatles' motion picture, *A Hard Day's Night* (1964), engaging four youngsters in zany escapades to help people in trouble. For his four principals, the producer auditioned several hundred performers, professionals and amateurs, adults and kids. The four finally selected were Davy Jones, Mike Nesmith, Peter Tork and Mickey Dolenz, each of whom bore a physical resemblance to one of the Beatles. The new quartet, baptized The Monkees, made its first television appearance in the fall of 1966. Capitalizing on the exposure The Monkees was getting, Colgems released the album, *The Monkees*, in October of that year. Mickey Dolenz, the lead vocalist, played the guitar and drums; Davy Jones sang and performed on the tambourine; Mike Nesmith played the guitar; and Peter Tork, who left the group early in 1969, played the bass. They had never before performed together, and both individually and collectively they were far from being highly esteemed rock artists. (Some skeptics even dropped broad hints that in the making of some of their records more experienced performers pinch-hit for them!). But their television coverage helped them sell records and establish themselves with their fans. In their very first season of recording, their initial album together with the singles "Last Train to Clarksville" (Tommy Boyce and Bobby Hart) and "I'm a Believer" (Neil Diamond) were gold records. Other gold records came in quick succession: for the singles "A Little Bit Me, a Little Bit You" (Neil Diamond), "Pleasant Valley Sunday" (Gerry Goffin and Carole King), "Daydream Believer" (John Stewart) and "Valleri" (Tommy

Boyce and Bobby Hart) and for their albums *Monkees Headquarters, Pisces, Aquarius, Capricorn and Jones, Ltd.*, and *The Birds, The Bees and The Monkees*.

The four members of The Mamas and the Papas organized the group in the Virgin Islands in 1965. They came to California a few months later where they won the support of Dunhill Records. Looking, dressing and behaving like hippies—at a time when a hippie was still a curiosity—they soon became the first American rock group to reestablish an American rock scene, and to counteract the British rock invasion. They reformed briefly in 1971 and 1972 but their album *Together Again for the First Time* did not sell as well as expected.

The star of The Mamas and Papas was "Mama" Cass Elliott. She was born in Baltimore, Maryland as Cassandra Elliott, and she turned to a singing career after failing to make progress in the New York theater. As a singer she served her initiation with The Big Three, the other two members being Denny Doherty and Tim Rose. After that she joined the Mugwumps which broke up because they failed to get a favorable public response (though the critics liked them). It was then that with Denny Doherty she helped form The Mamas and Papas with John Phillips and Michelle Phillips. All four members did the vocals, with John Phillips providing a guitar background and sometimes writing the songs for the group. With the "Papas" heard in the basic melody below the weaving sounds of the "Mamas", the group became famous for the way their voices blended into unique harmonies in the presentation of songs of love and peace. Their first singles and albums, all in 1966, were gold records on the Dunhill label: the singles, "California Dreaming" (John and Michelle Phillips), "Monday, Monday" (John Phillips); and the albums, *If You Can Believe Your Eyes and Ears* and *The Mamas and Papas*. A year or so later they received gold records for *The Mamas and Papas Deliver* and *Farewell to the First Golden Era* and attained the best-selling charts with a revival of "Dedicated to the One I Love" (Lowman Pauling and Ralph Bass), first popularized by The Shirelles in 1961. In 1968, The Mamas and the Papas broke up—John Phillips going on to advance his career as a writer, performer and producer, and "Mama" Cass Elliott appearing as a solo vocalist. Her success was virtually instantaneous with the hit records for Dunhill in 1968 of "Make Your Own Kind of Music" (Barry Mann and Cynthia Weil) and a revival from 1931 of "Dream a Little Dream of Me" (Gus Kahn—Wilbur Schwandt and Fabian Andre). She became a top attraction in concerts, over television, and on records, until her sudden death of a heart attack in her Mayfair apartment in London on July 29, 1974, following a highly successful two-week engagement at the Palladium.

The Doors was among the most disreputable of the new Los Angeles rock groups. Their leader was Jim Morrison—a tall, lean drug addict who wore tight black leather trousers and whose performances were tantrums of sadism and sexual exhibitionism. He gave his group the name of The Doors because, he explained, "there are things that are known and things that are unknown in and between the doors." He shrieked, slobbered, writhed, grimaced. His lewd exhibitions carried the sexual implications of Mick Jagger to their ultimate conclusions. Such stage behavior entangled him with the law in New Haven and Miami just before his life ended in 1970 through overindulgence in drugs.

The three other members of The Doors were Ray Manzarek at the organ, Robby Krieger at the guitar, and John Densmore at the drums. All four men released the darker dreams lurking in the subconscious of the young, and this was why to so many The Doors proved a favorite of favorites. At Ondine, at Steve Paul's The Scene, both in New York, their appeal at first was limited. Then came their first gold records all on Elektra: the album *The Doors* and the single "Light My Fire" (The Doors) in 1967, and the albums *Strange Days* and *Waiting for the Sun* in 1968. Their public appearances after that, until they dissolved in

1973, taxed the seating capacities of any auditorium in which the group performed—their young admirers coming as much to witness lascivious behavior as to listen to the music. Or they would rush to the shops to buy their records: the singles, "People Are Strange," "Love Me Two Times," "Unknown Soldier," "Hello, I Love You," "Touch Me", in the writing of which the four men were collaborators; and their albums, of which *Absolutely Live* in 1970, *L. A. Woman* and *The Doors' Greatest Hits* in 1971, and *13* in 1972, were gold records.

Three Dog Night was the creation in 1968 of Reb Foster Associates, an artist-managing firm in Los Angeles. Chuck Negron, Danny Hutton and Cory Wells were the singers (all of whom had earlier experience as lead singers with various rock groups) backed by Mike Allsup at the guitar, Floyd Sneed at the drums, and Joe Shermie at the bass and Jim Greenspoon at various keyboards. In a year's time Three Dog Night grew into one of the most prosperous rock groups since the Beatles and the Rolling Stones, with major engagements throughout the United States and best-selling recordings for Dunhill. Its first big records were the single "One" (Harry Nilsson) and the album *Three Dog Night*, both gold records, and the single "Eli's Coming" (Laura Nyro). Other of their albums were gold records, among these being *Live at the Forum*, *Naturally*, *Golden Bisquits*, *Harmony*, *Seven Separate Fools*, *Around the World*, *Cyan* and *Hard Labor*, while among their gold record singles were "Mama Told Me Not to Come" (Randy Newman), "Joy to the World" (Hoyt Axton) and "Shambala" (B. W. Stevenson and Daniel Moore). During the group's public appearances in the single year of 1971—1972 it grossed over five million dollars; at one of these in Rockingham, North Carolina it brought seven hundred thousand dollars into the box office for a single four-hour appearance. Such monumental success was realized without the antics, vulgarities or eccentricities of other groups, without a charismatic performer to capture and monopolize the limelight, and without featuring songs of its own creation.

Counteracting the strident sounds of hard or acid rock in Los Angeles was the low-key rock of The Carpenters. In time, the Carpenters would amass virtually a storehouse of gold records as specialists of pop, with occasional digressions into soft rock and country music. The Carpenters (Richard and Karen) was a brother and sister vocal and instrumental duo. They were born in New Haven, Connecticut where they early acquired a passion for popular music through their father, a record collector of Dixieland jazz, and the performances of the big bands of the 1930s and 1940s. In their teens, Richard and Karen were brought to Downey, California. There they soon formed the Carpenter Trio, the third member their friend, Wes Jacobs, who played the tuba and bass. The trio competed in the Hollywood Bowl Battle for Bands in 1966, coming out on top and, as a result, winning a record contract from RCA Victor. They made two records, neither of which was released because the recording officials felt that the soft-rock performance by The Carpenters had no market in an area dominated by hard-rock groups. In 1967, the Carpenters formed a new combo, this time a six-member group calling itself Spectrum. It performed in the Los Angeles area, including an appearance at the Whiskey-a-Go-Go. Its soft-voiced approach to rock was so much in contrast with the hard-rock performances generally heard at the Whiskey-a-Go-Go that the manager, fearing he might lose his clientele, canceled the engagement.

This time, the two Carpenters decided to go it alone, with Karen singing and Richard playing the keyboards and doing the arranging and some composing. They developed their own vocal style which synthesized that of the Beatles, the Beach Boys and several other rock groups, and they experimented with multitrack recordings. Herb Alpert, of A & M Records, became interested in them and signed them to a contract. Their first LP, *Offering*, in 1969 did only moderately well, but one of its cuts, "Ticket to Ride" (John Lennon and Paul McCartney) invaded the best-selling charts. Because of the success of this number, that first

LP by the Carpenters was renamed *Ticket to Ride* with impressive selling results. Their first gold records were not slow in coming—three of them in 1970: "Close to You" (Hal David—Burt Bacharach), "We've Only Just Begun" (Paul Williams and Roger Nichols) and the album *Close to You*. Their performing style was now refined and set, described by John Rockwell in the *New York Times* as "middle-of-the-road rather than rock. They sing pretty music prettily, even the rock and pop standards they appropriate into their repertory, and they project an image so clean that it glistens."

Gold records were translated into TV appearances and concerts to sold-out auditoriums. With their scrubbed faces, bright eyes and clean cut features they were a winning visual attraction. There were more gold records: four in 1971, including one for the LP *Carpenters* which arrived at its gold-record status only three weeks after release; three in 1972, including one for the album *A Song for You*; five in 1973, two coming for the albums *Class Clown* and *The Singles: 1969—1973*; *Horizon* in 1975 and *A Kind of Hush* in 1976. The Carpenters were awarded Grammys in 1970 as being the best new recording artists of the year and for recording the best contemporary vocal performance by a group ("Close to You"), and in 1971 for the best pop vocal performance by a group (for the album *Carpenters*). The Carpenters performed the Oscar winning song, "For All We Know" (Robb Wilson and Arthur James—Fred Karlin) on the sound track of the motion picture *Lovers and Other Strangers* (1970).

7

From other parts of the United States came more groups covering the spectrum of rock from soft to acid.

The Four Seasons was a vocal quartet from New Jersey headed by Bob Gaudio, a songwriter, with the other three members being Frankie Valli, Tommy De Vito and Nick Massi (later replaced by Joe Long). This singing group (whose hallmark was Frank Valli's falsetto) made a bid for the teenage trade with song material written by Gaudio, though sometimes with the collaboration of Bob Crewe, beginning with "Sherry", and "Big Girls Don't Cry" in 1962 and "Walk Like a Man" in 1963 on the Vee-Jay label, their first big sellers. Their first LP, *Born to Wander* (title song by Al Peterson) was released in January 1964. Within six years, The Four Seasons sold eight million records; their single, "Rag Doll" (Bob Crew and Bob Gaudio) was among their top releases, and their albums *Gold Vault of Hits* and *Second Gold Vault of Hits*, gold records. Their record sales went into a perceptible decline by the closing 1960s. Nevertheless, The Four Seasons continued to prosper in nightclubs and on college campuses. In 1972, the foursome appeared at Madison Square Garden for two successive evenings to sold-out houses.

The Association, from the Midwest, brought with their ingratiating vocal harmonies some of the fresh and salubrious air of the open spaces to clear out the smoke of drug-oriented rock. After their first big hit, "Along Came Mary" (Tandyn Almer) in 1966, came their first gold disk, a gentle, tender love ballad "Cherish" (Terry Kirkman) and their first gold albums, *Along Comes The Association* and *The Association's Greatest Hits*, all in 1966. After that their best sellers included the albums *Inside Out*, *The Association*, *The Association Live* and *Goodbye, Columbus*, the last the soundtrack they had recorded for the motion picture of the same name in 1969. The Association captured still another gold record for their single "Never My Love" (Don and Dick Adrisi).

The same wholesomeness and sweetness that characterized the Carpenters and The Association were attributes of The Rascals (originally The Young Rascals) who were outfitted in Lord Fauntleroy costumes. The original members of this Eastern vocal and instrumental group were Felix Cavaliere (organ), Dino Danelli (drums) and Eddie Brigati (vocals) to which Gene Cornish (guitar) was added. They hit it big with the single "Good Lovin'" (Rudy Clark and Arthur Resnick) and with appearances in New York night spots and at Madison Square Garden. On the Atlantic label, they boasted gold records with the albums *Groovin'*, *The Young Rascals*, *Freedom Suite*, and *The Rascals Greatest Hits*, and their singles "Groovin'," "People Got to Be Free" and "A Beautiful Morning" (all three by Felix Cavaliere and Edward Brigati). Their LP, *See*, in 1970 was a best seller. Their success might well be gauged by the way black groups imitated them. In 1971, The Rascals, with a changed personnel left Atlantic Records for Columbia. The duo of Cavaliere and Danelli was now augmented by three new members, Buzzy Feiten, Robert Popwell and Ann Sutton. This new group made its bow in 1971 with the LP *Peaceful World* which was a best seller as was their LP in 1972, *Island of Real*.

Blood, Sweat and Tears was made up of nine members whose personnel changed frequently. Through all the turnover, Blood, Sweat and Tears remained a vital influence in rock, due to Bobby Colomby, the drummer, the only original member of the group who remained with it throughout its existence and served as its catalyst. Blood, Sweat and Tears brought about a marriage between rock and jazz with a new kind of sound that emphasized the brass and in which the whole instrument group provided a subdued background to the vocalist. The band was the fruition of a dream by Al Kooper to expand the traditional rock quartet with a four-man horn section. Their first gold record came with the LP, *The Child Is Father to the Man*, in February 1968, where could be heard "I Can't Quit Her" (Al Kooper and I. Levine) "House in the Country" (Al Kooper). After Al Kooper left the group, Fred Kipsus, alto saxophonist, took over its direction and revitalized it. Blood, Sweat and Tears went on to new and greater successes, largely because of the addition of the Canadian singer, David Clayton-Thomas. These were their gold records: the singles "And When I Die" (Laura Nyro and Jerry Sears), "You've Made Me So Very Happy" (Berry Gordy, Jr., Patrice Hollo-way, Frank Wilson and Brenda Holloway) and "Spinning Wheel" (David Clayton-Thomas) and their albums *Blood Sweat and Tears*, *Blood, Sweat and Tears, 2*, *Blood, Sweat and Tears, 3*, and *Blood, Sweat and Tears, 4*. Later on, David Clayton-Thomas tried to pursue a solo career, and Blood, Sweat and Tears had to make three albums without him. But in 1975 he returned to the group and it released *New City*.

Among the further listings of gold records are those by other rock bands that have won acceptance in the crowded arena of rock music. The Allman Brothers Band, The Band, Sly and the Family Stone, Yes, Bread, Seals and Croft, Steppenwolf, the Zombies, Grand Funk Railroad, Santana, the Jimi Hendrix Experience, War, Credence Clearwater Revival, Deep Purple, the Grateful Dead, The Guess Who—the list could go on and on. Then there are the superstar groups formed to create "the great blend in music" by joining up established stars of different rock combos that broke up in or about 1970. Crosby, Stills and Nash (supplemented by Young) was one such, gaining particular notice with their albums *Déjà* in 1970 and *4 Way Street* in 1971, both gold records. On the strength of these releases, as well as successful public performances, Crosby, Stills and Nash received in 1970 the Interna-tional Award as the Best Group of the year from the magazine, *Melody Maker*.

8

Rock was king at the Monterey International Pop Festival in California, which first took place in 1967. A seventy-minute motion picture documentary released in 1969, *Monterey Pop*, provides testimony to the high quality of the rock performances given here, highlighting the art of Janis Joplin, Otis Redding, The Mamas and Papas, The Who, Jimi Hendrix, and

Jefferson Airplane. The festival proved a financial as well as an artistic success, inducing promoters throughout the United States to arrange similar rock festivals elsewhere, in Atlanta, Dallas, Atlantic City, Miami and Seattle. These were generally disciplined convocations, with tens of thousands congregating to hear rock music and pay tribute to their favorite rock performers.

But the Woodstock Music and Art Fair, near Bethel, New York, in August 1969, was a different story. Three hundred thousand young people—maybe thousands upon thousands more—paying almost half a million dollars for admission, swarmed over a six-hundred acre tract set aside for a giant three-day festival of "peace, love and rock." Neither crushing traffic jams, overcrowding, shortages of food and water, nor inadequate toilet facilities, could discourage these rabid devotees of rock. Superlative rock music—by Joan Baez, Jefferson Airplane, Sly and the Family Stone, Jimi Hendrix, The Who, Led Zeppelin, Janis Joplin and others—played before one of the largest audiences ever to attend a concert made Woodstock a landmark in rock-performing history. But a discordant note was injected by many in the audience who openly used drugs and sex as a stimulant to their music listening pleasures. These extraordinary proceedings were captured in the motion picture documentary, *Woodstock*, directed by Michael Wadleigh and released by Warner Brothers in 1970. In 1974, Joel Rosenman and John Roberts, the original promoters of the Woodstock Fair, with the collaboration of Robert Pilpel, published a book, *Young Men with Unlimited Capital*, which revealed the whole story of how the Fair came into existence and how it developed into a Frankenstein monster that in the end devoured those who had been its creators and promoters.

Notoriety also came to a rock festival in December 1969 at Altamont, California, an event that has already been described in connection with the Rolling Stones. After that, any announcement of an impending rock festival sent local residents into open revolt, with legal suits preventing many such events from taking place. During the year of 1970 numerous scheduled rock festivals were canceled by court order. At one of these, thousands of young people had already converged on Powder Ridge, near Middlefield, Connecticut only to learn that there would be no rock music at all—a fact that did not seem to dampen their enthusiasm for, or their participation in, other less desirable practices that characterized these events.

But rock festivals did not become extinct; Watkins Glen, in New York, in July 1973 proved that. Watkins Glen was the largest rock festival ever held in the United States, drawing six hundred thousand onto a ninety acre grass knoll. The box-office take was a million and a half dollars, but it should have been much more than that. Only 150,000 of those attending had paid the admission price of ten dollars, all the others were gate crashers. For twelve consecutive hours rock music was poured out. The Grateful Dead started the program at noon and continued for about four hours. Then The Band took over —interrupted but undaunted by a thundershower—for another four hours or so with the Allman Brothers Band concluding the festivities at 3:30 in the morning. Though the use of drugs and alcohol was widespread, sexual activities were far less conspicuous than they had been elsewhere, and order was basically maintained. However, some girls performed a topless dance, some men walked around naked, drugs were peddled as if they were soda pop, one person died, and one hundred and fifty were hospitalized. When the festival ended and six hundred thousand people were disgorged into untraversable highways, the grounds were left a giant garbage dump. The promoters decided to do a repeat at Watkins Glen the following September, but local authorities put a firm end to all such calculations.

A violent reaction against the indiscretions flaunted in the name of rock set in among some sections of the rock community itself. This was not yet a revolution, but it was most assuredly a dissent—a protest against the way in which drugs, obscenity, freakish attire and outlandish stage behavior had been contaminating the rock scene. There was a mounting impatience with rock numbers that glorified experiences produced by drugs or symbolic of drug experiences. Shock was beginning to be felt in the rock world at the way in which overindulgence in drugs had shortened the lives of Janis Joplin, Jimi Hendrix, and Jim Morrison among others. A feeling of revulsion was beginning to set in at the way rock music was being used by some of the more flamboyant performers to indulge in simulation of sexual practices onstage.

This reaction expressed itself in several ways, but most noticeably in the mounting interest of rock enthusiasts in folk and country music and in the growing stress in rock performances of subtle musical textures and designs and in poetic lyrics. This reaction was also reflected in the incorporation of religious subjects into rock, in such numbers as "Jesus Is a Soul Man" (Lawrence Reynolds and Jack Cardwell), in Bob Dylan's "Father of the Night," and in George Harrison's "My Sweet Lord"; also in the rock musicals, *Jesus Christ Superstar* and *Godspell*.

40

Rebels With a Cause

1

There was much for which Americans could well be proud in the 1960s. This was the decade in which man first walked on the moon; when America stood eyeball to eyeball with the Soviet Union during the Cuban missile crisis without flinching; when young men and women, motivated by idealism as well as adventure, joined a Peace Corps to help the underprivileged nations of the world.

But this was also a decade to raise doubts and questions, anger and hate. It seemed as if the fabric of the American dream was unraveling. America had lost its onetime innocence. It was reeling from the devasting triple blow of the assassinations of President John F. Kennedy, Senator Robert F. Kennedy and Martin Luther King. Nationwide cynicism was nurtured by the questionable morality and ethics of men in high places; by the incapacity of the law to cope with violence in the streets and with juvenile delinquency. The onetime implicit faith Americans had held in American power was corroded by the Bay of Pigs fiasco, by the apathetic American response to the building of the Berlin Wall, by the unleashing of American forces on a small and backward country in Indochina at an appalling price in manpower, wealth and morality without a suspicion of victory; by the capture of the S. S. *Pueblo* by North Korea, the first time an American warship was seized on the high seas in time of peace, with few overt reactions other than outraged words.

"Credibility gap" was a much bandied about phrase to suggest the skepticism of Americans about the information doled out from the highest authorities about Vietnam, from the "body count" to the "light at the end of the tunnel." Antiwar sentiment, which reached a climax with the Tet offensive that gave the lie to the inflated optimism of the Pentagon, and with the unprovoked attack by American forces on Cambodia, erupted into riots in the streets of Chicago during the Democratic convention of 1968. It was expressed in giant peace marches coverging on Washington, D.C. (where thousands were illegally herded off to jail); in student protests on college campuses; and in President Johnson's exit from the White House.

The mushroom cloud of the atom bomb and the smoke from the devastation in Vietnam hung menacingly over all. The antiwar movement deeply involved the young. In revolt, they became "flower children." Flowers became for the young of the 1960s the symbol for peace; flowers were painted on their cars, clothes and even bodies. The young became "love children" or the "love generation," once again partly as a rebellion to death and war. "Make love not war," or "God is Love" were slogans blazoned on their bumper stickers, posters and buttons. The young began to make love promiscuously, openly, at weekend "love-ins," free-form gatherings, communal living quarters, rock festivals, as well as in the privacy of their own pads. The young squealed with delight when their favorite rock performers indulged in obscenity and displays of eroticism. And drugs provided the young not only with an escape from a gloomy and unfriendly world threatened by atomic annihilation but also with a panacea for all other evils. In Boston, Dr. Timothy Leary helped form the League for Spiritual Discovery, a name shortened to LSD, which was adopted for mind-expanding drugs which were promoted as a new way of life. LSD, marijuana and hard drugs, sharpened or distorted the senses, extended the mind's capacity to appreciate the beautiful, opened up altogether new and formerly unexplored worlds of emotional and psychic experiences.

Next to Vietnam, the greatest single concern of the American people in the 1960s was the civil rights movement. Racial fires burned in Watts, California, and in Washington, D. C. In the south, demonstrations by black freedom riders brought on indiscriminate arrests, murder, bombing attacks, the unleashing of police dogs and the brandishing of electric "prod" poles. Governor Wallace of Alabama stood proudly in front of the doors of the University of Alabama to prevent two Negro students from entering; Lester G. Maddox (later become Governor, then Lieutenant Governor, of Georgia) held axe in hand to keep black customers from his restaurant. Violence bred violence. The cry of "black power" was sounded as a defiant answer to white antiblack power. Black hate was pitted against white hate. A new organization, the Black Panthers, was dedicated to open violence, as opposed to the nonviolent stand of the National Association for the Advancement of Colored People.

Another uprising involved the young of all colors in a revolt against a society for which they had little sympathy, against values for which they had no respect, and a morality which they deemed outmoded. The status symbols of their elders were decisively rejected: wealth, social position, culture, physical attractiveness, economic security. The young wore their shabby uniforms as a symbol of freedom: long hair and beards, faded jeans, tattered tee shirts, no shoes. They lived and socialized in drab pads. They held in disdain cosmetics, expensive jewelry, swank nightclubs and restaurants and all the other appurtenances and refinements of the affluent society. They indulged openly in sex practices in defiance of the moral codes of their parents, and preferred open to formal marriages. They smoked marijuana and indulged in hard drugs. They were antiestablishment, antiauthority, antiwar, antirace discrimination, antipollution, antinuclear proliferation, antiarmament races, and most of all antiVietnam war. They burned draft cards and either renounced military service for prison or fled to Canada. They participated loudly, and often violently, in protest rallies and marches, barricading or destroying buildings on campuses and in the streets, coming into direct confrontation with the police. The young were, in short, rebels—but unlike the young of the 1950s, rebels with a cause.

2

The rebellion of the young found its voice in folk music. The guitar became the young person's favorite instrument (much in the same way that the ukulele had been in the 1920s). Singing songs with folk themes to strumming guitar chords became a favored form of entertainment in college dorms, on the beach, and in pads from Greenwich Village to Haight-Ashbury. When they were not making folk music, the young were listening to it through the records of the Kingston Trio, the Chad Mitchell Trio, the Limeliters, the New Christy Minstrels, all of whose best-selling records were of the folk song variety.

The young would crowd into hot, darkened coffee houses which dotted the country in the 1960s catering to the demand of the young for folk music. The Limeliters made their debut in a coffee house in Hollywood, California, before they embarked upon their successful engagement at the "hungry i" in San Francisco. Buffy Sainte-Marie first tasted success at the Gaslight Café, a coffee house in Greenwich Village.

Besides the coffee house, intimate nightclubs provided a haven for folk songs and folk singers: places like the "hungry i," Gerde's Folk City, the Bitter End, the Purple Onion, the Crooked Ear, Ballad Room, the Golden Vanity, Ten O'Clock Scholar, Casino Alley, the Unicorn, Club '47, the Know Where and many others with names equally picturesque. In places such as these Joni Mitchell (originally Roberta Joan Anderson) first drew attention to herself. She had come from MacLeod, Saskatchewan, in the Alberta hills of Canada, where she was born in 1943, and from Saskatoon where she attended high school. A talent for art led her to enter the Alberta College of Art in Calgary after she had finished high school. Her hobby was to sing songs to her own accompaniment on a ukuele, and occasionally she performed in small coffee houses in Calgary. By the time she was nineteen, she lost interest in art, and decided to make her way in music. The first song she wrote was a blues, "Day after Day."

Moving to Toronto, she supported herself by working as a salesgirl while writing songs and singing them in Toronto coffee houses. In one of them, in 1965, she met Chuck Mitchell, a cabaret entertainer. They fell in love, got married that June, and a year later went to live in Detroit where they separated permanently. As Joni Mitchell, she appeared in Detroit and New York night spots and signed a recording contract with Reprise. The albums *Clouds* in 1969 and *Ladies of the Canyon* in 1970 became best-sellers, and the album *Blue* (in which she sang ten of her own numbers) was one of the top releases of 1971. Meanwhile, she had created something of a furor in January 1969 at the Miami Pop Festival, found a swelling army of admirers on her concert tour of Eastern United States and Canada in March 1969, and enhanced her fame in April 1969 over television in shows starring Bob Dylan and Johnny Cash.

In 1972 she left Reprise for Asylum Records for whom she recorded *Court and Spark*, a gold record in 1974, *Miles of Aisles*, a gold record in 1974 even before it was shipped to the stores, her own "Help Me" which was nominated for a Grammy as the record of the year in 1975, and *The Hissing of Summer Lawns*, a gold record in 1975. *Hejira*, in 1976, was an instant best-seller. On August 9, 1975 she was voted the best female vocalist at the Rock Music Awards presented at the Santa Monica Civic Auditorium and telecast over the CBS network.

Among her best songs—many of them tormented with frustrations, others subtle expressions of moods, feelings and scenes, and the later ones turning to social commentary—were: "Woodstock," "Both Sides Now," "Urge for Going," "Let the Wind Carry Me," "Rainy Night House," "Help Me," "The Arrangement," "I Had a King," "Woman of Heart and Mind," "Cactus Tree." "Joni exorcises her demons by writing those songs," says the guitarist, Stephen Stills, "and in so doing she reaches way down and grabs the essence of something very private and personal to women."

In the hot summer weeks, devotees of folk music abandoned the coffee house and the night spots to converge on Newport, Rhode Island for an annual festival of folk music. The Newport Folk Festival was sponsored by George Wein as an arm of his now-successful Newport Jazz Festival, and it was coproduced by Wein and Albert Grossman. Its first season in 1959 attracted to its platform not only distinguished folk singers (Pete Seeger and Oscar Brand) and folk musicologists (John Jacob Niles) but also pop folk groups (the Kingston Trio) and many other distinguished participants in folk and folk pop, one of whom was Joan Baez. In 1960, new attractions were added to its programs: Theodore Bikel, Mahalia Jackson and The Weavers. Riots by unruly audiences, combined with financial problems, temporarily halted the festival after 1960, but in 1963 it was revived with forty thousand attending the three days of events, and it continued to prosper throughout the 1960s with an attendance exceeding eighty thousand by the end of the decade.

Joan Baez, "queen of folksingers," began her professional career with traditional American folk songs: "Barbara Allen," "All My Trials," "Lonesome Road," "Wildwood Flower." But her pacifist convictions and her unshakable belief in nonviolence inevitably sucked her into the vortex of the social and political crises that oppressed the 1960s. With a sublime indifference to money, and the fortune that her professional appearances could command at will, she dedicated her life and art to the struggle for a better society. Every one of her concerts was in some way related to a cause, "and all of the causes are as close to radical nonviolence as I can get," she told Don Heckman of the *New York Times*. Income from her concerts were siphoned into the treasuries of those causes in which she believed. "I think it pointless," she told Heckman, "to have stored up a million amounts of dollars when they could be put to use somewhere." She sang in the streets, at rallies and demonstrations, and benefits furthering the civil rights movement or helping exploited farmers or financing the Institute for Nonviolence in Big Sur, California, which she helped to found, or supporting the Georgia Draft Resistance. As part of her struggle for the new world she sang "We Shall Overcome," "Birmingham Sunday," "Joe Hill," "Saigon Bride" and Bob Dylan's "Hard Rain's A-Gonna Fall" and "I Shall be Released." "There isn't any way to separate my political life . . . from my career, because it's the same thing," she says. She was imprisoned several times for civil disobedience. She stood atop the barricades in the fight to ban the nuclear bomb and to oppose the Vietnam war, and she fought just as bitterly against those who would use violence in such an opposition. In her nonviolent way she organized and participated in peace marches; she dedicated her autobiography, *Daybreak*, "with love, admiration and gratefulness to the men who find themselves facing imprisonment for resisting the draft." She refused to pay a good part of her federal income tax because this money was being used for war. She saw her young husband, David Harris (who had resigned as president of the student body of Stanford University to devote himself full time to the Resistance-to-the-war movement) imprisoned for draft evasion. That marriage, incidentally, was a casualty of the Vietnam war. Once Harris was released from prison, neither he nor Joan could bind up the broken strands of their relationship. They parted permanently—Joan to write the song, "Myths," about their breakup.

She was born in Staten Island, New York in 1941. Her father was a physicist, her mother a professor of dramatic art. The recorded music of the classical masters could always be heard in the Baez home. When, in her twelfth year, she acquired a guitar, she used it to accompany herself in rock 'n' roll. After graduating from high school in Palo Alto, California in 1958, she moved with her family to Boston. One evening her father took her to Tulla's Coffee Grinder, a coffee shop where amateur folk singers performed. This was her first taste of folk music, the beginning of an insatiable appetite. She began moving more and more in a circle of folk singers from whom she acquired a repertory and learned stylistic details of vocal production and technique. This was her Conservatory; she never took a formal lesson or did any musicological study of folklore.

For two years, she sang regularly in coffee houses in the Boston area, at the Golden Vanity, the Ballad Room, Club '47. There she acquired the enthusiastic following both of Harvard students and of professional folksingers Theodore Bikel and Harry Belafonte, the latter of whom invited her to sing with his own group.

During a visit to Chicago, Joan Baez appeared at the Gate of Horn, a night spot specializing in folk music. Bob Gibson, himself a folksinger, was so impressed by her performance that he had her participate at the first Newport Folk Festival in 1959. She appeared on the program unlisted, and sent an audience of over ten thousand jumping to its feet with enthusiasm.

She returned to the Newport Folk Festival in 1960, this time billed as a star, and in the same year recorded her first album, *Joan Baez*, for Vanguard. It became the best-selling folk album ever recorded by a female singer and Jack Elliott, the record critic, called it the best first album in his listening experience. She was now invited to sing on campuses and in concert halls throughout the country, and on November 13, 1961, she gave a highly acclaimed recital at Town Hall, New York. She also appeared on guest shots over television. But she was avaricious neither for fame nor money. She turned down more offers than she accepted, would make only one record album a year, refused outright to appear either in the movies or on Broadway, and limited her public appearances to two months a year.

"Her voice," said *Time* in a cover story on November 23, 1962, "is as clear as air in the autumn, a vibrant, strong, untrained and thrilling soprano. She wears no makeup, and her long black hair hangs like a drapery, parted around her long almond face. . . . she comes on, walks straight to the microphone, and begins to sing. No patter. No show business. . . . The purity of her voice suggests purity of approach. She is . . . palpably nubile. But there is little sex in that clear flow of sound. It is haunted and plaintive, a mother's voice, and it has in it distant reminders of black women wailing in the night, of detached madrigal singers performing calmly at court, and of saddened gypsies trying to charm death into leaving their Spanish caves."

She involved herself in political causes. In 1963 she refused to appear on the weekly television folk program over ABC, the "Hootenanny," because Pete Seeger had been turned down for his left-wing political affiliations. In 1964 she was heard at Berkeley, California, at a rally for the Free Speech Movement. She also included in her programs—though sparingly—songs touching on the momentous issues of the day. A few of these were early protest songs by Bob Dylan, for whose talent she had expressed intense admiration—that is, until he moved on from pure folk music to folk rock—and whose songs she was among the first folksingers to promote.

She continued to release an album a year: *Joan Baez*, Vol. 2 in 1961; *Joan Baez in Concert*, in 1962; *Joan Baez in Concert, Vol. 2* in 1963; *Joan Baez/5* in 1964 . . . and so on. *Joan Baez, Joan Baez 2* and *Joan Baez in the Concert Hall* earned her gold records as did *Blessed Are* and *Any Day Now* in 1972. All these were released by Vanguard. Then in 1972 she shifted to A. & M for whom she recorded *From the Shadows* in 1972 and *Where Are You My Son?* in 1973.

With the shrill protesting voices of the late sixties became muted in the early seventies, sales of Joan Baez's recordings went into a sharp decline. Joan Baez now had to reevaluate herself as an artist. As a human being she remained unchanged in her political and social persuasions, but as a songwriter and performer she decided the time had come to descend from the soapbox if she were not to lose her audience. "I was fading into oblivion," she told an interviewer. . . . I realized . . . music was a very big part of my life. It really mattered to me. I didn't want it to end." This new attitude, she insists, was just "coming to terms with myself" rather than going the commercial route for the sake of selling records. And so, she recorded *Diamonds and Rust* which contained personalized songs of emotional involvement. In the title number and in "Winds of the Old Days," for example, she reflected on her onetime love affair with Bob Dylan. *Diamonds and Rust*, which became a gold record in 1975, marked Joan Baez's return to the winning circle. The success of her summer tour in 1975 (which resulted in still another best-selling album, *From Every Stage*, recorded live during the tour) further confirmed her return to popularity.

Where Joan Baez was primarily a performer, Bob Dylan was a songwriter as well as performer. In both areas he has been a giant figure in the urban folk music and in the protest movement of the sixties. His sympathy was with the underdog of society and he liked to sing about him. Born in Duluth, Minnesota, as Robert Zimmerman in 1941, he became Bob Dylan when he entered upon a singing career by adopting half the name of his favorite poet, Dylan Thomas. Most of Bob Dylan's boyhood and early adult years were spent away from home, traveling about in boxcars or by foot or hitchhiking—from Minnesota to the Dakotas and westward to California. During these travels he learned firsthand the meaning of personal deprivation and suffering, social injustice and inequality, and man's cruelty to man. His first significant musical impression came to him from listening to a black man singing a rhythm and blues number. Dylan was so fascinated that he followed the black man around for days. Another wandering minstrel presented him with a battered old guitar, which Dylan soon mastered sufficiently to be able to accompany himself in his own tentative efforts at making music. When he was eleven, Dylan came under the influence of Big Joe Williams, a blues singer. Dylan's first attempt at songwriting, however, was not a blues, but a ballad honoring Brigitte Bardot, that French sex kitten of the cinema.

His first job as a professional singer was in a striptease joint in Central City, Colorado. Dylan's folk song performances were not the kind of material people came to hear in a striptease joint, and after one week, he was fired. For another six months he attended the University of Minnesota, but his nervous restlessness made it impossible for him to discipline himself to a classroom and textbooks.

While his life was drifting toward an uncertain destination, Dylan experienced the greatest single influence of his life—that of folk singer, Woody Guthrie. Guthrie's songs of protest, with which Dylan had become acquainted through records, had long stirred him deeply. A Guthrie concert in California had proved an experience he could not forget. Dylan and Guthrie are reputed to have met personally for the first time while Guthrie was bedridden in hospital with a rare disease that was destroying him. That meeting with the man he admired is said to have given Dylan the direction he needed; Guthrie is believed to have convinced him to pursue a career as a folksinger and writer of songs protesting against the abuses society inflicted on the underprivileged and the downtrodden.

With a goal now clearly in mind, Dylan came to Greenwich Village and made the

rounds of its small coffee houses and cafés singing folk songs, accompanying himself sometimes on the piano, sometimes on the guitar, and sometimes on a harmonica attached to the
neck of his guitar. He developed an individual singing style: a gruff and technically imprecise
voice rich with the emotion of the message he was conveying to his listeners. He was
discovered by Robert Shelton who wrote in the *New York Times* on September 29, 1961: "A
bright new face in folk music is appearing at Gerde's Folk City. Although only twenty years
old, Bob Dylan is one of the most distinctive stylists to play in Manhattan cabarets in
months. Resembling a cross between a choir boy and a beatnik, Mr. Dylan has a cherubic
look and a mop of tousled hair he partly covers with a Huck Finn black corduroy cap. His
clothes may need a bit of tailoring, but when he works his guitar, harmonica, or piano and
composes new songs faster than he can remember them, there is no doubt that he is bursting
at the seams with talent."

A month later, Dylan recorded for Columbia his first album, *Bob Dylan*. None of its
songs were by Dylan himself. In his second album, *Freewheelin' Bob Dylan*, a year later,
several of his own bitter songs lamenting social evils began to be heard. "Master of War" was
an attack against munition makers; "Hard Rain's a-Gonna Fall," against the hydrogen bomb;
"Talking World War III Blues," against warmongers; "I Shall Be Free," against the despotic
forces that would rob man of his basic rights of freedom; and "Blowin' in the Wind," his most
successful song, against racial prejudice, injustice and bigotry. To the young, "Blowin' in the
Wind" became their hymn of dissent against society. The number's first major success came
in a Warner recording by Peter, Paul and Mary which sold over two million disks and
received Grammy awards as the best performance by a vocal group and as the best folk
recording. Records of this song were also pressed by sixty other artists, among them Marlene
Dietrich, Sam Cooke, Duke Ellington, Percy Faith, and the New Christy Minstrels. When
Bob Dylan sang it at the Newport Folk Festival in 1962 he received such a thunderous
ovation that Joan Baez and Pete Seeger sprang from the audience to the platform to join him
in a repeat performance.

When Dylan gave his first concert at the Carnegie Chapter Hall in New York on
November 4, 1961, only fifty-three were in the audience. Less than two years later, when on
April 12, 1963, he appeared in a concert in Town Hall, New York, the auditorium was
packed. For Dylan was now a star, and as such he was invited to appear on the Ed Sullivan
CBS-TV show on May 12. When, on that occasion, the authorities at CBS refused to permit
him to sing his "Talking John Birch Society" (with Ed Sullivan dissenting), Dylan withdrew
from the program. But other appearances on television, on college campuses and in concert
halls—and, to be sure, his recordings—provided him with ample forums in which to preach
his song gospel. He touched upon racial problems in "Ballad of Emmett Till"—Till being a
black boy who was lynched for having whistled at a white woman. "Only a Pawn in their
Game" was inspired by the murder of Medgar Evers, the civil-rights leader; "Lonesome
Death of Hattie Carroll" was about a black maid who was caned to death by her employer in
the recent South. Dylan sang about the generation gap and the sexual revolution in "The
Times They Are a-Changin'," "Don't Think Twice, It's All Right" and "All I Really Want to
Do." The horror of war, nuclear or otherwise, concerned him in "It's All Right Ma" and
"With God on Our Side." The murder of the innocent was the theme not only of "Lone-
some Death of Hattie Carroll" but also of "Ballad of Hollis Brown" and "Who Killed Davey
Moore?" Dylan was apprehensive about the future of the world in "When the Ship Comes
In." In "Lay Down Your Weary Tune" he paid a touching tribute to Woody Guthrie.

He was, in short, the conscience of the 1960s, and the young people of that decade
loved him for it. They also loved him because fame and wealth did not greatly change his

way of life. For him possessions had little value and he cared little about his personal appearance. He favored simple, functional clothes: denim jeans, a turtleneck shirt, a worn-out jacket, or work clothes with boots. He preferred to travel by motorcycle rather than in a limousine. In the limelight, as in his former obscurity, he remained a lonely, restless, introverted man ever vitally troubled by the wrongs of the world.

But Bob Dylan's followers soon became disenchanted with him. In the summer of 1964, Dylan recorded *Another Side of Bob Dylan*. This was the first clue he gave that he was ready to move in a new direction in which social viewpoints were replaced by personal themes in which he would search deep within himself for his identity rather than serve as a critical spectator of the political and social scene. Three songs in this new album expressed this attitude: "All I Really Want to Do," "My Back Pages," and "It Ain't Me, Babe." Within the framework of his former folk-song style he introduced rock and pop elements ("It Ain't Me, Babe" is rock) to produce a new Dylan idiom, that of folk rock. His lyrics were now more symbolic and avant-garde than topical. He went further along this path with the album *Bringing It All Back Home*, released in March 1965, in which he used electrified instruments. At the Newport Folk Festival on July 25, 1965, in the second half of the program, he abandoned his acoustical guitar for an electrified one in presenting numbers in his new folk-rock manner. To his onetime passionate followers and admirers all this represented betrayal, and they expressed their disapproval at the festival with hisses, boos and derogatory shouts.

"I got bored with my old songs," was his explanation. "I can't sing 'With God On Our Side' for fifteen years. I was doing fine, you know, singing and playing my guitar. It was a sure thing, don't you understand. . . . I was getting very bored with that. . . . I was thinking of quitting."

Despite the defections in the ranks of Dylan's admirers, his public kept growing with this change of direction. Though in 1965 he had had million-disk sales with two singles—"Like a Rolling Stone" and "Postively 4th Street"—and though his first albums had been best sellers, his largest sales came after he replaced his pure folk idiom for a more popular one. He received gold records for three albums in 1967 (*Blonde on Blonde, Highway 61*, and *Bringing It All Back Home*) and others between 1968 and 1973 (*Bob Dylan's Greatest Hits, Vol. I., Self Portrait, Bob Dylan's Greatest Hits Vol. II., John Wesley Harding, Nashville Skyline*, and *Dylan*). *New Morning*, in 1970, while not earning a gold record was on the best-selling charts for weeks.

One of Dylan's most successful songs since "Blowin' in the Wind" was "Mr. Tambourine Man," which appeared in his album *Bringing It All Back Home*. It reached the best-selling charts in seven countries, and it was with this number that The Byrds became singing stars.

In 1966 it seemed that fate, rather than any changing style, would bring an end to Dylan's successful career. In August of that year, while riding his motorcycle at breakneck speed, he lost control and plunged almost to his death. He was confined to a hospital for many months; it seemed unlikely that he would ever return to a professional life. But after leaving the hospital and going into temporary retirement with his family in Woodstock, New York, he returned to recording with a country style album, *John Wesley Harding*, released on January 5, 1968. It was a giant seller. The significant numbers in the album were "Dear Landlord," "Drifter's Escape," "I'll Be Your Baby Tonight," "I Am a Lonesome Hobo" and "I Dreamed I Saw St. Augustine."

His second album in a country rock style was *Nashville Skyline*, in April 1969. Then Dylan resumed his concert work and in spite of his fee of $50,000 an appearance against a

percentage of receipts, there was no dearth of bookings. In a 1969 performance on the Isle of
Wight, off the coast of England, he drew an audience of almost two hundred thousand from
all over Europe. He also appeared in the motion picture *Don't Look Back* (1967), wrote songs
for another motion picture, *Little Fauss and Big Haley* (1970) and published a book,
Tarantula (1970), a personal volume written in a stream of consciousness style. He was given
an honorary doctorate from Princeton University in 1970 which led him to write the song,
"Day of the Locusts," about a man like himself who had never been able to adjust to the
academic life.

Dylan's first concert tour since 1966 took place early in 1974. He was backed up by
The Band, a rock vocal and instrumental group comprising Robbie Robertson, Richard
Manuel, Garth Hudson, Rick Danko and Levon Helm. The Band first became prominent
with its initial record release, *Music from Big Pink* on Capitol Records released in August
1968 and become a gold record, and in personal appearances at the Woodstock Festival, San
Francisco's Winterland, New York's Fillmore East and with Bob Dylan at Carnegie Hall, all
in 1969. Its army of stalwart believers swelled with the success of later albums: *The Band*
(1969), *Stage Fright* (1970), *Rock of Ages* (1972) and *Cahoots* (1973). The Band called it a
day with a mammoth nine-hour concert called "The Last Waltz" in San Francisco on
November 26, 1976, in which Bob Dylan, Joni Mitchell, Ringo Starr and Neil Diamond
were some of the participants.

Bob Dylan and The Band opened at the Chicago Stadium on January 3 and closed in
Los Angeles on February 14. Between these two dates they were heard in forty concerts in
twenty-one cities, grossing over five million dollars. Many of those crowding the auditoriums
came to hear Bob Dylan in nostalgic recollection of the sixties. The audiences joined him
robustly in the singing of such early Dylan protest songs as "Blowin' in the Wind" and "Like
a Rolling Stone," clapping their hands in rhythm as he sang. The new Dylan, who had
become a singer of ballads about love and other personal sentiments, ignited far less of a fire.
But there was no more turning back for Dylan, as he explained to his audience in one of his
new songs, "Most Likely You Go Your Way, I'll Go Mine." "Yeah," he wrote in the notes
for his gold record album *Planet Waves* released with the backup of The Band under a new
label, Asylum, in 1973, "the ole days are gone forever and the new ones ain't far behind."
That album included several of his late love songs, the best of which were "Hazel," "Going,
Going, Gone," and "On a Night Like This." *Before the Flood* was Dylan's second album for
Asylum and brought him another gold record.

In 1975 he toured the Northeast with the Rolling Thunder Revue, appearing mostly
in small halls and auditoriums in middle-sized cities and college towns. (It ended its tour,
however, in a mammoth auditorium—Madison Square Garden in New York.) "The Thunder Revue," explained John Rockwell in *The New York Times*, "was widely described as an
attempt to break the dehumanizing big-concert ritual and return to a simpler, more communal kind of music-making." In the meantime, late in 1974, Dylan left Asylum Records to
return to the Columbia fold with the release of *Blood on the Tracks*, a gold-record album that
was noted the best in its class at the Rock Music Awards at Santa Monica Auditorium on
August 9, 1975 (telecast over the CBS network). And, in 1975, he recorded another gold
disk Columbia album, *Desire*. "Shelter from the Storm," "Idiot Wind," "Lily, Rosemary
and the Jack of Hearts" and "A Simple Twist of Fate" came out of the former album; and
"Hurricane Carter," "Joey," and "Sara" out of the latter. In these albums, in his tours, and
his first network TV special in 1976, Dylan reemerged in the 1970s as a "vital force in both
contemporary pop music and, perhaps in contemporary culture as well," in the words of
John Rockwell.

Judy Collins emulated Joan Baez in starting out as a folksinger of Anglo-American ballads, before becoming interested in urban folk music and joining the political activist movement. Then, affected by the turbulent Sixties, she began appearing in demonstrations and benefits promoting the civil-rights movement, including a visit to Mississippi in 1964 to assist in black voter registration. She was in the forefront of Vietnam War protests and participated in the making of a record album sponsored by the Woman's Strike for Peace in which she sang a duet with Joan Baez. She helped in the support of Joan Baez's Institute for the Study of Nonviolence and other activist groups. Her folk-song repertory now included Bob Dylan's "Masters of War" "Farewell"; and her own song protest against war, "The Dove"; "Hey Nelly Nelly" (Shel Silverstein and Jim Friedman); Pete Seeger's "Bells of Rhymney" (Idris Davies); "Turn! Turn! Turn!", words taken from the Book of Ecclesiastes, music adapted by Pete Seeger; and "Come Away Melinda" (Fred Hellerman and Fran Minkoff). All these can be found in her LP, *Judy Collins, No. 3* released in October 1963. The *Judy Collins Concert* LP., recorded live at Town Hall, New York, on March 23, 1964, included "Tear Down the Walls" (Fred Neil), Bob Dylan's "Lonesome Death of Hattie Carroll" and Tom Paxton's "Ramblin' Boy" and "Bottle of Wine."

Then, almost at the very time Bob Dylan did so, she extended her horizon by reaching out to songs largely out of the range of social commentary: theater songs, songs of self-revelation, introspection and soul searching. She now favored the poetic and sometimes brooding songs of the Canadian poet-composer, Leonard Cohen, who may be said to have been her discovery, and the poignant and wistful ballads of another Canadian, the songstress-composer, Joni Mitchell. She also wrote revelatory and personalized ballads of her own. She could now say to an interviewer that the only answer to the problems of the day was "to love and to get together and to be open." The new Judy Collins was heard in the record albums *My Life*, in 1967, *Wildflowers* and *Who Knows Where the Time Goes?* in 1968, *Living* in 1971, as well as in her debut concert at Carnegie Hall, New York and her tours to Australia, New Zealand, Poland, the Soviet Union and Japan in 1966 and 1967. Her Elektra single "Both Sides Now" received a Grammy award, and she acquired gold records for "Who Knows Where the Time Goes?" (Sandy Denny) in 1969, "Amazing Grace" in 1971, and the albums *Colors of this Day* and *Judith* in 1974 and 1975 respectively.

The daughter of Charles "Chuck" Collins, a blind master of ceremonies on the radio, Judy Collins was born in Seattle in 1939. At seven she started taking piano lessons and soon came to be regarded as a child prodigy. When her family moved to Denver, Colorado, she studied the piano with Antonia Brico (one of the world's few women symphonic conductors), made public appearances with local orchestras, and began making plans for a career as a virtuoso. But the demanding regimen of a prospective concert artist led her, when she was sixteen, to forget the concert stage and concentrate her music making on singing and playing the guitar. At seventeen she won first prize in Stars of Tomorrow, a singing contest sponsored by the Kiwanis Club Convention in Atlantic City, New Jersey. While attending the University of Colorado, she began to appear in small nightclubs and coffee houses (principally at the Exodus in Denver), in Chicago (at the Gate of Horn), in Cambridge, Massachusetts and New York City. At the Village Gate in New York in 1961, an executive of Elektra Records heard her and gave her a contract. She made her first appearance at the Newport Folk Festival in 1963, and after that not only appeared there annually but also served as a member of its board of directors. In 1964 she made her first appearances in concert halls. After a recital at Town Hall in New York, Robert Shelton wrote in *The New York Times* on March 23, 1964, that she "established herself without delay in the front rank of balladeers." Her appearance at Carnegie Hall in 1965 was the first of many performances there. In 1967,

Donald Mullen said in the Los Angeles *Times*: "Folk singer Judy Collins has a voice that makes the ten-year old want to go out and protest something, the thirty-year old restless in his dark pin stripes, and the forty-year old wonder what happened to those dreams of living in a Left Bank garret."

Buffy Sainte-Marie is a full-blooded Cree Indian. Some of her songs concern her oppressed people and the abuses they suffered at the hands of white men, of which the best known is "My Country 'Tis of Thy People You're Dying." She voiced her indignation at the monstrosity of war in "Universal Soldier," which became an unofficial anthem of the opponents of military conscription and the Vietnam war. In "Cod'ine" she spoke bitterly about drugs, to which she herself at one time became addicted after using it as medication for a throat ailment. Withdrawal proved long and harrowing. She promoted the brotherhood of man in "Seeds of Brotherhood."

But though her best known songs are part and parcel of the protest movements of the sixties, most of her others are far removed from political or social distress. These include country-type songs, simple folk ballads, love songs, city blues, and songs with foreign subjects: "Broke Down Girl," "Until It's Time for You to Go," "I'm Gonna Be a Country Girl Again," "Tall Trees in Georgia," "He's the Keeper of the Fire," "Cripple Creek," "Los Pescadores," "A Man," and "Café Molineau." Her album, *Changing Woman*, released in 1974 by MCA, is made up of love songs, the most notable of which is "A Man."

She was born (probably) in the Saskatchewan district of Canada in 1942. Orphaned as a child, she was raised by adopted parents in Wakefield, Massachusetts. She got her first guitar when she was seventeen. While attending various colleges, she initiated a folksinging career on college campuses and in small coffee houses. At a guest appearance at the Gaslight Café in New York's Greenwich Village in 1965, she impressed Robert Shelton of the *New York Times* as "one of the most promising new talents on the folk scene." He commented favorably on her "throaty sensual voice" and "her vibrant way of interpreting her songs." She also made a strong impression that night on Herbert S. Gart, a New York talent agent, who became her manager.

Her first recording was the Vanguard album, *It's My Way*, released in 1964. Four of its numbers remained ever popular with her audiences: "Now that the Buffalo's Gone," "It's My Way," "Incest Song" and "Universal Soldier." It was a best-seller; so were succeeding albums, *Many a Mile, Little Wheel, Spin and Spin, Fire and Fleet and Candlelight, I'm Gonna Be a Country Girl Again, Illuminations, Native North American Child: An Odyssey* and *Changing Woman*. After public appearances at New York's Carnegie Hall, the Newport Folk Festival, and London's Royal Albert Hall she became a commanding figure in the folk-song movement of the Sixties, with performances in all the major American cities as well as Canada and Europe, performances at the Helsinki Music Festival and Montreal's Expo '67, engagements in nightclubs, and spots on network television programs. In the *Saturday Review*, Irving Kolodin found she was "blessed with a rare command of the powers that communicate. . . . She can sing on, off, or around the pitch, as she chooses; her sense of phrasing is superb." In the New York *Daily News*, Walter C. Meyer provided another note about her: "She sings in a clear, husky-timbered voice that can be sweet, bitter, compassionate, sprightly, sexy, or wryly humorous. She can purr or belt, warm you into a smile or chill you with a trembling intensity."

Paul Simon's hostility to war, the armaments race, racial bigotry, are sometimes explicit but more often implicit in his songs. While his "7 O'Clock News/Silent Night" is not a song at all but a vehicle, it reveals how deeply he felt about the political climate in America at the time he wrote it, by juxtaposing the singing of the beloved Christmas hymn, "Silent

Night, Holy Night," with a news broadcast whose headlines represent a stark contradiction to the peaceful message of the carol. But basically, Paul Simon's songs—which for several years he and his singing partner, Art Garfunkel presented so effectively—speak of a different kind of revolt from that found in the music of Joan Baez, Bob Dylan, Judy Collins or Buffy Sainte-Marie. Simon's songs give voice to the protest of the young against the demands made upon them by the establishment: for the young person's dream fantasies; for his contempt for the false values of society; for his fear of tomorrow. Such thoughts are couched not only in poignant music but in imaginative and sometimes symbolic poetry. Simon sees the young—even as he views the principals in "The Dangling Conversation"—"like a poem poorly written, we are verses out of rhythm, couplets out of rhyme, in syncopated time." In his article on Simon in the *New York Times Magazine*, Josh Greenfield tells how Simon's message is "one of literate protest against the pangs of youth, the pathos of old age and the matter-of-fact hypocrisies of the middle-aged and the middle class in between." Simon reaches out with empathy to the young: "Hear my words that I might teach you; Take my arms that I might reach you," he says in "The Sound of Silence." "When tears are in your eyes, I'll dry them, I'm on your side, Oh, when times get rough," he exclaims in "Bridge Over Troubled Water."

Born in Newark, New Jersey, in 1942, Paul Simon grew up in Forest Hills, in Queens, New York. Only three streets from where the Simons lived in Queens was the home of Art Garfunkel, later to become Simon's singing partner. Their first meeting took place in public school, in the sixth grade, when they were both cast in the same school production. Their mutual interest in rock 'n' roll made them friends. They would listen to Alan Freed's radio program together and sometimes to Simon's guitar accompaniment would perform not only rock 'n' roll numbers but also Simon's early song efforts. They put two of those Simon songs on a demonstration record which brought them a contract from a small company named Big Records. Their first release was "Hey, Schoolgirl," a rock 'n' roll number with lyrics by Garfunkel to Simon's melody. This in turn brought them an invitation to appear on Dick Clark's radio program where they were billed as "Tom and Jerry." Neither this exposure, nor the Big Records releases, were encouraging. Big Records, in fact, went into bankruptcy. Though only sixteen, Simon and Garfunkel considered themselves failures and went on to plan a more practical future. Simon went to Queens College to complete his academic education by receiving a Bachelor of Arts degree; Garfunkel majored in architecture at Columbia College. Intermittently they continued to make music together, but now preferring folk music to rock 'n' roll. They even made a few appearances in Greenwich Village coffee houses.

Simon made his entry as a successful professional songwriter with a song influenced and inspired by the political scene and the struggle for racial equality. That song was "He Was My Brother." The "brother" in this protest song was Simon's classmate at Queens College, Andrew Goodman, a young socially conscious rebel, who had gone to Mississippi to participate in demonstrations for racial equality where he was murdered. This tragedy shook Simon. He now knew he could no longer go on writing "dumb teenage lyrics" (to use his own phrase), but had to write meaningful verses suitable for the stormy times in which he lived. "He Was My Brother" helped bring him a contract with Columbia Records. With Art Garfunkel as his singing partner, Simon recorded the album *Wednesday Morning, 3 a.m.* in October 1964. It did not sell well. (Reissued in 1969 after Simon and Garfunkel had become famous, it went on to sell a million albums!) Simon and Garfunkel now parted temporarily, Simon going off to England to continue singing folk songs.

While Simon was in England, a Miami disc jockey discovered one of the cuts in the

Simon and Garfunkel album, "Sounds of Silence." He started to feature it repeatedly on his program. This led Columbia to record and market it as a single, offering it as a folk-rock number with an instrumental rock background of drums, bass and electric guitar, instead of the acoustical guitar used in the album. The rock public seized upon it and so did devotees of folk music. It became the first gold record of Simon and Garfunkel.

Simon and Garfunkel now reunited to appear on network television and at concerts, and to make more records for Columbia. Their second album, named after their big hit song, *The Sounds of Silence*, appeared in February 1966. Together with the title number this album was distinguished by several other outstanding Simon songs, the most significant of which was "I Am a Rock." A third album—*Parsley, Sage, Rosemary and Thyme* in September 1966—gathered into a single attractive package some of Simon's choicest numbers up to this time: "Scarborough Fair/Canticle," "Flowers Never Bend with the Rainfall," "The Dangling Conversation," "The 59th Street Bridge" (sometimes also called "Feelin' Groovy") and "7 O'clock News/Silent Night, Holy Night." This album sold over a million copies.

When, in 1967, the motion picture *The Graduate*, directed by Mike Nichols, was released, Simon and Garfunkel were heard on the sound track singing "The Sounds of Silence," "Scarborough Fair/Canticle" and several new Simon numbers, including "Mrs. Robinson" which had become one of the top songs of 1968 and in a performance by Simon and Garfunkel received a Grammy as the record of the year. The protest, implied rather than explicit, in Simon's songs was by no means a negligible element in the overall artistic design and intent of that film. In its release as a sound track album, *The Graduate* brought Simon and Garfunkel another gold record, together with a Grammy for the best original score for a motion picture.

Bookends, another gold record, released in 1968, contained more Simon delights sung by Simon and Garfunkel. "A Hazy Shade of Winter," "At the Zoo," and "Save the Life of the Child" are memorable. But one of the greatest commercial successes enjoyed by Simon and Garfunkel came with their album *Bridge Over Troubled Water*, in 1969, whose sale reached the million mark on the day of its release, climbing to a six-million figure within two years. They received a seventh gold disk in 1972 with the album *Simon and Garfunkel's Greatest Hits*. This was the first time any performer had accumulated gold records for each one of his first seven albums. In addition to these, gold records were awarded to them for their singles "Mrs. Robinson," "59th Street Song," "Cecilia" and "Bridge Over Troubled Water," the last winning Grammys as the record of the year, the album of the year, and the song of the year.

In 1969, the partnership of Simon and Garfunkel broke up. One of the disruptive forces in their continuing relationship was Art Garfunkel's involvement in motion pictures in which he successfully played nonsinging roles in *Catch 22* (1970) and *Carnal Knowledge* (1971). Garfunkel's obligations to his screen commitments complicated the working schedule of Simon and Garfunkel. But Simon confessed to an interviewer that another important factor was responsible for their separation. "I didn't want to be always half of something," he explained. "You can't go for a long period of time as a partner, not anybody. You can't be one quarter of the deal and be somebody—you're always one quarter of the deal. You've got to stop—and then it's traumatic."

Besides his work in the movies, Art Garfunkel made his recording debut, divorced from Simon, in 1973 with *Angel Clare*, a fine album of contemporary and traditional ballads released by Columbia. Paul Simon went it alone in 1972 with the LP *Paul Simon*, following it in 1973 with *There Goes Rhymin' Simon*. That Simon was well able to stand on his own two feet as a performer was demonstrated by the two gold records he received for these albums (extending his own streak to nine consecutive gold records for nine albums). He also did well in his public appearances as a solo performer. He made his first such tour in 1973, opening an eleven-city engagement in Hartford, Connecticut, on May 4, and ending it with three performances in Carnegie Hall, New York, on June 1, 2, and 3—always playing to capacity houses.

In 1974, Simon received a gold record for his album, *Live Rhythmin'*. One year later, on October 18, 1975, when he appeared live as a guest artist on the "Saturday Night" program over NBC-TV he sent shock waves not only through the auditorium but across the country. After completing "Gone at Last," with Phoebe Snow, he went to the wings and drew to center stage his one-time partner, Art Garfunkel. This was their first reunion in some five years. They brought down the house singing some of their old numbers—"Scarborough Fair," "Bye, Bye Love," "The Boxer"—and introduced a new number by Paul Simon, "My Little Town." This piece, sung by Simon and Garfunkel, was later included in Paul Simon's album *Still Crazy After All These Years* and in Art Garfunkel's album *Breakaway*, both released by Columbia later in 1975 and both of them earning gold records. His recording of his song "Fifty Ways to Leave Your Lover" was a gold disk in 1976.

Simon picked up two more Grammys in 1976: for *Still Crazy After All These Years* as the best album of 1975, and as best pop male vocalist of that year.

American folk music, and specifically songs of protest, were Arlo Guthrie's birthright and heritage, since he is the son of Woody Guthrie. Born in Brooklyn, New York, in 1947, Arlo Guthrie was brought up in an environment where folk music flourished. From his earliest years, he was fired with the ambition to travel in his father's shoes. Arlo began performing publicly when he was a teenager, made his professional debut in 1966 and soon acquired his own following on college campuses and in coffee houses. At the Newport Folk Festival in 1967, he created something of an explosion with his performance of his own song, "Alice's Restaurant." This was a strange ballad beginning and ending with a simple sixteen-measure melody opening with the line "You can get anything you want at Alice's Restaurant." In between was a twenty minute recited monologue about how he was arrested on Thanksgiving Day for littering and his unhappy experiences at the hands of police, followed by even more painful adventures at the hands of the draft board—the police and the draft board serving as symbols of a despotic establishment. As for Alice's restaurant—that is the place he went to with his friend on Thanksgiving Day when he decided, as a friendly gesture, to remove some garbage to a city dump, a gesture that got him arrested. "This song is called 'Alice's Restaurant,' " Arlo Guthrie says in an explanatory note that has about it the air of surrealism that pervades the ballad, "It's about Alice and the restaurant, but Alice's Restaurant is not the name of the restaurant; that's just the name of the song, and that's why I call the song 'Alice's Restaurant.' " Guthrie's success at the Newport Folk Festival brought him a recording contract from Reprise, whose first release was the LP *Alice's Restaurant* in 1967. Two years later Guthrie performed his ballad in a motion picture that was named after it. Later Reprise recordings of Arlo Guthrie's songs added to his stature and influence. These included the single "The Motorcycle Song" and the albums *Arlo*, *Running Down the Road* and *Washington Country*.

3

Bob Dylan's "Blowin' in the Wind" became an anthem of the civil rights movement of the 1960s.

But "Blowin' in the Wind" was second in importance to another hymn which served the civil rights struggle so effectively that it has been described as "the Marseillaise of the integration movement." The song is "We Shall Overcome"—its melody come from an old religious folk tune which, in 1901, was fashioned by C. Albert Tindley into the Baptist hymn, "I'll Overcome Some Day." Sometime later, this was made into the worker's song, "We Will Overcome." Zilphia Horton, a member of the Highlander Folk School in Tennessee, learned this worker's song in 1947 from a union member. Thirteen years later, in 1960, she helped to adapt it (with the help of Frank Hamilton, Guy Carawan and Pete Seeger) into the civil rights anthem, "We Shall Overcome." In the early demonstrations, Guy Carawan, a West Coast folk singer, began teaching it to black students. Like all songs that come at the right time with the right message, the song spread like a conflagration, heard wherever civil rights meetings or demonstrations were held. During the singing, as Robert Shelton explained in *The New York Times* on July 23, 1963, the participants "cross arms in front of themselves, link hands with persons on each side and sway in rhythm to the music. Sometimes the song is 'lined out' between leader and congregation in call and response fashion, at other times sung in unison. Improvisations of melody and lyrics are widespread."

"We Are Marching to Victory" was another song often heard during the racial conflicts of the Sixties. This one came into being a decade earlier during the boycott of the buses by the blacks in Montgomery, Alabama, led by the Reverend Martin Luther King. The melody itself was that old Negro spiritual, "Give Me That Old Time Religion," while the new lyrics were the work of an unidentified writer.

Popular composers and singers contributed to the song literature of the black protest movement. Some of them were written by whites. "Now!" with words and music by Betty Comden and Adolph Green was set to the Israeli melody "Hava Nagila," adapted by Jule Styne and introduced by Lena Horne. "Freedom Is the Word" (E. Y. Harburg—Burton Lane) was sung in May 1964 by Robert Preston and a children's chorus on a closed circuit television show beamed to thirty-five cities sponsored by the National Association for the Advancement of Colored People.

But most of the songs that owe their existence to the racial tensions of the times came from blacks. The bombing of a Sunday school in Birmingham, Alabama, in which four girls were killed, led Nina Simone to write "Mississippi Goddam!" Pride in race and heritage, nurtured by the black revolt, inspired Curtis Mayfield's "I Am So Proud," "Choice of Colors" and "We're a Winner." Ella Fitzgerald dedicated her civil rights song, "It's Up to You and Me" to Martin Luther King.

Songs of protest against the Vietnam War were many and varied. Pete Seeger's "Waist Deep in the Big Muddy" was a parable about the politics of war escalation which was censored from the Smothers Brothers Comedy Hour when Pete Seeger made his first return to television on September 10, 1967 after having been blacklisted for seventeen years by the broadcasting establishment. Joan Baez's "Saigon Bride" is a poignant farewell of a South Vietnamese soldier to his bride as he goes out "to stem the tide." He inquires: "How many children must we kill, before we make the wave stand still?" Miss Baez was to have sung it at her concert at Constitution Hall in Washington, D. C. in August 1967. When the Daughters of the American Revolution cancelled her appearance, she sang it at a free performance at the foot of Washington Monument to an audience of thirty thousand. "The Vietnam Blues" (Kris Kristofferson), "Napalm" (Nalvina Reynolds), "Talking Vietnam" (Phil Ochs), "The War Is Over" (Phil Ochs) and John Prine's "Sam Stone" and "Diamond in the Rough," are representative of many other songs bitterly denouncing American military involvement in Vietnam. (One pro-Vietnam War song, however, did gain a modest commercial success in 1966. It was "Ballad of the Green Berets," by Staff Sergeant Barry Sadler who recorded it in a best-selling Victor release.)

When, in 1971, the Los Angeles chapter of the National Organization for Women sought a song expressing their aspirations for liberation, their selection was "I Am Woman" (Helen Reddy and R. Burton).

Helen Reddy has said: "I don't think of myself as a feminist. I'm a singer who has had my woman's consciousness raised." In spite of such a disavowal, there is no doubt that her way to superstardom came through her espousal of women's rights through song and her becoming (whether by accident or design) a symbol of the surging feminist movement of the 1960s.

She was a singer-composer from Australia, having been born in Melbourne in 1941 to a theatrical family. Her father was a producer, writer and actor; her mother, a popular actress; her older sister, an ingenue in musical comedies. Her own stage debut took place when she was only four when she appeared with members of her family in a vaudeville act at the Tivoli Theatre in Perth. As a young adult, she sang with a band in a Melbourne hotel and appeared regularly over television, becoming the star of her own show, "Helen Reddy Sings," in 1960. Winning, in 1966, a national talent contest sponsored by a television station in which over thirteen-hundred performers competed, enabled her to come to New York where she hoped her singing career would take a giant leap forward. She arrived with $230 and "all I could fit in two suitcases. . . ." A promised audition with Mercury Records never materialized because they were not in the market for female vocalists. For a time she supported herself by singing in bars, private clubs and small-time resorts. "I got down to twelve dollars. That was it, I told myself. But it was also my birthday. Some friends I'd made in New York gave me a party. Turned out to be a fund raiser—everybody contributed five dollars a head for me. . . . It was the night that changed my life. Jeff Wald crashed the party."

Jeff Wald was a talent agent for the William Morris Agency. He took Helen Reddy's career in hand as her agent; he also became her husband. Some TV guest appearances were arranged. On one of these, the Johnny Carson Show in March 1970, audience reaction was so enthusiastic that Capitol Records signed her up and had her do a few singles. Two of them did very well, indeed: "I Believe in Music" (Mac Davis) and "I Don't Know How to Love Him" (A. L. Webster and T. Rice), the latter from *Jesus Christ Superstar*. Her first album was also called *I Don't Know How to Love Him*; one of its tracks was "I Am Woman." After being used on the sound track of the motion picture *Stand Up and Be Counted* (1972) in Helen Reddy's rendition, "I Am Woman" was released as a single by Capitol to sell two million disks and to earn her, in 1973, a Grammy as the best female rock-pop-folk vocal performer. From this time on, she became one of the most sought after women singers at public concerts, in plush nightclubs, at music fairs and festivals. She also became a star on a major network television program and made her film debut in 1974 in *Airport, 1975*. Her record albums *I Am Woman, Long Hard Climb, Love Song for Jeffrey, I Don't Know How to Love Him*, and *Greatest Hits* were all gold records, and so were many of her singles. Among her best known singles are "Leave Me Alone" (Linda Laurie—Anne-Rachel), "Angie Baby" (Alan O'Day), "Love Song for Jeffrey" (Helen Reddy and P. Allen), "Delta Dawn" (A. Harvey and L. Collins) and "Westwind Circus" (Adam Miller).

In the song "Stand Up and Be Counted" (Ruth Batchelor), which has nothing to do with the motion picture of that name, Helen Reddy had another successful pop number promoting the women's liberation movement. But most of her monumental successes outside of "I Am Woman" came with songs removed from the social scene, songs strong in either dramatic content or personalized feelings.

As a prodigy songwriter, Janis Ian raised a shrill voice against society's ills. She was only about sixteen when "Society's Child" became a best-seller in her own recording on the Verve label—a song touching on the problem of interracial dating and bitterly denouncing adult injustice. She followed it with several more songs excoriating society for dishonesty, hypocrisy, exploitation, and the absence of proper communication between the young and the adult world: "Janey's Blues," "Honey Do Ya Think?" and "New Christ Cardiac Hero."

Born Janis Fink in New York City in 1951, the daughter of a music teacher, she was a sensitive child who suffered from being shunted from one apartment to another—she had thirteen different homes in New York and New Jersey in her first fifteen years. Such a nomadic existence made her a perpetual stranger to her schoolmates and, apparently, she regarded herself as a stranger at home as well. Music was a refuge. She began to study the piano when she was three, and the guitar eight years later. She was only twelve when she wrote her first song. While she was attending the High School of Music and Art in New York, her songwriting efforts were "the only things that kept me going as long as I did without totally freaking out," she has explained. "School was always absurd . . . but the whole fame thing was happening, and I was going to a school where most of the teachers were frustrated musicians—they didn't like it."

Fame at sixteen had come by way of "Society's Child" which she had written three years earlier. It brought her engagements in night spots and concert halls all over the United States, together with appearances on television and recordings. Verve released two albums, *Janis Ian* in 1967 and *For All the Seasons* in 1968. Then her success petered out. Her songs were too monochromatic in subject matter and in musical appeal to prevent boredom. While participating in a peace march in Washington, D. C., in 1967, she met a young fellow whom she married, and for a couple of years she went into retirement.

She tried to revive her career in 1970 with some new songs—among them "Hello Jerry" and "Present Company"—and with a new album, this time for Capitol, *Present Company* in 1971. Failure to duplicate her early success brought a second withdrawal from a professional career.

When she returned once again to songwriting, to recording, and to public appearances she was no longer a prodigy strumming on the single string of her creative lyre but a mature songwriter concerned with her own personal world and the stresses and emotional crises of young women like her. Three new albums—*Stars, Between the Lines* and *Aftertones*—and an appearance at Carnegie Hall on December 11, 1975, revealed that she had grown up artistically both in her lyrics and in her music. Songs like "Watercolors," "From Me to You," "When the Party's Over," "Bright Lights and Promises" and most of all "At Seventeen", wrote John Lissner in his review in *The New York Times*, "offer testimonial to Ian's impressive arranging, composing and singing talents. Each song has meticulously crafted melodic lines." Earning a gold record for *Between the Lines* and a Grammy in 1976 as the best pop female vocalist for "At Seventeen" provided evidence that Janis Ian had reemerged, as John Lissner further noted, "as a force in the recording field."

The title song of *Stars* touched poignantly on the pitfalls of her one-time fame, and in "At Seventeen," the principal number in *Between the Lines*, looks back reflectively on her past as "an ugly duckling." In *Aftertones*, in 1975, which many critics regard as her best album thus far, "bittersweet vignettes give way to self-assertion," as we read in *Rolling Stone*. "She expands her musical palette with excursions into salsa and the blues and shows a steadily improving ability; she presents a feistier persona than before, especially in songs like 'This Must Be Wrong' and 'Boy, I Really Tied One On.' "

When Janis Ian abandoned the political and social arena in her songwriting she was just following the lead of Bob Dylan, Paul Simon, Joan Baez and Helen Reddy. The times they are a-changin'. The seventies were less conducive to the fertilization of monumentally successful songs of protest than the sixties had been. The millenium had not yet arrived, to be sure. But the Vietnam War was over. Watergate had driven President Nixon out of the White House. Racial equality was no longer the impossible dream. The protesters and the dissenters no longer disturbed streets and campuses the way they had done some years earlier. The songwriters who had been rebels with a cause in the sixties, then, were impelled to direct their creativity into other channels.

For those who were less resilient, the changing times brought silence or, more tragic still, annihilation. This happened to Phil Ochs, a young man born in El Paso, Texas in 1940 and, twenty years later, spawned by the folk scene in New York's Greenwich Village. In the 1960s, at gatherings and marches where the fist and the voice were upraised in protest he was there with his guitar singing about the disturbed social scene, about President Kennedy's assassination, about racial intolerance, about Vietnam: "I Ain't Marchin' Anymore," "I Declare the War Is Over," "The Crucifixion," "Outside of a Small Circle of Friends," "Talking Vietnam," "The War Is Over." Having lost most of the forums where he could sing his songs, and much of the audience to whom he could sing them, Phil Ochs took his own life on April 9, 1976.

41

Nashville Alley— and Country Sounds Elsewhere

1

By 1970, music in Nashville, Tennessee, had become a $250 million-a-year industry. For Nashville was by now not only the capital of country and western music, but also the greatest single center of musical production in America. Four hundred and more performers of country music and nine hundred songwriters resided within the limits of Nashville, with seventeen hundred members enrolled in the local chapter of the American Federation of Musicians, seven hundred members in the local American Federation of Television and Radio Artists, and four hundred members of the Nashville Songwriters Association. In Nashville, three hundred publishers established offices, forty resident record producers issued disks on three hundred labels. In addition, there could now be found in Nashville some sixty recording studios, six record pressing and plating plants, five hundred record distributors, one hundred talent agencies, forty booking and management agencies, eight syndication firms and the regional offices of BMI and ASCAP. All these forces combined to create, promote and disseminate country music. More than half of all the recorded music originated in Nashville. Coast-to-coast special radio programs have had their origins in Nashville. Where just a decade ago there were only eighty-one radio stations devoted to country music, the number has expanded to eight hundred. The telecast of the Johnny Cash and Glen Campbell shows and the annual presentation of the Country Music Awards are only three of many programs which have emanated from Nashville. Other country shows are taped in Nashville for syndication to over three hundred independent television stations. Probably the most widely circulated of these has been "Hee Haw," which started out as a television network attraction in 1969 before being syndicated to hundreds of stations; Roy Clark—banjoist, guitarist and singer—is its star. Some fifty live road shows come out of Nashville to tour the United States in country shows.

In 1967, the Country Music Association instituted annual awards for various categories of country and western music. Eddy Arnold was honored as entertainer of the year; Loretta Lynn, female vocalist of the year; Jack Greene, male vocalist of the year; the Stonemans, vocal group of the year; Porter Wagoner and Dolly Parton, vocal duo of the year, the Buckaroos, instrumental group of the year. "There Goes My Everything" (Dallas Frazier) was picked as the outstanding single and outstanding song, Jack Greene's *There Goes My Everything*, outstanding album, and Chet Atkins, outstanding instrumentalist. Since 1967, the entertainer of the year awards went to Glen Campbell, Johnny Cash, Merle Haggard, Charley Pride, Loretta Lynn, Roy Clark and Mac Davis. Chet Atkinson was three times chosen instrumentalist of the year (1967, 1968, 1969), and Jerry Reed, twice (1970, 1971). Loretta Lynn was chosen four times as female vocalist (1967, 1972, 1973, 1974), and Tammy Wynette, three times (1968, 1969, 1970). Charley Pride was picked twice as male vocalist (1971, 1972), and Merle Haggard, three times as entertainer of the year (1970, 1973, 1974). Among the recipients of awards in 1976 were Mel Tillis, Dolly Parton, Roy Clark and Buck Trent.

In Nashville, awards were also instituted by ASCAP and BMI for the best country music by songwriters affiliated with each of these two organizations. ASCAP chose only four songs for its initial selections in 1963: "The End of the World" (Sylvia Dee—Arthur Kent), "Adios Amigo" (Ralph Freed—Jerry Livingston), "Does He Mean That Much to You?" (Jack Rollins and Don Robertson), and "I Sat Back and Let It Happen" (Paul Hampton). The number of ASCAP awards in country music has since then increased to about fifty. BMI has proved more generous in its allotment of annual awards, beginning with forty-one in 1967, and subsequently exceeding one hundred. In addition to these awards, BMI instituted the Robert J. Burton Award in 1970 to honor the most widely performed BMI country song of the year. Its first recipients were "Gentle On My Mind" (John Hartford), "I Never Promised You a Rose Garden" (Joe South) and "Help Me Make It Through the Night" (Kris Kristofferson).

As part and parcel of the growth of Nashville into the national center of country and western music was the opening of Opryland, U.S.A., a new fifteen-million-dollar auditorium for the Grand Ole Opry. Amid the most elaborate ceremonies ever attending country music—and in the presence of President and Mrs. Richard M. Nixon—the Grand Ole Opry presented its first show in its palatial new home on March 16, 1974, part of which was beamed throughout the United States by over a thousand radio stations and by a television network.

The motion picture industry took cognizance of Nashville as the capital of country and western music—and of country and western as America's prime popular music in the 1960s and 1970s—with the production of the film epic, *Nashville* (1975), produced and directed by Robert Altman. Altman here planned a social as well as musical document, a portrait of the decadence of American politics, morality ethics and way of life as seen behind the facade of the country and western music industry. But *Nashville* is primarily about country music—on stage and behind the scenes, as chronicled in the activities of twenty-four characters during a five-day span. The greed, cynicism, hysteria and razzle dazzle that are the warp and woof of country music in Nashville are captured in a series of sequences and scenes brilliantly directed with a keen sense for detail. But the music itself does not always rise to the occasion. The motion picture should have exploited both the best and the most

characteristic of country and western music. But some inexplicable motive led Robert Altman to have the score made up of songs written for the film by the actors and actresses
themselves, with the result that too much of what is sung sounds more like a parody than the
real thing. Rising above the overall mediocrity are such numbers as "Memphis" (Karen
Black), "My Idaho Home" (Ronee Blakely) and "For the Sake of the Children" (Richard
Baskin and R. Reicheg). The best of the musical crop is "I'm Easy" (Keith Carradine), which
won an "Oscar" and the Golden Globe Award in 1976 as the year's best screen song. The
score as a whole—its deficiencies notwithstanding—was nominated for a Grammy in 1976.

2

During the sixties, and into the seventies, more and more stars began filling the galaxy of
country and western music.

Roy Clark, whom we have mentioned earlier in conjunction with the television
program "Hee Haw," was born in 1933 in Meaherrin, Virginia, the son of a government
employee who played the banjo and guitar. The father gave Roy instruction on both instruments when the boy was fourteen. Roy Clark won first prize in the National Country Banjo
Championship in 1948 and again in 1949, which opened the doors for his television debut
on a local station on the program "Hayloft Conservatory of Musical Interpretation" and an
appearance at the Grand Ole Opry.

In the early fifties, Clark moved on to Washington, D.C. where he made some
public and television appearances with Jimmy Dean. Clark's talent as an instrumentalist of
country music brought him a guest spot on the Arthur Godfrey Show on a national television
hookup in 1956 and numerous public appearances throughout the country.

In 1960 he appeared with the country singer, Wanda Jackson, at the Golden Nugget
in Las Vegas, and soon after that provided the instrumental backing for several of her
recordings. He was now given his first recording contract by Capitol as an instrumental
soloist. His first albums, *Lightning* and *Tip of My Fingers*, and the single "The Tip of My
Fingers" (Bill Anderson) brought Clark representation on the country charts. His stature kept
growing after that through appearances with Andy Williams both on the state fair circuit and
over network television, as a member of the Andy Griffith Spectacular in Las Vegas in 1966,
performances at the Grand Ole Opry, and appearances on the television syndicated country
program, "Swingin' Country."

He branched out from being a virtuoso on the banjo and the guitar to singing and
being a comedian. "Hee Haw," in which he was co-starred with Buck Owens beginning with
1969, made him a superstar. It was this vehicle, as Neil Hickey wrote in *TV Guide*, "that
brought him from the penumbral half-light of minor celebrity to the blinding glare of public
favor. Today he is a walking conglomerate with vast interests in real estate, cattle ranching,
broadcasting, music publishing, advertising and records. He will spend three hundred days
away from his home in Davidsonville, Maryland, performing at fairs, rodeos, livestock
expositions; making albums in the recording studios of Nashville; videotaping 'Hee Haw'
programs . . . and doing his nightclub act in places like Reno, Lake Tahoe, and Las Vegas."

He has been a frequent visitor to the Johnny Carson, Merv Griffin, Mike Douglas
and Flip Wilson shows, among others. As a recording artist he has enjoyed best-sellers (now
on the Dot label) with the albums *Happy to Be Unhappy, Do You Believe This, Urban,
Suburban, Greatest!, Everlovin' Soul* and *Superpicker*, and the single "Yesterday When I
Was Young" (Charles Aznavour). The Academy of Country and Western Music selected
him in 1970 as comedian of the year, and in 1973 both as entertainer of the year and as TV
personality of the year.

Roger Miller was born in Fort Worth, Texas, in 1936 and raised in Oklahoma. His boyhood days were spent working on a ranch and riding bulls in rodeos. He learned to play the guitar and acquired a repertory of country music by listening to Hank Williams' recordings. During the Korean War, he enlisted in the Army which assigned him to a hillbilly band entertaining American troops in Korea. After his discharge, he worked for a while as a fireman in Amarillo, Texas. By then, music had become all-important in his life. Determined to make his way as a performer and composer, he went to Nashville where he supported himself by working as a bellboy at the Andrew Jackson Hotel. In time he succeeded in getting a small record company to sign him up, but Roger Miller's first three releases were such failures that the contract was allowed to expire.

At this low point in Miller's life, he met Ray Price, guitarist, singer and composer of country music, who was a power in Nashville by virtue of his successes at the Grand Ole Opry, his hit records for Columbia, and his position as impresario and star of his own traveling show. Price hired Miller to appear with his company, then used his influence to get Miller to record the Miller song, "Invitation to the Blues." On the strength of the modest success of this release, Miller found a publisher for some of his songs, the Tree Publishing Company, which issued his "Half a Mind," a best-seller in 1958 in Ernest Tubbs' recording. Miller was also given a contract by Victor for whom he recorded his own songs "You Don't Want My Love," "Sorry Willie," "Teardrops," "Hitch-Hiker," "Hey, Little Star," "I Catch Myself Crying" and "Lock, Stock and Teardrops," among many other numbers. The last of these, in 1963, was Miller's last successful recording for Victor. After that his recording company was Smash, with whom he climbed to the uppermost echelon of the charts. "Dang Me" (backed by "Chug-a-Lug") in 1964 sold over a million disks and was given Grammys as the best country song of the year and the best male country performance. Three other Grammys came Miller's way that year for the best country and western single, best country and western album, and best new country and western artist.

"King of the Road" was the song and the recording that placed Miller permanently among Nashville's country and western stars. Written and recorded in 1965, it was a hobo song in the simplistic style of a folk tune of the twenties. It sold over two million disks in Miller's own recording, captured five Grammys (including those for best single of the year and best male performance). In addition, "King of the Road" was recorded by over one hundred and twenty-five other performers and was translated into more than thirty languages. A parody with new words by Mary Taylor but using Miller's melody intact—"Queen of the House"—was published in 1965, successfully recorded by Jody Miller for Capitol, and became the recipient of a Grammy Award. (In 1965, Roger Miller acquired a sixth Grammy for that year with his album *The Return of Roger Miller*, giving him the unprecedented total of eleven Grammys in two years.)

Roger Miller had many more resounding best-sellers after "The King of the Road" with his own recordings of his songs: "Engine, Engine, No. 9," "The Last Word in Lonesome Is Me," "England Swings," "One Dying and a-Burying," "Husbands and Wives," "My Uncle Used to Love Me but She Died," "Walking in the Sunshine," and "Little Green Apples." Andy Williams' recording of Miller's "In the Summertime" sold over two million disks.

His career came to an abrupt halt in the late 1960s due to his dependence on drugs. "I decided one day I was going to be a man and not a vegetable," he said, and he overcame his addiction in 1969 to resume an active career.

Glen Campbell's career was one of several instances in which a country performer achieved immediate success in Nashville with a single record. That recording by Campbell, on the Capitol label, was "Gentle On My Mind" (John Hartford) in 1967. From then on,

Campbell could not miss, whether on records, in concerts and over television (including his own network series). He acquired gold records for "Gentle On My Mind"; for "By the Time I Get to Phoenix" (Jim Webb) which brought him a Grammy as the year's best vocal performance; for Jim Webb's "Wichita Lineman" and "Galveston"; and for "Rhinestone Cowboy" (Larry Weiss), picked in 1976 by the Country Music Association as the year's best song and selected that year at the ABC-TV Bicentennial Music Awards as the best pop-rock single and the best country single; also for the albums *Galveston, Glen Campbell Live, Try a Little Kindness, Glen Campbell's Greatest Hits* and *Rhinestone Cowboy*. In 1969 he appeared in the motion picture *True Grit,* starring John Wayne.

Born in Delight, Arkansas, in 1938, Campbell got his first guitar when he was five by ordering it from a Sears Roebuck catalogue. He abandoned schooling in his fourteenth year to join a three piece band in a tour of Wyoming, playing in hillbilly clubs and bars. After appearing over the radio as a member of Dick Bills and the Sandia Mountain Boys, he organized the Glen Campbell and the Western Wranglers. In 1960 he headed for Hollywood where he was much in demand as a guitar sideman at recording sessions for top artists. For five years he was employed by various recording studios, earning a good deal of money, but getting little personal satisfaction from his work. The few records he himself had cut as a singer for Capitol, and which had moderate sales, convinced him that there might be far more fertile lands for him to till than those of a sideman. He was thinking of Nashville and he came there in 1967. His friendship for the composer John Hartford led him to record Hartford's "Gentle On My Mind" which immediately raised Campbell to star status. His top hit records, other than those already mentioned, included Jim Webb's "Where's the Playground Susie," "Dreams of the Everyday Housewife" (Chris Gantry), "I Wanna Live" (John D. Loudermilk), "True Grit" (Don Black—Elmer Bernstein) and "Try a Little Kindness" (Bobby Allen Austin and Thomas Curt Sapaugh).

Kris Kristofferson, whose music has been described as "progressive Nashville," knew rejection and frustration before he achieved triple fame as a composer, singer and motion picture actor. In many of his songs he has strummed poignant autobiographical strains. His personal struggles during the breakup of his first marriage is the subject of "For the Good Times." In "The Pilgrim—Chapter 33" he speaks of himself (in the third person) as a "walking contradiction, partly truth and partly fiction, taking every wrong direction on his lonely way back home." In "To Beat the Devil" he is the troubadour who is always "singin' to the people who don't listen to the things that I am sayin'." Lonesomeness and frustration stalk ghostlike in "Sunday Mornin' Comin' Down" (a best-selling record by Johnny Cash) and in "Me and Bobby McGee" (made famous by Janis Joplin, Roger Miller and others).

Kristofferson's life touched many bases before he slid home with the winning run. He had been a boxer, helicopter pilot, janitor, bartender, football player, Rhodes scholar, army officer, and novelist. Only then did he go on to become one of the most important songwriters to come out of Nashville. He was the son of an Air Force major, born in 1936 in Brownsville, Texas, where his father was stationed. After attending Pomona College in California—where he was a football star, a Golden Gloves boxer, and a sports reporter for his school paper—he went to Oxford, England, on a Rhodes scholarship to study English literature. In England he started to write a novel (his second such attempt) and began dabbing with songwriting, modeling his song efforts after Hank Williams who was his idol. Calling himself Kris Carson he appeared on English TV as a rock 'n' roll singer. Though he received top grades in literature and philosophy at Oxford, he dropped out of school, married his childhood sweetheart, then joined the U.S. Army to get assigned as a helicopter pilot in

Germany. In 1965, the Army redirected him to West Point to teach English at the Academy. On his trip back from England to the United States he stopped off at Nashville to meet some friends. They were sufficiently impressed with his songs to urge him to drop out of the Army for good and specialize in music. One of them, "Vietnam Blues" was published. While thus involved creatively in songwriting, he worked in Nashville as a janitor, ditch digger and bartender. Times were difficult. His son was born with a defective esophagus and doctor bills mounted astronomically. To help pay them he flew helicopters on oil rigs in New Orleans two weeks a month. His marriage was going sour and he was getting nowhere at all in his songwriting career. Disgusted with the way he was betraying his native intelligence by drifting from one endeavor to another, his parents practically disowned him. "They called me a dope fiend and a hippie and a Communist," he will tell you. When, at long last, he got a record contract and pressed some of his songs into his first album, *Kristofferson*, the company removed the album from the market soon after it was released without offering an explanation.

Then, in 1969, he published in Nashville the song, "Me and Bobby McGee," which he wrote with Fred Foster. This was a number about two lonely wanderers, the composer and a girl, Bobby McGee. "Freedom's just another word for nothin' left to lose"; in recollection, he knew he would trade all of his tomorrows "for a single yesterday, holdin' Bobby's body next to mine." Janis Joplin was only one of many who recorded this number and sent it flying in the charts. Because of its success, Monument re-released Kristofferson's first album, re-named it *Me and Bobby McGee*, and included in it the title song. That title number helped make it a best-seller, but other cuts also became popular: "For the Good Times," "To Beat the Devil," "Help Me Make It Through the Night" and "The Other Side of Nowhere."

To gain hearings for his songs, he became his own performer not only on records but at the Newport Folk Festival in 1969, on Johnny Cash's TV show in 1970, and at the Troubadour Club in Los Angeles with his own band in June 1970. In October 1970, Kristofferson received the Country Music Association's song of the year award for "Sunday Mornin' Comin' Down," and the following January (and again in 1974) he was named by the Nashville Songwriters Association songwriter of the year. He received his first Grammy in March 1971 for the best country song, "Help Me Make It Through the Night." Another Grammy came in 1973 for the best country duo, with his wife, Rita Coolidge whom he married on August 19, 1973. In 1973, Kristofferson received gold records for the single "Why Me" and the albums, *Silver Tongued Devil and I* and *Jesus Christ was a Capricorn*. In 1974, "From the Bottom to the Bottom," performed with his wife, was chosen by BMI as "the best country vocal performance by a duo or group." Their album, *Full Moon*, in 1975, received a gold record, and their album *Breakway* was a best-seller. In 1976, Kristofferson and Rita Coolidge received a Grammy for the best country vocal performance by a group.

He has gathered additional laurels in motion pictures: *The Last Movie* (1971); *The Fat City* (1972) for which he recorded "Help Me Make It Through the Night"; *Silver-Tongued Devil* (1972); *Cisco Pike* (1972); as Billy the Kid in *Pat Garrett and Billy the Kid* (1973); *Blume in Love* (1973); *Bring Me the Head of Alfred Garcia* (1974); *Alice Doesn't Live Here Anymore* (1975); *The Sailor Who Fell From Grace with the Sea* (1976); and *A Star Is Born* (1977) where he was co-starred with Barbra Streisand.

Charley Pride had the distinction of becoming the first black man to become successful in country music. But his prodigious artistic and commercial success has since given only tangential significance to the racial implications of Charley Pride's career. Charley Pride has become one of the greats of Nashville Alley, and the honors heaped upon him since 1970 have made him an elect in his chosen performing field. On May 6, 1974, *Time* noted: "He has sold more records for RCA than any singer since Elvis Presley"; and by that time he was reputed to have earned several million dollars from twenty-one of his records.

He had his first gold record in 1970 for his Victor album, *The Best of Charley Pride*. More gold records were earned in 1971 with *Tenth Album, Just Plain Charley* and *Charley Pride—In Person*. In 1970 he was the winner of the *Billboard* Trendsetter Award, and one year later he was chosen the year's leading male vocalist and the entertainer of the year by the Country Music Association. Then more gold records: "Kiss an Angel Good Morning" (Ben Peters), and the album *Charley Pride Sings Heart Songs* in 1972, the albums *Sensational, From Me to You,* and *The Country Way* in 1973, and *Did You Think to Pray* in 1975. In 1973 he was the recipient of a Grammy for the best male country performance *(Charley Pride Sings Heart Songs)*. Grammys also came to him for *Did You Think to Pray* and for the gospel "Let Me Live." In 1974, the first American Music Awards competition, based on a poll of the record-buying public, placed him as the top country male vocalist, and his *A Sunshiny Day* as the top country album.

Certainly he has become one of the biggest selling recording country artists. Just as certainly he is one of the best: a sweet-singing, sensitive artist who is neither black nor white in his country styling but uniquely himself.

His early ambition was to become a major league baseball player and he had given a good account of himself with semi-pro and minor-league teams. But the singing of country music had also been a passion from boyhood on. Born in 1938 in Sledge, Mississippi, where his father was a sharecropper, Charley learned to love country music by listening to the radio, and most particularly to the broadcasts of the Grand Ole Opry. When he was fourteen he used his savings from picking cotton to buy a guitar upon which he learned to play proficiently without instruction. Upon graduating from Sledge Junior High School, Pride went to Memphis in 1955 to join the Negro American Baseball League. Except for a two-year stint in the Army between 1956 and 1958, he was a professional ball player for a number of years, as a member of the Birmingham Black Barons, the Memphis Red Sox, and the Timberjacks and Amvets in Montana. In Montana, he supplemented playing ball with working in a tin smelter of the Anaconda Mining Company. He was also singing in night-clubs during the weekends, and at the ball park over the public address system before games.

Not until 1964 did he finally decide to forget baseball for music. On the advice and encouragement of Red Sovine—a successful guitarist and songwriter who was a regular of the Grand Ole Opry—Charlie Pride came to Nashville in February 1964. There he got a long-term singing contract from Victor. Some of his early singles reached the best-seller list in 1966–1967, among them "Does My Ring Hurt Your Finger?" (Don Robertson, John Crutchfield and Doris Clement) and "I Know One" (Jack H. Clement); so did his first album, *Country Charlie Pride,* released in 1967, which became a gold record some years later. "Just Between You and Me" (Jack H. Clement) got a Grammy nomination in 1966 as the best country and western male performance.

Pride first confronted the incongruity of being a black man in a field almost totally white when, in 1966, he drove from Montana to Detroit to appear at a gala country show before an audience of ten thousand people, none of whom were probably aware that he was black before his entrance on the stage. "I came out of the shadows and into the light," he has recalled, "and it wasn't that they suddenly stopped applauding, it was more like someone had turned down the volume. Then there was silence. Finally I said 'I realize this is kind of unique—me coming out here on a country show wearing a permanent tan.' " That remark won him the sympathy of his audience. They listened tolerantly—and liked what they heard.

"I kept saying that kind of thing for quite a while," Pride continues, "until it wasn't necessary. I mean now, after more than twenty albums, I don't have to say anything."

On October 16, 1972, Loretta Lynn became the first woman named entertainer of the year by the Country Music Association (She was so named three times more in 1972, 1973 and 1974.) Two more awards came to her that evening, as female vocalist and (with Conway Twitty) top vocal duo. These rewards were earned. For a decade, Loretta Lynn had been the foremost woman performer of country music; as far back as 1964 the *Record World* and *Music Business* had singled her out as the top country female vocalist of the year, and in 1967 and 1968 *Billboard* gave her a similar honor.

She came out of Butcher Hollow, Kentucky, born Loretta Webb in the early 1930s, probably 1932. Her father was a coal miner; a firsthand knowledge of coal mining later led her to write one of her best known songs, "Coal Miner's Daughter." As a child, she walked several miles each day to the one-room schoolhouse where she received an education that was terminated in the eighth grade. When she was fourteen she met and fell in love with Mooney Lynn, an army veteran and former coal miner seven years her senior. They got married and went to live in Custer, in the state of Washington. By the time she was eighteen she was raising four children and helping to contribute to the support of her family by washing other people's clothes and picking strawberries with migrant workers.

Since she loved singing to her children, her husband bought her a seventeen-dollar guitar upon which she learned those basic chords needed to accompany herself in the folk songs she had learned as a child in Kentucky and others she herself invented. One evening, in a grange hall in Custer, her husband jumped on a table and announced that his wife was a better singer than any of the performers heard in that hall. There and then, Loretta Lynn made her public debut. In 1960, she appeared over radio station KPUG in Custer and was so well regarded that she was asked to sing nightly in the public auditorium. In 1961, she organized her own band with which she appeared as vocalist and for which she wrote songs. Her first to get recorded was "I'm a Honky Tonk Girl," issued by Zero, a small house in Vancouver, British Columbia. To promote this record, she and her husband bought a secondhand Ford and traveled eighty thousand miles all over the country propagandizing it to disc jockeys and helping to make a sale of some fifty thousand disks. In time, Loretta Lynn became so well known that she was engaged to appear with the Grand Ole Opry, where she stayed on for a twenty-week engagement.

By the fall of 1961, Nashville became her permanent home. With her husband acting as her business manager, she signed a lifetime contract with Decca Records. Her first important Decca release was "Success" (Johnny Mullins) and soon after that came "Before I'm Over You" (Betty Sue Perry), "Wine, Woman and Song" (Betty Sue Perry), "Blue Kentucky Girl" (Johnny Mullins), and "The Home You're Tearing Down" (Betty Sue Perry). Her best-sellers included songs of her own writing: "Don't Come Home a Drinkin' " (in collaboration with Peggy Sue Wells), "You Ain't Woman Enough," "Dear Uncle Sam," "First City," and "The Pill," the last of these, a hit in 1975, banned from several radio stations because of its provocative subject matter. A long succession of best-selling LPs was begun with *Loretta Lynn* and brought her gold records for *Loretta Lynn Greatest Hits* and *Don't Come Home a Drinkin'*. In 1971 and 1974 she received a Grammy with Conway Twitty for the best country vocal performance by a duo. Her autobiography, *Loretta Lynn: Coal Miner's Daughter*, written in collaboration with George Vecsey, was published in 1976.

Three times selected female vocalist of the year by the Country Music Association —and holding gold records in one hand and Grammys in another—Tammy Wynette has often been called the "first lady in country music" both in the United States and in England. She came from Itawamba County in Mississippi, where she was born in 1942. Her father, a guitarist, died when she was eight months old, and since her mother had to find a job in Birmingham, Alabama, Tammy was raised by her grandparents, for whom she picked cotton and baled hay as one of the hired hands on the farm. After World War II, she got married, gave birth to three children, and then got divorced. To support her family—and to pay the medical bills for her youngest daughter afflicted with spinal meningitis—she worked in a beauty shop in Birmingham and added to her weekly income by singing over the local radio and TV stations. In 1966, she made her first public stage appearance at the Playhouse in Atlanta, Georgia. A year later she came to Nashville hoping to break in as a recording artist. There she was discovered by Billy Sherrill, head of production for Columbia and Epic Records. Her second release, "Your Good Girl's Gonna Go Bad" (Billy Sherrill and Glenn Sutton) reached the Number One spot on the national charts and "I Don't Wanna Play House" (Billy Sherrill and Glenn Sutton) earned a Grammy in 1967 as the best country and western female solo performance. One of her biggest hits, "D-I-V-O-R-C-E" (Bobby Braddock and Curly Putnam) came in 1968, and its success helped her become the top Female Vocalist in the Country Music Association Awards. This was followed in 1969 by another of her big records, "Stand By Your Man" (Billy Sherrill and Tammy Wynette); its two-million disk sale is believed to be the largest by any woman country singer up to that time. In 1970, her album *Tammy Wynette: Greatest Hits* was a gold record.

In 1969 she married George Jones, a singer with whom she made many professional appearances including some at the Grand Ole Opry, and with whom she made several recordings. They were divorced in 1975. Man-woman relationship is a recurring theme in the songs she has written, sometimes in celebration ("I'll See Him Through," "He Loves Me All the Way," "We Sure Can Love Each Other," "You're My Man," "Stand By Your Man" and "Till I Can Make It On My Own") and sometimes in condemnation ("D-I-V-O-R-C-E," "I Don't Wanna Play House," "Run, Woman, Run," "Your Good Girl's Gonna Go Bad"). Tammy Wynette was heard singing "Stand By Your Man" on the sound track of the motion picture *Five Easy Pieces* (1970). "To a lot of people Tammy Wynette is country music," wrote the writer, editor and lecturer, John Gabree. "She has had a greater impact on country and its image than any other woman . . . she has a strong, clear voice, maybe the best female voice in Nashville, and she knows how to wield it with great dramatic and emotional effect."

Lynn Anderson, who came to Nashville in the 1960s, realized a spectacular success in 1970 with her Columbia recording of "I Never Promised You a Rose Garden" (Joe South), receiving a Grammy for the best country vocal performance and, in 1971, a gold record for her album *I Never Promised You a Rose Garden*. That number received internationally fourteen gold records and one platinum.

Born in Grand Forks, North Dakota, in 1947, Lynn Anderson was born to parents both of whom had been successful in popular music: her father, Casey Anderson, was a music publisher; her mother, Liz, was a singer and songwriter. Lynn started her career as a singer in Sacramento on a local radio station. Then, coming to Nashville in 1965, she made some recordings for Chart Records. There she met, fell in love with and married Glen Sutton, a songwriter who was also a producer at Columbia and Epic Records. He wrote some of the songs which she recorded for Columbia and with which she earned her first success: "Stay There 'Til I Get There" and "You're My Man" before "I Never Promised You a Rose Garden" made her a recording star.

3

Bakersfield, California—a honky-tonk kind of city—is sometimes called "Nashville West." Oil workers and farm hands from nearby communities stream nightly into Bakersfield for their fun, and country music gets heard at dances, in nightclubs and over local radio and television. In the late 1930s, guitarist Bill Woods, a refugee from the Texas Dust Bowl, came to Bakersfield where he entertained oil-riggers and farmers. This was Bakersfield's beginnings with country music. By the late 1960s, Bakersfield had become the home of ten music publishing houses, three recording companies, five recording studios, two booking agencies, and two hundred musicians and thirty-five songwriters.

The most outstanding of these musicians and songwriters is Alvis Edgar Owens, Jr., better known to music lovers as Buck Owens. So popular is he in Bakersfield—and so influential—that devotees of country music have nicknamed the city Buckersfield. Born in Sherman, Texas, in 1929, Buck Owens hauled produce between Arizona and the San Joaquin Valley near San Francisco while perfecting himself as guitarist and singer. The quickening musical life of Bakersfield appealed to him when he was twenty and he made it his home. In short order he played in local bands and appeared on the local television station. His talent as a guitarist brought him assignments from recording companies to accompany country artists and, in 1956, led to a contract with Capitol Records which allowed his talents as a singing performer and songwriter to blossom. He had his first hit record in 1959 with "Under Your Spell Again," which he wrote with Dusty Rhodes. (This number was also recorded successfully by Ray Price for Columbia.) This initial success for Owens marked the beginning of a road that, stretching into the 1970s, led to twenty-three songwriting awards from BMI, twenty-two single records that reached the top place in either one or all of the principal country-music charts, and brought in a gross of forty million dollars in sales for twenty-five of his albums.

In 1963, he formed a country music group, the Buckaroos, which traveled on the back of a Chevrolet truck to fill two hundred and fifty engagements a year. A decade later, he and his Buckaroos filled between seventy or eighty dates a year, with the rest of his time devoted to making records and appearing on television. He has been cohost with Roy Clark on one of the most popular syndicated television country shows, "Hee Haw," reaching over three hundred markets, he was the star of his own syndicated color television show carried to forty markets, and of special performances such as one at the White House for President Johnson. The red, white and blue guitar he plays has become a personal trademark—a symbol of his pronounced patriotism.

Most of the best-selling records are of his own songs. These include "Together Again" (which was also recorded by forty other artists), "Love's Gonna Live Here Again," "Only You," "Open Up Your Heart," "How Long Will My Baby Be Gone?", "Your Tender Loving Care," "Sweet Rosie Jones," "Let the World Keep On a Turnin'," and "Who's Gonna Mow Your Grass?"; "Foolin' 'Round," "Excuse Me," "Under the Influence of Love" and "I've Got a Tiger by the Tail," which he wrote with Harlan Howard; "Waitin' In Your Welfare Line," written with Nat Stuckey and Don Rich; "Sam's Place," written with Red Simpson and "Before You Go," with Don Rich.

As a top ranking country performer Buck Owens has also recorded hit songs by other writers which became best-sellers. These include "Above and Beyond" (Harlan Howard), "Act Naturally" (Vonie Morrison—Johnny Russell), "Kickin Our Hearts Around" (Wanda Jackson) and "Think of Me" (Estella Olsen—Don Rich).

Buck Owens extended his influence in "Nashville West" by founding a publishing house and a record company, operating several radio stations and a record shop and heading a booking agency, all in addition to the ownership of several ranches and apartment houses.

Buck Owens' principal rival as composer-performer in Bakersfield is Merle Haggard, called by Pete Axthelm in *Newsweek* "the outstanding symbol of the troubled genre of country music." Haggard's grandfather had been a popular hillbilly fiddler in Oklahoma; Haggard's parents were Okies who came from Oklahoma to Bakersfield during the Depression of the 1930s. There his father found employment on the Santa Fe Railroad. Merle was born in 1937 in a converted refrigerator car just a stone's throw from the railroad main line. His schooling ended with the ninth grade. After that he took on any job he could find —pitching hay, sacking potatoes, working on a freight. "I was a general screw-up from the time I was fourteen," he confesses. Between his eighteenth and twenty-third years he spent more time in jail than out of it. Car theft sent him to the Ventura County Jail for ten months. Raiding a scrap metal yard brought another ninety-day sentence. An unsuccessful attempt to burglarize a roadhouse despatched him to San Quentin for two years and nine months. In San Quentin he reexamined his life and came to the conclusion it needed changing. He became a model prisoner and was employed in the prison textile mill. When he left San Quentin it was as if he were reborn.

Soon after his release from San Quentin in 1960 he came under the influence of Fuzzy Owens, a country and western performer who now gave Haggard a purpose in life. Also a direction in music—for country music and playing the guitar had been for Haggard a pet avocation from boyhood on. Fuzzy Owens, a recording artist for Tally, arranged to have Haggard make some records for that company. "Sing a Sad Song" (Wynn Stewart) did so well that Capitol Records signed him up. His first Capitol release, "Strangers" (Liz Anderson) was a best seller.

But Merle Haggard's principal fame comes from his performances of his own songs, many of which are autobiographical and provide glimpses into his tumultuous experiences and emotional upheavals—songs about prison, loneliness, tormented love: "I've Done it All," "Things Aren't Funny Anymore," "The Bottle Let Me Down," "Workin' Man Blues," "The Fighting Side of Me," "Mama Tried," "Hungry Eyes." But his most celebrated song, "Okie from Muskogee" (written with Roy Edward Burris), is no personal lament but a diatribe against hippies, marijuana, LSD, and the burning of draft cards, with a tip of the hat to "Ol' Glory down at the courthouse." Recorded by Haggard in 1969 it sold a quarter of a million disks in its first year, with close to a million copy sale for the album, *Okie from Muskogee*. It made Haggard a spokesman for the political right wing and earned him an invitation from President Nixon to sing at the White House in March 1973. It was also a favorite of the young—as good an indication as any that the youth of the nation was beginning to move in a new direction.

Merle Haggard married Bonnie Owens, a country and western singer, in 1965. Her surname came from the fact that she had previously been married to Buck Owens, whom she divorced a dozen years before she married Haggard. Together, Haggard and his wife recorded a best-selling LP, *Just Between the Two of Us*, released in 1966, the year they were selected as the best vocal group by the Academy of Country and Western Music, while at the same time Bonnie Owens herself was named top female vocalist. In 1970, Merle Haggard was chosen entertainer of the year by the Country Music Association, while his album, *Okie from Muskogee*, was picked as the year's best. In 1974 the LP, *The Best of Merle Haggard*, was a gold record.

Reviewing Haggard's *His Thirtieth Album*, released in 1974, Jim Miller wrote in the New York *Post*: "Haggard shapes his music as a singer, songwriter and bandleader. . . . As a singer, he evokes Lefty Frizzell and George Jones, two of modern country's central stylists; like both, he is at ease on the up-tempo material as well as ballads. His voice has a distinctive pungency to it, a kind of breaking point where his resonant delivery slips into a brittle half-whine. Haggard uses this device to telling effect, particularly on bittersweet laments. As a writer, Haggard has mined a wide range of themes that by now form an outlook every bit as consistent and arresting as Hank Williams. He started his career fixated on alcohol ("Swinging Doors"), moved into a desperado phase ("I'm a Lonesome Fugitive") and finally settled into assertive but confessional statements of belief and pride ("Mama Tried," "I Take a Lot of Pride in What I Am"). In more recent years he has composed some of modern country-western's finest love songs, direct and traditional, yet understated and simply sung ("Today I Started Loving You Again," "It's Not Love But It's Not Bad")."

4

Elsewhere in California, and further south, country music found two more creative voices: those of Jim Webb and Bobbie Gentry.

Jim Webb, the oldest son of a Baptist minister, was born in Elk City, Oklahoma, in 1946. His family came to California when Jimmy was still a child. There he soon learned to play the organ and piano. When he was eleven, he performed the organ in his father's church; at thirteen, he started writing songs. To find an outlet for his songwriting ambitions, Webb came to Hollywood where, for a time, he worked in a recording studio transcribing songs for various performers.

The first two songs on which his impressive song-writing career rests came in 1967, inspired by frustrated love affairs, and both become blockbusters. "By the Time I Get to Phoenix," was an expression of Webb's own yearnings for a Phoenix girl with long blonde hair and little canvas shoes. "Up, Up and Away" was written after another of his girl friends left him to marry another man. "By the Time I Get to Phoenix" was Glen Campbell's monumental success in a Capitol recording. "Up, Up and Away" (written for a motion picture that never materialized) earned a gold record in the Soul City recording by the 5th Dimension and received Grammys as the song of the year and the record of the year.

In 1968, Richard Harris recorded an album of Webb's songs, one of whose numbers was a seven-minute song, "MacArthur Park." Despite its length, "MacArthur Park" was widely promoted by disc jockeys which sent the album flying off to a million-dollar sale within a few weeks' time. Later the same year, Webb recorded an album of his own—his disk debut as a performer. Called *Jim Webb Sings Jim Webb* it contained his three big hits ("By the Time I Get to Phoenix," "Up, Up and Away" and "MacArthur Park") together with "You're So Young, I Need You," "Our Time is Running Out," and "I Can Do It On My Own." Other albums of Jim Webb singing Webb were *Jim Webb: Words and Music* in 1970, *Jimmy Webb and So On* in 1971, and *Land's End* in 1974.

Prestigious performers besides those already noted were also singing Webb: Glenn Campbell recorded "Where's the Playground, Susie," "Wichita Lineman" and "Galveston"; Art Garfunkel, "All I Know" (a gold record), "Brooklyn Bridge," "The Worst that Could Happen"; the 5th Dimension, "Paper Cup."

Jim Webb wrote the music for several motion pictures, among these being *How Sweet It Is* (1968), *Peter Pan* (1970), *Doc* (1971) and *Tell Them Will Boy Is Here* (1972). On Broadway, his music was heard in *His Own Dark City* (1970). Webb also toured concert halls and clubs throughout the United States from 1970 on, including an appearance at the Dorothy Chandler Pavilion in Los Angeles in February 1970. He was starred on major television networks, including a Special entitled "Jimmy Webb and his Friends."

Bobbie Gentry came to California from her native state of Mississippi when she was thirteen, having been born in Chickasaw County in 1944. Two years after settling in Los Angeles, she performed her own songs in fashionable clubs in Palm Springs where she was heard and encouraged by Bob Hope, Hoagy Carmichael, and Phil Harris. She then studied the guitar at the Los Angeles Conservatory of Music while supporting herself by appearing in small night spots on weekends, usually presenting her own songs. In 1967 she made a demonstration record of her "Mississippi Delta" which brought her a contract with Capitol Records. Her first Capitol recording in 1967 catapulted her to fame and wealth. It was "Ode to Billy Joe," a seven-minute ballad written one morning after she read a line in a notebook in which she always scribbled sudden thoughts and ideas. The line read: "Billy Joe jumped off the Tallahatchie Bridge." She used this as material for a story-ballad in which a preacher, Brother Taylor, sees Billy Joe and his girl throw an object off the bridge whose identity remains a dark mystery.

Within four months of its release, her own recording of this ballad usurped top place in the charts, selling over a million disks and capturing three Grammys in 1967 as best vocal female performance, best new artist, and best contemporary solo vocal female performance. Three million other disks by sixty other performers were also sold within a few years. By 1976, the worldwide sale of the record passed the twenty-seven million mark. *Ode to Billy Joe* was made into a motion picture in 1976 in which Bobbie Gentry did not appear but sang her ballad in the sound track.

Now a celebrity, Bobbie Gentry appeared on major network television shows; was chosen in 1968 by the Country Music Association as the entertainer of the year, and represented the United States at the San Remo song festival in Italy where she received the Italian Press Award. Two years after "Ode to Billy Joe," Bobbie Gentry had another huge hit in "Fancy," which she recorded for Capitol, and which received the ASCAP Country Music Award in 1970. Meanwhile, in 1969, Miss Gentry toured Europe to garner further success. She filmed fourteen Specials for BBC-TV, made numerous guest appearances on other English TV productions and was a guest of honor at the Dutch Grand Gala in Holland.

Among other notable songs by Miss Gentry are "I Saw an Angel Die," "Oklahoma River Bottom Band," "Louisiana Man," "Sweet Peony," "Mornin' Glory" (this one to words by Glen Campbell), "Chickasaw," "Touch 'em With Love," "Big Boss Man" and "All I Have to Do Is Dream."

5

Charlie Rich, "the Silver Fox," who was one of those who helped carry the blues into country music, made the big time in 1973 by receiving awards from the Academy of Country Music for the record single on Epic, "Behind Closed Doors" (Kenneth O'Dell), a song that was banned by some country stations because of its illicit lyrics, and for the album, *Behind Closed Doors*. Both the single and the album became gold records while his recording of "Behind Closed Doors" also brought him a Grammy as the best male country vocalist. One of the cuts from his album, "The Most Beautiful Girl" (Rory Bourke, Norris Wilson, and Billy Sherrill) was then released as a single to sell over two million disks. This was followed by the release of Charley Rich's next Epic album, *Very Special Love Songs*, and that too become a gold record, as did his single "There Won't Be Anymore." In 1974, Rich received the award of the Country Music Association as entertainer of the year. In 1975, he received the triple crown from the Country Music Association: favorite male country vocalist; top single, "The Most Beautiful Girl in the World"; and top country-pop album, *Behind Closed Doors*.

Fame and prosperity have come to many another country performer with a single recording—but not to Charlie Rich. Behind 1973 stretched many years when the recognition he now had won so conclusively seemed elusive. The son of a Gospel-singing Baptist, he was a southerner from Colt, Arkansas, born in 1932. Before he turned to singing as a profession he had been a cotton farmer. Both his father, an alcoholic, and his mother, a strict Baptist, encouraged his interest in singing, but as he put it, they did not approve "of the places I was singin' in." After a year in college, and some time on tour with the Air Force, he married Margaret Ann and settled down on a cotton farm in Arkansas where they remained two and a half years. Coming to the realization that there was no money in farming, he left for Memphis where he found work at Sun Records as a background musician.

His first single as a singing performer was a rock number recorded in 1958 for Sun. A minor success was realized two years later with his own song, "Lonely Weekends." Only moderately successful, too, were his recordings in the mid-1960s for Smash of "Mohair Sam" (Dallas Frazier) and "Big Boss Man" (Al Smith and Luther Dixon).

These and others of his well-stocked repository of recordings in the 1960s gave indications of a versatility that easily carried him from rock to country music, with stopovers at jazz, pop and Soul. Twenty-four of his early records, rereleased in a Mercury double album, reveal the wide scope of his stylings. "This jack of all trades," wrote an unidentified interviewer for the Chicago *Sun-Times* News Service, "is also a master of all, because he brings both taste and deep feeling to everything he tries. He is living proof that a singer can be both masculine and sensitive."

But the going was hard—and to smooth the bumps in his road to fulfillment as an artist Rich reached for the bottle and drugs. At one point, his wife bundled up their three children and left him. But then things took a dramatic turn for the better. A changeover to Epic Records—and the shrewd guidance of its producer, Billy Sherrill—spelled the difference between nagging failures and frustrations and, at long last, triumph.

From a Chicago suburb came John Prine, perhaps the most talented of the younger set of country music singing-composers. In Maywood, Illinois, west of Chicago, where he was born in 1948, he grew up listening to the country music broadcast from Nashville, and early became a devotee of Hank Williams, Jimmie Rodgers, and the Carter Family. From savings accumulated by working Saturday nights as a pew duster in an Episcopal Church he was able to buy a guitar from a mail-order house when he was fourteen. His grandfather (a gentleman from Kentucky who had personally known and sung with Merle Travis and Ike Everly) and his older brother gave him guitar lessons. It did not take Prine long to realize that he much preferred singing songs of his own invention; his first were an unabashed imitation of Hank Williams.

Upon graduating from high school, Prine worked in the post office for two years until 1966 when he enlisted in the Army and served in Stuttgart, Germany. He came back to America to his post office job and married his high school sweetheart, setting up home in Melrose Park, Illinois, near Chicago. In 1970, he began singing professionally for the first time in a coffee house in the Old Town section of Chicago. A year after that, Kris Kristofferson and Paul Anka used their influence on his behalf. Anka, in fact, became his manager, and got Prine a recording contract from Atlantic Records in Memphis that resulted in the albums, *John Prine, Diamonds in the Rough, Sweet Revenge* and *Common Sense*.

His songs evoke poignant memories of his own past, of his life in the Army ("Donald and Lydia"), of his childhood visits to Kentucky ("Paradise"), of his confusions and lonesomeness ("Rocky Mountain Times"). He also sings of the problems of others: of the Vietnam veteran who dies of an overdose of heroin ("Sam Stone") or the one who refused to answer any questions about his medals, preferring to give his conscience a rest ("Diamonds in the Rough"); or the chilling loneliness of the elderly couple ("Hell in There"). "His deceptive, genial songs," said *Time*, "deal with the disillusioned fringe of Middle America, hauntingly evoking the world of fluorescent-lit truck stops, overladen knicknack shelves, gravel-dusty Army posts and lost loves. In a plangent baritone that makes him sound like a young Johnny Cash, he squeezes poetry out of the anguished longing of empty lives."

Many of Prine's songs have become known not only through his own recordings but also in those of Joan Baez, Kris Kristofferson, Bob Dylan, Carly Simon and Bette Midler.

6

Out of the hills of Kentucky has come a country music known as Bluegrass. It was popularized in the 1960s by the rural music of Earl Scruggs and Lester Flatt (and their Foggy Mountain Boys) at the Grand Ole Opry, at the first Newport Folk Festival, in coffee houses, over radio and on records. And it was brought to college campuses by the Osborne Brothers.

Bluegrass music, however, owes a profound debt to the predecessor of Scruggs and Flatt and the Osborne Brothers. He was William "Bill" Monroe, its most significant pioneer voice.

In an essay for Folkways Records, Mike Seeger describes Bluegrass music as follows: "Vocally, the style is characterized by high-pitched emotional singing. . . . Instrumentally, Bluegrass music is a direct outgrowth of traditional hill music, its two most distinctive features being that it has no electrified instrument, that it uses a five-string banjo for lead or background in all songs. . . . The songs themselves are mostly built on traditional patterns. . . . The subject matter is most usually unsuccessful love but also covers home, Mother, catastrophes, religion and almost anything else under the sun. . . . Bluegrass is directly related to the old corn-shucking party banjo and fiddle music as well as the ballad songs and religious music of the southern mountains."

Bluegrass music first realized its subsequent style and format after World War II, and William "Bill" Monroe was the one most responsible for this development. Born in Rosine, Kentucky, in 1911, Bill Monroe early learned to play stringed instruments, guided by a mother who was a fiddler, and who died when Monroe was ten. By the time he was in his twenties, Monroe played the guitar at country fairs and dances, frequently in performances of his own compositions. Then he specialized on the mandolin, on which he became an outstanding virtuoso. In the mid 1920s he teamed up with his older brothers, Charlie and Birch, and performed Bluegrass music throughout the South and Midwest and over local radio stations. When Birch left the group, Bill and Charlie continued on as the Monroe Brothers, recording gospel and country music for Bluebird in a style anticipating Bluegrass. One of their best albums was *Early Blue Grass Music by the Monroe Brothers*, released by Camden. In 1934, Bill Monroe had his first significant success as a songwriter with "Kentucky Waltz" which he recorded successfully for Columbia and which, in 1951, was revived by Eddy Arnold in a best-selling Victor release. After that came such Monroe Bluegrass instrumentals as "Get Up, John," "Blue Grass Ramble" and "Memories of You."

In 1938, the brothers split up, with Bill carrying on the Bluegrass tradition with the Bluegrass Boys. In 1939, he appeared at the Grand Ole Opry with his band. As a performer and composer, Bill Monroe remained active until the early 1960s. His "Blue Moon of Kentucky," which he himself performed for Decca in 1947, later became one of Elvis Presley's early disks.

Monroe and his Bluegrass music retained their popularity in the 1960s through record releases, appearances at folk festivals, and performances on the ABC-TV Hootenanny program. In 1970 Bill Monroe was elected to the Country Music Hall of Fame.

In 1944, Lester Flatt joined Bill Monroe's Bluegrass Boys at the Grand Ole Opry as guitarist and one year later, Earl Scruggs, a banjoist, also became a member of this troupe. By 1948, Flatt and Scruggs decided to form their own group which found engagements over southern radio stations and began making recordings for Mercury. In 1951, they left Mercury for Columbia with whom they enjoyed successes with *Foggy Mountain Breakdown, Pike County Breakdown, Earl's Breakdown* and *Flint Hill Special*. In 1953, Flatt and Scruggs became featured artists at the Grand Ole Opry. Between 1955 and 1958 they were voted top instrumental group in the Country and Western Music Jamboree Poll for four successive years. Their Columbia recording of "Go Home" (Onie Wheeler) in 1961 was a best-seller, and a year later their recording of "Ballad of Jed Clampett" (Paul Henning)—the theme of the top-rated television situation comedy series, "The Beverly Hillbillies"—achieved top place in country and western charts. Among their other record successes in the 1960s were "Pearl, Pearl, Pearl" (Paul Henning) and "Petticoat Junction" (Paul Henning and Curt Massey), the latter once again the theme of a popular television series. In addition to their recordings, they popularized Bluegrass music on college campuses, at folk festivals and fairs, in night spots and auditoriums until they split up in March 1969.

The Osborne Brothers made their first appearance on a campus at Antioch College in Ohio in 1959—the first time that Bluegrass music was formally performed in a college setting. After that they gave numerous Bluegrass concerts on college campuses around the country; they were frequently starred at the Grand Ole Opry and at summer Bluegrass festivals; they became the first Bluegrass country group to perform at Harrah's Club at Lake Tahoe (in 1973) where they surpassed the attendance records held for many years by Sammy Davis, Jr.; they also performed at the White House.

The brothers were both born in Hyden, Kentucky; Bob, in 1931, and Sonny, in 1937. Both were raised on Bluegrass and country music. By the time they entered high school they had become proficient on the five-string banjo and the mandolin. When Sonny was only sixteen, the brothers made their first appearance on radio, on station WROL in Kentucky. Moving on to Detroit in 1954 they made concert appearances throughout the Midwest and in 1956—at Wheeling, West Virginia—they became regulars on the Wheeling Jamboree over WWVA and signed their first record contract (with MGM). Then, with Benny Birchfield joining them as a performer on the five-string banjo, and guitar and as lead singer, the Osborne Brothers came to Antioch College where their success instantly brought them engagements from other colleges. Bluegrass now became a passion with college kids everywhere.

Purists might condemn the Osborne Brothers for using electrified instruments and commercializing Bluegrass music. Nevertheless, few have done as much as they to make Bluegrass popular with the masses, both through their public appearances and on records. Their best earlier LPs were *Blue Grass Music by the Osbornes* and *Blue Grass Instrumentals*; their most successful later albums, for MCA, include *Fastest Grass Alive, Pickin' Grass and Singin' Country* and *Osborne Brothers—The Best*.

7

Country music is so indigenously American and so deeply rooted in American folk music, that it would seem that any attempt by a foreign artist to invade the country music field would be an intrusion. Olivia Newton-John, born in Cambridge, England, and in her early years raised in Australia, attempted such an invasion in the early seventies—and, despite opposition, conquered decisively. When, in 1973, she captured her first Grammy as best country vocalist with "Let Me Be There" (John Rostill) on the MCA label and when, one year later, the Country Music Association named her the female vocalist of the year, a veritable brouhaha erupted in country circles. They resented her being a foreigner and insisted that she was not a country singer at all but a pop singer. Attractive to look at—appearing to one writer as "part nymph and part schoolgirl"—and just as pleasing to listen to, Olivia Newton-John brought to her songs the kind of sentimental sweet music filled with emotion (that, however, never descends into bathos), the kind of innocence and at times coquettishness, and that fastidious attention to the lyrics that belonged more legitimately to pop music than to country. As a result of the controversy over Olivia Newton-John, the Association for Country Entertainers was founded in 1974 to promote traditional country music; it was meant to serve as an antidote to *ersatz* country.

Olivia Newton-John herself does not like being labeled country, pop, or anything else specifically. She says: "I don't put myself in any category, although probably my earliest influence was folk music. . . . I prefer folk . . . compared to straight-out pop. I like the simplicity, the basic quality, the pretty melodies and the good words. But I like all kinds of music."

But whether she comes to be regarded as country or as pop—actually her singing represents the middle ground between the two—there can be no question that she has become one of the most successful female singers to come out of England. She accumulated five gold records in 1974: for the single "If You Love Me" (John Rostill) and the album that bore the same title; for "I Honestly Love You" (Peter Allen and Jeff Barry), for "Let Me Be There" (John Rostill) and the album *Let Me Be There*. In 1975, she added five more gold records to her collection with "Have You Never Been Mellow" (John Farrar) and for the album of the same name, as well as for the albums *Please, Mister, Please, Clearly Love* and *Rock of Westies*. In 1975 she was awarded two Grammys—for "I Honestly Love You," both as the record of the year and as the best female vocal pop. Additionally, she was named "rising star of the year" by the American Guild of Variety Artists, honored as the "favorite female vocalist in pop–rock and country music" by the Bicentennial American Music Awards presented over the ABC-TV network in February 1976, and was called "the hottest pipes in pop" by *People* magazine.

The granddaughter of Max Born, winner of the Nobel Prize for physics, and the daughter of a schoolteacher, Olivia Newton-John was, early in life, brought from England to Australia where her father had become the headmaster of a school. Olivia's ambition for some time fluctuated between becoming a schoolteacher or a prima donna. Then she decided to become a folk singer. Leaving school, she began her career in a coffee-shop owned by her brother-in-law and made her TV debut on a daytime program. Winning first prize in a talent show enabled her to come to London while she was still in her teens. There she teamed up with another young Australian singing hopeful, Pat Carroll, in an act that found engagements in cabarets and over BBC-TV. When the expiration of Pat Carroll's visa forced her to return to Australia, Olivia joined a singing group and made a movie that turned out to be a disaster.

Now nineteen years old, she decided to stay in London and try to promote herself as a solo vocalist. She found some jobs singing in working men's clubs, and in 1971 she made her first recording.

With her first Grammy in 1973, and her invasion of the American country scene with new recordings, engagements in plush nightclubs (including her first appearance in Nashville in 1975) and on American television, she became one of the most valuable properties on the popular musical scene—country or otherwise.

42

Black Power—and Soul

1

They *did* overcome—not completely, to be sure, but to a degree that even the dreamers among black civil rights leaders of the 1950s did not dare to anticipate. Blacks finally realized opportunities they had never before known: as students in integrated schools; as employers and employees in industry and the arts; as residents in integrated neighborhoods and apartment houses.

In the world of entertainment, many barriers to racial acceptance had been surmounted. In television, in the 1950s, the black performer had been relegated almost exclusively to guest spots on the programs of whites, or—as in the case of Rochester on the Jack Benny Show—to stereotypes of black people. Blacks could not command programs of their own—even when their fame and talent equaled that of a Nat King Cole or Sammy Davis, Jr.—and upon those rare occasions when they were given programs they were unable to survive for lack of sponsors. Who could have foretold that within two decades Sanford and Son would be one of a half dozen of the most highly rated situation comedies on television? Or that other situation comedies on television ("Good Times," "That's My Mama," "The Jeffersons") and situation dramas ("Sounder") would devote themselves to black characters. Who could have guessed that one of the most highly esteemed and financial profitable variety shows of the early 1970s would be built around Flip Wilson? Who could have foreseen that the television screen would welcome a Diahann Carroll with open arms in a series, "Julia," which made her the first black actress to star on her own TV show; that Godfrey Cambridge, Bill Cosby, Sammy Davis, Jr. would also be the stars of their own TV

675

programs; that even in lesser roles—whether in dramas, comedies, variety shows or just commercials—blacks would be liberally represented; that the TV networks would open their airwaves to soap opera for blacks with black performers, as in "Sounds of the City"?

The musical theater, on and Off-Broadway, responded to black power with musicals deeply rooted in black traditions—which is something completely different from musical comedies, musical plays or revues with all-Negro casts: musicals such as *Ain't Supposed to Die a Natural Death* and *Don't Bother Me I Can't Cope, The Wiz* and *Raisin.*

In motion pictures, from the inception of talking pictures into the 1950s, black men were invariably assigned Uncle Tom roles or compelled to offer slow-footed, slow-tongued and sleepy-eyed characters such as Stepin Fetchit portrayed on the screen. Who would have dared to prophesy the eruption of completely black oriented movies of the 1960s and 1970s? *Sounder, Shaft, Lady Sings the Blues, Super Fly, Sweet Sweetback's Baadasss Song, Claudine, Uptown Saturday Night, Sounder Part 2, Sparkle,* were all solid box-office attractions and represent only a handful of films flowing out of motion picture studios. Who would have dared to say yesterday that some of the most important music for the screen today would be the work of blacks—of Quincy Jones, Isaac Hayes, Curtis Mayfield?

Never before were there so many black radio stations, featuring black disc jockeys, catering to black audiences. Never before had there come into existence recording firms owned exclusively by blacks, marketing only the music of blacks. Some of these recording companies have become giants in the industry.

This was black power, and it was experienced in the world of popular music through the resurgence of rhythm and blues, the expanding popularity of gospel and folk music, and through their evolution into Soul.

2

In the mid-1950s, rhythm and blues had been superseded by rock 'n' roll. Much of rhythm and blues had been confiscated and adulterated by white performers catering to white audiences. In the process, rhythm and blues lost much of its black identity. For a number of years so fine a line was being drawn to separate rhythm and blues from rock 'n' roll that the charts stopped using a separate listing for each and lumped both under the heading of rock 'n' roll.

A slow return to the older traditions of rhythm and blues was made in the late 1950s by English rock groups who incorporated into their repertory some of the rhythm and blues classics of earlier years. In the 1960s, in the advance of the civil rights movement, black men were increasingly conscious and increasingly proud of their heritage. Determined to separate themselves from a white man's culture, they began referring to each other as "soul brothers." Black performers and black songwriters—who in the 1950s had strayed over into the predominantly white camp of rock 'n' roll—returned to the fold. They reverted to the idiomatic techniques and methods basic to rhythm and blues as they had been conceived in earlier decades. Aware of this growing tendency, *Billboard,* in July 1964, reinstated the listing of rhythm and blues as a separate entity on its record charts, expanding it half a year later by listing the top forty in this category (all of them by black performers).

Gospel, the religious songs of blacks for church performances, was another facet of the black power in popular music. The queen of the gospel singers was Mahalia Jackson. The daughter of a New Orleans stevedore who worked as a barber at night and was the pastor of his church on Sundays, Mahalia Jackson—born in New Orleans in 1911—began singing gospel in her father's church when she was only five. In her early years she came to know and admire the blues singing of Bessie Smith, whom she always regarded as a prime influence in her own singing career. When she was sixteen, she came to Chicago, worked as a laundress and as a maid, while singing in the choir of the Greater Salem Baptist Church. She then became the leading member of a gospel quartet touring black churches. As the years passed, she advanced her social and economic status by engaging in real estate transactions. But she did not desert singing, continuing to appear in churches, and in 1945 she began making records for Apollo, a small outfit. Two years later, with the gospel number, "Move On Up a Little Higher," she realized a million-disk sale and with it the solidification of her fame as a gospel singer. The rich, vibrant, dark hues of her voice glowed with spiritual exaltation. Her fame continued to grow during the next two decades with appearances not only in churches, but also in concert halls and stadiums in America and Europe, in Columbia recordings, and in appearances at the Newport Jazz Festival where she participated in an afternoon gospel session in 1957 and where, in 1958, she collaborated with Duke Ellington in the performance of his *Black, Brown and Beige*. In 1954, she was heard on a regular, unsponsored Sunday evening radio program of gospel music, and in 1959 she was invited to the White House to perform for President Eisenhower on his birthday. She was featured in the motion picture, *Jazz on a Summer's Day*, and was the author of an autobiography, *Movin' On Up*. During the last decade of her life she was deeply involved in the civil rights movement. She died in 1972.

Though she devoted her immense talent almost exclusively to sacred music, Mahalia Jackson's success and her impact on the black community could not fail to impress black performers of rhythm and blues. These secular performers also became aware of such gospels as "He's Got the Whole World in His Hand," which since the mid-1950s had been recorded by numerous black artists, and the gospel, "Oh, Happy Day," recorded in 1969 for Buddah by the Edwin Hawkin Singers to become one of the few gospel records to reach the million mark in sales. The gospels which Reverend James Cleveland recorded for Savoy and the gospel-oriented rhythm and blues of the Staple Singers for Buddah, also had an effect on popular black singers.

Odetta is not a gospel singer, but a singer of spirituals, work songs and blues. Her fervent renditions, sometimes accompanied by rhythmic clapping of her hands, of "He's Got the Whole World in His Hand," or "Take This Hammer," or "Water Boy," have an intensity that performers of rhythm and blues—and later on of Soul—tried to capture in their own performances.

Odetta (full name, Odetta Felious Gordon) was born in Birmingham, Alabama, in 1930. In her childhood she was taken to Los Angeles where her interest in music was early developed through piano and vocal lessons and through singing with the high school glee club. To finance her night studies at the Los Angeles City College, where she majored in music, she worked as a housekeeper. She found a job in the chorus of the Los Angeles production of *Finian's Rainbow* in 1969. At about this time she heard her friends sing some Negro folk music which was responsible for introducing her to that musical area which she would cultivate so fruitfully. To further herself as a folk singer she began studying the guitar. An extended engagement at the Tin Angel in San Francisco and a month at the Blue Angel in New York marked the beginnings of a rich career which encompassed the movies (singing the chantey "Santy Anno" in *Cinerama Holiday*), theaters, nightclubs, concert halls, television, recordings and frequent appearances at the Newport Folk Festival.

3

In trying to capture the fervor of gospels in their secular numbers, rhythm and blues artists have helped to develop Soul.

The definitions of Soul are as varied as they are numerous. To Otis Redding, Soul was "something that you really have to bring up from the heart . . . really something that you think of and you can get in your mind and you *see* it and *feel* it."

As far as it goes, this statement helps to explain Soul, but it does not go far enough. More to the point, perhaps, is a statement by Bobbie Jean Lewis: "Soul communicates the soulfulness of the Negro people"; or the explanation of Ray Charles that Soul is "like electricity that can light a room"; or the definition of Soul by Ralph J. Gleason in the San Francisco *Chronicle* that it "is like a cross between church music and modern jazz with a flavor of rhythm and blues mixed in."

Though white performers can have Soul, this form of rhythm and blues is basically the music of black people for blacks. To reduce the explanation to simplicity: Soul is rhythm and blues with the religious fervor of gospel.

The word Soul was used in popular music before it became identified as a form of rhythm and blues. Jazz musicians sometimes employed it as a term of praise, sometimes to distinguish the music of jazzmen such as Charlie Mingus and Cannonball Adderley, who were more faithful to the black traditions of rhythm and blues than was the cool jazz spawned on the West Coast. In 1962, King Curtis wrote a Twist number with the title "Soul Twist." When, in 1964, a black disc jockey, Magnificent Montague, was asked to distinguish between black and white disc jockeys, he replied: "It's Soul, man, Soul. . . . The black brothers are the mainstay of our pop music today. Artists like Otis Redding and others are heavy on Soul—one thing that our English friends can't imitate."

As an accepted term for a specific kind of popular music, Soul came into general usage between 1967 and 1968. At that time, radio station WOL in Washington, D. C., featured a program for blacks in which the disc jockey sometimes referred to a rhythm and blues number as "Soul music." In June 1967 *Billboard* published the first of an annual series of volumes, *The World of Soul*, whose purpose was to record "the impact of blues and rhythm and blues upon our musical culture." Within a year, *Esquire* featured an article "Introduction of Soul," and *Time*, in a feature story on Aretha Franklin, identified her as "Lady Soul." At about the same time, a journal, *Soul*, was founded to devote itself exclusively to this form of music.

4

En route from rhythm and blues to Soul there are found several all-important transitional figures in black music who suggest the nature Soul would eventually assume.

James Brown called himself "America's No. 1 Soul Brother," while his followers dubbed him "Mr. Dynamite." He was a man with a high piercing voice, nimble dancing feet and a stage behavior suggesting demonic possession. In *The World of Soul*, Arnold Shaw points to another facet of James Brown's performances, his "quasi-religious quality." Shaw adds: "Whether one regards his style as orgiastic religion or sanctified sex, it is compounded of extremes of emotion, excitement and expression that are characteristic of gospel meets."

Brown's childhood in Augusta, Georgia, was spent picking cotton, washing cars, shining shoes and picking up coins thrown to him for dancing in the streets. He spent three of his teenage years in a reform school, having been convicted of car theft. Then, on parole, he sang in a church choir. After that he became a member of gospel groups, at which time he learned to play the drums and organ. He was discovered by an executive of King Records while he was singing in black theaters and nightclubs on the rhythm and blues circuit with his backup group, the Famous Flames. "Please, Please, Please" (James Brown and John Terry) in 1956 was his first big record release; "Try Me" (James Brown) in 1958 was another.

Each is believed to have sold a million disks or more, almost entirely to a black audience. In the 1960s, his recordings were often listed among the top ten and top forty in the rhythm and blues charts, some of them in first place. Among these were "Think" (Lowman Pauling), "Baby You're Right" (James Brown and Joe Tex), "Prisoner of Love" (Leo Robin—Russ Columbo and Clarence Gaskill), "Papa's Got a Brand New Bag" (James Brown) which won a Grammy in 1965 as the best rhythm and blues recording, "It's a Man's, Man's, Man's World" (James Brown and Betty Jean Newsome), "Don't Be a Drop-Out" (James Brown and Nat Jones), "Say It Loud" (James Brown and Alfred Ellis) in which he proudly and emphatically asserted his black identity, "Mother Popcorn" (James Brown and Alfred Ellis), "Give It Up or Turn It Loose" (C. Bobbitt), and "I Don't Want Nobody to Give Me Nothing" (James Brown); also the albums *Grit and Soul, James Brown Plays James Brown Today and Yesterday, Pure Dynamite, Raw Soul* and *Nothing but Soul*.

Though he made many public appearances in many different places (practically every day in the year it seemed) his audiences were basically the black population whose loyalty helped make him one of the most powerful black men in the music business, a fact recognized by *Cash Box* when it named him the leading male rhythm and blues vocalist of 1968, and by *Look* which featured him in a cover story in February 1969. In 1968, his earnings from recordings and public appearances, together with other investments, grossed him four and a half million dollars—his other investments included two record companies, a music publishing house, real estate and restaurants.

While James Brown has remained faithful to the spirit and letter of Soul, Ray Charles, so his severest critics maintain, has sold not only his own soul, but Soul as well, by reaching for success with country hits and standards of the Tin Pan Alley and Broadway variety. Certainly, in April 1962, Charles struck a rich payload with the country "I Can't Stop Loving You" (Don Gibson) which as a single sold over two million disks while the LP in which it can also be found, *Modern Sounds in Country and Western Music*, brought him another gold record.

It is also true that in wandering away so frequently from rhythm and blues and Soul, to win a far larger public than had formerly been his, Ray Charles is an artist commanding admiration. Whatever medium he embraced—be it pop, rock, jazz, blues, country, rhythm and blues, gospel or Soul—he has never lowered the high standards of musicianship and good taste that have always personalized his styling and characterized his work from the mid-1950s on.

This, too, is true: Ray Charles also achieves greatness when he brings the feeling of gospel into rhythm and blues to create Soul. As a singer of Soul, as Arnold Shaw has written, Ray Charles is the "sandy-voiced celebrant of the pleasures of the flesh and the agonizing frustrations and loneliness of the sightless"; and Charles is also, in the words of James Baldwin, the distinguished black writer, "a great tragic artist [who] makes a genuinely religious confession something triumphant and liberating."

If you are likely to encounter torment and despair in the best of Ray Charles it is because he has experienced both in his life, far in excess of the usual dose meted out to a black man reared in a hostile white southern society. For, in addition to being black, Ray Charles was blind from his seventh year, a victim of glaucoma. In addition, since adolescence he was an orphan forced to make his own way in the world, and from his late boyhood he was also a drug addict.

He was born in Albany, Georgia, probably in 1930, where his father was a railroad laborer and mechanic and his mother did housework and cooking for the white folks. He attended the St. Augustine School for the blind, a state institution in Florida, where he learned to read braille, got a good grounding in classical music, and received lessons on the clarinet and piano (later he studied the sax and trumpet as well). Gospel music, which he had heard his fellow blacks sing from his childhood on, was a profound early influence, and it remained a permanent one.

He stayed on at the St. Augustine School for nine years until the death of his parents made it necessary for him to earn his own living. He went to live with distant cousins in Jacksonville, Florida, earning his way by playing the piano, singing and making arrangements for small jazz bands. His first important job was with a hillbilly band in Tampa. In Seattle, Washington, he formed a trio of his own for which he played the piano and sang and where he became a faint carbon copy of Nat King Cole. Eventually he came to realize that walking in somebody else's footsteps was inhibiting to his progress. The blues had long since begun to appeal to him and by blending blues with the shouting gospel he was gradually able to develop his own sound and style.

He began making records for a small-time unit called Swingtime. His first release, "Confessin' the Blues" (Jay McShann and Walter Brown) was technically a dud. But gradually his records began to find their way onto the charts, one of which was "Baby, Let Me Hold Your Hand" (Ray Charles) in 1951. Atlantic Records now bought out his contract. It was in 1954–1955 that he began adding gospel to the blues to help evolve the beginnings of Soul with "I Got a Woman," "This Little Girl of Mine," and "Come Back, Baby," all of them written by Charles. Ahmet Ertegun, the president of Atlantic Records, says: "What makes these . . . historically important is that this was the first time that someone had the audacity to mix sacred and secular black music. Ray had taken the gospel hymn, 'My Jesus Is All the World to Me,' and rewrote it as 'I Got a Woman.' He had taken another gospel song made famous by Clara Ward, 'This Little Light of Mine' and converted it into 'This Little Girl of Mine.' "

We find this marriage of gospel and the blues in "Don't You Know" (Ray Charles) and "Greenbacks" (Renald Richard). In 1956, these and other Ray Charles favorites were gathered into his first best-selling album, originally called simply *Ray Charles* but later renamed *Hallelujah, I Love You So*. In this album, the title number was by Charles and so were "Ain't that Love," "Don't You Know," "Funny," "A Fool for You" and "Mary Ann."

During the next few years, Charles remained one of the finest and most successful rhythm and blues singers around. One of his recordings. "I Believe to My Soul" (Ray Charles) in 1959, is a rarity not only among Charles' recordings but in the entire recorded world of rhythm and blues. Here Charles not only sings the number but also, in falsetto, dubs in the voices of four female singers as accompaniment in a strict four-part harmony. Necessity was the mother of this invention. The accompaniment was supposed to have been provided by the Raelets, a girl quartet which often sang with Charles in concerts and on records. When the Raelets failed to show up for the recording session Charles decided to fill in their voices himself, recording them one at a time while listening to the surrounding sounds through earphones. The trick comes off remarkably well. Listening to the record one is not aware of a stunt but of an unusual musical experience.

But Charles was too versatile to confine himself to any single style. In 1959, he left Atlantic Records for ABC-Paramount, a far less specialized organization than Atlantic, one that allowed him to identify himself not only with rhythm and blues but also with pop, rock, country and other forms of popular music. After 1962, ABC-Paramount created a new subsidiary for Charles, Tangerine, under his complete artistic control, but subsequently Charles recorded under his own label, Crossover.

Hoagy Carmichael's "Georgia On My Mind" (Stuart Gorrell) became Charles' first giant success for ABC-Paramount. This release brought him a Grammy in 1960 for the best vocal male performance on a single record; at the same time his LP, *Genius of Ray Charles*, was picked as the best vocal male performance in an album. In country and western he recorded two albums, *Modern Sounds in Country and Western Music*, volumes 1 and 2, both in 1962. The first, recipient of a gold record, included "I Can't Stop Loving You" and the second his moving rendition of a country standard, "You Are My Sunshine" (Jimmie Davis and Charles Mitchell). Charles now became the first black man ever chosen by the Country Music Association of Nashville as one of the top ten country and western performers.

Rhythm and blues was not neglected. Charles' recording of "Let the Good Times Roll" (Sam Theard and Fleecie Moore) received a Grammy in the rhythm and blues department in 1960, and so did "Hit the Road, Jack" (Percy Mayfield) in 1961, "I Can't Stop Loving You" in 1962 and "Busted" (Harlan Howard) in 1963. Three years later, "Crying Time" (Buck Owens) brought him two more Grammys, for the best rhythm and blues recording and the best rhythm and blues solo performance.

In the early 1960s, Ray Charles' success assumed international dimensions. In 1961 he sold out the Palais des Sports in Paris for five consecutive nights; then, because of the seemingly insatiable demand, he gave two extra concerts. In 1964, he toured the world, appearing in ninety concerts in nine weeks before audiences totaling half a million.

In the United States he appeared extensively over television, in nightclubs and theaters, at concerts and jazz festivals. In 1961 he wrote a footnote to the social history of the times by performing before the first integrated audience ever to attend a municipally owned and operated auditorium in Memphis, Tennessee. He had informed the authorities in no uncertain terms that he would not appear before a segregated audience. In May 1963 he gave two concerts in a sold-out Carnegie Hall, New York, even including the standing room.

Through all these personal victories, he was able to bear the affliction of blindness far better than the curse of his addiction to drugs. Time and again law enforcement agents made his life miserable and twice he was arrested. His second arrest took place in Boston in 1964. One year later, at his own request, he was admitted to a California clinic for rehabilitation. Conscious of this rehabilitation, as well as out of respect for his monumental contribution to American popular music, the House of Representatives, in Washington, D. C.—on the occasion of his twentieth anniversary as a performer—honored him in 1966 with a special resolution in which the following lines appear: "The pain of his early life, and the hardships he has overcome, are part of the Ray Charles sound."

Sam Cooke's childhood was even more filled with gospels than that of Ray Charles. Cooke, born in Chicago in 1935, was the son of a Baptist minister. When he was nine, he joined two of his brothers and two of his sisters in forming the Singing Children, a group that appeared at Baptist church socials. After graduating from high school, in Chicago, Cooke became a member of a gospel group, the Soul Stirrers, for which he wrote spirituals. After one of their concerts at the Shrine Auditorium in Los Angeles, Cooke was approached by an executive from Specialty Records who signed him to his first record contract. His initial release, "I'll Come Running Back to You" (L. C. Cooke) in 1957 did well enough to make the rhythm and blues charts. But the insistence of the record producer that he concentrate more on gospel and less on rhythm and blues sent Cooke on to Keen, a recording outfit formed by a defecting employee of Specialty Records. Cooke's debut with Keen was a winner: a blues-type ballad, "You Send Me" (L. C. Cooke) which sold two million disks and sent Cooke's star soaring. Here, as later, Cooke was no belter or shouter in the way James Brown was, but a sensuous crooner. Cooke brought Keen further successes in 1958 and 1959 with

"Lonely Island" (Eden Ahbez), "Win Your Love for Me" (L. C. Cooke), "Love You Most of All" (Barbara Campbell) and "Everybody Loves to Cha Cha Cha" (Barbara Campbell).

His success brought him into the fold of RCA Victor in 1960 for whom, in the next few years, he enjoyed other formidable successes with his own songs, "Twistin' the Night Away," "Another Saturday Night," "Having a Party," "Bring It On Home to Me," "Good News" and "Shake." His albums were also best-sellers. Among them were the two volumes of *The Best of Sam Cooke*, the two volumes of *This Is Sam Cooke*, *Mr. Soul*, *Unforgettable Sam Cooke*, *Two Sides of Sam Cooke* and *The Man Who Invented Soul*.

He was well on his way toward the top when on December 10, 1964, at the age of twenty-nine, he was fatally shot by a female motel operator who claimed he was about to attack her and who was exonerated in court on the grounds of justifiable homicide.

Otis Redding was influenced by Sam Cooke, and Cooke's recordings had been his inspiration. Redding was the big gun in the arsenal of Stax-Volt Records; and Stax-Volt was the company which made the city of Memphis, Tennessee, one of the two principal towns from which Soul flowed (the other being Detroit). Stax Records originated when Jim Stewart, a country fiddler and bank teller, and Fred Bylar, a disc jockey, joined forces in 1956 to manufacture records in a garage. The venture collapsed after a loss of a thousand dollars. With fresh funds provided by his sister, Stewart then opened a recording studio in a movie theater in the heart of Memphis. Its first hit came in 1962 with "Green Onions" (Booker T. Jones, Steve Cropper, Al Jackson, Jr., and Lewie Steinberg), a novelty pop instrumental number recorded by Booker T. and The MG's. That same year, Otis Redding came under their wing, and it was with Redding that Stax Records became a force in the recording business as a giant dispenser of Soul.

Redding, like Cooke, was the son of a Baptist minister, and he, too, was raised on gospel, having sung in the church choir in his early years. Born in Macon, Georgia, in 1941, Redding's ambition to become a performer was awakened when he heard Little Richard, whose singing style he imitated in his own first album, *Pain In My Heart*, in 1963. Redding's equally ardent admiration for Ray Charles and Sam Cooke kept that ambition alive. In 1962, chance provided him with his first opening as a solo performer. He chauffeured a band —Johnny Jenkins and the Pinetroopers, for whom he served as vocalist and road manager —from Macon to Memphis for an audition for Stax Records. Stewart, the head of Stax, recalls his first meeting with Redding, an event that was so fateful to Stax, Redding and Soul. "He was a shy old country boy. . . . After the band recorded, someone suggested that Otis be given a chance to sing. He did one of those Heh, heh baby things. . . . I told him the world didn't need another Little Richard. Then someone suggested he do a slow one. He did. . . . No one flipped over it."

But Stewart apparently had faith in Redding's potentialities for he signed him to a contract. With his first Volt recordings, Redding's career really opened up and Soul came into being: "Ole Man Trouble," "I've Been Loving You Too Long," "Respect," "Fa-Fa-Fa-Fa-Fa" (sometimes called the "Sad Song"), "I Can't Turn You Loose," "Mr. Pitiful," "I've Got Dreams to Remember," "Sweet Soul Music" and "The Dock of the Bay," all of them written by Redding, sometimes in collaboration with others.

Redding did not sell his disks in such volume as others did; his only giant success came after his death. But if, during his lifetime, the sales of his records were comparatively limited, his influence proved profound even outside Soul. Janis Joplin's admiration for Redding touched the borders of idolatry. Redding was also capable of creating a storm in his public appearances, including a historic one at the Olympia in Paris in 1967 and another that same year at the Monterey Pop Festival where his grunting, groaning, sweating, stamping rendition of Sam Cooke's "Shake" had a cyclonic effect on the audience. "In person," said the jazz critic, Ralph J. Gleason, "everything Redding does is all-out powerhouse, total emotional explosion. He may start singing 'Try a Little Tenderness' with tenderness, but it always ends up 'Sock it to me, baby'. . . ."

In the fall of 1967, the English magazine, *Melody Maker*, selected him as the world's foremost male vocalist, usurping the place that had been held by Elvis Presley for a decade and which seemed to have become Presley's by squatter's rights. Only two months after this tribute, Otis Redding was dead. He was only twenty-nine when on December 10, 1967, he died in a crash over Lake Monona in Wisconsin in his private plane. He never lived to witness the triumph of "The Dock of the Bay" (Otis Redding and Steve Cropper), which he had recorded only two and a half weeks before his death and which was released posthumously. For a year it stayed on the charts, amassing a four-million disk sale. It received a Grammy as the year's best rhythm and blues number and another one for Redding himself for the best rhythm and blues performance. Said Jerry Wexler of Atlantic Records, ". . . It proves that a singer can do his own thing and still be commercially successful. Otis is tremendously responsible for the fact that . . . the young white audience now digs Soul the way the black does."

With his Volt recordings, Otis Redding not only helped to create Soul, but he was also responsible for producing the "Memphis Sound," something which became exclusive with Stax-Volt Records through its stable of artists. We hear the "Memphis Sound" not only with Redding but also with Booker T. and The MG's, whose best recordings were "Midnight Hour," "Green Onions," "Soul Limbo" and "Knock on Wood," which they wrote themselves.

Al Bell, executive at Stax Records, told how the "Memphis Sound" came to be: "In Memphis, we like for the artists to be able to *feel* what's in the lyrics of a song, to live with them and to interpret them in their own fashion. Here, when we get a group of musicians together in a studio, there are no written arrangements. The song has been sketched out by the writer or producer and the musicians go over and over it, adding their own ideas, working it over until everybody begins to feel it, then they begin recording it and it's the spontaneity of the whole thing that brings about the Memphis Sound, because this thing called Soul, as I define it, is based on an emotional experience."

5

Aretha Franklin has often been called a high priestess of Soul, and belongs with that imperial race of black singers that has numbered Ma Rainey, Bessie Smith, Billie Holiday, Dinah Washington and Mahalia Jackson. The daughter of a revivalist Baptist preacher, Aretha Franklin was born in 1942 in Memphis, Tennessee, but grew up in Detroit where her father became the pastor of the New Bethel Baptist Church when she was seven. A year or so later she taught herself to play the piano and then was tutored in music by the Reverend James Cleveland—who later became known as the king of Soul—who lived with the Franklin family. With the Reverend Cleveland's help she formed a singing group with her sister and two friends that performed gospels in local churches, her first public appearances. She also sang in the choir of her father's church, was featured as a singer with an evangelist group headed by her father that toured the country, and made some recordings of gospels. Since her home was a rendezvous for famous and aspiring black artists she early came to know and admire Mahalia Jackson, Sam Cooke and others, and from them learned valuable lessons in the projection of a song. Her father, however, was her greatest influence at the time. "Most of what I learned vocally came from him," she says.

In 1960, she came to New York, and one year later signed a contract with Columbia, for which she recorded nine albums of popular standards, jazz, and novelty tunes which were well received by the critics but which had only moderate sales. It was for one of these albums that Byron Roberts, writing in the Washington *Post* on March 22, 1964, praised her singing for its Soul, the first time the term was applied to her. But those early Columbia records failed for the most part to reveal her true artistic stature. When some of these releases were reassembled by Columbia into an album called *The First Twelve Sides*, issued in 1973, Clayton Riley noted in the *New York Times* that it failed "to challenge Aretha's gifted instrument on even terms."

In addition to her records, she made public appearances in intimate night spots, and was heard in 1963 at the Newport Jazz Festival and the Lower Ohio Jazz Festival.

Her career was limping, and she knew it. She knew something else: She was not fulfilling herself with the kind of material she was then using nor in the ways she was then using it. Therefore, when Columbia offered her a new contract, late in 1966, she turned it down to become affiliated with Atlantic Records, a smaller house specializing in black music. That change made all the difference. Under the skillful guidance of Jerry Wexler, the company's vice president, she found Soul and uncovered for herself new resources and new emotional depths. In addition, she was allowed to develop her talent as a pianist. Her first Atlantic single, in 1967, "I Never Loved a Man" (Ronny Shannon) reached the top place on the rhythm and blues charts and stayed there seven weeks. This was her first gold record. After that her best-sellers and gold records came in rapid succession. That same year she received gold records for the singles "Respect" (Otis Redding)—winner in 1967 of two Grammys for the best rhythm and blues recording and the best rhythm and blues solo female vocal performance—and "Baby, I Love You" (Ronny Shannon), and for the albums, *Lady Soul* and *I Never Loved a Man*. One after another her singles made the charts: "Chains of Love" (Don Covay), "Dr. Feelgood" (Aretha Franklin and Ted White), "Seesaw" (Don Conway and Steve Cropper), "Ain't No Way" (Caroline Franklin), "Don't Play that Song" (Ahmet Ertegun and Betty Nelson), "Since You've Been Gone" (Aretha Franklin and Ted White), "I Say a Little Prayer" (Hal David—Burt Bacharach), "Share Your Love with Me" (Al Braggs and Deadric Malone). In 1967 she was called the "top female vocalist" by *Cash Box*, *Billboard* and *Record World*, and in 1971 a poll among disc jockeys conducted by *Record World* still found her in the top spot among female singers. On the concert circuit, in nightclubs, and with television Specials and guest shots she was received as a superstar. Her long stretch of singles and albums through the years brought her gold records; her winning albums included *Aretha Live at Fillmore West*, *Amazing Grace*, *Aretha Franklin's Greatest Hits*, volumes 1 and 2, *Aretha Now*, *Spirit in the Dark*, *Hey Now, Hey*, *Young, Gifted and Black*, *With Everything I Feel in Me* and *You*.

When, in 1967, "Respect" brought her her first two Grammys, she could hardly have anticipated that each year until 1975 without interruption, her recordings would be picked for Grammys in the field of rhythm and blues female vocal performance: "Chain of Fools," "Share Your Love with Me," "Don't Play that Song," "Bridge Over Troubled Water" (Paul Simon), the LP album, *Young, Gifted and Black*, "Master of Eyes," "Ain't Nothing Like the Real Thing." No artist has ever equaled or approached such an unbroken succession of Grammy awards. In 1972 she received another Grammy, this time in the field of Soul Gospel, for the LP *Amazing Grace*.

Time magazine singled out intensity and conviction as the prime attributes of Aretha Franklin's vocal performances. It explained: "Her vocal technique is simple enough: a direct, natural style of delivery that ranges over a full four octaves, and the breath control to spin out long phrases that curl sinuously around the beat and dangle tantalizingly from blues notes. But what really accounts for her impact goes beyond technique; it is her fierce, gritty conviction. She flexes her rich, cutting voice like a whip; she lashes her listeners—in her words—'to the bone, for deepness.' "

Nina Simone is another singer who has often been called a high priestess of Soul. Born Eunice Kathleen Waymon in Tryon, North Carolina, in 1933, she was early affected by the gospels she heard in church where her father (a handyman during the week) preached on Sundays as an ordained Methodist minister. At seven she began learning to play the piano and organ by herself. She found a patron in a local music teacher who gave her free music lessons and prepared her for several local piano recitals. After graduating from Allen High School for Girls in Asheville, North Carolina, where she was the valedictorian of her class, Nina Simone studied the piano with Carl Friedberg at the Juilliard School of Music in New York and with Vladimir Sokoloff at the Curtis Institute in Philadelphia. To support herself, she worked as a piano accompanist and gave piano lessons. One summer, in 1954, she found a job in a nightclub in Atlantic City, New Jersey. She expected to perform on the piano, but the owner of the club, thinking he had hired a singer, insisted she sing. Though she had never before appeared in public as a vocalist, she hurriedly prepared a program of spiritual and popular ballads which delighted her audience. It was for this appearance that she assumed the name of Nina Simone so that her parents would not learn she was appearing in a nightclub.

That appearance rerouted her career from the concert stage, as a pianist, to the nightclub, as a singer of popular songs. A successful recording of George Gershwin's "I Loves You Porgy" (Ira Gershwin and Du Bose Heyward) in 1959 for Bethleham was followed by appearances in Greenwich Village cafés, in Town Hall and Carnegie Hall in New York, at the Newport Jazz Festivals, on television, and in tours of Europe.

She made her mark in Soul with a long string of successful LPs released by RCA Victor: *Nina Simone Sings the Blues, Silk and Soul, 'Nuff Said, High Priestess of Soul, Best of Nina Simone, To Love Somebody, Black and Gold, I Put a Spell on You, Here Comes the Sun, A Portrait of Nina, It Is Finished.* Her singing is a blend of many styles, including folk, popular and jazz. In his review of *It Is Finished*, Peter Reilly, writing in *Stereo Review*, describes Nina Simone as "prowling through her repertoire like a fastidious tigress, When she comes across a song such as Hoyt Axton's powerful 'The Pusher' she spits and snarls the lyrics, building to a stinging climax of contempt and loathing for those who profit from the lives—if they may be so called—of the helpless and totally defeated. . . . When she is feeling more playful, however, she bats . . . with the mocking, ferocious, claw-retracted tenderness of a mama tiger boxing with her cubs. . . . What we get from Simone is *style*, a uniquely individual mode of expression honed to a glittering edge."

Many of her own compositions are angry voices in the black protest movement: "Four Women," "If You Knew," "Come Ye," "Turning Point," "Go Limp." "To Be Young, Gifted and Black" was a song tribute to her playwright friend, Lorraine Hansberry. "Her extraordinary faculty for communicating," says Leonard Feather, "is based in part on the urgent topicality of her songs, and in equal measure, on the power, sometimes tantamount to fury, with which she drives home her point. . . . Though anger is by no means her only emotion, a great proportion of the material she uses . . . carries an urgent social message."

"Will Natalie Cole Be the New Queen of Soul?" headlined the story by Stephen Holden in *The New York Times* on November 21, 1976. In the article, Holden states that

Natalie Cole has become "the only serious contender for the 'Queen of Soul' crown worn by Aretha Franklin for the past decade." Natalie is the daughter of Nat King Cole, but her world is not ballads, but Soul and Soul-pop.

Miss Cole made her record debut with an album, *Inseparable*, on the Capitol label in 1975, which received a gold record and two Grammys (best new artist of the year and best female rhythm and blues performer). A second album, *Natalie* (1976) also received a gold record.

6

Though Al Green is adept at both pop and rock, his success rests most securely on Soul: on "Tired of Being Alone," one of his own numbers which in a Hi recording in 1970 became his first gold record; on his own "Let's Stay Together," which sold over two million disks and was selected in 1972 by *Billboard* as top Soul song, with Green himself designated as top singles male artist; on his other gold records of 1972, "Look What You Done for Me," "Power of Love," and "I'm Still in Love with You," all by Green, and the albums *Let's Stay Together* and *I'm Still in Love with You*; on his 1973 gold records, the single "Call Me," by Green, and the album of the same name; on his gold record album in 1974, *Livin' for You*; and on his gold records in 1975 for "Fire" and the album *Explore Your Mind*.

Green describes his singing style as "velvet funk," while commenting on his own songs as follows: "Love, emotional relationships, man-woman involvements. . . . My songs are of these basic relationships. . . . I don't talk in symbols very much. I try to sing and write what I mean."

One of ten children in an impoverished family in Forrest City, Arkansas, where he was born in 1946, Green began his singing career in his ninth year by joining his four brothers in performances of gospels in church. In high school he formed a singing group called Al Greene (original spelling) and the Creations, heard for about three years in mid-western and southern schools and clubs; this group was later reorganized as Al Green and the Soul Mates. His first successful recording came from Hot Line in 1967, "Back Up Train" (Curtis Rogers—Palmer E. Jones), its authors members of Al Greene and the Creations. From then on, Green preferred writing his own songs, all of them variations on the theme of love. His first hit on the Hi label was "I Can't Get Next to You" which reached a top spot in the Soul charts in 1971; his first Hi album, also a success, was *Al Green Gets Next to You*. Now just twenty-six, he was a star both on records and in public appearances. "What really makes him special," wrote Peter Bailey in *The New York Times*, "is that as a singer and a performer he's a throwback to the old days when voice and delivery, rather than tones of an electronic equipment, were all-important." And commenting upon Al Green's concert at Philharmonic Hall (now Avery Fisher Hall) in New York's Lincoln Center, Bailey said further: "Green's sensuous voice, clear and controlled, soared as he sang, his outstretched arms reaching out as if to embrace the audience. He expertly used all the techniques that black singers have made famous: repetition, the stretching of words so that a one-syllable 'yes' can become a five-or-six syllable word, the pauses, the falsetto voice that pierces right through to the soul, and the total use of the body to act out a song. The effect of all this on Green's fans is devastating."

Like Al Green, Isaac Hayes is both a performer and a composer of Soul. In 1971 he won an Oscar for his "Theme from *Shaft*" which then became one of the most frequently played rhythm and blues numbers between 1970 and 1972, while his recording for Enterprise brought in more than two million dollars and twice topped the charts of *Cash Box*. The sound track recording of the motion picture *Shaft* (1971) received two Grammys, one for instrumental arrangement (by Isaac Hayes and Johnny Allen) and another for the best original score for motion pictures; this release sold over a million albums. This score also earned Hayes an award as the best-selling movie sound track from the National Association of Record Merchandisers in 1972, and two others, as the best-selling male Soul artist and the best-selling jazz artist.

Isaac Hayes—his fans call him "Black Moses"—has risen from origins as a sharecropper in Tennessee, where he was born in Covington, near Memphis, in 1943. His was a long and hard road. With his mother dead when he was just under two, and his father disappearing at about the same time, Isaac was raised by his grandparents in Memphis. He combined his schooling with work in the cotton fields. The death of his grandfather, when Isaac was eleven, made it necessary for him to work for a living. Besides picking cotton, he worked as a dishwasher in a restaurant and a stockboy in a grocery store. On one occasion he was arrested on a false burglary charge. These obstacles notwithstanding, he managed to graduate from high school and to develop his native talent for music by singing with a gospel and a Soul group. After leaving high school, he led a group called Sir Isaac and the Doodads which played in small night spots in and around Memphis.

He was hired as pianist for Stax-Volt Records in Memphis for an Otis Redding recording session. This affiliation turned him to writing songs. His first, "You and the Mistletoe and Me," would have been recorded by Nat King Cole had not Cole died. Then, in 1962, Hayes initiated a songwriting collaboration with David Porter as his lyricist. When the Soul singing duo, Sam and Dave, came to Memphis to make some records at Stax-Volt, Hayes and Porter wrote some of the songs they recorded. "You Don't Know Like I Know" was a minor hit. "Hold On, I'm Coming" was a major one in Soul. "Soul Man" won for Sam and Dave a gold record. Hayes and Porter also wrote songs for other recording performers: "B-A-B-Y" and "Let Me Be Good to You" for Carla Thomas, and "I've Got to Love Sombody Baby" and "I Had a Dream" for Johnny Taylor. In all, Porter and Hayes wrote about two hundred numbers.

Isaac Hayes became his own performer for the first time when, after a drinking session with the vice-president of Stax-Volt, they suddenly decided to go to the studio and see how Hayes sounded on a record. The sound, apparently, was good, for Isaac Hayes soon after that recorded his first album, *Presenting Isaac Hayes*. Its successor, *Hot Buttered Soul*, released on the Enterprise label (a Stax subsidiary), in 1969, went on to become Hayes' first gold record. Now an esteemed performer as well as composer, Hayes recorded many more best-selling LPs: *Isaac Hayes Movement*, *Isaac Hayes. . . . To Be Continued*, *Black Moses*, *In the Beginning*, *Live at the Sahara Tahoe* and *Chocolate Chip* (the last receiving a gold record in 1975). As songwriter, performer—and later producer—Hayes became an all-important influence in developing the "Memphis Sound" at the Stax-Volt studios before he left that company to record for ABC.

7

There was the "Memphis Sound" produced by Stax-Volt Records in Memphis. And there was also the "Detroit Sound" that came out of Motown Records in Detroit, the first, and at one time the largest, completely black owned and operated recording company in the United States (with sales in excess of forty million dollars a year) and a force of incalculable importance in the world of Soul. The name "Motown" is a contraction of "Motor Town," and the company was founded by Berry Gordy, Jr., a ninety-dollar a week chrome trimmer at the Ford assembly plant. Gordy spent his spare time writing songs, some of which were used by local singers. In 1959, Gordy's friends induced him to start his own company in order to record a group which he had discovered and wanted to promote, The Miracles, headed by "Smokey" Robinson. With a small sum borrowed from his family's Credit Union—seven hundred dollars in all—Gordy formed Gordy Records. Its first release, by The Miracles, was one of Gordy's own songs, "Way Over There" and one by "Smokey" Robinson, "Mama Done Told Me." The company did well enough to spawn two smaller subsidiaries, Tamla and Motown. On the Tamla label, in 1961, Gordy had his first substantial winner in "Shop Around," performed by The Miracles and written by Gordy in collaboration with "Smokey" Robinson. Before the year ended, Tamla Records could boast its first million-disk sale with "Please Mr. Postman" (Brian Holland and Freddy C. Gorman) recorded by The Marvelettes. Mary Wells, one of the first females to become a top-selling rhythm and blues performer, entered the Gordy stable in 1962 to record for Motown "You Beat Me to the Punch" (William Robinson and Ronald White). It was Number One on the rhythm and blues charts that year. So was "Do You Love Me?" (Berry Gordy, Jr.) recorded by The Contours on the Gordy label.

Twelve-year-old Little Stevie Wonder—that prodigiously versatile screaming and finger snapping singing phenomenon of Soul, who accompanied himself by banging the bongos and drums and also performing on the piano, harmonica, clarinet and organ —exploded with his first Tamla album. It was appropriately named *Little Stevie Wonder: Twelve-Year Old Genius*, and it contained "Fingertips" (Henry Cosby and Clarence Paul), which, when released as a single, went on to sell well over a million-and-a-half disks. Stevie Wonder (originally Steveland Judkins) was born blind in Saginaw, Michigan, in 1950. When he was still an infant, his parents separated. His mother brought her children to Detroit, and there Little Stevie started to play the piano when he was four. Soon afterwards he tried to produce tunes on a four-hole harmonica and rhythmic sounds on toy drums. Fascinated by the rhythm and blues numbers he regularly heard over the radio on a program called "Sundown," he was soon a total convert to this kind of music as he continued studying the piano and progressed from toys to a real harmonica, drums and bongos. One day, when he was nine, he was expelled from the church choir of which he was then a member, because church members found him performing rock 'n' roll for other children.

Ronnie White, a member of The Miracles, brought Stevie to the studios of Motown Records when Stevie was about nine. From then on, every day after school, Stevie would barge into the studios and play on any instrument he could find. Hanging around until dark, he frequently made a nuisance of himself by interfering with recording sessions. Because he could play so many instruments and because he was already writing songs (his first song, "Lonely Boy," was written when he was ten) the people at the studio kept calling him "the little wonder boy." When Motown signed him to his first contract, it gave him the new name of Little Stevie Wonder.

He received his academic education in public schools and at the Michigan School for the Blind where he was taught classical piano. His second home and school was the Motown studio, and its singing stars became his second family and teachers. By the time he was twelve, Stevie Wonder was becoming one of Motown's valuable singing properties, his first album for Tamla became a smash success, and the single, "Fingertips," bringing him the first of many gold records. The force of his slick black sound was further unleashed during the next few years in other best-selling singles: "Uptight" (Sylvia Moy, Henry Cosby and Stevie Wonder), "Travelin' Man" (Ronald Miller—Bryan Wells), "I Don't Know Why" (Stevie Wonder, Paul Rise, Dom Hunter and Lula Hardaway), "Shoo-Be-Doo-Be-Doo-Da-Day" (Sylvia Moy, Henry Cosby and Stevie Wonder), "My Cherie Amour" (Sylvia Moy, Henry Cosby and Stevie Wonder), "For Once in My Life" (Orlando Murden), "I Was Made to Love Her" (Sylvia Moy, Henry Cosby, Lula Hardaway and Stevie Wonder), Bob Dylan's "Blowin' in the Wind," "A Place in the Sun" (Ronald Miller—Bryan Wells), and "Yester-me, Yester-you, Yesterday" (Ronald Miller—Bryan Wells). He also piled up sales with his many LP releases, among them A *Tribute to Uncle Ray* ("Uncle Ray" being Ray Charles), *The Jazz/Soul of Little Stevie, Fingertips, Uptight* and *Stevie Wonder's Greatest Hits*.

His record successes brought him engagements in nightclubs throughout the country, including the Copacabana in New York and in concert auditoriums. At the Philharmonic Hall (now Avery Fisher Hall) in New York City in April 1970 his virtuosity on the harmonica was almost as great an attraction as his piercing renditions of Soul. A versatile performer, he was an artist who became, as Jack Slater noted in the *New York Times Magazine* "all things to all who hear him: the child prodigy who made the transition to adulthood as a productive musician, the blind seer apocalyptically exposing America's injustices, the sightless man-child who still manages to smile, the musician who refused to accept the tyranny and paternalism of corporate recording interests, the black flower-child ruled by visions and astrological signs, the blind nature-boy telling us that the only thing that matters is to love and be loved in return, the black brother who 'made it,' who is still 'for real' and still funky and finally—and perhaps most burdensome of all—the young man who has become, as some whites tell him, an example and an inspiration for his people."

After 1966, his name began appearing in the credits of many of the songs he was performing and the creative Stevie Wonder began sharing the spotlight with the performing Stevie Wonder. The first LP which he produced himself—*Signed, Sealed and Delivered* in 1970—contained many of his own songs. *Where I'm Coming From*, in 1970, was an LP made up entirely of his songs which he had written in collaboration with his songwriting wife, Syretta Wright (a writing partnership that continued even after their divorce in 1974).

Where I'm Coming From was Stevie Wonder's last album under his second five-year contractual arrangement with Motown. He was twenty-one and the time had come, he felt, to free himself from the stereotyped material Motown had insisted he record and to venture into new and sometimes experimental directions in his music making. He took one quarter of the million dollars that up to now had been held in trust for him and invested it in a New York recording studio where he could experiment with new recording techniques. He now became interested in such electronic instruments as the Moog and ARP synthesizers whose unusual sound effects, he said, gave the voice to "what's inside my head." He also evolved the "one man" album in which he wrote his own songs, made his own arrangements, did the vocals, and played most of the instrumental accompaniments on the piano, drums, harmonica, organ and electronic instruments. The first such album was *Music of My Mind* in 1971.

Music of My Mind was brought out by Tamla Records in 1972 under a new arrangement which Wonder negotiated with Motown in which he became his own record producer, was given complete artistic control over all his future recordings, together with a larger share of the royalties. *Talking Book*, a second "one-man album," came later in 1972, a volume that contained two Stevie Wonder songs which, as singles, became gold records, "Superstition" and "You Are the Sunshine of My Life." When Grammys were distributed on March 2, 1974 for the best records of the preceding year, Stevie Wonder received one for his own release of "You Are the Sunshine of My Life" as the best male pop vocal, another for the same record as a rhythm and blues vocal, and a third one for "Superstition" as the best rhythm and blues song. In addition, he was awarded a fourth Grammy for the album *Innervisions*, which had been released in the summer of 1973. Among its best cuts were such hit songs as "Living for the City," "Higher Ground" and "All in Love Is Fair." (Wonder had been nominated that year for six Grammy awards, the first time such a thing had ever happened in the sixteen-year history of the National Academy of Recording Arts and Sciences.)

Supplementing these honors that year were two more given him by the American Broadcasting Company as the consequence of a poll conducted among record buyers: He was named the favorite male vocalist and his recording of "Supersitition" was selected as the best singing recording in the Soul division.

Early in 1972, Stevie Wonder organized Wonderlove, a backup group for his public appearances. With it he toured the United States for several months. That summer he also became the opening act for the Rolling Stones during its own tour. On February 3, 1973, Stevie Wonder made a triumphant debut at Carnegie Hall in New York, and in the fall of 1974 he and his band toured thirty American cities.

He was one of the mainstays of the Tamla catalogue at Motown, which up to that time had sold close to forty-million of his records, when a near-fatal accident almost ended his career permanently when he was only twenty-two. On August 6, 1973, the car in which he was riding crashed into a logging truck on a road in North Carolina. He was coming from a concert in Greenville, South Carolina, to perform at Duke University in Durham, North Carolina. He suffered a brain contusion, was in a coma for several days, and lay near death in hospitals in North Carolina and California. When he finally recovered he had a new outlook on life itself and on his career. "The accident," he said, "opened up my ears to many things around me." He grew more religious than ever before, more mystical, and at the same time more concerned than ever to fulfill himself artistically as completely as he could. His career now acquired new dimensions.

His first public appearances following his recovery took place in Boston and in Raleigh, North Carolina, in November 1973. He went on to give concerts in London, England, and Paris, in January and February of 1974, and to make a hero's return to New York with a mammoth concert at Madison Square Garden on March 25, 1974. His first album released since his accident became a gold record: *Fulfillingness' First Finale*, whose songs were by turns meditative, introspective, mystical, religious and sentimental.

In 1974, Wonder was chosen as the best-selling male Soul artist of the year by the National Association of Recording Merchandisers and he was given the American Music Award for "Superstition" as the best Soul vocalist and the best Soul single.

Four more Grammys came his way in 1975: for *Fulfillingness' First Finale* as the year's best album; for "Fulfillingness' First Finale," as the best pop male vocal; for "Boogie on Reggae Woman" as the best rhythm and blues male performance; and for "Living for the City" as the best rhythm and blues song. When, on August 9, the first Rock Music Awards were distributed at the Santa Monica Civic Auditorium, Wonder was singled out as leading male vocalist. In 1977 he was given the American Music Award as top Soul performer.

As a reward for such achievements, Stevie Wonder signed a new contract with Motown in 1975 that gave him the highest guarantee in the history of the recording industry: thirteen million for the next seven years during which time he agreed to record one LP a year.

It is no surprise, then, that in writing of him in a cover story *Newsweek* said: "He is recognized as the most creative—and popular—pop musician of his generation. With a career that already spans half his life and that has piled up sales of forty million records . . . Stevie is the favorite of young, old, black, white, the hip and the square."

But let us return to Motown: the year 1963, when Little Stevie Wonder first became one of Motown's shining lights, was also the time when Martha and The Vandellas recorded

"Heat Wave" (Eddie Holland, Brian Holland and Lamont Dozier) on the Gordy label and when Marvin Gaye recorded "Pride and Joy" (Marvin Gaye, William Stevenson and Norman Whitfield) for Tamla.

In 1964, the Gordy enterprise lured into its fold The Four Tops with "Baby, I Need Your Loving" (Eddie Holland, Brian Holland and Lamont Dozier); The Temptations with "The Way You Do the Things You Do" (William Robinson and Bobby Rogers); and The Supremes (with Diana Ross) with the single "Where Did Our Love Go" (Brian Holland, Eddie Holland and Lamont Dozier) and with the Motown album, *Meet the Supremes*.

By this time, 1964, the company occupied seven brick bungalows on both sides of Woodward Avenue in Detroit, and was selling over twelve million records a year. The sales figures and the profits kept growing—together with the expanding importance and influence of Motown. In 1965 and 1966, almost forty percent of all the best-selling recordings came from the Motown combine. In 1969, Motown left Detroit for Hollywood, having now become a conglomerate embracing not only its recording interests but also a motion picture and television division (its first production, *Lady Sings the Blues*, the screen biography of Billie Holiday starring Diana Ross), a publishing company and a talent agency.

In *The Guardian* (published in London)—on May 1, 1972—Geoffrey Cannon spoke of one of the major contributions made by Motown to popular music: "Most of the black groups who were successful up to the 1960s in America were owned by white business men who turned their singing towards comedy or novelty, on the prima facie sensible notion that any sound that smacked of gospel music would be unfamiliar and unattractive to the predominantly white national audience. It took Berry Gordy, a black man who has always put business first, to break a gospel sound out of this ethnic barrier."

Still another of Motown's achievements in the world of Soul was the creation of a new sound: the "Detroit" or "Motown" Sound. Phil Spector, later a recording executive but at that time a disc jockey, is believed to have been the first to use the term "Detroit Sound" to describe the new kind of music being pressed on Motown Records. He did so for The Four Tops' recording for Motown of "Reach Out I'll Be There" (Brian Holland, Eddie Holland and Lamont Dozier) in 1966. The "Motown" or "Detroit" Sound was worked out by Gordy with the help of his three house composers—Brian Holland, Eddie Holland and Lamont Dozier—and was brought to life by the company's leading performers. It was a Sound preferring discipline and control to the spontaneity of the "Memphis Sound." It diluted the strong Soul brew of the "Memphis Sound" to make it into "soft Soul," more palatable to white audiences. Yet the beat remained strong, with emphasis on percussion and bass, and the vocal parts retained gospel fervor. Bass sounds were built upon a foundation of rhythm and blues. Gordy himself described the new Sound as a "happy" one, "a big happy beat with a good strong bass with tambourine giving it a gospel flavor."

The Supremes was the strongest package in the Motown inventory. And as long as Diana Ross was its lead singer, it was the quintessence of Motown's "sweet Soul."

Diana Ross was one of six children. She was born in Detroit, Michigan, in 1944, and raised in a low-income development in one of Detroit's poorer neighborhoods. Young Diana not only sang in church but, in her early girlhood, appeared in little shows which she produced on the back porches of her friends' homes. The only vocal lessons she ever received, beyond some coaching in the performance of popular songs by an older cousin, was from a church choir leader.

She attended Cass Technical High School and after school hours worked as a busgirl in a cafeteria. With two of her Detroit friends—Mary Wilson and Florence Ballard—she formed a singing trio, the Primettes, which appeared at local functions and won first prize in a talent contest. During a two-week period in which she worked as an assistant secretary to Berry Gordy, she tried to induce him to make a commercial recording of the Primettes. He was interested, but insisted that Diana Ross first finish school. When that happened, Gordy used the Primettes as background to recordings by Mary Wells, Marvin Gaye and several other Motown performers. When Gordy finally decided to feature the three girls in their own recordings, he had them go through a processing in which they were instructed in charm, proper grooming and deportment. He then gave them the name of The Supremes.

Their first eight records, between 1961 and 1964, did only fairly well on the rhythm and blues charts. Then, in 1964, Gordy had his staff songwriters—Brian and Eddie Holland and Dozier—write special song material for The Supremes and at the same time to use their know-how in molding the trio's singing style. That spelled the difference. "Where Did Our Love Go" came first and with it came the first gold record for The Supremes and their first bid for stardom. "Where Did Our Love Go" was the third single released by Motown to get the Number One position on the national charts; it sold over two million disks.

One year later, The Supremes became the first singing group to be awarded six consecutive gold records within a single year: for "Baby Love," "Come See About Me," "Stop! In the Name of Love," "Back in My Arms Again," "I Hear a Symphony," and "You Can't Hurry Love," all of them written by Brian and Eddie Holland and Dozier.

Taken under the wing of the International Talent Management, a Motown subsidiary, The Supremes began in 1965 to circulate on the plush nightclub circuit from the Empire Room and the Copacabana in New York to Eden Roc in Miami Beach and the Coconut Grove in Los Angeles; also to tour the United States and Europe in concerts. Their earnings soared; they often received $25,000 a week in nightclubs and sometimes $100,000 for a single concert. In step with their success in personal appearances was the phenomenal sale of their recordings: the singles, "The Happening" (Brian Holland, Eddie Holland and Lamont Dozier), "In and Out of Love" (Brian Holland, Eddie Holland and Lamont Dozier), "Love Child" (Pam Sawyer, R. Dean Taylor, Frank Wilson and Deke Richards), "Forever Came Today" (Brian Holland, Eddie Holland and Lamont Dozier), "Some Things You Never Get Used To" (Nicholas Ashford and Valerie Simpson); and the albums, *At the Copa*, *Bit of Liverpool*, *Country, Western and Pop*, *Greatest Hits*, volumes, 1, 2 and 3, *More Hits*, *Cream of the Crop*, *Let the Sunshine In*, *Farewell*.

By 1968, when they recorded "Love Child," The Supremes had a change of personnel, with Cindy Birdsong replacing Florence Ballard. At the same time they acquired new billing, that of Diana Ross and The Supremes, in recognition of the increasing importance of Miss Ross in this singing partnership.

Then, being carefully groomed by Motown to go solo, Diana Ross decided to leave The Supremes. Her last recording with them was "Someday We'll Be Together" (Jackey Beavers, Johnny Bristol and Harvey Fuqua) in 1969, and her last public appearance with her singing colleagues took place in January of 1970 at the Frontier in Las Vegas. For The Supremes, this parting of the ways (with Jean Terrell taking over for Diana Ross) meant an artistic and financial decline. But for Diana Ross it spelled the making of a superstar. In her recordings and nightclub appearances she extended her repertory with pop numbers and show tunes to which she brought the same elegance of style and aristocracy of manner that had characterized her performances of "sweet Soul." She was given a Grammy and an award from *Billboard* in 1970 as the leading female vocalist of the year. In April 1971, she was the star of a TV Special, "Diana." One year later, in her first motion picture, she played Billie Holiday in *The Lady Sings the Blues*, a film produced by Berry Gordy that was criticized for its clichés and stereotypes, but which was a personal victory for Diana Ross. "She captured," wrote Judith Crist in *New York*, "the high pitch and girlishness of the early Holiday songs and the pure Soul sound she developed." *Cue* Magazine selected her entertainer of the year for this performance, for which she also received the Golden Globe Award. The sound track album of this motion picture was a best-seller, as was a later Diana Ross LP, *Touch Me in the Morning*. Diana Ross was once again singled out for special praise when she was starred in her second motion picture, in the title role of *Mahogany* (1975).

8

Roberta Flack, Dionne Warwick, and Della Reese also carried black power into the popular music. Among the most prestigious female vocalists of recent times, all three have revealed a wide gamut of style and materials, but are most famous for their "sweet Soul."

Roberta Flack was a teacher of music in the public schools of Washington, D. C. when, in 1967, she decided to embark upon a new career as a popular singer. In half a dozen years or so her "soft Soul" style captured numerous Grammys, a handful of gold records, and she was made the star of her own Special, "The First Time Ever," over ABC-TV in June 1973. In 1974 she was named top female vocalist in the Soul division by the American Music Awards competition in its first poll of the nation's record-buying public.

Born in Black Mountain, near Asheville, North Carolina, in 1939, she was brought up in Arlington, Virginia, a suburb of Washington, D. C. Since both her mother and father played the piano she was soon drawn to that instrument. She took her first lessons when she was nine, and at thirteen she captured second prize in a piano competition among black students in Virginia. After graduating from high school, she attended Howard University on a scholarship, specializing in music education. By this time, singing had begun to appeal to her strongly. She organized choral groups that performed in churches and public concerts. After receiving her Bachelor of Arts degree in music education in 1958, she took on a job teaching English and music in Farmville, North Carolina. A year later, she joined the public school system in Washington, D. C. where for the next half-dozen years she taught music in junior high schools. Her extracurricular musical activities included playing the organ, serving as an accompanist for several opera singers, directing church choirs, coaching vocal students, and receiving some vocal instruction from Frederick Wilkerson.

Wilkerson was the first to urge her to leave school and become a professional singer of popular tunes. It took a number of years for this advice to bear fruit. But reinforced by successful appearances at the 1520 Club in Washington, D. C. and at the Sunday brunches at Henry Yaffe's Club on Capitol Hill, Roberta Flack, in 1967, made the step that carried her across the threshold of greatness as a popular vocalist.

Her first appearances, in the fall of 1967, were at Mr. Henry's, a nightclub in the Georgetown section of Washington operated by Henry Yaffe. Owing to her instant popularity, Yaffee opened a special room for her. She was also signed to make recordings for Atlantic. The first LP, *First Take*, sold one hundred thousand albums in the first few months and, in time, brought her the first of several gold records. Other gold records came for the albums *Chapter Two, Quiet Fire, Killing Me Softly* and *Feel Like Makin' Love*, and for the single "Killing Me Softly with His Song" (Norman Gimbel and Charles Fox). "Killing Me Softly with His Song" also brought her a Grammy as the top female vocalist. In 1972 she captured a Grammy for "The First Time Ever I Saw Your Face" (Ewan McColl), chosen record of the year, and she shared a second Grammy with Donny Hathaway for the best pop vocal performance of a duo, "Where Is Love." Roberta Flack's recording of "The First Time Ever I Saw Your Face" was used on the sound track of the motion picture *Play Misty for Me* (1971).

She was a top box-office attraction in her public appearances at various festivals, in swank nightclubs throughout the United States and at her concert debut at Avery Fisher Hall in New York's Lincoln Center in December 1970. *Downbeat* named her the leading female vocalist of 1971, a title usurped from Ella Fitzgerald who had held it for eighteen consecutive years.

By 1975, Roberta Flack became weary of her continual recording sessions and her one-night performing stands. She had been at it for five years without interruption. "All of a sudden," she explained, "you get that rush of 20,000, 30,000, 50,000 people—the world. All these people love me, you think. Then you're back in a hotel room by yourself in Missouri, your stomach hurts, and your humanness just overwhelms you." For almost a year and a half she withdrew from her professional life as a singer to go back to the piano, and to study anew the piano music of the masters. She returned to the recording studio as a Soul performer with the album *Feel Like Makin' Love*, in which she was not only her own producer but also occasionally was heard as pianist (listed as Rubina Flake) in the background music. She had left recording a year and a half earlier while she was on the top, and she returned on the top. *Feel Like Makin' Love* was acclaimed by the critics as one of Roberta Flack's best, and it brought her one more gold record.

No singer has ever been identified so completely with the work of a single songwriter, or songwriting team, as Dionne Warwick—the songwriters being Burt Bacharach, composer, and Hal David, lyricist. Miss Warwick was a member of a singing group, the Gospelaires, which provided background music for a recording by the Drifters, when Burt Bacharach, who was directing the session, first caught sight and sound of her. "Just the way she carries herself, the way she works, her flow and feeling for the music—it was there when I first met her," Bacharach has said. "She had . . . a kind of elegance, a grace that very few people have."

When, some months later, Bacharach wanted to make demonstration records of two of his songs, he remembered Dionne Warwick and asked her to record them. Bacharach then submitted his songs to Scepter Records who were so taken with Dionne's performance that they signed her up for the company and engaged Bacharach as her producer. Her first Scepter record was "Don't Make Me Over" by David-Bacharach in 1963. It made the best-selling charts. From then on, Bacharach and David wrote many of their songs expressly for Dionne Warwick, and in public appearances and on records Dionne sang virtually everything Bacharach and David wrote. "It's a wonderful kind of progressive up-the-ladder sort of success story for the three of us—to have found a singer who is capable of being such an exponent of what you write, and being so musical, and to sing just about anything, and any way, and to work to her dimensions which are unlimited, and then to be able to write for her as she grows," Bacharach has written. As for Dionne Warwick, she had confided: "We're a team and the three of us belong together. . . . These men and their songs have been the best friends I ever had. They made me aware of the beauty of the world as well as the heartaches—helped me to know how to handle both extremes of living. . . . We're on the same wave length, wanting to say the same things about life and the living of it." Unfortunately, this long harmonious relationship received a sharp jolt in the fall of 1975 when Miss Warwick sued Bacharach and David for six million dollars for alleged violation of an agreement to produce for her and deliver to Warner Brothers a new album.

When she was born in Orange, New Jersey, in 1940, her name was Marie Dionne Warrick, but when she signed her first recording contract it was misspelled as "Warwick." Adding a final "e" to that name, and omitting the first name of Marie, she adopted Dionne Warwicke, but in time she reverted to Warwick. Her father was the head of the Drinkard

Singers, a group specializing in gospel music, successfully touring the United States, appearing at the Newport Jazz Festival and making recordings for RCA Victor. Dionne played the organ accompaniments for this group from time to time. Occasionally, when one of the members fell ill, Dionne became a handy replacement. After that, in 1954, she formed a vocal trio of her own, the Gospelaires—with her sister and their cousin—which gave concerts over a seven-year period.

On a scholarship, Dionne Warwick attended the Hartt College of Music at the University of Hartford in Connecticut, as a student of voice, piano and theory. During summers she continued singing with the Gospelaires who, in addition to performing gospels, provided vocal accompaniments for various singers and groups.

Her recording of "Don't Make Me Over" deflected her from teaching to professional singing as a solo vocalist. (She continued to study at Hartt College through the years with the hope of ultimately getting a Doctor's degree in music.) Other best-selling records of songs by Bacharach and David followed in short order: "Anyone Who Had a Heart," "Walk On By," "Always Something to Remind Me," the last two written for her. "Walk On By," recorded in 1964, reached the top ten in the charts not only in the United States but also abroad.

She was also becoming a star in nightclubs, and at concerts and festivals. Marlene Dietrich personally introduced her at one of her own concerts at the Olympia Theater, in Paris. From then on Dionne Warwick became the darling of the Parisian public which dubbed her "Paris's Black Pearl." Paris was the first stop of a tour that carried her throughout the Continent and England that year. Miss Warwick's first major American nightclub appearance (at the Basin Street East in New York in 1964) was a failure, but her first concert performance in the United States, at Lincoln Center in New York in 1966, was a success of the first magnitude. In 1965 and 1966 she began making frequent appearances on television network programs. *Cash Box* chose her as leading rhythm and blues recording artist in America in 1966, while giving her the Number Two place among pop singers. In 1969, Dionne Warwick was featured in a motion picture, *Slaves*.

By 1970, her recordings had sold over five million singles and six and a half million albums. She had received gold records for the single, "I Say a Little Prayer" (Hal David —Burt Bacharach) and for the albums *Dionne Warwicke's Golden Hits*, *Here Where There Is Love* and *Valley of the Dolls*. She received Grammys for her recordings of the single "Do You Know the Way to San Jose?" (Hal David—Burt Bacharach) as the best female contemporary performer and in 1970 for her album *I'll Never Fall in Love Again*.

She has, of course, made best-selling records with songs by writers other than Hal David and Burt Bacharach. Her album, *The Valley of the Dolls*, had songs by André Previn, with lyrics by Previn's wife, Dory. These songs were written for the motion picture, *Valley of the Dolls* (1967), where they were sung on the sound track by Miss Warwick. In 1974, she earned a gold record for the single, "Then Came You" (Sherman Marshall and Philip Pugh) in which she was backed by the Spinners.

But most of her recording successes (originally for Scepter, and later on for Warner Brothers) came to her with songs by David and Bacharach, many of which owe much of their enormous popularity to her performances either on singles or in albums: "I Just Don't Know What to Do with Myself," "Alfie," "Anyone Who Had a Heart," "Do You Know the Way to San Jose?", "Wishin' and Hopin'," "The Windows of the World," "Raindrops Keep Fallin' On My Head," "Message to Michael," "Trains and Boats and Planes," "I Say a Little Prayer" and many others. Although Dionne Warwick was not cast in the David-Bacharach Broadway musical, *Promises, Promises*, (1968), it was her recording that made the title number and "What Do You Get When You Fall in Love" giant hits. But the first huge record sales of the

David-Bacharach song, "What the World Needs Now Is Love" was earned not by Miss Warwick but by Jackie De Shannon in an Imperial recording that received a gold disk. Not that Miss Warwick was not given first choice on the song. But, as she has explained: "Burt and Hal brought it to me first, of course, but at the time the way it was written it didn't sound the way it sounds today—which is like a natural million seller. I should have known that it would be changed in the recording process, but I really felt that it wasn't for me. So Jackie had the million-selling single. I recorded it later, in an album, and we used exactly the same arrangement Jackie had."

Among the best-selling albums by Dionne Warwick in which the songs of Hal David and Burt Bacharach appear (as well as songs by others), in addition to those already mentioned, are *Sensitive Sound*, *Dionne Warwick's Gold Hits*, volume 2, *Promises, Promises*, *Soulful*, *I'll Never Fall In Love Again*, *Dionne*, *Very Dionne*, *The Dionne Warwick Story* and *The Love Machine*. The last of these was the sound track for the motion picture of the same name (1971) based on the novel by Jacqueline Susann.

Gospel is the source of Della Reese's intense delivery of the blues, jump tunes and even ballads. Born Doloreese Patricia Early in Detroit, Michigan, in 1932, she began singing in the junior choir of the Baptist Church when she was six, and soon after that was assigned solo parts. Mahalia Jackson, came to Detroit for a concert, became interested in her when Della was thirteen and engaged her to sing with her gospel choir on tours for the next five summers.

In the fall of 1949, Della Reese enrolled in Wayne State University in Detroit to major in psychology. The death of her mother, and the serious illness of her father, forced her to drop school after her freshman year and work for a living. For a number of years she was employed as a receptionist, a switchboard operator and a taxicab driver, but without abandoning her singing of gospels. She organized and sang with the Meditation Singers, as well as with several other gospel groups.

She made her first appearances as a solo vocalist in pop music in a bowling alley in Detroit in the early 1950s, after which she was given her first professional nightclub engagement in that city. An eighteen-week engagement at the Flame Showbar in Detroit brought her to the notice of Lee Magid, a New York theatrical agent, who became her manager. He brought her to New York where for nine months in 1953 she was a vocalist with Erskine Hawkins' orchestra. In 1953 she signed a recording contract with Jubilee; her first release, Cole Porter's "In the Still of the Night," sold half a million disks. Her first gold record came in 1957 with "And that Reminds Me" or "My Heart Reminds Me" (Al Stillman—Camillo Bargoni), the year when *Billboard*, *Variety* and *Cash Box* all selected her as the year's most promising female singer. Appearances on network television programs, including the Ed Sullivan Show on several occasions and the Jackie Gleason Show, and performances in plush nightclubs, intimate rooms in important hotels and supper clubs throughout the United States—where she sometimes introduced the singing of gospel together with pop numbers—lifted her to stardom. In 1958 she was featured in the motion picture *Let's Rock*.

Della Reese got her second gold record in 1959 with her RCA Victor recording of the ballad "Don't You Know" (Bobby Worth) adapted from Puccini's "Musetta's Waltz" from the opera *La Bohème*. Her album *Della: The Lady Is a Tramp*, was a best-seller in 1960; so were such subsequent LPs as *Story of the Blues*, *Classic Della*, *Della by Starlight*, *Della With Brass*, *Della on Strings of Blue*, and *Black Is Beautiful*.

In 1960, Della Reese became the first black singer to perform "The Star-Spangled Banner" at an annual All-Star baseball game. Two years later, she toured with the Meditation Singers in a show, *Portrait of Della Reese*, which was recorded by RCA Victor and taped for television by the National Telefilm Associates. After more than three hundred TV appearances, she was given her own TV Variety show in 1969, "Della," two hundred and fifty hour-long segments of which were syndicated five days a week to major stations.

9

In the early 1960s, several combos began carrying gospel into jazz. Among them were Horace Silver's Quintet, Horace Silver being the composer of "Senor Blues," "The Preacher" and "Song for My Father" among other jazz items. There was also Cannonball Adderley's Quintet (later Sextet). And there was Ornette Coleman, that saxophonist *par excellence* who played with various groups from the mid-1950s on and became influential in the sixties in night spots, at festivals in Newport and Monterey, and as a recording artist for Atlantic. Coleman's most ambitious composition was "Free Jazz," a thirty-seven minute free-form improvisational work.

If there is any such thing as "instrumental Soul" it can best be applied to the music of John William Coltrane, popularly known as "Trane," one of the most significant forces in jazz in the 1960s. He died in 1967 when he was forty—at a time when he was still growing and developing as a composer. But already he had written much music which led jazz on in new directions. An avant-gardist, Coltrane drew for his musical materials from Indian, African and French impressionist as well as from jazz sources, Coltrane worked within free forms that allowed his musical ideas to move in whatever direction they wished and to expand without confinement to structural patterns or to constriction to formal rhythmic and harmonic procedures. His writing had an improvisational character filled with passages of harsh sounds which some have called "angry black music," and some have named "the new black music," but which can reasonably be identified as instrumental Soul. His most famous composition probably is "A Love Supreme," a four-part "jazz prayer." It was chosen by *Downbeat* in 1965 as the record of the year with Coltrane at the same time named Jazzman of the year and top tenor saxophonist.

The son of a tailor, Coltrane was born in Hamlet, North Carolina, in 1926. After his family moved to Philadelphia, Coltrane studied the E-flat alto horn, clarinet and saxophone while attending high school. When he was eighteen he attended the Ornstein School of Music in Philadelphia, then, after service in the Army, he worked as a sideman in bands led by Dizzy Gillespie, Johnny Hodges and others. In 1955 and again in 1958 he was a member of the Miles Davis Quintet, and in 1957 he appeared with Thelonious Monk at the Five Spot in New York. He was now beginning to make records on his own. His album, *Giant Steps*, brought him forcefully to the attention of jazz buffs.

His prime importance in jazz began in 1961 when he formed his own quartet comprising besides himself, McCoy Tyner (piano), Jimmy Garrison (bass) and Elvin Jones (drums). With this group, and through his own compositions, he began producing the avant-garde jazz sounds that made him one of the most important jazzmen of his time. As Jimmy Garrison recalls: "Trane had started hearing other voices, other ways of doing things. He was the sort of man who was always learning, always practicing, even between sets. He was one big piece of music and he knew there had to be more roads to cover." Of Coltrane's thirty-eight minute free-form improvisational composition, "Ascension," Archie Shepp, sometimes picked as the heir to the Coltrane tradition, said: "It builds in intensity through all the solo passages, brass and reeds, until it gets to the final section where the rhythm section takes over and brings it back down to the level it started at." To this comment, A. B. Spellman, author of the liner notes to the Coltrane album *Ascension*, adds: "By that time your nervous system has been dissected, overhauled and reassembled."

Coltrane died in a hospital in Huntington, Long Island, on July 17, 1967. During his last two months he performed little, and though he was under medical care, he refused to be hospitalized until his last day when it was too late. He left behind a heritage of some forty albums with which the world of jazz has been immeasurably enriched. The best of these are *Coltrane Sound, Standard Coltrane, John Coltrane, The Last Trane, Coltrane Plays the Blues,* and *The Best of John Coltrane,* volumes 1 and 2. Some years after his death, in 1975, two biographies of him appeared: *Chasin' the Trane: The Music and the Mystique of John Coltrane* by J. C. Thomas and *Coltrane: A Biography* by C. O. Simpkins. A third, *John Coltrane* by Bill Cole followed in 1976. In reviewing the first two of these volumes, Gary Giddins said this of Coltrane which might well serve as that great jazzman's epitaph: "Not since Charlie Parker has a soloist offered a musical conception so compelling and self-sustaining that virtually thousands of musicians, professional and amateur, looked to his every record for sustenance in their own music."

43

Today's Troubadours— The Performing Composer

1

There was a time when songwriters were content to devote their full energies to writing the best songs they could, and to allow others, specialists in their own field, to do the performing. But in country and western music, rock, and soul, many songwriters have become their own performers. Many of these performing composers have already been spoken about in preceding chapters; but many more must now be considered. For what was first just a tendency and then a trend has, since the 1960s, become a sweeping movement in popular music. Recording companies are more likely than not to turn a receptive ear to writers who can promote their own songs by appearances at concerts, nightclubs and on television.

Burt Bacharach belongs in this ever-expanding army of composer performers. Burt Bacharach's creativity is of such originality and mass appeal that his songs easily would have found exposure in motion pictures, on records, and over television by performers other than himself. It is as a composer that he received two Academy Awards in 1969: for his background music for *Butch Cassidy and the Sundance Kid*, and for its song, "Raindrops Keep Fallin' On My Head" (Hal David). It was as a composer that he received a Tony award and another from the New York Drama Critics Circle as the season's best songwriter (with lyricist Hal David) for his score for *Promises, Promises* (1968), at the same time that that Broadway production captured another Tony as the season's best musical. It was as a composer that he earned two Grammys: in 1969 for the best original score for a motion picture (*Butch Cassidy and the Sundance Kid*) and for the best score of an original-cast album (*Promises, Promises*). His songs (all with Hal David's lyrics), recorded by some of the most gifted artists of our time, continually invaded the best-seller charts. Dionne Warwick's best-selling recordings of Bacharach's songs have already been discussed. B. J. Thomas' release of "Raindrops Keep Fallin' On My Head" alone sold three million records. Jack Jones received a Grammy for his recording of "Wives and Lovers." Aretha Franklin's recording of "I Say a Little Prayer" was a gold disk, and so were the recordings of the 5th Dimension of "One Less Bell to Answer," and of Tom Jones' recording of "I'll Never Fall in Love Again" and Jackie De Shannon's disk rendition of "What the World Needs Now Is Love." Other distinguished performers who have successfully recorded Bacharach's songs include Perry Como, Herb Alpert, Dusty Springfield, Sandi Shaw, Billy J. Kramer and the Dakotas, Gene Pitney, Marty Robbins, Cher and Bobby Vinton.

Yes, Burt Bacharach would have easily found his place with the best popular songwriters of the past quarter of a century even if he were not a performer. But being a performer of his own music has proved to be a powerful element in his success story. As a recording artist, conducting an orchestra in his own arrangements of his music, he received Grammys for his albums *Alfie*, *Butch Cassidy and the Sundance Kid*, *Make It Easy on Yourself*, *Reach Out* and *Burt Bacharach*. In addition, he has been starred as a performer composer in TV Specials year after year. One of them, "The Sound of Bacharach" in 1970, earned an Emmy for its director, while "The First Bacharach Special" in 1971 won another Emmy as the season's best musical variety program. And Bacharach has been a star in nightclubs and at concerts. His own music, of course, is the principal magnet, but he himself is also one. He is attractive, in a virile sort of way, and his boyish grin is infectious. At these personal appearances he plays the piano, conducts the orchestra, sings, and makes informal verbal comments—an impressive performance that fully displays his abundant charm. He is one of the very few songwriters who has been able to conquer the fleshpots of Las Vegas.

The appeal of Bacharach's songs is broad even though their sentiments and chiseled beauty are not always readily assimilated at first hearing. He avoids stereotyped patterns, changing his structure from song to song, now to exclude an opening verse, now to have a verse of just four or eight measures, now to follow the chorus of a song with an instrumental epilogue, and now to present his entire musical message in a seventy-eight measure chorus without any preliminary verse or concluding coda. He changes time values and meters freely and often, indulges in quixotic chromatics and unusual accents, and is not afraid to employ unconventional harmonies, to change his dynamics dramatically, or to allow a melody to progress toward unexpected intervals and finish with unorthodox cadences. His are not the kind of melodies that are easy to hum.

But in spite of their intricacies and subtleties, these songs have had a universal appeal, probably because Bacharach is never content to remain fixed in any single area of popular music. He borrows from rock, country, Soul and bop whatever serves him to create a polyglot language uniquely his, one which by the variety of its idioms can reach and satisfy the different tastes of a large public.

Though born in Kansas City, Missouri, in 1928—the son of Bert Bacharach, a distinguished author and journalist—Burt was brought up in Forest Hills, Queens, New York. He came to music early, by learning to play the cello, then the drums and finally the piano. He detested formal music study, preferring to spend his free time playing with his friends in the streets. He dreamed of becoming a football player. But, having become a rabid bebop devotee while attending high school, he kept on with his piano lessons and soon was able to play with various dance bands and jazz groups, one of which he himself organized and took on a USO tour of Army hospitals. This active participation in the making of popular music stimulated his musical appetite. He now hungered for additional instruction, a hunger satisfied at the David Mannes School of Music, the Berkshire Music Center, the Music Academy of the West in Santa Barbara, and for three years by study with the world-renown French master, Darius Milhaud.

After a two-year stint with the armed forces between 1950 and 1952, where most of his duties were musical, he found employment as a piano accompanist for various popular singers, occasionally doing some of their arrangements. He was working for the Ames Brothers when he decided to confine his talent to writing songs. Renting a cubbyhole in the Brill Building in New York, which overflowed with songwriters, he spent ten industrious months scribbling notes on manuscript paper. None of these songs interested publishers, record companies or performers, and necessity compelled him to return to piano playing to support himself. While working for Steve Lawrence, Vic Damone, Georgia Gibbs, Polly Bergen, Joel Grey and Marlene Dietrich, he also did arrangements for Famous Music Corporation. Then, in 1957, one of his songs, "The Story of My Life," was published by Famous Music. This number was typical of later Bacharach songs in its unorthodoxy. It had no verse; the chorus extended for fifty-two measures; and it required the performer to whistle as well as sing, concluding with a whistling passage. Marty Robbins' Columbia recording was a best-seller. Bacharach's second best-selling record came the same year with "Magic Moments," recorded by Perry Como for RCA Victor.

The lyricist for Bacharach's first two song successes was Hal David, a younger brother of Mack David, who was also a songwriter as well as popular performer. Born in 1921, in Brooklyn, New York, but raised on New York's East Side, Hal David aspired from boyhood to become a writer. After leaving high school and the School of Journalism at New York University, he served in the armed forces during World War II, writing humorous sketches and songs for Army productions in a unit headed by Maurice Evans, the distinguished actor. After the war, Maurice Evans had him work on several theatrical projects, none of which did much to further David's writing career. Then, in 1949, "Four Winds and Seven Seas," for which he wrote the lyrics to Don Rodney's music, was recorded by Sammy Kaye. Others of his lyrics were now being sung by major artists. Frank Sinatra recorded "American Beauty Rose" (music by Redd Evans and Arthur Altman) in 1950; Teresa Brewer, "Bell Bottom Blues" (music by Leon Carr) in 1953; Val Anthony, "The Heart of a Fool" (music by Frank Weldon) in 1954; Carl Dobkins, Jr., "My Heart Is an Open Book" (music by Lee Pockriss) in 1957.

Some of Hal David's songs were published by Famous Music Corporation and it was at its office that he met Bacharach and formed a working relationship with him. Their initial efforts were failures but before discouragement set in "The Story of My Life" and "Magic Moments" sent them winging towards success.

The songs of Bacharach and David proliferated through the 1960s; the best were collected in *The Bacharach and David Song Book* (1970). Between 1962 and 1963 they wrote the title songs for two movies—*Forever My Love* and *Wonderful to Be Young*—while two other films became the inspirations for "The Man Who Shot Liberty Valance," and "Wives and Lovers." Still in 1962–1963, "Make It Easy on Yourself" was successfully recorded by Jerry Butler; "Don't Make Me Over" and "A Message to Michael" by Dionne Warwick; "Only Love Can Break a Heart" and "Twenty-Four Hours from Tulsa" by Gene Pitney; "Wishin' and Hopin' " by Dusty Springfield; and "Blue on Blue" by Bobby Vinton. The string of hit records of Bacharach songs by major performing artists remained unbroken in the next few years. In addition, in 1965 and 1966, Bacharach and David wrote their first complete scores for motion pictures—*What's New Pussycat?* and *Alfie*. The title song of *What's New Pussycat?* was sung on the sound track by Tom Jones in one of his first significant bids for recognition, and that of *Alfie* was recorded by numerous performers and was nominated for an Academy Award. "The Look of Love" from the motion picture *Casino Royale* (1967) was also nominated for an Academy Award, and was circulated in the best-selling recording of Dusty Springfield who had introduced it in the movie. "Do You Know the Way to San Jose?" was one of the song hits of 1967, and in 1969, "Raindrops Keep Fallin' On My Head" won the Academy Award. Meanwhile, in 1965, Bacharach married the motion-picture star, Angie Dickinson. (They separated in 1976.)

In 1968, Bacharach and David made their first bow in the Broadway musical theater with an opulent score for *Promises, Promises*.

2

The songs for which Neil Diamond is most famous are those which reflect the insecurity of his early years. The frustrations of his childhood in a middle-class Jewish family in Brooklyn, New York, where he was born in 1941, were never forgotten. Within his family circle he always felt an outsider. As he told an interviewer: "I grew up in a family where everyone else seemed to be something special. A cousin was the smartest kid in school. My brother was an electronics genius and so forth. I was sort of a black sheep." Since his family moved about a great deal, he attended nine different schools, and was a stranger in all. "I was never accepted as a kid," he said. Music was an escape. When he was ten he sang in the streets with a group calling itself the Memphis Backstreet Boys. Three years later he toured the coffee-house circuit with the Roadrunners, a folk group he had organized.

When he was sixteen he took some guitar lessons which, in turn, led him to write his first song, "Hear Them Bells." "It was like taking your finger out of the dike," he explains about his creative experience. "I wrote night and day, on anything I could find. Shopping bags." He also said; "It was an outlet for a great deal of frustrations. Writing songs finally gave me something of my own."

He attended Brooklyn grammar and high schools, then entered New York University to prepare himself for medical school. In 1962, just six months before he was to get his college degree, he made some demonstration records of his songs which he sent around to publishers. One of them, Sunbeam Music, offered him a job writing songs for fifty dollars a week. That ended once and for all his plan to go to medical school. But the job turned out to be hack work and he quit. He found other jobs, no more satisfying, with other publishers and quit them, too. After four such years, he rented an office, a storage room above Birdland, and spent a year there turning out one song after another. In all, he spent seven years of failure from the time he left college, "seven years of knocking around New York. It's very difficult to accept seven years of failing without it doing something to you. And what it did was to close me up as a person." He encountered failure in his personal life as well; his marriage to a childhood sweetheart was breaking up, even though they had two daughters.

His first professional break came in the form of a recording contract from a small company, Bang. His initial releases in 1966—his own songs "Solitary Man," "I Got the Feelin' " and "Cherry, Cherry"—were best-sellers. He continued recording for Bang in 1967, "bubble gum" numbers slanted for the teenage market, and all of them profitable: "Girl, You'll Be a Woman Now," "Kentucky Woman," "Thank the Lord for the Night Time" and "You Got to Me." But he was growing restive with this kind of sophomoric material, aspiring to write adult songs with a more personalized slant, songs rising from past heartbreaks. The first of these was "Shilo"; another, "I'm a Believer" which the Monkees recorded for Colgems in 1966 to achieve a million-disk sale.

Analysis helped Diamond find himself creatively; and a new marriage in 1969 made it possible for him to rehabilitate his personal life.

Since Bang records was indifferent to the new course he was taking as a songwriter, Diamond left that company in 1968 after having recorded "I Am. . . . I Said" coupled with "Done Too Soon." He went on to record for Uni, beginning with "Brooklyn Roads" and "Two-Bit Manchild" and continued in 1969 with "Brother Love's Traveling Salvation Show," "Holly Holy," and "Sweet Caroline," the last being a gold record in 1969, Diamond's first as a composer-performer, and in 1970 with "He Ain't Heavy, He's My Brother." He was awarded other gold records for "Cracklin' Rose" and the album *Touching You, Touching Me* in 1970, for *Tap Root Manuscript* in 1971, and, in 1972, for "Song Sung Blue" "Play Me" and the album *Moods*.

On the strength of his sales, Diamond signed a five-million dollar contract with Columbia. Its first Diamond release came in 1973, the sound track music for the motion picture *Jonathan Livingston Seagull*, an album that piled up a million-dollar sale before its release date, and went on to become a platinum record, and to receive a Grammy and the Golden Globe Award in 1974.

In writing the music for his first motion picture, *Jonathan Livingston Seagull*, Diamond was aiming not at functional background music but at a score of symphonic dimensions. Hal Bartlett, producer of the film, in sympathy with Diamond's ambitious aims, allowed him to prepare forty-eight minutes of music. However, when the film was first released, some of Diamond's music was cut from the sound track which sent Diamond to the law courts in a victorious suit to restore the deleted parts.

Neil Diamond acquired two more gold records in 1974 for the LPs *Twelve Greatest Hits* and *Serenade*. *Hot August Night*, a giant seller in 1975, seemed destined to become another.

Inevitably, Diamond graduated from records to television, and after that to the stage where he proved himself a born showman in the presentation of his own material. At the Saratoga Arts Center, in the summer of 1972, he offered *Diamond's Greatest Hits* backed by a seven-piece band. That fall he brought this production to Broadway, selling out the Winter Garden for each performance of the two-week engagement. "Up front," wrote Grace Lichtenstein in *The New York Times*, "Diamond is totally in command, belting out the tunes in a rich baritone with a nice sincere ache in it, hips swaying gracefully but not graphically. Call him an urban Elvis, a *haimish* Tom Jones. He's a rock singer a girl could take her parents to see."

For about forty months, beginning with late fall 1972, Neil Diamond withdrew from all public appearances. He secluded himself at his home in Malibu Beach, California, with his wife, Marcia, and their son, Jesse. When he was not composing songs and working on other musical projects, he spent his time fishing, riding his motor bike to the hills, or looking out of his window at the Pacific. His return to the stage took place in Utah in February 1976, the beginning of a world tour. Three appearances at the then newly opened Aladdin Hotel Theater for the Performing Arts in Las Vegas, in July 1976 (his Las Vegas debut), brought him the unprecedented fee of five hundred thousand dollars. His later albums *Seranada* and *Beautiful Noise* became giant best-sellers. His first TV Special was televised over the NBC network on February 21, 1977.

3

Of Turkish descent, Neil Sedaka emerged from Brooklyn, New York, where he was born in

1939. He was the son of a taxi driver who, as a competent pianist, did everything he could to encourage his son's obvious talent for music. Music was Neil's refuge from the rejection of the neighborhood kids because he had braces on his teeth, wore glasses and found pleasure in practicing the piano. He started writing popular songs when he was thirteen. A year later he began using the lyrics of his friend, Howard Greenfield, a collaboration that remained fruitful for many years. At Lincoln High School in Brooklyn, Sedaka won several awards for writing pop tunes for school productions. He organized, played in and was the arranger for a pop quartet, The Tokens. During the summers he worked as music director in vacation camps. After graduating from high school he enrolled in the Juilliard School of Music on a scholarship won in a New York piano competition at which Arthur Rubinstein, that giant among concert pianists of the twentieth century, was one of the judges. He now seemed headed for a career as a virtuoso. But his first success as a songwriter deflected him from the piano. It was "Stupid Cupid" (Howard Greenfield) which Connie Francis made into a best-selling MGM record in 1958. Sedaka now left Juilliard to concentrate on writing songs with Greenfield. When Don Kirshner, a publisher, heard one of Sedaka's songs in a demo performed by Sedaka himself, he was even more enthusiastic about the performance than about the song and convinced Sedaka he should combine songwriting with performing. That demo had been made in the studios of RCA Victor, whose A and R man, Steve Sholes, agreed with Kirshner's opinion and signed Sedaka to an exclusive performing contract.

"The Diary," (backed with "No Vacancy"), which Sedaka recorded for RCA Victor was a best-seller in 1959. During the next few years, his songs—slanted for the teenage "bubble gum" trade—sold over twenty million copies: "I Go Ape" in 1959 and "Breaking Up Is Hard To Do," in 1962, were gold records. Sedaka's hits—always with Greenfield's lyrics—recorded by him for RCA Victor included "Happy Birthday, Sweet Sixteen," "Calendar Girl," "Let's Go Steady Again" and "Oh, Carol." The last was written for and dedicated to his then girl friend, Carole King, herself a distinguished composer performer. His best songs up to this time were gathered in the LPs *Little Devil and Others* in 1961 and *Neil Sedaka* in 1963.

During all this time, Sedaka made numerous appearances on network television programs and at concerts. With Greenfield as his lyricist he wrote songs for the motion picture *Where the Boys Are* (1961) in which Connie Francis made her screen debut.

In a five year period up to 1962, his songs sold twenty-five million records. Then the halcyon days were over, seemingly for good. "I overdid it," he explained years later. "I overdid the sound. Plus there were the record executives. They said 'You've got a winning formula and you have to stay with it.'" But something else was proving destructive to Sedaka's kind of song and to his success. The popularity of hard rock made the young public turn away from the kind of teenage songs Sedaka had been dispensing in favor of the sturdier stuff dispensed by the Beatles, the Rolling Stones and the new American rock groups in San Francisco and Los Angeles. With his career as a performing composer seemingly over, Neil Sedaka appeared in a nightclub act and did scoring for films. He now depended upon established singing stars, usually in the pop field, to record his songs and to help him reestablish himself as a songwriter. Eydie Gorme recorded "My World Keeps Getting Smaller"; Andy Williams, "One Day in My Life"; Tom Jones, "Puppy Man"; Davy Jones, "Rainy Jane"; Peggy Lee, "One More Ride on the Merry-Go-Round"; Johnny Mathis, "The World I Threw Away"; the 5th Dimension, "Working on a Groovy Thing." All the lyrics were by Howard Greenfield.

In 1970, Neil Sedaka moved with his Chinese doll-like wife, Leba, and their children to London, England. An English promoter found some bookings for Sedaka in clubs in northern England. Then Sedaka met Elton John who had him record for his company the album *Sedaka's Back*. This started Sedaka off on a comeback which saw him once again become a top-selling recording artist-composer. His "Laughter in the Rain" (Philip Cody) reached the Number One position on the English charts and just stopped thirty thousand disks short of becoming a gold record. It also became a best-seller in the United States. On the strength of the renewal of his popularity as a performing composer, Neil Sedaka returned in 1974 to make his first extended American tour in many years. On the nightclub circuit, particularly in Las Vegas, he became a bigger star than ever and his 1976 album *Steppin' Out* was a best-seller. He was also doing extraordinarily well as a songwriter. His "Love Will Keep Us Together" (Howard Greenfield) made top stars of the until then little known duo, Captain and Tennille; their recordings of the single and the album bearing the song title earned Grammys and became gold records in 1975. "Bad Blood" (Phil Cody), with Elton John providing a vocal background, also achieved the gold-record status in 1975 in a release by MCA, while "Lonely Night," for which Sedaka wrote his own lyrics, brought Captain and Tennille a new best-seller.

4

Harry Nilsson is a phenomenon among performing composers in that for a long time he scrupulously avoided appearing in public. Though he was catapulted to fame by singing "Everybody's Talkin' " (Fred Neil) on the sound track of the motion picture *Midnight Cowboy* (1969), he refused for a number of years to accept a major assignment for the movies and shunned public appearances, preferring to confine his talent to records. He explained: "I get the same feeling of excitement in a studio that many get on the stage. . . . You can't change anything in a concert. . . . And I'm a perfectionist in some areas of my life, even if I leave my socks on the floor. I can stop the tape in the studio. If I went on the stage and things didn't work out I'd probably say let's do it another time and walk off."

As a singer of other people's music, he is heard at his best in the album *A Little Touch of Schmilsson in the Night*, released in June of 1973. Here he concentrated entirely on such standards as "As Time Goes By" (Herman Hupfeld), "I Wonder Who's Kissing Her Now" (Will M. Hough and Frank R. Adams—Joseph E. Howard and Harold Orlob), Irving Berlin's "What'll I Do?" and "For Me and My Gal" (Edgar Leslie and E. Ray Goetz—George W. Meyer.) In these he was very good, indeed. But he has been far better in albums offering his own songs, songs that cover a wide range of styles from rock to ballads.

Robert Kimball and Abigail Kuflik wrote in *Stereo Review*: "He has a fine, flexible, unmannered tenor voice that occasionally evokes the late Nat King Cole, a fabulous range, and a clear unforced tone that appears to be especially secure on high, soaring top notes. At times, with multipart harmonies achieved through painstaking overdubbing of tapes in the studio, Nilsson sounds as if he were a singing group."

Nilsson hints at the tragedy that rocked his life in his early years in the song "1941," which happens to have been the year of his birth in Brooklyn, New York. This number is found in his first RCA Victor album, *Pandemonium Shadow Show*, released in November 1967. The subject is the desertion of a wife and son by a father who becomes a clown; and the repetition of this situation a generation later when the son deserts his wife and child also to become a clown. Nilsson's own parents were divorced when Harry was still very young, and he was himself divorced from his wife when his son was still an infant. In 1958, when he was seventeen, Nilsson was brought by his mother to southern California where for a while he attended the St. John Vianney's Parochial School in Los Angeles. After graduation, he worked first as an usher then as assistant manager in a movie house. When the theater closed down he took a course in programming, which made him eligible for a job with the Security First National Bank in Van Nuys where he worked for seven years with computers. His interest in music was awakened in his teenage years by listening to the radio. When he was seventeen he got a ukulele as a gift and learned to play it by ear. A year later, he bought himself a guitar "and everything came together then," he says.

While working at the bank, he wrote jingles and commercials (for Ban Deodorant, Sea and Ski lotion) and songs (some of which were recorded by the Ronettes and the Modern Folk Quartet). He often spent all night at such endeavors. Among his first song efforts were "1941," "Without Her," "Cuddly Toy" and "Ten Little Indians," all later included in his first record album. "Without Her," a soft rock number, was successfully recorded by Blood, Sweat and Tears in 1968 and by Herb Alpert in 1969. More successful still was the Monkees recording of Nilsson's "Cuddly Toy" in one of their albums, which brought Nilsson a royalty of $40,000. This, together with a three-year contract from RCA Victor with a down payment of $35,000 on signing, was the assurance Nilsson needed that he could get along very well without his bank job. After his first album was released he resigned from the bank to become a full time writer of songs.

His second album, *Aerial Ballet*, in 1968, contained Nilsson's "Don't Leave Me" and the Fred Neil song, "Everybody's Talkin'." In *Harry*, in 1969, we find Nilsson's "The Puppy Song," "Nobody Cares About the Railroads Anymore" and "Simon Smith and the Amazing Bear" among others. More albums followed, each filled with outstanding Nilsson songs. The soft rock album, *Nilsson Schmilsson* in 1971 brought in over a million dollars to become Nilsson's first gold record. Among its numbers were "Gotta Get Up," "Driving Along," "The Moonbeam Song," "Down," "Jump Into the Fire," and "I'll Never Leave You." *The Point*, another LP in 1971, contained the music Nilsson had written for a TV animated program of that name. 1971 was also the year in which Nilsson recorded the successful single, "Me and My Arrow" and the LP, *Aerial Pandemonium Ballet*.

A second soft and hard rock album, *Son of Schmilsson*, in 1972, did almost as well as its predecessor; this one had "You're Breaking My Heart," "Turn on Your Radio" and "The Lottery Song." "Without You" (a song originally done by the British rock group Badfinger and written by members of that group) brought Nilsson in 1972, in his own release, both a gold record and a Grammy.

There is heartache and desolation in songs such as "Driving Along" in which Nilsson sees the human race rushing to nowhere; or "Mr. Tinker" about a tailor who has outlived his usefulness; or "Mr. Richard's Favorite Song" about a onetime successful pop singer whom time has thrown into discard. "I Guess the Lord Must Be in New York City" (which he wrote for *Midnight Cowboy* but which was rejected) points up the sad truth that everybody seems to want to be somewhere except where he is; "Turn on Your Radio" finds the successful rock performer too busy to dispense love except in his songs; and "Mornin' Glory," is a lament from one whose life had lost its meaning.

But in other songs there is hope, as in "Don't Leave Me" which refuses to accept the fact that days of peace and joy are ended forever; or "The Wailing of the Willow" which carries with it the assurance that "love will call again."

Nilsson feels that even in his sadder and more brooding numbers there is an undercurrent of optimism. He says: "I do believe that most men live lives of desperation. For despair, optimism is the only practical solution. Hope is practical. Hope at least gives you the option of living."

In 1968, Nilsson's resistance to exhibiting himself before an audience was partly broken when he played a cameo role in the Otto Preminger motion picture *Skidoo*, starring

Jackie Gleason, for which he also wrote the score. Nilsson assumed a more prominent role as motion-picture actor when he starred in the funky *Son of Dracula* (1974), for which he wrote seven songs, the best of which, "Remember," was used as a recurrent melody.

During the late 1960s, Nilsson befriended Randy Newman, a young songwriter, some of whose early songs Nilsson began to include in his own repertory. In 1970, he recorded a complete album of Newman's songs, *Nilsson Sings Newman*. Good as this album is—good as are the performances of other Randy Newman songs by such artists as Judy Collins, Joni Mitchell, Peggy Lee and Three Dog Night—Newman's songs usually come off best in his own performances, with his highly personalized phrasings which point up the subtle ironies of his lyrics, and his individual raspy blues manner of vocal delivery that is so compatible with his creative song style. Newman started singing his own songs after many others had done so, first because he was not always sympathetic with the way some of his numbers were presented, but primarily because his record company, Reprise, pushed him into the stage limelight to help promote disk sales. Appearances in such intimate night spots as The Bitter End and guest shots on television, including one on the Liza Minnelli Special in 1970, helped focus interest on Newman's songs.

His gentle rock numbers, partly derived from the Beatles and partly from the folk rock style of Bob Dylan, with a transfusion of the pop style of George Gershwin and Cole Porter, are often touched with wit, cynicism and irony. In his songs, Newman likes to place weird characters in strange story settings, "A lot of the people in my songs are obviously offensive," he told Susan Lydon for the *New York Times Magazine*. "They're sometimes stupid, or they have no sense of morality. But they condemn themselves by their statements. . . . I've always been interested in things that were faintly abnormal, slight aberrations one way or the other. I write non-heroic things rather than 'The Impossible Dream.' "

He covers a wider spectrum of subjects in his song literature than do most other popular songwriters: racism ("Old Kentucky Home"), man's inhumanity to children ("Davy the Fat Boy"), nuclear explosion ("Political Science"), sex ("Maybe I'm Doing It Wrong"), old age and death ("Old Man), perverts ("Let's Burn Down the Cornfield"), humdrum middle-aged marital life ("Love Story"), parent-son relationships ("So Long, Dad" and "Memo to My Son"), pollution ("Burn On, Big River, Burn On"), American experiences ("Illinois," and "Cowboy," and "Dayton, Ohio—1903"). Sometimes his sardonic laughter is replaced by a blues-like lamentation, as in "I Think It's Going to Rain Today." Sometimes he is offbeat as in "Yellow Man." Sometimes he ventures into the absurd, as in "Mama Told Me Not to Come." "Whether straight blues or comically ominous," said Hubert Saal in *Newsweek*, "Newman's is a vision of the world that reflects its sadness, its terrors and its injustices, even when he sings with the innocence of an idiot savant."

Writing music was a heritage from two of his uncles, Alfred and Lionel Newman, both of whom were preeminently successful as composers for the screen. Randy Newman arrived at the writing of popular songs by way of a formal training in serious music. He was born in Los Angeles in 1943, began studying the piano when he was seven, and spent many boyhood hours on Hollywood sound stages listening to the recording of screen music by his uncles. Randy Newman began writing songs during his teens encouraged by Lenny Waronker, a close friend who later became his producer at Reprise Records. When he was seventeen, Randy Newman was paid $150 a month by Metric Music to provide it with musical material. This was a hack assignment, but Newman satisfied his conscience by writing for his own pleasure songs on offbeat subjects.

He left the University of California in Los Angeles, where he had been trained in composition and musical theory, without a formal degree because he never bothered to fulfill the performance requirement. He now divided his time between writing songs and day-dreaming. In 1967, he got married, and a year later had a son.

Major performers, on the hunt for material off the beaten track, began to record his songs successfully and to bring his name and music to public attention. In 1967, Judy Collins included "I Think It's Going to Rain" in her album *In My Life* and then released it as a best-selling single. Three Dog Night had a smash hit with Newman's "Mama Told Me Not to Come" and Peggy Lee with "Love Story" in 1969-1970. *Nilsson Sings Newman* was a best-selling LP in 1970. Many other artists were also singing Newman's songs in public and on records, among them Blood Sweat and Tears, Dusty Springfield, Ella Fitzgerald, the Everly Brothers, Trini Lopez, Fats Domino, Vikki Carr and Joni Mitchell. Randy Newman himself recorded his first LP in 1969, *Randy Newman Creates Something New Under the Sun* for Reprise, an album that contained "Davy the Fat Boy" and "I Think It's Going to Rain." The sales were modest and so were those of his next album *12 Songs* whose quality, said Susan Lydon, "was on a par with the best rock records ever offered to the public."

But later recordings by Randy Newman began to find an expanding market, reaching the Top 40 charts. Among these were the LPs *Randy Newman Live* (recorded at The Bitter End), *Sail Away* and *Good Old Boys* (the last, a concept album of life in the South as seen through the eyes of a factory worker).

5

Rod McKuen has distinguished himself not only as a preeminent performer composer but also commercially as the most successful poet of all time. Up through 1976, sixteen million copies of his books were in print, something no poet before him ever achieved in his lifetime. He has also done well as a poet on records. In 1968 he was the only author with three recorded albums of poems on the best-seller lists, with *Lonesome Cities* getting both a gold record and a Grammy in the category of the spoken word.

But he is hardly less famous as a songwriter, what with his songs selling over one hundred million records by 1976, and as a performer of these songs in concerts and over television. He was born in Oakland, California in 1933 and was raised by his mother, since his father deserted his family soon after Rod was born. (In later years, Rod McKuen went to great lengths to locate his father, but to no avail. He wrote a book about that search, *Finding My Father*, published in 1976.) Since his mother kept moving about from one western state to another, working at various menial occupations, the boy led a nomadic existence allowing for little formal schooling. He was eleven when his mother married a construction worker. For the next few years Rod worked as a logger, cattle herder, lumberjack, bulldogger with a rodeo, rod man on a surveyor unit—and then as a singer and disc jockey over radio station KROW in Oakland, California. All this time he was writing poems and songs. He soon began the practice of reading his own poems and singing his own songs over the air, receiving the Blue Ribbon Award from the San Francisco *Examiner* as the most promising newcomer.

Service in the Army occupied two years between 1953 and 1955. In Japan, when off duty, he appeared as a singer in a Ginza Strip night spot, and he acted in six motion pictures filmed in Japan. After his discharge from the Army he was hired by the Purple Onion in San Francisco to sing ballads—many of his own composition—at intermission time. There he was discovered by Cobina Wright, Sr., a columnist, who got him an assignment in a Hollywood nightclub and a job in the movies. Between 1956 and 1958 he appeared in four films at the Universal-International studios, for some of which he wrote the background music. He also tried writing songs for films. One was "Sing, Boy, Sing," written in collaboration with Tommy Sands, who introduced it in the motion picture of the same name in 1957 and recorded it.

In 1959, Rod McKuen came to New York where, for a time, he wrote and conducted music for Albert McCleary's CBS Workshop, prepared special material for various performing artists, and appeared as a singer in nightclubs and discotheques. His many appearances as a singer put such a strain on his vocal cords that his physician warned him he was in danger of losing his voice. To rest, he went back to Hollywood to concentrate on the creative side of his life by writing poems and songs. He himself published a volume of his verses, *Stanyan Street and Other Sorrows*, which realized the unusual sale of sixty-five thousand copies. The powerful publishing company, Random House, took over the publication of this and succeeding volumes of poetry, whose sales figures were astronomical.

As a songwriter, in which he was no less prolific, McKuen was also beginning to make important headway. Major performing artists began to use and record his songs: Jimmy Rodgers recorded "The World I Used to Know"; Petula Clark, "Because We Love"; Glen Yarborough, "Each of Us Alone," "The Lonely Things," and the *Rod McKuen Song Book*; Damita Jo, "If You Go Away"; Frank Sinatra, *A Man Alone*, an album made up entirely of McKuen's songs topped by the title number. But Rod McKuen's songs did best in his own recordings after he signed a contract with RCA Victor in 1965. That year RCA Victor released his first album, *Rod McKuen Sings His Own*, a best-seller, following it with *Loner and Other Kinds of Songs* in 1966, *Listen to the Warm* and *Thru European Windows* in 1967 and *Single Man* in 1968. In 1968 McKuen shifted to the Warner Brothers label with *Lonesome Cities*, followed by *Love's Been Good to Me* and *Greatest Hits*, volumes 1 and 2, among other LPs. All of McKuen's subsequent giant record sales were achieved on his own label, Stanyan.

Among his best known songs, in addition to those already mentioned, are "Love Be Good to Me," "Seasons in the Sun" (a Number One song in the recording of Terry Jacks), "Listen to the Warm," "Lonesome Cities," "The Ever Constant Sea" and "Jean." The last was written for the motion picture *The Prime of Miss Jean Brodie* (1969), was nominated for an Academy Award, received the Golden Globe Award for the best song of the year, and was made into a best-selling single by Oliver. *Joanna* (1968), *Me, Natalie* (1969), *Scandalous John* (1969) and *A Boy Named Charlie Brown* (1969) are some of the other motion pictures for which McKuen provided excellent songs or background music. He has also spread his wings as a composer by completing a classical suite, *The Plains of My Country*, which was used in 1976 as background music for a dance performed by the Pittsburgh Ballet. He has even written a full-length opera, *The Black Eagle*.

Over television (in numerous network Specials and in guest spots on major programs), in concerts (of which he gives about eighty a year throughout the United States), in nightclubs, theaters and casinos, Rod McKuen has proved to be a potent salesman of his song wares. He has given command performances for President Rhee of Korea, President John F. Kennedy, and Queen Elizabeth of England. His concert in Johannesburg became the first ever given in South Africa before an integrated audience. He has also given over three hundred performances for convicts, interested as he is in prison reform. In his public appearances, singing his songs in the easy, relaxed chansonnier style he had learned from the French during an extended stay in Paris in 1963 and 1964, he is a major box-office draw. If the numbers of those who attend his concerts are fewer than those of other popular singing performers, it is mainly because he prefers to appear in auditoriums with no larger seating capacity than three thousand.

6

Leonard Cohen is a Canadian who, like Rod McKuen, is basically a poet. He often turns to the writing of songs with visions of love and alienation, revolt and suffering. Cohen's own presentations of his songs on Columbia Records, and in sporadic public appearances in the United States, have had a profound impact on the American young who regard him as their spokesman. Born in Montreal in 1934 to a prosperous mercantile family, Cohen learned to play the guitar when he was sixteen while spending the summer in a socialist camp. Only a year later he was appearing in cafés in Montreal, singing his own songs to his own guitar accompaniment. "I've been on the outlaw scene since I was fifteen," he once told an interviewer in touching on his unconventional life style that included drugs, illicit sex relationships, footloose wanderings and sublime disinterest in social or financial status. Nevertheless, he did manage to complete his schooling at McGill University where he received the MacNaughton Prize in creative writing and from which he was graduated in 1955 with the degree of Bachelor of Arts. And he was able soon after that to forge his way in the world of literature. His first volume of poems, *Spice Box of Earth*, was published in Canada in 1961 (and in United States in 1966) and was succeeded by three more highly acclaimed volumes of verses, *Let Us Compare Mythologies*, *Flowers for Hitler* and *Parasites of Earth*. His first novel, *The Favorite Game*, appeared in the United States in 1963 and was followed three years later both in Canada and the United States by *Beautiful Losers. Selected Poems, 1956–1968* appeared in the United States in 1968. Meanwhile his talent was recognized in Canada in 1960 and 1961 through grants by a Canadian Council and in 1964 with the winning of the Quebec Prize for literature. Then, in 1967, the National Film Board of Canada released a documentary film, "Ladies and Gentlemen. . . Mr. Leonard Cohen," based on his concert tours and appearances on college campuses. This brought Cohen assignments to write music for other films produced by the National Film Board, in one of which, *The Ernie Game* (1968), he assumed a speaking role.

All this while he was also writing songs purely for his own delight and for the pleasure of his friends. Judy Collins was so taken with some of his songs that she included several in her albums between 1967 and 1969: "Sisters of Mercy" in *Wildflowers*, "Suzanne" in *In My Life*, "Birds on the Wire" in *Who Knows Where the Time Goes*. Judy Collins also convinced Cohen to make personal appearances in the United States. In 1967 he was heard at the Newport Folk Festival and at concerts at New York City's Central Park. He also made appearances on television. His first album, *The Songs of Leonard Cohen*, was released by Columbia in 1968 and sold so well that a second album, *Songs from a Room*, was not slow in coming. Reviewing the second album, Ritchie Yorke described Cohen's performance as "mournful, moody, and at time excruciatingly personal, almost as though this was Cohen writing, then singing for himself." Other LPs followed: *Songs of Love and Hate* in 1971 and *Songs from a Room* and *Live Songs* between 1972 and 1973.

For many years he made his home on the Greek island of Hydra, which drastically limited the number of his public appearances and recordings. Nevertheless, in that time, he did produce another record album, *Songs of Love and Hate*, and his voice was heard on the sound track of the motion picture *McCabe and Mrs. Miller* singing his own "Sisters of Mercy," "The Stranger Song," and "Winter Lady."

7

Don McLean's "American Pie" was one of the most valuable song properties of 1972. When it burst upon the musical scene, McLean had been a folksinger of limited fame, a composer yet unknown to the general public. But one song—"American Pie"—made him a person of considerable consequence in the music business. It brought McLean two gold records, one for the single he recorded for United Artists and a second for the album named for the title song.

In New Rochelle, New York, where he was born in 1945, McLean was a sickly child and a loner who was educated in Catholic schools. He loved singing from the time he was one, and when he was still very young he became infatuated with the rock music of Buddy Holly. Having learned to play the guitar and the banjo, and having participated in schoolboy ensembles, McLean appeared in solo gigs at coffee houses and parties. In 1966 he entered Iona College for night courses mainly in philosophy and theology but without abandoning his singing career. He performed in a café in Saratoga Springs, New York; in 1968 he toured the Hudson River Valley, appearing in fifty-six towns, singing some fifty songs a day and become known as the "Hudson River Troubadour." In 1969 he joined Pete Seeger's sloop, *Clearwater*, which sailed on the Hudson River propagandizing the need for pollution control. To raise money for a boat, McLean, Seeger and others gave dockside concerts of folk music that year in twenty-seven cities and towns along the Hudson to some hundred thousand people. One byproduct of this river tour was a Special, "The Sloop of Nyack," produced by National Educational Television; another, an anthology, *Songs and Sketches of the First Clearwater Crew*, edited by McLean.

McLean's debut as a performing composer was made with the album *Tapestry*, recorded in 1970 by a small company, Mediarts. (This album should not be confused with one with the same title by Carole King which came out about a year later.) McLean's album consisted primarily of songs of social protest. It failed to attract much interest when first released. When Mediarts went into bankruptcy, it was reissued by United Artists and, while still failing to make much of a mark commercially, it did get hearings on disc jockey programs.

One would not have expected that a song like "American Pie" could spell the difference between obscurity and fame for its composer performer. It is a song of unusual length (lasting eight minutes) and is highly unconventional in its lyrics which are full of symbolic implications and metaphoric allusions. McLean himself refused to provide a clue to the song's meaning, insisting that it must be interpreted by the listener for himself. The lyrics are sprinkled with phrases, titles and names and nicknames which reveal or just hint at the identity of people and places in popular music and youth culture of the 1950s and 1960s. The untimely death of McLean's idol, Buddy Holly, casts a shadow over the song which might be said to be a dirge to Holly or to rock music in general. Within each verse is found the line "the day music died," each time appearing within a different context.

This unique adventure in songwriting leaped to the Number One place in the *Billboard* Top 100 chart seven weeks after it was released. Before many months passed, its million-disk sale was certified, and McLean found himself a millionaire. The album, *American Pie*, included together with its now famous title song, a tribute to Vincent Van Gogh ("Vincent"), an autobiographical piece ("Crossroads"), together with several other attractive items, such as "Everbody Loves Me, Baby," "Empty Chairs," "The Grave," and "Babylon."

McLean was no one-shot phenomenon. Some of the songs of his next two albums—*Don McLean* and *Playin' Favorites*—gave proof of that. They demonstrated the wide range of his versatility: "Dreidel," "Narcissma," "Bronco Bill's Lament," "Oh My, What a Shame," "If We Try" and "On the Amazon." In these albums, as in *American Pie*, the songs benefit considerably from the disarming charm of McLean's performance. "McLean cannot be praised too highly for his abilities as a performer," wrote Don Heckman in *The New York Times* following McLean's concert at Carnegie Hall in February 1972. "His voice is sweet and articulate; its only flaw is an occasional tendency to croon too much, as though he were listening to the loveliness of his tone rather than the meaning of his words.

His guitar and banjo are superb, a genuine masterful exposition and extension of the folk styles on which they are based."

One of Don McLean's best LPs is *Homeless Brother*, issued by United Artists in 1974, and one of its strongest numbers is "The Legend of Andrew McCrew." This song was inspired by a bizarre episode. Andrew McCrew was a one-legged, black hobo who met his death by falling off a freight train in Marlin, Texas in 1913. His body was embalmed in a funeral home, and when relatives failed to show up to claim it, members of a carnival acquired it, dressed it up in a tuxedo, and, as the "Amazing Petrified Man," made it one of its attractions. Once this attraction stopped making money, the carnival troupe disposed of the body, and it rested for several years in the basement of a warehouse in Houston, Texas. At long last, in May 1973, the body was buried. McLean's ballad drew national attention to this strange adventure of a black mummified corpse and impelled an unidentified Chicagoan to donate the money for a headstone which was unveiled on McCrew's grave in Dallas, Texas on December 8, 1974 and on which is chiseled the fourth verse of McLean's song.

8

Don McLean's album *Tapestry* was more or less a failure. Carole King's *Tapestry*—a compilation of her own songs—is one of the great success stories in recorded-music history. Its sale of well over thirteen and a half million albums has made it the best-selling LP of all time. It received a Grammy as the best album of the year with Miss King claiming a second Grammy as the year's top female vocalist. She received two more Grammys that year, to bring up her total to four: for her song, "It's Too Late," chosen as the year's best song (which in turn brought James Taylor a Grammy for best male vocal performance on his own recording).

Tapestry was a sleeper when it was released by Ode in 1971, even though Carole King was then no novice as a songwriter. In the early 1960s, with her then husband Gerry Goffin writing the lyrics, she had been responsible for many a soft rock number that climbed to national fame. But as the gentle and reflective balladeer singing of home, friendship, lost youth, sensitive love affairs and painful separations—in "Tapestry," "Beautiful," "Way Over Yonder," "It's Too Late," "I Feel the Earth Move," "Will You Love Me Tomorrow" and "A Natural Woman"—she was now singing with an incandescent style. In *Tapestry*, Carole King was strumming on a new creative lyre. Well—not altogether new. Her previous album, *Carole King: Writer* (her first LP), touched on similar strains in a similar way.

Like Neil Diamond, she came from a middle-class Jewish family in Brooklyn, New York, where she was born in 1942 and went through the Brooklyn public schools. During her adolescence she became a devotee of the rock music of Bill Haley, Elvis Presley and Fats Domino. By the time she left high school she was writing rock numbers of her own. She then attended Queens College in New York for a year where she was a classmate of Neil Diamond and Paul Simon. Her formal schooling ended when she married Gerry Goffin, an aspiring chemist and an amateur song lyricist. Since Carole liked to spin out melodies of her own, they joined creative forces—their first step toward matrimony. Neil Sedaka, who had dated Carole before she married Goffin, and who was already a songwriter of consequence, was so taken with her songs that he brought her to his own publisher, Don Kirshner. Kirshner paid Carole and her husband a weekly stipend to write songs. The first to make money was "Will You Love Me Tomorrow," made successful in 1960 by the Shirelles on the Scepter label and reaching the Number One position on the *Billboard* charts in January 1961. "Take Good Care of My Baby" was recorded by Bobby Vee in 1961.

In 1962, Carole King made a demo of her song "It Might as Well Rain Until September." This was her first serious attempt at performing one of her own songs. Kirshner was so pleased with her singing that he released the performance on the Dimension label. It became a top hit in England, and in America it stayed on the charts for nine weeks. Despite this recognition, Carole King preferred specializing in songwriting rather than singing. For the next two years, her songs, with her husband's lyrics, were placed in the hit class by various eminent performers: "Up on the Roof" and "Some Kind-a Wonderful" by The Drifters; "He's a Rebel" by The Crystals; "Go, Away, Little Girl" by Steve Lawrence; "One Fine Day" by The Chiffons; "Loco-Motion" by Little Eva; "Halfway to Paradise" by Bobby Vinton; "Oh, No, Not My Baby," by the Byrds; "Wasn't Born to Follow" by the Righteous Brothers; "Just Once in My Life" by Herman's Hermits and "Take Good Care of My Baby" by Bobby Vee.

The vogue for hard rock in the mid-1960s sparked by the Beatles and other visiting English rock groups, threw Carole King's soft rock numbers into the shade. For a number of years, her songwriting career went downhill.

In 1968, her marriage to Gerry Goffin ended in divorce, and she took her two daughters to California, hoping to carve a new career for herself there. She formed a Los Angeles group, The City, for whom she played the piano and with whom she occasionally contributed vocals; they recorded an album for Ode which did poorly. (The bass player, Charles Larkey, became her husband and the father of two more of her children.) She also performed on tour with James Taylor, the songwriter singer, and drew attention for the first time to the charisma of her vocalizations. Taylor was the one who convinced her to do more singing.

Lou Adler, head of Ode Records, signed her for her first album as a performer composer, *Carole King: Writer*, a gathering of ten Carole King songs, many of them with Gerry Goffin's lyrics. Despite its failure in the marketplace, Lou Adler was so taken with her performance and with her songs that he personally produced her second album, *Tapestry*. During the year that Tapestry was *released*, 1971, Carole King made a nationwide tour with James Taylor, climaxed by a concert at Carnegie Hall in New York when some critics spoke of her as the "queen of rock" in succession to Janis Joplin. "Hers is far from a great natural voice," said a critic for *The New York Times*, "but it has the deceptive thin strength of a whip antenna. Its basic hue is a Canarsie twang that suggests Judy Holliday negotiating 'The Party's Over.' But hue is one thing and cry another, as proved by Carole's pile driving thrust."

What do you do for an encore after *Tapestry*? If you have the creative and performing resources of Carole King you go on to the albums *Music*, (which became a gold record as soon as it was released), *Rhymes and Reason*, *Fantasy*, *Diamond Girl*, *Wrap Around Joy*, *Really Rosie* (the soundtrack of a TV Special) and *Carole King Thoroughbred*. *Music*, *Fantasy* and *Diamond Girl* were all gold records and *Carole King Thoroughbred* received a Grammy award. These albums added stature to Carole King's creativity. In them are new songs to remember and cherish: "You Light Up My Life," "Child of Mine," "Song of Long Ago," "Surely," "Brother, Brother," "Carry Your Load," "Back to California," "Believe in Humanity," "You've Been Around Too Long," "A Night This Side of Dying," "You Go Your Way, I'll Go Mine," "Change of Mind, Change of Heart" and "There's a Space Between Us."

"Her total conception," wrote Don Heckman in *The New York Times*, "is what makes everything work: hard piano rhythms, chugging percussion and roving contrapuntal bass all combine to provide a pulsating and roving contrapuntal vehicle for her gospel-blues vocals."

Fantasy (so-called because, as she said, "in fantasy I can be black or white, woman or man") represented a new direction for Carole King by being a "concept" album. Throughout she sounds the refrains of dangers of drug addiction, pleas for greater compassion and tolerance and condemnation of sexual and racial inequality.

9

The closing years of the 1960–1970 decade brought another female composer-performer to prominence. She was Laura Nyro, who tapped many different veins in her songwriting: folk, soul, rock, blues, jazz, show tunes. On October 6, 1968, in *The New York Times*, William Kloman called her "the hippiest—and maybe the hottest" of the newer songwriting performers. She is, said Kloman, "perhaps the first fully urban composer to emerge from popular music," whose love of New York found expression "in the convulsively shifting moods of her music. When she sings the blues, it is an apartment house wall, untouched by the levee or the plantation. Her melodies capture the city's tempo the way Mozart's quartets captured the spicy nuances of eighteenth-century drawing rooms. Strains of Gershwin and Bernstein flash through Laura's songs, racing her city-soul voice through its three-octave range. But it is Bernstein without Bernstein's sentimentality, and Gershwin perhaps on acid."

The daughter of a Jewish mother and an American Italian father who played the trumpet, Laura Nyro was born in the Bronx, New York, in 1947. She made her first attempt at songwriting when she was eight, and kept on with it while completing her elementary school education and after that while attending the High School of Music and Art in Manhattan.

Her first public appearance, in 1967 at the Monterey Pop Festival, was a fiasco: A pop and jazz singer was sadly out of joint where acid rock was a fetish. It took her two years before she would try performing again in public.

But she was beginning to make headway as a songwriter. "Stoned Soul Picnic" reached the top place on the national charts in 1968 in a Soul City recording by the 5th Dimension. This was one of thirteen songs about the growing-up problems of a young girl in *Eli and the Thirteenth Confession*, which was Laura Nyro's first LP; Columbia released it in April 1968. "Eli's Coming," earned a gold record for Three Dog Night in 1969. Laura's own first album was slowly plodding its way up the charts and so was her second album, *New York Tendaberry* (late in 1968) which included "Save the Country," "Time and Love," "You Don't Love Me When I Cry" and some of whose songs reflected her growing social consciousness.

Now under the managerial wing of David Geffen, Laura Nyro was carefully shepherded through public appearances around the country culminating with a sold-out performance at the Dorothy Chandler Pavilion in Los Angeles in December 1970. Her third album was beginning to reach out to a large market and beginning to touch the upper regions of the charts. It was *Christmas and the Beads of Sweat* in 1970, a sardonic political-conscious commentary on the contradiction between the spirit of Christmas and the dissension, strife and cynicism afflicting America during the late years of the Vietnam war and the years of racial conflict. More successful still was an album of Soul standards, *Gonna Take a Miracle*, in 1971, none of whose songs were by Miss Nyro.

Hers was a strident, husky, soulful singing voice that rose from rich contralto tones to high soprano, sometimes given to sentimentalization, sometimes touching the melodramatic through repeated use of falsetto.

While she was singing her songs well enough, and doing satisfactorily in the sale of her records, it took other performers to earn gold records with her songs: the 5th Dimension with "Wedding Bell Blues"; Blood, Sweat and Tears with "And When I Die"; Barbra Streisand with "Stoney End."

In 1973, Laura Nyro decided she was through. Some of the dog-eat-dog aspects of the music business revolted her and she had broken with her manager, David Geffen. She wanted to escape from the madding crowd with her husband, whom she had married in October 1971 (and whom she would divorce a few years later). She needed time for reading, for contemplation, for soul-searching. Part of the time she lived in New England, and part of the time she traveled to Europe and the Orient.

She made her comeback in 1976 with a tour that began in Hartford, Connecticut, on February 5 and ended at Carnegie Hall, New York, on March 31. She also recorded a new album for Columbia, *Smile*, which contained one or two songs that had been influenced by her visit to the Orient ("Children of the Junks" and the title song which featured a koto solo), in which she spoke hauntingly of her broken marriage ("Stormy Love") and of loneliness and disenchantment ("Money," "I Am the Blues," "The Cat-Song"). These songs were every bit as good as those she had been writing a few years earlier. It was in her performance that she had grown. She was now more disciplined, more restrained, and more subtle in creating an emotional impact.

10

In 1971, many writers were calling James Taylor the first pop music superstar of the seventies. And with good reason. His Warner Brothers album, *Sweet Baby James*, was selling over a million and a half copies, and one of its cuts, released as a single, "Fire and Rain," was also a giant best-seller. In January 1971, Taylor made triumphant appearances at Fillmore East and Lincoln Center in New York. On March 10, 1971, Madison Square Garden burst at the seams with the thousands come to hear his concert. Before the year's end, he appeared in a motion picture, *Two-Lane Blacktop*, embarked on a national tour of twenty-seven cities that was a sellout, received a cover story in *Time* and feature stories in *Newsweek* and *The New York Times Magazine*, and issued a new album, *Mud Slide Slim*, which brought him a gold record.

His songs are soft rock, compounded of country and western strains, some folk music and some blues. Though he is capable of tender sentiments, as in his lullaby "Sweet Baby James," he usually draws deep from the well of his experiences in songs filled with fear, despair and loneliness. "I've seen fire, and I've seen rain. . . . I've seen lonely times when I could not find a friend," he sang in "Fire and Rain." He knew the frustration and bitterness of failure and the self-contempt of underachievement. He had suffered from drug addiction. Some of his love affairs had left him with open wounds. He was so close to nervous breakdowns that twice he committed himself to institutions. "I sing," he once said, "because I don't know how to talk." Introspective, introverted and painfully shy, he sang of his harrowing doubts and pains—and an anxiety-ridden young generation found in his singing an echo of its own torments.

All the conditions were right for a serene, happy and well adjusted childhood and boyhood. He was born in Boston, in 1948, to a family that was independently wealthy and had social and cultural position, since his father was the dean of the medical school at Chapel Hill, North Carolina, and his mother had studied to be an opera singer at the New England Conservatory. He lived in surroundings of natural beauty, during the winter on a twenty-eight-acre ranch outside Chapel Hill and in summers at Chilmark on Martha's Vineyard. But apparently there were subtle pressures too severe for an oversensitive child and boy to bear, which negated the blessings of the good life that wealth and social station could provide. James Taylor is reticent about his early years and makes no effort to explain why they were for him times of sheer misery. A clue comes from his brother Livingston: "The basic orientation in my family was that simply because you were a Taylor, you could and should be able to accomplish anything."

There were five Taylor children. All received instruction on the violin, cello and piano; all were musical, though each early gave up the discipline of formal instruction; four of them—Alex, James, Livingston and Kate—became professional pop singers and made recordings.

When James was fifteen, he won a hootenanny contest with his friend Danny Kortchmar soon to be known as Danny Kootch, singing folk songs to their own guitar and harmonica accompaniment, the award being a week's engagement in a coffee house.

At Milton Academy, an exclusive boarding school outside Boston, James Taylor was a misfit. "There were things going in my head other than what the Milton people thought was right and proper." The dean of the school explained further: "We just weren't ready for him. James was more sensitive and less goal-oriented than most students of his day."

At one point in his schooling at Milton, James dropped out to join a rock 'n' roll band, The Fabulous Corsayers. Back at Milton, in his senior year he felt he was coming apart, and contemplated suicide. On the advice of a psychiatrist, he committed himself to McClean Hospital, a mental institution in Belmont, Massachusetts. "McClean set me free," he says. "I felt ties to my family breaking." The disciplined life there was one to which he could conform. It provided him with the peace of mind with which to reflect, to discover who he was and what he wanted to be. He was able to graduate from a high school attached to the hospital.

After nine months, James left McClean and with his friend, "Kootch" Kortchmar, formed a rock group, The Flying Machine; James played the guitar, did the vocals and wrote some of the songs. One of these was "Knocking 'Round the Zoo," about his experiences in a mental hospital. This, and two other personal songs, "Rainy Day Man" and "Night Owl," were included in Taylor's first record album later.

The Flying Machine came to New York and appeared at the Night Owl. Taylor lived by himself in an impoverished pad in uptown New York, sleeping on a mattress on the floor. As Kortchmar remembers it, Taylor "got hung up on taking in weird people—runaway teenagers and people like that." Taylor also found refuge in drugs, mostly heroin, and, as he himself confesses, "nearly died of social diseases." A year and a half of this sordid life and Taylor drifted on to England in January 1968. There he sent a demo of one of his songs in his own performance to Peter Asher (formerly of Peter and Gordon), the talented director of Apple Records which had just been founded by the Beatles. Asher thought it so good that he signed Taylor to a three-year contract. For Apple, Taylor recorded his first album, *James Taylor*. When released in January 1969 it was well reviewed, but did not sell well.

Before the album came into the market, Taylor returned to the United States in a state of physical and mental exhaustion, more dependent than ever on drugs. Once again he had himself institutionalized, this time at Austen Riggs in Stockbridge, Massachusetts. There he wrote one of his finest and most self-revelatory songs, "Fire and Rain," upon discovering that a girl patient at Austen Riggs, with whom he was believed to have been in love, had committed suicide.

When, in the United States, Peter Asher became James Taylor's manager, Taylor's career suddenly began to flower. He got a recording contract with Warner Brothers that resulted at once in the phenomenally successful LP *Sweet Baby James*, *Mud Slide Slim* (which included "You've Got a Friend"), *One Man Dog*, *Walking Man*, *Gorilla*; also the best-selling singles "Don't Let Me Be Lonely Tonight," "Long Ago, Far Away" and a duet, "Mockingbird," which he sang with his wife, Carly Simon, in her album *Hotcakes*.

Asher brought Taylor into the movies, first in *Two Lane Backtop* and immediately after that in *Easy Rider* (1969). And Asher started him off on a concert career as a performing composer. In July 1969, Taylor was a sensation at the Newport Folk Festival. In March 1970 he was starred at the Gaslight, a basement coffee house in New York's Greenwich Village, where many were turned away each evening for lack of space. Then, early in 1971, there took place his tour of twenty-seven cities invariably to sold-out auditoriums.

He had climbed the heights, and now he felt the need to catch his breath. He withdrew for a two-year period of comparative retirement during which he achieved mental equilibrium and release from drug addiction. His marriage to Carly Simon (herself an exceptional singer composer) on November 4, 1972, was mutually beneficial in eventually bringing to both a stability each had not known before. They settled down to domesticity in an apartment on Manhattan's East Side and raised a daughter, Sarah.

When he returned to the concert stage in 1974, with a month-long American tour that ended in Carnegie Hall on May 26, and recorded his fourth album, *Walking Man*, new facets of his artistic personality were uncovered. Wrote Lorraine Alterman in *The New York Times*, Taylor was now "a musician who colors his perceptions about life with great sensitivity, humor and thoughtfulness. . . . The quiet glow that permeates both his music and his vocals makes all the more winning the intimate quality Taylor has achieved as a performer. . . . The final cut in this album, 'Fading Away,' appears to sum up Taylor's feelings about his current state of mind. . . . He seems to be stating that he's bowed out of the rat race of fame and is concentrating on his life and love." The richer and deeper veins in Taylor's productivity were further topped in 1976 with the single "Shower the People," and the album, *In the Pocket*, the latter a gold record.

Carly Simon and James Taylor had something in common beside their respective talents as composers and performers. Both were born to families with financial and social status, and both spent their early years in misery. The Simons were a family of exceptional achievers and doers. Carly's father, Richard, was a founder of the publishing house, Simon and Schuster. Three of Carly's uncles earned distinction in various fields of music: George, as an authority on jazz; Henry, as a musicologist and book editor; Alfred, as the music director of a classical radio station. Carly's older sister, Joanna, eventually developed into a distinguished opera and concert singer. Surrounded by such accomplishments, Carly felt totally inadequate. Born in New York City in 1945 and raised in the affluent New York suburb of Riverdale, she early became convinced of her shortcomings and tried to gain attention through rebellion and underachievement. If classical music was close to a religion in the Simon household, then Carly would make a fetish of rock. If the Simons were intellectuals, Carly would be a clown; specializing in imitations of Al Jolson. She told an interviewer, "I felt a desire to break away from what my parents felt was important. For instance, my father was a book publisher and I did my damndest never to read a book. . . . For a long time I was feeling that the only way I could get anyone's attention or love was by being the black sheep who wasn't making any money, didn't have a job, didn't fit."

She went through the motions of an academic education at the Riverdale Country School and for two years at Sarah Lawrence College. Her interest in singing came mainly from listening to the folksinger, Odetta. After her second year at Sarah Lawrence, she and her sister Lucy organized a singing duo, The Simon Sisters, which made a record album for Kapp, *The Simon Sisters* (later rereleased by Elektra as *Early Simon*). Nothing much came of it and the duo dissolved when Lucy married a physician.

Albert Grossman, the manager of Janis Joplin and other rock stars, advised Carly to go it alone and try to develop herself as "A Jewish Bob Dylan." But, she explained, "I couldn't sing like Dylan." For several years she did the best she could to keep herself busy, by working as a secretary writing commercial jingles and teaching guitar. She was going no-where, not even to that comfortable marriage toward which her parents were trying so painfully to direct her. She fled to southern France to live with her boyfriend in what she hoped would be a love idyll in a moving picture setting. It turned out to be a horror, since she developed tremors which sent her back home and into the care of a psychiatrist for four years. The tremors disappeared—at first she thought it was the result of the benefits of psychiatry that had explained them as a severe anxiety attack. But, on a return trip to France, she discovered that the tremors returned because she was allergic to French wine.

For some time she had been writing songs. One of her friends, Jacob Brackman, encouraged her to devote herself more seriously to what up till then had been a haphazard avocation. He had her make a demonstration record which brought her a recording contract from Elektra Records. He also wrote for her the lyrics of "That's the Way I've Always Heard It Should Be," a song in which the heroine sings of couples who "cling and claw and drown in love's debris," who knows full well that "soon you'll cage me on your shelf," but who in the end submits meekly and quietly to marriage. Carly Simon insists that in this number she is not saying that "marriage is the best thing. I am asking, 'What is a better way?' I guess I was trying to fight against the pattern established when we were children, growing up with bride dolls and having Mother say marriage is your goal in life." Released in 1971, in Carly Simon's performance, "That the Way I've Always Heard It Should Be" was a best-seller that brought her a Grammy as the best new artist. The song was also the highlight of her first album, *Carly Simon*, also issued that year.

She was about to make an appearance at the Troubadour in Los Angeles on April 6, 1971, when she learned that James Taylor was in the audience. She had known him when they were youngsters summering in Martha's Vineyard, but after that their paths had diverged. After her performance, Taylor went to her dressing room to congratulate her. It was the beginning of a romance that culminated in marriage seven months later.

After 1971, three of Carly Simon's releases received gold records: the single "You're So Vain" and her second and third albums, *Anticipation* and *No Secrets* (both made up mostly of her own songs, some to Jacob Brackman's lyrics). Considerable speculation has been aroused as to who Carly Simon had in mind when she wrote "You're So Vain." Some maintain it was the actor, Warren Beatty; others, that it was Mick Jagger (who sings backup vocal in the song); still others, that it was James Taylor. Carly Simon herself refuses to provide clarification, maintaining: "I don't want anyone to be named because the song is so nasty." Besides "You're So Vain," the best songs in these two albums include "Anticipa-tion," "Legend in Your Own Time," "Share the End," "The Garden," "Three Days," "Our First Day Together," "The Right Thing to Do" and "When You Close Your Eyes."

Most of her songs in these three albums are about male-female relationships. "They are a strange set of love songs," wrote Stephen Davis in *The Rolling Stone*, "more like a cycle of the wide range of the emotional pulls and tugs that love connotes. She sings sometimes as an acute observer of the life conditions of a fellow human, sometimes as an equal partner in a shattered affair, sometimes as a bemused annotator of losing battles and the highly charged moment flying away."

Her successes continued into 1974, 1975 and 1976 with her albums *Hotcakes* (a gold record) and *Playing Possum*, in both of which James Taylor participated, and with *Another Passenger*. In *Hotcakes* were found several more treasurable soft rock numbers: "Mind on My Man," "Mockingbird," "Haven't Got Time," "Safe and Sound," "Misfit" and "Forever My

Love." Here, as in "After the Storm" in *Playing Possum*, her art has become more mellow, her theme less inclined toward self-pity.

11

John Denver is another young composer singer of the early seventies who has become a superstar. In his public appearances, he may not have the charisma of a James Taylor or the lean and hungry look of a Rod McKuen. His is a boyish, smiling face. He wears gold-rimmed eyeglasses; his haystack hair is worn collar length; he avoids eccentric clothes or behavior; he looks like the kid you would like your sister to date. But, for all his apparent lack of glamor, he comes over remarkably well onstage before audiences ranging in age from adolescents to senior citizens, all of them well in the palm of his hand. He has done equally well on television in many Specials in England and the United States and in top spots on American network programs. Wholesome, sincere, infectiously lighthearted at times, sometimes almost corny, he comes across as the voice of Middle America. "If people want to get stoned and trip out on acid or Jesus," he has said, "that's their business. But if those things don't work, I've got something that will: love, appreciation and sincerity." His folk-oriented songs reflect this personal philosophy. They are simple both in structure and in emotional appeal; they are generally optimistic, and sometimes saccharine; they are consistently filled with sentiment, wearing their hearts on their sleeves. And the way he presents his songs with a fresh and easy delivery, with an acoustic guitar accompaniment tasteful in its discretion, adds to their popular appeal.

As a recording artist he has joined the top sellers. His single, "Take Me Home, Country Roads," was a gold record in 1971. He gathered two more gold records in 1973 for his LPs *John Denver's Greatest Hits* and *Farewell Andromeda*, and after that other gold records for the albums *Aerie, Rocky Mountain High, Poems, Prayers and Promises, Windsong, Back Home Again* (the last, which includes "Annie's Song" and was voted Album of the Year by the Academy of Country Music, at the same time that Denver was named Vocalist of the Year), *An Evening with John Denver* and *Rocky Mountain Christmas*. In fact, *John Denver's Greatest Hits* sold over two million albums by May 1974, while in the first four months of that year this album and two others (*Rocky Mountain High* and *Poems, Prayers and Promises*) had sold two and a half million units. His single "Sunshine on My Shoulders," sold over a million and a half disks, and the singles "Back Home Again," "I'm Sorry" and "Thank God I'm a Country Boy" a million disks each.

He was born in Roswell, New Mexico, as Henry John Deutschendorf, Jr. in 1943, and acquired his first guitar when he was in the seventh grade. He took lessons for a year, then quit. But listening to Elvis Presley stimulated him to return to the guitar, and from then on he was not only always singing to his own accompaniment but also writing songs. At Texas Tech University at Lubbock, where he majored in architecture, he was spending most of his spare time performing as a folk-singer on the campus and in local clubs. After two and a half years at the University, he decided to drop out of school and concentrate his efforts on music. He came to Southern California in 1964 where he changed his name to John Denver. A year later, in New York, he joined the Chad Mitchell Trio, replacing Mitchell as lead vocalist and touring with the group in their folk-music performances for four years. He went solo in 1969, and at that time signed a contract with RCA Victor.

In 1967, Peter, Paul and Mary had made a best-selling record for Warner Brothers of Denver's "Leaving on a Jet Plane" (which he had written from his experience of continual travel with the Chad Mitchell Trio). It enjoyed a giant sale two years later. In 1972, Mary

Travers included "Follow Me" in her Warner Brothers solo album *Mary*. But it was Denver himself who was the best salesman of his own songs. In 1969 he had a best-seller in *Rhymes and Reason*, his first LP. After that came the accumulation of gold records in the early 1970s, as well as public appearances to standing-room audiences across the country from the Greek Theatre in Los Angeles to Madison Square Garden and Carnegie Hall in New York. He made his motion picture debut in a remake of *Mr. Smith Goes to Washington*. With all this his place among the most successful composing performing artists of his time became secure. This fact became further recognized in 1975 when the Country Music Association presented him with two awards (as country entertainer of the year and for his song "Back Home Again"); when, in the year-end listings of *Billboard* in 1975, Denver emerged as Number One on four different charts (tops singles artist, overall pop artist, easy listening artist and country album); and when, in February 1976 the Bicentennial American Music Awards over ABC-TV gave him three awards (best male vocalist in pop-rock, best male vocalist in country music and for his album *Back Home Again*.)

12

Paul Williams also has that wholesome look of the kid-next-door. A cherubic-faced little fellow who stands only five feet two, he appears no more than sixteen years old, though he is well over twice that age. He wears oversized dark glasses perched on the bridge of his nose. An incurable romantic, he likes to write and sing love songs that, as he put it to an interviewer, "make positive statements. . . as opposed to negative ones."

He began writing his own songs because he could not read music nor had he the technique to perform other people's music. As his own songwriter, he has done exceptionally well, both with the partnership of Roger Nichols and alone. His smash hits have included "We've Only Just Begun," "Old Fashioned Love Song," Rainy Days and Mondays," "Cried Like a Baby," "Out in the Country," "You and Me Against the World," "So Many People" and "Talk It Over in the Morning." He has sung his own songs on records and television, in nightclubs and theaters. Others have also sung them: Tom Jones, Helen Reddy, Andy Williams, Dionne Warwick, Johnny Mathis and The Monkees, to mention a few. His songs by other performers have garnered four gold records: "We've Only Just Begun" and "Rainy Days and Mondays" by the Carpenters; "Old Fashioned Love Song" by Three Dog Night; "Cried Like a Baby" by Bobby Sherman. He himself earned a gold record for his album *Old Fashioned Love Song*. He was nominated for an Oscar for the song ballad "Nice to Be Around" in *Cinderella Liberty* (1974), for which he wrote only the lyrics with John Williams supplying the music, and for the score for a film satirizing the rock culture, *Phantom of Paradise* (1974), in which he was also starred.

He was born in Omaha, Nebraska, in 1940, the second of three sons of an architect. A brother, Mentor, also became a songwriter. The family moved about a great deal in the Midwest; Paul attended nine different grade schools by the time he reached the ninth grade. "I was always the newest kid in school—and the smallest," he recalls. He also remembers having sung from childhood, but the singing stopped, at least temporarily, when tragedy struck the Williams family with the death of his father in an automobile accident. Paul was fourteen then. For the next four years he lived with an aunt and uncle in Long Beach, California. At eighteen, he left home to begin his *Wanderjahre*. For a year or so he was employed as a houseboy in Denver. Then he went on to Albuquerque where he worked for an insurance company researching insurance titles and where, in 1959, he became a resident actor in the Albuquerque Playhouse. His dream of becoming an actor brought him to Hollywood in 1961. There he soon appeared in two films, *The Loved Ones* (1965) starring

Tony Richardson, and *The Chase* (1966) starring Marlon Brando. While working on this film he began to learn the guitar and as soon as he had mastered the basic chords with which to accompany himself he started writing songs. A few were written with Biff Rose, the first of which, "Fill Your Heart," was recorded by Tiny Tim. Then, beginning with "It's So Hard to Say Goodbye"—recorded by Claudine Longet—he began working with Roger Nicholas, with whom he was destined to write some of his biggest numbers.

He never aspired to be a singer, but kept making demos only to promote his songs. Finally, Herb Alpert of A & M Records had him make one of the cuts in Michel Colombier's album *Wings*. To promote this album, Williams filled a guest shot on the Tonight Show over television and a club date. "By then I was totally addicted. I knew I had to stick with this." With a group called The Mackerels, Paul Williams recorded an album for Warner Brothers, and in his second Warner album, *Someday Man*, Williams soloed in a group of Williams-Nichols songs. Both albums were failures. "Nobody knew who I was," Williams lamented.

The first hit song by Williams and Nicholas, "We've Only Just Begun," started out as a commercial for the Crocker Bank in Los Angeles. When the number began to attract the interest of several performers, Williams and Nichols added a verse to it, made some minor changes, and developed it into a song. The Carpenters recorded it for A & M Records and it went on to sell a million disks. Other hit records now established Paul Williams solidly as a performing songwriter, and led to his signing a contract with A & M Records. *Old Fashioned Love Song* became Williams' first gold disk, a collection of tender, wistful, intimate love songs. It was followed by other successful LPs including A *Little Bit of Love*, whose finest cuts are "Nice to Be Around" and "She Sings for Free."

<h3 style="text-align:center">13</h3>

The songs of Jim Croce are vibrant with descriptive power and contemplative beauty, alive with the truth of a man singing of his own experiences. Born in Philadelphia in 1942, Croce started learning to play the accordion when he was six. He was employed in a toy store a dozen years later when he acquired his first guitar and started playing and singing the blues. While attending the University of Villanova, he was master-of-ceremonies for a folk and blues radio show.

He graduated from Villanova in 1965, and in 1966 he got married. That summer he taught ceramics and guitar at a summer camp in Pennsylvania, and the following fall he took on a teaching job in a junior high school in South Philadelphia. Having won a fellowship for the study of Mexican pottery, he was soon off to Mexico with his wife, Ingrid. In 1967, they were back in the United States, with Jim Croce trying to make his living by singing blues and folk songs in intimate night spots, coffee houses and colleges in or near New York. At this time he made his first record album, in collaboration with his wife—*Another Day, Another Time*. Released by Capitol it was such a commercial failure that Croce decided to abandon singing. With his wife, he settled down on a farm near Philadelphia and took on various menial jobs, including one as a truck driver. He always carried with him a notebook or a tape recorder to jot down song ideas and random observations. "Croce looked at the common stuff and saw the wildness in it," said Noel Coppage in *Stereo Review*. "Croce learned the hard way to live in the present. Now his music does."

He returned to a musical career in the fall of 1971 by recording some of his own songs at the Hit Factory in New York City, assisted by Maury Muehleisen as lead guitarist. A year later, Croce issued an album for ABC-Dunhill, *You Don't Mess Around with Jim*, which sold between forty and fifty thousand copies. The title song also sold well as a single.

"Operator," one of his best ballads, did equally well as a single later the same year. His next LP, *Jim Croce: Life and Times*, did far better than its predecessor, with a sale of a quarter of a million copies. In it were included "Time in a Bottle," "Alabama Rain," and Croce's best-known song, "Bad, Bad Leroy Brown" which, as a single reached the top place in the charts in 1973. His last album, *I've Got a Name,* was completed just eight days before his death, a gathering of musical garlands that included "Lover's Cross," "Age," "I'll Have to Say I Love You in a Song," "The Hard Way Every Time" and the title song.

Croce was only thirty when his single engine craft, on a takeoff in Louisiana, crashed into a tree on September 20, 1973. Almost as soon as he was buried, Croce's popularity as a performer composer took on new dimensions. His last album, *I've Got a Name,* sold over a million copies and started the Jim Croce cult that helped send his three previous albums into the million-copy sale class. Other Jim Croce albums released posthumously were all best-sellers; one of them—*Photographs and Memories*, released by ABC-Dunhill in 1974—assembled some of Croce's greatest hits. A single, lifted from *I've Got a Name*, "I Have to Say I Love You in a Song," also sold a million copies, and so did theLPs, *Jim Croce: His Greatest Hits* and *Time in a Bottle*. In 1975, Lifesong Records released *The Faces I've Seen*, an album of previously unreleased material reaching back into the early sixties.

"A Tribute to Jim Croce," a ninety-minute show, was syndicated over television as a Special; it featured a seven-minute film of Croce that was also used on an ABC news program. The Sonny and Cher show on CBS-TV used a cartoon characterization of "Bad, Bad Leroy Brown." On the sound track of the motion picture, *The Adventures of the Last American* (1973), Croce sang "I've Got a Name." "Time in a Bottle" was the theme song of an ABC Television movie, *She Lives*, late in 1973, and became a gold record as a single.

After his death, many learned what only a handful had known when Croce was still living, that he was, as Noel Coppage put it, "one of the voices of America, spokesman for some real people who live out there somewhere or just about everywhere . . . the interior people who, by sheer numbers, define what America is like."

44

On Broadway—and Off

1

What have the years since 1960 brought and meant to those who had already so richly cultivated and fertilized the fields of the Broadway musical theater?·

To Richard Rodgers it meant the fruitless search for another writing collaborator of the stature of Lorenz Hart and Oscar Hammerstein II.

For Irving Berlin it marked the end of the road for a man who had been closely identified with the American musical theater for half a century.

To Stephen Sondheim it brought the transformation of a highly gifted lyricist into an even more gifted lyricist composer.

To Jerry Bock, the satisfaction and rewards gained from the most successful musical production in Broadway history.

For Jerry Styne, Meredith Willson, Harold Rome and Burton Lane it meant a harvest of musicals—some good, others only fair; some highly successful, others less so.

2

Almost sixty years old, Richard Rodgers, for the first time in seventeen years, had to work with a lyricist and librettist other than Oscar Hammerstein II, who died in 1960. They had been sensitively attuned to each other's moods, ideas, and thinking and working habits. Now that Hammerstein was dead, Rodgers had to find a new partner if he were to survive creatively. At first he found it impossible to consider working with a Hammerstein replacement. When the screen musical, *State Fair*, was refilmed and called for several new songs,

Rodgers decided to serve as his own lyricist for four tunes. For a new stage project he again wrote his own lyrics, while working on a libretto by Samuel Taylor. The new musical was *No Strings* (1962). As with many of Rodgers' musicals, the subject was an unusual one. In Paris, two Americans become emotionally involved. One is a white Pulitzer Prizewinning novelist, the other, a beautiful black model. The relationship between two highly attractive people is developed naturally without undue concern for interracial problems. But this open, tolerant attitude towards a love affair between black and white is not all that makes *No Strings* different from other musicals. In his attempt to overcome limitations imposed on the theater by tradition, Rodgers placed his orchestra (without any strings) not in the pit but unseen on the sides of the stage. Wind instruments provided both the accompaniment to the songs and a background for some of the dialogue. Occasionally, one, two or more musicians drifted to the stage to find a place near the characters, offering a soft musical commentary on what was happening or being said. Scenery was reduced to a minimum, while the performers themselves moved the sets and props as part of the action. "In short," as Walter Kerr explained in his review in *The New York Times*, "the composer's hirelings are used to support rather than to intercept the principals. . . . Mr. Rodgers' impudent resettlement works."

No Strings was much more than just an excursion into innovation. With such delightful songs as "The Sweetest Sounds" (heard on a darkened stage, sung by the two principals, in place of an overture), "Nobody Told Me" and the title number, and with refreshing performances by Richard Kiley and Diahann Carroll, *No Strings* provided an evening of enchantment. As a result of a poll among the country's leading critics, *Variety* selected Rodgers as the best composer of the theatrical season because of *No Strings*, and he also received a Grammy award for the original cast recording.

After *No Strings*, with an idea for a musical about extrasensory perception, Richard Rodgers got together with Alan Jay Lerner for a musical tentatively called *I Picked a Daisy*. The collaborators, however, could not agree how the text should be worked out and Rodgers politely bowed out of the picture, relinquishing the project to Lerner. With music by Burton Lane it eventually came to Broadway as *On a Clear Day You Can See Forever*.

Not until 1965 was another Richard Rodgers musical mounted on Broadway. With Arthur Laurents as librettist, adapting his own stage play, *The Time of the Cuckoo*, and with lyrics by Stephen Sondheim, *Do I Hear a Waltz?* used Venice as a setting, and as its central theme the ill-fated romance of an American female tourist with a handsome Venetian shopkeeper who turns out to be married. This was a slow-moving play and the resulting ennui was rarely relieved by Rodgers' score. Its best song, built up into the main production sequence (the highest of the musical) was the title number.

In July 1969, Rodgers suffered a heart attack, from which he recovered to work on his new musical, *Two by Two*, in Peter Stone's adaptation of Clifford Odets' stage play *The Flowering Peach*, with lyrics by Martin Charnin. Opening on Broadway on November 10, 1970, it starred Danny Kaye as the biblical Noah in Kaye's first return to the Broadway theater in thirty years. In this frequently amusing, sometimes touching, occasionally philosophical retelling of the biblical story of Noah and the flood, the text touched upon such universal themes and problems as the generation gap, the nature of man and some of his inclinations that pertain as much to the twentieth century as to biblical times. Throwing visuals of masterwork paintings on a background screen became an ingenious way for Noah to communicate with God. Danny Kaye's performance, first as a six-hundred-year-old patriarch and then as a lusty youth of ninety years, was resilient and energetic. Rodgers' appealing songs included the ballad "I Do Not Know a Day I Did Not Love You," "Something, Somewhere" and the title number.

In April 1975, Richard Rogers had to undergo a laryngectomy. Therapy finally enabled him to master what is known as esophageal speech. With that indomitable will to survive and create, which he had displayed not once but several times in the preceding quarter of a century, Rodgers would not permit his physical disability to arrest the flow of his theatrical activities. He assisted in the production of *Rodgers and Hart*, that "musical celebration" that came to Broadway in May 1975, was in attendance at the rehearsals of *Oklahoma!* before its revival at Jones Beach in New York that summer, completed the writing of his autobiography, *Musical Stages* (1975), and worked on the score and assisted in the overall production of a new Broadway musical, *Rex*. Regrettably, *Rex*—which involved a king, Henry VIII of England, in his marital problems—was no *King and I*. With book by Sherman Yellen and lyrics by Sheldon Harnick, it came to the Lunt-Fontanne Theater on April 25, 1976, where it expired after only forty-two performances.

On February 22, 1975, over the NBC television network, Richard Rodgers became one of four to receive the 1975 award from the Entertainment Hall of Fame (the others were Bob Hope, Fred Astaire and George Balanchine), selected by a vote of newspaper entertainment editors.

Mr. President (1962), Irving Berlin's last musical, had a book by Russel Crouse and Howard Lindsay. The man in the White House was played by Robert Ryan; the First Lady, by Nanette Fabray. Washington politics, international diplomacy between the United States and the Soviet Union, and a romance between the President's daughter and a former Secret Service agent were the basis of a synthetic libretto fashioned along traditional musical-comedy lines. Early in the musical, the Twist was danced in the Oval Room, and the musical ends with a rousing finale to country and flag, "This Is a Great Country." The best numbers from a serviceable score are the duets "Empty Pockets Filled with Love" and "Meat and Potatoes."

Frank Loesser's return to Broadway after *The Most Happy Fella*, and an absence of four years, came with *Greenwillow* (1960), a musical play to his own libretto (with the assistance of Lesser Samuels) which was a failure.

If Loesser lost heart at this setback, it was not for long. *How to Suceed in Business Without Really Trying* (1961) became his greatest success in the theater, with a run of over one thousand performances, the capture of the Pulitzer Prize in drama, and the Tony and Drama Critics Circle awards as the season's best musical. In 1967 it was made into a highly successful motion picture. Based on a satire of the same name by Shepherd Mead (adapted by Abe Burrows, Jack Weinstock and Willie Gilbert), *How to Succeed* was Loesser's return to musical comedy with the kind of songs, comedy, characterizations and routines that invariably spell success. The central character was a lowly window cleaner, infectiously performed by Robert Morse with the proper mixture of innocence and gall, who through ruthlessness, perseverance and guile rises to the position of chairman of the board of World Wide Wickets. The main musical numbers were "I Believe in You" (the hero's affirmation of self-confidence), "Brotherhood of Man" and "Grand Old Ivy."

How to Succeed should have been Loesser's grand finale in the musical theater. Regrettably, it was not, since it was followed in 1965 by *Pleasures and Palaces*, a dismal production that opened and closed out of town. Loesser died of cancer in New York City in 1969, and at his request, his ashes were strewn over the sea.

Stephen Sondheim, who served as lyricist for Richard Rodgers in *Do I Hear a Waltz?* had become a composer on his own for the first time three years earlier, in 1962, with a bawdy farce set in ancient Rome. *A Funny Thing Happened on the Way to the Forum*, whose text was loosely based on plays on Plautus, received a Tony. Zero Mostel appeared as a slave trying to bribe his owner into giving him his freedom by procuring for him a lovely courtesan. The fact that a warrior has prior claim to her provides the complications which the slave manages to surmount through elaborately concocted intrigues. The stress was on broad comedy which often slipped into burlesque. A *Funny Thing* was a fast-moving, noisy, earthy, hilarious show and audiences loved every minute of it. The ballad, "Love, I Hear"; a travesty on ballads, "Lovely"; and the witty "Everybody Ought to Have a Maid" and "That Dirty Old Man"—all these revealed that Sondheim's gift for writing music was as professional as that in fashioning lyrics.

Sondheim wrote his own music again for *Anyone Can Whistle* (1964), which closed after only eight performances. For a time after that Sondheim returned to his earlier role as lyricist for other composers. Not until 1970 did he reappear on Broadway as a composer lyricist, this time to assert himself forcefully in *Company* (1970) as one of the major composers, as well as lyricists, in the theater of the 1970s.

Company was selected by the Drama Critics Circle and the Antoinette Perry (Tony) awards as the best musical of the season. The critics were equally enthusiastic about this musical play that exposed the raw nerves and tissues of life in New York. "From the moment Boris Aronson's inspired steel and Plexiglas gymnasium setting and the sophisticated babble of New York's swinging couples begins to bounce around the theater," wrote Henry Hewes in the *Saturday Review*, "we sense how completely book writer George Furth and lyricist-composer Stephen Sondheim have caught the tone of casual, impersonal Gotham." The main thread of the text is the attempt by well-meaning friends to marry off an attractive middle-aged bachelor. But the subsidiary plots proved most intriguing, and these traced the marital difficulties of these respectable, well-meaning friends. Sondheim's score was top drawer throughout, whether in a satirical or romantic vein, with the best numbers being "Another Hundred People" (a touching comment on the way some girls suffer loneliness in the great city), the satirical, "The Ladies Who Lunch," "Someone Is Waiting," "You Could Drive a Person Crazy," and "The Little Things You Do Together."

Sondheim's *Follies* (1971), chosen by the New York Drama Critics Circle as the season's best musical, encouraged nostalgia. In an about-to-be-demolished theater (presumably the New Amsterdam, once the home of the *Ziegfeld Follies*) former Follies girls hold a reunion after several decades, with their producer, Dimitri Weismann (who is meant to be Florenz Ziegfeld), as host. Old memories come to life. Old romantic involvements are briefly reawakened as the principals, all unhappily married now, revert to their former selves. Old stage routines of *Follies* shows are revived in a musical extravaganza, "Loveland," in which each of the four principals reenacts her own personal folly. The cast was studded with old-time stars, adding to the pervading nostalgia. There were Dorothy Collins, graduate of "Your Hit Parade"; Ethel Shutta, who had appeared in the *Ziegfeld Follies*; and Alexis Smith, Gene Nelson and Yvonne De Carlo, veterans of motion pictures. Misses Collins, Smith and De Carlo were making their Broadway debuts. In his music Sondheim sometimes looked back to the twenties and thirties by writing a torch song ("Losing My Mind"), a blues ("The God-Why-Don't-You-Love-Me Blues"), and a De Sylva, Brown and Henderson type of ballad ("Broadway Baby"). Other songs are of present-day vintage, the best being "I'm Still Here," "Could I Leave You?" and "Who's that Woman?".

In 1973, as in 1970, a Stephen Sondheim musical, *A Little Night Music*, received the Tony. The Swedish motion picture classic, *Smiles of a Summer Night*, directed by Ingmar Bergman, contributed the "suggestion"—and some of the bare bones of the plot—which Hugh Wheeler elaborated into his libretto. The three characters, in Sweden at the turn of the century, were a middle-aged prosperous lawyer; his child wife, who remains a virgin eleven months after their marriage; and an actress who had once been the lawyer's mistress and with whom he is still in love.

The fact that each of Sondheim's seventeen numbers is in waltz meter has led some critics to speak of A *Little Night Music* as an operetta. But it has none of the visual trappings nor the established ritual of operetta. A *Little Night Music* is a sensitive, unhurried, subdued mood piece sustained throughout an evening. In it, the music and the lyrics are inextricably intertwined with the play. "This is," noted *Time*, "a jeweled music box of a show; lovely to look at, delightful to listen to, and perhaps too exquisite, fragile and muted ever to be quite humanly affecting. It is a victory of technique over texture, and one leaves it in the odd mental state of unbridled admiration and untouched feelings." "Send in the Clowns" (enchantingly sung by Glynis Johns) is the leading song; it earned a Grammy in 1976 as "the song of the year." "The Miller's Son" and "Liaisons" were two other principal numbers. Most of the musical numbers are what Sondheim described as "inner monologue songs," that is one in which the character presents through song his deepest emotions and thoughts without revealing them to anybody else.

Company, *Follies* and A *Little Night Music* have been designated by the critics as "concept musicals," by which is meant that a subject of some consequence is discussed from every possible theatrical and emotional angle. In each of these musicals, Stephen Sondheim as composer-lyricist and Harold Prince as producer-director, have shown a flair for innovation by addressing themselves to the subject, and encasing it within a structure, both of which are fresh and novel. As a concept musical, *Pacific Overtures* (1976) proved to be the most daring and unorthodox of the Sondheim–Prince adventures into unfamiliar territory by carrying over the traditions and stylizations of the Japanese Kabuki theater onto the Broadway stage. John Weidman's book (with additional material by Hugh Wheeler) deals with the Westernization of Japan after the arrival of Commodore Perry and a trade mission in 1853. We witness old Japan, splendid in centuries old isolation from the Western World, in the first act, together with the apprehension of the Japanese that the imminent arrival of Commodore Perry might have on their time-honored way of life. The impact of the Western World on Japan is the material for the second act, while in the finale the modernization of Japan becomes complete.

In the traditions of the Kabuki theater, the large cast in *Pacific Overtures* is all male (males assuming the female roles). For the most part this cast is either Asiatic or Asian-American. A Kabuki-like "reciter" serves as narrator. Haiku chants (form of Japanese poetry), a trio of Japanese musicians in one of the theater's boxes performing on taiko drums to supplement the Western music provided by an orchestra in the pit and Patricia Birch's choreography in the "Lion Dance" are further reminders of Japanese art forms. Stephen Sondheim's music—"Pretty Lady," "There Is No Other Way" and "Someone in a Tree" are the best songs—so successfully "interrelates the Western and Eastern elements," says Irving Kolodin in the *Saturday Review*, that the score may very well be "the truly pacific achievement in the venture."

A production that wanders so far afield from the norm in the Broadway musical theater invariably inspires sharply divergent opinions. There were those critics who considered *Pacific Overtures* ravishingly beautiful to eye and ear, an exhilarating theatrical experience, an opening of new vistas. There were other critics who regarded it as stilted, slow-moving and lacking in sustained theatrical interest. Except for a nod to Boris Aronson as scenic designer, the Tony Awards ignored *Pacific Overtures* completely; while the Drama

Critics Circle selected it as the best musical of the year. The public apparently sided with the negative reports. *Pacific Overtures* closed after 193 performances and a financial loss of a quarter of a million dollars.

Camelot (1960) was the Lerner and Loewe successor to *My Fair Lady*. Here there were assembled many of the ingredients that worked so magically in *My Fair Lady*: Lerner wrote the book and lyrics, and Loewe the music; Julie Andrews was the female star; Moss Hart directed; Hanya Holm did the choreography; Oliver Smith prepared the scenery. Other veterans of *My Fair Lady* lent their helping hands and talents to the new production: Franz Allers as conductor; Robert Russell Bennett as orchestrator; Robert Coote, playing a secondary role. Yet for all these ample borrowings, *Camelot* was no *My Fair Lady*. *Camelot* expended too much energy on lavish scenes and costumes, and too little on those subtleties of dialogue, characterization, humor and plot development that distinguished *My Fair Lady*. The story is developed with a heavy hand, often with a lack of cohesiveness and clarity, usually with little humor. But it was a good show—though most assuredly not a great one—good to the eye and the ear. The thrice-familiar plot came from the saga of King Arthur and his Round Table in Camelot as told in T. H. White's novel, *The Once and Future King*. In Alan Jay Lerner's adaptation, we get a retelling of the story of the marriage of King Arthur (played by Richard Burton) to Guenevere (Julie Andrews) in Camelot; the establishment of the Round Table, one of whose members is Young Lancelot, a role in which Robert Goulet made his Broadway debut; Lancelot's winning of the love of Guenevere and his enforced flight with her to France. The stage became illuminated with a suspicion of the radiance of *My Fair Lady* when Richard Burton sang the title song and "How to Handle a Woman," when Julie Andrews was heard in "The Simple Joys of Maidenhood" and "The Lusty Month of May," when she joined Richard Burton in presenting "What do the Simple Folk Do?," and when Robert Goulet brought his baritone voice to "If Ever I Would Leave You."

For many of those involved with *Camelot* it was a child of sorrow. During the writing, such violent misunderstandings and altercations broke out between Lerner and Loewe that they swore never again to work together. (They kept that vow for over a decade.) While the show had its tryout in Toronto, Alan Jay Lerner suffered bleeding ulcers and had to be hospitalized. For Moss Hart, *Camelot* was the final curtain. About a year after it opened on Broadway, Hart, who had suffered a heart attack during rehearsal, suffered a fatal second heart attack in Palm Springs, California, on December 20, 1961.

When the differences between Lerner and Loewe led to what seemed a permanent break, Lerner went on to work with other composers, while Loewe remained creatively silent, enjoying his wealth in Palm Springs, in New York, and on the Riviera. But a decade after *Camelot*, the two partners were reunited to write the score for a motion picture, *The Little Prince* (1974), and then to adapt their screen triumph, *Gigi*, into a Broadway musical. The stage *Gigi* opened on November 13, 1973, with the same characters, the same situations, and most of the same songs which had helped to make it a film classic. Though it received more or less kind notices from the critics, together with a Tony for the score, the public, who seemed to have had enough of *Gigi* through its earlier screen treatment, rejected the stage production.

Having captured the Pulitzer Prize in drama with *Fiorello!* in 1959, Jerry Bock (with his lyricist, Sheldon Harnick) returned in his next musical to the scene of their first triumph—that of New York City of a bygone day. Their new musical was *Tenderloin* (1960), adapted by Jerome Weidman and George Abbott from the novel of that name by Samuel Hopkins Adams, with Abbott also serving as director. A fictional rather than a historical character is the central interest. He is the Reverend Brock (played by Maurice Evans of Shavian and Shakespearean renown) who is out to purge the Tenderloin district of New York City of its moral decay.

Though not a *Fiorello!*, *Tenderloin* had much to recommend it, including neatly contrived dance routines by Joe Layton, George Abbott's brisk direction, Cecil Beaton's sets and costumes and the songs "Artificial Flowers" and "The Picture of Happiness."

It is a long way from the turn-of-the-century New York of *Fiorello!* and *Tenderloin* to Anatevka, in Czarist Russia. But in taking that route, Jerry Bock was able to achieve a destination thus far unrealized by any other American stage composer. He has participated in the most momentous triumph in American stage history, that of *Fiddler on the Roof* (1964). No other Broadway production has equalled its run of 3,242 performances, eighteen more than *Life with Father*, and sixty more than *Tobacco Road*, both non-musicals, and five hundred and twenty-five more than its rival among musicals, *My Fair Lady*. The New York box-office receipts from *Fiddler on the Roof* were without precedent, well beyond twenty million dollars to which still another fifteen million dollars or so were added by companies touring the United States. It scooped up nine Tony awards (including that of best musical), as well as the New York Drama Critics Award. Only one year after subsidiary leasing was available in the United States and Canada, there took place over one thousand productions by professional and amateur groups. But *Fiddler on the Roof* was not exclusively an American phenomenon. There were fifteen different productions in Finland alone, and two in Great Britain. Other companies presented it in France, Austria, Holland, West Germany, East Berlin, Spain, Switzerland, Czechoslovakia, Hungary, Yugoslavia, Greece, Israel, Turkey, Iceland, Norway, Sweden, Denmark, Moscow, Mexico, Argentina, Brazil, South Africa, Rhodesia, Australia, New Zealand, Japan and probably several other spots on the globe as well. Almost forty million people saw the stage show. Many, many millions more viewed the splendid screen version directed by Norman Jewison, starring Topol, released in 1971—especially after it was telecast over the ABC-TV network, in September 1974. Millions bought albums of the complete score in forty-three versions, eighteen of them with the original casts in various languages. A biography of this fabulous production, *The Making of a Musical*, was written by Richard Altman, assistant director of the New York production, and Mervyn Kaufman (1971).

Fiddler on the Roof achieved universal acclaim because it was very much more than just a faithful recreation of Yiddish stories by Sholom Aleichem which Joseph Stein adapted into a libretto. The rituals, ideals and way of life of religious Jews in an East-European *shtetl* were only the surface beneath which lay profound truths applicable to our own times. *Fiddler on the Roof* turned out to be far more than just a picture of old-world Jewish society, an ambiance faithfully reproduced not only in text, lyrics and music but also in the direction and choreography of Jerome Robbins, which stayed uncompromisingly true to the source. This was not only the tale of Tevye, a simple, devout, impoverished tradition-bound dairy farmer, marrying off his five daughters in a tiny Jewish village in Russia in 1905. It was also the tragedy of anti-Semitism culminating in a pogrom that drives the simple people out of their homes to search for a new life elsewhere. As Robert Altman explains in *The Making of a Musical*: "At its heart, it's about the enduring strength of the human spirit—and man's ability to grow, to change, to overcome adversity." Though tradition is the anchor that keeps the pious Jews of Anatevka moored to their strict religious beliefs, Tevye (who maintains a running conversation with God when problems beset him) finds that willy-nilly he must break loose from tradition so that his daughters can find happiness in marriages which both he and his wife oppose. The crumbling of tradition before the onslaught of twentieth-century liberalism, the gap between generations, the harassment of a minority by an intolerant authority—these are themes that strike home whether sounded in New York, Rhodesia or Tokyo. What happened in Tokyo is perhaps typical. A Japanese gentleman told Joseph Stein he could never understand how *Fiddler on the Roof* could be understood and appreciated in New York since it was basically so Japanese!

Without trying to create ethnic music, Jerry Bock succeeded in bringing the old-world Hebraic minor-mode sound and feeling into his songs, the most appealing of which was the ballad, "Sunrise, Sunset," the amusing "If I Were a Rich Man," the robust "L'Chaim" ("To Life"), and the tender "Do You Love Me?"

Almost two years after *Fiddler on the Roof*, Jerry Bock and Sheldon Harnick reappeared on Broadway with *The Apple Tree* (1966), a radical change of pace for them. It was made up of three satirical one-act musicals, each taken from three different short stories (by Mark Twain, Frank R. Stockton, and Jules Feiffer). Bock and Harnick made their own stage adaptations. The central theme of all three musicals is Woman. In the first, *The Diary of Adam and Eve*, Woman is Eve in the Garden of Eden; in the second, *The Lady or the Tiger*, she is Princess Barbara in a semi-barbaric kingdom of long ago; and in the third, *Passionella*, she is a present-day motion picture sex symbol. In the first musical two fine songs are heard, "Eve" and the ballad "What Makes Me Love Him?" The sardonic "I've Got What You Want" is the musical highlight of the second musical. In the third, effective use is made of film sequences by Richard Williams to provide a montage of stills and footage of the antics of La Passionella, a movie sex queen. Barbara Harris, who played the female role in all three musicals, emerged in this production as a star who was described by Walter Kerr in *The New York Times* as "exquisite, alarming, seductive, out of her mind, irresistible and from now on unavoidable." Much of the success of this more or less unconventional production, which had a Broadway run of 463 performances, was due to her performance.

On October 18, 1970, a Jerry Bock-Sheldon Harnick musical with a Jewish oriented text and score came to Broadway. It was *The Rothschilds*, taken from the best-selling history, *The Rothschilds*, by Frederic Morton, adapted by Sherman Yellen. The musical traces the history of Meyer Rothschild from his beginnings as a peddler in a ghetto in Frankfort, Germany, in the eighteenth century, to a position of immense financial and social eminence; also that of his five sons, who are coached by their father to become world powers in finance. The oppression of the Jew in an anti-Semitic world is again a basic thread, as it was in *Fiddler on the Roof*. The ingratiating warmth of Jewish family life is also a leaf torn from the book of *Fiddler on the Roof*, and so is the Jewish identity of the song "He Tossed a Coin," in which the father of the Rothschild household remembers his past as a peddler, and "In My Own Lifetime." *The Rothschilds* was a production with "wit, moral force and style," in the words of Clive Barnes in *The New York Times*, and it was enthusiastically received by audiences who helped make it a standout box-office attraction.

Jule Styne had a blockbuster of his own in the 1960s in *Funny Girl* (1964). This was four years after he had known a modest succes with *Do Re Mi* (1960), which starred Phil Silvers, and just two months after he suffered a setback with *Fade Out–Fade In* (1964) starring Carol Burnett. *Funny Girl*, which enjoyed a Broadway run of 1,348 performances before becoming a highly successful movie, is the musical biography of Fanny Brice in which Barbra Streisand became a superstar. Her performance was no caricature, nor was it a mimic's imitation, but a characterization in depth, revealing the tragedienne lurking behind the facade of the comedienne, with comedy surfacing even in the presence of tragedy. Adding her own puckish and whimsical charm to Fanny Brice's legendary gift for switching in a split second from the tragic to burlesque, Barbra Streisand gave a performance that remains one of the most memorable achievements in the musical theater, a performance that made her one of the supreme show-business personalities.

Ten years passed from the time *Funny Girl* was just a gleam in the eye of Ray Stark, the producer who was Fanny Brice's son-in-law, and its actual birth in 1964. One of the stumbling blocks had been finding the right person to play Fanny. Barbra Streisand was the answer, and once she was cast the wheels of production began moving. In planning her characterization, Miss Streisand had no intention of being a carbon copy of Fanny Brice, whom she had never seen on stage, and whose records, old movies and radio tapes she refused to research. She created a character of her own. But in the process, by some mysterious osmosis, she *became* Fanny Brice, in voice, gesture, inflection and sometimes even in appearance.

"My Man" (Channing Pollock—Maurice Yvain), the tearful ballad with which Fanny Brice mesmerized *Follies* audiences in 1921, not only for her poignant rendition but also because its subject so closely paralleled her own tragedy, was not in the musical, whose score was an original one by Styne. (It was, however, interpolated into the motion picture together with Styne's songs.) "The Music that Makes Me Dance" was a substitute. Three other numbers, given the Streisand treatment, were musical standouts: "People," "I'm the Greatest Star" and "Don't Rain on My Parade." All the lyrics were by Bob Merrill.

Hallelujah, Baby! (1967), in which Betty Comden and Adolph Green once again provided Styne with lyrics and book, was an ambitious attempt to encompass sixty years of life in show business and black participation in it, with a side-glance at the racial problems besetting each different period. The overall idea and its treatment are novel, but it is burdened by stock racial characters and situations. But for all its shortcomings, which doomed it to less than a three-hundred-performance run, *Hallelujah, Baby!* was selected for a Tony. Some of Styne's songs evoke the style and mood of the twenties and thirties: "Feet Do Yo' Stuff" and "Smile, Smile," the twenties; "Now's the Time," the thirties. Among the other numbers were "My Own Morning," "I Don't Know Where She Got It" and "Not Mine."

Styne's next two musicals were losers: *Darling of the Day* (1968), adapted from Arnold Bennett's novel, *Buried Alive*, with E. Y. Harburg as his lyricist, and *Look to the Lilies* (1970), lifted from the motion picture, *Lilies of the Field* (1963), in which Styne resumed his interrupted collaboration with the lyricist, Sammy Cahn. Then with *Sugar* (1972) and *Lorelei* (1974), Styne resumed his winning stride.

Sugar had Robert Morse and Tony Roberts appearing in drag throughout the musical, since they are fugitives from Chicago gangsters determined to obliterate them because they witnessed the St. Valentine's Day massacre. To conceal themselves, the pair become members of an all-girls jazz band headed for Miami. Matters get out of hand when one of them falls in love with a blond vocalist and the other is pursued by an aging millionaire rake. This is the same material that served Tony Curtis, Jack Lemmon and Marilyn Monroe so hilariously in the Billy Wilder motion picture, *Some Like It Hot* (1959). Peter Stone wrote the musical comedy text and Bob Merrill was Styne's lyricist. As Richard Watts noted in his review in the *Post*, "transvestism in the theatre can present problems." However, Robert Morse and Tony Roberts "are not only so hilarious and always tasteful, but look so utterly preposterous in their women's clothing and their attempts to seem girlish that they are a joy to watch." The song material was more serviceable than distinguished, the leading number being the title song; others were "We Could Be Close," "Beautiful Through and Through" and "When You Meet a Man in Chicago." An asset in the musical was the parody of the all-girl bands in vogue in the 1920s. Pleasurable, too, were Gower Champion's choreography for "Tear the Town Apart" and a terpischorean "conversation" among Chicago hoodlums through the rhythms of tap dancing.

Lorelei was (if you will) a sequel or, to be more accurate, a repeat of *Gentlemen Prefer Blondes*, the successful Styne musical from 1949. Like its predecessor, *Lorelei* starred Carol Channing as the baby-faced, baby-voiced Lorelei Lee, one of the symbols of the Roaring Twenties. Through the flashback technique much of the old show was recalled by the simple expedient of placing Lorelei, now a middle-aged widow, at Pier 14 in New York City recalling her adventures in the 1920s. The introduction and the epilogue were new; the rest was the same as before. The song classics of the 1949 production reappeared, "Diamonds Are a Girl's Best Friend," "A Little Girl from Little Rock," and "Bye Bye Baby," all with lyrics by Leo Robin. The four new numbers sounded as if they might have been written for the former production, but they were not and they offered little competition to the older tunes. Besides the title song, the new numbers were "Men," "Looking Back" and "I Won't Let You Get Away," lyrics by Betty Comden and Adolph Green. But the overall impression of *Lorelei* was that of *déjà vu*. If *Lorelei* proved good entertainment in 1972, as it did, it was because of the character of Lorelei Lee, played by Carol Channing with the incomparable vitality, spontaneity and charm she had brought to it in 1949.

Meredith Willson, the "music man" who had been his own lyricist and librettist for *The Music Man* (1957), left the writing of the text of *The Unsinkable Molly Brown* (1960) to Richard Morris, and concentrated on lyrics and music. A Molly Brown actually had lived in a mining town in Colorado where she became a legend because of her indomitable spirit. A rough-and-tumble girl from an impoverished family, confident some day she would grow into a proud and rich lady, Molly was a human cyclone, and this is what most impressed Richard Morris when he wrote his musical comedy text, and Meredith Willson, when he expressed willingness to serve as composer lyricist. Tammy Grimes was Molly, and she gave a stirring rendition of the show's principal song, "I Ain't Down Yet." The play's leading ballad was "Dolce Far Niente."

Harold Rome's only successful entry into the Broadway musical comedy sweepstakes since the 1960s was *I Can Get It for You Wholesale* (1962). It comes from Jerome Weidman's novel of the same name, which Weidman himself adapted for a musical comedy book. Harold Rome, as has been customary with him, was his own lyricist. The action takes place in New York's garment district in 1937 where Harry Bogen, a ruthless go-getter, uses every trick in the trade, and some of his own devising, to become a success. He achieves his goal, but in the process he even two-times his lifelong girl friend. The hard line of this callous get-rich-quick book is softened by the presence of Harry's mother, a gentle, humane Jewish lady touchingly performed by Lillian Roth in her comeback to the theater following her prolonged battle with alcoholism. Elliott Gould (long before his eminence in motion pictures) was Harry Bogen, giving here every indication that this was just the beginning of a lustrous acting career. But Elliott Gould was not the only one in the cast who was on the eve of celebrity. In the part of Miss Marmelstein, Bogen's secretary, Barbra Streisand appeared in her stage debut, already revealing her potential as a comedienne and singer in the song "Miss Marmelstein." Of the more serious numbers in this score, one of the best was the ballad "Have I Told You Lately?" the love song of husband and wife.

After 1960, Burton Lane was represented in the musical theater with *On a Clear Day You Can See Forever* (1965). This was the musical in which Alan Jay Lerner and Richard Rodgers tried to work together. When they failed to agree on textual matters, Rodgers withdrew from the collaboration, and Burton Lane replaced him for his first significant return to Broadway since *Finian's Rainbow* in 1947. Barbara Harris' performance as Daisy was the strong suit of the musical. She played the part of a girl with extrasensory perception who undergoes psychiatric treatment to cure herself of her addiction to tobacco. In one of these sessions, while under hypnosis, Daisy reveals she is the reincarnation of an eighteenth-century girl, Melinda.

The title song became a nationwide hit when Robert Goulet sang it over television and made it into a best-selling recording for Columbia. Three other songs had interest: "Melinda," "Come Back to Me" and "What Did I Have that I Don't Have?"

The original cast recording received a Grammy as the year's best release of a musical comedy score. When *On a Clear Day You Can See Forever* was made into a movie, and released in 1970, Barbra Streisand replaced Barbara Harris as Daisy.

3

What of the new composers for the Broadway musical stage since 1960?

Jerry Herman was one. Though born in New York City, in 1932, Herman was brought up in Jersey City, New Jersey, where he learned to play the piano competently by ear and began writing songs. Despite his flair for music, he was being directed toward a career as an interior decorator. For this purpose he enrolled at the Parsons School of Design in New York. The sale of his first song for two hundred dollars put songwriting at the top of his vocations. After completing his course of study at Parsons, Herman attended the University of Miami where he majored in drama. A varsity show which he initiated won a prize for playwriting. After graduating in 1954 with a Bachelor of Arts degree, Herman made his home in New York City with the ambition of becoming a professional writer for the theater. While supporting himself by playing the piano in a nightclub, he managed to place special material with several television performers, including Jane Froman, Garry Moore and Ray Bolger. Before 1954 was over, he was represented in the theater with an Off Broadway production, *I Feel Wonderful*, for which he had written text, lyrics and music while he was still a student at the University of Miami. "It is safe to say," reported William Hawkins in the New York *World-Telegram*, "that this twenty-two year old will be heard from in the future." But it took six years for Herman to make another contribution to the musical theater. Once again this happened Off Broadway with *Parade* (1960) a revue that came and went unnoticed.

Then, with *Milk and Honey* (1961), Herman finally arrived not only on Broadway itself but at success as well. This was the first American musical to take advantage of the colorful and at times exotic background of modern-day Israel. Don Appell wrote the book while Herman wrote his own lyrics. Two American tourists become romantically involved in each other; they set up a home in a kibbutz but their happiness is short-lived since both are tormented by their consciences.

What set *Milk and Honey* apart from other musicals was the way in which it caught and fixed the spirit of Israel through local backgrounds, dances and ceremonies. The title song and "Shalom" helped to develop the feel and exuberance of life in Israel, the reason Herman was awarded a Tony as the season's leading composer and lyricist.

With a year's run on Broadway, and a healthy tour of the country with a national company, *Milk and Honey* gave Herman a respected position in the American musical theater. Within less than three years he graduated from success to triumph with *Hello, Dolly!* (1964). This was an old-fashioned kind of musical in which neither the plot nor the characters carried much conviction, nor strayed far from a well-beaten path, both serving as an excuse for songs, dances and production numbers. What gave this musical class, and its formidable audience appeal, was the performance of Carol Channing as Dolly, the choreography of Gower Champion, and the phenomenal popularity of the title song. These three assets added up to a winning ticket that brought many rewards: a Broadway run of 2,844 performances (up to then the longest of any musical in Broadway history though soon to be surpassed by *Fiddler on the Roof*) and the gross of twenty-seven million dollars in New York (sixty million or so, worldwide); ten Tony awards, including that of best musical and another for Jerry Herman as lyricist composer; and the New York Drama Critics Circle Award. Jerry Herman won top place among stage composers in a poll conducted by *Variety*; the original cast recording became a gold record; and the title song received over seventy different recordings in the United States and thirty-five in Europe. It became a gold record in the United States, and the winner of a Grammy in Louis Armstrong's recording, and, after appropriate lyrics were written for it, was adopted as the song for Lyndon B. Johnson during the Presidential campaign of 1964.

Hello, Dolly! is Thornton Wilder's stage play, *The Matchmaker* (1955), bedecked by librettist Michael Stewart with the expected paraphernalia of traditional musical comedy. Dolly Gallagher Levi is a wealthy widow in New York in 1898 who has become a marriage broker and while pretending to arrange a desirable marriage for the wealthy Yonkers merchant, Horace Vandergelder, captures him for herself.

The plot is a convenient framework for songs, dances, humor and lavish production numbers. Of these, the most important takes place in the fashionable Harmonia Gardens where a resplendently garbed Dolly appears for the first time since her husband's death. She is given a rousing welcome in which the entire place participates lustily, singing the song "Hello, Dolly!" that stole the show.

Jerry Herman never expected this song to dominate the production, let alone win its way outside the theater to a nationwide popularity equaled by few theater songs. All he wanted to do was write a formal period piece, "a kind of Lillian Russell turn-of-the-century production number very 1890s," as he described it. What lifted the song far above its functional role in the play into a song blockbuster was Louis Armstrong's recording for Kapp. "Louis Armstrong recorded the song as if it were written for *him*," says Herman. "And it's Mr. Armstrong's version that really knocked everybody out. . . . I went to a cast party where they had the first cut of the recording. Before then I never expected it would have any popular market, but the way the other members of the company loved it, I began to realize that it was going to be something special."

Among the other good tunes from *Hello, Dolly!* were "So Long, Dearie," "Before the Parade Passes By," "Put on Your Sunday Clothes" and "Ribbons Down My Back."

With *Hello, Dolly!* installed at the St. James theater apparently in perpetuity, and with tickets for each performance at a premium, a second company, made up entirely of blacks, headed by Pearl Bailey and Cab Calloway, was also a sellout during this period. Some critics preferred the all black version to its white predecessor, agreeing with Clive Barnes when he wrote in *The New York Times* that the black production "goes like a rocket in a shower of sparks."

Mame (1966), Jerry Herman's next musical, proved an energetic and boisterous affair. Jerome Lawrence and Robert E. Lee prepared the musical stage version from *Auntie Mame*, Patrick Dennis's best-selling novel and from a non-musical stage production they had adapted. Angela Lansbury, in the title role of the eccentric Mame, gave one of her best performances. As the saga of Auntie Mame unfolds from 1928 to 1946 it carries her (and the orphaned nephew she "inherits" and tries to raise according to her own peculiar ideas) through picaresque adventures. The big song was the title number, with "If He Walked into My Life" and "My Best Girl" also of interest. *Mame* received the Tony as the season's best musical and a Grammy for the original cast recording. When *Mame* was made into a movie, in 1974, Lucille Ball took over the title role, but none too happily.

For Charles Strouse, *Bye Bye Birdie* (1960) was both his first score for Broadway and his first success. This was a musical about a singing rock idol called Conrad Birdie who looks, behaves and sings suspiciously like Elvis Presley.

Born in New York City in 1928, Charles Strouse was a serious music student who had attended the Eastman School of Music in Rochester, New York, before studying composition with Aaron Copland and, in Paris, with Nadia Boulanger. In 1950 he became a friend of Lee Adams. Since Adams had a way with verses and Strouse nursed a lifelong passion for jazz and other forms of popular music, they decided to become a songwriting pair. Beginning in 1955 they placed some of their numbers in intimate revues in New York. Most of these were box-office failures, and Strouse supported himself by playing the piano at club dates and making vocal arrangements for Jane Morgan, Dick Shawn, Carol Burnett and others.

In 1960, his nondescript fortunes took a dramatic turn for the better with his first Broadway musical comedy, *Bye Bye Birdie*. At first, not much was expected from it. Both Strouse and Adams were unknown as songwriters, and none of the principals in the cast could be looked upon as box-office attractions. Dick Gautier, as Birdie, was making his Broadway debut, and Dick Van Dyke, before his television fame, was still to achieve his first Broadway success. Gower Champion was new at stage directing, and the producer, Edward Padula, was also a newcomer.

But the rock 'n' roll fever of the 1950s in general, and Elvis Presley in particular, cried out for satiric treatment. Since Michael Stewart's text, and the songs of Strouse and Adams, filled this bill completely, *Bye Bye Birdie* won the Tony as the season's best musical, enjoyed a Broadway run of 607 performances, went on national tour, and was made into a slick movie in 1963.

"One Last Kiss" is a good rock number. Most of the other songs also fit neatly into the overall pattern and are more recognizably good show tunes than rock: "A Lot of Livin' to Do," "Kids" and "Baby, Talk to Me."

Golden Boy (1964) was the musical version of Clifford Odets' stage play of 1937, partly prepared by Clifford Odets just before his death, and then by William Gibson. In the transformation, the principal character no longer is an Italian-American who plays the violin and becomes a boxer, but a black man hungry for the self-esteem and power that ring championship can bring. Sammy Davis, Jr. was the "golden boy" to whom Strouse and Adams assigned the three best songs in their score: "No More," "Night Song" and "I Want to Be with You."

After a futile attempt to bring the characters and situations of the comic strip, *Superman*, to the Broadway stage in *It's a Bird, It's a Plane, It's Superman* (1966), Strouse and Adams waited four years before returning to Broadway. When they did, it was with *Applause* (1970), their greatest stage success. Like the source from which it was derived—a story by Mary Orr and the motion picture *All About Eve* (1950) that starred Bette Davis and which was made into a musical comedy by Betty Comden and Adolph Green—*Applause* was a behind-the-scenes story of show business with accents on ruthlessness, double dealing, jealousy, infidelity and opportunism. All of these unsavory traits are embodied in the character of Eve Harrington, a young, lovely and innocent-faced stagestruck girl who worms her way into the confidence and employ of Margo Channing, a famous actress, only to employ wiles and deceit to attain her dream of becoming a star.

Lauren Bacall's virtuoso performance as Margo was the generator charging the musical with much of its electricity, a performance winning her a Tony. The choreography of Ron Field—particularly in an elaborately contrived routine built around the title song and set in a gypsy hangout—contributed electric currents of its own. Besides the title number, the leading songs, all of them neatly integrated into the story, included "But Alive," "The Best Night of My Life," "Good Friends" and "One of a Kind."

The way in which songs, production numbers and dance routines evolve naturally from a text and flow smoothly through the different scenes puts *Applause* into the category of musical play rather than musical comedy. This was even more true of *Cabaret* (1966), one of the most momentous experiences the musical stage has brought us since 1960.

Its composer was John Kander, born in Kansas City, Missouri in 1927. His musical background was enriched by an intensive period of study at the Oberlin Conservatory where he wrote the music for two school productions, and at Columbia University where his teachers in music included Douglas Moore and Otto Luening. After serving in the Army and the Merchant Marine Corps, Kander found jobs as conductor, choral director or pianist with out-of-town theater groups, and in 1959 and 1960 he made musical arrangements for the Broadway musicals *Gypsy* and *Irma La Douce*. Kander made his bow as a Broadway composer with *A Family Affair* (1962), the first musical directed by Harold Prince. That same year, Kander was introduced by his publisher to a young lyricist, Fred Ebb, with whom he wrote "My Coloring Book," which was popularized by Sandy Stewart, Kitty Kallen and Barbra Streisand in their respective recordings, and "I Don't Care Much," introduced and popularized by Miss Streisand.

The first musical comedy for which Kander and Ebb wrote songs was *Flora, the Red Menace* (1965), a satire on Greenwich Village radicals in the thirties, directed by George Abbott. Liza Minnelli, in her Broadway stage debut, received a Tony for her performance, but *Flora* did not do well, in spite of Miss Minnelli's virtuoso performance. But in their very next musical, *Cabaret* (1966), Kander and Ebb had the Broadway world in their hands.

Cabaret was a picture of decadent, degenerate Berlin in Germany in the 1920s, the years just before the Nazi *putsch*. The picture was first drawn in a series of sketches by Christopher Isherwood, *Berlin Stories*, and made into a Broadway stage play, *I Am a Camera* (1951). Joe Masteroff adapted the Isherwood book and the Broadway play into a musical play text. The book made no attempt to compromise with its lurid material. As a musical—and later (1972) as a stunning motion picture with Liza Minnelli and Joel Grey—*Cabaret* was no escapist musical theater. It revealed the malodorous facets of life in a city in a state of moral and political decay. As Walter Kerr remarked in *The New York Times*: "It [*Cabaret*] has elected to wrap its arms around all that was troubling and all that was intolerable with a demonic grin, an insidious slink, and the painted-on charm that keeps revelers up until midnight making false faces at the hangman."

All the rewards for success came to *Cabaret*: an extended Broadway run of 1,165 performances; both the Tony and the New York Drama Critics Circle Awards as the season's best musical; the selection of John Kander as leading stage composer of the year by a poll of New York critics; a national company touring for several years; productions throughout Europe; a Grammy for the original cast recording; and, finally, the magnificent movie that commanded the highest price yet paid by television for a screen musical, reputed to be nine million dollars (eight million dollars more than the same network, ABC, paid for the rights to telecast *Fiddler on the Roof*).

The score included a nationwide song hit in the title number, popularized in recordings by Marilyn Maye for Victor and by Herb Alpert and the Tijuana Brass for A and M. The best of the other songs were "Willkommen," "It Couldn't Please Me More," "If You Could See Her," "Why Should I Wake Up?" and "What Would You Do?".

Two musicals with Kander's songs in 1968 deserve mention: *The Happy Time* and *Zorba*. Robert Goulet was starred in *The Happy Time*, which was N. Richard Nash's adaptation of Robert L. Fontaine's book and Samuel Taylor's Broadway play of the same name. Goulet played Jacques Bonnard, a globe-trotting photographer, who reminisces about a visit to his lovable family in a small French-Canadian town, and his romance with the local schoolmistress. "The Life of the Party," a song in which the grandfather recalls what a devil of a fellow he once was, invariably brought down the house. "A Certain Girl" and "Without Me" were two other attractive numbers with lyrics by Ebb.

Zorba came from Nikos Kazantzakis' best-selling novel, *Zorba the Greek*, and from the movie that was made from it in 1964. The setting is Crete and the time is 1924. Nikos, a studious youngster, is planning to rebuild an abandoned mine he has inherited. In this task he is aided by Zorba, a lovable, simple-minded Greek who believes in enjoying life to the full. The ethnic Greek element is strongly stressed in the dances, one at the opening of the musical accompanied by the song "Life Is" and another toward the end of the play; also in songs stylistically influenced by Cretan music, "I Am Free," "Only Love," "Why Can't I Speak?" with lyrics by Ebb.

In 1975, John Kander and Fred Ebb provided songs for *Chicago*, the musicalization by Fred Ebb and Bob Fosse of a play with the same title by Maurine Dallis Watkins, which had been successfully staged on Broadway in 1926 before becoming *Roxie Hart*, a movie in 1942 starring Ginger Rogers. In the musical (as in the play and the movie) the lurid, cynical 1920s are recalled in a plot in which Roxie Hart, a honky-tonk entertainer, is imprisoned for shooting her lover only to win acquittal through the slick maneuvers of her glib mouthpiece. Bob Fosse, choreographer and stage director, keeps the production moving briskly, often with cabaret or vaudeville routines and episodes reminiscent of his own work in *Cabaret*. "His style," said *Time*, "is a mod expressionism laced with instant-replay slow motion, dislocating spasms of joints, a sultry moiling of the pelvic powerhouse. It's show biz, but there's vision behind it." Gwen Verdon as Roxie Hart, and Chita Rivera as Velma (her sister-in-crime) emit sparks in their singing and dancing that continually erupt into flame. (The flame was still burning when, in the summer of 1975, Liza Minnelli stepped in as a substitute for the temporarily ailing Miss Verdon.) And the songs of Kander and Ebb cleverly conjure up memories of the songs of the twenties, some of which carry overtones of Chicago jazz, others the echoes of the ballads of crooners and torch singers. "All I Care About" is a tribute to such singers as Al Jolson and Bing Crosby, and "I Can't Do It Alone" is a satiric glance at the Pollyanna themes of oldtime operettas. "When You're Good to Mama" and "Razzle Dazzle" are two other outstanding musical numbers.

Cy Coleman, born Cy Kaufman in Bronx, New York, in 1929, had achieved top rating as a composer of popular songs by the time he wrote his first Broadway score. A piano prodigy, Coleman gave recitals in New York City when he was six, and for three consecutive years, 1934–1936, he received the Music Education League Interborough Award. His music study took place at the New York College of Music and with private teachers while he was employed as pianist at servicemen's clubs. After graduating from the High School of Music and Art in New York in 1947, he switched from serious to popular music by forming a trio that appeared in night spots. For a decade after that he wrote music for many TV and radio programs, together with popular songs to the lyrics of Joseph A. McCarthy. "I'm Gonna Laugh You Out of My Life" was popularized by Nat King Cole, "Why Try to Change Me

Now?" was introduced by Frank Sinatra, and "Tin Pan Alley" was interpolated into the Broadway revue John Murray Anderson's *Almanac* (1953).

In 1957, Coleman began working with the lyricist, Carolyn Leigh. She was an advertising copywriter who had also written the words for several songs used in the Broadway production of *Peter Pan* starring Mary Martin in 1950. Their first song together was "A Moment of Madness" which Sammy Davis later recorded. After that came more songs, including their giant hit, "Witchcraft," which Frank Sinatra made famous in 1957. "Firefly" and "It Amazes Me" were both recorded by Tony Bennett a year later.

Wildcat (1960) was their first full-length score. This was a musical starring Lucille Ball, who appeared as a wildcat promoter in Centavo City in 1912. This production was all too obviously tailor-made for Miss Ball. But it was not well sewn: the seams not only showed, at times they unraveled. One of its songs, "Hey, Look Me Over," did far better than the show itself which folded after 172 performances.

After *Wildcat*, Coleman and Leigh wrote the songs for *Little Me* (1962), book by Neil Simon based on a novel by Patrick Dennis. Sid Caesar was the star, portraying several different and unusual characters all vitally involved with Belle Poitrine, a young lady of questionable virtue who rises from Drifters Row in a small town in Illinois to wealth and social position in Southampton, Long Island. Here, too, one of the songs proved more durable than the overall production, "Real Live Girl," which Jack Jones helped make popular.

When the fruitful partnership of Coleman and Leigh broke up, the composer acquired a new lyricist in the veteran Dorothy Fields, with whom he wrote the songs for his greatest Broadway success, *Sweet Charity* (1966). Neil Simon's book came from the Federico Fellini motion picture, *Nights of Cabiria* (1957). In the transformation into a musical, a Roman streetwalker becomes a warmhearted American dance hall hostess, generous to a fault, who is ever on the search for true love. She is Charity Hope Valentine, portrayed by the dynamic and irrepressible Gwen Verdon.

From the first rise of the curtain, when she dances in silhouette under an electric sign reading "The Story of a Girl Who Wanted to be Loved" to the final scene of frustration, Miss Verdon galvanized the production and her audiences. One of the many high points of her performance was her rendition in song and dance of "If My Friends Could See Me Now," a top hat tipped rakishly over one eye, a cane slung under her arm. "Where Am I Going?" and "I'm a Brass Band" were two other numbers profiting from her electrifying delivery. Other outstanding numbers in the show were "There's Gotta Be Something Better than This," "Big Spender" and "Baby Dream Your Dreams."

The two-character play by William Gibson, *Two for the Seesaw* (1958) was swollen into a musical, *Seesaw* (1973), with a cast of more than fifty, and was further augmented with blackouts, dance routines and many superfluous production numbers. Michael Bennett wrote the book, with songs by Coleman and Fields. The central theme—the relationship of Gittel and Jerry Ryan come to New York City to escape a domineering wife—remained the same as in the play, and when the musical hewed closely to the plot line and to its two principal characters it proved a highly diverting attraction, though not a profitable one at the box office. The musical highlights were "I'm Way Ahead," which Gittel sings alone as the final curtain descends, "Nobody Does It Like Me," "He's Good for Me" and "It's Not Where You Start."

Seesaw was Dorothy Fields' nineteenth Broadway musical and her last. She died of a heart attack at her apartment on Central Park West on the evening of March 28, 1974; that afternoon she had watched a road company rehearsal of *Seesaw*.

Both André Previn and Burt Bacharach were hardy veterans as popular-song composers and writers of music for the screen when each made his first entrance into the Broadway theater. Previn did it with *Coco*, Bacharach with *Promises, Promises*.

Coco (1969) was reputedly the life of Gabrielle Chanel, the distinguished Parisian dress designer known to her friends as "Coco." The book and lyrics were by Alan Jay Lerner. This was a musical with little story interest or change of pace and even less charm and humor. Its greatest asset was Katharine Hepburn as Coco who could make dull lines crisp and bright, humorless situations amusing, and (without much of a singing voice) the seven songs assigned to her more exciting than they actually were. The story covered Coco's later successful years, beginning in 1954 when she was seventy-one, and after she had seen a precipitous decline in her fortunes because of World War II. Though no song stood out prominently, some were an assist to a limping libretto: "A Woman Is How She Loves," "Fiasco," "When Your Lover Says Goodbye" and "Let's Go Home."

Bacharach came off far better than Previn in his Broadway debut, for *Promises, Promises* (1968) presented one of Bacharach's greatest song hits in "I'll Never Fall in Love Again," together with a few more delectable song items, such as the title number, "Whoever You Are,'" and "Where Can You Take a Girl?", all to lyrics by Hal David.

A Billy Wilder screen comedy, *The Apartment* (1960) which starred Jack Lemmon and Shirley MacLaine, was the source of *Promises, Promises*, with Neil Simon serving as the librettist. This musical recognized a fact too often ignored, that what had been a good film story should still be a good story for a stage musical, and called for no elaborate face-lifting.

Pippin (1972) was Stephen Schwartz' first venture as a composer lyricist for the Broadway musical theater, but before then he had already attracted admiration Off Broadway. He was only twenty-three when *Godspell* pushed him into the theatrical limelight Off-Broadway, and twenty-four when *Pippin* opened on Broadway to rhapsodies by the critics. Schwartz was a native of Long Island and an alumnus of the preparatory division of the Juilliard School of Music, and Carnegie-Mellon where he received a Bachelor of Fine Arts degree. He produced the original cast albums of several Off Broadway productions, including his own *Godspell*; he collaborated on the lyrics and libretto for Leonard Bernstein's *Mass*, and he was the composer of the title song for the motion picture *Butterflies Are Free* (1972).

Pippin, played without an intermission, had a book by Roger O. Hirson. A present-day theatrical troupe is rehearsing a musical about the growing years of Pippin, the son of Charlemagne. We are thrust back to the eighth century to confront Pippin, a young man weary of sex, war and revolution, and bored with the idea of succeeding his father as ruler of the Holy Roman Empire. Bob Fosse's staging and choreography added enormously to the excitement of the production. "From the first moment until almost the last. . . . Mr. Fosse never loses his silk and velvet grasp on the show," reported Clive Barnes in *The New York Times*. "He gives the show the pace of a roller derby and the finesse of a conjuror. Yet nothing seems strained or exaggerated. Mr. Fosse has achieved complete continuity between his staging and choreography, and his dances themselves have art and imagination. They swing with life." For some of these choreographic sequences Stephen Schwartz provided appropriate song material: the opening "Magic to Do," "War Is Science," "No Time at All," and "Spread a Little Sunshine." As the formal master of ceremonies, referred to as "Leading Player," Ben Vereen (graduating from his role as Judas in *Jesus Christ, Superstar*) became the shining star among the performers. For him Stephen Schwartz wrote "Simple Joys," "Glory" and "On the Right Track."

For Harvey Schmidt, as for Stephen Schwartz, the route to Broadway started Off

Broadway. Born in 1929 in Dallas, Texas, Schmidt, son of a Methodist minister, learned to play the piano by ear and became interested in the theater. As a student at the University of Texas he collaborated with Tom Jones (not the singer but a fellow student with the same name) in writing two college shows. After graduating from the University in 1952 with a Bachelor of Fine Arts degree, Schmidt served in the Army, afterward settling in New York as a commercial artist. Songwriting was his pet hobby. With Tom Jones as his lyricist he wrote some songs used in a nightclub revue produced by Julius Monk and in a modest Off Broadway musical, *The Shoestring Revue* (1955). Schmidt and Jones became a major team in the theater with *The Fantasticks*, produced Off Broadway in 1960, about which more will be said later. This led to their first Broadway musical, *110 in the Shade* (1963), book by N. Richard Nash based on his own stage play, *The Rainmaker* (1954). Inga Swenson here made her Broadway debut, and presented the best songs in the score: "Love, Don't Turn Away," "Is It Really Me?" and "Raunchy." Equally attractive were two other numbers: "Everything Beautiful Happens at Night" and "Another Hot Day."

Three years later, Harvey Schmidt and Tom Jones wrote the songs for the first musical ever to call for just two characters. *I Do! I Do!* (1966) was adapted by Jones from Jan de Hartog's stage play, *The Fourposter* (1951). The two characters are Michael and Agnes, portrayed by Robert Preston and Mary Martin. The story of their marriage takes them from their wedding day and carries them through the many misunderstandings, jealousies, vicissitudes of fortune, and conflicts big and small that make up marital life, until old age brings them to terms with life and each other. The songs are beautifully integrated with the play and lend it much of its charm, particularly through the infectious performances of the two principals. In the wedding night scene, Robert Preston does a barefoot tap dance to the strains of a love song to his wife, "I Love My Wife," wearing the incongruous costume of a dressing gown and top hat. Mary Martin is equally arresting when, later in life, she insists that her blood is still hot in "Flaming Agnes." "My Cup Runneth Over," "Together Forever," "Where Are the Snows," "All the Dearly Beloved" and "A Well Known Fact" are more numbers to charm the heart and ear.

It took the courage and the innocence of a stranger to Broadway to think of making a musical play out of the signing of the Declaration of Independence. Sherman Edwards, a one-time history teacher, was both courageous and innocent when he undertook the project. The original concept of *1776* (1969) was his—though the libretto was finally written by Peter Stone—and so were the lyrics and the music.

It hardly seemed likely that Stone could build up interest and suspense in an event whose final denouement—the signing of the Declaration and the birth of a new nation—were familiar to everybody in the audience before the curtain went up. But the historic figures of 1776 came vividly to life with all their foibles and idiosyncrasies—Benjamin Franklin, Thomas Jefferson, John Dickinson and others—as the resolution of their doubts, fears and differences made for a taut drama, even though the conclusion could never be in question. The songs were an inseparable part of the fabric, no single one capable of surviving outside the production, but together adding depth and dimension to both the characters and the play: the opening number where John Adams complains about the lackadaisical behavior of the Continental Congress, "Sit Down, John"; the anti-war song, "Momma, Look Sharp"; the comic tribute to a venerable Southern family in "The Lees of Old Virginia"; and the song by the leaders of freedom, "But, Mr. Adams."

Despite the fact that *1776* carried a history lesson into the theater, that it had no stars in the cast, no production numbers, no chorus, no choreography—and an uncommercial title—it was a financial success as well as an artistic one. It ran on Broadway for 1,217 performances and then was made into a movie (1972) which, regrettably, proved insufferably dull. It also won a Tony as the season's best musical, and became the first musical ever presented in its entirety at the White House, before President and Mrs. Nixon and their guests on February 22, 1970.

Another page torn out of the American history book—this time covering the Civil War period—became the theme of *Shenandoah* (1975). *Shenandoah* came to Broadway after a successful summer tryout at the Goodspeed Opera House in East Haddam, Connecticut. The book, by James Lee Barrett, Philip Rose and Peter Udell, was adapted from a motion picture of the same name (1965) starring James Stewart. Gary Geld wrote the music and Peter Udell the lyrics. This was their second successful Broadway musical. The first, *Purlie*, is discussed later in this chapter with other black-oriented musicals.

In both the motion picture and the stage musical, the dominating character of *Shenandoah* is Charlie Anderson, a proud, courageous, independent-thinking farmer in Virginia's Shenandoah Valley, a widower with five sons and a daughter. An isolationist, he refuses to get involved in the Civil War which he stubbornly feels is none of his business. But the war comes to his very doorstep to involve both him and his family.

The book, winner of a Tony, is made up of a series of episodes separated by songs, some comedy, and a few dances. The dancing (choreographed by Robert Tucker) consists of two or three stereotyped mountain-folk routines, and there is little musical staging to speak of. *Shenandoah* had two strong assets. One of them was John Cullum who both vocally and histrionically gave Charlie Anderson dimension. His performance was rewarded with a Tony. The other asset was the songs, also earning for their creators a Tony. When performer and songs became one, *Shenandoah* became a musical with charm. "I've Heard It All Before," "The Pickers Are Comin' " and "Meditation" are songs with appealing sentiment. Other songs are also attractive: "Raise the Flag of Dixie," a tune typical of Civil War martial ballads, "Violets and Silverbells," "We Make a Beautiful Pair" and the choral "The Only Home I Know."

4

New writers, and experimental or offbeat musicals, finding Broadway a closed door because of astronomic production costs and overhead, could sometimes get a hearing in one of the many small theaters scattered around New York outside the periphery of Broadway. Off Broadway did not call for expensive casts, staging, costuming or choreography, which Broadway theatergoers generally demand in their musicals. Modestly projected with limited budgets, Off Broadway musicals could afford to welcome the unknown, the inexperienced, and the unconventional. It was also able to nurse a production to a long, successful run following a stumbling beginning.

Off Broadway presented a valuable revival of Kurt Weill's *Threepenny Opera*, with a revitalized text by Marc Blitzstein, which began a 2,611-performance run in 1954; also Jerome Kern's 1917 musical, *Leave It to Jane*, whose 928-performance run in downtown New York began in 1959. Off Broadway also was the scene for new musicals well off the beaten track.

The most successful original Off Broadway musical before 1960 was *Little Mary Sunshine* (1959), with a run of 1,143 performances. Book, lyrics and music were all the work of Rick Besoyan. This was a spoof on old-fashioned operettas of the Sigmund Romberg and Rudolf Friml variety, but most especially of Friml's *Rose-Marie*. The setting of *Little Mary Sunshine* was the Rocky Mountains at the turn of the present century. Among the characters were the Forest Rangers, who open the musical with a robust song about their profession,

"The Forest Rangers." The main love duet was named "Colorado Love Call." The troubles of little Mary when the mortgage on her home is foreclosed, and when she is attacked by an Indian, are par for the operetta course, as is her romantic interest in the Ranger, Captain Big Jim Warrington.

A new decade on Off Broadway brought with it the greatest box-office success ever known there by any musical, and up to this writing the longest running production in the history of the American theater. Yet when *The Fantasticks* (1960), with music and lyrics by Harvey Schmidt and Tom Jones, first opened at the Sullivan Theater on May 3, on an original investment of $16,500, it played for three months to half-empty houses, even though the seating capacity of the theater was less than one hundred and fifty. But since the producer had faith in his show, and the financial loss so far had been minimal, he stubbornly kept it going, trusting to the power of word-of-mouth enthusiasm and the kind words of the critics. These helped, and so did winning the Vernon Rice Award for the leading Off Broadway production of the year. Business picked up briskly until capacity houses became the rule rather than the exception. Sixteen years later, after 6,668 performances, it was still prospering. In that time it grossed four million two hundred dollars, bringing one and a half million dollars to each investor of $16,500. In addition to its phenomenal New York run, thousands of other performances were given throughout the United States by professional, semi-professional, stock and amateur companies, as well as professional productions in Europe, the Middle East, Africa, Scandinavia, Mexico and other countries. October 18, 1964, marked the first time that a still-running stage production in New York was also being offered by the same company in a television adaptation (on tape over NBC).

In creating *The Fantasticks*, Tom Jones adapted Edmond Rostand's *Les Romanesques*. Utilizing the most economical resources in staging, *The Fantasticks* called for a single set, no scenery, and elementary props. A stick represented a wall, a cardboard moon attached to a pole suggested nighttime. The tale itself is a fable of two youngsters, Matt and Luisa, who pass through disillusion to find fulfillment in love.

Musically, the production opens with best foot forward, with "Try to Remember" (since become a standard following a best-selling recording by The Brothers Four for Columbia). "Much More" and "Soon It's Gonna Rain" were two songs from the score popularized by Barbra Streisand in Columbia recordings.

After *The Fantasticks*, Schmidt and Jones realized successes on Broadway itself with *110 in the Shade* and *I Do! I Do!*. They returned to the Off-Broadway scene in 1975 with *Philemon*, an intimate musical produced at the Portfolio Studio, which in its modest aims and pervading charm was reminiscent of *The Fantasticks*. As in the earlier work, Schmidt and Jones wrote their own libretto. "Schmidt's score," wrote Martin Gottfried in his review in the New York *Post*, "is dazzling, ranging from spine-tingling rhythmic songs to a gorgeous love duet. His combination of soaring melody, theatricality and musicianship has never been more impressive."

Man of La Mancha, with songs by Mitch Leigh and Joe Darion, also born Off-Broadway, has become one of the glories of the American musical theater. It was first tried out at the Goodspeed Opera House in Connecticut before slipping, without any warning of potential triumph, into the Washington Square Theater on November 22, 1965. The production was transferred to the Martin Beck Theater in March 1968 to accumulate a total run of 2,328 performances. The critics, taken by surprise at the presence of a stage masterpiece, set into motion one of the greatest success stories in American musical-stage history with their glowing reviews. Besides achieving its monumental run, *Man of La Mancha* received both the Tony and the New York Drama Critics Awards. The musical was successfully performed all over the United States by touring companies and was seen in principal cities in Europe, East Germany, Israel, Japan, Mexico and Australia. The original cast recording earned a gold record and the sheet-music sale of the hit songs sold over two million copies. *Man of La Mancha* was also sold to the movies on a five million dollar deal (though the final production hardly justified the expenditure).

The plot, in a text by Dale Wasserman, tells the story of Cervantes and his writing of *Don Quixote*, with Don Quixote becoming Cervantes' alter ego. As Dale Wasserman explained, "I wanted to interweave and merge their identities. Miguel Cervantes was Don Quixote." The entire musical is given without intermission. Simple props are changed to meet the demands of the plot. The adventures of Don Quixote come to life, including the championing of Aldonza, a strumpet whom the Don looks upon as Dulcinea, a lady of high social station. Imagination in the staging, choreography, direction and acting endowed the text with a depth of perception together with, at times, an ingratiating humor, and at other moments, pathos. The choreographic highlight is the seduction of Aldonza by muleteers; the musical high point comes with the singing of "The Impossible Dream" (also known as "The Quest") by Cervantes, played by Richard Kiley. "The Impossible Dream" became a major hit song in recordings by Jack Jones, Roger Williams, The Hesitations and many others. "Dulcinea" and the title number are also distinctive.

The music of *Man of La Mancha* by Mitch Leigh was his first theater score. He was born in Brooklyn, New York, in 1928, and educated in New York's public schools and at Yale University where he received degrees of Bachelor of Arts and Master of Arts and where he attended Paul Hindemith's class in composition. In 1954, Leigh sold a TV commercial to Revlon. This started him off on a highly profitable career as a writer of musical commercials—as president and creative director of Music Makers, Inc., which he organized. His commercials won virtually every major radio and television award in the field. In the early 1960s he expanded his activities to include the writing of incidental music for several Broadway plays. This was the extent of his background as a popular composer when he and his lyricist, Joe Darion, were engaged to write the songs for *Man of La Mancha*. Joe Darion, however, had had considerable experience as a lyricist. Some of his songs in the 1950s were highly successful, among them "Ricochet" (music by Larry Coleman and Norman Gimbel), a major success in Teresa Brewer's recording for Coral, and "Changing Partners" (music by Larry Coleman), popularized by Patti Page in her Mercury recording. In the 1950s, Darion also wrote the book and lyrics, in collaboration with Mel Brooks, for the Broadway production *Shinbone Alley* (1957).

You're a Good Man, Charlie Brown (1967) also ranks among the longest running Off-Broadway productions with 1,597 performances. This musical was an extension to the stage of the popular *Peanuts* comic strip of Charles M. Schulz. Lyrics and music were by Clark Gesner, who did the adaptation under the pen name of John Gordon. The whimsy, non-sequiturs and irrelevancies that make the comic strip a delight to millions were carried over into a musical production which was more of a revue than a plot musical. The different scenes detail the problems of Charlie Brown in school, with baseball, kites, redheads, and so forth, on one of his typical days. The familiar cartoon characters are here with all their engaging absurdities: Linus, Lucy, Schroeder, Patty and Snoopy the dog. The songs are in the spirit of the cartoon strip. In "My Blanket and Me," Linus explains how much his security blanket means to him; in "Kite," Charlie Brown reveals his delight at flying kites; in "Book Report" he gives his reaction to a book report written on *Peter Rabbit*; and in "Little Known Facts," Lucy discloses how much misinformation Linus has been meting out to her.

In *Your Own Thing* (1968), rock is carried into a modern-day book by Donald Driver that was suggested by Shakespeare's *Twelfth Night*, with lyrics and music by Hal Hester and Danny Apolinar. In Shakespeare's play, Viola loves Duke Orsino who seeks Olivia, and poses as a boy page to be near him. Viola's twin brother, Sebastian, is attracted to Olivia. When Sebastian reveals the true sex of his sister, Viola and the Duke become emotionally involved, as do Olivia and Sebastian. All these happenings assume modern trappings in the musical. Orsino, the duke, becomes Orson, a booking agent handling a rock group, the Apocalypse. Olivia is the operator of a discotheque. Orson conceives the idea of dressing up Viola as a male rock 'n' roll artist to replace a missing member of the Apocalypse. The amatory entanglements of the four principals take place in Manhattan of the 1960s. With the vitality of youth to energize the whole production, the rock numbers contribute additional dynamism. The music maintains a breathless pace from opening to final curtain, with amusing timely comments interposed cinematically on the screen by Humphrey Bogart, Queen Elizabeth, Shakespeare, God, John Wayne, the Pope, and Shirley Temple among others. "Baby! Baby!", "I'm Me!" and "Do Your Thing" are all solid rock numbers.

Though *Godspell* (1971) was produced five months before *Jesus Christ, Superstar*, it was undoubtedly spawned by that remarkable English rock opera which had started life as a best-selling record to become (after the opening of *Godspell*) a sensational stage production and a spectacular motion picture. Both *Godspell* and *Jesus Christ, Superstar* were products of the spiritual revival that took place in the early 1970s among the young. That revival expressed itself in the growing popularity of gospel, the spread of evangelism in the streets, and in the "Jesus Revolution," all a reaction against and a rejection of the drug and sexual excesses of the youth of the 1960s. "I would like to revitalize people's interest in religion," said John-Michael Tebelak, one of the originators of *Godspell*, as well as its director. "I would want to bring more celebration into religion."

Godspell was the conception of youngsters at Carnegie Technical Institute in Pittsburgh, the idea being developed there by John-Michael Tebelak, a graduate student. Later on Ellen Stewart tried it out at the La Mama Theater in New York where it attracted the interest of Edgar Lansbury, a producer who enlisted the cooperation of two more producers. Stephen Schwartz was then called in to write the lyrics and music of a new score. *Godspell* arrived at the Cherry Lane Theater, Off Broadway, on May 17, 1971, and moved to the Promenade Theater three months later. Productions throughout the United States increased its popularity.

Its aim was to present Jesus Christ to a contemporary audience and to give relevance to the Gospel of St. Matthew. Using the argot of modern youth, and set to music in a rock idiom, *Godspell* gives Christianity meaning for the present in a manner and method that might be regarded by some as blasphemy or sacrilege. Jesus appears as a clown with a red nose and is dressed in a Superman shirt and multi-colored striped baggy trousers held up by suspenders. His faithful apostles are similarly dressed as clowns, their costumes comprising colored tennis shoes, floppy hats, fringed pants, patchwork shirts and sweatshirts bearing the names of philosophers. The apostles take turns in acting out the parables. Each parable is narrated with a different technique, sometimes mimed as in The Prodigal Son, sometimes through unique histrionic devices as in the Good Samaritan whose characters are represented by fingers walking along on a broom handle held high. As these episodes unfold, Jesus, atop a table, explains his teachings while his disciples go through routines filled with witticisms, slapstick humor, impressions, mugging. A dramatic climax is reached with the Last Supper and the Crucifixion. The message of the play is that since the real meaning of Christ's teachings of goodness, charity and forgiveness have long been lost, what is most needed today is the loving simplicity and humor of a clown. "As set to Stephen Schwartz's joyous rock score," said Arthur Knight in the *Saturday Review*, "it projects all the innocent faith and fervor of early Christianity. . . . *Godspell*, with no religious trappings whatsoever, provides a religious experience of extraordinary intensity." The top number in Schwartz's score is "Day by Day" (lyric by St. Richard of Chichester), though "Save the People," "Bless the Lord" and "All Good Gifts" are no less distinguished. Another fine song is an interpolation: "By My Side" (Jay Hamburger—Peggy Gordon). After five years Off-Broadway, *Godspell* moved to Broadway—the Broadhurst Theater—on June 22, 1976.

Grease (1972) takes a backward glance at the 1950s and seems to enjoy to the full what it sees. This is a rock musical by Jim Jacobs and Warren Casey which opened Off Broadway at the Eden Theater on Second Avenue before moving on to Broadway where it was still playing in 1977. The action—such as there is—transpires in what appears to be a midwestern high school, Rydell High; the main characters are lower middle-class teenagers of the class of '59, representing the culture, mores and fetishes of the 1950s. Cult figures of the fifties are recalled—Elvis Presley, Pat Boone, Jerry Lee Lewis, Sandra Dee, Annette Funicello—and so are the rock music, jive, dances, jargon and dress of the younger set. One of the best satirical numbers is "Look at Me, I'm Sandra Dee" with "Beauty School Dropout" a close second. "Alone at a Drive-In Movie" and "It's Raining on Prom Night" reflect the more serious moods of adolescents, and "Greased Lightin' " explodes into a hilarious production number.

With *A Chorus Line* (1975), Off Broadway again gave birth to a musical that became not only a monumental box-office success but also a treasured addition to musical theater. This is a backstage story, the idea for which was born with Michael Bennett, a Broadway producer, choreographer, writer and director. His purpose, as he expressed it, was "to do something on the stage that would show people being honest with one another." One evening he gathered twenty-four dancers in a rehearsal studio on 21st Street in Manhattan and asked them to speak as truthfully as they could about "the whys and hows of their careers." He explained further, "I brought along a tape recorder and we talked for hours about what we were doing, what we're after. . . ." This "rap session" lasted through the night, and several others followed. The result was some thirty hours of tape-recorded reminiscences to which Bennett added copiously from his own experiences. With this as raw material, Bennett called in Nicholas Dante to work it into a script. Some time later James Kirkwood was recruited to help Dante give the script professional shape and form; Marvin Hamlisch, who in Hollywood had recently captured triple Oscars in a single year, was to write the music with Edward Kleban as his lyricist; and Joseph Papp was to be induced to open up his purse strings.

One year and a half after the first "rap session"—on May 21, 1975—*A Chorus Line* opened at the Public (Newman) Theatre on Lafayette Street. Both the staging and the choreography were by Michael Bennett. Opening night had been preceded by several previews from which came the word-of-mouth report that a very special theatrical happening was taking place on Lafayette Street. The critics—all the leading ones were there—provided confirmation with ecstatic reviews. As *Variety* noted in the opening lines of its report: "The problem is to find superlatives to convey something of the enjoyment and excitement of *A Chorus Line*. . . . It is one of the best musicals in recent years."

The playbill provided a clue to the intentions of the creators with the following note: "The show is dedicated to anyone who has ever danced in a chorus or marched in step . . . anywhere." "I tried," added Bennett, "to show the audience exactly what Broadway dancing is all about, on all its levels."

There is no principal character or set of characters, nor is there a basic story line.

What happens on the stage is an audition at which twenty-four dancers try out for eight parts. This number is immediately cut to eighteen. The producer now invites the remaining number to tell him frankly about themselves. They do so in autobiographical vignettes which lay bare personal dreams, struggles, frustrations; homosexual experiences, the agony of keeping a hopeless marriage together, the release from life's dreariness through dancing, the self-esteem gained through silicone. Some stories are tragedies, other are trivia. But what emerges from these revelations is not just the personal histories of theater dancers but the struggle of everybody everywhere to survive. The involvement of the audience with each of the characters becomes total, one of the many reasons why night after night the finale brought a standing ovation and cheers.

The production was innovative and creative. Walter Kerr in *The New York Times* found much to admire in the "lightning-stroke severity, the percussive yet infinitely varied discipline creator-choreographer Michael Bennett has imposed upon his open, scenically empty stage. Except for revolving mirrors against the back wall and five or six cheval glasses that can be whipped in place the space is bare. To fill it, sharply outlined slivers of light dart from the heavens to pick out faces trained to grin, faces quivering in fear, bodies contorted in rhythmic ecstasy or in private humiliation and terror."

The dancing, the songs and background music continuously provided intriguing commentaries for eyes and ears. "The Music and the Mirror" became electric in Donna McKechnie's show-stopping rendition. Priscilla Lopez gave a hilarious portrait of a student actress incapable of "feeling" herself as a table or a sports car in "Nothing," and in "Dance: Ten; Looks: Three," Pamela Blair opined on the possibility of improving her status at an audition by using silicone. Other memorable musical numbers were "One," "What I Did for Love," "At the Ballet" and "Hello Twelve, Hello Thirteen, Hello Love".

On July 25, a month after it had opened Off-Broadway, *A Chorus Line* moved uptown to Broadway, to the Shubert Theater, to become "the hottest ticket in town." Within a few months three new companies were put into production: a second one for Broadway, opening on April 26, 1976; an international touring company come to Toronto on May 3; and a national company which began its cross-country tour in San-Francisco on May 11. By that time, *A Chorus Line* had captured the Pulitzer Prize for drama, nine Tony awards (including one for the best play and another for the best musical score), and had received five and a half million dollars from Universal Pictures for the cinema rights.

5

Grease, Godspell, and *Your Own Thing* are rock musicals, a new genre in the American musical theater that first became influential with *Hair* (1967), dubbed an "American tribal love-rock musical" by its authors, Gerome Regni and James Rado, librettists and lyricists, and composer Galt MacDermot. More than that, *Hair* was the voice of rebellion against war, racism, the draft, and the conventions and values of middle-class society as to morals, cleanliness, propriety of behavior and language. This was the musical that made the first significant inroads in the legitimate theater in the presentation of total nudity on the stage and was one of the first to speak so openly of sexual practices. The total nudity came in the first-act finale, "Be In." Sex is discussed without inhibitions in "White Boys" (about interracial sex relationships), "I Got Life" (glorifying the naked body) and "Sodomy" (dealing with sexual perversions). In "Colored Spade" a black singer parades all the distasteful expletives directed at people of his race.

Hair was first produced by the New York Shakespeare Festival Theater, under Joseph Papp's direction, at the Florence Sutro Anspacher Theater, Off-Broadway, on October 29, 1967. After eight weeks it moved to a onetime discotheque uptown. After that the musical underwent a giant overhauling, omitting whatever plot it once had, introducing nudity together with many new songs, routines and production details.

The final product came to the Biltmore Theater on Broadway on April 29, 1968. The show opened and closed with its two best musical numbers, each receiving wide circulation outside the theater. The opening was "Aquarius" where, with the help of electronic sounds, a new age is being proclaimed in which peace will guide the planets and love will steer the stars. The 5th Dimension helped bring this song to the best-selling record charts, a Soul City release that received a Grammy as the best record of the year. The closing number was the exultantly optimistic "Let the Sunshine In," which was on the flip side of the 5th Dimension record of "Aquarius."

Besides the opening and closing numbers, and some of the satirical songs already alluded to, the score was further enriched by "Frank Mills," "Good Morning, Starshine," "I Got Life," "Easy to Be Hard," "Where Do I Go?" and "Ain't Got No."

In 1970, *Hair* celebrated its second birthday with an open-air performance at the Central Park Mall in New York attended by over ten thousand. By that time, on an investment of $150,000, the musical had earned a profit of over two million dollars from the New York run alone, a profit greatly swelled by successful runs by other companies in Los Angeles, San Francisco, Chicago, Toronto, London, Manchester, Paris, Amsterdam, Lisbon, Munich, Copenhagen, Zagreb, Tokyo and other world centers.

Two Gentlemen of Verona (1971) was Shakespeare embellished with rock music, the updating done by John Guare and Mel Shapiro with music by Galt MacDermot to Guare's lyrics. Some of Shakespeare's text is retained, and a good deal of his mocking spirit in treating love and sexuality. The pairs of lovers are scrambled among Puerto Ricans and blacks —Proteus and Julia being Puerto Rican, and Silvia and Valentine, black. The whole evening had a quality of an improvisation. MacDermot's prolix score (comprising over thirty numbers) was more versatile and subtler than that for *Hair*, attesting to his musical growth as a theater composer. Conscious of the ethnic overtones of the text, he goes on to write a fetching calypso or a samba with as skilled a hand as he does a blues, rock, gospel or Soul. "Night Letter," sung by Silvia and Valentine, is the song that mesmerized audiences. Almost as good were "I Am Not Interested in Love," "Love's Revenge," "Who Is Silvia?", "Love Me" and "What a Nice Idea."

6

When an all-black company presented on Broadway a production of *Hello, Dolly!* following the original white one, it was just a case of a white man's musical comedy changing color. This had been true as far back as 1939 when a black cast, headed by Bill Robinson, brought zest and rhythm to Gilbert and Sullivan's *The Mikado* in *The Hot Mikado*. But several vibrant, cogent, inventive all black musicals since 1970 have offered us the world of the black man authentically and indigenously.

Purlie (1970) was a musical comedy whose book, by Ossie Davis, Philip Rose and Peter Udell, was taken from Ossie Davis' 1961 stage play, *Purlie Victorious*. The lyrics were by Udell to Gary Geld's music. *Purlie*, like so many other black musicals of recent date, did not hesitate to comment upon the racial struggle in America's South, but it did so with humor and kindliness rather than vitriol, ending, not on a note of frustration and despair, but on hope and optimism.

The setting is the cotton plantation country in Georgia in the "recent past." Purlie, a preacher, is a garrulous and conniving fellow who aspires to see his people freed from the ruthless exploitation of Ol' Cap'n, a bigot. The musical opens in the full sunlight of this hope as Big Bethel, Purlie's new temple, is being dedicated, and the joy of freedom is hymned in the gospel, "Walk Him Up the Stairs," which at the same time offers a prayer for the soul of the dead Ol' Cap'n. The next two acts, in flashback, describe the devious ways and means by which Purlie proved victorious over Ol' Cap'n and was able to get his own new church. In an epilogue, the congregation sings of its faith in the future by repeating "Walk Him Up the Stairs." The romance in the musical is provided by Purlie and Lutiebelle, who was given a luminous performance by Melba Moore (a graduate from *Hair*, where she had been the only black leading lady), a performance that forthwith placed her among the new singing stars of the 1970s. One of the songs that brought her this distinction was the title number in which she reveals how much she loves Purlie.

With electrified guitars in the orchestra much of the music is soft rock, but a good deal of it is in the style of gospel and Negro folk songs. What come most strongly to mind are "Down Home," "The World Is Comin' to a Start," "I Got Love" and "New Fangled Preacher Man."

But there is more bitterness than humor and more anger than good feeling in the two black musicals of Melvin Van Peebles that, in 1971 and 1972, presented the society of the black ghetto with uncompromising truth. Melvin Van Peebles is many things: actor, promoter, author, composer, lyricist, librettist, singer, film director and publicist. He was born on the South Side of Chicago in 1932 and grew up in Phoenix, Illinois. In 1953 he received a Bachelor of Arts degree from Ohio Wesleyan University. After three and half years in the Air Force he lived in San Francisco, supporting his family by working as a gripman in a cable car, while spending odd hours writing the text for a picture book about cable cars published in 1957. From this he went on to publish several novels and to write and produce several motion pictures. *Sweet Sweetback's Baadasss Song* was his third movie, and he not only wrote both the scenario and the music but he also directed and produced it and was its star. It became the highest grossing independent black movie ever made, earning several million dollars profit from the black trade before white audiences discovered it. Its success helped to spawn many imitations, some of which were also moneymakers.

Van Peeble's first black musical on Broadway was *Ain't Supposed To Die a Natural Death* (1971), for which he wrote text, lyrics, and music. This is a collection of songs, dances and soliloquies against a musical background portraying life in the black ghetto of a large city among prostitutes, lesbians, junkies, transvestites, corrupt law officers, thieves, procurers and others victimized by their backgrounds and upbringing. The songs are actually free-verse poems and set to rock music: as, for example, "Just Don't Make No Sense" which opens the show and "Put a Curse on You," which closes it with a bitter attack against mankind.

Van Peebles not only wrote text, lyrics and music of *Don't Play Us Cheap* (1972), but he also produced, directed and financed it. This is a parable in which demons come to earth disguised as cockroaches and rats. "The theme is a universal one," said Clive Barnes in the *New York Times*, "concerning people learning to be themselves, to avoid cant, hypocrisy and pretentiousness, and not only do their own thing, but even more to be their own thing." The rock score included "Saturday Night," "It Makes No Difference," "Ain't Love Grand," "Know Your Business" and "Feast on Me."

Don't Bother Me I Can't Cope (1972) is a black revue written entirely by Micki Grant who was also one of its principal performers. It places considerable stress on the racial question without losing entertainment values nor a sense of humor. The overall mood is ironic; the ways and standards of white men are contemplated and puzzled over. The best songs are "It Takes a Whole Lot of Human Feeling," "I Gotta Keep Moving," "Harlem Streets" and "Love Power."

Lorraine Hansberry's poignant stage drama of 1958, A *Raisin in the Sun*, became enriched in emotional and human values in its transfer to the musical stage as *Raisin* (1973), winner of a Tony as the season's best musical, and of a Grammy for the original cast album recording. The book was written by Robert Nemiroff and Charlotte Zaltsberg (with Joseph Stein contributing an uncredited assist), while Judd Woldin wrote the music and Robert Brittan, the lyrics. Donald McKayle, whose brilliant choreography and direction brought him favorable comparison with Jerome Robbins, became the first black man to fill the role of choreographer director on Broadway. Walter Kerr said of his work that he "snatches every orchestrated opportunity to propel the evening from its musical set-pieces into open drama."

It took some four years for *Raisin* to jell before it anticipated its Broadway run with a performance at the Arena Stage in Washington, D.C. in June 1972. Playing there to capacity houses and to the praises of critics, *Raisin* promised much at its New York opening, and fulfilled it. All the warmth, sweetness and pathos of the stage play are captured in depicting the attempt of a black family, through the inheritance of a ten thousand dollar insurance policy payment, to abandon the slums for a respectable, middle-class white neighborhood. Though the text is generally stronger and more eloquent than the music, "Who's Little Angry Man," "A Whole Lotta Sunlight," "Measure the Valley" and "Sidewalk Tree" are some of the songs that contribute to the overall emotional impact. "Booze" serves as the musical background for an excitingly conceived and projected African dance. "He Comes Down this Morning," a stirring gospel, also received effective choreographic treatment.

The Wiz (1975) is the black man's musical version of L. Frank Baum's children's classic, *The Wonderful World of Oz*. The original idea to make Baum's fantasy into a black musical was Ken Harper's, but the adaptation was made by William F. Brown, with music and lyrics by Charlie Smalls and with the choreography, direction and costuming by Geoffrey Holder. In plot, the musical stayed faithful to its source. Using black characters exclusively, and interpolating into the text references to drugs, sex, black urban encounters, the black man's slang, and his kind of music, dancing and humor, *The Wiz*, though springing out of the literature of white people, emerged as a totally black experience on the stage of the Majestic Theater on January 5, 1975. And as a black experience it monopolized seven Tony awards (not only as best musical and best musical score, but also for supporting actor and actress, direction, choreography and costume design), in addition to five Drama Desk Awards from the New York critics and feature writers. Thus *The Wiz* became one of the big success stories in the season's theater, as well as one of its most exciting theatrical adventures. The excitement was visual, through stunning choreography by Geoffrey Holder, of which the Tornado Ballet was the most spectacular, and with extraordinarily picturesque costuming. The excitement was dramatic through stunning performances not only in the principal roles but also in subsidiary ones, with the Tonys going to Ted Rose as the Cowardly Lion and to Dee Dee Bridgewater as Good Witch Glinda. Equally superlative performances were given by Stephanie Mills as Dorothy, Andre De Shields as the Wiz, and Tiger Haynes as the Tin Woodman. And the excitement was aural as well, in the music of Charlie Smalls, whose best songs were "Don't Nobody Bring Me No Bad News," "Ease on Down the Road," "I Was Born on the Day Before Yesterday" and "What Would I Do If I Could Feel."

The all-black musical, *Bubbling Brown Sugar* (1976), was billed as a revue but it used a slim story line to justify the presentation of exuberant dances and nostalgic songs. In today's Harlem, three black showpeople of former days meet a young white and a young black couple. The oldtime trio becomes the guide to conduct these two pairs through a tour of Harlem between 1920 and 1940. The book was by Loften Mitchell based on a concept by

Rosetta LeNoire and the choreography and staging was by Billy Wilson. The music (thirty-four numbers) was made up exclusively of standards by black songwriters, reaching as far back as 1905 to that Bert Williams specialty, "Nobody" (Alex Rogers—Bert Williams). Duke Ellington is represented by "Sophisticated Lady" (Mitchell Parish and Irving Mills), "It Don't Mean a Thing" (Irving Mills) and "I Got It Bad and that Ain't Good" (Paul Francis Webster) among other numbers, while the Duke Ellington orchestra is remembered through Billy Strayhorn's *Take the A Train*. Many other song classics by black composers and lyricists add to the musical delights, such as "Honeysuckle Rose" (Andy Razaf—Thomas "Fats" Waller), "Sweet Georgia Brown" (Ben Bernie, Maceo Pinkard and Kenneth Casey) with which Vivian Reed provided some stunning singing, "Some of These Days" (Shelton Brooks) and "Love Will Find a Way" (Noble Sissle and Eubie Blake).

7

In the early 1970s, the musical theater embarked on a nostalgia kick. The early 1970s was truly a time of anxiety. Crime was on the sharp ascent, and city streets were more dangerous than ever. Dope traffic was less controllable. New sex permissiveness invaded literature, the movies and the theater. College campuses were restive with anti-Vietnam War demonstrations. The one at Kent State University on May 4, 1970, led to the fatal shooting of four students by National Guardsmen after the ROTC building had earlier been burned to the ground by protesters. Then when peace—or, more accurately, the involvement of American troops—came to end collegiate defiance, it turned out to be no peace at all, and ended up with a Communist victory. In the mid-East, an outbreak of conflict on Yom Kippur day in October 1973 brought America and the Soviet Union on a collision course for several terrifying tension-filled hours. Watergate was releasing its shocking revelations, with the possible impeachment of a President of the United States becoming more and more of a reality until it was finally forestalled by resignation, the first in the history of the American Presidency. And before that happened, a Vice President had resigned as a self-confessed criminal. On top of all this was a spiraling inflation that could not be stopped, a plunging stock market, and a recession that threatened to grow into a depression.

In contrast to all this, preceding decades had seemed a time of wine and roses, even the war years of the 1940s which had been disturbing in their own way. And so, a flight into the past, from the grim events of the present, was much in order. The musical theater provided such an avenue of escape, first with a revival of Vincent Youmans' *No, No, Nanette* of 1925, which became one of the greatest successes in the history of theatrical revivals (861 performances). It is now recorded history—painstakingly recorded by Donald H. Dunn in *The Making of No, No, Nanette*—how before the revival reached Broadway on January 19, 1971, it was devastated by internecine warfare in which people were hired and fired quixotically, in which bitter charges and countercharges were exchanged, and in which blistering feuds erupted. It hardly seemed likely the revival could survive such disastrous inner conflicts. But survive them it did to become a stage triumph. With a greatly altered text by Burt Shevelove, and a cast topped by Ruby Keeler, a star of early talking pictures, the new *No, No, Nanette* was seen, was heard, and it conquered. It deserved the accolades heaped upon it by the critics, and the queues that stretched from the box office not only in New York but wherever it played. For it brought with it a warm, glowing recollection of the twenties, adorned with a lovable score by Vincent Youmans; and it represented a welcome return to a time of adolescent innocence in the American theater when tuneful songs, agile tap dances, arresting choreographic sequences, ingenuous comedy and sentimental romance were a prime source of entertainment.

Irene was the next vessel to come sailing in from the past (1919), arriving at the newly opened Minskoff Theater on Broadway on March 15, 1973 for a prolonged dockage, carrying in its hold the song for which it had always been remembered, "Alice Blue Gown" (Joseph McCarthy—Harry Tierney). Harry Rigby, who had conceived the project of reviving *No, No, Nanette*, was also responsible for the return of *Irene*. His adaptation of the original play by James Montgomery was overhauled by Hugh Wheeler and Joseph Stein to make it more palatable to a 1973 audience. From the original score by Harry Tierney, with lyrics by Joseph McCarthy, five numbers were retained, "Alice Blue Gown," and the title number, being the most famous. Eight other numbers were interpolated, two of which were old chestnuts of 1913 and 1917, "You Made Me Love You" (Joseph McCarthy—James V. Monaco) and "They Go Wild, Simply Wild Over Me" (Joseph McCarthy—Fred Fisher), together with several new songs. As Irene, Debbie Reynolds was making her Broadway debut after having starred in some thirty motion pictures, in numerous television Specials, in nightclubs, and after having received gold records for her MGM release of 'The Aba Daba Honeymoon" (Arthur Fields and Walter Donovan) and her Coral release of "Tammy" (Jay Livingston and Ray Evans). This diminutive lady proved to be a whirlwind, and the inevitable calm that followed when she was not on the stage was a letdown.

Next came *Good News* (1974), a revival of the college musical of 1927 by De Sylva, Brown and Henderson. It toured the country for about a year before settling in New York at the St. James Theater in December 1974. For its Broadway return after almost half a century, *Good News* starred Alice Faye and Gene Nelson. From the original score of sixteen songs, eleven were retained, to which were added the title song from the motion picture *Sunny Side Up*, "Button Up Your Overcoat" from the stage musical *Follow Thru*, "You're the Cream in My Coffee" from *Hold Everything*, "Life Is Just a Bowl of Cherries" from the *George White's Scandals of 1931*, and "Together," which had been published independently, all of them songs by De Sylva, Brown and Henderson. But song riches do not a successful revival make. *Good News* turned out to be, as Martin Gottfried reported in the New York *Post*, "a joyless, mechanical reproduction. . . that misses the whole point of nostalgia shows, which is to look at a sweet and simple past entertainment from an oblique and affectionate angle." Its slapdash plot, stilted dialogue and humor that continually missed the target, gave *Good News* a short life and an unlamented passing.

Very Good Eddie came back to Broadway after an absence of over half a century, and it seemed every bit as delightful to the audiences of the seventies as it had been in 1915. "It is a delight," attested Clive Barnes in *The New York Times*, reviewing the opening night performance of December 21, 1975. "It takes off, It flies. And it lands in a territory of innocence that we all think we ought to remember. But never do." About Jerome Kern's songs in 1975, Walter Kerr had this to say in the Sunday edition of the *Times*: "I was overwhelmed by their freshness, as though dawn had come calling, and only the first birds were up yet. If a melody is a melody, it doesn't matter whether it's old or new, whether you've heard it or not. It's still honey, and it pleaseth the ear."

Also cresting on this nostalgia wave were revivals on Broadway of other musicals, one from the twenties, one from the forties, four from the fifties and two more from the sixties: Sigmund Romberg's *Desert Song*, *Pal Joey* by Rodgers and Hart, Leonard Bernstein's *Candide*, Jule Styne's *Gypsy*, *My Fair Lady* by Lerner and Loewe and Frank Loesser's *Guys and Dolls*, Stephen Sondheim's *A Funny Thing Happened on the Way to the Forum* and Jerry Herman's *Hello, Dolly!* Off-Broadway proved even more receptive to the old musicals with Frank Loesser's *How to Succeed in Business Without Really Trying*, Cole Porter's *Du Barry Was a Lady*, the revue *One for the Money* in 1972, Irving Berlin's *Call Me Madam* in

1973, Jerome Kern's *Oh, Lady! Lady!* and Frank Loesser's *Where's Charley?* in 1974, and Jerry Bock's *Tenderloin* and Victor Herbert's *Naughty Marietta* in 1975—to single out a representative group.

There was plenty of nostalgia as well in some of the new musicals since 1960. Stephen Sondheim's *Follies*, the rock musical, *Grease*, John Kander's *Chicago* and the all-black revue, *Bubbling Brown Sugar* have already been described. *Over Here* (1974) recalled World War II on the American home front. It was an unashamed excursion into nostalgia even to the point of bringing back to professional life the beloved singing Andrews Sisters of the 1930s and 1940s (that is, only two of the Andrews Sisters, Patty and Maxine, since the third, La Verne, was dead). Will Holt's book dealt primarily with a trainload of soldiers and civilians bound for an embarkation center in New York en route to the European fighting front. "Everything seems nostalgically authentic," reported Clive Barnes in *The New York Times*, "from the tackiness of scenery and costumes to the high-key patriotism and the homespun sophistication and humor." The entire score was the work of Richard M. Sherman and Robert B. Sherman, whose seventeen songs sound as if they were lifted out of the trunk of a composer of the 1940s. "Wait for Me, Marlene," a takeoff on "Lili Marlene," stopped the show; "Where Did the Good Times Go?", "Since You're Not Around" and "My Dream for Tomorrow" also were appealing for all their derivativeness. After the final curtain calls, the Andrews Sisters carried their audiences further back to yesterday by offering a potpourri of the songs which they made famous (none, of course, by the Shermans and all of them dating from the late 1930s and early 1940s).

Still more Broadway musical productions were strong on nostalgia. In 1972, the leading hit songs of Arthur Schwartz and Howard Dietz were assembled for a stage presentation named after one of their numbers, *That's Entertainment*. (Not to be confused with the two motion picture anthologies of the same name made up of musical gems from MGM screen musicals, films released in 1974 and 1976.) In 1974, a new musical production with book by Alan Jay Lerner offered some of the best popular songs written in America over an eighty-year period, including the song treasures of Jerome Kern, George Gershwin, Rodgers and Hart, Rodgers and Hammerstein, Walter Donaldson, Vincent Youmans, Harold Arlen, Jule Styne, Lerner and Loewe and Galt MacDermot. This fascinating panorama entitled *Music! Music!*, was presented for a limited engagement by the City Center of Music and Drama in a production staged and directed by Martin Charnin. During the same month of April when *Music! Music!* was seen and heard, Sammy Cahn, the lyricist, took his admirers down memory lane in *Words and Music* in which he traced his own career through the presentation of his greatest songs, and also through an informal, engaging and at times highly witty stockpile of anecdotes on how these songs came into being. After he closed on Broadway, he took his production to London, England, and Las Vegas. On May 13, 1975, a survey of the age of Rodgers and Hart was given at the Helen Hayes Theater in a concept by Richard Lewine and John Fearnley named *Rodgers and Hart*. Burt Shevelove did the staging and Donald Saddler, the choreography. With almost no dialogue, no master of ceremonies to provide either identification for the songs or overall unification, ninety-six songs (the unfamiliar as well as the famous) were heard, none of them intact, many in brief quotations, most in medleys. The production as a whole made for a delightful stage divertissement, an evening to bring back reminders of the 1920s and 1930s.

A *Musical Jubilee* (1975) was another musical production to bring back a cornucopia of popular song classics to the Broadway stage, this time not from one pair of songwriters or some any single decade or two as had been the case with *Rodgers and Hart*. The time span in A *Musical Jubilee* was a full century and about fifty songwriters was represented. Planned as an American Bicentennial celebration of the American musical theater, this show originated in a more modest form in the summer of 1975 as a Theater Guild cruise ship production. Greatly expanded in its musical repertory and stage-production procedures, and with a cast headed by Patrice Munsel, John Raitt, Tammy Grimes, Dick Shawn, Larry Kert, Cyril Ritchard and Lillian Gish, A *Musical Jubilee* drew a chorus of delight from the critics when it arrived at the St. James Theater in November 1975 after a tryout in Washington, D. C. Morton Da Costa did the staging, John Lesko the direction, and Robert Tucker the choreography, with continuity written by Max Wilk and the musical supervision assumed by Lehman Engel. All these participants as well as the leading performers were top-drawer, but it was the songs—fifty eight of them—that provided the real thunder. The oldest songs in the score preceded the Civil War and included famous Civil War ballads; the latest song was "You Go to My Head" (Haven Gillespie—J. Fred Coots) in 1938. There were songs of the World War I era, and those from Broadway, Hollywood, Tin Pan Alley and even London.

8

The musical theater since 1960 has been the stepping stone to stardom for four young female performers as singing stylists on records, over television, at concerts and in nightclubs. Barbra Streisand, Liza Minnelli and Melba Moore made their stage debuts respectively in *I Can Get It for You Wholesale, Flora, the Red Menace* and *Hair*. Bette Midler was in *Fiddler on the Roof* for three years (1967–1969), appearing as Tzeitel, one of Tevye's daughters.

When Barbra Streisand stepped into the role of Miss Marmelstein in *I Can Get It for You Wholesale*, she was realizing what she had long thought was an impossible dream. In the Williamsburg section of Brooklyn, where she was born in 1942, she lived through a fantasy in which she was a stage star. She would lock herself in the bathroom, put on false eyelashes and makeup, and perform TV commercials in front of her mirror. Her real life was less glamorous. Her father, a high school teacher, died when Barbra was fifteen months old, leaving her and her brother to be raised by a working mother. Six years later, her mother remarried. The disagreeable relationship between Barbra and her stepfather was just one element in what appears to have been an unhappy life. She was an unattractive girl with a nose and mouth both too large, and legs too skinny. Gawky and awkward, painfully self-conscious about her appearance, and inclined to do the unexpected and to say the unconventional, she made few close friends, especially of the opposite sex. At school, where she did remarkably well at her grades, and at home, where there was little love, she was a loner. "That is why I wanted to become an actress, I guess," she has said. "I felt I could get the attention I missed as a child." She was hounded by ills, imaginary and real. In her later successful years, her chain-smoking and nail-biting, her outbursts of hostility and frequent antisocial, nonconformist behavior may possibly have been the consequence of those distressing early years.

Acting, then, was her goal, and toward it she proceeded with determination undimished by the fact that with her appearance the cards were stacked against her. As a girl, she went to work in a Chinese restaurant to earn money to study acting. When she was fourteen, she spent her summer vacations working in a summer theater in Malden, New York, and a year later she attended two acting schools. All this time she was attending Erasmus Hall High School in Brooklyn where she was making top grades in all her subjects, in spite of the fact that she spent far more of her free time going to the movies and watching TV, in reading fan magazines, in studying acting and in daydreaming about being a star than with school books. Graduating from high school in 1959, she left home for good, moving to Manhattan and living with a girl friend. Work in the theater, she soon discovered, was elusive. "I had this old raincoat," she recalls, "and I wore black tights and I couldn't get hired to play a beatnik. I went to auditions and readings and was usually abruptly dismissed. I was humiliated—people looking at you like you're crazy." She supported herself by working as a theater usher, then as a switchboard operator. Many times she was without a job. She was so broke that more than once she had to scrounge for a place to sleep and sometimes for something to eat.

At that time she was thinking in terms of acting rather than singing. Then she heard of a talent contest for singers in a Greenwich Village night spot, the winner to receive fifty dollars for a one-week engagement as well as suppers. Though she had never sung publicly she became a contestant by performing "A Sleepin' Bee" (Harold Arlen and Truman Capote—Harold Arlen). When she first tried out this song for some of her friends she was so self-conscious that she faced a wall rather than her audience. "When I finished and turned around, I remember I couldn't understand why they had tears in their eyes."

She won that contest and went on to make regular nightly appearances at the Bon Soir in Greenwich Village. She wore an outlandish dress which she found in a thrift shop where she continued to buy her clothes long after she could afford to go elsewhere. Her four-dollar outfit was made up of a frayed white lace jacket that looked very 1890s, and pink satin shoes with oversized buckles that came from the 1920s. She looked like a caricature as she stood there singing "Who's Afraid of the Big Bad Wolf?" (Frank E. Churchill and Ann Ronell). In spite of her strange getup and looks far different from the norm for nightclub singers, she made a sensational impact. This was because she was, by natural endowment, a vocalist in full command of her resources and, by instinct and intelligence, capable of projecting any mood or nuance she wanted. She was intent on making every song she performed a human experience, sometimes even an autobiographical experience. It is all very well to note that much of the success of "Who's Afraid of the Big Bad Wolf?" in the early 1930s came about because the searing years of the Depression were at hand and the song introduced a note of optimism in the face of disaster. But the song was written for a Walt Disney cartoon, and as most singers like to present it, it was a light and playful tune. To Barbra Streisand who had long since met her own big bad wolf and had still to overcome it, the song became a lament. Those who heard her were amazed to find themselves moved so profoundly.

It did not take long for Barbra Streisand to build a large personal following at the Blue Angel nightclub where she appeared late in 1961. Her exceptional vocalism, combined with her personal involvement in her songs, had an inescapable impact. When she sang "Happy Days Are Here Again" (Jack Yellen—Milton Ager) she made it obvious that if happy days were here for her, sad days had preceded them. Interpreting "Cry Me a River" (Arthur Hamilton) she had a specific face in mind, she tells us. "I tried to recreate in my mind the details of his face. The song no longer works for me as well, mostly because I don't feel that way toward that person anymore." No less personalized was the way she delivered "Who Will Buy?" (Lionel Bart) and the standard from 1922, "My Honey's Lovin' Arms" (Herman Ruby—Joseph Meyer).

David Merrick, the producer, heard her at the Blue Angel and engaged her for his musical, *I Can Get It for You Wholesale* (1962). Her leading man was Elliott Gould, who would soon become her husband, and who then allowed his own acting career to mark time while his young wife zoomed to success. Her comedic performance as Miss Marmelstein in *I Can Get It for You Wholesale* almost stole the show. She was also now beginning to make appearances as a singer on many major network television programs and in fashionable nightclubs. In May 1963 she was invited to the White House to perform before President and Mrs. John F. Kennedy. By the time her first Columbia album, *Barbra Streisand*, appeared in March 1963 she was something of a cult among many of her admirers. That first release became the best-selling album by a woman singer up to then and brought her a gold record. Her next two albums in 1963 and 1964—*The Second Barbra Streisand Album* and *The Third Barbra Streisand Album*—were also gold records, as were the albums that followed, among which were *People, My Name is Barbra, Color Me Barbra, The Way We Were, Live at the Forum, Butterfly* and *Lazy Afternoon. My Name is Barbra* was the sound track of the first of her TV Specials, in 1965.

Funny Girl (1964), in which she appeared as Fanny Brice, had an advance sale of almost one million dollars only because she was its star. Now only twenty-three, hers was one of the most extravagant success stories in show business history. For the one year and nine months of its 1,348 run, *Funny Girl* filled the Winter Garden to capacity because of her. She went on to Hollywood to star in the screen adaptation, and after that, on a multi-million dollar deal, to star in three more musicals (*Hello, Dolly!* in 1969, *On a Clear Day You Can See Forever* in 1970, and *Funny Lady* in 1974, the last a none too impressive sequel to *Funny Girl*), as well as in several non-musical films. In 1964, she signed a ten-year contract with CBS for appearances in one Special a year over which she had complete artistic control and for which she received five million dollars. She now commanded $50,000 a week for a concert or nightclub appearance, and when she starred at the opening of the International Hotel in Las Vegas she drew one hundred thousand dollars a week. Perhaps even more startling than her sudden dazzling popularity and prosperity was how she succeeded in contributing a new image to feminine beauty. The Streisand nose, the Streisand mouth, the Streisand hairdo, the Streisand eye makeup—all of which would have been regarded by beauticians with disdain a few years earlier—became the hallmarks of a new beauty which young women everywhere were copying. In appearance, as well as in her vocal ability and her talent at song styling, she was that rarity in any society, a true "original," as Emory Lewis, editor of *Cue* pointed out when he presented her with his magazine's Entertainer of the Year Award in 1963. She remained an "original" even when called upon to appear as a comedienne in non-singing starring roles in the movies: *What's Up, Doc?* (1972), *The Way We Were* (1973), and *For Pete's Sake* (1974). And, of course, she was the true "original" in her poignant renditions of new songs—"People" (Bob Merrill—Jule Styne), "Stony End" (Laura Nyro), "I Don't Know Where I Stand" (Joni Mitchell), "Let Me Go" (Randy Newman)—and of such hardy standards as "My Melancholy Baby" (George A. Norton——Ernie Burnett), "My Man" (Channing Pollock—Maurice Yvain), "As Time Goes By" (Herman Hupfeld) and "Right as the Rain" (E. Y. Harburg—Harold Arlen).

The name of Barbra Streisand is often brought into play when Bette Midler is written about. For Bette Midler not only has Miss Streisand's capacity to dramatize and personalize songs but also, like Streisand, she often allows satire, impishness and buffoonery to filter into some of her performances. Born in Paterson, New Jersey, in the 1940s, Miss Midler spent her formative years in Hawaii at rural Aiea, near the United States Naval Base where her father was employed as house painter. In her first grade at school she received a prize for singing "Silent Night, Holy Night," and after that she was featured in school and amateur productions.

She left the University of Hawaii after a year and supported herself at various jobs, one in a pineapple cannery and another as secretary at a radio station. Her ultimate goal was show business. After several unsuccessful and frustrating attempts to find a place for herself as a performer, in 1965 she landed a small role in the movie *Hawaii* (1966), then being filmed in that country. With the money she saved from this assignment, she traveled to New York to promote her career in the theater. For a time she worked in a children's theater, in revues in the Catskill Mountains in New York, and as a go-go dancer in Union City, New Jersey. In

1966 she auditioned successfully for the part of Tzeitel in *Fiddler on the Roof*, a role she played for three years.

Listening to recordings of blues, pop numbers and Soul by Bessie Smith, Aretha Franklin and Billie Holiday brought her into the orbit of popular music. She acquired a repertory—which included that Billie Holiday specialty, "God Bless the Child" (Arthur Herzog, Jr. and Billie Holiday)—which Miss Midler sang publicly for the first time at Improvisation, a small New York nightclub which paid nothing to its performers but gave them an opportunity to get heard. The owner of the club grew interested in her, became her manager, and helped her get some television appearances. She was also hired for fifty dollars a week to sing during weekends at the Continental Baths which catered to a homosexual clientele. There she developed both her repertory—which ranged from blues to Soul, from ballads of the 1890s to show tunes of a later era—as well as her individual style of performance. Word spread quickly around the theater district that she was something special, and show people began visiting the Continental Baths just to hear her sing. A guest spot on the Johnny Carson "Tonight" show proved so successful that she was reengaged on that program intermittently for the next eighteen months, bringing her a nationwide audience for the first time. A two-week engagement at the Downstairs on West 56th Street, New York, her first important debut in nightclubs, had to be extended to ten. In 1972 she appeared with Johnny Carson at the Sahara in Las Vegas, sang in a sold-out Carnegie Hall on June 23, was one of the stars at the Schaefer Music Festival in New York's Central Park in August and made two appearances at the Lincoln Center on New Year's Eve.

Her first record album, *The Divine Miss M*, released by Atlantic in November 1972, was an instant best-seller. In this, and in later LPs, she presented those personalized song interpretations which made her perhaps the most famous white song stylist since Miss Streisand: "Boogie Woogie Bugle Boy" (Don Raye and Hughie Prince), "Chapel of Love" (Phil Spector, Ellie Greenwich and Jeff Barry), "Leader of the Pack" (George Morton, Jeff Barry and Ellie Greenwich), "Do You Want to Dance?" (Bobby Freeman), Bob Dylan's "I Shall Be Released," "In the Mood" (Andy Razaf—Joe Garland), Hoagy Carmichael's "Skylark" (Johnny Mercer), "Am I Blue" (Grant Clarke—Harry Akst), "Lullaby of Broadway" (Al Dubin—Harry Warren). In recognition of her now strongly-entrenched position, *After Dark* presented her with its award for the Performer of the Year in April 1973 and the Antoinette Perry Awards presented her with a special Tony as an entertainer in 1974.

In an article in *The New York Times*, Henry Edwards spoke of Miss Midler as "the first white show woman of the current pop era." He went on to add: "Her dramatic commitment to her material enables her to transform tunes of the past into songs of the present and to offer totally unexpected readings of contemporary songs that we've heard many times again." Once again in *The New York Times*, Chris Chase singled out another quality that distinguished Miss Midler's performances, a puckish trait that seemed to bring a twinkle to her voice. "Her raffishness seems to come from a deep well of merriment, she has a gaiety and sweetness one seldom finds in a comic man or woman."

After appearing at the Palace Theater in New York in December 1973, Bette Midler went into temporary retirement for over a year. "I read, wrote and watched TV," she explained. "I went to Paris. I swam." Her only commitment was to record a duet with Paul Simon. Then on April 14, 1975 she appeared at the Minskoff Theater in New York in *Bette Midler's Clams on the Half Shell Revue* in which her song routines and verbal and humorous asides were showcased in a fully staged and choreographed production. Tony Walton designed the sets and costumes and Joe Layton was choreographer and stage director. In this revue she remained, as Clive Barnes described her in *The New York Times*, "a modern phenomenon, the low priestess of her own juke-box subculture, an explosion of energy and minutely calculated bad taste, a drizzle of dazzle, a lady both brash and vulnerable, a grinning waif singing with a strident plaintiveness of friendship and love. . . . her singing rock to ballad, from bebop to gospel, is individual, fascinating and usually self-explosive in its mockery."

For Liza Minnelli, the Tony for her performance in *Flora, the Red Menace* was only the first of many awards that declared her a queen among performers in her own right and not by virtue of royal heritage from a regal mother—Judy Garland. Within a few years after receiving that Tony, she held an Oscar in hand for her performance as Sally Bowles in *Cabaret* (1972), an Emmy for her TV Special, "Liza with a Z," and a Grammy for her record album of that telecast. (She also received a special Tony in 1974.) All this added up to making her one of the greatest draws at concerts and nightclubs, a singing star of rare eminence. Once she freed herself of that vocal vibrato and those tear-stained deliveries so reminiscent of her mother, Liza Minnelli's artistry was cut to her own measure, with a stage presence, an appearance, a delivery and a styling uniquely hers.

The daughter of Judy Garland and the film director Vincente Minnelli (who were divorced when Liza was five), Liza was born in Hollywood, California, in 1946. The daughter of distinguished show people, she grew up in a hothouse atmosphere where future stars are grown. She did a walk-on in one of her mother's movies when two and a half. At seven, she did a dance on the stage of the Palace Theater while her mother sang George Gershwin's "Swanee" (Irving Caesar). Other girls played with friends and dolls. But when she was not at school, Liza lived on the sets where her father was directing motion pictures, and in rehearsal halls watching and studying the dance techniques of Fred Astaire, Gene Kelly and Cyd Charisse, or in the theater and nightclub watching her mother perform.

If, as Judy Garlands's daughter, Liza knew the exaltation of living in the presence of greatness, she also absorbed the sufferings that robbed her of a normal childhood and often placed on her young shoulders adult responsibilities. As a child she was in the eye of the hurricane that destroyed the marriage of her parents. She saw her mother disintegrate as a woman and artist through excessive indulgence in alcohol and drugs and through depressions that brought on several attempts at suicide. Liza's home was disorganized. Sometimes there was no money to pay bills.

Once Judy Garland and Vincente Minnelli were divorced, Judy and her children moved around spasmodically from one home to another, in places as far apart as New York's Scarsdale is from Whittingham in London. Liza shifted from one school to another in America and Europe (twenty in all) without the time to take root in any one place. But whereever she went she remained determined to become a performer. At Scarsdale High School she played the lead in *The Diary of Anne Frank* in 1962. This led to an engagement in summer stock at the Hyannisport Summer Playhouse where she appeared in two musicals, *Take Me Along* and *Flower Drum Song*.

Liza saw her North star over New York City, and there she headed when she was sixteen and had given up all schooling after a few months at the Sorbonne in Paris. Those were hard times for her, since both her parents had made it clear that she was now entirely on her own. One time she was evicted from her hotel room for failing to pay the bill and all her clothes were confiscated.

Her first break in the theater came in 1963 when she had a leading role in an Off Broadway revival of the musical *Best Foot Forward*, for which *Theater World* gave her a

Promising Personality Award. Some appearances on network television followed, and after that her first recordings (including her first Capitol LP, *Liza, Liza*, which sold half a million copies) and appearances on the road in several musicals.

She had a taste of triumph at the London Palladium in 1964 when she shared the stage with her mother and, surprisingly, almost stole the limelight from her. That performance was recorded by Capitol and televised for American distribution. Her starring role in *Flora, the Red Menace* was her bow in the Broadway theater (a role, incidentally, for which she was cast over the objection of its director, George Abbott). The musical was a failure, but Liza's performance was noticed and admired.

Fred Ebb, the lyricist for *Flora, the Red Menace*, helped Liza prepare a nightclub act which opened with a graceful tribute to her mother through a series of songs Judy had taught her. Liza's nightclub debut—and the real beginning of stardom—came at the Blue Room of the Shoreham Hotel in Washington, D. C., in September 1965. A few months later, on February 9, 1966, she opened at the Persian Room of New York's Plaza Hotel. The nightclub trail then led her to some of the glamour palaces of the world: Monte Carlo, the Olympia Music Hall in Paris, Los Angeles' Coconut Grove, the Riviera Hotel in Las Vegas, the Eden Roc Hotel in Miami Beach. Gradually she carved her own identity singing blues, ballads, rock and show tunes, while scrupulously avoiding the numbers with which her mother had been associated. She became the wide-eyed pixie of the nightclub circuit with a gamin haircut; her histrionic talent, sharpened from a number of starring appearances in non-singing roles in the movies, made each of her songs an emotional or dramatic experience, as her eloquently expressive hands fluttered like butterflies. She sang, danced, and strutted about the stage with an intensity she sustained until the final note had been sung and the last bow made. "She swayed, pranced and rocked in the spotlight like a shapely pressure cooker threatening to explode," is the way S. K. Oberbeck described one of her nightclub appearances in *Newsweek*. "She warbled, she bellowed, she ached and enticed with a quivering voice and a quivering body that worked together like Nureyev and Fonteyn."

Some of the songs she sang were new but many were old: "Mr. Bojangles" (Ron Crosby); that Al Jolson specialty, "My Mammy" (Joe Young and Sam Lewis—Walter Donaldson); "You'd Better Sit Down Kids" (Sonny Bono); "Stormy Weather" (Ted Koehler —Harold Arlen), the Billie Holiday tour de force, "God Bless the Child" (Arthur Herzog, Jr. and Billie Holiday); "Liza with a Z" (Fred Ebb—John Kander), a tongue-twisting number written for her; Cole Porter's "Love for Sale"; Burt Bacharach's "The Look of Love" (Hal David). Her stunningly effective renditions of these were sui generis. With her television Special, "Liza with a Z," her remarkable performance as Sally Bowles in the motion picture *Cabaret*, and her formidable three-week appearance as a one-woman show at New York's Winter Garden in 1974, she was truly a star of stars, a fact acknowledged as early as 1972 when both *Time* and *Newsweek* made her the subject of a cover story on the same date (February 28).

1975 brought her a new starring role in motion pictures, in *Lucky Lady*, which while not a musical contained a cabaret scene that allowed her to sing a new number by John Kander and Fred Ebb, "Get While the Getting's Good"; and that same year brought her back to the Broadway stage as a temporary replacement for Gwen Verdon in *Chicago* while Miss Verdon was recuperating from a minor throat operation.

Melba Moore's journey to success as an interpreter of Soul, rock and soft-spoken ballads began in *Hair* in 1968. Born in New York City's Harlem in 1945 she was the daughter of two musicians: her mother, a professional singer, and her father, a saxophonist. Melba Moore received her early musical training in high school, then earned a Bachelor of

Arts degree in musical education at the State Teachers College in Montclair, New Jersey. For a time she taught music in the public schools of Newark, New Jersey, but her eye was fixed on show business. Her first professional experience came as pianist and vocalist with Voices, Inc., as a solo singer in cocktail lounges in hotels in the Catskill Mountains of New York, and in cafés in New Jersey, and by providing background music for recordings. At one of her recording sessions, Galt MacDermot heard her and induced her to join the cast of *Hair* which was then making its move to Broadway. Her theater debut—and the start of her professional life as a major solo vocalist—took place at the Biltmore Theater on April 29, 1968. From bit parts, one of which was a burlesque of the rock group, the Supremes, Melba Moore rose to female lead, the role of Sheila. *Hair*, said Hubert Saal in *Newsweek*, was "her emancipation."

The starring role of Lutiebelle in *Purlie* came in 1970, a performance bringing her a Tony and citations from the American Guild of Variety Artists and *Cue* Magazine. Before 1970 ended she won further acclaim as singer with her first album, *Learning to Give*, released by Mercury, some of whose cuts included "Let the Sunshine In" (Gerome Ragni and James Rado—Galt MacDermot) from *Hair* and "To Me and Love" (Laura Nyro). Greater sophistication and more subtle inflections together with increased versatility marked her next albums—*Look What You're Doing to the Man* and *Live!*—as well as in her television and nightclub and concert appearances. When she made her bow at the Empire Room of the Waldorf-Astoria in New York, in June of 1971, Hubert Saal wrote in *Newsweek*: "She started out quietly enough, hymnally. Suddenly, out of that child came this mountain of a voice, big and strong. . . . Almost every song began softly and sweetly and then all hell broke loose and she exploded high notes without restraint. . . . She used. . . a variety of registers, a range of colors, and a mixture of styles—gospel, blues, rock, pop."

45

The Decline
and Fall
of the Hollywood
Empire

1

It was the end of the Hollywood empire; the end of the great studios with their stables of stars, directors, writers and composers; the end of moguls who ruled like feudal lords over their respective estates; the end of the glitter and gloss that passed for glamour in the movie capital. In short, it was the end of an era in the history of motion pictures. It was television that brought this about.

There were more than fifty million television sets in American homes by the early 1960s; watching TV had become a way of life that, for many, supplanted the theater, or spending an evening in conversation with friends. Americans were becoming mesmerized by the tube which disgorged spectacles, variety entertainment, news and documentaries, sport events, talk shows, situation comedies, Westerns, programs involving doctors, lawyers and law enforcement agents and music. America's greatest and most high priced entertainers were now visitors to the American home at the flip of a dial. Variety shows from 1960 on were hosted by Ed Sullivan, Andy Williams, Dinah Shore, Donald O'Connor, Edie Adams, Steve Lawrence, Tom Jones, Glen Campbell, Merv Griffin, Red Skelton, Danny Kaye, Jackie Gleason, Flip Wilson, Julie Andrews, the Smothers Brothers and many others. Specials brought hours of watching and listening pleasure from Fred Astaire, Bob Hope, Ella Fitzgerald, Maurice Chevalier, Judy Garland, Harry Belafonte, Frank Sinatra, Barbra Streisand, Johnny Cash, Bill Cosby and Burt Bacharach. Spectaculars offered Broadway musicals, and special events. History in the making had an audience of many millions: the Presidential campaigns of 1960, 1964, 1968 (with its street battles in Chicago), 1972 and

1976; the assassination and funeral of President Kennedy; the funerals of Martin Luther King and Presidents Eisenhower and Johnson; the "abdication" speech of President Johnson; the war in Vietnam; the impeachment hearings of the Judicial Committee of the House of Representatives; the resignation speeches of Vice President Agnew and President Nixon. For those still partial to motion picture entertainment, there was Saturday Night at the Movies (the first such program given in prime time) to supplement the Late Show, and the Late Late Show, and after that movies every night of the week to fill the bill.

Emmy Awards rewarded the deserved in television. In the category of Variety entertainment they went to "Astaire Time," the Garry Moore Show, the Andy Williams Show, the Danny Kaye Show, the Sid Caesar Show, the David Frost Show, the Flip Wilson Show, the Carol Burnett Show and the Julie Andrews Hour. Specials honored with Emmys were "Julie and Carol at Carnegie Hall" (Julie Andrews and Carol Burnett), "My Name is Barbra" (Barbra Streisand), "Frank Sinatra—The Man and his Music," *Brigadoon*, the Bill Cosby Special, "Singer Presents Burt Bacharach," " 'S Wonderful, 'S Marvelous, 'S Gershwin" and "Liza with a Z" starring Liza Minnelli. For special distinction in musical composition for television, Emmys were presented to Richard Rodgers for his score to the documentary series on Sir Winston Churchill, "The Valiant Years," to Earl Hagen for a segment of "I Spy," John T. Williams for *Heidi* and *Jane Eyre*, Morton Stevens for a segment of "Hawaii Five-O," David Rose for a segment of "Bonanza!" Walter Scharf for "The Tragedy of the Red Salmon," Pete Rugolo for a segment of "The Bold Ones," Ray Charles for "The Funny Side," and Alex North for his score for *Rich Man, Poor Man*.

Peabody Awards in the field of television were bestowed on "The Fabulous Fifties," the Carol Burnett Show, the Danny Kaye Show, the Julie Andrews Hour, "My Name is Barbra," "Frank Sinatra—the Man and His Music," "Color Me Barbra," " 'S Wonderful, 'S Marvelous, 'S Gershwin," "Liza with a Z," "The Timex All-Star Swing Festival," the Flip Wilson Show, "The Carpenters—Live in Concert," and "Helen Reddy—Live In Concert."

Though the emphasis of the Golden Globes Awards was on motion pictures, some went to distinctive television programs, those in the musical and Variety categories being the Pat Boone Show, the Dinah Shore Show, the Ed Sullivan Show, the Danny Kaye Show and the Carol Burnett Show.

2

The magic tube replaced the motion picture theater as a prime source of entertainment. The attrition at the box office created an economic crisis that permanently destroyed the old order in Hollywood, creating a new one. New young (and comparatively low salaried) personalities took over choice roles, once the monopoly of established stars. The huge yearly output of films was drastically curtailed. Contract performers, composers, writers, lyricists, and directors had to look for work (and often found it in television).

In spite of the financial storm signals in Hollywood, and the economies they imposed, screen musicals (which had gone into a decline after World War II) took on a new lease on life beginning in 1960. The big money in Hollywood was being earned by giant musicals. In the 1977 tabulation by *Variety* of the highest gross in rentals in the United States and Canada of films of all time, eighteen of the twenty-two screen musicals grossing over ten million dollars all came out since 1960, with *The Sound of Music* reaching a hundred million dollars, and *Mary Poppins*, *Fiddler on the Roof*, *Funny Girl*, *American Graffiti*, *Cabaret* and *West Side Story* all surpassing twenty million dollars. (It should be remarked that the high box-office grosses since 1960 do not reflect an increase in attendance but inflated admission prices.) The other musicals in the more than ten million dollar rental returns are: *Funny Lady*, *Oliver!*, *Thoroughly Modern Millie*, *Tommy*, *Hello, Dolly!*, *Paint Your Wagon*, *Camelot*, *Irma La Douce* and *My Fair Lady*. This being the case, the largest financial investments were available for musicals. The 1960s, continuing into the 1970s, proved to be a rerun of the golden age of the screen musical of the early 1930s and the 1950s. Year after year, in the sixties and seventies, big musicals followed each other in a splendiferous parade. Some were cinematic masterpieces; some, huge money-makers; some pleasing entertainment; some, unconventional and offbeat; others, mere duds.

Two of the better screen musicals released in 1960, *Bells Are Ringing* and *Can-Can*, indicated one of the directions screen musicals would take. Both were adaptations of Broadway stage productions; the Broadway musical now dominated the motion picture studio as it had rarely done previously. Both remained sufficiently faithful to the original stage product as to text and music to be recognizable.

Both *Bells Are Ringing* and *Can-Can* were produced on a several-million dollar budget, with no expense spared in the making of spectacular productions headed by recognized stars. Despite the belt tightening which its economic depression induced in Hollywood, money seemed plentiful for good musical properties. In remaining faithful to the stage production, the motion picture, *Bells Are Ringing*, borrowed Judy Holliday to star in the role of Ella Peterson she had created on Broadway. And on the screen, as on the stage, she was most of the show.

Can-Can brought together Frank Sinatra, Maurice Chevalier, Shirley MacLaine and Louis Jourdan in a bountiful production whose Cole Porter stage score was further enriched with Porter songs from other musicals, such as "It's All Right With Me," "Just One of Those Things," "Let's Do It" and "You Do Something to Me."

Among the musicals of the 1960s and 1970s some came close to greatness, while one or two were unqualified masterpieces.

West Side Story (1961), with Natalie Wood, Richard Beymer and Rita Moreno, won ten Academy Awards, a sweep without precedent, including those for the year's best picture and another for the musical scoring (by John Green, Saul Chaplin, Sid Ramin and Irwin Kostal). Bosley Crowther had no hesitancy in calling *West Side Story* a "cinema masterpiece," when he reviewed it for *The New York Times*. "In every respect," he wrote, "the recreation of the Arthur-Laurents-Leonard Bernstein musical in the dynamic form of motion pictures is superbly and appropriately achieved."

Though Julie Andrews was replaced by Audrey Hepburn in the screening of *My Fair Lady* (1963), others from the original stage production were used to splendid advantage. Rex Harrison was once again Professor Higgins, and Stanley Holloway reenacted Alfred P. Doolittle, the bibulous father of Eliza. Produced at a cost of seventeen million dollars, *My Fair Lady* carried this legendary musical to new heights of popularity through its stunning sets, costuming, choreography and color photography. For its efforts, the film was rewarded with Oscars for the picture itself as the best of the year; to Rex Harrison as best actor; and to André Previn for the best adaptation score. Marni Nixon sang on the sound track for Miss Hepburn, and "On the Street Where You Live" (Alan Jay Lerner—Frederick Loewe) was sung on the sound track by Bill Shirley for Jeremy Britt.

The Sound of Music (1965) could be called old fashioned in its sentimentality and likeness to the operetta form. But the elements that brought it such an overwhelming success on the stage were retained by the producer-director, Robert Wise, in the film translation: what Bosley Crowther referred to in *The New York Times* as "a cheerful abundance of the kirche-küche-kinder sentiment and the general melodic felicity of the. . . musical score." To these was added the power of a moving camera to capture breathtakingly beautiful vistas of the Austrian Alps and the rococo charms of Salzburg and environs. *The Sound of Music* received four Oscars, including one for the best picture of the year and another to Irwin Kostal for the scoring. It became one of the two or three greatest money-makers in motion picture history, both at box offices all over the world and in record shops where it established the all-time figure of over fifteen million albums (in both the original stage cast and the film sound track recordings). For its female star, Julie Andrews, *The Sound of Music* represented a victory of another kind. Having been bypassed by Warner Brothers for the female lead in *My Fair Lady* in its screen adaptation (the role to which she had brought such splendor and beauty on the stage) she went on, first in *Mary Poppins* (1964) and then in *The Sound of Music* to give such ebullient, zestful and charismatic performances as to cause no small embarrassment to the powers at Warner Brothers who had slighted her. Certainly her share in the triumph of the screen version of *The Sound of Music* was a giant one.

Oliver! (1968) was the English musical based on Charles Dickens' *Oliver Twist* that had had a run of many years both in London and in New York. Filmed in England with an English cast, *Oliver!* was furnished with the magnificent trappings afforded by a multimillion dollar production. It captured the Oscar as the year's best motion picture, with additional awards going to director Carol Reed, to John Green for his adaptation scoring, and a special one to Oona White for choreography.

Once again the word "operetta" had the sting of opprobrium when some critics applied it to the screen version of *Fiddler on the Roof* (1971). They felt that Norman Jewison, as director-producer, placed too much stress on big scenes that changed the character of this musical, even while adhering to details, from a simple, poignant human drama into a spectacular. One such scene was the wedding of Motel and Tzeitel which, all things considered, was cinematically effective; another was the ill-advised graveyard scene. In other instances, the motion picture remained true to its stage model: in the characterizations; in the Jerome Robbins choreography; in the fidelity to authentic settings and esoteric ethnic rituals; and in Topol's performance as Tevye.

Cabaret (1972) was the screen musical in which Liza Minnelli, as Sally Bowles, became one of the superstars of the seventies. She was brilliantly supported by Joel Grey, who carried over to the screen his inimitable characterization of a cabaret master of ceremonies. Both Miss Minnelli and Joel Grey won Oscars for their performances. Though the screen musical derives more from *Berlin Stories* by Christopher Isherwood than from the stage musical, Bob Fosse's sensitive direction admirably captured the essence of the Broadway production in depicting the decadence of life in Berlin in the years immediately preceding World War II, with a mixture of stinging irony and exquisite tenderness. The picture stresses far more than did the play the momentous political and social upheaval that was rumbling in the background like a threatening volcano. And a more conscious effort was made in the movie to make each song a "plot number," developing logically from the play's context, and serving as a sometimes bitter and sometimes penetrating commentary on what was happening to Berlin society. The better to realize this complete integration of music and play, all the songs, with one minor exception, are sung during the cabaret scene. For the movie, John Kander, composer, and his lyricist Fred Ebb, added four numbers not found in the stage production, "Tomorrow Belongs to Me," "Money," "Mein Herr" and "Maybe This Time."

Though they were no masterpieces, or even near-masterpieces, many other screen musicals since 1960 adapted from the Broadway stage proved superior vehicles of entertainment, each a credit to the art of filmmaking: *Flower Drum Song* (1961), *The Music Man* (1962), *Bye Bye Birdie* (1963), *The Unsinkable Molly Brown* (1964), *How to Succeed in*

Business Without Really Trying (1966), *A Funny Thing Happened On the Way to the Forum* (1966), *Camelot* (1967), *Funny Girl* (1968), *Sweet Charity* (1968), *Hello, Dolly!* (1969), *On a Clear Day You Can See Forever* (1969), *Song of Norway* (1970), *Godspell* (1973), *Jesus Christ, Superstar* (1973), *Mame* (1974), *The Rothschilds* (1974) and *Tommy* (1975).

Original screen musicals (or screen plays with enough songs to warrant classifying them as musicals) have been plentiful and generally less rewarding than those taken from Broadway musicals. Several good ones were produced in England by the Buena Vista-Walt Disney studios for family consumption, with scores by the brothers Sherman—Richard and Robert. They were the sons of a prolific songwriter, Al Sherman (1897–1973), who had come to the United States from his native Prague in 1911 and had contributed musical numbers to many Broadway revues including the *Ziegfeld Follies* and the *George White's Scandals*. Both boys were born in New York City, Robert in 1925, Richard, three years later. Both attended the University of Southern California in Los Angeles and Bard College. First successes came with two popular songs recorded by Annette between 1958 and 1960: "Tall Paul" (written with Bob Roberts) and "Pineapple Princess." Annette was Annette Funicello, singing star of the Walt Disney children's TV show, The Mouseketeers. The association of Annette and the Sherman brothers brought the songwriting team into the Disney fold. After writing songs for *The Parent Trap* (1961) and *Summer Magic* (1963), the Shermans enjoyed a substantial success with their score for *Mary Poppins*, starring Julie Andrews and Dick Van Dyke, with Miss Andrews winning an Oscar for her performance. The notable songs in this captivating musical were "Chim Chim Cheree," "A Spoonful of Sugar" and "Supercali-fragilisticexpialidocious." For their score, the Shermans received a BMI Award, also a Grammy for the sound track recording. Five years later, the Shermans were nominated for a second Oscar for the title number of *Chitty Chitty Bang Bang* (1968). In between, they wrote songs for other Disney productions, among them *That Darn Cat* (1965), *Winnie the Pooh* (1965), *Jungle Book* (1967), and *The Happiest Millionaire* (1967). After *Chitty Chitty Bang Bang*, their songs appeared in *Bedknobs and Broomsticks* (1972), where "The Age of Not Believing" received an Academy Award nomination; *Charlotte's Web* (1972); *Tom Sawyer* (1973); *Marco* (1973); *Huckleberry Finn* (1974); *Cinderella* (1975) and *The Slipper and the Rose* (1976). For *Tom Sawyer, Huckleberry Finn, Cinderella* and *The Slipper and the Rose*, the Shermans wrote their own screenplays (in the last with the assistance of Bryan Forbes). In addition to their work for the movies they were affiliated for nine years with the television series," The Wonderful World of Disney," wrote music for the NBC-TV Special, "Goldilocks" in 1970, and made their first appearance in the Broadway theater with their score for *Over Here* (1974).

The vogue for screen biographies of musical notables declined sharply after 1960, but there were three worthy entries in this category: the story of Fanny Brice as told in *Funny Girl* (1968) in which Barbra Streisand repeated her successful stage characterization (followed in 1975 by its far less successful and entertaining sequel, *Funny Lady*, once again with Barbra Streisand), the biography of Billie Holiday as enacted by Diana Ross in *Lady Sings the Blues* (1972) and the story of Woody Guthrie, *Bound for Glory* (1976), starring David Carradine.

Another fine original screen musical, *Thoroughly Modern Millie*, is the biography of an entire decade—the flapper years of the roaring twenties. Four great ladies of show business—Julie Andrews, Beatrice Lillie, Carol Channing and Mary Tyler Moore—are involved in a gay, abandoned spoof of the times, customs and clichés of the twenties. Though the title song was original (Sammy Cahn—James Van Heusen) and good enough to win a nomination for an Academy Award, most of the songs were standards interpolated as period pieces to evoke the spirit of the decade. For his scoring, Elmer Bernstein was awarded an Oscar.

3

Though *Thoroughly Modern Millie* is partly satiric and partly burlesque—and not at all romantic or sentimental—it anticipated by a few years the nostalgic bath in which the movies, and its audiences, luxuriated in the closing sixties and in the early and mid-seventies with such successful motion pictures as *The Last Picture Show, Summer of '42, The Great Gatsby, The Sting, The Godfather* (parts I and II), *They Shoot Horses, Don't They?, The Way We Were, Save the Tiger, American Graffiti, The Day of the Locust, Lucky Lady, Next Stop, Greenwich Village, The Lords of Flatbush, W. C. Fields and Me, Funny Girl, Funny Lady, The Boy Friend* and *That's Entertainment* (Parts I and II).

The last five of these are musicals. *Funny Girl* (1968) and its sequel *Funny Lady* are biographies of Fanny Brice with Barbra Streisand as Miss Brice. *Funny Girl* had an original stage score by Bob Merrill, lyrics, and Jule Styne, music, plus the interpolation of several numbers with which Fanny Brice was identified, notably "Second Hand Rose" (Grant Clarke—James F. Hanley) and "My Man" (Channing Pollack—Maurice Yvain). *Funny Lady*, which did not come from Broadway but was a screen original, also boasted an original score, this time the work of Fred Ebb, lyricist, and John Kander, composer, but here the interpolations of standards of the 1920s and early 1930s were not Fanny Brice's specialities but were numbers in the writing of which Billy Rose (Fanny Brice's second husband) had a hand such as: "Me and My Shadow" (Billy Rose—Al Jolson and Dave Dreyer), "More Than You Know" (Billy Rose and E. Y. Harburg—Harold Arlen). The sound track recordings of both *Funny Girl* and *Funny Lady* became gold records, the former in 1968, and the latter in 1975.

The Boy Friend was based on an English-produced and English-written stage musical satirizing the twenties with which Julie Andrews made her American stage debut in 1954. Together with Sandy Wilson's stage score, the MGM screen production starring Twiggy offered some reminders of a bygone Hollywood with the Nacio Herb Brown-Arthur Freed standards, "All I Do Is Dream of You" and "You Are My Lucky Star."

That's Entertainment represented something new in screen musicals: an anthology. It was a retrospective glance at the high moments from screen musicals produced by the MGM studios from 1929 through 1958. Produced and directed by Jack Haley, Jr., *That's Entertainment* was a 132-minute cavalcade of great song and dance numbers lifted from many of the films that helped shape the history of motion picture musicals. And what magic moments were recalled! Judy Garland in "You Made Me Love You" (Joe McCarthy—James V. Monaco); Jeanette MacDonald and Nelson Eddy in "Indian Love Call" (Otto Harbach and Oscar Hammerstein II—Rudolf Friml); Lena Horne in "Honeysuckle Rose" (Andy Razaf—Thomas "Fats" Waller); Mario Lanza in "Be My Love" (Sammy Cahn—Nicholas Brodszky); Debbie Reynolds in "The Aba Dabba Honeymoon" (Arthur Fields and Walter Donovan); Fred Astaire and Eleanor Powell in Cole Porter's "Begin the Beguine". . . . *That's Entertainment* was far more than a paste-up of clips. It was a production carefully thought out and creatively conceived. Frank Sinatra opened and closed the proceedings with appropriate remarks. James Stewart, Liza Minnelli, Fred Astaire, Bing Crosby, Debbie Reynolds, Elizabeth Taylor and Mickey Rooney are some of those who served as commentators. Skillful montages abound, now presenting different versions of the song "Singin' in the Rain" (Arthur Freed—Nacio Herb Brown) from the time it was introduced by Ukulele "Ike" Edwards in the *Hollywood Revue of 1929* through Gene Kelly's celebrated rendition in

Singin' in the Rain, and now charting the careers of Fred Astaire and Judy Garland. And there were also surprises as when James Stewart sang Cole Porter's "Easy to Love" and Clark Gable hoofed with top hat and cane in Irving Berlin's "Puttin' on the Ritz" in *Idiots Delight*.

 With the kind of critical accolades and box-office profits accumulated by *That's Entertainment!*, a sequel became inevitable. Once again the creators of *That's Entertainment* dug deeply into the archives of MGM, not only the musical this time but also the nonmusical productions. *That's Entertainment, Part II* (1976) tapped seventy-two MGM features. Like its predecessor, the sequel proved to be a bountiful source of heart-warming nostalgia and show-business magic. Fred Astaire and Gene Kelly were here recruited to serve as the hosts tying the various segments together into an attractive package (in the process of which, for the first time in over thirty years, they were reunited briefly as dancing partners). This package yielded varied delights: Lena Horne in "The Lady Is a Tramp" (Lorenz Hart—Richard Rodgers) from *Words and Music*; Judy Garland joining Gene Kelly in "Be a Clown" (Cole Porter) from *The Pirate*; Nelson Eddy and Jeanette MacDonald in "Lover, Come Back to Me" (Oscar Hammerstein II—Sigmund Romberg) from *The New Moon*; Fred Astaire and Cyd Charisse in "All of You" (Cole Porter) from *Silk Stockings*; Judy Garland and Fred Astaire in "A Couple of Swells" (Irving Berlin) from *Easter Parade*; Gene Kelly's roller-skating sequence from *It's Always Fair Weather*; Grace Kelly in "You're Sensational" (Cole Porter) from *High Society*. All this—and sights and sounds of Frank Sinatra, Bing Crosby, Ethel Waters, Dinah Shore, Maurice Chevalier, Eleanor Powell, Esther Williams, together with Robert Taylor singing and Greta Garbo dancing! And the whole was topped off with a reprise from the first *That's Entertainment!* of the title song (Howard Dietz—Arthur Schwartz).

 Thoroughly Modern Millie also renewed a practice abandoned by the screen for some years, that of using the songs of a given period to create the ambience and the atmosphere of the time of the screen story. *They Shoot Horses, Don't They?* (1969), for which John Green was nominated for an Oscar for the scoring, starred Jane Fonda and Gig Young in a story about a seven-hundred hour dance marathon in a shabby Los Angeles ballroom in the early thirties. Old-time song favorites in the background music were combined with the singing of numerous standards of the early thirties, including two by John Green himself, "Easy Come, Easy Go" and "Out of Nowhere," both of them to Edward Heyman's lyrics. *M*A*S*H* (1969), which managed to find a good deal of uproarious comedy in the Mobile Army Surgical Hospital during the Korean War (together with many gory scenes in the operating room) funneled through the hospital intercom system many old American songs for the diversion of the American medical troops. *The Godfather* (1972), set in the years immediately following World War II, has as one of its characters a singer possibly modeled on Frank Sinatra. As a performer at the wedding of the daughter of Don Corleone, the godfather, the singer clutches a microphone to sing an old tune made popular by Frank Sinatra, "I Have But One Heart" (Marty Symes—Johnny Farrow), adapted from the Italian ballad "O Marenariello" as teenagers squeal with delight. "All My Life," an Irving Berlin ballad from 1944, was revived for the background music and so were such other favorites of the forties as "Mona Lisa" (Jay Livingston and Ray Evans), "Have Yourself a Merry Little Christmas," (Ralph Blane—Hugh Martin), and "Santa Claus Is Coming to Town" (Haven Gillespie—J. Fred Coots). *The Way We Were* (1973), with Barbra Streisand and Robert Redford, looked back to the thirties with songs such as "On the Sunny Side of the Street" (Dorothy Fields —Jimmy McHugh), "I've Got My Love to Keep Me Warm" (Irving Berlin), "The Glory of Love" (Billy Hill), "Paper Doll" (Johnny Black), "In the Mood" (Andy Razaf—Joe Garland), "Red Sails in the Sunset" (Jimmy Kennedy—Will Grosz) and "River Stay 'Way from My

Door" (Mort Dixon—Harry Woods). But the title song was new (Alan and Marilyn Bergman—Marvin Hamlisch) and it won an Oscar. *The Great Gatsby* (1974) was the highly publicized new screen version of F. Scott Fitzgerald's novel of a tycoon with a cast headed by Robert Redford and Mia Farrow. Songs of the twenties were counted upon heavily to recreate the pulse and beat of those times, with Irving Berlin's "What'll I Do?" serving as a kind of leitmotif. Seventy-six-year-old Nick Lucas (though he was not identified in the screen credits) sang "I'm Gonna Charleston Back to Charleston" (Roy Turk—Lou Handman), "When You and I Were Seventeen" (Gus Kahn—Charles Rosoff) and "Five Feet Two, Eyes of Blue" (Sam M. Lewis and Joe Young—Ray Henderson). In *California Split* (1974) Phyllis Shotwell is heard singing "Mean to Me" (Roy Turk—Fred E. Ahlert), "Georgia on My Mind (Stuart Gorrell—Hoagy Carmichael) and "You're an Old Smoothie" (B. G. De Sylva——Nacio Herb Brown), and George Segal revives a 1905 ragtime song, "What You Goin' to Do when the Rent Comes 'Round?" (Andrew B. Sterling—Harry von Tilzer). *Lucky Lady* (1975), a film about rum-runners during the early thirties, starring Liza Minnelli and Burt Reynolds and with a basic score by Fred Ebb as lyricist and John Kander as composer, recalled some of the song hits of the period. Among them were "If I Had a Talking Picture of You" (De Sylva, Brown and Henderson), "All I Do Is Dream of You" (Arthur Freed—Nacio Herb Brown) and a brief comedic treatment by Burt Reynolds of "Ain't Misbehavin' " (Andy Razaf—"Fats" Waller and Harry Brooks).

In a calculated move to make memories of bygone years more vivid, some major nonmusical motion pictures since 1970 have used old recordings on their sound tracks, usually those with which the songs first became famous. In the Mike Nichols film, *Carnal Knowledge* (1971), Glenn Miller's recording of "Moonlight Serenade" (Glenn Miller) is heard under the opening titles, and Tommy Dorsey's recording of "I'm Getting Sentimental Over You" (Ned Washington—George Bassman) is played under the opening scene, while during the picture itself, Glenn Miller's recording of "Tuxedo Junction" (Buddy Feyne —Erskine Hawkins, William Johnson and Julian Dash) is interpolated. Other old-time favorites, all of them reproduced from old records, were "Amapola" (Al Dubin—Harry Warren) and "Dream a Little Dream of Me" (Gus Kahn—Wilbur Schwandt and Fabian Andre). The sound track of Peter Bogdanovich's *The Last Picture Show* (1972) makes extensive use of Hank Williams' recordings of some of his best known numbers ("Half As Much," "Kaw-Liga," "Cold, Cold, Heart," "Lovesick Blues," "Jambalaya," "Faded Love," "I Can't Help It," "Hey, Good Lookin' " and "Why Don't He Love Me?"). Also heard on the same sound track are other recordings: those of Tony Bennett of "Solitaire" (Reneé Borek and Carl Nutter—King Guion) and "Blue Velvet" (Bernie Wayne and Lee Morris); of Eddie Fisher, "Wish You Were Here" (Harold Rome); of Pee Wee King, "Slow Poke" (Pee Wee King, Redd Stewart and Chilton Price); of Frankie Laine, "Rose, Rose, I Love You" (words by Wilfred Thomas, music adapted from a Chinese melody); of Johnnie Ray, "Mr. Snow" (Oscar Hammerstein II—Richard Rodgers); of Hank Snow, "A Fool Such as I" (Bill Trader); and of Jo Stafford, "You Belong to Me" (Pee Wee King, Redd Stewart and Chilton Price). In *Ash Wednesday* (1973), starring Elizabeth Taylor, old recordings of "Ruby" (Mitchell Parish —Heinz Roemhold) as sung by Ray Charles and "The Nearness of You" (Ned Washington—Hoagy Carmichael) are combined with an original score by Maurice Jarre. Old recordings are prominently played on the sound track of *Paper Moon* (1973) in which Ryan O'Neil and his nine-year old daughter, Tatum, become partners in a confidence game in the Kansas-Missouri farmlands. (Young Tatum received the Oscar for her performance, the youngest performer ever to be so honored.) The title number, of course, comes from Harold Arlen's "It's Only a Paper Moon" (Billy Rose and E. Y. Harburg); it is heard under the opening titles. During the picture itself old recordings are omnipresent, including such standards as "One Hour with You" (Leo Robin—Richard A. Whiting), sung by Eddie Cantor (this same Eddie Cantor recording was also used on the sound track of *Bonnie and Clyde* in 1967); "Picture Me Without You" (Ted Koehler—Jimmy McHugh); "Happy Days Are Here Again" (Jack Yellen—Milton Ager); "Just One More Chance" (Sam Coslow —Arthur Johnston); and "I Found a Million Dollar Baby in a Five and Ten Cent Store" (Dorothy Fields—Jimmy McHugh). "Sunny Side Up" (De Sylva, Brown and Henderson) was played under the closing titles. In *Save the Tiger* (1973) the hero—enacted by Jack Lemmon in an Oscar winning performance—clings to his memories of earlier years to cope with the harsh realities of an unethical present. These memories are supported by the historic recording of Bunny Berigan and his orchestra of "I Can't Get Started with You" (Ira Gershwin—Vernon Duke) which is heard throughout the film as a recurring theme; also Benny Goodman's equally celebrated recording of "Stompin' at the Savoy" (Andy Razaf —Benny Goodman, Chick Webb and Edgard Sampson). Since *American Graffiti* (1973) reflects on the rock era of 1962 in a suburb of San Francisco, the sound track is made up of rock records of the fifties still very much in favor in the sixties. "Rock Around the Clock" (Max C. Freedman and Jimmy De Knight) was heard in the recording of Bill Haley and his Comets under the opening titles and the first scene. After that came "Why Do Fools Fall in Love?" (Frankie Lymon and George Goldner); the Platters recording of "The Great Pretender" (Jack Ramm) and "Only You" (Buck Ram and Ande Rand); "You're Sixteen, You're Beautiful and You're Mine" (Dick Sherman and Bob Sherman); and Neil Sedaka's recording of "Happy Birthday, Sweet Sixteen" (Neil Sedaka and Howard Greenfield). In *Lenny* (1974), the screen biography of Lenny Bruce, jazz recordings of Miles Davis are heard on the soundtrack. Alice Faye sings "You'll Never Know" (Mack Gordon—Harry Warren) on the sound track of *Alice Doesn't Live Here Anymore* (1974) under the opening credits—a performance, in turn, taken from the sound track of the 1943 film musical, *Hello, Frisco, Hello*. Since *The Day of the Locust* (1975) recalls the movie world of Hollywood in the late 1930s, old recordings help evoke the period. From the old song catalogues of Paramount are heard "June in January" (Leo Robin—Ralph Rainger), "Who's Your Little Whozis?" (Ben Bernie, Al Goering and Walter Hirsch), "Hot Voodoo" (Leo Robin—Sam Coslow), "Isn't It Romantic?" (Lorenz Hart—Richard Rodgers), "Dancing on a Dime" (Frank Loesser—Burton Lane), "Sing You Sinners" (Sam Coslow—W. Franke Harling), "I Wished on the Moon" (Dorothy Parker—Ralph Rainger) and the unforgettable Louis Armstrong recording of "Jeepers, Creepers" (Johnny Mercer—Harry Warren). Since *Stardust* (1975), like *American Graffiti*, takes us back to the rock years of the 1960s, its score is made up of forty-five of the original hit recordings of Bobby Darin, the Beach Boys, The Righteous Brothers, Neil Sedaka, The Drifters and many others. Frank Sinatra's old recording of "Young at Heart" (Carolyn Leigh—Cy Coleman) was used on the sound track for the opening montage and the closing titles of *The Front* (1976) starring Woody Allen.

Many a nonmusical motion picture began to use standards for humorous or ironic effects. Stanley Kubrick did so in *Dr. Strangelove* (1964) with "Try a Little Tenderness" (Harry Woods, Jimmy Campbell and Reg Connelly) played under the opening titles and "We'll Meet Again" (Ken Darby and Lionel Newman) sung by Vera Lynn, a British singing star of World War II, whose vocal presence is used to identify the period and the mood as the world disintegrates into a huge mushroom cloud. Kubrick once again used a song standard with ironic effect in *A Clockwork Orange* (1971) by introducing Gene Kelly's recording of "Singin' in the Rain" (Arthur Freed—Nacio Herb Brown). The implication of Burt Bacharach's "What the World Needs Now Is Love" (Hal David), sung on the sound track for the final scene of *Bob and Carol, Ted and Alice* (1969) is obvious in a film about two swinging couples who end up in bed together; and so is the orchestral outburst of "Love Is a Many-Splendored Thing" (Paul Francis Webster—Sammy Fain) when the aged Harry meets a delectable hooker in *Harry and Tonto* (1974). Tongue is also in cheek when Roberta Flack sings "When You're Smiling" (Mark Fisher, Joe Goodwin and Larry Shay) on the sound track of $ (1971) under the closing scene; when "Love Is a Many-Splendored Thing" is recalled orchestrally in *The Marriage of a Young Stockbroker* (1971); and when Bette Midler sings her own "Friends" under the end titles of *The Last of Sheila* (1973). Dinah Shore's old recording of "I'll Be Seeing You" (Irving Kahal—Sammy Fain) on the sound track of *Fuzz* (1972) is an amusing reminder of the real life romantic interest between Burt Reynolds, the star of the movie, and Miss Shore, also of the way in which Reynolds acquired nationwide notoriety by allowing himself to be photographed in the nude for the center fold of a woman's magazine.

Sometimes a standard proved highly serviceable in summing up the sentiment or message of a picture. This proved particularly true in *Guess Who's Coming to Dinner* (1967), the interracial romance in which the white Katharine Houghton was paired off with the black Sidney Poitier. Billy Hill's "The Glory of Love," sung on the sound track was utilized with powerful impact throughout the film as a recurrent theme and also under the final scene.

4

If Hollywood was borrowing something old for its screen music after 1960 it was adding much that was new as well. Though the ranks of veterans creating original music for the screen were thinning (as were the opportunities for their employment), some of them were still productive in the writing of screen music and were having their best efforts rewarded with Oscars. In the field of scoring, whether original or adaptations, the old hands at this game were scooping up trophies at the annual Oscar ceremonies: Ray Heindorf *(The Music Man)*; André Previn (*My Fair Lady, Irma La Douce*); Alfred Newman and Ken Darby (*Camelot*); John Green (*West Side Story, Oliver!*); Ernest Gold (*Exodus*); Morris Stoloff (*Song Without End*); Burt Bacharach *(Butch Cassidy and the Sundance Kid)*; Leonard Rosenman *(Barry Lyndon)*. The veterans were also well represented when Oscars were given out for the best screen songs: James Van Heusen, with Sammy Cahn as lyricist, for "Call Me Irresponsible" in *Papa's Delicate Condition*; Johnny Mandel, with Paul Francis Webster as lyricist, for "The Shadow of Your Smile" in *The Sandpiper* (which also won a Grammy as the song of the year); Burt Bacharach, with Hal David as lyricist, for "Raindrops Keep Fallin' On My Head" in *Butch Cassidy and the Sundance Kid*.

Henry Mancini gathered an armful of Oscars both for songs and for background music in the early 1960s. Upon returning to the motion picture studio in 1960, after having worked for television, Mancini wrote the background music for *High Time* (1960) *The Great Imposter* (1961), *Bachelor in Paradise* (1961) and *Breakfast at Tiffany's* (1961). The last was the screen adaptation of a Truman Capote story starring Audrey Hepburn; for it Mancini wrote not only the background music but also the song "Moon River" (Johnny Mercer), sung under the titles by Andy Williams. These efforts sent him twice to the platform at the Academy Awards ceremonies in 1961 for dual Oscars. "Moon River" was Mancini's first song hit and his first to become a standard. It brought him several Grammys for the best song, best record (in Mancini's own performance), best arrangement (by Mancini), best sound track album. The Victor LP *Moon River*, conducted by Mancini, sold over two million albums and Andy Williams' Columbia recording of the song earned him a gold record. (Williams henceforth became so closely identified with this song that he used it as the theme for his TV series.) In addition to the recordings by Henry Mancini and Andy Williams, "Moon River" enjoyed almost five hundred other disk releases. It also sold about a million copies of sheet music.

Mancini became the first composer ever to win Oscars in two successive years when, in 1962, he received one for the title number for *Days of Wine and Roses* (Johnny Mercer) which starred Jack Lemmon and Lee Remick. Andy Williams sang it on the sound track under the titles and earned a gold record for his Columbia recording. And again the song was honored with several Grammys as song of the year, record of the year (in Mancini's own recording), and best background arrangement (by Mancini).

Mancini's background music for the movies, and his arrangements, were often honored by Grammy awards after that; by 1977 he had accumulated twenty Grammys, something without precedent for any single performer. These awards came to him for his arrangement of "Baby Elephant Walk" in *Hatari* (1962); for the best instrumental arrangement for the "Theme" from *The Pink Panther* (1964); for the best instrumental arrangement of the "Love Theme" from *Romeo and Juliet* (1968); for the best contemporary instrumental performance of the "Theme" from *Z* (1969). His background music to *The Pink Panther*, *Sunflower* (1971) and *Darling Lili* (1971) was nominated for Academy Awards, and so were his title songs for *Charade* (Johnny Mercer) and *Dear Heart* (Jay Livingston and Ray Evans), and the songs "Sweetheart Tree" (Johnny Mercer) from *The Great Race* (1965), "Whistling Away the Dark" (Johnny Mercer) from *Darling Lili* and "All His Children" (Alan and Marilyn Bergman) from *Sometimes a Great Notion* (1972). Mancini subsequently contributed scores for *The Party* (1974), *The Return of the Pink Panther* (1975), *The Great Waldo Pepper* (1975) and *W. C. Fields and Me* (1976). A monumental compilation of Mancini's music on disks was released by the Reader's Digest Association in 1976. Within an eight-disk album, one hundred and eleven of Mancini's songs and arrangements were gathered, with Mancini conducting the orchestra and chorus.

New faces, as well as familiar ones, appeared among Oscar winners since 1960. Fred Karlin received it in 1970 for the song "For All We Know" (Robb Wilson and Arthur James) from *Lovers and Other Strangers*. One year earlier he had been nominated for "Come Saturday Night" (Dory Previn) from *The Sterile Cuckoo*; in 1970 he was nominated for his score to *The Baby Maker* and in 1972 for the song, "Come Follow, Follow Me" (Marsha Karlin) from *The Little Ark*. As a boy in Chicago, where he was born in 1936, Fred Karlin aspired to become a tennis player, but when he was fifteen he saw the movie, *Young Man with a Horn*, which featured Harry James playing the trumpet on the sound track. Karlin's fascination was aroused for music in general and the trumpet in particular. After graduating from Amherst College, he played the trumpet in a Chicago jazz band and wrote music for several jazz organizations. In New York, he later worked as an arranger at the Radio City Music Hall. Before winning his first Oscar for a song, together with his first Oscar nomination for a score, in 1970, he had written the background music for *Up the Down Staircase* (1967) and *The Sterile Cuckoo* (1970), among others.

In an extended and highly productive career in Hollywood, Lionel Newman won an Oscar for his adaptation scoring for *Hello, Dolly!* (with Lennie Hayton) in 1969. He also gathered about a dozen Oscar nominations. Some came in the 1950s with his background music for *I'll Get By* (1950), *The Best Things in Life Are Free* (1956), *Mardi Gras* (1958), *Say One for Me* (1959) and the song "Never" (Eliot Daniel) from *Golden Girl* (1951). Others came in the 1960s: *Let's Make Love* (1960) which he wrote with Earl H. Hagen, *Pleasure Seekers* (1965) and *Dr. Doolittle* (1967), the last written with Alexander Courage. In addition, Newman's song "Again" (Dorcas Cochrane) enjoyed a sixteen-week stay on "Your Hit

Parade" in 1948, was heard in the motion picture *Road House* (1948) and was successfully recorded by Vic Damone, Gordon Jenkins and others.

Newman has long worn two hats, that of executive general music director for 20th Century-Fox and that of musical creator. The younger brother of Alfred Newman by fifteen years. Lionel Newman was born in New Haven, Connecticut, in 1916. He studied music extensively and when he was sixteen he initiated his professional career by working as a rehearsal pianist for the *Earl Carroll Vanities*. Newman did various other piano chores before turning to the writing of arrangements for Mae West and Gypsy Rose Lee, and arranging and conducting for Earl Carroll. In the mid-1930s Newman moved to California where he wrote or arranged special material at the Paramount studios. After that he was employed as rehearsal pianist at 20th Century-Fox where his brother, Alfred, was music director (a post Lionel took over when his brother resigned in 1960). Lionel Newman gradually became involved in other, more demanding, assignments at the studio than playing the piano, including composing and conducting. In time he wrote songs or did the scoring for some two hundred motion pictures, including (besides those already mentioned) *Gentlemen Prefer Blondes* (1953), *There's No Business Like Show Business* (1954), *Love Me Tender* (1956), *North to Alaska* (1960) and *Move Over Darling* (1963).

John Williams has made a specialty of writing pictorial, highly dramatized scores for disaster films. He received an Oscar for his scoring for *The Poseidon Affair* (1971). Since then he contributed scores to *Earthquake* (1974), *The Towering Inferno* (1974), for which he received his tenth Academy Award nomination, and to *Jaws* (1975) which brought him the Golden Globe Award, a Grammy and an Oscar. Born in Long Island, New York, in 1932, he was the son of a drummer who had been a member of Raymond Scott's Quintet. John Williams attended the University of California, and studied music privately with Bobby Van Eps. While serving for three years with the Air Force, he conducted several service bands and made some orchestrations. Leaving the service he continued his music at the Juilliard School of Music in the piano class of Rosina Lhevinne and he studied composition privately with Mario Castelnuovo-Tedesco. In 1955, Williams found employment as a piano accompanist for Vic Damone. Three years later, Williams did the scoring for the motion picture *Because They're Young* (1960), the first film for which he received writing credit. Within the next ten years he picked up the Academy Award for his scoring for *Fiddler on the Roof* (1971), and nominations for his scores to *Valley of the Dolls* (1967), *Goodbye, Mr. Chips* (1969), *The Reivers* (1969), *Images* (1972) and *Cinderella Liberty* (1973). He received still another Academy Award nomination for the song "You're So Nice to Be Around" (Paul Williams) from *Cinderella Liberty*. His music was also heard in *The Cowboys* (1972), *The Paper Chase* (1973), *The Missouri Breaks* (1976) and *Family Plot* (1976).

Williams also worked fruitfully for television, earning Emmys for his music for the specials *Heidi* and *Jane Eyre*, and contributing music to such major TV productions as Playhouse 90, the Kraft Suspense Theater, Alcoa Theater, "Checkmate," "Gilligan's Island" and "Bachelor Father."

In 1974, Marvin Hamlisch became the first to make a full sweep of all the music awards at the Oscar ceremonies, for his title song "The Way We Were" (Alan and Marilyn Bergman), for his original background music to the motion picture *The Sting* (1973), and for his adaptation scoring of several of Scott Joplin's ragtime numbers also for *The Sting*. One year later, his talent for garnering multiple awards was once again evidenced when he captured four Grammys: the song of the year, "The Way We Were"; best new artist; best pop instrumental, "The Entertainer"; and the best original film score, *The Way We Were*. "The Way We Were" was also chosen by the Golden Globe Awards as the year's best song, and the album of the sound track of that film became a gold record. In 1976, the phenomenally successful Broadway musical, A *Chorus Line*, for which he wrote the music, received the Pulitzer Prize.

Marvin Hamlisch was a musical prodigy in New York City where he was born in 1944. His father had a small band which specialized in salon music for restaurants and in which he played the accordion. Revealing perfect pitch when he was four, Marvin was immediately led to music study. At seven, after an audition in which he played "Goodnight Irene" (Huddie Ledbetter and John Lomax) on the piano in seven different keys, he became the youngest student ever enrolled at the Juilliard School of Music, and at eight he wrote his first song (which was never published). At the time his goal was not songwriting but the concert stage as pianist. In his teens he gave some recitals in and around New York but soon was forced to give up the idea of becoming a virtuoso because of nerves. As he later confided to an interviewer: "Before every recital, I would violently throw up, lose weight, the veins in my hands would stand out. By the time I was thirteen or fourteen, it became obvious it was going to kill me."

While attending Juilliard, he worked in a girl's summer camp in Lake Geneva, New York, and it was there that his songs first got performed. One of them was "Travelin' Man" which his friend Liza Minnelli included in her first record album. He had his first song hit when he was about sixteen with "Sunshine, Lollipops and Rainbows" (Howard Liebling), successfully recorded in 1965 by Lesley Gore for Mercury. At eighteen, he worked as an assistant vocal arranger for the Broadway musical *Funny Girl*.

After graduating from Queens College in New York with a Bachelor of Arts degree (cum laude), Hamlisch worked for three years as a rehearsal pianist and arranger for the Bell Telephone Hour over TV. He also made dance music arrangements for two Broadway shows. When he was twenty-four he made his move to Hollywood. At a party he attracted the interest of producer Sam Spiegel with his own music. Spiegel told him he was looking for a musical theme for his next production, *The Swimmer* (1968). Hamlisch brought him that theme three days later and it was bought. This led to scoring assignments for other motion pictures: *April Fools* (1969); two Woody Allen comedies, *Take the Money and Run* (1969) and *Bananas* (1971); *Move* (1970); *Kotch* (1971); *Fat City* (1972); *Save the Tiger* (1973); *The Prisoner of Second Avenue* (1974). In 1971 he got the first nod of recognition from the Academy of Motion Picture Arts and Sciences when his song "Life Is What You Make It" (Johnny Mercer) from *Kotch* was nominated. He also wrote special material for the Las Vegas acts of Liza Minnelli, Joel Grey and Ann-Margret; toured the nightclub and college circuit as pianist and straight man for Groucho Marx; starred in a nightclub act in Las Vegas and elsewhere. In 1975 he wrote music for the TV dramatic series *Beacon Hill* and *Hot L Baltimore*, and in 1976 for a much-praised TV musical starring Jack Lemmon, "The Entertainer." Another of his TV credits is the signature for the daily ABC-TV show, "Good Morning, America."

Among the winners of Oscars are two distinguished French composers, each of whom has made impressive contributions to American screen music. Maurice Jarre had come from Lyons, France, where he was born in 1924. In his own country he enjoyed extended and varied experience as a conductor in Parisian theaters and as a composer of music for French films and TV. Numerous awards and honors came his way including the decoration of Chevalier des Arts et Lettres, the International Harriet Cohen Award for film music and the Grand Prix for recording of l'Académie Charles Cros. In 1962, as a writer of screen music for Hollywood films, he won the Oscar for his background music to *Lawrence of Arabia*, following it up in 1965 with his second Oscar for his music to *Doctor Zhivago* with its popular "Lara's Theme" which, with words by Paul Francis Webster, became the song "Somewhere My Love." Jarre also received Oscar nominations for his music to *Sundays and Cybele* (1963) and in 1971 for the song "Marmalade, Molasses and Honey" (Marilyn and Alan Bergman) from *The Life and Times of Judge Roy Bean* (1972). Among his later films were *Ash Wednesday* (1973), *Shout at the Devil* (1976) and *Mohammed* (1977).

Michel Legrand, born in Paris in 1932, worked for several years as piano accompanist for entertainers, among whom were Bing Crosby, Gene Kelly and Jacqueline François. He also made some successful recordings and wrote music for the French films, the best of which was *Les Parapluies de Cherbourg*, distributed in the United States as *The Umbrellas of Cherbourg* in 1964. "I Will Wait for You," from that picture, written with Norman Gimbel, brought Legrand his first nomination from the academy of Motion Picture Arts and Sciences. Assignments for American films inevitably followed. In 1968 he had his first Oscar in hand with the song "The Windmills of Your Mind" (Marilyn and Alan Bergman) from *The Thomas Crown Affair* (1968). His second Oscar was for his original background music to *Summer of '42* in 1971 which differed from the moody, romantic and sentimental writing with which he was identified by being in a piano ragtime style; its theme became a worldwide best-seller on records and in 1972 received a Grammy as the year's best instrumental composition. Oscar nominations came to Legrand in 1969 for the song "What Are You Doing the Rest of Your Life?" (Marilyn and Alan Bergman) from *The Happy Ending* and in 1970 for the title song of *Pieces of Dreams* (Marilyn and Alan Bergman). One of Legrand's most beautiful scores was heard in *Brian's Song* (1970), a Grammy winner in 1973. He did the scoring for *Gulliver's Travels* (1976) and *Ode to Billy Joe* (1976) and wrote the music for *Gable and Lombard* (1976).

From England came John Barry (born in New York in 1933) to contribute other notable screen music. In England he was the leader of the John Barry 7 Pop Group before turning to the writing of background music for English films. Working for American financed motion pictures he wrote the scores for several James Bond features—*From Russia with Love* (1964), *Goldfinger* (1964), *Thunderball* (1965). He won two Oscars in 1966 for the background music to *Born Free* and for the title song, lyrics by Don Black. A third Oscar came in 1968 with his background music to the remarkable English-made film, *The Lion in Winter*, and in 1971 he received an Academy Award nomination for his score to *Mary, Queen of Scots*. Among other films for which Barry wrote the background music or did the scoring are *Diamonds Are Forever* (1972), *The Tamarind Seed* (1974), *The Day of the Locust* (1975), *Robin and Marian* (1976) and *King Kong* (1976).

Dipping into the lists of nominations for the Academy Awards in music, one comes upon several names, none of which, at this writing, has received an Oscar but whose work nonetheless has been of unquestioned importance.

Lalo Schifrin and Quincy Jones both served their musical apprenticeships in jazz before coming to Hollywood, and both have often combined the techniques and idioms of jazz with those of classical music in scoring for films. Schifrin (named Lalo, after the French Romantic composer, Edouard Lalo) was born in Buenos Aires in 1932 to a musical family. His father was the concertmaster of the Buenos Aires Symphony for thirty years, and an uncle was its first cellist. Lalo Schifrin began his musical education in his native Argentina and steeped himself in classical music. But when he was sixteen he discovered jazz and became a devotee of the music of Dizzy Gillespie, Thelonious Monk and Charlie Parker. "Jazz," he says, "was the strongest influence on me because it was my own discovery, it helped me find myself." Nevertheless, his study of serious music was not interrupted, continuing at the Paris Conservatory in France where, as a student of Charles Koechlin and

Olivier Messiaen, he received first prizes in harmony, counterpoint and orchestration. Back in Buenos Aires in 1956, he wrote music for the theater, television and for a movie short, and he founded and played in a jazz band. Dizzy Gillespie, on tour for the State Department, came to Buenos Aires in 1957 and was so impressed with Schifrin's jazz that he encouraged him to come to New York as his arranger. Schifrin did so in 1958, worked for a while with Gillespie, and then as an arranger for Xavier Cugat and Count Basie. After going to Hollywood, he scored music for numerous major television programs, receiving Emmy nominations for his music to "The Making of a President," "Mission Impossible," "The Seal" and "The Heir Apparent," and gaining accolades for his music for "Mannix," "The Virginian," "Medical Center," "Mission: Impossible," "Planet of the Apes," "Petrocelli" and "The Young Lawyers." He also made some recordings: *The Cat* and *Jazz Suite on the Mass Texts* received Grammys in 1964 and 1965 as the best recorded original jazz composition of their respective years. In 1967 he won two more Grammys, for the best instrumental theme and for best original score for motion pictures or television ("Mission Impossible"). His first assignment to score for a major American motion picture came with *The Cincinnati Kid* (1965). He has since had numerous screen credits: among them *The President's Analyst* (1967), *Bullitt* (1968), *Coogan's Bluff* (1968), *Dirty Harry* (1972), *Enter the Dragon* (1973), *The Four Musketeers* (1974), *The Master Gunman* (1975) and *St. Ives* (1976). For two scores he received Academy Award nominations, *Cool Hand Luke* (1967) and *The Fox* (1968).

Touching upon Schifrin's frequently novel and inventive approach to scoring Charles Higham wrote in *The New York Times*: "For *Cool Hand Luke*, a prison drama set in the South, Schifrin used a jagged banjo theme as his central motif; in *Enter the Dragon*, a Kung-Fu thriller, he rejected the usual windbells-and-tinsel approach of Hollywood composers to Chinese scores and instead based his score on an entensive study of Chinese music at U.C.L.A. In Richard Lester's *The Four Musketeers*, he effectively mirrored late Renaissance music, providing cunningly distorted sonorities with a very large orchestra in which the characteristic instruments of the period were wittily employed to reflect the acid, comic style of Lester's direction. Spirited gallops, triumphal marches, and muted pizzicati all create an impression of largeness undercut by a strong satirical sense."

Quincy Jones, born on Chicago's South Side in 1933, received his academic education at Seattle University, and his musical training at the Berklee School of Music in Boston, the Boston Conservatory, and, in Paris, with Nadia Boulanger. In his teens, in Seattle, he formed a combo with Ray Charles, playing the trumpet while Charles played the piano, and alternating with Charles in doing vocals. In the early 1950s, Jones played the trumpet in Lionel Hampton's band and with Dizzy Gillespie. During those years, Jones distinguished himself for his arrangements for Sarah Vaughan, Sammy Davis, Jr., Frank Sinatra, Andy Williams, Dinah Washington, Count Basie and Dizzy Gillespie. With his own orchestra, formed in 1959, he toured Europe and made numerous appearances in American nightclubs and concert halls as well as over radio and television. In 1961 he was made music director of Mercury Records, rising to the post of vice-president three years later. *The Pawnbroker* (1965) was the first movie for which he wrote background music and was the first movie to give full screen credit to a black composer. From this time on, writing music for the films became his principal activity. He was nominated for Oscars for his background music to *In Cold Blood* (1967), for the song "The Eyes of Love" (Bob Russell) in *Banning* (1967) and the title song of *For Love of Ivy* (Bob Russell) in 1968. He also wrote the background music for *Mirage* (1965), *The Slender Thread* (1965), *Walk Don't Run* (1966), *In the Heat of the Night* (1967), *Bob and Carol and Ted and Alice* (1969), *John and Mary* (1969), *Cactus Flower* (1970), *$* (1971), *The Hot Rock* (1972), *The New Centurions* (1972) and *The Anderson Tapes* (1972), among others. His television credits include the music for "Sanford and Son," "Ironside," and his Emmy award for "The Bill Cosby Show." *Smackwater Jack* brought him a Grammy in 1972 as the best popular instrumental performance, and *Summer in the City* a Grammy in 1974 as the best instrumental arrangement. In 1974, he received a gold record for his album, *Body Heat*.

The five nominations Jerry (Jerrald) Goldsmith has received for his background music to A *Patch of Blue* (1963), *Planet of the Apes* (1968), *Patton* (1971), *Papillon* (1973) and *The Wind and the Lion* (1975) place him in the forefront of writers of screen music. He was educated in the city of his birth, Los Angeles, at the University of Southern California, and studied piano privately with Jakob Gimpel. In 1950, Goldsmith found work as a clerk-typist at the music department of the CBS West Coast headquarters. There his musical talent was noticed and he was assigned to compose and conduct music for several radio shows. He moved on to television, and by the end of the 1950s he was one of its topflight composers, his music being heard on programs of "Playhouse 90," "The Twilight Zone," "Gunsmoke," "Studio One," "Perry Mason" and "Climax." He has since continued writing for television, producing either the theme or original music or both for "The Waltons," "Police Story," "Marcus Welby, M. D.," "Room 222," "Barnaby Jones," and he collected Emmy Awards for "Thriller," "The Man from U.N.C.L.E.," "Dr. Kildare" and "The Red Pony." His "Theme from Dr. Kildare" became a song hit as "Three Stars Will Shine Tonight" (written with Pete Rugolo to the lyrics of Hal Winn) in Richard Chamberlain's MGM recording. In addition to the motion pictures for which he received Academy Award nominations, he wrote the background music for *The Sand Pebbles* (1965), *The Blue Max* (1966), *Tora! Tora! Tora!* (1970), *Klute* (1971), *Escape from the Planet of the Apes* (1973), *Chinatown* (1974), *The Last Hard Men* (1976), *Islands in the Stream* (1976) and *Logan's Run* (1976).

Laurence Rosenthal received an Academy Award nomination for his atmospheric music to the motion picture *Becket* (1964) which skillfully combined medieval idioms and style with contemporary writing. Born in Detroit in 1926, Rosenthal received his extensive musical training at the Eastman School of Music in Rochester, New York (where he received the degrees of Bachelor of Music in 1948, and Master of Music in 1951), the Mozarteum in Salzburg, the National Conservatory in Paris and with Nadia Boulanger in Paris and Fontainbleau. While serving in the Air Force between 1951 and 1955, Rosenthal worked as a composer with a unit preparing documentary and historical films. Upon his separation from the armed forces, he wrote incidental music for the Broadway stage productions of A *Clearing in the Woods* (1957), *Rashomon* (1959) and *Becket* (1960); made dance music arrangements for *The Music Man* (1957) and *Goldilocks* (1958); and prepared music for the ballet sequences of *Take Me Along* (1959) and *Donnybrook!* (1961). He first distinguished himself as a composer of screen music in A *Raisin in the Sun* (1961), *The Miracle Worker* (1962) and *Requiem for a Heavyweight* (1962). After winning an Academy Award nomination for *Becket*, his background music was heard in *Hotel Paradiso* (1966), *The Comedians* (1967), *Three* (1969), A *Gunfight* (1971) and several other films.

5

Hollywood is crowded with composers who are masters of their craft and who possess the creative imagination to produce distinctive, distinguished screen music. Some of the screen songs and background music of recent years are of more than passing merit. Most of it, however, is not. A discouraging deterioration in the quality and importance, of motion picture music has been taking place. As year by year we have been listening to the songs nominated for the Academy Award and the annual presentation festivities, we have become increasingly aware that, with occasional exceptions, mediocrity has overtaken screen songwriting. Few are the screen songs since 1960 that are likely to survive as standards in the way that the best screen songs of earlier decades have done. Most of the songs winning the Academy Award since 1960 have already entered into limbo.

As for background music, the revival in the early 1970s of recordings of some of the screen music of yesteryear by Max Steiner, Erich Wolfgang Korngold and some of their colleagues has been a harsh reminder of how good screen music could be and how inadequate, synthetic and pedestrian by comparison screen music has become.

Where does the trouble lie? The blame does not rest with the composers themselves, since many of them are men of uncommon talent who, when given the opportunity and a free hand, have fully demonstrated of what they are capable. The fault lies with the producers who seem to have forgotten that the primary aim of music for the screen is to intensify emotion, point up the action, build up suspense, create moods, help delineate character—in short to sound those subtle undertones which words and pictures cannot. What concerns many producers far more than providing the screen with music that is an ally of the play is the capacity of this music to sell phonograph records and tapes to feed the huge market of record buyers. "Now the phonograph is the barometer," says John Green, "not the dramaturgical needs of the picture."

In seeking out music for any given screen play, the producer finds it hard to forget the enormous profits rolled up by hit recordings. He remembers what happened to a motion picture like *Easy Rider* (1969), an outstanding Columbia release that floundered at the box office. However, it made so much money through numerous recorded versions of its background rock score that *Easy Rider* became a financial bonanza capable of rescuing Columbia Pictures, then in financial distress, from disaster.

With rock, Soul, and country and western so marketable in the record shops, the producers frequently have called upon composers to transplant one of these idioms into their background writing whether it fits or not. Not that rock, Soul, or country and western are incapable of producing good screen music—far from it! But these styles are applicable only when the story on the screen calls for them. But rock, Soul and country and western sell records, and so these styles are often brought to the sound track even if the musical material is totally irrelevant to story, characters and setting. A composer noted for rock, Soul, or country and western is engaged by the producer because of his success on records and not because his is the kind of music the screen play requires. Since many of these composers are short-winded creatively, and do not have the technique or the experience to maintain a sustained, elaborate musical concept, they come up with scraps and snatches which then need the efforts of numerous arrangers for enlargement and development into what Elmer Bernstein prefers to designate as a "nonscore." Haste is of the essence in the production of this music. Time was when a composer was allowed ten weeks to prepare his score. Now the assignment must be filled in days. "They don't want it good," is the favorite remark of Hollywood composers. "They want it Thursday."

The producer, in seeking a song that has best-selling record potential, is likely as not to slip into his production a song even when its presence makes little sense. Good as is Burt Bacharach's song "Raindrops Keep Fallin' On My Head" (Hal David), its relevance or value to *Butch Cassidy and the Sundance Kid* is highly questionable. Title or theme songs can prove to be a wonderful reservoir of hit records. Producers, consequently, now seek out those composers who are in vogue, and performers who are leaders in the record charts. These songs are used under the opening and closing credits (a practice known as "book-ending") and are repeated (sometimes ad nauseam) throughout the picture, as happened, say, in *Love*

Story (1970), for whose background music Francis Lai received an Academy Award. (The main theme music from *Love Story* not only sold well on records as an instrumental, but also as a song, "Where Do I Begin?" with superimposed lyrics by Carl Sigman.)

Regrettably, the screen composer has for the most part been robbed of his dignity and artistic significance. His work gets scrambled, rewritten, abbreviated at the whim of the director or producer in this insatiable hunger for music that is highly marketable in the record shops. Neil Diamond had to go to the law courts to get the studio to use his complete score for *Jonathan Livingston Seagull* (1974). Jim Webb, who had been contracted to write the music for *Love Story*, and Lalo Schifrin who completed a score for *The Exorcist* (1974) were both bypassed for a more commercial product than either man could or did produce.

Motion-picture music has also suffered through the declining importance of the conductor, a decline brought about through the advance in technology. "The recording engineer with his fourteen track boards, innumerable microphones, electronic metronomes and echo chambers is the conductor of today," wrote Harry Sosnick in *Variety* (January 5, 1977). "In addition . . . we have an untold number of electrically amplified instruments as well as many newly invented electronic keyboard instruments with totally new sounds." The result has been, as Sosnick maintains, "the human emotions, the warmth that can be created by an intelligent and experienced conductor is no longer a part of the music track. It is all manufactured and packaged computer music."

But the outlook for screen music need not be pessimistic. Bountiful creative talent is available. From time to time we do get excellent, even remarkable, background music from musicians of great skill and integrity when a producer stands willing to allow them to keep both eyes focused on the screen, and not one eye on the record charts. Let the record business plough its own musical fields! And let the screen composer fertilize for himself that area that is solely cinematic! Once this becomes standard procedure again, the age of Max Steiner, Erich Wolfgang Korngold, Dimitri Tiomkin, John Green, Bernard Herrman and Henry Mancini of earlier decades need no longer be looked back upon longingly as a great age of motion picture music but only the prelude of still richer and more productive eras.

INDEX

Note: The principal page references to persons and topics are in **boldface**. For references to albums, see under the name of the performer, group, or composer.